THE OFFICIAL ®
PRICE GUIDE TO
BOTTLES
OLD & NEW

FROM THE EDITORS
OF THE HOUSE OF COLLECTIBLES

TENTH EDITION

THE HOUSE OF COLLECTIBLES
NEW YORK, NEW YORK 10022

© 1986 The House of Collectibles

All rights reserved under International and Pan-American Copyright Conventions.

Published by: The House of Collectibles
201 East 50th Street
New York, New York 10022

Distributed by Ballantine Books, a division of Random House, Inc., New York and simultaneously in Canada by Random House of Canada Limited, Toronto.

Manufactured in the United States of America

Library of Congress Catalog Card Number: 84-643005

ISBN: 0-87637-521-2

10 9 8 7 6 5 4 3 2 1

TABLE OF CONTENTS

ACKNOWLEDGMENTS

For their assistance, the House of Collectibles extends sincere gratitude to the following: Ralph Riovo of Alburtis, PA 18011 for his extensive work on our dairy section; Tom and Deena Caniff of Steubenville, OH 43952 for our fruit jars section; Harold Barkley of Barkley's Museum, Taylor, MO 63471; Ralph Lazore of Utica, NY 13501; Ole Severson of Huntington, CT 06484; Chuck Pauls of Charleston, SC 29402; Ken Cornell of Leroy, NY 14482; Roy Warren of Getzville, NY 14068; Sven Stau of Buffalo, NY 14225; Tony Natelli of Howard Beach, NY 11414; and Noel Tomas of the Federation of Historical Bottle Clubs, Glastonbury, CT 06033.

A big thanks to Mr. Robert Snyder, author of three volumes of *Bottles in Miniature,* for his assistance in our new mini-bottle section.

Also, a big thanks to Jim Hagenbuch of East Greenville, PA 18041. Jim is the publisher of *Antique Bottle & Glass Collector* and is also the head of Glass Works auctions. He is one of the most knowledgeable bottle men around.

NOTE TO READERS

MARKET REVIEW

Bottle collectors have been very busy lately. Considering the vast number of shows, auctions, and club meetings, it's safe to assume that bottle collectors don't stay home very much. Record prices are being set and interest in new fields is growing rapidly. Many interesting trends have developed.

Inks are continuing their strong performance. Especially strong are teakettle inks and pontiled or embossed inks. French and English inks are also doing well, as are inks in unusual colors. One of the most interesting auctions of the recent past featured the ink collection of Mrs. Annette Latker. It was held at Glass Works auctions in East Greenville, Pennsylvania in January of 1986. A crown shaped teakettle ink in amethyst sold for $1,400.00. Another interesting sale at that auction was a teakettle ink shaped like a lounging cat in clear glass. Probably of French manufacture, it brought in $650.00. But the really exceptional ink sale that day was a bottle embossed "FINE / BLACK INK / MADE & SOLD BY / J.L. THOMPSON / TROY N-Y" in yellow-amber with an open pontil that took in $2,100.00. However, most inks are still available at very reasonable prices, so there is still a lot of room for the average collector.

Patent Proprietary medicines are also doing quite well. Color remains the most important criteria in this area, but other factors such as age or being pontiled are always considered. Of all the sub-groupings in this area, cures seem to be the strongest. Medicine bottles are also doing well. Although not common at the auction houses, private sale reported to House of Collectibles recently included an "I. NEWTON'S PANACEA PURIFIER OF THE BLOOD GREENWICH, VERMONT" that was pontiled, in an olivy-amber that sold for $1,500.00. A "GIBBS BONE LINIMENT", pontiled, in an olive-green, also did well at $550.00.

Bitters bottles are rebounding from the boom of 1983–84. Prices are dropping slowly but many collectors and dealers, including Jim Hagenbuch (publisher of *Antique Bottle & Glass Collector* and one of the most knowledgeable dealers active today), feel that the prices now being realized reflect a more realistic market value. Mr. Hagenbuch feels that the '83–'84 peak was artificially induced by a sudden influx of money from a single source. It had no lasting effects on the market but the cycle is coming full-swing and the market is now in a downturn. No crash is expected, but caution is advised. A collector should be sure a bitters bottle is of very good quality before investing in it. Skinner Auctions of Bolton, Massachusetts recently held a sale that showed some good bitters. Highlights from that sale included a

"McKEEVER'S ARMY BITTERS" in the shape of a civil war drum with a grouping of cannon balls making up the shoulder and neck that sold for $1,200.00. Also sold that day was a lighthouse-shaped bottle embossed "SOL FRANK'S PANACEA BITTERS" in amber that was taken home for $1,500.00. At the January, 1986 auction at Glass Works, a "E. DEXTER LOVERIDGE / WAHOO BITTERS / PATD / XXX—1863" in a fabulous deep-green sold for a strong $2,900.00.

Poison bottles, although a relatively small area, is showing a lot of activity. Prices are strong and collector interest is very high. It's also one of the few types of American bottles popular abroad, especially in Great Britain. Conversely, English poison bottles have flooded the U.S. market and are not doing well. Rarity and color are both strong factors in determining the value of poisons. Amber and green are common, but aqua is hard to find and remains valuable. Clear poison flasks from 18th century Europe are also doing quite well. Two outstanding private sales recently reported were of a skull-shaped poison in cobalt-blue, 4¼" high that sold for $450.00. An embossed coffin poison also in cobalt-blue, 7½" high did nicely at $375.00. Poison prices are not in the range of other bottle specialities but supplies are also smaller. Further growth can be expected.

Antique flasks are also showing strength. An amber, pin, GX-27 American flag flask from New Granite Glass Works, Stoddard N.H. sold at Skinner's recently for $2,900.00. A deep sapphire-blue GIV-3 masonic flask with an embossed American eagle, but a small potstone crack sold at Skinner's in March of 1986 for an outstanding $4,500.00. Again, many flasks are priced affordably and continued collector growth can be expected.

What can you say about dairy bottles? This area is growing faster than anyone can keep up with. The Milk Route, of Westport, Connecticut is now a national magazine and is looking to expand the hobby. The low-priced milk bottles ($2–$6) are staying stable, but the sectors of the market higher in price are expanding rapidly. World War II bottles are scarce and are widely sought as are embossed bottles; particularly those with Walt Disney characters. Where is the milk hobby headed? In the words of the sage, hold on to your hats, we're going up!

Beer bottles are a specialty that's impossible to pin down. It is so much a regional interest that how beer bottles are doing often will depend on what town a collector lives in. Generally, beer bottle prices are staying stable. Early iron-pontiled beers are popular as are beer bottles in green and especially cobalt-blue. Paneled bottles are also very strong.

Fruit jars have long been one of the largest fields of interest in bottles and collector interest continues to grow. Prices, however, are not sharing in the expansion. Low and middle priced bottles are soft. High priced bottles ($1,000.00 or more) continue to show stability. A pint "BODINE AND BROTHER NE PLUS ULTRA AIRTIGHT FRUIT JAR" in aqua, iron-pontiled, sold at Skinner's recently for $1,500.00. The market is still out there, but the collector should do the necessary research before buying.

Spirits bottles are also doing well. Two sales at the March, 1986 Skinner's auction that illustrate this were a 14″ cannon-shaped whiskey embossed "J.T. GAYEN, ALTONA" in amber that went for $425.00 and a "GEORGE NOAR LOUISVILLE, KY. BOURBON WHISKEY" in amber, iron pontiled with an applied handle, that brought down $500.00. Again, spirit bottle prices do not reach the heights that, for example, antique flasks do. Prices are affordable throughout the hobby.

Last, but certainly not least of the antique bottles, sodas are bringing in good prices. At the Glass Works auction, a "TAYLOR / NEVER / SURRENDERS — UNION GLASS WORKS" in cobalt-blue, iron-pontiled, went for $1,450.00. At the same sale, a "G.D. COGGESHALL / 421 PEARL ST. — NEW YORK — SODA WATER" sold for a whopping $2,900.00. Good bottles were offered at the Glass Works auction house and collectors responded with outstanding prices. Sodas should continue their strong showing.

Modern bottles continue to spark strong interest. Private transactions are the rule with modern bottles, so speaking about specific prices isn't generally possible. Jim Beam bottles remain the leader in the field. Clubs specifically devoted to Beam bottles spring up constantly and collector interest is growing at an unparalleled rate. Everyone knows that the Beam hobby will continue to grow.

Bottles are a healthy hobby. Good prices, high interest, and great people make this varied field very special. No matter what your specialty is, enjoy the bottles; but most of all, enjoy the people who share your interest. Consult the club listings in the back of this book. If there's a club in your area, join it. If there is no club listed that is convenient for you, consult our dealer listings. Call one close to you and find out what's happening in bottles. You'll be glad you did.

HISTORY OF BOTTLES

Obviously, the history of bottles is closely linked to the history and development of retail merchandising in this country. In spite of the extent to which this subject has been studied, much remains to be learned.

American business firms were the leaders in bottle packaging in the

19th and 20th centuries. Many kinds of merchandise, foodstuffs, medicines, etc., that were sold by other means in foreign countries, came in bottles in the U.S. Pills, for example, were still being dispensed in cartons and tins in most parts of Europe long after bottled pills had become commonplace in the United States. American manufacturers and retailers depended more on bottles for packaging merchandise suitably, than on any other kind of container. Subsequently, the extent and variety of American bottles available to the collector is enormous. As early as 1870, many items purchased in the average general store in any U.S. town were supplied pre-packaged in bottles. Commercially packaged foodstuffs in bottles were not available in many areas of the world until after World War II.

What came *before* bottles? Obviously, the grocer of Ben Franklin's day did not sell his milk in paper bags. "Portion selling" was the sole method of merchandising in early America. The customer was expected to bring his own container when purchasing liquids or other hard-to-package items. If he wanted milk, he brought his own jar to the store. The grocer would fill it with a ladle from his milk can or barrel. Easily handled items were weighed out, or sold by the piece, and wrapped in paper. Packaging was only meant to get the item home safely, not to serve as a long-range storage container.

If there was a bottlemaker nearby, successful merchants had bottles specially made for specific products. Ready-packaged merchandise added slightly to the merchant's cost, but it saved a lot of time and work. It also increased the shelf life of perishables. Even the most old-fashioned of shopkeepers gradually came to bless the bottle.

As bottles became commonplace, distribution extended to every corner of the continent. Bottles from the east were carried overland by early settlers. Most were discarded or lost at many points along the way. This is why old bottles turn up just about anywhere—sometimes in the most unlikely locations.

A good indication as to the extent of merchandise sold pre-packaged in bottles can be gleaned from Sears Roebuck catalogs of the 1890s and early 1900s. This was without question the golden age of bottle packaging. These catalogs contain *thousands* of items sold in bottles. Reprint editions are available and invaluable to the collector.

The sales of soft drinks in bottles ushered in another important era in the history of commercial bottle making. Collecting early soft drink bottles from all different retailers has become one of the major specialties of the hobbyist. Prices on many of the more historic soft drink bottles have risen to extraordinary heights, due to the combination of scarcity and high demand. Millions were made, but probably only one in a thousand were saved. No more thought was given to saving them than to the soft drink bottles of today. One reason soft drink bottles are so popular among collectors is the long history of the manufacturing companies. This makes it possible to form a collection exhibiting changes in bottle design. There is no other kind of bottle that lends itself so well to a "developmental" collection.

BEGINNING A COLLECTION

An individual's approach to bottle collecting is apt to be determined, or at least influenced by, personal finances, available spare time, space in the home for whatever bottles are to be stored and/or displayed, and in what directions the hobbyist's personal taste happens to run. The collector can choose to concentrate on bitters bottles, soft drink bottles, milk bottles, or one of the other popular specialties covered in this book. By purchasing according to place of origin, time period, or because the bottle is intriguing, the hobbyist will have a combination of many different types of bottles within his collection, which is perfectly acceptable.

Most collectors, however, choose to specialize because of its distinct advantages. Approximately 70% of active bottle enthusiasts are specialists. A comprehensive representation of every kind of bottle would result in a huge collection. Specialization narrows the field and gives a collection a sense of continuity. Since all the specimens relate to one another, the study and research of their origin can be better organized. The collector can quickly become an authority on bottles in a chosen specialty. Knowledge gained about one maker can be very helpful in researching another. When examining bottles in a shop or at a convention, the collector will very often be in a position of having more knowledge than the seller. A general collector, on the other hand, constantly encounters bottles which he is inclined to buy, but about which he knows next to nothing. The specialist can spot "sleepers" and underpriced items better by having expert knowledge of one or two groups of bottles.

Another benefit in being a specialist is that swapping becomes possible. It is easy to find another collector with the same interest who has duplicates or other unwanted bottles. By specializing in the same type, both parties will know the value of the items to be traded. Bottle collecting has a way of bringing people together, and many collectors become good friends.

A good collection in just about any line can be started without spending a great deal per bottle. Even with a ceiling price of $10 per purchase, it is possible to make impressive inroads into nearly all of the popular groups, especially since many bottles are selling at less than their fair retail values. It would not be worthwhile to venture into a field where most of the better items are very expensive. Coke bottles and 19th century flasks are not for the lean wallet. A collector must be able to compete on an equal financial footing with other buyers. It is best for him to begin on the "ground floor" in specialties that have not yet attracted great hordes of buyers, such as ink bottles and many varieties of food bottles. The prices on these are likely to rise in the future, just as Coke and flask prices skyrocketed from the 1950s to the present time. Every antique dealer knows that old Coke bottles are potentially very valuable. A dealer will not price such an item without checking the value. But many dealers are unaware of the potential value of the less publicized bottles, and may just mark them up at a percentage over the cost price. It is possible to find bottles worth $20 selling for $2 and similar buys, if the collector's field of specialty is a little off the beaten path.

In choosing a type of bottle in which to specialize, the hobbyist must consider what features or aspects of bottles intrigue him the most. Is it the color, shape, printed label, artistic value, historic significance, or impending research that peaks his curiosity? There are collectible bottles to suit every taste and personality. Collecting a certain kind of bottle just because someone else does, or because the local antiques shop happens to have a good stock, is fairly unrewarding. Whatever specialty is chosen, the sources of supply for bottles are endless.

Available display space must be a consideration to the serious collector. Where is the collection going to be kept? Approximately how many bottles will the space hold? Is there room for expansion? Space limitations can influence the choice of a specialty. A collector may wish to invest in a moderately expensive class of bottles, and make purchases only occasionally to keep his collection relatively small. Certain kinds of bottles are larger than others and require more space. A hundred ink bottles can be kept in a space that would be used up by half as many soft drink bottles.

Old vs. New. Old bottles are obviously not the only kinds suitable to collect. The Avons, Jim Beams and other figurals of recent and current vintage are not only collectible, but made to be collected. In terms of artistry and as decorative objects, they clearly outshine 1880s bitters bottles and old milk bottles. There are many hobbyists who object to "instant" collectors' items, and prefer bottles which have acquired interest by being preserved over long periods of time. The older bottles have history on their side, and a collection of "oldies" will be much more original than one of limited editions. These two groups are so different in every respect that it should be no problem for any potential collector to decide where his preferences lie.

Technically, there is no clear-cut definition of what separates an "old" from a "new" bottle. Some of the Avons are quite old. By the same token, recent Coke bottles are collected as evolutionary links in the history of Coke bottle manufacturing. The term "antique," though frequently applied to bottles even in this book, really has little practical use in this hobby. By accepted definition, an antique is any article more than one hundred years old. Quite a few of the bottles listed in this book are over one hundred years old, and could deservedly be called antiques; but other bottles, which are just as collectible and sometimes worth even more, are not antiques. There may be a certain magic attached to other collectors' items that rank as antiques, but it makes no difference with bottles. Perhaps this is because bottle making has been going on for 2,000 years, and even a one hundred-year-old specimen is fairly modern. The background, history, use, design, and scarcity of a bottle count with collectors far more than whether it falls in front of or behind the one hundred year mark.

DETERMINING VALUE

What makes a bottle valuable? No simple answer can be given. Prices are set by supply and demand: the availability of any given bottle on the market versus the number of buyers who want it. Certain bottles are more scarce than others. Demand occurs for some bottles more because of collectors' tastes. Many scarce bottles sell for modest prices simply because they are labeled "slow movers." Dealers have no choice but to mark it low, because there are few customers for that particular kind of bottle. These are the "sleepers," whose values can, and probably will in time, adjust in line with their scarcity. If all buyers had the same tastes and goals in collecting, it would be very easy to say what makes a bottle valuable; but such certainty would also create a very dull hobby.

The variety of old bottles available to the collector is considerably greater than that of new or recent specimens. This is because old bottles need not be fancy or decorative to have collector appeal; they can simply be *old.* Nevertheless, many old bottles have unusual shapes and command premium prices. An odd or artistically shaped bottle from the 1800s was not made for sale to collectors, but rather to stimulate sale of the product. This is one of the reasons why "old fancies" are, in the opinion of the devotees, more collectible than "modern fancies." In many instances, these "old fancies" were manufactured in greater quantities than modern Jim Beams or Avons, as they were not limited editions; however, the number in existence have a rather low survival rate. With "store bottles," the rate is particularly low because most fell into the hands of people who had absolutely no interest in them, so they were discarded when empty. Only a small percentage of the "fancies" made before 1900 survives today. With "non-fancies" the survival rate is even lower, since they were the ones most frequently discarded. The following is a list of additional factors that will increase the value of a specimen.

Unusual Shape. Shape is the contour or physical outline of the bottle itself. Shapely bottles were produced for expensive products and gift giving. They are collected by topic, such as fish and animals, etc.

Unusual Size. Size is important if very large or very small.

Artistic Design. Design is not the same as shape. A bottle may be of standard shape and still be artistic, usually as a result of carrying a design raised on the surface (bas-relief). These ancient bottles were blown in a mold. They were used frequently for store goods in 19th century America, since they had a tendency to promote sales and the cost was no more than that required to make plain bottles. Once the mold was made, the bottles could be produced as inexpensively as non-decorative specimens. Labor costs in the 19th century were so low that the price of special molds could be easily absorbed. Spirits flasks are the most familiar 19th century bottles with artistic designs. Numerous motifs can be found. Political subjects are common, including portraits of Presidents. Railroad trains and animals are also frequently encountered. Like bottles of unusual shape, artistically designed bottles lend themselves to topical collecting.

Presence of Background Information. An old bottle that carries the name and place of business, or other details relating to the manufacturer will have greater appeal for hobbyists and carry a higher price than if such information were absent. A dated bottle will increase in value, as there are collectors who specialize in certain dates and will buy them regardless of the product or bottle shape, etc. Dates prior to 1900 are especially desirable. The mere presence of this information will not turn a fairly common item into an expensive collectible. Other factors must also be considered. The value will depend on the overall desirability of the bottle.

Presence of Printed Label. There are many collectors specializing in bottles with printed paper labels. Such bottles were manufactured in great quantities, but certain kinds, such as *very* old ones or those with highly decorative labels, are not plentiful. The artwork on early labels, especially on tonic bottles, is very original and appealing. The label should not be torn or stained. Fading is expected as an inevitable result of age.

Presence of Original Contents. An old bottle containing a portion of its original contents has a certain attraction for some collectors. It is questionable, however, whether any great premium should be given for such specimens; it is often impossible to know, with any degree of assurance, if the contents *are* original. By the same token, it is possible that evaporation may occur in time. The feature for which a premium was paid will, quite literally, go up in thin air.

BUYING

Collectible bottles are all around and they are just about endless. Bottles that interest collectors turn up in antiques shops, flea markets, antiques shows and conventions, swap meets, secondhand and salvage stores, pawn shops, Salvation Army thrift shops, in attics and under old front porches.

The beginning collector should realize that the source of a bottle does not contribute to, or detract from, its desirability and value. Once the bottle has left the place where it was found, it matters very little whether it was bought from a posh antiques shop, or was dug from a gravel heap. Many specimens in antiques shops were unearthed by bottle diggers.

The bottle itself is the important thing, not the source, nor the price. The retail selling prices for all the bottles listed in this book are the average sums for which they sell at the top of the market. There are numerous opportunities, however, to buy for much lower prices, as well as to obtain scarce and desirable bottles absolutely free, if the collector knows what to look for and where to find it. To most bottle collectors, the hunt and chase is as thrilling as the capture. The emotional stimulation and reward of buying a specimen off the counter, in a transaction as routine and uninspiring as buying groceries, does not equal that of making a "find." In this hobby, unlike many others, the collector *can* make "finds," and conceivably build a whole collection. Some bottle buffs own very impressive collections, and have never paid the full retail value for a single specimen.

Listed are some of the possible sources for bottles and the potential they hold.

Retail Dealers. This category includes all dealers who sell collectible bottles at or near the full market prices. Some of them specialize in bottles exclusively while others carry glassware with bottles comprising the majority of their stock. A number of dealers operate storefronts; others trade only by mail, through pricelists or advertisements in the various collectors' publications.

When buying from such a dealer, the collector will pay a price similar to that listed in this book. Dealers are well informed on the values of all kinds of collectible bottles and rarely make a significant mistake. If they come into possession of a bottle of whose value they are not sure, they put it aside rather than offering it for sale, until they can research the value. They will use this book, as well as the lists from other dealers, to arrive at a price. Even if they bought the bottle for $1, they will price it for $75, if this seems to be the fair retail value. They have a large clientele for bottles and have no trouble making sales at the full retail price.

These specialist dealers serve an important purpose. They offer a huge selection of bottles in an orderly manner. Often their price lists contain helpful background information and details. In buying from a specialist, the collector can be fairly confident that the specimen has been thoroughly examined, is authentic, and that the price has been set in accordance with any flaws or imperfections it may bear. These individuals are expert at noticing damage of all kinds, and they will not try to sell an inferior bottle for the price of a mint one. If a certain bottle is needed to fill out a collection, and time is of the essence, the collector should seek a specialist dealer.

To build an entire collection with purchases from specialists is not only expensive, but also boring. Lists can be obtained from such dealers that detail merchandise being offered in the bottle market. A stamped self-addressed envelope is all that need be sent in most cases. A charge of $1 is sometimes imposed, to defray preparation costs, but is usually refundable on the first purchase.

Specialist dealers purchase their bottles from the public, from auction sales, and often from other dealers. Like the more active private collectors, they keep their eyes and ears open for favorable opportunities. They visit the non-specialist antique dealers in the area to check on new arrivals. Bottles are also brought to them by diggers and collectors who have duplicates of which they wish to dispose, or who want to sell their entire collection. These dealers make some very favorable purchases by knowing exactly what the material is worth and having ready cash when opportunity knocks. Also among their sources of supply are the local auction sales. If the dealer handles rare and costly material in the $200-and-over category, he will undoubtedly be a subscriber to the catalogs of major auction houses, such as Sotheby/Parke-Bernet and Christie in New York, and will place bids on whatever appears to be suitable for his business. When a dealer bids in an auction, he is careful not to go as high as a private collector; he must take his operating expenses and margin of profit into account. Even when a dealer knows for certain that he can sell a bottle at the full retail price, he will not pay more than 60% of the value. A dealer will sometimes bid for a collector, as an agent, in an auction sale. The collector will pay the bill from the auction house, plus expenses and the dealer's service charge of approximately 10%.

Nonspecialist Dealers. All general antiques shops, which do not specialize in bottles, fall into this category. Many very fine bottles, as good as those handled by the specialists, pass through these shops. The difference is that their selections are not as comprehensive.

Because these dealers are not as knowledgeable as the specialists, they might incorrectly identify a bottle, or overlook damage. This can work to the collector's disadvantage, if he paid for a mint specimen and discovered it was flawed, or advantage, if he finds bottles selling well below the full retail level. The pricing policies of nonspecialist dealers vary. If the shop is large, prestigious, and the location is good, the dealer will ask the full retail price. On the other hand, the item may be offered at a discount if his clientele is not composed solely of bottle collectors. He must offer a bit of inducement to make a sale. If the full retail price is charged, odds are quite good that the bottle will sit for months, tying up capital, and end up being discounted anyway. Some dealers will place the full retail price on newly arrived merchandise, but bring it down quickly if there are no takers. The collector can decide whether he wants to buy at the first price, or gamble that the item will be available in the future at a discount. He should become familiar with the dealer's pricing policies and other methods of doing business.

Often the nonspecialist dealers do not have a great deal of reference material on hand. They will have one or two general price guides on antiques which they use in an effort to price everything. If the specific item does not appear in the book, they will try to estimate a price by adding a percentage on to the cost. If they buy a certain bottle for $5 and are not aware of the retail value, they may ask $10 for it. A specialist may be selling the same bottle for $7.50 or as much as $50. If the collector is knowledgeable of market values, he will be able to avoid the overpriced items offered by non-specialist dealers, and take advantage of the opportunities to pick up underpriced merchandise.

Auction Sales. Bottles come up for sale in almost every auction of antiques and general estate contents. Some collectors do a great deal of buying at auction. This is especially suitable if several good auction houses are within driving distance. Making absentee purchases of bottles by auction is a bit risky, because the collector does not have the opportunity to examine the material that the auctioneer describes briefly without taking note of the item's physical condition or other details of collector interest. This list is prepared for the bidders who attend the sale so that they can keep track of the various lots. Frequently, the auctioneer is not a bottle authority and cannot even identify the specimens being sold; he merely lists them as "Lot 121—6 flasks." It may be possible to obtain additional information by calling or writing the auctioneer.

When bidding at a major sale, whether in person or as an absentee, the collector is in competition with hundreds of other collectors, dealers, museums, etc. It is rarely possible to get an item for a bargain price. At a small sale, such as a country auction, where there are no bottle people in attendance, he can just about name his price on whatever he choses to purchase. It is certainly worth attending any sales in the area, especially if the announcement does not mention bottles. Chances are dealers who specialize in bottles are not likely to be in attendance.

A collector should not be afraid to bid against dealers. Dealers may have plenty of cash, but they will not bid up to the full retail price or anywhere near it. They are looking to buy only those items for which they can get a favorable price and make a reasonable profit.

By attending the presale exhibition, a collector can critically examine the bottles for sale, checking for flaws, signs of repair, or missing components. Observations should be noted on the auction list, not committed to memory. It is wise to jot down the highest bid for each desired bottle to insure a wise purchase.

Secondary Sources. Secondhand shops, salvage stores, flea markets, thrift stores, etc. are often located near other shops which carry old, used and other miscellaneous merchandise of all kinds. Wherever miscellaneous household items are found, so are bottles. The vast majority of what they will have is not in the collectible category, but when they do turn up at these sources, prices are much less than those at an antique shop or auction. These shops must be visited frequently as different merchandise arrives daily. The manager should know which days have the heaviest arrival of material. The specific items a collector wishes to buy should never be mentioned to the manager, as this may lead to a higher price. A collector must rely on his own knowledge of items and their value and not take any written materials along when he shops.

Other Collectors. There are other collectors and bottle clubs that hold swap meets from which bottles can be obtained. Many collectors, especially those who go digging have duplicate or unwanted bottles that they are willing to sell or trade. When buying from another collector, the chances are very good that he knows the exact retail value of the bottles he has. He may give you a substantial break compared to the price charged by a dealer in a shop. A fair price when buying from a private collector is 80% of the full retail value.

The way to get bargains is to know more about the value of bottle than the person selling it. As we pointed out, you will often be in a position of buying a bottle from a dealer (at a flea market, garage sale, junkshop, etc.) who knows absolutely nothing about the bottle or its value. To him, it's just an old bottle and he wants to sell it for as much as he can get. You can end up paying more than you need to in these situations. Never let on that you're a collector. Wear old clothes. Learn to act dumb. The seller may try to get an opinion from you on the bottle's value, directly or indirectly. He may say for example, "That sure is an old one, isn't it?," or "You don't see many like them," or "You must be a collector, to have picked that one out." All of these queries can be effectively dodged. You should have some useful lines up your own sleeve, such as "Hope this one is cheap," "This ought to make a good present for my mother-in-law—I don't want to spend much on her," and "My friend paid $2.50 for one like this—hope you aren't charging that much." Never admit to *liking* the bottle you're about to buy. Never admit to knowing anything about it—or even caring. If the seller should mention something about its age or beauty or anything that would contribute to the price, just brush aside such comments with a casual, "Well, I wouldn't know, and since I'm only going to use it for varnish it doesn't make much difference. Varnish keeps a lot better in glass, you know . . ." In other words, you meet every thrust with a parry. This may be a little damaging to the ego, when you know the complete history of that bottle and could enrapture the seller with half an hour's worth of conversation about it. But it's very healthy on the wallet.

CONDUCTING A DIG

Prospecting for bottles has become one of the favorite pastimes for collectors. Old and collectible bottles are buried in all parts of the country. There is no possible way to imagine the wealth of bottles that is waiting for the enthusiastic prospector.

Bottles are buried along with the discards of past generations. What was junk at one time has become today's treasure. This is true of many old bottles which have often been preserved much better underground than can be imagined. Many bottles were thrown away because they were broken, but some went into the ground whole and stayed that way. The soft earth and sand acted as a cushioning agent to protect them against breakage.

Bringing the science of archaeology to the hobby of bottle collecting represents a big advance. Through the efforts of diggers, many historically and artistically important bottles are coming to light, and valuable information is being learned about the history of bottlemaking in this country.

Although these amateur digs have been going on in earnest for more than a decade, the surface has only been scratched. More bottles have yet to be found, and the odds are quite good that the quest will never end. Since bottles are still being discarded, future generations will probably be digging the ones thrown away today. There is a better chance of finding interesting bottles now than for the prospector of 100 years ago. Trash disposal methods were not sophisticated in the 19th and early 20th centuries. Many bottles that would be destroyed today laid for decades in city dumps.

How *did* so many old bottles succeed in being preserved beneath the earth? Ancient artifacts from the Greek, Roman, Egyptian and other ancient civilizations are being found in the Old World today. They were preserved as the result of cities being abandoned and new cities growing up atop the old ones. With the passage of centuries, layers of soil and sand covered them with the help of the wind, rain, and other actions of nature. Man covered them further with cobblestones and then cement.

The same process has occurred in the United States, but on a smaller scale. Instead of 2,000 years, the time span has been no more than a hundred years. A bottle may be thrown in a ditch and, in time, the ditch becomes partially filled with sand and covers the bottle. Bottles left on beaches are buried as each incoming tide deposits sand and silt. Bottles buried in this manner come under the heading of "accidental burials."

Street paving is an example of an "intentional burial." When a dirt road is being paved, no effort is made to remove any articles mixed in the soil. As bottles are often discarded along roadways, any dirt road is sure to have many of them. In paving the road, bottles and other possible collectors' items are sealed up as if in a tomb. Opportunities to explore sites of this kind occur when the old pavement, which may be forty to fifty years old, is being broken up to lay pipelines or for other maintenance work. Many bottles may be uncovered and are free for the taking; therefore, a chance to check out a site of this type should never be missed.

Sometimes, town dumps have been covered over to become parks or playgrounds. These present golden opportunities. A bit more work on a site of this nature may be necessary, but the results are usually well worth the effort. If the town is old, quite likely the dump has been there for many years. The practice of having town or city dumps goes all the way back to colonial times before the Revolution. Nearly all the junk thrown in them would be collectors' items today. The only problem is that a lot of old dumps were leveled—the contents were taken away and dumped in the ocean or used elsewhere for landfill—before converting the site to its present use. Those that were not leveled were paved with concrete, putting a rather formidable obstacle before the collector. Thorough investigation, however, will help to locate an old dump suitable for digging.

Finding Sites. It is not profitable to attempt random digging. To go into a field and dig, on the chance that bottles may be lying beneath the surface, is an extremely hit and miss affair. Sites must be investigated thoroughly before any actual spadework is done. The best sites are not necessarily those that have already been dug. The success or failure of a "dig" will depend mostly on the decision of where to dig.

A bottle collector who has conducted a successful dig is reluctant to reveal the exact location of his finds. He will not supply specific information on finding the site, because each digger considers his sites personal property. He wishes to rework the site without competition from others. This is understandable since a fertile site may not be located until weeks or months of probing have been completed.

The following suggestions may prove to be helpful in finding a fruitful digging site. First of all, the collector must learn as much as possible about the area in which he lives. Libraries have books on the history of each town, county, or surrounding counties. Old town directories will point out where the business districts used to be. Maps of what the area looked like in the past are available and may help to locate the sites of abandoned dumps. People who have lived in the town for half a century or more should certainly have some recollections that will be helpful. If the town is a big city like New York or Chicago, most of the streets have been paved over for as far back as anyone can remember; but there may be outlying areas of the town, such as the Bronx in New York, which still have vacant lots and dumps.

Some sites may be located by walking or driving through a town. Fairgrounds or reunion grounds are likely to be worthwhile places to investigate further. The areas around ballparks and sandlots are also particularly good, especially if the town is old and these sites have been in use for a long time. Generations of people brought bottles to these places, or purchased them on the spot, and discarded them nearby. Beaches are particularly fertile sites for bottle digging. People have been bringing beverage bottles to beaches for well over 100 years. Odd to say, but the litterbug of yesteryear performed a great service for the collector of today. If all garbage down through the ages had been properly disposed of, not much would remain today in the way of collectors' items.

There are many other types of locations worth exploring. Old abandoned mine shafts have yielded great quantities of collectible bottles.

The miners carelessly left bottles for decades, and residents of the area used the mines for pitching in their trash. Extreme care must be taken when exploring sites such as these. This type of exploration is not recommended unless the collector has an expert knowledge of caves.

Ghost towns are high on the list of localities with good potential. The only difficulty is that most of them have been heavily worked over by collectors within recent years and nearly everything worthwhile has been taken. Quite possibly, however, the collectors visiting that site took away only surface material, and did not bother to dig. One of the best places to poke around in a ghost town is the saloon area, where bottles will most likely be found. Not to be overlooked are cabins, general stores, railway stations, and carriage depots.

Frequently old bottles are found beside houses, either a few feet under the lawn's surface or beneath porches. It was a common habit in the Midwest during the late 19th and early 20th centuries for people to dispose of bottles by placing them beneath the front porch. Valuable bottles, often by the dozens, have been discovered underneath porches in Illinois, Wisconsin, Minnesota and other states of that region. It would be smart to check beneath the porch of *any* house, regardless of location, that appears to be at least seventy-five to one hundred years old. The bottles found in this fashion will be from soft drinks, as the beverage was consumed on the porch and the bottle stashed under it when empty. If any are pre-1920 Coke bottles, a fine "strike" has been made.

Prospecting Equipment. A metal detector is a valuable tool for the bottle prospector. Although it will not react to the bottles themselves, it will locate areas where metal objects are buried. Wherever metal objects have been discarded or lost, bottles can often be found. Although a metal detector may cost anywhere from $200 to $300, none of the other equipment needed in bottle digging is very expensive. Following is a list of the essentials plus some extras that are very useful to have along. Some bottle diggers use nothing but a shovel, while others have extensive equipment. How thoroughly a prospective wishes to outfit himself is a matter of personal choice.

Shovel
Potato Rake (3 or 4 prong)
Small short-handled rake (3 prongs)
Thin steel probing rod
Hunting knife
Hedge shears for cutting roots that get in the way of digging
Bow saw for cutting thicker roots
Tablespoon

Newspaper for wrapping specimens
Hard bristle brush
Canvas sack or wicker basket for carrying specimens
Pad and pencil for making notes and drawing maps

Depending on the terrain, it may be necessary to take along insect repellent, a snakebite kit, and a general first-aid kit.

Here are a few tips on personal safety: heavy-duty canvas type gloves must be worn at all times. They may take getting used to when picking things up, but the protection is well worth the inconvenience. Even with gloves, it is not a good idea to reach under rocks or into holes in the ground where there may be broken glass, wasps, or other animals who do not appreciate the intrusion. Instead, use one of the tools to probe in an area that cannot be seen. Sturdy shoes are also essential. If the area might be inhabited by snakes, tall boots are in order, not to mention rugged clothing.

The prospector must never overestimate his ability to climb, leap, swim, or survive in the wilds. The experienced collector never takes any unnecessary chances. Whenever possible, he should form a digging party rather than going out alone, especially when going into woods, deserts, or other unpopulated areas. If he must go alone, he should leave word with someone as to his whereabouts and what time he should be home. When arriving at the digging site, he should take note of the location of the nearest phone.

When digging begins, the prospector starts by clearing away several shovelfuls of earth at a given spot. If no bottles appear, but other man-made relics turn up, further digging should be carried out at that spot; not only deeper into the ground, but in a wider area. Where there are man-made relics of fairly substantial age, there are usually bottles. If nothing turns up within one-and-a-half feet, it is time to move to another spot. The perimeter of the area should be covered first and then work toward the center. It may be necessary to make many test diggings at a site before anything is found, or until it is concluded that the site will be unproductive. Some sites that should contain bottles do not. It is also possible that the sites may have been well researched and pinpointed accurately; but digging may be just thirty or forty yards from where the bottles are located. An enthusiast never becomes discouraged. Even professional archaeologists come up empty-handed.

When a bottle is found, **digging must stop!** The bottle must be lifted out gently by hand. If the bottle is embedded in the soil, the surrounding dirt must be removed bit by bit, using the hands or a small tool, such as a spoon, until the bottle is loosened. In dry soil, a brush sometimes does the trick. The bottle must be handled gingerly since it will be fragile when first exposed to air and sunlight after its many years of burial. It should be wrapped in paper and placed aside. Cleaning of the specimen should never be attempted in the field. It is unusual for a single old bottle to turn up at a site, so when one has been found, there are probably more. Unless absolutely certain that a bottle is worthless, all specimens should be taken home.

BOTTLE CARE

Compared to many other kinds of collectors' items, bottles require very little care and upkeep. Once the hobbyist has learned to clean his bottles properly and safely, he will have few maintenance problems. Storage and display problems are minimal because bottles are not damaged by sunlight, moisture, or insects.

How to Clean Bottles. There is a difference of opinion among collectors as to which is the best technique for cleaning bottles. While some will use abrasives to get their bottles as clean and shiny as when new, others object to harsh cleaning procedures and would rather let some signs of age remain. It should be noted, however, that the general consensus of opinion is that patina (acquired layers of grime) does *not* contribute to desirability. If the collector does not like the looks of it, he need not be concerned about reducing a specimen's value by removing it.

Bottles bought from an antique dealer will usually have already been cleaned in order to enhance their sales potential. Dealers may do a rather slapdash job, however, and the specimen may need to be recleaned before it can be placed in a collection. In the case of freshly dug bottles, the cleaning task can be challenging.

Cleaning approaches must be varied in some cases. If a bottle is enameled, or surface painted, extreme care must be taken not to remove any of the enamel. The same is true of bottles with paper labels. Any damage to the label will reduce the bottle's value. Leaving a little dirt is preferable to damaging the label. If immersed in water, the label will dry out; but solvents ought to be avoided, as well as any rubbing or scrubbing across the label. Some collectors prefer to merely wipe such specimens with rubbing alcohol on a soft cloth, taking care not to touch the label. Wringing out the cloth will prevent any dripping or splashing. This procedure should be repeated several times, allowing the bottle to dry thoroughly between treatments.

Fortunately, most collectible bottles are not enameled and have no label. More rigorous cleaning techniques can be used, but some restraint must still be exercised. Overly enthusiastic cleaning efforts can result in broken bottles.

When a freshly dug bottle has been brought in from the field, the surface condition is likely to be so miserable that it offers very little encouragement of ever being successfully cleaned. Most bottles will clean up well with a bit of patience and hard work. The first step is to remove loose surface particles (sand, small stones, etc.) with a brush. An artist's brush is good for this kind of job. The bottle should soak in lukewarm water for a while to remove surface dirt.

To soften and break down the tough impacted grime, the bottle must soak in something stronger than plain water. A solution of two tablespoons of bleach in a gallon of lukewarm water can be used. It must be stirred thoroughly before introducing the bottle; otherwise, damage could result. Straight ammonia is also a possibility if there is good ventilation in the room. Kerosene is recommended by some collectors. Bottles should never be put into hot or boiling liquid as they could crack. The length of soaking time will depend on how dirty the specimen is, and how good a job the solvent is doing. A badly caked specimen may need to soak for a week or longer. It will be much more difficult to clean the inside of a bottle. The outside may be spotless, but the bottle may still need to soak for several days. Periodic checks must be made and the solution changed from time to time.

Bottles can, of course, be cleaned with steel wool or a stiff brush. The bottle should be soaked in one of the solutions mentioned above for a couple of hours before scrubbing. It may be necessary to soak it again afterwards and repeat this procedure several times before satisfactory results are achieved.

When the bottle has gotten as clean as can reasonably be expected, it should be soaked again in lukewarm water for a few hours to remove any traces of the cleaning agent. All that remains then is to dry the bottle, which can be done with a rag or by allowing it to air-dry. The bottle can be buffed with oil to give the glass a shinier appearance. This will be successful only if the bottle came very clean.

If minor traces of dirt or grime remain after cleaning, the collector need not worry. It is better to live with a little dirt than to destroy the bottle in an effort to clean it.

How to Display Bottles. The chief consideration in display is to prevent breakage while allowing the specimens to be viewed and handled. The collector may wish to keep his bottles in a cabinet, on wall shelving, or distributed at random about the house to provide decorative touches. While certainly appealing, the last approach tends to be riskier. When a collection is not grouped together in one place or one part of the house, it becomes more difficult to guard against accident. This is especially true if pets or small children are around.

When a collection is within a cabinet or on shelves, it is out of harm's way.

Almost any kind of cabinet is suitable for a bottle collection. Choice will depend on personal taste, room decor, size of the collection, and the cost of the unit. An ordinary bookcase with glass doors or grillwork will do, *if* it has adjustable shelves and is not too small. A case with wooden sides will not provide as much visibility or light penetration to the inside. With very little expense and trouble, however, a lighting fixture can be installed inside. Cabinets with glass sides are ideal for displaying bottles, and can often be picked up at antiques shops or from used furniture dealers.

The usual practice in stocking a display cabinet is according to size —the largest bottles on the bottom shelf, the smallest ones on top. This not only gives a better sense of proportion, but also places the smallest specimens at eye level where their details can be closely examined. Very large specimens can be placed atop the cabinet to provide aesthetic balance. If the collection consists of different kinds of bottles, one shelf can be used for flasks, another for milk bottles, and so forth.

It is important not to overcrowd the shelves by not standing bottles in front of one another. Visibility is reduced and accidents may occur when removing or replacing a specimen. A unit should be large enough to accommodate a growing collection. Any remaining space can always be used for books or curios.

How to Store Bottles. Occasionally bottles may have to be stored rather than displayed. This happens when a collection exceeds the available display space, or when a collector is moving to a new residence. There is no real danger of breakage if reasonable care is exercised. Each bottle should be wrapped in layers of newspaper, and each package taped securely. Extra protection must be given to bottles of unusual shape or with small, delicate components. Placing plenty of crumpled newspaper on the bottom of a sturdy carton and between each bottle will prevent them from knocking against each other. The largest or heaviest bottles must be on the bottom and the lighter ones on top.

This approach, however, is *not suitable* for mailing. Extra protection must be provided when bottles are to be mailed or sent by some other kind of carrier. Each package intended for shipment should contain no more than one bottle. A double carton (one inside the other) should be cushioned with packing material. The bottle should be wrapped and packed securely in the inner carton. The outer carton must be well sealed and tied with strong twine. The address is written directly on the carton, because a label could become detached.

Keeping a Collection Record. A hobbyist should begin to keep a record of his collection as soon as possible. Delay can only mean that the necessary information will be forgotten. A collection record can be kept on index cards, using one card for each specimen. The card identifies the specimen and gives details as to how and when it was obtained. It should include the dealer's name and the purchase price, or the location and date if the specimen was found while digging. Each bottle can also be assigned a number for cataloging. Such a record is vital for insurance purposes, and will prove enormously useful and informative.

INVESTING

Collectible bottles definitely have investment potential. In the past two years, the retail values of some bottles have increased twofold or more. Even those investors who paid full retail value at the peak of the bottle market in 1979 would profit by selling their bottles today. When compared to the number of investors in stamps, coins and some other collectibles, there is little doubt that the number of investors and speculators will grow as the general public becomes more aware of the increased prices of certain collectible bottles.

Bottle collecting is obviously not a fad. This hobby has established definite patterns of activity and is growing steadily. The number of bottle collectors, dealers, and auction sales increases each year. While some specimens are found by digging, the majority of them are purchased from dealers or through auction sales. As the demand increases for desirable bottles, prices are forced upward. Many bottles that might have been considered expensive at $10 in 1970 are eagerly purchased today for $100 or more. This situation shows every indication of continuing in the future. The prices of today will seem just as inexpensive in 1991 as those of 1970 seem now.

Anyone interested in buying bottles for investment should study the market. An investor must learn to interpret trends and do a bit of forecasting. Not all bottles advance in value at the same rate. Those showing the best gains in the past will not necessarily score well in the future. A smart investor will buy the underpublicized, underpriced bottles in any given group, rather than put his money into those which have already attained high price levels. As the star items in each category become too expensive for the average hobbyists, more and more investors will be turning their attention to bottles that are not heavily collected at the moment.

It would be rash to assume that a certain bottle whose price advanced 200% in the past five years will gain another 200% in the next five. It rarely works that way, for various reasons. Coke bottles "shot up" in the 1960's because they were undercollected and underpriced before then. They were selling for much less than their projected value. Then when the wave of Coke collecting came around 1962, prices jumped. By the early 1970's collectors demand was as strong as it had been in the early sixties. As collectors who had "bought cheap" cashed in their holdings, more and more Coke bottles began to flood the market. This increase in supply, as well as demand, helped to keep prices from soaring any higher. Today, Coke bottle prices are just as high as ever, but they are not likely to skyrocket again. There are not enough new Coke collectors to create another rush on the market; only enough to push prices up approximately 10% a year. Anyone investing in Coke bottles today can not hope to do as well as if he had been buying the same bottles in 1960 or earlier.

Beer bottles appear to be underpriced at the moment. Many old specimens can be picked up for under $5. This is because "beer collectors" prefer cans to bottles, since the value of cans has surpassed that of bottles. Other soft drink bottles have already been affected by the Coke boom and it is probable that their values will increase further in the years to come.

As far as other types of bottles are concerned, early noncommemorative figurals are a good bet for price increases. Not too many of them are around, and they seldom turn up at "digs." The most collectible milk bottles are those of the small manufacturers—not those of the large companies such as Borden or Sheffield. They should be pre-1940 and in mint condition. Ink bottles have a good steady market, but are not an attractive investment item at the moment. Early bitters bottles are "blue chips" since they hold their value as well as any collectors' item; however, whether any profit can be made by investing in them, now that prices are high, is questionable. Some speculation might be worthwhile in the inexpensive ($10–20) machine-made bitters bottles. Once shunned by collectors, these bottles have acquired a following now that the rarer bitters bottles are costly and beyond the budgets of most buyers.

The more popular groups of non-antique bottles, such as Avon, Luxardo and the rest, have been collected at the top market for many years. Somewhat undercollected have been Kikukawa and Kamotsuru (Japanese) bottles, Garnie, Bardi, and Bralatta, just to name a few.

SELLING

Undoubtedly every collector will have the occasion to sell all or part of his bottle collection. The need to sell often arises when a collector changes direction and decides to specialize in a group of bottles different than those he had been buying. All collectible bottles are saleable. A profit can be made on most, depending on how they were acquired and the length of time they have been owned.

A collector must think before he sells. If space is not a problem or cash is not needed immediately, he might be better off to hold on to his bottles for a while longer. If they were purchased recently at full retail value, either from a specialist dealer or at a highly competitive auction sale, the odds are against recouping the full amount of the investment. By checking future editions of this book, as well as price lists and catalogues from dealers, the collector can evaluate the market and sell when the values have advanced far enough for him to break even. There is absolutely no reason for the seller to take a loss. Bottles are collectors' items of established growth and their potential value *will* eventually rise.

There are many different methods of selling. The inexperienced or uninformed seller may take his bottles to a local antiques shop and accept whatever is offered. In addition to neighborhood antiques shops, there are specialist dealers, auctions, and other collectors.

Selling to a Dealer. A specialist dealer will generally give a higher price than a general antique dealer. Since he deals with customers looking specifically for bottles, he can afford to invest more money in his purchases. He knows just how much he can get for a particular bottle and roughly how long it will take to sell. Usually he will not object to taking some duplicate specimens of scarce bottles, but will not accept an unlimited number of the same item.

Except in rare cases, a specialist dealer sells his bottles at 100% of the retail value. Naturally he tries to obtain his merchandise at the lowest possible prices, since he must pay shop rent, utilities, employee salaries, etc., in addition to turning a reasonable profit. The best prices are received when the seller exhibits his knowledge of the material. The dealer will often ask him to name a price so he must know the current market value of the item. Bargaining should begin at 80% of the retail value. An offer of 60% is considered quite fair and is generally the best that can be expected. Sometimes the offer may be lower if the dealer does not have the clientele interested in that particular item.

Specialists have fairly high standards in the matter of condition. They are not likely to buy any damaged or repaired bottles, and in the case of inexpensive bottles, they may not want any in less than mint condition. Dealers are constantly bombarded with bottle offers and they have to be selective in what they buy; otherwise, their shops would become junkpiles.

Non-specialist dealers might be more flexible on condition, but will probably pay much less for what they buy. They pay on the basis of what they can safely afford to invest. A non-specialist may have very few customers for bottles. Even if an item is desirable, he may hesitate to buy, because he does not know how long it will take to sell. Most often he will not pay more than 40% of the retail value.

If there are no specialist dealers in a certain area, the seller can check the classified phone directories of other surrounding communities. A list of names and addresses of bottle dealers, such as the one in the back of this book, can be found in the hobby magazines and newspapers. Even with the task of packing and the expense of postage, the seller may still be farther ahead by not selling to a local non-specialist.

Selling by Auction. Auction selling is unpredictable. Unless the sale is being conducted with reserves (minimum selling prices), there is no way to guard against disappointing, or sometimes disastrous, prices. The risks can be minimized somewhat if the collection is consigned to an auctioneer who handles glassware regularly, and has an established reputation for selling collectible bottles. The results of his past sales will indicate to the seller how his own bottles will fare.

Auctioneers who handle only estate sales are not suitable for selling bottles. One must be found who holds sales of antiques. The odds are quite good that his sales are composed of material put up by many different consignors. He will undoubtedly agree to include, in one of his future auctions, any collection consisting of bottles in the moderate to high price range. It may be difficult to locate an auctioneer willing to sell items that are in the low price category. Auctioneers are paid on commission according to the prices realized by each lot. They do not want to handle inexpensive material because it means little or no profit for them.

Of course, a valuable collection should be consigned to one of the major fine-art auctioneers, such as Sotheby/Parke-Bernet which has offices in New York and Los Angeles. This type of firm allows the collector to place reserves on his consigned items—price, of course, must be agreeable to both parties. They produce lavishly illustrated catalogues that afford the material the best possible chance of selling at a high price.

Selling to Another Collector. Although the best prices are obtained by selling to another collector, the seller should not expect to receive full retail value. If a collector wants to pay top dollar, he will buy from a specialist dealer. Selling to a collector at 80% of the value is far more lucrative than selling to a dealer who has to make a profit. Sometimes collectors can be contacted by taking out ads in the bottle publications, in the general hobby press, or even in the classified section of the local newspaper. The seller will then be contacted by only those collectors interested in his types of bottles.

BOTTLE AGE

Free Blown Bottles. B.C. to 1860—some are still free blown today.

Pontil. 1618–1866; also some modern hand blown bottles.

Raised Letters. 1790 to date.

Three Part Mold. 1806–1889.

Amethyst or Sun Colored Glass. 1800 to date.

Sheared Lip. 1800–1830 (the top has been sheared off).

Machine-Made Bottles. 1903 to date (Mold Line runs from base through the top).

Black or Dark Olive Green Glass. 1700–1880 approx.

Blob Top. thick rounded lip, on most soda and mineral water bottles.

Crown Cap or Top. 1895 to date.

BOTTLE AGE AS DETERMINED BY MOLD LINE

—1800+   —1880+   —1890+   —1903+   1910 To Date

BOTTLE SHAPES

Cone Ink

Glue

8-sided Conical

Conical

Cylindrical

Old Beer

New Beer

Old Soda

New Soda

Shoe Polish

Hutchinson

Tear Drop

Round Bottom

Old Whiskey

New Whisk

Broken Pontil

Sheared Lip (1800's)

18 "Seal"

Graphite Pontil

2 Part Mold

3 Part Mold

Side Mold

Lady Leg Neck

Old Medicine

New Medicine

Free Blown

**Medicine or
Bitters, label**

Ten Pin

Fire Extinguisher

Squat or Onion

Scroll

Wide Mouth Case Bottle

TRADEMARKS

FOREIGN

A in a Circle: Alembic Glass, Industries Bangalore, India.

Big A in Center of it GM: Australian Glass Mfg. Co. Kilkenny So. Australia.

A.B.C.: Albion Bottle Co. Ltd., Oldbury, Nr. Birmingham, England.

A.G.W.: Alloa Glass Limited, Alloa, Scotland.

A G B Co: Albion Glass Bottle Co., England, trademark is found under Lea & Perrins, circa 1880 to 1900.

AVH-A.: Van Hoboken & Co., Rotterdam, The Netherlands, 1800–1898.

B & Co. L: Bagley & Co. Ltd. Est. 1832 still operating (England).

Beaver: Beaver Flint Glass Co., Toronto, Ontario, Canada, circa 1897 to 1920.

Bottle in Frame: Veb Glasvoerk Drebkau Drebkau, N.L. Germany.

Crown with 3 Dots: Crown Glass, Waterloo, N.S. Wales.

Crown with Figure of a Crown: Excelsior Glass Co., St. Johns, Quebec and later Diamond Glass Co., Montreal, Quebec, Canada, circa 1879 to 1913.

CS & Co.: —Cannington, Shaw & Co., St. Helens, England, circa 1872 to 1916.

D in Center of a Diamond: Cominion Glass Co., Montreal, Que.

D.B.: in a book frame, Dale Brown & Co., Ltd., Mesborough, Yorks, England.

Excelsior: Excelsior Glass Co., St. John, Quebec, Canada, 1878–1883.

Fish: Veb Glasvoerk Stralau, Berlin.

Hamilton: Hamilton Glass Works, Hamilton, Ontario, Canada, 1865–1872.

Hat: Brougba, (Bulgaria).

HH: Werk Hermannshutte, Czechoslovakia.

Hunyadi Janos: Andreas Saxlehner, Buda-Pesth, Austria-Hungary, circa 1863 to 1900.

IYGE: all in a circle, The Irish Glass Bottle, Ltd., Dublin.

KH: Kastrupog Holmeqaads, Copenhagen.

L.: on a bell, Lambert S.A. (Belgium).

LIP: Lea & Perrins, London, England, 1880–1900.

LS: in a circle, Lax & Shaw, Ltd. Leeds, York, England.

M: in a circle, cristales Mexicanos, Monterey, Mexico.

N: in a diamond, Tippon Glass Co., Ltd. Tokyo, Japan.

NAGC: North American Glass Co., Montreal, Quebec, Canada, 1883–1890.

PG: Verreries De Puy De Dome, S.A. Paris.

R: Louit Freres & Co., France, circa 1870 to 1890.

S: in a circle, Vetreria Savonese. A. Voglienzone, S.A. Milano, Italy.

S.A.V.A.: all in a circle, Asmara, Ethipia.

S & M: Sykes & Macvey, Castleford, England, 1860–1888.

T: in a circle, Tokyo Seibin Co., Ltd. Tokyo, Japan.

vFo: Vidreria Ind. Figuerras Oliveiras (Brazil).

VT: Ve-Tri S.p.a., Vetrerie Triventa Vicenza, Italy.

VX: Usine de Vauxrot, France.

WECK: in a frame, Weck Glaswerk G. mb.H, ofligen, in Bonn.

Y: in a circle, Etairia Lipasmaton, Athens, Greece.

U.S.

The words and letters in bold are only a representation or brief description of the trademark as it appeared on a bottle. This is followed by the complete name and location of the company and the approximate period of time in which the trademark was in use.

A: John Agnew & Son, Pittsburgh, PA, 1854–1866.

A in a Circle: American Glass Works, Richmond, VA and Paden City, WV, circa 1909 to 1936.

A in a Circle: Armstrong Cork Co., Glass Division, Lancaster, PA, 1938–1968.

A & B Together (AB): Adolphus Busch Glass Manufacturing Co., Belleville, IL and St. Louis, MO, circa 1904 to 1907.

A B Co.: American Bottle Co., Chicago, IL, 1905–1930.

A B G M Co.: Adolphus Busch Glass Manufacturing Co, Bellville, IL and St. Louis, MO, circa 1886 to 1928.

A & Co.: John Agnew & Co., Pittsburgh, PA, Indian Queen, Ear of Corn and other flasks, circa 1854 to 1892.

A C M E: Acme Glass Co., Olean, NY, circa 1920 to 1930.

A & D H C: A. & D.H. Chambers, Pittsburgh, PA, Union flasks, circa 1842 to 1886.

AGEE and Agee in Script: Hazel Atlas Glass Co., Wheeling, WV, circa 1921 to 1925.

A.G.W. Co.: American Glass Works Ltd., 1880 to 1905.

AGW: American Glass Works, circa 1880.

Anchor Figure with H in Center: Anchor Hocking Glass Corp., Lancaster, OH, circa 1955.

A.R.S.: A.R. Samuels Glass Co., Philadelphia, PA, circa 1855 to 1872.

A S F W W Va.: A.S. Frank Glass Co., Wellsburg, WV, circa 1859.

ATLAS: Atlas Glass Co., Washington, PA, and later Hazel Atlas Glass Co., 1896–1965.

AVH: A. Van Hoboken & Co., Rotterdam, The Netherlands, 1800–1898.

Ball and Ball in Script: Ball Bros. Glass Manufacturing Co., Muncie, IN and later Ball Corp., 1887–1973.

Bernardin in Script: W.J. Latchford Glass Co., Los Angeles, CA, circa 1932 to 1938.

The Best: Gillender & Sons, Philadelphia, PA, circa 1867 to 1870.

B F B Co.: Bell Fruit Bottle Co., Fairmount, IN, circa 1910.

B.G. Co.: Belleville Glass Co. IL, circa 1882.

Bishop's: Bishop & Co., San Diego and Los Angeles, CA, 1890 to 1920.

B K: Benedict Kimber, Bridgeport and Brownsville, PA, circa 1822 to 1840.

Boyds in Script: Illinois Glass Co., Alton, IL, circa 1900 to 1930.

Brelle (in Script) Jar: Brelle Fruit Jar Manufacturing Co., San Jose, CA, circa 1912 to 1916.

Brilliantine: Jefferis Glass Co., Fairton, NJ and Rochester, PA, circa 1900 to 1905.

C in a Circle: Chattanooga Bottle & Glass Co. and later Chattanooga Glass Co., since 1927.

C in a Square: Crystal Glass Co., Los Angeles, CA, circa 1921 to 1929.

C in a Star: Star City Glass Co., Star City, WV, since 1949.

Canton Domestic Fruit Jar: Canton Glass Co., Canton, OH, circa 1890 to 1904.

C & Co. or C Co.: Cunninghams & Co., Pittsburgh, PA, 1880–1907.

CCCo: C. Conrad & Co. (Beer) 1878–1883.

C.V. Co. No. 1 & No. 2: Milwaukee, Wis. 1880–1881.

C C Co.: Carl Conrad & Co., St. Louis, MO, 1876–1883.

C C G Co.: Cream City Glass Co., Milwaukee, WI, 1888–1893.

C.F.C.A.: California Fruit Canners Association, Sacramento, CA, circa 1899 to 1916.

C G M Co.: Campbell Glass Manufacturing Co., West Berkeley, CA, 1885.

C G W: Campbell Glass Works, West Berkeley, CA, 1884–1885.

C & H: Coffin & Hay, Winslow, NJ, circa 1838 to 1842.

C L G Co.: Carr-Lowrey Glass Co., Baltimore, MD, circa 1889 to 1920.

Clyde, N.Y.: Clyde Glass Works, Clyde, N.Y, circa 1870 to 1882.

The Clyde in Script: Clyde Glass Works, Clyde, N.Y, circa 1895.

C Milw: Chase Valley Glass Co., Milwaukee, WI, circa 1880.

Cohansey: Cohansey Glass Manufacturing Co., Philadelphia, PA, 1870–1900.

CS & Co.: Cannington, Shaw & Co., St. Helens, England, circa 1872 to 1916.

DB: Du Bois Brewing Co., Pittsburgh, PA, circa 1918.

Dexter: Franklin Flint Glass Works, Philadelphia, PA, circa 1861 to 1880.

Diamond: (plain) Diamond Glass Co. since 1924.

The Dictator: William McCully & Co., Pittsburgh, PA, circa 1855 to 1869.

Dictator: same as above only circa 1869 to 1885.

D & O: Cumberland Glass Mfg. Co., Bridgeton, NJ, circa 1890 to 1900.

D O C: D.O. Cunningham Glass Co., Pittsburgh, PA, circa 1883 to 1937.

D S G Co.: De Steiger Glass Co., LaSalle, IL, circa 1867 to 1896.

Duffield: Duffield, Parke & Co., Detroit, MI, 1866–1875.

Dyottsville: Dyottsville Glass Works, Philadelphia, PA, 1833–1923.

Economy (in Script) Trade Mark: Kerr Glass Manufacturing Co., Portland, OR, 1903–1912.

Electric Trade Mark in Script: Gayner Glass Works, Salem, NJ, circa 1910.

Electric Trade Mark: same as above only circa 1900 to 1910.

Erd & Co., E R Durkee: E.R. Durkee & Co., New York, NY, post-1874.

E R Durkee & Co: same as above only circa 1850 to 1860.

Eureka 17: Eurkee Jar Co., Dunbar, WV, circa 1864.

Eureka in Script: same as above only 1900–1910.

Everlasting (in Script) Jar: Illinois Pacific Glass Co., San Francisco, CA, circa 1904.

Excelsior: Excelsior Glass Co., St. John, Quebec, Canada, 1878–1883.

F Inside of a Jar Outline: C.L. Flaccus Glass Co., Pittsburgh, PA, circa 1900 to 1928.

F & A: Fahnstock & Albree, Pittsburgh, PA, 1860–1862.

FL or FL & Co.: Frederick Lorenz & Co., Pittsburgh, PA, circa 1819 to 1841.

G E M: Hero Glass Works, Philadelphia, PA, circa 1884 to 1909.

G & H: Gray & Hemingray, Cincinnati, OH, circa 1848 to 1864.

Gilberds: Gilberds Butter Tub Co., Jamestown, NY, circa 1883 to 1890.

Greenfield: Greenfield Fruit Jar & Bottle Co., Greenfield, IN, circa 1888 to 1912.

H (with Varying Numerals): Holt Glass Works, West Berkeley, CA, circa 1893 to 1906.

Hamilton: Hamilton Glass Works, Hamilton, Ontario, Canada, 1865–1872.

Hazel: Hazel Glass Co., Wellsburg, WV, 1886–1902.

Helme: Geo. W. Helme Co., Jersey City, NJ, circa 1870 to 1895.

Hemingray: Hemingray Brothers & Co. and later Hemingray Glass Co., Covington KY, since 1864.

Heinz & Noble: same as above only circa 1869 to 1872.

F. & J. Heinz: same as above only circa 1876 to 1888.

H.J. Heinz: H.J. Heinz Co., Pittsburgh, PA, circa 1860 to 1869.

H.J. Heinz Co.: same as above only since 1888.

HS in a Circle: Twitchell & Schoolcraft, Keene, NH, 1815–1816.

Hunyadi Janos: Andreas Saxlehner, Buda-Pesth, Austria-Hungary, circa 1863 to 1900.

I G Co.: Ihmsen Glass Co., Pittsburgh, PA, circa 1870 to 1898.

I.G. Co.: Ihmsen Glass Co. circa 1895.

I.G. Co.: monogram, IL. Glass Co. on fruit jar 1914.

I G: Illinois Glass F inside of a jar outline, C.L. Flaccus ½ glass ½ co., Pittsburg, PA, circa 1900 to 1928.

I G: Illinois Glass Co., Alton, IL, before 1890.

IG Co in a Diamond: same as above only circa 1900 to 1916.

Ill. Glass Co.: 1916 to 1929.

Improved G E M: Hero Glass Works, Philadelphia, PA, circa 1868.

I.P.G.: in diamond, IL. Pacific Glass Corp. 1925 to 1930.

I P G: Illinois Pacific Glass Co., San Francisco, CA, 1902–1932.

JAF & Co., Pioneer and Folger: J. A. Folger & Co., San Francisco, CA, since 1850.

J D 26 S: Jogn Duncan & Sons, New York, NY, circa 1880 to 1900.

J R: Stourbridge Flint Glass Works, Pittsburgh, PA, circa 1823 to 1828.

JSB Monogram: Joseph Schlitz Brewing Co., Milwaukee, WI, circa 1900.

J T: Mantua Glass Works and later Mantua Glass Co., Mantua, OH, circa 1824.

J T & Co.: Brownsville Glass Works, Brownsville, PA, circa 1824 to 1828.

Kensington Glass Works: Kensington Glass Works, Philadelphia, PA, circa 1822 to 1932.

Kerr in Script: Kerr Glass Manufacturing Co. and later Alexander H. Kerr Glass Co., Portland, OR; Sand Spring, OK; Chicago, IL; Los Angeles, CA, since 1912.

K H & G: Kearns, Herdman & Gorsuch, Zanesville, OH, 1876–1884.

K & M: Knoz & McKee, Wheeling, WV, 1824–1829.

K Y G W and KYGW Co: Kentucky Glass Works Co., Louisville, KY, 1849–1855.

Lamb: Lamb Glass Co., Mt. Vernon, OH, 1855–1964.

L G Co: Louisville Glass Works, Louisville, KY, circa 1880.

Lightning: Henry W. Putnam, Bennington, VT, 1875–1890.

L I P: Lea & Perrins, London, England, 1880–1900.

L K Y G W: Louisville Kentucky Glass Works, Louisville, KY, circa 1873 to 1890.

L & W: Lorenz & Wightman, PA. 1862 to 1871.

"Mascot," "Mason" and M F G Co: Mason Fruit Jar Co., Philadelphia, PA, all circa 1885 to 1900.

Mastadon: Thomas A. Evans Mastadon Works, and later Wm. McCully & Co., Pittsburgh, PA, 1855–1887.

MG: slant letters, Maywood Glass, Maywood, CA 1930 to 1950.

M.G. CO.: Missouri Glass Co. 1900.

M.G. Co: Modes Glass Co., IN 1895 to 1904.

M. G. W.: Middletown Glass Co. NY, circa 1889.

Moore Bros.: Moore Bros., Clayton, NJ, 1864–1880.

N B B G Co: North Baltimore Bottle Glass Co., North Baltimore, OH, 1885–1930.

O: Owen Bottle Co.

O-D-1 O & Diamond & I: Owens Ill. Pacific Coast Co., CA, 1932 to 1943. Mark of Owen-Ill. Glass Co. merger in 1930.

P G W: Pacific Glass Works, San Francisco, CA, 1862–1876.

Premium: Premium Glass Co., Coffeyville, KS, circa 1908 to 1914.

Putnam Glass Works in a Circle: Putnam Flint Glass Works, Putnam, OH, circa 1852 to 1871.

P & W: Perry & Wood and later Perry & Wheeler, Keene, NH, circa 1822 to 1830.

Queen (in Script) Trade Mark all in a Shield: Smalley, Kivlan & Onthank, Boston, MA, 1906–1919.

R: Louit Freres & Co., France, circa 1870 to 1890.

Rau's: Fairmount Glass Works, Fairmount, IN, circa 1898 to 1908.

R & C Co: Roth & Co., San Francisco, CA, 1879–1888.

Red with a Key Through It: Safe Glass Co., Upland, IN, circa 1892 to 1898.

R G Co: Renton Glass Co., Renton, WA, 1911.

Root: Root Glass Co., Terre Haute, IN, 1901–1932.

S: In a side of a star-Southern Glass Co. L.A. 1920 to 1929.

S.B. & G. Co.: Streator Bottle & Glass Co., IL 1881 to 1905.

S.F. & P.G.W.: John Wieland's extra pale Cac. cal. Bottling Works S.F.

S & C: Stebbins & Chamberlain or Coventry Glass Works, Coventry, CT, circa 1825 to 1830.

S F G W: San Francisco Glass Works, San Francisco, CA, 1869–1876.

S & M: Sykes & Macvey, Castleford, England, 1860–1888.

Squibb: E.R. Squibb, M.D., Brooklyn, NY, 1858–1895.

Standard (in script, Mason): Standard Coop. Glass Co. and later Standard Glass Co., Marion, IN, circa 1894 to 1932.

Star Glass Co.: Star Glass Co., New Albany, IN, circa 1860 to 1900.

Swayzee: Swayzee Glass Co., Swayzee, IN, 1894–1906.

T C W: T.C. Wheaton Co., Millville, NJ, since 1888.

T S: Coventry Glass Works, Coventry, CT, 1820–1824.

W & CO: Thomas Wightman & Co., Pottsburgh, PA, circa 1880 to 1889.

W C G Co: West Coast Glass Co., Los Angeles, CA, 1908–1930.

WF & S MILW: William Franzen & Son, Milwaukee, WI, 1900–1929.

W G W: Woodbury Glass Works, Woodbury, NJ, 1882–1900.

W T & Co: Whitall-Tatum & Co., Millville, NJ, 1857–1935.

GLOSSARY

AMBER COLORED GLASS: Nickel was added in glass production to obtain this common bottle color. The theory was that the dark color would prevent the sun from spoiling the contents of the bottle.

AMETHYST COLORED GLASS: This is clear glass that has been exposed to the sun or a very bright light for a period of time, and has turned a light purple color. NOTE: Only glass containing manganese will turn purple. This glass has remained in production since 1800.

APPLIED LIP: On older bottles (pre-1880), after removal from the blowpipe, the neck was applied, therefore the seams ended below the top of the lip. This helps distinguish Old Bottles from New—if the seam ends below the top of the lip it is usually a hand-blown applied top. If it runs to the very top of the lip, the bottle was probably machine-made.

AQUA COLORED GLASS: This is the natural color of glass. The shades of aqua depend on the iron oxide contained in the sand used in glass production. This type of glass was produced until the 1930s.

BLACK GLASS: Carbon was added in glass production to obtain this dark, olive green color. This type of glass was produced between 1700–1880.

BLOB SEALS: A popular way of identifying an unembossed bottle was to apply a molten coin-shaped blob of glass to the shoulder of the bottle, into which a seal with the logo, or name of the distiller, date, or product name was impressed.

BLOB TOP: A large thick blob of glass was placed around the lip of Soda or Mineral Water bottles, the wire that held the stopper was seated below the blob, and anchored the wire when the stopper was closed, to prevent carbonation from escaping.

BLOWPIPE: This is a long tube used by the blower to pick up the molten glass which is then either blown in mold or Free Blown outside a mold to create unlimited varieties of shapes.

COBALT COLORED GLASS: This color was used in the days of patented medicines and poisons to distinguish them from the rest of the bottles.

GROUND PONTIL: This is the pontil scar that has been ground off.

IMPERFECTIONS: Bubbles of all sizes and shapes, bent shapes and necks, imperfect seams, errors in spelling, and embossing, increase rather than decrease the value of Old Bottle, providing these imperfections were formed as a part of the natural production of the bottle. The more imperfections, the greater the value.

KICK-UP BOTTOM: An indented bottom of any bottle is known as a "Kick-up." This can vary from deep indentations to a very slight impression. Wine bottles as a group are usually indented.

LADY'S LEG: These were called by the manufacturers "long bulbous neck." The shape of the neck earned this type of bottle its nickname.

MILK GLASS: Tin is added in glass production to obtain this color primarily used for cosmetic bottles.

MOLD, FULL HEIGHT 3 PIECE: The entire bottle was formed in the mold, and the 2 seams run the height of the bottle to below the lip on both sides.

MOLD, THREE PIECE DIP: In this mold the bottom part of the bottle mold was one piece, and the top, from the shoulder up, was two separate pieces. Mold seams appear circling the bottle at the shoulder, and on each side of the neck. These bottles date from 1806–1889.

OPALIZATION: This is the frosty bottle or variated color bottle, that has been buried in the earth, or in mud or silt, and minerals in these substances have interacted with the glass of the bottle to create these effects. Many collectors have a high value on bottles of this type.

PONTIL MARKS: To remove the newly blown bottle from the blow-pipe, an iron rod with a small amount of molten glass was applied to the bottom of the bottle after the neck and lip were finished. A sharp tap removed the bottle from the pontil, leaving a jagged glass scar. This "Pontil Scar" can be either round, solid, or ring-shaped. On better bottles, the jagged edges were ground down. These marks date from 1618–1866; also some modern hand blown bottles have them.

PUMPKIN SEED: A small round flat flask, often found in the western areas. Generally made of clear glass, the shape resembled nothing more than the seed of the grown pumpkin. These bottles are also known as "Mickies," "Saddle Flasks," or "Two-Bit Ponies."

ROUND BOTTOMS: Many soda bottles containing carbonated beverages were made of heavy glass, designed in the shape of a torpedo. This enabled the bottle to lie on its side, keeping the liquid in contact with the cork, and preventing the cork from drying, and popping out of the bottle.

SHEARED LIP: In the early years of bottle making, after the bottle was blown, a pair of scissor-like shears clipped the hot glass from the blowpipe. Frequently no top was applied, and sometimes a slight flange was created. The Sheared Top is a usual feature of Old Patriotic Flasks. These bottles were produced from 1800–1830.

SNAP: A more effective way of detaching the blown bottle from the blowpipe was the "Snap." This device, which made it's appearance in the 1860s, was used to grip the blown bottle in a spring cradle in which a cup held the bottom of the bottle. The bottles, held in a Snap during manufacture, have no pontil scars, or marks, but may have grip marks on the side.

TURN MOLD BOTTLES: These are bottles which were turned in forming, in a mold containing a special solvent. The action of turning, and the solvent, erased all seams and mold marks, and imparted a high luster to the finished bottle. As a group, most old wine bottles were made this way.

"WHITTLE MOLD," or "WHITTLE MARKS": Many molds used in the 1800s, and earlier, were carved of wood. Bottles formed in these molds have genuine "Whittle Marks." The same effect was also caused by forming hot glass in early morning cold molds, this combination caused "goose pimples" on the surface of these bottles. As the mold warmed the later bottles were smooth. "Whittle Mold," and "Whittle Mark" bottles are in demand, and command higher prices.

HOW TO USE THIS BOOK

This book is divided into old and new bottles. The Old Bottles section is categorized by bottle type such as ale and beer, flasks or inks. The listings are organized alphabetically by trade name or subject. The listings include the written material exactly as it appears on the bottle and a bottle description.

The New Bottle section is arranged alphabetically by manufacturer. Some of the most popular modern bottle companies in the collector market are listed including Avon, Jim Beam, Ezra Brooks, Ski Country and Old Commonwealth. The listings are organized alphabetically by trade name or subject. The bottle's description is given in each listing.

Read the printed descriptions carefully in both sections. The prices given are for the specific bottles listed. A bottle which is similar might have a higher or lower value than the item which appears in this book.

The prices given in both sections range from good to mint condition. A bottle in very poor condition would bring less than the values stated.

For your convenience, use the following record keeping system to note the condition of your bottles in the checklist boxes that precede each listing.

☐ *MINT M—* An empty bottle complete with new intact labels. Color bright and clean, no chips, or scrapes, or wear. Tax stamp like new, but cut. Box in like new condition. All stoppers, handles, spouts like new.

☐ *EXTRA FINE EF—* A bottle complete with labels, stamps, etc. All color clean and clear, slight wear on labels and tax strip, gold or silver embellishments perfect. Stoppers, handles, spouts in fine condition. Box or Container missing. **WORTH 10% LESS THAN LISTED RETAIL PRICE.**

☐ *FINE F—* The bottle shows slight wear, but color is clear and bright overall. Tax stamp complete but worn. Labels can be missing. Gold or silver embellishments perfect. Stoppers, handles, spouts complete and undamaged. No box or container. **WORTH 15% LESS THAN LISTED RETAIL PRICE.**

☐ *VERY GOOD VG—* The bottle shows some wear, gold or silver slightly worn. Labels missing, Tax stamp missing. Stoppers, handles, spouts complete. No box or container. **WORTH 25% LESS THAN LISTED RETAIL PRICE.**

☐ *GOOD G—* The bottle shows wear, complete but color faded. Gold or silver shows wear. Labels and tax stamp missing. Stoppers, handles, spouts complete. No box or container. **WORTH 40% LESS THAN LISTED RETAIL PRICE.**

☐ *FAIR FR—* The bottle color is worn and the gold or silver embellishments are faded. Labels and tax stamp missing. Stoppers, handles, spouts complete but worn. An undesirable category. No box or container. **WORTH 50% TO 75% LESS THAN LISTED RETAIL PRICE.**

OLD BOTTLES

ALE AND GIN

Not heavily collected until recent years, ale and gin bottles have become one of the more popular specialties in the hobby. Their dark, bold colors and distinctive shapes give them special appeal even though the majority were not made to be collected. These bottles have a definite masculine character and seem to reflect the ruggedness of their original owners. Superb opportunities still prevail to acquire many of these specimens at low prices.

	Price Range	
☐ **ABMYERSAM**		
Rock Rose, New Haven, Md., dark green, 9⅛″	7.00	10.00
☐ **A & D.H.C.**		
Yellow-amber, 9½″	14.00	20.00
☐ **AFRICAN GIN**		
Name embossed on one side, dark green, 9″ ..	17.00	25.00
☐ **A.H.**		
In seal, roll top, green amber, 11⅜″	38.00	52.00
☐ **A.I.**		
With an anchor in seal on shoulder, honey amber, 8¾″	36.00	49.00
☐ **ALE**		
Label, dark green, turn mold, 9½″	5.00	8.00
☐ **ALE**		
Label, olive, turn mold, kick-up, 8½″	5.00	8.00
☐ **ALE**		
Label, green, kick-up, 6″	5.00	8.00
☐ **ALE**		
Label, c. 1916 A under bottom, olive, 9½″	3.00	5.00
☐ **ALE**		
Label, aqua, 9½″	4.00	6.00
☐ **ALE**		
Label, aqua, kick-up, 8″	3.00	4.00
☐ **ALE**		
Label, aqua, Root under bottom, 11¾″	4.00	6.00
☐ **ALE**		
Label, dark olive, turn mold, 9½″	9.00	12.00

Price Range

☐ **ALE**
Label, amber, ground pontil, 11¼" 32.00 41.00
☐ **ALE**
Label, amber, 8¾" 17.00 23.00
☐ **ALE**
Label, light green, small kick-up pontil, 9" 18.00 26.00
☐ **ALE**
Label, olive, kick-up, 7½" 19.00 27.00
☐ **ALE**
Label, olive, kick-up with broken pontil, 12" ... 18.00 26.00
☐ **ALE**
Label, olive, kick-up pontil, three-part mold, 8¾" 22.00 30.00
☐ **ALE**
Label, amber, pontil, 9" 31.00 42.00
☐ **ALE**
Label, milk glass, 11" 18.00 26.00
☐ **ALE**
Label, five dots under bottom, small kick-up,
black, 10" 7.00 10.00
☐ **ALE**
Label, light aqua, 9½" 4.00 6.00
☐ **ALE OR WINE**
Label, three-part mold, B under bottom, dark
olive, 10" 7.00 10.00
☐ **ALE OR WINE**
Label, kick-up, dark olive, 9½" 3.00 5.00
☐ **ALE OR WINE**
Label, kick-up, dark olive, 10" 3.00 5.00
☐ **ALE**
Plain, 7¼", free-blown, 2" diameter, pontil, crude
top 22.00 32.00
☐ **ALE**
Plain, aqua, free-blown, kick-up, pontil, light-
weight bottle, very crude top, 2¾" diameter, 9½" 27.00 38.00
☐ **ALE**
Plain, free-blown, aqua, kick-up, pontil, 2¼" di-
ameter, crude top, 8½" 22.00 32.00
☐ **ALE**
Plain, quart, 3" neck, very crude applied top, pon-
til in kick-up, very light blue, 6" 25.00 35.00
☐ **ALE**
Plain, eight panels, graphite pontil, green, 7" .. 23.00 33.00

Price Range

☐ **ALE**
Plain pottery, brown and white, 8½" 5.00 8.00
☐ **ALE**
Plain pottery, white, 8½" 7.00 10.00
☐ **ALE**
Plain, white, pottery, 11½" 7.00 10.00
☐ **S. ALVARES**
On seal, clear, kick-up, 11½" 11.00 15.00
☐ **AMELIORATED SCHIEDAM HOLLAND GIN**
Amber, 9½" 19.00 27.00
☐ **ANTEDILUVIAN LUYTIES BROTHERS**
New York, small kick-up, olive, 12" 9.00 12.00
☐ **ASCR**
In a seal, olive, kick-up, pontil or plain, 10½" .. 50.00 65.00
☐ **ASPARAGUS GIN**
THE ROTHENBERG CO. on front in circle, slug
plate, San Francisco, CA., same shape as a Duffy
malt, graduated collar, aqua, 10⅛" 21.00 29.00
☐ **AVAN HOBOKEN & CO.**
On front, seal on shoulder AVH, case bottle,
olive, 11¼" 33.00 43.00
☐ **BAIRD DANIELS CO. DRY GIN**
Taped and ring top, aqua, 9" 10.00 15.00
☐ Same as above, except MISTLETOE DRY GIN,
8½", clear or amethyst 10.00 15.00
☐ Same as above, except CORONET under bottom,
aqua 12.00 18.00
☐ **BART E.L.**
In Old English type on one line, on the other Dry
Gin, light green, 8½" 7.00 10.00
☐ **BASS' PALE ALE**
Label, three-part mold, amber, 9½" 5.00 8.00
☐ **B.B. EXTRA SUPERIOR**
Whiskey, amber, 10½" 18.00 24.00
☐ **B. C. W.**
Dark olive, pontil, 9" 60.00 80.00
☐ **BENEDICTINE**
Dark green, kick-up, F22 on bottom, 8¾" 14.00 20.00
☐ **BERGOMASTER**
Geneva Gin, Cobb Hersey Co., Boston on round
label, also ship on bottom of label, case type,
10½", olive 12.00 16.00

Price Range

☐ **BERRY BROS.**
323 E. 38th St. N.Y. in circle on front, aqua, 11¼″   **4.00**   **6.00**

☐ **BILL & DUNLOP**
Dark olive, 11½″ **28.00**   **38.00**

☐ **BLACK BOTTLE**
Beer or Ale, three-part mold, kick-up with one dot,
4½″ body, 2″ neck, crude top, bottom 3″, dark
olive, 7¾″ **15.00**   **21.00**

☐ **BLACK BOTTLE**
4¾″ body, 2″ neck, 3″ bottom, three-part old,
kick-up, dark olive **15.00**   **21.00**

☐ **BLACK BOTTLE**
5½″ body, 2½″ lady's leg neck, improved pontil,
2¾″ bottom, crude top **15.00**   **21.00**

☐ **BLACK BOTTLE**
Beer or ale, three-part mold, 6½″ body, 3″ neck,
2½″ bottom, dark olive **10.00**   **15.00**

☐ **BLACK GLASS**
Plain, three-part mold, kick-up, 7¾″ **7.00**   **10.00**

☐ **BLACK GLASS**
C.W. & Co. under bottom, three-part mold, kick-
up **7.00**   **10.00**

☐ **BLAKE BROS PALE ALE**
Langport label, P & R B under bottom, three-part
mold, olive, 9½″ **12.00**   **16.00**

☐ **BLANKENHEYM & NOLET**
On front, ½″ letters, case bottle, olive, 9½″ . . . **28.00**   **35.00**

☐ **BLANKENHEYM & NOLET**
Dark olive, 7½″ **20.00**   **30.00**

☐ **BLANKENHEYM & NOLET**
Green or amber, 9½″ **16.00**   **23.00**
☐ Same as above, except brown or amber, 8½″ . . **16.00**   **23.00**
☐ Same as above, except brown, 7⅞″ **18.00**   **27.00**
☐ Same as above, except clear, 9⅜″ **12.00**   **16.00**
☐ Same as above, except green, 9½″ **25.00**   **35.00**

☐ **BOUVIER'S BUCHU GIN**
On front, on back, Louisville, KY., square fancy
shoulder and neck, purple **13.00**   **19.00**

☐ **DR. C. BOUVIER'S BUCHU GIN**
Vertical in two lines, fancy quart bottle, 11¾″   **15.00**   **22.00**

☐ **BOUVIER'S BUCHU GIN**
Clear or amethyst, 11¾″ **7.00**   **10.00**

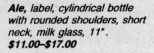

Ale, *label, cylindrical bottle with rounded shoulders, short neck, milk glass, 11".* **$11.00–$17.00**

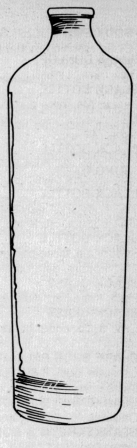

Blake Bros. Pale Ale, *Langport, label, cylindrical bottle with rounded shoulders, long neck, p & RB on bottom, three-part mold, olive color, 9½".* **$12.00–$16.00**

Price Range

☐ **BOUVIER'S BUCHU GIN**
Clear, machine made, 6″ 4.00   6.00

☐ **BOWER & TUFT'S**
New Albany, IN., around bottom in ten panels,
L & W under bottom, dark amber, 9½″ 30.00   40.00

☐ **E.J.F. BRANDS** (ale)
In seal, case type, ribbed sides, tapered top, 9½″   30.00   40.00

☐ **B. R. P. CO.**
Mold-blown, tapered top, green or amber, 8⅞″   16.00   23.00

☐ **BUNGALOW**
Gin label, tapered top, amber, 10½″ 12.00   17.00

☐ **BURROUGH'S BEEFEATER**
Gin, London distilled dry gin. Colorful label fea-
tures English "Beefeater." Sides embossed with
James Burrough LTD. London, Established 1820.
James Burrough-London England embossed on
bottom, clear glass 5.00   8.00

☐ **C.A. & C. DOS VINHOS DO PORTO**
Vertical, whittle mold, olive, amber, 11¾″ 13.00   17.00

☐ **CARL MAMPE**
Berlin Ale, small kick-up, tapered top 16.00   23.00

☐ **CASE BOTTLE**
Two dots under bottom, crude applied top, 9½″   18.00   27.00

☐ **CASE BOTTLE**
Plain, broken pontil, curved bottom, dark olive,
short neck, 10″ 55.00   70.00

☐ **CASE BOTTLE**
Plain, curved bottom, dark olive, crude applied
top, full of bubbles, short neck, 9¼″ 19.00   27.00

☐ **CASE BOTTLE**
Plain, clear, long neck, on front, sunken circle, 9″   13.00   17.00

☐ **CASE BOTTLE**
Plain, five dots under bottom, short neck, crude
top, olive, 10½″ 16.00   23.00

☐ **CASE BOTTLE**
Plain, short neck, crude top, olive, 10½″ 16.00   23.00

☐ **CASE BOTTLE**
Plain, small kick-up, dark olive, 9½″ 16.00   23.00

☐ **CASE BOTTLE**
Plain, milk glass, roof type shoulder, 2″ neck and
top, 1¼″ deep circle under bottom, 9½″ 50.00   65.00

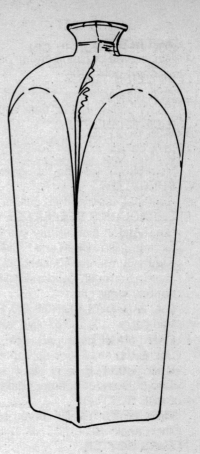

Case Gin, label, squared shoulders, short neck, pontil, 10", black glass.
$30.00–$40.00

Bower & Tuft's, New Albany, Indiana circling bottom in ten panels, L & W on bottom, Cream Ale on front, dark amber color, 9½".
$30.00–$40.00

Price Range

☐ **CASE BOTTLE**
Plain, curved or plain bottom, dark olive, tapered
top, short neck, 10″ **16.00   23.00**

☐ **CASE BOTTLE**
Plain, curved or plain bottom, dark olive, tapered
top, short neck, 3⅞″ **16.00   23.00**

☐ **CASE BOTTLE**
Plain, curved or plain bottom, brown-olive, light
olive, tapered top, short neck, 10″ **16.00   23.00**

☐ **CASE BOTTLE**
Label, black, 8″ **13.00   17.00**

☐ **CASE GIN**
Label, green, cross on bottom, 10″ **19.00   27.00**

☐ **CASE GIN**
Label, pontil, black, 10″ **30.00   40.00**

☐ **CASE GIN**
Label, dark olive, green, 9″ **25.00   35.00**

☐ **CROWN SEAL**
Label, kick-up, aqua, 11″ **7.00   10.00**

☐ **C.S. & CO.**
Under bottom, three-part mold, olive, 10″ **11.00   15.00**

☐ **C.W. & CO.**
Under bottom, kick-up, dot in center, three-part
mold, 5″ body, 2″ bob neck type, 3″ bottom, dark
olive **12.00   17.00**

☐ **JOHN DE KUYPER & SON**
Olive, 10¼″ **14.00   19.00**

☐ **DE KUYPER GIN**
Label, dark amber, 10½″ **10.00   15.00**

☐ **DE KUYPER, L.G. CO.**
Square face gin, dark green, 7⅜″ **13.00   17.00**

☐ **DEMIJOHN**
Sample label, clear or amethyst, 4″ **11.00   15.00**

☐ **DEMIJOHN**
Olive, 12″ **12.00   16.00**

☐ **DEMIJOHN**
Label, cobalt, 12″ **28.00   37.00**

☐ **DEMIJOHN**
Pontil, dark green, 16½″ x 6½″ x 8″ **45.00   60.00**

☐ **DE MONDARIZ V.H.P. ACUAR**
A round shoulder, snap-on top, olive, machine
made, 8½″ **7.00   10.00**

Price Range

☐ **DOUBLE EAGLE SEAL**
Kick-up on bottom, turn mold, ring top, light
green, 9¾" 16.00 23.00

☐ **DREWS DOPPEL KRONENBIER**
Squat bottle, ale, dark amber, 8" 18.00 27.00

☐ **D^R K**
In center of a circle with INTRODUCED ON
MERIT around edge of circle, on bottom, Established D^R K 1851 inside a circle, applied top, quart
size, amber 30.00 42.00

☐ **D-SEARS**
In a seal, ale, tapered collar, olive, 10½" 29.00 38.00

☐ **DUB & G**
In seal, olive, 8¼" and 6½" 50.00 65.00

☐ **DUNMORE OR SQUAT**
Label, different sizes and heights, dark olive,
green, pontil, free-blown 130.00 170.00

☐ **J. & R. DUNSTER**
On front panel, tapered top, olive green, 9½"   30.00 42.00

☐ **F. DUSCH, RICHMOND, VA., T.B.I.N.S.**
Reverse side XXX Porter, squat type, aqua, 6¾" 38.00 50.00

☐ **DUTCH ONIONS**
Ale, free-blown, open pontil, olive 135.00 170.00

☐ **DYOTTVILLE GLASS WORKS**
Phila. under bottom, three-part mold, olive, graphite pontil, 11" 22.00 32.00

☐ **DYOTTVILLE GLASS WORKS**
Phila. under bottom, three-part mold, amber, 11" 15.00 22.00

☐ **W. EAGLE**
Canal St, NY. (Missing period after N); Philadelphia Porter 1860 on back, ice blue, 7" 23.00 31.00

☐ **EMON COLL**
In seal, kick-up, olive, 11½" 25.00 32.00

☐ **D.H. EVANS**
St. Louis ale, three-piece mold, tapered top and
ring, quart, black glass 30.00 40.00

☐ F under bottom, label, amber, 6" 5.00   8.00

☐ **FABRICADE GIJON**
Under bottom, dark olive, 11" 7.00   10.00

☐ **F.C.G. CO.**
Lou., KY under bottom, amber, 12" 10.00 15.00

Price Range

☐ **F E S & CO. GIN**
Aqua, 9¾″ 12.00   17.00
☐ **FINEST OLD WINDMILL GIN**
Tapered top, clear, 10½″ 25.00   35.00
☐ **FLORA TEMPLE HARNESS TROT 219**
Horse on front, amber, 8½″ 100.00   130.00
☐ **GARNET DRY GIN**
Clear, 8¾″ 9.00   12.00
☐ **GINEBRA DE LA CAMPANA**
In center a bell in seal, dog bottle, a Star of David
on base, TRADE MARCA REGISTRADA, ta-
pered case gin, green, 9⅛″ 45.00   60.00
☐ **GIN**
Label, free-blown, open pontil, wide collar, green,
11″ 19.00   25.00
☐ **GIN**
Label, free-blown, flared lip, open pontil, amber
green, 13″ 19.00   25.00
☐ **GIN**
Label, free-blown, roll lip, pontil, green or amber,
15½″ 60.00   80.00
☐ **GIN**
Label, free-blown, improved pontil, dark green,
8½″ 25.00   34.00
☐ **GIN**
Label, clear or amethyst, 9½″ 5.00   8.00
☐ **GIN**
Label, green, 10½″ 7.00   10.00
☐ **GIN**
Plain, clear, 3¼″ 4.00   6.00
☐ **GOLDEN SPRAY**
Clear or amethyst, 9½″ 7.00   10.00
☐ **GORDON'S DRY GIN**
On front, on one side, England, the other London,
under bottom in sunken circle a wild boar, green
or clear, seam to top, 8½″ or 8⅝″ 6.00   9.00
☐ Same except seam to top ring, the boar is a little
different, amber 8.00   11.00
☐ **GRAVES GIN**
Label, clear, 6″ 5.00   8.00
☐ **H D B & C**
Roll lip, green or amber, 6¼″ 16.00   22.00

Price Range

☐ **P. F. HEERING**
Amber, 11″ 29.00 41.00

☐ **P. F. HEERING**
On a seal, amber, 10¼″ 29.00 41.00

☐ **P.F. HEERING**
On ribbon, shield, kick-up, double ring top, dark
green, 8¾″ 50.00 65.00

☐ **J.H. HENKES**
Delfshaven, tapered top, green, 8½″ 16.00 23.00

☐ **J.H. HENKES**
Tapered top, green, 10⅜″ 21.00 28.00

☐ **HIGHEST MEDAL**
Vienna 1873, in circle, head in circle, green, 8¼″ 50.00 65.00

☐ **I.C. HOFFMAN**
In seal, kick-up, dark olive, 9″ 45.00 55.00

☐ **P. HOPPE**
Schiedam, in seal, flared top, improved pontil,
dark green, 9⅜″ 35.00 45.00
☐ Same as above, green, 9½″ 35.00 45.00

☐ **A. HOUTMAN & CO.**
Schiedam, same on reverse side, roll lip, amber
green, 11″ 32.00 42.00

☐ **V. HOYTEMA & C.**
Gin, name embossed sideways on one side, dark
olive green, 9¼″ 17.00 25.00

☐ **H.T. & CO.**
London & NY, under bottom, capacity 24½ oz on
shoulder, sheared top, aqua 7.00 10.00

☐ **HERMAN JANSEN**
Schiedam, Holland, in seal, dark green, 9⅜″ .. 23.00 32.00

☐ **C.A. JOURDE BORDEAUX**
Dots under bottom, olive, 10½″ 11.00 15.00

☐ **JUNIPER BERRY GIN**
Bottled by Quinine Whiskey Co., Louisville, KY.
Wide ring top, aqua, 10½″ 22.00 30.00

☐ **JUNIPER LEAF GIN**
Case type, amber, 10½″ 16.00 23.00

☐ **KAISERBRAUEREI**
Bremen, vertically in ¾″ letters, olive, inside
screw top, 9¼″ 16.00 23.00

☐ **KEY SEAL**
Dark olive, 9½″ 40.00 52.00

Price Range

☐ **E. KIDERLEN**
  Dark olive, 5¾" **22.00 31.00**
☐ **H.B. KIRK & CO.**
  NY, "Bottle Remains The Property Of" in back,
  right face, amber, 11" **14.00 19.00**
☐ Same as above, except left face **14.00 19.00**
☐ **A.B. KNOLL**
  Registered Erie, PA., amber, 9½" **13.00 18.00**
☐ **KOPPITZ MELCHERS**
  Detroit, MI., A B & Co under bottom, aqua, 9½" **13.00 18.00**
☐ **L.M.G. CO.**
  In seal, flared top, improved pontil, brown, green,
  9½" **50.00 65.00**
☐ **LONDON JOCKEY**
  N's in London backward, Club House Gin on one
  side, man riding a horse on back, dark olive, 9¾" **125.00 150.00**
☐ Same except N is correct **60.00 80.00**
☐ **LONG NECK PORTER**
  Free-blown, open pontil, olive **45.00 60.00**
☐ **P. LOOPUYT & CO. DISTILLERS**
  Schiedam, dark olive, 9½" **33.00 42.00**
☐ **LOTHARINGEN**
  Pontil, dark olive, 10" x 18" **120.00 150.00**
☐ **L & T Gin**
  Anchor on front, olive, 9" **40.00 53.00**
☐ **MADISON ORIGINAL ALE**
  John Fennell Louisville, KY. on front, tapered ring
  top, star under bottom, amber, 7⅛" **15.00 20.00**
☐ **THE MALTINE M'F'G CO.**
  New York, amber, 6" **13.00 18.00**
☐ **V. MARKEN & CO.**
  Semi-script, tapered top, green or amber, 9⅜" **23.00 32.00**
☐ **V. MARKEN & CO.**
  Gin, name embossed sideways on front of one
  side. Large "1" embossed on bottom, dark olive
  green, 9¼" **17.00 25.00**
☐ **J. MEBUS**
  In seal, olive 9¾" **42.00 60.00**
☐ **MEDER & ZOON**
  Swan with W.P. in center, all in a seal, amber or
  green, 9¼" **38.00 48.00**

Price Range

☐ **J. MEEUS**
Anchor with J.M. over it, improved pontil, clear or
amber, 9¾" **43.00 55.00**

☐ **L. MEEUS**
Antwerp, key in center, green, brown, 10¼" ... **43.00 55.00**

☐ **V. MEIER**
Indianapolis, IN, dark amber, 8¾" **28.00 37.00**

☐ **MELCHER GIN**
Label, dark olive, 10¾" **13.00 18.00**

☐ **J.J. MELCHERSWZ COSMOPOLIET**
On top, J.J. Melcherswz under, in center, a man
holding a bottle, on base Schiedam, case type,
short neck, tapered top, dot under bottom, dark
olive, 10" **55.00 70.00**

☐ **MONK**
Label, amber, 10" **60.00 80.00**

☐ **NATHAN BROS**
c. 1863 Phila., amber, 9½" **115.00 145.00**

☐ **A.C.A. NOLET**
Schiedam, greenish brown, 8⅞" **31.00 39.00**

☐ **I.A.I NOLET**
Schiedam, dark green, amber, 8¼" **33.00 42.00**

☐ **NOLETS MISTLETOE BRAND**
Dark green, amber **55.00 70.00**

☐ **PALMBOOM**
With palm tree, in a seal, Ilyes & Co., Schiedam,
improved pontil, green, 11" **65.00 85.00**

☐ **P & C**
Tapered top, green, 11¾" **17.00 24.00**

☐ **J.J. PETERS**
On one side, Hamburg other side, sunken panel
under bottom, green, 8½" x 3¼" x 3¾" **45.00 60.00**

☐ **J.J.W. PETERS**
Tapered top, figure of dog on one side, green,
7¾" x 2½" x 2½" **65.00 85.00**

☐ **J.J.W. PETERS**
Hamburg, on bottom, dog figure, tapered lip, two-
piece mold, oval, amber, 7¾" **80.00 110.00**
☐ Same as above, except dark amber, 8¼" **80.00 110.00**

☐ **J.J.W. PETERS**
In vertical line, tapered lip, case type, dog figure,
green, 10½" x 3¼" x 3" **75.00 100.00**

Price Range

☐ **P.G. & OLD BRISTOL**
Seal, pontil, dark olive, 9″ 110.00 150.00

☐ **PHILANTROP**
Only imported by Lrucipsoila Demerara Mein,
crown over head, amber, green, 10¾″ 55.00 75.00

☐ **G.W. PORTER, XX PORTER & ALE**
Hollow P on reverse side, tapered top with ring,
light green, 7¼″ 75.00 95.00

☐ **POSEN, WRONKERSTR. NO 6, HARTWIG
KANTOROWIC**
Eagle under bottom, amber, 10″ 35.00 50.00

☐ **P.S.**
In seal, ale, double ring top, pontil, olive, 10″ .. 31.00 42.00

☐ **JAMES RAY**
Savannah, GA, in front, in back, XX Ale, 4″ body,
2¾″ neck, blob top, aqua 45.00 60.00

☐ **T.M. REEVE**
c. 1732, in a seal on shoulder, square, refined
pontil, olive, 10″ 65.00 85.00

☐ **RELYEA, CARTER & CO'S**
On one side Royal, other side Schiedam
Schnapps, olive, 9½″ 45.00 60.00

☐ **ROMAN BOTTLE**
Teardrop catcher, free-blown, aqua, 4″ 45.00 65.00

☐ **ROMAN BOTTLE**
Teardrop catcher, pontil, aqua, 4½″ 45.00 65.00

☐ **ROSS'S IRISH GIN**
Label, three-part mold, quart, aqua 7.00 10.00

☐ **ROYAL CHAMPI**
Dark olive, 8¾″ 30.00 40.00

☐ **RUCKER DRY GIN**
1 under bottom, aqua, 9″ 12.00 17.00

☐ **R.W.**
In a seal on shoulder, squat body, ale, long neck,
olive, 6¼″ 55.00 75.00

☐ **JOHN RYAN**
Savannah, GA, two dots under a, in front, XX Philadelphia Porter on back, cobalt, improved pontil,
6½″ 70.00 90.00

Price Range

☐ **JOHN RYAN**
In 1″ letters around bottle, ½″ letters under John
Ryan, XX Porter & Ale, Philadelphia, blue, ground
pontil, 7¾″ 75.00 100.00

☐ **JOHN RYAN**
c. 1886, in 1″ hollow letters around bottle, ½″
under J.R., XX Porter & Ale, Philada, blue, 4¾″ 70.00 90.00

☐ **JOHN RYAN**
c. 1866, Savannah, GA, in front, Philadelphia XXX
Star on each side of Ale on back, squat body,
blue, 7¼″ 70.00 90.00

☐ **JOHN RYAN**
c. 1866, Savannah, GA, in front, Philadelphia XXX
Star on each side of Porter on back, squat body,
blue, 7¼″ 60.00 80.00

☐ **JOHN RYAN PORTER & ALE, PHILADA, XX**
(c. 1859) graphite pontil, cobalt, 7″ 65.00 85.00

☐ **SAMPLE**
Label, square, free-blown, black glass, 6″ 22.00 32.00

☐ **SARGENT**
c. 1830 (Reverse 3 on front), dark amber, 8½″ 100.00 130.00

☐ **SEAHORSE HOLLANDS GIN**
Tapered top, three dots under bottom, green,
9⅝″ 30.00 45.00

☐ **ST. ANGELINE**
#1136 under bottom, dark amber, 11″ 50.00 65.00

☐ **ST. DOMINIC**
Indentation in back for label, dark olive, 9¼″ .. 30.00 45.00

☐ **T.C.C.R.**
In a seal at the base, three-piece mold, dark
green, 11″ 32.00 48.00

☐ **A. THELLER**
Label, Theller Arnold under bottom, dark olive,
8¾″ 13.00 18.00

☐ **VANDENBURGH & CO**
Bell in a seal on shoulder of bottle, case gin, avocado or olive, crude top, 11″ 90.00 110.00

☐ Same except 9″ 90.00 110.00

☐ **VANDENBURGH & CO.**
Bell with ribbon in center, flared top, dark amber,
8⅞″ 45.00 60.00

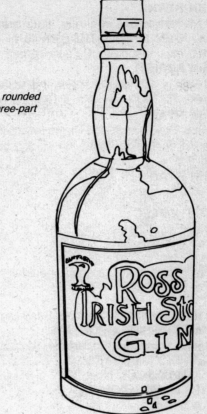

Ross's Irish Gin, *label, rounded shoulders, long neck, three-part mold, one quart, aqua.*
$7.00–$10.00

	Price Range	
☐ **VANDENBURGH & CO.** Bell with ribbon in center, improved pontil, green or amber, 9″	80.00	100.00
☐ **J. VANDERVALK & CO,** Rotterdam, green, 9½″	37.00	48.00
☐ **VANDERVEER'S MEDICATED GIN OR REAL SCHIEDAM SCHNAPPS** Flared top, amber, 8½″	17.00	24.00
☐ **VAN DUNCK'S GENEVER, TRADE MARK** Ware & Schmitz in back, amber, 9″	140.00	180.00

	Price Range	

☐ **S. VAN DYKE**
Amsterdam, cross in center, dark green, 10¼″   25.00   35.00

☐ **H. VAN EMDEN POSTHOORN GIN**
M in a ring under bottom, clear or amethyst, 10⅝″   19.00   26.00

☐ **J.H. VANGENT**
Schiedam, tapered top, three dots under bottom,
brown, 9⅜″ 22.00   29.00

☐ **A. VANPRAAG & CO'S. SURINAM GIN**
Dark green, 9¾″ 30.00   40.00

☐ Same except dark amber 30.00   40.00

☐ **V.G.& C.**
Flared top, pontil, green or amber, 10″ 32.00   43.00

☐ **VH & C**
Under bottom, dark olive, 9½″ 23.00   31.00

☐ **VHOYTEMAEC**
Vertical, case bottle, 2¼″ x 2¼″, short neck, tapered top, dark olive, 9″ 40.00   50.00

☐ **V.H.P.**
Aquas De Mondariz around shoulder, three-part
mold, olive, 6½″ 22.00   30.00

☐ **VIII**
Pontil, dark olive, 9″ 65.00   85.00

☐ **DANIEL VISSER & ZONEN**
Schiedam, tapered top, amber, 9″ 27.00   36.00

☐ **WARNERS IMPORTED**
B Gin in back, sky blue, 9″ 26.00   35.00

☐ **WATSON BILTONPARK**
Olive, 9″ 120.00   150.00

☐ **WEISS BIER**
On front, KARL HUTTER, N.Y. on bottom, blob
top, 7¼″ 10.00   15.00

☐ **R. WHITE & SONS LD**
London, around a W on bottle top, on bottom J
in a shield, whittle mark, dark olive, 10¼″ 23.00   31.00

☐ **WOODMAN'S**
Pontil, three-part mold, black glass, 8″ 150.00   180.00

BEER

Beer bottles were among the least popular of the collectible bottles for many years. The similarity of design of beer bottles detracted
from their collector appeal, as well as the fact that old beer bottles

were considered to be so common that they could never achieve any real value. This, of course, has now changed. A number of specimens command double-digit prices, and beer bottle devotees claim that these sums will appear ridiculously low in the not-too-distant future. Their commonness may be misjudged. Certainly enormous quantities were manufactured, but the percentage that were saved cannot be too great. Oddly enough, beer bottle collecting was mainly stimulated (in the early 1970s) by interest in beer can collecting—a rare instance of a newer version of a product exciting interest before its predecessor.

You will search in vain for American beer bottles dating before the mid–19th century. Despite the large amounts of beer consumed in this country up to 1850, beer bottles did not exist. All the beer at that time was either made in the home or drank at taverns, where it was dispensed from wood barrels.

The first bottles used for beer in the U.S. were made of pottery. Glass became dominant following the Civil War. The average beer bottle of 1870 was made of glass, contained a quart of beer and was cork stoppered. Breweries did not emboss their names and emblems on bottles until early 1870.

Commercial sale of bottled beer naturally led to advertising wars between manufacturers, as with other products. Makers concentrated very much on extolling the medicinal virtues and purity of their beers. David Nicholson of St. Louis called his beer "liquid bread." The only common ingredient was yeast. Hoff's Malt Extract (beer was not always called beer, for fear the word might offend the genteel) was advertised as "a remedy recommended by European Physicians for complaints of the chest, dyspepsia, obstinate cough, hoarseness, and especially consumption."

C. Conrad and Company, a wholesaler for Adolphus Busch in St. Louis, sold the original Budweiser from 1877 to 1890. The Budweiser name was a trademark of C. Conrad but in 1891 the company sold it to the Anheuser-Busch Brewing Association. By that time Adolphus Busch, founder of the company, had already established two companies to make beer bottles. In addition to furnishing bottles for Budweiser, they supplied other breweries from about 1880 to 1910.

Corks were replaced as stoppers on beer bottles with the invention by William Painter in 1891 of the "crown cork closure," containing a thin slice of cork within a tight-fitting metal cap. This continues to be used today.

Until the 1930s beer was customarily retailed in green glass bottles. There were some exceptions, such as the aforementioned David Nicholson, who used cobalt blue glass. When production of beer was resumed following Prohibition, green glass was abandoned in favor of brown. It was believed that brown glass would repel sun rays better and thereby prolong freshness.

	Price Range	
☐ **ABC Co.**		
Aqua, 9½"	3.50	5.50
☐ **A.B.G.M. CO.**		
E27 on bottom in circle, aqua, 11½"	6.00	10.00
☐ **A.B.G.M. CO.**		
C13 under bottom, aqua, 9½"	3.50	5.50
☐ **A.B.G.M. CO.**		
S4 under bottom, aqua, 10"	5.00	8.00
☐ **A.B.G.M. CO.**		
In a circle under bottom, in center E27, aqua, 11¼"	5.00	7.00
☐ **A.B.G.M. CO.**		
Under bottom, aqua, 9¾"	4.00	7.00
☐ **ABERDEEN BREWING CO.**		
Aberdeen, WA., blob top, amber, clear, 9¼"	8.00	12.00
☐ **AB6G**		
4 under bottom, aqua, 9½"	3.00	5.00
☐ **A.661**		
2 under bottom, aqua, 9½"	3.00	5.00
☐ **ACME BREWING COMPANY**		
Aqua, 9½"	10.00	14.00
☐ **ALABAMA BREWING CO.**		
Birmingham, AL, Aqua, 9½"	8.00	12.00
☐ **AMERICAN BREWING CO.**		
Rochester, NY "This Bottle Not To Be Sold" on rear, blob top, amber, 9½"	40.00	45.00
☐ **AMERICAN BREWING CO.**		
Rochester, NY, "This Bottle Not To Be Sold" on rear, blob top, aqua, 9½"	25.00	35.00
☐ **AMERICAN BREWING & C. I. CO.**		
Baker City, OR, crown top, amber, 11¼"	7.00	11.00
☐ **ANHEUSER BUSCH INC.**		
Amber, machine made, 9½"	3.00	6.00
☐ **ARNAS**		
Under bottom, amber, round, 8"	3.00	4.00
☐ **AROMA**		
F under bottom, amber	4.00	7.00

Price Range

☐ **AUGUST STOEHR**
Milwaukee Lager, Manchester, NH, slug plate,
"This Bottle Not to be Sold," blob top, honey-
amber, 9½" **16.00 22.00**

☐ **AUGUSTA BREWING CO.**
Augusta, GA, around outside of circle, in center
of circle, a large A with bottle shape embossed
over A, crown top, aqua, 9¼" **7.00 11.00**

☐ Same except Hutchinson Bottle, 7" **20.00 28.00**

☐ **THE BAKER CO.**
Dayton, OH, on front in oval slug plate, blob top,
quart, amber, 11¼" **8.00 12.00**

☐ **BARTHOLOMY BREW CO.**
Rochester NY, with trademark, blob top, amber,
10" **40.00 50.00**

☐ **BARTHOLOMAY BREWING CO.**
Rochester NY, on rear "To Fill or Sell This Bottle
is a Criminal Offense", on the bottom is a winged
wheel figure B, blob top, yellow-green **55.00 65.00**

☐ **BEADLESTON & WOERZ**
Excelsior Empire Brewery in a circle, in center of
it two ladies, eagle, monogram, New York. "This
Bottle Not To Be Sold," round, aqua, 9" **9.00 12.00**

☐ **BECHER & CO. BOTTLE BEER**
Lancaster, OR, blob top, aqua, 10½" **8.00 12.00**

☐ **THE GEORGE BECHTEL BREWING CO.**
"This Bottle Not to be Sold" on back, aqua, 9" **8.00 12.00**

☐ **BEER**
Amber, A.B.G.M. Co. in center, K 17 all under bottom of bottle, opalescent, 9½" **4.00 7.00**

☐ **BEER**
Label, M.G. Co. under bottom, amber, 9¼" ... **3.00 5.00**

☐ **BEER**
Label, star under bottom, amber, 7¾" **8.00 12.00**

☐ **BEER**
Label, dark green, 9" **8.00 12.00**

☐ **BEER**
Label, on bottom, I inside ring, clear or amethyst,
9½" **3.00 5.00**

☐ **BEER**
Label, Root 8 on bottom, amber, 9½" **3.00 5.00**

Price Range

☐ **BEER**
Label, crown top, amber, 11½" 3.00   5.00

☐ **BEER**
Label, blob top, 9½" 7.00   11.00

☐ **BEER**
Label, pontil, aqua, 10½" 20.00   30.00

☐ **BEER**
Milk glass, wine type, crown top, ABM, 10¼" .. 12.00   18.00

☐ **E. BENSWANGER**
Philadelphia, PA, Bartholomay's Rochester Beer,
blob top, amber, 10¼" 25.00   30.00

☐ **BERGHOFF**
On shoulder, FT. WAYNE, IND. at base, crown
top, ABM, aqua 3.00   4.00

☐ **BERGHOFF**
Fort Wayne, IN, blob top, amber 9" 10.00   16.00

☐ **B. 42**
On bottom, dark green, turn mold, 9½" 5.00   8.00

☐ **BIERBAUER BREWING CO.**
Cana—Joharie, NY, on front in slug plate, blob
top, aqua, 9⅜" 6.00   9.00

☐ **BLATZ**
Milwaukee, on shoulder, olive, 9¼" 3.00   5.00

☐ **BLATZ**
Old Heidelberg, stubby bottle, amber 9" 10.00   16.00

☐ **BLATZ**
Pilsner, Amber, 10½" 4.00   6.00

☐ **BLATZ VAL BREWING CO.**
Milwaukee, on shoulder in a star VB, under bottom V.B. & CO., Milw., Blob top, amber, 12" ... 8.00   12.00

☐ **BOHEMIAN LAGER BEER, BODIE BOTTLING WORK**
Bodie, CA, crown top, aqua 9.00   12.00

☐ **BORN & CO.**
Columbus, OH, in a diamond shape, blob top,
quart, amber 6.00   9.00

☐ **BOSCH LAKE**
Linden, MI, on front, T.B.N.T.B.S. on bottom, blob
top, amber, 12" 6.00   9.00

☐ **BOSCH LAKE**
Linden, MI, T.B.N.T.B.S., on bottom, blob top,
amber, 12" 7.00   11.00

Anheuser Busch, Inc.,
cylindrical bottle, rounded
shoulders, long neck, stopper
made of wire and porcelain,
clear glass, 9½".
$3.00–$6.00

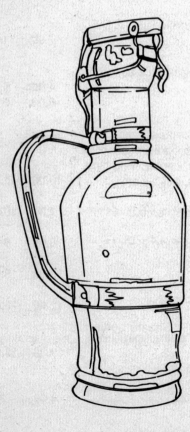

Beer, label, short bottle with
rounded shoulders, belt around
mid section and neck, wire
stopper, dark green color, 9½".
$8.00–$12.00

Price Range

☐ **BOSCH LAKE**
  Linden, MI, blob top, quart, amber 4.00   6.00
☐ **R. BOVEE**
  Large block outline of a B, Troy, N.Y., reverse
  T.B.N.T.B.S., N.B.B. & Co., aqua, 12″ 7.00   10.00
☐ **BUFFALO BREWING CO.**
  Sacramento, CA, in form of circle, horseshoe with
  buffalo jumping through, blob top, quart, amber,
  12″ 15.00   25.00
☐ **BUFFALO BREWING CO., S.F. AGENCY, BB
  CO.**
  Monogram, crown top, amber, 9⅛″ 15.00   25.00
☐ **E & J BURKE**
  E & B on bottom (Cat), ABM, amber, 8″ 3.00   5.00
☐ **C.W. BURR**
  Richmond, VA, in a circle, reverse T.B.N.T.B.S.,
  blob top, aqua, 9¼″ 7.00   11.00
☐ **CAIRO BREWING CO.**
  On shoulder, amber, round, wire-porcelain stop-
  per, clear, 9″ 4.00   6.00
☐ Same as above except aqua 5.00   8.00
☐ **CALLIE & CO. LIMITED**
  In semi-circle appears above center, center is a
  1½″ diam. circle with Dogs Head embossed in
  it, St. Helens appears below center, ring-type
  blob top, dark green, 8¼″ tall, 2⅝″ diam 10.00   16.00
☐ **CALUMET BREWING CO.**
  Calumet, Mich in circle on front, amber, 11⅞″   7.00   10.00
☐ **CAMDEN CITY BREWERY**
  Amber, various numbers on bottom, 9″ 5.00   9.00
☐ **CANTON, OH**
  Star under bottom, aqua, 9¾″ 12.00   18.00
☐ **CAS-CAR-RIA BOTTLE**
  With 45 in a circle, amber, 9¼″ 12.00   18.00
☐ **CB CO.**
  Monogram in circle, under it, Chattanooga, Tenn.,
  light amber, 11½″ 10.00   16.00
☐ **CB CO.**
  Monogram near shoulder, under it, Chattanooga,
  Tenn., amber, 11¼″ 4.00   7.00

Price Range

☐ **THE CENTRAL BRAND EXTRA LAGER BEER**
Label, aqua, 9¼" 3.00   5.00

☐ **CHAS JOLY**
Phila on back, amber, 9¼" 7.00   10.00

☐ **CHARLESTON BOTTLING COMPANY**
Charleston, SC, crown top, amber 4.00   8.00

☐ **CHATTAHOOCHEE BREWING CO.**
"This Bottle Not To Be Sold, Phoenix City, Ala."
on back, aqua, 9½" 8.00   12.00

☐ **CHATTAHOOCHEE BREWING CO.**
Columbus, GA, aqua, 9½" 8.00   12.00

☐ **CHATTAHOOCHEE BREWING CO.**
Brownsville, AL, aqua, 9½" 8.00   12.00

☐ **CHATTANOOGA BREWING CO.**
Aqua, 9½", C on bottom 5.00   8.00

☐ **CLAUSSEN BREWING ASS'N.**
Seattle, WA, crown top, 9½", clear amber 9.00   12.00

☐ **CLAUSSEN BREWING CO.**
Charleston, SC, Palmetto Tree, blob top, aqua 8.00   12.00

☐ **CLAUSSEN SWEENEY BREWING CO.**
Blob top, 10½", aqua 6.00   9.00

☐ **THE CLEVELAND & SANDUSKY BREWING CO.**
Under bottom M, in center of bottle C.S.B.C.
monogram, blob top, aqua, 9" 9.00   12.00

☐ **COBALT BLUE BEER**
Label, graduated and flared band collar, 9¾" .. 20.00   28.00

☐ **COLUMBIA WEISS BEER B'WY**
St. Louis, MO, Imported Berliner, "This Bottle
Never Sold" on rear, blob top, emerald green,
10" 30.00   40.00

☐ **THE CONNECTICUT BREWERIES CO.**
The Connecticut, Bridgeport, Conn. in a circle, in
center Breweries Co., blue green, 9½" 3.00   4.00

☐ Same except Registered on shoulder 8.00   11.00

☐ **C. CONRAD & CO.**
Original "Budweiser," U.S. Patent no. 6376,
under bottom CCCO, short tapered top with ring,
aqua, 9¼" 12.00   18.00

Price Range

☐ **CONSUMER B.B.E.**
Charleston, SC, Anheuser Eagle, blob top,
amber, 9^1/$_6$″ 4.00 8.00

☐ **CONSUMERS B.B.E.**
Charleston, SC, Anheuser Eagle on back, crown
top, amber, 9¼″ 4.00 8.00

☐ **CONSUMERS ICE CO.**
Hygeia Water, Memphis, Tenn., around lower bottom, round, tapers, to small neck, 10″ tall, base
4¼″, porcelain-spring stopper 6.00 9.00

☐ **THE COOK & BERNHEIMER CO.**
On one side, other side "Refilling Of This Bottle
Prohibited," on the bottom, C&B. Co. Bottling,
2¼″, x 4″, amber, 6¾″ 10.00 16.00

☐ **THE COOK & BERNHEIMER COMPANY**
"Refilling Of This Bottle Prohibited" other side,
amber 12.00 18.00

☐ **COOK BOCK BEER**
Label, amber, 9¼″ 3.00 5.00

☐ **COOKS 500 ALE**
Label, amber, 9½″ 5.00 8.00

☐ **T.P. COSTELLO**
Charleston, SC, crown top, amber 4.00 8.00

☐ **CROWN**
On shoulder, label, applied lip, twisted neck, deep
grooves, three-piece mold, iron pontil, dark olive,
8½″ 20.00 25.00

☐ **CRYSTAL BREWAGE**
Baltimore, MD, amber, 10½″ 8.00 11.00

☐ **C 6 CO.**
1 on bottom, aqua, 9¼″ 3.00 5.00

☐ **DALLAS BREWERY**
Clear or amethyst, 9″ 6.00 9.00

☐ **M. DAVIES**
Manchester, at top of bottle, center is a shield
with a mason's shield emblem embossed in the
shield, Malveren Street City Road, Cornbrook
Manchester appears on back of bottle, S.Y.C.B.
Co. appears on bottom of bottle, two raised rings
on neck, blob top, aqua, 7¼″ tall, 2¾″ diam. 22.00 30.00

☐ **DAYTON BREWERIES**
amber, 9½″ 7.00 10.00

	Price Range	

☐ **J. DEMANGEOT**
Lancaster, NY, slug plate, "This Bottle Not to be
Sold" on rear, blob top, aqua, 10" **15.00 22.00**

☐ **DIAMOND JIMS BEER**
Label, aqua, 9¼" **5.00 8.00**

☐ **DIXIE BREWERY, PHENIX [sic] CITY, ALA,**
aqua, 9½" **8.00 11.00**

☐ **DOBLER BREWERY**
Written in large letters in arc with very large D in
circle, "This Bottle Not to be Sold" on bottom,
light green, 9½" **5.00 8.00**

☐ **D. C. DOWNING & CO.**
Holyoke, MA, slug plate, blob top, emerald green,
9¼" **30.00 40.00**

☐ **A. DRINGEMANN**
Leroy, NY, slug plate, amber, 10" **15.00 20.00**

☐ **DU BOIS**
Blob top, 8", amber **6.00 9.00**

☐ **DUBUQUE BRG. & MALTING CO.**
Dubuque, 1A under bottom, amber, 8¾" **8.00 11.00**

☐ **DUKEHART & CO.**
"Maryland Brewery, Baltimore" on front, three
lines, squat body, long neck, amber, round, 8" **15.00 25.00**

☐ **EAGLE SPRING DISTILLERY CO.**
On front, rectangular, amethyst, 7" **4.00 6.00**

☐ **E.B. CO.**
ESCANABA, MI., amber, 8½" **8.00 9.00**

☐ **E.B. & CO. LD 11614**
On bottom, aqua, 12" **5.00 8.00**

☐ **E.G. BARTHEL & CO.**
"Gardner, Mass" written on front, white porcelain
stopper, clear, 9½" **7.00 10.00**

☐ **E.P. FRANCIS**
Fall River, Mass. written in oval plate, metal stop-
per, clear, 9½" **6.00 10.00**

☐ **THE EBLING BREWING CO.**
New York, USA on front, crown top, aqua, 9¼" **6.00 9.00**
☐ Same as above except blob top **9.00 13.00**

☐ **THE JOHN EICHLER BREWING CO.**
New York, Registered, (written fancy) on front,
blob top, aqua, 9" **7.00 10.00**

Price Range

☐ **EL DORADO BREWING CO.**
E.B.D. Co. monogram, Stockton, CA, crown top,
four-piece mold, quart, amber, 12″ 20.00 28.00
☐ **EL PASO BREWERY**
Amber, 8″ 8.00 12.00
☐ Same as above except aqua 8.00 12.00
☐ **ENGEL & WOLF'S NO. 26 & 28**
Dillwyn St., Phila., PA, applied lip, graphite pontil,
blue green, 7¼″ 23.00 32.00
☐ **ENTERPRISE BREWING CO.**
San Francisco CA., vertical on front, four-piece
mold, quart, blob top, light amber, 11¾″ 12.00 17.00
☐ **C.H. EVANS & SONS ALE**
On shoulder, crown top, amber, 9″ 4.00 6.00
☐ **EXCELSIOR**
Lager bier, H. Thimig 288 Atlantic St., Brooklyn,
NY, with trademark, blob top, aqua, 9½″ 10.00 15.00
☐ **EXCELSIOR LAGER BEER**
Slug plate, "This Bottle Never Sold" on rear,
aqua, 9½″ 15.00 20.00
☐ **EXCELSIOR LAGER BIER FROM**
VALENTINE BLATZ BOTTLING DEPT.
Chicago, in a circle, blob top, T.B.I.N.S. on re-
verse side, aqua, 9″ 12.00 18.00
☐ **FALSTAFF LEMP**
St. Louis, inside of shield, crown top, aqua, 9″ 5.00 8.00
☐ **FEE BROS.**
Rochester, NY, Bel Isle, 8 fl. oz., 6″ 6.00 9.00
☐ **JOHN E. FELDMAN**
Richfield Springs, NY, in oval slug plate, blob top,
9¼″, clear 7.00 10.00
☐ **FEIGENSPAN & CO.**
Newark, NJ, "This Bottle Not To Be Sold" on
rear, with trademark, blob top, amber, 10″ 15.00 20.00
☐ **F.H.G.W.S.**
Tapered top with ring, blob neck, 12″ 7.00 10.00
☐ **FINLEY BREWING CO.**
Toledo, OH, under bottom, trademark, an F in a
diamond on shoulder, blob top, quart, aqua ... 7.00 10.00

Price Range

☐ **FINLEY BREWING CO.**
Toledo, OH, trademark on top of diamond shape
in center of which is an F, all on bottom, aqua,
10¾" 7.00 10.00

☐ **FITZGERALD BROS. BRG. CO.**
Troy NY, slug plate, on rear "This Bottle Not to
be Sold," blob top, aqua, 9½" 15.00 20.00

☐ **THE FLORIDA BREWING CO.**
Tampa, FL, in sunken panel, aqua, under bottom
F.B. Co., 6¾" 5.00 8.00

☐ **THE FOSS-SCHNEIDER BREWING CO.**
Aqua, 7½" 6.00 9.00

☐ **THE FOSS-SCHNEIDER CO.**
In a horseshoe shape, under it "BREWING CO.,
CINCINNATI, O.," crown top, aqua, 11" 7.00 10.00

☐ **J. GAHM**
Boston, MA, with trademark of beer stein with
embossed initials, J.G., blob top, amethyst, 10½" 20.00 25.00

☐ **J. GAHM**
Boston, MA, on back "Joseph Schlitz's Milwaukee Lager Beer," with trademark, blob top, light
green, 10" 25.00 30.00

☐ **J. GAHM**
Boston, MA, on rear "JOSEPH SCHLITZ'S, MIL-
WAUKEE," lager beer, with trademark, blob top,
amber 18.00 25.00

☐ **GALLITZIN BOTTLING CO.**
326 under bottom, clear, 10" 6.00 9.00

☐ **GALVESTON BREWING CO.**
Guaranteed Pure, Galveston, Tex., aqua, round,
7¾" 5.00 8.00

☐ **GALVESTON BREWING**
Galveston, TX, reverse T.B.N.T.B.S., aqua, 9½" 7.00 10.00

☐ **G-B-S (with arrow)**
Baltimore, MD, trademark on the shoulder, clear,
round, porcelain wire top, 9¼" 8.00 12.00

☐ **JOHN L. GEBHARDT**
Boston, MA, with trademark, blob top, emerald
green, 10" 30.00 40.00

Price Range

☐ **GEO. CH. GEMUNDEN**
Savannah, GA, in a circle in center, Lager Beer
on back, "This Bottle Is Loaned Only" in three
lines, blob top, 8" 20.00   25.00

☐ **GEORGE GRIFFIN**
Camden, NJ written in large letters on front, large
star embossed in center, in small letters at lower
part of bottle "This Bottle Not To Be Sold," clear,
9¾" 9.00   12.00

☐ **GEORGE SIMMERMACHER**
Hoboken, NJ, in round slug plate on front, written
on bottom XIN- K. Hutter, N.Y., light green, 9¾"   7.00   10.00

☐ **GEORGIA BREWING ASSOCIATION**
Aqua, 9¾" 7.00   10.00

☐ **THE GERMANIA BREWING CO.**
Aqua, 7½" 8.00   11.00

☐ **GERMANIA BREWING CO.**
Charleston, SC, crown top, amber 4.00   8.00

☐ **GERMANIA BREWING CO.**
Charleston, SC, crown top, aqua, 7⅞" 4.00   8.00

☐ **GERMANIA BREWING CO.**
Charleston, SC, writing in script, crown top, aqua
9½" 4.00   8.00

☐ **A. GETTLEMAN BREWING CO.**
Pure Malt & Hops, Milwaukee, round, hand holding hops, amber, 9¼" 10.00   15.00

☐ **GREAT SEAL STYRON, BEGGS & CO.**
Newark, OH, round, clear, 9" 6.00   9.00

☐ **CHARLES S. GROVE CO.**
78 & 80 Merimac Street, Boston, Sparkling Lager
Beer, with CSG Co. monogram all inside of
diamond-shaped panel on front, blob top, clear,
9" 9.00   12.00

☐ **GUTSCH BREW CO.**
13 under bottom, red or amber, 8½" 12.00   18.00

☐ **A. HAAS BREWING CO.**
Houghton, MI, in circle on front, blob top, large
size, REGISTERED at base, amber, 12" 5.00   8.00

☐ **A. HAAS BREWING CO.**
Written fancy at slant, blob top, amber, 9½" .. 6.00   9.00

Price Range

☐ **HAFFENREFFER & CO.**
Boylston Brewery, Boston, MA, written in script
at angle across bottle, metal cap, clear, 9¾" ..　　7.00　10.00

☐ **THE JOHN HAUCK BREWING CO.**
Cincinnati, OH, on the bottom A.B. Co., round,
clear or amber, 11⅜" ....　10.00　16.00

☐ **THE HENNING BREWING CO.**
Written in center of bottle, Mendota, Ills. in oval
slug plate, green, 11¼" ....　7.00　10.00

☐ **HENNINGER**
Machine made, amber, 11½" ....　5.00　8.00

☐ **HENRY ELIAS BREWING CO.**
New York, lager beer, on rear "FAIRBANKS &
SNYDER BOSTON MASS.," blob top, yellow-
amber, 9½" ....　30.00　35.00

☐ **HEUSTIS' E.M.**
Main St., Charleston, MA, "This Bottle Not To Be
Sold," Registered, aqua, round, 9" ....　5.00　8.00

☐ **H.G. CO.**
on base, tapered top, blob top, amber, 9½" ...　7.00　10.00

☐ **HOME BREWING CO.**
Richmond, VA, on shoulder, number under bottom, aqua, 9½" ....　10.00　16.00

☐ **HOME BREWING CO.**
Indianapolis, blob top, clear ....　8.00　12.00

☐ **HOSTER CO**
OH, 665 and mark under bottom, amber, 11¾"　8.00　12.00

☐ **HOSTER'S**
In script, Columbus, OH, Weiner Beer blob top,
quart, amber ....　7.00　10.00

☐ Same as above, except dark amber, 7½" .....　7.00　10.00

☐ **HOUSTON ICE & BREWING CO.**
Crown top, ABM, aqua, 7¾" ....　7.00　10.00

☐ **EVANS ALE**
Hudson, NY, on shoulder, crown top, ABM,
amber, 10" ....　3.00　4.00

☐ **A. HUPFEL'S SON'S**
161 St. & 3rd Ave. New York, blob top, amber,
9⅜" ....　5.00　7.00

☐ Same as above except crown top, 9" ....　4.00　6.00

Price Range

☐ **INDEPENDENT BR'G ASS'N**
On bottom in circle form with big E and building
on top and small B at bottom of E, amber, 11¼" 9.00 12.00

☐ **INDEPENDENT BREWING CO. OF PITTSBURGH**
On front, crown top, light amber, 9" 4.00 6.00

☐ Same as above, except PITTSBURGH misspelled
PITTSBRUGH 15.00 25.00

☐ **INDIANAPOLIS BREWING CO.**
R.C. Co. under bottom, amber, 7¼" 6.00 9.00

☐ **INDIANAPOLIS BREWING CO.**
Indianapolis, IN, angel holding a glass of beer, sitting on a wheel on world, USA, all on front, aqua,
9½" 15.00 25.00

☐ **IROQUOIS BRG. CO.**
Buffalo, inside of circle, INDIAN HEAD in center,
crown top, ABM, amber 7.00 10.00

☐ **THE ISENGART BREWING CO.**
Troy, NY, written in a circle on front, small lip on
blob top, green, 9" 6.00 9.00

☐ **J. JEPSEN**
Escanaba, MI, on front, small inner lip on blob
top, green, 11¾" 7.00 10.00

☐ **J.N. BOURGAULT & CO.**
Winchendon, MA, "This Bottle Not To Be Sold"
in arc at top, clear, 9¼" 6.00 10.00

☐ **JACKSON & CO.**
Hop leaves with B in center, YONKERS, N.Y. on
front, 1904 on bottom, blob top, clear, 9½" . . . 7.00 10.00

☐ **JACOB JACKSON**
803 & 805 Dickinson St., Phila. blob top, reverse
T.B.N.T.B.S., aqua, 9½" 7.00 10.00

☐ **F. W. JESSEN BOTTLING WORKS**
Charleston, SC, Anheuser Eagle on back, crown
top, amber, 9½" 4.00 8.00

☐ **F. W. JESSEN BOTTLING WORKS**
Charleston, SC, crown top, aqua 4.00 8.00

☐ **F. W. JESSEN**
Charleston, SC, large initial J, blob top, aqua . . 6.00 10.00

☐ **A. KANHOUSE**
Dover, NJ written on front, on bottom, Karl Hut-
ton, New York, aqua, 9½" 6.00 10.00

	Price Range	

☐ **THE KANSAS CITY BREWERIES CO.**
On front, crown top, amber, 9″ **7.00 10.00**
☐ **KAUFMAN BEV. CO.**
Cincinnati, OH, clear, 7″ **7.00 10.00**
☐ **A.W. KEMISON CO.**
In horseshoe shape, blob top, blob neck, amber,
7¾″ **7.00 10.00**
☐ **KESSLER MALT EXTRACT**
Squat body, crown top, amber **7.00 10.00**
☐ **KOPPITZ-MELCHERS BREWING CO.**
Trademark star in center, Reg. Detroit Mich. in a
circle slug plate, blob top, aqua, 11¼″ **10.00 16.00**
☐ **M. KRESS**
Redwood City, T.B.N.T.B.S................... **10.00 16.00**
☐ **THE KRESS WEISS BEER CO.**
Amber, 7¼″ **6.00 9.00**
☐ **C.A. KRUEGER**
D.O.C. 36 under bottom, amber, 9¾″ **10.00 16.00**
☐ **K.S.**
Monogram, KUEBELER STRONG, SANDUSKY,
OHIO, blob top, aqua, 7½″ **6.00 9.00**
☐ Same as above, except 11″ **8.00 11.00**
☐ **K.S.**
Monogram on front, crown top, ABM, aqua, 9″ **3.00 4.00**
☐ **THE JOHN KUHLMAN BREWING CO.**
Ellenville, NY, aqua, 7″ **6.00 9.00**
☐ **JOHN KUHLMAN BREWING CO.**
Ellenville, NY, on front in oval slug plate, crown
top, aqua, 9¼″ **5.00 8.00**
☐ **LAKE ERIE BOTTLING WORKS**
Toledo, OH, in a circle, aqua, 10½″ **8.00 11.00**
☐ **LARGE AQUA BOTTLE**
Round blobtop, "This Bottle Loaned Not Sold,"
SIX PINTS, near base, place for large label, 13¼″ **7.00 10.00**
☐ **JOHN HENRY LEES**
In semi-circle above center, center is a large em-
bossed anchor with rope and letter H entwined,
Old Trafford appears on bottom front of bottle, in-
side screw thread, dark green, 8⅛″ tall, 2⅝″
diam. **12.00 18.00**
☐ **LEECHEN BEER**
Germany, label, amber, 9¼″ **5.00 8.00**

Price Range

☐ **LEISY**
Peoria, IL on back, amber, 9½" 6.00   9.00
☐ **LEMP**
AB Co. under bottom, aqua, 9½" 3.00   4.00
☐ **LEXINGTON BREWING CO.**
Lexington, KY, blob top, S.B. & CO. under bottom,
amber, 12" 9.00   12.00
☐ **LIMP**
St. Louis, in a shield, blob top, amber, 8¾" . . .   7.00   10.00
☐ **J.D. LINXWEILER**
Leroy, NY, "This Bottle Not Sold" on rear, slug
plate, blob top, aqua, 9½" 15.00   22.00
☐ **D. LUTZ & SON BREWING CO.**
Allegheny, PA, on front in oval slug plate, blob
top, 9¾" 10.00   16.00
☐ **MALZBIER BEER GERMAN**
Amber, 8½" 5.00   8.00
☐ **THE MARYLAND BREWING COMPANY**
Amber, 9" 12.00   18.00
☐ **MASSACHUSETTS BREWERIES CO.**
Boston, MA, crown top, amber, 9½" 3.00   5.00
☐ **M. MAYER**
"This Bottle Not To Be Sold" in back, 4 under bot-
tom, aqua, 9" 7.00   10.00
☐ **McAVOY BREWING CO., LAGER BEER**
Chicago, IL, blob top, aqua, 9½" 7.00   10.00
☐ **D.W. McCARTHY**
D.W. McC. monogram, STOCKTON, CAL. on
front, blob top, four-piece mold, quart, amber, 12"   12.00   18.00
☐ Same as above, except 9½" 12.00   18.00
☐ **McLYMAN & BRADY**
Toledo, OH, blob top, aqua, 11½" 7.00   10.00
☐ **GEORGE MEYER BEER**
Aqua, 7½" 7.00   10.00
☐ **GEORGE MEYER**
Savannah, GA, aqua, 9½" 20.00   28.00
☐ **C. & J. MICHEL BREWING CO.**
Lacrosse, WI, reverse side B.N.T.B.S., blob top,
amber, 7½" 10.00   15.00

Price Range

☐ **MILLER BECKER CO.**
On back "Send Me Home When I Am Empty,"
on base "This Bottle Not to be Sold," machine
made, aqua, 11½" 7.00   10.00

☐ **MILWAUKEE LAGER BEER**
"J. Gahm 83 State St., Boston, Mass.," with
trademark of beer stein with embossed initials
J.G., blob top, honey-amber, 10" 20.00   25.00

☐ **MINERAL SPRING BEER**
Label, aqua, 9" 3.00   5.00

☐ **MOBILE BREWERY**
Mobile, AL, aqua, 10" 9.00   12.00

☐ **THE CHRISTIAN MOERLEIN BREWING CO.**
Cincinnati, OH, in a circle, in center of circle
monogram M, aqua, 9½" 5.00   8.00

☐ **THE CHRISTIAN MOERLEIN BREWING CO.**
Cincinnati, OH, in four lines, amber, fifth, blob top,
blob neck 9.00   12.00

☐ **MOFFATS-ALE BREWERY-INC.**
On both sides, large M on bottom, ABM, crown
top, grass green, 9⅜" 4.00   6.00

☐ **MUNCHNER BAVARIAN TYPE BEER**
Aqua, 9¼" 7.00   10.00

☐ **NATIONAL LAGER BEER, H.**
ROLTRBACHER AGT.,
Stockton, CA, H.R. monogram all on front, four-
piece mold, blob top, amber, 11½" 9.00   12.00
☐ Same as above, except pint size 12.00   18.00
☐ Same as above, except 8" 12.00   18.00

☐ **NEBRASKA BREWING CO.**
Omaha, NB, in a circle, amber, 9" 8.00   11.00
☐ Same except clear 5.00   8.00
☐ Same except red or amber 15.00   25.00

☐ **T.L. NEFF'S SONS**
Case bottle trademark on back, aqua, 11" 12.00   18.00

☐ **DYSON NELSON**
Trademark, round, aqua, inside screw, 6¾" ... 12.00   18.00

☐ **NORFOLK BREWERY, HABICH & CO.**
Boston, MA, written in large letters on front, blob
top has inner lip, clear, 9¾" 9.00   12.00

Price Range

☐ **OAKLAND BOTTLING CO.**
Oakland, CA. around shoulder, blob top, amber,
9″ **12.00 18.00**

☐ **O.B. CO.**
Under bottom, label, amber, 9¾″ **5.00 8.00**

☐ **OCONTO BREWING CO.**
Blob top, amber **7.00 10.00**

☐ **THE PROPERTY OF OHLSSON'S CAPE BREWERY**
Inside screw cap **15.00 25.00**

☐ **W. OLMSTED & CO.**
On one side, reverse NEW YORK, roof type
shoulders, on roof in front CONSTITUTION, pon-
til, 10½″ **65.00 85.00**

☐ **OTTO A. SCHOLZ**
New Haven, CT, written in circle on front, clear
or amethyst, 9½″ **6.00 9.00**

☐ **PABST BREWING CO. OF MILWAUKEE**
Amber, 12″ **7.00 10.00**

☐ **PABST**
Milwaukee, WI, in circle in center, leaves and in
circle big P, Trademark under it, on bottom Registered, "This Bottle Not To Be Sold," amber, 9¼″ **7.00 10.00**

☐ **THE PALMETTO BREWING COMPANY**
Charleston, SC, blob top, aqua 7¾″ **4.00 8.00**

☐ **THE PALMETTO BREWING CO**
Charleston, SC in a circle in center, large monogram P, aqua, 7¾″ **7.00 10.00**

☐ Same except no P, crown top, aqua, 9½″ **4.00 6.00**

☐ **THE PALMETTO BREWING CO.**
Charleston, SC, palmetto tree, blob top, aqua,
7¾″ **8.00 12.00**

☐ **C. PFEIFFER BREWING CO., C.P.B. CO.**
Detroit, MI, in circle on shoulder, blob top, amber,
9¼″ **6.00 9.00**

☐ **WM. PFEIFER**
Chicago, with trademark, blob top, emerald
green, 10″ **30.00 40.00**

☐ **PHIL SCHEUERMANN BREWERY**
Hancock, MI written on front, amber, 11¾″ ... **7.00 10.00**

☐ **PHOENIX BREWING CO.**
An eagle with trademark under it, Victoria, B.C.,
tapered top, amber, 8¼″ **15.00   25.00**

☐ **PIEL BROS**
P.B. and arrow in shield, East New York Brewery,
all on front, crown top, amber, 9¼″ **6.00   9.00**

☐ Same as above, except dark aqua **6.00   9.00**

☐ **PIEL BROS**
Above P.B. inside of circle, under the East New
York Brewery, aqua, 9″ **7.00   10.00**

☐ **PITTSBURGH BREWING CO.**
Crown top, amber, 12¼″ **7.00   10.00**

☐ **PAUL POHL**
Chicago, IL, diamond with "D" on bottom. Blob
top, amber, 7½″ **15.00   20.00**

☐ **ROBERT PORTNER BREWING CO.**
Amber, 7¼″ **15.00   25.00**

☐ **PROSPECT BREWERY, CHAS WOLTER'S
PHILA**
Reverse T.B.N.T.B.S., blob top, amber, 8″ **15.00   25.00**

☐ Same as above, except 7¼″ **10.00   15.00**

☐ **W.O. PUTNAM**
Clear, 9½″ **6.00   9.00**

☐ **QUANDT BREWING CO.**
Troy, NY, with trademark of running man, blob
top, emerald green, 10″ **60.00   70.00**

☐ **JOHN RAPP & SON**
San Francisco, CA, on front, blob top, quart, light
amber, 11½″ **10.00   15.00**

☐ Same as above, except 9½″ **12.00   18.00**

☐ Same as above, except 8¼″ **7.00   10.00**

☐ **RENO BREWING CO.**
Reno, NV, tapered top, amber, 10¾″ **7.00   11.00**

☐ **R.G. WALSH & CO.**
256 Central St., Winchendon, MA, written on
front. "This Bottle Not To Be Sold" written at top
in arc, metal stopper, clear, 9½″ **7.00   10.00**

☐ **F. ROBINSON UNICORN BREWERY**
In semi-circle at top of bottle, "Stockport" appears below, center of bottle is an embossed uni-

Rochester Brewing Co.,
Old Topper Ale.
$5.00–$8.00

Rochester Brewing Co.,
R in script on front, wire
stopper, amber.
$15.00–$18.00

corn, raised ground, "trade" and "mark" appear on either side, bowed neck, blob top, medium dark green, 8″ tall. 2½″ diam. **12.00 18.00**

☐ **ROSE NECK BREWING CO.**
Richmond, VA, embossed star, round, crown top, aqua, 9¾″ **7.00 10.00**

☐ **ROSESSLE BREWERY**
Boston, MA, T.B.T.B.R. on front, Premium Lager on back, crown top, aqua, 9″ **5.00 8.00**

☐ **L. C. A. ROSSLER**
Charleston, SC, Anheuser Eagle on back, crown top, amber, 9¼″ **6.00 10.00**

☐ **JOHN ROTHWELL**
In semi-circle across top, "Mayor Street, Bolton" in semi-circle at bottom, shield and lamb design similar to "William Rothwell" also on this page, but shape of shield and lamb is different, blob top, aqua, 8½″ tall, 3″ diam. **9.00 16.00**

☐ **WILLIAM ROTHWELL**
In semi-circle across top, "Mayor Street, Bolton" in semi-circle at bottom, in the center of the bottle appears a shield with a lamb embossed on it, "Registered" appears above lamb, trademark appears below, all within shield, blob top, aqua, 7⅝″ tall, 2½″ diam. **8.00 15.00**

☐ **ROYAL RED**
"Not To Be Refilled, No Deposit No Return," on base, ABM, red, 9½″ **20.00 28.00**

☐ **RUBSAM & HORRMANN BREWG. CO.**
In horseshoe shape in center, Staten Island, N.Y., Registered, in four lines on back near bottom "This Bottle Not To Be Sold," blob top, under bottom KH, 1906, aqua, 9″ **7.00 10.00**

☐ **JACOB RUPPERT BREWER**
New York, on shoulder in circle, crown top, yellowish green or amber, 9¼″ **5.00 8.00**

☐ **SAKURA BEER**
on base, foreign writing on back, dark amber, 11¼″ **6.00 9.00**

☐ **SANTA CLARA COUNTY BOTTLING CO.**
San Jose, four-piece mold, ½ pint, light amber, 7¾″ **7.00 10.00**

Price Range

☐ **F. & M. SCHAEFER MFR'G CO.**
New York, around base on front, crown top, aqua,
9″ 3.00   5.00

☐ **THE SCHAEFER-MEYER BRO. CO.,**
Louisville, KY. trademark, in a shield, amber, 11″   12.00   18.00

☐ **SCHEFFEL & CO.**
Chicago, blob top, olive-green, 9″ 40.00   50.00

☐ **SCHLITZ BEER DEPOT**
Charleston, SC, crown top, amber 6.00   10.00

☐ **SCHLITZ**
Charleston, SC, man holding world, crown top,
amber 6.00   10.00

☐ **C. SCNEER & CO.**
In horseshoe letters, under it "SACRAMENTO,
CAL.", blob top, blob neck, amber, 7½″ 7.00   10.00

☐ **JOHN SCHUSLER**
Brewing Co., Buffalo, NY, with trademark bearing
the logo "THE FINEST," blob top, amber, 10″   30.00   40.00

☐ **SCHWARZENBACH**
Brewing Co., Germania, PA, with trademark, slug
plate, blob top, amber, 9½″ 20.00   25.00

☐ **CHAS SEILER,**
Milwaukee, Beer in two lines on front, on back
"Empty Bottle to be Returned," blob top, aqua,
8″ 7.00   10.00

☐ **G.B. SELMER, CALIFORNIA POP BEER**
Reverse Pat. Oct. 29, 1872, tapered top, amber,
10½″ 25.00   35.00

☐ **SIEGLER & SCHIEMANN BREWING CO.**
Chicago, IL, blob top, with trademark, green, 9½″   40.00   45.00

☐ **SMITH BROS. BREWERS, NEW BEDFORD,
MASS.**
Inside of slug plate, "TO BE WASHED AND RE-
TURNED" on front also, blob top, clear 6.00   9.00

☐ **SOUTHERN BREWING CO.**
Machine made, green, 9½″ 3.00   4.00

☐ **L..SPEIDEL & CO.**
Boston, MA, hop leaf and B on center front, Registered LS Co. monogram on back, blob top,
clear, 9″ 12.00   18.00

Rock River Brewing Co.,
*Blackhawk Beer, portrait of
Indian in center.*
$5.00–$8.00

Schepps Brewing Co.,
Stein Gold Beer.
$5.00–$8.00

Price Range

☐ **SPRINGFIELD BREWERIES CO.**
Boston Branch, Boston, MA, Trademark S.B. Co.
monogram, blob top, clear, 9" 6.00   9.00

☐ **JOHN STANTON BREWING CO.**
Troy, NY, with trademark, blob top, amber, 10"   18.00   24.00

☐ **A.F. STEDWELL**
"121 S. Water St., Philada." written on front,
clear, 9¾" 4.00   7.00

☐ **STETTNER & THOMAS**
Weiss Beer Brewers, St. Louis, MO, blob top,
amber, 9½" 12.00   18.00

☐ **ST. MARY'S BOTTLING WORKS**
St. Mary's, OH, in a circle, quart, blob top, aqua   9.00   13.00

☐ **JOHN STROHM**
Jackson, CA, J.S. monogram on front, four-piece
mold, light amber, 7¾" 12.00   18.00

☐ **PETER STUMPF**
"This Bottle Not For Sale" on back, amber, 8½"   12.00   18.00

☐ **TEIKOKU BEER**
Japanese writing on back, graduated collar and
ring, amber, 11¾" 6.00   9.00

☐ **TERRE HAUTE BREWING CO.**
2½" diameter, "R.G. CO." on bottom, aqua, 9½"   6.00   9.00

☐ **FRANK S. TERRY BOTTLING WORKS**
Crown top, amber 4.00   8.00

☐ **THOS BRAZELL**
201 & 205 Pleasant St., West Gardner, MA, in
oval plate, clear 9¼" 6.00   10.00

☐ **GEO. A. TICOULET SAC.**
On front four-piece mold, amber, 7¾" 7.00   10.00

☐ **TOLEDO BREWING & MALTING CO.**
Amber, 9½" 5.00   8.00

☐ **JOHN TONS**
JT monogram, "STOCKTON, CAL," on front,
four-piece mold, blob top, quart, amber, 11½"   9.00   13.00

☐ **S.A. TORINO**
Gray snake around bottle, RED EYE, RED
TONG, clear, 12¼" 15.00   25.00

☐ Same as above, except aqua 12.00   18.00

☐ **TROMMER'S EVERGREEN BR'Y**
Aqua, 9¼" 8.00   11.00

Price Range

☐ **UNION BREWING CO., LTD.**
Beer, Tarrs, PA, on bottom "Union Made C & CO.,
brown, 8" 7.00 10.00
☐ **UNITED STATES BREWING CO.**
Chicago, IL, aqua, 9" 7.00 10.00
☐ **VA. BREWING CO.**
Aqua, 9¾" 6.00 9.00
☐ **A.G. VAN NOSTRAND**
Charlestown, MA inside of ribbon, "BUNKER
HILL LAGER, BUNKER HILL BREWERIES, EST.
1821 REG.", amber, 9¾" 20.00 28.00
☐ **C.J. VATH & CO.**
San Jose, on front in slug plate, blob top, amber,
12" 11.00 16.00
☐ **VICTORIA BREWING CO.**
On base "Not To Be Sold," Victoria, B.C., amber,
9" 10.00 16.00
☐ Same except red amber 10.00 16.00
☐ **W. STREETER**
Gardner, MA. in round slug plate, registered in arc
at top, porcelain stopper, clear, 9¼" 6.00 10.00
☐ **THE WACKER & BIRK BREWING CO.**
Chicago, IL, reverse T.B.N.T.B.S., aqua, 9½" .. 7.00 10.00
☐ **SIDNEY O. WAGNER**
On shoulder, crown top, 11¼" 3.00 5.00
☐ **THE J. WALKER BREWING CO.**
Cincinnati, OH, in a circle, amber, 11¼" 5.00 8.00
☐ **HENRY K. WAMPOLE & CO.**
Phila., PA, around shoulder, graduated collar and
ring, light amber, 8½" 8.00 12.00
☐ **WASHINGTON BREWING CO.**
Trademark with picture of eagle, Reg. Wash.
D.C., aqua, 9¼" 15.00 25.00
☐ **WEST END**
Written fancy, Brg. Co. Utica, N.Y., crown top,
ABM, amber, 9½" 8.00 11.00
☐ **W.F. & G.P MIL**
Under bottom, clear, 9¼" 5.00 8.00
☐ **W.F. & S.**
On bottom, crown top, aqua, 9½" 3.00 4.00

Price Range

☐ **W.F. & S MIL**
   Under bottom, aqua, 9″ 3.00   5.00
☐ Same except #39 and amber 3.00   5.00
☐ **WIEDEMANN**
   0179 under bottom, amber, 9½″ 8.00 11.00
☐ **WISCONSIN SELECT BEER**
   Aqua, 9¼″ 5.00   8.00
☐ **THE P.H. WOLTERS BREWING CO.**
   "This Bottle Never Sold" in back, aqua, 9½″ . .   6.00   9.00
☐ **WUNDER BOTTLING CO.**
   W.B. Co. monogram, "SAN FRANCISCO, CAL.,"
   on front, amber, 7⅝″ 7.00 10.00
☐ Same as above, except "OAKLAND" 7.00 10.00
☐ **Y**
   Under bottom label, amber, 9¾″ 7.00 10.00
☐ **YOERG BREWING CO.**
   St. Paul, MN, aqua, 9½″ 6.00   9.00
☐ **GEO. YOUNG CALIFORNIA POP BEER**
   Reverse Pat. 29th 1872, amber, 10½″ 25.00 35.00
☐ **THEO. YOUNG**
   With large stars, hop leaves, buds, in a mono-
   gram, "T.Y. Union Ave., 165th & 166th St., NY,"
   all on front, crown top, amber, 9″ 7.00 10.00
☐ **WELDE & THOMAS**
   Vacuum Purified, lager beer, Bottle Establish-
   ment, 1348 & 50 Kates St., blob top, aqua 20.00 25.00
☐ **WESTMACOTT & SON**
   In semi-circle above center, center is an old sailing ship with the word "trade" etched above and
   the word "mark" etched below, "Manchester"
   appears below center, slightly recessed bottom,
   blob top, olive-green 10.00 15.00

BITTERS

   Bitters bottles have long ranked as favorites in the bottle hobby.
In fact, they were being saved and admired ("collected" might not be
the right word) before most other kinds of cold bottles. Some people—certainly not the majority but some here and there—who bought
bitters in the 19th century used the bottles for display in their homes
after their contents had been consumed. This was not the case with

most bottles of that time. Hence, bitters bottles have survived in somewhat greater numbers than most other old bottles, but demand for them is so great that prices are strong nevertheless.

Bitters was a liquor of varying alcoholic content, popular first in England and then in America. It was advertised primarily as a tonic and could be bought from supply houses and stores that did not sell other kinds of liquor—as well as from liquor dealers.

The decorative shapes of some bitters were likewise intended to promote sales, thus providing yet another excuse for their purchase. The more creative ones featured likenesses of pigs, fish, cannons, drums, ears of corn and the like. Generally, the bitters collector will either specialize in these "figurals," or in the bottles of a particular manufacturer, such as Hostetter.

Jacob Hostetter of Lancaster County, Pennsylvania, was a physician who made his own bitters and used it for his patients. Upon his retirement in 1853, he gave his son, David, permission to manufacture it commercially. Thus began the most successful bitters firm in the nation.

Over 1,000 types of bitters bottles are known, most of them produced from 1860 to 1905. In addition to the figurals already mentioned, shapes included round, square, rectangle, barrel-shaped, gin bottle shaped, twelve-sided, and flask-shaped, as well as others. Figurals are the scarcest and, in general, the most desirable to collectors.

Bitters bottles were usually embossed with a design and the manufacturer's name. Many carried paper labels. The embossed variety are generally older, scarcer, and more valuable. By the 1880s it had become a common practice to sell the bottles in cardboard boxes, which carried illustrations and lengthy maker-to-buyers messages. The boxes are collectible, too, but very few were preserved. Pictures in early Sears Roebuck catalogues give an idea of what they looked like.

The most common color for bitters bottles was amber in various shades, ranging from pale golden yellow to dark amber-brown. Next was aqua (light blue). Green and clear glass bottles were sometimes used. The rarest colors are dark blue, amethyst, milk glass, and puce.

Since many collectors of bitters bottles specialize by manufacturer, certain specimens have become more valuable than they might be expected to on grounds of design or scarcity. Generally speaking, the American-made bitters bottles will command higher prices than those of foreign origin when sold in this country if design and color are similar.

Note: The great popularity of bitters bottles as a collectors' item has encouraged the making of reproductions. Some are of quite good quality and can fool an inexperienced buyer. Take care, and do not buy unless you can be certain of the specimen's authenticity.

	Price Range	
☐ **ABBOTT'S BITTERS**		
C.W. Abbott & Co. Baltimore, round bottle, amber, machine made	6.00	10.00
☐ **ABBOTT'S BITTERS**		
On base, "C. W. Abbott & Co., Baltimore" on shoulder, machine made, amber, 8"	6.00	8.00
☐ **ABBOTT'S BITTERS**		
6½", machine made	6.00	8.00
☐ **DR. ABELL'S SPICE BITTERS**		
Label, pontil, aqua, 7½"	70.00	80.00
☐ **ACORN BITTERS**		
Amber, tapered lip, 9"	150.00	250.00
☐ **AFRICAN STOMACH BITTERS**		
In three lines near shoulder, amber, 9½"	30.00	65.00
☐ **AFRICAN STOMACH BITTERS**		
In three lines near shoulder, amber, round, under "Bitters" small letters "Spruance Stanley & Co., 9½"	45.00	70.00
☐ **AIMAR'S SARRACENIA BITTERS**		
On back "Charleston SC," aqua, 7½"	40.00	50.00
☐ **AIMAR'S SARRACENIA FLY TRAP BITTERS**		
Label, on back embossed "A. S. B. Charleston SC," aqua, 7¼"	125.00	150.00
☐ **ALEX VON HUMBOLDT'S**		
On back "Stomach Bitters," tapered neck, ring top, amber, 9¾"	60.00	95.00
☐ **ALPINE HERB BITTERS**		
In two lines in front, in back in a shield "TT&CO," amber, 9¾"	100.00	250.00
☐ **WILLIAM ALLEN'S CONGRESS BITTERS**		
Rectangular bottle, deep green, clear, light amber, 10"	200.00	300.00
Same except pontil, amethyst, 7¾"	200.00	300.00
☐ **DR. ALTHER'S BITTERS**		
Lady's leg shape, clear, 5"	20.00	50.00
☐ **AMAZON BITTERS**		
Reverse side "Peter McQuade, NY," amber, 9¼"	150.00	250.00

Price Range

☐ **AMERICAN CELEBRATED STOMACH BITTERS**
Amber, 9¼" 100.00 200.00

☐ **AMERICAN LIFE BITTERS**
Back same, "P. Eiler Mfg. Tiffin, Ohio," log effect, cabin type bottle, tapered lip, light amber to amber 175.00 200.00

☐ **AMERICAN LIFE BITTERS**
Same as above, except Omaha, NB 175.00 200.00

☐ **AMERICAN STOMACH BITTERS**
Amber, 8½" 75.00 100.00

☐ **DR. ANDREW MUNSO BITTERS**
Lady's leg shape, amber, 11¼" 85.00 110.00

☐ **DAVID ANDREW'S VEG. JAUNDICE BITTERS**
Open pontil, aqua 85.00 110.00

☐ **ANGOSTURA**
Bitters on back, "Rheinstorom Bros, NY & Cin." on bottom, amber 35.00 75.00

☐ **ANGOSTURA BARK BITTERS**
Clear or aqua, 9½" 35.00 60.00

☐ **ANGOSTURA BARK BITTERS**
Figural bottle, "EAGLE LIQUOR DISTILLERIES", amber, 7" 50.00 65.00

☐ **ANGOSTURA BITTERS**
On base, green, 7¾" 30.00 38.00

☐ **APPETINE BITTERS**
Geo. Benz & Sons, St. Paul, MN MFG., label, amber, 7¼" 250.00 350.00

☐ **ARABIAN BITTERS**
In back, "Lawrence & Weicesslbaum, Savannah, GA," square, tapered top, amber, 9½", rare ... 110.00 150.00

☐ **ARGYLE BITTERS**
E. B. Wheelock, NO., tapered lip, amber, 9¾" 150.00 250.00

☐ **AROMATIC ORANGE STOMACH BITTERS**
Square bottle, amber 50.00 62.00

☐ **ARPS STOMACH BITTERS**
Ernest L. Arp & Kiel, label, round, aqua, 11¼" 20.00 30.00

☐ **ASPARAGIN BITTERS CO.**
Clear to aqua, 11" 45.00 60.00

Price Range

□ **ATHERTON'S DEW DROP BOTTLES**
On base "1866 Lowell Mass.," ringed shoulder,
short tapered top, amber, 10" 700.00 775.00

□ **ATWELL'S WILD CHERRY BITTERS**
Label, oval bottle, aqua, 8" 10.00 20.00

□ **ATWOOD'S GENUINE BITTERS**
Round bottle, aqua, 6½" 8.00 11.00

□ **ATWOOD'S QUININE TONIC BOTTLES**
Rectangular bottle, aqua, 8½" 30.00 35.00

□ **ATWOOD'S BITTERS—VEGETABLE
JAUNDICE**
Round bottle, aqua, Moses F. Atwood 10.00 14.00

□ **ATWOOD GENUINE PHYS. JAUNDICE
BITTERS**
Georgetown, MA, 12-sided, aqua, 6½" 10.00 20.00

□ **ATWOOD JAUNDICE BITTERS**
"by Moses Atwood" on panels, clear or aqua, 6" 5.00 12.00
□ Same as above, except pontil 15.00 20.00

□ **ATWOOD JAUNDICE BITTERS**
Formerly made by Moses Atwood, clear or aqua,
6" 5.00 10.00

□ **ATWOOD JAUNDICE BITTERS**
Machine made, clear or aqua, 6" 7.00 4.50

□ **ATWOOD'S / GENUINE / BITTERS**
Marked on base, "N. WOOD SOLE PROPRI-
ETOR" on domed shoulder, aqua, round, 6" .. 15.00 20.00

□ **ATWOOD'S / JAUNDICE BITTERS / M.C.
ARTER & SON**
Georgetown, MA, aqua, 12-sided, ring top, 6" 10.00 20.00

□ **ATWOOD JAUNDICE BITTER**
Formerly made by Moses Atwood, clear or aqua,
screw top, 6" 20.00 30.00

□ **ATWOOD'S VEGETABLE DYSPEPTIC
BITTERS**
Pontil, short tapered top, aqua, 6½" 55.00 70.00

□ **AUNT CHARITY'S BITTERS**
Label, Geo. A. Jameson Druggist, Bridgeport, CT,
clear and amber, 8½" 10.00 20.00

□ **DR. AURENT IXL STOMACH BITTERS,
BARKERS, MOORE & MEIN**
Mfg. Wholesale Merch. Phila., clear, 8½" 20.00 35.00

Price Range

☐ **AYOLA MEXICAN BITTERS**
On back "M. Rothenberg & Co. San Francisco,
CA", long collar with ring, amber, 9½", rare ... **100.00 150.00**

☐ **DR. M. C. AYERS RESTORATIVE BITTERS**
Aqua, 8½", rare **100.00 150.00**

☐ **E. L. BAILEY'S KIDNEY AND LIVER
BITTERS**
On back "Best Blood Purifier," amber, 7¾" ... **60.00 80.00**

☐ **BAKER'S HIGH LIFE BITTERS**
"The Great Nerve Tonic" embossed on back, tapered top, machine made, pint **15.00 25.00**

☐ **BAKERS ORANGE GROVE**
On back "Bitters," roped corners, tapered top,
amber, 9½" **95.00 125.00**

☐ Same as above, except yellow **175.00 225.00**

☐ **BAKERS STOMACH BITTERS**
Label, lady's leg shape, amber, 11¼" **55.00 70.00**

☐ **E. BAKERS PREMIUM BITTERS**
Richmond, VA, aqua, 6¾" **60.00 100.00**

☐ **DR. BALLS VEGETABLE STOMACH
BITTERS**
Pontil, aqua, 7", rare **100.00 150.00**

☐ **BALSDONS GOLDEN BITTERS**
"1856 NY" other side, amber, 10½" **100.00 125.00**

☐ **BARBER'S INDIAN VEGETABLE JAUNDICE
BITTERS**
12-sided, aqua, 6¼" **100.00 130.00**

☐ **BARTLETT'S EXCELSIOR BITTERS**
On bottom "BARTLETT BROS. NY", 8-sided,
aqua and amber, 7¾" **175.00 300.00**

☐ **BARTO'S GREAT GUN BITTERS**
In circle in center "Reading, PA", cannon shop
bottles, amber, olive amber, 11" x 3¼" **800.00 1100.00**

☐ **BAVARIAN BITTERS**
Hoffheimer Brothers other side, amber, 9½" .. **100.00 135.00**

☐ **BAXTER'S MANDRAKE BITTERS**
"Lord Bros. Prop. Burlington, VT." on vertical
panels, amethyst, 6½" **10.00 20.00**

☐ **BEECHAM BITTERS**
Woodward Drug Co. Portland, OR, label, amber,
8¼" **10.00 18.00**

Price Range

☐ **BEGG'S DANDELION BITTERS**
Rectangular bottle, clear, 8" 80.00 100.00

☐ **BEGG'S DANDELION BITTERS**
Square bottle, amber, 9¼" 65.00 85.00

☐ **BEGG'S DANDELION BITTERS**
"Chicago, IL" other side, amber, 9" 60.00 80.00

☐ **BEGG'S DANDELION BITTERS**
In 3 lines, tapered top, base to neck a plain band,
amber, 7¾" 21.00 26.00

☐ **BELLS COCKTAIL BITTERS**
Lady's leg shape, amber, 10¾" 125.00 175.00

☐ **BELMONT'S TONIC HERB BITTERS**
Amber, 9½", rare 100.00 200.00

☐ **BEN-HUR CELEBRATED STOMACH
BITTERS**
"New Orleans" in 3 lines, same in back, tapered
top, 9" 100.00 150.00

☐ **BENDER'S BITTERS**
Aqua, 10½", rare 100.00 150.00

☐ **BENNETTS CELEBRATED STOMACH
BITTERS**
Amber, 9¼" 85.00 100.00

☐ **BENNETTS WILD CHERRY STOMACH
BITTERS**
Amber, 9¼" 100.00 150.00

☐ **BERKSHIRE-BITTERS, AMANN & CO.**
Cincinnati, OH, ground top, dark amber, 10½" 800.00 1100.00

☐ **BERLINER MAGEN BITTERS**
"S. B. Rothenberg sole agents S. F.," label,
green, 9½" 90.00 115.00

☐ **BERLINER MAGEN BITTERS**
Amber, 9½" 40.00 60.00

☐ **DR. L. Y. BERTRAMS LONG LIFE
AROMATIC STOMACH BITTERS**
Aqua, 9" 85.00 100.00

☐ **BERRY'S VEGETABLE BITTERS**
Labeled only, square bottle, amber, iron pontil,
9½" 15.00 20.00

☐ **THE BEST BITTERS OF AMERICA**
Cabin shape, amber, 9¾" 750.00 850.00

☐ **BILLING'S MANDRAKE TONIC BITTERS**
Labeled only, rectangular bottle, aqua, 8" 10.00 15.00

Price Range

☐ **BIRD BITTERS**
"Philadelphia Proprietor," clear, 4¾" 20.00   30.00
☐ **DR. BIRMINGHAM ANTI BILIOUS BLOOD PURIFYING BITTERS**
Round, green, 9¼" 75.00 125.00
☐ **DR. BISHOPS WAHOO BITTERS**
Amber, 10¼" 115.00 145.00
☐ **BISMARCK BITTERS**
½" pint, amber 100.00 150.00
☐ **BOTANIC STOMACH BITTERS**
Same on reverse, paper label, amber, 9" 50.00   75.00
☐ Same as above, except back reads "BACH MEESE & CO. S.F.", amber, 9" 50.00   75.00
☐ **BOURBON WHISKEY BITTERS**
Barrel, bright puce, 9" 175.00 225.00
☐ **BOURBON WHISKEY BITTERS**
Barrel, yellow olive, 9" 175.00 225.00
☐ **BOWES CASCARA BITTERS**
"Has No Equal, P. F. BOWES, Waterbury, Conn. U.S.A.", clear, 9¼" 80.00 120.00
☐ **DR. BOYCE'S TONIC BITTERS**
"Francis Fenn Prop. Rutland, VT." on panels, bottle has twelve panels, aqua blue, 7¼" 40.00   50.00
☐ **DR. BOYCE'S TONIC BITTERS**
Label, sample size, twelve panels, aqua, 4½" 10.00   15.00
☐ **BOYER'S STOMACH BITTERS**
Bottle in shape of an arch, fancy bottle, round, clear, 11" 100.00 150.00
☐ **BOYER'S STOMACH BITTERS CINCINNATI**
Whiskey shape bottle, fluted shoulder and round base, clear 115.00 140.00
☐ **BITTER DE**
2 Lions Bordeaus in a seal on shoulder, tapered top ring, piece mold, Dr. Olive, 12¼" .... 50.00 · 80.00
☐ **BITTER**
Secrestat in a seal, turn mold, Dr. Olive, 12" .. 50.00   80.00
☐ **THE BITTER'S PHARMACY**
Label, clear, 4½" 4.00   6.00
☐ **DR. BLAKE'S AROMATIC BITTERS N.Y.**
Aqua, pontil, 7¼" 70.00   90.00
☐ **BLAKE'S TONIC & DUERETIC BITTERS**
Round, aqua, 10¼" 20.00   30.00

Price Range

☐ **DR. BOERHAVES STOMACH BITTERS**
Olive amber, 9¼" 50.00 85.00

☐ **BOERHAVES HOLLAND BITTERS**
One side "B. Page Jr.", other side "Pittsburg,
PA", aqua, 8" 50.00 80.00

☐ **BOSTON MALT BITTERS**
Round, green, 9½" 20.00 30.00

☐ **BRADY'S FAMILY BITTERS**
On three sunken panels, amber, 9½" 50.00 90.00

☐ **BROWN, N.K.**
On other side Burlington, Vt., on front "Iron & Quinine Bitters", ring top, aqua, 7¼" 40.00 75.00

☐ **BROWN'S CELEBRATED INDIAN HERB
BITTERS**
In a shield shaped panel at base on left side, on
base "Patented-Feb. 11-1867," Indian Maiden,
amber, golden amber, other shades of amber
which are common for this bottle 450.00 550.00

☐ Rare in green, clear, aqua 1000.00 1500.00

☐ **BROWN'S AROMATIC BITTERS**
Oval bottle, aqua, 8½" 50.00 80.00

☐ **BROWN CHEMICAL CO.**
Brown Iron Bitters on other side, amber, 8" ... 10.00 15.00

☐ **F. BROWN BOSTON SARSAPARILLA
STOMACH BITTERS**
Pontil, aqua, 9¼" 100.00 150.00

☐ **DR. BROWN'S BERRY BITTERS**
Aqua or clear, 8¼" 30.00 55.00

☐ **BROWN'S CASTILIA BITTERS**
Round, tapered, amber, 10" 70.00 90.00

☐ **BROWN'S CELEBRATED INDIAN HERB
BITTERS**
Indian maiden figural, back, 12½" 345.00 440.00

☐ **BROWN'S INDIAN QUEEN BITTERS**
Figural Indian maiden, 12½" 150.00 200.00

☐ **BROWN'S INDIAN QUEEN BITTERS**
Reddish amber, 12½" 250.00 335.00

☐ **BRYANT'S**
"Stomach Bitters" on three panels, green, small
kick-up with dot 500.00 600.00

☐ **BRYANT'S STOMACH BITTERS**
On two panels, 8 sided, pontil, olive, 11¾" 500.00 600.00

Price Range

☐ **GEO. J. BYRNE:**
"Professor-New York," on 1 panel in back. "The
Great-Universal-Compound-Stomach-Bitters-
Patented-1890," all in fancy panels, very fancy
decor bottle, amber, 10" 700.00 1000.00
☐ Same as above, clear or amethyst 350.00 425.00
☐ **H. E. BUCKLEN & CO.**
"Electric Brand Bitter" on each side, amber, 9" 18.00 23.00
☐ Same except no Electric 18.00 23.00
☐ **BURDOCK BLOOD BITTERS**
Canadian type early ABM, clear, 8½" 10.00 18.00
☐ **BURDOCK BLOOD BITTERS**
"T. Milburn & Co. Toronto, Ont." on back, tapered
neck, aqua blue, 8½" 20.00 40.00
☐ **BURDOCK BLOOD BITTERS**
"Foster Milburn Co." on one side, other side
"Buffalo, NY," clear, 8" 22.00 27.00
☐ **DR. BURNHAM'S TIMBER BITTERS**
With contents and box, blown in mold, rectangu-
lar, amber, 9" 25.00 35.00
☐ **BITTERS**
Label, McC on bottom, gold, 9½" 6.00 8.00
☐ **BITTERS**
Label, under glass in circle, bar bottle, clear,
12¼" 15.00 20.00
☐ **BITTERS**
Label, crock, light olive brown trim, 10¼" 15.00 30.00
☐ **CALDWELL'S HERB BITTERS**
Multi-sided bottle, "GREAT TONIC," amber, pon-
til, 12⅝" 175.00 225.00
☐ **DR. CALLENDER & SONS LIVER BITTERS**
Square bottle "CELEBRATED LIVER BITTERS,"
light amber, 9⅝" 80.00 100.00
☐ **CALIFORNIA FIG BITTERS**
Square bottle, "CALIFORNIA EXTRACT OF FIG
CO.," amber, 9⅝" 50.00 80.00
☐ Same as above, except Fig & Herb Bitters, black 180.00 230.00
☐ **CALIFORNIA WINE BITTERS**
"M. KELLER, L.A." in shield on shoulder, "M. K."
around bottle, olive green, 12¼" 75.00 100.00
☐ **CAMBELL DR. SCOTCH BITTERS**
Flask, amber, 6½" 100.00 150.00

Price Range

☐ **CANTON BITTERS**
Amber, 11½" 100.00 125.00

☐ **CAPITAL BITTERS**
One side, "Dr. M. M. Fenner's Fredonia, NY" on
reverse side, aqua, 10½" 35.00 47.00

☐ **CARACAS BITTERS**
Amber to emerald green, 8¼" 40.00 50.00

☐ Same as above, in dark green 45.00 60.00

☐ **CARMELITE BITTERS**
"For the Kidney and Liver Complaints" on one
side, on back, "Carmelite, Frank R. Leonori & Co.
Proprietors, New York," square, amber, olive,
10½" 60.00 80.00

☐ **CARMELITER KIDNEY & LIVER BITTERS**
Square bottle, "CARMELITER STOMACH BIT-
TERS CO.-NEW YORK", amber, 10⅝" 50.00 60.00

☐ **CARONI BITTERS**
½ pint, green 15.00 20.00

☐ **CARPATHIAN HERB BITTERS**
"Hollander Drug Co. Braddock P." on other side,
amber, 8½" 30.00 50.00

☐ **CARPENTER & BURROWS**
Cincinnati, OH, in 2 lines, cabin type bottle, tapered top, amber, label stated bitters-S is reverse
in Burrows, 9½" 225.00 300.00

☐ **CARTER'S LIVER BITTERS**
Oval bottle, label, amber, 8⅝" 50.00 90.00

☐ **CASSINS GRAPE BRANDY BITTERS**
Triple ringed top, dark olive green, 10" 200.00 300.00

☐ **CASTILIAN BITTERS**
In vertical letters, round shape and tapered from
bottom to neck, narrow square top and ring in
center of neck, light amber, 10" 80.00 120.00

☐ **CATAWBA WINE BITTERS**
Cluster of grapes in front and back, green, 9" 200.00 300.00

☐ **CELEBRATED BERLIN STOMACH BITTERS**
Square bottle, light green, 9½" 95.00 115.00

☐ **CELEBRATED CROWN BITTERS**
"F. Chevalier & Co. Sole Agents," amber, 9¼" 100.00 150.00

☐ **CELEBRATED HEALTH RESTORING
BITTERS**
"Dr. Stephen Jewetts", pontil, aqua, 9½" 40.00 60.00

Price Range

☐ **CELEBRATED PARKERS BITTERS—STOMACH**
In 3 lines, side mold, amber, tapered top, 8¼″   **90.00 115.00**

☐ **CELERY & CHAMOMILE BITTERS**
Label, square, amber, 10″ **10.00 20.00**

☐ **CHALMER'S**
On shoulder on base "Proprietors" in center, "Catawka Wine Bitters," ¼ moon letters under it Trademark, center of it circle with mill tree, under it in ¼ moon letters "Sutters Old Mill. Spurance Stanley & Co.," round, ring tapered top, aqua, 11½″ **85.00 105.00**

☐ **CHANDER'S, DR., JAMAICA GINGER ROOT BITTERS**
All in 4 lines, barrel type bottle, on shoulder in 2 lines "Chas. Nichols Jr. & Co. Props. Lowell Mass.," amber, double ring top, 10″ **750.00 850.00**

☐ **CHRISTIAN XANDER'S STOMACH BITTERS**
Label, Washington, DC, amber, 12″ **15.00 20.00**

☐ **CINTORIA BITTER WINE**
On shoulder, amber, 11″ **18.00 23.00**

☐ **CLARKE'S COMPOUND MANDRAKE BITTERS**
In 3 lines, aqua, ring top, 7⅝″ **40.00 60.00**

☐ **CLARKE'S GIANT BITTERS**
Rectangular bottle, ring top, "PHILADA. PA." aqua, 6¾″ **30.00 53.00**

☐ **E. R. CLARKE'S SARSPARILLA BITTERS**
Sharon, MA, rectangular bottle, aqua, pontil, 7⅞″ **120.00 130.00**

☐ **CLAYTON & RUSSELL'S BITTERS**
Labeled only, square bottle, "CELEBRATED STOMACH BITTERS", amber, 8⅞″ **10.00 25.00**

☐ **CLARKES SHERRY WINE BITTERS**
Clear, blue green pontil, 8″ **20.00 37.00**

☐ **CLARKE'S SHERRY WINE BITTERS**
Only 25-, pontil, blue green, 8″ **90.00 115.00**

☐ **CLARKS VEGETABLE BITTERS**
Only 75-, pontil, aqua, 8″ **100.00 130.00**

☐ **CLAW BITTERS**
Label, light amber, 4¾″ **20.00 30.00**

Price Range

☐ **CLIMAX BITTERS**
On back "S. F. CA.," golden amber, square, 9½",
rare **100.00 150.00**

☐ **CLOTWORTHY'S**
"Oriental Tonic Bitter" on back, amber, 10" ... **85.00 105.00**

☐ **COCA BITTERS ANDES MTS.**
Trademark, picture of Indian carrying man across
stream, also "THE BEST TONIC" **100.00 130.00**

☐ **COCAMOKE BITTERS**
Hartford, CT., square bottle, amber, tapered top,
9" **50.00 80.00**

☐ **COCKTAIL BITTERS**
"Cribbs Davidson & Co.," other side, 9¼" **125.00 145.00**

☐ **COLE'S PERUVIAN**
Bark and wild cherry bitters **150.00 200.00**

☐ **DR. A. W. COLEMAN'S ANTIDYSPEPTIC
TONIC BITTERS**
Pontil, ground pontil, green **90.00 115.00**

☐ **COLLETON BITTERS**
Pontil, aqua, 6½" **60.00 80.00**
☐ Same as above, without pontil **15.00 23.00**

☐ **COLUMBO PEPTIC BITTERS**
On back "L. E. Junc, New Orleans, LA," square
bottle, under bottom SB&CO, amber, 8¾" **20.00 30.00**

☐ **COMPOUND HEPATICA BITTERS**
H.F.S. monogram, oval bottle, "H.F. SHAW
M.D.," aqua, ring top, Mt. Vernon, ME, 8⅜" ... **65.00 85.00**

☐ **COMPOUND CALISAYA BITTERS**
In 2 lines, tapered top, square, amber, 9½" ... **14.00 18.00**

☐ **COMUS STOMACH BITTERS**
In 2 lines, "Back Clerc Bros & Co. Limited sole
proprietors, New Orleans, LA" in 3 lines, tapered
top, amber, 9" **50.00 75.00**

☐ **CONGRESS**
On other side, "Bitters," amber or clear, tapered
top, 9" **100.00 125.00**

☐ **CONSTITUTION BITTERS**
Rectangular bottle, "SEWARD & BENTLEY",
Buffalo, NY, green, round. Below shoulder A.M.S.
2 at base 1864, 9½" **150.00 250.00**

☐ **CONSTITUTION BITTERS 1880**
Bodeker Bros Prop. Rich. VA, amber, 7" **115.00 145.00**

	Price Range	

☐ **CORN JUICE BITTERS**
Flask-shaped bottle, quart, aqua, pint also **70.00 90.00**

☐ **CORWITZ STOMACH BITTERS**
Amber, 7½″ **50.00 75.00**

☐ **CRIMEAN BITTERS**
Under it on base, "Patent 1863," on other side
"Romaines Crimean Bitters," amber, 10¼″ **175.00 225.00**

☐ **H.M. CROOKESS**
Stomach bitters, letters separated from the
mould seam, round big blob neck, long tapered
top, small kick up olive green, 10½″ **325.00 400.00**

☐ **CUNDERANGO BITTERS**
Same on back side, greenish amber, 7¾″ **50.00 80.00**

☐ **CURTIS CORDIAL CALISAYA, THE GREAT
STOMACH BITTERS**
Tapered neck, amber, 11½″ **300.00 400.00**

☐ **DAMIANA BITTERS**
"Baja, Calif." on back, 8-pointed star under bottom, "Lewis Hess Manufr." on shoulder, aqua,
11½″ **70.00 90.00**

☐ **DAMIANA**
Same as above, except no "Lewis Hess Manufr."
on shoulder **25.00 48.00**

☐ **DANDELION BITTERS**
Rectangular bottle, clear, amber, tapered top, 8″ **25.00 48.00**

☐ **DANDELION XXX BITTERS**
Aqua or clear, 7″ **50.00 80.00**

☐ **DEMUTH'S STOMACH BITTERS**
Philada., square bottle, amber, 9⅝″ **30.00 45.00**

☐ **DEVIL-CERT STOMACH BITTERS**
Round bottle, clear, ABM, 8″ **30.00 60.00**

☐ **DEXTER LOVERIDGE WAHOO BITTERS,
DWD**
"1863 XXX" on roof tapered top, eagle faces
down to left with arrow. dark amber, 10″ **150.00 200.00**

☐ Same as above, except eagle faces up to right,
light yellow **95.00 120.00**

☐ **DIGESTINE BITTERS**
"P.J. Bowlin Liquor Co. sole proprietors-St. Paul,
Minn." in lines, tapered top, amber, 8½″ **275.00 325.00**

Price Range

☐ **DIMMITT'S 50CTS BITTERS**
Flask bottle, "ST. LOUIS," amber, tapered top,
6½" 125.00 175.00

☐ **DeWITTS STOMACH BITTERS**
Chicago, amber, 8" 55.00   75.00

☐ **DeWITTS STOMACH BITTERS**
Chicago, amber, 9¾" 55.00   75.00

☐ **DOC DUNNING OLD HOME BITTERS**
Greensboro, NC, dark red, amber, 13" 75.00   95.00

☐ **DOYLE'S HOP BITTERS**
Cabin shape, "1872" on roof, several shades of
amber and many variants of colors 20.00   40.00

☐ **ST. DRAKES**
On top of roof panel, 1860 plantation on next
panel, Bitters on next, reverse center panel "Patented 1862" with six logs, front plain for label,
other covered with logs, some have five logs and
the earliest have four logs, amber the most common, others: citron, pale yellow, green, scarce in
olive green, 10" 150.00 250.00

☐ **EAGLE AROMATIC BITTERS**
Round bottle, "EAGLE LIQUOR DISTILLERIES,"
yellow amber, 6¾" 20.00   40.00

☐ **EAST INDIA ROOT BITTERS**
Geo. P. Clapp, sole Prop., gin shaped bottle,
"BOSTON MASS," amber, 9⅝" 110.00 140.00

☐ **EMERSON'S EXCELSIOR BOTANIC BITTERS**
Oval, aqua, labeled, 8¼" 50.00   75.00

☐ **EMERSON EXCELSIOR BOTANIC BITTERS**
Rectangular bottle, "E.H. Burns-Augusta-Maine,"
amber, 9" 10.00   15.00

☐ **DR. E.P. EASTMAN'S YELLOW DOCK**
Pontil, rectangular bottle, "LYNN, MASS," aqua,
tapered top, 7¾" 70.00   90.00

☐ **ELECTRIC BITTERS**
Square bottle, "H.E. BUCKLEN & CO., CHI-
CAGO, ILL," amber, 9" 50.00   60.00

☐ **ELECTRIC BITTERS**
"H.E. Bucklen & Co., Chicago, Ill," with contents,
label, seal, and box, square, amber, 9" 55.00   65.00

Price Range

☐ **EGON BRAUN HAMBURS**
Embossed on shoulder, "Universal Mercantile
Co. San Francisco, Original Amargo Bitters, etc.,"
all on label, double ring top, green, 5" 30.00   40.00

☐ **ENGLISH FEMALE BITTERS**
On reverse "Dromgoole," Louisville, KY, clear or
amber, 8½" 30.00   50.00

☐ **EXCELSIOR**
On back "Bitters," tapered top, amber, 9" 80.00   120.00

☐ **EXCELSIOR HERB BITTERS**
J.V. Mattison, Washington, NJ, rectangular,
roofed shoulder, amber, 10" 115.00   145.00

☐ **FAVORITE BITTERS**
Powell & Stutenroth, barrel shape with swirl ribbing, amber, 9¼" 500.00   1000.00

☐ **FEINSTER STUTTGARIES MAGEN BITTERS**
Brand Bros. Co., label, 3-sided bottle, long neck
and ring top, amber, 10" 45.00   75.00

☐ **FER-KINA GALENO**
"Bitters" on shoulder, beer type bottle, brown,
machine made, 10⅛" 10.00   15.00

☐ **FERNET GIGLIANI BITTERS**
San Francisco, label, wine type bottle, kick-up
bottom, green 15.00   20.00

☐ **FERRO QUINA STOMACH BITTERS BLOOD
MAKER**
Dogliani Italia, D.P. Rossi, 1400 Dupont St. S.E.
sole agents, U.S.A. & Canada, lady's leg type
neck, amber, 9¼" 70.00   90.00

☐ **THE FISH BITTERS**
On side of eye, on reverse "W.H. Ware Patented
1866," on base "W.H. Ware Patented 1866,"
plain rolled top, amber, 11½" x 3½" x 2½" ...1500.00   2500.00

☐ Same as above, except clear 400.00   575.00

☐ **FITZPATRICK & CO.**
Shape of stubby ear of corn, amber, 10" 220.00   275.00

☐ **A.H. FLANDERS M.D. RUSH'S BITTERS**
Clear, amethyst, amber, 9" 30.00   50.00

Price Range

☐ **DR. FLINT'S**
Back side is embossed "PROVIDENCE, R.I."
rectangular, blown in mold, ring top, with label,
aqua, 9¾" 40.00   50.00
☐ Same as above, in amber 40.00   50.00
☐ **FISCHER'S-N.E., COUGH BITTERS**
"Atlanta, GA." all in 3 lines, tapered top, aqua,
6" 30.00   50.00
☐ **DR. FORMANECK'S BITTER WINE**
Amber, round, 10½" 10.00   15.00
☐ **FOWLER'S STOMACH BITTERS**
Fancy bottle, square, light amber, "STOMACH
BITTERS," 10" 250.00 350.00
☐ **FRANK'S LAXITIVE TONIC BITTERS**
Flask type, on bottom 502, amber, tapered top,
6¼" 90.00 115.00
☐ **FRANCKS PANACEA BITTERS**
"Frank Hayman & Rhine Sole Proprietors,"
round, light house, amber, 10" 500.00 750.00
☐ **FRENCH AROMATIQE**
The finest stomach bitters in 4 lines on shoulder,
ring top, aqua, 7⅜" 40.00   80.00
☐ **GARRY, OWEN STRENGTHENING BITTERS**
On one side "Sole Proprietor's," on other side
"Ball & Lyon's," New Orleans, LA, front plain,
under bottom "W.McC & Co. Pitts.," amber, 9"   80.00 100.00
☐ **GERMAN BALSAM BITTERS, W. M.
WATSON & CO.**
Sole agents for U.S., milk glass, 9" 300.00 400.00
☐ **GERMAN HOP BITTERS**
Square, amber, "READING, MICH.," 9½" 45.00   60.00
☐ **GERMAN TONIC BITTERS**
Pontil, square, aqua, "BOGGS, COTMAN &
CO.," 9¾" 75.00   90.00
☐ **GEO. C. GODWINS**
Reverse Indian Vegetable Sarsaparilla, each side
reads "Bitters," all lettering reads vertically, pon-
til, aqua, 8¼" 160.00 200.00
☐ **THE GLOBE TONIC BITTERS**
Tapered top, square bottle, amber, 10" 70.00   90.00

Price Range

☐ **GLOBE BITTERS**
Manufactured only by Byrne Bros. & Co., New
York, fluted tapered neck, amber, 11″ 135.00 170.00

☐ **GLOBE BITTERS**
Manufactured only by John W. Perkins & Co.,
Sole Proprietors, Portland, ME, amber, 10″ 165.00 210.00

☐ **DR. GODDIN'S BITTERS**
Square, aqua, "GENTIAN BITTERS," 10″ 185.00 230.00

☐ **GOLDEN SEAL BITTERS**
Square bottle, amber, 9″ 100.00 130.00

☐ **GODFREYS CELEBRATED CORDIAL BITTERS**
Iron pontil, aqua, 10″ 30.00 50.00

☐ **GOFF'S BITTERS**
Label, Camden, NJ., aqua 5.00 18.00

☐ **GOFF'S BITTERS**
H on bottom, machine made, clear and amber,
5¾″ 7.00 10.00

☐ **GOLD LION BITTERS**
Round bottle, labeled, clear, 6″ 10.00 20.00

☐ **DR. GOODHUE'S ROOT & HERB BITTERS**
Rectangular bottle, "J.H. RUSSELL & CO.,"
aqua, 10⅜″ 50.00 75.00

☐ **ST. GOTTHARD HERB BITTERS**
"Mette & Kanne Bros. St. Louis, MO" in vertical
line on front, tapered top, 8¾″ 75.00 80.00

☐ **GRANGER BITTERS**
Clear flask bottle, amber, anchor on front, 7⅞″ 10.00 20.00

☐ **W.H. GREEG LORIMER'S JUNIPER TAR BITTERS**
Almira, NY, blue green, 9½″ 80.00 100.00

☐ **GREELEY'S BOURBON BITTERS**
Amber, puce, 9½″ 175.00 225.00

☐ **GREER'S ECLIPSE BITTERS**
"Louisville, KY" on side, amber, 9″ 100.00 130.00

☐ Same as above except puce 140.00 170.00

☐ **GRIEL'S HERB BITTERS**
Lancastle, PA, round bottle, "GRIEL & YOUNG,"
aqua, 9½″ 70.00 90.00

☐ **J. GROSSMAN**
"Old Hickory Celebrated Stomach Bitters" on
back, amber, 4½″ 20.00 30.00

Price Range

☐ **J. GROSSMAN**
"Old Hickory Celebrated Stomach Bitters,"
amber, 8¾" 100.00 125.00

☐ **J. GROSSMAN**
"Old Celebrated Stomach Bitters" on other side,
amber, 8¼" 75.00 100.00

☐ **DR. GRUESSIE ALTHER'S KRAUTER
BITTERS**
Label, B under bottom, amber, 10½" 80.00 100.00

☐ **GUNCKELS EAGLE BITTERS**
Square bottle, labeled only, amber, 9⅜" 10.00 20.00

☐ **HAGANS BITTERS**
Amber, 9½", rare 75.00 100.00

☐ **E. E. HALL, NEW HAVEN**
"Established 1842" on base, amber 10¼" 80.00 95.00

☐ **HALL'S BITTERS**
"E.E. Hall, New Haven, Established 1842" on
back, barrel shape, amber, 9¼" 170.00 220.00

☐ **DR. T. HALL'S, CALIF. PEPSIN WINE
BITTERS**
In three lines, amber, tapered top, 9¼" 85.00 105.00

☐ **DR. THOS. HALL'S/CALIFORNIA/PEPSIN
WINE BITTERS**
Vertically on three lines on front, light amber, 9"
tall, 2½" base 75.00 90.00

☐ **HANSARD'S HOP BITTERS**
Crock, tan and green, 8" 75.00 90.00

☐ **DR. MANLEY HARDY'S GENUINE JAUNDICE
BITTERS**
Boston, MA, long tapered neck, aqua, 7½" ... 90.00 115.00

☐ Same as above, except Bangor, ME 90.00 115.00

☐ Same as above, except 6½" 80.00 105.00

☐ Same as above, except no pontil 25.00 32.00

☐ **DR. HARTER'S WILD CHERRY BITTERS**
St. Louis or Dayton, OH, rectangular, amber, 7¾" 28.00 37.00

☐ Same except miniature 28.00 37.00

☐ **DR. HARTER'S WILD CHERRY BITTERS**
Dayton, OH, four sunken panels, rectangular,
4¾" 35.00 47.00

☐ **DR. HARTER'S WILD CHERRY BITTERS**
"St. Louis" all in four lines, embossed cherries on
both side panels, 2 under bottom, amber, 7¼" 160.00 210.00

Right: **H.A. Graef's Son
Canteen, N.Y.,** whiskey flask,
rounded canteen shape with two
handles, square mouth, smooth
base, 6½". **$210.00–$310.00;**
Bottom: **Berkshire Bitters
Bottle,** pig, amber, 9½".
$800.00–$1200.00

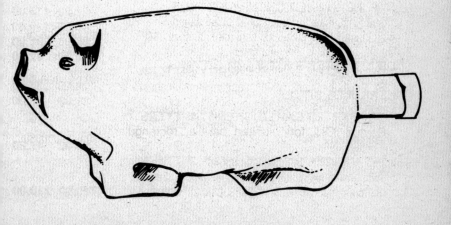

Price Range

☐ **HARTWIG'S CELEBRATED ALPINE BITTERS**
Base Wm. Mc. & Co., Pittsburgh, PA, square bottle, "ST. JOSEPH, MO.," golden amber, 9⅜" . . 100.00 120.00

☐ **HARTWIG KANTOROWICZ**
Posen, Germany, case type bottle, milk glass, 4" 50.00 75.00

☐ Same as above, except 9½" 50.00 70.00

☐ **HARZER KRANTER BITTERS**
Reverse Herman C. Asendorf, Brooklyn, NY, amber, 9½" 30.00 50.00

☐ **HAVIS IRON BITTERS**
In base "THE WILLIAMSBURG DRUG CO.," square bottle, "WILLIAMSBURG, KY," amber, 8" 85.00 110.00

☐ **H.H. HAY CO.**
"Selling Agents Portland, ME." on back, on bottom "L.F. Atwood," in center "L.F.," 6¾" 5.00 10.00

☐ **HENDERSON'S CAROLINA BITTERS**
Trademark H.C.B., square bottle, amber, 9⅝" 85.00 110.00

☐ **DR. HENLEY'S CALIFORNIA IXL** (in oval) **BITTERS**
"W. Frank & Sons, Pitt." reverse side, sky blue 60.00 80.00

☐ **DR. HENLEY'S SPICED WINE**
OK in a circle, Bitters label, reverse OK Bitters, round bottle, ring top, bluish aqua, 12" 25.00 50.00

☐ **DR. HENLEY'S WILD GRAPE ROOT**
Reverse IXL in an oval, Bitters under it, tapered and ring top, square bottle, under bottom "W. F. G. Sons," amber, 12" 60.00 80.00

☐ **HENTZ'S CURATIVE BITTERS**
Phila., label, embossed, clear, 9½" 50.00 100.00

☐ **H. P. HERB WILD CHERRY BITTERS**
"Reading, PA.," in back wild cherry and tree, Bitters on all four sides of the roof, amber, 10" . . 150.00 175.00

☐ Same as above, except green 150.00 200.00

☐ **DR. I. HESTER'S STOMACH BITTERS**
Amber, 8¾" 80.00 100.00

☐ **HERKULES BITTER**
Monogram, G.A. inside of circle, figural-ball shape bottle, "1 QUART," labeled, also 1 pint, deep green, 7¾" 250.00 300.00

National Bitters Bottle, *ear of corn design, burgundy, 12½".*
$400.00–$500.00

S.T. Drake's Plantation Bitters Jar, *square body, expanded lip, golden amber, 9½".*
$150.00–$250.00

Price Range

☐ **DR. R.F. HIBBARD'S WILD CHERRY BITTERS**
Proprietor, NY, round bottle,
"C.N.CRITTENTON," aqua, 8" 95.00 120.00

☐ **HIERAPICRA BITTERS**
Reverse side "Extract of Fig, Botanical Society,"
other side "California," aqua, 6½" 90.00 100.00

☐ **HIGHLAND BITTERS & SCOTCH TONIC**
Barrel-shaped bottle, ring top, amber, 9½" 160.00 200.00
☐ Same as above, except olive 185.00 230.00

☐ **HI HI BITTER CO.**
Triangular shape, amber, 9½" 50.00 60.00

☐ **HILL'S HOREHOUND BITTERS**
Round bottle, labeled only, "IRISH MOSS," 6½" 10.00 15.00

☐ **HILL'S MOUNTAIN BITTERS**
Rectangular bottle, "EMBOSSED INDIANA
DRUG SPECIALTY COMPANY," amber, tapered
top, 7¾" 20.00 30.00

☐ **HOBOKEN AVAN BITTERS**
Olive, 9¼" 20.00 30.00

☐ **HOFFHEIMER BROS.**
Reverse "BAVARIAN BITTERS," amber, 9½" 100.00 150.00

☐ **DR. HOFFMAN'S GOLDEN BITTERS**
Label, "ACW" under bottom, amber, 9" 10.00 15.00

☐ **HOLTZERMANN'S PATENT STOMACH BITTERS**
On the roof of cabin-shaped bottle, shingle roof,
tapered top, amber, 9¾" 350.00 450.00

☐ **HOLTZERMANN'S PATENT STOMACH BITTERS**
Label, amber, 4¼" 125.00 150.00
☐ Same as above, except 9¾" 140.00 170.00

☐ **HOME BITTERS**
On the side, "Saint Louis, MO," square, beveled
corners, long tapered top, 9", amber 70.00 90.00

☐ **DR. HOOFLAND'S GERMAN BITTERS**
Rectangular bottle, aqua, pint, pontil, in back
"C.M. Jackson, Phila.," 4" 25.00 50.00

☐ **HOP & IRON BITTERS**
Square bottle, in back "Utica, NY," amber, tapered top, 8⅝" 30.00 50.00

Price Range

☐ **DR. VON HOPFS CURACO BITTERS**
In back "Chamberlain & Co., Des Moines, Iowa,"
tapered top, amber, 9¼".................... 95.00 120.00
☐ Same as above, in a flask type bottle 70.00   90.00
☐ **HOPS & MALT BITTERS**
Roofed shoulder, Trademark (Sheafil Grain),
square bottle, yellow amber, amber, tapered top,
9⅝".. 80.00 100.00
☐ **DR. A.S. HOPPINS**
"Union stomach bitters," in three lines, tapered
top, off shade of amber, beveled corners, 9¾" 30.00   50.00
☐ **HORSE SHOW BITTERS**
Amber, square, 10"......................... 125.00 140.00
☐ **HORSE SHOE BITTERS**
"Horse Shoe Med. Co., Base Pat. App. for,"
Horseshoe shape, amber, COLLINSVILLE, ILL.",
12"..1500.00 2000.00
☐ **DR. J. HOSTETTER'S STOMACH BITTERS**
Square, light amber, amber, 9"............. 10.00   15.00
☐ Same except yellow green................... 75.00 125.00
☐ Same except machine made 5.00   10.00
☐ **DR. J. HOSTETTER'S STOMACH BITTERS**
With two labels, seal, square, amber, 8¾" 20.00   30.00
☐ **DR. HOSTETTER'S STOMACH BITTERS**
On base I.G.L., square, amber, 9"........... 5.00   10.00
☐ Same as above, except on back 18 Fluid ox., 8¾" 10.00   15.00
☐ Same as above, machine made 10.00   15.00
☐ **DR. J. HOSTETTER'S STOMACH BITTERS**
(J is backwards), amber, 8½".............. 75.00 125.00
☐ **DR. J. HOSTETTER'S STOMACH BITTERS**
L & W 10 on base, yellow amber, 9½" 15.00   20.00
☐ Same as above, except dark amber........... 15.00   20.00
☐ Same as above, except S. McKEE & CO., 2 on
base...................................... 15.00   20.00
☐ Same as above, except #2 on base 15.00   20.00
☐ **HUA**
On base, small lady's leg, amber, 7½" 15.00   20.00
☐ **H.U.A.**
Monogram on bottom, Bitters label, lady's leg
shape, amber, 10½"....................... 20.00   30.00
☐ **HUBBARD'S THEUMATIC SYRUP**
Square, amber, in original box, amber, 9¼" ... 25.00   35.00

Price Range

☐ **GEO. C. HUBBEL & CO.**
On each side, blank front and back, tapered top,
aqua, golden bitters, 10½" 160.00 210.00

☐ **HUTCHINS**
On side, "DYSPEPSIA BITTERS" on front, "New
York" on other side, tapered top, aqua, pontil,
8½" 125.00 150.00

☐ **J.W. HUTCHINSON'S**
Reverse Tonic Bitters, Mobile, AL, aqua, 8¾" 130.00 150.00

☐ **HYGEIA BITTERS**
Square bottle, "FOX & CO.," amber, tapered top,
base L & W, 9" 50.00 80.00

☐ **IMPERIAL RUSSIAN TONIC BITTERS**
Rope design on sides, clear or aqua, 9¼" 90.00 115.00

☐ **I.N.C. BITTERS**
Reedy, PA, round, long neck, barrel shape,
amber, 10" 90.00 115.00

☐ **IMPERIAL BITTERS**
One side, "Victor Rivaud," other side, "Louisville,
KY," amber, 10½" 100.00 125.00

☐ **INDIAN VEGETABLE SARSAPARILLA**
"Reverse Bitters, Boston," all vertical lettering,
pontil, aqua, 8¼", rare 100.00 130.00

☐ **IRON BITTERS**
Square bottle, "BROWN CHEMICAL CO.," 8⅝" 15.00 23.00

☐ **ISAACSON SEIXAS & CO. BITTERS**
CO. with eye in center, monogram, square, light
amber, "66 & 68 COMMON ST." Push up with
five star pontil, etc. 160.00 210.00

☐ **JACOB'S CABIN TONIC BITTERS**
Cabin shape bottle, "LABORATORY-
PHILADELPHIA," clear glass, pontil, 7⅜"... 8000.00 12000.00

☐ **DR. JACOB'S BITTERS**
S. A. Spencer, rectangular bottle, "NEW
HAVEN," aqua, 10" 100.00 130.00

☐ **JENKINS STOMACH BITTERS**
In two lines, under bottom, "W.McC & Co.," tapered top, amber 70.00 90.00

☐ **JEWEL BITTERS**
Reverse "John S. Bowman & Co.," amber, 9" 50.00 75.00

Price Range

☐ **JEWEL BITTERS**
On side, "John S. Bowman & Co., California" on
back, tapered top, quart, amber 30.00 50.00

☐ **JOCKEY CLUB HOUSE BITTERS**
J. H. Dudley & Co., green, 9½" 50.00 75.00

☐ **A. H. JOHNSON & CO.**
On the side "Collingwood, Ont.," on front "Johnson's Tonic Bitters," clear or amethyst, double
ring top, 8¾" 30.00 50.00

☐ **JOHNSON'S INDIAN DYSPEPTIC BITTERS**
Each on four sides, rectangular, aqua, tapered
top, pontil, ring top, 6¼" 70.00 90.00

☐ **A.H. JOHNSON & CO.**
Other side "Collingwood, Ont.," on front "Johnson's Tonic Bitters," clear or amethyst, double
top, 8¾" 15.00 20.00

☐ **JONES INDIAN SPECIFIC HERB BITTERS**
SW. Jones-Prop., Phila; square, amber, "PA-
TENT," 1868, tapered top, 9" 80.00 120.00

☐ **DR. HERBERT JOHN'S INDIAN BITTERS**
Great Indian Discoveries; amber, 8½" 70.00 90.00

☐ **JOHNSON'S CALISAYA BITTERS**
Reverse "Burlington, VT," tapered top, amber,
10" 20.00 30.00

☐ **KAISER WILHELM BITTERS CO.**
Sandusky, OH, bulged neck, ringed top, round
bottle, amber, clear, 10" 225.00 300.00

☐ **KELLY'S OLD CABIN BITTERS**
"Patd March 1863" on one side; green, 10" . . . 350.00 450.00

☐ **KELLY'S OLD CABIN BITTERS**
"Patented 1868 or 1870" on each side of roof,
amber, 9¼" 275.00 350.00

☐ **KENNEDY'S EAST INDIA BITTERS**
Clear, Omaha, NB., 6½" 55.00 70.00

☐ **KEYSTONE BITTERS**
Barrel-shaped bottle, ringed top, amber, 10" . . . 175.00 225.00

☐ **KIMBALL'S** (has backward S) **JAUNDICE
BITTERS**
"Troy, NH" on side; tapered top, pontil, dark
amber, 6¾" 175.00 225.00

Price Range

☐ **KIMBALL'S JAUNDICE**
On other side "Troy, NH," beveled corners, rectangular, olive green, tapered top, pontil, 7¼" x 2¾" x 2" 115.00 140.00

☐ **KING SOLOMON BITTERS**
Seattle, WA, rectangular bottle, amber, 8½" ... 95.00 115.00

☐ **KING SOLOMON'S BITTERS**
Other side "Seattle, Washington," rectangular, amber, 10 oz. 75.00 90.00

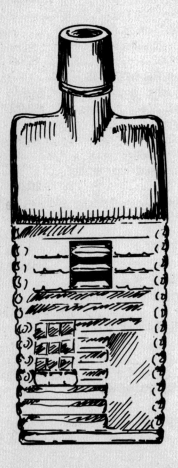

Kelly's Old Cabin Bitters, rectangular shaped, smooth base, sloping mouth, olive green, 9". $350.00–$450.00

Price Range

☐ **KLAS'S OREGON PEACH BITTERS**
In large letters on shoulder, round, aqua, 11½″,
rare 100.00 150.00

☐ **KOEHLER & HENRICH RED STAR
STOMACH BITTERS**
"St. Paul, Minn." in a circle, label in red, black and
white circle; 1908, 11½″ 175.00 225.00

☐ **KOEHLERS STOMACH BITTERS CO.**
Amber, 12½″ 20.00 30.00

☐ **LANDSBERG'S CENTURY BITTERS**
In three lines; over it a bird or eagle; in back "The
Ader Company, St. Louis" also in three lines; 13
stars around shoulder, also 1776 & 1876; corner
diamond effect, very decorative bottle, tapered
top and ring, 11½″ 375.00 500.00

☐ **LACOUR'S BITTERS**
Sarsoparipher, round fancy bottle, amber, yellow-
green, 9⅛″ 300.00 400.00

☐ **DR. LANGLEY'S ROOT & HERB BITTERS**
"76 Union St. Boston" on front; round, ringed top,
light green, 6¾″ 35.00 48.00

☐ **DR. LANGLEY'S ROOT & HERB BITTERS**
"99 Union St. Boston" on front; ringed top,
amber, 8½″ 45.00 60.00

☐ Same as above, but embossing in indented panel 45.00 60.00

☐ **LASH'S BITTERS CO.**
NY, Chicago, San Francisco; round, clear, dark
amber, amethyst, 10¾″ and 11″ x 3″ 15.00 20.00

☐ Also with label Cordol Bitter 5.00 6.00

☐ **LASH'S, BITTERS CO., NEW YORK,
CHICAGO, SAN FRANCISCO**
Amber, round, ABM only 5.00 10.00

☐ **LASH'S BITTERS CO. N.Y., CHICAGO, SAN
FRANCISCO**
Round, fluted neck and shoulder, tapered top and
ring, amber, 10½″ 15.00 20.00

☐ **LASH'S KIDNEY & LIVER BITTERS AND
BLOOD PURIFIER**
In back, square, tapered top and ring, amber, bev-
eled corners, 9½″ 20.00 30.00

Price Range

☐ **LASH'S BITTERS**
With circle between words "KIDNEY" and "LIVER," on back in two lines, "The Best Cathartic and Blood Purifier," 2¾" x 2¾", amber, 9" 8.00 10.00
☐ Same except 1" x 1" x 3" 5.00 10.00
☐ **LASH'S LIVER BITTERS**
"Nature's Tonic Laxative" on back, machine made, amber, 7½" 5.00 8.00
☐ Same as above, except screw top 10.00 15.00
☐ **LEAK KIDNEY & LIVER BITTERS**
Reverse side "The Best Blood Purifier and Cathartec," amber, 9" 60.00 80.00
☐ **LEDIARDS**
On side "Celebrated Stomach," on back "Bitters," tapered top, sea green, 10" 125.00 175.00
☐ **LEIPZIGER BURGUNDER WEIN BITTERS**
All in a circle in center "A" around it, The Hockstadter Co. all under bottom, ring & tapered top. Round, 3pt. mould, green 20.00 30.00
☐ **LEWIS RED JACKET BITTERS**
Around bottom, three-piece mold, amber, 11" 60.00 75.00
☐ **LIPPMAN'S GREAT GERMAN BITTERS**
Other side NY & Savannah, GO., amber, 9¾" 120.00 150.00
☐ **LITTHAUER STOMACH BITTERS**
In center "Invented 1884 by Josef Lowenthal, Berlin" in vertical lines, tapered top, milk glass, 9¾" 100.00 130.00
☐ Same as above, except Berlin omitted 70.00 90.00
☐ Same as above, except clear and "J" is backward, Invented, 7" 130.00 170.00
☐ **LINCOLN BITTERS**
Rectangular bottle, labeled only, clear glass, 9⅜" 10.00 15.00
☐ **LOHENGRIN BITTERS**
Adolph Marcus, Van Buton German, square-gin shape, milk glass, 9½" 200.00 250.00
☐ **LOWELL'S INVIGORATING BITTERS**
Square bottle, "BOSTON, MASS," aqua, 8¼" 75.00 100.00
☐ **DR. LOEW'S CELEBRATED STOMACH BITTERS & NERVE TONIC**
Amber, 3½" 75.00 100.00

American Life Bitters Bottle, cabin design, amber, 9". $160.00–$190.00

The Fish Bitters (on side of eye), on reverse W.H. Ware Patented 1866, on base W.H. Ware Patented 1866, tail is bottom with a smooth base, fish mouth is also tooled mouth of bottle, clear glass, 11½". $400.00–$575.00

Price Range

☐ **DR. LOEW'S CELEBRATED STOMACH BITTERS & NERVE TONIC**
Reverse "The Loew & Son Co.," tapered top and swirled ribbed neck, fancy bottle, apple green, 9½" 170.00 220.00

☐ **LORD BROS., DR. MANDRAKE BAXTO'S BITTERS**
Amber, 12" 25.00 33.00

☐ Same as above, except clear or amber 10.00 15.00

☐ **LORENTZ MED CO. TRADEMARK**
Around shoulder, bitters label, amber, 9¾" 10.00 15.00

☐ **LORENTZ MED CO.**
On bitters label, "Trade To-Ni-Ta Mark" around shoulder, amber, 10" 10.00 15.00

☐ **LORIMER'S JUNIPER BITTERS**
Blue green, square, 9½", 2¼" 80.00 110.00

☐ **DR. XX LOVEGOODS FAMILY BITTERS**
On roof of cabin-shaped bottle, tapered neck, amber, 10½" 500.00 600.00

☐ **DR. LOVEGOODS FAMILY BITTERS**
(E left out of BITTERS), amber, 9½" 500.00 600.00

☐ **E. DEXTER LOVERIDGE WAHOO BITTERS DWD**
"1863 XXX" on roof, tapered top, eagle faces down and left with one arrow, dark amber, 10" 200.00 300.00

☐ Same except eagle faces up to right, light yellow 125.00 150.00

☐ **LOWELL'S INVIGORATING BITTERS**
Square bottle, "BOSTON-MASS," aqua, 8¼" .. 40.00 60.00

☐ **LUTZ**
Isaac D, Reading, PA, red amber, double ring top, label stated bitters, 7¼" 40.00 60.00

☐ **DR. LYFORD'S BITTERS**
C.D. Herrick, Tilton, NH, on bottom "W.T. & Co. C," ringed top, aqua, 8" 40.00 60.00

☐ **E. G. LYONS & CO.**
Mfg. San. F. CA." (n in SAN is backward), tapered top, amber, 9" 60.00 80.00

☐ **MACK'S SARSAPARILLA BITTERS**
In back "Mack & Co., Prop's S.F., amber, 9¼" 100.00 150.00

☐ **MAGADOR BITTERS**
"E. J. Rose's" in back, superior tonic, cathartic and blood purifier, amber, 9" 90.00 115.00

Price Range

☐ **MAGIC BITTERS**
Prepared by Minetree & Jackson, Petersburg, VA, two panels and rounded sides, tapered top, olive, 14½″ 150.00 250.00

☐ **MALARION BITTERS**
Snyder Gue & Condell, St. Louis, MO, amber, 8½″ 75.00 125.00

☐ **MALT BITTERS CO.**
"Boston, U.S.A." under bottom, round, emerald green, 8½″ 20.00 40.00

☐ **MAMPE BITTERS**
Label, back embossed same with "Carl Mampe, Berlin," dark green, 6″ 40.00 50.00

☐ **PROFESSOR B.E. MANNS ORIENTAL STOMACH BITTERS**
Amber, 10¼″ 75.00 100.00

☐ **MARSHALL'S BITTERS**
"The Best Laxative and Blood Purifier" on back, amber, 8¾″ 20.00 35.00

☐ **McNEIL'S INDIAN VEGETABLE BITTERS**
Oval bottle, labeled only, aqua, 6¾″ 10.00 20.00

☐ **McKEEVER'S ARMY BITTERS**
On shoulder, drum-shaped bottom, cannonballs stacked on top, tapered top, amber, 10¼″ 700.00 775.00

☐ **MILLS BITTERS**
A. M. Gilman, sole prop., lady's leg shape, ringed top, 6 ounce, amber 35.00 50.00

☐ Same except sample size, 2 ounce 35.00 50.00

☐ **MISHLER'S HERB BITTERS**
"S. B. Hartman & Co." in back, under bottom "Stoeckels Grad Pat. Feb. 6, 66," tapered top, amber, 8¾″ 30.00 60.00

☐ Same as above, except back reads Wm. McC & CO. 30.00 50.00

☐ **MITCHELL'S (DR. F.A.) SAN GENTO BITTERS**
Amber, square 8⅞″ 75.00 100.00

☐ **MOHICA BITTERS**
On back "Roth & Co. S. F.," ringed top, amber, 9″ 30.00 50.00

Price Range

☐ **MORNING STAR BITTERS**
With Iron Pontil, fancy triangular, amber, "INCEP-
TUM 5869," Patented (curve) 5869, 13" ...... | 175.00 225.00
☐ Same without pontil .... | 90.00 115.00
☐ **G. N. MORRISON'S**
"Invigorating" other side, "G.N. Morrison, New
Orleans," amber, tapered top, 9¼" .... | 190.00 235.00
☐ **MOULTONS OLOROSO BITTERS**
Trade (Pineapple) mark, round, aqua, ribbed bot-
tle, 11½" .... | 100.00 140.00
☐ **MURRAY'S PURIFYING BITTERS**
Rectangular bottle, labeled only, aqua, 8" ..... | 10.00 20.00
☐ **NATIONAL BITTERS, EAR OF CORN**
"Patent 1867" under bottom, amber, corn, 12¼" | 400.00 500.00
☐ **NATIONAL TONIC BITTERS**
Amber, square, pat. 1867, 8½" .... | 50.00 75.00
☐ **NEW YORK HOP BITTERS CO.**
Tapered top, aqua, 9" .... | 140.00 200.00
☐ **DR. NISKIAN'S STOMACH BITTERS**
On one side, "Morrin-Powers, Merc.-sole
agents"-"Kansas City, MO." on other side, other
two plain, tapered top, clear, 8¼" .... | 150.00 190.00
☐ **NIGHTCAP BITTERS, SCHMIDLOPP & CO.**
"Distillers, Cincinnati, OH, a good Beverage,"
multi-sided bottle, tapered top with ring, clear, 9" | 100.00 125.00
☐ **NORMAN BITTERS**
In back "Dr. Bohlins," clear, 8¾" .... | 25.00 41.00
☐ **NORTHCRAFTS BOTANIC BITTERS**
Square bottle, labeled only, machine made,
amber, 9¼" .... | 10.00 14.00
☐ **O.K. PLANTATION**
Triangular shape, amber, 11" .... | 275.00 350.00
☐ **OLD ABE'S AQUE & STOMACH BITTERS**
In three lines, ring top, under bottom in a clove
lief-H B & C, 0–12 oz., aqua, 7¼" .... | 20.00 34.00
☐ **OLD CABIN BITTERS**
Schnudlapp & Co., Cincinnati, OH, etx., cabin-
shape bottle, "PATENTED 1863," amber, 9" .. | 350.00 450.00
☐ **OLD DR. SOLOMON'S INDIAN WINE
BITTERS**
Rectangular bottle, aqua, 8½" .... | 65.00 85.00

Price Range

☐ **OLD HICKORY CELEBRATED STOMACH BITTERS**
On other side "J. Grossman, N.O., LA," amber, 4½" **100.00 130.00**

☐ **OLD HOMESTEAD WILD CHERRY BITTERS**
Cabin shape, golden amber, clapboards not logs and shingled roof, 10" **170.00 220.00**

☐ **OLD HOMESTEAD WILD CHERRY BITTERS**
Cabin shape, amber, 10" **160.00 180.00**

☐ Same except "PATENT" on roof, clapboards not logs and shingled roof, amber, 10" **110.00 120.00**

☐ Same except cobalt blue **500.00 675.00**

☐ Same except inside thread, marked on top "PAT. 1861" **175.00 225.00**

☐ **OLD KENTUCKY BITTERS**
Amber, square, 9" **75.00 100.00**

☐ **OLD SACHEM BITTERS & WIGHAM TONIC**
Barrel type bottle, ringed top, puce, amber, yellow amber, 9¾" **150.00 250.00**

☐ Same except green **150.00 250.00**

☐ Same except with label "MERRICK & MOORS OLD SACHEM BITTERS & WIGWAM TONIC, NEW HAVEN, CONN." **120.00 150.00**

☐ **OLD SOL BITTERS**
Round, figural shoulders looked something like elephant, 7½" **475.00 550.00**

☐ **O'LEARY'S 20th CENTURY BITTERS**
In vertical line, tapered top, light amber, 8½" .. **100.00 130.00**

☐ **ORANGE BITTERS**
Round bottle, labeled only, machine made, pale green, six-pointed star with 3 dots on base, 11¾" **10.00 14.00**

☐ **OREGON GRAPE ROOT BITTERS**
Round, clear, 9¾" **100.00 130.00**

☐ **ORIGINAL POCAHONTAS BITTERS**
In center above it 10 hoops and 10 below, barrel shape, short neck, ring top, aqua, 9½" **1000.00 1300.00**

☐ **ORIZABA BITTERS**
On back "J. Maristany Jr.," round bottle, tapered top, amber, 9½" **75.00 100.00**

☐ **ORRUSO BITTERS**
Around shoulder, round, ABM, dark green, 11¼" **15.00 20.00**

Price Range

☐ **OXYGENATED BITTERS**
Pontil, aqua, 6¾ " 50.00   75.00
☐ **PAINE'S CELERY COMPOUND BITTERS**
Rectangular bottle, amber, 8" 20.00   30.00
☐ Same as above, clear glass 15.00   20.00
☐ **DR. PALMERS TONIC BITTERS**
Square bottle, labeled only, aqua, 8¾" 10.00   14.00
☐ **PARKER. R. MASON-CHICAGO**
In two lines, other side "Aromatic-Golden Bitters," amber, tapered top, 9¼" 110.00 135.00
☐ **PATENTED BITTERS**
T. Pirters & Co., 31 & 33 Mich. Ave., Chicago, square bottle, "CHICAGO," amber, 9¼ " 75.00   95.00
☐ **PAWNEE BITTERS**
Indian Medicine Co. S.F., amber, 11¼" 70.00   90.00
☐ **DR. PELZOLDS GENUINE GERMAN BITTERS**
Cabin type bottle, amber 120.00 150.00
☐ **PENNS BITTERS FOR THE LIVER**
On front panel, square, beveled edge, amber, 6½" 60.00   75.00
☐ **PEPSIN BITTERS**
On one side, with R.W. Davis Drug Co., Chicago, U.S.A. in two lines on other side, shoulder and neck are raised, but not on ends, sunken panels on front and back, yellow green, 8¼" tall, 4¼" x 2⅛" 80.00   100.00
☐ **PEPSIN CALISAYA BITTERS**
In two lines, opposite side Dr. Russell Med. Co., rectangular, green, olive green, beveled corners with three vertical ribs, 7½" tall, 4¼" x 2¼" . . 25.00   34.00
☐ **PERRINS APPLE GINGER, PHILA.**
Embossed apple on front, cabin type bottle, amber, 10¼" 90.00   115.00
☐ **PERUVIAN BITTERS**
On shoulder, in black in shield "P.B. CO.," square bottle, amber, 9¼" 30.00   40.00
☐ **DR. D.S. PERRY & CO.**
On other side New York Excelsior Aromatic Bitters, roofed shoulder, tapered top, amber, 10½" 110.00 140.00
☐ **JOHN A PERRY'S, DR. WARREN'S BILIOUS BITTERS**
Boston, MA., aqua, 10" 70.00   90.00

Price Range

☐ **PETER VIERLING'S BLOOD PURIFYING BITTERS**
Evansville, IN, square bottle, amber, 10″ 70.00 90.00

☐ **DR. PETZOLD'S CABIN BITTERS**
Except 1862, amber, 11″ 125.00 150.00

☐ **PEYCHAUD'S AMERICAN AROMATIC BITTERS CORDIAL**
"L.E. JUNG, SOLE PROP. N.O.," round tapered
top, amber, 10½″ 25.00 30.00

☐ **PHILADELPHIA HOP BITTERS**
In three lines, top of it a man holding a bottle, roof
shoulder, tapered top, aqua, 10¼″ 175.00 225.00

☐ **PHOENIX BITTERS**
On back "J.N. Moffat," on one side "Price
$1.00," other side "N.Y.," pontil, dark olive, 5″ 175.00 225.00

☐ **DR. GEO. PIERCES INDIAN RESTORATIVE BITTERS**
On side "Lowell, Mass.," tapered top, aqua, pontil, 7½″ 30.00 50.00

☐ **PINEAPPLE BOTTLE**
Bitters label, light amber, 9¼″ 200.00 300.00
☐ Same except yellow green 400.00 475.00

☐ **PIPER BITTERS**
In a seal on shoulder, tapered top and ring, Dr.
Olive, 3 Pt. mold, 12¼″ 75.00 90.00

☐ **DR. PLANETTS BITTERS**
Iron pontil, aqua, 9¾″ 90.00 110.00

☐ **PLOW'S SHERRY BITTERS**
A large leaf on back of label, amber, 7¾″ 350.00 425.00

☐ **POLO CLUB STOMACH BITTERS**
Amber, 9½″ 75.00 100.00

☐ **POMLO BITTERS CO.**
"N.Y." on back, tapered top and ring, light green,
11½″ 65.00 85.00

☐ **POND'S BITTERS CO.**
Chicago, label, "Ponds Genuine Ginger Brandy"
on back, clear, 11½″ 35.00 45.00

☐ **POND'S BITTERS**
Reverse side "Unexcelled Laxative," on base 76,
amber, 9¾″ 42.00 47.00
☐ Same except machine made, clear 18.00 24.00

Price Range

☐ **POOR MAN'S FAMILY BITTERS**
Ringed top, aqua, 6½″ **30.00 52.00**

☐ Same except label reads "POOR MAN'S BIT-
TERS CO., OSWEGO N.Y.," Entered according
to Act of Congress in 1870" **50.00 75.00**

☐ **DR. POTER'S STOMACH BITTERS**
(Dr. Poter New York), rectangular bottle, labeled,
clear glass, embossed, round bound top, 5½″ **15.00 20.00**

☐ **R.W. POWERS & CO. AROMATIC PERUVIAN
BITTERS**
Rich., VA 1881, amber, 10½″ **75.00 95.00**

☐ **PRICKLEY ASH BITTER CO.**
In two lines in sunken panel, other sides are flat
for labels, beveled corners, 2¾″ x 2¾″, 10″ .. **20.00 25.00**

☐ **PRUSSIAN BITTERS**
Tapered top, amber, 9½″ **55.00 75.00**

☐ **PRUNE STOMACH & LIVER BITTERS**
"The best cathartic & blood purifier," square,
amber, on base 2280, tapered top, 9″ **85.00 105.00**

☐ **THE QUININE BITTER CO.**
184–196 Congress St., Chicago, IL U.S.A., dia-
mond shape, concave sides, clear, 8½″ **60.00 80.00**

☐ **RAMSEY'S TRINIDAD BITTER**
On shoulder, bitters misspelled on bottom, dark
olive, 8¼″ **80.00 100.00**

☐ **RAMSEY'S TRINIDAD BITTERS**
Round, dark olive, body 5″, 3¼″ neck on a shoulder, under bottom, "Ramsey Trinidad Bitter" (no
date) **45.00 60.00**

☐ **DR. MILLER'S RATAFIA,** (Sphinx)
Under it, "Damiana Silbe Bros. Jr. Plagemann,
S.F. sole agents," Pacific Coast, round bottle, ta-
pered and ringed top, amber, 12″ **60.00 80.00**

☐ **RED CLOUD BITTERS**
Square bottle, "TAYLOR & WRIGHT Chicago,"
green, also amber, 9½″ **100.00 120.00**

☐ **RED JACKET BITTERS**
Square bottle, "BENNET & PIETERS," amber,
9½″ **65.00 98.00**

☐ **RED JACKET BITTERS**
Rectangular bottle, "MON-HEIMER & CO.,"
amber, 8½″ **50.00 70.00**

Price Range

☐ **REED'S BITTERS**
In back curved letters "Reed's Bitters", round,
lady's leg neck, on ring, 12½" 200.00 250.00

☐ **DR. RENZ'S HERB BITTERS**
Tapered and ring top, light green, 9" 75.00 120.00

☐ **REX BITTERS CO.**
Chicago, whiskey shape, amber, clear, 10¼" .. 35.00 48.00

☐ **REX KIDNEY & LIVER BITTERS**
Square bottle, in back "LAXATIVE & BLOOD PU-
RIFIER," red amber, 10" 55.00 75.00

☐ **RICHARDS, C.A. & Co.**
18 & 20 Kilby St., Boston, MA., amber, label
stated wine bitters, 9½", with label 55.00 75.00

☐ Same as above, without label 30.00 40.00

☐ **RISING SUN BITTERS**
Amber, 9½" 75.00 125.00

☐ **S.O. RICHARDSON**
Vertically on front, "Bitters So. Reading" on side,
other side "Mass.," flared top, pontil, light green,
6½" 75.00 80.00

☐ **R.C. RIDGWAY & PHILA.**
Big 3 under bottom, amber, 11" 80.00 105.00

☐ **RIVAUD'S** (reverse apostrophe) **IMPERIAL
BITTERS**
"Victor Rivaud" on side, "Louisville, KY" on other
side, amber, 10½" 85.00 110.00

☐ **RIVENBURG'S (DR.) INDIAN VEGETABLE
BITTERS**
Rectangular, aqua, 8⅝" 85.00 100.00

☐ **DR. C.W. ROBACKS**
Cincinnati, OH in small circle in center, "Stomach
Bitters," dark brown, barrel shape, ten ribs on top,
ten ribs on base, 9¾" 160.00 215.00

☐ **ROCK CITY BITTERS**
"50¢ size" in two lines, side mold, amber, 7½" 70.00 90.00

☐ **ROHRER'S**
On one side "Lancaster, PA," on the other side
"Expectoral-Wild Cherry Tonic," 10½" 90.00 115.00

☐ **ROMAINES CRIMEAN BITTERS**
Fancy square, amber, "PATEND 1863," on base,
10" 160.00 210.00

Price Range

☐ **E.J. ROSE'S**
"Superior Tonic, Cathartic and Blood Purifier" on
back, amber, 9" 60.00   75.00
☐ **ROSSWINKLE'S CROWN BITTERS**
Square bottle, amber, tapered top, 8¾" 75.00   80.00
☐ **S.B. ROTHENBERG**
In a semicircle inside of which is "SOLE/
AGENT/U.S./," the reverse has an applied
blob seal stamped "PAT. APPLIED FOR,"
bottle is in the shape of a square face gin, milk
glass color, top, 8½" tall, 2" at base, 3" at shoul-
der. 70.00   90.00
☐ **ROYAL ITALIAN BITTERS**
Round, tall, red amber, wine type bottle, 13½"   250.00 350.00
☐ **ROYAL PEPSIN STOMACH BITTERS**
Amber, 8½" 75.00   95.00
☐ Same as above, except no embossing 15.00   20.00
☐ **W.L. RUCHARDSON'S BITTERS**
Pontil, rectangular bottle, "MASS.," aqua, 7" . .   80.00   100.00
☐ Same except no pontil 50.00   70.00
☐ **RUSH'S BITTERS**
Square bottle, "A.H. FLANDERS, M.D. N.Y.,"
aqua, pint size 20.00   30.00
☐ Same as above, amber, 9" 30.00   40.00
☐ **RUSS'S ST. DOMINGO BITTERS**
Square bottle, "NEW YORK," amber, also olive
green, 10" 70.00   90.00
☐ **DR. RUSSELL'S ANGOSTURA BITTERS**
Round tapered top, amber, medium green, clear,
7¾" 90.00   115.00
☐ Same except olive green (rare) 85.00   110.00
☐ **SAIDSCHITSER-FURSTLICH-LOBKOWITZ
BITTER WASSER**
In circle, tan crock, four panels, round bottom,
9½" 30.00   50.00
☐ **SAINSEVINS WINE BITTERS**
Label, ringed top, aqua, 12" 18.00   24.00
☐ **SALMON'S PERFECT STOMACH BITTERS**
Tapered top, square beveled corners, amber,
9½" 80.00   100.00

Price Range

☐ **SANBORN'S KIDNEY & LIVER VEGETABLE LAXATIVE BITTERS**
On bottom B, tapered bottle to paneled shoulder with fluted neck, amber, 10″ 90.00 115.00

☐ **SAN JOAQUIN WINE BITTERS**
On back at bottom "B. F. C. Co.," deep kick-up in base, amber, 9¾″ 125.00 175.00

☐ **SARRACENIA STOMACH BITTERS**
Amber, square, 9⅛″ 100.00 125.00

☐ **SARSAPARILLA BITTERS**
On side "E. M. Rusha," back side "Dr. De Andrews," amber, 10″ 75.00 100.00

☐ **SAZERAC AROMATIC BITTERS**
In a circle on shoulder in monogram "DPH & Co.," milk glass, also in blue, green, 12½″ 250.00 325.00

☐ **SAZERAC AROMATIC BITTERS**
"D.P.H." in seal, lady's leg shape, light amber, 10¼″ 175.00 235.00

☐ **DR. S.B. & CO.**
"ML" under bottom, clear or amethyst, 7¼″ ... 3.00 5.00

☐ **SCHROEDER'S BITTERS**
"Louisville, KY" in three lines, base in one line, "Ky.G.W.Co.," lady's leg, ring top, amber, 11½″ 100.00 200.00
☐ Same except tapered top and ring, 5½″ 215.00 270.00

☐ **SEAWORTH BITTERS ROUND FIGURAL LIGHTHOUSE**
Amber, 11½″ 250.00 300.00

☐ **SEGRESTAT BITTERS** in seal
Kick-up bottom, dark olive, 11¾″ 80.00 100.00

☐ **SEGUR'S GOLDEN SEAL BITTERS**
Springfield, MA, Pontil, aqua, 8″ 85.00 110.00

☐ **W. F. SEVERA**
On back "Stomach Bitters," tapered top, red amber, 10″ 35.00 48.00

☐ **SHARP'S MOUNTAIN HERB BITTERS**
Amber, square, 9½″ 75.00 100.00

☐ **SHERMAN BITTERS**
Myer Bros. Drug. Co., St. Louis, label, amber, 7¾″ 10.00 14.00

☐ **DR. B.F. SHERMAN'S PRICKLY ASH BITTERS**
Machine made, amber, 10″ 20.00 30.00

Price Range

☐ **DR. SHOOP'S FAMILY MEDICINES**
"Racine, Wis." embossed on sides, rectangular,
blown in mold, clear, 6½" 25.00   35.00

☐ **SIMONS AROMATIC STOMACH BITTERS**
Clear or amber, 7¼" 70.00   90.00

☐ **SIMONS CENTENNIAL BITTERS TRADE
MARK**
Bust shape bottle, double ring top, amber, clear
or aqua, 10¼" 600.00 900.00

☐ **DR. SKINNER'S CELEBRATED 25 CENT
BITTERS**
So. Reading, MA, pontil, aqua, 9½" 80.00   100.00

☐ **DR. SKINNER'S SHERRY WINE BITTERS**
Rectangular bottle, "SO. READING, MASS.,"
aqua, pontil, 8½" 85.00   110.00

☐ **S.C. SMITH'S DRUID BITTERS**
Barrel shape bottle, brown, 9½" 165.00 200.00

☐ **DR. SMITH'S COLUMBO BITTERS**
Label and embossed, amber, 9¾" 40.00   60.00

☐ **SMITH'S TONIC BITTERS**
Amber, square, 9" 150.00 175.00

☐ **S.N. BITTERS**
Amber, square, 8" 75.00   90.00

☐ **SNYDER BITTERS**
Jonesboro, AK, tapered top, amber, 9½" 75.00   90.00

☐ **SOMER'S STOMACH BITTERS**
Square shape bottle, amber, 9½" 65.00   80.00

☐ **SOLOMON'S STRENGTHENING &
INVIGORATING BITTER**
On one sunken panel, on the other "Savannah,
Ga.", on other side, sunken panels, back flat,
roofed shoulders, beveled corner, cobalt, 9½" 200.00 250.00

☐ **DR. SPERRY'S FEMALE STRENGTHENING
BITTERS**
Waterbury, CT, label and embossed, 10" 90.00   115.00

☐ **SPICE BITTERS**
Amber, 9" 175.00 200.00

☐ **STAAKE'S ORIGINAL VITAL-TONE BITTERS**
Around shoulder, ringed top, clear, 8¼" 65.00   85.00

Price Range

☐ **STANDARD AMERICAN AROMATIC
BITTERS CORDIAL**
"Yochim Bros" in seven lines, New Orleans,
round bottle, tapered top and ring, quart, amber,
10½" 20.00   30.00

☐ **STAR KIDNEY & LIVER BITTERS**
Tapered top, amber, 9½" 40.00   60.00

☐ Same as above with label 40.00   60.00

☐ **STEINFIELD'S BITTERS**
Light amber, tapered top, in back on shoulder
"First Prize-Paris," 10" 700.00 800.00

☐ **DR. STEWARTS TONIC BITTERS**
"Columbus, Ohio" under bottom, amber, 8" ... 65.00   80.00

☐ **STONGHTON BITTERS**
Clear, 7" 20.00   30.00

☐ **DR. STOEVER'S BITTERS**
Established 1837, square, "KRYER & CO.,"
amber, 9" 75.00   95.00

☐ **SUFFOLK BITTERS**
Other side Philbrook & Tucker, Boston, shape of
a pig, ground lip, light amber, 9½" x 3½" 400.00 550.00

☐ **SUMTER BITTERS**
On front and back "Charleston S.C.," on back
"Dowie Moise & Davis Wholesale Druggist,"
amber, 9½" 90.00 115.00

☐ **SUN KIDNEY & LIVER BITTERS**
Square bottle, "VEGETABLE LAXATIVE,"
amber, machine made, 9½" 75.00   95.00

☐ **SWAN'S, C.H.**
On back "Bourbon Bitters," square, tapered top,
beveled corners, amber, 9" 100.00 115.00

☐ **DR. SWEET STRENGTHENING BITTERS**
Long tapered top, aqua, 8¼" 65.00   80.00

☐ **THORN'S HOP & BURDOCK TONIC BITTERS**
Square bottle, "BRATTLEBORO, VT," amber,
label states this is a bitters, 8" 10.00   15.00

☐ **DR. TILTON'S COMPOUND DANDELION
BITTERS**
Amber, round, 10" 200.00 250.00

☐ **TIP-TOP BITTERS**
Multi-sided bottle, labeled only, amber, 8½" ... 10.00   15.00

Price Range

☐ **TIPPECANOE**
Amber, aqua, 9″ 135.00 145.00
☐ Same as above, clear 140.00 160.00
☐ **TIPPECANOE**
Misspelled Rochester under bottom, amber, 9″ 80.00 105.00
☐ **TODD'S BITTERS**
Machine made, clear, 8¼″ 20.00 30.00
☐ **TONOLA BITTERS**
Trademark Eagle, square, aqua, "PHILADEL-
PHIA," 8″ 60.00 75.00
☐ **TONECO STOMACH BITTERS**
Square bottle, tapered top, "APPETIZER &
TONIC," clear glass, ABM 20.00 30.00
☐ **TONECO BITTERS**
Clear, under bottom a diamond shape with num-
ber 20.00 30.00
☐ **OLD DR. TOWNSEND CELEBRATED**
STOMACH BITTERS
In six lines, handled jug, amber, plain band, pontil,
8¾″ 1100.00 1600.00
☐ **TRAVELLERS BITTERS**
A man with a cane standing up, oval, amber,
1834–1870, 10½″ 2200.00 2600.00
☐ **TRAVELLERS BITTERS**
Amber, rectangular, 10½″ 1000.00 1500.00
☐ **TUFTS ANGOSTURA BITTERS**
Label, green, 9¾″ 10.00 20.00
☐ **TUFTS TONIC BITTERS**
Rectangular bottle, labeled only, aqua, 9″ 5.00 10.00
☐ **TURNER'S BITTERS**
Rectangular, clear glass, 8″ 60.00 75.00
☐ **TURNER BROTHERS N.Y.**
Buffalo, NY, San Francisco, CA, tapered top, pon-
til, amber, 9½″ 100.00 210.00
☐ **TYLER'S STANDARD AMERICAN BITTERS**
Square bottle, amber, 9″ 85.00 110.00
☐ **THE ULLMAN**
Einstein Co., Cleveland, OH, Germania Mager
Bitters, back and front labels, complete label in-
formation, under bottom a diamond in center of
it, #337, golden amber, ring top, round shoulder,
3 blob in neck 115.00 140.00

Price Range

☐ **ULMER MT. ASH BITTERS**
Aqua, 7″ 85.00 110.00
☐ **UNCLE TOM'S BITTERS**
Square bottle, "THOMAS FOULD & SON," Tre-
vorton, PA, pale amber, tapered top, 10″ 125.00 175.00
☐ **UNDERBERG-ALBRECHT**
On base H.U.A., round bottle, labeled, red-amber,
lady's leg neck, also ABM, 12″ 10.00 20.00
☐ **UNIVERSAL BITTERS**
Pontil, aqua 100.00 125.00
☐ **UNIVERSAL BITTERS**
Mfg. by Aug. Horstmann, Sole Agent F.J. Schae-
fer, 231 Market St., Louisville, KY, lady's leg
shape, emerald green, 12″ 450.00 550.00
☐ **UNKA**
Within a ball on front, picture of an eagle on top
of the ball, Army & Navy around all this, "Unka
Bitters 1895" under all this, label, tapered and
ringed top, amber, 8½″ 25.00 34.00
☐ **USAACSON SEIXAS & CO.**
Other side reads "66 & 68 Common St., C.O."
With eye, bitters monogram under it, bulged neck,
tapered and ring top, kick-up 75.00 95.00

COSMETIC

The cosmetic category includes all bottles that contained products to improve or beautify personal appearance, as well as perfume bottles. Because of the nature of their contents, and the class of people who purchased them, these bottles were frequently designed to be eye-appealing. Not only would an attractive bottle promote impulse sales, it stood to be selected over others for its decorative contributions to milady's dressing table. Thus, competition was keen among manufacturers not only to have the best products, but also (and sometimes more so) to sell them in the most appealing containers.

The European cosmetic industry had a long head start on America's, and the U.S. manufacturers mostly styled their products, as well as the containers for them, after foreign prototypes. It is sometimes claimed that cosmetics, in the form of perfume, were the earliest products to be stored or distributed in bottles. This may or may not be so; certainly, wine was kept in bottles in the distant past. In any event, glass bottles known to have contained perfumes and sweet oils used in embalming can be traced to the 18th dynasty of Egypt (3,000 B.C., or 5,000 years ago).

The most celebrated American maker of perfume bottles in the 18th century was Casper Wistar, whose factory was founded in New Jersey in 1739. Martha Washington's perfume bottle, which she carried at all times, is said to have been made by Wistar. Another well-known domestic manufacturer of perfume bottles in the 18th century was Henry William Stiegel. He entered the trade in 1763. While Wistar's bottles were mainly plain and functional, those of Stiegel include many decorative specimens that appeal greatly to collectors.

In the 1840s Solon Palmer of Cincinnati began to manufacture and sell perfumes. A few had rather unusual names, Jockey Club and Baby Ruth among them. Though Jockey Club definitely carried sporting overtones, Baby Ruth had no connection with the Yankee baseball star. It was introduced well before his time and referred to Ruth Cleveland, baby daughter of President Cleveland. In 1871, Solon Palmer moved to New York and by 1879 his products were being retailed in drugstores throughout the country. Palmer bottles are appealing to collectors, because of their brilliant emerald green color.

So-called "Charley Ross Bottles," containing perfume, appeared around 1880. Those are of great interest to collectors for their historical overtone. Young Charley Ross was kidnapped in Pennsylvania in 1874 and was never heard from again. The case became one of the major news stories. Charley Ross perfume bottles were sponsored by the child's father, who saw this as a means of reminding the public of his son's name and thereby perhaps finding clues or leads. The bottles carry a likeness of a youth's face, but it was to no avail.

Perfumes for men became popular in the second half of the 19th century. Left to themselves, American males might not have adopted the use of colognes and other fragrances this early, but they were very popular in Europe, and whatever was current or fashionable in Europe was sure to be copied in the U.S. Just as manufacturers of bitters and other preparations often overstated their virtues, makers of perfumes and colognes were guilty of this as well. A trade card for Florida Water, an after-shave-lotion, claimed it to be "the richest, most lasting, yet most delicate of all perfumes for use on the handkerchief, at the toilette and in the bath, delightful and healthful in the sickroom. Relieves weakness, fatigue, prostration, nervousness, and headache."

Price Range

☐ **AUBRY SISTERS**
"Pat Aug 22, 1911" under bottom, milk glass, 1"   2.00   3.00

Price Range

☐ **AYER'S HAIR VIGOR**
Deep blue, rectangular, 6½″ 16.00 20.00

☐ **BAKER'S PERFUME**
Ring top, clear, 3″ 4.50 6.50

☐ **BALDWINS QUEEN BESS PERFUME**
Reverse side "Sample Baldwins Perfume," label,
ring top, 5½″ 8.00 12.00

☐ **BARBER BOTTLE**
Bell-shaped, enameled floral design, sheared lip,
open pontil, stoppered, 8″ 120.00 145.00

☐ **BARBER BOTTLE**
Long cylinder neck, flattened bulbous body,
green leaf and vine motif 90.00 110.00

☐ **BARBER BOTTLE**
Long cylinder neck, waisted bulbous body, green,
7″ 80.00 100.00

☐ **BARBER BOTTLE**
Long cylinder neck with ring in center, bulbous
body, footed, 7¾″ 100.00 130.00

☐ **BARBER BOTTLE**
Long fluted neck, bulbous fluted body, yellow, 7″ 65.00 75.00

☐ **BARBER BOTTLE**
Long narrow neck, barrel shaped body, floral
motif, stoppered, blue, 7½″ 250.00 300.00

☐ **BARBER BOTTLE**
Long neck with globular body, thumbprint design,
stoppered, cranberry, 7″ 120.00 145.00

☐ **BARBER BOTTLE**
Long neck, bulbous body, footed, floral and vine
motif, stoppered, 8″ 75.00 95.00

☐ **BARBER BOTTLE**
Long neck, bulbous body, jigsaw motif, blue, stoppered, 6¾″ 100.00 120.00

☐ **BARBER BOTTLE**
Long neck with bulbous middle, bulbous body,
stoppered, purple, 7″ 125.00 135.00

☐ **BARBER BOTTLE**
Milk glass, ring top, 4¾″ x 2½″, sunken panel on
front of bottle for label, round, 9″ 18.00 24.00

Price Range

☐ **BARBER BOTTLE**
Narrow cylinder shaped neck, cone shape body, palm tree motif in foreground, mountain motif in background, lavender, 8″ 175.00 210.00

☐ **BARBER BOTTLE**
Narrow fluted neck, fluted bulbous body, blue, 6½″ 75.00 95.00

☐ **BARBER BOTTLE**
Narrow neck, bulbous body, hunting scene on front, 7½″ 75.00 85.00

☐ **BARBER BOTTLE**
Plain, red, 3½″ 18.00 24.00

☐ **BARBER BOTTLE**
Tiered shape with cylinder shape mouth, floral motif, green, 8″ 350.00 400.00

☐ **BAY RUM**
On one panel, Barber bottle, six 1¾″ panels, root type shoulder, lady's leg neck, neck 3¼″, ring top, milk glass, body, neck and shoulder 4½″ 25.00 35.00

☐ **BELL**
Plain, perfume, clear, 2″ round, 3″ 6.00 9.00

☐ **BOOT**
Perfume label, clear or amethyst, 3½″ 13.00 18.00

☐ **BRUNO COURT PERFUMEUR**
Green with gold neck, 5½″ 10.00 14.00

☐ **C & C**
Blue, 5″ 3.50 5.50

☐ **CALIF. PERFUME CO.**
Fruit flavors on the front of panel, rectangular, amethyst, 5½″ 18.00 24.00

☐ **CARD COLOGNE or OPIUM SQUARE**
Decorated, frosted, tapered 4.50 7.00

☐ **C CO.**
Perfume, fancy shape, screw top, clear, 3¼″ .. 4.50 7.00

☐ **CHAPOTEAUT**
Reverse side "Paris," "BL4063" on bottom, clear or amethyst, 2¾″ 3.00 4.00

☐ **CHAPOTEAUT**
On back "Paris," clear 3.00 4.00

☐ **CHRISTIAN DIOR**
Clear, 4″ 8.00 11.00

Price Range

☐ **CHRISTIANI DE PARIS**
Perfume, fancy shape, thin flared lip, open pontil,
aqua, 3⅜″ 32.00 40.00

☐ **CLARKE & CO.**
"Woodard" under bottom, cosmetic, square, cobalt, 4¼″ 6.00 9.00

☐ **C.M.**
Label, clear, 1¾″ 3.00 4.00

☐ **COLGATE & CO.**
Clear or amethyst, 6¼″ 6.00 8.00

☐ **COLGATE & CO.**
New York, in a circle, through center of circle
"PERFUMERS," clear or amethyst, 3⅝″ 3.00 4.00

☐ **COLGATE & CO.**
"New York" on back, clear, 4¾″ 6.00 10.00

☐ **COLGATE & CO.**
New York on bottom, fancy shape, five concave
panels on side, step on shoulder, ring collar, amethyst, 5¼″ 6.00 8.00

☐ **COLGATE & CO. N.Y. COLEO SHAMPOO**
X on sides, flask, AMB, amethyst 3.50 6.00

☐ **COLGATE & CO. PERFUMERS**
New York, rectangular, long neck, amethyst, 3⅝″ 4.00 5.75

☐ **COLGATE AND CO. PERFUMERS**
"New York" on one panel, rectangular, amethyst
or clear, 3¾″ 6.00 8.00

☐ **COLOGNE**
Decorated trunk and shoulder, applied lip, six
panels, amethyst or clear, 5¼″ 4.00 6.00

☐ **COLOGNE**
Cathedral type, ring top, 1¼″ square at bottom,
improved pontil, cobalt, 5¾″ 80.00 100.00

☐ **COLOGNE**
Label, fancy shape, panels, milk glass, 7¼″ ... 22.00 28.00

☐ **COLOGNE**
Label, fancy shape, open pontil, flared lip, aqua,
4¾″ 28.00 38.00

☐ **COLOGNE**
Label, 603 on bottom, clear or amethyst, 3″ ... 3.00 4.00

☐ **COLOGNE or PEPPERSAUCE**
Label, five stars on three panels, light green, 7½″ 11.00 15.00

Price Range

☐ **COLOGNE**
Label, pontil, cobalt, 8¾″ 18.00 24.00

☐ **COLOGNE**
Plain, round, clear or opalescent, 2¾″ 1.35 2.25

☐ **COLOGNE**
Round, tapered, blue, 7¾″ 110.00 125.00

☐ **COLOGNE**
Shaped like monument, blue, 11¾″ 275.00 300.00

☐ **COLOGNE**
Twelve sided, amethyst, 4″ 150.00 175.00

☐ **COLOGNE**
Twelve sided, blue, 7¼″ 150.00 200.00

☐ **COLOGNE**
Violin shape, blue, 5½″ 500.00 600.00

☐ **COSMETIC JAR**
Round, cream, 1¾″ base 2¼″ 4.00 5.75

☐ **COSMETIC**
Plain, square, metal screw top, cobalt, 6″ 1.30 2.20

☐ **CREAM**
Label, milk glass, 2¼″ 1.30 2.20

☐ **CREAM**
Label, milk glass, 2″ 1.30 2.20

☐ **CREAM**
Label, tan, 2″ 2.50 3.50

☐ **CREAM**
Label, milk glass, 2″ 2.50 3.50

☐ **CREAM**
Label, milk glass, 2½″ 2.50 3.50

☐ **CREAM**
Label, tan, 2¾″ 2.50 3.50

☐ **CREAM**
Label, milk glass, 2½″ 2.50 3.50

☐ **CREAM**
Label, milk glass, 2¾″ 2.50 3.50

☐ **CREAM**
Label, milk glass, 1¾″ 2.50 3.50

☐ **CREAM**
Label, tan, 3¼″ 2.50 3.50

☐ **CREAM**
Label, milk glass, 2¾″ 2.50 3.50

Toilet Water, *fluted panels from mid section to bottom to form a smooth base, flower designs embossed across top with one flower drawing attention in the center, medium size neck, clear glass.*
$20.00–$30.00

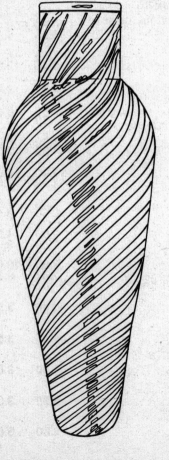

Cologne, *bottle for vanity or dresser contained cologne and ammonia, swirled ribbing on mold-blown glass, rounded shoulders, medium neck, smooth mouth, smooth base.*
$20.00–$30.00

Price Range

☐ **CREME SIMON**
"J.S. 80" under bottom, milk glass, sheared top,
2½" 4.00 6.00

☐ **THE CROWN PERFUMERY CO.**
Amber, 2½" 4.00 6.00

☐ **CRUSELLASH**
Wood marks, aqua, 11½" 12.00 18.00

☐ **CUTEX**
Rectangular, frosted, 1½" x 1¾" x 2½" 2.35 3.25

☐ **DAGGETT & RAMSDELL**
"Perfect Cold Cream, Trademark Made in
U.S.A." on base, round, screw top, clear, 2¾" 1.25 2.15

☐ **DAYBROOKS DETROIT PERFUMERS**
On top in a round design, 3 on bottom, clear or
amethyst, 6" 4.00 6.00

☐ **DEPAS PERFUME**
Clear, 4" 8.00 12.00

☐ **DERWILLO**
On the front panel, "For The Complexion" on the
back, tapered to shoulders, square, clear, 3¾" 7.00 10.00

☐ **DE VRY'S DANDERO-OFF HAIR TONIC**
Label, clear, 6½" 5.00 7.00

☐ **DOLL**
Figural, perfume, clear, 2½" 12.00 18.00

☐ **DRYDEN & PALMER**
D&P under bottom, clear, 7½" 5.00 7.00

☐ **EAGLE BRAND NOVA**
Milk glass, 1½" 3.00 4.00

☐ **MARIE EARLE, PARIS**
Under bottom, clear, 2¾" 7.00 10.00

☐ **EAU DENTIFRICE DU DOCTEUR, JEAU-PARIS**
In four lines, clear or amethyst, 3" 3.00 4.00

☐ **ELCAYA**
Milk glass 2.35 3.20

☐ **EMPRESS JOSEPHINE TOILET CO.**
Milk glass, 6¼" 9.00 12.00

☐ **FACE CREAM**
Label, cream and black, 1½" 2.35 3.20

☐ **FLORIDA WATER**
Label, clear, 568 on bottom, 7¼" 4.00 6.00

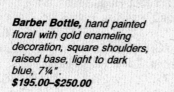

Barber Bottle, *hand painted floral with gold enameling decoration, square shoulders, raised base, light to dark blue, 7¼".*
$195.00–$250.00

Barber Bottle, *hobnail, pineapple shaped, long, ribbed neck leads to wide, sheared lip, light blue, cranberry or amber, 6¾".*
$55.00–$80.00

Price Range

☐ **FLORIDA WATER**
Label, pontil, aqua, 8" 7.00 10.00

☐ **FRANCO AMERICAN HYGIENIC CO.**
Chicago, on front panel, "Toilet Requisites" on
left side, "Franco-American" on the right side,
rectangular, amethyst, 6" 6.00 8.00

☐ **FRANCO AMERICAN HYGIENIC CO.**
Other side "Franco American Toilet Requisites,"
clear, 1½" x 1½" base, 7" 6.00 8.00

☐ **FROSTILLA**
On front panel, "Elmira N.Y., U.S.A." on side, Fra-
grant Lotion on other side, clear, 4½" 5.00 7.00

☐ **FROSTILLA FRAGRANCE**
Clear, 4½" 3.50 5.50

☐ **GERMAN ENAMELLED BOTTLE**
On front, painted on panels: a girl drinking from
a glass, in back: five lines in German script, on
each side on a panel: flowers, seven panels in all,
pontil, small crude neck, OF BOSTON, On bottom, cold cream, eight panels, screw top, amethyst, 2½" 3.00 4.00

☐ **GERMAN ENAMELLED BOTTLE**
Hand painted, pontil, around 1650, blue green,
5½" 160.00 200.00

☐ **GOURAUD'S ORIENTAL CREAM**
"New York" on side, "London" other side, machine made 4¼" 3.00 4.00

☐ **L.L.E. GRAND**
"P.L." on bottom, clear 3½" 6.00 8.00

☐ **GRIMAULT & Cᴵᴱ PARIS**
Reverse side "PHARMACIE, DY," pontil, clear,
4" 20.00 30.00

☐ **GUERLAIN PARIS**
"Depose" in black, clear, 6¾" 5.00 7.00

☐ **GURRLAIN**
"Eau Lustrale LUS" other side, broken pontil,
raspberry, 6¼" 24.00 30.00

☐ **HAGANS MAGNOLIA BALM**
In three lines on front, beveled corners, ring top,
milk glass, 5" 11.00 15.00

☐ Same as above, except turned-under top, 4½" 10.00 14.00

Price Range

☐ **HAIR OIL**
Label on back, amber, 10¼″ 45.00 55.00

☐ **HARMONY OF BOSTON**
On bottom, cold cream, eight panels, screw top,
amethyst, 2½″ 3.00 4.00

☐ **HARRISON'S COLUMBIAN PERFUMERY**
Clear, 2¾″ 6.00 8.00

☐ **J. HAUEL**
Reverse Philadelphia, on side "Perfumer,"
square, flared lip, open pontil, aua, 3″ 25.00 35.00

☐ **H.B. & H. N.Y.**
On shoulder, clear, 3½″ 6.00 8.00

☐ **C. HEEMSTREET & CO.**
Troy, NY, eight panels, ring top, pontil, blue, 7″ 40.00 50.00

☐ **HESSIG-ELLIS CHEMIST**
Memphis, TN, "Q Ban For The Hair" on back,
clear, 6½″ 7.00 10.00

☐ **HILBERT'S DELUXE PERFUMERY**
Flattened heart shape with long neck, clear, 3¼″ 6.00 8.00

☐ **H.J.**
Perfume label, 2¼″ 3.50 4.50

☐ **HOGG & CO.**
Three-cornered bottle, 8″ 7.00 10.00

☐ **HOLT'S NICKEL COLOGNE**
In a sunken front panel, round, amethyst or clear,
2⅞″ 4.00 6.00

☐ **HOMATROPIN**
Perfume dropper, blue, 2″ 12.00 18.00

☐ **F HOYT & CO. PERFUMERS**
Phila, PA, in sunken panel, round, amethyst, 3″ 5.00 7.00

☐ **HOYT'S**
Clear, 3¼″ 3.50 4.50

☐ **HUBBARD, HARRIET**
Ayer, NY, in a square with monogram, 3¾″
ounces on the trunk, square, screw top, clear,
4¾″ 2.35 3.20

☐ **HUBBARD, HARRIET**
Ayer, NY, cosmetic jar, milk glass, square, screw
top, 1½″ or 2½″ 5.00 7.00

☐ **RICHARD HUDNUT**
NY, monogram, 4 fl. Ozs. Net, rectangular, clear,
5¾″ 2.35 3.20

Left to Right: **Extrait d'Eau de Lavender**, paper label in color shows peasant girl and goat framed by leaves and grapes, cylindrical shaped, rolled mouth, pontil mark, light blue, 6¾". **$50.00–$60.00; Cologne**, broad body with raised panels on side, long neck leads to flanged mouth, flowers in vase embossed in panel on front, ribbed panel on back, clear glass, 6⅞". **$50.00–$70.00; Cologne**, long, thin body, raised panels along sides, short neck with narrow ring at mouth, ribbed in V pattern on front, clear glass, 6¼". **$30.00–$50.00**

Price Range

☐ **RICHARD HUDNUT, N.Y. U.S.A.**
With eagle and monogram, tapered neck, round,
clear, 5¼″ 5.00   7.00

☐ **RICHARD HUDNUT PERFUMER**
NY, square, amethyst, 3″ or 3½″ 3.00   4.50

☐ **RICHARD HUDNUT**
Clear or amethyst, 3″ 4.00   6.00

☐ **RICHARD HUDNUT**
Machine made, clear, 4″ 2.35   3.20

☐ **C.W. HUTCHINS PERFUMER**
New York, clear, 3¼″ 3.00   4.00

☐ **HYACINTHIA TOILET HAIR DRESSING**
Crude applied lip, open pontil, rectangular, aqua,
6″ 28.00   38.00

☐ **IMPERIAL CROWN PERFUMERY & CO.**
Clear, 5″ 6.00   8.00

☐ **INGRAMS MILKWEED CREAM**
On shoulder, screw top, milk glass jar, white, 2¼″ 1.30   2.15

☐ **INGRAMS SHAVING CREAM**
On shoulder, screw top, round, cobalt, 2¼″ ... 5.00   7.00

☐ **JEWELETTE LABORATORIES, PERFUMERS**
Chicago, clear, 8″ 8.00   11.00

☐ **JUILLET 1827, 28, 29, 30,**
Perfume, shaped like a harp with a rooster at
base, improved pontil, double coated with a turquoise milk glass effect on the outside and a brilliant ultramarine effect on the inside, 5¼″ 150.00   175.00

☐ **D. KERKOFF**
Paris, tapered, footed, rectangular, amethyst,
3¼″ 1.30   2.15

☐ **KERKOFF**
Clear or amethyst, 5¼″ 4.00   6.00

☐ **KIKEN**
St. Louis, under bottom, label, clear or amethyst,
8¼″ 7.00   10.00

☐ **DR. KOCH'S TOILET ARTICLES**
Winona, MN, ring top, clear or amethyst, 5¼″ 5.00   7.00

☐ **KRANKS COLD CREAM**
Jar, milk glass, round, screw top, 2¾″ 3.00   4.00

☐ **G.W. LAIRD**
Milk glass, 4¾″ 9.00   12.00

Price Range

☐ **LARKIN CO.**
Dark green, 1½" x 1¼" base, 3" 7.00 10.00

☐ **LARKIN CO.**
Under bottom, milk glass, 2" 6.00 10.00

☐ **L B**
Under bottom, clear or amethyst, 4" 6.00 8.00

☐ **DR. H. HOWARD LEVY**
Milk glass, 1" 3.00 4.00

☐ **L. H.**
On bottom, shape of a slipper, perfume, improved
pontil, flared lip, clear, 3½" long 32.00 42.00

☐ **LIGHTNER'S HELIOTROPE PERFUMES**
Lightning on back, in center, hollow letters L.E.N.
& Co. Detroit, MI, milk glass, 6½" 18.00 24.00

☐ **LIGHTNER'S JOCKEY CLUB PERFUMES**
Lightning on back, in center, hollow letters L.E.N.
& Co. Detroit, MI, milk glass, 6½" 18.00 24.00

☐ **LIGHTNER'S MAID OF THE MIST**
Lightning on back, in center, hollow letters L.E.N.
& Co. Detroit, MI, milk glass, 6½" 18.00 24.00

☐ **LIGHTNER'S WHITE ROSE PERFUMES**
Lightning on back, in center, hollow letters L.E.N.
& Co., Detroit, MI, milk glass, 6½" 15.00 20.00

☐ **LIT. PIVER**
Paris, under bottom, clear or amethyst, 3" 3.00 4.00

☐ **LUBIN**
Clear, 1½" diameter, 3" 3.00 4.00

☐ **LUBIN PARFUMERS**
Paris, pontil, clear, 3½" 18.00 24.00

☐ **LYON'S POWDER**
New York, round, purple, 6½" 60.00 70.00

☐ **MACK'S FLORIDA WATER**
Tapered top, aqua, 8½" 6.00 8.00

☐ **MEADE & BAKER CARBOLIC MOUTH WASH
ANTISEPTIC GARGLE**
Amethyst, 5" 2.50 4.50

☐ **MELBA**
Label, machine made, clear, 4¾" 4.00 6.00

☐ **MINERALAVA FACE FINISH**
NY, "Scotts Face Finish" on back, clear, 5¼" 6.00 8.00

Price Range

☐ **MONELL'S TEETHING CORDIAL**
NY, on three of eight panels, aqua, 1⅛" round
5" 5.00 7.00

☐ **MORTON, CARPENTER CO., COLONITE**
Boston, MA, square, amethyst or clear, 4" 4.00 6.00

☐ **MURRAY & LANMAN**
Machine made, aqua 3.00 4.50

☐ **MURRAY & LANMAN, AGUA DE FLORIDA**
New York, 6" or 9" 5.00 6.50

☐ **MURRAY & LANMAN, AGUA DE FLORIDA,**
No. 69 Water St., NY, pontil, aqua, 9" 20.00 28.00

☐ **MURRAY & LANMAN DRUGGISTS, FLORIDA
WATER**
New York, in four vertical lines, aqua, 5½" body,
3¾" neck 5.00 7.00

☐ Same as above, except smaller bottle 5.00 7.00

☐ **NEWTON**
London, shape of a schoolhouse, flared lip, milk
glass, 2⅝" 45.00 60.00

☐ **THEO NOEL**
Aqua, 4½" 4.00 6.00

☐ **NUIT DE MONE**
Around top, black glass, 3¾" 18.00 24.00

☐ **OBOL**
Under bottom in sunken panel, front and back
1¼" panels, plain, on each side three panels,
three-part mold with short round neck facing out,
½" open on one side, milk glass, 2⅛" x ¾", 4¼" 12.00 18.00

☐ Same as above, except no writing, flat bottom, 2" 10.00 13.00

☐ **ORIENTAL CREAM**
On side, "Gourands, New York," square bottle
with short neck, clear or amethyst, 5¼" 5.00 7.00

☐ **ORIZA-OIL L. LEGRAND PARIS**
"Modele Exclush Depose" on back, clear, 5¼" 3.50 4.75

☐ **PALANGIE**
BL 2874 under bottom, clear, 5¾" 3.50 4.75

☐ **PALMER**
In script, vertically on flat sides, some round bottles, emerald green, 4½" 12.00 18.00

☐ **PALMER**
Metal crown, with "Salon Palmer Perfumer" and
two stars, fancy shape, ribbed shoulders, emer-

Price Range

ald green, 5¾" 14.00   19.00

☐ Same as above, except with rings instead of ribs, glass stopper, "Salon Palmer Perfumer" on shoulder, 4½" 13.00   18.00

☐ **PALMER**
In script in center of bottle, ring top, 2" round, 4½" body, 2" neck 12.00   18.00

☐ Same as above, except oval, 7¼" 12.00   18.00

☐ **PALMER**
Clear or amethyst, 3¼" 4.00   6.00

☐ **PALMER**
Clear, 2½" 4.00   6.00

☐ **PALMER**
Flat front, round back, blue green, 4¾" 12.00   16.00

☐ **PALMER**
C2 under bottom, oval shape, blue green, 5" .. 11.00   15.00

☐ **PARIS PERFUME CO.**
Jersey City, NJ, Guaranteed full 2 oz. Ring top, clear or amethyst, 6" 5.00   7.00

☐ **PARKET'S HAIR BALSAM**
Aqua, 8" 2.00   4.00

☐ **L. PAUTAUBERGE PHARMACIEU**
Paris, in three lines, on bottom R 6, 5862, beveled corners, cobalt, 2¼" square base, 6" body, 2" neck 16.00   21.00

☐ **P.D.**
On base, aqua, 4¾" 11.00   15.00

☐ **PERFUME**
Fancy shape, four sides, round ribs on three sides, one plain ring, ring top, ring vase type body, 3¼" tall, 2" neck 11.00   15.00

☐ **PERFUME**
Fancy shape, clear, 3" 9.00   12.00

☐ **PERFUME**
Label, aqua, 6½" 13.00   18.00

☐ **PERFUME**
Label, clear or amethyst, 6¼" 3.50   4.25

☐ **PERFUME**
Label, blue, 2¾" 4.00   6.00

☐ **PERFUME**
Label, fancy shape, clear, 3¼" 4.00   6.00

Price Range

☐ **PERFUME**
Label, clear, 6½" 6.00   8.00
☐ **PERFUME**
Label, clear, 5½" 3.50   4.25
☐ **PERFUME**
Label, clear or amethyst, 3" 3.50   4.25
☐ **PERFUME**
Label, clear, 2¾" 4.00   6.00
☐ **PERFUME**
Label, various colored stripes around bottle, 2"   8.00   11.00
☐ **PERFUME**
Label, clear or amethyst, 3" 2.35   3.15
☐ **PERFUME**
Label, aqua, 6" 4.00   6.00
☐ **PERFUME**
Label, clear, sheared top, 2½" 6.00   11.00
☐ **PERFUME**
Label, pontil, clear or amethyst, 4" 14.00   19.00
☐ **PERFUME**
Label, aqua, 7½" 6.00   9.00
☐ **PERFUME**
Label, clear or amethyst, 4¾" 4.00   6.00
☐ **PERFUME**
Label, eight panels, clear or amethyst, 1¾" ... 3.50   4.25
☐ **PERFUME**
Label, pontil, aqua, 3¾" 16.00   21.00
☐ **PERFUME**
Label, clear, 5¼" 4.00   6.00
☐ **PERFUME**
Label, clear or amethyst, 5½" 20.00   28.00
☐ **PERFUME**
Label, pinch bottle, pontil, green, 6" 20.00   28.00
☐ **PERFUME**
Label, gold frame around bottle with marble on
each corner, aqua, 4" 16.00   21.00
☐ **PERFUME**
Label, flat front, round back, clear, 6½" 6.00   8.00
☐ **PERFUME**
Label, pontil, clear, 12¼" 16.00   21.00
☐ **PERFUME**
Label, clear, 6½" 13.00   18.00

Price Range

☐ **PERFUME**
Label, cut glass flower satin glass, sheared top,
5″ 6.00 9.00

☐ **PERFUME**
Label, clear, 4″ 3.50 4.25

☐ **PERFUME**
Label, clear, 6½″ 12.00 16.00

☐ **PERFUME**
Label, pontil, cobalt, 5″ 45.00 55.00

☐ **PERFUME**
Label, snail design, machine made, satin, clear,
7½″ 6.00 8.00

☐ **PERFUME**
Label, flowers around bottle, square, milk glass,
pontil, 5″ 20.00 28.00

☐ **PERFUME**
Label, cobalt, 5½″ 10.00 14.00

☐ **PERFUME**
Label, fancy shape, clear or amethyst, 3¼″ ... 3.50 5.00

☐ **PERFUME**
Label, fancy shape, clear or amethyst, 3¼″ ... 5.00 7.00

☐ **PERFUME**
Label, clear or amethyst, 3¾″ 8.00 11.00

☐ **PERFUME**
½ bell shaped, clear or amethyst, 3″ 8.00 11.00

☐ **PERFUME**
Eight vertical panels, ring collar, glass stopper,
improved pontil, clear, 3⅛″ 14.00 19.00

☐ **PERFUME**
Fancy hand-painted gold-lead design, open pontil, deep purple appears black, 6½″ 32.00 42.00

☐ **PERFUME**
Very ornate, fancy scroll work around gothic letter
M, reverse side has blank oval area for label,
flared lip, open pontil, clear, 4″ 42.00 52.00

☐ **PERFUME**
Shaped like a clam shell, still has partial paper
label with round mirror glue to label, very crude,
open pontil, clear, 3½″ 50.00 65.00

Price Range

☐ **PERFUME**
Shaped like a woven basket with handles, small
oval circle on front for paper label, open pontil,
aqua, 2⅞" **32.00 42.00**

☐ **PERFUME**
Figure of an Indian maiden sowing seeds on front,
each side has a potted plant, fancy shape, fluted
neck, clear, 4⅞" **25.00 32.00**

☐ **PERFUME**
Violin or corset shaped, flared lip, open pontil,
clear, 5⅜" **50.00 60.00**

☐ **PERFUME**
Picture of an Indian holding a spear between
gothic arches, open pontil, turquoise, 4" **40.00 50.00**

☐ **PERFUMERIE**
Clear, 3½" **3.00 5.00**

☐ **J. PICARD**
Clear, 3¼" **2.35 3.15**

☐ **ED PINAUD**
Clear or amethyst, 7" **5.00 7.00**

☐ **ED PINAUD**
Aqua, 6" **4.00 6.00**

☐ **ED PINAUD**
Clear, 3¾" **2.35 3.15**

☐ **PINCH BOTTLE SHAPED**
Plain, light amber, 3½" body, 4½" neck **12.00 16.00**

☐ Same as above, except smaller **8.00 10.00**

☐ **POMPEIAN MASSAGE CREAM**
Clear or amethyst, 2¾" **4.00 6.00**

☐ **POMPEIAN MFG. CO.**
Machine made, clear or amethyst, 3¼" **3.00 4.00**

☐ **POND'S EXTRACT**
"1846" on bottom, machine made, clear, 5½" **4.00 6.00**

☐ **PREPARED BY N. SMITH PRENTISS, ESPRIT
DE _____**
New York, perfume, fancy shape, picture of
young girl with an armful of flowers on front, on
reverse an embossed vase and plant, open pon-
til, flared lip, aqua, 5½" **55.00 70.00**

Price Range

☐ **BY N. PRENTISS**
Reverse "28 John St. N. York," one side "Bear-
soil," other side "Perfumes," square, flared lip,
open pontil, clear, 2¾" 40.00   55.00

☐ **PUMPKIN SEED**
Perfume, plain, clear or amethyst, 3¼" 3.00   4.00

☐ **PUMPKIN SEED**
Label, side strap, clear or amethyst, 3½" 6.00   8.00

☐ **QUENTIN**
Clear, 3" 3.50   4.25

☐ **Q.T.**
On base, perfume, monument shaped with round
ball supported by eagles, flared lip, open pontil,
clear, 5" 42.00   52.00

☐ **RICKSECKER'S**
Clear, 3½" 4.00   6.00

☐ **RIEGER'S CALIFORNIA PERFUMES**
Crooked neck, clear, 3¼" 7.00   10.00

☐ **R & M**
Shoe shaped, clear, 3½" 12.00   18.00

☐ **ROGER & GALLET**
Clear or amethyst, 1¾" 4.00   6.00

☐ **ROGER & GALLET**
Paris, on back, 8897 H.P. under bottom, clear or
amethyst, 5½" 5.00   7.00

☐ **ROGER & GALLET**
Clear or amethyst, 4¼" 4.00   6.00

☐ **J. ROIG**
Clear, 3¼" 3.50   4.25

☐ **CHARLEY ROSS**
Picture of a boy, four sizes 42.00   52.00

☐ **C.H. SELICK, PERFUMER**
NY, ring top, clear, 2⅝" 5.00   7.00

☐ **SCENT**
Seahorse shape, clear with white swirls, 2½" .. 90.00   120.00

☐ **SCENT**
Vertically ribbed, yellow, 3" 90.00   110.00

☐ **STIEGEL**
Teardrop shaped, sixteen swirls to the left, improved pontil, clear, 3⅛" 42.00   52.00

☐ **SWANSON'S ANTISEPTIC**
Clear, 6" 20.00   24.00

Price Range

☐ **TOILET WATER**
Blown three mold, tooled mouth, smooth base,
6" 200.00 250.00

☐ **TOILET WATER**
Blown three mold, blue, 6" 200.00 240.00

☐ **TOILET WATER**
On one panel of a six-paneled bottle, roof type
shoulder, lady's leg neck, barber bottle, milk
glass, 3¼" body, neck and shoulder 4½" 25.00 35.00

☐ **TOILET WATER**
Label, amber, 7¼" 3.00 4.00

☐ **T.P.S. & CO.**
NY, on base, man's head figural, three-part mold,
metal cap, 7" 45.00 55.00

☐ **TREVILLE PARIS**
Green, 8¼" 7.00 10.00

☐ **VAIL BROS**
Green, 3" 8.00 11.00

☐ **VALENTINES**
Green, 2¾" 4.00 6.00

☐ **VAN BUSKIRB'S**
Aqua, 5" 2.50 3.35

☐ **VELVETINA**
"Velvetina Skin Beautifier Goodrich Drug Co
Omaha" on back, milk glass, 5¼" 18.00 24.00

☐ **VIN DE CHAPOTEAUT PARIS**
Clear or amethyst, 10½" 3.25 4.50

☐ **VIOLET DULCE VANISHING CREAM**
Eight panels, 2½" 4.00 6.00

☐ **VOGN**
In script, in two lines "Perfumery Co. New York,"
case type body, seam end at collar, clear, 7¾" 7.00 10.00

☐ **W.B. & CO.**
Under bottom, aqua, 3½" 5.00 7.00

☐ **W & H. WALKER**
Clear, 8¾" 6.00 8.00

☐ **WHITE ROSE**
Label, second label picture of a bird holding a
note which reads "Faith and Love," cucumber
shaped, turquoise green, 4⅜" long 30.00 40.00

☐ **WITCH HAZEL**
Milk glass, 9¼" 15.00 20.00

Price Range

☐ **ALFRED WRIGHT, PERFUMER**
Rochester, NY, cobalt or amber, 7½" 14.00 20.00

☐ **W.T. & CO.**
V in center, U.S.A. under bottom, beveled corners, ring top, milk glass, 5" 8.00 11.00

CROCKS

Crocks are not made of glass, but pottery. Because many collectors of glass bottles are collectors of crocks, we have included a brief
selection of them. Many more styles, types and manufacturers exist
than we have space to list.

Crocks are appealing for their variety of shapes, painted or stenciled
decorations and lustrous finishes. Of ancient origin—older than
glass—they were used extensively in the sale of store products in
America during the 19th century and into the 20th. Alcoholic beverages were only one of many products kept in crocks; nevertheless,
the association became so well planted that the term "old crock"
came to refer to perpetual imbibers.

Pottery containers were made in the U.S. as early as 1641 in Massachusetts, just 21 years after the Mayflower. They might have taken
the place of glass for widespread commercial use but for several
drawbacks. One of these was that the products could not be seen
through the bottle, as it could with glass. This not only hurt sales, but
made it difficult for consumers to know when the bottle was getting
empty. There was also some problem in convincing the public about
the cleanliness of pottery bottles, since the interior was not visible.
One big plus in their favor was that they could be manufactured more
cheaply than glass. Pottery bottles also kept beverages cooler and
presumably extended shelf life as they prevented entry of light.

The pottery industry in early America usually followed the move-
ment of immigrants from one territory to another. The pioneer settlers
in Pennsylvania and Ohio were famous for their pottery: bottles, jugs
and mugs of fired clay made for holding beverages, medicines, condi-
ments and inks. Many early jugs were imaginatively hand painted and
rank as prime examples of folk or primitive art.

A very differently styled group of crocks, in all sizes and designed
for all purposes, was brought to the U.S. by the first major wave of
Chinese immigrants. They arrived in California and set up communities
there, then spread out to establish additional communities elsewhere
(notably in Vancouver, British Columbia). Nearly all of their household
goods, foodstuffs and medicines were carried about in pottery crocks,

bearing delicately enameled or shaped designs. Of course, the art of pottery making was very old in China by then, and had reached levels of achievement that Americans could not hope to duplicate. While American designers derived some inspiration from these Chinese specimens, they were well aware that they could not successfully imitate them and rarely tried. Chinese crocks are eminently collectible, but because of their foreign origin they fall outside the scope of this book. See *The Official Price Guide to Oriental Collectibles* for a comprehensive listing of such articles.

Most household pottery jars were made in the 19th century. Jugs glazed on the inside date to after 1900. The advent of the automatic glassblowing machine in 1903 made glass bottles cheaper and easier to produce and the use of pottery declined.

	Price Range	
☐ **ALASKAN YUKON 1909 PACIFIC EXPO OF SEATTLE**		
Flower on shoulder, jug, 2¾″	30.00	40.00
☐ **P. H. ALDERS, COMPLIMENTS OF THE EAGLE SALOON**		
St. Joseph, MO, Cream and brown, 3″	35.00	45.00
☐ **ALE**		
Label, tan, 8½″	15.00	25.00
☐ **ALE**		
Label, brown, 6″	8.00	12.00
☐ **THE ALTMAYOR & FLATAU LIQUOR CO., FINE LIQUORS**		
Macon, GA, round, tan, 6½″	38.00	48.00
☐ **ALLEN & HANBURY'S LTD. BYNOL MALT & OIL**		
Black on prints, enormous amount of writing	15.00	25.00
☐ **AMERICAN STONE WARE**		
In 2 lines, blue letters also near top a large 6, 14 x 13, gray, 13½″	32.00	42.00
☐ **F.A. AMES & CO.**		
"Owensboro, KY" in back, flat, tan and brown, 3½″	38.00	48.00
☐ **ANDERSON'S WEISS BEERS**		
7¼″	10.00	16.00
☐ **ARMOUR & COMPANY**		
Chicago, IL, jug, pouring spout, white, 7¼″	25.00	32.00
☐ **B. & J. ARNOLD**		
London, England, Master Ink, dark brown, 9″	15.00	25.00

Price Range

☐ **B & H**
Cream, 3″ 30.00 40.00

☐ **BASS & CO.**
NY, cream, 9½″ 18.00 24.00

☐ **BEAN POT**
Label, light blue, 4¼″ 5.00 8.00

☐ **L. BEARD**
On shoulder, cream & blue, blob top, 8½ 20.00 28.00

☐ **BELLARMINE JUG**
Superb mask, two horseshoe decorations below
mask, 13″ 25.00 35.00

☐ **BISCUIT SLIP GLAZE STONE PORTER**
Blob top with small impressed ring for string.
Firmly impressed towards base J, Heginbotham,
Kings Arms, Stayley Bridge. Reserve has other
letters impressed below shoulder which cannot
be clearly deciphered: UBL?T ??? ?EA TODY. Towards base are a further possible 14 characters
which cannot be deciphered. MINT STATE &
EARLY 1800s, 9½″ 50.00 70.00

☐ **COMPLIMENTS OF BENISS & THOMPSON**
Shelbyville, KY, tan and brown, 3¾″ 30.00 42.00

☐ **JAS. BENJAMIN, STONEWARE DEPOT**
Cincinnati, OH, blue stencil lettering, mottled tan,
9″ 38.00 48.00

☐ Same as above, except tan, 13½″ 38.00 48.00

☐ **BLACK'S FAMILY LIQUOR STORE, H.P.**
BLACK
2042–43 Fresno in blue glaze letters, 1 Gal. Jug,
ivory and dark brown 30.00 40.00

☐ **BITTER**
Label, olive, brown trim, 10¼″ 35.00 50.00

☐ **B. B. BITTER MINERAL WATER**
Bowling Green, MO, white, five gallon, 15″ 35.00 50.00

☐ **BLACK FAMILY LIQUOR STORE**
Stamped in blue glaze, brown and tan, gallon 20.00 28.00

☐ **BLANCHFLOWER & SONS, HOMEMADE**
4 Prize Medals, GT, Yarmouth, Norfolk, cream
with black, 6 sided lid 20.00 28.00

☐ **BLUE PICTURE PRINT GINGER JAR**
Picture extends entire circumference of jar, building and junk in sail, 3½″ 25.00 35.00

Price Range

☐ **BLUE PRINT OINTMENT POT BEACH & BARNICOTT**
Successors to Dr. Roberts Bridport, Poor Man's
Friend, crisp print 12.00 18.00

☐ **BLUE TOP & PRINT CREAM POT**
Golden Pastures, Thick Rich Cream, Chard, picture of maid milking cow 15.00 25.00

☐ **BROWNINGS PALE ALE**
Lewes, sparkled biscuit glazed finish, string rim at
neck. Cork closure, impressed: 8¾" 18.00 24.00

☐ **BROWNINGS PALE ALE**
Lewes, Potters mark: STEPHEN GREEN'S LAM-
BETH 18.00 24.00

☐ **BOSTON BAKED BEANS**
"HHH" on back, brick color, 1½" 6.00 10.00

☐ **BOSTON BAKED BEANS**
"OK" on back, brick color, 1½" 6.00 10.00

☐ **BOWERS THREE THISTLES SNUFF**
Cream color with blue lettering, two to three gallon 40.00 55.00

☐ **BURGESS, JOHN & SON, ANCHOVY PASTE, WAREHOUSE 107 STAND**
Black print on white, 3½", curved shoulder type,
print 2 x 2¾" 30.00 40.00

☐ **BRYANT & WOODRUFF**
Pittsfield, ME, handled jug, blue gray, 7" 28.00 38.00

☐ **BYNOL MALT & OIL, ALLEN & HANBURY'S**
Black on white, print 2¾" x 3¾", height, lots of
writing on this pot, 4¹/₅" 20.00 30.00

☐ **BUTTER CROCK**
No label, handle, blue-gray decoration, 4" 28.00 38.00

☐ **BUTTER CROCK**
No label, blue-gray decoration, 5¼" 20.00 28.00

☐ **CALIFORNIA POP**
Pat. Dec. 29, 1872, blob top, tan, 10½" 60.00 80.00

☐ **CALIFORNIA COUGH BALM**
Dose teaspoon full, children ½, 10- brown, crock
jug with handle, 3¼" 95.00 125.00

☐ **CAMBRIDGE SPRINGS MINERAL WATER**
In 2 lines, 2½", brown & tan 20.00 30.00

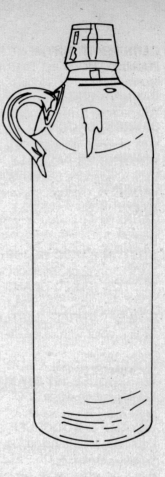

Crock Bottle, *Amsterdam seal,*
narrow body, one handle on side,
sloping mouth with narrow
opening, light brown, 12".
$8.50–$11.00

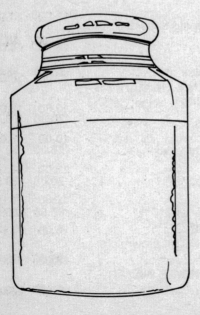

Crock, *squared shoulders,*
rolled mouth with wide opening,
light brown and cream, 6¾".
$8.50–$11.00

Price Range

☐ **CANNING CROCK**
Inscribed "Hold Fast That Which is Good," dark
brown, 6½" 28.00 38.00
☐ **CANNING CROCK**
Wax sealer, 6" 24.00 34.00
☐ **CANNING CROCK**
Wax sealer, reddish brown, 8" 24.00 34.00
☐ **CANNING CROCK**
Blue with a gray decorative design, 8½" 24.00 34.00
☐ **CANNING CROCK**
Mustard color, 7" 20.00 28.00
☐ **CANNING CROCK**
Maple leaf design in lid, caramel color, 6" 12.00 18.00
☐ **CANNING CROCK**
Brown, 5" 18.00 24.00
☐ **CANNING CROCK**
Wax channel, brown, 8½" 18.00 24.00
☐ **CANNING CROCK**
Reddish brown, green on the inside, 6¾" 20.00 28.00
☐ **CANNING CROCK**
Crude, brown, 4" 12.00 18.00
☐ **CANNING CROCK**
Wax sealer, dark brown, 5½" 18.00 24.00
☐ **CANNING CROCK**
Wax sealer, tan, 5½" 18.00 24.00
☐ **CANNING CROCK**
Wax sealer, dark brown, 5½" 12.00 18.00
☐ **CANNING CROCK**
Wax sealer, dark brown, 6½" 10.00 16.00
☐ **CANNING CROCK**
Wax sealer, mottled gray, 5" 10.00 16.00
☐ **CANNING CROCK**
Wax sealer, brown, 5½" 12.00 18.00
☐ **CANNING CROCK**
Barrel, dark brown, 5½" 12.00 18.00
☐ **CANNING CROCK**
Lid, star design, dark brown, 8¾" 20.00 28.00
☐ **CANNING CROCK**
Dark brown, 7½" 18.00 24.00
☐ **CANNING CROCK**
Tan, 9" 20.00 28.00

Price Range

☐ **CANNING CROCK**
Wax channel, brown, 7½" 20.00 28.00

☐ **CASPER CO., FROM THE, WINSTON-SALEM, LOWEST PRICE WHISKEY HOUSE**
Write for confidential list, tan crockery, blue letters, with wire handle, 9¾" 65.00 85.00

☐ **18th CENTURY BELLARMINE**
Superb large decorative mark approx. 2½" x 2½", large star decoration beneath contained in oval with decorative border, 9¼" 250.00 325.00

☐ **GEO. M. CHERNAUCKAS BUFFET, TELEPHONE CANAL 1756**
1900 S. Union St., Corner 19th St., Chicago, large hall, etc., in a square under it ½ gal. liquid measure, gal. brown & white, black lettering, 8½" .. 45.00 60.00

☐ **CHINESE CROCK JUG**
Vase, wide, flared mouth, black or dark brown, 6" 12.00 18.00
☐ Same as above, except Federal Law Forbids ... 4.00 6.00

☐ **CHRIS MORLEY'S**
Under it in a scroll, "Ginger Beer," under it Victorias B.C., brown & cream, inside screw, 7¾" .. 20.00 28.00

☐ **CLARK BROS.**
Pat. May 17, 1899, Zanesville, Ohio, brown, 7½" 20.00 28.00

☐ **CLARK BROS. GROCERS**
Birmingham, AL, handle, jug, white and brown, 10½" 22.00 30.00

☐ **JOHN CLIPP & CO.,**
Lambeth in a circle on base, lt. brown (crock), 5¾" 20.00 28.00

☐ **COMMEMORATIVE WHISKEY/SPIRIT JUG**
By Copeland Spode & bearing their marks on base. Underglazed transfer in band around neck reads: "CORONATION OF KING GEORGE 5TH & QUEEN MARY, June 22, 1911." Distillers, Edinburgh, 8½". Main body in Royal Blue with 2 inch band at neck in grey, ¾" bottom ornamental white embossed relief Royal Crown with 2 flags, the left bearing portrait of King George V on background of Union Jack & the right bearing Portrait of Queen Mary on background of Royal Standard. Whole measures Approx. 3¾" x 3¾", reverse of jug: Crowned Royal Coat of Arms surrounded by

Price Range

Garter. Thistle to left top. Rose to right top. Shamrock either side of base. Rose thistle & shamrock relief in white around top of neck 90.00 110.00

☐ **COMPLIMENTS OF M. A. CLAUTON**
26 Farm St., brown and tan, 3″ 25.00 35.00

☐ **COMPLIMENTS OF MARTIN COLLINS**
Cartersville, GA, brown and tan, 3″ 30.00 40.00

☐ **COMPLIMENTS OF COLUMBIA LIQUOR COMPANY**
Augusta, GA, handle, tan and brown, 3″ 28.00 38.00

☐ **CONNER'S BLOOD REMEDY**
Cream, 6⅜″ 12.00 18.00

☐ **COMPLIMENTS OF J.R. COPELAND**
781 24th St., miniature jug, brown and white, blue lettering, 5¼″ 20.00 28.00

☐ **COOK FAIRBANK & CO.**
Akron, OH, on shoulder, 11 x 6½″ with handle, gray 15.00 25.00

☐ **COOPER'S FRANK SEVILLE MARMALADE,**
Black on white, 3¾″, large print with lots of writing 8.00 12.00

☐ **CORNISH MEAD CO., LTD.**
Penzance, Cornwall, one pint two tone stone jar with handle, Underglaze Mary-print on side: "The Honey-moon Drink, Ye Olde Mead." 25% Proof, black top 20.00 26.00

☐ **COWDEN & CO.,**
Harrisburg, PA, dark brown, 6½″ 40.00 50.00

☐ **CRAMER'S KIDNEY CURE**
Albany NY, N's are backward, aqua, 4½″ 40.00 50.00

☐ **CROCK BOTTLE**
Gray, 10″ 10.00 16.00

☐ **CROCK**
Label, cathedral type, brown and tan, 8½″ 35.00 45.00

☐ **CROCK FLASK**
Red and brown glaze, 7½″ 50.00 65.00

☐ **CROCK**
Label, brown, green and tan, 7″ 12.00 18.00

☐ **CROCK**
Label, light gray, 6½″ 15.00 25.00

☐ **CROCK**
Label, brown, 7″ 12.00 18.00

Price Range

☐ **CROCK**
With seal, Amsterdam, tan, 12″ 18.00 24.00

☐ **CROCK**
Label, tan and cream, 6¾″ 10.00 16.00

☐ **CROCK**
Label, tan and cream, 5½″ 10.00 16.00

☐ **CROCK**
Plain, ring top, two tone, tan and cream, 8½″ 6.00 10.00

☐ **CROCK**
Plain, Kinney on base, ring top, two tone, tan and
cream, 8½″ 12.00 18.00

☐ **CROCK**
Plain, bottle type, tapered crown, cream and tan,
7½″ 10.00 16.00

☐ **CROCK**
Plain, roof type shoulder, cream and tan, 8″ ... 8.00 12.00

☐ **DR. CRONK'S SARSAPARILLA BAR**
Blob top, sand color, 9½″ 20.00 28.00

☐ **CROWOUS, J.W. DRUG CO., 1 lb. MERCURY**
Dallas, TX. in 4 lines, tan crock, ring top, 2¾″ 40.00 50.00

☐ **CROWN GINGER BEER CO.**
Cleveland, OH, in a circle in center, brown, 6¾″ 12.00 18.00

☐ **CRUISKEEN LAWN**
Cream and brown, 8″ 20.00 30.00

☐ **PRESENTED BY, P.J. CURRIN, A MERRY
CHRISTMAS AND HAPPY NEW YEAR**
Pint jug, brown and tan with blue stencil lettering,
6½″ 25.00 35.00

☐ **DAWSON SALTS & WATER CO.
DISTRIBUTORS HAMBY SALTS, IRON AND
LITHIA WATER**
Dawson Springs, KY, large 5 above, jug, brown
and white, blue lettering, 18″ 30.00 40.00

☐ **D.C.**
Gray, 11″ 10.00 16.00

☐ Same as above, except tan, 10½″ 10.00 16.00

☐ **THE D.C.L. SCOTCH WHISKEY DISTILLERS
LIMITED**
London, Edinburgh, Glasgow, Gold Medals, Edin-
burgh 1886, under bottom Bengimark, Doulton,
Shicon, England 55.00 70.00

Price Range

☐ **DEACON BROWN VINEGAR**
In 3 lines, tan & brown, 3¼" 30.00 40.00

☐ **GEO. A. DICKEL & CO., CASCASE**
DISTILLERY HAND MADE SOUR MASH
TENNESSEE WHISKEY
White with black lettering, blue bands, 9½" ... 25.00 35.00

☐ **D.J. AND CO.**
No. 2A Lumber Street, N.Y., 1795, preserves
crock, seal top, salt glaze, 5" 100.00 130.00

☐ **A.P. DONAGHHO**
Parkersburg, WV, canning crock, tan, blue stencil, 8" 25.00 35.00

☐ **A.P. DONAGHHO**
Parkersburg, WV, written at a slant, blue-gray
stencil, 8" 25.00 35.00

☐ **DOSTER-NORTHINGTON DRUG CO.**
Birmingham, AL, jug with handle, white and
brown, 11" 20.00 28.00

☐ **DOSTER-NORTHINGTON DRUG CO.**
Birmingham, AL, brown and cream, ½ gallon .. 20.00 28.00

☐ **DOTRICK DISTILLING CO.**
Dayton, O. MOTTO JUG, "EAT, DRINK AND BE
MERRY," in 3 lines, crock brown & cream with
hand, 5½" 40.00 55.00

☐ **COMPLIMENTS OF A.J. DRESEL**
Second & Magnolia Ave., Louisville, KY, brown
and tan, 2¼" 30.00 40.00

☐ **DRINKOMETER**
In back, tan, 5" 10.00 16.00

☐ **EAGLE LIQUEUR DIS.**
Cincinnati, OH, ring top, eagle and shield in center, green, 2¼" 30.00 40.00

☐ **EELAARKI, ADRSV.**
Schiedarn, crock with handle, ring around bottom, tan, 4" 20.00 28.00

☐ Same as above, except 12" 10.00 16.00

☐ **ENGLAND NATOINE**
In two lines on base, four rings near shoulder,
spout, brick brown, 10" 10.00 16.00

☐ Same as above, except in all colors and sizes,
some with panels, some with plain tops 10.00 16.00

Price Range

☐ **ETRUIA STONE CHIN**
2518 under bottom, syrup label, tan, 6″ 20.00 28.00

☐ **J. W. M. FIELD & SONS WHOLESALE LIQUORS**
Owensboro, KY, cream, 3¼″ 30.00 40.00

☐ **FOCKIN, WYNAND**
Amsterdam, beer jug with handle, tan, 12″ 18.00 24.00

☐ **FOWLKES & MYATT CO. CIDER VINEGAR**
Miniature jug, brown and white, blue lettering, 3″ 30.00 40.00

☐ **FRANC, L. & CO.**
Toledo, Ohio, M.C. Kingon Hand Made Sour
Mash Whiskey in a frame, blue letters, tapered
top & ring, 10½″ 20.00 28.00

☐ **FREIBERG & KAHN DISTILLERIES, METROPOLITAN CLUE**
In a form in 4 lines, tan & cream, 3½″ 18.00 24.00

☐ **J FRIEDER**
Hand-painted picture, ring around bottom, tan,
12″ 30.00 40.00

☐ **FROG**
Sheared top, coming out of mouth, green, 6½″ 18.00 24.00

☐ Same as above, except B. FRANKFER 30.00 40.00

☐ **G.W. FULPER & BROS.**
Flemington, NJ, tan and blue decorations, 11¼″ 30.00 40.00

☐ **GALLAGHER & O'GARA, DEALERS IN FINE WHISKEY**
Bessemer, AL, tan 20.00 30.00

☐ **GALLOWAY'S EVERLASTING JAR**
Pat'd Feb. 8th Pat. Applied for 1870, canning
crock with wax sealer, gray, 7¾″ 20.00 30.00

☐ **GINGER POT**
Fancy decoration, no lettering, turquoise, 3½″ 10.00 16.00

☐ **GOLD TESTER**
Crock, 4″ 8.00 12.00

☐ **CHARLES S. GOVE COMPANY, WHOLESALE LIQUOR DEALERS**
Boston, MA, jug with handle, brown top and
cream base, 9″ 20.00 28.00

☐ **COMPLIMENTS OF H. GRAFF & CO., FRESNO, CAL**
In three lines, jug with handle, letters stamped in
blue glaze, ivory and dark brown, 3½″ 28.00 38.00

Price Range

☐ **H. GRAFF & CO.**
Compliments of Fresno, CA, in 3 lines, blue glaze
letters, cream brown, 3¼", with handle 20.00   28.00
☐ **GRASSELLI ARSENATE OF LEAD**
Poison crock, cream, 6½" 20.00   28.00
☐ **THE O. L. GREGORY VINEGAR CO.**
Tan and brown, 3½" 20.00   28.00
☐ **H. G. NASH**
Brushed bird decoration, 1 gallon, covered,
ovoid, 8¾" 225.00   265.00
☐ **HAILWOODS MANCHESTER**
Brown Top Cream Pot, outline picture of cow at
center, height 4" 25.00   35.00
☐ **HAMMERSLEY'S CREAMERY**
Blue Print Cream Pot broughton, three hammers
pictured at center, 4" 20.00   28.00
☐ Same but height 3" 30.00   40.00
☐ **HAPPY PATTY**
With handle, brown and tan, 8½" 20.00   28.00
☐ **I. W. HARPER**
Nelson Co., KY, cream, 3¼" 40.00   58.00
☐ **HARPER, I. W.**
Nelson Co., KT, "Wluses & many doz. a ribbing
etc." on front of jug with handle, tan neck, etc.
ring top, cream, 7½" 80.00   110.00
☐ **I. W. HARPER, GOLD MEDAL WHISKEY**
Square base, long twisted neck, cobalt, 8¾" ..   40.00   55.00
☐ **W. P. HARTLEY**
Liverpool & London, London Tower in center,
under it "Trademark Reg.," eleven panels, tan,
4" 10.00   16.00
☐ **VINCENT HATHAWAY & CO.**
Blob top, tan, 9½" 12.00   18.00
☐ **HAYNER LOCK**
Box 290, Dayton, OH, white, 8" 25.00   35.00
☐ **HELMENT RYE**
Blue lettering, cream, 3" 20.00   28.00
☐ **HESSIG-ELLIS DRUG CO.**
Memphis, TN, 1 lb. Mercury, Cream, ring top ..   18.00   24.00

Price Range

☐ **DISTILLED BY JAMES R. HOGO, JIM WHISKEY**
Popular Bluff, MO, white and brown, blue lettering, 9¾″ 45.00   65.00

☐ **COMPLIMENTS OF HOLBERG**
Mobile and Cincinnati, brown and white, 3¼″ .. 30.00   40.00

☐ **E. J. HOLLIDGE**
Label, cream, 6″ 10.00   16.00

☐ **HOLLOWAY'S FAMILY OINTMENT FOR THE CURE OF CTC.**
8 lines (London), 1″ x 1½″ round crock, in back 7 lines, ring top 20.00   28.00

☐ **HOLLOWAY'S OINTMENT, GOUT & RHEUMATISM,**
Height 1½″ 12.00   18.00

☐ **J.W. HOOPER & BRO., GROCERIES AND LIQUORS**
Nashville, TN, jug, tan with brown top and blue lettering, 8¼″ 30.00   40.00

☐ **HORTON CATO MFG. CO. ROYAL SALAD DRESSING**
Detroit, MI, wide mouth jug, white and brown with black lettering, 10¼″ 25.00   35.00

☐ **R.M. HUGHES & CO'S**
Monogram, VINEGAR, blue label, white, 9¼″ .. 30.00   40.00

☐ **HUMPHREY & MARTIN**
Tan and brown crock, 8¾″ 30.00   40.00

☐ **INK CROCK**
Conical, light gray, 2¾″ 10.00   16.00

☐ **INK CROCK**
Round pouring lip, cream, 10¾″ 10.00   16.00

☐ **INK CROCK**
Round pouring lip, brown, 7¾″ 10.00   16.00

☐ **INK CROCK**
Plain, roof type shoulder, pouring lip, 6″ 15.00   25.00

☐ **INK CROCK**
Plain, tan, 2¾″ 10.00   16.00

☐ **INK CROCK**
Plain, no neck, round collar, brown, 1¾″ round, 1¾″ tall 12.00   18.00

☐ **INK CROCK**
Label, light gray, 5¾″ 12.00   18.00

	Price Range	

☐ **INK CROCK**
Label, tan, 2¼" **12.00** **18.00**

☐ **INK CROCK**
Label, tan, 2½" **12.00** **18.00**

☐ **INK CROCK**
Label, tan, 2¾" **12.00** **18.00**

☐ **INK CROCK**
Label, tan, 7" **12.00** **18.00**

☐ **INK CROCK**
Label, cream, 5" **12.00** **18.00**

☐ **INK POTTERY**
Light blue, short neck **12.00** **18.00**

☐ **INK POTTERY**
Some have embossing, brick brown, 10" **12.00** **18.00**

☐ **INK POTTERY**
Plain, conical, light gray, 2¾" around bottom,
2⅛" tall **10.00** **16.00**

☐ Same as above, except brown **10.00** **16.00**

☐ **INK POTTERY**
Plain, ring top, light brown, 1¾" round, ¼" neck **10.00** **16.00**

☐ **JONES BROS. & CO.**
Brown and tan, 3½" **30.00** **40.00**

☐ **JONES BROS., COMPLIMENTS OF J. CARR
MFG.'S OF HIGH GRADE CIDER & VING.**
Louisville, KY, tan and cream, 3½" **30.00** **40.00**

☐ **JORDAN & STANLEY, WINE & SPIRIT
MERCHANTS**
Newport, I.W., Spirit jug, cork closure, brown top,
light fawn bottom, incised across top front, handle at neck, 8", round section jug with waist towards bottom third, 8" **20.00** **28.00**

☐ **JUG**
Very crude bell shape, red and tan, 7" **10.00** **16.00**

☐ **KABBENBEER LTD.**
London, pattened one litre lidded beer jug, white
glaze, handle at side, impressed below neck, IL.
base impressed "W", black underglaze printed lid
reads "THIS JUG IS THE PROPERTY OF KAB-
BENBEER, LTD., LONDON, PATENTED." Han-
dle at side, brass thumb plate for opening lid, over
center brass clip to keep lid closed, 9¼", hairline

Price Range

crack extends 3½" down from neck on one side
only. Unusual Brewery item. No other damage except defect mentioned 40.00 50.00

☐ **KAEHLER BROS**
Fresno, CA, in a circle with a medicine trademark,
ivory and brown, gallon 20.00 28.00

☐ **KAN 2**
In seal on shoulder, ring neck, ring top, handle,
tan, 12", round 30.00 40.00

☐ **JAMES KEILLER & SONS, DUNDEE
MARMALADE**
London, (c. 1862), Great Britain, gray, 4" 10.00 16.00

☐ **KENNEDY**
Tan and beige, 8½" 12.00 18.00

☐ **THE KINTORE**
Cream and brown, 8¼" 20.00 28.00

☐ **C.B. KIRBY, LATE R. CROOK & CO.**
Hervey Street, Ipswich, tan and cream, two gallon 28.00 38.00

☐ **J.W. KOLB & SON**
4471 St. Louis Ave., St. Louis, MO, jug, stamped
letters, dark brown and cream, 3¼" 30.00 40.00

☐ **RETURN TO KUTNER & GOLDSTEIN & CO.**
Wholesale Grocers, Fresno, CA, wire handle,
cream, gallon 28.00 38.00

☐ **KUTNER GOLDSTEIN & CO., RETURN TO**
Wholesale Grocers Fresno, Calif. in 4 lines in blue
glaze letters, bucket type handle, 1 gal., cream 28.00 38.00

☐ **LAMBRECHT** in script, **BUTTER**
White and blue lettering, 2⅞" 10.00 16.00

☐ **LITTLE BROWN JUG**
Engraved, brown pottery, 2¾" 30.00 40.00

☐ **LITTLE BROWN JUG 1876**
Dark brown, 3" 30.00 40.00

☐ **LIVERPOOL**
On base, brown and white, tapered top, 7¼" .. 12.00 18.00

☐ **LYMANS CLARE & CO.**
384 & 386 St. Paul Street, Montreal, tan, blue in-
cising, 6" 20.00 28.00

Price Range

☐ **HAILWOODS PURE RICH CREAM,**
Manchester, cream pot, stone color, creamery,
Broughton, 4″ 15.00 25.00
☐ Same but height 3¼″ 25.00 35.00
☐ **COMPLIMENTS OF J.C. MAYFIELD MFG. CO.**
Birmingham, AL, tan, 3¼″ 45.00 65.00
☐ **MAYFIELD VINEGAR & CIDER CO.,**
THE FAMILY & PICKLING VINEGAR
Mayfield, KY, cream, 3¼″ 40.00 58.00
☐ **McCOMB POTTERY**
"Pottery Pat. Pend." on bottom, canning crock,
tan and brown, 6″ 25.00 35.00
☐ **McCOMB POTTERY & CO.**
Pat. Jan. 24, 1899, canning crock, white, 7″ ... 20.00 28.00
☐ **COMPLIMENTS OF, McDONNEL, JOHN A.**
269 Conception St. in 4 lines, crock with handle,
cream, 3″ 45.00 65.00
☐ **THE MEDENHALL HOTEL BATHS**
Claremore, OK, Radium Water from, Cures rheu-
matism, stomach trouble, eczema and other ail-
ments, letters in blue, 1 gal. jug, ivory and brown
with handle 25.00 35.00
☐ **MELCHERS, J. J. WZ—SCHIEDORM—**
"Honey Suckle, Old Gin" in 4 lines on base, tan,
12½″ x 2¾″ with handle, ring top 18.00 24.00
☐ **M.H. MELICK**
Roseville, OH, canning crock, gray, 8¼″ 18.00 24.00
☐ **MERCURY**
Tan and white crock, 5″ 10.00 16.00
☐ **MERCURY SPURLOCK NEAL CO.**
Nashville, TN, jug, white and blue lettering, 3¼″ 45.00 65.00
☐ **MEREDITH'S DIAMOND CLUB PURE RYE**
WHISKEY
White, 8″ 50.00 70.00
☐ **METROPOLITAN CLUB, FREBERG & KAHN**
DISTILLERS
Miniature jug, brown and white, blue lettering,
3¼″ 30.00 40.00
☐ **MILLER, C. J.,**
"Fine Whiskies, Vicksburg, Miss." in 3 lines,
crock jug with handle, brown, tan, 7½″, qt. 25.00 35.00

Price Range

☐ **MINN. STONEWARE CO.**
Red Wing, MN, on bottom, wide mouth, reddish
brown, 7″ 25.00 35.00

☐ **MINN. STONEWARE CO. SAFETY VALVE
PAT.**
Canning crock, white and blue markings, 8½″ 20.00 28.00

☐ **CHRISTIAN MOERLEIN BREWING CO.**
Cincinatti, OH, in a circle on shoulder, "TRADE-
MARK" on top of it in center, "MOERLEINS OLD
JUG LAGER RUN BEER" with fancy design
around it, dark brown, 8″ 30.00 40.00

☐ **COMPLIMENTS OF D. MONROE, SR.**
303–305 South 18th St., brown and tan, 3½″ 45.00 65.00

☐ **MOTTO JUG "AS I GO UP THE HILL OF
PROSPERITY, MAY I NEVER MEET A
FRIEND,"**
Dotrick Distillery Co., Dayton, OH, brown and
cream crock with handle, 4½″ 45.00 65.00

☐ **MOUTH WASH**
Letters running bottom left to top right with 3 leaf
clover, applied top, elephant stopper, pale blue,
5″ 12.00 18.00

☐ **MOUTARDE DESSAUZ FILS ORLEANS
FRANCE**
On back, cream, 4″ 12.00 18.00

☐ **WM. J. MOXLEY'S SPECIAL
OLEOMARGARINE**
"The Taste is the Test," Pat. 6–2–14, white and
black lettering blue bands, 7½″ 20.00 28.00

☐ **GRAPE JUICE PREPARED BY MYERS,
BENTON & CO.**
Cleveland, tan, 5½″ 35.00 45.00

☐ **N.K.A.**
In a circle near shoulder, tan with handle, short
neck, double ring top, tan, 11¼″ 18.00 24.00

☐ **D. NEWMAN**
Tan and white crock, 7″ 10.00 16.00

☐ **NORDJAUSEN KORNSCHNAPPS**
Tan and cream, 7½″ 20.00 28.00

☐ **NORTON & CO., J.**
Bennington, VT, with #2 and flower Dis. (blue)
Sand color, 2 gal., flat ring top 150.00 200.00

Price Range

☐ **COMPLIMENTS OF NORTON & NORTON**
Savannah, GA, brown and tan, 3¼″ 40.00   50.00

☐ **E. & L. P. NORTON**
Bennington, VA, gray with blue decorative design,
8″ 75.00   125.00

☐ **E.B. NORTON & CO.,**
Worcester, MA, handle, gray with blue decorative
design, 14″ 75.00   125.00

☐ **JOHN H. OELKERS**
730 S. Rampart St., N.O. LA, tan and brown, 4½″   30.00   40.00

☐ **OLD**
In center a picture of a Jug on it, Rye, Jug, tan,
3½″ 30.00   40.00

☐ **OLD CONTINENTAL WHISKEY**
Miniature size, brown and tan, 3¼″ 30.00   40.00

☐ Same as above, except cream 30.00   40.00

☐ **OLD CONTINENTAL WHISKEY**
Brown and cream, 3″ 30.00   40.00

☐ **OLD CUTTER RYE, A.E. CAMPBELL**
CATERING CO.
Birmingham, AL, tan, 3¼″ 30.00   40.00

☐ **OLD DEXTER DIS. CO.**
Butler, KY, dis. in a circle a flower in center in
back Pat. Aug. 11, 1919, The Old Dexter Jug
Whiskey, rib side, round jug with handle and vase
bottom, 8″ 60.00   80.00

☐ **OLD JUG, BOURBON, G. HANNEMAN**
Portland, OR, in 4 lines, handle, silver-plated,
pouring spout, 10½″ 110.00   140.00

☐ **OLD JUG LAGER**
"The Fashionable Beverage of the Day, Brilliant
in Color, Absolutely Pure, Stimulating, Rejuvenat-
ing, Truly Cultured, Veritable Luxury, Nashville,
Tenn." all in ornate lettering, cream, 8¾″ 20.00   28.00

☐ **OLD NECTAR RYE**
R.P. Blalack, Mobile, Ala., cream, 3″ 30.00   40.00

☐ **OLD PRIVATE STOCK PURE RYE**
In 2 lines, brown and gray crock with handle, double ring top, 3¼″ 32.00   42.00

☐ **OLD TAYLOR**
On side, reverse "S.H. TAYLOR & SONS DIST.,
FRANKFORT, KY.," tan, quart 25.00   35.00

Price Range

□ **OREGON IMPORT COMPANY**
Portland, OR, with handle, brown and cream
crock, ½ gal. 32.00   42.00

□ **D.L. ORMSBY, 1850**
With star in a circle, reverse at base in shield Patent Pressed W. Smith NY, twelve-sided, very
crude, tan, ½ pint 20.00   28.00

□ **OTTMAN BROS. & CO.**
Fort Edward, NY, blue bird, gray with cobalt decoration, 11″ 75.00   100.00

□ **J.W. PALMER**
Tan, 3″ 30.00   40.00

□ **PAIN & BAYLOR**
Tan and white, 7″ 10.00   16.00

□ **RICHARD PEARCE**
Tan, 7″ 10.00   16.00

□ **PEWTRESS, S. L.**
Conn, #2, Blue Flower Dis., tapered ring top,
same color................................... 100.00   130.00

□ **G.W. PIPER**
Cream, 7¼″ 10.00   16.00

□ **PRICE & BRISTOL**
On base, brown and white, tapered top, 7¼″ .. 12.00   18.00

□ **M. QUINN, WHOLESALE GROCER**
Kansas City, MO, wire handle with wooden grip,
white with blue lettering, 10″ 28.00   38.00

□ **WM. RADAM'S MICROBE KILLER NO. 1**
Handle on jug, white with blue lettering, 10¾″   40.00   55.00

□ **RANDOLPH & CO.**
Brown and tan, 3″ 30.00   40.00

□ **THEO RECTANUS CO.**
"Pure Old Hand Made Sour Mash Louisville,"
brown and cream, 3¼″ 30.00   40.00

□ **RELIABLE MIDDLE QUALITY FRUIT PRESERVES**
Gray with black lettering, 6″ 20.00   28.00

□ **JACOB RICHTER CO.**
Fresno, CA, Best Wines & Liquors $5 per gal. in
four lines, brown and ivory, gallon 40.00   50.00

Price Range

☐ **H.E.N. ROSS**
In a circle, In a circle under it a cross and cross flag, under it in one line Phein Preussen, Pottery or Crock on shoulder, handle, tan, 12″ tall, 3¼″ round **15.00   25.00**

☐ **ROYAL DOULTON DEWARS WHISKEY**
With Scottish figure, crock jug, qt. **45.00   60.00**

☐ **RUSSELL, M.C. & SON,**
"Corner 3rd & Market Sts., Maryville, KY." in a frame, brown and sand with handle, 6″ **30.00   40.00**

☐ **SAINSBURY'S BLOATER PASTE,**
Black or white, 3″ **8.00   12.00**

☐ **SATTERLEE & MORY**
Ft. Edwards, NY, gray with blue decorative design, 7½″ **40.00   50.00**

☐ **JAMES SCHAM**
Pat. July 13, 1909, embossed "Sherwood," canning crock, glass lid, white, 7½″ **20.00   28.00**

☐ **CHRISTIAN SCHMIDT**
Shenandoah, PA, cream, 7″ **15.00   25.00**

☐ **COMP. OF H. SCHRODER**
401 & 403 Broughton, brown and tan, 3½″ ... **30.00   40.00**

☐ **SHUSTER, BEN J., COMPLIMENTS OF**
Selma, AL in 3 lines, beige and brown with handle, 3¾″ **30.00   40.00**

☐ **FRED L. SCHWANTZ, UP-TO-DATE GROCER, FINE LIQUOR**
63 Beale St., Memphis, TN, jug, tan with brown top, 8½″ **30.00   40.00**

☐ **SCOTLAND EXPORT CO. LTD. CHIVAS REGAL**
Tan, 12″ **30.00   40.00**

☐ **B.J. SIMOND'S**
Blob top, 10″ **50.00   70.00**

☐ **SIMPLEX HEKTOGRAPH,**
Composition for Hall's Patent Simplex, large picture of hatted man blowing trumpet, very large print 3″ x 3″, printed at rear with instructions "For Use" **20.00   28.00**

☐ **D.F. SMITH & SNOWS**
Whitefoot, Pat. July 17, 66, blob top, tan, 10″ **50.00   65.00**

Price Range

☐ **J. L. SMITH**
Inside under lip, crude Southern pottery, brown,
11″ 20.00 28.00

☐ **SMOKY MT. 1880**
Vinegar jar, brown, 5″ 18.00 24.00

☐ **COMP. OF SOUTHERN GRO. CO.**
114 Bernard St., brown and tan, 3½″ 30.00 40.00

☐ **SOY SAUCE**
Pottery jug, short neck, ring top, side spout,
brown, 5″ 12.00 18.00

☐ **SOYER'S PERFECT SAUCE**
Meadville, PA, on front in 3 lines, crock with handle, ring top, 7½″ 18.00 24.00

☐ **W. M. SPENCER**
"Clarks improved, Pat. May 19th 92, Zanesville,
Ohio" on bottom, white with blue lettering, 9″   25.00 35.00

☐ **STONE MASON PAT'D APPLIED FOR**
On shoulder, canning crock, tan and brown ... 20.00 28.00

☐ **THE WEIR STONEWALL FRUIT JAR, PAT.**
1892
Tan and brown, 6½″ 18.00 24.00

☐ **STOUT & GINGER BEER**
Tan and brown, 6″, a cross in center 10.00 18.00

☐ **E. SWASEY & CO.**
Portland, ME, butter crock, white and brown, 3½″ 20.00 28.00

☐ **DR. SWETT'S ORIGINAL ROOT BEER,**
REGISTERED,
Boston, MA, brown and tan, 7¾″ 10.00 16.00

☐ **E.B. TAYLOR**
Richmond, VA, at an angle, gray with blue stencil
lettering, 8″ 30.00 40.00

☐ **THWAITES DUBLIN**
Tan tapered, top, short neck, 6¾″ 10.00 16.00

☐ **TIGER GLAZED & 17th CENTURY**
8½″, large oval decoration below composed of
shield with 5 ears of corn erect above, 2½″ in
height by 1¾″ in width, salt glaze 300.00 375.00

☐ **TIMOTHY WHITE CO., LTD. EXTRACT OF**
MALT & COD LIVER OIL
Black on white, $5^3/_5$″, print size 3½″ x 3¼″,
crisply printed 18.00 24.00

Price Range

☐ **TODE BROS.**
T.B. and arrow through a ring on bottom, dark tan   **10.00**   **16.00**

☐ **N.M.URI & CO. R.H. PARKER**
Tan, 2¾″ **45.00**   **65.00**

☐ **VASE**
Label, 3½″ **10.00**   **16.00**

☐ **VOODOO FACE JUG**
2 under bottom, gray, 6″ x 6″ **45.00**   **65.00**

☐ **VITREOUS STONE BOTTLING, J. BOURNE & SON**
Patentees Denby Pottery, near Derby P&J Arnold Sondon, 4¼″ x 2½″, pouring lip, brown **18.00**   **24.00**

☐ **WHITES**
Jug, 2 gallon, orchid design, 14″ **200.00** **250.00**

☐ **WHITES**
Jug, orchid design, 1 gallon, straight sides, 11½″   **160.00** **200.00**

☐ **WHITES**
Jug, fantail bird design, 2 gallon, slightly bulbous, 12½″ **375.00** **425.00**

☐ **WHITES**
Ovoid crock, 2 gallon, c. 1840, floral bouquet design, 10″ **200.00** **240.00**

☐ **WHITES**
Jug, 3 gallon, floral design, 15½″ **200.00** **250.00**

☐ **WHITES BUTTER**
Orchid design, 1 gallon, covered, slightly waisted, 7½″ **200.00** **250.00**

☐ **WHITES**
Utica, 1 gallon jug, beehive design, 11″ **140.00** **165.00**

☐ **WHITES**
Jug, 2 gallon, floral design, area of design is larger than usual, 13½″ **200.00** **225.00**

☐ **WHITES AND WOOD**
Longtail bird design, flared lip, straight sides, 3 gallon, 10½″ **400.00** **500.00**

☐ **F. WOODWORTH**
Burlington, VT, scrolled dandelion design, covered, 22″ **400.00** **470.00**

CURE

Cure bottles serve as documentary evidence of how the public was fooled in the 19th and early 20th centuries when tonics and other preparations were advertised to cure all manner of physical and emotional problems. Strict modern laws enforced by the Food and Drug Administration, and Federal Trade Commission, do not allow the sale of such products any longer.

Patent medicine cures became such big business that road shows were organized around them. They worked not only out of wagons, but were booked into vaudeville theatres throughout the country. Various forms of entertainment were offered along with sales pitches for the product. Generally, the cast included several persons who had been "chronic sufferers" but due to repeated use of the cure, were totally healed. They came forward to tell their stories in long monologues. The show traditionally closed with cases of the product being carried onstage for the public to come up and purchase by the case or bottle. Patent medicine shows were extremely successful. They often realized better profits than the legitimate theatre, since they collected both from an admission fee and sale of the product (and, sometimes, sales of books and quack appliances). Theatrical managers were always glad to book medicine shows into their theatres.

Manufacturers made a game of inventing bizarre product names. Some used foreign-sounding names or blatantly claimed that their product was of foreign origin. This was commonplace in retailing in the 19th century, not only for medicinal cures but other products. Coffee was customarily called Brazillian, leather Moroccan, rubber Indian, silk Persian, and tea Chinese, even if domestically produced. To suggest that something was imported not only lent charm but implied that it was better. So far as medicines were concerned, slapping on foreign names gave the impression that somebody, somewhere in the world, had an inside track on curing ailments that baffled American science. One example of this was Carey's Chinese Cure (a very collectible bottle). Catarrh was the old-fashioned name for headcold. For all the American public knew, they were sneezing while 10,000 miles away the Chinese were merely downing this simple remedy whenever a cold struck. Of course, there was no cold cure in China—or anyplace else, but it sounded good, and it sold.

Some cures were supposedly composed of Indian medicine. It was widely known that indians did not visit the white man's physicians, did not take their medicines, but made cures of their own from closely-guarded recipes. Quite likely, if commercially sold "Indian cures" had followed the authentic recipes, some good might have been accomplished. But they merely used the name to sell worthless potions. They included the Ka-Ton-Ka Cure, and Kickapoo Indian Cough Cure.

Price Range

☐ **A NO. 1**
Self cure, the specific-(label), aqua, 5″ 6.00 10.00

☐ **ABBOTT-BROS.—RHEUMATIC CURE**
Estd. 1888, amber, 7¾″ 14.00 21.00

☐ **ABBOTT-BROS.—RHEUMATIC CURE EST 1888**
Side Rheumatic Cure, side Abbot Bro's., taper top, amber, 7½″ 15.00 20.00

☐ Same except side embossed SAMPLE BOTTLE, amber, 5″ 20.00 25.00

☐ Same front panel on oval bottle, no side embossing, amber, 5½″ 10.00 15.00

☐ **ABC BLOOD CURE**
On SNAKE entwined through ABC MONOGRAM, manufactured by ABC Chemical Co., Richmond, VA, ring top, aqua, 7½″ 25.00 35.00

☐ **ACID CURE SOLUTION, EMPIRE MFG. CO.**
Akron, OH, in a circle, crock, white, 4¾″ 9.00 12.00

☐ **ACID CURE SOLUTION EMPIRE**
White crockery, taper top, 4⅞″ round 15.00 20.00

☐ **DR. ADAMS, COUGH CURE**
Prepared by E.J. Parker, Cortland, NY all in 4 lines, flat ring top, beveled corner, clear, 5½″ 14.00 21.00

☐ **DR. AGNEWS CURE FOR THE HEART**
Ring top, clear, 8½″ 12.00 15.00

☐ **ALEXANDER'S ASTHMA CURE**
The G. F. Alexander Co., Portland, ME. all on front, ring top, amber, 6¼″ 15.00 20.00

☐ **ALEXANDER'S SURE CURE FOR MALARIA, Akron**
Other side ALEXANDER'S LIVER & KIDNEY TONIC, Akron, OH, ring top and ring in center of neck, amber, 7¾″ 20.00 30.00

☐ **ALKAVIS SURE CURE FOR MALARIA**
Label, ring top, amber, 8¼″ 7.00 10.00

☐ **ALMYR SYSTEM OF TREATMENT FOR CATARRH**
ALMYR CATARRH CURE in three lines, aqua, ring top, 8¼″ 30.00 35.00

Price Range

☐ **AMERICAN**
On one side, "COUGH CURE" other, front Howard Bros., aqua, 6½" 12.00 16.00

☐ Same as above, except Prepared by W. B. Jones, M.D. 12.00 16.00

☐ **ANCHOR WEAKNESS CURE**
Amber, 8¼" 15.00 20.00

☐ **ANDERSON'S POOR MANS COUGH CURE**
Ring top, aqua, 5¾" 12.00 18.00

☐ **ANTI-APOPLECTINE**
On side, "THE ONLY APOPLEXY PREVENTATIVE AND PARALYSIS CURE" on front, other side "DR. F. S. HUTCHISON CO.," double ring top, aqua, 9¼" 20.00 25.00

☐ **ANTIBRULE CHEMICAL CO.**
Other side "St. Louis, MO. U.S.A.," on front "ANTIBULE CURES BURRUS-WOUNDS-SKIN DISEASES-AND ALL INFLAMMATION" in three lines, clear, 6¼" 15.00 20.00

☐ **ANTICEPHALALGINE THE GREAT HEADACHE CURE**
Ring top, aqua, 3½" 8.00 10.00

☐ **ANTIMIGRAINE CURE EVERY VARIETY OF HEADACHE**
Clear or amethyst, 5¼" 7.00 10.00

☐ **ARCTIC FROSTBITE CURE**
Label, ring top, clear or amber, 2¾" 7.00 10.00

☐ **ARMISTEAD'S FAMOUS AGUE CURE**
On shoulder, taper top, aqua, 6" 10.00 15.00

☐ **ARTHUR'S ELIXER OF SULPHUR POSITIVELY CURES ALL THROAT and LUNG DISEASES and CATARRH**
Ring top, aqua, 8¼" 45.00 65.00

☐ **ARZY'S PAINLESS CORN CURE**
Ring top, aqua, 2½" 8.00 10.00

☐ **ATLAS KIDNEY & LIVER CURE, ATLAS MEDICINE CO.**
Henderson, N.C., U.S.A., with fancy monogram, AM CO. in sunken panel, honey amber, 9" 5.00 8.00

☐ **DR. F. G. ATWOODS NO 2 COLIC CURE DOSE ½ OZ**
Laboratory New Haven, CT, ring top, amber, 5" 15.00 20.00

Price Range

☐ **AYER'S**
In sunken panel, one side "AQUE CURE," other
"Lowell, Mass.," aqua, pontil, 7" 100.00 120.00
☐ Same as above, except no pontil 8.00 11.00
☐ **B.H. BACON, OTTO'S CURE**
Rochester NY, clear, 2½" 3.00 5.00
☐ **BAKER'S VEGETABLE BLOOD AND LIVER
CURE**
Lookout Mountain Medicine Co. Mfgrs & Props.
Greensville, TN, double ring top, amber, 9¾" .. 100.00 120.00
☐ Same except SPENCER MEDICINE CO. 100.00 120.00
☐ **DR. BAKER'S GRAPE CURE**
Embossed "B" on front lower neck, blown in
mold, rectangular, with contents and box, amber,
9¼" 45.00 55.00
☐ **DR. BALL'S HUSTENA, GREATEST OF ALL
COUGH CURES**
Ring top, clear, 4⅞" 5.00 8.00
☐ **BAUER'S COUGH CURE**
On front, clear, 4⅞" 2.00 5.00
☐ **BAUER'S INSTANT COUGH CURE**
Mt. Morris, NY in three lines, tapered top, aqua,
7" 10.00 15.00
☐ **BECK'S STRUDEL VICHI CURES
HEADACHES**
Ring top, round, clear, 2⅝" 15.00 20.00
☐ **DR. BEEBE'S CATARRH & ASTHMA CURE,
OTTO L. HOFFMAN MFGR.**
Columbus, OH, ring top, amber, 5" 15.00 20.00
☐ Same except M.C. Beeb's etc. 15.00 20.00
☐ **P.A. BENJAMIN'S LIVER & KIDNEY CURE**
Tapered top, aqua, 7½" 10.00 20.00
☐ **DR. BENNETT'S**
Other side "A.L. Scovill & Co.," front, quick cure,
aqua, 4½" 15.00 21.00
☐ **BENNET'S MAGIC CURE**
Ring top, cobalt blue, 5⅛ 80.00 160.00
☐ **BENSON'S CURE FOR RHEUMATISM**
In three lines, three ring top, pontil, aqua, 6½" 100.00 125.00
☐ **BERRY'S CANKER CURE**
Side "CUTLER BROS. & Co.," side "BOSTON,"
ring top, aqua, 5" 4.00 8.00

Price Range

☐ **BIRD'S LUNG CURE**
In two lines vertical, ring top, aqua, 2½" 16.00 22.00

☐ **BISHOP'S GRANULAR CITRATE OF CAFFEINE**
On two beveled corners "HEADACHES CURED," ring top, corn flower blue, 5 and 6⅛" 15.00 25.00

☐ **THE BLISS REMEDY CO., BLISS LIVER & KIDNEY CURE**
Stockton, CA, aqua, 9¼" 15.00 20.00

☐ **DR. BOSANKO'S RHEUMATIC CURE**
Aqua, 5¾" 6.00 9.00

☐ **BRADYCROTINE A CURE FOR ALL HEADACHES**
Ring top, clear, 4¼" 6.00 10.00

☐ **BREEDEN'S RHEUMATIC CURE**
Label, "BREEDEN MEDICINE CO., CHATTA-NOOGA, TN," on front, aqua, 6½" 4.00 8.00

☐ **BREWERS LUNG RESTORER/CERTAIN PERMANENT CURE**
In two circles, front side, "CURE BRONCHITIS" side "CURES CONSUMPTION," double ring top, amber, 9½" 75.00 125.00

☐ **BRIGGS TONIC PILLS, NEVER FAIL TO CURE**
M.A. Briggs, Valdosta, Ga., clear, 3" 6.00 9.00

☐ **M.A. & H.G. BRIGGS, VALDOSTA, GA**
Side "Never FAIL TO CURE," reverse "TRADE-MARK NUNN BETTER," side "TONIC PILLS," ring top, amber, 2⅝" 8.00 12.00

☐ Same except aqua 5.00 8.00

☐ **BRIGHTSBANE THE GREAT KIDNEY AND LIVER CURE**
Taper top, aqua 75.00 100.00

☐ Same except KIDNEY AND STOMACH CURE 90.00 120.00

☐ **BRIGHTSBANE, THE GREAT KIDNEY AND LIVER CURE**
Vertical on front, square beveled corners, light amber, 8⅞" 50.00 75.00

☐ **BROWN'S BLOOD CURE**
Philadelphia, green, 6½" 50.00 75.00

Price Range

☐ **BROWN'S BLOOD CURE**
Philadelphia, ring top, green, 6¼" 75.00 100.00
☐ Same except amber 15.00 20.00
☐ **DR. L. BURDICK'S KIDNEY CURE**
In two lines, amber, ring top, 7¼" 20.00 27.00
☐ Same as above, except with Lodewick 16.00 22.00
☐ **DR. L. BURDICK'S KIDNEY CURE**
Side "J.E. JACKSON & CO PROPS.," side
"WOODBURY, NJ," ring top, aqua, 6¾" 10.00 15.00
☐ **DR. SAN JAC BURNHAM'S**
"KIDNEY CURE" in three lines vertical, on shoul-
der, Chicago, ring top, clear, 7¼" 15.00 21.00
☐ **BURNS' CATARRH CURE** (fancy letters)
Taper top, aqua, 9" 30.00 40.00
☐ **MRS. BUSH**
"SIDE FRONT SPECIFIC CURE FOR BURNS &
SCALDS," side "WINDER, GA," ring top, clear
or aqua, 5" 6.00 10.00
☐ Same except "JUG TAVERN, GA." 15.00 20.00
☐ **BUXTON'S RHEUMATIC CURE**
Aqua, 8½" 10.00 15.00
☐ **THE DR. D. M. BYE OIL CURE CO.**
Reverse side, "316 N. Illinois St.," other side "In-
dianapolis, Ind.," ring top, clear, 6½" 15.00 20.00
☐ **C (small letters) ubeb, ouch, ure**
All in one word, vertical, double ring top, clear,
5¼" 12.00 18.00
☐ **CALCURA side, SOLVENT side**
Double ring top, aqua, 8½" 10.00 15.00
☐ **CAMPBELL & LYON**
On one side, other "Detroit, MI," front
"UMATILLA-INDIAN-COUGH CURE" in two
lines, vertical, tapered top, aqua, 5½" 21.00 30.00
☐ **CANADIAN BOASTER HAIR TONIC**
Reverse side Dandruff Cure, clear, 8¼" 7.00 10.00
☐ **CAPUDINE HEADACHE CURE**
Oval, aqua, 3⅜" 2.00 4.00
☐ **CARSON'S AGUE CURE**
"Jamestown, NY" in three lines vertical, ring top,
aqua, 7¼" 15.00 21.00
☐ **CAULKS ABSCESS CURE**
Ring top, aqua, 1⅝" round 8.00 10.00

Price Range

☐ **CENTURY side, CATARRH CURE side**
Ring top, clear, 3½" 5.00   8.00

☐ **CERTAIN CURE FOR RHEUMATISM**
Vertical on front in sunken panel, "Chas. Dennin"
on side, "Brooklyn" on opposite side, aqua, 6¾"   11.00   15.00

☐ **CHAMBERLAINS CURE FOR CONSUMPTION**
Aqua, 5" 7.00   10.00

☐ **CHASE'S DYSPEPSIA CURE**
"Newburgh, NY" in three lines vertical, double
ring top, aqua, 8¾" 15.00   21.00

☐ **CHAUL-MOO-GRA THE EAST INDIA CURE**
Ring top, aqua, 6¼" 10.00   15.00

☐ **CHALMOOGRA DR GOERSS' THE EAST
INDIA CURE**
Side "FRANZ C.A. GOERSS M.D." in fancy
script, ring top, amber, 6¼" 20.00   30.00

☐ **CILL'S CATARRH CURE**
Vertical on front, sheared top, round bottom,
clear, 3¼" 11.00   15.00

☐ **CLAYS SURE CURE FOR RHEUMATISM, E.
J. KIEFFER. PROPRIETOR**
Savannah, GA, ring top, amber, 8" 15.00   20.00

☐ **CLEM'S SUMMER CURE**
Reverse "HOWE'S & CO. PROPRIETORS," ring
top, aqua, 4⅞" 20.00   30.00

☐ **CLEWLEYS MIRACULOUS CURE FOR
RHEUMATISM**
(Picture of nuns head) side "OFFICE 66 LIBERTY
ST, NEW YORK," side "SHAW PHARMACAL
CO.," ring top, aqua, 7¼" or 6" 75.00   125.00

☐ **THE CLINIC KIDNEY & LIVER CURE**
In two lines, on back "M'fr'd by Foley & Co., Stu-
benville, OH & Chicago," amber, tapered top,
9½" 30.00   40.00

☐ **DR. J.W. COBLENTZ CURE**
Ft. Wayne, IN, label, cobalt, 7¾" 6.00   10.00

☐ **COE'S DYSPEPSIA CURE, THE C. G. CLARK
CO., NEW HAVEN, CONN. U.S.A.**
Clear or aqua, 7½" 11.00   15.00

☐ **COKE DANDRUFF CURE**
On bottom, large ring top, clear, 6½" 5.00   8.00

	Price Range	

☐ **DR. COLE'S CATARRH CURE**
Ring top, aqua, 2½" **3.00** **5.00**
☐ **COLLINS (DANIEL) SURE CURE LINIMENT**
Taper top, clear, 6¾" **20.00** **25.00**
☐ **CONVERSE'S (MRS M.E.) SURE CURE FOR EPILEPSY**
Ring top, aqua, 6½" **35.00** **50.00**
☐ **MRS. M.E. CONVERSE'S SURE CURE FOR EPILEPSY**
Ring top, clear, 6¾" **25.00** **35.00**
☐ **C.C.C. (CORN CURE) BY MENDENHELL CO., EVANSVILLE, IND.**
Ring top, clear or aqua, 4¼" **13.00** **19.00**
☐ **COX'S CURE**
On side, FOR CONSUMPTION on front W.H. MOOERS side, ring top, aqua, 5⅛" **5.00** **8.00**
☐ **"COX'S" side, "CURE" side**
Ring top, clear, 4⅜" **3.00** **5.00**
☐ Also C.C.C. (Certain Cough Cure) **13.00** **19.00**
☐ **CRAIG'S KIDNEY**
c. 1887, in ½ moon circle, under it "Liver Cure Company," amber, double ring top, bottle same as Warner Safe Cure, 9½" **75.00** **100.00**
☐ **DR. CRAIG'S COUGH & CONSUMPTION CURE**
In four lines vertical, double ring top, amber, 8" **140.00** **190.00**
☐ **CRAMER'S COUGH CURE**
In two lines, ring top, aqua, 6¼" **15.00** **21.00**
☐ **CRAMERS KIDNEY & LIVER, CURE**
In 3 lines, ring top, aqua, 7" **12.00** **17.00**
☐ **CRAMER'S KIDNEY CURE SAMPLE**
Albany, N.Y. in four lines, ring top, round bottle, aqua, 4½" **7.00** **10.00**
☐ **CRISWELL'S BROMO-PEPSIN CURES HEADACHE**
Vertical, round, ring top, amber, 2½" **5.00** **10.00**
☐ **CRISWELL'S BROMO-PEPSIN CURES HEADACHE AND DIGESTION**
Vertical on front, amber, 4¾" **10.00** **14.00**
☐ **CROSBY-5-MINUTE CURE**
In three lines vertical, ring top, amber, 2¾" ... **8.00** **12.00**

Price Range

☐ **CROW'S CHILL CURE**
In two lines vertical, tapered top, aqua, 9½" .. **20.00 25.00**

☐ **CRYSTALINA THE MAGIC SKIN CURE A.S. HULL**
Hinesburgh, VT, ring top, clear, 5" **12.00 15.00**

☐ **CURTIS COUGH CURE**
"C.C.C." on each side, J. J. Mack & Co.-sole Proprietors, San Francisco, CA, ring top, aqua, 7" **15.00 20.00**

☐ **J.M. CURTIS CURE FOR THE BALDNESS**
Providence, RI, flared top, aqua, ½ pint **10.00 14.00**

☐ **THE CUTICURA SYSTEM OF CURING CONSTITUTIONAL HUMORS**
On front of panel, "Potter Drug and Chemical Corp. Boston, Mass, U.S.A." on reverse of panel, rectangular, aqua, 9¼" **10.00 14.00**

☐ **DA COSTA'S RADICAL CURE**
On 3 panels "Morris & Heritage" on one side other "Philadelphia," SSS monogram at top, in back panels, ring top, 8¼", aqua **55.00 70.00**

☐ **DA COSTA'S RADICAL CURE**
Side "SYRUP OF TAR," side "DR. MORRIS'," ring top, aqua, 5⅜" **30.00 35.00**

☐ **DR. DANIEL'S COLIC CURE**
Ring top, clear or amethyst, 3¾" **2.00 5.00**

☐ **DR. DANIEL'S COLIC CURE NO. 1**
On front, square, clear, 3½" **2.00 5.00**

☐ **DR. DANIEL'S COLIC CURE NO. 2**
Same as above **2.00 5.00**

☐ **DR. DANIEL'S VETERINARY COLIC CURE NO. 1**
On front, square, clear, 3½" **3.00 6.00**

☐ **DR. DANIEL'S VETERINARY COLIC CURE NO. 2**
Same as above **3.00 6.00**

☐ **DR. DANIEL'S WONDER WORKER LINIMENT NATURES CURE FOR MAN OR BEAST**
Ring top, clear, 6½" **7.00 10.00**

☐ **DATILMA-A RADICAL CURE FOR PAIN**
In three lines vertical, clear, ring top, 4½" **8.00 12.00**

Price Range

☐ **DEAN'S KIDNEY CURE**
"The Langham Med. Co. LeRoy, NY" in 3 lines,
ring top, 7¼", aqua **11.00   15.00**

☐ **DEERING & BERRY—GREAT KIDNEY CURE**
"Saco, ME in three lines vertical, ring top and ring
on neck, clear, 6⅛" **10.00   15.00**

☐ **DeWITTS COLIC & CHOLERA CURE**
Aqua, 4½" **6.00   9.00**

☐ **DR. DeWITT'S LIVER, BLOOD, & KIDNEY
CURE**
Amber, 8½" **55.00   70.00**

☐ **DR. DeWITT'S**
Eclectic Cure, W.J. Parker & Co. Baltimore, MD,
tapered top, aqua, 6½" **10.00   15.00**

☐ **D.K.&B. CURE**
Side, BRO. MED. CO. side, ring top, aqua, 5½"   **3.00   7.00**

☐ **E. C. DeWITT & CO., ONE MINUTE COUGH
CURE**
Chicago, U.S.A., tapered top, aqua, 4½" **7.00   10.00**

☐ **W. H. DOLF'S SURE CURE FOR COLIC**
Flat ring top, "T.C.W. & Co." under bottom, aqua,
3½" **10.00   15.00**

☐ **DUFFY'S TOWER MINT CURE (TRADEMARK
EST 1842)**
Tapered bottle, wide ring top, embossed tower
and flag, amber, 6½" **100.00 125.00**

☐ **DUNLAPS COLIC KIDNEY CURE**
Side "FOR HORSES," side "FOR MULES,"
taper top, clear, 6⅛" **20.00   30.00**

☐ **EDLIS DANDRUFF CURE AND HAIR
INVIGORATOR**
Pittsburg, PA, ring top, clear, 5½" **6.00   10.00**

☐ **ELECTRICITY IN A BOTTLE**
Around shoulder, on base, "The West Electric
Cure Co.," ring top, blue, 2½" **40.00   60.00**

☐ **ELEPIZONE, A CERTAIN CURE FOR FITS
AND EPILEPSY, ELEPIZONE, H.G. ROOT
M.C.**
"183 Pearl St., New York" on front, ring top,
aqua, 8½" **40.00   50.00**

Price Range

☐ **"ELEPIZONE" A CERTAIN CURE FOR FITS
& EPILEPSY H.G. ROOT M.C.**
183 Pearl St., New York, ring top, aqua, 6" 25.00 30.00

☐ **DR. ELLIOT'S, SPEEDY CURE**
Ring top with lower ring, aqua, 7" 12.00 18.00

☐ **ELLIS'S SPAVIN CURE**
In two lines vertical, ring top, aqua, 8" 15.00 21.00

☐ **A.D. ELMERS IT CURES LIKE A CHARM**
Side "PAINKILLING," side "NALM," ring top,
aqua, 5" 10.00 15.00

☐ **EMERSON'S RHEUMATIC CURE**
"Emerson Pharmaceutical Company, Baltimore,
MD" in five lines, ring top, amber, 5" 20.00 25.00

☐ **EMERSON'S SARSAPARILLA 3-BOTTLES
GUARANTEED TO CURE -3**
Kansas City, MO, ring top, clear, 8¼" 35.00 50.00

☐ **FAILING'S RHEUMATIC CURE**
Albany, NY, ring top, clear, 6¼" 15.00 20.00

☐ **FALEY'S [sic] KIDNEY & BLADDER CURE**
On front, "Foley's & Co." on-one side, "Chicago,
U.S.A." on reverse, amber, 9½" 7.00 10.00

☐ **DR. M.M. FENNER'S PEOPLE REMEDIES**
Fredonia, NY, USA, Kidney and backache cure,
in original box, amber, 10¼" 40.00 50.00

☐ **DR. FENNER'S KIDNEY & BACKACHE CURE**
All on shoulder, taper top, amber, 10¼" 20.00 25.00

☐ **DR. M.M. FENNER'S PEOPLES REMEDIES
KIDNEY & BACKACHE CURE**
Fredonia, NY, U.S.A. 1872–1898 all front Taper
top, amber, 10⅛" 20.00 25.00

☐ **DR. M.M. FENNER'S PEOPLES REMEDIES,
NY, U.S.A., KIDNEY & BACKACHE CURE
1872–1898**
All on front horizontally, amber, 10½" 25.00 35.00

☐ **FENNINGS FEVER CURER**
Ring top, aqua, 6¼" 8.00 12.00

☐ **FITZGERALD'S MEMBRANE CURE**
Vertical on front in sunken panel, aqua 12.00 17.00

☐ **FLORAPLEXION CURES DYSPEPSIA LIVER
COMPLAINT AND CONSUMPTION**
Double ring, aqua, 6", round 12.00 18.00

Dr. M.M. Fenner's Peoples Remedies, Fredonia, N.Y., amber, 10". **$25.00–$35.00**

	Price Range	
☐ **FLORAPLEXION CURES DYSPEPSIA LIVER COMPLAINT AND CONSUMPTION** Side "FRANKLIN HART," side "NEW YORK," double ring top, aqua, 6"	8.00	12.00
☐ **FOLEY'S KIDNEY & BLADDER CURE** On front, on one side "Foley & Co.," reverse "Chicago U.S.A.," double ring top, amber, 7½"	9.00	13.00
☐ **SAMPLE BOTTLE FOLEY'S KIDNEY CURE, FOLEY & CO.** Chicago, U.S.A., vertical around bottle, aqua, 4¼"	7.00	10.00

Price Range

☐ **FOLEY'S SAFE DIARRHEA & COLIC CURE**
Chicago, panels, aqua, 5½" 7.00 10.00

☐ **FONTAINE'S CURE**
One side, other "FOR THROAT & LUNG DIS-
EASES," front in three lines "FRANKLIN COIT,
Brooklyn, NY, U.S.A." ring top, aqua, 5½" 10.00 15.00

☐ **FOOD shoulder, CURE opposite shoulder**
Ring top, aqua, 6¼" 8.00 12.00

☐ **H.D. FOWLE**
Boston, MA, in back, label, "Fowle's Pile &
Humor Cure," ring top, aqua 5½" 9.00 13.00

☐ **DR. FRANK, TURKEY FEBRIFUGE FOR THE
CURE OF FEVER AND AGUE**
Pontil, aqua, 6" 100.00 125.00

☐ **FRAZIER'S DISTEMPER CURE, NAPPANEE,
IND.**
Ring top, clear, 4¾" 3.00 7.00

☐ **FREE SAMPLE CRAMERS KIDNEY CURE**
N's in Albany and NY are reversed, aqua, 4¼" 11.00 16.00

☐ **FRENCHS**
Under it a crown, on each side Trademark, under
it "Kidney & Liver & Dropsy Cure Co.," on base
Price 1.00-all on front, round corners double ring
top, Trademark in reverse, 9½", amber 100.00 125.00

☐ **FROG POND CHILL & FEVER CURE**
Flat ring top, amber, 7" 40.00 50.00

☐ **G.R. & N. CURE &, MAGICAL PAIN,
EXTRACTOR**
In 3 lines on front, ring top, aqua, 4¼" 12.00 18.00

☐ **GANTER'S L. F., MAGIC CHICKEN
CHOLERA CURE**
"L. P. Ganter Medicine Co.-Glascow, NY, U.S.A."
in nine lines, ring top, amber, 6¾" 40.00 60.00

☐ **GARGET CURE, C.T. WHIPPLE PROP**
Portland, ME, ring top, aqua, 5¾" 7.00 10.00

☐ **DR. A.F. GEOGHEGAN CURE FOR
SCROFULA**
Louisville, KY, graphite pontil, green, 9¼" 100.00 125.00

☐ **GILBERT'S CURE FOR CHOLERA
INFANTUM**
Ring top, aqua, 6⅛" 25.00 35.00

Price Range

☐ **GLOVER'S IMPERIAL DISTEMPER CURE, H. CLAY GLOVER**
New York, vertical on front, amber, 5" 7.00 10.00

☐ **GLOVERS IMPERIAL MANGE CURE**
"H. Clay Glover DU'S" one side, "New York" on other side, amber, 7" 7.00 10.00

☐ **GOLD DANDRUFF CURE**
Vertical on center front, ring top, clear, 7½" ... 10.00 15.00

☐ **GOLDEN ROB LOTION, A SAFE AND CERTAIN CURE**
Amber, 6" 15.00 20.00

☐ **GOWAN'S CURE**
On base, ring top, clear, 2⅝" 2.00 5.00

☐ **DR. GRAVES HEART REGULATOR, CURES HEART DISEASE**
Ring top, aqua, 5¾" 10.00 15.00

☐ **GRAY'S BALSAM, BEST COUGH CURE**
In 2 lines, one side "S.K. Pierson," other "LeRoy, NY," tapered top, clear, 6½" 15.00 22.00

☐ **GRAY'S BALSAM BEST COUGH CURE**
Side "S.K. PIERSON," side "LEROY, NY," taper top, clear, 6⅜" 8.00 12.00

☐ **GREAT BLOOD & RHEUMATISM CURE NO. 6088 MATT.J. JOHNSON CO.**
"West Superior, WI," all front, double ring top, aqua, 9" 20.00 25.00

☐ Same except ST. PAUL, MN 20.00 25.00

☐ **THE GREAT SOUTH AMERICAN NERVINE TONIC AND STOMACH & LIVER CURE**
(LARGE MONOGRAM CID) all front, double ring top, clear, 9¾" 50.00 75.00

☐ **GREGORY'S INSTANT CURE**
Pontil, aqua, 4" and 6" 100.00 125.00

☐ **S. GROVER GRAHAM'S DYSPEPSIA CURE**
Newburg, NY, vertical on front in large letters, amethyst, 8¼" 13.00 18.00

☐ **GROVE'S CHRONIC CHILL CURE**
All on front in 2 lines, ring top, clear, 7¼" 20.00 25.00

☐ **DR. B. W. HAIR'S ASTHMA CURE**
"Hamilton, OH in three lines, tapered top, aqua, 8" 20.00 25.00

Price Range

☐ **DR. HALES HOUSEHOLD COUGH CURE**
Double ring top, aqua, 6" 2.00 6.00
☐ **HALL'S CATARRH CURE**
Aqua, 4½" 3.00 6.00
☐ **HALL'S PAINLESS CORN CURE**
Ring top, clear, 2" 10.00 15.00
☐ **HAMILTON'S MEDICINES CURE**
All inside of a 7 pt. star, under it, "Auburn, NY,"
rectangular, ring top, aqua, 8½" 16.00 23.00
☐ **HANDYSIDES CONSUMPTION CURE**
Double taper top, green, 7⅛" 100.00 140.00
☐ **DR. HANFORD'S CELERY CURE OR NERVE FOOD CURE**
"Rheumatism-neuralgia-insomnia & C & C" all in
nine lines on front, double ring top, aqua, 7½" 25.00 35.00
☐ **DR. HARDING'S**
"Celebrated, Catarrh Cure," in 3 lines on front,
ring top, clear, 3" 12.00 17.00
☐ **HARTS HONEY & HAREHOUND**
"Cure, coughs, colds, croup," 4 lines on front on
one side "Lincoln, IL U.S. Other Harts Med. Co."
ring top, clear 7" 12.00 17.00
☐ **HART'S SWEDISH ASTHMA CURE**
"Buffalo, NY" on side, rectangular, beveled cor-
ners, light amber, 6⅝" 7.00 10.00
☐ **HAWKER DYSPEPSIA CURE THE HAWKER MEDICINE, CO.**
St. John, NB, ring top, clear, 4¼" 10.00 15.00
☐ **HEALY & BIGELOWS KICKAPOO INDIAN COUGH CURE**
On panels, ring top, aqua, 6¼" 6.00 9.00
☐ **HEBBARD'S, DR. CURE FOR FITS**
"New York" in three lines, vertical, ring top, clear,
8½" 30.00 40.00
☐ **DR. J.B. HENIONS**
Reverse side "Sure Cure For Malaria," cobalt,
6¼" 100.00 125.00
☐ **HENRY'S RED GUM COUGH REMEDY GUARANTEED TO CURE**
Ring top, clear, 5½" 8.00 12.00

Price Range

☐ **HENTZ'S CURATIVE BITTERS**
"FREE SAMPLE" all front, double taper, aqua or
clear, 4¼" **25.00 35.00**

☐ **HENTZ'S side, CURATIVE BITTERS front,**
"PHILADELPHIA" side, double taper top, clear or
aqua, 9⅜" **35.00 50.00**

☐ **HEPATICURE FOR BLOOD, LIVER &
KIDNEYS**
In 2 lines on front, on one side "Marshall Med.
Co.," other "Kansas City, MO," ring top, clear or
amethyst, 9½" **30.00 45.00**

☐ **DR. HERMAN'S**
"Vegetable, Catarrh Cure" on round type bottle
in 3 lines, ring top, clear, 2¾" **12.00 17.00**

☐ **HERMANUS GERMANY'S INFALLIABLE
DYSPEPSIA CURE**
Reverse "PREPARED FOR THE U.S. BY L. AND
N. ADLER, READING, PA, USA," side "PICTURE
OF ROMAN SOLDIER WITH RAISED SWORD,"
double taper top, amber, 8¾" **100.00 150.00**

☐ **DR. HERNDON'S**
On one side, other "Gypsey Gift Bank," plain
front, in over lap letter "H.G.G." inside of a circle
under it in 5 lines. "That is medicine which cures,
Balt, MD." rectangular, long neck & ring top,
clear, 6½" **15.00 22.00**

☐ **HERRICK'S HOREHOUND SYRUP**
"Cures all throat and lung infections" all in 3 lines,
ring neck & top, aqua, 6" **15.00 22.00**

☐ **HICK'S CAPUDINE CURES ALL
HEADACHES, ETC.**
Amber, 5¾" **6.00 12.00**

☐ **HILLEMANS AMERICAN CHICKEN
CHOLERA CURE**
Arlington, MN, flared top, cobalt, 6½" **100.00 125.00**

☐ **DR. HILLER'S COUGH CURE**
Tapered top, aqua, 7½" **9.00 12.00**

☐ **HILLS**
With block H letters and arrow, under it "DYS-
PEP-CU-CURES CHRONIC DYSPEPSIA, IN-
DIAN DRUG SPECIALTY CO., St. Louis, India-
napolis" on front, tapered top, amber, 8½" ... **45.00 55.00**

Price Range

☐ **HIMALAYA, THE KOLA COMPOUND,**
NATURES CURE FOR ASTHMA
New York, CI, embossed horizontally on indented
front panels, square, amber, 7½" 12.00 18.00

☐ **HIRES**
On front on one side "Cough Cure," other side
"Phila.," ring top, aqua, 4½" 15.00 20.00

☐ **HITE'S PAIN CURE**
"Staunton, VA." 2 lines on front, ring top, clear,
5½" 12.00 17.00

☐ **THE H.K.B. SAFE CURE FOR THE HEART**
KIDNEY AND BLADDER
All on slant, double ring top, clear, 8¾" 40.00 55.00

☐ **HOLLENSWORTH'S RUPTURE CURE**
In three lines, aqua, ring top, 6¼" 20.00 25.00

☐ **HOLLOWAY'S—CORN CURE**
In two lines running vertically, ring top, clear, 2½" 10.00 25.00

☐ **HOLME'S SURE CURE MOUTH WASH**
"PICTURE OF DENTURES PREPARED
SOLELY BY DR. W. R. HOLMES MACON, GA,"
ring top, clear, 6¼" 20.00 30.00
☐ Same, "NO DENTURES," 3½" 5.00 8.00

☐ **HOOD'S PILLS CURE LIVER ILLS**
All in a circle, ring top, sim. round bottle, 1" ... 6.00 9.00

☐ **HOWARD BROS.**
On front, one side "AMERICAN," other "COUGH
CURE," aqua, 6½" 12.00 17.00

☐ **HOWARD BROS.**
On front, on one side "Cough Cure," other side
"Pettit's American," tapered top, aqua, 7" 12.00 17.00

☐ **C. H. HOWE**
On the other side "CURE," ring top, aqua, 7¼" 9.00 12.00

☐ **DR. HOXSIE'S**
On the side "Buffalo, NY, Certain Croup Cure" in
two lines, clear, ring top, 4¾" 7.00 10.00

☐ **HUFFMAN'S**
In script, "GOITRE CURE-NAPANEE, ONT." in
three lines vertical, ring top, clear, 7" 50.00 60.00

☐ **HUNNICUTT'S**
Reverse side "Rheumatic Cure," ring top, aqua,
8" 15.00 20.00

Price Range

☐ **IDEAL DANDRUFF CURE CO.**
Side, "F.W. FITCH'S" side, ring top, clear, 7" 8.00 10.00
☐ **INDIAN MED. CO., KICKAPOO INDIAN COUGH CURE**
Clintonville, CT, aqua, 5¾" 10.00 15.00
☐ **DR. H. A. INGHAM'S**
Side, "PAINCURAL side," ring top, aqua, 6¾" 5.00 8.00
☐ **JOHNSON'S CHILL & FEVER TONIC, GUARANTEED TO CURE A.B. GIRARDEAU**
Sav'h, GA, ring top, aqua, 5¾" 2.00 7.00
☐ **W. M. JOHNSON'S PURE HERB TONIC, SURE CURE FOR ALL MALARIAL DISEASES**
Vertical lettering, amber, 8½" 50.00 60.00
☐ **K.K.K., KAY'S KENTUCKY KURE OR LINIMENT**
Vertical around bottle, aqua, 3¾" 20.00 27.00
☐ **DR. J. KAUFFMAN'S ANGELINE INTERNAL RHEUMATISM CURE**
Hamilton, OH, ring top, amber, 8" 35.00 50.00
☐ **DR. J. KAUFFMAN'S ANGELINE, INTERNAL RHEUMATISM CURE**
Hamilton, OH, vertical in three lines on front, flared top, clear, 7⅞" 15.00 22.00
☐ **DR. L. E. KEELEY, KEELEY'S CURE FOR DRUNKNESS**
"Etc., Dwight, ILL," ring top, clear or amethyst, 5½" 50.00 75.00
☐ **DR. L.E. KEELEY'S DOUBLE CHLORIDE OF GOLD CURE FOR DRUNKENNESS, TESTED AND INFALLIBLE REMEDY DISCOVERED BY DR. L.E. KEELEY**
Dwight, IL, ring top, clear, 5½" 65.00 90.00
☐ Same except "NEURASTHENIA CURE" 100.00 125.00
☐ Same except "OPIUM HABIT CURE" 100.00 125.00
☐ Same except "TOBACCO HABIT CURE" 100.00 125.00
☐ **KEESLING CHICKEN CHOLERA CURE C.C.C.**
Package 25 cents, B. F. Keeslings, Logansport, IN 9.00 12.00
☐ **KELLUM'S—SURE CURE FOR INDIGESTION AND DYSPEPSIA**
In six lines, ring top, clear, 6¾" 15.00 22.00

Price Range

☐ **KENDALL'S SPAVIN CURE**
Around shoulders, "Enosburgh Falls, VT" on bottom, twelve vertical panels, amber, 5½" 7.00 10.00

☐ **KENDALL'S SPAVIN CURE FOR HUMAN FLESH**
Vertical on two panels, ten vertical panels, aqua, 5¼" 7.00 10.00

☐ **KICKAPOO COUGH CURE**
Vertical on indented panel, round, aqua, 6¼" .. 9.00 13.00

☐ **E. J. KIEFFER, PERUVIAN CURE**
Savannah, GA, aqua, 4" 9.00 13.00

☐ **DR. KILMER'S COUGH CURE CONSUMPTION OIL**
In embossed lung shape panel, "CATARRH SPECIFIC all on front, "BINGHAMTON, NY" on side, rectangular, aqua, double band collar, 8¾" 125.00 150.00

☐ **DR. KILMER'S INDIAN COUGH CURE CONSUMPTION OIL**
Vertical on front, "BINGHAMTON, NY" on side, rectangular, aqua, double band collar, 5⅝" 18.00 23.00

☐ **DR. KILMER'S INDIAN COUGH CURE CONSUMPTION OIL**
Vertical on front, "BINGHAMTON, NY" on side, rectangular, aqua, square collar, ball neck, 7⅛" 12.00 17.00

☐ **DR. KILMER'S SURE HEADACHE CURE**
25 doses in a box 6.00 9.00

☐ **DR. KILMER'S SWAMPROOT KIDNEY LIVER AND BLADDER CURE**
"BINGHAMTON, NY, USA" embossed on front, rectangular, aqua, double band collar, 7" 15.00 20.00

☐ Same as above, only square band collaring neck, 7¼" 7.00 10.00

☐ **DR. KILMER'S SWAMPROOT KIDNEY LIVER AND BLADDER CURE**
"London, E.C." vertical on front, rectangular, aqua, double band top, 5¾" 15.00 22.00

☐ Same as above, only 7¼" 15.00 22.00

☐ **THE GREAT/DR. KILMER'S SWAMPROOT KIDNEY LIVER AND BLADDER CURE**
In embossed kidney shape panel "SPECIFIC,"

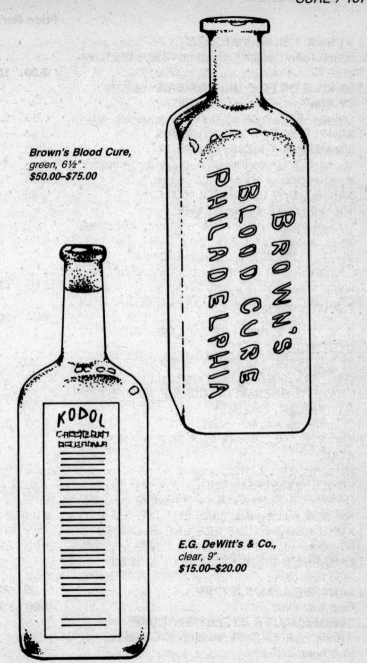

Brown's Blood Cure,
green, 6½".
$50.00–$75.00

E.G. DeWitt's & Co.,
clear, 9".
$15.00–$20.00

Price Range

on front, "BINGHAMTON, NY" on side, aqua, double band collar, rectangle, 8¼″, 8⅛″, 8″, 8½″, 9″ 8.00 12.00

☐ **SAMPLE BOTTLE DR. KILMER'S SWAMPROOT KIDNEY CURE**
London, E.C., aqua, cylindrical, square top, 3¼″ 8.00 12.00

☐ **SAMPLE BOTTLE DR. KILMER'S SWAMPROOT KIDNEY CURE**
"London, E.C." vertical on front, aqua, cylindrical, square collar, 4⅛″ 8.00 12.00

☐ **SAMPLE BOTTLE DR. KILMER'S SWAMPROOT KIDNEY CURE**
"Binghamton, NY" vertical on front, cylindrical, aqua, square collar, 4⅜″, 3⅛″, 4⅛″, 4¼″ 5.00 8.00

☐ **DR. T. J. KILMER'S COUGH CURE**
"Schoharie, NY" vertical on front, rectangular, aqua, square band collar, 5⅝″ 12.00 17.00

☐ **DR. KING'S NEW CURE FOR CONSUMPTION**
Clear or aqua, 6″ 7.00 10.00

☐ **K. K. CURE'S BRIGHTS DISEASE AND CYSTITIS**
All in six lines, one side "K. K. Med. Co.," other side "New Jersey," aqua, tapered top, 7½″ ... 20.00 25.00

☐ **KNIGHT'S RHEUMATIC CURE PREP'D BY A.P. KNIGHT, CHEMIST**
Chicago, IL, ring top, clear, 6⅜″ 8.00 12.00

☐ **KNOX'S CHILL, CURE FOR FEVER AND AGUE**
Memphis, TN, ring top, aqua, 6½″ 25.00 35.00

☐ **KODOL DYSPEPSIA CURE**
On side, "E. C. DeWitt & Co., Chicago" on opposite side, rectangular, aqua, 6⅞″ 8.00 11.00

☐ **KUKU KOUGH KURE ERB ERB IN CROSS**
Ring top, aqua, 6″ 35.00 50.00

☐ **LABAREE'S COLIC CURE NO 1 or NO 2**
Ring top, clear, 3¼″ 2.00 5.00

☐ **LABAREE'S MANGE CURE**
Ring top, clear, 5¼″ 2.00 5.00

☐ **LANGENBACH'S DYSENTERY CURE**
Vertical on front, San Francisco, CA, round bottle, blob type, amber, 6″ 30.00 35.00

Price Range

☐ **LASH'S KIDNEY & LIVER CURE**
Amber, 9" 50.00 75.00

☐ **LAWSON'S side, CURATIVE side**
Double ring top, aqua, 9½" 18.00 25.00

☐ **JARABE DE LEONARDI**
"Para La Tos Creostodado, Leonardi Cough Cure
Creosoted, New York and Tampa, FL" in four
lines in sunken panel, plain back, plain sunken
side panels, aqua, under bottom "W. T. Co 4,"
U.S.A., 5¼" 6.00 9.00

☐ **LEONARDI'S**
Side, "GOLDEN EYE LOTION CURE WITHOUT
PAIN" front, "TAMPA, FLA" side, ring top, aqua,
4¼" 6.00 12.00

☐ **DR. LESURES COLIC CURE NO 1 or 2**
Ring top, clear, 3¼" 2.00 5.00

☐ **LEWIS ANTI-MALARIAL & CHILL CURE**
Ring top, clear, 6¼" 12.00 18.00

☐ **DR. L.G.S. & CO.**
Side, "DYSENTERY CURE" front, "AVON, NY"
side, ring top, clear, cathedral panels, 4⅝" 4.00 9.00

☐ **LIEBIG'S FIT CURE—AN ENGLISH REMEDY**
"Dr. A. B. Meserole, 96 John St., NY" in five lines,
ring top, aqua, 5½" 25.00 30.00

☐ **LIGHTNING KIDNEY AND LIVER CURE,**
"No Relief, No Pay," in 2 lines on front, on one
side Herb "Med. Co." other "Weston, W Va",
double ring top, aqua, 9½" 55.00 65.00

☐ **LIGHTNING OIL**
On one side, other Oil, front sure cure, back plain,
rectangular, ring top, aqua, 5½" 12.00 17.00

☐ **THE H.C. LINDERMAN CO MEXICAN
KIDNEY AND LIVER CURE**
Atlanta, GA, ring top, clear, 7½" 75.00 100.00

☐ **LIQUIFRUTA side, COUGH CURE side**
Double ring top, light green, 5⅜" 8.00 12.00

☐ **LITTLE GIANT CATARRH CURE**
In two lines back, Warsaw, NY, one side only Mfd.
by A. F. Mann, ring top, amber, 3½" 16.00 22.00

☐ **LONG'S STANDARD MALARIA CURE CO**
Rochester, NY, in six lines amber, double ring
top, 7½" 100.00 125.00

Price Range

☐ **DR. W.H. LONG'S VEGETABLE COUGH CURE 25 CENTS**
Ring top, aqua, 6" 8.00 12.00

☐ **LOUDEN'S & COS CURE FOR PILES**
Reverse "PHILA," taper top, aqua, open pontil,
6¾" 100.00 125.00

☐ **LUCAS, D. D. CO. BOHEMIAN CATARRH CURE**
Vineland, NJ, ring top, clear, 3¼" 6.00 9.00

☐ **J.J. MACK & CO., CURTIS COUGH CURE, C.C.C.**
"SF, CA" on both sides, 7" 11.00 16.00

☐ **DR. MACKENZIES CATARRH CURE**
"SMELLING BOTTLE" all on base, ring top,
green, 3¾" ball top 15.00 20.00

☐ **MAGIC CURE LINIMENT front**
Side "E.I. BARNETT," side "EASTON, PA,"
taper top, aqua, 6¼" 18.00 25.00

☐ **MAGIC MOSQUITO BITE CURE & INSECT EXTERMINATOR, SALLADE & CO.**
"NY," on front, oval, tapered collar, aqua, 7⅞" 10.00 15.00

☐ **MALAY, OIL H.F.M.**
In leaf, "Instant Relief Cure Rheumatism," clear,
4¾" 15.00 20.00

☐ **MARNE'S FAMOUS ANISEED CURE**
In two lines, clear, ring top, 5" 15.00 22.00

☐ **MARVINIS CHERRY COUGH CURE**
Label, tapered top, amber, 9½" 15.00 22.00

☐ **MATTISON'S NEW CURE FOR HEADACHE**
Ring top, aqua, 4¾" 5.00 8.00

☐ **MAYER'S MAGNETIC CATARRH CURE**
In two lines vertical, ring top, clear, 3½" 9.00 13.00

☐ **MC CLURE & EATON**
Side, "PAIN CURE OIL" front, "READING, PA."
side, taper top, aqua, 5½" 25.00 35.00

☐ **DR. J.H. MC LEANS CHILLS AND FEVER CURE**
Double ring top, aqua, 6" 8.00 15.00

☐ **J.A. MELVIN'S RHEUMATIC & DYSPEPSIA CURE**
Ring top, aqua, 6" 12.00 18.00

Price Range

☐ **MERRILL'S (script) NEW CENTURY CATARRH CURE MERRILL DRUG CO**
Brewer, ME, ring top, aqua, 5⅜″ 18.00 25.00

☐ **MERTOL DANDRUFF CURE**
Clear, 5½″ 7.00 10.00

☐ **METZERS CATARRH CURE**
Ring top, aqua, 7¼″ 8.00 10.00

☐ **METZER'S AFRICAN CATARRH CURE**
Ring top, aqua, 7¼″ 10.00 15.00

☐ **DR. MILES NEW HEART CURE**
Vertical on front in sunken panel, double band collar, aqua, 8½″ 11.00 15.00

☐ Same as above, free sample size, 4¼″ 12.00 16.00

☐ **DR MILES RESTORATIVE NERVINE**
Reverse "CURE ALL NERVOUS TROUBLE, SEE WRAPPER," ring top, aqua, 4″ 7.00 10.00

☐ **MINER'S DAMIANA NERVE DISEASE CURE**
Embossed woman, amber, 8¼″ 100.00 125.00

☐ **PETER P. MINIOTTIS—RHEUMATISM CURE**
In center, in a circle man with a bear around it—"Great West Indian Discovery, etc.—10 Wyckoff St., Brooklyn, N.Y. Registered," under bottom "21," tapered top, aqua, label only, 10″ ... 12.00 16.00

☐ **MORRIS-MORTON DRUG CO.**
On one side, other, "Ft. Smith, Ark." on front, "SWAMP-CHILL AND FEVER CURE" in four lines, tapered top, clear or amethyst, 6½″ 25.00 35.00

☐ **MOXIE CATARRH CURE**
Around flat watch type bottle, clear, 1½″ 20.00 30.00

☐ **MUNYON'S INHALER, CURES COLDS, CATARRH AND ALL THROAT & LUNG DISEASES**
On front, "Patented," "Fill to the Line" on back, round, olive green, 4⅛″ 15.00 20.00

☐ **MYSTERIOUS PAIN CURE—A SCOTCH REMEDY**
In three lines, vertical, ring top, clear, 5½″ 9.00 12.00

☐ **MYSTIC CURE**
Other side "MYSTIC CURE," on front "for Rheumatism and Neuralgia," ring top, clear, 6¼″ ... 12.00 18.00

☐ **NATIONAL KIDNEY AND LIVER CURE**
Taper top, amber, 9″ 40.00 50.00

Price Range

☐ **NAU'S DYSPEPSIA CURE**
  Amber, 5″ 15.00   20.00
☐ **NORWOOD COLIC CURE NO 1 or 2**
  Ring top, clear, 3¼″ 2.00   5.00
☐ **ONE MINUTE COUGH CURE**
  Vertical on front in sunken panel, "E.C. DeWitt &
  Co." on one side, "Chicago, U.S.A." on opposite
  side, rectangular, aqua, 5½″ 9.00   13.00
☐ **ONE MINUTE COUGH CURE**
  Vertical on front, "E.C. DeWitt & Co." "Chicago,
  U.S.A." vertical on back, rectangular, aqua, 4¼″   7.00   10.00
☐ **ONE NIGHT COUGH CURE KOHLER M'FG
  CO BALTIMORE, MD.**
  Ring top, aqua, 3½″ 5.00   10.00
☐ **THE ORIGINAL COPPER CURE**
  In 2 script lines, oval shape bottle, ring top,
  amber, 7¾″ 45.00   60.00
☐ **THE ORIGINAL—DR. CRAIG'S—KIDNEY
  CURE (c. 1889)**
  In three lines, on base "Rochester, N.Y.," double
  ring top, amber, bottle same as Warner Safe
  Cure, 9½″ 100.00 125.00
☐ **OTTO'S CURE FOR THE THROAT & LUNGS**
  On front indented panel, "B.H. Bacon" on right
  panel, "Rochester, N.Y." on reverse side, aqua,
  6″ 7.00   10.00
☐ **OTTO'S CURE FOR THE THROAT & LUNGS**
  Vertical on front indented panel, oval, aqua, 2¾″   6.00   9.00
☐ **PANTINA COUGH & CONSUMPTION CURE
  E. SCHMIDT & CO.**
  Baltimore, ring top, aqua, 5¾″ 5.00   10.00
☐ **PARKS KIDNEY & LIVER CURE**
  Side "FRANK O. REDDISH & CO.," side
  "LEROY, N.Y.," taper top, amber, 9¾″ 90.00 120.00
☐ **PARKS KIDNEY & LIVER CURE**
  Side "GEO. H. WELLS," side "LEROY, N.Y.,"
  taper top, aqua, 9¾″ 80.00 110.00
☐ **PARK'S SURE CURE (KIDNEY CURE)**
  Aqua, 6½″ 9.00   12.00

Price Range

☐ **DR. PARK'S COUGH SYRUP**
Geo. H. Wells, other side "Le Roy, N.Y.," tapered
top, label reads "The Throat & Lungs—A Positive
Guarantee of Cure of Any Throat or Lung Dis-
ease, etc.," aqua, 6¼" .... | 11.00 | 15.00

☐ **DR. PARKER'S & SONS CO.**
Batavia, NY, "RED CHERRY COUGH CURE
FOR CONSUMPTION" all in four lines, running
vertically, ring top, aqua, 5½" .... | 11.00 | 15.00

☐ **DR. PARKER'S COUGH CURE**
Ring top, aqua, 6" .... | 7.00 | 10.00

☐ **DR. PARKERS SONS DYSPEPSIA CURE**
Akron, NY, ring top, aqua, 5" .... | 10.00 | 15.00

☐ **DR. PARKERS SURE CURE FOR HEADACHE
MANF'D BY DR. PARKERS SONS CO**
Batavia, NY, Ring top, aqua, 4" .... | 9.00 | 12.00

☐ **PECKHAMS CROUP REMEDY, THE
CHILDRENS COUGH CURE**
Taper top, aqua, 6¼" .... | 8.00 | 12.00

☐ **PERUVIANA-NATURE'S KIDNEY CURE**
"Peruviana Herbal Remedy Co.—Cincinnati,
Ohio" in four lines vertical, tapered top, amber | 45.00 | 60.00

☐ **CURECHILINE, PINKSTONES CURECHILINE
CURES CATTLE DISEASES**
Ball top, aqua, 7½" .... | 35.00 | 50.00

☐ **PISO'S CURE**
On side, "FOR CONSUMPTION" on front, other
side "HAZELTONE & CO"., emerald green, 5" | 7.00 | 10.00
☐ Same as above, except clear or aqua .... | 6.00 | 9.00

☐ **POLAR STAR (STAR) COUGH CURE**
Ring top, aqua, 7" .... | 10.00 | 15.00

☐ **POLAR STAR COUGH CURE**
With embossed star in center, vertical on front in
sunken panels, rectangular, aqua, 5¾" .... | 6.00 | 9.00
☐ Same as above, except 4" .... | 6.00 | 9.00

☐ **POLAR STAR (STAR) DIARRHEA CURE**
Ring top, aqua, 5" .... | 12.00 | 18.00

☐ **POLKS DIPTHERIA CURE**
(Diptheria on slant) ring top, clear, 4" .... | 8.00 | 12.00

☐ **POND'S COUGH CURE**
Taper top, aqua, 6¼" .... | 8.00 | 12.00

Price Range

☐ **PORTER'S CURE OF PAIN**
Cleveland, OH, clear, 6½" 7.00 10.00

☐ **PORTERS**
Front, "CURE OF PAIN" side "BUNDYSBURG,
OH" double ring top, aqua, open or graphite pon-
til, 6⅝" 100.00 125.00

☐ **PRATT FOOD CO.**
"Phila. U.S.A." in two lines vertical, "PRATT'S
BLOAT CURE" in two lines vertical, double ring
top and ring in neck, aqua, 6½" 22.00 30.00

☐ **PRATT'S DISTEMPER & PINK EYE CURE**
Amber, 7" 20.00 25.00

☐ **PRATT'S DISTEMPER CURE, PRATT FOOD
CO.**
Phila, PA, ring top, amber, 7" 11.00 15.00

☐ **PRESTONS *HED-AKE* CURES YOU
"WHILE YOU WAIT"**
Ring top, aqua, 4" 10.00 15.00

☐ **DR. CHARLES T. PRICE**
"THE CURE FOR FIT—67 William St.-New York"
in 5 lines, ring top, clear, 8½" 45.00 60.00

☐ **PRIMLEY'S SPEEDY CURE**
"For Coughs and Colds," all on front, rectangular,
ring top, aqua, 6½" 15.00 20.00

☐ **PUS CURE**
Ring top, clear, 1⅞" 10.00 15.00

☐ **QUICK HEADACHE CURE, B.F. KEESLING**
Logansport, IN. 9.00 13.00

☐ **RADAMS MICROBE KILLER CURES ALL
DISEASE, GERM BACTERIA & FUNGUS
DESTROYER**
Picture of man with spiked mace beating off skel-
eton, shear top, amber, 10¼" all on front 60.00 80.00

☐ **RAY'S GERMICIDE CURES MANY DISEASES**
On front in gold paint, hand painted flowers on
top half, top half is white, lower half is brown pottery somewhat glazed, sheared type, handle, jug
shape, 8½" 40.00 50.00

☐ **RED FLAG OIL FAMOUS PAIN CURE E.
SCHMIDT & CO.**
Baltimore, ring top, aqua, 5¾" 15.00 20.00

Price Range

☐ **RED STAR COUGH CURE**
On one side, other side "THE CHARLES A. VO-
GELER CO.," "Baltimore, U.S.A." on base, ta-
pered top, aqua, 7½" 9.00   12.00

☐ **REEVE'S COMP. TEREBENE COUGH CURE**
Clear, 4" 7.00   10.00

☐ Same as above, except 6" 7.00   10.00

☐ **REEVE'S COMP TEREBENE COUGH CURE**
Ring top, aqua, 6" 8.00   10.00

☐ **3913—RHEUMATISM CURE**
In two lines, ring top, clear or aqua, 5¾" 11.00   15.00

☐ **RHODE'S FEVER & AGUE CURE**
Embossed on sides, blown in mold, rectangular,
with contents, label, and box, aqua, 8¼" 40.00   50.00

☐ **RHODE'S**
Other side FEVER & AGUE CURE, front, "Antidote to Malaria" in three lines, aqua, tapered top,
8½" 35.00   47.00

☐ **RICKSECKERS SKIN SOAP HEALS CURES**
Ring top, aqua, 2⁶/₈" 8.00   15.00

☐ **RIVER SWAMP, THE**
Under it "chill and alligator fever cure" under it
"Augusta, GA." flat ring top, amber, 7" 125.00 175.00

☐ **DR. C.C. ROC'S CHILL & FEVER CURE**
Side "CULLEN & NEWMAN," side KNOXVILLE,
TENN.," ring top with ring below, aqua, 8" 25.00   30.00

☐ Same except "LIVER RHEUMATIC AND NEU-
RALGIC CURE" 25.00   30.00

☐ **ROCK'S COUGH & COLD CURE, CHAS. A.
DARBY**
NY, vertical on front in sunken panel, rectangular,
aqua, 5⁵/₈" 9.00   13.00

☐ **ROGER'S ROYAL HERBS LIQUID**
A liver and kidney cure, blown in mold, square,
with contents and box, clear, 7¾" 35.00   45.00

☐ **DR. ROGERS**
Other side "CURE", front, "INDIAN FEVER,"
clear, tapered top, aqua, 7" 60.00   80.00

☐ **ROLL'S SYRUP WILD CHERRY WHITE PINE
AND TAR, CURES COUGHS AND COLDS**
Flared top, clear 15.00   20.00

Price Range

☐ **H. G. ROOT M.C.**
183 Pearl St. N.Y.," ELEPIZONE, A CERTAIN
CURE FOR FITS AND EPILEPSY," ring top,
amber, 8½" 35.00   50.00

☐ **ROSEWOOD DANDRUFF CURE, PREPARED
BY J.R. REEVES CO.**
Anderson, IN, vertical on front, rectangular, pan-
eling on collar, amethyst, 6½" 11.00   15.00

☐ **ROSEWOOD DANDRUFF CURE**
Ring top, clear, 7" 8.00   10.00

☐ **RUBY REMEDY THAT CURES**
Ring top, clear, round bottom, 4½" 10.00   15.00

☐ **RUPTURINE CURES RUPTURE
HERNIA CURE CO**
Westbrook, ME, on four panels of ten sided bot-
tle, ring top, clear, 6" 50.00   65.00

☐ **SALLADE & CO. MAGIC MOSQUITO BITE
CURE & INSECT DESTROYER**
Oval, blown in mold, aqua, 7¾" 15.00   20.00

☐ **SAMPLE SHILOH'S CURE**
Vertical on front, rectangular, aqua, 4¼" 7.00   10.00

☐ **SANFORD'S**
On one side, "RADICAL CURE," on opposite
side, rectangular, cobalt blue, 7¾" 18.00   25.00

☐ **SANO RHEUMATIC CURE AND SYSTEM
TONIC**
(TRADE SANO MARK IN SHIELD), ring top,
clear, 7½" 15.00   20.00

☐ **SAVE-THE-HORSE, REGISTERED TRADE
MARK, SPAVIN CURE, TROY CHEMICAL CO.**
Binghamton, NY, on front, ring top, aqua, 6½" 7.00   10.00
☐ Same as above, except "TROY, N.J." 12.00   16.00

☐ **SHILOH'S CURE SAMPLE**
In two lines, aqua, ring top, 4½" 11.00   15.00

☐ **SAWYER, DR. A. P.**
One side, other "CHICAGO," front "FAMILY
CURE," double ring top, aqua, 7½" 22.00   30.00

☐ **S.B. CATARRH CURE**
On shoulder, base "SMITH BROS S.B.C.C.
FRESNO, CAL," ring top, aqua, 8" 5.00   10.00

Price Range

☐ **SHILOH'S CONSUMPTION CURE**
In three lines, "S. C. Wells & Co." other side,
"Leroy, N.Y.," aqua, was made in three sizes, ta-
pered top, 8" 15.00 20.00
☐ Same as above, except "S.C. Wells," 6½" 9.00 13.00
☐ **DR. SHOOP'S COUGH CURE**
Clear, 6½" 5.00 7.00
☐ **SIMONDS**
Other side PAIN CURER, ring top, aqua, 4¾" and
6" 12.00 17.00
☐ **SKABCURA DIP CO.**
Chicago, IL, ring top, aqua, 5¼" 5.00 10.00
☐ **SLOANS SURE COLIC CURE**
Ring top, clear or amethyst, 4¾" 7.00 10.00
☐ **SMITH'S CHILL & FEVER TONIC
GUARANTEED TO CURE, COLUMBIA DRUG
CO**
Savannah, GA, (C.D. CO. in triangle), ring top,
clear, 5⅞" 20.00 30.00
☐ **H. K. SMITH CURE ALL**
All in two lines, ring top, aqua, 5" 8.00 12.00
☐ **DR. JAMES SOLOMON JR'S**
Side, "COUGH CURE" side, ring top, aqua, 7" 7.00 10.00
☐ **SPARKS KIDNEY & LIVER CURE, BUST**
Camden, NJ, ring top, amber, 9¾" 100.00 125.00
☐ **SPEEDY CURE FOR COUGHS AND COLDS**
On one side "Jones & Primley Co.," other side
"Elkhart, Ind.," ring top, clear, 8" 15.00 20.00
☐ **THE SPEICHER DANDRUFF CURE CO.**
Philadelphia "TRADE STC MONO MARK," ring
top with ring below, clear, 7¾" 20.00 25.00
☐ **SPOHN'S DISTEMPER CURE SPOHN
MEDICAL CO.**
Goshen, IN, ring top, aqua, 7" 5.00 8.00
☐ **SPOHN'S DISTEMPER CURE, SPOHN
MEDICAL COMPANY**
Goshen, IN, vertical on front in sunken panel,
aqua, 5" 7.00 10.00
☐ **DR. STANLEYS AFRICAN RHEUMATIC &
NEURALGIC CURE**
21 Debrosses St., NY, ring top, aqua, 6¾" 30.00 35.00

Price Range

☐ **STERN'S ALPINE ASTHMA CURE 3X**
Ring top, aqua, 7¼" 30.00   40.00

☐ **STEWART D. HOWE'S—ARABIAN MILK CURE**
In three lines, vertical, one side "For Consumption," other "New York," aqua, ring top, 7½" . .   22.00   30.00

☐ **DR. STINSON'S CATARRH CURE LONDON SUPPLY CO.**
New York, London, ring top, clear, 4⅛" 10.00   15.00

☐ **DR. I.L. ST JOHN'S**
Side "MAGNETIC OIL CURES RHEUMATISM NEURALGIA AND" side "HEADACHE," ring top, clear, 6¼" 10.00   15.00

☐ **DR. STRUBLES KIDNEY CURE**
In a circle, under it "Himrode, N. Y.," ring top, cobalt, 6½" 100.00   120.00

☐ **SUNFLOWER CHOLERA CURE**
Side "W.J. ROBERTS MED. CO.," side "COLDWATER, MICH.," ring top with ring below, clear, 5½" 20.00   30.00

☐ **SWANSON RHEUMATIC CURE CO. 5 DROPS**
Side "300 DOSES $1.00," side "CHEAPEST MEDICINE MADE," double ring top, aqua, 5⅝"   8.00   12.00

☐ **DR. SYKES SURE CURE FOR CATARRH**
In front, four-part mold, aqua, round, short neck, 6¾" 15.00   20.00

☐ **SYLVAN REMEDY CO.**
"Peoria, ILL." in back, "REIDS-GERMAN COUGH & KIDNEY CURE," one side "No Danger from Overdose," other "Contains no Poison," aqua, 5½" 12.00   18.00

☐ **TA-HA COUGH CURE**
In two lines vertical, ring top and ring on neck, aqua, 6" 15.00   20.00

☐ **TAMALON SAFE ANIMAL CURE**
Amber, 11¼" 100.00   125.00

☐ **DR. TAYLOR'S SURE CHILL CURE**
Side, "RICHARDSON TAYLOR MED. CO." side, ring top, aqua, 5½" 5.00   10.00

☐ **E. E. TAYLOR'S CATARRH CURE**
All in a circle, in center a star, ring top, clear, 2¾"   9.00   13.00

Price Range

☐ **TAYLOR'S HOSPITAL CURE FOR CATARRH**
"N.Y. WT Co. U.S.A." under bottom, clear or amethyst, 6¼" **15.00   20.00**
☐ **WARNER'S SAFE KIDNEY & LIVER CURE**
Rochester, NY, with embossed safe, amber, 9½" **10.00   15.00**

DAIRY

The history of the milk bottles is quite short. Milk used to be delivered door-to-door directly from the farmer's cow or goat, or by the more sophisticated churn. Then in 1884, Dr. Harvey D. Thatcher, a druggist from Pottsdam, New York invented the first milk bottle. Appropriately titled the "Thatcher Milk Protector," it pictured a Quaker farmer sitting on a three-legged stool milking a cow. The words "Absolutely Pure Milk" were embossed into the glass on the shoulder of the bottle. Reproductions have been made but the original bottles are extremely rare.

Shortly after, dairies of all sizes started bottling their own milk. Usually the bottles were made of clear glass but on rare occasions amber or green glass was used on the theory that dark glass would prevent the milk from spoiling. The dairies had their names embossed and later, advertised their slogans on the bottles by a silk screen process.

Sterilized milk in the early bottles was sealed by "swing stoppers," a lightning type of closure. By 1900, this was replaced by wax tagboard discs that would fit into formed grooves to create a seal at the mouth of the bottle.

With the birth of the milk bottle came the birth of the milkman. As early as 1878, a Brooklyn milkman is reported to have been delivering milk around the neighborhood.

Milk bottles were not in popular use in America or Europe until post-World War I. Waxed paper containers began replacing milk bottles in the early 1950s and they have all but disappeared except for a few instances in England.

Interest in milk bottles is fairly recent, but growing at a fast pace. Twentieth century clear glass bottles can still be found for reasonable prices, but the pre-1900 green glass bottles are very rare and valuable.

Price Range

☐ **ABBOTTS ALDERNEY DAIRIES**
Round, embossed, quart tin-top **15.00   22.00**

Price Range

☐ **ABBOTTS' ALDERNEY DAIRIES**
Round, embossed, tall pint 12.00 18.00

☐ **ABBOTTS ALDERNEY DAIRIES**
Sun-colored amethyst, round, tall, ribbed, embossed half-pint 10.00 15.00

☐ **ACME DAIRY**
Massillon, OH, round, red pyroglazed quart, cream-separator 57.00 63.00

☐ **ALAMITO**
Omaha's pioneer dairy, round, brown and gold pyroglaze quart, picture of covered wagon and pioneer family 15.00 21.00

☐ **ALLEGHENY DAIRY COMPANY**
Round, embossed, quart, crude picture of full cow 8.00 12.00

☐ **ALTO**
Georgia, State TB Sanatorium, round, embossed half pint 18.00 22.00

☐ **AMBOY**
"Amboy Dairy, Syracuse, N.Y." on front, square, clear, quart 3.00 5.00

☐ **ANCKER HOSPITAL**
Round, embossed half-pint 12.00 16.00

☐ **ARDEN FARMS**
Round, red pyroglazed quart with neck ribs 10.00 12.00

☐ **AVONDALE FARMS**
Square red pyroglazed creamer 5.00 7.00

☐ **A. S. H.**
Allentown State Hospital, round, embossed half-pint 7.00 10.00

☐ **B. BALL**
"A.B. Ball Dairy Product," picture of baseball, "Buffalo, N.Y." on front, square, clear, quart ... 3.00 5.00

☐ **B. BALL DAIRY**
Picture of baseball, round, embossed quart 11.00 13.00

☐ **BABBLIN BROOK**
Clear, pint 2.50 4.00

☐ **BANGOR**
Bangor Dairy, Bangor, MI, round, clear, quart .. 3.50 5.00

☐ **BAPTISTE DAIRY**
Koloa, Kauai, round, red pyroglazed pint 14.00 16.00

Price Range

☐ **BARTON'S BEE GARDENS AND DAIRY FARMS**
Davison, MI, round, embossed pint **14.00** **16.00**

☐ **BASA**
Basa Goat's Milk, 10 mile Rd. & Northwestern, round, embossed quart **28.00** **32.00**

☐ **BELLEVUE**
"Please Return Me Promptly to Bellevue Dairy, Inc., Syracuse, N.Y." on front, square, clear, ½ gallon **2.00** **5.00**

☐ **BETHANY COLLEGE**
Bethany, WVA, round embossed half-pint **16.00** **20.00**

☐ **BILLING'S DAIRY**
Green pyroglazed ½ oz. creamer **5.00** **7.00**

☐ **BIRELEY'S TRADEMARK REG.**
Hollywood, CA, clear, 5¼" **4.00** **6.00**

☐ **BLAKE-HART**
Chehalis, WA, embossed square quart **33.00** **37.00**

☐ **BLUE RIBBON CREAMERY**
3¢, South Boston, VA, round, embossed half-pint   **3.00** **5.00**

☐ **BORDEN'S**
Borden's Milk embossed on front, amber, quart   **6.00** **8.00**

☐ **BORDEN'S**
"If It's Borden's It's Got To Be Good!," picture of Elsie the Cow, "Deposit" on front, jug, clear, one gallon **3.00** **5.00**

☐ **BORDEN'S**
"If It's Borden's It's Got To Be Good!," picture of Elsie the Cow on front, square, clear, ½ gallon   **2.00** **5.00**

☐ **BORDEN'S**
Picture of Elsie the Cow on front, round, clear, quart **3.50** **6.00**

☐ **BORDEN'S**
Picture of Elsie the Cow on front, square, clear, quart **3.00** **5.00**

☐ **BORDEN'S CONDENSED MILK CO.**
Round, embossed, quart, tin-top, sun-colored amethyst **28.00** **37.50**

☐ **BRALEY'S CREAMERY**
Red pyroglaze ¾ oz. creamer **7.50** **9.50**

Price Range

☐ **BREWERS**
Brewers Dairy, Augusta, ME, Pasteurized Milk & Cream. Red round pyroglazed quart **4.00 6.00**

☐ **BREYER ICE CREAM CO.**
Round, embossed quart **14.00 16.00**

☐ **BRIDGEMAN**
Picture of little girl with pail on front, square, clear, ½ pint **1.50 3.00**

☐ **BRIDGEMAN**
Picture of little girl with pail on front, square, clear, quart **3.00 5.00**

☐ **BRIDGEMAN**
Picture of little girl with pail on front, square with grip indentation, clear, ½ gallon **3.00 5.00**

☐ **BROCK-HALL**
Red pyroglaze ¾ oz. creamer **6.50 8.50**

☐ **BROOKFIELD/BABY TOP**
Two-face bottle, clear embossed quart **22.00 32.00**

☐ **BROOKFIELD DAIRY**
Red pyroglaze ¾ oz. creamer **7.00 9.00**

☐ **BROWN'S DAIRY**
Brown pyroglaze 1 oz. creamer **11.00 13.00**

☐ **BUFFALO MILK CO.**
Embossed buffalo, round, embossed quart **16.00 18.00**

☐ **CACOOSING DAIRY**
Square, orange pyroglaze creamer **5.00 8.00**

☐ **CALLOW'S**
"Be Sure Callow's Dairy, Electro-Pure, Memominee, Michigan" on front, square, clear, tall quart **2.00 4.00**

☐ **CARNATION**
"Fresh Milk Carnation Company" on front, square, clear, ½ pint **2.50 4.00**

☐ **CARNATION**
"Fresh Milk Carnation Company, One Gallon" on front, jug, clear, one gallon **3.00 5.00**

☐ **CATHERWOOD'S**
"Catherwood's Milk Lowell," with MA seal. "Catherwood's Cream Lowell" on reverse. Maroon round pyroglazed quart **4.00 6.00**

Alta Crest Farms, fluted collar, green glass. **$400.00–$600.00**

Golan and Murphy Dairy Farm, Binghamton, N.Y. on front, square, clear, tall quart. **$2.00–$4.00**

Price Range

☐ **CHEWTON DAIRY**
Chewton, PA, round, embossed quart, embossed
picture of Lincoln 10.00   15.00
☐ **CLARKSBURG DAIRY**
With war slogan, round, red pyroglazed quart . .   17.00   19.00
☐ **CLOVER CREAM TOP DAIRIES**
Bayville, NJ, round, embossed, quart cream-top   10.00   13.00
☐ **CLOVERDALE**
"Hoppy's Favorite," square, red and black
pyroglazed quart 27.00   33.00
☐ **CLOVER MEADOW**
Green pyroglaze on milk glass ¾ oz. creamer   10.00   12.00
☐ **COLEMAN, L.E.**
"Coleman, L.E., Belvidere, Ill." in a circle in cen-
ter, clear, pint 18.00   24.00
☐ **COLLINWOOD DAIRY**
J & N Vanderplate, Port Jefferson, NY, round em-
bossed quart 7.00   9.00
☐ **CONEY ISLAND MILK CO. INC.**
Coney Island, NY, round, embossed 32 oz. 9.00   12.00
☐ **CORNELL UNIVERSITY**
Ithaca, NY, square, red pyroglaze pint 12.00   15.00
☐ **COUNTRY BOY**
Country Boy Dairy, picture of boy carrying Coun-
try Boy milk jug on front, square, clear, quart . .   3.00   5.00
☐ **CRESCENT**
Orange pyroglaze ¾ oz. creamer 4.50   6.50
☐ **CURLES NECK DAIRY**
Thrift Top, square, embossed, quart cop-the-
cream 18.00   22.00
☐ **DAILEY'S DAIRY**
Elmira, NY, round, orange pyroglaze half-pint,
war slogan 14.00   16.00
☐ **DAIRYLEA**
"Hoppy's Favorite," square, red and black
pyroglaze quart 22.00   26.00
☐ **DANVILLE PRODUCER'S DAIRY**
Danville, IL, with war slogan, round, orange
pyroglazed quart 17.00   19.00
☐ **DARICRAFT**
Square, red pyroglaze creamer 5.00   8.00

Price Range

☐ **DECKERS DAIRY**
Hightstown, NJ, milk bottle with arms, legs and face. "If I'm Sent Home Today I'll Return With More Milk Tomorrow." Dacro top with Decker metal cap. Square pyroglazed quart 4.00 6.00

☐ **DOUGLASTON MANOR FARM**
Pulaski, NY, round, black pyroglaze quart, picture of flying goose 15.00 18.00

☐ **DYKE'S DAIRY**
Youngsville-Warren, PA, with war slogan, round, red pyroglazed quart 28.00 32.00

☐ **DE. F. MAYER**
Phone Glen'd 3887R, 289 Hollenbeck St., round, embossed, amber quart 32.00 48.00

☐ **EL CAMINO CREAMERY**
San Bruno, CA, round, green pyroglazed quarter pint 8.00 10.00

☐ **ELMWOOD FARM**
Wrentham, MA, round, embossed, pint tin-top 30.00 42.00

☐ **ESSEX CO. INDUSTRIAL FARM**
Middletown, MA, round, embossed, half-pint ... 13.00 15.00

☐ **ESSEX COUNTY DAIRY**
Salem, MA, round embossed ½ pint 4.00 6.00

☐ **FARMER'S CO-OP DAIRY**
Connellsville, PA, square, orange pyroglaze creamer 7.00 12.00

☐ **FOOTMAN'S DAIRY**
"School Bottle." Scene with factory Footman's Dairy Brewer on reverse. Round pyroglazed ½ pint 9.00 11.00

☐ **FOUR OAKS DAIRY**
Four Oaks Dairy C. H. Carroll & Son, Auburn, ME. Oak leaves and acorns. "Use More Of Our Pure Cream" on reverse. Round pyroglazed ½ pint 8.00 12.00

☐ **FRANKLIN CO-OP**
Dripless, brick design around neck, round, embossed half-pint 10.00 12.00

☐ **FREEMANS DAIRY**
Red pyroglaze ½ oz. creamer 3.50 5.50

☐ **FREEMAN'S DAIRY**
Red pyroglaze ¾ oz. creamer 4.00 6.00

	Price Range	

☐ **FREEMAN'S MILK**
Round, red pyroglaze, quart, war slogan on reverse **10.00** **12.00**

☐ **GARDEN STATE**
Vineland, NJ, with war slogan, round, orange pyroglazed quart **43.00** **47.00**

☐ **GERBER'S CENTRAL**
Red pyroglazed ¾ oz. creamer **8.00** **10.00**

☐ **GENERAL ICE CREAM**
Round, embossed cream-top pint **10.00** **14.00**

☐ **GETTYSBURG ICE & STORAGE COMPANY**
Round, embossed pint **5.00** **7.00**

☐ **GLENSIDE DAIRY**
Deep Water, NJ, square, brown pyroglaze, quart cop-the-cream **25.00** **30.00**

☐ **GLENSIDE DAIRY**
Deep Water, NJ, round, brown pyroglaze, quart cop-the-cream **50.00** **60.00**

☐ **GOLDEN HEALTH**
"Deposit Bottle, Brickley Dairy Farms, Inc., Michigan" on front, square with one ring at neck, amber, one quart **3.00** **5.00**

☐ **GRADY FARMS**
"Grady Farms Dairy, Waterloo, Iowa" on front, jug, clear, one gallon **3.00** **5.00**

☐ **GRATZER**
"Gratzer Dairy, Syracuse, NY" on front, square, clear, ½ gallon **2.00** **5.00**

☐ **GROVE DAIRY**
Grove Dairy-Urbana, OH "No Bottle-No Milk," one pint.................................... **4.00** **6.00**

☐ **HERSHEY CHOCOLATE CORP.**
Hershey, PA, round, embossed pint **5.00** **6.00**

☐ **HIDDEN ACRES**
Hidden Acres Dairy, Farmington, ME. Full cow on reverse. Orange round pyroglazed quart **5.00** **7.00**

☐ **HIGHLAND**
Coatesville, PA, round, embossed, half-pint, baby top **38.00** **42.00**

☐ **HIGHLAND**
Coatesville, PA, round, embossed quart, baby top **28.00** **32.00**

Price Range

☐ **HI-LAN DAIRY**
Des Moines, IA, round, orange pyroglaze, modern
top **20.00** **24.00**

☐ **HILAND DAIRY**
Black pyroglaze ¾ oz. creamer **8.00** **10.00**

☐ **HILLMAN DAIRY**
Hillman Dairy Sunnydale Farms. Sunrise scene.
"Sunnydale Milk The Finest Under The Sun",
round pyroglazed ½ pint **2.00** **4.00**

☐ **CHAS. A. HOAK**
Round, embossed pint cream top **8.00** **10.00**

☐ **HODGDON**
"Property of & Filled By Hodgdon Dairy Co.,
Quincy, ILL" in oval slug plate, eagle on branch
above. Bottle is paneled with stripes, embossed
"H" on bottom. Half pint **8.00** **12.00**

☐ **HOFFMAN'S**
Telford, PA, orange pyroglaze creamer, 1 oz .. **11.00** **13.00**

☐ **HOFFMAN'S**
Square, orange pyroglaze creamer **7.00** **9.00**

☐ **HOME DAIRY**
Eureka, CA, round, orange pyroglazed quarter
pint **6.50** **8.50**

☐ **HORNSTRA'S DAIRY**
"Hornstra's Dairy Farm Hingman, Bottled At The
Farm." Stork carrying baby. "Listen Pal! I Hope
They Use Hornstra's Milk Where You're Taking
Me" on reverse. Square pyroglazed quart **3.00** **5.00**

☐ **HUNT'S**
"Hunt's Dairy, Dial GR-2604, Skowhegan, ME"
on front, square, clear, pint **1.50** **3.00**

☐ **HYCREST FARMS**
Sterling, MA, orange pyroglaze ¾ oz. creamer **9.00** **11.00**

☐ **HY CREST FARMS**
Sterling, MA, orange pyroglaze ¾ oz. creamer **8.00** **10.00**

☐ **HYGIENIC DAIRY CO.**
Round, red pyroglaze quarter-pint **3.00** **4.00**

☐ **IMPERIAL DAIRY PRODUCTS**
Square black pyroglaze creamer **9.00** **11.00**

Price Range

☐ **INDIAN HILL FARM**
Indian Hill Farm Dairy, Greenville, ME, picture of
Indian in headdress, partial telephone number on
front, orange pyroglaze, round, clear, quart 3.50   5.00

☐ **IMPERIAL DAIRY PRODUCTS**
Round, embossed, quart cream-top, picture of
crown 9.00   12.00

☐ **H.W. JENNINGS**
"H.W. Jennings, Battle Creek, Michigan" on
front, square, clear, quart 3.00   5.00

☐ **KALEVACO**
Kalevaco Oprative ASSN., Maynard, MA, pure
milk, round embossed pint 4.00   6.00

☐ **R. W. KESPOHL DAIRY**
"R. W. Kespohl Dairy, 2705 Oak, Quincy, ILL,
Phone 4133-J," with clover leaf design on round
slug plate. Large embossed three leaf clover on
bottom. One quart 10.00   15.00

☐ **KEYSTONE DAIRY CO.**
New York, Brooklyn, and New Jersey, round, embossed, square 8 oz. cream bottle 3.50   6.00

☐ **KIRSCH**
"Kirsch Dairy, Inc.," the letter K enclosed in a diamond shape, "Syracuse, N.Y." on front, square,
clear, ½ gallon 2.00   5.00

☐ **KLEASNER P.C.**
"Kleasner P.C., Belvidere, Ill., Pure Milk" in a circle on front, the letter K on base, clear 12.00   18.00

☐ **KORNELY**
"Kornely Guernsey Farms Dairy, Drink Milk For
Good Health, Manitowoc, Wis." on front, square,
clear, ½ pint 1.50   3.00

☐ **KORNELY**
"Kornely Guernsey Farms Dairy, Manitowoc,
Wis." on front, jug, clear, one gallon 3.00   5.00

☐ **KREMELINE**
Centralia, WA, blue round pyroglazed quart 28.00   32.00

☐ **LAKE PLACID CLUB DIARY**
Round, embossed half-pint 5.00   7.50

☐ **LAMB'S DAIRY**
Susquehanna, PA, red pyroglaze ¾ oz. creamer   8.00   10.00

Price Range

☐ **LANTZ BROS.**
Follansbee, W. VA, round, embossed pint cream-
separator **65.00   75.00**

☐ **LANTZ BROS.**
Follansbee, WVA, round, embossed, quart cream
separator **25.00   35.00**

☐ **LAWRENCE BROTHERS**
"Lawrence Bros., Conklin Road, Binghamton,
N.Y., Since 1850" on front, square, clear, ½ gal-
lon **2.00   5.00**

☐ **LEDERLE**
Bacillus acidophilus milk, round, embossed quart   **6.00   10.00**

☐ **LEWE'S**
"Lewe's Dairy, Inc.," picture of cow, "Buy it by the
Gallon" on front, jug, clear, one gallon **3.00   5.00**

☐ **LIBERTY MILK CO., INC.**
Buffalo, NY, embossed Statue of Liberty, round,
embossed half-pint **4.00   6.00**

☐ **LIBERTY MILK CO., INC.**
Buffalo, NY, round, embossed pint, picture of
Statue of Liberty **6.00   8.00**

☐ **LINAIR DAIRY AND POULTRY FARMS**
Round, embossed pint **8.00   10.00**

☐ **LINCOLN**
"Lincoln Dairy and Ice Cream Co., Lincoln, NEB."
on front, square, clear, pint **2.50   4.00**

☐ **LINK'S**
Randolph, NY, red pyroglaze 1 oz. creamer . . .   **10.00   12.00**

☐ **LITTLETON DAIRY**
"Littleton Dairy Inc. Littleton, NH, Let Us Serve
You. Milk & Cream, Buttermilk, Cottage Cheese,
Chocolate Drink, Orange Drink," on reverse.
Black letters on red background, embossed on
base. Pat. Nov. 22, 1927. Round pyro quart . . .   **8.00   12.00**

☐ **LIVE OAK RIVIERA FARMS**
Round, red pyroglaze half-pint, picture of United
States food emblem on back **15.00   18.00**

☐ **MAINE CREAMERY CO.**
"Cannot be supplied by milkmen. Return bottle
to your grocer." Round, embossed, half-pint tin-
top, aqua and crude **100.00   125.00**

Price Range

☐ **MANCHESTER**
Manchester Dairy Store, round embossed ½ pint   1.00   3.00

☐ **MANSFIELD DAIRY**
Stowe, VT, round, green pyroglaze quart, picture
of comic cow on skis 20.00   23.00

☐ **MAPLEWOOD DAIRY**
Two sides white pyroglaze, square, amber quart   18.00   22.00

☐ **MARINETTE PRODUCE**
"Marinette Produce Twin Cities Finest Pasteurized Dairy Products, Marinette, Wis." on front,
square, clear, tall quart 2.00   4.00

☐ **MARSHALL DAIRY CO.**
Ithaca, NY, round, embossed, pint cream-top ..   8.00   12.00

☐ **MARTIN**
"Martin Dairy Farms, Newark, N.J." on front,
square, clear, quart 3.00   5.00

☐ **MASHAMURKET FARM**
Round, embossed, half-pint tin-top 15.00   20.00

☐ **MATUELLA'S**
Hazelton, PA, Cop-the-Cream, round, embossed
quart 38.00   42.00

☐ **MEADOW GOLD**
Red pyroglaze ¾ oz. creamer 7.00   9.00

☐ **MERRILL DAIRY**
Keeseville, NY, with war slogan, round, orange
pyroglazed quart 28.00   32.00

☐ **MIFFLIN CO. HARDWARE CO.**
Lewistown, PA, round, embossed pint 17.00   19.00

☐ **MILLER'S**
"Miller's Finer Dairy Products" on front, square,
clear, pint 1.50   3.00

☐ **MONSON**
"Monson Milk Co. Est. 1921. Health in Every Bottle" on reverse. Scene with 2½" cow, orange and
maroon on both sides. Round pyroglazed quart   8.00   12.00

☐ **MONT CLARE**
Round, embossed cream top pint 7.00   11.00

☐ **MOORE MILK**
Red pyroglaze ½ oz. creamer 6.00   8.00

Price Range

☐ **MT. DESSERT ISLAND DAIRIES**
Bar Harbor, ME, with picture of Indian, round, maroon pyroglazed quart 15.00 17.00

☐ **MT. HERMON BOY'S SCHOOL**
Mt. Hermon, MA, round, embossed quart 16.00 18.00

☐ **MOWRER'S CREAM**
Orange pyroglaze 1 oz. creamer 11.00 13.00

☐ **MUMPER' DAIRY**
Elizabethtown, round, orange pyroglaze half-pint, war slogan 12.00 14.00

☐ **NATIONAL DAIRY**
Honolulu, round, red pyroglazed quart 14.00 16.00

☐ **NEPONSET VALLEY**
Neponset Valley Farms, Norwood, MA, round embossed quart 6.00 10.00

☐ **NORTHRUP FARM CREAMERY**
F. D. Jackson Prop, 91 Hudson St., Hoboken, NJ, round, embossed, pint, tin-top 30.00 45.00

☐ **OAK PARK**
Oak Park Dairy, Eau Claire, WI, picture of oak tree leaves on front, square, clear, tall quart 2.00 4.00

☐ **OAKHURST DAIRY**
Oakhurst Dairy Co, Bath, ME, store bottle, round embossed ½ pint 4.00 6.00

☐ **OLDS DAIRY**
Maroon pyroglaze ½ oz. creamer 6.00 8.00

☐ **PARAMOUNT**
Ice Cream Co., Ogden, UT, round, embossed half-pint 12.00 15.00

☐ **PAULUS**
Red pyroglaze ¾ oz. creamer 4.50 6.50

☐ **PENINSULA DAIRY**
"Toothache," square, embossed quart 33.00 37.00

☐ **PEOPLES MILK CO.**
70–78 E. Perry St., round, embossed amber quart 20.00 30.00

☐ **PIEDMONT SANATORIUM**
Round, embossed half-pint 10.00 15.00

☐ **PILLSBURY'S**
"Pillsbury's Dairy, Phillips, Maine" on front, square, clear, tall quart 2.00 4.00

Price Range

☐ **PILLSBURY'S**
"Morn, Noon Or Night Drink Pillsbury's Milk," picture of milk glass on front, square, clear, tall quart   2.00   4.00

☐ **PINE HILL FARM**
S. O. Sargent, Concord, NH, Ayrshire Milk, round, red pyroglaze half-pint, picture of Ayrshires 5.00   6.00

☐ **PLATTSBURG DAIRY**
"Plattsburg Dairy Plattsburg, NY. For Your Next Salad Try Our Delicious Cottage Cheese. Delightful! Appetizing!" on reverse. Red round pyroglazed quart 4.00   6.00

☐ **POTOMAC FARMS**
Square orange pyroglaze creamer 7.00   9.00

☐ **POTOMAC STATE COLLEGE**
Keyser, WVA, square, red pyroglazed half-pint   18.00   22.00

☐ **PURVIN DAIRY CO.**
Maroon pyroglaze ¾ oz. creamer 8.00   10.00

☐ **PURITY MILK CORP.**
Phone 313, Phillipsburg, PA, square, red pyroglaze creamer 7.00   9.00

☐ **P.S.C. DAIRY DEPT.**
State College, PA, round, embossed half-pint ..   9.00   11.00

☐ **QUALITY AND SERVICE DAIRY**
Red Lion, PA, square, red pyroglazed, quart, square top 26.00   30.00

☐ **QUINCY SANITARY MILK CO.**
"Quincy Sanitary Milk Co., Quincy, ILL" in oval slug plate. "Pat. Aug. 1901" embossed on bottom, one pint 8.00   12.00

☐ **RICHVALE FARM**
"Richvale Farm Golden Guernsey Milk, Farmington, Maine. Production Supervised by Golden Guernsey Inc.," on reverse. Orange and brown milk can, round pyroglazed quart 7.00   9.00

☐ **RIECK'S**
Round, embossed amber quart 60.00   70.00

☐ **RILEY'S**
Pitman, NJ, round, embossed quarter-pint 6.00   8.00

☐ **RIVERSIDE**
"Riverside Dairy Bar, First in Quality, Kirkwood, N.Y. 13795" on front, square, clear, ½ gallon   2.00   5.00

Price Range

☐ **RIVERSIDE FARM**
Emile Labrecque Livermore Falls, farm scene silo, barns. "A Bottle Of Milk Is A Bottle of Health" with milk bottle and boy drinking glass of milk on reverse. Orange round pyroglazed quart 7.00 9.00

☐ **ROETS**
Roets is Home Dairy, Waupon, WI, picture of flag flying on flagpole in the sea, square, clear, ½ gallon 2.00 5.00

☐ **ROSEBUD CREAMERY**
Picture of rose, square, maroon pyroglazed creamer 5.00 7.00

☐ **ROTHERMEL'S**
Minersville, PA, round, embossed, quart, cream separator 45.00 55.00

☐ **ROYALE DAIRY**
Keyser, WVA, square red pyroglazed creamer 8.00 10.00

☐ **S. A. GEIST**
Ayrshire milk, Topton, PA, round, embossed pint 12.00 17.00

☐ **SANITARIUM DAIRY**
Boulder, CO, round, embossed pint 18.00 22.00

☐ **SANITARY DAIRY**
Sanitary Dairy Chisholm, ME. "Morn, Noon or Night Drink Milk," on reverse. Read square quart cream top 11.00 13.00

☐ **SAYLES' DAIRY**
A. W. Evans No. Attleboro, with MA. seal. "Sayles' Dairy Farms" on reverse. Cows head, maroon with "STORE" in orange. Round pyroglazed quart 7.00 9.00

☐ **SHAMROCK DAIRY**
Tucson, AZ, round, brown pyroglaze cream-top 30.00 35.00

☐ **SHERMAN COLLEGE INN**
Round, embossed, half-pint, cobalt blue 100.00 150.00

☐ **SHORE DAIRIES INC.**
Square orange pyroglaze creamer 6.00 8.00

☐ **STAFFORD'S**
"Stafford's Dairy, Quality Dairy Products, Peoria, Illinois" on front, square, clear, ½ gallon 2.50 5.00

☐ **STATE COLLEGE CREAMERY**
State College, PA, round, red pyroglaze quart 10.00 15.00

Price Range

☐ **STONY HILL FARM**
Blue pyroglaze ½ oz. creamer 6.50 8.50

☐ **ST. JOSEPH'S HOSPITAL**
Round, black pyroglaze half-pint 10.00 12.00

☐ **ST. PAUL'S POLY. INST.**
Lawrenceville, VA, round, embossed half-pint .. 20.00 24.00

☐ **SUNLITE**
"Sunlite Dairy Milk Builds Sturdy Bodies," picture
of cow and milk bottle enclosed in a badge, "Soo.
Mich" on front, round, clear, quart 3.50 5.00

☐ **SWAINS DAIRY**
"Tel Laconia, 1431–W2. Produced On Our Own
Farm. A Delicious Drink, A Nutritious Food Pasteurized Milk," on reverse. Red round pyroglazed
quart 5.00 7.00

☐ **SWEET CLOVER**
"Sweet Clover Dairy, Depere, Wis." on front,
square, clear, tall quart 2.00 4.00

☐ **TEMPLE FARMS**
Picture of cow, "N. Midler Ave., E. Syracuse,
N.Y." on front, square, clear, ½ gallon 2.00 5.00

☐ **TRU-LI-PURE-SEALTEST**
Red pyroglaze ½ oz. creamer 5.50 7.50

☐ **TUSCAN DAIRY**
Red pyroglaze ¾ oz. creamer 4.00 7.00

☐ **UVM**
University of Vermont, white pyroglaze amber
quart 42.00 48.00

☐ **UNITED FARMERS**
United Farmers, A Real Co-operative Bost, MA,
dacro top, square quart, red 9.00 11.00

☐ **UNION MEMORIAL HOSPITAL**
Round, embossed quart 13.00 15.00

☐ **UNIVERSITY OF CONNECTICUT**
Storrs, square, blue pyroglaze quart 12.00 15.00

☐ **UNIVERSITY OF CONNECTICUT**
Round-embossed half pint 7.00 9.00

☐ **VALLEY FARM DAIRY**
"John H. Bowen, Pikesville, Md." in center on
front, "MTC" on back, the letter E and #28 in circle on base, ring on neck and ring top, clear, quart 5.00 8.00

☐ **VAN NUYS**
"Please Return Promptly to Van Nuys Quality
Dairy, I Belong To Your Dairy Not In Your Environ-
ment," picture of animated milk bottle on front,
square, clear, quart 3.00   5.00

☐ **WAKEFIELD DAIRY**
Embossed picture of George Washington, round,
embossed quarter pint 9.00   11.00

☐ **WALDORF LUNCH**
Coffee, round, embossed half-pint 16.00   22.00

☐ **WAYSIDE**
"Wayside Dairy, Belgium, Wis." on front, jug,
clear, one gallon 3.00   5.00

☐ **WEBER'S**
"Weber's, Joliet, Illinois" on front, "Best By The
Glass" on front and side, round, clear, quart . .   3.50   5.00

☐ **WHITE DOTTE FARMS**
Dairy Bar, orange pyroglaze ¾ oz. creamer . . .   6.00   9.00

☐ **WILLOW FARMS DAIRY**
Warner, Westminster, MD, round, embossed,
half-pint cream-top 4.50   6.00

☐ **WM. WECKERLE AND SONS, INC.**
Buffalo, NY, round, embossed amber quart 39.00   49.00

FLASKS

Flasks have become one of the most popular varieties of bottles
in the hobby. Their myriad designs and shapes, and their mottos re-
flecting sentiments of the past make them important artistic, as well
as historical objects. Prices have attained very high levels for the most
desirable examples. This is not due to rarity, but that flasks have long
been collected and demand has been building up for many years.

Today we think of a flask as a small, rather flat spirits bottle that
can be carried in the pocket. Many of those on the collector market
fit the description, but others are of figural shape and various sizes.
All were made to contain whiskey. It would be easy to assume that
they were created as collectors' items, but this was not the case. Their
attractive designs and the presence of slogans or sayings were merely
intended to catch the eye and hopefully promote sales.

Mottos were numerous. They included such popular patriotic sayings as "Don't tread on me," coined by the revolutionists of '76 and
deeply ingrained into our language by the 19th century.

The earliest American flasks were probably those of the Pitkin Glasshouse, set up in 1783 near Hartford, Connecticut. At first, they were freeblown, or made without aid of a mold. By 1850, some 400 design variations had been used. These flasks have black graphite pontil marks. The pontil was coated with powdered iron to enable the flask's bottom to be broken away without damaging the glass. The several hundred additional types made between 1850 and 1870 carry no such markings, thanks to invention of the snapcase. This was a spring device to cradle the flask in the finishing process.

Competition to devise the most original designs and slogans in the flask trade was intense. Plagiarism of mold designs by rival companies occurred frequently.

Thomas W. Dyott, an English immigrant who had worked as a boot-black, became proprietor of the Philadelphia and Kensington Glass Works, one of the major flask manufacturers. Among his portrait flasks was one picturing himself, along with a likeness of Benjamin Franklin on the reverse.

Masonic flasks were plentiful. Many bore the order's emblems on one side and the symbolic American eagle on the other. George Washington was a perennially popular subject for flasks.

The Presidential elections of 1824 and 1828 produced a number of special flasks promoting Andrew Jackson and his rival, John Quincy Adams.

Price Range

☐ **JOHN Q. ADAMS**
In a circle, Eagle facing to right, on base "J.T. & CO.," beaded edge, sheared top, pontil, green, pint 800.00 1050.00

☐ **A.G.W.L.**
Under bottom, saddle flask, amber, ½ pint 18.00 27.00

☐ **ALL SEEING EYE**
Star and large eye in center, under it "A.D.," in back, six-pointed star with arms, Masonic emblem, under it "G.R.J.A.," pontil, sheared top, amber, pint 240.00 320.00

☐ **ANCHOR FLASK**
Double ring, amber or clear, ½ pint, quart 35.00 45.00

☐ **AQUAMARINE**
Pint 45.00 55.00

☐ **BALTIMORE GLASS WORKS**
Aqua, very thin glass, pontil, on back a stack of wheat 160.00 220.00

Price Range

☐ **BALTIMORE MONUMENT**
And under it Balto. door with step railing, in back
sloop with pennant flying, sailing to right above
it Fells below point, ½ pt. 3 ribbed on side, plain
top, pontil, aqua, qt. (c. 1840) 135.00 190.00
Same as above, except plain bottom, ... 125.00 155.00

☐ **B.P. & B.**
Yellow green, ½ pint 50.00 65.00

☐ **BRIDGETON**
New Jersey, around a man facing to left, in back
a man facing to the left with Washington around
it, ribbed sides, sheared top, pontil, aqua, pint 85.00 110.00

☐ **BRYON & SCOTT**
One picture of each, Byron on front and Scott in
back, ribbed sides, sheared top, pontil, 5½"
amber 210.00 260.00

☐ **CABIN**
Sheared top, pontil, blue, pint 3600.00 4600.00

☐ **CALABASH**
Hunter and fisherman, aqua, quart 50.00 65.00

☐ **CANNON FLASK**
Cannon and balls lengthwise of flask, cannon
balls at left of wheel in foreground, rammer and
swab beneath, A rammer leans against cannon
in front of right wheel. In horseshoe circle around
cannon "GEN. TAYLOR NEVER SURREN-
DERS." Vine and grapes for a frame in center of
it. "A LITTLE MORE GRAPE CAPT BRAGG,"
vertically ribbed with heavy medial rib, plain top,
pontil, puce, ½ pint, aqua 385.00 465.00

☐ **CHAPMAN P.**
Baltimore, MD, soldier with a gun on front, a girl
dancing on a bar in back, sheared top, aqua, pint 170.00 220.00

☐ **CLASPED HANDS**
Eagle Flask (c. 1860–75), Union 13 stars, clasped
hands, eagle above banner mark, "E", Wormer
& Co., Pittsburg, aqua, quart 110.00 140.00

☐ **CLASPED HANDS**
Eagle Flask (c. 1860–75), deep golden amber, ½
pint 120.00 160.00

Price Range

☐ **CLASPED HANDS**
Flask (c. 1860–75), one with eagle and banner,
above oval marked "Pittsburgh, PA.," other can-
non to left, flag and cannonballs, aqua, pint ...   85.00   110.00

☐ **COLUMBIA**
Eagle Flask (c. 1820–50), Columbia with Liberty
Cap facing left, 13 stars—half moon circle around
bust, in back eagle facing right under eagle "B &
W", plain top, pontil, yellow, pint 300.00   375.00

☐ Same as above, except aqua (c. 1830) 300.00   375.00

☐ **CORN FOR THE WORLD**
c. 1835, in half moon around ear of corn, in back
design on large oval panels, Baltimore Monument
and under it "BALTIMORE," the step railing of
the entrance door facing left, pontil, round top,
golden yellow, quart 325.00   400.00

☐ Same as above, except the door is facing right, ½
pt. smooth edge, sheared top, pontil, aqua. (c.
1840) 90.00   120.00

☐ **CORNUCOPIA**
Designs on oval panels, beading on edges and
at top, inverted cornucopia coiled to left and filled
with produce, in back large circular, in center of
it large geometric star around it 8 petalled rosette—under it palm (6), plain top, pontil, light
blue green, ½ pint 1450.00 1850.00

☐ **CORNUCOPIA**
Cornucopia coiled to the left and filled with produce, urn in back with 6 bars and filled with pro-
duce, pontil, plain top, light amber, ½ pint 75.00   100.00

☐ Same as above, except aqua 75.00   100.00

☐ Same as above, except olive amber, pint 75.00   100.00

☐ **CORN FOR THE WORLD**
Amber, 8¼″ 200.00   250.00

☐ **CORNUCOPIA**
Emerald green, pint 55.00   70.00

☐ **CORNUCOPIA AND EAGLE**
Kensington Glass Works, aqua, ½ pint 75.00   125.00

☐ Same as above, except inverted cornucopia ...   250.00   350.00

☐ **CORNUCOPIA and URN**
Olive, pint 65.00   80.00

Price Range

☐ **CORNUCOPIA and URN**
Amber, ½ pint 65.00 80.00
☐ **CORNUCOPIA and URN**
With twig, open pontil, olive or amber, ½ pint .. 75.00 95.00
☐ **CUNNINGHAM**
Pittsburgh, PA, Indian, hunter and eagle 125.00 140.00
☐ Delicate powder blue, ½ pint 45.00 55.00
☐ 18 diamond quilted flask, green, 6¼″ 125.00 145.00
☐ **DOG**
In center, in back man in uniform on a horse, pontil, sheared top, aqua, quart 130.00 165.00
☐ **DOUBLE EAGLE**
Eagles lengthwise, open pontil, olive green 103.00 115.00
☐ **DOUBLE EAGLE**
Sheared mouth, aqua, pint 110.00 135.00
☐ **DOUBLE EAGLE**
Light green, pint 95.00 115.00
☐ **DOUBLE EAGLE**
Beneath unembossed oval, sheared top, pontil, amber, 6¼″ 40.00 50.00
☐ **DOUBLE EAGLE**
NH, olive or amber, pint 85.00 110.00
☐ **DUCK FLASK**
Picture of a duck in water, under duck "SWIM," above duck "WILL YOU HAVE A DRINK," aqua, pint 150.00 170.00
☐ **AMERICAN EAGLE**
Facing left, shield with bars on breast, above eagle 13 stars, 3 arrows in right talons, branch in left, back big bunch of grapes and smaller one at right, above it two large leaves, qt., aqua—fine vertical ribbing, pontil, plain top, (c. 1835) 95.00 115.00
☐ **EAGLE FLASK**
Circle below eagle, aqua, 6″ 70.00 90.00
☐ **EAGLE**
Facing left, shield with eight vertical bars on breast, 4 arrows in left. Claw large branch in right, 23 sun rays around head. Eagle stand on oval frame in side frame 20 small pearls, a bar connects the claw, back same, pt. aqua, 3 side ribbed, pontil, plain top, c. 1840 .... 95.00 115.00

Price Range

☐ **EAGLE**
Facing to right resting on a shield and rock pile,
aqua, pint 70.00 90.00

☐ **EAGLE**
Facing left, ribbon held in back with 5 star extending to the right, below eagle large stellar
Motif—same in back, all in Designs on oval panels, qt. corrugated horz. with vertical rib., aqua,
plain top, pontil (c. 1845) 140.00 170.00

☐ **EAGLE and MASONIC FLASK**
Large eagle with rays over head and "OHIO" in
a circle under eagle, under that "J. SHEPARD &
CO.," on shoulder "ZANESVILLE," reverse Masonic arch, ornaments under arch, pontil, green,
amber or olive, pint 250.00 300.00

☐ **EAGLE**
Resting on arrows and olive branch with ribbon
in beak, an oval panel under eagle, "CUNNING-
HAM & CO., PITTSBURGH, PA.," ring neck, olive
green, quart 150.00 170.00

☐ **EAGLE**
And Clasped Hands, aqua, pint 55.00 70.00

☐ **EAGLE**
And Cornucopia, clear, pontil, aqua, ½ pint 200.00 250.00

☐ **EAGLE and DYOTTVILLE G.W.**
Aqua, pint 115.00 160.00

☐ **EAGLE TREE**
Eagle head turned to left, shield with 8 vertical
bars on breast, large olive branch in right, etc.,
in back large tree in foliage, plain top, pontil,
aqua, Kensington Glass Works, common flask,
pint 150.00 200.00

☐ **EAGLE**
And flag, aqua, pint, pontil, (c. 1830) 150.00 180.00

☐ **EAGLE**
And girl on bicycle, A & DHA, aqua, pint 85.00 105.00

☐ **EAGLE**
Grape and scroll, sheared mouth, pontil, aqua,
quart 70.00 90.00

☐ **EAGLE**
And Morning Glory, (1840–1860) stoneware, pint 300.00 375.00

Price Range

☐ **EAGLE**
Head to the left, wing partly up, large shield with
6 bars on breast, above eagle liberty, eagle
stands on wreath branches, in back 4 lines Willington Glass co. West Willington, Conn., qt. ta-
pered top, plain base, dark olive green (c. 1860)   110.00 150.00

☐ **EAGLE**
Kensington Glass Works, blue green, pint 85.00 105.00

☐ **EAGLE**
On oval panels, 25 sun rays in ¼ circle around
eagle head, 8 vertical bars on shield. End of olive
branch & arrows under claws in oval frame with
23 small pearls around. T.W.D., in back full sailing
to right. U.S. flag at reas., waves beneath frigate
and in semi-circle beneath Franklin pt. 3 vertically
ribbed on side, sheared top, pontil, aqua, (c.
1830) 135.00 185.00

☐ **EAGLE**
And Stag, aqua, ½ pint 200.00 250.00

☐ **EAGLE**
And Tree, Kensington Glass Works, aqua, pint   95.00 125.00

☐ **FLASK**
Plain, amber, ½ pint 10.00 15.00

☐ **FLASK**
Plain, bulbous neck, ½ pint, 6¾" 8.00 12.00

☐ **FLASK**
Plain, bulbous neck, ½ pint, 7" 10.00 15.00

☐ **FLASK**
Label, pontil, very pale olive, 6" 50.00 65.00

☐ **FLASK**
Label, dark olive, 5½" 18.00 23.00

☐ **FLASK**
Label, ribbed base, clear, 6¾" 15.00 20.00

☐ **FLASK**
Label, amber, 7½" 15.00 20.00

☐ **FLASK**
Round Label, amber, 6½" 15.00 20.00

☐ **FLASK**
Label, pontil, clear, 6¾" 23.00 32.00

☐ **FLASK**
plain, sheared top, pontil, green, pint 160.00 210.00

☐ Same as above, except clear 160.00 210.00

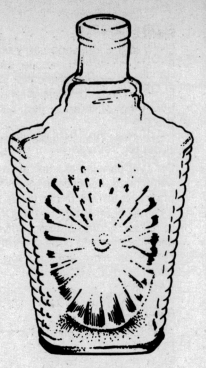

Keene Marlboro Street Glassworks, *sunburst design, green.* **$310.00–$390.00**

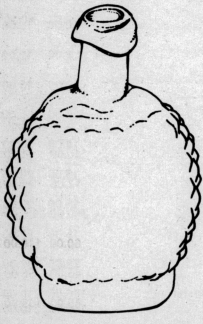

Poison Flask, *diamond motif, 4".* **$55.00–$75.00**

Price Range

☐ **FLORA TEMPLE**
Aqua, pint 210.00 260.00
☐ **FLORA TEMPLE**
Handle, puce or amber, pint 210.00 260.00
☐ **FLORIDA UNIVERSAL STORE BOTTLE**
Clear, pint 8.00 12.00
☐ **H. FRANK**
Pat'd. Aug. 6th 1879, under bottom, two circles
in center, reverse plain, ring top, ribs on sides 45.00 55.00
☐ **H. FRANK**
Pat. Aug. 6, 1872, all on bottom, circular shaped
flask, two circles in center on front, reverse side
plain, wide rib on sides, ring neck, aqua, pint .. 50.00 70.00
☐ **FRANKLIN AND DYOTT**
Kensington Glass Works, sheared mouth, pontil,
aqua, pint 110.00 160.00
☐ **FRANKLIN & FRANKLIN**
Aqua, quart 140.00 180.00
☐ **GEN. MACARTHUR and GOD BLESS
AMERICA**
Purple or green, ½ pint 13.00 21.00
☐ **G.H.A.**
Concord, NY 1865, aqua, ½ pint 23.00 32.00
☐ **GIRL FOR JOE**
Girl on bicycle, aqua, pint 75.00 95.00
☐ **GRANITE GLASS CO.**
In three lines, reverse Stoddard, NH, sheared top,
olive, pint 155.00 210.00
☐ **GUARANTEED FLASK**
Clear or amethyst, 6¼" 8.00 12.00
☐ **GUARANTEED FULL**
Clear, 6½" 10.00 14.00
☐ **HISTORY FLASK**
Label, aqua, side panels, 7¼" 17.00 25.00
☐ **HUNTER**
And Dog, puce, pint 310.00 385.00
☐ **HORSEMAN**
And Dog, aqua, ½ pint 60.00 110.00
☐ **IRON**
Pontil, double collared, pint 45.00 55.00
☐ **ISABELLA G.W.**
Sheaf of wheat, pint 85.00 105.00

Price Range

☐ **GENERAL JACKSON**
Eagle Flask. Jackson, three-quarter view facing
left in semi-circle above bust, in back -eagle head
turned to right, laurel branch in eagle's beak, nine
stars above eagle. Eagle stands on oval frame
with inner band of 16 large pearls, J.R. in oval
frame below eagle, in semi-circle below oval
frame "-LAIRD. SC.PITT," Edge horizontal bead-
ing rib, plain top, pontil, aqua, pint 1100.00 1400.00

☐ **JENNY LIND**
With wreath, reverse picture of glass works,
above is "FISLERVILLE GLASS WORKS," wavy
line on neck, pontil, tapered top, aqua, quart ..   120.00   160.00

☐ Same as above, except "S. HUFFSY" 65.00   85.00

☐ **JENNY LIND LYRE**
Aqua, pint 115.00   160.00

☐ **KEEN**
P & W, SUNBURST FLASK (c. 1814–30), olive
amber, ½ pint 220.00   300.00

☐ **KEENE**
Masonic, tooled lip, pontil, pint 220.00   300.00

☐ **KEENE**
Sunburst, green 310.00   390.00

☐ **LAFAYETTE**
Large bust in uniform, face slightly to the right,
General-LA-Fayette in ¾ circle around bust.
Back, on edges, "Republican Gratitude-
Kensington Glass Works, Philadelphia," under
eagle facing left in oval frame T.W.D. Pontil, aqua,
pt., (c. 1830) 400.00   500.00

☐ **LAFAYETTE**
And Eagle, amber 85.00   120.00

☐ **LAFAYETTE**
And Eagle, Kensington, open pontil, aqua, pint   140.00   170.00

☐ **LAFAYETTE**
And Dewitt Clinton, olive, amber, ½ pint 325.00   475.00

☐ **LAFAYETTE**
And Liberty Cap, aqua, pint 130.00   160.00

☐ **LAFAYETTE**
And Masonic, ½ pint 210.00   270.00

Price Range

☐ **LC. & R. CO.**
On bottom, Eagle in a circle, reverse plain, clear,
½ pint 45.00   55.00

☐ **LEGENDARY GRANDFATHER**
Broken swirl pattern, reddish amber 120.00 170.00

☐ **LIBERTY & UNION**
In three lines, in back Baltimore Monument, in
above semi-circle "BALTIMORE," entrance to
door is without step railing, edges smooth, plain
lip, pontil, yellow olive, pint 3675.00 4375.00

☐ **LOUISVILLE G.W.**
And eagle, aqua, ½ pint 110.00 140.00

☐ **LOUISVILLE, KY. GLASS WORKS**
In lower part of flask, rectangular panel, near
shoulder, in oval panel, American eagle, facing
right, wings raised above and paralleled to body,
eagle rests on shield, no bars, in eagle's beak
narrow ribbon extending upward above eagle and
below, through shield, in back no design or inscription all covered with decidedly angular vertical ribbing, eagles vertical, ribbing plain with laid
on ring, base plain, yellow green, pint 120.00 160.00

☐ **LOWELL R.R.**
Olive, amber, ½ pint 160.00 185.00

☐ **LYNDEBORO, LG. CO.,**
PATENT on shoulder, aqua, pint 22.00   30.00

☐ **LYNDEBORO, L.G. CO.**
Golden amber, quart 38.00   48.00

☐ **MAN**
With a gun and bag, reverse side running dogs,
double ring top, aqua, pint 150.00 190.00

☐ **MAN**
With a gun and bag and a feather in hat, reverse
side grape vine, with bunches of grapes and
leaves, ribbed sides, sheared top, pontil 110.00 150.00

☐ **MARKED DOUBLE EAGLE**
Olive or amber, pint 80.00 100.00

☐ **MASONIC ARCH**
Pillars & pavement, no stars etc., pt. 2 rings at
shoulders, fine horizontal corrugations around
flask etc. sheared top, pontil O., amber, in back
eagle head turning left. shield with bars and tiny

Price Range

dots on breast, 3 arrows in its left claw. Olive branch in right, plain ribbon above head, plain oval frame below eagle (c. 1825) **1100.00 1400.00**

☐ **MASONIC ARCH**
Pillars & pavement, 6 stars surrounding quarter moon & without comet at right of pillars, Eagle facing left. No shield on breast., etc. under it in plain oval frame KCCNC. pt. O. amber, one single vertical rib. Sheared top, pontil, (c. 1825) **135.00 185.00**

☐ **MASONIC**
Eagle Flask, pillars and pavement, except 6 stars surrounding quarter moon and without comet to right of pillars, in back, eagle facing to left KCCNC in oval frame, mold work error should read KEENE, olive amber, pint (c. 1814–50) **235.00 260.00**

☐ Same as above, except clear **420.00 520.00**

☐ **MASONIC**
And Eagle, pint, pontil, green **535.00 610.00**

☐ **MASONIC**
And Eagle, olive or amber, pint **110.00 135.00**

☐ **MASONIC**
And Eagle, pontil, pint, blue green **110.00 135.00**

☐ **MONUMENT**
And corn in a circle under this, BALTIMORE, reverse side a large ear of corn, aqua, quart **140.00 170.00**

☐ Same as above, except amber **160.00 210.00**

☐ **MOUNTED**
Soldier and dog, citron, quart **260.00 310.00**

☐ **NEW GRANITE GLASS WORKS**
In horse shoe letters, in center of it "Stoddard, N.H." in back on a pole a flag with 13 stars and 9 stripes flying to the right, rib sides, sheared top, pontil, amber, 5¾" **110.00 160.00**

☐ **"NEW LONDON GLASSWORK"**
Anchor Eagle Flask, golden amber, pint, (c. 1860–66) **420.00 550.00**

☐ **PIKE'S PEAK**
Man with pack and cane walking to left, reverse eagle with ribbon in beak in oval panel, aqua, pint **100.00 150.00**

☐ Same as above, except several colors **75.00 95.00**

Price Range

☐ **FOR PIKE'S PEAK**
Reverse side, man shooting a gun at a deer,
aqua, 9½″ 35.00   45.00
☐ **FOR PIKE'S PEAK**
Old rye, aqua, pint 40.00   50.00
☐ **PIKE'S PEAK**
Traveler and hunter, olive, amber, pint 200.00 250.00
☐ **PIKE'S PEAK HISTORICAL FLASK—Penn.**
(c. 1859–70) Ring top, Eagle—Prospector to
right, under it "For Pike's Peak", yellow amber,
pint 570.00 685.00
☐ Same as above, except aqua, ½ pint 110.00 135.00
☐ **PITTSBURGH**
Double eagle, citron, pint 210.00 260.00
☐ **PITTSBURGH**
Double eagle, aqua, pint 35.00   45.00
☐ **PITTSBURGH, PA.**
In raised oval circle at base, with an eagle on
front, back same except plain for label, aqua, ap-
plied ring at top, pint, 7½″ 45.00   55.00
☐ **PITKIN**
Type, light green, pint 85.00 135.00
☐ **POTTERY FLASK**
Figure of a man and horse, same on reverse side,
pint 300.00 375.00
☐ **QUILTED**
Pattern Flask, sheared top, pontil, reddish brown,
amber, green, olive amber, ½ pint 525.00 650.00
☐ Same as above, except amethyst 650.00 850.00
☐ Same as above, except white bluish cast 200.00 250.00
☐ **RAILROAD**
Eagle flask, amber, pint (c. 1830–48) 170.00 215.00
☐ **RAILROAD FLASK**
On oval panels, horse drawing long cart on rail
to right. Cart filled with barrels and boxes, under
it "Lowell" and above it "Railroad" in back eagle
facing left. Shield with 7 vertical & 2 horizontal
bars on breast, 3 arrows in eagles left claw, olive
branch in right, 13 large stars surround edge, ½
pt. 3 ver. ribbed on side, sheared top, pontil, O.
amber (c. 1860) 120.00 170.00

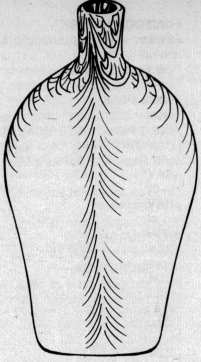

Nailsea Flask,
blue with white
loopings, 7".
$200.00–$250.00

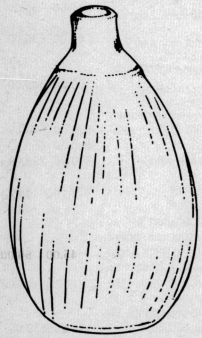

Pitkin Flask,
vertical ribbing,
amber, 7".
$55.00–$75.00

Price Range

☐ **RAILROAD FLASK**
Designs on oval panels, crude locomotive to left
on rail, embossed success to the Railroad, reading around locomotive-back but the line connect-
ing the tender with rear wheel shows a slight
break and E in success carries a convex dot attached to the upper bar pt. 3 vertically ribbed on
size, sheared top O. amber, (c. 1830) 160.00   200.00

☐ **RAVENNA GLASS WORKS**
Star flask, OH, aqua, pint (c. 1857–60) 160.00   200.00

☐ **RAVENNA GLASS WORKS**
In three lines, ring top, yellow green, pint 140.00   185.00

☐ **RAVENNA**
In center, anchor with rope, under it "GLASS
COMPANY," ring top, aqua, pint 150.00   185.00

☐ **RAVENNA TRAVELERS COMPANION**
Pontil, amber, quart 265.00   365.00

☐ **REHM BROS**
"Bush & Buchanan Sts & O'Farrel & Mason Sts,"
in a sunken circle, ribbed bottom, two rings near
shoulder, coffin type, metal and cork cap, clear
or amethyst, ½ pint 110.00   155.00

☐ **RIBBED FLASK**
Fluted base to shoulder, sheared top, pontil,
aqua, ½ pint 170.00   210.00

☐ Same as above, except yellow or amber 210.00   260.00

☐ **SAILING VESSEL AND COLUMBIAN
JUBILEE**
Amber, pint 95.00   130.00

☐ **SAILOR BOTTLE**
Dancing sailor on back, amber, 7½" 75.00   100.00

☐ **SCROLL**
One star, smooth base, aqua, 7" 15.00   25.00

☐ Same as above, except two stars 35.00   45.00

☐ **SCROLL**
One star, clear, aqua or amber, pontil, ½ pint to
quart 45.00   60.00

☐ Same as above, except two stars CIX-17, (c.
1855) 120.00   145.00

☐ **STAR**
Cornucopia Flask, oval panels banded at top,
sides by same on edge, inverted cornucopia,

Price Range

coiled to left and filled with produce, in back—large circle in center, star-shaped design with six ribbed points and in center circle with small eight-petalled rosette, under it medallion modified symmetrical palm motif rising from pointed oval with hatching, plain top, pontil, horizontal beading edges, light blue green, ½ pint   **2690.00 3690.00**

☐ **STAR**

With a circle around it on shoulder, light amber, saddle flask, ½ pint **14.00 20.00**

☐ **STODDARD**

Double eagle, Granite Glass Co., Stoddard, NH, pontil, golden amber, pint **110.00 140.00**

☐ **STODDARD, NH**

In panel under eagle facing left, reverse same except blank panel, sheared top, pontil, amber, pint   **135.00 185.00**

☐ **STODDARD, NH**

In 2 lines, in back 3 lines "Granite Glass Co." tapered top, light amber, plain bottom **110.00 140.00**

☐ Same as above, except tapered top, olive green   **130.00 160.00**

☐ **STRONGMAN**

And two gentlemen, clear, ½ pint **130.00 160.00**

☐ **S.T.R.A.**

In a five point star, reverse plain, ring collared top, amber, ½ pint **125.00 150.00**

☐ Same as above, except double ring top **110.00 150.00**

☐ **SUNBURST FLASK**

CT, olive amber, pontil, ½ pint (c. 1813–30) ...   **110.00 150.00**

☐ Same as above, except clear **185.00 240.00**

☐ Same as above, except olive green **350.00 450.00**

☐ **SUCCESS TO THE RAILROAD**

With a horse and a cart on rail around it, same on reverse side, sheared top, pontil, olive or aqua, pint **235.00 300.00**

☐ **SUCCESS TO THE RAILROAD**

Around it a horse and cart on a rail, in back an eagle with wings spread, also an arrow and a branch, 17 stars around this, sheared lip and pontil, amber, ½ pint **260.00 310.00**

Price Range

☐ **SUCCESS TO R.R.**
Eagle, olive, pint, pontil (c. 1850) **135.00 160.00**
☐ Same as above, except aqua, pint **155.00 175.00**
☐ Same as above, except olive green or amber, pint **120.00 150.00**
☐ **SUCCESS TO RAILROAD**
NH, Keene Glassworks, olive, amber, pint (c.
1830–50) **160.00 210.00**
☐ **SUMMER and WINTER FLASK**
Aqua, ½ pint **100.00 130.00**
☐ Same as above, except quart **100.00 130.00**
☐ **SUMMER TREE**
Tapered collared lip, pontil, aqua, pint, rare **70.00 110.00**
☐ **SUNBURST**
Large elliptical sunburst 26 triangles, sectioned
rays, flatted at ends forming closed ellipse in center, back same, edges horizontally corrugated,
extending around flask at juncture of neck and
body, tapered top, three rings around neck at
shoulder, pontil, olive amber, ½ pint **1690.00 2290.00**
☐ **SUNBURST FLASK**
Large elliptical sunburst ($4^1/_6$ x 2½″) 24 rounded
rays rounding downward to surface of flask and
forming ellipse, back same. . . pt. Horizontal cor-
rugation extends around side at base & around
upper part between neck & squared and concave
shoulder (three rings), sheared top, pontil, olive
green, (c. 1820) **350.00 450.00**
☐ **SUNBURST FLASK**
Aqua, pint **95.00 130.00**
☐ **SUNBURST, KEENE**
Olive or amber, pint **155.00 195.00**
☐ **SUNBURST, KEENE P & W**
Olive or amber, pint **210.00 260.00**
☐ **SUNBURST, KEENE**
Amber, ½ pint **210.00 260.00**
☐ **SWIRLED PITKIN**
Amber **160.00 185.00**
☐ **SWIRLED PITKIN**
Blue green, pint **85.00 105.00**

Price Range

☐ **TAYLOR—CORNSTALK**
Baltimore Glass Works, MD, clear or amethyst,
large mouth, pint (c. 1800–52) 1050.00 1350.00
☐ Same as above, aqua 225.00 425.00
☐ **TAYLOR, GENL**
Facing right in one-quarter moon circle, bust in
uniform, back, "Fells point" in semi circle above
monument under it Balto, pt. ver. 3 ribbed, with
heavy medial rib., aqua, pontil, plain top, Mary-
land (c. 1850) 95.00 120.00
☐ **TAYLOR & RINGGOLD**
Pontil, plaintop, aqua, pint (c. 1845) 105.00 125.00
☐ **TRAVELERS**
In center a sunflower, under it "COMPANION,"
in back Ravenna, in center sunflower, under it
"Glass Co.," sheared top, amber, pint 125.00 165.00
☐ **TRAVELERS COMPANION**
And sheaf, amber, quart 105.00 130.00
☐ **TRAVELERS COMPANION**
And star, aqua, ½ pint 75.00 95.00
☐ **UNION**
Side mold, ball and cannon on back, aqua, 7½" 100.00 130.00
☐ **UNION**
Clasped hands in shield, eagle with banner on re-
verse side, pint 70.00 90.00
☐ **U 2266**
On bottom, clear or amethyst, 5" 8.00 12.00
☐ **VIOLIN FLASK**
Curled ornaments in a heart shape, with a panel
with two stars and a C, reverse same except no
C, collared neck, green, pint 185.00 235.00
☐ **VERTICALLY RIBBED SUNBURST FLASK (c.
1810–50)**
Light blue green, ½ pint 210.00 260.00
☐ **WARRANTED FLASK**
Clear or amethyst, 7½" 12.00 18.00
☐ **G. WASHINGTON**
Prune color, pontil, 10½" 120.00 160.00
☐ **WASHINGTON AND ALBANY**
Aqua, ½ pint 150.00 190.00
☐ **G. WASHINGTON AND A. JACKSON**
Olive green, pint 160.00 185.00

Price Range

☐ **G. WASHINGTON AND T. JEFFERSON**
Dark amber, pint **160.00 210.00**

☐ **WASHINGTON G.**
In half moon circle above bust, in back eagle fac-
ing right, pontil, plain top, beading edge, pt., aqua
(G1–10) **75.00 95.00**

☐ **WASHINGTON, GENERAL**
In ¾" moon circle above bust facing left in back
eagle facing right, "E. Pluribus Unum" above sun
rays, T.W.D. in oval frame near base, vertically
ribbed and inscription "July 4, A.D. 1776, Kensington Glass Works, Phila.," three star 1776, pt.,
aqua, pontil, plain top **185.00 235.00**

☐ **G. WASHINGTON**
And sheaf of wheat, aqua, pint **150.00 195.00**

☐ **WASHINGTON (c. 1810–52)**
Bust facing left, Fells above bust below point,
back, Baltimore Monument, under it, "BALTO.,"
plain top, pontil, aqua, pint, qt., (c. 1810–52) ... **260.00 360.00**

☐ **WASHINGTON—JACKSON**
Sheared mouth, pontil scar, aqua, pint (c.
1830–50) **85.00 105.00**

☐ **WASHINGTON—TAYLOR**
No inscription around Washington bust, facing
right, in back "Baltimore X Glass Woks," (r omitted), in center Taylor facing right, heavy vertical
medial rib with narrow rib each side and two narrow ribs forming out edge of each panel, plain top,
pontil, deep puce, quart, (c. 1820–40) **1490.00 1790.00**

☐ **WASHINGTON—TAYLOR FLASK**
Washington bust facing left without queue, in
back Taylor facing left in uniform, smooth edge,
deep yellow green, tapered top and ring, quart **260.00 360.00**

☐ **WASHINGTON—TAYLOR FLASK**
Dyottville Glass Work, Washington facing left,
Taylor facing left, in uniform, four buttons on coat,
light blue, quart, (c. 1860–75) **220.00 320.00**

☐ **WASHINGTON**
In half moon circle above bust in back eagle facing left, B.K. in oval frame near base, P.T., edge,
vertical ribbing, pontil, plain top, yellow green .. **65.00 85.00**

Price Range

☐ **WASHINGTON**
Above bust in three-quarter circle, "The Father
of His Country" in back "I have endeavour, D. Do
my duty" above bust in three-quarter circle, qt.
plain edge, plain top, aqua 80.00 130.00

☐ **WASHINGTON BUST**
In back tree, Calabash flask, qt., aqua sloping collared with ring, vertical fluting, pontil, (c. 1850) 80.00 130.00

☐ **WASHINGTON FLASK**
"Father of His Country" around bust, back plain,
NY, plain top, light green, pint, (c. 1840–60) ... 105.00 150.00

☐ **WASHINGTON—TAYLOR**
Washington facing left, back, Taylor facing left,
deep blue green, quart, (c. 1833–60) 225.00 325.00

☐ **WASHINGTON**
Bust, Washington in half moon circle, above bust,
back Gen. Z. Taylor in half moon circle above
bust, qt. smooth edge, aqua, plain top, (c. 1850) 75.00 95.00

☐ **WASHINGTON**
Facing left in half moon circle above bust, in back
"Baltimore Glass Works" in ¾″ around monument, side 3 ribbed, pontil, plain top, pale blue
green, (c. 1840) 185.00 225.00

☐ **WASHINGTON—TAYLOR**
Washington facing left, in back Taylor facing left,
deep sapphire blue, pint 275.00 325.00

☐ Same as above, except yellow green, plain back,
double ring top 140.00 175.00

☐ **WASHINGTON**
Facing right, in ¾″ moon circle above bust unknown bust facing right, in ¾″ moon circle, above
bust Bridgetown, New Jersey, side 3 ribbed with
heavy medial rib, deep wine, pontil, plain top,
quart, (c. 1830) 1200.00 1400.00

☐ **WASHINGTON**
Facing right in half moon circle, bust, back Jackson facing left-half moon circle, bust ½ pint, pontil, plain top, conventry Glass Work, Conn., olive
amber, (c. 1840) 115.00 145.00

Price Range

☐ **WASHINGTON**
Facing right, fells, above bust below point, buck
Balto, below Monument, pontil, plain top, aqua,
quart, (c. 1840) 150.00 200.00

☐ **WESTFORD**
Eagle head turned to left, shield on breast, eagle
stands on large laurel wreath, above eagle "LIB-
ERTY," in back "Westford Glass Co. Westford,
Conn.," double ring top, pontil, olive amber, ½
pint 95.00 125.00

☐ **WESTFORD GLASS CO.**
In half circle, under it "WESTFORD, CONN.," reverse side a stack of wheat, green, pint 80.00 120.00

☐ **WHEELING, VA**
A bust facing to the right, in a horseshoe shape
"WHEAT PRICE & CO., WHEELING, VA.," reverse a building, around it "FAIRVIEW WORKS,"
sheared top, pontil, green 425.00 500.00

☐ **WHISKBROOM**
Clear, 7½″ 15.00 22.00

☐ **WHISKEY FLASK**
Quilt design, clear or amethyst, 8″ 12.00 18.00

☐ **WILL YOU TAKE A DRINK? WILL A DUCK
SWIM?**
Aqua, pint 150.00 175.00

☐ **WILLINGTON**
Eagle Flask, bright green, pint, (c. 1860–72) ... 100.00 130.00
☐ Same as above, except olive amber, ½ pint ... 100.00 130.00

☐ **WILLINGTON GLASS CO.**
West Willington, CT, on four lines, reverse eagle
and shield, under it a wreath, on shoulder "LIB-
ERTY," amber, pint 100.00 130.00

☐ **WINTER AND SUMMER FLASK**
Tree with leaves and a bird on right side, above
it "SUMMER," reverse side tree without leaves
and bird, above it "WINTER," tapered top, aqua,
quart and pint............................... 85.00 115.00
☐ Same as above, but with "Summer" on front and
"Winter" on back 75.00 95.00

☐ **ZANESVILLE CITY GLASS WORKS**
In oval panel, reverse plain, ring top, amber ... 100.00 130.00
☐ Same as above, except aqua 65.00 85.00

FOOD

Food bottles are defined as those made for commercial sale of all consumable food items, as well as cooking aids such as oil, but excluding beverages of most kinds.

This is one of the largest fields in bottle collecting, as well as one of the most diversified. It is, therefore, ideal for beginners. Since food bottles on the whole have not been heavily collected until recently, many are still underpriced in relation to scarcity and interest. Additionally, you will find that antique dealers—except for specialists—sometimes fail to realize the value of certain food bottles and price them very low.

The amateur historian, particularly, will enjoy food bottle collecting. The pages of 19th and early 20th century magazines, as well as newspapers, are filled with pictorial ads for the products sold in these bottles. Some food bottle collectors keep scrapbooks of these ads. They serve as an excellent source for placing approximate dates on specimens.

It was not considered wise to go to any great expense in making food bottles, since most customers were only interested in the contents and the lowest-priced brand was likely to be the best seller. Nevertheless, many very interesting and collectible specimens were created, because each manufacturer tried to make his bottles distinguishable from those of the competition. Certain shapes came to signify certain products. In time, these bottles began to carry slogans and/or advertising messages, either through embossing or (later) paper labels.

Peppersauce bottles were fashioned in the shape of Gothic cathedrals with arches and windows on each side. Most were made between 1860 and 1890, the earlier ones being pontil scarred. Apparently, the use of this motif relates to the popularity of peppersauce (hot sauce) in central Europe where Gothic architecture is common. These bottles are in shades of green. Tomato sauce bottles were made of clear glass.

Mustard jars came in various shapes. Differences include varying numbers of rings around the jar and sizes of jar mouths. Colors were green or clear. Older mustard jars have pontil scars. Some are embossed, as are some chili sauce bottles. One chili sauce bottle bears a Maltese cross.

Cooking oil was not commonly sold in bottles until 1890. The early specimens are tall and slim. A few are embossed, though embossing was largely discontinued at the turn of the century. Paper labels were not only less expensive, they could carry lengthy messages that would be impossible to emboss.

Though round bottles traveled better in shipments because they could withstand more pressure, manufacturers sometimes departed from the standard round shape. Pickle or chutney bottles were large and square. Spice bottles, too, were a risk in transit due to their concave front and back panels. Both early pickle and spice bottles have pontil scars.

Worcestershire sauce, originally made in Worcester, England, was as much in demand in the 19th century as today. C.W. Dyson Perrins, director of the Lea and Perrins sauce company, parlayed Worcestershire sauce into a great fortune—much of which he used to indulge his interest in art, antiques, and rare books. These bottles are quite common. Most are in shades of green.

Henry J. Heinz began manufacturing "Good Things for the Table" in 1869. This Pittsburgh, Pennsylvania company started on a small scale. Its goal was to instill public confidence in pre-packaged foodstuffs. One of the company's innovations was using clear glass instead of colored.

	Price Range	
☐ **A-1 SAUCE & CO.**		
Aqua, 7½"	3.00	5.00
☐ **THE ABNER ROYCE CO.**		
"The Abner Royce Co. Pure Fruit Flavor, Cleveland, Ohio" in back, clear, 5¼"	6.00	12.00
☐ **THE ABNER ROYCE CO.**		
Aqua, 5½"	6.00	9.00
☐ **A.E.B.B., PURE OLIVE, DEPOSE FRANCE**		
Aqua, 10"	3.50	5.00
☐ **A.G. 5 & CO.**		
4-Patented April 5, 1898, clear, quart	15.00	22.00
☐ **ALART & McGUIRE TRADEMARK "OK" PICKLES**		
Amber, 7"	6.00	9.00
☐ **ALART & McGUIRE**		
NY, under bottom, aqua, 5"	10.00	14.00
☐ **ALEXIS GODILLOT JEUNE**		
Bordeaux on back panel, eight panels, green, 6¼"	14.00	20.00

Price Range

☐ **AMERICAN GROCERY CO. PAT APP. FOR NY**
Under bottom, clear, 10″ **4.00 5.50**

☐ **ANCHOR**
Screw top, clear or amethyst, quart, 9″ **10.00 13.00**

☐ **ARMOUR AND COMPANY**
Chicago, in four lines on cathedral type panels, round corner, lady's leg neck, milk glass, 5¼″ **14.00 20.00**

☐ **ARMOUR & CO.**
Aqua, 4″ **3.50 5.00**

☐ **ARMOUR & CO.**
Milk glass, 5¼″ **12.00 16.00**

☐ **ARMOUR & CO. PACKERS**
Chicago, under bottom, milk glass, 2¼″ **3.00 4.00**

☐ **ARMOUR'S TOP NOTCH BRAND**
Chicago, under bottom, clear or amethyst, 5¾″ **9.00 13.00**

☐ **A-10**
Under bottom, clear or amethyst, 8″ **4.00 5.50**

☐ **BAKER'S**
Aqua, 4¾″ **5.00 7.00**

☐ **BAKER'S FLAVORING EXTRACTS, BAKER EXTRACTS CO.**
On one side "Strength & Purity," on the other side "Full Measure," machine made, clear **3.50 5.00**

☐ **BANQUET BRAND CHARLES GULDEN**
NY, on slug plate, flare lip, amethyst, 5⅛″ **4.50 5.75**

☐ **BARREL MUSTARD**
Plain, two rings on top, three on bottom, amethyst or clear, 4½″ **4.00 5.25**

☐ **BARREL MUSTARD**
Plain, three rings on top and bottom, clear or amethyst, 4½″ **4.00 5.25**

☐ **B.B.G. CO. 326**
Under bottom, clear or amethyst, 8″ **1.50 2.25**

☐ **B.B.G. CO. 78**
On bottom, clear or amethyst, 7½″ **2.60 3.40**

☐ **B & CO. LD. B**
13 under bottom, aqua, 8½″ **2.50 3.40**

☐ **B C CO.**
Clear or amethyst, 4½″ **5.00 7.00**

☐ **BECKER'S PURE HORSE-RADISH**
Buffalo, aqua, 4¼″ **10.00 14.00**

Price Range

☐ **B.F.B. CO. 109**
2845 on bottom, aqua, 8″ **2.50** **3.25**
☐ **B & FB CO.**
2445 under bottom, aqua, 8″ **2.50** **3.25**
☐ **BISHOP & COMPANY**
Under bottom, clear or amethyst, 5½″ **10.00** **14.00**
☐ **BISHOP & COMPANY**
On bottom, 14 vertical panels, ring at base, amethyst, 9¾″ **4.00** **6.00**
☐ Same as above, except 7⅝″ **4.00** **6.00**
☐ **B & L**
Embossed barrel, 5¼″ **15.00** **20.00**
☐ **A. BOOTH & CO.**
Baltimore, label, "Oyster Cocktail Catsup Salad Dressing" under bottom, clear or amethyst, 7½″ **4.00** **5.50**
☐ Same as above, except 6″ **1.50** **2.50**
☐ **BREAST PUMP**
Sheared top, clear, 4″ **5.00** **7.00**
☐ **H. B. BROOKS**
Amber, 10¼″ **20.00** **26.00**
☐ Same as above, except clear **7.00** **12.00**
☐ **B-33**
On bottom, aqua, 5″ **1.35** **2.30**
☐ **BURNETT'S STANDARD FLAVORING EXTRACTS**
In sunken panel, aqua, 5¼″ **2.75** **3.50**
☐ **BURNETT'S STANDARD FLAVORING EXTRACTS**
Long neck, medicine bottle type, clear or amethyst, 4½″ **5.00** **7.00**
☐ Same as above, except 5⅝″ **5.00** **7.00**
☐ **BWCA**
In monogram, eight panels, clear or amethyst, 10″ **4.00** **5.25**
☐ **JOSEPH CAMPBELL PRESERVE CO.**
Clear or amethyst, 8″ **5.00** **7.00**
☐ **CANDY BROS MFG. CO. CONFECTIONERS**
Label, aqua, 12″ **7.00** **9.00**
☐ **CANNON BOTTLE**
Amber or olive, 9½″ **30.00** **40.00**

Price Range

☐ **CAPER**
Plain, green, 6½" 10.00 14.00
☐ Same as above, except machine made 2.60 3.50
☐ **CAPER BOTTLES**
Several different sizes and colors, some em-
bossed, some not 12.00 18.00
☐ **CAPERS**
Eight indented panels in neck, two-ring top, three
sizes 14.00 20.00
☐ **DON CARLOS CYLINDER**
"Pat. June 19, 1894 N.Y." under bottom, clear,
5¼" 7.00 9.00
☐ **CATSUP**
Plain, clear or amethyst, 7½" 1.75 2.50
☐ **CATSUP**
Ten panels, amethyst or clear, 8" or 9¾" 3.50 5.00
☐ **CATSUP**
Ten panels, top and bottom panels alternate,
clear or amethyst, 10" 3.50 5.00
☐ **CATSUP**
Two mid-sections, ten panels, clear or amethyst,
8" 5.00 7.00
☐ **CATSUP**
Plain, tapered body, ring at shoulder, tapered
neck, ring top, clear or amethyst, 7½" 5.50 7.50
☐ **CATSUP**
Plain, clear or amethyst, 10" tall, 2½" diameter 6.00 8.00
☐ **CATSUP**
Label, 1600 on bottom, clear or amethyst, 10" 1.60 2.35
☐ **CATSUP**
Label, clear or amethyst, 9¾" 3.50 4.50
☐ **CATSUP**
Plain, clear or amethyst, 9" 9.00 13.00
☐ **CATSUP**
Plain, clear or amethyst, 8½" 6.00 8.50
☐ **CATSUP**
Label, 403 on bottom, clear or amethyst, 7½" 2.50 4.00
☐ **CATSUP**
Label, aqua, panels, 8" 8.00 11.00
☐ **CATSUP**
Plain, clear or amethyst, 8½" 6.00 8.00

Price Range

☐ **CATSUP**
Label, clear or amethyst, 10½" 6.00 8.00

☐ **CATSUP**
Label, swirl design, clear or amethyst, 8" 6.00 8.00

☐ **CATSUP**
Label, 10F under bottom, clear or amethyst ... 6.00 8.00

☐ **CATSUP**
Label, clear, 9½" 5.00 7.00

☐ **CATSUP AND PRESERVE BOTTLES**
Embossed 4.00 5.00

☐ **C B B**
Under bottom, aqua, 8" 5.00 7.00

☐ **C.B.K.**
And 1233 on bottom, aqua, 7¼" 3.00 4.00

☐ **C B W**
Under bottom, clear or amethyst, 10¼" 5.00 7.00

☐ **C & D**
Under bottom, aqua, 7¾" 12.00 18.00

☐ **CENTRAL MFG. COMPANY**
Clear or amethyst, 5" 5.00 7.00

☐ **CHAMPAGNE CATSUP**
Round, screw top, amethyst or clear, 7½" 3.50 5.00

☐ **CHAMPAGNE CATSUP**
Applied top, one ring, amethyst, 9¾" 4.00 5.50

☐ **CHAMPION VERMONT MAPLE SYRUP**
Label, clear or amethyst, 8½" 7.00 9.00

☐ **CHAMPION'S VINEGAR**
Aqua, 14½" 27.00 33.00

☐ **CHAMPION'S VINEGAR**
Aqua, 15½" 25.00 31.00

☐ **R.C. CHANCE'S SONS, TABLE TALK
KETCHUP**
Phila, label, clear or amethyst, 9¼" 6.00 8.00

☐ **CHERRY**
Label, B under bottom, clear, 4½" 2.00 2.50

☐ **CHERRY**
Plain, 33 and a star on bottom, clear or amethyst,
6¼" 2.00 2.50

☐ **CHERRY PICKLE**
Plain, clear or amethyst, 6" 2.00 2.50

Price Range

☐ **THE C.I. CO. LTD.**
This Trademark Registered, Maple Sap & Boiled Cider Vinegar, on front, East Ridge, NH, three rings near base, flint shoulder, tapered neck and ring top, cobalt, 11½" 35.00   45.00

☐ **THE J.M. CLARK PICKLE CO.**
Louisville, KY, round, clear, 5" 6.00   8.00

☐ **N.L. CLARK & CO., PERUVIAN SYRUP**
Aqua, 8½" 7.00   9.00

☐ **THE COOPERATIVE**
"Ideal Feeder" in three lines, in center of one side ounces table, other table spoon, oblong—bottle and turn up top, 6¼ long (English) 22.00   30.00

☐ **COTTAGE CHEESE**
Ten panels, clear or amethyst, 4½" 6.00   8.00

☐ **COURTENAY & CO.**
A & P under bottom, clear or amethyst, 7" 7.00   9.00

☐ **COURTENAY & CO.**
Clear or amber, 7" 5.00   7.00

☐ **C.R.B.**
Under bottom, label, aqua, 8" 4.00   6.00

☐ **CROWN**
Under bottom, pickle label, 14" 10.00   13.00

☐ **CRUIKSHANK BROS & CO.**
Allegheny, PA., under bottom, clear or amethyst, 8" 3.00   4.00

☐ **C.S. & CO. LD5302**
On bottom, eight panels, aqua, 6½" 3.00   4.00

☐ **CURTICE BROTHERS CO.**
"1613" under bottom, 8", 2¼" round, clear or amethyst 6.00   9.00

☐ **CURTICE BROS.**
Machine made, clear or amethyst, 10" 4.00   6.00

☐ **CURTICE BROS. CO.**
Preserves on the shoulders, ridges all around, amethyst or clear, 7¼" 4.00   6.00

☐ **CURTICE BROTHERS CO. PRESERVES**
ROCHESTER, NY, in circle on tapered neck, 8", 10½" or 12¼" 7.00   9.00

☐ **CURTIS BROS. PRESERVES**
Clear, 10½" or 12½" 7.00   9.00

Price Range

☐ **GEORGE M. CURTIS, PURE OLIVE OIL**
Clear, 17" **3.50** **5.50**
☐ **GEO. M. CURTIS, PURE OLIVE OIL**
Slim, round **2.00** **2.50**
☐ **CURTIS & MOORE**
Clear or amethyst, 2¼" x 2¼", 10" **9.00** **12.00**
☐ **DAVIS OK BAKING POWDER**
Round, aqua, 4½" **4.00** **6.00**
☐ **DAWSON'S PICKLES**
Ten panels, clear or amethyst, 7½" **5.00** **7.00**
☐ **D. & C.**
Pontil, clear or amethyst, 11½" **13.00** **17.00**
☐ **D. & CO**
Mustard, clear or amethyst, 4½" **3.00** **4.00**
☐ **DIXIE under bottom**
Clear, 7¾" **3.50** **5.50**
☐ **DODSON & HILS MFG CO.**
Aqua, 8" **5.00** **7.00**
☐ **DUNDEE**
Gray **9.00** **12.00**
☐ **J. DUPIT BORDEAUX ELIXIR DE SOULAC LES BAINS**
Amber, 3" **8.00** **11.00**
☐ **A. DURANT & FILS BORDEAUX**
Round, aqua and blue, 7⅛" **5.00** **7.00**
☐ Same as above, except no embossing, fancy .. **4.00** **6.00**
☐ **E. R. DURKEE & CO.**
NY, pontil, aqua, 4½" **20.00** **26.00**
☐ **E. R. DURKEE & CO. CHALLENGE SAUCE**
Sample, amethyst, 4" **7.00** **9.00**
☐ **E.R. DURKEE & CO. SALAD DRESSING**
NY, vertically, "Bottle Patented April 17, 1877"
on bottom, round, amethyst, 6½" **5.00** **7.00**
☐ **E.R. DURKEE & CO.**
NY, round, screw top, amethyst, 3½" **2.00** **3.00**
☐ **E.R. DURKEE & CO., SALAD DRESSING**
NY, round shoulder, "Patented April 17, 1877" on
the bottom, round, clear, 4½" or 7¾" **2.00** **3.00**
☐ **E.R. DURKEE & CO.**
New York, in vertical lines, clear or amethyst, 5",
6¾" or 8¼" **3.00** **4.00**

Price Range

☐ **E. R. DURKEE AND CO.**
Sheared top, eight panels, clear or amethyst, 4″   4.00   6.00

☐ **E. R. DURKEE & CO.**
Clear or amethyst, 6″ 7.00   9.00

☐ **E.R. DURKEE & CO.**
Clear or amethyst, 7″ 5.00   7.00

☐ **E. R. DURKEE & CO.**
Clear or amethyst, 1½″ diameter, 4″ 7.00   9.00

☐ **E.E. DYER & CO. EXTRACT OF COFFEE**
Boston, MA, graphite pontil, green, 6″ 35.00   45.00

☐ **E.H.V.B.**
Graphite pontil, six panels, light blue, 9½″ 45.00   56.00

☐ **EIFFEL TOWER LEMONADE**
"G. Foster Clark & Co. Manufacturer" on opposite side, clear, 2¾″ 4.00   6.00

☐ **CHARLES ELLIS SON & CO.**
Phila., aqua, 6″ 5.00   7.00

☐ **ENO'S FRUIT SALT**
"W" on bottom, 7″ tall, 1½″ x 2½″ 6.00   8.00

☐ **ESKAY'S**
"pat. J11-93 Albumenized 163 Food" on bottom, sheared top, amber, 7½″ 4.00   6.00

☐ **ESKAY'S**
"pat July 93 Albumenized 179 Food" on bottom, machine made, amber, 7½″ 4.00   6.00

☐ **EVANGELINE PEPPERSAUCE**
"Made in St. Martinville, La., U.S.A." on one side panel, twelve panels, tiny screw top, 5¼″ 3.00   4.00

☐ **EXTRACT TABASCO**
Under bottom, clear, 4¾″ 3.00   4.00

☐ **F**
In center of bottle, Refined pontil, clear, 5″ 9.00   13.00

☐ **FANCY OLIVE OIL**
Small base with five rings, six rings at shoulder, long bulbous neck, aqua, 7″ 7.00   9.00

☐ **F.G.W.**
Under bottom, clear, 7¾″ 4.00   6.00

☐ **J.A. FOLGER & CO.**
"Golden Gate High Grade Flavoring Extracts, 2 oz Full Measure" on front panel, rectangular, amethyst, 5½″ 3.00   4.00

Price Range

☐ **FOLGERS GOLDEN GATE FLAVORING**
On panel, rectangular, amethyst, 5¼″ 5.00   7.00
☐ **FORBES DELICIOUS FLAVORING EXTRACTS**
"Made by Forbes Bros. & Co, St. Louis" on front
panel, rectangular, clear, 4¾″ 5.00   7.00
☐ **4N**
Under bottom, clear or amethyst, 9¾″ 4.00   6.00
☐ **THE FRANK TEA & SPICE CO.**
Machine made, clear, 5½″ 4.00   6.00
☐ **FRANK TEA & SPICE CO**
Cincinnati, OH, Jumbo Peanut Butter, Made from
No. 1 Spanish and No. 1 VA Peanuts, Salt Added,
5 oz, embossed head of elephant, round ridges
on bottle, clear 4.00   6.00
☐ **LOUIT FRERES & CO. BORDEAUX**
Mustard barrel, three rings at base and shoulder,
crude ring collar, open pontil, amethyst, 4¾″ ..   6.00   9.00
☐ Same as above, except graphite pontil 17.00   24.00
☐ **G.A.J.**
Under bottom, sheared top, 7″ 4.00   6.00
☐ **GARRETTS FOOD PRODUCTS**
Garrett & Co. Inc. Monticello, NY, St. Louis Est.
U.S. Pat. Off., round, green, 10½″ and 12⅛″ ..   6.00   9.00
☐ **GEBHARDT EAGLE**
On the side panel, "chili powder" on the opposite
panel, eagle embossed on the front with trade-
mark, screw top, rectangular, clear or amethyst,
3½″ or 5½″ 6.00   12.00
☐ **THE M.A. GEDREY PICKLING CO.**
Aqua, 9¼″ 6.00   8.00
☐ **GIBBS**
B on bottom, clear or amethyst, 8¼″ 4.00   5.50
☐ **GOLDBERG-BOWEN & CO.**
Sierra Madre Olive Oil San Francisco, CA,
shaped like a gin bottle, flared collar, bulbous
type neck, amethyst, quart, 11¼″ 5.00   7.00
☐ **GOLDEN TREE PURE SYRUP**
Crown top, aqua, 11¼″ 4.00   5.50
☐ **THE GRADUATED NURSING BOTTLE**
Clear, 6¾″ 14.00   20.00

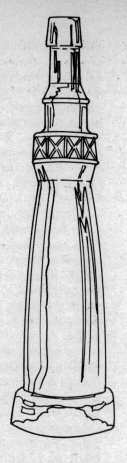

Left to Right: **Heinz's Chili Sauce,** *cylindrical bottle with rounded shoulders and thick, flared base, clear glass, $4.00–$6.00;* **Heinz Gold Medal Worcester Sauce,** *cylindrical bottle, long neck, glass stopper, clear glass, $5.00–$10.00;* **Skilton Foote & Co.,** *Bunker Hill Pickles, narrow body without the usual gothic cathedral arches, long neck, small mouth makes a narrow opening, thick, round base, green, 11½".* **$27.00–$35.00**

Price Range

☐ **GRAPE JUICE**
Plain, aqua, 6" 4.00 5.50

☐ **GRAPETTE PRODUCTS CO. CAMDEN ARK.**
Under bottom, ABM, clear, 7¼" 7.00 9.00

☐ **GRARY & CO**
Stag head on shoulder, "Worcestershire Sauce"
on side, a stag on neck, clear or amethyst 6.00 8.00

☐ **CHARLES GULDEN**
Clear or amethyst, 4¾" 4.00 5.50

☐ **CHAS. GULDEN**
"New York" on bottom, pickle jar, four large bulbous rings, flared collar, clear, 5½" 5.00 7.00

☐ **CHAS. GULDEN**
"16" under bottom, aqua or clear, 8½" 6.00 8.00

☐ **CHAS. GULDEN**
New York, four rings on base, three on shoulder,
mustard barrel, amethyst, 4⅝" 5.00 7.00

☐ **CHAS. GULDEN**
NY, under bottom, clear, 4¼" 6.00 9.00

☐ **CHAS. GULDEN**
NY, under bottom, clear or amethyst, 4¼" 4.00 5.50

☐ **H**
Under bottom, clear, 4½" 3.00 4.00

☐ **HALFORD LEIGESTERSHINE**
Aqua, 7⅛" 3.00 4.00

☐ **HANANC**
Aqua, 6" 5.00 7.00

☐ **THOMAS L. HARDIN CO.**
Clear or amethyst, 7" 6.00 9.00

☐ **GEO. HARM**
"This Bottle To Be Washed and Returned, Not
To Be Bought Or Sold" on back, clear, quart .. 13.00 20.00

☐ **H.J. HEINZ CO. NO. 37 GOTHIC
HORSERADISH**
Aqua, 6" 3.50 5.00

☐ **H.J. HEINZ CO.**
On bottom, also large notch on bottom, 18 panels, round, clear, 8¾" 5.00 7.00

☐ **H.J. HEINZ CO.**
"Patent" on the bottom, eight panels, amethyst,
9¼" 5.00 7.00

Price Range

☐ **H.J. HEINZ CO. 69 PATD.**
Under bottom, clear, 6″ 6.00   9.00
☐ **H.J. HEINZ CO.**
"Patd" under bottom, ten panels, clear or ame-
thyst, 4¾″ 4.00   5.50
☐ **H.J. HEINZ CO.**
"7 Patented" and an "X" on bottom, clear or am-
ethyst, 8¼″ 4.00   5.50
☐ **HEINZ**
Clear or amethyst, 6″ 5.00   7.00
☐ **HEINZ**
"No. 28" under bottom, aqua, 7¼″ 3.00   4.00
☐ **HEISEY RELISH**
Label, eight panels, lead glass, clear or amethyst,
4″ 6.00   8.00
☐ **HERB JUICE**
On panel, rectangular, clear, 8⅜″ 4.00   5.50
☐ **HILL'S**
Label, machine made, L.B. CO monogram on
back, aqua, 11″ 7.00   9.00
☐ **HIRES IMPROVED ROOT BEER**
Panel, "Mfg. by The Charles Hires Co.," panel,
"Philadelphia, PA, U.S.A.," panel, "Make Five
Gallons of a Delicious Drink," aqua, 4¾″ 5.00   7.00
☐ **HOLBROOK & CO.**
P.B. on bottom, aqua, 7½″ 4.50   5.50
☐ **HOLBROOK & CO.**
Aqua, 4½″ 6.00   9.00
☐ **HOLBROOK & CO.**
R.B.B. under bottom, aqua, 8¾″ 12.00   16.00
☐ **HONEY**
Clear or amethyst, 8″ 10.00   14.00
☐ **HONEYWELL**
Sauce type bottle, rolled lip, concave panels,
front and back, three concave on sides, open
pontil, aqua, 6¾″ 17.00   25.00
☐ **HORLICK'S TRADEMARK**
Racine, WI., Malted Milk M.M. U.S.A. 1 Gal.
round, clear, 10¾″ 3.00   4.00
☐ **HORLICK'S**
Twice on shoulders, round, screw top, clear, 2¾″   1.60   2.50

Price Range

☐ **HORLICK'S**
Clear or amethyst, 5" 3.50 5.00

☐ **HORLICK'S**
Aqua, different sizes 3.50 5.00

☐ **HORTON-CATO MFG CO**
DETROIT, MI, in three lines, three round panels,
on bottom T.P., clear, 5½" 6.00 9.00

☐ **HORTON-CATO CO.**
Clear, 7" 4.00 5.50

☐ **HORTON-CATO & CO.**
Detroit, MI, reverse side "Crown Celery Salt,"
gold, 8" 22.00 30.00

☐ **HORTON-CATO MFG. CO.**
"Detroit, MI," under bottom, clear, 6" 4.00 6.00

☐ **J.W. HUNNEWELL & CO.**
On side, "Boston" on opposite side, three con-
cave panels, aqua, 1½" 4.00 5.50
☐ Same as above, except aqua green 6.00 8.00

☐ **H.W.P. 394**
Under bottom, sheared top, clear, 6" 5.00 7.00

☐ **HYMAN PICKLE CO.**
"Louisville, KY" under bottom, yellow, 8" 6.00 8.00

☐ **INDIA PACKING CO.**
Portland, OR, moon in center, aqua, 6" 9.00 13.00

☐ **JELLY**
Label, "Patented June 9-03 June 23 03" under
bottom, clear, 3½" 3.00 4.00

☐ **JELLY**
Label, 2 under bottom, clear or amethyst, 4¾" 1.00 4.00

☐ **JELLY**
Label, sheared top, 2¼" 3.00 4.00

☐ **JELLY**
Label, "Patented June 9-03 June 23 03" under
bottom, clear or amethyst, 2½" 3.00 4.00

☐ **JOSLYN'S MAPLE SYRUP**
Eight sides, ground lip, aqua, 8" 6.00 9.00

☐ **J.P.S.**
Under bottom, clear or amethyst, 7¼" 3.00 4.00

☐ **J.P.S.**
Under bottom, pickles, green, 6" 6.00 9.00

☐ **J.P.S.**
Under bottom, green, 6" 6.00 9.00

Price Range

☐ **J.P.S.**
Under bottom, clear or amethyst, 5" 4.00 5.00

☐ **J. Wm JUNKINS CATSUP**
Baltimore, MD clear or amethyst, 8" 12.00 16.00

☐ **KELLOGGS**
On base, oval, clear, 4¼", 6" or 7" 2.00 3.00

☐ **KEPLER**
On four sides on shoulder, tapered bottle, ring
top, under bottom "Snowhill RW&CO," London,
green, 1¾" x 2¼", 1¼" neck, 5¼" 9.00 13.00

☐ Same as above, except no Kepler on shoulder,
7½" tall, 2¼" x 3¼" 10.00 14.00

☐ **KARL KIEFER PAT**
In glass lid to fit pickle bottle, round, amethyst or
clear, 6" 5.00 7.00

☐ **KITCHEN BOUQUET**
On bottom, round, ABM, aqua, 5¾" 3.00 4.00

☐ **LAM A & F**
Under bottom, green, 9¼" 17.00 25.00

☐ **LAMP CANDY BOTTLE**
Aqua, 3" 6.00 9.00

☐ **LEA & PERRINS**
"J10D,S" on bottom, aqua, 11½" 4.00 5.50

☐ Same as above, except 8½" 4.00 5.50

☐ Same as above, except 7¼" 3.00 4.00

☐ **LEA & PERRINS**
Worcestershire sauce, blue, 7" 1.00 3.00

☐ **LEVER BROS. CO.**
New York, label, amber, 10" 9.00 13.00

☐ **LINCOLN BANK BOTTLE**
On base, "Pat 1959 Lincoln Foods Inc. Lawrance
Mass 3-17-3" under bottom, clear, 8½" 11.00 15.00

☐ **LIPTON**
Number on bottom, aqua, 8½" 5.00 7.00

☐ **JOSHUA LONGFIELD**
North of England Sauce around shoulder, aqua,
7" 6.00 9.00

☐ **LONG SYRUP REFINING CO.**
San Francisco, CA, wine color, 4¾" 7.00 9.00

☐ **LUNDBORG**
Clear or amethyst, 2½" 4.00 5.00

Price Range

□ **E.G. LYONS & RAAS CO.**
Clear or amethyst, 4" 6.00 8.00
□ **M**
Under bottom, amber, 6½" 6.00 9.00
□ **MANDER WEAVER & CO.**
Cream crock, 4" 10.00 13.00
□ **MANSFIELD DAIRY**
Clear, quart.............................. 11.00 15.00
□ **SGDG GRAND MARNIER**
On back, snap on, machine made, light amber,
6" 13.00 19.00
□ **D. MAURER & SON**
Under bottom, 3" 3.00 4.00
□ **F.E. McALLISTER'S**
Aqua, 7" 4.00 5.00
□ **McCORMICK & CO. SPICE GRINDERS**
Baltimore, MD, eight panels, sheared top, clear
or amethyst, 3¾" 4.50 6.50
□ **McCORMICK & CO., EXTRACTS, SPICES & ETC.**
Baltimore, MD, clear, 4½" 4.50 6.50
□ **McCORMICK & CO.**
Baltimore, MD, triangular, clear, 3½" 4.50 6.50
□ **McCORMICK & CO.**
Clear or amethyst, 4¾" 5.00 7.00
□ **McCORMICK & CO.**
Clear, 5¼" 4.00 5.50
□ **McCORMICK & CO.**
Round, aqua, 5¼" 4.00 5.50
□ **McILHENNY CO.**
Avery Island, LA, clear or amethyst, 8" 6.00 8.00
□ **McILHENNY CO.**
Avery Island, LA, swirl pattern, clear, 8" 12.00 18.00
□ **MELLINS FOOD, FREE SAMPLE**
P on bottom, aqua, 3¾" 4.25 5.00
□ **MENLEY-JAMES LIMITED**
"N.Y.," London on bottom, milk glass, 1¾" ... 3.00 4.00
□ **M&M**
On one line, "T" in center, "CO" on bottom line,
pumpkin seed type bottle, clear, 3¾" 3.50 5.00

Price Range

☐ **MOUTARDE DIAPHANE / LOUIT FRERES & CO.**
Mustard barrel, three rings at base and shoulders, crude ring collar, graphite pontil, amethyst, 5″   16.00   24.00

☐ Same as above, except clear 14.00   20.00

☐ **MUSKOGEE WHO. GRO. CO.**
Clear, 8¼″ 5.00   7.00

☐ **MUSTARD**
Label, clear or amethyst, 4½″ 3.00   4.00

☐ **MUSTARD**
Label, small kick-up, six-part mold, clear or amethyst, 5½″ 3.00   4.00

☐ **MUSTARD**
Label, "Patented" under bottom, twelve panels, clear or amethyst, 4¾″ 3.00   4.00

☐ **MUSTARD BARREL**
Plain, three rings at top and bottom, sheared top, clear or amethyst, 1¾″ round 5.00   7.00

☐ Same as above, except no sheared top, 4½″ ..   3.50   5.50

☐ **MY WIFE'S SALAD DRESSING**
Machine made, blue green, 8″ 6.00   9.00

☐ **BIBO NEWMAN & KENBERG**
BNI monogram, San Francisco, CA, round, ring collar, clear, 5¼″ 6.00   9.00

☐ **NUT HOUSE**
Figure of house and other writing, store jar, ball shape, clear 14.00   20.00

☐ **OLD DUFFY'S 1842 5 YEAR OLD APPLE JUICE VINEGAR**
On top shoulder, "Duffy's" in diamond shape and 1842 in circle on neck, eight panels, amber, 6¾″   17.00   25.00

☐ **OLIVE OIL**
Long neck, ring collar, graphite pontil, light aqua, 12½″ 10.00   14.00

☐ **OLIVE OIL**
Plain, old flared lip, round with tapered neck, aqua, 11¼″ 6.00   9.00

☐ **OLIVE OIL**
Plain, three-part mold, flat ring top, under bottom, sunken circle, cobalt, 4¼″ tapered body, 2½″ neck 12.00   16.00

	Price Range	

☐ **OLIVE OIL**
Amber, 1½″ round, 6¼″ tall, 2½″ neck **4.50 5.50**

☐ **OLIVE OIL**
Slim, bulbous neck, clear or aqua, three sizes,
7¼″ to 12½″ **6.00 8.00**

☐ **OLIVE OIL**
Label, aqua, 7½″ **5.00 7.00**

☐ **OLIVE OIL**
Aqua, 10¼″ **3.00 5.00**

☐ **OLIVE OIL**
Free-blown, pontil, small kick-up, aqua, 10″ ... **13.00 19.00**

☐ **OLIVE OIL**
Label, clear, 6½″ **3.00 4.00**

☐ **OLIVE OIL**
Label, kick-up, aqua, 12¾″ **8.00 11.00**

☐ **OLIVE OIL**
Label, clear or amethyst, 8″ **4.00 5.00**

☐ **OLIVE OIL**
Aqua, 10″ **5.00 7.00**

☐ **OLIVE OIL**
Label, clear or amethyst, 5½″ **3.00 4.00**

☐ **OLIVE OIL**
Label, free-blown, pontil, aqua, 13½″ **17.00 24.00**

☐ **OLIVE OIL**
Label, free-blown, pontil, aqua, 10″ **17.00 24.00**

☐ **OLIVE OIL**
Label, applied ring top, deep kick-up, aqua, 9½″ **6.00 9.00**

☐ **J. M. OLIVER & SONS**
On blob seal, Olive oil, aqua, 7″ **6.00 9.00**

☐ **F.A. OSTEN'S PURE SALAD OIL**
Eight-ring top, long neck, flared bottom, aqua .. **8.00 11.00**

☐ **PARKER BROS.**
Vertically, on shoulder, "London Club Sauce,"
crude top, round, aqua, 7¼″ **6.00 9.00**

☐ **PASKOLA'S, THE PRE-DIGESTED FOOD
CO., TRADEMARK**
Embossed Pineapple, amber, 6″ **6.00 9.00**

☐ **PEPPERMINT**
Marble in center of neck, aqua, 7¼″ **10.00 13.00**

☐ **PEPPERSAUCE**
20 rings around bottle, round, space for label,
clear or aqua, 6¼″ **9.00 13.00**

E.R. Durkee & Co., embossed gauntlet on front of bottle, round bottle with screw top, clear or amethyst. **$4.00–$6.00**

Planters Peanuts, peanut shaped bottle, glass top with peanut nob, clear. **$40.00–$55.00**

Price Range

☐ **PEPPERSAUCE**
22 rings around bottle, space for label, oval, clear
or aqua, 7″ 9.00 13.00

☐ **PEPPERSAUCE**
Tooled lip, smooth base, green, 7¾″ 32.00 42.00

☐ **PEPPERSAUCE**
Tooled lip, smooth base, aqua, 7¾″ 32.00 42.00

☐ **PEPPERSAUCE**
Tooled lip, smooth base, blue, 7¾″ 32.00 42.00

☐ **PEPPERSAUCE**
Tooled lip, smooth base, aqua, 8¼″ 32.00 42.00

☐ **PEPPERSAUCE**
Tooled lip, smooth base, amethyst, 8¼″ 32.00 42.00

☐ **PEPPERSAUCE**
Tooled lip, smooth base, green, 8½″ 13.00 18.00

☐ **PEPPERSAUCE**
Tooled lip, smooth base, aqua, 8½″ 13.00 18.00

☐ **PEPPERSAUCE**
Tooled lip, smooth base, blue, 8½″ 13.00 18.00

☐ **PEPPERSAUCE**
Cathedral, gothic arch in lower half of six panels
two windows in upper half of each panel, aqua,
8½″ 20.00 26.00

☐ **PEPPERSAUCE**
Cathedral design, hexagon, 8¾″ 22.00 32.00

☐ **PEPPERSAUCE**
Cathedral design, pontil scars, hexagon, aqua,
8¾″ 53.00 73.00

☐ **PEPPERSAUCE**
Cathedral design, pontil scars, hexagon, gray,
8¾″ 53.00 73.00

☐ **PEPPERSAUCE**
Cathedral design, square, aqua, 8¾″ 22.00 32.00

☐ **PEPPERSAUCE**
Clear, 8″ 8.00 11.00

☐ **PEPPERSAUCE**
Amethyst, 19 rings, 6″ 4.00 6.00

☐ **PEPPERSAUCE**
Label, "X" on bottom, aqua, 9″ 10.00 13.00

☐ **PEPPERSAUCE**
Clear or amethyst, 1½″ square, 6½″ 10.00 13.00

Price Range

☐ **PEPPERSAUCE**
Aqua, 8" 2.25 4.25

☐ **PEPPERSAUCE**
Label, aqua, 7" 5.00 7.00

☐ **PEPPERSAUCE**
Label, aqua, 10½" 10.00 14.00

☐ **PEPPERSAUCE**
Clear, 6¼" 2.00 4.00

☐ **PEPPERSAUCE**
Label, "NYMM" and monogram under bottom,
aqua 10.00 14.00

☐ **PEPPERSAUCE**
Clear, 10" 14.00 18.00

☐ **PEPPERSAUCE**
Label, leaded glass, clear or amethyst, 7¼" ... 6.00 9.00

☐ **PEPPERSAUCE**
Label, swirl pattern, clear or amethyst, 8½" ... 6.00 8.00

☐ **PEPPERSAUCE**
Fifteen rings, cathedral type, "G.C.O. Pat. Sept
26, 1875" on base, double ring top, aqua, 8½" 20.00 26.00

☐ **PEPPERSAUCE**
Clear, 22 rings, 8" 4.25 6.25

☐ **PEPPERSAUCE**
Label, "C & B" on base, clear or amethyst, 7½" 14.00 20.00

☐ **PEPPERSAUCE**
Label, "D.E." under bottom, aqua, 8" 6.00 10.00

☐ **PEPSINE CHAPOTEAUT**
Ten panels, clear or amethyst, 3½" 4.00 5.00

☐ **PEPTOGENIC MILK POWDER**
Around shoulder, machine made, tin measure
top, amber, 5¾" 5.00 7.00

☐ **PHOENIX BRAND**
Machine made, clear, 6" 5.00 7.00

☐ **PICKLE**
Cathedral design, cobalt, ½" square, 5½" 34.00 44.00

☐ **PICKLE**
Cathedral design, smooth base, square, aqua,
7¼" 110.00 160.00

☐ **PICKLE**
Cathedral design, smooth base, square, aqua,
7¾" 110.00 160.00

Price Range

☐ **PICKLE**
Cathedral design, square, aqua, 8½″ 65.00 85.00

☐ **PICKLE**
Cathedral design, square, green, 11″ 400.00 450.00

☐ **PICKLE**
Cathedral design with clock, square, green, 11″ 340.00 400.00

☐ **PICKLE**
Cathedral design, smooth base, square, blue
green, 11½″ 360.00 435.00

☐ **PICKLE**
Cathedral design, smooth base, hexagon, blue
green, 12¾″ 420.00 500.00

☐ **PICKLE**
Cathedral design, smooth base, hexagon, aqua,
13″ 160.00 200.00

☐ **PICKLE**
Label, cathedral design, blue green, 13½″ 90.00 120.00

☐ **PICKLE**
Cathedral design, smooth base, square, aqua,
13½″ 120.00 150.00

☐ **PICKLE**
Cathedral design, smooth base, square, green,
13½″ 485.00 550.00

☐ **PICKLE**
Cathedral design, smooth base, square, green,
13¾″ 500.00 550.00

☐ **PICKLE**
Cathedral design, smooth base, square, aqua,
14″ 400.00 450.00

☐ **PICKLE**
Plain, paneled corner, tapered neck, yellow, 2½″
square, 7¼″ 14.00 20.00

☐ Same as above, except no panel, under bottom
"Pat. Apr 4 1882, Heinz 16" in circle, aqua 5.00 7.00

☐ **PICKLE**
Label, clear or amethyst, 3¾″ square, 13½″ .. 6.00 9.00

☐ **PICKLE**
Label, machine made, 165 under bottom, clear
or amethyst, 7″ 3.00 4.00

☐ **PICKLE**
Label, pontil, aqua, 10″ 13.00 19.00

Price Range

☐ **PICKLE**
Label, broken pontil, aqua, 7¼" 75.00   95.00

☐ **PICKLE**
Label, kick-up, pontil, aqua, 8½" 21.00   30.00

☐ **PICKLE**
Label, "W.T. & CO." under bottom, aqua, 6¼"   2.00   3.00

☐ **PICKLE**
Label, aqua, 8¼" 5.00   7.00

☐ **PICKLE**
Label, aqua, 6½" 4.00   5.00

☐ **PICKLE**
Label, green, 11" 6.00   8.00

☐ **PICKLE**
Label, clear or amethyst, 6¾" 8.00   11.00

☐ **PICKLE**
Label, small kick-up, aqua, 9" 7.00   10.00

☐ **PICKLE**
Label, clear or amethyst, 7½" 4.00   5.00

☐ **PICKLE**
Label, "Patented Aug. 20, 1901" under bottom,
clear or amethyst, 7" 2.00   3.00

☐ **PICKLE**
Label, "Pat Applied For #16" under bottom,
clear, 11¼" 5.00   7.00

☐ **PICKLE**
Label, "Pat July 11th 1893" under bottom,
sheared top, clear, 7" 4.00   5.50

☐ **PICKLE**
Label, 3 under bottom, aqua, 3½" 6.00   9.00

☐ **PICKLE**
Label, sheared top, clear or amethyst, 5" 5.00   7.00

☐ **PICKLE**
Label, sheared top, aqua, 12¾" 22.00   30.00

☐ **PICKLE**
Label, aqua, 10½" 8.00   12.00

☐ **PICKLE**
Label, clear or amethyst, 5" 6.00   8.00

☐ **PICKLE**
Label, small kick-up, green, 7½" 14.00   20.00

☐ **PICKLE**
Label, eight panels, clear or amethyst, 6½" . . .   4.00   5.50

Price Range

☐ **PICKLE**
Label, amber, 6¾" 14.00 18.00

☐ **PICKLE**
Label, clear, 7" 6.00 9.00

☐ **PICKLE**
Label, clear or amethyst, 11" tall, 2½" x 3¼" 6.00 9.00

☐ **PICKLE**
Label, green, 5½" 5.00 7.00

☐ **PICKLE**
Label, ten panels, clear or amethyst, 10¼" ... 4.00 5.50

☐ **PICKLE**
"AM" on bottom, clear 3.50 4.50

☐ **PICKLE**
Label, "Pat Apr. 20, 1901" on bottom, clear or
amethyst, 8¼" 3.50 4.50

☐ **PICKLE**
Label, "Pat O.P. 1900" on bottom, clear or amethyst, 6" 4.50 5.50

☐ **PICKLE**
Label, sunken bottom, aqua, 2½" diameter, 9" 4.00 5.50

☐ **PICKLE**
Label, aqua, 8½" 8.00 11.00

☐ **PICKLE**
Label, pontil, aqua, 9" 1.00 10.00

☐ **PICKLE**
Label, clear, 4½" 4.50 5.50

☐ **PICKLE**
Label, broken pontil, aqua, 6½" 19.00 25.00

☐ **PICKLE**
Label, improved pontil, amber, 10" 30.00 37.00

☐ **PICKLE**
Label, sheared top, green, 3¼" 5.00 7.00

☐ **PICKLE**
Label, small kick-up, amber, 7½" 6.00 9.00

☐ **PICKLE**
Label, four side panels, pontil, aqua, 6¼" 30.00 37.00

☐ **PICKLE**
Label, green, 8½" 6.00 9.00

☐ **PICKLE**
Label, "Pat. App. For" under bottom, aqua, 9¼" 8.00 11.00

☐ **PICKLE**
Label, pontil, aqua, 7½" 15.00 22.00

Price Range

☐ **PICKLE**
Label, three-piece mold, light blue, 12″ 6.00 9.00

☐ **PICKLE**
Label, aqua, 9″ 4.00 5.50

☐ **PICKLE**
Label, ten panels halfway down, small kick-up,
aqua, 12″ 6.00 9.00

☐ **PICKLE or CHERRY**
Label, "Pat. App. For" under bottom, clear or amethyst, 5″ 5.50 8.00

☐ **PICKMAN'S CHOCOLATE**
Machine made, aqua 4.00 5.50

☐ **PIN MONEY**
Clear, 5¼″ 6.00 9.00

☐ **E. D. PINAUD**
Aqua, 2¼″ 5.00 7.00

☐ **PLANTERS**
Same in back, peanut figures on each corner,
glass top with a peanut nob, clear 82.00 115.00

☐ **PLANTERS**
Same in back, square, glass top with peanut
nobs, clear 30.00 40.00

☐ **PLANTERS**
Same in back on base, glass top with peanut nob,
clear 43.00 53.00

☐ **PLANTERS**
Same in back on base, glass top with peanut nob,
clear 22.00 30.00

☐ **PLANTERS**
On shoulder, "PENNANT 5c SALTED PEA-
NUTS" on front, on each side a Planters Peanut
Man figure, glass top with peanut nob, clear ... 55.00 70.00

☐ **PLANTERS SALTED PEANUTS**
Same in back, glass top with peanut nob, clear 43.00 53.00

☐ **P/P CO.**
Under bottom, clear, 1¾″ diameter, 5″ 3.00 5.00

☐ **DR. PRICE'S**
Clear or amethyst, 5¾″ 3.00 4.00

☐ **PRICE-BOOKER MFG. CO.**
Clear or amethyst, 8″ 5.00 7.00

☐ **PRIDE OF LONG ISLAND**
Clear or amethyst, 9¾″ 5.00 7.00

Price Range

☐ **POMPEIAN BRAND VIRGIN LUCCA OLIVE OIL**

In four lines, aqua, 7½″ 5.00 7.00

☐ Same as above, except other sizes 5.00 7.00

☐ **THE POTTER PARLIN CO.**

Under bottom, sheared top, clear or amethyst, 4″ 6.00 8.00

☐ **PRIMROSE SALAD OIL WESTERN MEAT CO.**

Vertically on one panel, aqua, 9½″ 5.00 7.50

☐ Same as above, except quart 6.00 8.00

☐ **PURE OLIVE OIL S.S.P.**

Bulb shaped base, long neck, amethyst, 7¼″ 5.00 7.50

☐ **QUERUS**

Pontil, aqua, 5¼″ 22.00 30.00

☐ **RADISH**

Label, eight panels, clear or amethyst 5.00 7.00

☐ **RADISH**

Label, ten panels, clear, 4½″ 3.50 4.50

☐ **RADISH**

Label, square on bottom, clear or amethyst, 7″ 4.00 5.25

☐ **RADISH**

Label, 2 on bottom, sheared top, clear or amethyst, 10¾″ 5.00 7.00

☐ **RADISH**

Label, green, 5½″ 4.00 5.25

☐ **RADISH**

Label, clear or amethyst, 9½″ 3.00 4.00

☐ **RADISH**

Label, clear or amethyst, 5¼″ 3.00 5.00

☐ **RADISH**

Label, Pat April 2nd, 1901 under bottom, clear or amethyst, 5½″ 4.00 5.00

☐ **RADISH**

Label, ribbed base, clear or amethyst, 7½″ ... 4.00 5.00

☐ **RADISH**

Label, eight panels, clear or amethyst, 6½″ ... 4.00 5.00

☐ **RADISH**

Label, "169" under bottom, clear or amethyst, 8¾″ 3.00 4.00

☐ **RADISH**

Label, clear or amethyst, 6″ 3.50 5.00

Price Range

☐ **RADISH**
Label, clear or amethyst, 5¾" 3.50 5.00
☐ **RADISH**
Label, "56S" in triangle under bottom, clear, 4½" 3.00 4.00
☐ **RED SNAPPER SAUCE CO.**
Memphis, TN, six sides, clear, 9½" 9.00 13.00
☐ **RED SNAPPER**
Clear or amethyst, 7½" 4.50 5.50
☐ **RESTORFF & BETTMANN**
"NY," under bottom, light green, 4½" 5.00 7.00
☐ **RESTORFF & BETTMANN F.F.**
"NY" under bottom, Mustard, aqua, 4½" 6.00 9.00
☐ **R.J. RITTER CONSERVE CO.**
Under bottom, clear, 8¼" or 10½" 6.00 8.00
☐ **ROWAT & CO.**
Same in back, light green, 10" 6.00 9.00
☐ **ROYAL IUNCHEON CHEESE**
Milk glass, 2½" 3.00 4.00
☐ **ROYAL LUNCHEON CHEESE**
Under bottom, milk glass, 3" 3.00 4.00
☐ **SALAD DRESSING**
Label, clear or amethyst, 6¼" 5.00 7.00
☐ **M. SALZMAN CO., PURITY ABOVE ALL**
855 under bottom, amber, 10½" 13.00 19.00
☐ **SAUCE**
Round, tapered neck, sixteen concave vertical
panels all around, aqua, 8" 6.00 9.00
☐ **SAUCE**
Coffin shape, ring on base and top of neck, clear,
8¼" 4.00 5.00
☐ **SAUCE**
Olive oil shape, round, tapered neck, graduated
collar, pontil, aqua, 5¾" 10.00 13.00
☐ **SAUCE**
Square, tapered neck, sixteen rings, sunken
panel on front, aqua, 8⅜" 5.00 7.00
☐ **SAUCE**
Tapered neck, 23 rings, oval, sunken panel on
front, ABM, aqua, 8" 4.00 5.50

Price Range

☐ **SAUCE**
Triangular, tapered neck, diamond shape down center on all three sides, crude collar, amethyst, 8¾" 6.00 8.00

☐ **SKILTON FOOTE & COS., BUNKER HILL PICKLES**
Light olive, 11½" 27.00 35.00

☐ **SKILTON FOOTE & COS., BUNKER HILL PICKLES**
In outer ring, picture of pickle barrels, trees, fence, tower, all in center, round, aqua, 6⅜" .. 8.00 11.00

☐ Same as above, except gold, 7½" 17.00 23.00

☐ **SNOWHILL B.W. & CO.**
"London" on bottom, amber, 6½" 4.00 5.50

☐ **SOCIETE HYGIENIQUE, NO. 5 RUE J.J. ROUSSEAU**
"Paris" vertically around bottle, cylindrical, graphite pontil, clear, 6⅜" 20.00 26.00

☐ **STRONG COBB & CO.**
Cleveland, OH, "Pure Concentrated Flavoring Extracts" embossed, clear, 6½" 6.00 8.00

☐ **TILLMANN'S**
In small panel at top, star with "T" in center in circular panel, "OIL" in square panel at base, square, aqua, 8" 6.00 8.00

☐ **TABASCO or DRY FOOD**
Wide mouth, 2½" opening, pontil, dark green, 7½" 27.00 35.00

☐ **TOURNADES KITCHEN BOUQUET**
Clear or amethyst, 5¼" 4.00 5.50

☐ **TRAPPEY'S TABASCO PEPPERS**
On center panels, vertical panels on upper and lower half, four large rings divide the panels, crown top, oval, ABM, clear, 6¾" 4.00 5.50

☐ **WILLIAM UNDERWOOD & COMPANY**
Around bottom, aqua, 10" 12.00 16.00

☐ **U. S. NAVY**
Pepper, eight panels, aqua 17.00 22.00

☐ **VALENTINES**
Amber, 3¼" 6.00 9.00

☐ **V.D. CO.**
Pat April 27, 1875 under bottom, aqua, 7" 6.00 9.00

	Price Range	

☐ **VINEGAR**
Label, milk glass, 5½ " 6.00   9.00
☐ **VIRGINIA FRUIT JUICE CO., NORFOLK, VA.**
In script on front, machine made, tenpin shape,
clear or amethyst, 7½ " 4.00   5.50
☐ **M.T. WALLACE & CO. PROP. BROOKLYN
N.Y.**
Brasst's Purifying Extract 1850, pontil, aqua, 9½ "   42.00   53.00
☐ **WM. R. WARNER & CO.**
Clear, 8¼ " 8.00   11.00
☐ **WARSAW PICKLE CO.**
Aqua, 8¾ " 8.00   11.00
☐ **WATERS BROS. OLIVE OIL AND
EXTRACTS, OAKLAND, CAL.**
Round, light aqua, 11½ " 6.00   9.00
☐ **WDS N.Y.**
Graphite pontil, dark green, 8" 45.00   57.00
☐ **C. WEISBECKER, MANHATTAN MARKET,
NEW YORK**
Pickle jar, corner panels, square, ring on neck,
square collar, aqua, 6¼ " 6.00   9.00
☐ **WELLCOME CHEMICAL WORKS**
Under bottom, "Kepler" around top, machine
made, amber, 6½ " 4.00   5.50
☐ **THE J. WELLER CO.**
Clear or amethyst, 7½ " 6.00   8.00
☐ **WELLS & RICHARDSON CO.**
"Cereal Milk" on each side, amber, 7¾ " 10.00   13.00
☐ **H. WICKERT**
Aqua, 7¼ " 6.00   9.00
☐ **THE WILLIAMS BROS CO.**
Pickle label, clear, 7½ " 4.00   5.00
☐ **WOOD COOPER PURE OLIVE OIL**
Santa Barbara, CA inside of crude blob seal on
shoulder, band collar, round, aqua, 11" 6.00   9.00

FRUIT JARS

Fruit jars, as defined by collectors, are jars originally sold empty, intended for use in home preservation of foodstuffs.

During the 1800s when many kinds of foodstuffs were not available from stores in a preserved state, home canning served an important purpose. Many varieties of fruit jars are available to the collector, ranging from the mid 19th century to recent date. They are distinctively different in character than most other kinds of bottles since they carry no product name or advertising. However, they cannot be termed "plain," as the bottle maker's name is usually in large lettering along with (sometimes) the patent date. Ornamental motifs on fruit jars are not common, but will be encountered on some. There are also specimens on which the maker's name appears in artistic lettering. When grouped together as a collection, they can make a handsome display. Prices are still very modest, on the whole, for fruit jars. Excellent buys will be found by anyone touring the flea markets, garage sales and thrift stores. Another plus in their favor is that fruit jars haven't been extensively copied, hence there is little danger of acquiring reproductions.

The origin of fruit jars dates to the 18th century. The problem of preserving perishable foodstuffs seemed to be unsolvable for generations. Food was often put on blocks of ice, but the ice was not always available; there were no refrigeration devices in those days to manufacture it. The problem was especially acute when traveling. Military troops in battle ate very poorly, because there was no way of supplying them with a variety of fresh foods. Napoleon Bonaparte, recognizing that a well-nourished army was likely to have an advantage over the enemy, proposed a competition with a prize of 12,000 francs to anyone who could develop a means of effectively preserving food. Some 14 years later, Nicolas Appert claimed the prize. His method was incredibly simple: enclose the food in a glass container, seal it, then boil to destroy bacteria. His findings were published in book form in New York in 1812. The volume created a sensation and the public soon clamored for glass preserving jars.

Thomas W. Dyott, a prestigious bottle maker, was selling fruit jars by 1829 and possibly earlier. It was his advertising campaign that gave preserving bottles the name "fruit jars."

The most common closure used on fruit jars in the first 50 years of their production was cork sealed with wax. The process was improved upon in 1855 when Robert Arthur invented an inverted saucer-like lid, which was inserted into the jar. This provided greater air tightness.

There was strong competition to arrive at a better fruit jar which presumably would earn a fortune for whoever took out the patent. This was seemingly achieved in 1858, just two years later, when a zinc lid for fruit jars was patented by John Landis Mason. At first, they were widely hailed and Mason had trouble making them fast enough to meet orders. It was then observed by the medical profession that zinc coming into contact with foodstuffs could be potentially harmful. This problem was resolved by a patent issued to Lewis R. Boyd in 1869 for a glass liner for zinc lids. After Mason's patent rights ran out many glass companies, large and small, made jars to his patent, embossed with the famous legend "MASON'S PATENT NOV. 30TH 1858." Although many jar closures were developed, Mason's zinc-lidded shoulder seal jars predominated until about 1915 when the metal lid and band closure was introduced by the Kerr Glass Co. Yesterday's collectible jars number well over 3,000, taking into account all of the size, color and embossing variations.

Several product jars are included in this listing, since a number of food packers utilized the basic fruit jar designs for their containers. Many of these product jars even carried labels telling the homemaker that the jar, when empty, could be used for home canning.

Price Range

☐ **A. B. C.**
Aqua quart, glass lid and iron yoke clamp **300.00 350.00**
☐ **ABGA MASON PERFECT**
In script, blue-aqua quart, glass lid and screw band (c. 1910) **20.00 25.00**
☐ **ACME**
Across shield, clear quart, glass lid and lightning wire clamp (c. 1910) **3.00 5.00**
☐ **ACME SEAL**
In script, clear quart, glass lid and screw band **20.00 25.00**
☐ **ADAMS & CO. MANUFACTURERS**
Pittsburgh, PA, aqua quart, glass stopper **300.00 325.00**
☐ **AGEE MASON JAR**
Clear quart, zinc screw cap, Australian (c. 1930) **15.00 20.00**
☐ **AGEE SPECIAL**
Amber quart, wide mouth, zinc screw cap (c. 1930) **25.00 30.00**
☐ **AGNEW & CO. PAT APLD. FOR 1887**
"Pittsburgh," all lettering on base, clear quart, groove-ring wax sealer, tin lid **50.00 75.00**
☐ **A. G. W. L.**
"Pitts, PA" all on base, aqua quart, groove-ring wax sealer, tin lid **15.00 20.00**
☐ **AIRTIGHT**
Clear quart, glass lid & lightning wire clamp . . . **30.00 35.00**

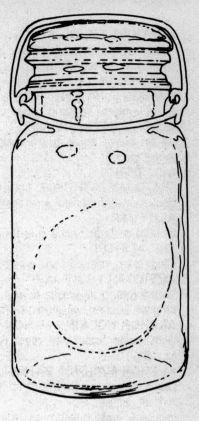

Amazon Swift Seal, in 2 lines in a circle embossed on front, smooth top with lightning seal, aqua.
$4.50–$7.00

Anchor, anchor emblem diagonally on front, smooth top with screw lid, quart, 9″.
$35.00–$45.00

Price Range

☐ **AIR TIGHT FRUIT JAR**
Aqua barrel-shaped quart, groove-ring wax
sealer, tin lid (c. 1860) 400.00 500.00

☐ **THE AKRON**
"MASON'S PATENT 1858" on reverse, clear
quart, smooth lip, zinc screw cap 450.00 500.00

☐ **ALLEN'S PAT. JUNE 1871**
All on base, aqua quart, square, glass lid and
metal clamp 150.00 200.00

☐ **ALL RIGHT**
"PATD JAN 28TH 1868" on reverse, aqua quart,
domed metal lid and wire clamp 125.00 150.00

☐ **ALMY JAR**
Double outlined, aqua quart, glass screw lid ... 125.00 150.00

☐ **THE ALSTON**
Clear quart, metal lid and wire bail clamp (c. 1910) 150.00 175.00

☐ **AMERICAN FRUIT JAR**
With eagle, green-aqua quart, glass lid and lightning wire clamp, wide mouth, Australian (c. 1910) 125.00 150.00

☐ **ANCHOR HOCKING MASON**
With anchor, clear pint, glass lid and screw band
(c. 1940) 4.00 6.00

☐ **ANCHOR MASON'S PATENT**
Clear pint, zinc screw cap (c. 1909) 35.00 40.00

☐ **A R S**
In script, aqua quart, glass Kline stopper 50.00 60.00

☐ **ATLAS CAN OR FREEZE**
Clear half-pint, tapered, metal lid and screw band
(c. 1960) 10.00 15.00

☐ **"ATLAS E-Z SEAL"**
Aqua quart, glass lid and lightning wire clamp (c.
1920) 1.00 2.00

☐ **ATLAS E-Z SEAL**
Cornflower blue quart, glass lid and wire clamp
(c. 1930) 12.00 18.00

☐ **ATLAS E-Z SEAL**
Amber quart, glass lid and lightning wire clamp
(c. 1930) 25.00 30.00

☐ **ATLAS GOOD LUCK**
With clover, clear quart, glass lid and lightning
wire clamp (c. 1940) 3.00 5.00

Price Range

☐ **ATLAS JUNIOR MASON**
Clear ¾ pint, metal lid and screw band (c. 1952) 5.00 8.00
☐ **ATLAS HA MASON**
Miniature bank, clear, slotted metal lid & screw
band 6.00 8.00
☐ **ATLAS- MASON FRUIT JAR**
Clear quart, zinc screw cap 25.00 30.00
☐ **ATLAS MASON IMPROVED PAT'D**
Aqua quart, glass lid and screw band (c. 1915) 3.00 4.00
☐ **ATLAS SPECIAL MASON**
Green quart, zinc screw cap, wide mouth (c.
1920) 18.00 20.00
☐ **ATLAS STRONG SHOULDER MASON**
Cornflower blue quart, zinc screw cap (c. 1930) 18.00 23.00
☐ **ATLAS STRONG SHOULDER MASON**
Olive green quart, zinc screw cap 10.00 15.00
☐ **ATLAS WHOLEFRUIT JAR**
Clear pint, glass lid and wire clamp, wide mouth
(c. 1945) 5.00 7.00
☐ **THE AUTOMATIC SEALER**
Aqua quart, glass lid and coiled wire bail (c. 1888) 125.00 150.00
☐ **BALL**
Underlined with loop, aqua quart, zinc screw cap 3.00 4.00
☐ **BALL**
Underlined, clear, 2⅛″ high, child's jelly jar, 63
mm. metal lid and screw band 20.00 25.00
☐ **BALL DELUXE JAR**
Clear quart, glass lid and lightning wire clamp (c.
1929) 7.00 10.00
☐ **BALL ECLIPSE**
Clear quart, glass lid and lightning wire clamp (c.
1925) 4.00 6.00
☐ **BALL ECLIPSE WIDE MOUTH**
Clear quart, glass lid and lightning wire clamp (c.
1930) 3.00 5.00
☐ **BALL BBGM CO. FRUIT JAR**
Monogram, aqua quart, glass lid and screw band,
(c. 1883) 700.00 1000.00
☐ **BALL HALF-PINT**
Clear half-pint, tapered, metal lid and screw band,
(c. 1956) 15.00 20.00

Price Range

☐ **BALL HAPPY HOLIDAY CARTERET PLANT 1962**
Deep green quart, specially made jar, metal lid
and screw band, wide mouth 40.00   45.00

☐ **BALL IDEAL**
"PROPERTY OF SOUTHERN METHODIST OR-
PHANS HOME" on reverse, clear half-gallon
only, glass lid and wire clamp 35.00   40.00

☐ **BALL IDEAL**
"BICENTENNIAL CELEBRATION 1776 * 1976
MADE IN U.S.A." on reverse with eagle and
stars, blue aqua quart, glass lid and lightning wire
clamp 4.00   6.00

☐ **BALL IMPROVED**
Blue aqua quart, glass lid and screw band, (c.
1920) 3.00   5.00

☐ **BALL IMPROVED MASON'S PATENT 1858**
Aqua quart, zinc screw cap, (c. 1900) 5.00   7.00

☐ **THE BALL JAR MASON'S PATENT 1858**
Aqua quart, zinc screw cap, (c. 1895) 10.00   12.00

☐ **BALL (over ghosted ROOT) MASON**
Green-aqua half-gallon, zinc screw cap 20.00   23.00

☐ **THE BALL MASON**
"THE" in first loop of "MASON", aqua quart, zinc
screw cap 7.00   10.00

☐ **BALL MASON'S PATENT**
Clear quart, zinc screw cap (c. 1928) 5.00   8.00

☐ **THE BALL MASON'S PATENT 1858**
In script, "PAT. APLD. FOR" ghosted through
"MASON'S," aqua quart, zinc screw cap 15.00   20.00

☐ **THE BALL**
In script "PAT. APLD. FOR", aqua quart, metal
lid and wire bail clamp (c. 1898) 150.00 175.00

☐ **BALL PERFECTION**
Blue-aqua quart, glass lid and screw band (c.
1914) 75.00 100.00

☐ **BALL PERFECT MASON**
Blue-aqua, zinc screw cap (c. 1920) 1.00   2.00

☐ **BALL PERFECT MASON**
Amber half-gallon, rounded square, made for use
in thermos containers 20.00   25.00

Price Range

☐ **BALL PERFECT MASON**
Amber pint, rounded square, metal lid and band   **250.00 300.00**

☐ **BALL SANITARY SURE SEAL**
Blue-aqua quart, glass lid and lightning wire
clamp (c. 1914) **4.00 6.00**

☐ **BALL SPECIAL**
Blue-aqua half-gallon, zinc screw cap, wide
mouth **15.00 20.00**

☐ **BALL SPECIAL MADE IN U.S.A.**
Clear quart, zinc screw cap (c. 1940) **2.00 5.00**

☐ **BALL STANDARD**
Aqua quart, groove-ring wax sealer, tin cap (c.
1912) **4.00 7.00**

☐ **BALL SURE SEAL**
Blue-aqua pint, glass lid and lightning wire clamp
(c. 1915) **5.00 7.00**

☐ **BALL SURE SEAL**
Below "PACKED IN ST. JOHNSBURY, VT" "BY
THE TOWLE MAPLE PRODUCTS CO." on reverse, Blue-aqua 22 oz. jar, glass lid and wire
clamp **35.00 40.00**

☐ **BALL TAPERED MASON**
Clear pint, metal lid and screw band (c. 1956)   **20.00 30.00**

☐ **BAMBERGER'S MASON JAR**
Blue-aqua, zinc screw cap (c. 1922) **15.00 18.00**

☐ **B B G M CO.**
Monogram, aqua quart, glass lid and screw band,
(c. 1885) **33.00 38.00**

☐ **B B G M CO.**
Monogram, on base: "AN HISTORIC REPRO-
DUCTION MUNCIE, INDIANA 1976 NO. 1 THE
AMBER BUFFALO JAR" around "BALL" amber
quart, glass lid and screw band **15.00 20.00**

☐ **BEAVER**
Below beaver facing right clear quart, glass lid
and screw band **20.00 25.00**

☐ **BELLAIRE STAMPING CO.**
Bellaire, OH, clear quart, glass lid and screw
band, (c. 1888) **400.00 500.00**

☐ **TRADEMARK BEEHIVE**
With beehive, aqua half-gallon, glass lid and
screw band **125.00 150.00**

Ball Ideal Patd July 14, 1908,
smooth top with lightning seal,
aqua.
$4.00–$8.00

Price Range

☐ **BERNARDIN MASON**
  Clear pint, metal lid and screw band, (c. 1948) 7.00 9.00
☐ **BEST**
  Amber quart, glass lid and screw band (c. 1900) 300.00 350.00
☐ **"THE BEST" FRUIT-KEEPER**
  Aqua pint, glass lid and wire clamp (c. 1900) .. 55.00 60.00
☐ **B. G. CO.**
  On base, aqua quart, groove-ring wax sealer, tin
  lid 7.00 10.00
☐ **BOSTON DAGGER BRAND TRADE MARK**
  With dagger, green-aqua quart, glass lid and light-
  ning wire clamp, wide mouth, Australian 150.00 175.00

Price Range

☐ **B. P. & CO.**
On base, aqua quart, groove-ring wax sealer, tin
lid **7.00   10.00**

☐ **BRAUN SAFETEE MASON**
Clear pint, metal lid and screw band, (c. 1945)   **8.00   10.00**

☐ **A. E. BRAY PAT. PEND'G**
Clover, amber quart, glass lid and screw band, (c.
1901) **700.00 800.00**

☐ **BRIGHTON**
Clear quart, glass lid and double cam wire clamp,
(c. 1890) **70.00   75.00**

☐ **BROCKWAY CLEAR-VU MASON**
Clear pint, round, glass lid and screw band, (c.
1943) **7.00   9.00**

☐ **BROCKWAY SUR-GRIP MASON**
Clear half-pint, zinc screw cap, (c. 1933) **20.00   23.00**

☐ **BROCKWAY SUR-GRIP SQUARE MASON**
Clear half-gallon, zinc screw cap, (c. 1933) **8.00   10.00**

☐ **GEO. D. BROWN & CO.**
Below shoulder, clear pint, glass lid and 3-armed
metal clamp **75.00   85.00**

☐ **BUCKEYE**
Aqua quart, glass lid and iron yoke clamp (c.
1865) **175.00 200.00**

☐ **CADIZ JAR**
Aqua half-gallon, glass screw lid (c. 1884) **350.00 500.00**

☐ **CALCUTT'S PAT'S. APR 11TH NOV 7TH
1893**
On base, clear quart, glass screw lid **45.00   50.00**

☐ **THE CANTON DOMESTIC FRUIT JAR**
Clear quart, finned glass lid and wire clamp (c.
1895) **70.00   75.00**

☐ **THE CANTON ELECTRIC FRUIT JAR**
Clear quart, finned glass lid and wire clamp (c.
1890) **100.00 125.00**

☐ **THE CANTON FRUIT JAR**
Clear half-gallon, glass screw lid, wide mouth (c.
1890) **85.00   100.00**

☐ **A. & D. H. CHAMBERS UNION FRUIT JAR**
Pittsburgh, PA, aqua quart, groove-ring wax
sealer, tin lid **8.00   10.00**

Price Range

☐ **THE CHAMPION PAT. AUG. 31, 1869**
Aqua quart, glass lid, yoke clamp and thumb-
screw 125.00 150.00

☐ **CHEF TRADE MARK THE BERDAN CO.**
Chef, clear pint, glass lid and lightning wire clamp 7.00 10.00

☐ **"CHICAGO" FRUIT JAR**
Aqua quart, glass lid and wire clamp, Australian
(c. 1910) 125.00 150.00

☐ **THE CHIEF**
Aqua pint, tinned iron lid with soldered wire clamp
(c. 1870) 800.00 850.00

☐ **CLARKE'S CAM LEVER**
Aqua quart, glass lid, cam-lever clamp and wire 500.00 600.00

☐ **THE CLYDE**
Clear quart, glass lid and lightning wire clamp (c.
1900) 6.00 8.00

☐ **COHANSEY**
Aqua pint, glass lid with encircled wire clamp (c.
1888) 15.00 20.00

☐ **COHANSEY GLASS MFG. CO. PAT. MAR. 20
77**
On base, aqua barrel-shaped quart, groove-ring
wax sealer, tin or glass lid 80.00 100.00

☐ **COLLINS & CHAPMAN**
Wheeling, WV, aqua quart, metal ring around
neck forms groove for wax sealing, tin lid (c.
1867) 800.00 900.00

☐ **COLUMBIA**
Aqua pint, ramped glass lid and wire clamp (c.
1910) 30.00 35.00

☐ **COMMON SENSE**
Aqua quart, glass lid and iron cam-lever clamp (c.
1879) 200.00 250.00

☐ **CONSERVE JAR**
Clear pint, glass lid and lightning wire clamp (c.
1900) 8.00 10.00

☐ **CROWN**
Crown figure, aqua quart, glass lid and screw
band, many styles, most common, Canadian .. 2.00 4.00

☐ **CRYSTAL**
Aqua quart, glass screw lid (c. 1878) 65.00 75.00

Price Range

☐ **CRYSTAL MASON**
Clear pint, zinc screw cap 25.00 30.00
☐ **CUNNINGHAMS & IHMSEN**
"Pittsburgh, PA" on base, aqua quart, groove-
ring wax sealer, tin lid 7.00 10.00
☐ **THE DAISY F. E. WARD & CO.**
Aqua pint, glass lid and lightning wire clamp ... 8.00 12.00
☐ **TRADEMARK THE DANDY**
Amber quart, glass lid and lightning wire clamp 90.00 110.00
☐ **THE DENVER JAR**
Green-aqua, zinc screw cap (c. 1890) 200.00 300.00
☐ **DEXTER IMPROVED**
Circle of fruit, aqua quart, glass lid and screw
band 55.00 65.00
☐ **D G CO.**
(Dual lined monogram), aqua quart, glass lid and
screw band 40.00 50.00
☐ **DOANES GREAT AIR TIGHT JAR**
Aqua quart, wingnut and metal disks stopper (c.
1868) 1200.00 1500.00
☐ **D. O. C.**
On base, amber quart, groove-ring wax sealer, tin
lid 150.00 175.00
☐ **DOCTOR RAMSAY'S**
Aqua quart, glass lid (c. 1868) 1200.00 1400.00
☐ **DOME**
Clear quart, glass lid and wire clamp (c. 1885) 150.00 200.00
☐ **DOUBLE SAFETY**
Clear pint, glass lid and side toggle clamps 8.00 12.00
☐ **DOUBLE SEAL MASON**
Clear pint, zinc screw cap (c. 1920) 10.00 12.00
☐ **DREY PAT'D 1920 IMPROVED EVER SEAL**
Clear quart, glass lid and wire clamp 3.00 5.00
☐ **D. S. G. CO.**
On base, amber quart, groove-ring wax sealer, tin
lid 75.00 100.00
☐ **ECLIPSE JAR**
Aqua quart, glass screw lid (c. 1885) 250.00 300.00
☐ **ECONOMY SEALER PATD SEPT 13TH 1858**
Ghosted, aqua quart, groove-ring wax sealer, tin
lid 12.00 15.00

Price Range

☐ **E. H. E.**
On lower front, aqua quart, groove ring wax
sealer, tin lid 15.00 20.00

☐ **TRADEMARK ELECTRIC**
Aqua quart, glass lid and lightning wire clamp (c.
1910) 8.00 10.00

☐ **ERIE**
Clear quart, glass lid and screw band (c. 1895) 20.00 23.00

☐ **EUREKA**
Clear quart, glass lid and flat metal clamp (c.
1926) 8.00 10.00

☐ **EUREKA 1 PATD DEC. 27TH 1864**
Aqua pint, metal press-down lid 100.00 150.00

☐ **E-Z SEAL**
Aqua quart, glass lid and lightning wire clamp 15.00 18.00

☐ **FARM FAMILY BUCK GLASS CO.**
"Baltimore, MD" on lid, clear pint, glass lid and
metal snap clips 5.00 10.00

☐ **FAVORITE**
Aqua quart, iron lid and attached yoke clamp (c.
1875) 1000.00 1200.00

☐ **FAVORITE TRADEMARK**
Aqua quart, glass lid and screw band (c. 1908) 15.00 20.00

☐ **F. B. CO.**
On base, amber quart, groove-ring wax sealer, tin
lid 60.00 75.00

☐ **FEDERAL FRUIT JAR**
Eagle, green-aqua half-gallon, glass lid and lightning wire clamp, Australian 100.00 125.00

☐ **F. H. G. W.**
On base, aqua quart, groove-ring wax sealer, tin
lid 10.00 12.00

☐ **FLACCUS BROS. STEERS HEAD**
Steer's head, fruit jar, clear pint, glass Simplex
screw lid 25.00 35.00

☐ **E. C. FLACCUS CO. TRADEMARK**
Stag's head, amber pint, milk glass lid and screw
band 225.00 250.00

☐ **C. L. FLACCUS**
"Pittsburgh" on base, clear quart, groove-ring
wax sealer, tin lid 30.00 35.00

Price Range

☐ **THE FORSTER JAR**
Clear quart, glass lid and screw band, English   **15.00   20.00**

☐ **FOWLER'S NO. 20**
On heel, clear quart, metal press-down lid and flat
metal clamp, English **20.00   25.00**

☐ **WM. FRANK & SONS**
"Pitts" on base, aqua quart, groove-ring wax
sealer, tin lid.................................   **8.00   12.00**

☐ **FRANKLIN NO. 1 FRUIT JAR**
Aqua quart, glass lid and screw band (c. 1867)   **125.00 150.00**

☐ **FRISCO A-1 TRADEMARK F L CO.**
Crown, monogram, fruit jar, green-aqua quart,
glass lid and wire clamp **150.00 175.00**

☐ **FRUIT-KEEPER G J CO.**
Monogram, aqua pint, glass lid and double cam
metal and wire clamp **40.00   45.00**

☐ **F & S**
Aqua quart, glass lid and lightning wire clamp   **8.00   10.00**

☐ **GARDEN QUEEN BUCK GLASS CO.**
"Baltimore, MD" on lid, clear pint, glass lid and
metal snap clips **5.00   10.00**

☐ **1908 GEM**
Clear quart, glass lid and screw band **10.00   15.00**

☐ **GETZBEST**
Clear quart, glass lid and lightning wire clamp (c.
1920) **30.00   35.00**

☐ **GILBERDS JAR**
Star, aqua quart, glass lid and wire clamp which
encircles jar from lid to base **125.00 150.00**

☐ **GILBERDS IMPROVED JAR**
Star, aqua quart, glass lid and wire clamp **100.00 125.00**

☐ **G J CO.**
Monogram, aqua pint, zinc cap with milk glass
fruit depressor liner **30.00   35.00**

☐ **GLOBE**
Amber quart, glass lid, ball cam-lever clamp and
wire (c. 1900) **35.00   40.00**

☐ **GLOBE**
Sun-colored, amethyst half-gallon, glass lid, ball
cam-lever clamp and wire **35.00   40.00**

☐ **GOLDEN HARVEST MASON**
Cornucopia, clear pint, metal lid and screw band   **1.00   2.00**

Price Range

☐ **THE GREAT EASTERN PHILADA E. T. WHITEHEAD**
Green-aqua, threaded glass stopper-like lid 1200.00 1500.00

☐ **GREEN MOUNTAIN C. A. CO.**
Clear half-pint, glass lid and wire clamp (c. 1910)　30.00　35.00

☐ **GRIFFEN'S PATENT OCT. 7 1862**
On lid, aqua quart, glass lid and iron clamp ... 100.00 125.00

☐ **HAINES COMBINATION**
Aqua quart, glass lid and wire clamp 125.00 150.00

☐ **HAINES PATENT MARCH 1ST 1870**
Aqua quart, glass lid and wire clamp 90.00 100.00

☐ **C. K. HALLE & CO.**
121 Water St., Cleveland, OH aqua quart, glass Kline stopper 150.00 175.00

☐ **MRS. G. E. HALLER PATD FEB 25 73 (on stopper)**
On stopper, aqua quart, hollow glass stopper .. 100.00 150.00

☐ **HAMILTON**
Clear quart, glass lid and flat metal clamp (c. 1890) .... 60.00　75.00

☐ **HARTELL'S GLASS AIR TIGHT COVER PATENTED**
"Oct. 19, 1858" around side of cap, aqua quart, glass screw cap .... 50.00　60.00

☐ **HARTFORD FRUIT JAR COMPANY**
On base, clear quart, glass lid and screw band　20.00　25.00

☐ **HARVEST MASON**
Clear pint, glass lid and screw band (c. 1940)　20.00　25.00

☐ **HAWLEY GLASS CO.**
"Hawley, PA" on base, aqua pint, zinc screw cap　10.00　12.00

☐ **THE HAZEL**
On milk glass lid, amber quart, glass lid and screw band .... 75.00　85.00

☐ **HAZEL-ATLAS E Z SEAL**
Aqua quart, glass lid and lightning wire clamp (c. 1906) .... 10.00　12.00

☐ **HAZEL HA PRESERVE JAR**
Clear pint, glass lid and lightning wire clamp (c. 1925) .... 12.00　14.00

☐ **H & C**
Aqua quart, glass lid and lightning wire clamp　10.00　12.00

Price Range

☐ **HELMES RAILROAD MILLS**
Amber pint, glass lid and screw band 15.00   18.00

☐ **THE HERO**
Aqua quart, glass lid and screw band (c. 1880)   15.00   25.00

☐ **HERO IMPROVED**
Aqua quart, glass lid inside metal lid and screw
band (c. 1875) 30.00   35.00

☐ **HEROINE**
Olive-green quart, tinned-iron lid and screw band
(c. 1867) 100.00   125.00

☐ **HOLLIEANNA MASON**
Clear quart, zinc screw cap (c. 1932) 25.00   30.00

☐ **THE "HOME" PRESERVING JAR 1**
Clear quart, glass or metal lid and screw band,
English 18.00   22.00

☐ **HONEST MASON JAR PAT. 1858**
Clear quart, zinc screw cap 12.00   15.00

☐ **HOOSIER JAR**
Aqua half-gallon, glass screw cap (c. 1885) ... 750.00   800.00

☐ **THE HOWE JAR**
Scranton, PA, aqua quart, glass lid and wire bail
clamp (c. 1890) 60.00   75.00

☐ **M. B. HUMPHREY**
Phila, PA, aqua quart, Cohansey glass lid/wire (c.
1885) 50.00   60.00

☐ **J. W. HUNTER,**
Wheeling, WV, clear pint, glass lid and screw
band 75.00   85.00

☐ **H. W. P.**
On base, aqua quart, glass lid and lightning wire
clamp..................................... 5.00   8.00

☐ **IDEAL C & E CO.**
Monogram, light green quart, glass lid and screw
band 15.00   20.00

☐ **THE IDEAL IMPERIAL QUART**
Aqua quart, glass lid and screw band 18.00   20.00

☐ **I. G. CO.**
On base, aqua quart, groove-ring wax sealer, tin
lid 7.00   10.00

☐ **C. IHMSEN & SONS**
"Pittsburgh, PA" on base, aqua quart, groove-
ring wax sealer, tin lid 7.00   10.00

Price Range

☐ **THE E G CO. IMPERIAL**
Monogram, aqua quart, glass lid and screw band   10.00   12.00

☐ **IMPERIAL PAT. APRIL 20TH 1886 COULTER MFG. CO.**
"St. Joseph, MO" on base, aqua quart, glass lid
and wire clamp 50.00   55.00

☐ **KEYSTONE IMPROVED**
Aqua quart, glass lid and screw band 10.00   15.00

☐ **IMPROVED CROWN**
Crown, clear quart, glass lid and screw band ..   7.00   10.00

☐ **IMPROVED GEM**
Reverse: L G CO. monogram, aqua quart, glass
lid and screw band 200.00 250.00

☐ **IMPROVED JAM**
Reverse: L G CO. monogram, aqua quart, glass
lid and screw band 80.00 100.00

☐ **IMPROVED JEWEL**
Made in Canada, clear quart, glass lid and screw
band 2.00   4.00

☐ **IMPROVED MASON JAR**
Clear quart, zinc screw cap 6.00   8.00

☐ **INDICATOR**
Aqua quart, tinned iron lid and band 600.00 800.00

☐ **INSTANT SEAL**
Clear quart, rubber-covered metal lid (c. 1940)   8.00   10.00

☐ **INSTANT SEAL CONSERVA-JAR MFG FOR PHILCO**
Clear quart, rubber-covered metal lid 8.00   12.00

☐ **J & B FRUIT JAR PAT'D JUNE 14, 1889**
Aqua quart, octagon-topped zinc screw cap ... 60.00   75.00

☐ **JAR SALT DETROIT SALT CO. MASON'S PAT.**
Aqua quart, zinc screw cap 18.00   20.00

☐ **JEWEL JAR**
Made in Canada, clear quart, glass lid and screw
band (c. 1940) 2.00   4.00

☐ **J F N CO**
"Boston" on milk glass lid, amber quart, glass lid
and screw band wide mouth 60.00   65.00

☐ **J H F**
Monogram, base: Trademark lightning Putnam
aqua half gallon, glass lid and wire clamp 10.00   12.00

Price Range

☐ **JOHNSON & JOHNSON**
New York, cobalt quart, glass lid and screw band
(c. 1895) 90.00 100.00

☐ **JOHNSON & JOHNSON**
New York, amber quart, glass lid and safety valve
clamp 25.00 30.00

☐ **JOHNSON'S 2 PATENT JAN. 7TH 1868**
Aqua quart, special zinc screw cap 400.00 500.00

☐ **J. H. JONES & CO. TOOWOOMBA**
Aqua quart, glass lid and lightning wire clamp
wide mouth, Australian 125.00 150.00

☐ **THE JULES JAR**
Clear pint, glass lid and screw band (c. 1915) 40.00 50.00

☐ **K MONROE COUNTY**
Ohio, green-aqua quart, groove-ring wax sealer,
tin lid 10.00 12.00

☐ **KC FINEST QUALITY MASON SQUARE
SPACESAVER STYLE**
Clear pint, metal lid and screw band 8.00 10.00

☐ **KERR ECONOMY TRADEMARK**
Clear quart, metal lid and flat metal clamp 4.00 6.00

☐ **KERR "SELF SEALING" MASON**
Blue-streaked clear quart, anniversary jar, metal
lid and screw band (c. 1968) 18.00 22.00

☐ **KERR "SELF SEALING" MASON**
Gold-painted quart, anniversary jar, metal lid and
screw band (c. 1968) 20.00 25.00

☐ **KERR "SELF SEALING"**
Reverse: "UNITED STATES BICENTENNIAL
1776–1976," ruby red quart, Liberty Bell shape,
metal lid and screw band, special issue 25.00 28.00

☐ **KEYSTONE**
Aqua quart, cast-iron cap (c. 1860) 600.00 800.00

☐ **K. G. W. CO.**
On base, aqua quart, groove-ring wax sealer, tin
lid 10.00 12.00

☐ **K. H. & G. Z. O.**
On base, aqua quart, groove-ring wax sealer, tin
lid 10.00 12.00

☐ **KARL KIEFER PAT. NOV. 25 1913**
On lid, clear in varying sizes, product jar, glass lid
and twin metal clamps 5.00 10.00

Price Range

☐ **THE "KILNER" FRUIT JAR**
Green-aqua quart, glass lid and screw band (c.
1915) 20.00 22.00

☐ **THE KING PAT. NOV. 2, 1869**
Aqua quart, glass lid and iron thumbscrew/yoke
clamp 150.00 175.00

☐ **KINSELLA 1874 TRUE MASON**
Clear quart, product jar, metal lid and screw band
(c. 1940) 8.00 10.00

☐ **A. KLINE PATD OCT. 27 1863 USE PIN**
On stopper, aqua quart, glass stopper 25.00 30.00

☐ **KNOWLTON VACUUM FRUIT JAR**
Star, aqua pint, glass lid and zinc screw cap with
six holes 35.00 40.00

☐ **KNOX GENUINE MASON**
Clear pint, glass lid and screw band (c. 1950) 15.00 18.00

☐ **KNOX MASON**
In script, clear quart, zinc screw cap 40.00 50.00

☐ **KOHRS**
Davenport, IA, clear quart, metal screw cap ... 4.00 6.00

☐ **KOLD PROSSO CANNER**
Woman & kettle, clear quart, glass lid & twin toggle clamps 80.00 100.00

☐ **LA ABEJA PAT'D JULY 14, 1908**
Clear quart, glass lid and lightning wire clamp 20.00 30.00

☐ **THE LAFAYETTE**
In block letters, aqua quart, glass stopper and
iron cam-lever clamp device 400.00 450.00

☐ **LAFAYETTE**
Profile of man, aqua quart, glass stopper and iron
cam-lever clamp device 500.00 600.00

☐ **LAMB MASON**
Clear round quart, glass lid and screw band (c.
1940) 5.00 6.00

☐ **THE LEADER**
Amber quart, glass lid and wire cam clamp (c.
1892) 100.00 125.00

☐ **LEADER FRUIT JAR IMPROVED**
TRADEMARK
On base, clear pint, glass lid and lightning wire
clamp 6.00 8.00

Price Range

☐ **J. ELLWOOD LEE CO.**
"Conshohocken, PA, U.S.A." on lid, amber quart,
glass lid and screw band, gauze jar 25.00 30.00

☐ **LEGRAND IDEAL TRADEMARK LIJ CO.**
PAT'D. 7-5-98 VACUUM JAR
Aqua quart, aluminum stopper-type lid 125.00 150.00

☐ **LEOTRIC**
Clear pint, glass lid and lightning wire clamp (c.
1910) 10.00 12.00

☐ **LE PARFAIT SUPER**
Clear pint, hinged glass lid and toggle clamp .. 5.00 8.00

☐ **L. G. CO.**
Crown on base, amber quart, groove-ring wax
sealer, tin lid............................... 90.00 100.00

☐ **L'IDEALE**
Green-aqua quart, hinged glass lid and wire toggle clamp, French (c. 1925) 20.00 22.00

☐ **LINDELL GLASS CO.**
On base, aqua quart, groove-ring wax sealer, tin
lid 7.00 10.00

☐ **THE LINCOLN JAR**
Aqua quart, unknown closure, ground lip 500.00 1000.00

☐ **LONGLIFE WIDE MOUTH**
Amber quart, wire screen and screw band, seed
sprouter product jar (c. 1980) 15.00 18.00

☐ **P. LORRILARD & CO.**
On base, amber pint, Cohansey glass lid and wire
closure, snuff jar 12.00 15.00

☐ **LOU KY G. W.**
On base, aqua quart, groove-ring wax sealer, tin
lid 10.00 12.00

☐ **L & S**
On base, blue-aqua quart, glass lid and lightning
wire clamp 4.00 5.00

☐ **LUDLOW'S PATENT JUNE 28, 1859 &**
AUGUST 6, 1861
On lid, aqua quart, glass lid and iron yoke clamp 125.00 150.00

☐ **L & W**
Aqua quart, groove-ring wax sealer, tin lid (c.
1870) 18.00 25.00

Price Range

☐ **L & W**
Reverse: "HOLCOMB'S" near heel, aqua quart,
metal lid and wire clamp 50.00 60.00

☐ **L & W'S X L**
Aqua quart, groove-ring wax sealer, tin lid 20.00 28.00

☐ **LYNCHBURG STANDARD MASON**
Aqua quart, zinc screw cap (c. 1925) 15.00 18.00

☐ **MACOMB POTTERY CO. PAT APL FOR**
On base, pottery quart, zinc screw cap 15.00 18.00

☐ **MADE IN CANADA CANADIAN KING**
Clear quart, glass lid and lightning wire clamp 25.00 30.00

☐ **MADE IN CANADA CROWN ½ IMPERIAL PINT**
Crown, clear half-pint, glass lid and screw band 15.00 18.00

☐ **MADE IN CANADA PERFECT SEAL WIDE MOUTH ADJUSTABLE**
Clear quart, glass lid and lightning wire clamp 2.00 6.00

☐ **MAGIC TM MASON**
Clear pint, metal lid and screw band (c. 1977) 1.00 2.00

☐ **MANSFIELD**
Aqua quart, glass lid and zinc screw cap (c. 1908) 50.00 60.00

☐ **MANSFIELD MASON**
Aqua quart, zinc screw cap (c. 1908) 25.00 30.00

☐ **MANUFACTURED BY INDPLS. GLASS WORKS**
"Indianapolis, IN", on base, aqua quart, groove-
ring wax sealer, tin lid 15.00 20.00

☐ **MANUFACTURED FOR N. O. FANSLER**
Cleveland, OH, aqua quart, glass Kline stopper 130.00 150.00

☐ **MANUFACTURED FOR J. T. KINNEY**
Trenton, NJ, aqua quart, glass Kline stopper .. 130.00 150.00

☐ **MASCOT DISK IMMERSER**
Aqua quart, milk glass disk immerser and screw
band (c. 1980) 200.00 250.00

☐ **"MASCOT" IMPROVED**
Immerser figure, clear half-gallon, milk glass disk
immerser and screw band 400.00 500.00

☐ **THE "MASCOT" TRADEMARK PAT'D IMPROVED**
Clear quart, milk glass disk immerser and screw
band 150.00 175.00

Price Range

☐ **MASON**
Reverse: 1776 1976, clear quart, metal lid and
band 1.00 3.00

☐ **MASON**
Underlined with loop, clear pint, zinc screw cap 8.00 10.00

☐ **MASON**
Flagtail underline, clear quart, zinc screw cap .. 7.00 9.00

☐ **MASON**
With shepherd's crook, aqua pint, zinc screw lid 8.00 10.00

☐ **MASON**
Amber pint, zinc screw cap 40.00 45.00

☐ **MASON**
Base: "GILBERDS", aqua quart, zinc screw cap 18.00 20.00

☐ **THE MASON**
"THE" in curve of "M", aqua quart, zinc screw
cap 7.00 9.00

☐ **THE MASON AIRTITE**
Clear quart, zinc screw cap 20.00 25.00

☐ **MASON FRUIT JAR**
Amber pint, zinc screw cap (c. 1920) 90.00 100.00

☐ **MASON FRUIT JAR**
Keystone, aqua quart, zinc screw cap 12.00 15.00

☐ **MASON FRUIT JAR PATENTED NOV. 30TH
1858**
Keystone, aqua half-gallon, zinc screw cap 10.00 14.00

☐ **MASON IMPROVED**
Aqua quart, glass lid and screw band 10.00 12.00

☐ **MASON IMPROVED A.B.G.A.**
Aqua quart, glass lid and screw band (c. 1915) 15.00 20.00

☐ **MASON JAR**
Near heel, clear pint, metal lid and screw band 4.00 7.00

☐ **MASON JAR**
Star, clear quart, metal lid and screw band 1.00 2.00

☐ **MASON JAR**
Star, clear pint, glass lid and lightning wire clamp 4.00 5.00

☐ **THE MASON JAR OF 1872**
Aqua quart, glass lid and screw band 40.00 45.00

☐ **THE MASON JAR PAT. SEP 24TH 1872**
Aqua quart, glass lid and metal screw band ... 50.00 60.00

☐ **MASON PATENT NOV. 30TH 1858**
"EHE" on reverse, clear quart, zinc screw cap 20.00 25.00

Price Range

☐ **MASON PAT'D 1858**
"WHITNEY" ghosted above, aqua quart, zinc
screw cap 6.00   8.00

☐ **"MASON" PATENT NOV. 30TH 1880**
Aqua quart, zinc screw cap with milk glass disk
immerser liner 90.00   100.00

☐ **MASON PORCELAIN LINED**
Aqua quart, zinc screw cap 40.00   45.00

☐ **MASON Q G**
Monogram, clear quart, zinc screw cap 40.00   50.00

☐ **MASON S G W**
Monogram, clear quart, zinc screw cap 40.00   50.00

☐ **MASON VACUUM KNOWLTON PATENT
JUNE 9TH 1908**
Aqua quart, glass lid and wire clamp 60.00   63.00

☐ **MASON W G CO.**
Monogram, aqua quart, zinc screw cap 40.00   50.00

☐ **MASON'S**
With two triangular designs, aqua quart, zinc
screw cap 35.00   40.00

☐ **MASON'S IMPROVED**
H G W monogram on reverse, aqua quart, glass
lid and screw band 20.00   25.00

☐ **THE "MASON'S" IMPROVED**
Amber half-gallon, glass lid and screw band ... 90.00   120.00

☐ **MASON'S CFJ CO. IMPROVED**
Aqua quart, glass lid and screw band 5.00   7.00

☐ **MASON'S CFJ CO. IMPROVED**
"Clyde, NY" on reverse, aqua quart, glass lid and
screw band 6.00   8.00

☐ **MASON'S IMPROVED**
Cross, aqua quart, glass lid and screw band ... 5.00   7.00

☐ **MASON'S IMPROVED**
Cross, aqua quart, glass lid and screw band ... 5.00   7.00

☐ **MASON'S IMPROVED**
Keystone, aqua quart, glass lid and screw band 10.00   12.00

☐ **MASON'S L G W IMPROVED**
Monogram, aqua quart, glass lid and screw band 18.00   20.00

☐ **MASON'S IMPROVED JAR**
Aqua quart, zinc screw cap 10.00   12.00

Price Range

☐ **MASON'S IMPROVED TRADEMARK**
"CFJ CO." monogram on reverse, aqua quart,
glass lid and screw band 8.00   10.00

☐ **MASON'S JAR**
Ghosted "HOOSIER" aqua, half-gallon, zinc
screw cap 75.00   80.00

☐ **MASON'S KEYSTONE**
Keystone, aqua half-gallon, metal lid and screw
band 300.00 400.00

☐ **MASON'S PATENT**
Aqua quart, zinc screw cap 6.00   8.00

☐ **MASON'S PATENT 1858**
"PORT" on reverse, aqua quart, zinc screw cap 8.00   10.00

☐ **MASON'S PATENT 1858**
"BALL" over ghosted "PORT" on reverse, aqua
pint, zinc screw cap 12.00   18.00

☐ **S MASON'S PATENT 1858**
Aqua quart, zinc screw cap 6.00   8.00

☐ **MASON'S PATENTED JUNE 27TH 1876**
Aqua quart, zinc screw cap 100.00 150.00

☐ **MASON'S PATENT NOV. 30TH 58**
Aqua quart, zinc screw cap 8.00   10.00

☐ **MASON'S PATENT NOV. 30TH 58** (fancy
letters)
Aqua pint, zinc screw cap, "Christmas Mason" 50.00   55.00

☐ **MASON'S PATENT NOV. 30TH 58** (fancy
letters)
Fancy letters, "BALL" on reverse, aqua pint, zinc
screw cap, "Christmas Mason" 60.00   65.00

☐ **MASON'S PATENT NOV. 30TH 58** (fancy
letters)
Fancy letters, aqua pint, glass lid and screw band
"Christmas Mason" 60.00   65.00

☐ **MASON'S PATENT NOV. 30TH 1858**
In circle, aqua "midget" pint, zinc screw cap .. 150.00 200.00

☐ **MASON'S PATENT NOV. 30TH 1858**
Amber "midget" pint, no closure 1970s reproduction, 3 vertical seams 12.00   15.00

☐ **MASON'S PATENT NOV. 30TH 1858**
Milk glass half-gallon, no closure, reproduction 30.00   35.00

☐ **MASON'S PATENT NOV. 30TH 1858**
Aqua pint, glass lid and screw band 8.00   10.00

Price Range

☐ **MASON'S PATENT NOV. 30TH 1858**
Aqua quart, zinc screw cap 2.00   4.00

☐ **MASON'S PATENT NOV. 30TH 1858**
Cross, aqua pint, zinc screw cap 6.00   8.00

☐ **MASON'S PATENT NOV. 30TH 1858**
Keystone, aqua quart, zinc screw cap 8.00   10.00

☐ **THE MARION JAR MASON'S PATENT NOV. 30TH 1858**
Aqua pint, zinc screw cap 15.00   18.00

☐ **RED MASON'S PATENT NOV. 30TH 1858**
Over key, aqua quart, zinc screw cap 12.00   15.00

☐ **MASON'S -C- PATENT NOV. 30TH 1858**
DUPONT on reverse, aqua quart, zinc screw cap   80.00 100.00

☐ **MASON'S CFJ CO. PATENT NOV. 30TH 1858**
Monogram, aqua quart, zinc screw cap 5.00   7.00

☐ **MASON'S CFJ CO. PATENT NOV. 30TH 1858**
Monogram, amber quart, zinc screw cap 100.00 125.00

☐ **MASON'S PATENT NOV. 30TH 1858**
Cross, aqua pint, zinc screw cap 7.00   9.00

☐ **MASON'S PATENT NOV. 30TH 1858**
Cross, amber quart, zinc screw cap 75.00   90.00

☐ **MASON'S G C CO. PATENT NOV. 30TH 1858**
Monogram, aqua pint, zinc screw cap 8.00   10.00

☐ **MASON'S J G PATENT NOV. 30TH 1858**
Monogram, aqua quart, zinc screw cap 18.00   20.00

☐ **MASON'S PATENT NOV. 30TH 1858**
Keystone, amber quart, zinc screw cap 300.00 400.00

☐ **MASON'S KGB CO. PATENT NOV. 30TH 1858**
Monogram, aqua quart, zinc screw cap 10.00   15.00

☐ **MASON'S N PATENT NOV. 30TH 1858**
"PORT" on base, green-aqua pint, zinc screw
cap 12.00   15.00

☐ **MASON'S OI PATENT NOV. 30TH 1858**
Monogram, aqua quart, zinc screw cap 8.00   10.00

☐ **MASON'S OVG CO. PATENT NOV. 30TH 1858**
Monogram, aqua quart, zinc screw cap 200.00 250.00

☐ **MASON'S SG CO. PATENT NOV. 30TH 1858**
Monogram, aqua quart, zinc screw cap 6.00   8.00

☐ **MASON'S PATENT NOV. 30TH 1858**
"EVERETT" on base, aqua quart, zinc screw cap   20.00   25.00

Price Range

☐ **MASON'S PATENT NOV. 30TH 1858**
"L&W" on base, aqua quart, zinc screw cap ...   8.00   12.00
☐ **MASON'S PATENT NOV. 30TH 1858**
"MOORE" on base, Bro's Glass Co., Clayton, NJ,
aqua pint, zinc screw cap 8.00   12.00
☐ **MASON'S PATENT NOV. 30TH 1858**
"Pat. NOV. 26 67" on base, aqua quart, zinc
screw cap 6.00   8.00
☐ **MASON'S PATENT NOV. 30TH 1858**
"S R & CO." on base, aqua quart, zinc screw cap   10.00 15.00
☐ **MASON'S PATENT NOV. 30TH 1858**
"TIGNER G CO. XENIA, IND." on base, green-
aqua quart, zinc screw cap 10.00 12.00
☐ **MASON'S PATENT NOV. 30TH 1858**
"T W & CO." on base, aqua quart, zinc screw cap   15.00 20.00

GINGER BEERS

Though Ginger Beer originated in the early 1800s in Great Britain, this section features only American Ginger Beer bottles. The heyday for Ginger Beer was from 1890 to the 1920s when the new production of grain beer won many fans. Some non alcoholic Ginger Beer is still made today, however. Unless otherwise noted in the description, the ginger beer bottles listed are made of stoneware.

The bottles and prices in this section were furnished by Sven Stau of Buffalo, NY. For further information on Ginger Beer bottles, please refer to *The Illustrated Stone Ginger Beer* by Sven Stau, P.O. Box 1135, Buffalo, NY 14211.

Price Range

☐ **ACE**
Ginger Beer, contents 7½ oz., brown glass ...   4.00   6.00
☐ **ALBANY BOTTLING COMPANY**
Albany, NY 13.00 18.00
☐ **ANDERSON'S**
Ginger Beer, registered, brown glass 4.00   7.00
☐ **ATLANTIC BOTTLING WORKS**
Buffalo, NY, Ginger Beer, green glass 3.00   7.00
☐ **ATLANTIC BOTTLING WORKS**
Buffalo, NY, pottery 95.00 110.00
☐ **BARNUM'S**
Niagara Falls, NY, Brewed Ginger Beer 20.00 30.00

The Double Eagle Bottling Co., $3.00–$7.00

Sir Arthurs Ginger Beer, Rex Water Co., **$10.00–$15.00**

Price Range

☐ **C. BAUMGARTNER**
McKeesport, PA, Ginger Beer 18.00 24.00
☐ **BRADFORD GINGER BEER**
Bradford, PA, BGB 12.00 18.00
☐ **HENRY BROWN CO.**
Glendale, CA, Sierra Club Ginger Beer 22.00 26.00
☐ **A. CARPENTER AND CO.**
Eastman Springs, MI/Chicago, IL, U.S.A., Stone
Ginger Beer 22.00 27.00
☐ **CHELMSFORD SPRING CO.**
Chelmsford, MA, Old English Ginger Beer 33.00 38.00
☐ **COBURN, LANG AND CO.**
Ginger Beer, incised, quart 60.00 70.00
☐ **COCK 'N' BULL**
Ginger Beer, painted glass 6.00 9.00
☐ **CRESCENT BOTTLING CO.**
Alleghany, PA, The Original Brewed Ginger Beer,
2233 Wayne St. 18.00 24.00
☐ **DR. BROWN'S**
New York, NY, Ginger Pop, incised 27.00 34.00
☐ **DOUBLE A**
Brewed Ginger Beer 10.00 14.00
☐ **THE DOUBLE EAGLE BOTTLING CO.**
Cleveland, OH, with picture of double eagles,
painted label, brown glass 3.00 7.00
☐ **ENNIS BROS.**
Ginger Beer, Utica, NY 22.00 28.00
☐ **ERIE BOTTLING WORKS**
Home-brewed Ginger brew, Utica, NY 17.00 23.00
☐ **ADRIAN FEYH**
New York City, NY, incised 11.00 15.00
☐ **FLANIGAN AND MURPHY**
Syracuse, NY, Brewed Ginger Beer 18.00 24.00
☐ **FRIEDLER'S**
Rochester, NY, High Grade English Brewed Gin-
ger Beer 18.00 24.00
☐ **GARDNER'S**
Elmira, NY, Gardner's Old English Style Ginger
Beer 18.00 24.00
☐ **GERNHARDT'S**
Ginger Beer, Mansfield, OH 12.00 18.00

Price Range

☐ **J.F. Giering**
Ginger Beer, contents 8 oz., Youngstown, OH   8.00   12.00

☐ **A. GOLDSTEIN**
Rochester, NY, Celebrated Ginger Beer 25.00   35.00

☐ **JOHN J. HALLORAN CO.**
High-grade English-brewed Ginger Beer, Syracuse, NY 16.00   22.00

☐ **HENNESSEY'S BREWED**
Ginger Beer, Syracuse, NY 17.00   23.00

☐ **HENRY BROWN**
Sierra Club Ginger Beer, Glendale, CA 22.00   27.00

☐ **HEYWORTH**
New Bedford, PA, Brewed Ginger Beer 22.00   28.00

☐ **HOUSE'S**
Ginger Beer, Lyons, NY, label is painted, green glass 4.00   7.00

☐ **HUDOR**
Brewed Ginger Beer, Buffalo, NY, tapered collar top 13.00   18.00

☐ **HUGHES & POTICHER**
Johnston, PA, English Brewed Ginger Beer 22.00   30.00

☐ **INTERNATIONAL DRUG CO.**
Calais, ME, Old Homestead Ginger Beer, height 6¾" 13.00   18.00

☐ **JACOB GUTTENBERG**
Medina, NY 15.00   21.00

☐ **JOHNNY BULL**
Ginger Beer, green glass 4.00   7.00

☐ **JOHN'S ENGLISH BREW**
Ginger Beer, The So There English Ginger Beer Co., Jacksonville, FL, 5½" 22.00   30.00

☐ **JUMBO BOTTLING WORKS**
Cincinnati, OH, Ginger Beer, with picture of elephant 48.00   56.00

☐ **KILGORE'S**
Ginger Beer, Greeneburg, PA 17.00   23.00

☐ **LATTER AND CO.**
Seattle, WA, Home Brewed Ginger Beer 18.00   30.00

☐ **LEE & GREEN CO.**
English-brewed Ginger Beer, Syracuse and Buffalo, NY 10.00   14.00

Price Range

☐ **MAURICE LEWIS**
Rochester, NY, High Grade English Style Ginger
Beer, brown glass 8.00 12.00
☐ **MAURICE LEWIS**
Rochester, NY, High Grade English Brewed Gin-
ger Beer 50.00 65.00
☐ **McCOY AND BUSHNELL**
Watertown, NY 13.00 18.00
☐ **McLAUGHLIN'S GINGER SHANDY**
Buffalo, NY, this company eventually became
Canada Dry 65.00 75.00
☐ **MIDDLETON'S**
Home-brewed Stone Ginger Beer 22.00 28.00
☐ **NIAGARA BOTTLING CO.**
Buffalo, NY, Brewed F&M Ginger Beer 20.00 25.00
☐ **OHIO GINGER BEER CO.**
Toledo, OH, O. Ginger Beer, Brewed by English
Process 16.00 22.00
☐ **OLD HOMESTEAD**
Ginger Beer, Calais, ME, 8⅜" 32.00 39.00
☐ **OLD HOMESTEAD**
Ginger Beer, Calais, ME, 6¾" 12.00 18.00
☐ **J. OLIVER**
Savannah, GA, Ginger Pop, incised 28.00 35.00
☐ **J. PABST**
Baltimore, MD 13.00 18.00
☐ **PAINESVILLE MINERAL SPRINGS CO.**
Painesville, OH 10.00 16.00
☐ **QUALTOP**
Ginger Beer, English style, brown glass 4.00 6.00
☐ **R.D.**
High-grade European-style Ginger Beer, Syra-
cuse, NY, brown glass 4.00 6.00
☐ **RAMROTH**
Troy, NY, Ginger Beer, green glass 3.00 7.00
☐ **REX WATER CO.**
New York, NY, Sir Arthur's Original Ginger Beer
English Brew, Non-Alcoholic 22.00 29.00
☐ **ROCHESTER SODA AND MINERAL WATER
CO.**
Rochester, NY, English Brewed Ginger Beer .. 18.00 25.00

Price Range

☐ **RYCROFT ARCTIC SODA CO., LTD.**
Honolulu, HI, Rycroft's Old Fashioned Ginger
Beer, 9 fluid ounces 150.00 300.00
☐ **THE M. SHOULER BOTTLING WORKS**
Akron, OH, English Brewed Ginger Beer, Keep
Cool 13.00 19.00
☐ **SIR ARTHURS**
Ginger Beer, English brew, NY, USA, non-
alcoholic 10.00 15.00
☐ **SMITH AND CLODY**
Buffalo, NY, Brewed Ginger Beer, Monogram
Brand 10.00 15.00
☐ **SOUTHERN ENGLISH GINGER BEER CO.**
Jacksonville, FL, John's English Brew Ginger
Beer, with man holding mug, height 5½" 20.00 30.00
☐ **STANDARD WATER CO.**
Buffalo, NY, Ginger Beer 45.00 55.00
☐ **STAPLETON BROTHERS**
English-brewed Ginger Beer, Auburn, NY, 10 fluid
oz. 15.00 21.00
☐ **STONE JUG BEVERAGE CO.**
Buffalo, NY, All American Gingerbru, painted
label, brown glass 3.00 7.00
☐ **SUSPENSION BRIDGE BOTTLING CO.**
Niagara Falls, NY 22.00 28.00
☐ **DR. SWETT'S ROOT BEER**
Boston, MA, Original Root Beer, Registered ... 13.00 18.00
☐ **VARTRAY**
Buffalo, NY, Brewed Ginger Beer, Keep Cold .. 10.00 15.00
☐ **WASHINGTON BOTTLING CO.**
Baltimore, MD, Genuine Brewed Ginger Beer
English Process 13.00 18.00
☐ **WESTERN BOTTLING CO.**
Buffalo, NY, WB 13.00 18.00
☐ **WINTER BROS. CO.**
Ginger Beer, Buffalo, NY 11.00 15.00

HUTCHINSON

Charles A. Hutchinson of Chicago developed a novel and revolutionary kind of bottle in the late 1870s, the rights for which were sold
to a number of manufacturers and resulted in great proliferation of the

Hutchinson Bottle. The Hutchinson Bottle had the distinction of originating the phrase "pop bottle," and this is how soda came to be known as "pop." That's exactly what the Hutchinson bottles did—they popped when being opened.

It wasn't really the Hutchinson bottle that was different, but the stopper. Hutchinson patented the stopper on April 8, 1879. It was intended as an improvement on cork stoppers, which could shrink and allow air to seep into the bottle. It consisted of a rubber disc held between two metallic plates, attached to a spring stem. This spring stem was a figure eight in shape, the upper loop being larger than the lower to prevent the stem from falling into the bottle. The lower loop could pass through the bottle's neck to push down the attached disc and permit filling or pouring from the bottle. After filling, the bottle was sealed by pulling the disc up to the bottle's shoulders, where it made a tight fit. To open, the spring was hit—thereby creating the "POP" sound. Three different lengths and five sizes of gaskets were made to fit bottles of various proportions. Hutchinson bottles ceased to be made when health authorities warned of the dangers of metal poisoning from consuming beverages sold in them. They were last manufactured in 1912, but they had already become obsolete by that time.

As curiosities, the Hutchinson bottles rank high, and they enjoy a strong following among collectors. In the main, they are not decorative, and, of course, figurals were not made (it was tough enough adapting this device to a standard shape bottle).

Prices on Hutchinson bottles tend to vary more sharply by geographical locale than prices of most other collector bottles. Specimens that are scarce and highly priced in one part of the country are sometimes common and inexpensive in another.

Hutchinson bottles often carried abbreviations, in the form of a series of initial letters spelling out a message. They include the following:

TBNTBS — this bottle not to be sold
T.B.M.B.R. — this bottle must be returned
T.B.I.N.S. — this bottle is not sold

These instructions or warnings to the customer were not without their purpose. Hutchinson bottles were easily reusable, and manufacturing firms wanted to be certain that beverage companies would buy only from them rather than from the public. This problem was later solved by the "deposit bottle," after the Hutchinson era.

Price Range

☐ **ABA**

"Forgo, ND," all in a circle, light blue, 7" **27.00   35.00**

Price Range

☐ **A.B.A.**
"Grand Forks, ND," all in a circle, panels base
aqua, 7" 15.00 20.00

☐ **A.B. CO.**
"Alliance OH", all in a circle, aqua, 6½" 12.00 17.00

☐ **ACME BOTTLING WORKS, J.J. RUTISHAUSER,**
"Fernandina, FLA." all in a circle aqua, 7" 12.00 17.00

☐ **ACME, THE WATER CO, REGISTERED**
Pittsburgh, PA, in back "W.A.S. Co." in hollow letters. clear or aqua, 6½" 12.00 17.00

☐ **A.D. HUESING,**
"Rock Island, IL" in circle, light green, 6¾" ... 12.00 18.00

☐ **AETNA BOTTLING**
"Concord, NH," all in a circle, aqua, 6¾" 12.00 17.00

☐ **A.F. LUCAS,**
Wilmington, NC, all in a circle, aqua, 6⅞" 12.00 17.00

☐ **ALABAMA BOTTLING CO.**
"a" under bottom, a bid in a circle "This Bottle
Prop. of A.B. Co. Not To Be Sold," aqua, 7½" 11.00 15.00

☐ **ALAMEDA SODA WATER COMPANY**
Show clasped hard, light green, 6½" 17.00 24.00

☐ **ALBUQUERQUE BOTTLING WORKS**
All in a circle, aqua, 6¼" 15.00 20.00

☐ **ALLEN, WM. T. & SON, PETERSON, N.J. REG'S**
In 5 lines "Live & Let Live," trademark, clear, 6½" 17.00 24.00

☐ **ALHOUN & BRASWELL**
Stanford, Florida, all in a circle, in center trademarks, registered, on base. registered #33 under
bottom in back a harp, clear, 7" 15.00 20.00

☐ **AMAN, H. CHEYENNE, WYO.**
All in a circle, aqua, 6½" 15.00 20.00

☐ **AMAN, H. CHEYENNE, WYO.**
All in a circle, Clear, 6½" 12.00 17.00

☐ **AMERICAN BOTTLING WORKS**
In horse shape under it "Alboirn, and Detroit,
Mich." clear, 6½" 12.00 17.00

Price Range

☐ **AMERICAN BOTTLING CO. 323–325**
Sarasota all in a circle, on bottom "AB Co." aqua,
7" **15.00 20.00**

☐ **AMERICAN BOTTLING CO.**
Springfield, Mass, in oval slug plate, number on
bottom, light green, 7" **10.00 15.00**

☐ **AMERICAN**
In center a flag under it soda works, S.F. clear,
6½" **12.00 17.00**

☐ **AMERICAN SODA FOUNTAIN CO.**
All on front, aqua, 6¾" **15.00 20.00**

☐ **AMORY L.B. BOTTLER**
Grafton, AL., on base "T.B.N.T.B.S." light blue,
6¾" **12.00 17.00**

☐ **ANCHOR STEAM BOTTLING WORKS**
In center, an anchor, "Shawnee, OT" all in a circle, on base anchor, aqua, 6¾" **110.00 140.00**

☐ **A ANCHOR UNDER IT BOTTLING WORKS**
All in a circle. Shawnee, OK., aqua, 6¾" **15.00 20.00**

☐ **ANCHOR, THE BOTTLING WORKS**
Cincinnati, OH, all in a circle in center of it an anchor, in back registered bottle never sold in 2
lines, on base D, panels base 6¾" aqua **17.00 24.00**

☐ **ANCHOR, THE BOTTLING WORKS**
Cincinnati, OH all in a circle, in center, anchor,
aqua, 7" **15.00 20.00**

☐ **ANCHOR STEAM BOTTLING WORKS**
Shawnee, OK, all in a circle, in center an anchor,
anchor on base, clear, 6¾" **15.00 20.00**

☐ **ANDRAE**
G. PORT HURON, MI All in a circle blue, 6¾" **25.00 35.00**

☐ **ANNESTON, AL.**
"Coca-cola" in block letters, aqua, 7¾" **100.00 130.00**

☐ **ARCO, CAPE, SODA WORKS**
Marshfield, OR all in 3 lines, aqua, 7¾" **17.00 24.00**

☐ **ARDMORE BOTTLING & MFG. CO.**
"ARDMORE, I.T." under bottom O.F., aqua, 6¾" **140.00 190.00**
☐ Same as above, except "O" under bottom **140.00 190.00**

☐ **ARDMORE BOTTLING WORKS**
All on front, aqua, 7" **27.00 36.00**

Price Range

☐ **ARDMORE BOTTLING WORKS, ARDMORE, I.T.**
All in a horse shoe (5 lines) letters aqua **140.00 190.00**

☐ **ARIZONA BOTTLING WORKS**
Phoenix, AR all in a circle, aqua on base, 329, 6⅞" **15.00 20.00**

☐ **ARIZONA BOTTLING WORKS**
Phoenix, AR all in a circle, aqua, 7" **15.00 20.00**

☐ **A.R.O.**
Mel around shoulder in side of horse shoe. Eclispe carbonating company, on base "St. Louis," in center monogram EC. Co., amber, 6¼" **23.00 34.00**

☐ **ARTESIAN BOTTLING WORKS**
Dublin, GA, in sunken circle, with panels, C.C. Co. on one panel, aqua or clear, 7" **13.00 18.00**

☐ **ARTIC SODA WORKS**
Honolulu, HI on vertical panels, clear, 7" **17.00 24.00**

☐ **ASHLAND BOTTLING WORKS**
All in a circle, amber, 7" **25.00 35.00**

☐ **ASTLEY**
Lyman Cheyenne, WY. All in 3 lines, aqua, 7" **30.00 45.00**

☐ **ASTORG SPRINGS MINERAL WATER**
S.F., CAL. all in 5 lines, light green, 6½" **15.00 20.00**

☐ **A.T.G.**
On base, amber, 7" **32.00 43.00**

☐ **ATLANTA COCA-COLA**
Atlanta, GA, all in block letters, clear, 6½" **130.00 180.00**

☐ **ATLANTA CONSOLIDATED BOTTLING CO.**
All on front, aqua, 7½" **12.00 17.00**

☐ **AUGUSTA B.C.**
"Augusta, GA," all in a circle in center large a with bottle in center, aqua, 9½" **15.00 20.00**

☐ Same as above, except, 7" **12.00 17.00**

☐ **AUSTIN BOTTLE WORKS**
"MN," all in a circle, clear, 6¾" **16.00 23.00**

☐ **AUSTIN BOTTLE WORKS**
"Austin, TX" All on front, clear, 7" **10.00 20.00**

☐ **AUSTIN ICE & BOTTLING, REG.**
Must not be sold on back, 71 under bottom, aqua, 7¼" **12.00 17.00**

Price Range

☐ **A. & W. H. BEAUMONT**
In ½ moon letters under it in 2 lines Atlanta, GA,
5 points star under bottom. Semi round base panels base & shoulder, aqua, 7″ 14.00   21.00

☐ **A. WOOD**
"Kingston, NY" in round slug plate, aqua, 7¼″   10.00   15.00

☐ **AYLMER, WM. FARGO**
In 2 lines, blue, 7″ 32.00   45.00

☐ **AYLMER, WM. FARGO**
In 3 lines O.T., blue, 6½″ 130.00   180.00

☐ **BACON'S SODA WORKS**
In horse shoe letters, under it Sonora, Cal., lt.
blue, 7″ 15.00   20.00

☐ **BAILEY & ZEA**
Cloversville, NY in a circle, light green, 7″ 12.00   17.00

☐ **J. ED BAKER**
Clear, 9½″ 6.00   9.00

☐ **BARTH F.E.**
In ½ moon under it Green Port, LINY under it
Reg., aqua, 7½″ 11.00   16.00

☐ **BARTLESVILLE BOTTLING WORKS**
Coombs & Martin Prop., aqua, 7″ 14.00   21.00

☐ **BARTLESVILLE BOTTLING WORKS**
Coombs & Martin Prop, aqua 7″ 14.00   22.00

☐ **BARTNER, E.D.**
"Glenville, PA" all in a circle, on base D.O.C. 54,
aqua, 6¼″ 14.00   22.00

☐ **BARTOW**
"Fla. Coca-Cola" in black letters, clear, 7″ 125.00   175.00

☐ **BATE'S, DR.**
Trademark National Tonic Beer, 1876, green 8″   37.00   46.00

☐ **BATT BROTHERS BOTTLING WORKS**
"Tonawanda, NY" all in a circle, light blue, 6⅛″   14.00   22.00

☐ **BAUER, L.J.**
"Woodsfield, OH." all in a circle, aqua, 6″ 11.00   16.00

☐ **BAUMON F.**
"Santa-Maria, CA" all in a circle, aqua or clear,
7″ 14.00   22.00

☐ **BAY CITY BOTTLING WORK**
All in a circle, aqua, 6¼″ 12.00   21.00

☐ **BAYVIEW BOTTLING WORKS**
"Seattle," all in a circle, clear, 7″ 24.00   36.00

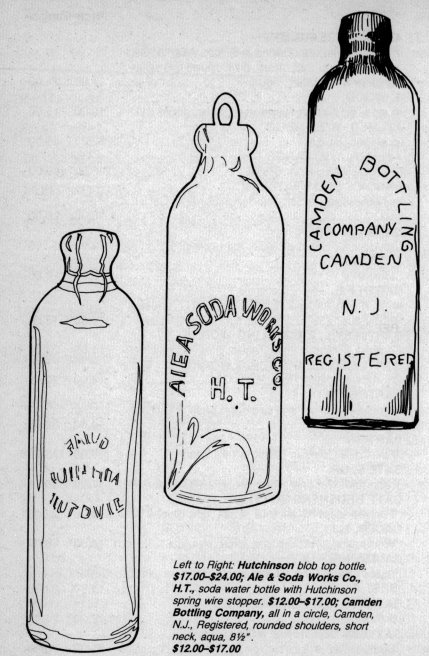

Left to Right: **Hutchinson** *blob top bottle.* **$17.00–$24.00; Ale & Soda Works Co., H.T.,** *soda water bottle with Hutchinson spring wire stopper.* **$12.00–$17.00; Camden Bottling Company,** *all in a circle, Camden, N.J., Registered, rounded shoulders, short neck, aqua, 8½".* **$12.00–$17.00**

Price Range

☐ **B & B BOTTLING WORKS**
"Hawkinsville, GA." all in a circle, aqua, 6¼" .. 11.00 16.00

☐ **B.B. & M.F.G. CO.**
All on front, in back on base "T.B.N.T.B.S." under
bottom "S", aqua, 7" 12.00 17.00

☐ **B.B. & W. BOTTLING WORKS**
"Hattiesburg, Miss." all in a circle, 7" 22.00 32.00

☐ **R.M. BECKER'S**
"B" under bottom, aqua, 6½" 12.00 17.00

☐ **R.M. BECKER'S**
"B" on bottom, aqua, 7¼" 11.00 15.00

☐ **BECKER R.M.**
"Waterford, Miss." all in a circle, aqua, 7" 9.00 13.00

☐ **BECKER, HENRY**
In a horse shoe letters, in center of it, Terre
Haute, IN, aqua, 6½" 14.00 22.00

☐ **BEEBETAFT & CO.**
"Wardner, Idaho Ter." all in a circle on base 33,
clear or aqua, 6¼" 130.00 170.00

☐ **BEEBETAFT & CO.**
"Colfax, Washington Ter." all in a circle, under
bottom 33, aqua, 6¾" 115.00 160.00

☐ **BENSON BOTTLING CO.**
"Minneapolis" all in a circle on back
"T.B.N.T.B.S.," aqua, 8" 16.00 23.00

☐ **BENNETTVILLE BOTTLING WORKS**
"Bennettville, SC" all in a circle, registered on
base "T.B.N.T.B.S.," 6½" 11.00 16.00

☐ **BENSON BOTTLING CO.**
"Minneapolis" all in a circle, in back
"T.B.N.T.B.S.," aqua, 8" 14.00 23.00

☐ **BERGER, JOHN M.**
"Bottle Works" in center "Felk Point, Baltimore"
all in a circle aqua, 8" 12.00 19.00

☐ **BESSEMER COCA—COLA.**
Inscript AL all in a circle, aqua, 6½" 190.00 265.00

☐ **BEST A.**
"Cincinnati" all in a circle, aqua, 6½" 11.00 16.00

☐ **BICKAL JAS. P.**
"Stuebenville, OH" all in a circle, under bottom
J.B.P., aqua, 6½" 11.00 16.00

Price Range

☐ **BICKAL JAS. P.**
"Steubenville, OH," all in a circle, aqua, 6½" .. **11.00 16.00**

☐ **BIEDENHARN COUNTY CO.**
All in a circle, "B" under bottom, 7¼" **80.00 105.00**

☐ **BIEDENHARN CANDY CO.**
All in a circle B.C.C., under bottom, aqua, 7¼" **45.00 60.00**

☐ **BIEDENHARN CANDY CO.**
"Vicksburg, Miss. aqua **70.00 100.00**

☐ **BILLINGS E.L.**
Under it "Sac City," in back Geyser soda, aqua,
6¾" **12.00 17.00**

☐ **BINDER, CHAR**
C.B. Mongroft C.B., all in a circle in back, under
bottom C.B., aqua, 7" **12.00 17.00**

☐ **BIRMINGHAM BOTTLING WORKS**
"Birmingham, AL" all in a water mellow letters
under it T.B.M.B.R., aqua, 8" **12.00 17.00**

☐ **BIRMINGHAM COCO—COLA**
In script "Bottling A." all in a circle, aqua, 7" .. **200.00 275.00**

☐ **BISMARKS, REMINGTON, P.C.**
All in a circle, clear, 7" **16.00 22.00**

☐ **BIWABIK BOTTLING WORKS**
Biwabik, MN all in a circle, under bottom N & L,
clear, 7" **12.00 17.00**

☐ **BLACK DIAMONDZ**
A T in center "Soda Works" all in a circle, under
bottom "P.C.G.W.," aqua, 6¾" **16.00 22.00**

☐ **BLACKWELL BOTTLING**
In horse shoe letters in center works "W.S.,"
under it "Blackwell O.T." panel base, aqua, 6⅜" **130.00 170.00**

☐ **BLACK & ROGERS, BOTTLERS OKLAHOMA**
"Ter." all in a circle (Guthrie, O.T.) under bottom
B & R panel base, yellow aqua, 6⅝" **115.00 155.00**

☐ **BLACK R.W.**
"Oklahoma Ter." in a circle, panel base, aqua,
6¼" **130.00 170.00**

☐ **WM. BLANCHFIELD REGISTERED SALEM,
N.Y.**
All in tombstone slug plate, light blue, 6⅞" **8.00 12.00**

☐ **BLISS, CHAS. F.**
In ½ moon under it "Racine, WI," star & 8 under
bottom, light blue, 6¾" **12.00 17.00**

Price Range

☐ **BLUFF CITY BOTTLING**
All in horse shoe letters in center Co., under it
"Memphis, Tenn.," panels base, light aqua, 7″   **14.00**   **19.00**

☐ **BLAIR, J.R.**
"Bottler Oklahoma City, O.T." all in a circle, light
aqua, 6¾″ **130.00 170.00**

☐ **BOARD T.M.**
"Coshocton, OH." all in a circle, clear, 7″ **12.00**   **17.00**

☐ **BODE NO. 5**
All in a circle, plain back, clear, 6¾″ **12.00**   **17.00**

☐ **BODE, GA., BOTTLERS EXTRACTS**
"Chicago," in a circle, clear, 6¾″ **12.00**   **17.00**

☐ **BOISE**
"Idaho" on front, paneled base, aqua, 7″ **26.00**   **37.00**

☐ **BOISE J.H.**
"Idaho" all in a circle, aqua, 7″ **32.00**   **45.00**

☐ **BOKOSHE BOTTLING WORKS G.W. GILES,
PROFS.**
All in a circle, Bokoshe, OK, aqua, 6⅜″ **17.00**   **24.00**

☐ **BONANZA BOTTLING CO.**
In ½ moon letters under it, Dawson N.W.T.,
greenish, 7¾″ **130.00 170.00**

☐ **BORTNER E.D., GLENVILLE, PA.**
All in a circle, on base D.O.C.54, clear, 6½″ .. **12.00**   **17.00**

☐ **BOSTELMANN, D.W.**
In ½ moon circle, under it trade anchor mark, Chicago, IL, aqua, 6½″ **16.00**   **23.00**

☐ **BOTTLE MADE FOR HUTCHINSON'S
PATENT, SPRING STOPPER**
All in a circle, plain back, aqua, 6¾″ **15.00**   **20.00**

☐ **BOTTLING: P.S.: CO.**
"Spartanburg, SC" all in a circle in back, TB-
NTBS, aqua 6½″ **21.00**   **27.00**

☐ **BOONVILLE MINERAL SPRINGS**
"NY" all in a circle, amber, 6½″ **28.00**   **42.00**

☐ **BOWDEN, D.**
"Boonton, NJ" in 3 lines, panels, base clear or
light blue, 7½″ **15.00**   **20.00**

☐ **BOWLING GREEN, BOTTLING WORKS**
"Bowling Green, OH" all in a circle, aqua, 7″ .. **15.00**   **20.00**

Price Range

☐ **BOYLAN & STURR BOTTLING CO.**
Paterson, NJ, registered 1902, in four lines vertical, slug plate in back, large letters B & S under
it, registered under bottom B & S, light blue, 6½″   **15.00   20.00**

☐ **BOYLE, DAVID, CO.**
"Paterson, NJ" in center of it "65 & 87 Washington St. 1904" all in a circle, on base registered,
aqua, 9″ **15.00   20.00**

☐ **BOYLAN & STURR BOTTLING CO.**
"Paterson, N.J. Re. 1902" in 4 lines vertical in
slug plate in black large B & S under it Reg. under
bottom B & S, light blue, 7½″ **15.00   20.00**

☐ **BOYNTON**
In ½ moon letters under it in 4 lines bottler, North
Hampton, MA. Reg. B under bottom, aqua, 6¾″   **12.00   17.00**

☐ **BRADCOCK J.M.**
"Pawnee, OK" all in a circle, aqua, 6½″ **12.00   17.00**

☐ **BRANHAWL & CO.**
In ½ moon, under it Woodfield, OH. in block
D.O.C., aqua, 6⅜″ **15.00   20.00**

☐ **BRANDON, THOS**
"Topeka, KS" all in a circle, clear, 6¾″ **27.00   34.00**

☐ **BRAZELL, THOS.**
"201–205 Pleasant St., West Yardner, MA" all in
horse shoe letters, panels under it Reg., clear,
6¼″ **12.00   17.00**
Same as above, except words all in a circle and
reg. on shoulder, amethyst, 6½″ **12.00   17.00**

☐ **BRENNAN & MC GRATH**
In ½ moon letters under it "Naugatuck, Conn.,"
dark aqua, 6½″ **15.00   20.00**

☐ **BRIG & SCHAFFER S.F.**
In 2 lines over it a fish, lt. green, 6¼″ **17.00   23.00**

☐ **BROADWAY**
In ½ moon letters, under it "Bottling Works, Silver
City, N.M., clear, 6″ **17.00   23.00**

☐ **BROADWAY BOTTLING WORKS**
"Silver City, N.M." all in a circle, star under bottom, aqua, 6⅛″ **17.00   23.00**

Price Range

☐ **BROE & GORMAN**
In a horseshoe letters under it in 3 lines, "404–6
East 60th St., New York," in back B.G. under it
registered, clear, 6¾" **12.00 17.00**

☐ **BROE & GORMAN**
In horse shoe letters under it in three lines.
"404–6 East 60th St. NY" in back B.C. under it
reg., clear, 6¾" **12.00 17.00**

☐ **BROOKS BOTTLING WORKS**
"Durant, I.T." all in a circle, aqua, 6⅞" **135.00 185.00**

☐ **E.D. BROOKS**
Port Henry, NY, name and location in circle slug
plate on front, #25 embossed on bottom, aqua,
6⅞" **7.00 11.00**

☐ **BROUGH, THE CO.**
"Contents mfg. by," in 2¼" moon letters under
it Trademark Eagle, under it "Reg. Cleveland,
OH, aqua, 6¾" **18.00 27.00**

☐ **BROWN'S VALLEY BOTTLING CO.**
All in a circle, clear, 7" **12.00 17.00**

☐ **BRUNSWICK**
"Coca-Cola Bottling Co. Brunswick, GA" all in a
water mellow letters, under bottom Reg, aqua, 8" **125.00 160.00**

☐ **BRUNSWICK COCA—COLA**
"Brunswick, GA" all in block letters, clear **125.00 160.00**

☐ **BUFFALO**
In center "Trademark Reg." under it "T.B.N.S.,"
aqua, 6½" **15.00 20.00**

☐ **BURNS & ARMSTRONG**
Running vertical, in center of double round ring
an arm holding scale, clear or aqua, 7" **15.00 20.00**

☐ **BURK J., MACON BOTTLING WORK**
"Macon, GA" all in a circle. Panel base, light blue,
7½" **15.00 20.00**

☐ **BURGIE J.L.**
"Dyesburg, TN", all in 3 lines, aqua, 6¾" **17.00 23.00**

☐ **BURGOYNE, P.M.**
"Memphis, TN" all in a circle, 25 under bottom,
aqua, 6⅝" **15.00 20.00**

☐ **BURKHARDT, HENRY**
H.B. under bottom, 6¾" **11.00 15.00**

Left to Right: **Capital, S.W. Co.**, Columbus, Ohio, rounded shoulders, short neck, stopper, aqua, 7¼", **$12.00–$17.00**; **Delta Mfg. Co. Trademark, Delta** (in triangle), Greenville, Miss., rounded shoulders, short neck stopper, aqua, 7½", **$10.00–$12.00**; **Elephant Steam Bottling Works**, Birmingham, Ala., all on front under line drawing of elephant, aqua, 6½", **$14.00–$19.00**

Price Range

☐ **BURN'S T.**
"Tucson, AZ" in a circle, under bottom
"T.B.N.S," clear, 6½″ 17.00 23.00

☐ **BURN'S T.**
"Tucson, AZ" in a circle, "T.B.N.S." on base,
clear, 6¾″ 17.00 23.00

☐ **BUSCH, HENRY**
"Minnemucca, NY" all in a circle, should be "Win-
nemucca, 33″ under bottom, aqua, 6⅞″ 22.00 31.00

☐ **C.B. CO.**
"Concord, NH" all in a circle, aqua, 6¾″ 17.00 23.00

☐ **C.C.S. & M CO. 270T0274**
"Royal New Orleans T.B.N.S." in 4 lines, vertical,
¼ moon on base, aqua, 7¾″ 15.00 20.00

☐ **C. HOFFMAN & CO.**
"Lakeview, IL" in circle, large "H" on bottom,
aqua, 6½″ 12.00 17.00

☐ **C & O**
"Wellston, OH" in 3 lines, aqua, 7″ 12.00 17.00

☐ **CALESBURY BOTTLING WORKS**
A. Davis Prop's Calesbury, IL, panels base, aqua,
6½″ 12.00 17.00

☐ **CALIFORNIA BOTTLING WORKS**
"T. Blauth, 407 K St. Sacramento" in 5 lines, light
green 6¾″ 17.00 23.00

☐ **CALIFORNIA SODA WORKS**
In a circle, eagle in center, aqua, 7″ 24.00 33.00

☐ **CALWIN, JAMES**
In center Monogram "J.C., Lowel, MA." all in a
circle, Reg. near shoulder, aqua, 8½″ 15.00 20.00
☐ Same as above, no monogram 12.00 17.00
☐ Same as above, under it center, Lowell, MA in a
circle, Mispelled Calvin 23.00 33.00

☐ **CALUMENT BOTTLING WORKS**
"M. Cols-West Pullman, IL all in a circle. Panels
base under bottom C.B.W., clear, 7¾″ 15.00 20.00

☐ **CALVERT W.H.**
Brownsville, PA all in a circle. Panels base, aqua,
6¾″ 12.00 17.00

☐ **CALVIN BOTTLING WORKS**
Calvin, IT all in a circle on base, big "H 3" top,
3 bottom in the big H. Yellowish aqua, 6½″ ... 130.00 180.00

Price Range

☐ **CALVIN BOTTLING WORKS**
Calvin, OK All in a circle on base, 3 on top 3 bottom in "Big H.," aqua, 6½" **15.00 20.00**

☐ **CALVIN JAMES (CALVIN)**
Lowell, MA all in a circle, aqua, 3½" **16.00 23.00**

☐ **CAMDEN BOTTLING COMPANY**
All in a circle, aqua, 8½" **12.00 17.00**

☐ **CAMEL BOTTLING WORK**
Clear, 7" **12.00 17.00**

☐ **CAMMON BOTTLING WORKS**
Scammon, KS all in a circle under it Artificial Flavor and color, clear, 6½" **16.00 23.00**

☐ **CAMBELL, C.H.**
Asheville, NC all in a circle, aqua, 7" **12.00 17.00**

☐ **CAMBELL C.H.**
Asheville, NC all in a circle, under bottom Pat. 85, aqua, 7" **16.00 23.00**

☐ **CANTON ICE FACTORY**
Canton, MI Clear **60.00 70.00**

☐ **CAPE ARCO**
In ½ moon under it in 2 lines, "Soda Works, Marshfield, OR," light green, 7" **15.00 20.00**

☐ **CAPE ARCO**
"Soda Work Marshfield" all in 3 lines, aqua, 7" **15.00 20.00**

☐ **CAPITOL BOTTLING WORKS**
Jackson, MI aqua **100.00 150.00**

☐ **CAPITAL CITY BOTTLING WORK**
Atlanta, GA all in a circle, under bottom a diamond, aqua, 7" **12.00 17.00**

☐ **CAPITAL, S.W. CO.**
Aqua, 8½" **12.00 17.00**

☐ **CARDEN BROS.**
Little Falls, NY all in a circle, clear, 6⅞" **15.00 20.00**

☐ **CARMEN BOTTLING WORKS**
Carmen O.T., aqua, 6⅜" **125.00 160.00**

☐ **CARR P.**
Phila., PA in 2 lines, light green, 7½" **15.00 20.00**

☐ **CARRE E.**
Mobile, ALA all in a circle, aqua, 7¼" **12.00 17.00**

☐ **CARROLL**
Newburgh, NY in 3 lines, C under bottom, light aqua, 6½" **12.00 17.00**

Price Range

☐ **P. CARROL**
"Mt. Vernon, NY" in circular slug plate, in center
of slug plate are initials "CP" and "Trademark,"
near bottom of bottle appears "Registered," light
green, 6⅞" **8.00 11.00**

☐ **H. W. CASE**
"Amsterdam, NY" all in circle, large "C" embossed on bottom, aqua, 6⅝" **8.00 12.00**

☐ **CASEY & CRONAR'S**
In ½ moon letters, under it in two lines, "Eagle
Soda Works," aqua, 7½" **12.00 17.00**

☐ **CASEY & CRONAR'S**
In ½ moon letters, under it "Eagle, Soda Works,"
light green 7¼" **12.00 17.00**

☐ **CASEY, HUGH**
"Eagle Soda Works" all in 3 lines, aqua, 7" ... **15.00 20.00**

☐ **CASEY HUGH**
Eagle, Soda Works, 50 K St. Sacramento, Cal. all
in 6 lines, aqua, 7" **16.00 23.00**

☐ **CASEY, HUGH**
Eagle Soda Works in large letters 3 lines, light
green 7" **12.00 17.00**

☐ **CAWLEY, W.H., D.B.W.**
Phillipsburg, NJ all in a water mellow letters under
it T.B.N.T.B.S. on shoulder Reg., aqua, 6¾" ... **15.00 20.00**

☐ **CAWLEY, W.H., CO D.B.W.**
"Dover, NJ" all in a circle above it Registered on
base T.B.N.T.B.S. on base C, aqua, 6¾" **15.00 20.00**

☐ **CAWLEY, THE W.H. CO S.B.W.**
"Somerville, NJ" all in a circle, top Reg. on base
T.B.N.T.B.S., aqua 6¾" **15.00 20.00**
☐ Same as above, except blue **20.00 30.00**

☐ **CAWLEY, THE W.H., SOMERVILLE DOVER**
"Flemington, NJ T.B.N.T.B.S." in 8 lines under
bottom "C", aqua, 6½" **15.00 20.00**

☐ **CEDAR POINT, PLEASURE, RESORT CO.**
All in a circle, aqua, 7¾" **16.00 23.00**

☐ **CENTRAL BOTTLING WORKS**
"Detroit, MI" all in a circle, under bottom J.J.G.,
blue, 7" **30.00 40.00**

Price Range

☐ **CHICAGO CONSOLIDATED BOTTLING CO.**
"14 to 18, Lomax Place Chicago, IL" all in 6 lines
in back Trademark in center Mary C.C.B. Co.
under it Reg. on base "T.B.I.N.S. & M.E.R.E.,
B.B.Co. 1900," aqua 6" 16.00   23.00

☐ **CHICAGO CONSOLIDATED BOTTLING CO.**
"14 to 18 Charles Place, Chicago, IL" in 6 lines,
in back Trademark & Reg., aqua, 6½" 15.00   20.00

☐ **CHACTAW BOTTLING WORKS**
All in front, aqua or clear, 6¾" 15.00   20.00

☐ **CHAMPION**
In center "Soda Works," under it, "PLYMOUTH,
CAL." aqua 7" 15.00   20.00

☐ **CHAMPION BOTTLING WORKS**
All in ½ moon letters under bottom Ironton, OH,
aqua, 6½" 12.00   17.00

☐ **CHAMPION BOTTLING WORKS**
"Ironton, Ohio," all on front, aqua, 6¾" 15.00   20.00

☐ **CHAMPION SODA WORKS**
"Plymouth, CA" all in a water mellow letters,
clear, 6¾" 15.00   20.00

☐ **CHARLESTON BOTTLING WORKS**
"Charleston, WV" all in a circle, aqua, 6¾" . . .   15.00   20.00

☐ **CHEADLE N.F.**
"Guthrie, OK" all in 3 lines on base C, aqua, 6½"   12.00   17.00

☐ **CHECOTAH BOTTLING WORKS**
"Checotah, IT" all in a circle, on base C, 6¾"   135.00   180.00

☐ **CHICKASAW BOTTLING CO.**
"Pauls Valley, OK" all in a circle, on base S.B.,
light aqua, 7⅛" 15.00   20.00

☐ **CHICKASAW BOTTLING WORKS**
"S. Bros. Props." all in a circle S.B. on base,
Pauls Valley, OK, aqua, 7½" 15.00   20.00

☐ **CHICKASHA**
In one line under it in ½ moon letters Bottling
Works, under it "Chickasha, IT," aqua, 6⅜" . . .   135.00   180.00

☐ **CHICKASHA BOTTLING WORKS**
"Chickasha, IT" all in a circle, aqua, 6⅜" 135.00   180.00

☐ **CHICO SODA WORKS**
In 2 lines, clear, 6¼" 11.00   15.00

☐ **CHICO SODA WORKS**
In large letters in 2 lines, clear, 6½" 15.00   20.00

Price Range

☐ **CHILLICOTHE, THE, BOTTLING WORKS**
"Chillicothe, OH" all in a circle, aqua, 6½" 15.00 20.00

☐ **CILLEY, H.D.**
"Lanconia, NH" in horse shoe letters on base C,
36, light aqua, 6¾" 15.00 20.00

☐ **CINCINNATI, THE, SODA WATER & GINGER
ALE CO.**
In a horse shoe letters in center 5 pt. stars
through it Trade choice marks, on base
"T.B.I.N.S.," clear, 6⅝" 15.00 20.00

☐ **CIRCLEVILLE, MINERAL WATER CO.**
"Circleville, OH" all in a circle, in back "K.C.B.
Co.," clear 6⅝" 15.00 20.00

☐ **CITY BOTTLING CO.**
In ½ moon letters in center, "LIMITED," under
it in 4 lines 322 to 332 S. Liberty St., New Orleans,
LA on base "T.B.N.T.B.S.," aqua, 7¾" 12.00 17.00

☐ **CITY BOTTLING CO. LIMITED**
"69 & 71 South Liberty St., New Orleans, LA" in
5 lines on base A.C.G. Co. T.B.N.T.B.S., on bottom 6 leaves flower, 7⅞" 15.00 20.00

☐ **CITY BOTTLING WORKS**
In large letters, "Horizon" in 3 lines on back.
M.G.W. in back in 3 lines "City Bottling Works To-
ledo, OH" under bottom C.B.W., aqua, 6⅞" ... 15.00 20.00

☐ **CITY BOTTLING WORKS**
"Braddock, PA" all in a circle, aqua, 6½" 12.00 17.00

☐ **CITY BREWING CO.**
Wapakonet, OH in moon letter, aqua, 7" 12.00 17.00

☐ **CITY ICE**
In center, "& Bottling Works, Georgetown,"
under it "Texas," all in a circle, aqua, 6½" 12.00 17.00

☐ **CITY ICE & BOTTLING WORKS**
"Georgetown, TX" all in a circle, aqua, 6½" ... 15.00 20.00

☐ **CLAREMORE BOTTLING WORKS**
"Claremore, IT," all in 5 lines, aqua, 6½" 135.00 180.00

☐ **CLARKSBURG BOTTLING WORKS**
Clarksburg, WV, aqua, 6¾" 15.00 20.00

☐ **CLEBURNE BOTTLING WORKS**
"Cleburne, Texas" all in a circle, aqua, 7½" ... 12.00 17.00

Price Range

☐ **CLEVELAND LIQUOR LEAGUE**
In horse shoe letters in center a horse head, under it "Bottling Work C.", aqua, 6¾" .... | 15.00 | 20.00

☐ **CLING & LUDWIG**
"Brunswick, GA" in horse shoe letters in slug plate, under bottom Dixon in back T.B.T.B.R., clear, 7½" .... | 15.00 | 20.00

☐ **CLINTONDALE ELIXIR SPRING WATER**
Name and location in circular slug plate, "Registered" appears below, "number 3" on bottom, clear glass, 7⅜" .... | 7.00 | 11.00

☐ **CLOVERSVILLE BOTTLING WORKS**
Name appears in oval slug plate, large fancy "C" in center, clear glass, 6⅞" .... | 7.00 | 11.00

☐ **COALGATE BOTTLING WORKS**
"Coalgate, IT" all in a circle, 6⅝" .... | 135.00 | 180.00

☐ **COBB, ROB. T.**
"Welmington, NC" all in a circle, aqua, 6½" ... | 30.00 | 40.00

☐ **COCA—COLA BOTTLING CO.**
"Chattanooga, TN" all in a circle, block letters, light green, 7" .... | 150.00 | 200.00

☐ **COCA—COLA BOTTLING CO.**
"Tuskegee, AL" all in a circle, block letters, clear, 7" .... | 150.00 | 200.00

☐ **COLDMAN BROS.**
In center (mong. 1 & H.) "Trenton, NJ" in a circle, Panels base, under bottom 674, aqua, 8¾" ... | 15.00 | 20.00

☐ **COLE'S SODA**
By N.J. Cole, So. Action, MA, clear, 7½" ..... | 12.00 | 17.00

☐ **COLLINS JNA**
"Groveton, TX" all in a circle, clear or aqua, 6½" | 12.00 | 17.00

☐ **COLONY BOTTLING WORKS**
"Colony, OK" all in a circle, aqua, 6½" .... | 15.00 | 20.00

☐ **COLUMBIA BOTTLING WORKS**
Columbia, MI, aqua .... | 100.00 | 130.00

☐ **COMANCHE BOTTLING WORKS**
"Comanche, IT" all in a circle, 6¾" .... | 135.00 | 180.00

☐ **COMANCHE BOTTLING WORKS**
"Miller & Co. Comanche, IT" all in a circle on base M & Co. Panels base, aqua, 7⅛" .... | 170.00 | 220.00

☐ **CONCHO BOTTLING WORKS**
"San Angelo, Texas" all in a circle, aqua, 7½" | 15.00 | 20.00

Price Range

☐ **CONCORD BOTTLING CO.**
In a horse shoe shape letters, under it "Concord, NH," aqua, 6⅝" **16.00** **23.00**

☐ Same as above, except a star in center **16.00** **23.00**

☐ **CONCORD BOTTLING CO.**
In horse shoe letters, under it "Concord, NH," aqua, 6½" **12.00** **17.00**

☐ **CONCORD BOTTLING CO.**
Concord, NH star in center, aqua, 6¾" **12.00** **17.00**

☐ **CONSOLIDATED BOTTLING CO.**
"Huron SD" all in a circle, Panels base, clear or aqua, 6¾" **15.00** **20.00**

☐ Same as above, except AB 126 under bottom .. **19.00** **25.00**

☐ **CONSOLIDATED, THE, BOTTLING CO.**
Lima, Ohio all in a circle aqua, 6½" **12.00** **17.00**

☐ **CONSUMERS BOTTLING CO.**
"Key West, Fla" in 4 lines all in a circle, clear, 7" **11.00** **15.00**

☐ **CONSUMERS BOTTLING CO.**
"Key West, Fla" all in a circle on base Reg. etc., clear, 6¼" **12.00** **17.00**

☐ **CONSUMERS S & M**
"Waters Mfg. Co. Ltd. New Orleans, LA." in 5 lines, on base "Y.B.N.T.B.S.," under bottom "M," clear, 6¾" **16.00** **23.00**

☐ **CONSUMERS SAND. M. WATER MFG. CO. LIMITED**
"New Orleans, LA" in 4 lines, vertical, aqua, 6¼" **16.00** **23.00**

☐ **COOK H.E. WHEELING, W. VA.**
"Wheeling, WV," all in a circle, clear, 6½" **15.00** **20.00**

☐ **COOS BAY SODA WORKS**
"J.A. Golden, Marshfield, OR" in 4 lines, aqua, 6⅝" **15.00** **20.00**

☐ **CORBETT, JOHN DEMING, N.M.**
Deming, NM all in a circle, clear, 6⅜" **15.00** **20.00**

☐ **CORDOVA BOTTLING WORKS**
Aqua, 6¾" **12.00** **17.00**

☐ **CORONETT & CO.**
"Wheeling, WVA." all in a circle in center of it a 6 pt. star. Trademark, clear 6½" **16.00** **23.00**

☐ **CORTES, H. & CO.**
"Prop Tx Bottling Works Galveston, TX," around base A & D.H.C., aqua, 8" **12.00** **17.00**

Price Range

☐ **CRAMER JACKY**
In ½ moon letters, under it Phillipsburg, mon., aqua, 6½" **12.00 17.00**

☐ **CRAWLEY, W.A.**
"Clarksdale, Miss." all in a circle, clear, 7¼" .. **12.00 17.00**

☐ **CRIPPLE CREEK**
In center of it "Bottling Works, Cripple Creek, Colo." all in a circle, aqua, 6¾" **16.00 23.00**

☐ **CRIPPLE CREEK BOTTLING WORKS**
Cripple Creek, Colo. all in a circle, clear, 6¾" **16.00 23.00**

☐ **CRIPPLE CREEK BOTTLING WORKS**
Cripple Creek, Colo. all in a circle, aqua, 6¾" **20.00 30.00**

☐ **CRIPPLE CREEK BOTTLING WORKS**
Cripple Creek, Colo all in a circle, "V.P." under bottom, clear, 6½" **16.00 23.00**

☐ **CROGAN, J.F.**
"Lexington, KY" all in a front, blue, 7½" **16.00 23.00**

☐ **CRONAR, M.**
"230 K St., Sacramento" in 3 lines, aqua, 6½" **15.00 20.00**

☐ **CROSS J.C.**
"Kingfisher OT" in 3 lines, aqua, 6¼" **130.00 175.00**

☐ **CROWN BOTTLING CO.**
"Buffalo, NY" all in a circle in a crown. Panels base, aqua, 7⅛" **15.00 20.00**

☐ **CROWN BOTTLING & MFG. CO.**
All in front aqua, 6½" **12.00 17.00**

☐ **CROWN BOTTLING & MFG. CO.**
In center a crown, "Ardmore, IT" all in a circle, big Y under bottom (120), aqua, 6¾" **135.00 175.00**

☐ **CROWN BOTTLING & MFG. CO.**
Ardmore, OK., crown in center, on base "C", clear, 6¼" **15.00 20.00**

☐ **CROWN BOTTLING WORKS**
In horse shoe letters, under it "Sandusky, OH," aqua, 7" **12.00 17.00**

☐ **CROWN BOTTLING WORKS**
In horse shoe letters in center of it, a crown, under it Ardmore, I.T., G on base, clear, 6½" .. **135.00 175.00**

☐ **CROWN BOTTLING WORKS**
"Delaware, OH" all in a circle, aqua, 7" **15.00 20.00**

☐ **CROWN BOTTLING WORKS**
"Hugo, IT" all in a circle B & D, aqua, 7⅛" ... **135.00 175.00**

Price Range

☐ **CROWN BOTTLING WORKS**
"Muskogee, IT" all in a circle, aqua, 6⅝" **135.00 175.00**

☐ **CROZIER**
In center an elk, Orangeville, Ont., clear or aqua,
6¾" **15.00 20.00**

☐ **CRUSELLASH**
Wood marks, aqua, 11½" **14.00 19.00**

☐ **CRYSTAL BOTTLING CO.**
"Charleston, W. VA" all in a circle, aqua, 6¾" **15.00 20.00**

☐ **CRYSTAL BOTTLING WORKS**
"Lehigh, IT" all in a circle "S" on base, aqua,
6½" **130.00 170.00**

☐ **CRYSTAL S.W. CO. S.F.**
In 3 lines, diamond under bottom, Dr. aqua, 6¼" **16.00 23.00**

☐ **CRYSTAL SODA WATER CO.**
"SF" in 3 lines, 7¼" **15.00 20.00**

☐ **CRYSTAL SODA WORKS**
Honolulu, HI aqua, 7½" **45.00 60.00**

☐ **CRYSTAL SODA WORKS**
Honolulu, HI Trademark J.A.P. under bottom
aqua, 6½" **22.00 31.00**

☐ **CRYSTAL SPRING BOTTLING CO.**
"Barnet, VT" all in a circle, clear, 6½" **16.00 23.00**

☐ **CRYSTAL SPRING BOTTLING CO.**
"Barnet, VT" all in a circle, clear, 7½" **16.00 23.00**

☐ **CRYSTAL SPRING BOTTLING WORKS**
"Columbus, KS" all in a circle, light blue, 7" ... **16.00 23.00**

☐ **CRYSTAL WATER CO.**
"Johnstown, PA" All in a circle, Cak. 8 oz. Reg.,
under bottom L & H., aqua, 6¼" **12.00 17.00**

☐ **CUMAER BARKMAN**
"Port Jervis, NY" in 4 lines, aqua, 6¾" **15.00 20.00**

☐ **CUMMINGS, T.D.**
In ½ moon circle under it "Phila," in black large
"C" under it, T.B. is Regst., light green, 6½" .. **15.00 20.00**

☐ **CUNNINGHAM SUPPLY CO.**
"Phila." in scripts under it. "Regst. #1907" under
bottom, in back (Mong.) large "C.S.C.," clear,
7½" **15.00 20.00**

☐ **CUNNINGHAM SUPPLY CO.**
"518 Locust St., Phila., PA." all in 5 lines on base
T.B.N.T.B.S. under bottom 1895, aqua, 7¼" ... **14.00 19.00**

Price Range

☐ **CUNNINGHAM WESLEY, REG.**
"Hampton, VA" all in a water mellow circle, aqua, 6½" 15.00   20.00

☐ **CUSHING BOTTLING WORK G.F. KNOWLES**
"Cushing, OK." all in a circle, aqua, 6¼" 15.00   20.00

☐ **CUSHING CROWN BOTTLING, THE, CO. W. CORLIS PROP.**
"Cushing, Okla," all in a circle, aqua, 6¼" 15.00   20.00

☐ **CURRIERS**
"Orange phosphate" all in a horse shoe letters, aqua, 6¾" 15.00   20.00

☐ **CURRIERS VANILLA**
All in a circle, aqua, 7" 12.00   17.00

☐ **CUTTING, THE, MINERAL WATER BOTTLING CO.**
In horse shoe letters, in center Trademark, C.M.W. Co. (Mong.) Regs. 422 Morres St. Phila., clear, 7¼" 15.00   20.00

☐ **DAHLSTROM, JOHN**
"Ishkeming, MI" all in a circle, light blue, quart 18.00   25.00

☐ **DAHLSTOM, JOHN**
"Ishikeming, MI" all in a circle, 10 panels base, aqua, 7" 12.00   17.00

☐ **DALINGER J.E.**
Tacoma all in a circle, aqua, 7" 12.00   17.00

☐ **DARLING W.H., & SON**
In a horse shoe letters under it, "Newport, VT.," aqua, 7" 16.00   23.00

☐ **DAVIS BOTTLING**
In ½ moon letters in center works under it Davis L.T. bottom M. yellowish aqua, 6½" 110.00   140.00

☐ **DAVIS & WORCHESTER, EHE CO.**
All in a circle, on base No. 3, aqua, green, 6½" 15.00   20.00

☐ **DEAMEP**
In a hollow letters, under it "Grass Valley," back W.E.J., 7½" 12.00   17.00

☐ **DEAN, H.E.**
"Great Bend, Kans." all in a circle, clear or amber 18.00   25.00

☐ **DECKER BOTTLING**
"Dayton, OH." on 3 panels bottle, aqua, 7" ... 19.00   25.00

☐ **DEIS & TIBBALS**
"Lima, OH" all in a circle, aqua, 7" 12.00   17.00

Price Range

☐ **DELANEY & CO. BOTTLERS**
"Plattsburg, NY" all in a circle, aqua, 7" 12.00   17.00

☐ **DELANEY & YOUNG**
"Eureka, Cal" all in a circle, pale blue, 6½" ...   15.00   20.00

☐ **DELTA BOTTLING WORKS**
"Yazoo City, Miss." in 4 lines, Panel base, aqua,
7¼" 10.00   12.00

☐ **DELTA MFG. CO., "DELTA"**
In a triangle under bottom, aqua, 7¼" 12.00   17.00

☐ **DELTA MFG. CO.**
"Greenville, Miss." all in a circle, aqua, 6½" ..   10.00   12.00

☐ **DENHALTER, H.**
"Salt Lake City, UT." in 4 lines, clear, 6½" 15.00   20.00

☐ **DENHALTER & SON**
"Salt Lake City, UT." all on front, aqua, 6½" ..   15.00   20.00

☐ **DENNALTER, THE, BOTTLER**
"Salt Lake, UT." all in a circle & a shield, clear,
6¾" 12.00   17.00

☐ **DENNAULTER H.G. SON**
In ½ moon circle under it "Salt Lake City, UT,"
aqua, 6½" 22.00   30.00

☐ **DEWAR JAMES**
In ½ moon letters under it, "Elko, Nev.," aqua,
6¾" 16.00   23.00

☐ **DIAMOND BOTTLING WORKS**
"Columbus, Kans." all in a circle, aqua, 7½" ..   16.00   23.00

☐ **DIAMOND BOTTLING WORKS**
"Miami, Oklahoma" all in a circle under bottom
"M.," aqua, 7⅜" 15.00   20.00

☐ **DIAMOND BOTTLING WORKS**
"Miami, OK. T." all in a circle under bottom "M.,"
panels base, aqua, 7¼" 80.00   105.00

☐ **DIAMOND BOTTLING WORKS**
"Miami, Oklahoma" all in a circle. Panels base,
"M" under bottom, aqua, 7" 15.00   20.00

☐ **DIEHL & DANBURY, D**
In back on shoulder, "D" under bottom, 6½" ..   12.00   17.00

☐ **DIEHL & LORD**
In hollow letters, under it "Nashville, Tenn.,"
under bottom a star, aqua, 7" 15.00   20.00

Price Range

☐ **DIETZ, A.F.**
In ½ moon letters in center "Knowersville, NY,"
aqua, 7" .... | **12.00** **17.00**

☐ **DIETZ, A.F.**
"Altamont, NY Reg." all in a circle, clear, 7" .. | **12.00** **17.00**

☐ **DISBORO YEO & CO.**
"Chicago" all in a circle, clear, 6¾" .... | **22.00** **30.00**

☐ **DISTILLED SODA WATER CO.**
"Of Alaska" all in a circle, panel base, light aqua,
7¼" .... | **22.00** **30.00**

☐ **D.J. WHELAN**
"Troy, NY" in large letters at angle across bottle,
large W on bottom, aqua, 7⅛" .... | **12.00** **18.00**

☐ **DOBBS FERRY, MINERAL WATER CO.**
"Dobbs Ferry, NY" all in a circle, aqua, 6½" .. | **12.00** **17.00**

☐ **DONAT & MOTIS**
"Chicago, ILL." all in a circle in center through it
"576, W. 19th St." in back on base "D.O.C."
under bottom "Big D," aqua or clear, 6½" .... | **12.00** **17.00**

☐ **DOOLEY & MULLEN**
"Belvidere, ILL." all in a circle, "511" on back,
aqua, 6¾" .... | **12.00** **17.00**

☐ **DUNCAN BOTTLING WORKS**
"Duncan, Okla." all in a circle, panels base under
bottom "S," aqua, 7¼" .... | **16.00** **23.00**

☐ **DURANT, PROPERTY OF, BOTTLING
WORKS**
"Durant, IT" all in a circle, aqua, 7" .... | **130.00 160.00**

☐ **DURESEN, JOHN**
"Minneapolis, Minn" all in a circle, panels base,
clear, 7¼" .... | **15.00** **20.00**

☐ **E.B. CO.**
"Evarnsville, Ind" all in a circle, aqua, 7" ...... | **12.00** **17.00**

☐ **E.B. CO.**
"Evansville, Ind." "B" under bottom panels bot-
tle, aqua, 7" .... | **12.00** **17.00**

☐ **E.O.H.**
"Parkersburg, W. VA." all in a circle, aqua, 6¾" | **12.00** **17.00**

☐ **EAGLE**
Under it an "Eagle, Soda Water and Bottling Co.
Santa Cruz, California." All in 4 lines, on base
"T.B.N.S.," aqua, 6½" .... | **15.00** **20.00**

Price Range

☐ **EAGLE BOTTLE WORKS**
"Knoxville, Tenn." all in a circle, in center of it an
eagle, in back B.N.S., aqua, 7¼" **16.00   23.00**

☐ **EAGLE BOTTLING WORKS**
In center spray wing eagle on one side "J.," other
"L., Davenport, LA" all in a circle, under bottom
"J & L" all in a circle. aqua, 6¾" **15.00   20.00**

☐ **EAGLE BOTTLING WORKS**
In center eagle and flag, etc., "Tacoma, Washing-
ton" in a circle, aqua, 6½" **15.00   20.00**

☐ **EAGLE BOTTLING WORKS**
"Lawton, OT" all in a circle, yellow aqua, 6¾"   **130.00 175.00**

☐ **EAGLE SODA WATER & BOTTLING CO.**
Santa Cruz, CA under eagle in a spray wing, eagle
on base T.B.N.S., aqua, 6½" **12.00   17.00**

☐ **EAST, THE, IND. BOTTLING WORKS**
In a horse shoe letters in center in 3 lines, F.V.
Cleveland, OH, clear, 6⅞" **12.00   17.00**

☐ **EASTERN**
"Chicago" in center, through it "Bottling Works,"
under bottom "E.B.W.," aqua, 6½" **12.00   17.00**

☐ **EASTON, ALEX**
"Fairfield, Iowa" all in a circle, aqua, 6½" **15.00   20.00**

☐ **EASTERN BOTTLE WORKS**
"Chicago," all in a circle, back Trademark, "ship
Reg. T.B.N.S." under bottom, "E.B.W.," aqua,
6½" **15.00   20.00**

☐ **EBNER P.**
In ½ moon letters, under it "bottle Wil, Del." in
back in large hollow letters, "P.E.," under bottom
"P.E.," panels base, aqua, 7½" **16.00   23.00**

☐ **ECLIPSE CARBONATIONS COMPANY**
In horse shoe in center "E.C., Co.," under it "St.
Louis," on shoulder "ARO," in back "M.E.L., 2½
cents deposit Required for Return of this bottle,"
under bottom "E.C. Co." amber, 6⅜" **30.00   40.00**

☐ **EL PROGRESSO DU, LA.**
Havana arsenal in four lines (Cuba), light aqua,
6⅞" **30.00   40.00**

☐ **EL RENO**
1 line under it in ½ moon letters "Bottling Works,"
under it in 2 lines "El Rind, OT," aqua **135.00 180.00**

Price Range

☐ **EL RENO BOTTLING WORKS**
All in a circle, "El Reno, OT," clear, 6½" 135.00 180.00

☐ **ELECTRIC BOTTLING CO.**
In ½ moon letters under it "T.B.L.M.B.R.W." in
4 lines, on base "Valdosta, GA," aqua, 7" 12.00 17.00

☐ **ELECTRIC BOTTLING WORKS**
"West Point, Miss." all in a circle, aqua, 6½" .. 12.00 17.00

☐ **ELEPHANT BOTTLING CO.**
On base D.O.C., under bottom "D", aqua, 8" .. 12.00 17.00

☐ **ELEPHANT ON SHOULDER BOTTLING
WORKS**
"Chicago, M. Levin, Prop." in 3 lines, in back a
ship, over it Trademark, under it "Reg. T.B.N.S.,"
aqua, 6½" 15.00 20.00

☐ **ELEPHANT STEAM BOTTLING WORKS**
All on front under bottom "D", aqua, 6½" 14.00 19.00

☐ **ELK VALLEY BOTTLING WORKS**
"Larimore, ND" all in a circle, aqua, 6½" 16.00 23.00

☐ **ELKO BOTTLING WORKS**
"Elko, Nev." all in a circle, aqua, 6½" 40.00 40.00

☐ **ELWICK C.L.Z.**
"Lincoln, Neb." all in a water mellow circle, on
base 8-13-33, aqua, 6¾" 16.00 23.00

☐ **ELWICK**
"Neb, Lincoln, Neb" all in a circle, aqua, 6¾" 15.00 20.00

☐ **EMPIRE SODA WORK**
"Vallyo, Cal" all on front, aqua, 6¾" 12.00 17.00

☐ **ENGEL, DAVID**
Under it a horse shoe, in it "Mineral Trademark,"
under it "Cincinnati, O.T.B.I.N.S." in 3 lines, aqua,
7" 15.00 20.00

☐ **ENGLAND, NEW BOTTLING CO.**
"Minneapolis" all in a circle, under bottom
T.B.N.T.B.S., aqua, 6¾" 12.00 17.00

☐ **ENGLE F.E., F.E.**
"Lancaster, PA" in 3 lines, 8 fl. ozs. on shoulder,
aqua, 6¾" 12.00 17.00

☐ **ERIE BOTTLING WORKS**
"Utica, NY" all in a circle, on base Reg. clear,
6¾" 12.00 17.00

Price Range

☐ **ERTEL JOHN M.**
Under bottom "B & E," clear, 6¾" **12.00 17.00**

☐ **J.M. ERTS**
"Poughkeepsie, NY" all in oval slug plate on
front, "REGISTERED" appears below this, large
"E" embossed on bottom, clear, 7" **7.00 11.00**

☐ **ESPOSITO G., PHIADE.**
All in a circle, aqua, 6¾" **12.00 17.00**

☐ **ESPOSITO, J.**
812 & 814 Washington Ave., Kaca Kola, aqua,
7½" **12.00 17.00**

☐ **ETTA BOTTLING WORK**
Lafayette, LA, clear, 6¾" **12.00 17.00**

☐ **EUREKA BOTTLING WORKS**
Ft. Smith, AR, the words "stolen from" are at the
top, aqua, 7" **15.00 20.00**

☐ **EUREKA CALIFORNIA SODA WATER CO.**
S.F., in center of it, a bird, light green, 6¾" ... **16.00 23.00**

☐ **EVENCHIK, BROS. BOTTLING WORKS**
Cleveland, OH, in center an eagle, all in a circle,
aqua, 7" **15.00 20.00**

☐ **EWA BOTTLING WORK**
In a horse shoe letters, under it "H.T.," panels
base, clear, 7½" **75.00 95.00**

☐ also aqua **85.00 110.00**

☐ **EXCELSIOR BOTTLING CO.**
"Bloomington, Ill" all in a circle, under bottom
"E.B. Co.," aqua, 7" **14.00 19.00**

☐ **EXCELSIOR BOTTLING CO**
"Clarksburg, W. VA" all in a circle, aqua, 6¾" **12.00 17.00**

☐ **EXCELSIOR BOTTLING WORKS**
"Houston, Texas" all in a circle, aqua, 7¼" ... **15.00 20.00**

☐ **F.A.B.**
In a large horse shoe, in center, "Galveston, TX"
near base, aqua, 7½" **12.00 17.00**

☐ **FARGO, THE MINERAL SPRINGS CO.**
In a horse shoe letters, in center of it "Pure &
Clean, Warren, OH," clear, 6⅝" **12.00 17.00**

☐ **FELBRATH, H**
"Peoria, Ill" all in a circle at base S.B. & Co., aqua,
7" **12.00 17.00**

Price Range

☐ **FIDELITY BOTTLING WORKS**
"Reg. Monroe, LA" all in a circle, panels base,
under bottom, "Fidelity," aqua, 7" 15.00   20.00

☐ **5TH WARD BOTTLING WORKS**
"Houston, TX" All in a water mellow letters, in
center "5th Ward," aqua, 7¾" 15.00   20.00

☐ **FINLEY & SON**
In ½ moon letters in center 1893, under it "Bot-
tlers, 1806 D St. N.W. Washington, D.C." in back,
"T.B.N.T.B.S.," under bottom F, aqua, 6½" . . .   15.00   20.00

☐ **FISCHER & CO.**
"Santa Fe, NM" all in a circle, aqua, 6¼" 15.00   20.00

☐ **F.K. & SON**
"Socarro, NM" all in a circle, aqua, 6½" 30.00   40.00

☐ **FLADUNG & SONS**
"Reg. Reading, Ohio" all in a circle, aqua, 7½"   15.00   20.00

☐ **FLA. BREWING CO.**
"Fostoria, Ohio" all in a circle, aqua, 7" 15.00   20.00

☐ **FLETCHER, H.W.**
"Bellair, OH." all in a circle, aqua, 6½" 15.00   20.00

☐ **FLECKENSTEIN'S BOTTLING WORKS**
"Columbia, PA" in an oval on top & Reg. under
it, panel base, aqua, 6¾" 15.00   20.00

☐ **THE FLORIDA BREWING CO.**
"Tampa, Fla." all in a circle, on base F.B. Co.,
aqua, 6½" 15.00   20.00

☐ **FREIDMAN, WM.**
"Champion, Soda Factory, Key West, Fla." all in
a circle, on base "Reg. Etc.," clear, 6¾" 15.00   20.00

☐ **FOLGER'S BOTTLING WORKS**
"Grand Rapids, Mich" all on front in 5 lines, aqua,
6½" 15.00   20.00

☐ **FONDA D.C.**
"Boulder, Colo." all in a circle, aqua, 7" 15.00   20.00

☐ **FORSTER & POLHEMUS**
"Poughkeepsie, NY" All in 4 lines, clear, 7" . . .   15.00   20.00

☐ **FORTHOFEER, JOHN**
In ½ moon letters under it "Mt. Vernon, Ind.,"
light aqua, 6½" 15.00   20.00

☐ **FOSTORIA BOTTLING WORKS**
"Fostoria, Ohio" all in a circle, aqua, 7" 15.00   20.00

Price Range

☐ **FORT TOWSON BOTTLING WORKS**
"Fort Towson, Okla" all in a circle, under bottom
B & D, Panel base, aqua, 7½" 15.00 20.00

☐ **FURA, J., BOTTLING CO.**
All in a circle, aqua, 6½" 15.00 20.00

☐ **G.A.K.**
In large block letters in center of bottle, aqua,
6¾" 15.00 20.00

☐ **GADSEN BOTTLING WORK**
"Gadsen, Ala" all in a circle, clear, 6½" 15.00 20.00

☐ **GADSEN COCA—COLA**
"Gadsen, Ala" in block letters, clear, 7" 170.00 225.00

☐ **GALLAGER & CO.**
In ½ moon circle under it "Philade," in back Big
"C", in side of it "& Co.," light blue, 6⅞" 22.00 32.00

☐ **GALLUP BOTTLING WORKS**
"Gallup, NM" all in a circle, light aqua, 6½" ... 22.00 32.00

☐ **GAPERA BOTTLING**
"Ft. Worth, Texas" all in a circle, clear, 6½" .. 15.00 20.00

☐ **GARRISON, E.J.**
"Paterson, NJ" all in a circle, aqua or clear, 5¼" 15.00 20.00

☐ **GEARY BOTTLING WORKS**
"Geary, OT" all in a circle, yellow aqua, 6⅜" .. 170.00 225.00

☐ **GEARY BOTTLING WORKS**
"Geary, Okla" all in a circle, aqua, 6⅞" 45.00 65.00

☐ **GENTSCH, E.**
"Buffalo, NY" in three lines under bottom "G",
squat type bottle, light amber, 5¾" 15.00 20.00

☐ **GEORGIA BOTTLING CO.**
"Atlanta, GA" all in a circle, aqua, 7" 15.00 20.00

☐ **JOS GFROERER & CO.**
In ½ moon letters under it "Millbank D.T.," quart,
aqua 140.00 180.00

☐ **GIERING J.F.**
Youngstown, OH, clear, 6⅝" 15.00 20.00

☐ Same as above, except aqua 15.00 20.00

☐ **GILBERT BOTTLING WORKS**
"Minn." all in a circle, clear, 7½" 15.00 20.00

☐ **GILBERT BOTTLING WORKS,**
"Gilbert, Minn" all in a circle, bottom "R.," aqua,
6¾" 15.00 20.00

Price Range

☐ **GILLIGAN, A.C.**
In ½ moon letters under it, "Cincinnati, O.,
T.B.I.N.S." in back, eagle, under it "Trademark,
E.H.E. Co.," aqua, 7½" 15.00 20.00

☐ **GIMLICH & WHITE**
"Pittsfield, Mass" all in a circle, aqua, 7" 15.00 20.00

☐ **GLASSER & REASBECK**
"Bellaire, O." all in a circle, aqua, 6½" 15.00 20.00

☐ **GLENN & BARTOY**
"New Ulm, Texas" all in a circle, aqua, 6¾" .. 15.00 20.00

☐ **GOLDEN WEST SODA WORKS, BRUNS & NASH**
"Mountain View, Cal." all in 5 lines, light green,
7" 15.00 20.00

☐ **GORDON, A., HALF WAY HOUSE**
"Tannerville N.Y.," in a circle, under it registered,
on base in back, "Not to be Sold," clear, 6¾" 12.00 20.00

☐ **GORNY, A.**
In center "Trade A.G. Mark, Chicago, Ill." under
it, "R.T.B." on bottom "AG," aqua, 7" 12.00 17.00

☐ **GRAFTON BOTTLING WORKS**
Grafton, ND, clear, 6¾" 12.00 17.00

☐ **GRAFTON BOTTLING WORKS**
"Grafton, ND, Ill." in a circle, clear, 6¾" 15.00 20.00

☐ **GRAMERCY, BOTTLING WORKS**
Gramercy, LA, clear, 7" 12.00 17.00

☐ **GRAMERCY BOTTLING WORKS**
Gramercy, LA, aqua, 7" 15.00 20.00

☐ **GRANT, C.E.**
"Ohio" in 2 lines, aqua, 6½" 12.00 17.00

☐ **GRANT & UPTON**
In ½ moon letters, under it in 2 lines "Columbus,
Ohio," aqua, 6½" 12.00 17.00

☐ **GREENHOUSE, L.**
"Newark, NJ" in a circle, in back T.B.N.T.B.S.,
aqua, 7" 15.00 20.00

☐ **GREENVILLE BOTTLING & MFG. CO.,**
"Greenville, Texas" all in a circle, bottom "G,"
aqua, 6¼" 16.00 23.00

☐ **GREENWOOD STEAM BOTTLING WORKS**
Greenwood, MI, aqua 30.00 40.00

Price Range

☐ **GRERA BOTTLING**
"Ft. Worth, Texas" all in a circle, clear **12.00** **17.00**

☐ **GROCERY & CANDY CO.**
In horse shoe letters, under it "Fairmont, W. Va.,"
clear, 8¼" **12.00** **17.00**

☐ **GRUBEL, GEO.**
In ½ moon letters, under it in 2 lines "Kansas
City, Kans.," aqua, 6¾" **12.00** **17.00**

☐ **GRUBEL, GEO.**
"Kansas City, Kansas" in three lines, aqua, 6½" **8.00** **15.00**

☐ **GRUBEL, GEO.**
"Kansas City, Kansas" in three lines, clear, 6½" **12.00** **17.00**

☐ **GUAYMAS BOTTLING WORKS**
"Guaymas, Mexico" in 4 lines, clear, 7¼" **32.00** **42.00**

☐ **GUILBER, YREKA**
In a circle, aqua, 7¼" **15.00** **20.00**

☐ **GUILBER, YREKA**
In a circle, clear, 7" **12.00** **17.00**

☐ **GULFPORT BOTTLING WORKS, F. FRANK
SMITH, PROP.**
Gulfport, MI, aqua **70.00** **85.00**

☐ **GUTEKUNST, O.J.**
"Registered" all on front, clear, 6¾" **12.00** **17.00**

☐ **GUYETTE & COMPANY**
"Detroit, Mich, Reg." in center, "G" under bot-
tom, cobalt blue, 6¼" **42.00** **55.00**

☐ **GWINN BOTTLING WORK**
"Mich." in 3 lines, clear **12.00** **17.00**

☐ **C. C. HALEY & CO.**
"Celebrated California Pop Beer, Trademark" all
on front of bottle. Back of bottle: "531 & 533 West
38th St., New York, Patented Oct. 29th 1872." On
bottom: "This bottle not to be sold." Aqua, 7½" **15.00** **22.00**

☐ **HARVEY BOTTLING WORKS, R. T. HARVEY**
"Registered, Calumet, Mich," all in oval circle,
aqua, 6¼" **10.00** **15.00**

☐ **HATTIESBURG BOTTLING WORKS**
Hattiesburg, MI, aqua **20.00** **25.00**

☐ **J. J. HEINRICH & CO.**
Memphis, TN, clear, 7¾" **6.00** **8.00**

Price Range

☐ **JOS. HLADOVEC**
"84 Fisk St., Chicago, IL," name in semi-circle, address in straight lines. Unusual back marking "Tato Lahev Se Musi Naratit Spatky." Aqua, 6⅝"   16.00   30.00

☐ **HOFMANN BROS.**
So. Green St., Chicago, pictorial featuring large eagle with outstretched wings in the center, light aqua, 6¾" 18.00   30.00

☐ **C. H. HUDSON**
Scranton, MI, aqua 60.00   75.00

☐ **ICE PLANT BOTTLING WORKS**
"Oklahoma City" all in a circle under bottom B, aqua, 6¾" 16.00   23.00

☐ **IDABEL MFG. & BOTTLING CO.**
"Idabel, Okla" all in a circle, aqua, 6¾" 16.00   23.00

☐ **IMPERIAL BOTTLING WORKS**
"Montgomery, Ala" all in 4 lines, aqua, 7" 12.00   17.00

☐ **INDEPENDENT BOTTLING WORK**
In center hand shake, "S. McAlester, Okla. Trade Mark, reg." all in a circle, aqua, 6¾" 16.00   23.00

☐ **INDEPENDENT BOTTLING WORKS**
In center "B.C. Chicago," under bottom "C.B.," light blue, green, 6¼" 16.00   23.00

☐ **INGO SODA WORKS**
In a horse shoe letters, under it "Bishop, Calif.," 6½" 15.00   20.00

☐ **IRELAND BROS.**
B.W., inter blocking Mong. "Bottling Works, Malleawan, N.Y." all in a circle, aqua, 9⅜" 15.00   20.00

☐ **IRON CITY**
"11" on bottom, "96" on base, aqua, 6½" 12.00   17.00

☐ **ISAAC CRANS & SONS**
Missiletown, NY, all in slug plate, pale aqua, 6¾" 12.00   17.00

☐ **ISAAC, MERKEL**
"Plattsburg, NY" all in a circle, on bottom "A.G.W.," panel base, aqua, 7¼" 12.00   17.00

☐ **ISIAH BUNN**
"Reg Riverside Bottling Works Warwick, N.Y." all in a circle, under bottom a star, clear, 6⅝" 18.00   27.00

Price Range

☐ **ISIAH BUNN**
(top Reg.) "Riverside Bottling Works. Warwick,
N.Y." all in a circle, in back "T.B.N.T.B.S.," quart,
clear, 8¾" **22.00   32.00**

☐ **IUKA MINERAL**
Spring all in a circle, aqua, 6¾" **16.00   23.00**

☐ **JACKSON BOTTLING WORKS**
"W.A. Lake," all on front, aqua, 7" **16.00   23.00**

☐ **JACOBS, J.L.**
"Cairo, NY" all in a circle, light aqua, 7" **12.00   17.00**

☐ **JOS. JAMES—BOTTLING WORKS**
"Red Jacket MICH." all in oval circle, aqua, 6⅜" **11.00   16.00**

☐ **JASPER COCA—COLA CO.**
"Jasper, Ala," all in block letters, 6¾" **130.00 165.00**

☐ **J & F BORDE**
"Tampico, Mexico" all in water mellow letters,
panels base, light blue **23.00   32.00**

☐ **JEFFERSON BOTTLING WORKS**
"Jefferson, Texas" all in a circle, aqua, 7½" .. **23.00   32.00**

☐ **J.J. FLYNN & CO.**
In arc, "Quincy, Ill." below in two straight lines,
large "F" on bottom, aqua, 7¼" **8.00   12.00**

☐ Same as above, except has backward Q in
Quincy, aqua **10.00   14.00**

☐ **JOHN & HUGH, O'REILLY**
"Staten Island" all in a circle, T.B.N.T.B.S., light
blue, 6⅞" **16.00   20.00**

☐ **JOHNSON & BROS.**
"Delta, PA" all in a circle, amber, 6½" **23.00   34.00**

☐ **JOHNSON & CORBETT**
In ½ moon letters, under it "Socorro, N.M.,"
aqua, 6¼" **16.00   23.00**

☐ **JONES, A.**
In 2 lines, aqua, 6¾" **12.00   17.00**

☐ **JONES GEO.**
In 2 lines, aqua, 7" **12.00   17.00**

☐ **JONES, LEWIS F.**
"Philips Burch, PA" all in a circle, in back
"T.B.N.S.," aqua, 7" **16.00   23.00**

☐ **JOYCE, A.L.**
"Bottling Work, Traverse City, Mich." all in a circle, aqua, 6½" **12.00   17.00**

Price Range

☐ **JOYCE BROS**
"Greenville, Mich" all in a water mellow circle,
panels base, aqua to light green, 6¼" 12.00 17.00

☐ **JUMBO BOTTLING WORK**
In ½ moon letters, in center elephant, under it
Trademark, Cincinnati, OH, aqua, 7" 16.00 23.00

☐ **JUMBO BR'G CO.**
"The Mineral Water Dept. Cincinnati, OH" all in
a circle, on base "J.B. Co.," aqua, 7" 16.00 23.00

☐ **KAMMERER, G.**
"A.G.W.L." on base, aqua, 7" 12.00 17.00

☐ **KANTER BROS AND CO.**
All in a circle, aqua, 7" 9.00 13.00

☐ **L. KARNAHRENS**
"A Star-Bottling Jacksonville, Fla." all in 4 lines,
aqua.. 12.00 17.00

☐ **KARSCH & SONS, JOHN**
Evansville, IN, aqua, 6½" 12.00 17.00

☐ **A. W. KAYE**
Meridian, MI, clear 15.00 20.00

☐ **KEARNEY WM., A.**
Shamokin, PA, amber, 7¼" 27.00 38.00

☐ **KEAVENY BUCKLEY & CO.**
"348 & 350 Bienville Street, New Orleans" in 4
lines, under bottom star, aqua, 7⅛" 15.00 20.00

☐ **KEE, GEORGE F.**
In center a key, "Congers, NY" all in a circle,
under it "T.B.N.T.B.S.," clear, 7" 12.00 17.00

☐ **KEE, GEORGE F.**
In center a key, "CONGERS, NY" all in a circle,
under it "T.B.N.T.B.S.," clear, 7" 12.00 17.00

☐ **KEENAN MFG. CO.**
"Butte, MT." in a circle, ten panels at base, aqua,
7¼" 18.00 27.00

☐ **KEENAN MFG. CO**
"Butte, Mont." all in a circle, aqua, 6¾" 18.00 27.00

☐ **KELLER'S BOTTLING CO.**
In horse shoe, letters in center "Big K," under it
"Cleveland, OH" clear, 7¼" 12.00 17.00

☐ **KELLY, T.H. & CO.**
"Eagle Bottling Works, Steubenville, O." all in a
circle, aqua, 6½" 12.00 17.00

Price Range

☐ **KELLY T.H. & CO.**
"Eagle Bottling Works, Steubenville, O." all in a
circle, on base C & Co. 3, aqua, 6¾" 12.00 15.00

☐ **KELLY, T.H., EAGLE BOTTLING WORKS**
"Steubenville, O." all in a circle, aqua, 6" 12.00 17.00

☐ **KENNEDY, C.H.**
"Butler, PA." in 2 lines in center, clear, 6½" .. 15.00 20.00

☐ **KENRICK, E.J. & SON**
In ½ moon circle, under it "Portsmouth, O.,"
aqua, 6½" 12.00 17.00

☐ **KING, N.Y.**
"Rogers, Ark." all in a circle, aqua, 6" 12.00 17.00

☐ **KING & JOYCE**
Chicago, on base "T.B.I.N.S." under bottom "K
& J," aqua, 7½" 12.00 17.00

☐ **KINGFISHER BOTTLING WORKS F.C.
BROWN**
"Kingfisher, OT" all in a circle, aqua, 6¾" 120.00 155.00

☐ **KINNEY BOTTLING WORKS**
"McCurtain, IT" all in a circle, aqua, 6½" 65.00 85.00

☐ **KINNEY'S BOTTLING WORKS**
"McCurtain, Okla." all in a circle, aqua, 6½" .. 16.00 23.00

☐ **KINGSTON BOTTLING WORK, I.V. WAGNER
PROP.**
"Kingston, NC" in a horse shoe, letters in back
"T.B.N.T.B.S.," clear, 7" 15.00 20.00

☐ **KLUETSCH, CHARLES**
In center (mong. KC) "Chicago, Ill." all in a circle,
Bolton CK., aqua, 6½" 16.00 23.00

☐ **KNOWN**
(besides what is listed in this book) Coca-Cola,
Tuskgee, Al, Brunswick, Ga., Atlanta, Ga., Gadsen, al., Chatt, Tenn., all in block letters, Jasper,
Al 150.00 350.00

☐ **KOEHLER, HENRY**
"Pomeroy, Ohio" all in a circle under it registered,
aqua, 7" 12.00 17.00

☐ **KREBS UNION**
In ½ moon letters, under it in 3 lines "Bottling
Works, Krebs, I.T.," clear, 6½" 120.00 155.00

☐ **KROGER BROS.**
"Butte, MT" in a circle, aqua, 8" 30.00 40.00

Price Range

☐ **KROGER BROS.**
"Butte, MT" all in a circle, clear, 6½" 185.00 235.00

☐ **KRUSLING & HUESMANN**
In a horse shoe, letters in center a flag on 3 strip,
Union Trademark, under it "Cincinnati," aqua, 7"   15.00   20.00

☐ **KUHLMAN THE JOHN BREWING CO.**
"Ellenville, NY" all in a circle, bottom "A & D,"
aqua, 7" 16.00   23.00

☐ **KULY BOTTLING WORKS**
"Decatur, Ill" all in a circle, bottom "A & D," aqua,
6½" 12.00   17.00

☐ **LA. PRULVA**
"Farrica de Aguss, Gasedsas, Jose Ma. Sam-
chez, Jerez, Zac" all in a circle, under bottom
"A.R.," aqua, 6¾" 16.00   23.00

☐ **LAKE W.W., JACKSON BOTTLING WORKS**
"Jackson, MI" in 3 lines, under bottom "L," aqua,
7" 12.00   17.00

☐ **LAYER, C.**
"Raton, NM" all in a circle, panel base, clear,
7¼" 16.00   23.00

☐ **LAUBE, JAS. X**
"Akron, O" all in a circle, blue, 6¾" 23.00   32.00

☐ **LAUGMONT BOTTLING WORKS**
All in a circle, clear or aqua, 6½" 12.00   17.00

☐ **LAUREL BOTTLING WORKS**
Laurel, MI, aqua 25.00   30.00

☐ **LAUTERBACK, JOHN**
In a horse shoe letters, under it "Springfield, Ill.,"
on base "N.B.B.G. Co.," 46, aqua, 7⅛" 12.00   17.00

☐ **LAVIN, M.F.**
"Ashley, PA" in a horse shoe letters, under it
"Reg.," light blue, 6¾" 12.00   17.00

☐ **LAWRENCE, LOUIS**
"Manaimo, B.C." all in a circle, aqua, 7½" 16.00   23.00

☐ **LEHIGH BOTTLING**
In horse shoe letters, "Works" under it, "Lehigh,
Ind. Ter.," aqua, 6½" 130.00 170.00

☐ **LEHIGH, BOTTLING WORKS**
"Lehigh, IT" all in a circle, light aqua, 6⅝" 130.00 170.00

Price Range

☐ **LEHIGH BOTTLING WORKS**
"Lehigh, Okla" all in a circle, under bottom "S,"
aqua, 6⅝" .... | 16.00 | 23.00

☐ **LEMAIRE**
On front 4 piece mold, aqua, 6½" .... | 12.00 | 17.00

☐ **LEMON BEER**
"Noona & Irmiger, Manitowac, Wisc.," all in 4
lines, amber, 6½" .... | 32.00 | 43.00

☐ **LEMON BEER**
"Moonan & Manitowac, Wisc" all in a circle,
amber, 6¼" .... | 32.00 | 43.00

☐ **LETTENMAYER O.**
"Keen, NH" All in a circle, "H 2–5" under bottom,
aqua, 6½" .... | 12.00 | 17.00

☐ **LINDSEY, J.A.**
A harp on back, "33" under bottom, aqua, 7" | 12.00 | 17.00
☐ Same except clear .... | 12.00 | 17.00

☐ **LIQUID THE**
In side of diamond, on bottom, on base "M.B. &
g. Co. 33," aqua, 6¾" .... | 12.00 | 17.00

☐ **LODI SODA WORKS**
"California" all in a circle, large letters, aqua,
6½", rare .... | 30.00 | 45.00

☐ **LOHR, ANDREW**
Ridge on back mold, on bottom "C. & Co. LIM,"
clear or aqua, 6½" .... | 12.00 | 17.00

☐ **LOMAX**
"Chicago, Etc." on front, in back "T.B.M.B.R.,"
cobalt, 7" .... | 55.00 | 75.00

☐ **LOMAX J.A.**
Ginger ale all on front, aqua, 6½" .... | 12.00 | 17.00

☐ **LOMAX J.A.**
"14–16 & 18 Charles Place, Chicago, Trademark
Reg." in a diamond square in center of it 4 bottle
in a diamond in center "J.A.L." all on front, base
"T.B.M.B.R.," bottom "J.L.," 6¾" .... | 60.00 | 80.00

☐ **LOMAX, K.A.**
"Chicago" all in a circle, cobalt, 7" .... | 45.00 | 60.00
☐ Same except in back "T.B.M.B.R." .... | 50.00 | 70.00

☐ **LONG, F.C., THE BOTTLING CO.**
"Chicago" in 3 lines, aqua, 6½" .... | 12.00 | 17.00

Price Range

☐ **LOW, JOHN**
"S" all in a circle, aqua, 7" 12.00   17.00
☐ **LUCAS, A.E.,**
"Wilmington, NC" all in a circle, 6⅞" . . . 16.00   23.00
☐ **LUDWIG A.**
"Napa, Cal." in 3 lines, clear or aqua, 6½" 16.00   23.00
☐ **LUDWIG, L.**
"Brunswick, GA" in horse shoe letters, in back
"T.B.T.B.R.," under bottom "Dixon," smoke
color, 7¼" 12.00   17.00
☐ **LUMBERTON BOTTLING WORKS**
Lumberton, MI, aqua 70.00   85.00
☐ **LUTHER & MYERS**
In ½ moon letters, under it "Albany, N.Y.," panels
base, under bottom, "L & M," aqua, 7" 16.00   23.00
☐ **LYMAN ASTLEY**
"Cheyenne, Wyo" all in a circle, 6¾" 25.00   34.00
☐ **M.B.W.**
"Minot, ND" all in a circle, aqua, 7¼" 12.00   17.00
☐ **M & M STAR BOTTLING CO.**
"Oskaloosa, IA" aqua, 6½" 15.00   23.00
☐ **MACON BOTTLING WORKS**
E.J. Burk, aqua, 6⅝" 12.00   17.00
☐ **MAGIC CITY BOTTLING WORKS**
Hattiesburg, MI, aqua 25.00   30.00
☐ **MADDEN, GEORGE E.**
Aqua, 7" 15.00   20.00
☐ **MAGIC CITY BOTTLING WORKS**
Hattiesburg, MI, aqua 25.00   30.00
☐ **MAGINNIS, GEO. T. & CO.**
All in a circle, aqua, 7" 12.00   17.00
☐ **MAHASKA BOTTLING WORKS**
All in a circle, clear, 7" 12.00   17.00
☐ **MAHASKA BOTTLING WORKS**
All in a circle, aqua, 6¾" 12.00   17.00
☐ **MANFIELD BOTTLE WORKS**
"Manfield, Ark" all in a circle, "M" etc. under bot-
tom, light green, 6½" 15.00   20.00
☐ **THE MANHATTAN BOTTLING CO.**
Chicago, IL, in center of it Trademark a horse
head, "Registered" under bottom "Trademark
Registered" in center head, aqua, 6¾" 16.00   23.00

Price Range

☐ **MANHATTAN, THE, BOTTLING CO.**
"Trademark registered Chicago, Ill." all in a circle, in center of it a horse head, aqua, 6½" **12.00   17.00**

☐ **MARIETTA BOTTLING WORKS**
"Marietta, GA" all in a circle, clear, 7" **12.00   17.00**

☐ **MARIETTA BOTTLING WORKS**
"Marietta, Okla." all in a circle, panels base, aqua, 7¼" **75.00 100.00**

☐ **MARION BOTTLING & ICE CREAM CO.**
"Made from Mo-Cola, original Coca-Cola Formula not an imitation, Ocala, Fla." all in a circle, aqua, 6¾" **12.00   17.00**

☐ **MARION BOTTLING & ICE CREAM CO.**
"Made from Mo-Cola original, Coca-Cola Formula, not an imitation," all in a circle, clear, 6¼" **55.00   75.00**

☐ **MARION BOTTLING WORKS**
"Fairmont, W.VA." all in a circle, aqua, 6¾" ... **12.00   17.00**

☐ **MARKOWITZ, L.**
"Brunswick, GA" in 3 lines in back "T.B.T.B.R.," aqua, 7⅝" **16.00   23.00**

☐ **MARSH, J.I.**
"Portmouth, O." all in a circle, aqua, green, 6¼" **12.00   17.00**

☐ **MARTIN BRAZELL**
"North Hoosick, NY" in round slug plate on front, blue, 7" **10.00   16.00**

☐ **MARTINS BOTTLING CO.**
"Minneapolis" in 3 lines, aqua, 6½" **12.00   17.00**

☐ **MATHIEU, JACOB**
"Byesville, O." all in a circle, aqua, 7" **12.00   17.00**

☐ **MAUSER G. & CO.**
"Adams, Mass. Registered" all in a circle, aqua, 7¼" **12.00   17.00**

☐ **MAYER & BERNSTEIN**
"Albany, NY Registered" in 3 lines, clear or aqua, 7" **12.00   17.00**

☐ **MAYER, CHAS. H. CO.**
Trademark large G D all in a ½ moon letters, under it "Registered, Hammond, Ind.," Registered "M" under bottom, light green, 7¼" **15.00   20.00**

Price Range

☐ **MAYER, CHAS. H.M. & CO.**
In ½ moon circle, in it Trade G.D., under it in 3 lines "Registered, Hammond, Ind.," also extra Registered panel base in back" T.B.I.N.S.," under bottom "M," light blue, 7″ **15.00 20.00**

☐ **MAYER, JACOB**
"Evansville, IN" under bottom, "J.M.," panels base, aqua, 6¼″ **12.00 17.00**

☐ **MAYFIELD**
In script "Celery Cola," not script "Standard Bottling Co. Atlanta, GA." all in a circle, panels base, aqua, 7″ **32.00 42.00**

☐ **MAYFIELD**
In script "Celery Cola," not script, "Rome Bottling Works, Rome, GA" all in a circle, aqua, 6½″ . . **32.00 42.00**

☐ **MAYFIELD, CELERY—COLA**
J.C. Mayfield Mfg. Co. Birmingham, AL., aqua, 6½″ **12.00 17.00**

☐ **McBRIDE EARL & POLLAND**
In a horse shoe letters, under it "Registered, Detroit, Mich.," aqua, 7″ **12.00 17.00**

☐ **McCARTHY**
"Perry, OT" all in a circle, bottom "77," panel base, aqua, 7¼″ **75.00 100.00**

☐ **McCARTHY**
"Ponoa City, OT" all in a circle, on bottom, "77," aqua, 7¼″ **75.00 100.00**

☐ **McCREEDY**
"Providence, RI" all in a circle, on shoulder "Registered," panels base, clear, 7″ **23.00 32.00**

☐ **McCREEDY, S.E.**
"Providence, RI" in a circle, panels base, aqua, 6¼″ **12.00 17.00**

☐ **McDONOUGH & COMPANY**
"First and Henderson, J.C." in 4 lines vertical, "No. 1" under bottom, aqua, 6½″ **12.00 17.00**

☐ **McGRATH BROS**
Hoosick Falls, NY, tombstone shape slug plate, number on bottom, aqua, 6⅝″ **8.00 12.00**

☐ **McGRAW, J.C.**
"Harper's Ferry, W. Va." all in a circle, clear, 7″ **12.00 17.00**

Price Range

☐ **McGUINESS**
Eagle in center, "Utica, NY" all in a circle, bottom
star, light aqua, 6⅞" 135.00 175.00

☐ **McMAHAN**
Paulsvilley, IT, clear, 6¾" 12.00 17.00

☐ **McNEIL B.**
"Wheeling, W. Va." In center mong, all in a circle,
clear, 6⅝" 12.00 17.00

☐ **McPALIN, DON**
"Park City, Utah" all in a circle, clear 6½" 16.00 23.00

☐ **GEORGE L. McREEVY**
In ½ moon letters, in center "GL & McCm" mong
letters, "trademark Reg. Baltimore, Md." all in a
circle, Registered in back "T.B.I.N.S.," bottom
"CL McC," aqua, 7" 12.00 17.00

☐ **MEEHAN BROS.**
"M" under bottom, light green, 6½" 12.00 17.00

☐ **MEISER BROS.**
"Pleasant City, O." all in a circle, in back M.B. &
G Co., aqua, 7" 16.00 23.00

☐ **MEMPHIS BOTTLING AND MFG. CO.**
"Memphis, Tenn." all in a circle, aqua, 6½" ... 16.00 23.00

☐ **MEMPHIS BOTTLING WORKS, R. M.
BECKER**
Aqua, 7¼" 8.00 10.00

☐ **MENDOCINO BOTTLING WORKS, A. L.
REYNOLDS**
All in 3 lines, light green, 7" 16.00 23.00

☐ **MENTON, M., BELTON**
Texas, in center a rooster, aqua, 6¾" 12.00 17.00

☐ **MERIDIAN STEAM BOTTLING CO.**
"(Miss)" all in a circle, clear, 6¾" 16.00 23.00

☐ **MERRIT MOORE, JR. BOTTLER**
All in a circle, back "T.B.N.T.B.S.," CLEAR, 7" 12.00 17.00

☐ **MERRIT MOORE JR. BOTTLER**
"This Bottle Not To Be Sold" on back, clear or
amethyst, 7" 12.00 17.00

☐ **MESSALL**
"(M.E. Mong.) Mark, Enid, O. T. Registered," all
in a circle, light aqua, 6⅝" 90.00 120.00

☐ **MESSALL, E.J.**
"Concordia, Kans." all in a circle, aqua, 6⅞" .. 18.00 26.00

Price Range

☐ **MESSALL AND MESSALL**
All in a circle, Guthrie, OK, aqua, 6¾" 80.00 105.00
☐ **METTE BROS.**
"Chicago, Ill." in 3 lines under bottom, mong.
"M.B.," clear or amethyst, 6½" 12.00   17.00
☐ **MEW, W.B., & LANGTON CO.**
All in a circle, green, 7" 16.00   23.00
☐ **MEYER & RADCLIFFE**
"Wheeling, W. Va." in center mong. all in a circle,
clear, 6⅝" 12.00   17.00
☐ **MILES, A.S.**
All on front, aqua, 6½" 12.00   17.00
☐ **MILLER, A.H.**
Aqua, 6½" 12.00   17.00
☐ **MILLER WM., BOTTLING WORKS**
"Montpelier, VT" all in a circle, bottom "E. 3,"
aqua, 6⅞" 16.00   23.00
☐ **MILLER, W.J.**
"Woodsfield, O." in center a star all in a circle,
clear, 6½" 12.00   17.00
☐ **MILLS BROS. & CO. IN ARC**
"Quincy, Ill" below in two straight lines. Large
"M" on bottom, aqua, 7" 11.00   15.00
☐ **MILWAUKEE BOTTLING CO.**
"N. Platte, Neb." in a sunken panel, aqua, 7¼"   16.00   23.00
☐ **THE MINERAL WATER MFG. CO.**
"Defiance, Ohio" all in a circle, under it registered
in back "T.B.I.N.T.B.S.," aqua, 7" 18.00   26.00
☐ **MINOT BOTTLING WORKS CO.**
"Minot, ND" all in a circle, aqua, 7" 16.00   23.00
☐ **MISSOULA BOTTLING WORKS**
Clear or aqua, 7" 12.00   17.00
☐ **MOE, J.M.**
"Tomahawk, Wis." in three lines, clear, 5¼" . .   14.00   19.00
☐ **MOE, J.M.**
"Tomahawk, Wis." in three lines, aqua, 6¾" . .   12.00   17.00
☐ **MOKELUMNE HILL SODA WORKS**
All in a circle, aqua, 6½" 12.00   17.00
☐ **MONROE BOTTLING**
In a horse shoe letters, under it "Works," Mon-
roe, LA. clear, 7¼" 12.00   17.00

Price Range

☐ **MONROE CIDER & VINEGAR**
"Eureka, Cal." all in 3 lines, aqua, 6¾" 12.00 17.00
☐ **MOORE JOHN R.**
"Swainsboro, GA" all in a circle under bottom
201, aqua, 6½" 12.00 17.00
☐ **MORJARITY & CARROLL**
All in a circle, aqua, 6½" 12.00 17.00
☐ **MORLEY C.**
"Victoria, BC" in 3 lines, under bottom diff Nos.,
aqua, 7½" 23.00 32.00
☐ **MORNINGSTAR D.**
"Salem, Ohio" all in a circle under it
"T.B.N.T.B.S.," aqua, 7" 12.00 17.00
☐ **MOULTON & SCOTT**
"Norton, Kans." all in a circle, clear, 6½" 15.00 20.00
☐ **MT. CARMEL ICE & BOTTLING CO. MT.**
"Carmel, Ill." all in a circle, aqua, 6¾" 12.00 17.00
☐ **MT. HOOD SODA WATER**
"Portland, Ore. Etc." all in a circle, panels base,
light green, 7" 16.00 23.00
☐ **MOXIE**
In large letters near shoulder, aqua, 6½" 45.00 60.00
☐ **MULLEN B.J.**
"Albany, NY" in 3 lines under bottom, (mong.)
"B.J.M.," clear, 7¼" 12.00 17.00
☐ **MULLEN B.J.E.**
In ¼ moon letters, in center mong. "M.B.J.E.,
1886," clear, 7¼" 12.00 17.00
☐ **MULLINS, J.**
In 1" hollow letters, under it "Buffalo, N.Y.,"
under bottom "M," on base "C & Co.," aqua,
6½" 11.00 15.00
☐ **MUSKOGEE BOTTLING WORKS**
Muskogee, IT, aqua or clear, 6½" 90.00 125.00
☐ **MUSKOGEE BOTTLING WORK**
"Muskogee, IT" all in a circle, bottom "E.R.R.,"
aqua, 6⅜" 100.00 130.00
☐ Same except panels base 120.00 155.00
☐ **MUSKOGEE BOTTLING WORKS**
"Muskogee, IT" all in a circle, bottom "S," light
aqua, 6¼" 115.00 140.00

Price Range

☐ **MUSKOGEE FRUIT CO.**
"Muskogee, IT" all in a circle, clear, 7" 100.00 130.00
☐ **MUSKEGON BOTTLING WORKS**
Muskegon, MI, panels base, dark aqua, 6½" .. 35.00 20.00
☐ **MUTCHLER & WEISER**
"Cherry Vale, Kans." all in a circle, clear, 6⅞" 16.00 23.00
☐ **CHAS. J. MUTH LIBERTY BOTTLING WORKS**
"Liberty, NY" all in tombstone shaped slug plate
on front, back of bottom has "This Bottle not to
be Sold," aqua, 6⅞" 8.00 12.00
☐ **NATIONAL BOTTLE WORKS**
"John J. Ball Prop. York, Pa." all in a circle, under
it reg. under bottom "#4," clear, 6½" 12.00 17.00
☐ **NATIONAL, DOPE CO.**
"Birmingham, AL" all in a water mellow letters,
under it "T.B.I.N.S.," aqua, 8" 18.00 25.00
☐ **NATIONAL SODA WATER**
All in a circle, aqua, 6½" 12.00 17.00
☐ **HOPE, NEW SELTZ & MINERAL WATER MFG. CO.**
"L. M. 350 Bienville's N.O. La." in 7 lines, vertical,
under bottom a anchor, aqua, 8" 12.00 17.00
☐ **NEW LIBERIA ICE & BOTTLING CO.**
In 4 lines, clear, 7" 12.00 17.00
☐ **NEW LIBERTY SODA CO.**
All in a circle, clear, 6½" 12.00 17.00
☐ **NEWMANN & FUNKE**
"Detroit, Mich." all in a circle, under bottom N &
F, aqua, 7" 12.00 17.00
☐ **NEWPORT MINERAL WATER CO.**
"Newport, KY." all in a circle, under it "Reg.," on
base "T.B.I.N.S. D.O.C. 92," under bottom "W.,"
light aqua, 6⅞" 12.00 17.00
☐ **NEW YORK BOTTLING WORKS**
"Fayette City" all in a circle, under it "SS," clear,
6½" 18.00 25.00
☐ **NEVADA CITY SODA WATER WORKS**
"E.T.R. Powell in 2 lines vertical lines, light green,
6¾" 12.00 17.00

Price Range

☐ **NEVADA CITY SODA WORKS**
In horse shoe letters, under it "E.T.R. Powell,"
aqua, 6½" 15.00 20.00

☐ **NEVADA CO.**
"Col." all in 5 lines, light green, 7" 12.00 17.00

☐ **NEVADA SODA WATER**
"Grass Valley" all in a circle, aqua, 6½" 12.00 17.00

☐ **NOCK'S BOTTLING WORKS**
"Niles, Ohio" all in a circle, clear, 7¼" 12.00 17.00

☐ **NORTHROP & STURGIS CO.**
"Portland, OR." in 4 lines, light blue, 6¼" 16.00 23.00

☐ **NORTHWESTERN BOTTLING CO.**
"Butte, Mont." all in a circle, aqua, 6½" 33.00 42.00

☐ **NORTHWESTERN BOTTLING WORKS**
Washington, D.C., in center "1601 5th St.
N.W.J.H. Schlueter," on back "Reg. N.T.B.S.,"
6½" 16.00 23.00

☐ **O.K. CITY BOTTLING WORKS C.G. FROST**
All in a circle, bottom "F.," aqua, 6⅜" 16.00 23.00

☐ **O.K. CITY BOTTLING WORKS C.G. FROST**
All in a circle, "F," under bottom, amber, 6¾" 45.00 60.00

☐ **OK MULGEE BOTTLING WORKS OK**
"Mulgee, IT" all in a circle, aqua, 6⅝" 170.00 225.00

☐ **O.P.S.W. CO.**
In center, "O" and a bottle, Trademark, under it
"Oakland, Al." Reg. on base "T.B.T.N.S.," aqua,
6½" 16.00 23.00

☐ **OAKLAND STEAM SODA WORKS**
In center, a sun and "1882," on bottom "B.N.S.,"
6¼" 16.00 23.00

☐ **OCEANVIEW BOTTLING WORKS**
"N & B Prop. Mendocino, Cal." all in a water mellow letters, aqua, 6½" 15.00 20.00

☐ **OGDEN, BOTTLING SODA WORKS**
"Ogden, Utah" all in a circle, clear, 6¾" 16.00 23.00

☐ **THE OHIO BOTTLING CO.**
"Cleveland, O." in a circle, in center eagle, Trademark Reg., aqua, 7¼" 16.00 23.00

☐ **OHIO BOTTLING WORKS**
In horse shoe letters in center, a mong. under it,
Sandusky, OH., light green, 5¼" 16.00 23.00
☐ Same except all in a circle, aqua, 5½" 12.00 17.00

Price Range

☐ **OHIO BOTTLING WORK**
In center mong. "O.N. Sandusky, O." all in a circle, aqua, 5½" 12.00 17.00

☐ **OHIO BOTTLING WORKS**
In ½ moon letters in center mong., under it in 1 line "Sandusky, O.," aqua, 7⅝" 12.00 17.00

☐ **OKLAHOMA CITY BOTTLING WORKS**
"Stiller Bros.," all in a circle, under bottom "S," aqua, 6¼" 16.00 23.00

☐ **OLIN & ORENDORFF**
"So. Pueblo, Col." all in a circle, aqua, 6¼" ... 16.00 23.00

☐ **OLIN & ORENDORFF**
"So. Pueblo, CO," aqua, 6½" 16.00 23.00

☐ **OMAHA BOTTLING CO.**
All in a circle, aqua, 6¼" 16.00 23.00

☐ **OMAHA BOTTLING CO.**
In 2½ moon lines, under it "Omaha Nebr." "O" under bottom, light aqua, 6½" 16.00 23.00

☐ **E. OTTENVILLE**
Nashville, TN, cobalt blue, 6¾" 125.00 150.00

☐ **OTTENVILLE, E. "MC"**
In 2 lines, under bottom "25," cobalt, 6" 70.00 90.00

☐ **OTTENVILLE**
"Nashville, Tenn." all in a circle, blue 33.00 42.00

☐ **OTTENVILLE, E.**
"McC" on base, "25" under bottom, cobalt, 6" 70.00 90.00

☐ **PABLO & CO.**
Man in a canoe and dog, T.B.N.S., etc. N.O., aqua, 7" 33.00 42.00

☐ **PABLO & CO. J.**
In center, man in canoe with dog, Trademark, on base "T.B.N.S. Seltzer & Mineral Mfg. Nos. 475–477 & 479 St. Claude, St. N.D." 17.00 23.00

☐ **PABST & SONS, J.**
In ½ moon, in center a big "P," under it "Hamilton," aqua, 6½" 15.00 20.00

☐ **PACIFIC BOTTLING WORKS**
In a horse shoe letters, under it "Tacoma, Wash.," light green, 6¾" 15.00 20.00

☐ **PACIFIC PUGET SOUND SODA WORKS**
"Seattle, WT" in 5 lines, under bottom a diamond with "A" in side of it, aqua, 6¾" 100.00 140.00

Price Range

☐ **THE PACOLET GRAPE JUICE CO.**
"Tryon, N.C." in a circle, cob. top, aqua, 7" ...   12.00   17.00

☐ **D. PALISER**
"Paliser" should be "Palliser" (misspelled), aqua,
6¼" 22.00   32.00

☐ **PALISRODE**
Eagle in center, on other side "Bottling Co.,"
shield and monogram in center, 6½" 12.00   17.00

☐ **D. PALLISERS SONS**
Aqua, 7" 12.00   17.00

☐ **PALMER S.C. WASHING CO.**
All in a circle, amber, 6¾" 60.00   80.00

☐ **PAPE, THE CHAS BOTTLING WORKS**
"Maritta, O." all in a circle, under it registered, in
back "T.B.I.N.S.," aqua, 7" 12.00   17.00

☐ **PARSON, T.**
"Salt Lake City" in 3 lines, light blue, 6½" 15.00   20.00

☐ **PASTOL, HENRY J.**
"Sacramento, Cal." all in 3 lines, aqua, 7" 12.00   17.00

☐ **PAWNEE ICE & COLD STORAGE CO.
BOTTLING WORKS**
"Pawnee, Okla." all in a circle, light aqua, 6¾"   16.00   23.00

☐ **PEARSON BROS.**
"Placerville" in 2 lines, aqua, 6½" 12.00   17.00

☐ **PENNSBORO BOTTLING WORKS**
"Pennsboro, W. Va." all in a circle, aqua, 6¾"   12.00   17.00

☐ **PENSACOLA BOTTLING WORKS**
"Pensacola, Fla." all in a circle, dark aqua, 6"   15.00   20.00

☐ **PEPSI-COLA**
In script, "PENSACOLA, FLA.," clear, 7" 235.00 315.00

☐ **PERKINS, P.W.**
Star in center, Tannerville, N.Y., under bottom K.
Hutter, 10 D.N.Y., aqua or clear, 6½" 12.00   17.00

☐ **PERKINS STEAM BOTTLING WORKS**
"L.O. Martz Proprietor, Perkins, Okla." all in a circle, aqua, 6½" 16.00   23.00

☐ **PAUL POMEROY**
Ludington, MI, aqua, 7" 12.00   17.00

☐ **PIONEER MINERAL & SODA WATER
WORKS**
Meridian, MI, aqua 30.00   40.00

Price Range

☐ **POND BOTTLING CO., A.J. ENCLERT**
"Pond Creek, OT" all in a circle, on shoulder "R,"
clear, 6¾" 140.00 190.00

☐ **POP BOTTLE**
Label, aqua, 7" 11.00 15.00

☐ **POPULAR SODA WORKS CO.**
All in a circle, aqua, 6½" 12.00 17.00

☐ **PORT BOTTLING CO.**
All in a circle, sold at sloe 85, aqua, 6¼" 12.00 17.00

☐ **PORTNER, ROBERT, BREW COMP**
In center a diamond with "Trade, Tivoli, Mark,"
under it "Alexandria, Va." all in a circle, clear,
7½" 15.00 20.00

☐ **POTEAU BOTTLING**
In horse shoe letters in center works, under it,
bottom "S. Poteau, I.T.," aqua, 6½" 140.00 190.00

☐ **POTEAU BOTTLING WORKS**
"Poteau, I.T." all in a circle, no sundy bottom,
aqua, 6⅝" 130.00 175.00

☐ **POTEAU BOTTLING WORKS**
"Poteau, I.T." All in a circle, under bottom "S,"
aqua, 6¾" 140.00 190.00

☐ **POUND CREEK BOTTLING CO., A.J.**
ENCLERT
"Pound Check," should be "Pound Creek, O.T.,"
clear, 6¾" 135.00 185.00

☐ **PRESCOTT BOTTLING WORKS**
Prescott, A.T. clear, 6¾" 150.00 210.00

☐ **PRIDE BOTTLING CO.**
All in a circle, aqua or clear, 6¼" 12.00 17.00

☐ **PROPERTY OF C.C. BOTTLING CO.**
Clear, 6¾" 150.00 210.00

☐ **PURDY BOTTLE CO.**
All in a circle, under bottom "P.," aqua, 6½" .. 12.00 17.00

☐ **QUERBES, ANDREW**
"Shreveport, LA." all in a circle, "Q" under bottom, aqua, 6¾" 15.00 20.00

☐ **R & W**
"Las Vegas, N.M." all in a circle, aqua, 7⅛" .. 16.00 23.00

☐ **R & W**
"Las Vegas, N.M." in a sunken panel, ten sided
base, aqua, 7½" 16.00 23.00

Price Range

☐ **RAINIER, SODA CO. BOTTLING WORKS**
"Seattle" all in a circle, clear, 7" 16.00 23.00

☐ **RALSTON BOTTLING WORKS**
Ralston, OT, clear, panel base, clear, 7¼" 135.00 180.00

☐ **RALU, H.A., COLON, R.P.**
All in a water mellow letters, in back
"T.B.N.T.B.S.," Panels base, clear, 8" 16.00 23.00

☐ **RANFTS BOTTLING WORKS**
"Joliet, Ill, Reimers & Voitik-successors," all in a
circle, aqua, 6½" 12.00 17.00

☐ **RAVENNA, O.**
In center "E.S.H. Bottling Works" all in a circle,
aqua, 6¾" 12.00 17.00

☐ **RAVENNA, O.S.**
In center "E.S.H. Bottling Works," all in a circle
on base "Reg. T.B.N.T.B.S., A.B. Co., 0191,"
under bottom "H.," clear 23.00 32.00

☐ **RAVIA BOTTLING WORKS**
Ravia, IT, under bottom "16," light aqua, 6¾" 130.00 175.00

☐ **RAY, JAS.**
"Savannah, GA" all in a circle, aqua, 6½" 16.00 23.00

☐ **REASBECK, C.J.**
"Martins Ferry, O" on 2 panels, 10 panels bottle,
aqua, 6⅞" 16.00 23.00

☐ **REASBECK, C.J.**
"Martins Ferry, O" all in a circle, aqua, 6⅞" . . . 12.00 17.00

☐ **REASBECK, P.H.**
Braddock, PA, clear or aqua, 7" 12.00 17.00

☐ **RED FOX BOTTLING WORKS**
"Steubenville, O." all in a circle, aqua, 6⅞" . . . 12.00 17.00

☐ **REED, J.R.**
"Fernandina, Fla." all in a circle, aqua, 6½" . . . 12.00 17.00

☐ **REEDER BOTTLING WORKS, REEDER, N.D.**
"Reeder, N.D." all in a circle, aqua, 6¾" 27.00 36.00

☐ **REICHERT, F.A., WASHINGTON C.H.**
"Ohio" all in a circle, under it Reg., aqua, 7" . . 12.00 17.00

☐ **RENFRO MFG. CO.**
"Atlanta, GA" all in a circle, panels base, under
bottom "A.C. Co." aqua, 7" 12.00 17.00

☐ **RICHARD & THALHEIMER**
Under bottom "Dixie," clear or amethyst, aqua,
7½" 12.00 17.00

Price Range

☐ **THE RICHARDSON BOTTLING CO.**
"Mansfield, O" all in a circle, aqua, 6¾" **12.00** **17.00**

☐ **RICHTER'S BOTTLING WORKS**
"Fresno, Cal" in 3 lines, "R" under bottom, aqua,
6¼" **12.00** **17.00**

☐ **RIDER C.W.**
"Watertown, NY" all in a circle, amber, 7" **23.00** **32.00**

☐ **RINN EMIL F.**
"Bottle Work," all in a circle, dark green, 6½"   **12.00** **17.00**

☐ **RIVIERA MINERAL WATER**
"Tyler, Texas" all in a circle, under bottom "X"
panels base, aqua, 7¼" **15.00** **20.00**

☐ **ROBERT J.**
"Union City, Tenn" on 2 panels, 10 panels bottle
on base "C & Co.," aqua, 6¾" **12.00** **17.00**

☐ **ROBINSON, A.B.**
"Bangor, ME" all in a circle, aqua, 7½" **16.00** **23.00**

☐ **THE ROCKY MOUNTAIN BOTTLE WORKS**
All in a circle, clear or aqua, 6½" **12.00** **17.00**

☐ **ROESEN, W.F.**
Jefferson City, MO, in center lady with glass &
banner riding, ale bottle on wheels, etc., aqua,
6¼" **16.00** **23.00**

☐ **ROGATZ H.**
"Chicago" in center, mong. "H. R." under bottom
"28," aqua, 16½" **12.00** **17.00**

☐ **ROLFE BOTTLING WORKS**
"Rolfe, IA" all in a circle, aqua, 6½" **12.00** **17.00**

☐ **ROLL, HENRY**
"Blue Island, Ill" in 3 lines, under bottom "H.R.,"
clear, 7¼" **12.00** **17.00**

☐ **ROSE BOTTLING WORKS**
"Reg. 1909, Cleveland, O." all in a circle, aqua,
7" **12.00** **17.00**

☐ **ROSE & CO. W.L.**
"Wheeling, W. Va." all in a circle, aqua, 6½" ..   **12.00** **17.00**

☐ **RUBIN BROS**
In center "R.B. Philade." all in a water mellow let-
ters, under it "Reg.," aqua, 7¾" **12.00** **17.00**

☐ **RUMFF, PETER**
"Spokane Fall," all in a circle, clear or aqua, 6¾"   **22.00** **31.00**

Price Range

☐ **RUMMEL, HENRY**
"Charleston, W. Va." all in a circle, aqua, 7" ..   12.00   17.00

☐ **RUMMEL, HENRY**
"Charleston, W. Va." all in a circle, aqua, 6¾"   12.00   17.00

☐ **RUONA, K.A. & CO.**
"Reg. Ishpeming, Mich." all in a circle, quart,
clear, 6¾" 15.00   20.00

☐ **RUSSELL, GEORGE**
"Aromatic, Gingerale, 369 Jay St. New Wil-
longhyde, Brooklyn" on 8 panels virtual, aqua,
6¾" 15.00   20.00

☐ **RYAN BOTTLING WORKS**
"Chicago, Ill." all in a circle, aqua, 6⅜" 12.00   17.00

☐ **RYAN BOTTLING WORKS**
"Trade, R.B.W., Mark, Chicago," aqua, 6¾" ...   15.00   20.00

☐ **S.C.O.N.M.W. ASS.**
In ½ moon in center Trademark, under it "registered Sacramento, Cal.," aqua, 6½" 12.00   17.00

☐ **ST. HELENA SODA WORKS**
In 2 lines, aqua or clear, 6¼" 16.00   23.00

☐ **ST. MARY'S BOTTLING WORKS**
"St. Mary, O." all in a circle, aqua, 7" 15.00   20.00

☐ **SALLISAW BOTTLING WORKS**
"Sallisaw, Okla." all in a circle, "33" on base,
aqua, 6¾" 15.00   20.00

☐ **SALT LAKE, UTAH**
In a circle in center of it in a shield, "The Dan-
halter Bottle Co.," under bottom in a shield 3
cross, "Denhalter," on base "40," clear, 6¾"   15.00   20.00

☐ **SALVO & BERDON**
Natchez, MI, aqua 25.00   35.00

☐ **SAN FRANCISCO SODA WORKS**
In 2 lines, aqua, 7" 12.00   17.00

☐ **SAN JOSE SODA WORKS**
"John Balzhouse, Prop. San Jose, Cal." all in a
water mellow circle, aqua, 7" 15.00   20.00

☐ **SAND**
"Altamont, NY" in three straight lines, on base,
8 oz., registered, blue, 7⅛" 12.00   18.00

☐ **SANDER, JOHN, L.**
On back "T.B.N.T.B.S.," aqua, 7" 12.00   17.00

Price Range

☐ **SANDBERG BROW**
In 2 lines, aqua, 6⅜″ **12.00** **17.00**

☐ **SANDERS, JOHN L.**
In Baltimore, MD in center a shield "J.L.S.," on
base Reg. semi-round bottle, aqua, 7″ **15.00** **20.00**

☐ **SANDUSKY BOTTLING WORKS**
In 3 lines, 12 panels, on base "G.H.," aqua, 6¾″ **16.00** **23.00**

☐ **SAPULPA BOTTLING WORKS**
"Sapulpa, IT" all in a circle, A.S., clear, 6½″ .. **200.00** **285.00**

☐ **SARATOGA BOTTLING WORKS**
In 2 lines, panels base, blue, 7″ **45.00** **60.00**

☐ **SASS & HAFNER**
In ¼ moon letters, in center of it trademark, under
it in 2 lines "S & H Chicago," frosted blue, 7″ **18.00** **25.00**

☐ **SATINSKEY B.**
In script, "338 So 4th Phila. Reg." all in 4 lines,
in back "T.B.N.T.B.S.," under bottom a star,
aqua, 3″ **12.00** **17.00**

☐ **SCAMMON BOTTLING WORKS**
"Scammon, Kans" all in a circle, clear, 7″ **16.00** **23.00**

☐ **SCHAUR, FRED B.**
Registered, Utica, NY, clear, 6¾″ **15.00** **20.00**

☐ **SCHARR FRED**
In 2 lines, 6½″ **12.00** **17.00**

☐ **SCHEMRICH, L.G.**
In center a big "S." Benwood, WV, clear, 6½″ **12.00** **17.00**

☐ **SCHERRER, JAS., MOLINE, ILL.**
"Moline, Ill" all in a circle, aqua, 6¾″ **12.00** **17.00**

☐ **SCHILLE, P.**
Center (mong.) "S.S. Columbus, O." all in a circle,
aqua, 7″ **15.00** **20.00**

☐ **SCHILLE P.**
Fancy script "S.B. Columbus, Ohio," aqua, 7″ **12.00** **17.00**

☐ **SCHINERS, C.**
"And Co., Sacramento, Cal. Capital Soda Works"
all in a circle, aqua, 6½″ **12.00** **17.00**

☐ **HENRY SCHINZ**
"Milwaukee," name and location embossed in
arc with "Bottling Co." in straight line in center,
large "H.S." on bottom, the lettering is crude,
clear glass, 7⅛″ **7.00** **11.00**

Price Range

☐ **SCHLEGED G.W., SCHELEGED**
"Chandler, OT" all in a circle, clear, 6¾" 130.00 170.00

☐ **SCHLEGEL G.W.**
In horse shoe letters, under it "Chandler O.T.,"
on base "S," light aqua, 6½" 160.00 215.00

☐ **SCHMIDT L.**
"Thomasville, GA" all in a circle, aqua, 6½" .. 14.00 19.00

☐ **SCHMUCK'S GINGER ALE**
In 2 lines, vertical, 12 panels, amber, 8" 28.00 37.00

☐ **SCHNERR, C.**
"Sacramento, Cal." in 3 lines, aqua, 7" 15.00 20.00

☐ **SCHRADER, A.W.**
In ½ moon letters, in center a bottle, under it
"Scranton, PA.," panels base, under bottom "S,"
in back "S," aqua, 6½" 16.00 23.00

☐ **SCHRAMM, HENRY**
Anvil in center, "Fullersburge, Ill." all in a circle,
aqua, 6¼" 12.00 17.00

☐ **SCHWCINHART, PITTSBURG**
In back "10th Ward Bottling Works," under bottom "J.J.," aqua, 6¾" 12.00 17.00

☐ **SCOTT, ED**
In center (mong.) "Trademark Parkenburg, W.
Va." all in a circle, aqua, 7" 15.00 20.00

☐ **SEATTLE SODA WORKS**
In a circle "#16" under bottom, aqua, 6¾" ... 12.00 17.00

☐ **SEATTLE SODA WORKS**
In 2 lines, aqua, 6¾" 16.00 23.00

☐ **SEETZ BROS.**
"Easton, PA." all in a circle, panel base, light
green, 6½" 15.00 20.00

☐ **SELMA PRODUCE CO.**
"Selma, AL," all in a circle, aqua, 6¾" 12.00 17.00

☐ **SERWAZI, P.J.**
"Managunk, PA." all in a circle, olive green, 7" 80.00 105.00

☐ **SESSETON BOTTLING WORKS**
In 2 lines, aqua, 6¾" 12.00 17.00

☐ **SEWELL BOTTLING WORKS**
"Sewell, W.Va." all in a circle, aqua, 6½" 15.00 20.00

☐ **SHAWEE BOTTLING WORKS F. SCHNEITER
& CO.**
"Shawee, Okla." all in a circle, aqua, 6⅞" 14.00 19.00

Price Range

□ **SHAWEE BOTTLING WORKS**
"Shawee, OT" all in a circle back, "this bottle not to be sold," under bottom "F.S.," yellow aqua, 6⅝" 160.00 215.00

□ **SHEEP**
In center of Trademark Reg., under it "T.B.N.S.," aqua, 6½" 15.00 20.00

□ **SHERIDAN BOTTLE WORK**
Sheridan, Ark, aqua, 6" 12.00 17.00

□ **SHEYNNE BOTTLING WORKS**
"Valley City, N.D. Stevens & Co. Prop." all in a circle panels base, aqua, 6¾" 15.00 20.00

□ **SHIPLEY S.J.**
"Wheeling, W. Va." all in a circle, aqua, 6⅞" .. 12.00 17.00

□ **SHONE, T.**
In one line, aqua, 6½" 12.00 17.00

□ **THE SHOULDER BOTTLING WORKS**
"Akron, O." all in a circle, aqua, 6¾" 12.00 17.00

□ **SING SING SODA WORKS**
In 3 lines in cathedral slug plate, aqua, 6½" ... 16.00 23.00

□ **SISTECK, FRANK**
In horse shoe letters, under it "Bottling Works, Irwin, PA.," panels base, on base "C & Co. LIM No. 6," aqua, 7" 15.00 20.00

□ **SMITH BERT**
"Brownsville, Tenn." all in a circle, aqua, 7" ... 32.00 41.00

□ **SMITH & BRIAN CO.**
"Pioneer Soda Works, Reno, Nev." all in 3 lines, 4 part mold, light blue green 80.00 105.00

□ **SMITH DAVID**
"Johnstown, NY" in a circle, panels base, under bottom "C26," aqua, 6¾" 12.00 17.00

□ **SMITH, DAVID**
"Johnstown, NY" in a circle letters, panels base, under bottom "C-26," aqua, 6¾" 15.00 20.00

□ **SMITH, H.D.**
"Tennille, GA." in a water mellow letters, on base "T.B.N.T.B.S.," clear, 6½" 12.00 17.00

Price Range

☐ **SMITH, H.D.**
"Tennille, GA" all in a circle, under it reg.
"T.B.N.T.B.S.," clear, 6½" 12.00   17.00

☐ **SMITH, H.D.**
"Tennille, GA." all in a circle, "no. 4" under bottom, clear, 7" 12.00   17.00

☐ **SMITH WATER**
"Rockwood, Tenn." all in a circle, aqua, 6¾"   16.00   23.00

☐ **SOMERSET ICE CO.**
"Under it Steam Bottling Works, Somerset, KY.,"
all in a horse shape letters panels, aqua, 7" ... 15.00   20.00

☐ **SOUTH BEND SODA BOTTLING WORKS**
In a circle, in center of it "South Bend, Wash.,"
aqua, 7" 12.00   17.00

☐ **SOUTH McALISTER**
In ½ moon letters, under it in 4 lines "Bottling
Works South McAlister, Ind. Ter.," aqua, 6½"   190.00   250.00

☐ **SOUTH RANGE BOTTLING WORKS**
"South Range, Mich.," all in a circle, aqua, 6¾"   12.00   17.00

☐ **SOUTHERN BOTTLING WORKS**
All in horse shoe letters, under it "F.J. Hyatt,
Prop. Houston, Tx." in 4 lines, aqua, 7¼" 16.00   23.00

☐ **SOUTHERN SODA WATER CO.**
"Nashville, Tenn." all in a circle, on base
"D.O.C.," 8 panels base, aqua, 7¼" 15.00   20.00

☐ **THE SOUTHWESTERN BOTTLING CO.**
Tulsa, IT, panels base, under bottom "S," aqua,
7⅛" 190.00   250.00

☐ **SPANCENBERGER, J. & W.**
In ½ moon letters, under it "Springfield, O.,"
aqua, 6¼" 15.00   20.00

☐ **SPARKS & CHARLES E.**
"Delaware," in center of it, "210 E 4th St., Wilmington" all in a circle on base reg., aqua, 7¼"   12.00   17.00

☐ **SPARKS & GRIFFITH**
"Lehigh, IT" all in a circle fluted base, aqua, 7¼"   115.00   140.00

☐ **SPEIDEL BROS.**
Boston, aqua, 6" 12.00   17.00

☐ **SPEIDEL, BROS**
"Wheeling W. Va." all in a circle, aqua, 7" 12.00   17.00

Price Range

☐ **SPENCER & BUTTLER**
"Des Moines, Iowa State Capital" all on front,
aqua, 7¼" 18.00 25.00

☐ **SPRENGER J.J.**
In a horse shoe shape letters, under it "Atlanta,
Ga.," aqua, 7" 12.00 17.00

☐ **SPRING ST. BOTTLING WORKS**
"J.A. Smith, Warwick, N.Y." all in a horse shoe
letters, on top "Reg.," aqua, 6¼" 12.00 17.00

☐ **STAMP ICE & FULL CO., STAMP, ARK.**
"Stamp, Ark." all in a circle, under bottom "S,"
aqua, 6¾" 15.00 20.00

☐ **STANDARD BOTTLING CO.**
Atlanta, in back, "T.B.T.B.R.," aqua, 8" 12.00 17.00

☐ **STANDARD BOTTLING CO.**
"Denver, Colo" in 2 vertical lines, base "S.B.
Co.," amethyst, 6⅛" 16.00 23.00
☐ Same except aqua 11.00 15.00

☐ **STANDARD BOTTLING CO.**
"Denver, Colo" all in a circle, clear or amethyst,
6½" 16.00 23.00

☐ **STANDARD BOTTLING CO.**
"Ft. Bragg" all in 3 lines, aqua, 7" 15.00 20.00

☐ **THE STANDARD BOTTLING CO.**
Odgen, UT, clear, 6¾" 16.00 23.00

☐ **STANDARD BOTTLING CO.**
"Silverton, Colo. Peter Orello, Prop." all in a circle, aqua, 6¾" 15.00 20.00

☐ **STANDARD BOTTLING**
"Denver, Colo." in 3 vertical lines, clear, 6¼" 22.00 31.00

☐ **STANDARD, THE, BOTTLING MFG.**
Cripple Creek, Colo." all in a circle, on bottom
"#20," clear, 6½" 18.00 27.00

☐ **STANDARD BOTTLING WORKS**
"Minneapolis, Minn." all in a circle, "K.R." under
bottom, amber, 6¼" 27.00 37.00

☐ **STANDARD BOTTLING WORKS**
"Minneapolis, Minn." all in a circle "H.R." on
base, amber, 6½" 55.00 75.00

☐ **STANDARD BOTTLING WORKS**
"Minneapolis, Minn." in 4 lines, amber, 6¾" ... 30.00 40.00

Price Range

☐ **STAR BOTTLING**
In center a star under it "Works Co.," under it
"Houston, Tx.," on shoulder 3 stars, aqua, 6½″ **12.00 17.00**

☐ **STAR BOTTLING WORKS**
In ½ moon letters in center a 5 points star in cen-
ter of it, (mong.) under it in 2 lines "Reg. New
Haven, Conn.," on base "T.B.N.T.B.S.," aqua, 6″ **12.00 17.00**

☐ **STAR BOTTLING WORKS**
Under it a star (mong.), in center of it "Reg. New
Haven, Conn.," on base "T.B.N.T.B.S.," aqua,
6½″ **12.00 17.00**

☐ **STAR BOTTLING WORKS**
Anadaro, OT "T & M, 16" on base, clear, 6⅝″ **170.00 220.00**

☐ **THE STAR BOTTLING WORKS**
Cincinnati, OH, in center a star with "KK Trademark" all in a circle, under it "Reg. T.B.N.T.B.S."
in 3 lines, aqua, 7″ **15.00 20.00**

☐ **STAR BOTTLING WORKS**
Galena, KS, panels bottom, star on base, aqua,
7¼″ **18.00 27.00**

☐ **STAR BOTTLING WORKS**
St. Paul, MN, "Con. 8 Fl. oz.," in back
"T.B.I.N.S.," aqua, 6¾″ **15.00 20.00**

☐ **STAR BOTTLING WORKS**
Laurel, MI, aqua **70.00 85.00**

☐ **STAR BOTTLING WORKS**
"Sandusky, O." all in a circle, aqua, 6¼″ **12.00 17.00**

☐ **THE STAR BOTTLING WORKS**
"Sandusky, O." around a star, aqua, 6¾″ **12.00 17.00**

☐ **STAR BOTTLING WORKS**
"Star, N.C." all in a circle, aqua, 6¾″ **32.00 42.00**

☐ **STAR BOTTLING WORKS CO.**
All in a water mellow letters, in center faceted
star, under it in 2 lines, "Houston, TX.," clear,
7¼″ **16.00 23.00**

☐ Same except flat star **12.00 17.00**

☐ Same except on shoulder 3 stars **16.00 23.00**

☐ **STEAM BOTTLING WORKS**
In center, anchor, "Trademark," in ½ moon let-
ters, under it "Reg. Shawnee, O.T.," aqua, 6½″ **170.00 230.00**

☐ **STENSON, HAS.**
In back "Chicago, Ill.," aqua, 6¼″ **12.00 17.00**

Price Range

☐ **STETSON, JAS**
"Chicago, Ill." in 2 panels, under bottom "J.S.,"
light blue, 6¾" **15.00   20.00**

☐ **STEPHEN, P.G.**
Hexagon shape (panels bottle), aqua, 7" **16.00   23.00**

☐ **STEPHENS & JOSE**
In ½ moon letters, under it "Virginia City, Ne-
vada," aqua, 7" **18.00   27.00**

☐ **STERLING SPRING MINERAL WATER CO.**
In (mong.) "PL" "Hancock, Mid" all in a circle
under bottom "PL," aqua, 6¾" **12.00   17.00**

☐ **STERLING SPRING MINERAL WATER CO.,
P.L.**
mong. "Hancock, Mich." all in a circle, under bottom "P.L.," aqua, 6¾" **12.00   17.00**

☐ **STEUBEN B.T.**
"Iowa" in 3 lines, aqua, 7" **12.00   17.00**

☐ **STEUBENVILLE BOTTLING**
In a horse shoe letters, in center "Works," under
it "J.W. Sharp," aqua, 6½" **15.00   20.00**

☐ **STEUBENVILLE BOTTLE WORKS, J.W.**
Sharp all in a horse shoe letters, aqua, 6½" .. **12.00   17.00**

☐ **STILLWATER BOTTLING WORKS**
G.F. Knowles, Stillwater, OK, aqua, 6¾" **16.00   23.00**

☐ **STILLWATER BOTTLING WORKS**
G.F. Knowles, Stillwater, OK, aqua, 6¾" **12.00   17.00**

☐ **STOCKDER, F.**
"Cannon City, Colo." all in a circle, aqua, 7" .. **12.00   17.00**

☐ **STOLEN FROM EUREKA BOTTLING WORKS**
Ft. Smith, AR "3" on base, aqua, 6¾" **12.00   17.00**

☐ **STROUD BOTTLING WORKS**
"Stroud, Okla." all in a circle, light aqua, 6½" **12.00   17.00**

☐ **STROUD BOTTLING WORKS STILLER
BROS.**
"Stroud, Okla." all in a circle, under bottom "S,"
light aqua, 6½" **12.00   17.00**

☐ **SUCCESS BOTTLING WORKS**
In 2 lines, clear, 6¼" **12.00   17.00**

☐ **SUMRALL BOTTLING WORKS**
Sumrall, MI, Aqua **100.00 150.00**

Price Range

☐ **SUMTER BOTTLER BOTTLING WORKS**
"Sumter, S.C." all in a circle, on base T.B.R.,
clear 7" 12.00   17.00

☐ **SUMTER BOTTLING WORKS**
"Sumter, S.C." all in a circle, aqua, 6½" 16.00   23.00

☐ **SUNSET BOTTLING WORKS**
All in a circle, aqua, 7" 12.00   17.00

☐ **SUPERIOR BOTTLING WORKS**
Superior, WI, aqua, 7½" 12.00   17.00

☐ **SUPERIOR BOTTLING WORKS**
"Superior, Wis." all in a circle, aqua, 6⅜" 12.00   17.00

☐ **SUTTON BOTTLING WORKS**
Sutton, WV, in center "Juepcene & Walker
Props.," mong. "J.W.," under it "T.B.N.T.B.S.,"
aqua, 7" 15.00   20.00

☐ **SWINDLER & BERNSTEIN**
"CHICAGO" all in a circle, "S.B." under bottom,
aqua, 6½" 16.00   23.00

☐ **T.H.**
Monogram, in side of slug plate, aqua, 6½" ... 12.00   17.00

☐ **T. & S. PORT TOWNSEND SODA WORKS**
P.T.W.T.
In 4 lines vert., greenish aqua, 6⅛" 22.00   32.00

☐ **TABLE WATER CO.**
"Reg. Hallett" all near top, in center an Indian
head, under it "Nonquit Trademark Bridgeport,
Conn.," on base "T.B.N.T.B.S.," clear, 7½" ... 16.00   23.00

☐ **TALLODEGA, AL**
"Coca-Cola" in block letters, clear, 7" 130.00   190.00

☐ **TAMPA BOTTLING WORKS**
"Tampa, Fla." all in a circle, clear, 6½" 12.00   17.00

☐ **TAMPA CIDER & VINEGAR CO.**
All in a circle, clear, 6" 12.00   17.00

☐ **TANNER, T.J.**
"Port Townsend, Wash." In 4 lines, aqua, 7" .. 35.00   50.00

☐ **TAWASENTHA SPRINGS CO.**
In 3 lines, under it "Indian maid Trademark,"
under it "Cincinnati, O.," aqua, 6¾" 15.00   20.00

☐ **TAYLOR, E.**
"Erie, Pa" around bottle, large "T" under bottom,
aqua, 6¼" 12.00   17.00

Price Range

☐ **TAYLOR, JAS., F.**
"New Bern, N.C." all on front, aqua, 6¾" 16.00 23.00

☐ **TAYLOR SODA WATER MFG. CO.**
"Boise, Ida." all in a circle, panels bottom, light
aqua, 6¼" 45.00 55.00

☐ **TEXAS PRODUCE CO.**
"Texarkana, Tex." all in a circle, clear, 6¼" ... 15.00 20.00

☐ **THIMELIN, THOS.**
"South Bridge, Mass." all in a circle, aqua, 6½" 15.00 20.00

☐ Same except pale aqua 12.00 17.00

☐ **THOMAS, W.Z.**
"Niles, Ohio" all in a circle, clear, 8" 12.00 17.00

☐ **THOMAS W.Z.**
"Niles, Ohio" all in a circle, "T.B.N.T.B.S." on
base, clear, 8¼" 15.00 20.00

☐ **TIMPSON BOTTLING WORKS**
"Timpson, Texas" all in a circle, panels base,
under bottom "J & B," aqua, 7" 16.00 23.00

☐ **TIC TAC BOTTLING WORKS, M & C**
"Greenwich, N.Y." all in a diamond shape letters,
in back "T.B.N.T.B.S.," aqua, 6½" 16.00 23.00

☐ **TIPTON BOTTLING WORKS**
Tipton, Iowa, in many diff. towns in Iowa, clear or
aqua, 7" 12.00 17.00

☐ **TOLLE BOTTLING WORKS, T.**
"Litchfield, Ill." all in a circle, clear, 6½" 12.00 17.00

☐ **TONOPAH SODA WORK**
"Nev" in 3 lines, clear, 6¾" 27.00 36.00

☐ Also greenish aqua 27.00 36.00

☐ **TRINIDAD**
In center "BOTTLING WORKS, Trinidad, Colo."
all in a circle, aqua, 7" 23.00 32.00

☐ **TRINIDAD BOTTLING WORKS**
All in a circle, clear or amethyst, 6½" 16.00 23.00

☐ **TULSA BOTTLING WORKS**
"Tulsa, I.T." all in a circle, aqua, 6⅛" 135.00 185.00

☐ **TUPELO ICE FACTORY**
Tupelo, MI. aqua 20.00 25.00

☐ **TUSKALOOSA BOTTLING WORKS, C.C.
SIMPSON**
"MGA Tuskaloosa, Ala." all in a circle, back
"T.B.N.T.B.S.," aqua, 6½" 12.00 17.00

Price Range

☐ **TUSKGEE, ALA**
In block letters, clear, 6¼″ 16.00   23.00

☐ **TUSKGEE COCA-COLA BOTTLING**
"(ALA)" all in a circle, clear, 6½″ 120.00 165.00

☐ **TUTTLE BROTHERS BLUFF CITY BOTTLING WORKS**
Natchez, MS, clear 20.00   30.00

☐ **TWIN CITY BOTTLING WORKS**
"Dennison, OH" all in a circle, aqua, 6½″ 12.00   17.00

☐ **TWIN SPRINGS BOTTLING WORKS**
"Kansas City, MO" all in a circle, under bottom
P.S., aqua, 9½″ 15.00   20.00

☐ **TYLER UNION BOTTLING WORKS**
All in a circle, aqua, 6¾″ 16.00   23.00

☐ **U.N. BOTTLING**
In center "WORKS, N.Y. Canandaiqua" all in a
circle under it "Reg;" in back, "T.B.N.T.B.S.,"
under bottom "33," clear, 6¾″ 12.00   17.00

☐ **UNAKA BOTTLING WORKS**
"Erwin, Tenn" all in a circle, on base "C.G. Co.,"
aqua, 7″ 15.00   20.00

☐ **UNION B. WORKS**
Houston, TX, interlocking "F.P. & Co." in triangle,
Trademark, aqua, 7½″ 16.00   23.00

☐ **J.T. WILCOX**
"Berlin, NY," name and location in oval slug plate
on front, "W.B." embossed on bottom, aqua, 7″   7.00   11.00

INK

Ink bottles have a lengthy history and quite likely have been made in a greater variety of designs than any other single class of bottles. Figurals are numerous among ink bottles, some of them of extremely imaginative shapes and high-quality modeling.

You might wonder why a product so cheap as ink would be retailed in decorative bottles. There is no mystery about this. Most other things sold in bottles were quickly used up and the bottle discarded; or the bottle and its contents were kept in a cupboard out of view. Ink bottles not only remained in the home for a while (one bottle might last for months or longer), they were prominently displayed on desks in offices, dens and studies. The manufacturers felt it was advantageous for ink bottles to be styled as ornamental objects and be suitable beside fine writing sets or any objets d'art that might be on the desk. Very likely, many buyers in the late 1800s chose their ink not by brand, but by the bottle's appeal.

Prior to the 18th century, ink was generally sold in copper or brass containers, and this is how the common people used it. Well-to-do persons transferred the contents of these jars into their ornate silver inkwells. The nobility of Europe and other wealthy individuals often owned magnificent inkwells on which their family coat of arms was engraved. These are now very desirable and costly collectors' items.

Ink was being sold in glass and pottery bottles in England in the 1700s, but the bottling was done by retailers rather than manufacturers. Hence, these bottles carry no brand names and often cannot be identified as having contained ink. The first patent for the commercial production of ink was granted in England in 1792. In America, the first patent for ink was given to Maynard and Noyes of Boston in 1816. Naturally, patents on ink only covered the specific recipe used by the maker or developer; patents did not prevent rivals from selling ink made from other formulas. Until 1816, most of the ink used in the U.S. had been imported from Britain and France and was fairly costly.

The first American-made master bottles—bottles containing a pint or quart of ink from which inkwells could be filled in offices and schools—were of poor quality glass containing many bubbles and other imperfections.

The early ink industry in America was hampered by the lack of good writing pens. Quills, which were awkward to use, continued to be used until the mid 19th century. Peregrine Williamson of Baltimore invented a metal pen (really a re-invention of the Egyptian stylus) in 1809, but it failed to win widespread acceptance until 1858. In that year, Richard Esterbrook opened a factory to make metal pens at Camden, New Jersey. These pens were not an immediate success, as they had to be dipped in the ink often having no ink supply of their own. This resulted in messy ink spills. Bottle manufacturers set about to create "untippable" bottles and this gave birth to many unusual shapes and designs. Umbrella-shaped ink bottles were popular, as were the tea-kettle shapes—complete with pouring spout. Other shapes included turtles, barrels, shoes, buildings, boats, schoolhouses and cathedrals.

A man named Hyde, from Reading, Pennsylvania, invented the fountain pen in 1830. But for one reason or another—lack of financing, or advice of people who thought the idea was silly—it was not commercially manufactured until 1884. As the fountain pen gained in use, ink bottles gradually became plainer. Since the pen now carried its own ink supply, it was not necessary to keep ink on the desk top. Bottles could be stored in drawers where they were out of sight. With nobody seeing them, it was unnecessary to make them fancy. Thus, the majority of decorative American ink bottles belong to the era dating from 1860 to about 1890.

Price Range

☐ **ALLING'S INK**
Triangular, green, 1⅞" x 2¼" 53.00 63.00
☐ **ALONZO FRENCH**
Barrel, Pat. March 1st, 1870, aqua, 2" tall, 2" long 22.00 30.00
☐ **ANTOINE ET FILS**
Straight top with pouring lip, brown pottery, 8⅜" 8.00 11.00
☐ **P & J ARNOLD**
Collar with pouring lip, brown, 9¼" 14.00 20.00
☐ **ARNOLD'S**
Round, clear or amethyst, 2½" 6.00 8.00
☐ **A3**
"Pat July 9, 1895" under bottom, aqua, 2¼" .. 12.00 16.00
☐ **B & G**
Square, vertical ribbing on three sides, two pen ledges, base embossed, burst top, aqua, 2⅜" 17.00 27.00
☐ **BELL**
Sheared top, clear or amethyst, 3" 6.00 8.00
☐ **BELL**
Label, crock, double ring top, tan 15.00 22.00
☐ **BELL TOP**
On side and under bottle "patd. Apr. 21st 1868," flare top, ring on base and shoulder, aqua, 2½" x 2¹/₁₆" 15.00 22.00
☐ **BERTINGUIOT**
Sheared top, amber, 2" 80.00 130.00
☐ **BERTINQUOIT**
Round, sheared lip, pontil base, yellow olive, 2½" 130.00 175.00
☐ **BILLING & CO.**
Banker's Writing Ink, "B" in center, aqua, 2" x 1½" 14.00 20.00
☐ **BILLING & CO.**
Banker's Writing Ink, "B" embossed in center on bottom, aqua, 2" 12.00 18.00
☐ **BILLINGS, J. T. & SON**
Sheared top, aqua, 1⅞" 6.00 9.00
☐ **BILLINGS/MAUVE INK**
Near base, dome shaped, sheared top, aqua, 1¾" tall, 2¹¹/₁₆" deep base 20.00 26.00

Price Range

☐ **BIRDCAGE-SHAPED INK**
Square base, embossed "M" on front panel,
aqua, 3¼" 110.00 190.00
☐ **S.M. BIXBY & CO.**
Aqua, 2½" 20.00 26.00
☐ **BIXBY**
On bottom, aqua, 2½" 4.00 5.00
☐ **BIXBY**
On bottom, clear or amethyst, 2½" 3.50 4.50
☐ **BIXBY**
Under bottom, ink or polish, "Patented Mch,"
"83" under shoulder, square base, round corners
slanting upward so the bottle gradually becomes
round, bulbous shoulder, amber, 4" tall, 1⅛"
base 6.00 9.00
☐ Same as above except plain, no BIXBY 5.00 7.00
☐ **BIXLEY MUSHROOM INK**
Aqua, 2" 17.00 27.00
☐ **C. BLACKMAN**
Green, 2½" 10.00 13.00
☐ **BLACKWOOD & CO.**
On one panel, under it on panel "London," 10
panels, aqua, snap top, 2¼" x 2" 14.00 18.00
☐ **BLACKSTONE'S, INK, U.S.A.**
Cones type bottle, ring shoulder and ring top,
clear, 2⅛" x 2⅛" 15.00 22.00
☐ **BOAT SHAPED**
Plain, blue, 1¾" 33.00 43.00
☐ Same as above except clear 22.00 32.00
☐ **BONNEY W.E. BARREL INK**
Aqua, 5½" 45.00 62.00
☐ **BONNEY CONE INK**
Bonney Premium French Ink, South Hanover,
MA, aqua, 5½" 44.00 55.00
☐ **W. E. BONNEY INK**
South Hanover, MA, aqua, 2¼" 10.00 13.00
☐ **W. E. BONNEY**
Aqua, 2½" x 3" x 1½" 100.00 135.00
☐ **J. BOURNE & SONS NEAR DERBY**
On base, "Carter's Ink," tan, 7" 13.00 17.00

Cottage Ink, "PATD MAR 14 1871" on base, applied lip, smooth base, aqua, 2⅜", **$300.00–$350.00** (Courtesy of Glass-Works Auctions, East Greenville, PA)

Locomotive Ink, "PAT. OCT. 1874—TRADEMARK," sheared ground lip, aqua, 2", **$550.00–$650.00** (Courtesy of Glass-Works Auctions, East Greenville, PA)

Farley's/Ink, eight-sided, open pontil, sheared lip, olive-amber, 1¾", **$300.00–$360.00** (Courtesy of Glass-Works Auctions, East Greenville, PA)

Price Range

☐ **J. BOURNE & SON, PATENTEES**
"Derby Pottery near Derby, P. J. Arnold, London, England" embossed near the base, pottery, round, pouring spout lip, light brown, 9½" tall, 3¾" diameter 80.00 90.00

☐ **BOURNE DERBY**
Crock, brown, 8½" 6.00 8.00

☐ **BRICKETT J. TAYLOR INK**
Cylindrical, flared lip, 4½" 52.00 62.00

☐ **D. B. BROOKS & CO. INK**
Blue green, 2⅛" 10.00 13.00

☐ **D. B. BROOKS & CO.**
Amber, 2" x 2½" 15.00 23.00

☐ **BULLDOG HEAD**
Milk glass, 4" 75.00 110.00

☐ **J. J. BUTLER**
Aqua, 2" 75.00 85.00

☐ **J.J. BUTLER**
Cincinnati, flared lip, smooth base, square, clear, 2⅝" 20.00 28.00

☐ **J.J. BUTLER**
Cincinnati, rolled lip, rectangular, aqua, 2¾" ... 107.00 122.00

☐ **CALUMBINE INK**
Between four pointed stars, ring top, aqua, 1¾" x 1½" x 1½" 24.00 35.00

☐ **CARDINAL BIRD INK**
Turtle, aqua 70.00 85.00

☐ **CARDINELL INK OU TRADE MARK, MONTCLAIR, N.J.**
"Cardinell Erado Trademark Montclair, N.J." on back, square, collar, ABM, amber, 1" x 2⅛" ... 3.50 5.00

☐ **CARTER**
"#11" under bottom, aqua, 2½" 5.00 7.00

☐ **CARTER**
Under bottom, milk glass, 3" 17.00 27.00

☐ **CARTER INK**
"Made in U.S.A." under bottom, tea kettle, clear, 2½" x 4" 48.00 68.00

☐ **CARTER INK**
Clear or amethyst, 2¼" 4.00 5.25

Price Range

☐ **CARTER'S**
On bottom, double V band collar, ring on shoulder
and base, round, aqua or amethyst, 2⅝" 4.50 5.50
☐ Same as above except "CARTER'S 7½ MADE IN
USA" on bottom, aqua 6.00 8.00
☐ **CARTER'S**
On bottom, cone, large and small raised ring at
base of neck, two round bands on collar, aqua,
2½" x 2⅞" 6.00 8.00
☐ **CARTER'S**
On lid, screw-on top, "13" embossed on bottom,
clear, 1⅛" 6.00 8.00
☐ **CARTER'S**
Cobalt, 6½" 12.00 16.00
☐ **CARTER'S**
Eight panels, aqua, 1¾" 10.00 15.00
☐ **CARTER'S**
On shoulder, three-part mold, ring collar and
pouring lip, light green, pint 17.00 28.00
☐ **CARTER'S**
One ring tapers at neck, round base, amethyst,
2¼" 4.00 5.50
☐ **CARTER'S**
Three dots close together under bottom, aqua,
2½" 5.00 7.00
☐ **CARTER'S CLOVER LEAF**
Smooth base, octagonal, blue, 3" 55.00 65.00
☐ **CARTER'S FULL ½ PINT**
On shoulder, applied ring, round, aqua, 6¼" .. 9.00 13.00
☐ **CARTER'S**
On back, "Full ½ Pint" on bottom, Pat Feb. 14-
99, 6" tall, 2½" round 8.00 13.00
☐ **CARTER'S FULL QUART**
On top shoulder, under that "Made in U.S.A.,"
aqua, 9½" 14.00 18.00
☐ **CARTER'S FULL QUART, MADE IN U.S.A.**
Around shoulder, Pat. Feb. 14, 99 on base, round,
applied lip, aqua, 9⅝" 13.00 17.00
☐ **CARTER'S**
Tooled lip, smooth base, cylindrical, cobalt blue,
9¾" 22.00 27.00

Price Range

☐ **CARTER'S**
House Ink, turtle, double door with two windows
on dome near spout, Ink, and below that, Carter's   **160.00 260.00**

☐ **CARTER'S INK**
Plain, three-part mold, round, pouring lip, light
green, ½ pint, quart, 10¼" tall, 3" bottom, 2¼"
neck **17.00   28.00**

☐ Same as above except ring collar, two-part mold   **17.00   28.00**

☐ **CARTER'S INK MADE IN U.S.A.**
Under bottom, label, aqua, 2¾" **6.00   8.00**

☐ **CARTER'S INK CO.**
Two porcelain bottles, one in the shape of a man
and one in the shape of a woman, woman has
red blouse, red and white skirt, black shoes, yellow hair, and rolling pin in her left hand, man has
tan trousers, blue jacket and red tie, 3⅝" **38.00   48.00**

☐ **CARTER'S KOAL BLK INK**
Label, machine made, clear, 2" **4.00   5.25**

☐ **CARTER'S MADE IN U.S.A.**
On shoulder, also Full Qt. Bulk Ink, aqua, 9¾"   **5.00   7.00**

☐ **CARTER'S**
Under bottom, ring base and ring shoulder, dou-
ble ring top, honey amber, 2⅛" x 2" **17.00   28.00**

☐ **CARTER'S MADE IN U.S.A.**
Under bottom, ring top, four pen ledge, aqua,
square, 1¼" x 2¼" **12.00   17.00**

☐ **CARTER'S**
On base Made in U.S.A. 1897, round base, tapers
at neck, one ring, green or aqua, 2½" tall, base
2⅜" **6.00   8.00**

☐ Same as above except brown **10.00   13.00**

☐ **CARTER'S/NON-
COPYING/CARMINE/WRITING/FLUID**
Imprinted on jug, The Carter's Ink Co., seal,
powderhorn, etc., brown and tan glaze, gallon   **23.00   28.00**

☐ **CARTER'S NO. 1**
On base, round, cobalt blue, 32 fluid ounces, 9½"   **17.00   28.00**

☐ **CARTER'S NO. 5 MADE IN U.S.A.**
On bottom, machine made, clear or amethyst   **6.00   8.00**

☐ **CARTER'S #6**
"Made in USA" on bottom, round, ring collar, ring
on shoulder and base, aqua, 2½" diameter, 3"   **5.00   6.50**

Price Range

☐ **CARTER'S #6½**
"Made in USA" on bottom, "16 FLUID OZ." on shoulder, sheared type collar and ring on neck, bulbous shoulder, ring at base, round, ABM, amethyst, 3" diameter, 7½" 14.00 20.00

☐ **CARTER'S #9 MADE IN USA**
On bottom, double ring collar, step on shoulder, amethyst, 2" x 2" x 2" 4.00 5.00

☐ **CARTER'S 1897**
On bottom, cone, wide and narrow raised rings, rings at base of neck, narrow, round band collar, aqua, 2½" 6.00 9.00

☐ **CARTER'S 1897**
"Made in USA" under bottom, cone, aqua 12.00 16.00

☐ **CARTER'S 1897**
"Made in USA" under bottom, cone, emerald .. 12.00 16.00

☐ **CARTER'S PENCRAFT COMBINED OFFICE & FOUNTAIN PEN FLUID**
Clear, 7½" 6.00 9.00

☐ **CARTER'S PRO WRITING FLUID**
Label, machine made, "G11 Sk No. 1" under bottom, on shoulder "32 Fl. Oz.," cobalt, 9½" 14.00 20.00

☐ **CARTER'S RYTO PERMANENT**
Blue-black ink for fountain pen and general use, The Carter's Ink Co., "Carter" embossed near base, The Cathedral, label, 9¾" 38.00 49.00

☐ **CARTER'S 2 C-101**
Under bottom, Cathedral type, in bottom of each window Ca, machine made, cobalt blue, 10", set of 4 .... 45.00 55.00

☐ Same as above except 8" 45.00 55.00

☐ **CAW'S INK**
"New York" on one side, circle on top of shoulder with raised square on top of circle, clear, aqua or light blue, 2¼" x 1¾" 6.00 9.00

☐ **CAW'S**
New York square collared mouth, smooth base, embossed square on front, aqua, 2¾" 3.00 7.00

☐ **CHALLENGE**
Green, 2¾" 9.00 14.00

Price Range

☐ **CHASE BROS.**
Excelsior Office Ink, Haverhill, MA., label, under
bottom "Feb. 15, 1886," cobalt, 9" 15.00   23.00

☐ **CLAR-O-TYPE CLEANER**
Label, "Clar-O-Type" embossed on each side, 3
under bottom, cobalt, 2½" 5.00   7.00

☐ **CLIMAX**
On shoulder, machine made, square, curved bot-
tom, clear, 3¾" 6.00   8.00

☐ **CLIMAX**
Rectangular inkwell, concave base, embossed
shoulder on front and back, clear, 3⅝" 3.00   5.00

☐ **THE CLUB INK CARTER HEXAGONAL**
Four-leaf clover, cobalt, 4 ounces 30.00   40.00

☐ **COCHRAN & CO.**
Liverpool, England, round, flared mouth with inside the lip pour spout, shoulder embossed, aqua,
6¼" 3.00   5.00

☐ **COMP. S.I. HOUSE INK BOTTLE**
On roof S.I. Comp., doors and windows around
square bottle, flat round top, fancy bottle, 2⅝" x
1¾" x 1½" 150.00   190.00

☐ **CONFEDERATE HAT INK WELL**
Copper and tin, 3¾" x 1½" 45.00   55.00

☐ **CONQUEROR**
Label, blue or aqua, 2¼" 10.00   14.00

☐ **CONTINENTAL JET BLACK INK MFG. CO.**
Philadelphia label, two dots under bottom, clear   5.00   7.00

☐ **CONTINENTAL INK**
Long tapered collar and pouring lip, aqua, 7¾"   12.00   16.00

☐ **COTTAGE**
Embossed windows and doors and peak roof,
Patd Mar 14 1871, aqua, 2⅜" h. 300.00   350.00

☐ **COTTAGE**
Base embossed "R. Mahony," with water barrel,
tiled roof, diamond pane windows, burst top,
aqua, 2½" 210.00   265.00

☐ **COTTAGE**
"LEVISON'S/INKS/ST. LOUIS," amber, 2½" h.,   170.00   200.00

☐ **COTTAGE**
With door appendage, tiled roof, burst top, with-
out embossing, aqua, 2½" 220.00   270.00

Price Range

☐ **COTTAGE**
Embossed windows and doors, aqua, 2½″ h.,   **200.00 240.00**

☐ **COTTAGE**
Without embossing, small tile roof with square
panes, burst top, aqua, 2½″ **270.00 325.00**

☐ **COVENTRY GEOMETRIC INK**
Open pontil, amber, 1⅝″ **75.00   90.00**

☐ **CROLIUS, C.**
Manufacturer, Manhattan, Wells, NY, round crock
with holder for pen, ring top, tapered shoulder,
gray and blue glaze, 2⅜″ x 3¼″ **1390.00 1790.00**

☐ **CROSS PEN CO.**
Aqua, 2¾″ **15.00   22.00**

☐ **CROSS PEN CO. INK**
CPC trademark, aqua, 2¾″ **17.00   28.00**

☐ **APPLE GREEN CROSS PEN CO.**
Embossed monogram, 2½″ **10.00   14.00**

☐ **CURRIER & HALL, CONCORD, N.H. POT INK**
Brown, quart **37.00   48.00**

☐ **CURRIER & HALL POTTERY MASTER INK**
Two-tone label **10.00   13.00**

☐ **CURRIER & HALL'S INK**
Concord, NH, 1840, label, twelve-sided, open
pontil, aqua, 2½″ **60.00   75.00**

☐ **DANSK DESIGNS, LTD**
"France IHQ" under bottom, wide ring top and
base, (A.B.M.) 2⅛″ x 2″ wide, flare top **14.00   19.00**

☐ **DAVID'S**
On base, "Turtle Ink," sheared top, aqua, 2″ x
2¼″ **33.00   43.00**

☐ **DAVID CO.**
NY Thad, square label, David's Red Ink, 1⅞″ x
1⅛″, ring top **16.00   22.00**

☐ **DAVID'S ELECTRO CHEMICAL WRITING
FLUID**
Label, "M3" under bottom, machine made, cobalt
blue, 9″ **14.00   20.00**

☐ **DAVID'S TURTLE INK**
Green **37.00   48.00**

☐ **THAD DAVID'S CO.**
"NY" on bottom, amber, 2¾″ **6.00   8.00**

Price Range

☐ **THAD DAVID'S INK**
Beveled edges, slope shoulder, green, 1¾"
square 7.00 10.00

☐ **THADDEUS DAVID'S CO.**
Pinched pouring lip, clear, 6⅜" 17.00 28.00

☐ **THADDEUS DAVID'S & CO.**
Label, "Writing Fluid, New York," cream crock,
5¾" 32.00 41.00

☐ **DAVIES**
Sheared top, "Patd Sept 4–80" under bottom,
clear or amethyst, 2½" 37.00 48.00

☐ **W.A. DAVIS CO.**
In back, "U.S. TREASURY" on front shoulder,
clear or amethyst 16.00 24.00

☐ **W.A. DAVIS CO/BOSTON**
"Mass USA" embossed on shoulder, decorated
cylinder with sixteen curved panels at top of body,
and sixteen near base of body, base pedestal
flared, double rings at base of neck, mold lines
end at base of neck, flared ring on lip, greenish
aqua, 8" 17.00 29.00

☐ **DIAMOND & ONYX**
Aqua, 9" 10.00 13.00

☐ **DIAMOND & ONYX**
Aqua, 3" and 5½" 8.00 11.00

☐ **DIAMOND INK CO**
"Milwaukee" in a circle under bottom, pinch type
bottle, in each pinch a diamond, round ring on
shoulder, ring at base, clear, ½" neck 14.00 20.00

☐ **DIAMOND INK CO.**
"Milwaukee" on base, Patented Dec 1st, 03, No.
622, square, amethyst, 1⅝" 5.00 6.50

☐ **DIAMOND INK CO.**
Clear, 1½" 5.00 6.50

☐ **DIAMOND INK CO.**
Wash pen point, one large and small connected
jar 12.00 17.00

☐ **DOULTON, LAMBETH**
Pouring lip, brown pottery, 4½" 8.00 12.00

Price Range

☐ **DOULTON LAMBETH**
Deeply imprinted at base of bottle, stoneware, jug-shape, no pouring spout, collared, cream color, 5″ tall, 2¾″ diam. at base **12.00   18.00**

☐ **DOVELL'S**
In ¼ moon, under it "Patent," cones type bottle, ring on shoulder, ring top, aqua, 2¼″ x 2¼″ . . **15.00   23.00**

☐ **DOVELL'S PATENT**
Cone, blue, 2½″ **8.00   12.00**

☐ **E. DUCK & CO.**
London, round, clock-shaped with Roman numerals from top to bottom on obverse and reverse sides, burst top, embossed base, aqua, 3⅜″ . . **85.00   105.00**

☐ **S.O. DUNBAR**
Stopper or cork, aqua, 2½″ **8.00   12.00**

☐ **S.O. DUNBAR**
Taunton, cone, eight-sided, open pontil, aqua . . **110.00 155.00**

☐ **S.O. DUNBAR**
Taunton, cone, eight-sided, open pontil, aqua . . **25.00   35.00**

☐ **S.O. DUNBAR**
"Taunton" on one panel in 2 lines, cone type bottle, ring top, pontil, aqua **65.00   45.00**

☐ **S.O. DUNBAR**
Taunton, MA, round, graduated collar, aqua, 5¾″ x 2¾″ **10.00   14.00**

☐ **EARLES INK CO.**
Pouring lip, crock, beige, 6⅛″ **8.00   11.00**

☐ **E.B.**
Inside threads, cone, clear or amethyst, 2⅛″ . . **6.00   8.00**

☐ **EDISON FOUNTAIN PEN INK**
Petersburg, VA, under bottom "A.C.W. 232," ring tip and neck, square, clear **9.00   11.00**

☐ **ESBINS INDELIBLE INK**
Aqua, small bottle **6.00   8.00**

☐ **ESTES, N.Y. INK**
Pontil, aqua, 6¾″ **20.00   29.00**

☐ **FARLEY'S INK**
Open pontil, olive or amber, 2″ x 2″ **200.00 245.00**

☐ **FARLEY'S INK**
Eight-sided, open pontil, aqua, 2″ x 2″ **75.00   95.00**

☐ **L.P. FARLEY CO**
Sheared top, dark green, 2″ **19.00   25.00**

Price Range

☐ **FIELD**
"London" is embossed below, white glazed stoneware, tapering neck, with pouring spout, British, 5⅞" 14.00 20.00

☐ **FIELD'S**
Field's Ink & Gum, RD No. 660694, slight concave circle in bottom with embossed "C," small raised collar on top. Aqua, 2" x 2" x 2⅜" 6.00 10.00

☐ **J. FIELD**
Schoolhouse type, sheared lip, name embossed on one side, "JH" embossed on bottom, aqua, 1½" x 1½" x 2" 5.00 8.00

☐ **FINE BLACK WRITING INK**
Label, pontil, aqua, 5" 15.00 22.00

☐ **PATENT FORTSCHMITT**
Canada, long metal cap with "P," clear, 6" 15.00 22.00

☐ **FOUNTAIN INK CO.**
NY, USA, clear, 3½" 13.00 17.00

☐ **FRANKLIN INK**
Aqua, 4" long, 2" at tallest part 45.00 55.00

☐ **FRENCH INK CO.**
Hanover, MA 25.00 33.00

☐ **FULLER'S BANNER INK**
Decatur, IL, Aqua, 8" 17.00 28.00

☐ **FUNNEL INKWELL**
Round thick glass, amethyst, 2⅜" h., ... 70.00 85.00

☐ **FUNNEL INKWELL**
Round with 25 vertical ribs, pontil scarred, clear glass, 1⅞" h., ... 80.00 100.00

☐ **GARGOYLE FACE**
Metal, figure sits on its haunches, grinning face, ears act as pen holders, hinged cover, 3¼" ... 65.00 75.00

☐ **GATES**
Round, clear, 6" 2.00 3.00

☐ **GEOMETRIC INKWELL**
3-mold quilted, light blue-green, 2" h., 2³/₁₆" dia., pontil scarred 650.00 740.00

☐ **GEOMETRIC INKWELL**
3-mold quilted, olive-amber, 2" h., 2⅛" dia., pontil scarred 90.00 100.00

Price Range

☐ **GEOMETRIC INKWELL**
3-mold quilted, olive-amber, $1^3/_{16}''$ h., 2¼' dia.,
pontil scarred 75.00   85.00

☐ **GEOMETRIC INKWELL**
3-mold quilted, dark olive-amber, $1^{13}/_{16}''$ h., 2⅝''
dia., pontil scarred 115.00 135.00

☐ **GEOMETRIC INKWELL**
3-mold quilted, dark olive-green, 1¾'' h., 2'' dia.,
pontil scarred 90.00 110.00

☐ **GLENN & CO.**
Round, clear, 1⅝'' 6.00   9.00

☐ **GLUE or INK**
Label, clear, 2¾'' 4.00   5.00

☐ **GLUE or INK**
Label, eight panels, aqua 8.00   11.00

☐ **G.M.W.C.A.A.S.**
Turtle, ink pen rest slot, oval, aqua 10.00   13.00

☐ **GREENWOOD'S**
Sheared top, under bottom "Patd March 22, 92,"
tapered, clear or aqua green, 1½'' 8.00   11.00

☐ **HALEY**
"Made in U.S.A., Ink Co." in 3 lines, ring shoulder
and base, ring top, aqua, 1¼'' x 1¼'' 17.00   26.00

☐ **HALEY INK CO.**
Aqua, 2¾'' 8.00   11.00
☐ Same as above except clear 6.00   8.00

☐ **HALEY INK CO.**
"Made in USA," two rings on shoulder, four rings
on base, clear or amethyst, 6¾'' 10.00   13.00
☐ Same as above except brass spout, aqua 13.00   17.00

☐ **HARRIS INK**
Label, pontil, black glass, 10½'' 24.00   31.00

☐ **HARRISON'S COLA INK 2**
Open pontil, aqua 58.00   75.00

☐ **HARRISON'S COLUMBIAN INK**
Eight-sided, rolled lip, aqua, 1½'' 63.00   83.00

☐ **HARRISON'S COLUMBIAN INK**
Eight-sided, rolled lip, yellow green, 1⅝'' 75.00   85.00

☐ **HARRISON'S COLUMBIAN INK**
Eight panels, pontil, aqua, 2'' 38.00   51.00

☐ **HARRISON'S COLUMBIAN INK**
Eight-sided, flared lip, aqua, 2½'' 22.00   45.00

Price Range

☐ **HARRISON'S COLUMBIAN INK**
Eight-sided, flared lip, aqua, 3" 49.00 59.00

☐ **HARRISON'S COLUMBIAN INK**
Cylindrical, sapphire blue, 4⅛" 130.00 150.00

☐ **HARRISON'S COLUMBIAN INK**
Cylindrical, flared lip, cobalt blue, 7¼" 365.00 415.00

☐ **HARRISON'S COLUMBIAN INK**
Twelve-sided, aqua, 11⅛" 395.00 405.00

☐ **HARRISON'S COLUMBIAN INK**
In 3 lines, round, ring top, pontil, cobalt, 4½" x
1¼" 100.00 130.00

☐ **HARRISON'S COLUMBIAN INK**
Eight-sided squat, open pontil, aqua, 1¾" tall,
1¾" base 50.00 65.00

☐ **HARRISON'S COLUMBIAN INK**
Open pontil, cobalt, 1½" x 1½" 120.00 145.00

☐ **HARRISON'S/COLUMBIAN INK**
Embossed vertically on three of twelve panels,
Patent embossed on shoulder, iron pontil, aqua
3⅛" x 1½" 40.00 55.00

☐ **G.E. HATCH**
Pat's Dec. 27, 1875, firey opalescent, pontil
scarred, 2½" h., 3¼" dia., figural pear and leaves
on top with original paint 200.00 240.00

☐ **PENN MFG. WORKS**
P. GARRETT & CO. "Philada" on base, inkwell
with stopper, firey opalescent, 2⅞" h. 8.00 12.00

☐ **HIGGINS DRAWING INK**
Under bottom, machine made, clear, 3" 4.00 5.00

☐ **HIGGINS INKS, BROOKLYN, N.Y.**
On bottom, round, squat, clear, 3¾" 6.00 8.00

☐ Same as above except ABM 3.00 4.00

☐ **HIGGINS INKS**
Brooklyn, NY, round, amethyst or clear, 2" 5.00 7.00

☐ **H.J.H. WRITING INK**
B.B. on panels, sheared top, clear or aqua, 2½" 18.00 23.00

☐ **HOGAN & THOMPSON**
Phila, cone, open pontil, aqua, 2" x ⅜" 110.00 160.00

☐ **JOHN HOLLAND**
Cincinnati, square bottle with rounded corners,
ring top and neck, aqua, 2¼" 6.00 8.00

Price Range

☐ **HOLLIOGE**
Square, sheared lip, name embossed on shoulder, pen groove one each side, one side smooth, other sides ribbed, small concave bottom, medium cobalt blue, 1¾" x 1¾" 12.00 16.00

☐ **HOOKER'S**
Sheared top, round, aqua, 2" 10.00 14.00

☐ **HOVER**
"Phila" on two panels, eight panels, umbrella shape, aqua, 2" 45.00 55.00

☐ **HOVER**
"Phila" in 2 lines on one panel, umbrella type bottle, ring top, pontil, ring top, blue-green, 2¼" x 2⅛" 33.00 43.00

☐ **HUNT MFG. CO., SPEEDBALL**
"U.S.A., Statesville, N.C." embossed on bottom, cone, clear, 2¾" 3.00 4.00

☐ **HUNT PEN CO. SPEEDBALL**
"U.S.A., Camden, N.J." embossed on bottom, round, clear, 2¾" 3.00 4.00

☐ **IGLOO INK**
Dome shaped, plain with neck on side, sheared top, 1¾" or 1¼" tall, 2" round, sapphire blue 185.00 240.00
☐ Same as above except cobalt 240.00 310.00

☐ **IMPROVED PROCESS BLUE CO.**
Aqua, 2⅜" 5.00 9.00

☐ **INK**
Boat shaped, sheared lip, indented grooves on each side of neck. Deep cobalt, 1⅞" wide x 2¼" long 25.00 35.00

☐ **INK**
Cone, ring collar, bulbous ring forms shoulder, ring on base of neck, amber, 2½" x 2½" 6.00 8.00

☐ **INK**
Round, cobalt blue, 2½" x 3" 6.00 8.00

☐ **INK**
Cone type, yet not a true cone, base is cone shape with two large graduated flared bands on shoulder and neck, sheared collar, aqua, 3⅜" 8.00 11.00

☐ **INK**
Cone, honey amber, 2½" 5.50 7.00

Price Range

☐ **INK**
Cone, tan, crock, 2½" 9.00   12.00
☐ **INK**
Cone, cobalt blue, 2½" 12.00   17.00
☐ **INK**
Cone, amber, 2⅝" 12.00   17.00
☐ **INK**
Cone, light blue, 2¾" 8.00   11.00
☐ **INK**
Cone, plain, clear or amethyst, 2½" 3.00   4.00
☐ Same as above except blue or amber 12.00   17.00
☐ **INK**
Cone, amethyst, 3" 6.00   8.00
☐ **INK**
Design "Patd. Feb 16th, 1886" under bottom in
sunken circle, five different size rings on top or
shoulder, one 1¼" ring on base, clear 12¼" .. 8.00   11.00
☐ Same as above except one ring near shoulder,
green 8.00   11.00
☐ **INK**
No emboss, 8 panels, umbrella type bottle, pontil,
plain top, brilliant blue, aqua, 2¼" x 2¼" 15.00   23.00
☐ **INK**
Three-piece mold, crude graduated collar, ice
blue, pint, 7⅜" 8.00   12.00
☐ **INK**
Ice cube shaped, solid glass, heavy, small well,
metal collar, desk type, clear, 2" x 2" x 2" 4.50   5.50
☐ **INK**
Label, three-part mold, aqua, 2¾" 8.00   11.00
☐ **INK**
Label, black, 7½" 25.00   35.00
☐ **INK**
Label, cone, ring shoulder, 2½" 7.00   9.00
☐ **INK**
Lable, crock, tapered neck, brick red, 4" 6.00   8.00
☐ **INK**
Label, aqua, 2¾" 5.00   7.00
☐ **INK**
Label, crock, green and white, 2½" x 2½" 12.00   17.00
☐ **INK**
Label, clear, 2½" 4.00   5.00

Price Range

☐ **INK**
Label, light blue, 2¾" 5.00 7.00

☐ **INK**
Label, tin box, 1½" 24.00 33.00

☐ **INK**
Label, dark aqua, 2¾" 5.00 7.00

☐ **INK**
Label, clear, 2½" at base tapering to 2" at top 14.00 18.00

☐ **INK**
Label, wood, brick red, 3" 12.00 17.00

☐ **INK**
Plain, checked bottom, clear, 3" tall, 1¾" x 1¾"
base 20.00 28.00

☐ **INK**
Label, three-part mold, green, 9¼" 15.00 23.00

☐ **INK**
Label, sheared top, pontil, clear, 2" 15.00 22.00

☐ **INK**
Label, desk bottle, sheared top, clear or amethyst, 1¾" 10.00 14.00

☐ **INK**
Label, "Pat Oct. 17, 1865" around bottom, clear
or amethyst, 2¾" 25.00 33.00

☐ **INK**
Label, desk bottle, sheared top, clear or amethyst, 1½" 10.00 13.00

☐ **INK**
Label, sheared top, panels on shoulder, clear or
amethyst, 1¼" x 1½" x 1½" 10.00 13.00

☐ **INK**
Label, green, 2½" 65.00 85.00

☐ **INK**
Label, broken pontil, green, 7½" 27.00 36.00

☐ **INK**
Label, sheared top, aqua, ½" tall, 5½" long ... 40.00 53.00

☐ **INK**
Label, long square body, neck on end, clear, 3¾"
x ¾" 14.00 18.00

☐ **INK**
Label, round, dark green, 2¼" 12.00 16.00

Price Range

☐ **INK**
Pen rest on both sides at shoulder, sheared collar, amethyst, 2⅝″ x 2⅜″ x 2⅜″ 7.00   9.00
☐ Same as above except aqua, 2″ x 2¼″ x 2¾″   7.00   9.00
☐ **INK or GLUE**
Plain, heavy ring forms shoulder, slightly raised ring above at base of neck, conical, aqua, 2¼″ tall, 2½″ base 4.00   5.00
☐ Same as above except brown or amber 5.00   7.00
☐ Same as above except green or blue 7.00   9.00
☐ Same as above except cobalt 8.00   11.00
☐ **INK**
Plain, has two deep rounded troughs on shoulder on either side of neck for pen rest, plain top, sunken bottom, clear or amethyst, 2¼″ x 2½″, neck ¾″ 10.00   13.00
☐ **INK**
Plain, ring encircling base, another forming shoulder, small ring on base of neck, round, clear, 2¼″ x 2″ 4.00   5.00
☐ Same as above except different colors 8.00   11.00
☐ **INK**
Plain, no emboss, flare lips, ring shoulder and base, round, clear, 2⅛″ x 2″ 12.00   16.00
☐ **INK**
Plain, 2¾″ round bottom, trench from shoulder to shoulder ¾″ wide for clamp of some kind, flat ring, ring at bottom of neck, 1½″ ring top, ½″ neck, machine made, clear 6.00   8.00
☐ **INK**
Plain, round, inside of flower stand, two prongs on left top to hold pen, all metal is gold color, clear, 2½″ tall, 3½″ round 24.00   34.00
☐ **INK**
Plain, round bottom, green, 9″ 8.00   11.00
☐ **INK**
Plain, square top, on top and bottom fancy gold colored metal stand, round base, clear, 2″ 14.00   23.00
☐ **INK**
Plain, square, green or clear, 2″ 4.00   5.50

Price Range

☐ **INK**
Tooled lip, "Penn Mfg. Works" on smooth base,
round, 2¼" 17.00   23.00

☐ **INK**
Sheared lip, smooth base, bell shape, 2¼" . . . 23.00   34.00

☐ **INK**
Square, squat, cobalt blue, 2⅜" 6.00   9.00

☐ **INK**
Square, amethyst or aqua, 2½" 4.00   5.00

☐ **INK**
"Patd./Mar 14/1871 embossed on base, cabin
shaped, square, 2½" 400.00 420.00

☐ **INK**
Square collared lip, twelve-sided, light blue, 6¾" 34.00   38.00

☐ **INK**
No embossing, flared lip, cylindrical, 7½" 165.00 185.00

☐ **INK**
Twelve-sided, square collared lip, smooth base,
8½" 22.00   32.00

☐ **INK**
2 oz. on short neck, square, rounded corners, machine made, cobalt, clear or blue, 2" x 2" 4.00   5.00

☐ **IRVING**
Square, aqua, 2½" 24.00   34.00

☐ **J & IEM**
Imprinted in each panel, Turtle with six panels, on
base Patd Oct 31, 1865, under bottom J, aqua   14.00   27.00
☐ Same as above except no patent date, amber . . 95.00   130.00
☐ Same as above except cobalt 320.00 420.00

☐ **J & IEM**
Turtle, tooled mouth, smooth base, aqua, 1¾"   14.00   20.00

☐ **JASMINE INK CORP.**
Norfolk, VA, square, labeled "Perfumed Jasmine
Ink," ABM, clear 4.00   5.00

☐ **J. M & S IGLOO INK**
Early 20.00   26.00

☐ **JOHNSON INK CO.**
Willington, CT. fancy label, Stoddard, tapered and
sheared top, dark green, 5⅞" 30.00   40.00

Price Range

☐ **JOSIAH JONSON'S**
"Japan, Writing Fluid, London," one word on each panel, teakettle type crock, 2½" x 2¼", gray and brown glazes 170.00 220.00

☐ **KEENE GEOMETRIC INK**
Open pontil, amber 90.00 115.00

☐ **KEENE UMBRELLA INK**
Eight-sided pontil, green 48.00 68.00

☐ **KELLER**
Double ring top, clear or amethyst, 2½" 7.00 9.00

☐ **KELLERS INK**
Under bottom, clear, 1¼" x 1½", ½" neck ... 14.00 18.00

☐ **F. KIDDER IMPROVED, INDELIBLE INK**
Around bottle, square, aqua, 2½" x 1½" x 1½" 33.00 43.00

☐ Same as above except 5", clear 30.00 40.00

☐ **F. KIDDER IMPROVED INDELIBLE INK**
Around bottle, flared mouth, rectangle, 2⅜" ... 60.00 65.00

☐ **KIRKLAND WRITING FLUID**
Ring on shoulder and base, aqua, 2¼" x 1½" 7.00 9.00

☐ **LAKE'S**
Cone, aqua, 2½" 22.00 30.00

☐ **LEVISON'S**
Machine made, clear, 7¼" 8.00 11.00

☐ **LOCOMOTIVE**
Shape embossed with train features "PAT. OCT. 1874-TRADE MARK," aqua, 2' h., C-715 ...... 550.00 630.00

☐ **LOMBARD'S LILAC INK**
Diamond shape label, house type, clear, 2⅜" 6.00 8.00

☐ **LOVATT & LOVATT LANGLEY MILL**
Imprinted in small lettering at base in two straight lines, stoneware, flaired top, pouring spout, brown, 4¾" tall, 2¼" diam at base 10.00 14.00

☐ **LOVATT & LOVATT NO. 77 LANGLEY MILL**
Imprinted at bottom, stoneware, high gloss glaze, pouring spout, dark brown, 6¼" tall, 2⅝" diam. at base 14.00 20.00

☐ **LYNDEBORO**
Rectangular, slots for two pens, aqua, 2¼" ... 12.00 17.00

☐ **LYNDEBORO**
Rectangular, slots for two pens, green, 2¼" x 2⅜" 10.00 14.00

Price Range

☐ **LYONS**
Square with vertical ribbing on three sides, two
pen ledges, base embossed, aqua, 2⅜″ 17.00 28.00

☐ **MABIE TODD AND CO.**
"London Base" embossed, swan in center,
square collared mouth, clear, 5¼″ 3.00 7.00

☐ **MAGNUS**
Tan pottery, 4⅝″ 8.00 11.00

☐ **CARL MAMPE BERLIN**
Amber, 2″ 14.00 22.00

☐ **MANN'S**
Label, Design Patd Feb 16, 1886 under bottom,
amber, 9¼″ 14.00 22.00

☐ **MASSACHUSETTS STANDARD RECORD INK**
On shoulder, clear, 7¾″ 13.00 17.00

☐ **MAURIN A. DEPOSE**
"Paris" in 3 lines, square bottle, ring top, clear,
2½″ x 1¼″ 24.00 38.00

☐ **MAYNARD & NOYES'**
Label only, flare top, pontil, olive green, 4¼″ x
1⅛″ 27.00 37.00

☐ **MAYNARD'S WRITING INK**
Sheared top, amber case, eight panels, umbrella
type, dark green, 2″ 32.00 43.00

☐ **JULES MIETTE**
Paris, sheared top, blue green, 2¾″ 20.00 26.00

☐ **MON-GRAM INK**
Round, clear or amethyst, 2½″ 6.00 8.00

☐ **MOORE & SON**
Sheared top, aqua or clear, 1⅝″ 8.00 11.00

☐ **MOORE J & IEM**
Igloo, round, 2½″ to 6½″, several other types
and sizes 27.00 38.00

☐ **MORDAN**
Bell-shaped, obverse embossing, burst top,
aqua, 5½″ 5.00 9.00

☐ **M.S. CO.**
"Sanford's #216" on bottom, clear 5.00 7.00

☐ **MT. WASHINGTON GLASS CO.**
New Bedford, MA, Bubble Ball Inkwell, clear, 2″ 33.00 43.00

☐ **MY LADY INK**
On base, Carbonine Ink Co., NY, aqua, 1⅜″ .. 8.00 11.00

Price Range

☐ **NA**
On one panel, 10 base panels concave, ring top,
aqua, clear, 2¼" x 2½" 35.00   45.00

☐ **NATIONAL INK N.W.W. & CO.**
Label, clear, 2" 4.00   5.00

☐ **NAYMARD & MOYES [sic]**
Boston, label, pontil, clear 45.00   55.00

☐ **P. NEWMAN & CO.**
Gilsum, NH, label, umbrella type, eight panels,
olive green, 1½" 20.00   30.00

☐ **NEWTON'S INK**
In 2 lines, ring shoulder and top, and ring base
of neck, sheared top, aqua, 2⅞" x 2¼" 12.00   17.00

☐ **NICHOLS & HALL**
Label, house type, clear, 2⅞" 8.00   11.00

☐ **OBLONG**
Two wells, two pen rests, covers, clear, 1⅜" .. 12.00   16.00

☐ **OCTAGON INK**
Mushroom shaped, pontil, aqua 26.00   34.00

☐ **1 X L**
Fancy ink, ring top, clear, 2½" 14.00   22.00

☐ **OPDYKE**
Barrel shaped bottle with four rings around it,
opening in center, clear, 2" 14.00   22.00

☐ Same as above except panels around bottom,
ring top, "Opdyke" under bottom, clear, 2¼" .. 24.00   32.00

☐ **OPDYKE BROS. INK**
Barrel with opening in center, ring top, aqua, 2½"
x 2⅜" 22.00   32.00

☐ **OPDYKE BROS. INK**
Barrel, patd March 11, 1870, opening in center,
aqua, 2½" x 2⅜" 24.00   33.00

☐ **P AND J ARNOLD**
London, cut stopper, flared mouth, embossed on
shoulder, clear, 6¾" 3.00   7.00

☐ **P & J ARNOLD**
Pour spout, collared, brown, 9¼" 14.00   20.00

☐ **PALMER**
Round, sheared top, golden amber, 4¼" 32.00   49.00

Price Range

☐ **PANTHEON BUILDING**
Stone inkwell shape of gray circular building, embossed with "Pantheon," tan and cream colored column area, 2⅝" 95.00 120.00

☐ **PARKER**
Panels on shoulder, ring top, ABM, clear, 2½" 10.00 13.00
☐ Same as above except Parker's "Quink" under bottom, Made in U.S.A. #1, ABM, 1½" 7.00 9.00

☐ **PAUL'S INKS**
"N.Y., Chicago" on back, cobalt, 9½" 20.00 24.00

☐ **PAUL'S SAFETY BOTTLE & INK CO.**
"NY" on shoulder, squat, ring top, clear, 1⅜" 14.00 22.00

☐ **PAUL'S WRITING FLUID**
NY, Chicago, flared neck, ring top, three-part mold, 5½" 14.00 22.00

☐ **PENN MFG. WORKS**
P. GARRETT & CO. "Philada" On base, inkwell with stopper, firey opalescent, 2⅞" h., ... 8.00 12.00

☐ **PEERLESS**
On two panels, eight panels, umbrella type, bulbous shoulder, sheared top, clear or amethyst 16.00 27.00

☐ **J.W. PENNELL**
Embossed on eight panels on base, round top, ring top, aqua, 2" 14.00 22.00

☐ **PENN. MFG. WORK**
Phila., eight flat sides, white, 2½" 40.00 55.00

☐ **PERRY & CO.**
"London, Patent" in two lines, on top ½" hole for ink and funnel hole for pen, flared ring bottom 3" to 2¼" top, sunken bottom, cream pottery, 3" round, 1¾" tall 27.00 38.00

☐ **PITKIN INKWELL**
36 ribs swirl left, double pattern with verticle ribbing, olive-green, 1½" h., 2⁵/₁₆" dia., pontil scarred, C-1123 .... 600.00 700.00

☐ **PITKIN INKWELL**
36 ribs swirl left, double pattern with verticle ribbing, pronounced mouth opening, olive-green, 2" h., 2⁷/₁₆" dia., C-1123 .... 420.00 480.00

☐ **PITKIN INKWELL**
36 ribs swirl left, olive green, 1¼' h., 2¼' dia., C-1147 .... 250.00 300.00

Pitkin Ink, open pontil, 36-rib mold, double patterned, olive-green, 2",
$300.00–$360.00 (Courtesy of Glass-Works Auctions, East Greenville, PA)

	Price Range	
☐ **PITKIN INKWELL** 36-rib mold, swirls to left, flared lip, lime green, 1¾" x 2½" x 2¼"	260.00	340.00
☐ **POMEROY INK** Newark, NY label, two rings on base and shoulder, ring top, aqua, 2¾"	8.00	11.00
☐ **G.A. POTTER** Pottery, tan, 9⅞"	17.00	28.00
☐ **PRICE** Bristol, England stoneware, cream, 5½"	7.00	11.00
☐ **RAVEN'S** Label, design "Patd Feb 16th 1886" under bottom, 7¾"	17.00	27.00
☐ **READING INK CO.** Reading, Mich., Superior Blue Ink, label, round, wide collar, flared top, aqua, 6³/₁₆" x 1⁹/₁₆"	10.00	15.00
☐ **READING INK CO.** Reading, Mich., diamond shaped label, on base "Pat. April 18, 1875," round, crude pouring lip, aqua, 6⅛"	12.00	17.00

Price Range

☐ **READING INK CO.**
Violet Ink, label, crude cone with pronounced
mold lines, 2¾″ x 2⅝″ 12.00 17.00
☐ **READS INKSTAND AND INK**
Pat. Nov. 25, 1872, ring top, aqua blue, 2″ 27.00 38.00
☐ **REXALL LIVER SALTS**
Square bottle with rounding sides, paper label,
bottom embossed "M-UD Co. 10." Cobalt blue,
5½″ 5.00 8.00
☐ **ROUND**
Free-blown, funnel mouth, pontil base, aqua, ⅞″ 14.00 20.00
☐ **ROUND BLOWN**
Rolled mouth, pontil base, aqua, 1½″ 12.00 16.00
☐ **ROUND INK**
Flared mouth with pour spout, without emboss-
ing, 5¾″ 3.00 5.00
☐ **ROUND MASTER INK**
Tooled mouth with pour spout, without emboss-
ing, clear, 9″ 3.00 5.00
☐ **ROUND TRAVEL**
With round rosewood case, cover, blown glass,
clear, 2⅛″ 20.00 26.00
☐ **SAFETY BOTTLE & INK CO.**
New York, patented July 9, 1895, swirl pattern
body, tooled mouth, embossed shoulder, clear,
2⅜″ 6.00 11.00
☐ **SANFORD'S**
Round, embossed "Sanford's" on base, aqua,
2⅜″ 3.00 5.00
☐ **SAFETY BOTTLE & INK CO.**
NY, "Paul's pat." on shoulder, diagonal swirls,
sunburst pattern on base, clear, 2⅛″ x 2⅜″ .. 14.00 22.00
☐ **SANFORD HORSE-SHOE INK**
Sanford 217 Pat. apl. for, aqua 10.00 15.00
☐ **SANFORD/INKS/ONE QUART/AND
LIBRARY PASTE**
Vertically, raised ¾″ ring around base and shoul-
der, round, square collar and ring, ABM, amber,
3¾″ diameter, 9⅜″ tall 7.00 9.00
☐ Same as above except embossing on pouring
cap, Pat. Feb. 27, 06, 10½″ 13.00 19.00

Price Range

☐ **SANFORD MFG. CO.**
Pat. May 23, 1899 on bottom, clear or amethyst,
3" .... | 4.00 | 5.00

☐ **SANFORD'S**
Bellwood, IL "Made in U.S.A. 44CC." embossed
on bottom, metal screw-on top, red plastic, 1½" | 9.00 | 11.00

☐ **SANFORD'S MFG. CO.**
Vertically in sunken panel, 1 oz. on next panel,
S.I. Co. monogram on next panel, square collar,
ABM, amethyst, 1½" x 2½" .... | 6.00 | 11.00

☐ **SANFORD'S FREE SAMPLE NEVER SOLD**
Sheared top, 3½" .... | 11.00 | 15.00

☐ **SANFORDS #6**
On bottom, 1½ oz. on one panel, large step on
shoulder, double band collar, clear, 1¾" x 2¼" | 3.50 | 4.50

☐ **SANFORD'S #8**
Under bottom, light green, 2½" .... | 5.00 | 7.00

☐ **SANFORD'S 25-8**
On bottom, aqua, 2½" .... | 5.00 | 7.00

☐ **SANFORD'S #29 PAT APP'D FOR**
On bottom, boat shaped, clear, 2" x 2¾" x 2¼" | 10.00 | 13.00

☐ **SANFORD'S 30 PATENT APPLIED FOR**
On bottom, boat shaped, aqua, 2" tall, 2¼" x
1¾" base .... | 12.00 | 16.00

☐ **SANFORD'S #39**
On bottom, large ring with deep groove at base
and shoulder, step on shoulder, small and large
ring collar, round, aqua or amethyst, 2" x 2⅜" | 4.50 | 5.00

☐ **SANFORD'S #88**
Bell shaped, sheared collar, amethyst, 2½" di-
ameter, 3⅜" tall .... | 8.00 | 11.00

☐ **SANFORD'S #89**
Somewhat conical, sheared collar, amethyst,
2¼" diameter, 2½" tall .... | 4.00 | 5.00

☐ **SANFORD'S #98**
Chicago, New York 1½ oz. on bottom, large ring
on base and shoulder, two rings on collar, round,
ABM, clear, 1¾" x 2½" .... | 3.50 | 4.00

☐ **SANFORD'S**
"CHICAGO, #187" under bottom, round, flared
top, clear, 1½" x 1½" .... | 17.00 | 28.00

Price Range

□ **SANFORD'S #219**
On bottom, large ring on base and shoulder, large ring and small ring collar, round, ABM, clear, 1⅞" x 2¼" 3.50 4.00

□ **SANFORD'S #276**
On bottom, S.I. Co. monogram in sunken bull's-eye panel, rings at base of neck, ABM: three other plain bull's-eyes, clear, 1⅞" x 2⅝" 3.50 4.00

□ **SANFORD'S PREMIUM WRITING FLUID**
Label, ABM, amber, 9" 7.00 9.00

□ **SCHLESINGER'S HYDRAULIC INK**
White and black crock, copper top, 6" 37.00 53.00

□ **SHEAFFER'S/SKRIP/THE SUCCESSOR TO INK**
Embossed on metal plate in top of wooden cylinder, container for an ink bottle, wooden threaded screw-on top, 3⅝" tall, 2⁷⁄₁₆" diameter 8.00 11.00

□ **DR. A. SHEET'S**
Dayton, OH, black ink, square collared lip, smooth base, aqua, 2¾" 27.00 48.00

□ **DR. SHEET'S INK**
Double collared lip, pour spout, smooth base, cylindrical, aqua, 8½" 58.00 69.00

□ **SHOE**
Label, clear, 6" long 10.00 13.00

□ **SHOE**
With buckle, clear, 3⅞" long 8.00 11.00

□ **SI**
Under bottom pontil, umbrella type bottle, 8 panels, plain top, pontil, aqua, 2¼" x 2½" 37.00 48.00

□ **SIGNET INK**
Threaded for screw top, cobalt blue, 7¾" 13.00 18.00

□ **S. SILL**
(cannot decipher balance) Chester, CT, blue label under bottom, 3¼" round ring at bottom and top, vase shaped, four different side holes to hold quill pens, in center top a bottle for ink, all wood, brown, 1¾" 27.00 38.00

□ **SISSON & CO.**
Sheared top, round, pale aqua green, 1⅝" 8.00 11.00

Price Range

☐ **SKRIP**
Tighten cap, tip bottle to fill the well on metal top, "Pat'd 1759866" on bottom, ink well, screw-on top, clear, 2¾" 13.00 17.00

☐ **S.M. CO 6**
Under bottom, aqua, 2¼" 1.50 11.00

☐ **T. SMITH & CO.**
"Old Kent Rd., London" all in oval design at base of bottle, jug-shape, no pouring spout, collared, mottled brown-black, 4¾" tall, 2¾" diam. at base 14.00 20.00

☐ **S. O. DUNBAR**
Taunton, Mass. round, sloping collared mouth, obverse embossing, aqua, 5¾" 5.00 9.00

☐ **SONNEBORN & ROBBINS**
Flared lip, cork stopper topped with brass, tan pottery, 5½" 8.00 11.00

☐ **SO. STAMP & STATIONERY CO., MFG. STATIONERS**
Richmond, VA amber, 9½" 32.00 42.00

☐ **SQUARE**
Paneled body with rounded corners, clear, 2" 5.00 9.00

☐ **SQUARE**
Vertically ribbed, funnel mouth, pontil base, three quill holes, clear, 1½" 43.00 53.00

☐ **SQUARE INK**
Vertical ribbing on three sides, two pen ledges, without embossing, turquoise, 2⅜" 17.00 28.00

☐ **SQUARE INKWELL**
Rounded corners, metal dome cover, clear, 2¾" 27.00 38.00

☐ **SQUARE TRAVEL**
Brass fitting, cover with flanged piece which un-screws to open, clear, 1⅛" 3.00 5.00

☐ **SSS**
Under bottom, 8 panels, umbrella type, bottle plain top, aqua, 2¼" x 2¼" 14.00 22.00

☐ **STAFFORD'S COMMERCIAL INK**
Round, Pat. Jan 13-85, S.M. CO, clear, 2" 10.00 13.00

☐ **STAFFORD'S INK**
In two lines running vertically, two rings on shoul-der and bottom, amber, 4¼" body, 2" neck ... 10.00 13.00

☐ **STAFFORD'S INK**
Tooled lip, smooth base, cylindrical, olive, 7¾" 22.00 27.00

Price Range

☐ **STAFFORD'S INK**
Green, 8″ 13.00 17.00

☐ **STAFFORD'S INK**
Round, aqua, 3″ 6.00 8.00

☐ **STAFFORD'S INK**
Near base, round bottle, aqua, 2⅛″ x 2¼″ 13.00 17.00

☐ **S.S. STAFFORD INK**
"Made in U.S.A." in two lines, in a sunken panel,
under it "This Bottle Contains One Full Quart,"
two rings on bottom, two on shoulder, short neck,
aqua, 2″ 17.00 27.00

☐ Same as above except 7″ 17.00 27.00

☐ Same as above except 6″ 13.00 20.00

☐ Same as above except 4¾″ 13.00 20.00

☐ **STAFFORD'S INKS**
Made in U.S.A., pouring spout, cobalt blue, 6″ 13.00 22.00

☐ **S.S. STAFFORD'S INKS**
Made in U.S.A., embossed, pour spout, colbalt
blue, 7″ 13.00 20.00

☐ **STAFFORD'S INK SS**
Made in U.S.A., in sunken panel, under it, "This
Bottle Contains One Full Qt.," aqua or light blue,
9½″ 7.00 9.00

☐ **STAFFORD'S NO. 5, PAT NOV. 17, 1896,
NOV. 22, 1892**
On base, shoe shaped, aqua, 2½″ neck, 3¼″ 14.00 20.00

☐ **STAFFORD'S VERMILION INK**
Two pen slots, aqua with blue label 10.00 14.00

☐ **STANFORD**
Square roof and 1½″ chimney, ½″ base, Stanford's Fountain Pen Inks, machine made, 2″ x 2″ 3.50 5.25

☐ **STANFORD'S BLUE INK**
Label around body, ring on base, neck and shoulder, 2⅜″ neck, 2″ tall, 2″ round 5.50 7.50

☐ **STEPHENS LONDON**
Imprinted in ¼″ letters near bottom of bottle,
stoneware, no pouring spout, flaired ring type top,
¾″ neck, glazed, brown, 5¾″ tall, 3⅛″ dia. at
base 14.00 20.00

☐ **HENRY C. STEPHENS, LTD.**
Pouring spout, dark brown, 9″ 8.00 11.00

Teakettle Ink, *embossed floral design, original paint and cap, fiery opalescent, 2",*
$600.00–$700.00 *(Courtesy of Glass-Works Auctions, East Greenville, PA)*

	Price Range	
☐ **STODDARD MASTER INK**		
Olive amber around pontil, 9⅜"	34.00	45.00
☐ **STODDARD UMBRELLA INK**		
Eight-sided, open pontil, amber	57.00	68.00
☐ **STONE INK**		
Square, indentation around mouth, gray, 2½"	17.00	28.00
☐ **STONEWARE**		
Inverted area at shoulder for dripwell, cream		
glaze, 3⅛"	17.00	28.00
☐ **STONE-SHAPED IRON**		
Square, footed, glazed top and base, 1⅞"	37.00	47.00
☐ **SUPERIOR INK**		
Tan and brown, 2"	8.00	11.00
☐ **SWIFT & PEARSON**		
Top and neck drawn out and shaped by hand,		
bulbous neck, dark green, 7⅝"	40.00	50.00
☐ **SYR-RHEL INK**		
Pontil, cobalt, 8"	53.00	69.00
☐ **BRICKETT J. TAYLOR INK**		
Cylindrical, flared lip, Keene, open pontil, 4½"	133.00	169.00

Price Range

☐ **TEA KETTLE**
In shape of a crown with embossings, amethyst, with original cap, 1⅞″ h. 1400.00 1500.00

☐ **TEA KETTLE**
In shape of lounging cat, "N.A. DEPOSE" on spout, clear glass, 1⅞″ h. 600.00 700.00

☐ **TEA KETTLE SANDWICH GLASSWORKS**
Domed and five protrusion shapes in clambroth, 2½″ h. 500.00 550.00

☐ **TEA KETTLE SHAPE**
Fiery opalescent with embossed floral designs, original paint and cap, 2⅜″ h 600.00 640.00

☐ **TEA KETTLE SHAPE**
Brilliant amethyst with original cap, 2¹/₁₆″ h. 500.00 525.00

☐ **TEA KETTLE SHAPE**
Cobalt blue, 2″ h., panelled, ... 140.00 180.00

☐ **TEA KETTLE SHAPE**
Brilliant green with original cap, panelled, 1⅞″ h. 875.00 950.00

☐ **TEA KETTLE SHAPE**
Yellow amber, panelled, 2⁹/₁₆″ h. 170.00 220.00

☐ **TEA KETTLE SHAPE**
Deep sapphire blue, panelled, with cap rim but no cap, 2⁵/₁₆″ h. 250.00 300.00

☐ **TEA KETTLE SHAPE**
Clear glass with original gold gilt floral decoration and flashed pink inside, with cap rim but no cap, 1⅝″ h. 610.00 670.00

☐ **TEA KETTLE SHAPE**
White porcelain, panelled, 2¼″ h. 110.00 170.00

☐ **TEA KETTLE SHAPE**
Floral designs embossed in dome and on sides in emerald green, 2½″ h. 410.00 470.00

☐ **TEA KETTLE SHAPE**
Original wooden stand with pen holder, cobalt blue, panelled, 2¼″ h. 240.00 290.00

☐ **TEA KETTLE SHAPE**
Amethyst with darker amethyst striations throughout, panelled, 2¼″ h. 200.00 250.00

☐ **TEA KETTLE INK**
Label, eight panels, 2½″ sheared top, cobalt, 2″ x 4″ 70.00 90.00

Price Range

☐ Same as above except clear 70.00 90.00
☐ Same as above except neck is close to the eight
panels, metal top aqua 70.00 90.00
☐ **THACKER**
London, round with vertically ribbed shoulders
and sides, label panel under pen ledge, burst top,
base embossed, light aqua, 2⅛" 35.00 45.00
☐ **THOMAS**
On bottom, cone, bulbous shoulder, double col-
lar, amethyst 7.00 9.00
☐ **L.H. THOMAS & CO.**
Clear or aqua, 2¼" x 3⅛" 4.00 6.00
☐ **L.H. THOMAS CHICAGO CO. #57**
On bottom, double band collar, large and small
ring on shoulder, large ring on base, round, aqua,
2½" 8.00 11.00
☐ **L.H. THOMAS INK**
Aqua, 5¼" 13.00 17.00
☐ **L.H. THOMAS INK**
Bell shaped, aqua, 2¾" 20.00 28.00
☐ **L.H. THOMAS INK**
"Pat. April 13, 1875" under bottom, aqua, 8" .. 13.00 18.00
☐ **W.B. TODD**
Ring top, round, green, 2⅞" 9.00 12.00
☐ **TRAVEL INK**
Label, with fitted hard leather case, six panels,
aqua, 2" 22.00 32.00
☐ **TURTLE**
Plain rim around bottle at bottom, spout extends
1¹/₁₆" on side, sheared top, aqua, 1½" wide, 2⅛"
tall 23.00 30.00
☐ **TURTLE**
Aqua, 2" x 4" 53.00 110.00
☐ **TURTLE**
Twelve lines lower half, granite, sheared top,
aqua, 1½" x 2" 35.00 45.00
☐ **UMBRELLA INK**
Tooled lip, amber, 2" 32.00 37.00
☐ **UMBRELLA INK**
Eight-sided, tapers into small round neck, open
pontil, olive amber, 2½" tall, 2½" base 68.00 85.00
☐ Same as above except brown 28.00 40.00

Umbrella Ink, sixteen-sided, open pontil, sheared lip, pinhead flake off side of lip, olive-amber, 2½", **$175.00–$225.00** (Courtesy of Glass-Works Auctions, East Greenville, PA)

	Price Range	
☐ Same as above except blue	**28.00**	**40.00**
☐ Same as above except no pontil..............	**20.00**	**29.00**
☐ Same as above except no pontil, brown or blue	**13.00**	**17.00**
☐ **UMBRELLA INK**		
Octagonal, rolled mouth, smooth base, without embossing, aqua, 2½"	**17.00**	**23.00**
☐ **UMBRELLA INK**		
Six panels, pontil, aqua or blue, 2½"	**65.00**	**85.00**
☐ Same as above except no pontil..............	**38.00**	**55.00**
☐ Same as above except smaller type	**28.00**	**39.00**
☐ **UMBRELLA INK**		
Rolled lip, eight vertical panels, aqua, 2⅝"	**12.00**	**17.00**
☐ **UMBRELLA INK**		
Rolled lip, open pontil, light amber, 2½" diameter, 2⅜" tall	**45.00**	**56.00**
☐ **UMBRELLA INK**		
Eight vertical panels, rolled lip, whittled effect, open pontil, emerald green, 2⅜"	**49.00**	**60.00**

Price Range

☐ **UMBRELLA INK**
Eight-sided, square, collared lip, smooth base,
amber, 2¾" **28.00 38.00**

☐ **UMBRELLA INK**
Label, twelve panels, open pontil, aqua **25.00 32.00**

☐ **UNDERWOOD**
Aqua, 3" **10.00 14.00**

☐ **UNDERWOOD INKS**
Cobalt blue, 6½" **43.00 60.00**

☐ **UNDERWOOD INKS**
Embossed, cylindrical, two pen rests on shoulder,
flared lip, cloudy, mold line ends at base of neck,
aqua, 1⅞" tall, 2⅛" base **22.00 26.00**

☐ **UNDERWOOD INKS**
Under bottom, circle or ring, tapered bottle, space
for label, aqua, 3¼" x 2¼" **48.00 60.00**

☐ **JOHN UNDERWOOD & CO.**
Cobalt blue, 9½" **13.00 41.00**

☐ **UNION INK CO.**
Ring top, aqua, 2¼" **10.00 13.00**

☐ **UNION INK CO.**
"Springfield, Mass." on sloping front, dome
shaped, sheared top, aqua, 1½" **23.00 30.00**

☐ **UNION INK CO.**
Springfield MA, aqua, 2" **14.00 20.00**

☐ **VOLGERS INK**
Label, house type, "T.C.V." under bottom, ring
top, clear, 2" **14.00 19.00**

☐ **WWW**
Enter lock large letters, under it trademark, flare
ring top, round, blue-green, 2⅞" x 2⅛" **20.00 28.00**

☐ **SAMUEL WARD & CO.**
Sheared top, clear, 3" **10.00 14.00**

☐ **WARD'S INK**
Pouring spout, round, olive green, 4¾" **10.00 14.00**

☐ **WATERLOW & SONS, LIMITED, COPYING
INK**
Label, crock, brown, 7½" **10.00 14.00**

☐ **L.E. WATERMAN CO.**
Squat band, ABM, aqua **3.00 4.00**

Price Range

☐ **WATERMAN'S WELLTOP**
2 oz., A.B.M., clear, square, screw top and well
top, clear, 3⅛″ x 1⅞″ 15.00 25.00

☐ **E. WATERS**
Vertically words, "Troy, N.Y.," round, amber,
6½″ 350.00 475.00

☐ **WATERS INK**
"Troy, N.Y." on panels, six panels, pontil, ring on
shoulder and ring top, tapered, aqua, 2½″ x 2″ 120.00 160.00

☐ **J.M. WHITALL**
Round, green, 1¾″ 7.00 10.00

☐ **WHITTEMORE BROS & CO.**
Dark green, 9½″ 9.00 12.00

☐ **WILBORS INK**
On shoulder, ring top and base, ring top, round,
aqua, 2½″ x 2″ 15.00 25.00

☐ **WILLIAMS & CARLETON**
Hartford, CT, round, aqua 18.00 23.00

☐ **GEORGE W. WILLIAMS & CO.**
Hartford, Conn., cone, aqua, 2½″ 25.00 35.00

☐ **WOODS**
Portland, Maine, black ink tapered, ring top, aqua,
2½″ 25.00 35.00

☐ **WORDEN & WYATT'S**
In 3 lines, in black 1 XL Fancy Inks, square, ring
top, clear, 2½″ x 1¼″ 30.00 40.00

☐ **WRIGHT-CLARKSON, MERC. CO.**
"Duluth, Minn." on base, clear, 6½″ 5.00 7.00

☐ **WRITEWELL & CO/INK/CHEMICALLY PURE**
Label, cobalt blue, 7¼″ x 2¹⁵/₁₆″ 12.00 17.00

☐ **YALE**
Dickinson & Co., Rutherford, NJ, amber, 1¾″ 6.00 8.00

MEDICINE

This category includes all patent medicines sold as medicine. It
excludes bitters, a liquor generally advertised as medicinal tonic, since
bitters collecting is a major specialty in itself (see the section on Bitters
Bottles). Likewise excluded are all bottles carrying the word "Cure,"
which also are collected as a specialty in themselves (see the section
on Cure Bottles).

Patent medicine refers to preparations whose formulas were covered by a patent registered with the U.S. Patent Office. In the 19th century, such patents could be obtained by anyone whether a licensed physician, pharmaceutical company or (as was generally the case) a fast-buck artist who knew nothing about medicine. So long as the ingredients were not deemed poisonous in ordinary dosages, the patent would be granted. They were treated as "products" rather than medicines. After passage of the Pure Food and Drug Act of 1907, most patent medicine companies went out of business. They were required to list ingredients on labels and upon learning the ingredients, few people wanted to buy them. Many consisted of nothing more than liquor diluted with ordinary water, sometimes with the addition of opiates. Others contained small amounts of strychnine or arsenic. Some quack manufacturers considered it good business to load up their preparations with powerful ingredients; they felt that if users experienced some kind of reaction, even if just dizziness or faintness, they'd believe in the product's effectiveness.

Not all medicines were patented. The U.S. Patent Office opened in 1790, but it was six years later before a patent was taken out for medicine. Many makers hesitated to take out patents as this required them to reveal the contents.

One of the oldest types of medicine bottles came out of England, the embossed Turlington's "Balsam of Life" bottles made between 1723 and 1900. The earliest American-made medicines came in plain bottles from domestic production. The first embossed U.S. medicine bottles date from around 1810. By 1906, the making of medicine bottles had become an $80,000,000 per year industry.

	Price Range	
□ **THE P.L. ABBEY CO.**		
Clear, 8¾"	**11.00**	**16.00**
□ **THE ABBOTT AIKAL CO.**		
"Chicago" in vertical lines, ring top, clear, 2⅝"	**5.00**	**8.00**
□ **THE ABBOTT AIKLORD CO.**		
Chicago, clear or aqua, 2⅝"	**7.00**	**12.00**
□ **ABBOTT BROS.**		
Chicago, reverse side "Rheumatic Remedy," amber, 6½"	**18.00**	**28.00**
□ **THE ABNER ROYCE CO.**		
Clear or amethyst, 5½"	**3.00**	**5.00**
□ **ABRAMS & CORROLLS ESSENCE OF JAMAICA GINGER**		
San Francisco, aqua, 5¼"	**12.00**	**18.00**

Price Range

☐ **ABSORBINE**
Springfield, MA, U.S.A., amber, 7½" 9.00 13.00

☐ **A & CO.**
Under bottom, label, amber, 5¼" 7.00 10.00

☐ **A.C. CO. COMFORT**
"Jacksonville, Fla." under bottom, clear, 5½" 3.00 5.00

☐ **ACEITE ORIENTAL RESSERT**
In back, cobalt, 3½" 20.00 28.00

☐ **ACEITE ORIENTAL RESSERT**
Moon and star on back, amber, 3½" 8.00 11.00

☐ **ACID IRON EARTH**
Reverse side "Mobile, Ala.," amber, 6¾" 15.00 22.00

☐ **DR. ACKER'S TU-BER-KU**
"Catarrh Of The Head" other side, clear, 8" ... 6.00 9.00

☐ **ACKER'S ELIXER, THE GREAT HEALTH RESTORER**
Label, amber, 6½" 5.00 8.00

☐ **AFFLECKS DRUG STORE**
Washington, D.C. clear or amethyst, 3¼" 5.00 8.00

☐ **AFRICANA**
In script, amber, 8" 15.00 22.00

☐ **AGUA PERUBINAT CONDAL**
Label, round, 10½" 6.00 9.00

☐ **AIMARS**
Reverse side "Charleston S.C.," reverse "Sarsa-parilla & Queens Delight," amber, 9⅝" 55.00 70.00

☐ **G. W. AIMAR AND CO.**
Charleston, SC, 409 King St., aqua, 5" 3.00 5.00

☐ **ALBANY CO. PHARMACY**
Laramie, WY., aqua 6.00 9.00

☐ **DR. ALEXANDER**
On side, "Lung Healer" on opposite side, rectan-gular, square collar, aqua blue, 6½" 6.00 9.00

☐ **DR. W. H. ALEXANDERS WONDERFUL HEALING OIL**
Label, aqua................................... 4.00 6.00

☐ **ALLAIRE WOODWARD & CO.**
Peoria, IL, reverse side "Elixir & Nutrans," amber, 10" 20.00 30.00

☐ **ALLAN ANTIFAT BOTANIC MED CO.**
Buffalo, NY, 1895, Aqua, 7½" 8.00 12.00

Price Range

☐ **MRS. A. ALLEN'S**
"World's Hair Restorer" one side, "New York"
other side, amber, 7½" 6.00 9.00

☐ **MRS. S.A. ALLEN'S**
"World's Hair Restorer, 355 Produce St., N.Y."
on two panels, dark purple, 7" 20.00 28.00

☐ **ALLEN'S ESSENCE OF JAMAICA GINGER**
Aqua, 5½" 7.00 10.00

☐ **ALLEN'S NERVE & BONE LINIMENT**
Vertical around bottle, square collar, round, aqua,
3⅞" 6.00 9.00

☐ **ALLEN'S SARSAPARILLA**
Vertical on front, oval shape, narrow square,
aqua, 8⅛" 18.00 24.00

☐ **ALLE-RHUME REMEDY CO.**
Machine made, clear, 7¾" 6.00 9.00

☐ **T.C. CAULK ALLOY**
On bottom, sunken panel, clear, 2¼" 4.00 6.00

☐ **AMERICAN DRUG STORE N.O.**
In center, tapered top, amber, 9¼" 45.00 60.00
☐ Same except sample size, 4¼" 50.00 65.00

☐ **AMER'S**
In vertical writing, clear or amethyst, 1¾" 4.00 7.00

☐ **SP. AMMON AR**
Clear, 9¼" 18.00 24.00

☐ **AMMONIA**
Flask, all sizes, aqua 3.00 5.00

☐ **AMMONIA**
Label, aqua, 10½" 4.00 7.00

☐ **SPOROTUS AMMONIAE**
Label, machine made, amber, 6½" 3.00 5.00

☐ **DR. H. ANDRES & CO.**
On each side, picture of face of sun, under it
"Haurieshal Fontevitale," ground top, pontil,
aqua, 9" 50.00 65.00

☐ **ANGIERS EMULSION**
Aqua, 7" 4.00 7.00

☐ **ANGIERS PETROLEUM EMULSION**
Under bottom in three lines, sunken panel in
front, back side is rounded, aqua, 7" 5.00 8.00

☐ **ANGIERS PETROLEUM EMULSION**
Aqua, 7" 4.00 7.00

Price Range

☐ **ANODYNE FOR INFANTS**
Vertical on front in sunken arch panel, "Dr. Groves" on side, "Philada" on opposite side, rectangular, clear, 5¾" 5.00 8.00

☐ **ANTHONY**
"501 Broadway, N.Y." on front, "Flint Varnish for Negatives" on label on back, round, clear, 5½" 4.00 6.00

☐ **E. ANTHONY**
"New York" vertical on front, oval, cobalt blue, 6" 7.00 11.00

☐ **APOTHECARY JARS**
Open pontil, round, ground stopper, aqua 8½" and 10" 7.00 11.00

☐ **APOTHECARY (drug store)**
Different sizes, clear, 2" and up 7.00 11.00

☐ **APOTHECARY (drug store)**
Different sizes, green, amber, light amber, blue, etc., 2" and up 8.00 12.00

☐ **APOTHECARY (drug store)**
Different sizes, pontil, 2" and up 15.00 22.00

☐ **APOTHECARY**
Label, 100 under bottom, amber, quart size ... 12.00 18.00

☐ **ARMOUR AND COMPANY**
"Chicago" in four lines on cathedral type panels, round corner, lady's leg type neck, taller than milk glass, 5¼" 20.00 28.00

☐ **ARMOUR AND COMPANY**
Chicago, fluted neck, milk glass, 8¼" 30.00 35.00

☐ **ARMOUR LABORATORIES'**
"Chicago" in egg shape circle in center, amber, 7¾" 10.00 14.00

☐ **ARMOUR LABORATORIES**
"Chicago" on fancy oval panel, rectangular, amber, 5" 14.00 17.00

☐ **ARMOUR'S VIGORALS**
Chicago, squat body, amber 3.00 5.00

☐ **ARNICA LINIMENT**
Embossed vertically on front, "J.R. BORDSALE'S" embossed on one side, "NEW YORK" on the other, pontiled, aqua, 5¼" 20.00 30.00

Price Range

☐ **ARNICA & OIL LINIMENT**
Vertical on two panels, eight vertical panels,
aqua, 6½" 3.00   5.00

☐ **DR. SETH ARNOLD'S BALSAM, GILMAN BROS.**
"Boston" on front and sides, rectangular, amethyst, 3¾" 6.00   9.00

☐ **DR. SETH ARNOLD'S BALSAM, GILMAN BROS.**
Boston, aqua, 7" 12.00   18.00

☐ **DR. SETH ARNOLD'S**
Embossed vertically on side, other side embossed "COUGH KILLER," rectangular, pontiled, aqua, 5½" 15.00   20.00

☐ **AROMATIC CATARRH & HEADACHE**
Embossed vertically on front, "DOC MARSHALL'S" embossed on one side, "SNUGG" embossed on the other, rectangular, pontiled, aqua, 3" 20.00   30.00

☐ **AROMATIC SCHNAPPS**
S is backwards, dark olive, 8" 32.00   42.00

☐ **A.D. ASHLEY'S' RED SEA BALSAM**
New Bedford, MA, twelve-sided, aqua, 4¼" ... 2.00   8.00

☐ **ASTER**
In script running up, "The Puritan Drug Co., Columbus, O." on base, aqua, 8¾" 7.00   10.00

☐ **ASTYPTODYAE CHEMICAL CO.**
Clear or amethyst, 4½" 3.00   5.00

☐ **ASTYPTODYAE CHEMICAL CO.**
In two lines, 3¾" body, 1" round, 1" neck, clear or amethyst 3.00   5.00

☐ **ATHIEU'S COUGH SYRUP** 3.00   5.00

☐ **DR. A. ATKINSON**
NY, pontil, aqua, 8¼" 18.00   24.00

☐ **THE ATLANTA CHEMICAL CO.**
"Atlanta, GA, U.S.A." on side, amber, 8½" 5.00   8.00

☐ **ATLAS MEDICINE CO.**
Henderson, NC, U.S.A. 1898, amber, 9¼" 12.00   18.00

☐ **ATRASK OINTMENT**
Square bottle, aqua, 2½" 1.50   2.50

Price Range

☐ **C. W. ATWELL**
"Portland, ME" vertical on front in large letters,
oval, light aqua, 8" 5.00   7.00

☐ **C. W. ATWELL**
Long tapered lip, vertical "C. W. Atwell, Portland,
ME," oval shape, open pontil, aqua, 7½" 18.00   24.00

☐ **ATWOODS JANNAICE LAXATIVE**
Machine made, clear, 6" 3.00   5.00

☐ **AYER'S AGUE CURE**
Lowell, MA, aqua, 5¾" 8.00   12.00

☐ **AYER'S CHERRY PECTORAL**
Lowell, MA, aqua, 7¼" 6.00   9.00

☐ **AYER'S HAIR VIGOR**
Label, aqua, 7½" 12.00   18.00
☐ Without label 4.00   7.00

☐ **AYER'S**
"Lowell, Mass, U.S.A." on back, 8½" 5.00   7.00

☐ **AYER'S PILLS**
Square, clear, 2⅜" 1.50   2.50

☐ **AYER'S PILLS**
Lowell, MA, rectangular, aqua, 2" 5.00   8.00

☐ **AYER'S**
In sunken panel, aqua, 6¼" 1.50   4.00

☐ **AYER'S SARSAPARILLA**
Lowell, MA, U.S.A., Compound Ext., aqua, 8½" 2.75   4.25

☐ **AYER'S**
Reverse side, "Lowell, Mass.," on side "Pecto-
ral," other side "Cherry," aqua, 7¼" 20.00   30.00

☐ **ELIXIR BABEK FOR MALARIA CHILLS FEVERS**
"Washington, D.C." vertical on front in sunken
panel, rectangular, clear, 6" 6.00   9.00

☐ **BABY EASE**
Aqua, 5½" 3.00   5.00

☐ **WM. A. BACON**
Ludlow, VT, pontil, aqua, 5½" 18.00   24.00

☐ **DR. BAKER'S PAIN PANACEA 1855**
Pontil, aqua, 5" 35.00   45.00

☐ **DR. IRA BAKER'S HONDURAS SARSAPARILLA**
Aqua or clear, 10½" 20.00   28.00

Price Range

☐ **JN. C. BAKER & CO.**
On one side 100 N. 3rd. St., on other side Phild.,
pontil, Aqua, 4¾″ 20.00 28.00
☐ **BALLARD SNOW LINIMENT CO.**
Clear or amethyst, 4½″ 4.00 9.00
☐ **BALL BALSAM OF HONEY**
Ringed top, pontil, aqua, 3½″ 20.00 28.00
☐ **BALSAM OF HONEY**
Pontil, aqua, 3¼″ 25.00 35.00
☐ **BALSAM VEGETABLE PULMONARY**
Around bottle, aqua, 5″ 6.00 9.00
☐ **DR. A.V. BANES MEDICINE CO.**
St. Joseph, MO, USA labels front and back, with
contents and box, rectangular, blown in mold,
aqua, 8¼″ 25.00 30.00
☐ **JNO. T. BARBEE & CO.**
Clear or amethyst, 6″ 5.00 8.00
☐ **JNO. T. BARBEE & CO.**
Clear or amethyst, machine made, 6″ 3.00 5.00
☐ **BARBER MEDICINE CO.**
Kansas City, MO, label, aqua, 7½″ 12.00 18.00
☐ **A. O. BARBOT AND SON**
Charleston, SC, 54 Broad St., clear, 4⅞″ 4.00 6.00
☐ **BARKER MOORE & MEIN MEDICINE CO.**
"Philadelphia" on front and side, rectangular,
aqua, 6⅜″ 4.00 6.00
☐ **BARKER MOORE & MEIN**
Vertical on front, "Druggist" on side, "Philadel-
phia" on opposite side, aqua, 5¼″ 4.00 6.00
☐ **WM. JAY BARKER**
"Hirsutus, New York" vertical on front in sunken
panel, pewter stopper, square collar, ABM, clear,
6⅝″ 6.00 9.00
☐ Same as above except aqua, 5¼″ 6.00 9.00
☐ **DR. BARKMAN'S NEVER FAILING LINIMENT**
On front, light green, 6¼″ 5.00 7.00
☐ **BARNES & PARKE, N.Y., BALSAM OF WILD
CHERRY & TAR**
7½″ 12.00 18.00
☐ Same as above except 6¼″ 12.00 18.00

Price Range

☐ **BARRY'S TRICOPHEROUS FOR THE SKIN & HAIR**
NY, pontil, 5¼" 15.00 22.00
☐ Same as above except five other different sizes 15.00 22.00
☐ **T.B. BARTON**
Clear or amethyst, 4½" 3.00 5.00
☐ **BARTOW DRUG CO.**
Clear or amethyst, 3½" 4.00 6.00
☐ **BATCHELOR'S**
Clear or amethyst, 3" 5.00 7.00
☐ **BATEMANS DROPS**
Vertical, cylindrical, amethyst, 5¼" 3.00 5.00
☐ **J. A. BAUER**
S. F., CAL., lime green, 8¼" 10.00 16.00
☐ **BAYER ASPIRIN**
In circles, "Bayer Aspirin" run up and down as cross sign, screw top, machine made, clear, buttle type bottle, 2½" 3.00 5.00
☐ **X-BAZIN SUCCRTO, E. ROUSSEL**
Philadelphia, six panels, sheared top, clear, 2¾" 6.00 9.00
☐ **B.B.B.**
Atlanta, GA, amber, 3¾" x 2¼" 10.00 16.00
☐ **BEASON'S VEGO SYRUP COMPOUND**
Smith Chemical Corp. Johnson City, TN, label, clear, 8½" 4.00 6.00
☐ **BEE-DEE MEDICINE CO.**
Chattanooga, TN, on one side "Bee Dee Liniment," double ring top, clear, 5½" 6.00 9.00
☐ **BEGGS CHERRY COUGH SYRUP**
Rectangular, aqua, 5¾" 3.00 4.00
☐ **BEGGS DIARRHOEA BALSAM**
Aqua, 5½" 6.00 9.00
☐ **DR. BELDING'S MEDICINE CO.**
On one side of sunken panel, other side "Minneapolis, Minn.," side sizes 1¾", 3" wide panel, one side plain for label, other in script, "Dr. Belding's Wild Cherry, Sarsaparilla," body 6", neck 3", aqua 20.00 28.00

Price Range

☐ **DR. BELDING'S WILD CHERRY SARSAPARILLA**
In sunken panel in front, back plain, "Dr. Belding Medicine Co." on one side in sunken panel, other side "Minneapolis, Minn.," aqua, 10" 12.00 18.00

☐ **BELL ANS**
On both sides, round, ABM, amber, 3¾" 3.00 4.00

☐ **BELL & COMPANY INC. MFG, CHEMISTS**
"New York" in three lines, ring top, bottom "M.B.W. U.S.A.," clear, 7" 7.00 10.00

☐ **BELL, PA PAY ANS BELL & CO. INC.**
"Orangeburg, NEW YORK, USA" on opposite sides, rectangular, ABM, amber, 2¾" 3.00 4.00

☐ **DR. BELL'S**
The E.E. Sutherland Medicine Co. Paducah, KY, Pine Tar Honey, aqua, 5½" 7.00 12.00

☐ **J.A. BERNARD DRUGGIST**
552 Westminister St., Providence, RI, rectangular, clear, flared lip, 5½" 5.00 7.00

☐ **BERRY BROS.**
"323 E. 38th St. N.Y." in circle on front, aqua, 11¼" 4.00 6.00

☐ **THE BETTES PHARMACY**
Label, clear, 4½" 3.50 5.50

☐ **BISM SUBNITR**
Clear, 5¼" 6.00 9.00

☐ **B-L TONIC, THE B-L-CO.**
Atlanta, GA, label, "B-L Made in U.S.A." embossed in back, amber, 10" 3.00 5.00

☐ **H.C. BLAIR**
"8th & Walnut Philada" on side of bottom, clear or amethyst, 6½" 5.00 8.00

☐ **E. BLOCH & CO.**
W.B. under bottom, clear, 3½" 5.00 8.00

☐ **BLOOD BALM CO.**
Label, amber, 9" 8.00 12.00

☐ **DR. E. BLRICKERS TONIC MIXTURE FOR FEVER AND CHILLS**
Small tapered top, aqua, 6" 25.00 35.00

☐ **BLUD-LIFE**
Clear or amethyst, machine made, 8½" 3.00 4.50

Price Range

☐ **DR. A. BOCHIE'S GERMAN SYRUP**
In two vertical lines, square, aqua, 6¾" 3.00   4.50
☐ **BOERICKE & RUNYON COMPANY**
In script on front, clear, 7¾" 2.50   3.25
☐ **BOERICKE & RUNYON CO.**
In large letters vertical on one panel, square, bev-
eled corner, amethyst, 8⅝" 4.00   6.00
☐ Same as above except sample size, amber, 2½"   4.00   6.00
☐ **BOLDWIN CHERRY PEPSIN & DANDELION
TONIC**
Amber, 8" 28.00   38.00
☐ **W. H. BONE CO. C.C. LINIMENT**
S.F., CA, U.S.A., aqua, 6½" 4.00   6.00
☐ **BON-OPTO FOR THE EYES**
Clear or amethyst, 3¼" 3.00   5.00
☐ **BOOTH'S HYOMEI**
Buffalo, NY, Rorterie, Canada, black, 3" 3.00   5.00
☐ **BORAX**
Clear, 5¼" 12.00   18.00
☐ **DR. BOSANKO'S PILE REMEDY**
Phila., PA, aqua, 2½" 3.00   5.00
☐ **DR. BOSANKO'S**
"Trial Size" on one side, aqua, 4" 3.00   5.00
☐ **DR. A. BOSCHEES GERMAN SYRUP**
In vertical lines, long neck, aqua, 6¾" 5.00   7.00
☐ **BOSTON, MASS**
On front panel, "Egyptian Chemical Co.," square,
clear, screw top, measured, 7½" 2.75   3.50
☐ **DR. C. BOUVIER'S**
Clear, 4½" 6.00   9.00
☐ **DR. M. BOWMAN'S HEALING BALSAM**
Rectangular, clear, 6½" 4.00   8.00
☐ **BRADFIELD'S**
Atlanta, GA, aqua, 8¾" 5.00   7.00
☐ **BRANDRIFF'S FOR AGUE**
On front, "Piqua, Ohio," ring top, aqua or green,
8" 8.00   11.00
☐ **BRANDRIFF'S VEGETABLE ANTIDOTE**
Piqua, OH, aqua, 8" 6.00   9.00

Price Range

☐ **BRANT'S INDIAN PULMONARY BALSAM, MT. WALLACE PROPRIETOR**
Vertical on three panels, 8″ wide vertical panels,
aqua, 6¾″ 42.00 58.00

☐ **BREIG & SHAFER**
On bottom, on top of it a fish, green 2.75 3.50

☐ **G.O. BRISTO BACKWAR**
Buffalo, six panels, pontil, 4¾″ 32.00 42.00

☐ **BRISTOL'S**
On one side in sunken panel, other side, "New
York," front panel plain for label, on back in
sunken panel "Genuine Sarsaparilla," under bottom in circle panel #18, 2¼″ neck, 3¾″ wide,
2¼″ thick, aqua 6.00 9.00

☐ **BRISTOL'S SARSAPARILLA**
Pontil, green 33.00 47.00

☐ **B & P**
Amber, "Lyons Powder" on shoulder of opposite
side, 4¼″ 3.00 5.00

☐ **B.P. CO.**
On front, also "BP" back to back with circle
around it, cobalt, oval, 3″ 12.00 18.00

☐ **B.P. CO.**
On front, also "BP" back to back with circle
around it, oval, 1½″ 10.00 14.00

☐ **BROMATED PEPSIN, HUMPHREY'S CHEMICAL CO.**
"New York" vertical on front, square, cobalt blue.
3¾″ 5.00 7.00

☐ **BROMO CAFFEINE**
Light blue. 3¼″ 3.00 5.00

☐ **BROMO LITHIA CHEMICAL CO.**
Amber, 4¼″ 2.75 3.50

☐ **BROMO LITHIA CHEMICAL CO.**
Amber, 3¼″ 3.00 5.00

☐ **BROMO-SELTZER**
On shoulder, round, machine made, cobalt, under
bottom M1 in a circle, 5″ 3.00 6.00

☐ **BROMO-SELTZER EMERSON DRUG**
"Baltimore, MD." on front, round, cobalt, 5″ ... 1.50 2.25

Price Range

☐ **BROMO-SELTZER EMERSON DRUG**
"Baltimore, MD." on front, round, cobalt, machine made, 5" 1.50 2.25

☐ **BROMO-SELTZER EMERSON DRUG**
"Baltimore, MD." on front, round, cobalt, machine made, 4" 1.50 2.25

☐ **BROMO-SELTZER EMERSON DRUG**
"Baltimore, MD." on front, round, cobalt, 5" ... 7.00 11.00

☐ **BROMO-SELTZER EMERSON DRUG**
"Baltimore, MD." on front, round, cobalt, machine made, 6½" 1.50 2.25

☐ **BROMO-SELTZER EMERSON DRUG**
"Baltimore, MD." on front, round, cobalt, machine made, 8" 1.50 2.25

☐ **BROMO-SELTZER EMERSON DRUG**
"Baltimore, MD." on front, round, cobalt, machine made, 2½" 1.50 2.25

☐ **BROMO-SELTZER EMERSON DRUG**
"Baltimore, MD." on front, round, cobalt, machine made, screw top, 4¾" 1.50 2.25

☐ **BROMO-SELTZER**
Around shoulder, machine made, screw top, cobalt 2.00 3.25

☐ **THE BROOKS DRUG CO.**
Battle Creek, MI., label, 887 under bottom, clear, 8" 3.00 5.00

☐ **BROOKS & POTTER DRUGGISTS**
Senatobia, MI., clear or amber, 7¼" 3.00 5.00

☐ **THE BROWNE PHARMACY**
"1st to 203 Union St., New Bedford, Mass.," B in wreath, rectangular, clear, flared lip, 4" 12.00 18.00

☐ **BROWN CO., W.T. & CO.**
Cobalt, 8" 7.00 10.00

☐ **DR. BROWN'S RUTERBA**
Side mold, amber, 8" 10.00 16.00

☐ **DR. C.F. BROWN, YOUNG AMERICAN LINIMENT**
New York, ring top, aqua, 4" 5.00 8.00

Price Range

☐ **F. BROWNS ESSENCE OF JAMAICA GINGER**
Philada., tapered top, pontil, aqua, 5½" 22.00 32.00
☐ Same except no pontil 8.00 12.00
☐ Same except no pontil and has ringed top 8.00 12.00
☐ **F. BROWN'S**
Aqua, 5½" 4.00 6.00
☐ **BROWN-FORMAN CO.**
Clear or amethyst, 4½" 3.00 5.00
☐ **BROWN HOUSEHOLD PANACEA AND FAMILY LINIMENT**
Vertical on front in sunken panel, "Curtis & Brown" on side, "Mfg. Co. L. D. New York" on opposite side, rectangular, aqua, 5⅛" 4.00 6.00
☐ **J. T. BROWN PREPARATION**
292 Washington St., Boston, pontil, aqua, 6" .. 18.00 24.00
☐ **DR. BROWNDER'S COMPOUND SYRUP OF INDIAN TURNIP**
Embossed vertically on front, rectangular, pontiled, aqua, 7" 100.00 110.00
☐ **DR. O. PHELPS BROWN**
Aqua, 3½" 4.00 6.00
☐ **DR. O. PHELPS BROWN**
On side "Jersey City, N.J.," ring top, aqua, 2½" 3.00 5.00
☐ **BROWN SARSAPARILLA**
Aqua, 3x1¾x9½" 6.00 9.00
☐ **W. E. BROWN DRUGGIST**
Manchester, IA, clear 5.00 8.00
☐ **W. E. BROWN DRUGGIST**
Manchester, IA, mixing jar and an eagle over it, clear, 5½" 6.00 8.00
☐ **BROWN'S INSTANT RELIEF FOR PAIN**
Aqua, embossed, 5¼" 3.00 5.00
☐ **B. S. #30**
Under bottom, drop bottle, clear, 3½" 7.00 10.00
☐ **BUCHAN'S HUNGARIAN BALSAM OF LIFE**
London, vertical lines "Kidney Cure," round short neck, green, 5¾" 20.00 28.00
☐ **BUCKINGHAM**
On one side, "Whisker Dye" on other side, brown, 4¾" 4.00 6.00

Price Range

☐ **A. H. BULL**
Embossed on side, on front "EXTRACT OF SAR-
SAPARILLA," on other side is embossed "HART-
FORD, CONN.," rectangular, pontiled, aqua, 7"   15.00   20.00

☐ **DR. BULL'S HERBS & IRON**
"Pat. Oct. 13, 85" on base, 9½" 20.00   28.00

☐ **DR. J. W. BULL'S VEG. BABY SYRUP**
Trademark, round, aqua, 5¼" 4.00   6.00

☐ **W. H. BULL MEDICINE CO.**
Amber, 9½" 5.00   8.00

☐ **W. H. BULL'S MEDICINE BOTTLE**
"Pat Oct 1885" under bottom, clear, 5¼" 4.00   6.00

☐ **DR. BULLOCK'S NEPHRETICURN**
Providence RI, aqua, 7" 10.00   14.00

☐ **BUMSTEADS WORM SYRUP**
Philada, aqua, 4½" 10.00   14.00

☐ **A. L. BURDOCK LIQUID FOOD**
"Boston, 12½ Percent Soluble Albumen" on four
consecutive panels, twelve vertical panels on
bottle, square collar, amber, 6" 7.00   10.00

☐ **J. A. BURGON**
Allegheny City, PA label on back, Dr. J.A. Burgon
standing and holding a bottle and table, clear,
8¼" 18.00   24.00

☐ **BURKE & JAMES**
"W.T. CO. A.A. U.S.A." under bottom, clear or
amethyst, 6¼" 7.00   10.00

☐ **E.A. BURKHOUT'S DUTCH LINIMENT**
Prep. at Mechanicville, Saratoga Co., NY, pontil,
aqua, 5¼" 90.00   120.00

☐ **BURLINGTON DRUG CO.**
Burlington, VT, label, clear, 5½" 8.00   11.00

☐ **BURNAM'S BEEF WINE E.J.B. & IRON**
On front, thumb print on back, oval, aqua, 9¼"   7.00   10.00

☐ **EDW. S. BURNHAM APOTHECARY**
Charleston, SC, aqua, 4⁵/₁₆" 5.00   7.00

☐ **BURNETT**
Clear, 6¾" 8.00   12.00

☐ **BURNETT**
"Boston" on other side, clear, 4¼" 8.00   12.00

Price Range

☐ **BURNETT**
On side, "Boston" on opposite side, beveled corners, square collar, oval shape, aqua, 6½" 10.00 16.00

☐ **BURNETTS COCAINE**
Vertical on front, "Burnetts" on side, "Boston" on opposite side, large beveled corners, tapered shoulders, aqua, 7⅜" 8.00 12.00

☐ **BURNETTS COCAINE**
Boston, ringed top, aqua, 7¼" 10.00 16.00

☐ **BURNETTS COCAINE, 1864–1900**
Ringed top, clear 12.00 18.00

☐ **BURNHAM'S BEEF WINE & IRON**
Aqua, 9½" 5.00 8.00

☐ **BURNHAM'S CLAM BOUILLON, E.S. BURNHAM CO.**
"New York" five lines, machine made, 4½" ... 3.00 4.00

☐ **BURNHAM'S**
Aqua, 4¾" 3.50 5.00

☐ **BURRINGTON'S VEGETABLE COUGH SYRUP**
"Providence, RI" vertical around bottle, ring collar, cylindrical, clear, 5½" 30.00 40.00

☐ Same as above except aqua 30.00 40.00

☐ **BURTON'S MALTHOP TONIQUE**
Label, three-part mold, dark olive, 7½" 5.00 8.00

☐ **BURWELL-DUNN**
"R.S.J., 969" under bottom, clear or amethyst, 3¾" 3.00 5.00

☐ **BUTLER'S BALSAM OF LIVERWORT**
Pontil, aqua, 4¼" 60.00 80.00

☐ **CABOT'S SULPHO-NATHOL**
Round, clear, 4¾" 4.00 8.00

☐ **CABOT'S SULPHO NAPTHOL**
Vertical on front, oval back, beveled corners, square collar, amber, 6½" and 4¾" 5.00 9.00

☐ **CABOT'S SULPHO NAPTHOL**
Written fancy, large beveled corners, oval back, square collar, aqua, 5⅛" 6.00 9.00

☐ **DR. W.B. CALDWELLS LAXATIVE SENNA**
Rectangular, indented panels, clear with a tinge of green, 7" 2.00 4.00

Price Range

☐ **CALDWELLS SYRUP PEPSIN**
Mfd by Pepsin Syrup Co., Monticello, IL, aqua,
rectangular, 3" 3.00   5.00

☐ **CALDWELLS SYRUP PEPSIN**
Mfd by Pepsin Syrup Co. Monticello, IL, aqua, rectangular, machine made, screw top, all sizes .. 1.35   2.15

☐ **CALIFORNIA FIG SYRUP CO.**
On front panel, "Louisville, KY" on left side, "San
Francisco, Calif." on right side, rectangular, ame-
thyst, 7¼" 3.00   5.00

☐ **CALIFORNIA FIG SYRUP CO.**
On front on side "Wheeling, W. Va.," 6" ABM,
clear 5.00   7.00

☐ **CALIFORNIA FIG. SYRUP CO.**
"San Francisco, Cal" vertical on front, "Syrup of
Figs" on both sides, rectangular, square collar,
amethyst, 6½" 5.00   8.00

☐ **CALIFORNIA FIG SYRUP CO.**
"Califig, Sterling Products (inc) Successor" on
front, rectangular, clear, 6¾" 3.00   5.00

☐ **CALIFORNIA FIG SYRUP CO.**
"Califig, Sterling Products (inc) Successor" on
front, rectangular machine made, screw top, all
sizes and colors 1.35   2.15

☐ **CALIFORNIA FIG. SYRUP CO.**
S.F., Cal., Syrup of Fig, clear or amber, 6¾" .. 3.00   4.50

☐ **PROF. CALLAN'S WORLD RENOWNED
BRAZILIAN GUM**
Vertical on one panel, square collar, aqua, 4⅛" 3.00   4.50

☐ **DR. CALLAN'S WORLD RENOWNED
BRAZILIAN GUM**
Clear, 4½" 3.00   4.50

☐ **CALVERT'S**
Clear or amethyst, 8" 20.00   30.00

☐ **THE CAMPBELL DRUG CO., THE GENERAL
STORE**
Fostoria, OH, on back "Camdrugo," green, 5¼" 7.00   10.00

☐ **CAMPBELL V. V.**
In script, the genuine always bears this signature
in the front panel, diamond shaped base, clear,
5⅛" 4.00   6.00

Price Range

☐ **CAPLION**
Label, clear, "TCWCO. U.S.A." on bottom, 5″   4.00   6.00

☐ **CAPUDINE CHEMICAL CO.**
"Raleigh, N.C." in center, "G" under bottom,
label, machine made, amber, 7½″ 2.50   3.25

☐ **CAPUDINE FOR HEADACHE**
On front panel, amber, oval, 3¼″ 1.35   2.10

☐ **DR. M. CARABALLO**
"Vermicida" in back, aqua, 4¼″ 5.00   7.00

☐ **CARBONA**
On the base, paneler, aqua, 5½″ and 6″ 8.00   12.00

☐ **CARBONA, CARBONA PRODUCTS CO.**
"Carbona" in three lines, hair oil, aqua, 6″ 5.00   10.00

☐ **CARBONA, CARBONA PRODUCTS CO.**
"Carbona" in three lines running vertically, round,
aqua, hair dressing, 6″ 8.00   12.00

☐ **CARBONA & CARBONA PRODUCTS CO.**
"Carbona" on three vertical panels, twelve pan-
els, square collar, aqua, 5⅛″ 10.00   16.00

☐ **DR. CAREY'S MARSH ROOT**
Embossed vertically on front, embossed on sides
"THE CAREY MEDICAL CORP'N ELMIRA,
N.Y.," rectangular, clear, 9¾″ 10.00   15.00

☐ **DR. CAREY'S MARSH ROOT**
Embossed vertically on front, "CAREY MEDICAL
CORPN. ELMIRA N.Y." on sides, rectangular,
clear, 7½″ 5.00   8.00

☐ **CARLES HYPO-COD.**
Clear, double ring top, one big under it small top,
8″ 15.00   22.00

☐ **CARLO ERBA MAINO, OLEO PICINO**
Clear or amber, 3¾″ 10.00   15.00

☐ **CARLSBAD AH**
Under bottom, sheared top, clear, 4″ 3.00   5.00

☐ **CARLSBAD RA**
Under bottom, sheared top, clear, 4″ 5.00   9.00

☐ **CARPENTER & WOOD, INC.**
"Est. 1883 Providence, R.I." with eagle and
shield on center front, glass stopper, round, clear
or amethyst, 2¼″ 3.00   5.00

☐ **CARTER'S SPANISH MIX**
Pontil, green, 8″ 150.00   200.00

Price Range

☐ **CARY GUM TREE COUGH SYRUP**
S. Fran., U.S.A., aqua blue, 7½" 12.00 18.00
☐ Same as above except lime green 15.00 22.00
☐ **CASSEBEER**
Reverse side "N.Y.," amber, 7½" 7.00 10.00
☐ **CASTOR OIL, PURE**
2 fl. oz., The Frank Tea & Co, cintion front, clear,
flask, 5¼" 7.00 10.00
☐ Also machine made and screw top, all sizes and
colors 1.50 2.20
☐ **CASTOR OIL**
4" body, 3" neck, 1¼" round bottle, cobalt blue 15.00 22.00
☐ Same, except smaller, some in different sizes .. 15.00 22.00
☐ Castor oil label, W.C. 3oz under bottom, cobalt,
8¼" 12.00 18.00
☐ **CHAMBERLAIN'S PAIN BALM**
Vertically on front, "CHAMBERLAIN MEDICINE
CO., DES MOINES, IA, USA" on sides, blown in
mold, rectangular, aqua, 6" 5.00 8.00
☐ **DR. J.F. CHURCHILL'S SPECIFIC REMEDY
FOR CONSUMPTION**
Vertically on front, "HYPOPHOSPHITES OF
LIME AND SODA" on sides 20.00 30.00
☐ **CITY DRUG COMPANY**
103 Main St., Anaconda, MT, clear, 4¼" 3.00 5.00
☐ **CITY DRUG COMPANY**
Meridian, TX, amethyst, rectangular, 3¼" 1.35 2.15
☐ **OTIS CLAPP & SONS MALT & COD LIVER
OIL COMPOUND**
Vertical on front in fancy lettering, large square
collar, amber, 7¼" 5.00 8.00
☐ **C. G. CLARK & CO.**
Restorative other side, aqua, 7¾" 4.00 7.00
☐ **THE C. G. CLARK CO.**
Vertical on one panel, "New Haven, Ct." on third
panel, twelve vertical panels, square collar, aqua,
5½" 3.50 5.00
☐ **CLARK'S CORDIAL**
On front in diamond shape panel, (Note: you can
see where the words "Clark's Calif. Cherry Cor-
dial" were slugged out of the mold), amber, 8¼" 27.00 36.00

Price Range

☐ **DR. J. S. CLARK'S, THROAT & LUNGS**
Reverse side "Balsam For The," aqua, 8½" .. 15.00 22.00

☐ **CLOUDS CORDIAL**
On each side, tapered type bottle, tapered top,
amber, 10¾" x 3" x 2" 24.00 33.00

☐ **W.W. CLARK**
16 N. 5th St. Phila, pontil, aqua, 5⅜" 15.00 22.00

☐ **CLEMENTS & CO.**
Rosadalis other side, aqua, 8½" 15.00 22.00

☐ **CREME DE CAMELIA FOR THE**
COMPLEXION
On side, "The Boradent Co. Inc., San Francisco"
on opposite side, beveled corners, rectangular,
flared collar, "New York" in slug plate, cobalt
blue, 5⅛" 7.00 10.00

☐ Same as above except "San Francisco" & "New
York" embossed 7.00 10.00

☐ **COBALT BLUE**
Unembossed, sloped ring-type top, sloping
rounded top of body of bottle where it joins neck,
recessed bottom, seam marks stop at base of
neck, 3⅞" 5.00 8.00

☐ **COD LIVER OIL**
Aqua, 9¾" 4.00 6.00

☐ **COD LIVER OIL**
Fish in center, screw top, machine made, two
sizes, amber, round 3.00 5.00

☐ **COD LIVER OIL**
In front with a fish in sunken panel, square,
amber, screw top, machine made, 9" 3.00 5.00

☐ **COD LIVER OIL**
In front with a fish in sunken panel, square,
amber, screw top, machine made, 6" 3.00 5.00

☐ **COD LIVER OIL-FISH**
Different sizes and many different colors, some
made in Italy 18.00 24.00

☐ **DR. P. M. COHAN**
Charleston, SC, Open pontil, aqua 70.00 80.00

☐ **COLLEGE HILL PHARMACY**
Clear or amethyst, 4½" 3.00 5.00

☐ **N.A. COLLINGS**
"WT Co. U.S.A." under bottom, clear, 6¼" 3.00 5.00

Price Range

☐ **COLUMBIA LINIMENT**
Clear, blown in mold, "THE F.C. STURTEVANT
CO., HARTFORD, CT.," with contents and box,
rectangular, clear, 6¾" 12.00 16.00

☐ **COLY TOOTH WASH**
Backward "S" in "WASH," clear, 4½" 15.00 22.00

☐ **COMPOUND ELIXIR**
Aqua, 8¾" 9.00 12.00

☐ **W. H. COMSTOCK**
On back "Moses Indian Root Pills," on side
"Dose 1 to 3," amber, 2½" 4.00 6.00

☐ **W.H. COMSTOCK, MORSE'S INDIAN ROOT
PILL, DOSE 2 to 4**
Rectangular, embossing, amber, 2½" 2.00 6.00

☐ **CONE ASTHMA CONQUEROR CO.**
Cincinnati, OH, clear, 8" 5.00 8.00

☐ **CONNELL'S BRAHMNICAL MOON PLANT
EAST INDIAN REMEDIES**
On base in back ten stars around a pair of feet,
under it trademark, amber, 7" 20.00 28.00

☐ **COOPER'S NEW DISCOVERY**
Tonic, label, aqua, 8¾" 8.00 12.00

☐ **CHAS. D. COOPER PHARMACIST**
Walden, NY, rectangular, amethyst, 4½" 5.00 7.00

☐ **COSTAR'S**
"NY" on shoulder, amber, 4" 6.00 9.00

☐ **GEORGE COSTER**
Side mold, aqua, 5½" 4.00 6.00

☐ **CREENSFELDER & LAUPHEIMER
DRUGGISTS**
"Baltimore, MD." on three panels, twelve panels,
on shoulder "A.R.B.," amber, 8½" 10.00 16.00

☐ **DALTON'S SARSAPARILLA AND NERVE
TONIC**
Embossed on front, "BELFAST, MAINE, USA"
on sides, rectangular, blown in mold, with contents, label, box, and flier, aqua, 9¼" 18.00 25.00

☐ **DAVIS**
Embossed horizontally on front, "VEGETABLE"
embossed on one side, "PAIN KILLER" embossed on the other, rectangular, pontiled, aqua,
4⅜" 20.00 30.00

Price Range

☐ **DELIGHT'S SPANISH LUSTRAL**
Embossed vertically on front, on rear "PRE-
PARED BY J.C. WALEIGH," rectangular, pon-
tiled, aqua, 6" 15.00 20.00

☐ **A.M. DINIMOR & CO., BINNINGERS OLD
DOMINIAN WHEAT TONIC**
Tapered top, amber, 9½" 20.00 28.00

☐ **MRS. DINMORE'S COUGH & CROUP
BALSAM**
Vertical on front in oval end of sunken panel, rec-
tangular, aqua, 6" 6.00 9.00

☐ **DIOXOGEN**
"The Oakland Chem C." on back, amber, 7¾" 4.00 7.00

☐ **DIPPER DANDY**
On neck, sheared bottom, 10 to 60 cc grad scale,
metal shaker bottom, clear, 6" 5.00 8.00

☐ **DR. E. E. DIXON**
Clear or amethyst, 6½" 4.00 7.00

☐ **DODGE & OLCOTT CO, NEW YORK, OIL
ERIGERON**
Label, cobalt, machine made, D & O under bot-
tom, 7" 6.00 9.00

☐ **DODSON'S**
On one side of panel, "Livertone" on other side,
aqua or amethyst, rectangular, 7" 5.00 8.00

☐ **DODSON & HILS**
St. Louis, U.S.A., amethyst, round, 8¼" 4.00 7.00

☐ **DONALD KENNEDY & CO.**
Roxbury, MA, label, aqua, 6½" 3.00 5.00

☐ **DONNELL'S RHEUMATIC LINIMENT**
Vertical on front, "J.T. Donnell & Co., St. Louis,
Mo." on opposite sides, rectangular, aqua blue,
7¼" 5.00 8.00

☐ **C. K. DONNELL, M.D.**
1809 Sabattus St., Lewiston, ME." vertical on
front in sunken panel, square collar, rectangular,
amethyst, 6¼" 3.00 5.00

☐ **GEORGE DOWDEN CHEMIST & DRUGGIST**
No. 175 Broad St. Rich. VA, pontil, aqua, 4½" 35.00 45.00

☐ **DOWIE, MOISE AND DAVIS WHOLESALE
DRUGGIST**
Charleston, SC, amber, 7$^{1}/_{16}$" 5.00 7.00

Price Range

☐ **REV. N. H. DOWN'S, VEGETABLE BALSAMIC ELIXER**
Vertical on four panels, twelve vertical panels in all, aqua, 5½" 5.00 8.00

☐ **DR. DOYEN STAPHYLASE DU**
Clear or amethyst, 8" 5.00 7.00

☐ **D.P.S. Co.**
Amber, 3½" 3.00 4.00

☐ **DRAKE'S PALMENTO WINE**
Embossed vertically on three sides, blown in mold, with label, contents, and box, square, clear, 9¼" 13.00 17.00

☐ **DR. DRAKE'S GERMAN CROUP REMEDY**
Vertical on front in sunken panel, "The Glessner Med. Co." on side, "Findlay, Ohio" on opposite side, square collar, rectangular, aqua, 6⅜" 7.00 10.00

☐ **DROP BOTTLE**
#45 under bottom, aqua, 4" 9.00 13.00

☐ **THE DRUGGISTS LINDSEY RUFFIN & CO.**
Senatobia, Ml., clear or amber, 6¼" 5.00 8.00

☐ **J. DUBOIS**
On other panels around bottle, "Great Pain Specific and Healing Balm, Kingston, N.Y.," aqua, 2¼" 6.00 9.00

☐ **DUCH POISON, ZUM K. VERSCHLUSS**
Under bottom, clear or amethyst, 8¼" 9.00 13.00

☐ **DR. DUFLOT**
Clear or amethyst, 4¼" 5.00 7.00

☐ **DRUG STORE MEAS. BOTTLE**
Clear with handle, long neck, body has Oz. Measure, 3⅛" x 7" 10.00 15.00

☐ **S. O. DUNBAR**
Taunton, MA., aqua, 6" 7.00 10.00

☐ **T. J. DUNBAR & CO.**
On side Cordial Schnapps, other side Schiedam, green, 10" 28.00 34.00

☐ **DUTTON'S VEGETABLE**
Other side "Discovery," aqua, 6" 4.00 6.00

☐ **DYER'S HEALING EMBROCATION**
Providence, RI, embossed, oval, pontiled, aqua, 5" 20.00 30.00

Price Range

☐ **THE EASOM MEDICINE CO.**
On back a house in center of trade mark, aqua,
2¼" 6.00 9.00

☐ **EASTMAN**
Rochester, NY, clear or amber, 6½" 3.00 5.00

☐ **A.W. ECKEL & CO. APOTHECARIES**
Charleston, SC, clear, 4" 4.00 6.00

☐ **EDDY & EDDY**
Clear, 1" x 1¾", 5" 3.00 5.00

☐ **EDDY & EDDY CHEMIST**
St. Louis, round, amethyst, 5" 4.00 6.00

☐ Same as above except clear, 6" 5.00 7.00

☐ **EDDY'S**
Round, green, 5¼" 4.00 6.00

☐ **W. EDWARDS & SON**
Clear, 5" 3.00 5.00

☐ **FRANK H. E. EGGLESTON**
Pharm., Laramie, WY, clear or amber 6.00 9.00

☐ **THE E.G.L. CO.**
Aqua, sheared top, 5¾" 7.00 10.00

☐ **E. H. CO. MO COCKTAILS**
Same on reverse side, three-sided bottle, dark
olive, 10" 110.00 145.00

☐ **EHRLICHER BROS. PHARMACISTS**
Pekin, IL, clear, 4¼" 5.00 8.00

☐ **E.L. & CO.**
Under bottom, amber, 7¼" 3.00 4.50

☐ **ELECTRIC BRAND LAXATIVE**
On label, blown in mold, square, with contents
and box, amber, 8" 12.00 20.00

☐ **ELECTRIC HAIR DYE**
Embossed on front, on side is embossed "BO-
GLES'S," on the other side is embossed "BOS-
TON," embossed on rear "NO. 2," rectangular,
pontiled, aqua, 2" 18.00 25.00

☐ **ELIXIR ALIMENTARE**
On side, "Ducro A. Paris" on opposite side, beveled corners, large square collar, rectangular,
light green, 8¼" 5.00 7.00

☐ **COMPOUND ELIXIR OF PHOSPHATES &
CALISAYA**
Aqua, 8¾" 8.00 11.00

Price Range

☐ **ELLEMAN'S ROYAL EMBROCATION FOR HORSE**
Aqua, 7½" **12.00 18.00**

☐ **CHARLES ELLIS, SON & CO.**
"Philada." vertical around bottle, round double
band, light green, 7" **5.00 7.00**

☐ **ELY'S CREAM BALM**
Ely Bros. New York, Hay Fever Catarrh on front
and sides, sheared lip, rectangular, amber, 2⅝" **4.00 6.00**

☐ Same as above except 3¼" **5.00 8.00**

☐ **ELYS CREAM BALM**
On front panel, rectangular, amber, 2½" **4.00 6.00**

☐ **EMBOSSED ANCHOR**
Anchor appears on recessed bottom, square
medicine tube, ¼" raised rim at top, seam line
stops at start of neck, deep cobalt blue, 4⅞" **8.00 12.00**

☐ **C.S. EMERSONS AMERICAN HAIR RESTORATIVE**
Cleveland, OH, pontil, clear or amber, 6½" **35.00 45.00**

☐ **EMPIRE STATE DRUG CO. LABORATORIES**
Aqua, 6½" **4.00 7.00**

☐ **THE EMPIRE MED CO.**
Rochester, NY, blob top, aqua, 8¼" **6.00 9.00**

☐ **EMPRESS**
Written on front, round, flared lip, amber, 3¾" **3.00 5.00**

☐ **E.R.S. & S. 3**
Under bottom, label, amber, 7½" **2.50 3.25**

☐ **E.R.S. & S.**
Under bottom, amber, 4½" **3.00 5.00**

☐ **ESCHERING**
Clear or amethyst, 5¼" **3.00 5.00**

☐ **E. ESTANTON**
"Sing Sing, N.Y." other side, Prepared by Block
Hunt's, aqua, pontil, 5" **35.00 45.00**

☐ **EUREKA HAIR RESTORATIVE**
P. J. Reilly, San Fran., dome-type bottle, aqua, 7" **10.00 15.00**

☐ **EUTIMEN**
Clear or amethyst, 5¼" **3.00 5.00**

☐ **D. EVANS CAMOMILE PILLS**
Pontil, aqua, 3¾" **25.00 35.00**

☐ **THE EVANS CHEMICAL CO.**
Clear or amethyst, round back, 6¼" **3.50 5.00**

Price Range

☐ **THE EVANS CHEMICAL CO. PROPRIETORS,**
"CINCINNATI, O. U.S.A." on front with big "G",
oval, clear, 5" 3.00 4.75

☐ **DR. W. EVANS TEETHING SYRUP**
Flared lip, pontil, aqua, 2½" 20.00 28.00

☐ **EYE CUP**
"S" under bottom, clear or amethyst, 2" 4.00 5.75

☐ **EYE-SE**
Around shoulder twice, on bottom Gilmer Texas,
decorated, round, aqua, 9¼" 3.00 5.00

☐ **G. FACCELLA**
On bottom, aqua, 6" 4.00 6.00

☐ **B.A. FAHNESTOCK'S VERMIFUGE**
Cylindrical, pontiled, aqua, 4" 15.00 25.00

☐ **DR. FAHRNEY'S**
Uterine other side, clear or amethyst, 8½" 18.00 28.00

☐ **DR. PETER FAHRNEY**
71 under bottom, clear, 6" 4.00 7.00

☐ **FARBENFABRIKEN OF ELBERFELD CO.**
"N.Y.C." label, "90" under bottom, amber, 4¼" 3.00 5.00

☐ **FARR'S GRAY HAIR RESTORER**
"Boston, Mass. 6 oz." all on front at a slant, beveled corners, ABM, amber, 5⅝" 3.00 5.00

☐ **H.G. FARRELLS ARABIAN LINIMENT**
Pontil, aqua, 4¼" 18.00 24.00

☐ **FATHER JOHN'S MEDICINE**
Lowell, MA, ring top, wide mouth, dark amber,
12" 7.00 10.00

☐ Same as above except 8¾" 8.00 11.00

☐ **FEBRILENE TRADEMARK**
On front, aqua, rectangular, 4½" 1.50 2.25

☐ **FELLOWS & CO. CHEMISTS**
St. John, NB. vertical on front, flask, 8" 6.00 9.00

☐ Same as above except ABM 3.50 4.75

☐ **FELLOW'S LAXATIVE TABLETS**
Clear or amber, 2½" 5.00 8.00

☐ **FELLOW'S SYRUP OF HYPOPHOSPHITS**
Deep indentation on lower trunk on face of bottle,
oval, aqua, 7¾" 5.00 8.00

☐ **DR. M. M. FENNER, ST. VITUS DANCE
SPECIFIC**
Fredonia, NY, ringed top, aqua, 4½" 8.00 11.00

Price Range

☐ **DR. M. M. FENNERS PEOPLES REMEDIES**
Vertical on front, "U.S.A. 1872–1898" on side, "Fredonia, N.Y." on opposite side, graduated collar, rectangular, amethyst, 6" .... 6.00　8.00

☐ **FERRO CHINA MELARO TONICO**
Lion embossed on three-sided bottle, tapered top with ring, green .... 35.00　45.00

☐ **FERROL THE IRON OIL FOOD**
One side "Iron & Phosphorus," other side "Cod Liver Oil," amber, 9¼" .... 10.00　15.00

☐ **B. W. FETTERS DRUGGIST**
Phila. Pat. Aug. 1, 1876, beer bottle shape, blue green, 8¾" .... 14.00　19.00

☐ **FIFIELD & CO.**
263 Main Street, Bangor, ME, rectangular, clear, 4¾" .... 7.00　11.00

☐ **FINDLEY-DICKS LTD.**
New Orleans, USA, Dick's Tasteless Castor Oil, oval, indented front panel, cobalt blue, 6" ..... 40.00　50.00

☐ **DR. S. S. FITCH & CO.**
714 Broadway, NY, pontil, aqua, 3¼" .... 25.00　35.00

☐ **DR. S. S. FITCH**
On side, "707 Broadway, N.Y." on opposite side, sheared collar, rectangular, beveled corners, pontil, aqua, 3¾" .... 35.00　45.00

☐ **DR. S. S. FITCH**
701 Broadway, NY, pontil, aqua, 1¾" .... 20.00　28.00
☐ Same as above except 6½" .... 20.00　28.00
☐ Same as above except tapered top, oval ...... 20.00　28.00

☐ **DR. S.S. FITCH**
"714 Broadway, NY" vertical on front, oval, aqua, 6½" .... 30.00　40.00

☐ **FIVE DROPS**
On side, "Chicago, USA" on opposite side, rectangular, aqua, 5½" .... 4.00　6.00

☐ **FLAGG'S GOOD SAMARITANS IMMEDIATE RELIEF**
Cincinnati, OH, pontil, five panels, aqua, 3¾" .. 20.00　28.00

☐ **A.H. FLANDERS, M.D.,**
"NY" on back, amber, 9" .... 55.00　70.00

Price Range

☐ **FLETCHERS VEGE-TONIO**
On front panel, beveled corner, 2½" square, amber, roof shoulder, under bottom, DOC, 8½" 13.00 18.00

☐ **FOLEY & CO.**
Clear or amethyst, 5½" 4.00 6.00

☐ **FOLEY & CO.**
Chicago, Foley's Kidney Pills, aqua, 2½" 3.00 5.00

☐ **FOLEY & CO.**
Chicago, U.S.A., sample bottle, Foley's Kidney Cure, round, aqua, 4½" 10.00 15.00

☐ **FOLEY'S CREAM**
On one side, "Foley & Co., Chicago, U.S.A." on opposite side, square, clear, 4¼" 3.00 5.00

☐ **FOLEY'S HONEY AND TAR, FOLEY & CO.**
"Chicago, USA" vertical on front, rectangular, sample size, aqua, 4¼" 4.00 6.00

☐ **FOLEY'S HONEY & TAR**
Foley's & Co., Chicago, aqua, 5¼" 6.00 9.00

☐ **FOLEY'S KIDNEY PILLS, FOLEY & CO.**
"Chicago" on front vertically, round, clear, 2½" 5.00 7.00

☐ **J. A. FOLGER & CO., ESSENCE OF JAMAICA GINGER**
San Fra., tapered top, aqua, 6¼" 10.00 15.00

☐ **J. A. FOLGER & CO., ESSENCE OF JAMAICA GINGER**
"San Francisco", vertical on front in oval slug plate, graduated collar, oval, aqua, 6" 5.00 8.00

☐ **DOCT. ROBT. FOLGER'S OLOSAONIAN**
"New York" embossed on front, pontiled, rectangular, 7" 30.00 40.00

☐ **DR. FOORD'S**
Embossed vertically on side, "RECTORAL SYRUP" embossed on front, on other side is embossed "NEW YORK," rectangular, pontiled, aqua, 7" 27.00 37.00

☐ **THE FORBES DIASTASE CO.**
Cincinnati, OH, amber, 7⅝" 8.00 12.00

☐ Same as above except clear 11.00 15.00

☐ **B. FOSGATES ANODYNE**
Round, flared top, aqua, 4½" 7.00 10.00

☐ Same except ringed top, 5" 5.00 8.00

Price Range

☐ **H. D. FOWLE**
Boston, aqua blue, 5½″ 7.00 10.00

☐ **DR. FRAGAS**
"Cuban Vermifuge" on two other panels, eight
panels, aqua, 3¾″ 6.00 9.00

☐ **FRANCO AMERICAN HYGENIC CO.**
"Perfumer Chicago" other side, clear, 3″ 4.00 6.00

☐ **G.E.S.S.**
Embossed vertically on front, "THE CAREY
MEDICINE CO., ELMIRA, N.Y." embossed on
sides, with contents and box, blown in mold, rectangular, clear, 9⅛″ 20.00 30.00

☐ **GRANULAR CITRATE OF MAGNESIA**
Kite with letter inside it, ring top, cobalt, 8″ 25.00 35.00
☐ Same except 6″ 25.00 35.00

☐ **GRAY'S CELEBRATED SPARKLING SPRAY
& EXQUISITE TONIC**
Blob top, clear 5.00 8.00

☐ **GRAY'S ELIXIR, GRAY LAB**
Amber, 7¼″ 3.00 5.00

☐ **GRAY'S SYRUP OF RED SPRUCE GUM**
On opposite sides, sunken panels, rectangular,
ABM, aqua, 5½″ 3.00 5.00

☐ **DR. T.W. GRAYDON**
"Cincinnati, O., Diseases of the Lungs" vertical
on front in slug plate, square collar, light amber,
5⅞″ 6.00 9.00

☐ **GREAT ENGLISH SWEENY**
Vertical on front in sunken panel, "Specific" on
side, "Carey & Co." on opposite side, rectangular, aqua, 6″ 4.00 6.00

☐ **L. M. GREEN**
Other side "Woodbury, N.J.," clear or amethyst,
4¼″ 3.00 5.00

☐ **S.L. GREEN, DRUGGIST**
"Camden, Ark., 3 iv" on shoulder, ring top, under
bottom, "W.T. & Co., U.S.A.," amber, 3″ 3.00 5.00

☐ **DRS. E.E. & J.A. GREENE**
N Y & Boston aqua, 7½″ 7.00 10.00

☐ **DRS. E.E. & J.A. GREEN**
On side, "New York & Boston" on opposite side,
square collar, rectangular, aqua, 7½″ 4.00 6.00

Price Range

☐ **GREEN'S AGUE MISSISSIPPI MIXTURE**
Jackson, MI, open pontil, green, 7¼" 350.00 400.00

☐ **J. HAVEL**
"Phila" embossed vertically on front, oval, pontiled, aqua, 3½" 13.00 22.00

☐ **HAY'S**
On side, "Hair Health" on opposite side, label on back, adopted April 1, 1912, ABM, amber, 7½" 4.00 7.00

☐ **CASWELL HAZARD & CO.**
Square, cobalt, 7½", 2¾" x 2¾" 7.00 10.00

☐ **CASWELL HAZARD & CO.**
In three lines near top, in center in a circle "Omnia Labor Vincit," under this in four lines "Chemists, New York & Newport," square, beveled corner, short neck, cobalt, 3¾", 7½" 12.00 18.00

☐ **HEALTH NURSER**
Clear or amber, $6^{1/3}$" 8.00 12.00

☐ **HEALTH SPECIALIST SPROULE**
Clear, 8¼" 5.00 8.00

☐ **HEALY & BIGELOW INDIAN SAGWA**
Embossed on sides, embossed Indian on front, rectangular, blown in mold, aqua, 9" 10.00 15.00

☐ **HECEMAN & CO.**
On front of panel, on one side "Chemists," other side "New York," 3" x 2" body, 6½" neck, aqua, 3¾" 6.00 9.00

☐ **HECEMAN & CO.**
Vertical in large letters on front, "Chemists" on side, "New York" on opposite side, rectangular, aqua, 10½" 4.00 6.00

☐ **G. F. HEDRICH APOTHECARY**
Charleston, SC, clear, 4⅜" 4.00 6.00

☐ **H. T. HELMBOLD**
"Philadelphia" on side, "Genuine Fluid Extracts" on front, side mold, aqua, 7¼" 6.00 9.00

☐ **H. T. HELMBOLD'S GENUINE PREPARATION**
Pontil, aqua, 6½" 22.00 32.00

☐ **H. T. HELMBOLD**
"Philadelphia" other side, "Genuine Fluid Extracts" front side, side mold, aqua, 6½" 10.00 16.00

☐ **HEMOGLOBINE DESCHIENS**
Cobalt, 7¾" 11.00 15.00

Price Range

☐ **HENRY'S CALCINED MAGNESIA**
Manchester, pontil, 4¼″ .... | 18.00 | 24.00

☐ **HENRY'S CALCINED MAGNESIA**
"Manchester," vertical on all four sides, rolled lip,
clear, 4¼″ .... | 7.00 | 10.00

☐ **HENRY'S THREE CHLORIDES**
Amber, 7¼″ .... | 3.00 | 5.00

☐ **THE HERB MED. CO.**
Springfield, OH, reverse side "Lightning Hot
Drops No Relief No Pay," aqua, 5″ .... | 6.00 | 9.00

☐ **HERB MED CO.**
Weston, W. VA, aqua, 9½″ .... | 6.00 | 9.00

☐ **HERBINE**
"St. Louis" on the left side, "Herbine Co." on the
right side, rectangular, clear, 6¾″ .... | 2.00 | 3.00

☐ **HERRINGS MEDICINE CO.**
Atlanta, GA, label, clear, 7¾″ .... | 3.00 | 5.00

☐ **H. 82**
Under bottom, green, 7¼″ .... | 3.00 | 5.00

☐ **H**
On bottom, amber, 4″ .... | 1.40 | 2.30

☐ **H.H.H. MEDICINE**
"The Celebrated" one side, "D.D.T. 1869" other
side, aqua .... | 7.00 | 10.00

☐ **HIAWATHA RESTORATIVE**
Embossed vertically on front, embossed on one
side is "MINEHAHA," on the other is "MUD-
JEKEE, WIS.," rectangular, pontiled, aqua, 7″ | 90.00 | 110.00

☐ **HICKS & JOHNSON**
"C.L.C. CO-2" under bottom, clear, 6½″ ...... | 4.00 | 7.00

☐ **HICKS' CAPUDINE**
Three different sizes, amber .... | 3.00 | 5.00

☐ **HICKS' CAPUDINE**
Amber, 5¾″ .... | 4.00 | 6.00

☐ **DR. H.H. HIGGINS SARSAPARILLA**
Romney, VA, pontil, aqua, 10″ .... | 29.00 | 42.00

☐ **DR. H.R. HIGGINS**
In back "Romney, Va.," on one side "Sarsaparilla," other side "Pure Extract," pontil, tapered
top, aqua, 10″ .... | 45.00 | 60.00

Price Range

☐ **HILL'S**
Vertical on front, "Hair Dye No. 1" on back,
square, oval sides, aqua, 3¼" 3.00 4.00

☐ **HILLSIDE CHEM. CO.**
On bottom, amber, 7½" 3.00 5.00

☐ **HIMALYA**
ring top, amber, 7½" 4.00 6.00

☐ **HIMALYA**
Amber, 7½" 3.00 5.00

☐ **HINDS HONEY AND ALMOND CREAM, A.S. HINDS CO.**
"Portland, Maine, USA, Improved the Complexion, Alcohol 7%" on front and sides, rectangular,
2⅞", clear 4.00 6.00

☐ **HIT**
Embossed vertically on front, "ELMIRA, N.Y." on
sides, rectangular, clear, 5½" 2.00 4.00

☐ **A. S. HINDS**
"Portland, Me" other side, clear, 5½" 4.00 6.00

☐ **HOBO MED. CO.**
"Beaumont, Texas Registered Trademark, H.B."
on the front panel in a diamond, rectangular,
clear, screw top, 8⅛" 3.00 5.00

☐ **HOFFMAN'S ANODYNE**
Label, rectangular, square collar, clear, 5" 3.00 4.00

☐ **HOFFMAN'S**
In center in large letters, "Great Find Trade
Make" in three lines on front, one ring in neck,
ring top, aqua, 6¼" 7.00 10.00

☐ **HOFF'S GERMAN LINIMENT**
"Goodrich & Jennings, Anoka, Minn." vertical on
three panels, twelve vertical panels, ring collar,
aqua, 5¾" 5.00 8.00

☐ **HOFF'S LINIMENT**
"Goodrich Drug Co., Anoka, Minn." vertical on
three panels, twelve vertical panels, ring collar,
ABM, aqua blue, 7" 4.00 6.00

☐ **DR. J.J. HOGAN**
"Next to post office, Vallejo, Cal." in circle, "W.T.
& CO. U.S.A." under bottom, ringed top, cobalt
blue, 7¼" 30.00 40.00

Price Range

☐ **HOLBROOK'S COMPOUND OF SARSAPARILLA**
Label, rectangular, blown in mold, with contents, aqua, 9¼" 20.00 30.00

☐ **HOLLAND**
Aqua, 3½" 3.00 5.00

☐ **HOLLAND DRUG CO.**
"Prescriptions A Specialty, Holland, Tx." on the front, on the bottom, "USP", rectangular, amethyst, 4¾" 1.35 2.25

☐ **HOLLIS BALM OF AMERICA**
Cylindrical, square collar, aqua, 5" 7.00 11.00

☐ **HOLMAN'S NATURES GRAND RESTORATIVE, J. B. HOLMAN, PROP.**
Boston, MA, pontil, olive green 250.00 300.00

☐ **HOLTONS ELECTRIC OIL**
On bottle vertically, round, amethyst, 3¼" 3.00 5.00

☐ **HOLTON'S ELECTRIC OIL**
Vertical on bottle, cylindrical, square collar, clear, 3¼" 5.00 8.00

☐ **THE HONDURAS CO'S. COMPOUND EXTRACT SARSAPARILLA, 1876**
Aqua, 10½" 28.00 38.00

☐ **HONDURAS MOUNTAIN TONIC CO.**
Fancy writing in sunken panel, double band collar, aqua, 9" 20.00 28.00

☐ **HONE DEURE**
On one panel, "Colours" on back panel, six panels, flared top, clear, t.p. pontils, small bottles, 2¾" 12.00 18.00

☐ **HOOD'S**
Machine made, clear, 8½" 3.00 5.00

☐ **HOOD'S TOOTH POWDER**
Clear, C.I. Hood & Co., Lowell, MA, 3½" 5.00 8.00

☐ **W.H. HOOKER [sic] & CO. PROPRIETORS**
"New York, U.S.A." vertical on front in sunken panel, "For the Throat and Lungs on side, Acker's English Remedy" on opposite side, cobalt, 5¾" 14.00 19.00

☐ Same as above except N.&S. Americars, 6½" 11.00 15.00

☐ Same except round and "Acker's Baby Soother," aqua... 7.00 11.00

Price Range

☐ **W. H. HOOPER & CO.**
"Proprietors New York, U.S.A." in three lines in
sunken panel, on one side in sunken panel
"Acker's English Remedy," on other "For The
Throat & Lungs," 1½" neck, ring top, cobalt, 5¾"   15.00   22.00

☐ **G. W. HOUSE CLEMENS INDIAN TONIC**
Ring top, aqua, 5" 65.00   85.00

☐ **HOUSEMAN'S GERMAN COUGH DROPS
PREPARED BY J.J. DAVIS**
Embossed vertically, cylindrical, pontiled, 5¾"   25.00   30.00

☐ **THE HOWARD DRUGS & MEDICINE CO.**
"Prepared By, Baltimore, Md., Frixie Hair Oil" in
sunken panel on front in script, six lines, clear or
amethyst 2¼" x 1" x 4" 3.00   5.00

☐ Same size as above except "Rubifoam For the
Teeth, Put Up By E.W. HOYTH & CO., Lowell
Mass" in six lines, not in sunken panel 5.00   8.00

☐ **HUGHEL'S DANDER-OFF HAIR TONIC
DANDRUFF REMEDY**
All on front side, square bottle, clear, 6¼" 6.00   9.00

☐ **HUMMEL AND HENDICH**
Charleston, SC, aqua 7.00   9.00

☐ **HUMPHREY'S**
"Humphrey's Homeophathic" on back, clear,
3½" 3.00   5.00

☐ **HUMPHREY'S MARVEL OF HEALING**
Clear or amethyst, 5½" 3.00   5.00

☐ **HUMPHREY'S MARVEL WITCHHAZEL**
Machine made, clear, 5½" 3.00   5.00

☐ **HUNGARIAN BALM**
Embossed vertically on front, "PERRY'S" embossed on one side, "FOR THE HAIR" embossed on the other, rectangular, pontiled aqua,
5¾" 20.00   30.00

☐ **HURD'S COUGH BALSAM**
Embossed vertically on front, rectangular, pontiled, aqua, 4½" 20.00   30.00

☐ **R. H. HURD PROP.**
No. Berwick, ME, U.S.A., Backer's Specific, clear,
4½" 6.00   9.00

Price Range

☐ **HUSBAND'S CALCINED MAGNESIA**
"Phila." vertical on all four sides, square, sheared
collar, aqua, 4¼" 4.00 6.00

☐ **HUSBAND'S CALCINED MAGNESIA**
"Phila." square, sheared lip, clear or amber, 4½" 5.00 8.00

☐ **HYATT'S**
Other side "LIFE BALSAM, N.Y.," on front "Pulmonic;" olive green, pontil, applied top, 12⅛" 65.00 85.00

☐ **HYATT'S**
On front, "Pulmonic" other side, "Life Balsam,
NY," aqua, applied top, pontil, 11" 50.00 65.00

☐ **I. G. CO.**
Under bottom, aqua, 7" 6.00 9.00

☐ **IMPERIAL HAIR/TRADEMARK**
Shield with crown in center, "Regenerator" vertical on front, "Imperial Chemical Manufacturing
Co." on side, "New York" on opposite side, rectangular, beveled corners, square collar, 4½",
light green, 4½" 6.00 9.00

☐ **INDIA CHOLAGOGUE**
Vertical on front, "Norwich, Conn. U.S.A." on
side, "Osgood's" on opposite side, rectangular,
beveled corners, machine made, aqua, 5½" ... 3.00 5.00

☐ Same as above except "NEW YORK" embossed
on side, not machine made, aqua, 5⅜" 5.00 8.00

☐ **DR. H.A. INGHAM'S VEGETABLE PAIN
EXTRACT**
Aqua, 4½" 5.00 7.00

☐ **IODINE**
Machine made, amber, 2¼" 3.00 5.00

☐ **I.R.**
Label, fancy bottle, graphite pontil, aqua, 6½" 18.00 24.00

☐ **ISCHIROGENO O BATTISTA FARMACIA
INGLESE DEL CERVO NAPOLI**
Amber, 7" 15.00 22.00

☐ **J & J**
Under bottom, sheared top, cobalt, 2½" 3.00 5.00

☐ **JACKSON MFG. CO.**
COLUMBUS, OH, ring top, clear, 6¼" 3.00 5.00

☐ **JACOB'S PHARMACY**
Other side "Atlanta, Ga., Compound Extract Pine
Splinters," clear, 7½" 3.00 5.00

Price Range

☐ **JACOB'S PHARMACY**
"W.T.&CO. C. U.S.A." under bottom, amber, 6" 5.00 8.00
☐ **ST. JACOB'S OEL, THE CHARLES A.
VOGELER COMPANY**
"BALTIMORE, MD., U.S.A." vertical around bot-
tle, cylindrical, aqua, 6⅝" 5.00 8.00
☐ Same as above except amethyst 5.00 8.00
☐ **JAD SALTS, WHITEHALL PHARMACY CO.**
N.Y., label, screw top, clear, 5¾" 3.00 4.00
☐ **JAMAICA GINGER**
Label, clear, 5¾" 3.00 4.00
☐ **JAMAICA GINGER FRUIT CORDIAL,
MANUFACTURED BY C.C. HINES & CO.**
"Boston, Mass." on two sides, square, clear,
6½" 3.00 5.00
☐ **DR. D. JAYNES TONIC VERMIFUGE**
"242 Chest St., Phila" on front, aqua, rectangular,
5½" 3.00 4.00
☐ **DR. D. JAYNES EXPECTORANT**
On front panel, on back "Philada" on each side,
three panels, short neck, aqua, pontil, 6¾" ... 20.00 28.00
☐ **DR. D. JAYNES EXPECTORANT**
Vertical on front in sunken panel, "Twenty Five
Cents" on side, "Quarter Size" on opposite side,
rectangular, square collar, aqua, 5¼" 4.00 6.00
☐ **DR. D. JAYNES**
"Half Dollar" on one side, "Half Size" on other
side. 5.00 8.00
☐ **DR. D. JAYNES**
Pontil, aqua, 7" 12.00 18.00
☐ **JAYNES & CO.**
Boston, screw top, amber, 9½" 6.00 9.00
☐ **T.E. JENKINS & CO., CHEMISTS**
Louisville, KY. graphite pontil, aqua, 7" 18.00 24.00
☐ **JOHNSON'S AMERICAN ANODYNE
LINIMENT**
Around bottle, aqua, 4½" or 6½" 3.00 5.00
☐ **JOHNSON'S AMERICAN ANODYNE
LINIMENT**
Vertical, round, aqua, 4¼" 3.00 5.00
☐ Same as above except 6½" 3.00 5.00

Price Range

☐ **JOHNSON & JOHNSON OIL**
Label, "C1637" under bottom, aqua, 5" 3.00   5.00

☐ **S. C. JOHNSON & SON**
"Racine, Wis." under bottom, clear, 3" 3.00   5.00

☐ **DR. E.S. JOHNSON BLOOD SYRUP**
"Farmington, ME." vertical on front in oval slug
plate, large square collar, oval, aqua, 9⅝" 9.00   12.00

☐ **DR. JOHNSON'S HORSE REMEDIES PREPARED BY NEW YORK VETERINARY HOSPITAL**
Vertical on front in slug plate, oval, flared collar,
aqua, 6¾" 7.00   10.00

☐ **JONES DRUG CO., NATIONAL PARK HOTEL BLDG.**
Vicksburg, MI, cylinder, blob top, emerald green,
8" 100.00   150.00

☐ **DR. JONES' AUSTRALIAN OIL**
"Not To Be Taken" on each side, amber, 5" ..   9.00   12.00

☐ **J.P.L.**
Under bottom, aqua, 7½" 3.00   5.00

☐ **DR. JUG'S MEDICINE FOR LUNGS, LIVER & BLOOD**
Brown, neck ¾", jug with handle, 6¼" x 3½"   20.00   28.00

☐ **L.E. JUNG**
Machine made, amber, 11" 3.00   5.00

☐ **JUNKET COLORS**
With monogram on one side, Little Falls, NY,
Chas. Hansen's Laboratory, square, aqua, 3½"   3.00   5.00

☐ **DR. JURNITZKI**
Aromatic Wire Grass Tonic, amber, 9½" 18.00   24.00

☐ **K-577**
Embossed on bottom, no other embossing, squat
round medicine, seam line ends ¼" from rim, medium cobalt blue, 2⅞" 4.00   7.00

☐ **KALO COMPOUND FOR DYSPEPSIA, BROWN MFG. CO.,**
"Greenville, Tenn." (N's in TENN. are backwards), all on front in oval end of sunken panel,
rectangular, square collar, amethyst, 9½" 18.00   24.00

☐ **KA:TON:KA, THE GREAT INDIAN REMEDY**
On opposite sides, rectangular, graduated collar,
aqua, 8¾" 8.00   12.00

Price Range

☐ **DR. KAY'S LUNG BALM**
Rectangular, aqua, 7¾" 5.00   8.00
☐ **KEASBEY & MATTISON CO. CHEMISTS**
"Ambler, PA." on front, light blue, rectangular, 5"   3.00   4.00
☐ **KEASBEY & MATTISON CO**
"Ambler, PA." on front, smoky blue, round, 5¾"   3.00   5.00
☐ **KEASBEY & MATTISON**
"Philadelphia" around shoulder, cylindrical, ring
collar, cobalt blue, 6" 7.00   10.00
☐ **THE KEELEY REMEDY NEUROTENE**
Discovered by Dr. L.E. Keeley Dwight, clear, 5⅝"   7.00   10.00
☐ **DR. KELLINGS PURE HERB MED.**
Pontil, green, 6" 20.00   28.00
☐ **J.W. KELLY & CO.**
C in triangle on bottom, clear or amethyst, 6"   3.00   5.00
☐ **KEMP'S**
"O.F. Woodward" on one side, "Leroy, N.Y." on
other side, light blue, 5½" 3.00   5.00
☐ **KEMP'S BALSAM**
Vertical on front, sample size, heavy glass, un-
usual flask shape, band collar, aqua, 2⅞" 4.00   6.00
☐ **KEMP'S BALSAM FOR THROAT AND
LUNGS**
"Leroy, N.Y., O.F. Woodward" front and sides,
rectangular, square band collar, aqua, 5¾" 4.00   6.00
☐ **KENDALL'S SPAVIN TREATMENT**
On shoulder, "Enosbury Falls, Vt." on base,
amber, twelve panels, 5½" 5.00   8.00
☐ **DR. KENDALL'S QUICK RELIEF**
Vertical on front in sunken panel, rectangular,
double band collar, aqua, 5" 3.00   5.00
☐ **DR. KENNEDY'S**
Aqua, side mold, 9" 4.00   6.00
☐ **DR. KENNEDY'S FAVORITE REMEDY**
"Kingston, N.Y., U.S.A." vertical on front in
sunken panel, clear, 7" 3.00   5.00
☐ **DR. D. KENNEDY'S**
On side, "Favorite Remedy" on front, "Kingston,
N.Y., U.S.A." on opposite side in sunken panels,
graduated collar, rectangular, amethyst, 8¾" . .   4.00   6.00
☐ Same as above except aqua 3.00   5.00

Price Range

☐ **DR. KENNEDY'S RHEUMATIC LINIMENT**
Roxbury, MA, rectangular, aqua, 6¾" 4.00 7.00

☐ **DR. KENNEY'S**
On other side, aqua, 9" 6.00 9.00

☐ **DR. M.G. KERR & BERTOLET**
Embossed vertically on front, on back is embossed "COMPOUND ASIATIC BALSAM," rectangular, pontiled, aqua, 4¾" 20.00 30.00

☐ **KEYSTONE DRUG CO.**
So. Boston, VA, tapered top, clear or amber, 9" 6.00 9.00

☐ **MRS. E. KIDDER CORDIAL**
Marked vertically "Mrs. E. Kidder Dysentery Cordial, Boston," round, open pontil, aqua, 8" 20.00 28.00

☐ **KIDNEY BOTTLE PILLS**
Label, kidney shape, ring top, clear, 5½" 11.00 15.00

☐ **E.J. KIEFFER & CO.**
Round back, clear or amethyst, 6½" 4.00 6.00

☐ **KILLINGER**
On front, aqua, square, 7⅞" 4.00 6.00

☐ **DR. KILMER'S**
"Swamp Root Kidney Liver and Bladder Remedy, Binghampton, N.Y., U.S.A." on front, aqua, rectangular, 7" 6.00 12.00

☐ **DR. KILMER'S**
"Swamp-Root, Kidney & Bladder Remedy" on front, "Binghampton, N.Y." on left, aqua, rectangular, 8" 5.00 9.00

☐ **DR. KILMER'S**
"Swamp-Root, Kidney Remedy, Binghampton, N.Y.," sample bottle, aqua, round, 4¼" 8.00 11.00

☐ **DR. KILMER'S SWAMP ROOT KIDNEY LIVER AND BLADDER CURE**
"Binghampton, N.Y., USA" aqua, 7" 4.00 10.00

☐ **DR. KILMERS SWAMP ROOT KIDNEY LIVER AND BLADDER CURE**
"Embossed, Binghampton, N.Y." on side, aqua, 8" 6.00 12.00

☐ **DR. KILMER'S U & O ANOINTMENT**
"Binghampton, N.Y." on front, round, aqua, 1¾" 3.00 5.00

☐ **DR. KILMER'S**
Clear, machine made, 7¼" 3.00 5.00

Price Range

☐ **KINA**
"Laroche" on back, aqua, 7¾" 3.00 5.00

☐ **DR. KING'S NEW DISCOVERY**
On front, "Chicago, Ill." on side, "H.E. Bucklem
& Co." on right side, rectangular, aqua, 4½" .. 4.00 6.00

☐ **DR. KING'S NEW DISCOVERY FOR COUGHS AND COLDS**
On front panel, clear, rectangular, 6¾" 5.00 8.00

☐ **DR. KING'S NEW LIFE PILLS**
On front, clear, square, 2½" 2.50 3.50

☐ **KINNEY & CO.**
Clear or amethyst, 3" 5.00 8.00

☐ **KLINKER'S HAIR TONIC**
"Cleveland" vertical on front in fancy panel, ring
collar, ring on neck, three ribs on side, base
crown shape, fancy shape, clear, 6" 6.00 9.00

☐ **KNAPPS**
Aqua, 4" 3.00 5.00

☐ **KNAPP'S EXTRACT OF ROOTS**
NY, rectangular, aqua, 5½" 6.00 12.00

☐ **KOBOLE TONIC MED. CO.**
Chicago, IL, milk glass, 8½" 25.00 35.00

☐ Same as above except amber or aqua 18.00 24.00

☐ **DR. KOCH'S REMEDIES, EXTRACTS & SPICES**
On one side "Dr. Koch Vegetable Tea Co.," other
"Winona, Minn.," clear, 9" 4.00 6.00

☐ **KODEL NERVE TONIC, FREE SAMPLE**
Under bottom "E. C. Dewich & Co., Chicago,"
wide ring top, aqua, 3¼" 3.00 5.00

☐ **KOKEN**
"St. Louis, U.S.A., 10 fl. oz." on front, clear,
round, 7" 1.40 2.15

☐ **KOLA-CARDINETTE**
On each side, "The Palisade Mfg. Co., Yonkers,
N.Y." under bottom, amber, 9" 4.00 7.00

☐ **KONING TILLY**
In vertical line, sheared top, round, aqua, ¾" .. 5.00 7.00

☐ **KONJOLA MOSBY MED. CO.**
"Cincinnati, U.S.A." on front, "Konjola" on left
and right panels, clear, rectangular, screw top,
8¼" 1.40 2.20

Price Range

☐ **DR. Wm KORONG HAIR COLORING MFG. CHEMIST**
"Louisville, KY." with teaspoon on each side, "3ii" on shoulder, "Simplex" in script, clear, double ring top, 4½" 9.00 12.00

☐ **THE KREBS-OLIVER CO.**
Amber, 5¾" 4.00 6.00

☐ **KUHLMAN'S**
"Knoxville, Tenn. W.&T. Co. U.S.A." under bottom, clear, 4½" 5.00 8.00

☐ **KUTNOW'S POWDER**
Vertical on front in large letters, rectangular, large square collar, corner panels, aqua, 4¾" 3.00 5.00

☐ **LA AMERICA**
Clear or amethyst 5.00 8.00

☐ **LACTO-MARROW CO.**
Other side "N.Y., U.S.A.," clear or amethyst, side mold, 9¼" 4.00 7.00

☐ **LACTOPEPTINE**
New York, clear or amethyst, 4" 3.00 5.00

☐ **LACTOPEPTINE FOR THE DIGESTIVE AILMENTS**
Around cross, dark green, sheared top, 3" 5.00 7.00

☐ **LA-CU-PIA**
Under bottom, aqua, four-part mold, 8¼" 4.00 6.00

☐ **LAINE CHEM CO.**
Amber, "341" under bottom, 6½" 4.00 6.00

☐ **GEO. L. LAIRD & CO.**
In horseshoe shape, "OLEO-CHYLE" in vertical line, cathedral type bottle, ring top, blue, 6¾" 25.00 35.00

☐ **THE LARAKOLA CO.**
"New York & Chicago" embossed, rectangular, aqua, 6¼" 2.00 4.00

☐ **LAKE SHORE SEED CO.**
"Dunkirk, N.Y." vertical on front in large sunken panels, rectangular, ring on neck, aqua, 5½" .. 3.00 5.00

☐ **LANGLEY & MICHAELS**
"San Francisco" vertical on front in round sunken panels, round graduated collar, aqua, 6¼" 7.00 10.00

☐ **LANMAN & KEMP**
One side, other side "N.Y.," aqua, 6" 3.00 5.00

Price Range

☐ **LANMAN & KEMP**
Aqua, "Cod Liver Oil" one side, other side "N.Y.,"
10½" 7.00 11.00

☐ **LARKIN SOAP CO., MODJESKA DERMA-BALM, MODJEST DERMA-BALM**
On three sides, square, flared lip, clear, 4¾" .. 6.00 9.00

☐ **LAUGHLIUS & BUSHFIELS WORM POWER**
Wheeling, VA, 1850, pontil, aqua, 3¼" 20.00 28.00

☐ **A.J. LAXOL**
"White, New York" in two indented panels on
front, oval back, triangular, round band collar, cobalt blue, 7" 12.00 18.00

☐ **LAXOL**
2½" neck, triangular, cobalt blue, 7" 10.00 16.00

☐ **L-C 1903**
On bottom, blue, sheared top, 4" 5.00 8.00

☐ **H. LEE'S TRICOPHEROUS FOR THE HAIR**
Vicksburg, MI, rectangular bottle, indented panels, rolled lip, 5⅜" 80.00 100.00

☐ **JOHN P. LEE**
Clear, 4½" 3.00 5.00

☐ **LEGRANDE'S ARABIAN CATARRH REMEDY**
"N.Y." embossed vertically, oval, aqua, 8" 8.00 12.00

☐ **LEGRANDE'S ARABIAN CATARRH REMEDY**
"N.Y." on front, flask type bottle, aqua, 9½" .. 9.00 12.00

☐ **LEHN & FINK**
"New York", on bottom, amber, seven-part mold,
7¼" 5.00 8.00

☐ **DR. H.C. LEMKE'S**
On other side, aqua, 10" 14.00 19.00

☐ **LEMON ELIXIR**
Under bottom, paper label reads "DR. H.
MOYEY'S LEMON ELIXIR HERB COMPOUND,
ATLANTA, GA.," aqua, 7¼" 6.00 9.00

☐ **LEONARDI'S**
On one side, other "New York, N.Y.," front "Golden Eye Lotion, relieves without pain" all in
sunken panels, aqua, 4½" 10.00 16.00

☐ Same except "Tampa, Fla." 10.00 16.00

☐ Same except A.B.M. 6.00 10.00

Price Range

☐ **LEONARDI'S BLOOD ELIXIR**
"The Great Blood Purifier, Tampa, Fla." all in 4
lines, beveled corners, ring top, amber, 8¼" .. **16.00 22.00**
☐ Same except "New York and Tampa, Fla." **16.00 22.00**
☐ **LEONARDI & CO.**
"Pharmacists, Jackson Black, Tampa, Fla." all in
3 lines, oval, thin tapered top, clear, 4¾" x 6¾" **9.00 12.00**
☐ **JARABE DE LEONARDI**
5 under bottom, aqua, 5½" **3.00 5.00**
☐ **LEONARDI, JARABE**
"De., Para Latos Creasotado, Leonardi's Cough
syrup creosated, New Rochelle, N.Y." all in 4
lines, ring top, clear and aqua, 5¼" **5.00 7.00**
☐ Same except "New York and Tampa, Fla." **5.00 7.00**
☐ **LEONARDI'S WORM SYRUP,**
"The Great Worm Killer, S. B. Leonardi & Co.,
N.Y. & Tampa, Fla." in 4 lines, square ring top,
aqua, 5¹/₁₆" **5.00 8.00**
☐ Same except "Prepared only by S.B.L. & Co., &
New York, aqua, 4¼" **5.00 7.00**
☐ **W.F. LEVERA**
On side, "Cedar Rapids, Iowa" on opposite side,
amber, 5½" **4.00 6.00**
☐ **J.A. LIMCRICK'S GREAT MASTER OF PAIN**
Rodney, MA., pontil, tapered top, aqua, 6¼" .. **25.00 32.00**
☐ **DR. LINDSEY'S BLOOD SEARCHER, DR.
J.M. LINDSEY**
Greenburg, PA, 1850, Sold by agent Robert
Emory Sellers & Co., Pittsburgh, 1880, clear, 8½" **20.00 28.00**
☐ **DR. LINICK'S MALT EXTRACT**
Vertical on front, ring collar, square, shaped like
pickle jar, clear, 6" **5.00 8.00**
☐ **LINIMENT OR OIL OF LIFE 16 OZ.**
On side in sunken arch panel, "C.C. TAYLOR"
on side, "Fairport, N.Y." on opposite side, rectan-
gular, graduated collar, clear, 10½" **6.00 9.00**
☐ Same as above except 5⅞" **6.00 9.00**
☐ **LIQUID FRANCONIA**
Leroy, NY, "O.F. Woodward" on front and sides,
rectangular, amethyst, 4¼" **3.00 5.00**

Price Range

☐ **LIQUID PEPTONOIDS, ARLINGTON CHEMICAL CO.**
"Yonkers, N.Y." sunken in arched panel, square,
amber, 7⅝" 3.00 5.00

☐ **LIQUID OPDELDOC**
Cylindrical, two-piece mold, square band collar,
aqua, 4½" 6.00 9.00

☐ **LIQUOZONE**
3" diameter, amber, 8" 3.00 5.00

☐ **LIQUID VENEER**
Under bottom, clear or amber, 6¼" 4.00 6.00

☐ **LISTERINE**
Near shoulder, at bottom "Lambert Pharmacal
Co." in two lines, three sizes, clear or amethyst 3.00 5.00

☐ Same except machine made 1.40 2.20

☐ **LITTLE GIANT SURE DEATH TO ALL KINDS OF BUGS**
Every bottle warranteed, Little Giant Co., New-
buryport, MA, aqua, 8½" 9.00 12.00

☐ **LIVE & LET LIVE CUT RATE DRUG CO.**
Chattanooga, TN., clear, 3½" 3.00 5.00

☐ **L.L.L.**
In front, ring top, aqua, 7¾" 5.00 8.00

☐ **LOG CABIN COUGH AND CONSUMPTION REMEDY**
Under bottom "Pat. Sept. 6th, 1887," amber .. 14.00 19.00

☐ **LOG CABIN EXTRACT**
Label, Rochester, NY, Pat'd. Sep. 6 1889, amber,
6¼" 65.00 85.00

☐ **LONDON**
Pontil, light green, 5½" 9.00 13.00

☐ **L.O.R. CO.**
Around an eye, tapered top, 4¾" 25.00 35.00

☐ **LORD'S OPDELDOC**
With embossed man breaking and tossing away
his crutches, on front in arched panel, oval,
square collar, aqua, 5" 15.00 22.00

☐ **DON LORENZO**
Same on reverse side, dark olive, 10" 18.00 24.00

☐ **J.M. LOTRIDGE**
"W.T. Co." under bottom, clear, 6¼" 3.00 5.00

Price Range

☐ **THE LOUIS DAUDELIN CO.**
Clear, 8¾" 3.00 5.00

☐ **LOUIT FRERES & CO, BOR DEAUX**
On front, mustard barrel, three rings at base and
shoulder, crude ring collar, amethyst, graphite
pontil, 4¾" 12.00 18.00

☐ **LUFKIN ECZEMA REMEDY**
Label, clear, 7" 5.00 8.00

☐ **LUNDBORG**
NY, teal blue, 8⅝" 5.00 7.00

☐ **LUYTIES**
Amber, 7" 5.00 8.00

☐ **LYMAN ASTLEY**
"Cheyene, Wyo." in a circular panel, aqua, 7" 9.00 13.00

☐ **DR. J.B. LYNAR & SON**
"Logansport, Ind., J.B.L." in seal on shoulder,
clear, 6" 9.00 13.00

☐ **DR. J.B. LYNAR & SON**
Clear or amethyst, 6" 5.00 8.00

☐ **LYON'S LAXATIVE SYRUP, LYON MED. CO.**
Reverse "Louisville, Ky.," clear, 6¼" 3.00 5.00

☐ **LYON'S FOR THE HAIR**
"Kat Hairon, New York" on front, back and sides,
sunken panels, rectangular, pontil, aqua, 6⅛" 35.00 42.00

☐ **LYON'S POWDER B & P**
NY, open pontil, whittled, round, purple, 4½" .. 62.00 70.00

☐ **LYON MFG. CO.**
"Mexican Mustang Liniment" on back, aqua,
7¾" 6.00 9.00

☐ **LYON MFG' CO.**
Same as above except 7½" 5.00 8.00

☐ **LYON'S**
Pontil, aqua, 6¼" 12.00 17.00

☐ **LYRIC 3—Y**
Under bottom, machine made, clear or amethyst,
4½" 1.45 2.25

☐ **MACASSAR OIL**
Embossed on front, rectangular, pontiled, aqua,
3½" 10.00 20.00

☐ **J. J. MACK & CO.**
San Francisco, Dr. A. E. Flint's Heart Remedy,
amber, 7½" 11.00 16.00

Price Range

☐ **J.B. MARCHISI, M.D.**
"Utica, N.Y." embossed on front, oval, blown in
mold, aqua, 7″ 15.00 25.00

☐ **MASTA'S INDIAN**
Embossed horizontally on front, embossed on
sides "PULMONIC, BALSAM," embossed on
rear "LOWELL, MASS.," rectangular, pontiled, 5″ 40.00 50.00

☐ **A. McECKRON'S R.B. LINIMENT**
"N.Y." embossed vertically on front, oval, pontiled, aqua, 6″ 30.00 40.00

☐ **MEDICAL DEPT. U.S.N.**
Reverse side "50c.c.," clear or amber, 4″ 16.00 22.00

☐ Same as above except 8½″ 16.00 22.00

☐ **MEDICATED WORM SYRUP**
Embossed on front, "HOBENSACK'S" embossed on one side, "PHILA." embossed on the
other, rectangular, pontiled, aqua, 9½″ 15.00 20.00

☐ **C.W. MERCHANT CHEMIST**
"Lockport, N.Y." in vertical lines, tapered top,
amber, 5¾″ 9.00 13.00

☐ **C.W. MERCHANT**
Lockport, NY, Oak Orchard Acid Springs, tapered
top, dark green, 9¼″ 32.00 42.00

☐ **THE WM. S. MERRELL CO.**
Label, amber, machine made, 7¾″ 4.00 6.00

☐ **THE WM. S. MERRELL CO.**
FGN on bottom, machine made, amber, 7¾″ .. 3.00 5.00

☐ **MERRICK'S VERMIFUGE**
"Milton, PA." embossed on three panels, 12-
sided, pontiled, aqua, 3½″ 45.00 55.00

☐ **THE MERZ CAPSULE CO.**
Clear, twelve panels, 3¾″ 3.00 4.00

☐ **MRS. S. METTLER'S MEDICINE**
Aqua, 6½″ 5.00 8.00

☐ **MEXICAN MUSTANG LINIMENT**
In three vertical lines, round, aqua, pontil, 4½″ 18.00 24.00

☐ Same except no pontil 3.00 5.00

☐ **MEXICAN MUSTANG LINIMENT**
On back, clear, 7½″ 7.00 10.00

☐ **MEYERS MFG. CO.**
Vertical on side, shaped like a miniature pop bottle, crown top, amethyst, 4″ 4.00 6.00

U.S.A./Hosp. Dept., *quart size, smooth base, collared mouth, yellow-olive, 9½"*, **$65.00–$85.00** *(Courtesy of Glass-Works Auctions, East Greenville, PA)*

	Price Range	
☐ **C. O. MICHAELIS APOTHECARY**		
Charleston, SC, aqua	5.00	7.00
☐ **DR. MILE'S RESTORATIVE NERVINE**		
On the front panel, rectangular, aqua, old bubbles, 8¼"	4.00	6.00
☐ **DR. MILE'S MEDICAL CO.**		
On the front panel, aqua, rectangular, 8¼"	3.00	4.00
☐ **DR. MILES MEDICAL CO.**		
Vertical in sunken panel on front, label on reverse side, "Dr. Miles Alterative Compound," picture of man with diagram of blood veins, double band collar, rectangular, ABM, aqua, 8¾"	9.00	12.00
☐ **DR. MILES RESTORATIVE BLOOD PURIFIER**		
Embossed vertically on front, machine-made, rectangular, with contents and label, clear, 8¼"	12.00	17.00
☐ **DR. J.R. MILLERS'**		
On side, "Balm" on opposite side, arch panels, rectangular, square collar, clear, 4¾"	5.00	9.00

Price Range

☐ **MINARD'S LINIMENT**
Boston, seven vertical panels on front half, back
plain, round, round band collar, amethyst, 5⅛″   4.00   6.00
☐ **MINARD'S**
Clear or amethyst, 5″ 4.00   6.00
☐ **MINARD'S LINIMENT**
Six panels, round back, clear or amethyst, 6″ ..   5.00   8.00
☐ **MITCHELL'S**
Cobalt, on side "Eye Salve" 5.00   8.00
☐ **M.J. & CO.**
Amber, 8″ 5.00   8.00
☐ **MOE HOSPITAL**
"Sioux Falls, So. Dak." vertical on front, side pan-
els show scales, oval back, fluting on back, ame-
thyst, 8¼″ 6.00   9.00
☐ **MONTECATINI SALTS**
Italy, amber, 4″ 7.00   10.00
☐ **GEORGE MOORE**
Clear, 5¾″ 4.00   6.00
☐ **DR. J. MOORE'S ESSENCE OF LIFE**
Embossed vertically on front, cylindrical, pontiled,
aqua, 3¾″ 15.00   20.00
☐ **MOORE'S REVEALED REMEDY**
Amber, 8¾″ 9.00   12.00
☐ **DR. MORENO**
Aqua, side mold, "W.T. & CO. 5 U.S.A." under
bottom, 8″ 7.00   10.00
☐ **E. MORGAN & SONS, SOLE PROPRIETORS**
"Providence, R.I." (E left out of Providence),
twelve panels, on shoulder "Dr. Haynes Arabian
Balsam," aqua, 7½″ 10.00   16.00
☐ **MORLEY BROS**
Label, aqua, 7″ 4.00   6.00
☐ **MORNING CALL-C. LEDIARD,**
St. Louis, olive amber, 10½″ 6.00   9.00
☐ **H.S. MORRELL**
N.Y., pontil, tapered top, aqua, 5¾″ 25.00   35.00
☐ **DR. MORSE'S CELEBRATED SYRUP**
Embossed vertically on front, on bottom is em-
bossed "1848," strap-sided, oval, aqua, 8¾″ ..   20.00   25.00

Price Range

☐ **MORSE'S CELEBRATED SYRUP**
Vertically, oval, long tapered neck, graphite pontil, 9½" 20.00 28.00

☐ **MORTON & CO.**
Clear or amethyst, 5½" 3.00 5.00

☐ **MORTON & CO., W.T. & CO.**
Tampa, FA, clear or amber, 4½" 4.00 6.00

☐ **MOUTARDE DIAPHANE LOUIT FRERES & CO.**
On front, mustard barrel, three rings at base and shoulders, amethyst, crude ring collar, graphito pontil, 5" 11.00 15.00

☐ **MOXIE NERVE FOOD, TRADEMARK REGISTERED**
"Moxie" on front and back, round, crown top, aqua, 10¼" 12.00 16.00

☐ **MOXIE NERVE FOOD**
"Lowell, Mass" thick embossed line, graduated collar, round, aqua, 10" 9.00 12.00

☐ **MOYER'S OIL OF GLADNESS**
"Bloomsburg, PA" vertical on front in sunken panel, graduated collar, aqua, 5⅝" 7.00 10.00

☐ **MUEGGE BAKER**
Oregon, "Muegge's" on reverse shoulder, green, 8" 10.00 15.00

☐ **MUL-EN-OL, F. A. DICKS**
"NATCHEZ, MISS." indented front panel, amber, 4¾" 5.00 10.00

☐ **MUNYON'S**
In one sunken side panel, other "Paw-Paw," in front on top a tree, two board lines with "Munyon's Paw-Paw," plain back, amber, long tapered top, 10" 16.00 22.00

☐ **MUNYON'S GERMICIDE SOLUTION**
Side mold, green, 3¼" 5.00 8.00

☐ **MUNYON'S GERMICIDE SOLUTION**
Green, 3½" 7.00 10.00

☐ **MURINE EYE REMEDY CO**
Chicago, U.S.A., round, clear, 3½" 4.00 6.00

☐ **MURPHY BROTHERS**
"Portland" on front in oval end panel, rectangular, square collar, aqua, 4⅞" 3.00 5.00

Price Range

☐ **SIR. J. MURRAY'S RE-CARBONATED PATENT MAGNESIA**
Vertical on front, crude band and small band collar, oval, light green, 7¼" 5.00 7.00

☐ **NANKINS SPECIFIC**
"Bordentown, N.Y." embossed vertically on front, "FOR THEUMATISM, FOUT AND LUMBACO" on sides, rectangular, aqua, 6½" 8.00 12.00

☐ **NELSON'S CHILL CURE**
Prepared by Natchez Drug Co., Natchez, MI, oval, clear, 6" 25.00 30.00

☐ **NERVE & BONE LINIMENT**
Round bottle, old type mold, aqua, 4¼" 5.00 8.00

☐ **NERVINE**
"Prepared by the Catarrhozone Co., Kinston, Ont." vertical on front in oval sunken panel, rectangular, square collar, amethyst, 5¼" 6.00 9.00

☐ **NEWBROS HERBICIDE KILL THE DANDRUFF GERM**
Ring top, clear or amber, 5½" 6.00 9.00

☐ **THE NEW YORK PHARMACAL ASSOCIATION**
In two lines in a sunken panel on one side, on other side "Lactopeptine," in front "The Best Remedial Agent In All Digestive Orders," round 6" body, 1½" neck, 2¾" square, corners, cobalt 18.00 24.00

☐ **N.Y. MEDICAL**
Reverse side "University City," cobalt, 7½" ... 18.00 24.00

☐ **NORTH**
Pontil, 6¼" 20.00 28.00

☐ **NORTON**
Clear or amethyst, 5" 3.00 5.00

☐ **NOYES, GRANULAR EFFERVESCENT MAGNESIA SULPHATE**
Vertical on front, rectangular, corner panels, square collar, aqua, 6" 5.00 8.00

☐ **NYAL'S EMULSION of COD LIVER OIL**
Amber, 9" 4.00 6.00

☐ **NYAL'S LINIMENT**
Amber, ring in neck 4.00 6.00

☐ **N.Y. PHARMACAL ASSOCIATION**
In two vertical lines, cobalt, 8½" 16.00 22.00

Price Range

☐ **THE OAKLAND CHEMICAL CO.**
Amber, 4¾″ 3.00 5.00

☐ **OD CHEM. CO.**
"New York" in two lines, amber, 6¾″ 3.00 4.00

☐ **ODOJ**
Under bottom, milk glass, "M632" on one panel,
4½″ 11.00 15.00

☐ **O.K. PLANTATION**
Triangular, amber, 11″ 220.00 260.00

☐ **OLD DR. TOWNSEND'S SARSAPARILLA**
Pontil, green 45.00 60.00

☐ **OLDRIDGE BALM OF COLUMBIA FOR RESTORING HAIR**
Aqua, 6¼″ 40.00 55.00

☐ **OLD DRUG STORE APOTHECARY JARS**
Open pontils, round, glass stoppers, 10½″ 9.00 12.00

☐ **OLEUM, DR. PETER'S**
In back, tree in center of it, "P-B" under it
"1783–1880," on base "Trademark," ring top,
clear, 5⅞″ 16.00 22.00

☐ **OLIVE OIL**
Open pontil, no embossing, 10½″ 9.00 12.00

☐ **OMEGA OIL CHEMICAL CO.**
"New York" in three lines at bottom, above bottom, a leaf with words "Omega Oil It's Green,"
ring under this with trademark, flared top with ring,
under bottom, various numbers in circle, light
green, 4½″ 10.00 15.00

☐ **OMEGA OIL IT'S GREEN, TRADEMARK**
All inside of leaf embossed on front, "THE
OMEGA CHEMICAL CO. NEW YORK" at base
on front, sheared collar, clear, 6″ 6.00 9.00
☐ Same as above except 4½″ 6.00 9.00
☐ Same as above except ABM, thread top, 6″ ... 3.00 4.00

☐ **OMEGA OIL**
Vertical on front, cylindrical, aqua, 3¼″ 3.00 4.00

☐ **OPIUM BOTTLES**
In different sizes, 1 drop to ½ ounce, most are
clear, some amethyst 9.00 13.00

☐ **OPIUM**
Aqua, 2½″ 9.00 13.00

Price Range

☐ **ORIENTAL CONDENSED COFFEE,**
TRADEMARK, ORIENTAL TEA COMPANY
"Boston, Mass." vertical on front in slug plate,
square collar, oval, aqua, 6½" 5.00   8.00

☐ **ORIENTAL CREAM, GOURAND'S**
"New York" on flat front, front panels and sides,
corner panels, flared lip, rectangular, clear, 5½"   5.00   8.00

☐ **OWL**
"J.B. Co., P.C. CO." in diamond shape on bottom,
clear, 3½" 7.00   10.00

☐ **OWL DRUG CO.**
Clear, 5¼" 7.00   10.00

☐ **THE OWL DRUG CO.**
"San Francisco" on bottom, double wing owl on
mortar on front, clear, 8⅜" 12.00   18.00

☐ **OWL BOTTLE**
Double wing owl on mortar, thread top, rectangu-
lar, clear, 3⅝" 4.00   6.00

☐ **THE OWL DRUG CO.**
On back, double wing owl, rectangular, square
collar, ABM, clear, 5¾" 4.00   6.00

☐ Same as above except 4" 7.00   10.00

☐ **THE OWL DRUG CO.**
On back, single wing owl, hair tonic type bottle,
ring collar, tapered neck, round, amethyst, 7" . .   7.00   10.00

☐ **OWL DRUG STORE**
Embossed owl in center, diamond and 2 under
bottom, clear, 1½" x 2³/₁₆" 7.00   10.00

☐ **OX**
Pontil, cobalt blue, 8½" 45.00   55.00

☐ **OXIEN PILLS, THE GIANT OXIEN**
Augusta, ME, clear, 2" 5.00   8.00

☐ **OXIEN PILLS**
The Giant Oxien Co., Augusta ME, clear, 2" . . .   4.00   6.00

☐ **OZOMULSION**
Amber, 5½" 3.00   5.00

☐ **OZON ANTISEPTIC DRESSING: W.H.**
DUNCAN, NATURES PINE REMEDY
Label, rectangular, square collar, ABM, clear, 6"   3.00   5.00

☐ **THE OZONE CO. OF TORONTO, LIMITED**
Same in back, double ring top, clear, 7" 7.00   10.00

Price Range

☐ **THE LIQUID OZONE CO.**
8 under bottom, amber, 8″ 7.00 10.00
☐ **PAINES CELERY COMPOUND**
Aqua, 10″ 7.00 10.00
☐ Same as above except amber 7.00 11.00
☐ **PAINE'S CELERY COMPOUND**
Vertically embossed on front and back, square,
sloping collared mouth with ring, smooth base,
amber, 9½″ 2.00 6.00
☐ **PALACE DRUG STORE**
Clear, 4½″ 3.00 5.00
☐ **PALACE DRUG STORE**
Clear or amethyst, 6″ 4.00 6.00
☐ **PALATINE MED. CO.**
Japanese Dropper, MAN'F'D By, tapered type
bottle, ring top, clear, 5¼″ 9.00 12.00
☐ **THE PALISADE MFG. CO.**
"Yonkers, N.Y." on bottom, clear or amethyst,
7¾″ 5.00 8.00
☐ **THE PALISADE MFG. CO.**
"Yonkers, N.Y." under bottom, amber, 7¼″ ... 5.00 9.00
☐ **JAS. PALMER & CO.**
Philada., one side "Wholesale," other side
"Druggists", aqua, 5″ 5.00 9.00
☐ **PALMETTO PHARMACY**
Charleston, S.C., 277 King St., aqua 4.00 6.00
☐ **PALMOLIVE SHAMPOO, B.J. JOHNSON**
Toronto Ont. CANADA On front and back, rectan-
gular, ring collar, ABM, clear, 7¼″ 5.00 8.00
☐ 10 panel, bluish, 4″ 5.00 9.00
☐ **PANKIN AND PHIN**
Round, open pontil, aqua, 7″ 18.00 24.00
☐ **PANOPETON/MADE BY/FAIR-CHILD BROS.**
& FOSTER
Vertically embossed, rectangular, label printed
"The Elm Pharmacy Cor. Elm and Westfield Strs.
W. Springfield, Mass.," flared mouth, smooth
base, amber, 7¾″ 2.00 6.00
☐ **PARDEE'S**
Other side is embossed "RHEUMATIC REM-
EDY," rectangular, labels on front and back,
blown in mold, with contents and box, aqua, 8½″ 15.00 20.00

Price Range

☐ **JOHN D. PARK**
"Cincinnati, O., Dr. Cuysotts Yellow Dock & Sarsaparilla" in five vertical lines on front, 8½" body, 2" neck, tapered top, graphite pontil, aqua, 2¼" x 4¼" 35.00 45.00

☐ **JOHN D. PARK**
Cincinnati, OH., Dr. Wistars Balsam of Wild Cherry, aqua, 7½" 12.00 18.00

☐ **PARKE DAVIS & CO.**
Label, amber, 5½" 3.00 5.00

☐ **PARKE DAVIS & CO.**
Label, "343" under bottom, amber 4.00 6.00

☐ **PARKE DAVIS & CO.**
Label, black glass, 3½" 5.00 8.00

☐ **PARKE DAVIS & CO.**
Label, "P.D. & CO. 274" under bottom, amber, 5¼" 3.00 5.00

☐ **PARKER**
On one side, "New York" other side, 17 under bottom, amber, 7" 3.00 5.00

☐ **PARKER'S HAIR BALSAM**
"New York" on front and sides in sunken oval panels, rectangular, ABM, amber, 7½" 5.00 8.00

☐ **PARKER'S HAIR BALSAM**
"New York" on front and sides, rectangular, amber, 6½" 4.00 7.00

☐ **DR. PARK'S INDIAN LINIMENT**
Wyanoke, clear, 5⅜" 4.00 7.00

☐ **PAUL WESTPHAL**
Clear or amethyst, 8" 5.00 8.00

☐ **PAWNEE INDIAN TA-HA**
Price 25¢, Jos. Herman Agt., aqua, 8½" 15.00 22.00

☐ **PAWNEE INDIAN, TOO-RE**
Vertical on front in sunken panel, plain sides and back, rectangular, aqua, 7¾" 9.00 12.00

☐ **P D & CO.**
Under bottom, amber, 3¼" 3.00 4.00

☐ **P D & CO. 119**
Under bottom, amber, 4" 3.00 4.00

☐ **P. D. & CO.**
Under bottom, amber, 3¾" 3.00 4.00

	Price Range	

☐ **P D & CO. 21.S**
Under bottom, machine made, amber, 2½″ ...   3.00   4.00
☐ **P D & CO. 334**
Under bottom, amber, 4¾″ 3.00   5.00
☐ **PEARL'S WHITE GLYCERINE**
Cobalt, 6¼″ 10.00   14.00
☐ **EBENEZER A. PEARL'S TINCTURE OF LIFE**
Vertical on front in sunken panels, rectangular,
aqua, 7¾″ 6.00   9.00
☐ **PEASE'S EYE WATER**
Newman, GA, aqua, 4¼″ 3.00   5.00
☐ **PROF. W.H. PEEK'S REMEDY**
NY, amber, 8″ 7.00   10.00
☐ **DR. H.F. PEERY'S**
On back "Dead Shot Vermifuce," amber, 4″ ...   4.00   7.00
☐ **DR. H.F. PEERY'S**
Clear or amethyst 3.00   5.00
☐ **WM. PENDELTON**
"Rockland, Me." vertical on three panels, twelve
panels, square collar, aqua, 4⅜″ 4.00   7.00
☐ **PEOPLES CHEMICAL CO., THE**
SCIENTIFICALLY PREPARED RED CROSS
With cross embossed in circle, "BEEF WINE &
IRON PROVIDENCE, R.I." all on front, flask
shape, flared collar, clear, 7½″ 7.00   10.00
☐ **PEPERAZINE EFFERVESCENTE MEDY**
In three vertical lines, amber, 2¾″ x 1¼″, 6¼″   4.00   6.00
☐ **PEPTENZYME**
Cobalt, 2½″ 12.00   18.00
☐ **PEPTENZYME**
At slant on front in sunken panel, cobalt blue,
3¼″ 7.00   10.00
☐ **PEPTO-MANGAN GUDE**
Six panels, aqua, 7″ 5.00   8.00
☐ **PEPTONOIDS, THE ARLINGTON CHEMISTS**
"Yonkers, NY, amber, 6″ 4.00   6.00
☐ **PERRIN & STEPHENSON NO PERCENTAGE**
PHARMACY PORTER BUILDING
San Jose, CA, rectangular, aqua, square collar,
4½″ 4.00   7.00

Price Range

☐ **DR. PETER'S KURIKO**
On one of the panels, "Prepared By Dr. Peter
Fahrney & Sons, Co., Chicago, Ill., U.S.A." on the
other side, amethyst, square, paneled, 9" 4.00 6.00

☐ **PETER MOLLER'S PURE COD LIVER OIL**
Label, clear, 5¾" 3.00 5.00

☐ **PETET'S AMERICAN COUGH CURE**
Howard Bros., rectangular, aqua, 7" 7.00 9.00

☐ **DR. J. PETTIT'S CANKER BALSAM**
Vertical on front, flask shape, clear, 3¼" 6.00 9.00

☐ **PURE COD LIVER OIL BYNE ATWOOD**
"Provincetown, MASS." vertical on front, oval,
aqua, 7" 5.00 8.00

☐ **PURE & GENUINE FOUR FOLD LINIMENT,
R. MATCHETTS**
On front and sides, rectangular, clear, 5¼" ... 3.00 5.00

☐ **PYNCHON**
At base on front, "Boston" on opposite side at
base, oval, aqua, 4¾" 5.00 8.00

☐ **Q BAN**
Machine made, amber, 6¾" 3.00 4.00

☐ **QUAKER HERB EXTRACT**
On label only, machine-made, rectangular, with
contents and box, clear, 8½" 10.00 15.00

☐ **R.R.R. RAILWAY & CO.**
"New York" embossed vertically on front, "ACT
OF CONGRESS" embossed on sides, rectangu-
lar, aqua, 6¼" 4.00 6.00

☐ **DEL DR. RABELL**
Reverse side "Emulsion," aqua, 9½" 3.00 5.00

☐ **R.R.R. RADWAY & CO.**
"New York, Entd. Accord. to Act of Congress" on
flat front panel and opposite sides in large letters,
rectangular, aqua, 6⅜" 6.00 9.00

☐ **RADWAY'S**
On side, "SARSAPARILLIAN RESOLVENT" on
front, "R.R.R." on opposite side, "Entd. Accord.
to Act of Congress," sunken panels, rectangular,
aqua, 7¼" 16.00 22.00

Price Range

☐ **RAMSON'S NERVE & BONE OIL, BROWN MFG. CO. PROPRIETORS**
Vertical on front in sunken panel, "Greenville, Tenn." on side, "New York, NY" on opposite side, rectangular, aqua 5¾" 7.00 10.00

☐ **RANSOM'S HIVE SYRUP & TOLU**
Buffalo, NY, square, aqua, 4½" 6.00 8.00

☐ **RAWLEIGH**
In vertical script, under it in ribbon, Trademark, clear or amethyst, 7⅝" 4.00 6.00

☐ **W.T. RAWLEIGH MED. CO.**
"Freeport, Ill" on other side, clear 8¼" 3.00 5.00

☐ **RAWLEIGH'S**
Embossed in script, rectangular, chamfered corners, amber, 8½" 2.00 4.00

☐ Rectangular, almost square, no embossing, pontil, aqua, 2½" 6.00 9.00

☐ Same as above, concave corner panels, crude flared lip pontil, aqua, 5¼" 6.00 9.00

☐ **RED BALSAM**
"Taunton, Mass." vertically embossed on two panels, twelve sided, screw type mouth, clear, 4¼" 2.00 4.00

☐ **RED CROSS FAMILY LINIMENT**
Label, "Cooperative Drug Mfg., Jackson, Tenn.," clear, 5½" 3.00 5.00

☐ **RED CROSS PHARMACY, W.T. CO. U.S.A.,**
"Savanah [sic] Ga.," clear, 5½" 9.00 12.00

☐ **REDINGTON & CO., ESSENCE OF JAMAICA GINGER**
"San Francisco" vertical on front, aqua, 5¼" .. 5.00 8.00

☐ **REED & CARNRICK**
"Jersey City, N.J." in three slanting lines, in back "Peptenzyme," cobalt, ring top, 2¾" x 2½" x 8½" 12.00 18.00

☐ Same, two smaller sides 10.00 14.00

☐ **REED & CARNRICK**
Same except 4½" 10.00 14.00

☐ **REED AND CARNRICK PHARMACISTS**
"New York" in five lines on front panel, amber, 7½" 6.00 9.00

Price Range

☐ **REED & CARNRICK**
"N.Y." on bottom, amber, 4¾" 5.00 8.00
☐ **REED & CARNRICK**
NY, dark blue, 6¼" 25.00 35.00
☐ **REED & CARNRICK**
New York, "Peptenzyme" on back, cobalt, 4½" 10.00 14.00
☐ **REESE CHEMICAL CO., BLOOD & SYSTEM TONIC**
Ring top, green, 3¾" 7.00 10.00
☐ **RENO'S NEW HEALTH UTERINE TONIC**
In center a lady head. "Prepared only by S.B.
Leonardi & Co., New York, N.Y." all in 8 lines on
front, ring top, 7½" aqua 16.00 22.00
☐ **RENO'S NEW HEALTH**
"Or Woman's Salvation, Prepared only by S.B.
Leonardi & Co. Tampa, Fla." all in 7 lines, 7½"
aqua 16.00 22.00
☐ **RENWAR**
On each side, ring top, cobalt, 6" 7.00 10.00
☐ **RESINAL BALTO. MD. CHEMICAL CO.**
Under bottom, milk glass, 3¼" 3.00 5.00
☐ **RESTORFF & BETTMAN**
NY, six panels, aqua, 4¼" 5.00 8.00
☐ **REXALL**
"3VIII" on shoulder, rectangular, flared lip, emer-
ald green, 6½" 7.00 10.00
☐ **RICH-LAX**
Label, aqua, 7½" 9.00 12.00
☐ **F.A. RICHTER & CO. MANUFACTURING, CHEMISTS**
"New York" with embossed anchor, vertical on
front, anchor on side, "Pain Expeller" on opposite
side, rectangular, aqua, 5" 7.00 10.00
☐ **RICKER HEGEMAN OR HEGENAK DRUG STORES**
In center, cobalt, 5½" 16.00 22.00
☐ **RIKER'S COMPOUND SARSAPARILLA**
Vertical in sunken panel on front, beveled cor-
ners, rectangular, sunken panels on all sides,
aqua blue, 10" 28.00 38.00

Price Range

☐ **C.B. RINCKERHOFFS, PRICE ONE DOLLAR**
On side, "Health Restorative, New York," tapered top, olive, 7¼" 70.00 90.00

☐ **THE RIVER SWAMP CHILL AND FEVER CURE**
With alligator in center, Augusta, GA, clear or aqua, 7" 35.00 50.00

☐ **JAMES S. ROBINSON**
Memphis, TN, clear, 7" 5.00 8.00

☐ **ROCHE'S EMBROCATION FOR THE WHOOPING COUGH, W. EDWARDS & SON**
On consecutive panels, flared lip, clear, 5" 7.00 10.00

☐ **RODERIC'S WILD CHERRY COUGH BALSAM**
Flared collar, ABM, clear, 5½" 6.00 9.00

☐ Same as above except amber, 4½" 5.00 8.00

☐ **ROOT JUICE MED. CO.**
Aqua, 9" 3.00 5.00

☐ **ROOT JUICE MED. CO.**
Label, clear or amethyst, 6" 3.00 5.00

☐ **DR. ROSE'S**
Philadel on other side, pontil, aqua 10.00 15.00

☐ **ROSHTON & ASPINWALL**
New York, on back "Compound Chlorine Tooth Wash," flared top, pontil, golden olive, 6" 170.00 220.00

☐ Round, crude ring collar, cylindrical, whittled effect, pontil, aqua blue 5¾" 7.00 10.00

☐ **V. ROUSSIN, DRUGGIST**
Muskegon, MI clear, 7¼" 5.00 8.00

☐ **ROWLAND'S MAGASSAR**
Embossed vertically on front, embossed on side "OIL," embossed on rear "NO. 20 HATTON GARDEN, LONDON," embossed on other side "THE ORIGINAL AND GENUINE," rectangular, pontiled, aqua, 3½" 30.00 45.00

☐ **ROYAL FOOT WASH, EATON DRUG CO.**
Atlanta, GA 7.00 10.00

☐ **ROYAL GALL REMEDY**
Machine made, dark amber, 7½" 7.00 10.00

Rohrer's Wild Cherry Tonic Medicine Bottle, *pyramid shape, amber, 10½".* **$20.00–$30.00**

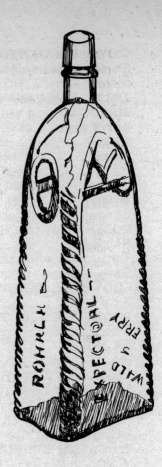

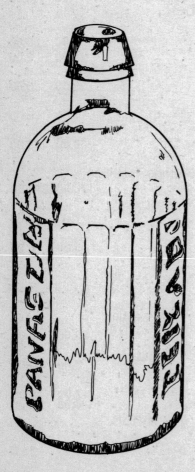

Swaim's Panacea Medicine Bottle, *yellow green, 8¼".* **$55.00–$80.00**

Price Range

☐ **ROYAL GERMETUER**
Same on reverse side, one side "Kings Royal
Germeturer Co.," other side "Atlanta Ga.
U.S.A.," amber, 8½" 18.00 24.00

☐ **RUBIFOAM FOR THE TEETH, PUT UP E.W.
HOYT & CO.,**
"Lowell, MA." all on front, oval, clear, 4" 5.00 8.00

☐ **RUSH'S**
On one side, **"REMEDY"** on reverse, other two
sides "A.H.F. Monthly," double ring top, aqua, 6" 7.00 10.00

☐ **RUSH'S**
Vertical on front in small rectangular panel,
"Lung" on side, "Balm" on opposite side, "A.H.
Flanders, MD." on back side, sunken panels, rec-
tangular, aqua, 7" 16.00 22.00

☐ **RUSHTON'S**
"F.V." on back, "Cod Liver Oil" on other side,
"N.Y." other side, ice blue, 10½" 10.00 15.00

☐ **RUSS'S AROMATIC**
Side panel "Schnapps," other side "N.Y.," dark
olive, 8" 25.00 35.00

☐ **JOHN RYAN CITRATE OF MAGNESIA**
"Savannah, GA." on front in four lines, aqua,
short neck, round, 7" 48.00 58.00

☐ **SKEYHAN PHARMACY**
"Rockford, IL" all in 3 lines on front, on shoulder
"3IV," on bottom "C.L.M. & Co.," 2½", clear .. 7.00 10.00

☐ **DR. SAGE'S**
On one side, on other side "Buffalo," "Catarrah
Remedy" on front, on back "Dr. Price Propr.," all
on sunken panels, "#1" under bottom, 2¼" .. 7.00 10.00

☐ **SALVATION OIL, AC MEYER & CO.**
"Baltimore, Md." in four lines in a sunken panel
in front, rounded sides, under bottom, letter "D,"
rectangular, 2¼" x 1" 5.00 8.00

☐ **SALVATION OIL, A.C. MEYER & CO., TRADE
MARK**
"Baltimore, Md., USA" all on front, arched panel,
rectangular, aqua, 6¾" 6.00 9.00

☐ **SALVATION TRADE MARK OIL, A.C. MEYER
& CO.**
"Balt. Md., U.S.A." ring top, aqua, 6¾" 6.00 9.00

Price Range

☐ **SAMMY'S MEDICINE**
Reverse side "Baltimore, Md., U.S.A.," under bottom "S.R. Scoggins," front side "Reaches through the Entire System," sky blue, 7" 7.00   10.00

☐ **SAND'S SARSAPARILLA**
New York, pontil, aqua, 6¼" 25.00   35.00

☐ **SANITAL DE MIDY**
Clear, twelve panels, 2¾" 4.00   6.00

☐ **THE SANITAS CO.**
Label, aqua, 9" 4.00   6.00

☐ **SANITOL**
"For the Teeth" on other side, clear, 4½" 5.00   8.00

☐ **DR. R. SAPPINGTON**
Reverse side "Flaxseed Syrup," ring top, aqua, 7½" 5.00   8.00

☐ **A. SARTORIUS & CO.**
"New York" on front, round, clear, 2¾" 3.00   5.00

☐ **SASSAFRAS**
Under it an eye cup, "Eye Lotion, Sassafras Eye Lotion Co., Maugh Chunk, Pa.", cobalt blue, 6"   16.00   22.00

☐ **SAVER**
Three-sided, amber, 3½" 18.00   24.00

☐ Same as above except aqua, 4½" 18.00   24.00

☐ **E.R. SCHAEFER'S**
Round back, clear, 4" 3.00   5.00

☐ **SCHEFFLER'S HAIR COLORINE, BEST IN THE WORLD**
On front, rectangular, beveled corners, clear, 4¼" 5.00   8.00

☐ **SCHENBS PULMONIC SYRUP**
Pontil 16.00   22.00

☐ **SCHENK'S PULMANIC SYRUP**
"Philadelphia" on four panels, eight sided, with contents, wrap-around paper label, in box, blown in mold, aqua, 7" 15.00   20.00

☐ **DR. SCHENCK'S PINE TAR FOR THROAT AND LUNGS**
Vertical in oval sunken end panel, rectangular, square collar, aqua, 6⅛" 9.00   12.00

☐ **SCHENCK'S SYRUP**
Vertical on front, oval end sunken panel, aqua, 6¼" 5.00   8.00

Price Range

☐ **SCHENCK'S SYRUP**
"Philada" on three panels, eight vertical panels,
aqua, 7¼" 7.00   10.00

☐ **SCHLOTTERBECK & FUSS CO.**
"Portland, Me." vertical on front in sunken panel,
rectangular, sheared collar, amber, 5" 5.00   8.00

☐ **SCHUTZEN STR. NO. 6**
"J. E. Gilke" on back panel, 10" 30.00   40.00

☐ **SCOTT'S EMULSION**
"Cod Liver Oil" on one side, "With Lime Soda"
on other side, aqua, various sizes 4.00   6.00

☐ **S. & D. 8**
Under bottom, amber, 6" 3.00   5.00

☐ **S & D 83 2**
Under bottom, sheared top, amber, 3½" 3.00   5.00

☐ **S & D 2S**
Under bottom, amber, 4½" 1.50   2.25

☐ **S & D 100**
Under bottom, sheared top, clear, 2½" 3.00   5.00

☐ **S & D 73**
Under bottom, amber, 6¼" 3.00   5.00

☐ **S & D 83**
Under bottom, amber, 3½" 1.50   2.25

☐ **SEABURY**
Cobalt, sheared top, 3¾" 5.00   8.00

☐ **SEABURY**
Sheared top, amber, 3¾" 5.00   8.00

☐ **R. N. SEARLES**
On side, "Athlophoros" on opposite side, rectangular, aqua, 6¾" 5.00   7.00

☐ **SHAKER CHERRY PECTORAL SYRUP**
Embossed vertically on side, other side embossed "CANTERBURY, N.H., NO. 1" rectangu-
lar, pontiled aqua, 5¼" 60.00   70.00

☐ **SHAKER FLUID**
Embossed vertically on side, on other side is embossed "EXTRACT VALERIAN," rectangular,
pontiled aqua, 3½" 50.00   60.00

☐ **DR. S.&H. AND CO.**
"P.R. Registered" on base, amethyst or aqua,
round, 9¼" 7.00   10.00

Price Range

☐ **SHARP & DOHME**
"Baltimore, Md." under bottom, amber, 5¾" ..   3.00   5.00

☐ **SHARP & DOHME**
Three corners, round back, cobalt, 3½" 5.00   8.00

☐ **SHECUTS SOUTHERN BALM FOR COUGHS, COLD 1840**
Aqua, 6¾" 20.00   28.00

☐ **WM. H. SHEPARD**
Marblehead, MA. label, aqua, 9" 9.00   12.00

☐ **J.T. SHINN**
Clear, 4¾" 3.00   5.00

☐ **S.H.K.C. EXT. P.C.**
Clear or amethyst, 4" 3.00   5.00

☐ **DR. SHOOP'S FAMILY MEDICINES**
Racine, WI, aqua, ring top, 5½" 5.00   8.00

☐ **DR. SHOOP'S FAMILY MEDICINES**
Racine, Wis. square, aqua, 7" 5.00   10.00

☐ **SHORES**
Label, clear, 9½" 3.00   5.00

☐ **SHORT STOP FOR COUGHS, H.M. O'NEIL**
"N.Y." vertical on front in sunken panel, square,
aqua, 4" 3.00   5.00

☐ **SCHULTZ**
"Dr. Shultz" on other side, aqua, 6½" 5.00   8.00

☐ **SHUPTXINE**
In script, "Druggist, Savannah, Ga." in two lines
on front flap panel, top "31V," panel each side,
round blank back, under bottom "Pat 18/17 C.L.
Co.," Freen, 5¼" tall, 2" x 1¼" 12.00   18.00

☐ Same as above, 3½" tall, 1½" x ¾" 7.00   10.00

☐ Same as above, 2½" tall, 1⅛" x ¾" 8.00   11.00

☐ **THE SILBURT CO., TRADEMARK**
Cleveland, Sixth City, clear, 4¼" long 5.00   8.00

☐ **SIMMON'S LIVER REGULATOR**
In three sunken panels on front, "Philadelphia"
on side, "Macon, Ga." on opposite side, "J.H.
Eeilin & Co." vertical on back, rectangular, aqua,
9" 6.00   9.00

☐ **DR. SIMMON'S SQUAW VINE WINE COMPOUND**
Vertical lines, tapered top, aqua, 8½" 5.00   8.00

Price Range

☐ **DR. M.A. SIMMON'S LIVER MEDICINE**
St. Louis, aqua, 5¾" 5.00   8.00

☐ **C. SINES**
One side, "Phila. Pa." reverse side, front side
"Tar Wild Cherry & Hoar Hound," pontil, aqua, 5"   20.00   28.00

☐ **SIPHON KUMY SGEN BOTTLE FOR PREPARING KUMYSS FROM REED & CARREIC**
N.Y., cobalt, 8¾" 28.00   38.00

☐ **S.J.S. FOR THE BLOOD**
On one side "L.G. Gerstle & Co.", other side
"Chattanooga, Tenn.", amber, 9" 9.00   13.00

☐ **SKABCURA DIP CO.**
Chicago, U.S.A., aqua, 5" 5.00   8.00

☐ **SKODA'S SARSAPARILLA**
On side "Skoda's", opposite side "Discovery"
with "Belfast, Me," on indented panel, front indented panel marked "Concentrated Extract Sa-
saparilla Compound," back panel has label,
amber, 9" 18.00   24.00

☐ Same as above except "Wolfville" on one side,
"Nova Scotia" on other side 18.00   24.00

☐ **DR. SLEDGE'S HOREHOUND PECTORAL**
"HOREHOUND PECTORAL" in indented front
panel, "Memphis, Tenn." one side, "Dr.
Sledge's" on other side, graphite pontil, aqua,
7¼" 22.00   30.00

☐ **SLOAN'S LINIMENT**
Clear or amethyst, 7" 5.00   8.00

☐ **SLOCUM'S COLTSFOOT EXPECTORANT**
On bottom, flask or oval shape, aqua, 2¼" ... 3.00   5.00

☐ **SLOCUM'S EXPECTORANT COLTSFOOT**
Under bottom, aqua, 2¼" 4.00   6.00

☐ **T.A. SLOCUM CO. MFG., CHEMISTS**
"N.Y. & London" with anchor seal, one side
reads "For Consumption", other side "Lung
Troubles," beveled corners, long collar, aqua,
9½" 15.00   22.00

☐ **T.A. SLOCUM MFG. CO., PSYCHINE CONSUMPTION**
181 Pearl St., N.Y., aqua, 8½" 5.00   8.00

Price Range

☐ **MFG. SLOUGH, ELLIMAN'S ROYAL EMBROCATION FOR HORSES**
Double ring top, aqua, 7½″ 9.00 13.00

☐ **SMITH'S GREEN MOUNTAIN RENOVATOR**
Tapered top & ring, green 9.00 13.00

☐ **S. SMITH, GREEN MOUNTAIN RENOVATOR**
"East Georgia, Vt." in 3 lines, tapered top, olive
& amber, pontil 25.00 30.00

☐ **SMITH'S GREEN MOUNTAIN RENOVATOR**
East Georgia, VT, oval, rounded shoulders, indented, smooth base, aqua, 7¾″ 40.00 50.00

☐ **SMITH GREEN MT. RENOVATORE**
E. Ga. Vt., olive amber, stoddard glass, 6⅛″ .. 175.00 220.00

☐ **T.B. SMITH KIDNEY TONIC**
Cynthiana, KY, aqua, 10½″ 12.00 18.00

☐ **SOLOMONS CO.**
In script, "Branch Drug Stores, Bull St., Savannah, GA.", in three lines in front, under bottom
"WTCo, U.S.A." in two lines, aqua or amethyst,
7″ 4.00 6.00

☐ Same only different sizes 4.00 6.00

☐ Same only cobalt 15.00 22.00

☐ **A.A. SOLOMONS & CO., DRUGGISTS MARKET SQUAE**
Misspelled Square, aqua, 3¾″ 15.00 22.00

☐ **SOZONDONT**
On each side, clear, 2½″ 3.00 5.00

☐ **SPARKLENE**
Registered on back, amber, 5″ 3.00 5.00

☐ **SPARKS PERFECT HEALTH**
"For Kidney & Liver Diseases," three lines in
sunken panel on front, round, aqua, 4″ 5.00 8.00

☐ **SPENCER MED. CO.**
On one side sunken panel, front "Nubian Tea and
Trademark," other side panel "Chattanooga
Tenn.", amber, square, 4″ 4.00 6.00

☐ **SPENCER MED CO.**
One side panel, "Chatt. Tenn., Nubian Tea" in
sunken panel on front, golden, 4″ 4.00 6.00

☐ **P.H. SPILLANE, PHARMACIST**
Cohoes, NY, "W. T. Co." under bottom, clear, 5″ 4.00 6.00

Price Range

☐ **SPITH SAN FRANCISCO PHARMACY**
11th & Railroad Avenues, flared lip, 5¼" 5.00 7.00

☐ **SPIRIT OF TURPENTINE**
Franklin, OH, label, "Pat April 21, 1896" under
bottom, clear, 8¾" 5.00 8.00

☐ **E.R. SQUIBB 1864**
Round, green, 6" 7.00 10.00

☐ **DR. L.R. STAFFORD OLIVE TAR**
Label, directions, "J.R. Stafford" on side, "Olive
Tar" opposite side, rectangular, double band col-
lar, clear, 6" 4.00 6.00

☐ **J.R. STAFFORD'S OLIVE TAR**
On opposite side, rectangular, aqua, 6" 4.00 6.00

☐ **STANDARD OIL CO.**
Vertical on front, "Cleveland, O." on one side,
"Favorite" on opposite side, rectangular, ame-
thyst, 6¼" 3.00 5.00

☐ **STAPHYLASE DU DR. DOYEN**
Clear, 7½" 4.00 6.00

☐ **STEIN & CO., APOTHECARIER**
Jersey City, "M-W U.S.A." under bottom, clear or
amethyst, 5⅜" 4.00 6.00

☐ **STEELMAN & ARCHER**
"Philadelphia, PA" on front, rectangular, clear, 5" 5.00 8.00

☐ **R.E. STIERAUX PILLS**
In front in form of circle about the size of a half
dollar, clear, 1¾" 3.00 5.00

☐ **A. STONE & CO.**
Inside screw top, 3 Philada on screw top, aqua,
7½" 20.00 28.00

☐ **DR. STONES OXFORD DROPS FOR
COUGHS & COLDS**
Embossed vertically on front, oval, pontiled,
aqua, 5" 45.00 55.00

☐ **F.E. SUIRE & CO.**
Cincinnati, reverse side "Waynes Duiretic Elixir,"
amber, 8" 9.00 12.00

☐ **SULTAN DRUG CO.**
"St. Louis & London" on other side, amber, 7¼" 5.00 8.00

Price Range

☐ **SUTHERLAND SISTERS HAIR GROWER**
All seven sisters on front in a sunken panel, "Sutherland Sisters" on the side, "New York" on opposite side, rectangular, ABM, clear, 5¼" ... 7.00 10.00

☐ **SUTHERLAND SISTERS HAIR GROWER**
Aqua, 6" 7.00 10.00

☐ **L.B. SUTTON**
Amber, 5½" 3.00 5.00

☐ **SWAIN'S VERMIFUGE**
Embossed vertically, on rear "DYSENTERY, CHOLERA, MARBUS, DYSPEPSIA, ETC.," oval, pontiled, aqua, 5¼" 30.00 40.00

☐ **SWIFTS**
Cobalt blue, 9" 20.00 28.00

☐ **DR. SYKES**
Specific Blood Medicine, Chicago, ILL, clear, 6½" 4.00 6.00

☐ **SYR:RHOEAD**
Cobalt blue, pontil, 8½" 32.00 42.00

☐ **SYRUP OF THEDFORD'S BLACK DROUGHT**
Vertical on front in sunken panel, rectangular, ABM, clear 3.00 4.00

☐ **DR. TAFT'S**
"Asthmalene, N.Y." on the front panel, rectangular, 3½" 3.00 5.00

☐ **TANGIN**
Same on reverse side, 9" 9.00 12.00

☐ **TARRANT & CO.**
Clear, 5¼" 5.00 8.00

☐ **TAYLOR'S CELEBRATED OIL**
On front, back plain, one side "Leraysville," other "Penn.," aqua, 6⅛" 9.00 12.00

☐ **TAYLOR'S DRUG STORE**
Clear or amethyst, 4" 3.00 5.00

☐ **TAYLOR'S DRUG STORE**
Clear, 4¾" 5.00 8.00

☐ **TAYLOR'S ESSENCE OF JAMAICA GINGER**
Clear, 5½" 7.00 10.00

☐ **TEABERRY FOR THE TEETH & BREATH**
Clear, 3½" 7.00 10.00

☐ **TERISSIER PREVOS A PARIS**
Graphite pontil, blue, 7½" 70.00 90.00

Price Range

☐ **A TEXAS WONDER, HALL'S GREAT DISCOVERY**
For Kidney, Bladder Troubles, E.W. Hall, St. Louis, MO, clear, 3½" 3.00   5.00

☐ **DR. THACHER'S**
"Liver and Blood Syrup, Chattanooga, Tenn." on the front panel, rectangular, amber, 7¼" and 8¼" 4.00   6.00

☐ **DR. THACHER'S LIVER AND BLOOD SYRUP**
On the front, "Chattanooga, Tenn." on one side of the panels, Sample on the opposite panel, amber, rectangular, 3½" 4.00   6.00

☐ **DR. H.S. THACHER'S DIARRHEA REMEDY**
"Chattanooga" on one of the panels, amethyst, square, 3⅜" 4.00   6.00

☐ **DR. THACHER'S VEGETABLE SYRUP**
"Chattanooga, Tenn." on the front, amethyst, rectangular, 7" 4.00   7.00

☐ **DR. H.S. THACHER'S WORM SYRUP**
On the side panel, "Chattanooga, Tenn." on other panel, aqua, square, 4¼" 4.00   7.00

☐ **DR. THACHER'S**
Olive, 3¼" 4.00   7.00

☐ **DR. THACHER'S**
"Chattanooga, Tenn." on side, aqua, 3¼" 3.75   6.00

☐ **DR. H.S. THACHER'S**
Amber, 2½" 4.00   6.00

☐ **HENRY THAYER**
Amber, 9½" 22.00   30.00

☐ **THOMAS ELECTRIC OIL**
Vertical on front in sunken panel, "Internal & External" on side, "Foster Milburn Co." on opposite side, rectangular, clear, 4¼" 3.00   5.00

☐ **DR. S.N. THOMAS ELECTRIC OIL**
Vertical on front, "External" on side, "Internal" on opposite side, "Northrum & Lyman, Toronto, Ont." on back, double band collar, rectangular, aqua, 5½" 3.00   5.00

☐ **THOMPSON'S DRUG STORE**
Opposite "The Market," clear, 5⅝" 7.00   10.00

☐ **THOMPSON'S HERBAL COMPOUND**
New York, label, clear or aqua, 6¾" 3.00   5.00

Price Range

☐ **DR. THOMPSON'S SARSAPARILLA, GREAT ENGLISH REMEDY**
On front indented panel, "Calais, Me. U.S.A." side, "St. Stephens, N.B." opposite side, rectangular, aqua, 9" 11.00   15.00

☐ **THOMPSON'S**
"Philada" other side, "Diarrhea syrup" on back, aqua 5.00   8.00

☐ **DR. THOMPSON'S**
Eye Water, New London, CT, aqua, round, pontil, 3¾" 27.00   30.00

☐ **THOMSON'S**
Embossed on one side, on front "COMPOUND SYRUP OF TAR," on other side "FOR CONSUMPTION" on rear "PHILA.," rectangular, pontiled, 5½" 35.00   45.00

☐ **THURSTON & KINGBURY TAK FLAVORING EXTRACT,**
"Bangor, Maine" vertical on front in oriental style letters, "Finest Quality Full Strength," clear, 5"   5.00   8.00

☐ **DR. TICHENOR'S**
Aqua, "Antiseptic" on other side, 3¾" 7.00   10.00

☐ **DR. TICHENOR'S**
On one side of panel, "Antiseptic" on the other side, rectangular, aqua, 5⅞" 3.00   5.00

☐ **DR. G.H. TICHENOR'S ANTISEPTIC REFRIGERANT**
One side "Sherrouse Medicine Co.," other side "Ltd., New Orleans La., aqua, 5¾" 9.00   13.00

☐ **TIKHELL**
Light blue, 6½" 5.00   8.00

☐ **TILDEN**
Under bottom, amber, 5" 3.00   5.00

☐ **TILDEN**
Amber, 7½" 3.00   5.00

☐ **CLAES TILLY**
Aqua, 3¾" 3.00   5.00

☐ **G.De KONING TILLY**
Oil, aqua, 1" 3.00   5.00

☐ **TIPPECANOE**
Amber, clear, aqua, 9" 80.00   100.00

Price Range

☐ **TIPPECANOE**
Misspelled "Rochester" under bottom, amber, 9″   **90.00 120.00**

☐ **DR. TOBIAS**
"New York" in large letters vertically on front, "Venetian Liniment" in large letters on back, large beveled corner panels, aqua, graduated collar, 6¼″ **4.00 6.00**

☐ **DR. TOBIAS**
"New York" vertical on front, same as above except oval, 4¼″ **4.00 6.00**

☐ **DR. TOBIAS**
"New York" aqua, 8″ **6.00 9.00**

☐ **DR. TOBIAS VENETIAN HORSE LINIMENT**
"New York" on front and back, rectangular, aqua, 8¼″ **7.00 10.00**

☐ **TOKA**
Reverse Blood Tonic, aqua, 8½″ **10.00 15.00**

☐ **T. TOMLINSON**
Aqua, 10½″ **7.00 10.00**

☐ **TONICIO ORIENTAL PARA EL CABELLO**
In three lines on sunken panel on front, on one side "New York," on other, "Lanman Y Kemp," both in sunken panels, under bottom #34, aqua, flat collar, ringed neck, 6″ **7.00 10.00**

☐ **TO-NI-TA LORENTS MED. CO. TRADEMARK**
Around shoulder, bitters label, amber, 9¾″ **9.00 13.00**

☐ **R.E. TOOMBS JR.**
Clear or amethyst, 5¼″ **3.00 5.00**

☐ **TOOTH POWDER**
Label, milk glass, 2″ **9.00 13.00**

☐ **DR. TOWNSEND**
Reverse Sarsaparilla, 1850, 9½″ **80.00 100.00**

☐ **DR. TOWNSEND**
"Sarsaparilla" on other sides, pontil, amber, 9½″   **100.00 125.00**

☐ **A. TRASKS**
"Magnetic Ointment" on back, aqua, 2½″ and 3¼″ **5.00 8.00**

☐ **M. TREGOR SONS**
Baltimore, MD., Wash. D.C., E.R.B., clear, 8″ ..   **6.00 9.00**

☐ **J. TRINER**
"Chicago" on one panel, six panels, clear, 5¼″   **7.00 10.00**

Price Range

☐ **TRUAX RHEUMATIC REMEDY, BEN O. AIDRICH**
Keene, NH label, clear 4.00   6.00

☐ **DR. TRUES ELIXIR ESTABLISHED 1851, DR. J.F. TRUE & CO. INC.**
"Auburn, Me., Worm Expeller, Family Laxative" on front and opposite side in sunken panel, rectangular, ABM, clear, 5½" 3.75   5.50

☐ Same as above except 7¾" 5.00   8.00

☐ **H.A. TUCKER M.D.**
Brooklyn, NY, MO, "DIAPHORTIC COMPOUND" on front, ring top, aqua, 5½" 5.00   8.00

☐ **J. TUCKER, DRUGGIST**
Reverse "Mobile," pontil, aqua, 7½" 25.00 35.00

☐ **NATHAN TUCKER M.D.**
"Star & Shield Specific for Asthma, Hay Fever and All Catarrhal Diseases Of The Respiratory Organs" all on front, round, clear, 4" 5.00   8.00

☐ **JOHN S. TUFTS APOTHECARY**
J. S. T. Monogram, Plymouth, NH, oval, clear, 6¾" 4.00   6.00

☐ **TURKISH FOOT BATH, GALLED ARMPITS & CO.** 7.00 10.00

☐ **TURKISH LINIMENT**
Aqua, 4¾" 3.00   5.00

☐ **ROBT. TURLINGTON**
"TURLINGTON" misspelled, on one side "June 14, 1775," other side "London," back side "By the Kings Royal Pat. Granted to," aqua, 2¾" .. 20.00 28.00

☐ **ROBT. TURLINGTON**
"By The Kings Royal Patent Granted" on back, aqua, 2¾" 30.00 40.00

☐ Same except no pontil 9.00 13.00

☐ **TURNER BROTHERS**
"New York, Buffalo, N.Y., San Francisco, Cal." on front, graphite pontil, tapered top, amber, 9½" 75.00 95.00

☐ **TUSSICON**
In one line vertical, Ring top, clear, 5" 7.00 10.00

☐ **DR. TUTT'S**
"New York" on other side, "Asparagine" on front, aqua, 10¼" 9.00 12.00

Price Range

☐ **DR. S.A. TUTTLE'S**
"Boston, Mass." on vertical panels, twelve vertical panels, aqua, 6¼" 6.00 9.00

☐ **TUTTLE'S ELIXIR CO.**
"Boston, Mass." on two vertical panels, twelve panels, amethyst, 6¼" 5.00 8.00

☐ **TYSON DRUG CO.**
Holly Springs, MI, flared lip, emerald green, 4¼" 50.00 75.00

☐ **DR. VON WERT'S BALSAM**
Embossed vertically on front, "VAN WERT CHEMICAL CO., WATERTOWN, N.Y." embossed on sides, rectangular, aqua, 6" 4.00 6.00

☐ **WALFOX BRAND**
Embossed in raised triangle, above this is embossed "Running Fox," all set in recessed round panel, smooth base bottom, cork type, applied top, medium cobalt blue, 11⅛" 15.00 22.00

☐ **WARNER'S SAFE NERVINE**
"ROCHESTER, N.Y." embossed safe, oval, blown in mold, with contents, amber, 7" 30.00 37.00

☐ **UDOLPHO WOLFE'S**
On front panel, on back "Aromatic Schnapps" in two lines, right side plain, left "Schiedam," 2¼" square, beveled corners, 1½" neck, golden amber 18.00 24.00

☐ Same except light amber, 9½" 13.00 20.00

☐ Same except olive 20.00 28.00

☐ **WYETH 119 6**
Under bottom in sunken panel, 1¾" x 1¹³/₁₆", clear, amethyst, 3⅝" 5.00 8.00

☐ **WYETH**
Under bottom, clear or amethyst, 3½" 3.00 5.00

☐ **WYETH**
Under bottom, amber, 3¼" 1.50 2.25

☐ **WYETH & BRO.**
"Philada" in a circle, saddle type flask, under bottom "226A," amber, 1½" neck, 7½" 3.00 5.00

☐ Same except cobalt blue 20.00 28.00

☐ **WYETH & BRO.**
Saddle type flask, amber, 7½" 5.00 8.00

☐ **JOHN WYETH & BRO. BEEF JUICE**
On front, round, amber, 3½" 3.00 5.00

Price Range

☐ **JOHN WYETH & BRO.**
"Pat May 16th 1899" under bottom, cobalt, 6½"   16.00   22.00
☐ Same except 3½" 9.00   12.00
☐ **JOHN WYETH & BROTHER**
Philadelphia, Liquid Extract Malt, squat body,
amber, 9" 7.00   10.00
☐ **JOHN WYETH & BROTHER**
Phila, 1870, round, blue, 9" 20.00   28.00
☐ **JOHN WYETH & BROTHER**
Saddle shape, clear, 7¾" 6.00   9.00
☐ **JOHN WYETH & BRO. TAKE NEXT DOSE AT**
Around base of neck, Pat. May 16, cap shows
hours 1 to 12, square, cobalt blue, 5¾" 14.00   20.00
☐ Same as above except ABM 5.00   8.00
☐ **X-LALIA**
Boston, MA, Clear or amethyst, 7¼" 5.00   8.00

MINERAL WATER

The bottling and selling of mineral water was a major industry in the U.S. in the 19th century. It was consumed by some for supposed health benefits, by others who simply liked the taste, and, to a large extent, by those who wanted to be chic. The mere fact that European royalty plus American aristocrats such as the Astors and Vanderbilts drank mineral water was enough recommendation for the public.

Mineral water was popular for nearly a full century, but the peak period was from about 1860 to 1900. The majority of collectible bottles, such as those listed below, fall into that era. Shapes of mineral water bottles are not extremely creative, but they all feature bold attractive lettering and, sometimes, designs—either with embossing or a paper label. The variety, in terms of manufacturers and places of origin, is enormous—so much so that the hobbyist may want to specialize by geographical locale. Another intriguing point about mineral water bottles is that the *sizes* vary greatly, from about 7 inches in height up to 14 inches. Although specimens with paper labels are not highly sought-after by some collectors because they're more recent in date than embossed bottles; the labels are often very colorful with entertaining messages.

The motive for drinking mineral water in the 19th century was somewhat different than that for using spring water today. Ordinary drinking water of that time did not contain the chemical additives to which some persons now object. It was essentially pure water, but mineral water—from mineral springs—had the supposed advantage of a higher mineral content which was thought to be healthful. Mineral water might be classified as a fad but, if so, it was one of long duration. The Greeks were extolling the virtues of mineral water as early as 400 B.C. Hippocrates, the Greek "father of medicine," mentioned it favorably in his writings. During the Italian Renaissance (c. 1400–1550 A.D.), when classical ideals came back into vogue, mineral water returned to popularity. For the next several centuries, Europe's well-to-do flocked to mineral springs in their leisure time, to swim in mineral water, bathe in it, relax in it, and drink it. In early times, it was possible to obtain mineral water for drinking only by visiting the springs. Visitors would gleefully fill their jugs, pack them into wagons, and hope that the supply would last until their next trip. Eventually, the popularity of mineral water reached such a point that shopkeepers made efforts to supply it. This was not easy at first since there were no distributors. The shopkeeper had to engage an agent at one of the spas to fill barrels or tubs with the water and ship it to him. Upon its arrival it was placed into bottles which the retailer had to buy empty from a glass manufacturer. This was a costly process, resulting in mineral water selling in such places as London and Paris for very high sums—more than most wine and spirits. The so-called "carriage trade" (customers who arrived in their own carriages) bought it and it became evident that the general public would, too, if prices could somehow be lowered.

Since America also was blessed with mineral springs, spas began opening up in the U.S. as early as colonial times. In 1767, a Boston spa started bottling its water. It was followed by one in Albany in 1800 and by a Philadelphia spa in 1819.

Competition naturally developed between the spas. Claims of the curative powers of the various bottled waters were often as outlandish as those of bottled medicines. The sparkling waters were believed to cure rheumatism, diabetes, kidney disorder, gout, nervous afflictions, and all sorts of other ailments. Doctors recommended it to their patients.

European immigrants to America were so convinced of the powers of these salted waters that they imported their favorite brands from the "old country." These arrived in crudely made pottery bottles. The first American bottles for mineral water were unadorned but made of glass.

Sellers of mineral water were quick to capitalize on stories about its powers. During the Civil War, it was said that wounded soldiers at Gettysburg made rapid recoveries by drinking the mineral water there. Almost as soon as the report had been circulated, Gettysburg Katalysine Spring Water was available in shops.

Bottled spring water began to replace mineral water in the late 19th century. Most collectible mineral water bottles were cork-stoppered.

Price Range

☐ **ABILENA NATURAL CATHARTIC WATER**
On the bottom, amber or brown, 11½" 7.00 9.00

☐ **ABILENA NATURAL CATHARTIC WATER**
On the bottom, blob top, amber, 10⅛" 9.00 12.00

☐ **ADIRONDACK SPRING**
Westport, NY, tapered top with "Reg.," plain bottom, quart, emerald green, (30.00) 42.00 52.00

☐ **AETNA MINERAL WATER**
Aqua, 11½" 6.00 9.00

☐ **AETNA SPOUTING SPRING**
In horseshoe letters in center, "A & E" in block letters, Saratoga, NY, aqua, pint 80.00 120.00

☐ **AKESION SPRINGS**
Owned By Sweet Springs Co., Saline Co., MO, amber, 8" 18.00 24.00

☐ **ALBERT CROOK**
"Saratoga Co. N.Y." in a circle, through center of it "Paradise Spring," tapered top, six rings, green or aqua, pint 80.00 100.00

☐ **ALEX EAGLE**
In center, "1861 MINERAL WATER," tapered top, aqua, 7¼" 16.00 22.00

☐ **ALHAMBRA NAT. MINERAL WATER CO.,**
Martinez, CA, applied top, aqua, 11¼" 15.00 22.00

☐ **ALLEGHANY SPRING**
VA, amber.................................. 15.00 22.00

☐ **ALLEN MINERAL WATER**
Horizontal letters placed vertically on bottle, blob top, golden amber, 11½" 12.00 16.00

☐ **ALLEN MINERAL WATER**
Big ring top, 7½" 12.00 16.00

☐ **AMERICAN KISSINGER WATER**
In vertical lines, tapered top and ring, aqua, pint 60.00 75.00

Price Range

☐ **AMERICAN MINERAL WATER CO.**
New York, M.S. monogram all inside slug plate,
"THIS BOTTLE NOT TO BE SOLD" at base, blob
top, aqua, 9¼" .... | 14.00 | 20.00

☐ **ARTESIAN BALLSTON SPA**
Green .... | 28.00 | 38.00

☐ **ARTESIAN SPRING CO.**
Ballston, NY, "Ballston Spa. Lithia Mineral Water
on back," dark aqua, 7¾" .... | 30.00 | 40.00

☐ **ARTESIAN WATER**
Pontil or plain, "Dupont" on back, dark olive, 7¾" | 60.00 | 75.00

☐ **ARTESIAN SPRING CO.**
In center an "S" super-imposed over an "A".
under it "Ballston, N.Y.," tapered top and ring pt.
emerald green .... | 40.00 | 50.00

☐ **ASTORG SPRINGS MINERAL WATER**
S.F., CA, blob top, green, 7" .... | 11.00 | 15.00

☐ **JOHN S. BAKER**
"Mineral Water, this bottle never sold" on panels,
blob top, eight panels, pontil, aqua .... | 42.00 | 52.00

☐ **BALLSTON SPA MINERAL WATER**
Artesian Spring Co., Ballston, with trademark like
a dollar sign, green, 8" .... | 25.00 | 30.00

☐ **BARTLETT SPRING MINERAL WATER**
"California" in a slug plate, blob top, 11⅝" ... | 15.00 | 22.00

☐ **BATTERMAN H.B.**
In ½ moon circle, in center, 1861, under it in 2
lines "Brooklyn, N.Y.," tapered top, ground pontil
(C1860), aqua, 7½" .... | 40.00 | 50.00

☐ **BAUMAN, N.**
"Pottsville, Pa." in 4 lines, slug plate, (c. 1860)
ground pontil, tapered top and ring, green, 7½" | 70.00 | 90.00

☐ **BEAR LITHIA WATER**
Aqua, 10" .... | 6.00 | 9.00

☐ **J. & A. BEARBOR, NEW YORK MINERAL
WATER**
Eight panels, star on reverse side, graphite pontil,
blue, 7¼" .... | 42.00 | 62.00

☐ **BEDFORD WATER**
Label in back, aqua, 14" .... | 5.00 | 9.00

Price Range

☐ **BITTERQUELLE SAXLEHNERS JANOS**
On bottom, whittle mark or plain, ring top, avocado green, 10½″ 5.00 8.00

☐ **BLOUNT SPRINGS NATURAL SULPHUR**
Cobalt, 8″ and 11″ 65.00 85.00

☐ **BLUE LICK WATER CO.**
KY, double ring top, pontil, pt. amber 110.00 135.00

☐ **J. BOARDMAN & CO. MINERAL WATER**
Eight panels, graphite pontil, cobalt, 7¾″ 80.00 120.00

☐ **BOLEY & CO.**
Sac. City, CA, reverse side "Union Glass Work,
Phila.", slug plate, blob top, graphite pontil, blue,
7½″ 70.00 90.00

☐ **J. BORN MINERAL WATER**
Cincinnati, reverse below B, "T.B.N.T.B.S.", blob
top, green, 7¾″ 15.00 22.00

☐ **J. BORN MINERAL WATER**
"Cincinnati" in three lines, reverse side large B
and T.B.N.T.B.S., blob top, blue, 7½″ 22.00 33.00

☐ **BOWDEN LITHIA WATER**
Under it a house and trees, under that "Lithia
Spring Ca.," blob top, aqua 12.00 17.00

☐ **BROWN DR**
"NY" in 1 line, vertical big B in back, tapered top,
pontil green, 7½″, (c. 1850) 70.00 90.00

☐ **BUCKHORN MINERAL WATER**
Label, aqua, 10¼″ 5.00 8.00

☐ **BUFFALO LICK SPRINGS**
Clear or amethyst, 10″ 6.00 9.00

☐ **BUFFALO LITHIA SPRING WATER**
Aqua, 10½″ 11.00 15.00

☐ **BUFFALO LUTHIS' WATER**
Natures Materia Medica, lady sitting with pitcher
in hand, under it, trademark, round, aqua, 11½″ 11.00 15.00

☐ **BYTHINIA WATER**
Tapered top, amber, 10¼″ 6.00 9.00

☐ **CAL. NAT. MINERAL WATER**
"Castalian" around shoulder, amber, 7¼″ 8.00 11.00

☐ **CALIFORNIA NATURAL SELTZER WATER**
Reverse side picture of a bear, H.&G., blob top,
aqua, 7¼″ 18.00 26.00

Price Range

☐ **CAMPBELL MINERAL WATER, C.**
Burlington, VT, (c. 1870), plain bottom, tapered
top and ring, aqua, quart 130.00 180.00

☐ **W. CANFIELD**
Agt. for S.H.G., graphite pontil, squat, blob top,
green, 6¼″ 55.00 70.00

☐ **CANTRELL, THOS. J.**
"Bellfast, Medicated aerated water," all in 5 vertical lines, blop top, round bottom, aqua, 9¼″, (c.
1900) 20.00 28.00

☐ **CARL H. SCHULTZ**
C-P M-S, NY, Vichy, pint, blue-green, 8″ 40.00 45.00

☐ **CARLSBAD L.S.**
Sheared collar, cylindrical, ground top, clear, 4″ 6.00 9.00

☐ **CARLSBAD L.S.**
On bottom, short tapered top, quart, green, 10¼″ 11.00 15.00

☐ **CARTERS SPANISH MIXTURE**
Pontil, 8½″ 50.00 65.00

☐ **C.C. & B., SAN FRANCISCO**
In two lines, reverse side "Superior Mineral
Water," ten-sided base, blob top, graphite pontil,
blue, 7″ 150.00 185.00

☐ **CHAMPION SPOUTING SPRING**
"Saratoga, N.Y." in four lines all on front, in back
in 2 lines "Champion Water," green, pint 110.00 140.00

☐ **CHAMPLAIN, SPRING**
Highgate, VT, tapered top & ring, emerald green,
qt. 60.00 80.00

☐ **CHASE & CO. MINERAL WATER**
"San Francisco, Stockton, Marysville, Cal." in
five lines, graphite pontil, blob top, green, 7¼″ 70.00 90.00

☐ **CITY BOTTLING WORK**
Under it a girl seated, Mt. Vernon, OH, tapered
top, clear, 11″ 28.00 38.00

☐ **C. CLARK MINERAL WATER**
Blue, Round, Pint, 8″ 35.00 45.00

☐ **C. CLARK MINERAL WATER**
Green, Round, Pint, 8″ 35.00 45.00

☐ **JOHN CLARKE**
"New York" around shoulder, two-piece mold,
pontil, olive, 9¼″ 60.00 80.00

**"Buffum—Sarsaparilla—Lemon—
Mineral Water—Pittsburg"** *ten-sided,
iron pontil, applied lip, aqua.*
$300.00–$360.00

**"M.T. Crawford/Springfield—Union
Glass Works Phila/Superior/Mineral
Water,"** *iron pontil, round with "mug"
base—applied top, deep cobalt-blue.*
$400.00–$475.00

Price Range

☐ **JOHN CLARK, N.Y. SPRING WATER**
Back "New York", green, pint, 7" 40.00 50.00
☐ **LYNCH CLARK**
NY, dark olive, pint 50.00 65.00
☐ **CLARK & WHITE**
New York, embossed "C", pint, olive green, 8" 30.00 40.00
☐ **CLARK & WHITE**
In horseshoe, in center big "C," in back "Mineral
Water," olive green, 9½" 13.00 18.00
☐ **CLARKE & CO.**
"N.Y." in two lines, tapered top and ring, pontil,
blue green, 7¾" 55.00 70.00
☐ **CLARKE & WHITE**
Wide mouth, dark olive, 7" x 3¾" 19.00 27.00
☐ **CLARKE & WHITE**
Olive, 8" 19.00 27.00
☐ **CLARK & WHITE**
New York, qt. & pt., olive green, tapered top with
ring 60.00 80.00
☐ **C. CLEMINSON SODA & MINERAL WATER**
Troy, NY, blob top, blue, 7¼" 20.00 28.00
☐ **COLUMBIA MINERAL WATER CO.**
St. Louis, MO, aqua, 7¼" 9.00 12.00
☐ **COLWOOD, B.C., HYGENIC MINERAL
WATER WORKS**
Blob top, crock, white and brown, 8" 20.00 28.00
☐ **CONGRESS & EMPIRE SPRING CO.**
"Hotchkiss Sons & Co. New York, Saratoga,
N.Y.," large hollow letters, "CW" in center, olive,
7" 55.00 68.00
☐ **CONGRESS & EMPIRE SPRING CO.**
Sarotoga, NY, reverse side "Congress Water,"
dark olive, 7¾" 38.00 48.00
☐ **CONGRESS & EMPIRE SPRING CO.**
In horseshoe shape, Big "C" in center, above it
"Hotchkiss Sons," under the big "C" New York,
Saratoga, N.Y., pint, under bottom two dots,
green, wood mold, 7¾" 30.00 40.00
☐ **CONGRESS & EMPIRE SPRING CO**
In a horseshoe shape, in center of it a big "C"
in frame, under it "Saratoga, N.Y.," tapered and
ring top, emerald green, 7¾" 55.00 75.00

Price Range

☐ **CONGRESS & EMPIRE SPRING CO.**
On back "Empire Water," dark green, under bottom a star, 3" diameter, 7½" 35.00 45.00

☐ **CONGRESS & EMPIRE SPRING CO.**
New York, Saratoga, Olive green, 7½" 24.00 32.00

☐ **CONGRESS & EMPIRE SPRING CO.**
In U, under it "Saratoga, N.Y." in center of big "C," Mineral Water, blue green, 9¼" 28.00 38.00

☐ **CONGRESS SPRING CO.**
Saratoga, NY, dark green, quart, tapered top and ring 35.00 45.00

☐ **CONGRESS SPRING CO.**
In horseshoe shape, in center large "C," under it "Saratoga, N.Y.," in back "Congress Water," quart, dark green, 7¾" 30.00 40.00

☐ **CONGRESS SPRINGS CO.**
S.S., N.Y. in a circle, under the bottle in center "#4", old beer type, wood mold, blue green, 9½" 12.00 18.00

☐ **CONGRESS SPRINGS CO.**
In horseshoe shape, in center a "G," Saratoga, NY, emerald green, tapered top and ring, 8" .. 42.00 52.00

☐ **CONGRESS WATER**
In two lines, tapered and ring top, green, 8" ... 42.00 52.00

☐ **CONNOR, C.**
In ½ moon letters, in back also "Union Glass Works, Phila.," tapered top with ring, pontil, green, 7½" (c. 1844) 70.00 90.00

☐ **CONONT'S, F.A.**
In ½ moon letters under it in 4 lines "Mineral Water, No. 252, Girod St., N.O.", ring top large "C" in background pontil aqua, 7" (c. 1850) ... 42.00 52.00

☐ **P. CONWAY, BOTTLER**
Phila, reverse side "No. 8 Hunty, 108 Filbert, Mineral Water," blob top, cobalt, 7¼" 28.00 38.00

☐ **COOPERS WELL WATER**
"BCOO" on back base, aqua, 9¾" 18.00 24.00

☐ **CORRY BELFAST**
In 2 hollow letters lines, ver. tea drop bottle, blob top, aqua, 9½" (c. 1910) 20.00 28.00

Price Range

☐ **COULEY'S FOUNTAIN OF HEALTH, NO. 38 BALTIMORE'S BALTIMORE**
Symbol of a fountain in the center, tall whiskey
bottle shape, pontil, aqua, 10″ 28.00 38.00

☐ **COURTLAND STREET 38**
NY, "T. Weddle's Celebrated Soda Mineral
Water" on back, graphite pontil, cobalt, 7½″ .. 80.00 100.00

☐ **COWLEY'S FOUNTAIN OF HEALTH**
Pontil, aqua, 9½″ 24.00 35.00

☐ **CROWN**
On shoulder, olive green, beer type bottle, 8½″ 7.00 10.00

☐ **CRYSTAL SPRING WATER**
In horseshoe shape, under it, "C.R. Brown Saratoga Springs, N.Y.," quart, green, 9½″ 100.00 135.00

☐ **CRYSTAL SPRING WATER CO.**
"N.Y." around base, aqua, 9½″ 6.00 9.00

☐ **DAWSON AND BLACKMAN**
Charleston, S.C., Union Glass Works, Phila, Superior Mineral Water, blue, 10-sided base, pint, 8″ 280.00 320.00

☐ **DAWSON AND BLACKMAN**
Charleston, S.C. Union Glass Works Phila, Supe-
rior Mineral Water, green, 10-sided base, pint, 8″ 280.00 320.00

☐ **DAWSON AND BLACKMAN**
Charleston, S. C. Union Glass Works Phila, Superior Mineral Water, teal, 10-sided base, pint, 8″ 280.00 365.00

☐ **DEARBORN, J & A**
In ¼ moon letters under it "New York," in back
"D" tapered blob top, pontil, blue, 7½″ (c. 1857) 80.00 100.00

☐ **DEEP SPRING**
Three-part mold, "C" in a diamond under bottom,
amber, 12¾″ 16.00 23.00

☐ **DOBBS FERRY MINERAL WATER CO.**
Dobbs Ferry, NY, aqua, 6½″ 6.00 9.00

☐ **DOBBS FERRY MINERAL WATER CO.**
"White Plains, NY" all inside slug plate, "CON-
TENTS 7 OZ. REGISTERED" on front at base,
amethyst and clear, 8″ 6.00 9.00

☐ **D.P.S. CO.**
Rochester, NY, U.S.A., amber, 3½″ 4.00 7.00

☐ **EAGLE SPRING DISTILLERY CO.**
On front, rectangular, amethyst, 7″ 5.00 7.00

Price Range

☐ **EAGLE'S W.E., SUPERIOR SODA &
MINERAL WATER**
All in 4 lines in black, large "W.E.," pontil, blob
top, blue, 7½" (c.1856) 90.00 110.00
☐ **G. EBBERWEIN**
"Savannah, Geo." in three lines on front, on back
between words "Mineral Water," monogram
"EGB," under bottom monogram "E," light blue,
blob top, 7½" 30.00 40.00
☐ Same except aqua 17.00 25.00
☐ Same except amber or dark blue 45.00 60.00
☐ Same except short neck, vertical in back Ginger
Ale, 8" 45.00 60.00
☐ Same except amber 25.00 34.00
☐ **ELK SPRING WATER CO.**
"Buffalo, N.Y." on front in oval slug plate, blob
top, ½ gallon, clear 17.00 25.00
☐ **C. ELLIS & CO.**
Phila., short neck, graphite pontil, green, 7" ... 50.00 65.00
☐ **EMPIRE SPRING CO.**
"E" in center, "Saratoga, N.Y.," back "Empire
Water," green, tapered top and ring, 7½" 30.00 40.00
☐ **EMPIRE WATER**
Pint, star under bottom, green 17.00 25.00
☐ **A.C. EVANS SUPᴿ MINERAL WATER**
"Wilmington, N.C." written vertically, graphite
pontil, green, 7½" 50.00 65.00
☐ **EXCELSIOR SPRINGS**
MO, "Roselle" under bottom, clear or amethyst,
8" 9.00 12.00
☐ **EXCELSIOR, SPRING**
Saratoga, NY, plain bottom, tapered top & ring,
emerald green, qt. (c.1870) 50.00 62.00
☐ **THE EXCELSIOR WATER**
Blue, ground pontil, 7" 50.00 62.00
☐ **THE EXCELSIOR WATER**
On eight panels, blob top, graphite pontil, green,
7¼" 70.00 90.00
☐ **FARREL'S MINERAL WATER**
Evansville, IN., graphite pontil, aqua, 7½" 52.00 62.00

Price Range

☐ **FRANKLIN SPRING, MINERAL WATER**
Ballston, SPA Saratoga Co. N.Y. Mineral Water
bottle, emerald green, pt. 110.00 145.00

☐ **FRIEDRICHSHALL, C. OPPEL & CO.**
On the bottom, label, blob top, green, 9" 8.00 11.00

☐ **J.N. GERDES**
S.F. Mineral Water, blob top, green, eight-sided,
7½" 35.00 45.00

☐ **J.N. GERDES S.F. MINERAL WATER**
Vertical on four panels, eight panels in all, blob
top, aqua blue, 7⅛" 35.00 45.00

☐ **GETTYSBURG KATALYSINE WATER**
X under bottom, green, 10" 23.00 29.00

☐ **GEYSER SPRING**
Saratoga Springs, State of NY, light blue, 7¾" 28.00 38.00

☐ **GEYSER SPRING SARATOGA SPRINGS**
State of New York, "THE SARATOGA SPOUTIN'
SPRING," pint, aqua, 7½" 30.00 40.00

☐ **GILBEY'S SPEY ROYAL**
Label, three dots and number under bottom, golden amber, 8" 13.00 18.00

☐ **GLACIER SPOUTING SPRING**
"Glacier" misspelled, in horseshoe shape, letters
under it "Saratoga Springs, N.Y.," in back a fountain, green, pint 145.00 175.00

☐ **GLENDALE SPRING CO., THIS BOTTLE NOT
TO BE SOLD,**
Blob top, aqua, 7" 11.00 16.00

☐ **GRANITE STATE SPRING WATER CO.**
Akinson Depot, NY, Trademark embossed, two
Indians taking water from stream and large gran-
ite rock, crown top, aqua, 10" 15.00 22.00

☐ **GREAT BEAR SPRING**
"Fulton, N.Y., This Bottle Is Loaned And Never
Sold" on bottom, aqua, 11½" 11.00 16.00

☐ **CHARLES S. GROVE & CO. SPARKLING
MINERAL WATER**
"No. 30 Canal St., Boston," in a diamond shape,
reverse side "T.B.N.S. Deposit On Same, Refund
When Returned," aqua, 7½" 20.00 28.00

☐ **GUILFORD MINERAL SPRING WATER**
Blue green, 9¾" 16.00 23.00

Price Range

☐ **GUILFORD MINERAL SPRING WATER**
Green 16.00   23.00
☐ **GUILFORD MINERAL, SPRING WATER**
Guilford, VT, tapered top with ring, yellow green,
qt. 80.00   100.00
☐ **GUILFORD & STAR SPRING**
Green or amber 16.00   23.00
☐ **GUILFORD MINERAL SPRING WATER**
Inside of a diamond in center, also "G.M.S.,"
under it "Guilford, Vt.," short neck, dark green,
10″ 32.00   42.00
☐ **HANBURY SMITH**
Light olive, 8″ 7.00   10.00
☐ **HANBURY SMITH'S MINERAL WATERS**
Dark green, 7¾″ 28.00   38.00
☐ **HARRIS**
Amber, 9¼″ 6.00   9.00
☐ **HARRIS ALBANY MINERAL WATERS**
Graphite pontil, tapered top, aqua, 7¼″ 28.00   38.00
☐ **DR. HARTLEY'S MINERAL WATER**
"Phila" in front, in back "Improved Patent," pon-
til, flared top, light emerald green, 6¾″ 55.00   70.00
☐ **HASKINS SPRINGS CO.**
Shutesbury, MA, on rear is embossed "H.S.G.,"
with "H" trademark, pint, emerald green, 7¼″ 150.00   170.00
☐ **HATHORN**
Saratoga, NY, Amber, 9¼″ 25.00   35.00
☐ **HAWTHORN SPRING**
Saratoga, NY, pint, amber, 8″ 20.00   25.00
☐ **HAWTHORN SPRING**
In horseshoe shape, under this "Saratoga, N.Y.,"
dark amber, under bottle a "drop" and a letter
"H," round, 7½″ 35.00   45.00
☐ Same except bottom plain, very dark green 35.00   45.00
☐ **HAWTHORN WATER**
Saratoga, NY, paper label, amber, 9½″ 5.00   8.00
☐ **HEADMAN**
In a dome shape, under it "Excelsior Mineral
Water," reverse "F.W.H." in hollow letters,
graphite pontil, green, 7½″ 45.00   65.00
☐ **HECKINGS MINERAL WATER**
Green 15.00   22.00

R. & J. Adams/Druggists/St. Louis—Superior/Mineral/Waters, round, iron pontil, applied top, aqua, **$100.00–$135.00**

Price Range

☐ **HIGH ROCK CONGRESS SPRING**
Saratoga, NY, tapered top & ring, qt., yellow olive
(c.1870) **70.00   90.00**
☐ **HIGHROCK CONGRESS SPRING**
"Rock," under it "C&W, SAT, NY," green **70.00   90.00**
☐ Same except amber **45.00   65.00**
☐ **HOLMES & CO. MINERAL WATER**
Ground pontil, blue, 7½" **45.00   65.00**
☐ **HOLMES & CO.**
Ground pontil, "Mineral Water" in back, light blue,
7¼" **45.00   65.00**
☐ **HONESDALE GLASS WORKS, AP**
"PA" backwards, "Mineral Water" in back, aqua,
7½" **22.00   29.00**
☐ **HONESDALE GLASS WORKS, PA.**
In a dome shape, reverse side "Mineral Water,"
graphite pontil, blob top, green **60.00   80.00**
☐ **J. HOPKINS**
Phila., pontil, short neck, dark aqua **24.00   32.00**

Price Range

☐ **HORAN P.**
"75 West 27th St., N.Y." all in 4 lines, pontil, blob
top, green, 7½", (c.1860) 55.00   75.00

☐ **HUBENER, J.**
In ¼ moon letters under it "New York," in back
"Mineral Water" big "H", tapered top, pontil,
blue, 8" 75.00   95.00

☐ **HYGEIA WATER**
"Cons. Ice Co., Memphis, Tenn." around base,
aqua, 9¾" 6.00   9.00

☐ **HYPERION SPOUTING SPRING**
In a horseshoe shape, under it "Saratoga, N.Y.,"
in back "American Kissinger Water," tapered and
ring top, aqua, pint 140.00   175.00

☐ **IMPROVED MINERAL WATER**
Short tapered top, graphite pontil, cobalt, 7½"   38.00   52.00

☐ **IMPROVED MINERAL WATER**
Blob top, graphite pontil, blue, 6¼" 31.00   40.00

☐ **INDIAN SPRING**
In center, Indian head under bottom, aqua, 10½"   15.00   22.00

☐ **IODINE SPRING, L.**
South Hero, VT, Qt. golden amber, tapered top,
with ring 175.00   200.00

☐ **JACKSON NAPA SODA**
On front, in back "Natural Mineral Water, Jack-
sons T.B.I.N.S.," aqua, 7½" 9.00   12.00

☐ **JACKSON'S NAPA SODA SPRING**
On front, reverse side "Natural Mineral Water,"
blob top, aqua, 7½" 8.00   12.00

☐ **JOHNSTON & CO.**
"Phila" in large block letters, on back large fancy
2" "J.," tapered top, sea green, 6¾" 15.00   22.00

☐ **JUBILEE SPRING WATER CO.**
"101" under bottom, "5 pt" on back, aqua, 11½"   15.00   22.00

☐ **J. KENNEDY, MINERAL WATER
"PITTSBURG"**
In three lines on back, script letters "J.K.," graph-
ite pontil, blob top, green, 7½" 38.00   48.00

☐ **KISSINGER WATER**
Dark olive, 6¼" 32.00   42.00

Price Range

☐ **KISSINGER WATER PATTERSON & BROZEAU**
Tapered top, olive, 7" 17.00 24.00

☐ **D.A. KNOWLTON**
In a dome shape, under it "Saratoga, N.Y.," tapered top, olive, 9½" 42.00 55.00

☐ **KNOWLTON, D.A.**
"Saratoga, N.Y." in 3 lines, tapered top & ring, em. green pt. (c.1850) 45.00 60.00
☐ Same except amber 150.00 200.00
☐ Same except blue 150.00 200.00

☐ **R.T. LACY, NEW KENT CO.**
"VA., PROP. BELMONT LITHIA WATER" in a circle, in center two men turning a hand drill, under that "DEUS AQUAM CREAVIT BIBAMUS" and "AD 1877," blue green. 10" 25.00 35.00

☐ **J. LAMPPIN & CO. MINERAL WATER**
MADISON, LA, in back "Madison Bottling Establishment," graphite pontil, blob top, blue green, 6½" 65.00 85.00

☐ **LIVITI DISTILLED WATER CO.**
"PASADENA, CAL." around base in small letters, crown top, "I.P.G. CO. 841 LIVITI" on bottom, round, ABM, tapered neck, aqua, 7¾" 5.00 8.00

☐ **J.A. LOMAX**
14 & 16 Charles Place, Chicago, four-piece mold, amber, 9¾" 15.00 22.00

☐ **LYNCH & CLARK, NEW YORK MINERAL WATER**
Tapered top & ring pontil, olive amber, pt. 110.00 140.00

☐ **LYTTON SPRING**
In center a pelican, "SWEET DRINKS" under it, in three lines "P.M.H. Co., San Francisco, C.H.B.," aqua, 6½" 15.00 22.00

☐ **MACNISH & SON**
"JAMAICA" In 2 ver. lines, semi round bottom, applied crown top, aqua, 9½" (c. 1910) 13.00 18.00

☐ **MADDEN MINERAL WATER CO.**
Label, aqua, 7" 9.00 12.00

Price Range

☐ **MADURO, I.L. CANAL ZONE**
All in a water mellow circle, marble bottle, applied
top, aqua, 9¼″ (c. 1910) 15.00 22.00
☐ Same except, "Jr." add to name 13.00 18.00
☐ **MAGEE'S**
Aqua, 10½″ 12.00 17.00
☐ **MAGNETIC SPRING**
Amber 29.00 40.00
☐ **MAGNETIC SPRING**
Henniker, NH, tapered top & ring, qt. Go. amber
plain bottom, (c. 1868) 90.00 110.00
☐ **J. MANKE & CO.**
"Savannah" in two lines, in back "Mineral
Water," blob top, aqua, 7″ 16.00 24.00
☐ **MASSENA SPRING, WATER, MINERAL
WATER**
Tapered top & ring, emerald green, qt. 60.00 80.00
☐ **FREDERICK MEINCKE**
In horseshoe shape, in center of horseshoe
"1882," under it in two lines, "Savannah, Geo.,"
on back 2″ monogram "F.M.," on top of it "Min-
eral Water," under it "Water," under bottom is
monogram M, cobalt, 7¾″ 42.00 62.00
☐ **MEINCKE & EBBERWEIN**
"Savannah, Geo." in horseshoe shape, in center
"1882," on back monogram between words
"Mineral Water," "M&E," under bottom mono-
gram "ME," cobalt, blob top 50.00 65.00
☐ **MERCHANT**
Lockport, NY, plain bottom tapered top & ring,
emerald green, qt., (c.1870) 55.00 70.00
☐ **MICUELPIRIS MINERAL WATER**
No. 334 Royal St., N.O., ground pontil, aqua, 7½″ 45.00 65.00
☐ **MIDDLETOWN HEALING SPRING**
Amber 25.00 35.00
☐ **MIDDLETOWN MINERAL SPRING, NATURE
REMEDY**
Middletown, VT, tapered top with rings, emerald
green, qt. 80.00 100.00
☐ **MIDDLETOWN SPRING**
VT, amber 18.00 25.00

Price Range

☐ **J. & D. MILLER**
Marietta, OH, reverse side "Mineral Water," blob.
top, aqua, 7½" 16.00   22.00

☐ **MILLS SELTZER SPRING**
Under bottom "M," blob top, aqua, 7½" 16.00   22.00

☐ **MINERAL WATER**
Tapered top, graphite pontil, green, 7¼" 35.00   45.00

☐ Same as above except cobalt 60.00   80.00

☐ **MINERAL WATER**
Tapered top, six panels, improved pontil, dark
green, 7" 28.00   39.00

☐ **MINERAL WATER**
Label, light green, 10¾" 6.00   9.00

☐ **MINERAL WATER**
Ground pontil, green, 7¼" 31.00   43.00

☐ **MINERAL WATER**
In ¼ moon letters, tapered top, pontil, 7", green
(c.1850) 31.00   43.00

☐ **MINERAL WATER**
Troy, NY, large entwined heavily embossed "CC"
on back, unusual bottom, lettering is "C. Clemin-
shaw" in wavy letters across center of bottom,
edge of bottom is embossed "vitating stopper -
PAT. OCT 11th 1864," aqua, 7", blob top 18.00   30.00

☐ **MISSISQUOI. A, SPRING, PAPOOSE**
MINERAL WATER
(c. 1868) Tapered top & ring, plain base, Y. olive,
qt. 145.00   175.00

☐ **MOSES POLAND WATER**
Figural Mineral Water bottle, tapered top, plain
bottom, aqua, qt. (c. 1875) 34.00   48.00

☐ Same except some have a screw cap, ABM (they
were made for Hiram Ricker Co., c.1885). Just a
few of the originals are left or survived, then came
in different sizes, colors are clear, green and
amber 38.00   48.00

☐ **MURTHA & CO.**
In front running ver., in back "Mineral Water" in
2 lines running ver., tapered top, pontil, green,
7½" (c.1842) 65.00   85.00

Price Range

☐ **NAPA SODA, PHIL CADUC**
Reverse "Natural Mineral Water," tapered neck,
blob top, blue, 7½" 30.00 40.00

☐ **NATURAL**
In center, a man with sleeping cap and handkerchief around neck, under it "MINERAI WATER,"
blob top, 7½" 15.00 22.00

☐ **NEW ALMADEN**
In a horseshoe shape, under it "MINERAL
WATER," blob top, aqua, 6¾" 14.00 20.00

☐ **NEW ALMADEN MINERAL WATER, W&W**
On panels, ten panels, tapered top, blob top,
graphite pontil, green, 7½" 42.00 62.00

☐ **N.Y. BOTTLING CO.**
NY, star on shoulder "10cts. Deposit" on back,
"This Bottle is Loaned, 10¢ Will Be Paid For Its
Return" under bottom, aqua, 12" 8.00 11.00

☐ **OAK ORCHARD ACID SPRING**
On shoulder "H.W. BOSTWICK AGT., NO. 574
BROADWAY, N.Y.," on bottom From "F. Hutchins Factory Glass, Lockport, N.Y.," light amber,
9" 38.00 48.00

☐ **O.K. BOTTLING CO.**
O.K., in center "526, 528, 530, W. 38th St., N.Y.,"
reverse side Indian holding a flag, aqua, 10¾" 20.00 28.00

☐ **O'KEEFE BROS. HIGH GRADE MINERAL
WATER**
Mattewan, NY, with monogram, crown top, ame-
thyst, 7¾" 6.00 9.00

☐ **OLYMPIA WATER CO.**
In a dome shape, under it "MINERAL WELLS,
TEX.," blob top, several different sizes, aqua .. 20.00 28.00

☐ **OLYMPIA WATER CO.**
Mineral Well, TX, aqua, 9½" 11.00 16.00

☐ **ORIGINAL CALIF. MINERAL WATER CO.**
Sweetwater Springs, San Diego, CA, aqua, 11" 16.00 23.00

☐ **E.O. OTTENVILLE**
Large "E.O." on front, reverse "Ottenville, Nashville, Tenn.," amber, 9¼" 28.00 38.00

☐ **P**
On base, round bottle, blob top, aqua, 9¾"
(c.1900) 8.00 11.00

Price Range

☐ **PABLO & CO.**
Mineral Water Factory on back, aqua, 7½" **14.00** **19.00**

☐ **PACIFIC CONGRESS WATER**
On bottom, crown top, four-piece mold, aqua, 8¼" **7.00** **10.00**

☐ **PACIFIC CONGRESS WATER**
In horseshoe shape, under it "WATER," applied top, light blue, 7" **11.00** **16.00**

☐ **PARAISO MINERAL WATER BOTTLED BY P. STEGELMAN**
"Salinas, Cal." on front, four-piece mold, crown top, aqua, 8¼" **7.00** **9.00**

☐ **PATTERSON & BRAZEAU, VICHY WATER**
NY, dark green, 6¾" **7.00** **9.00**

☐ **PAVILION & UNITED STATE SPRING CO.**
Dark olive, 3" diameter, 7¾" **28.00** **38.00**

☐ **PARIS, MIGUEL, MINERAL WATER**
"No. 334, Royal St., N.O." all in 5 lines, in back Big "P", blob ring top, pontil, aqua, 7½" (c.1850) **45.00** **65.00**

☐ **P.H. CRYSTAL SPRING WATER COMPANY**
"N.Y." around base, crown top, tenpin shape, aqua, 9¼" **7.00** **9.00**

☐ **POLAND WATER**
Aqua **30.00** **40.00**

☐ **PRIEST NATURAL SODA**
Aqua **8.00** **11.00**

☐ **PRIEST NAPA**
A natural mineral water recarbonated at St. Helena from The Priest, Mineral Spring, Napa Co., CA, applied crown, aqua, 7¼" **8.00** **11.00**

☐ **PURE NATURAL WATERS CO.**
"Pittsburg, PA." inside fancy shield, with house embossed in center, crown top, ABM, aqua, 12¼" **5.00** **8.00**

☐ **THE PURITAN WATER CO.**
NY, aqua, 12¼" **7.00** **9.00**

☐ **QUAKER SPRINGS, I.W. MEADER & CO., SARATOGA CO.**
"N.Y." all in 3 lines, tapered top & ring, plain bottom, green and teal blue, qt. (c. 1880) **100.00** **130.00**

Price Range

☐ **R.C. & T.**
In hollow letters under it "New York," tapered
top, pontil, green, 7½" (c. 1880) 65.00   90.00
☐ **ROCKBRIDGE ALUM WATER**
Aqua, 9½" 11.00   15.00
☐ **ROUND LAKE MINERAL WATER**
Saratoga, NY, amber 7¾" 90.00   110.00
☐ **RUTHERFORDS PREMIUM MINERAL
WATER**
Ground pontil, dark olive, 7½" 60.00   80.00
☐ **RUTHERFORD & KA**
On shoulder, three-piece mold, graduated collar,
olive amber, 10½" 28.00   38.00
☐ **JOHN RYAN**
"Excelsior Mineral water, Savannah" in front,
back "Unionglass Work, Phila. This Bottle Is
Never Sold," cobalt, improved pontil, 7" 45.00   65.00
☐ **ST. REGIS MASSENA WATER**
Green 12.00   17.00
☐ **SAN FRANCISCO GLASS WORKS**
Tapered neck, blob top, sea green, 6⅞" 14.00   19.00
☐ **SAN SOUCI SPOUTING SPRING**
In a horseshoe shape, in center a fountain and
"Ballston Spa, N.Y.," tapered top and ring, aqua,
pint or amber, quart 120.00   150.00
☐ **SARATOGA SPRING**
Honey amber, 9¾" 30.00   40.00
☐ **SARATOGA RED SPRING**
Green, 7½" 50.00   65.00
☐ **SARATOGA**
Under it a big "A," under it "Spring Co., N.Y.," ta-
pered top and ring, olive green, round, pint and
quart, 3¼" x 9" 80.00   100.00
☐ **SARATOGA SELTZER SPRING**
Olive green, quart, tapered top and ring, 8" . . .   32.00   42.00
☐ Same except pint, 6¼" 55.00   80.00
☐ **SARATOGA VICHY SPOUTING SPRING**
In a horseshoe shape, in center a hollow letter
"V," under it "Saratoga, N.Y.," tapered top, aqua,
7½" 40.00   50.00

Price Range

☐ **J. SCHWEPPE & CO.**
"51 Berners Street Oxford Street, Genuine Superior, Aerated Waters," around bottle, tear drop type, light green, 8½" 30.00 40.00

☐ **SEVEN SPRINGS MINERAL WATER CO.**
Goldsboro, NC, aqua, 8" 7.00 9.00

☐ **SHASTA WATER CO.**
Mineral Water Co., amber, 10½" 7.00 9.00

☐ **E.P. SHAW & CO. LTD. WAKEFIELD**
Paper label, green, 5" 6.00 9.00

☐ **SHOCO LITHIA SPRING CO.**
Lincoln, NB, crown top, aqua, 7¾" 6.00 9.00

☐ **SMITH AND CO.**
Charleston, SC, Union Glass Works Phila. Superior Mineral Water, 10-sided, bottom blue, pint, 8¹/₁₆" 180.00 215.00

☐ **S. SMITHS, KNICKERBOCKER MINERAL & SODA WATER**
NY, pontil, green, 7" 50.00 65.00

Carpenter—Cobb—Knickerbocker—Soda Water—Saratoga—Springs, ten-sided, iron pontil, applied lip, light green, **$300.00–$350.00**

Price Range

☐ **SPARKLING LONDONBERRY SPRING LETHA WATER**
Nashua, NH Label, green, 11⅝" 4.00 6.00

☐ **STAR SPRING**
Saratoga, NY, aqua 25.00 35.00

☐ **STAR SPRING CO.**
Saratoga, NY, with trademark of a star, pint, amber, 8" 27.00 35.00

☐ **STEINIKE & WEINLIG SCHUTZ MARKE**
Embossed hand holding some tools, "Seltzers" in large letters on back, three-piece mold, blob top, emerald green, 9¾" 13.00 20.00

☐ **STODDARD MAGNETIC SPRING**
Hennicker, NH, amber 50.00 65.00

☐ **SUMMIT MINERAL WATER**
"J.H." in three lines, blob top, green, 7½" 11.00 15.00

☐ **SUNSET SPRING WATER**
Catskill Mt., Hames Falls, NY, on base "This Bottle Loaned Please Return," aqua, 13" 13.00 20.00

☐ **SYRACUSE SPRINGS**
Different sizes, amber 42.00 52.00

☐ **TAYLOR**
"Never surrenders" in 3 lines, slug plate in back "Union Glass Works, Phila." in 2 lines, tapered top, pontil, blue, 7¼" (c. 1850) 120.00 150.00

☐ **THOMPSON'S**
In center "Premium Mineral Waters," tenpin shape, reverse side "Union Soda Works, San Francisco," blob top, aqua, 7½" 15.00 21.00

☐ **TOLENAS SODA SPRINGS**
Reverse side "Natural Mineral Water," tapered neck, blob top, aqua blue, 7" 15.00 21.00

☐ **TRITON SPOUTING SPRING**
In horseshoe shape, in center block letter "T," under it, "Saratoga, NY," in back "Triton Water," pint, aqua 90.00 115.00

☐ **TWEDDLES CELEBRATED SODA OR MINERAL WATER**
Reverse side "Courtland Street," in center "#38," under it "New York," tapered top, graphite pontil, cobalt, 7½" 50.00 65.00

Price Range

☐ **UNDERWOOD SPRING**
"Falmouth Foreside, ME." on front in oval slug
plate, crown top, 8⅞" 6.00   9.00

☐ **UNGARS OFNER BITTERWASSER**
Green, 9½" 6.00   9.00
☐ Same as above with no embossing 3.00   5.00

☐ **UNION GLASS WORKS**
"Phila," under it "SUPERIOR MINERAL
WATER," panel base, blob top, graphite pontil,
blue, 7" 50.00   65.00

☐ **UNION SPRING**
"Saratoga, N.Y." in a circle, green, 8" 80.00 120.00

☐ **UTE CHIEF OF MINERAL WATER**
"Maniton, Colo., U.T." on base, crown top, clear
or purple, 8" 5.00   8.00

☐ **VARUNA MINERAL WATER WELLS**
In a horseshoe shape, "Richwood, Ohio", under
it "I. Miller, Prop. T.B.N.S." and "must be returned," clear, 6½" 15.00   22.00

☐ **VERMONT SPRING SAXE & CO.**
Green 15.00   22.00

☐ **VERMONT SPRING, SAXE & CO.**
"Sheldon, VT," Qt., yellow green, tapered top
with rings 70.00   90.00
☐ Same except emerald green 70.00   90.00

☐ **VERONICA MEDICINAL SPRING WATER**
Amber, 10½" 7.00   9.00

☐ **VERONICA MINERAL WATER**
Around shoulder, square, amber, clear, 10¼" 8.00   11.00
☐ Same as above except ABM 6.00   9.00

☐ **VERONICA MINERAL WATER**
On square shoulder, square, amber, 10½" 8.00   11.00

☐ **VICHY ETAT**
Label, reverse side embossed "Establishment
Thermal De Vichy," cobalt, 6¾" 20.00   28.00

☐ **VICHY WATER CULLUMS SPRING**
Choctaw Co., AL, dark olive, 7¼" 35.00   45.00

☐ **VICHY WATER**
"Patterson & Brazeau, N.Y." vertically on front,
pint size, dark green, 6¾" 13.00   20.00

Price Range

☐ **WASHINGTON, SPRING**
"Saratoga, N.Y." in 4 lines, plain bottom, tapered
top & ring, O. green, pt. 50.00   68.00
☐ Same except single ring lip 50.00   68.00
☐ Also in green 50.00   68.00
☐ Also in amber 80.00 120.00
☐ **WASHINGTON SPRING**
Picture of Washington's head, pint, emerald
green, 6¼" 55.00   80.00
☐ Same except quart, 8¼" 30.00   40.00
☐ **WELLER BOTTLING WORKS**
Saratoga, NY, blob top, aqua 8.00   12.00
☐ **G.W. WESTON & CO.**
Saratoga, NY, pontil, pint, olive-green, 8" 30.00   40.00
☐ **WHELAN TROY**
Embossed tulips, Hutchinson, 7½" 11.00   15.00
☐ **D.J. WHELAN**
"Mineral Water" on back, aqua, 7½" 10.00   14.00
☐ **WHITE SULPHUR WATER**
Blue green, 8¾" 11.00   15.00
☐ **WITTER**
"Witter Medical Spring" under bottom, amber,
9½" 7.00   9.00
☐ **WITTER SPRING WATER**
"Witter Medical Springs Co." under bottom,
amber, 9½" 7.00   9.00
☐ **WITTER SPRING WATER, W.M.S. CO.**
"San Francisco" around shoulder and bottom,
amber, 9¼" 10.00   14.00
☐ **W.S.S. WATER**
Machine made, 9-2-8 O.I. with diamond shape
under bottom, green, 5½" 5.00   7.00
☐ **XXX($_{XXX}^X$)**
In two lines, blob top, graphite pontil, green, 7"   25.00   35.00
☐ **ADAM W. YOUNG**
"Canton, Ohio" in slug plate, squat shape, gradu-
ated collar, aqua, 9¼" 7.00   9.00
☐ **ZAREMBO MINERAL SPRING CO.**
Seattle, WA, blue, tapered top, 7½" 16.00   22.00

NAILSEA-TYPE BOTTLES

Nailsea-Type bottles are stunning creations. They are classic examples of the art of glassblowing. These beautiful bottles feature loopings or stripes and often applied glass beadings or rings. Shapes vary from flasks and bellow to powder horn and oval. Many bright colors are used including deep red, blue and green. Many Nailsea-Type bottles have stands.

The bottles in this section were made in England from the 1850s to the 1880s.

Price Range

☐ **BELLOWS BOTTLE**
Long narrow neck, bulbous body, footed on stand, applied beading on body, clear with white and pink looping, 10½" **220.00 260.00**

☐ **BELLOWS BOTTLE**
Long narrow neck, long teardrop shaped body, on stand, applied beading on sides, white and clear with blue loopings, 15" **175.00 195.00**

☐ **BELLOWS BOTTLE**
Small narrow neck, bulbous body, on stand, applied beading on body, clear with narrow red and white loopings, 10¾" **80.00 110.00**

☐ **BOOT BOTTLE**
Boot shaped, clear with narrow white loopings, 9" **120.00 140.00**

☐ **CARAFE**
Cylinder neck, bulbous body, applied shoulder ring, footed, clear with close white loopings, 10" **175.00 225.00**

☐ **FLASK**
Short neck, bulbous shoulders, narrow base, blue with narrow white loopings, 6½" **500.00 550.00**

☐ **FLASK**
Small neck, flat oval body, white with red and blue loopings, 7½" **130.00 150.00**

☐ **FLASK**
Small neck, teardrop shape, very narrow base, green with white loopings, 8¾" **150.00 200.00**

☐ **GEMEL BOTTLE**
Oval shape, two spouts, blue with wide white loopings, 8¾" **150.00 175.00**

Bellows Bottle, *long narrow neck, long teardrop shaped body, on stand, applied beading on side, white and clear with blue loopings, 15".*
$175.00–$195.00

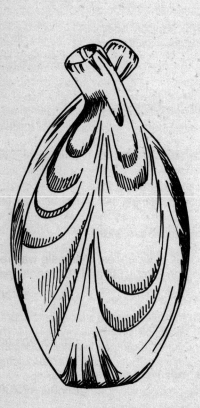

Gemel Bottle, *oval shape, two spouts, blue with wide white loopings, 8¾".*
$150.00–$175.00

Price Range

☐ **GEMEL BOTTLE**
Teardrop shape body, two spouts, on stand, applied decoration on side, clear with narrow white loopings, 10" 125.00 135.00
☐ **POWDER HORN BOTTLE**
Powder horn shape, applied ring decoration, on stand, clear with blue loopings, 12" 175.00 200.00
☐ **POWDER HORN BOTTLE**
Powder horn shape, applied ring decoration, on stand, clear with large white loopings and narrow red stripes, 13" 225.00 275.00

POISON

Poison bottles have become more popular in the collector market recently. The mere deadliness of their original contents gives poison bottles a special allure. Though it would have been senseless to promote sales of such products by using decorative bottles, quite a few poison bottles are ornamental—not for sales reasons, but to make them readily identifiable on the home shelf. The figural skull and crossbones or just the skull, is the most familiar. For many years, collectors were prejudice against these bottles to the point where they were almost offended by them. Today, it is quite a different story. They're recognized as historical and decorative objects, and no one is offended at the sight of them any longer.

The sale of poison in bottles dates back to very early times. For centuries, chemists dispensed toxic substances in vials stoppered with corks. The poisons of the ancients were chiefly derived from vegetable substances, such as the hemlock Socrates drank to carry out his death sentence. They were used (as were poisons of later times) in very small quantities as ingredients in medicine, usually as stimulants or relaxants.

Because of the abuse of poisonous substances, their sale was restricted or prohibited in much of Europe in the 18th and 19th centuries. There was the further danger of such products falling into the hands of children.

However, the society had a need for these preparations, and to prevent the sale of everything which could be poisonous was unfair to the public. Solvents used in cleaning, for example, were a necessity article in the Industrial Age. Attention was then focused on providing the containers with unmistakable identification, either by shape or a special texture or other means, to prevent accidental consumption.

As early as 1853, the American Pharmaceutical Association recommended national laws to identify poison bottles. The American Medical Association suggested in 1872 that poison containers be uniformly identified by a rough surface on one side and the word "poison" on the other. Despite much discussion and debate on the subject, no laws for uniform poison containers were ever enacted. Each manufacturer remained at liberty to identify his product and provide warning in whatever fashion he selected.

The skull and crossbones became the traditional symbol of poisonous substances, at first in the form of figural bottles then gradually being downplayed to the point where it ended up as a tiny symbol on bottle labels of the 20th century. The skull and crossbones were originally a Christian religious symbol, indicating life after death. It came to signify poison after pirates used it on their flags in the 18th century.

Most poison bottles are strong shades of blue or brown. Colorless specimens are very uncommon; there was too much danger of them being mistaken for tonic bottles (remember, literacy was not high in the 19th century—not everybody could read labels on bottles). In addition to the skull and crossbones, another shape sometimes used was the coffin, or sometimes "longbones." Containers were also likely to have quilted or ribbed surfaces to further distinguish them. This was probably intended as an aid to blind persons.

John Howell of Newton, New Jersey, designed the first safety closure in 1886. However, such closures were not considered vital until poison bottles began to be made in less identifiable shapes. This did not occur until well into the 20th century.

	Price Range	
□ **ACID,**		
Round, clear or green, 6⅜"	3.00	4.00
□ Amber, vertical ribs all around, rectangular, ring collar, ABM, 3¼"	5.00	8.00
□ **SP. AMMON AR.**		
Label, clear, 9½"	10.00	15.00
□ **BALTIMORE, MD.**		
Under bottom, amber, 3"	3.00	4.00
□ **BETUL-OL, W.T. CO. U.S.A.**		
Under bottom, clear, 4¼"	3.00	5.00
□ **BOWKERS PLROX**		
"670-2" under bottom, clear or amethyst, 4¼"	3.00	5.00
□ Same as above except 8"	14.00	19.00
□ **BOWMANS**		
In script, "Drug Stores" on side panels, ribs, hexagonal cobalt, 5¼"	35.00	50.00

Price Range

☐ **BROWNS RAT KILLER**
Under it "C. WAKEFIELD CO.", applied lip, aqua,
3" 7.00   11.00

☐ **BROWN**
Three-sided, ABM, 4½" 3.00   5.00

☐ **CARBOLIC ACID**
3 oz. on each side, poison crosses all around it,
ring top, cobalt, 5" 22.00   32.00

☐ Same as above except no carbolic acid, 8½" .. 38.00   48.00

☐ **THE CLARKE FLUID CO.**
Cincinnati "Poison" on side, "8 to 64 oz. graduated measure" on other side, clear or amethyst,
quart size 20.00   30.00

☐ **C.L.C. CO PATENT APPLIED FOR**
Under bottom, cobalt, 2¼" 5.00   8.00

☐ **C.L.C. & CO. PATENT APPLIED FOR**
Under bottom, hexagonal, emerald green, ½
ounce to 16 ounces 25.00   35.00

☐ Same as above except cobalt 35.00   50.00

☐ Cobalt blue, seven concave vertical panels on
front half, ½ oz. at top on front, square collar,
oval, ABM, 2⅞" 4.00   6.00

☐ **COCAINE HYDROCHLOR POISON**
Label, triangular, vertical ribs, ring top, amber, 5"   12.00   17.00

☐ **CROSSBONES & STAR**
Snap-on top, amber, 2½" 22.00   30.00

☐ **CURTICE BROS. PRESERVES, ROCHESTER, N.Y.**
Four-part mold, clear or amethyst, 7" 14.00   19.00

☐ **DAGGER**
On front, square, pouring lip, aqua, 5" 12.00   17.00

☐ **D.D.D.**
Clear or amethyst, 3¾" and 5½" 5.00   8.00

☐ **D.D. CHEMICAL CO**
NY, "SAMPLE" on front of panel, square, amber,
5" 2.00   3.00

☐ **DEAD STUCK**
"Non-poisonous, won't stain" in small letters,
"For Bugs" on same line but small letters, in cen-
ter a bug, on each side Trademark, under it "Got-

Price Range

tlieb Marshall & Co., Cersal, Germany, Philadelphia, Pa." in three lines, under bottle "X," aqua, 7" tall, 3½" x 1½" 22.00 32.00

☐ **DEPOSE**
On bottom, four-cornered, label reads "Riodine Organic Iodine 50 capsules," 4⅛" tall, 1¾" x ½" neck 6.00 9.00

☐ **FINLAY DICKS & CO DISTRIBUTORS**
New Orleans, LA Dick's Ant Destroyer, sheared top, clear or amethyst, 6½" 6.00 9.00

☐ **DPS**
Below skull and cross on front, "Poison" on each side, cross on four sides, ring top, cobalt 8.00 12.00

☐ **DURFREE EMBALMING FLUID CO.**
8 to 64 oz. graduated measure, clear or amethyst, ½ gallon 16.00 23.00

☐ **DURFREE EMBALMING FLUID CO.**
Clear or amethyst, 8¾" 20.00 28.00

☐ **ECORC:QUINGUINA PULV:**
Pontil, clear, painted brown, 5¾" 15.00 22.00

☐ **ELI LILLY & CO.**
"Poison" on each panel, amber, 2", four other different sizes 7.00 10.00

☐ **E.R.S.&S.**
Under bottom, vertical ribbing on all sides, space for label, double ring top, square, cobalt, 4½" 15.00 22.00

☐ **EVANS MEDICAL LTD., LIVERPOOL**
Label, Chloroform B.A., Poison, number and U.Y.B. under bottom, ABM, amber, 6½" 5.00 8.00

☐ **EXTRAIT FL: DE QUINQUINA**
Amber, 6½" 15.00 22.00

☐ **FERRIS & CO. LTD.**
"Bristol" near base, "poison" in center, vertical ribbing, wide ring top, aqua, 7½" 11.00 15.00

☐ **FORTUNE WARD DRUG CO.**
"Larkspur Lotion Poison, 119 Maderson, Memphis, Tenn." on label, on each side "For External Use Only," ring top, amber, 5½" 7.00 11.00

☐ **FREDERIA**
Vertical, flask type, hobnail clover, clear, ½ pint 55.00 75.00

Price Range

☐ **THE FROSER TABLET CO.**
St. Louis, NY, Brooklyn, Chicago, Sulphate poison tablets, label, ABM, clear, 5¾" 5.00 8.00

☐ **F.S. & CO. P.M.**
On base, POISON vertically, surrounded by dots, two sides plain, rectangular, ring top, amber, 2¾" 11.00 16.00

☐ **J.G. GODDING & CO, APOTHECARIES**
"Boston, Mass." in three lines in center, ribs on each side, ring top, cobalt, 4⅛" hexagon 18.00 25.00

☐ **GRASSELLI ARSENATE OF LEAD**
"POISON" on shoulder, different sizes 55.00 70.00

☐ **HB CO**
Under bottom within an indented circle, glass top ornaments with "Poison" around half of bottle, nobs and lines, very few lines or nobs in back, cobalt, 6½" 7.00 10.00

☐ Same as above except smaller, 3¼" 5.00 8.00

☐ Same as above except plain bottom 4.00 6.00

☐ **HOBNAIL POISON**
Collared neck, made using double gather, attributed to N. England, clear, 6" 65.00 85.00

☐ **IKEY EINSTEIN, POISON**
On each side of it, rectangular, ring top, clear, 3¾" 18.00 25.00

☐ **IODINE POISON TINCT.**
Machine made, amber, 2¼" 4.00 6.00

☐ **IODINE TINCT**
No embossing on bottle, but stopper in glass tube is embossed "THE S. H. WESTMORE CO./PAT. AUG. 19, 1919," square, ring collar, ABM, light amber, 3½" 4.00 7.00

☐ **JTM & CO.**
Under bottom, 1¼" slim letters "Poison," label reads "Milliken's Tri-Sept., Bernays No. 2 Unofficial Poison" on two panels, tablet container, amber, 3" 6.00 9.00

☐ **J.T.M. & CO.**
Under bottom, three-cornered, "Poison" on one side, two plain sides, ring top, amber, 10" 110.00 145.00

☐ **LIN, AMMONIAE**
Label, green, 6¾" 18.00 25.00

Price Range

☐ **LIN BELLAD**
Label, green, 7¾" 30.00 40.00
☐ **LIN BELLAD**
Label, cobalt, 7" 60.00 80.00
☐ **LIN BELLADON**
Label, under bottom "Y.G. CO.," green, 7" 18.00 25.00
☐ **LIN SAPONIS**
Label, green, 6¾" 18.00 25.00
☐ **LIQ. ARSENIC**
Label, green, 5¾" 18.00 25.00
☐ **LIQ:HYD: PERCHLOR POISON**
Label, green, 9" 22.00 33.00
☐ **LIQ. MORPH. HYDROCHL POISON**
Label, cobalt, 4½" 40.00 50.00
☐ **LIQ. STRYCH. HYD.**
Label, green, 6" 18.00 25.00
☐ **LRAY POISON**
Label, embossed ribs on edges, amber, 3½" .. 14.00 20.00
☐ **EDWARD R. MARSHALL CO.**
Deed Stuck Insecticide, green, 9" 35.00 50.00
☐ **McCORMICK & CO.**
"Registered Trademark., Balto, MD. Patented,
Three-sided, cobalt, 4" 7.00 10.00
☐ Same as above except "July 8th 1882" 8.00 11.00
☐ **McCORMICK & CO., BALTIMORE**
Three-sided, clear or amethyst, 3¾" 6.00 9.00
☐ **McCORMICK & CO.**
"BALTO." in a circle, in center a fly or bee under
it, "Patent Applied For," triangular, ring top, co-
balt, 1½" tall 6.00 9.00
☐ **MELVIN & BADGER, APOTHECARIES**
Boston, MA, ribbing on side, ring top, cobalt, 7½" 110.00 140.00
☐ **R.C. MILLINGS BED BUG POISON**
Charleston, SC, shoulder strap on side, clear,
6¼" 12.00 17.00
☐ **N 16 OZ.**
"Poison" label, cobalt, 6½" 30.00 40.00
☐ **N 8 OZ.**
Poison label, cobalt, 6" 12.00 17.00
☐ **NORWICK**
On base, coffin shape, "Poison" vertical down
center of front, also horizontal in back on shoul-

Price Range

der, covered with diamond embossing, amber,
7½" 12.00 17.00

☐ Same as above except ABM, cobalt 12.00 17.00

☐ Same as above except BIMAL 27.00 36.00

☐ **THE NORWICK PHARMACY CO.**
Norwick, NY label, "M" under bottom, ABM, cobalt, 3½" 11.00 16.00

☐ **NOT TO BE TAKEN**
In center vertically, vertical wide ribbing on sides, rectangular, ring top, cobalt, 6¾" 11.00 16.00

☐ **NOT TO BE TAKEN**
In center of bottle on each side in three vertical lines, "#12" under bottom, cobalt, 7¾" 50.00 70.00

☐ Same as above except in two lines "Poison, Not to Be Taken," cobalt 50.00 70.00

☐ Same as above except emerald green, clear ... 17.00 25.00

☐ **01. CAMPHOR FORTE**
Label, crystal glass, amber, 5" 30.00 40.00

☐ **01. EUCALYPTI**
Label, crystal glass, amber, 6½" 30.00 40.00

☐ **01. SINAP. AETH.**
Label, crystal glass, amber, 5" 30.00 40.00

☐ **ORGE MONDE**
Label, cut glass, blue 27.00 35.00

☐ **OWL POISON AMMONIA**
Label, three-cornered, cobalt, 5¼" 30.00 40.00

☐ **THE OWL DRUG CO.**
Poison other side, three-cornered, cobalt, 8" .. 110.00 140.00

☐ **POISON BOTTLE**
On one side, irregular diamond shape, ridges on three corners, amber, four sizes 5.00 8.00

☐ Some have "Poison" on two sides 7.00 10.00

☐ Same machine made 4.00 6.00

☐ **POISON**
On one panel, nobbed on three sides, 16 on bottom, round back, 3⁹/₁₆", also four other sizes .. 10.00 15.00

☐ **POISON**
On each side panel, no round back, four-cornered, three sides nobbed, other plain, amber, 2¾" 6.00 9.00

Price Range

☐ **POISON**
On each side panel, round back; three sides nobbed, machine made, amber, four different sizes ... 6.00 8.00

☐ **POISON, TINCTURE IODINE**
Under a skull and crossbones, "½" on one side of skull, "Oz." on the other, oval, 5 panels on front, under bottom At. 1–7–36, amber, 2¼" tall, ¾"x1" 9.00 13.00

☐ **POISON**
On each side, "P.D. & CO." on bottom, amber, 2½" 6.00 9.00

☐ **POISON**
Plain, cobalt, different sizes 13.00 18.00

☐ **POISON**
Label, dark blue, 8" 8.00 12.00

☐ **POISON**
Ribs in front, "90" under bottom, black back, cobalt, 13½" 100.00 130.00

☐ **POISON**
Casket type, hobnail finish, amber, 3½" 40.00 50.00

☐ Same except cobalt, 7½" 55.00 68.00

☐ **POISON**
"Use with Caution" on other side, cobalt, 8¾" 18.00 25.00

☐ **POISON DO NOT TAKE**
"N" in "Not" backward, DCP under bottom, 4¼" 20.00 28.00

☐ **POISON**
Label, cobalt, 8" 25.00 35.00

☐ **POISON**
Machine made, ground top, clear, 13½" 17.00 26.00

☐ **POISON**
"12" under bottom, "Not To Be Taken" on side, cobalt, 7¾" 50.00 65.00

☐ **POISON**
Label, three-cornered, "74" under bottom, cobalt, 2½" 4.00 6.00

☐ **POISON**
Label, cobalt, 5" 18.00 25.00

☐ **POISON**
Flask, made rough to avoid a mistake in the dark, sheared top, aqua, ½ pint 150.00 180.00

☐ Same as above except pontil, green 50.00 65.00

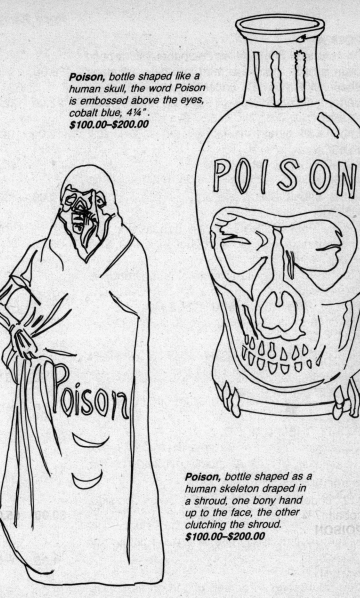

Poison, bottle shaped like a human skull, the word Poison is embossed above the eyes, cobalt blue, 4¼".
$100.00–$200.00

Poison, bottle shaped as a human skeleton draped in a shroud, one bony hand up to the face, the other clutching the shroud.
$100.00–$200.00

Price Range

☐ **POISON**
"X" around "POISON" in one panel, "X" around plain side, "1 oz. use with caution," diamond shape with letter "D" under bottom, ring top, cobalt, 3¼" 22.00 32.00

☐ **POISON**
Label, dark blue, 8" 12.00 18.00

☐ **POISON**
Label, cobalt or amber, 3½" 7.00 10.00

☐ **POISON**
Label, cobalt, 3¼" 9.00 13.00

☐ **POISON**
Skull, "Pat. Applied For" on bottom rim, "S" under bottom, ceramic reproduction, cobalt, 3½" 40.00 50.00

☐ **POISON**
Clear, 6½", embossed picture of rat on front, machine made 7.00 10.00

☐ **PYROX BOWKER INSECTICIDE CO.**
Boston & Baltimore, cream crock, glass top, 7½" 10.00 15.00

☐ **RAT POISON**
Horizontal on round bottle, clear or amethyst, 2½" 18.00 26.00

☐ **RIDDES**
"7073" under bottom, 6½", three-cornered with ribs or edges, ring top, aqua 18.00 26.00

☐ **REESE CHEMICAL CO.**
Cleveland, OH, "For External Use Only," etc., rectangular, 5½", sides ribbed, flat and ring top, cobalt, green, clear 16.00 24.00

☐ **RIGO**
Embossed on base, vertical on left panel, "Use with Caution," in center "Not to be Taken," right usage extreme with stars all around bottle, ring top, cobalt 30.00 40.00

☐ **ROMAN INC.**
Vertical in script in center, ribbed on each side, hexagonal, ring top, emerald green, 5¼" 20.00 28.00

☐ **S & D**
"173" under bottom, ABM, poison label, cobalt, 2½" 17.00 25.00

Price Range

☐ **SHARP & DOHM**
On one panel, "Phila" on other panel, label, "X126–1" under bottom, three cornered, cobalt, 2" 9.00 12.00

☐ **SHARP & DOHME**
"Baltimore" on two panels, six vertical panels, bulbous shoulder ring collar, amber, ABM, 2½" 4.00 6.00

☐ **SHARP & DOHME**
On one panel, Baltimore, MD, three cornered, cobalt, 3½" 6.00 9.00

☐ **SHARP & DOHME**
On one panel, other "Phila," label reads "Ergotole D & D," three cornered, 2", cobalt, under bottom "X–126–1" 9.00 12.00

☐ **SKULL & CROSSBONES**
On each of six vertical panels, also "GIFT" embossed on each panel, (gift means poison in German), aqua or clear, flared collar, 8⅛" 13.00 18.00

☐ **SKULL**
"POISON" on forehead, crossbones under bottom, 2" round, 3" tall, 1" neck, ring top, cobalt, "Pat. Appl'd For" on base in back 130.00 170.00

☐ **SPIRITS**
Silver and milk glass, 9" 28.00 38.00

☐ **SOL TRYPAFLAVIN**
1 + 49, crystal glass, amber, 5" 23.00 32.00

☐ **SYR: HYPOPH: CO.**
Green, 9" 21.00 29.00

☐ **SYR: FER: PA: CO.**
Cobalt, 7" 48.00 62.00

☐ **SYR: FER: IODID**
Cobalt, 7" 95.00 115.00

☐ **TEINTURE de COCHENILLE**
Label, amber, 7½" 14.00 20.00

☐ **F.A. THOMPSON & CO., DETROIT**
"Detroit" on front, "Poison" on sides, ribbed corner, coffin type, ring top, 3½" 40.00 50.00

☐ **TINCT CELLADON, POISON**
Round bottle, vertical ribbing, aqua and green 32.00 45.00

Price Range

☐ **TINCTURE IODINE**
In three lines under skull and crossbones, square,
flat ring and ring top, amber, ABM 6.00   9.00
☐ Same as above except "BIMAL" 9.00   13.00
☐ Same as above except 2¾" 6.00   9.00
☐ **TINCT. ACONITI**
Label, green, 6" 18.00   26.00
☐ **TINCT. ACONITI**
Label, green, 7¾", "Y.G. Co." under bottom . .   25.00   34.00
☐ **TINCT. CAMPH: CO. POISON**
Label, green, 9" 22.00   30.00
☐ **TINCT. CHLOROF. et MORPH CO.**
Label, green, 7¾" 25.00   34.00
☐ **TINCT. CONII, POISON**
Label, cobalt, 6" 32.00   43.00
☐ **TINCT. ERGOTAE. AMM**
Y.G. Co. under bottom, green, 7¾" 25.00   34.00
☐ **TINCT. IODI MIT.**
Label, green, 7¾" 25.00   34.00
☐ **TINCT. LOBELLIAE AETH**
Label, green, 6" 17.00   24.00
☐ **TINCT. NUX VOM**
Label, green, 6" 17.00   24.00
☐ Same except wide mouth and different label . . .   17.00   24.00
☐ **TINCT. OPII**
Label, green, 6" 17.00   24.00
☐ **TINCT. OPII.**
POISON on base, cobalt, 7" 40.00   50.00
☐ **TINCTURE: SENEGAE**
Label, under bottom number "6 U.G.B." ABM,
amber, 6" 10.00   15.00
☐ **TRILETS**
Vertical, other side "poison," triangular, cobalt,
3½", ribbed corner, ABM 7.00   10.00
☐ Same as above except BIMAL 12.00   17.00
☐ **TRILOIDS**
On one panel of triangular bottle, "Poison" on an-
other, the other plain, corners nobbed, number
under bottom, cobalt, 3¼" 6.00   9.00

☐ **TRI-SEPS, MILIKEN POISON**
One ribbed side, two for label, under bottom in
sunken panel "JTM & Co.," ring top, 1½"x 2" tall,
¾" neck, 1¼" letters "Poison" on side 6.00   8.00

☐ **U.D.O.**
On base, "Poison" vertically on two panels, triangular, 5¼", ring top, cross stitch around "Poi-
son," cobalt 18.00   25.00

☐ Same as above except 8½" 22.00   32.00

☐ **VAPO-CRESOLENE CO.**
Vertical on one panel with four rows of nail heads,
"Patd. U.S. July 1794 Eng. July 23, 94" on next
panel with nail heads, square, double band collar,
aqua, ABM, 5½" 1.50   5.00

☐ Same as above except clear, 4" 5.00   8.00

☐ Same as above except "S" is reversed, dated
"July 23, 94" 8.00   12.00

☐ **VICTORY CHEMICAL CO.**
Quick Death Insecticide, 148 Fairmont Ave.,
Phila, PA, 8 oz., clear, 7" 11.00   16.00

☐ **W.R.W. & CO.**
Under bottom, "Poison" on each side, ribbed cor-
ner, rectangular, 2½", ring top 12.00   17.00

☐ **JOHN WYETH & CO.**
"Phila" on front, oval, cobalt, 4", cross around
base and side, flat ring collar 6.00   9.00

☐ **JOHN WYETH & BROS.**
"Phila" in two lines on side, square, 2¼" 17.00   23.00

☐ **WYETH POISON**
Vertical in back, round ring base and top, cobalt,
2¼" 10.00   15.00

☐ Same as above except amber 6.00   9.00

SODA

Soda bottles probably attract as many collectors as any other
group of bottles on the hobby market. The only thing that has prevented prices from going higher is the relatively recent dates of most
specimens and the rather high preservation rate. Nevertheless, a
number of Coke bottles (and others) are already well into double digit

prices and the time may well be when soda bottles sell for as much on the average as 19th century flasks. The tremendous enthusiasm for them shows no sign of waning.

One of the intriguing aspects of soda bottle collecting is that the evolution of each maker's bottles can be traced down to the present time. It is possible to assemble complete collections showing every type of bottle in which any popular soft drink was retailed over the years.

Coca-Cola, the first really successful cola drink, was developed in 1886. On a May afternoon in 1886, "Doc" Pemberton of Atlanta diligently stirred a mixture in a three-legged pot in his back yard. When it was finished he sampled it, liked it, and brought a glassful to the local druggist for his opinion. Willis Venable, proprietor of Jacob's Drug Store, added ice and tap water to the syrup, tested it, and *he* liked it, too. Venable agreed to sell the drink as a headache cure. Only one customer bought a Coca-Cola that day, but sales have now reached 95 million daily, including bottles, cans and restaurant consumption. Poor Doc wasn't able to cash in on the international success of his invention. What became one of the major companies of the world yielded him just $50 in its first year.

When carbonated water was added to Coca-Cola, beginning in 1887, sales improved. Pemberton died in 1888, with "Coke" still in its infancy. It did not become a corporation until 1892. At that time, it was still being sold exclusively at druggists' fountains mainly in the South. It occurred to Joseph A. Biedenharn in 1894 that if he bottled Coca-Cola he could sell a great deal more of it. He loaded the bottles on his horse-drawn truck and peddled the beverage throughout the countryside around Vicksburg, Mississippi. Bottled Coke was a hit.

After bottling started, the references to Coke as a headache cure disappeared from advertising. Instead, it was claimed to be refreshing, invigorating and energy-building.

Alex Samuelson is credited with designing the familiar Coke bottle in 1915. A supervisor of the Root Glass Co. of Terre Haute, Indiana, he studied drawings of cola nuts, the brown bitter-tasting seeds from which Coca-Cola syrup was made. The result was the "hobble skirt" or "Mae West" bottle adopted by the Coca-Cola company in 1916. Though it was similar to the cola nut in shape, it was named "hobble skirt" after a ladies' fashion of the time. Except for a minor trimming in the middle, the bottle has remained the same. Prior to 1916, a variety of shapes can be found.

Many people tried cashing in on Coke's rising popularity by mixing their own cola drinks. The most successful of these was Caleb D. Bradham of New Bern, North Carolina, who began producing Brad's

Drink in 1890. In 1896, he changed its name to Pep-Kola and two years after to Pipi-Cola. Not until 1906 did it become known as Pepsi-Cola.

Most of the early soda bottlers made their own products and sold them locally. It was not until c. 1900 that these small local plants began going nationwide. Many early bottles can be found with pontil scars.

	Price Range	
□ **ABILENA**		
Label, "#1" under bottom, amber, 6"	6.00	9.00
□ **ALABAMA GROCERY CO.**		
"Register" on shoulder, clear, 8¼"	4.00	6.00
□ **C. ALFS SODA WATER**		
Charleston, SC, "This Bottle to be Returned," eight sided, iron pontil, blue, 8½"	550.00	650.00
□ **C. ALFS SODA WATER**		
Charleston, SC, "This Bottle to be Returned," eight sided, iron pontil, dark olive green, 8½"	550.00	650.00
□ **ALPHA**		
"B.H.A." in back, light green or aqua, 6"	4.00	6.00
□ **THE A.M. & CO.**		
Reg. Waco, Texas & St. Louis, MO, reverse side "We Pay For Evidence Conv. Thieves For Refilling Our Bottles," aqua, 8½"	10.00	14.00
□ **AQUA DIST & BOT CO.**		
Aqua, 8½"	6.00	9.00
□ **ARIZONA BOTTLING WORKS**		
"A" under bottom, "This Bottle Must Be Returned" on vase, aqua, 7"	7.00	10.00
□ **ARTER & WILSON, MANUF.**		
"Boston" in 4 vertical lines, tapered top, graphite pontil, light green, 7"	60.00	70.00
□ **AUGUSTIN VITALE**		
"Providence, R.I., A.V." monogram all in slug plate on front, blob top, clear, 9¼"	6.00	9.00
□ **B**		
On front, gravitating stopper made by John Matthews, "N.Y. Pat. Oct. 11, 1864" on bottom, blue aqua, 7¼"	6.00	9.00
□ **B & G**		
Large letters, under it "San Francisco" in 2 lines, blob top, 7½" base panels, iron pontil, cobalt blue	75.00	95.00

Price Range

☐ **BABB & CO.**
"San Francisco, CA" in three lines, graphite pontil, green, 7½" 60.00   80.00

☐ **DANIEL BAHR**
In three lines, graphite pontil, green, 7½" 6.00   9.00

☐ **BAKER, JOHN S., SODA WORK**
On 2 panels, panel bottle, aqua, 7¼" 35.00   50.00

☐ **JOHN C. BAKER & CO.**
Aqua, 7½" 6.00   9.00

☐ **J. ED BAKER**
"417 Washington St., Newburgh, N.Y." on front slug plate, aqua, 7⅛" 6.00   9.00

☐ **THE PROPERTY OF MRS. J. ED. BAKER**
"Newburgh, N.Y." on front in oval slug plate, blob top, clear, 9" 7.00   10.00

☐ **JOHN S. BAKER SODA WATER T.B.I.N.S.**
Eight-sided, green, 7½" 7.00   10.00

☐ **BARCLAY STREET**
In center "41, N.Y.," applied lip, green, 7" 12.00   18.00

☐ **BARTH, ELIAS**
In ¼ moon letters, under it in 2 lines "Burlington, N.J.," blob top, squat type bottle, aqua, 7" 20.00   30.00

☐ **BARTLETT BOTTLING WORK**
Clear or amethyst, 6½" 7.00   10.00

☐ **BARTOW BOTTLING WORKS**
Aqua, root under bottom, 7½" 5.00   8.00

☐ **F. BAUMAN**
"Santa Maria, Cal." in a circle, "SODA WORKS" in center, aqua, 7¼" 7.00   10.00

☐ **BATTERMAN, H.B.**
In ½ moon letters in center "1861," on base "Brooklyn, N.Y.," tapered top, aqua, 7½" 20.00   27.00

☐ **BAY CITY POP WORKS M.T.**
"Registered Bay City, Mich." on front in slug plate, "This Bottle Not To Be Sold" on opposite side, blob top, quart, apple green, 8¾" 9.00   12.00

☐ **BAY CITY SODA WATER CO., S.F.**
Star Symbol, blue, 7" 9.00   13.00

☐ **B. & C., S.F.**
Applied lip, cobalt, 7¼" 25.00   35.00

☐ **R.M. BECKER'S HYGEIA BOTTLE WORKS TRADEMARK**
In a shield, "B" on bottom, crown top, aqua, 7½" 7.00 10.00

☐ **THE BENNINGTON BOTTLE CO.**
"No. Bennington, VT." in a sunken panel, under bottom "E.S. & H.," ten-sided base, clear or amber, 7¾" 25.00 35.00

☐ **BELFAST COCHRAN & CO.**
On front and back of tear drop bottle, 7/16" size letters, aqua, 9¼" 12.00 18.00

☐ **BELFAST DUBLIN**
Cantrell, Cochrane, see that cork is branded around bottles on bottom, pop top, aqua, round bottom, 9½" 6.00 9.00

☐ **BELFAST**
Round bottom, aqua, 9¼" 12.00 18.00

☐ **BELFAST**
Plain flat bottom, aqua, 9" 4.00 7.00

☐ **BELFAST GINGER ALE, ARTHUR CHRISTIN**
"Chicago, Ill." large lettering embossed sideways across bottle, on the other side appears embossed initials "AC" entwined in fancy script, entwined initials also appear on bottom, "PAT. Apr. 13th, 1875-Arthur Christin" appears around the base, above this appears "A. & D.H.C.," unusual solid pull up hard composition stopper, blob top, aqua, 8" tall 15.00 25.00

☐ **BELFAST ROSS**
Round bottom, aqua, 9¼" 5.00 8.00

☐ **BELFAST ROSS**
Plain, aqua and clear, 9½" 5.00 8.00

☐ **C. BERRY & CO.**
"84 Levett St., Boston, Registered" on shoulder in oval slug plate, crown top, emerald green, 9⅜" 6.00 9.00

☐ **C. BERRY & CO.**
"84 Leverett St., Boston" in oval slug plate, crown top, clear, 9½" 3.00 5.00
☐ Same as above except amber, 9¼" 3.00 5.00
☐ Same as above except blob top, clear, 9" 6.00 9.00

☐ **SAMUEL BESKIN**
"Fishkill Landing, N.Y." on front in oval slug plate, blob top, aqua, 9⅜" 7.00 10.00

Price Range

☐ **BEVERAGE**
Plain, aqua, opalescent, pop type, 6¼″ 5.00 8.00

☐ **BEVERAGE**
Plain, Belfast type, aqua, 9″ 4.00 6.00

☐ **BEVERAGE**
Plain, clear, aqua 4.00 6.00

☐ **BIG 4 MF'G. CO.**
1120 and three dots under bottom, aqua, 7¾″ 7.00 10.00

☐ **BIG HOLLOW LETTER "B"**
Applied crown top, light green, 8½″ 7.00 10.00

☐ **E.L. BILLINGS**
Sac. City, CA, reverse "Geyser Soda," blob top,
blue, 7″ 10.00 15.00

☐ **BLACKHAWK GINGER ALE**
Dark green, 6½″ 6.00 9.00

☐ **J.A. BLAFFER & CO.**
"New Orleans" squat type, blob top, amber, 6½″ 20.00 30.00

☐ **T. BLAUTH, BOTTLING WORKS**
407 K. St., Sacramento, CA, aqua, 6¾″ 10.00 16.00

☐ **BLUDWINE BOTTLING CO.**
Aqua, machine made, 7½″ 10.00 16.00

☐ **BLUDWINE**
Clear or amethyst, 8″ 5.00 8.00

☐ **BLUFF CITY BOTTLING**
In horseshoe shape, in center of horseshoe "Co.
Memphis, Tenn.," on bottom, on one panel "B.G.
Co." in very small letters and next to it "199,"
aqua 7.00 10.00

☐ **BOARDMAN**
Blue, ground pontil, 7½″ 35.00 45.00

☐ **GEO. BOHLEN**
"Brooklyn," in a round slug plate, in center "358
Hart St.," blob top, aqua, 7¼″ 7.00 10.00

☐ **BOLEN & BYRNE**
In a dome shape, under it "EAST 54th ST. N.Y.,"
reverse "T.B.N.T.B.S.," aqua, 7¾″ 12.00 18.00

☐ **BOLEN & BYRNE**
Opposite side "N.Y.," aqua, 8¼″ 12.00 18.00

☐ **BOLEN & BYRNE**
New York, round bottom, aqua, 9″ 7.00 10.00

☐ **BOLEY & CO.**
Sac. City, CA, Union Glass Works, Phila., cobalt,
7½" **60.00   70.00**

☐ **BOLEY & CO.**
"Sac. City, Calif." all in 2 lines, tapered top, cobalt
blue, 7¼" **40.00   55.00**

☐ **BOLEY & CO.**
"Sac. City, Cal." in slug plate, reverse "Union
Glass Works, Phila.," graphite pontil, blob top, co-
balt, 7¼" **60.00   70.00**

☐ **BOLEY & CO.**
"Sac City, Calif." in 2 lines, blob top, graphite
pontil, cobalt, 7¼" **60.00   70.00**

☐ **THE BONHEUR CO. INC.**
"Syracuse, N.Y." in script, clear, "14 fl. ounces"
on bottom, under bottom diamond shape figure,
machine made, 7½" **7.00   10.00**

☐ **BONODE 5**
Clear or amber, 6¾" **6.00   9.00**

☐ **BORELLO BROS. CO., FRESNO (B.B. CO.)**
On bottom, crown top, light aqua blue, 7¾" ... **5.00   8.00**

☐ **R. BOVEE**
Troy, NY, clear, 7½" **7.00   10.00**

☐ **BOWLING TYPE BOTTLE**
Applied crown top, light green and dark green, 9" **30.00   40.00**
☐ Same except blob top, aqua **20.00   30.00**

☐ **W.H. BRACE**
"Avon, N.Y." on front in slug plate, blob top,
aqua, 9¼" **6.00   9.00**

☐ **C.W. BRACKETT & CO.**
"61 & 63 Andrew St., Lynn, Mass." on front in
oval slug plate, clear, 9⅛" **7.00   10.00**

☐ **H. BRADER & CO.**
"Penalty For Selling This Bottle, SLLR Soda
Work, 738 Broadway, S.F." on eight-panel, blob
top, aqua, 7¼" **15.00   25.00**

☐ **BREIG & SCHAFFER, S.F.**
Picture of a fish under it, aqua, 6½" **12.00   18.00**

☐ **BREMEKAMPF & REGAL**
Eureka, NV, clear or aqua, 7¼" **12.00   18.00**

☐ **BREMENKAMPF & REGLI**
In ½ moon letter under it "Eureka, Nev.," 7" .. **60.00   80.00**

Price Range

☐ **DWIGHT BRINTON**
"Falls Village, Conn." in oval slugplate, aqua,
7½" **10.00 15.00**

☐ **W.E. BROCKWAY**
In hollow letters, "NEW YORK," graphite pontil,
squat type, blob top, blue green, 6¾" **60.00 80.00**

☐ **BROWN BROS CHEMISTS**
Glasgow, round bottom, blob top, aqua, 9½" .. **7.00 10.00**

☐ **H.L. & J.W. BROWN**
In hollow letters, "HARTFORD, CT.," squat type,
tapered top, olive, 7" **70.00 80.00**

☐ **I. BROWNLEE**
In dome shaped lines, under it "NEW BED-
FORD," in back "T.B.N.S.," blob top, blue **10.00 15.00**

☐ **J. BRUNETT**
Big hollow letter "A," big "B," aqua, 7" **12.00 18.00**

☐ **THE BRUNNER BOTTLING CO.**
669 to 673 Grand St., Brooklyn, N.Y., 1889, Aug.,
blob top, 7½" **10.00 15.00**

☐ **FILLIPPO BRUNO & CO.**
"298–300 North St. & 50 Fleet St., Boston,
Mass." on front in oval slug plate on shoulder,
clear, 8⅞" **6.00 9.00**

☐ **BURGIN & SONS**
In one line over it in ½ moon letters "Philad.
Glass Works," tapered blob top, med. green,
7¼" **60.00 70.00**

☐ **BURKE**
"E & J" under bottom, amber, 7½" **6.00 9.00**

☐ **HENRY BURKHARDT**
"H.B." under bottom, aqua, 6¾" **6.00 9.00**

☐ **W.H. BURT**
San Francisco, blob top, graphite pontil, aqua,
6½" **45.00 55.00**

☐ **BURT, W.H.**
"San Francisco" in 2 lines, blob top, graphite
pontil, dark green, 7¼" **80.00 100.00**

☐ **J.G. BYARS**
In center "1882 No. Hoosick, N.Y.," reverse
"T.B.N.T.S.," aqua, 7" **12.00 18.00**

Price Range

☐ **CALHOUN FALLS**
In center, "BOTTLING WORKS, CALHOUN
FALLS, S.C.," clear or amber, 7½" 8.00   12.00

☐ **CALIFORNIA BOTTLING WORK, T. BLAUTH**
407 K St., Sacramento, clear, 7" 6.00   9.00

☐ **CALIFORNIA SODA WORKS**
With an arrow under it, "H. FICKEN, S.F.," in back
an embossed eagle, blob top, green, 7" 20.00   30.00

☐ **CALVERT BOTTLE WORKS**
Calvert, TX, aqua, soda water, 7¼" 5.00   8.00

☐ **D. CAMELIO CO.**
"10 Lewis St., Boston, Mass." on shoulder in oval
slug plate, clear, 2⅞" 7.00   10.00

☐ **CANADA DRY**
"141 Ginger Ale Incorporated" under bottom,
carnival glass, crown top, machine made, 10½"   14.00   20.00

☐ **P. CANTERBURY**
Galveston, TX, blob top, aqua, 6¼" 8.00   12.00

☐ **M. J. CANTRELL**
Yonkers, NY, "M.J.C." monogram, amethyst or
clear, 6½" or 11½" 7.00   10.00

☐ **CANTRELL & COCHRANE'S**
Aerated Water, Dublin & Belfast, aqua, round bot-
tom, 8¾" 6.00   9.00

☐ **CANTRELL & COCHRANE'S**
"Aerated Waters, Dublin & Belfast" runs up and
down, round bottom, aqua, 8¾" 7.00   10.00

☐ **CANTRELL & COCHRANE**
"Belfast & Dublin Medicated Aerated Water"
around bottle, round bottom, aqua, 9¼" 10.00   16.00

☐ **CANTRELL & COCHRANE**
"Belfast & Dublin" around bottle, round bottom,
aqua, 9" 10.00   16.00

☐ **N. CAPPELLI**
"327 Atwells Ave., Providence, R.I., Registered"
On front, blob top, clear, 8¼" 7.00   10.00

☐ **CAPRONI BROS. CO.**
"Prov., R.I., Registered" written inside of shield,
blob, top, clear, 9¼" 7.00   10.00

☐ **CARBONATING APPARATUS COMPANY**
Buffalo, NY, Reg., Marble inside bottle, clear . .   12.00   18.00

Price Range

☐ **M. CARNEY & CO.**
"Lawrence, Mass." with "MC & Co." monogram
all inside of slug plate circle, blob top, clear, 9¼" 7.00 10.00

☐ **HUGH CASEY EAGLE SODA WORKS**
"51 K St., Sac., Cal.," aqua, 7¼" 7.00 10.00

☐ **OWEN CASEY EAGLE SODA WORKS**
On front, "Sac. City" on back, blob top, aqua
blue, 7¼" 10.00 15.00

☐ **OWEN CASEY EAGLE SODA WORKS**
Dark blue, 7¼" 12.00 18.00

☐ **CASWELL & HAZARD & CO.**
"New York, Ginger Ale" in vertical line, round bot-
tom, blob top, aqua, 9" 12.00 18.00

☐ **C. B. SODA**
"Quality Coca Cola Bottling Co." on back, aqua,
machine made "St. Louis" on bottom, 8" 5.00 8.00

☐ **C.C.**
Portland, Or., T.M., Reg., T.B.N.T.B.S., amber,
7½" 9.00 13.00

☐ **C. C. S. & M. CO.**
1118 Toll 26 Royal St., New Orleans, crown top,
aqua, 8" 6.00 9.00

☐ **CELERY COLA**
"C" under bottom, amber, 7½" 7.00 10.00

☐ **CELERY COLA**
Clear or amethyst, 7½" 4.00 6.00

☐ **CENTRAL CITY BOTTLING CO.**
Clear or amethyst, 7¾" 5.00 8.00

☐ **CENTRAL CITY BOTTLING CO.**
On back "Bottle Not To Be Sold," clear or ame-
thyst, note misspelling, 7¾" 7.00 10.00

☐ **CENTRAL CITY BOTTLING CO.**
Note misspelled Selma, "Bottle Not To Be Sold"
on back, clear, 7¾" 17.00 23.00

☐ **CHADSEY & BRO.**
2" hollow letters, NY, blob top, graphite pontil, co-
balt, 7½" 60.00 80.00

☐ **CHAMPAGNE MEAD**
On 2 panels, 8 panels, blob top, aqua, 7" 25.00 35.00

☐ **CHCRO-COLA**
"Savannah, Ga." on back, aqua, 7½" 5.00 8.00

**"Crystal Palace/Premium/Soda
Water/W.E. Eagle/New York—An
Embossed Crystal Palace/Union Glass
Works/Phila,"** *round, iron pontil, applied
top, deep teal-blue,* **$625.00–$700.00**

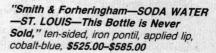

**"Smith & Forheringham—SODA WATER
—ST. LOUIS—This Bottle is Never
Sold,"** *ten-sided, iron pontil, applied lip,
cobalt-blue,* **$525.00–$585.00**

Price Range

☐ **CHECOTAH BOTTLING WORKS**
Checotah, IT, light blue, 7¼" 23.00 29.00

☐ **CHERO COLA BOTT. CO.**
Raised X pattern, Tyler, TX, aqua, 7⅝" 3.00 5.00

☐ **CHICAGO BOTTLING CO.**
Root on bottom, aqua, 7" 7.00 10.00

☐ **O. CHISOLM**
Round, iron pontil, green, 7½" 175.00 225.00

☐ **CHRISTIAN SCHLEPEGRELL & CO.**
Eight panels, ground pontil, blue, 8¼" 50.00 70.00

☐ **THE CINCINNATI**
On shoulder, under it in horseshoe letters "SODA
WATER & GINGER ALE CO." in center, aqua 7.00 10.00

☐ **THE CITY BOTTLING CO.**
On label, marble in center of neck, aqua, 7¼" 8.00 11.00

☐ **CITY BOTTLING WORKS**
Cleveland, OH, aqua, 7" 25.00 35.00

☐ **CITY BOTTLING WORK**
Detroit, MI, in back "G. Norris & Co.,"
"A.&D.H.G." on base, blob top, blue, 7¾" 18.00 24.00

☐ **CITY ICE & BOTTLING WORKS**
Aqua, 7½" 6.00 9.00

☐ **C & K**
In hollow letters, "EAGLE SODA WORK, SAC.
CITY," blob top, cobalt, 7" 45.00 55.00

☐ **C. CLARK**
Ground pontil, green, 7½" 38.00 48.00

☐ **C. CLARK**
Charleston, SC, slug plate, iron pontil, green,
7⁷/₁₆" 30.00 40.00

☐ **CHARLES CLARK**
Ground pontil, green, 7¾" 33.00 45.00

☐ **CHARLES CLARK, SODA WATER**
Charleston, SC, round, iron pontil, green, 7½" 35.00 45.00

☐ **CLAUSSEN BOTTLING WORKS**
Round, aqua, 6⅝" 6.00 10.00

☐ **CLEBURNE BOTTLING WORK**
Cleburne, TX, paneled trunk, wire "pop" stopper,
7¼" 7.00 10.00

☐ **CLYSNIC**
Under bottom, green, 7½" 3.00 5.00

Price Range

☐ **G. B. COATES**
"G.B.C." monogram, "LYNN, MASS." in a slug
plate, clear, 8½" 5.00 8.00

☐ **M.H. COBE & CO. BOTTLERS**
"Boston" in large letters on front, clear, 8⅛" .. 7.00 10.00

☐ **COCA COLA**
Christmas Coke, "Patd. Dec. 25, 1923, Zanesville, Ohio" on bottom, ABM, crown top, aqua,
7⅝" 20.00 30.00

☐ **COCA COLA CO.**
Seattle WA, clear or aqua, 8½" 6.00 9.00

☐ **COCA COLA IDEAL BRAIN TONIC SUMMER
& WINTERS BEVERAGE FOR HEADACHE
AND EXHAUSTION**
All on label, clear, 9½" 55.00 75.00

☐ **COCA COLA**
Toledo, OH, amber, 7" 20.00 30.00

☐ **COCA COLA BOTTLING WORKS**
Topeka, KS, aqua, 6" 7.00 10.00

☐ **COCA COLA**
Buffalo, NY, clear or amethyst, 7¾" 7.00 10.00

☐ **DAYTONA COCA COLA BOTTLING CO.**
Clear or amethyst, 8½" 10.00 16.00

☐ **COCA COLA**
"Wilmington, N.C." around bottom of bottle,
under it small letters "D.O.C. 173," aqua, clear,
7¼" 6.00 9.00

☐ **COCA COLA**
Macon, GA, "Property of the Coca Cola Bottling
Co" on back, aqua, 7¾" 10.00 14.00

☐ **COCA COLA BOTTLING CO.**
Rome, GA, "Trade Mark Reg." on back, "This
Bottle Not To Be Sold" on base, clear, 7½" .. 6.00 9.00

☐ **COCA COLA**
"Macon (reverse N), GA," aqua, 7" 15.00 25.00
☐ Same as above with different town in U.S.A. ... 6.00 9.00

☐ **COCA COLA**
In center of bottle, under it "Trademark Registered," around bottom of bottle "Waycross, Ga.,"
on back, in small letter, "O.B. Co.," aqua, clear,
7¼" 6.00 9.00
☐ Same as above with different towns in U.S.A. .. 6.00 9.00

Price Range

☐ **COCA COLA BOTTLING WORKS**
"6¼ Flu ozs" on lower trunk, also in center of
shoulder, clear or aqua, 7¼" or various sizes   6.00   9.00
☐ Also in amber, vertical arrow, under it the name of
different towns, some have only "Coca Cola"   12.00   18.00
☐ Also machine made 7.00   10.00
☐ **COCA COLA**
On crown top, amber, under the bottom "S B &
G CO. #2," diamond shape label, 7¼" 20.00   30.00
☐ **COCA COLA**
Name on shoulder in center, also on trunk, aqua,
clear, 7¾" 6.00   9.00
☐ **COCA COLA BOTTLING CO.**
"Charleston, S.C." on front of shoulder, other
side "Trademark Registered," under the bottle
"Root," aqua or clear, 7¼" 6.00   9.00
☐ **COCA COLA**
Not in script in center, clear or aqua, 8½" 6.00   9.00
☐ **COCA COLA**
Around bottom base "Trademark Registered,"
around shoulder "Portland, Oregon, this bottle
never sold," amber, 7½" 5.00   8.00
☐ **COCA COLA**
In ½ circle, under it "Berlin, N.H.," slim bottle,
around bottom "Contents 7 fl. oz.," machine
made, green, 8¾" 6.00   9.00
☐ **J. COSGROVE 1866**
Charleston, aqua, round, 7⅜" 25.00   30.00
☐ **J. COSGROVE 1866**
Charleston, blue, round, 7⅜" 32.00   38.00
☐ **J. COSGROVE**
Charleston, blue, round, 7⅜" 32.00   38.00
☐ **JAMES COSGROVE**
Charleston, SC, aqua, round, 7" 6.00   9.00
☐ **J. COSGROVE AND SON**
Charleston Trademark on back, blue, round, 7⅛"   32.00   38.00
☐ **JAMES COSGROVE AND SON**
Charleston, SC, aqua, round, 8¼" 6.00   9.00
☐ **COSGROVE AND KERNAN**
Charleston, SC, green, round, pint, 7¹/₁₆" 55.00   65.00
☐ **COSGROVE AND KERNAN**
Charleston, SC, green, round, 7¹/₁₆" 30.00   40.00

	Price Range	
☐ **JOHN COTTER**		
Aqua, 7¾″	**6.00**	**9.00**
☐ **COTTLE POST & CO.**		
Portland, blob top, blue, 7½″	**14.00**	**19.00**
☐ **COTTLE POST & CO.**		
In center an eagle under it, "PORTLAND, ORG."		
blob top, green, 7¼″	**20.00**	**30.00**
☐ **JOHN COYLE**		
"Newburgh, N.Y." inside of circular slug plate on		
front, "THIS BOTTLE NOT TO BE SOLD" also		
on front blob top, clear, 9¼″	**7.00**	**11.00**
☐ **C.R. CRAMER & JACKY**		
In a dome line under it "PHILLIPSBURG, MON.,"		
aqua, 6¾″	**7.00**	**11.00**
☐ **C.W. CRELL & CO.**		
Ground pontil, blue green	**55.00**	**75.00**
☐ **M. CRONAN**		
"2330 K St., Sacramento" on front, "Sac. Soda		
Works" on bottom, aqua, 6¾″	**9.00**	**13.00**
☐ **M. CRONAN**		
"230 K St., Sacramento, Soda Works," blob top,		
aqua, 6½″	**9.00**	**13.00**
☐ **CROWN BOTTLING WORKS**		
"Delaware, O." in a circle, light green, 6¾″ ...	**7.00**	**10.00**
☐ **THE CROWN CORK & SEAL CO.**		
Baltimore, crown top, sample, clear, 3¾″	**9.00**	**13.00**
☐ **CRYSTAL BOTTLING CO.**		
Charleston, W. VA, panel base, aqua, 7¼″	**7.00**	**10.00**
☐ **CRYSTAL BOTTLING WORKS**		
"C.B.W." under bottom, aqua, 7½″	**6.00**	**9.00**
☐ **CRYSTAL BOTTLING WORKS**		
"C.B.W." under bottom, aqua, 7¾″	**6.00**	**9.00**
☐ **CRYSTAL SODA WORKS CO.**		
SF, aqua or light green, 7¼″	**7.00**	**10.00**
☐ **CRYSTAL SPRING BOTTLING CO.**		
Barnet, VT, clear or amber, 7¼″	**7.00**	**10.00**
☐ **CRYSTAL** "Soda" in center, **WATER CO.**		
In back "Pat. No. 12–1872, Taylors U.S.P.T."		
blob top, blue, 7½″	**7.00**	**10.00**

Price Range

☐ **CUDDY GINGER ALE**
"Albany, N.Y." embossed sideways on length of
bottle, entwined initials on bottom, scalloped,
paneled from bottom of bottle to 2½" from top
ending in gothic style arches, aqua, 8" 15.00 25.00

☐ **CULVER HOUSE PURE NATURAL
LEMONADE SPECIALTY**
In back "Registered Trademark" with house in
center, golden amber, 9" 25.00 35.00

☐ **CUNNINGHAM & CO.**
Phila, blob top, aqua, 7" 7.00 10.00

☐ **T. & J. CUNNINGHAM**
Phila., blob top, green, 7" 9.00 12.00

☐ **JOHN CUNEO**
"269" under bottom, aqua, 9" 6.00 9.00

☐ **DR. DADIRRIAN'S ZOOLAK**
Vertical around neck in two lines, aqua, 7¼" .. 6.00 9.00

☐ **M.D'AGASTINO**
Aqua, "1223" under bottom, 7¼" 6.00 9.00

☐ **DANNENBURG BROS., C.C. T.M.R.**
In center "GOLDSBORO, N.C.," clear or aqua,
7¾" 10.00 15.00

☐ **E. DANNENBURG, AUTHORIZED BOTTLER
of C.C. WILSON**
"Goldsboro, N.C., U.S.A." in a circle on the
T.B.N.T.B.S., clear or amber, 8" 13.00 18.00

☐ **C. DAVIS**
"Phoenixville" in slug plate squat type, graphite
pontil, green, 7" 50.00 60.00

☐ **J. DAY & CO.**
In two lines blob top, aqua, 7¾" 7.00 10.00

☐ **DEACON BROWN MFG. CO.**
Montgomery, AL, on base "T.B.N.T.B.S.," aqua,
8¾" 5.00 8.00

☐ **DEAMER**
In hollow letters, "Glass Valley" in back,
"W.E.D." in hollow letters blob top, aqua, 7¼" 7.00 10.00

☐ **W. DEAN**
Small kick-up pontil, blue green, 6½" 25.00 35.00

☐ **WM. DEAN**
Pale blue, 7¾" 7.00 10.00

Price Range

☐ **DEARBORN**
83 3rd Ave, NY, blob top, green, 7″ 12.00 18.00

☐ **E.T. DELANEY & CO.**
In center "BOTTLERS PLATTSBURG, N.Y."
aqua, 7″ 7.00 10.00

☐ **H. DELMEYER**
In center, "1861 BROOKLYN" in back, "XX" in
hollow letters, Porter squat bottle, blob top, aqua,
6½″ 15.00 25.00

☐ **DeMOTT'S CELEBRATED SODA or MINERAL
WATER**
In back, Hudson County, NJ, cobalt, 7¼″ 28.00 38.00

☐ **G.V. DeMOTT'S**
Graphite pontil, green, 7½″ 50.00 60.00

☐ **DeMOTT'S PORTER & ALE**
Squat body, blob top, green, 6½″ 35.00 45.00

☐ **H. DENHALTER & SONS**
In a dome-shaped line in center "SALT," under
it "SALT LAKE CITY, UT." aqua, 7″ 8.00 12.00

☐ **D.G.W.**
Script type letters, blob top, aqua, 7¼″ 7.00 10.00

☐ **JOHN DIETZE**
"Winona, MI" on front inside of slug plate, crown
top, aqua, 8⅛″ 5.00 8.00

☐ **J. DINETS, SUPERIOR SODA WATER**
"Chicago" in panel, six panels, graphite pontil,
blue, 8″ 60.00 80.00

☐ **DISTILLED & AERATED WATER CO.**
Mitchell, SD, aqua, 3½″ 12.00 18.00

☐ **DIXIE CARBONATING CO.**
Thick bottom, clear or amethyst, 9″ 6.00 9.00

☐ **DIXIE CARBONATING CO.**
Back shoulder "Trademark, Augusta, Ga.," clear
or amethyst, 8″ 6.00 9.00

☐ **DIXIE CARBONATING CO.**
Aqua, 8″ 6.00 9.00

☐ **HENRY DOWNES**
On back "The City Bottling Works of New York,"
aqua, 7½″ 6.00 9.00

☐ **DOOLY**
Cordele, GA, panel base, clear, 7″ 8.00 12.00

Price Range

☐ **DR. PEPPER**
Label, aqua, 7″ 3.00   5.00
☐ **DR. PEPPER KING OF BEVERAGE**
Reg. Dallas Bottling Co., Dallas, TX, amethyst,
8¼″ 7.00   10.00
☐ **DR. PEPPER**
In script, under it "King of Beverages," on shoul-
der "Registered," on base "Artesian Mfg. & Bot.
Co., Waco, Tex.," clear, amethyst 7.00   10.00
☐ **D.S. & CO.**
San Francisco, blob top, cobalt blue, 7″ 20.00   30.00
☐ **E. DUFFY & SON**
Green, 7″ 20.00   30.00
☐ **FRANCIS DUSCH, T.B.N.T.B.S., 1866**
Blob top, blue, 7¼″ 14.00   19.00
☐ **DUTCHESS BRAND BEVERAGES MADE IN VERBANK VILLAGE**
"7 oz" on front, amethyst, 8½″ 4.00   6.00
☐ **JAMES N. DYER**
Catskill, NY, "This Bottle Not To Be Sold," aqua,
6½″ 8.00   12.00
☐ **DYOTTVILLE GLASS WORKS**
Phila, squat type, graphite pontil, green, 6¼″ .. 60.00   80.00
☐ **EAGLE SYMBOL**
In a circle, marble closure, aqua, 8″ 12.00   18.00
☐ **EAGLE ON SHIELD AND FLAGS**
"Superior Soda Water" on back, blue, round, pint,
7¾″ 110.00   140.00
☐ **EAGLE ON SHIELD AND FLAGS**
"Superior Soda Water" on back green, 7¾″,
round, pint 130.00   160.00
☐ **EAGLE ON SHIELD AND FLAGS**
"Superior Soda Water" on back, dark olive-
green, round, pint, 7¾″ 180.00   215.00
☐ **EAGLE ON SHIELD AND FLAGS**
Blue, round, pint, 7¼″ 90.00   110.00
☐ **EAGLE ON SHIELD AND FLAGS**
Green, round, pint, 7¼″ 110.00   135.00
☐ **EAGLE ON SHIELD AND FLAGS**
Dark olive-green, round, pint, 7¼″ 160.00   200.00
☐ **WM. EAGLE, N.Y. PREMIUM SODA WATER**
Paneled, blob top, graphite pontil, cobalt, 7¼″   65.00   85.00

☐ **W. EAGLE**
"Canal St., N.Y." reverse side "Phila. Porter,"
blob top, squat types, dark green, 6¾" 60.00 70.00
☐ **EAGLE BOTTLING WORKS**
"D" under bottom, clear, 7¾" 6.00 9.00
☐ **EAGLE BOTTLING WORKS**
Birmingham, AL, eagle symbol, crown top, aqua,
8" 8.00 12.00
☐ **ALEX EASTON**
"Fairfield, Iowa" in a circle, Hutchinson, aqua,
6½" 14.00 19.00
☐ **E.B. CO.**
Evansville, IN, "B" under bottom, panels around
bottle, aqua, 7" 6.00 9.00
☐ **G. EBBERWEIN**
"Savannah, Geo." on front, "Ginger Ale" vertical
on back, short neck, amber, 7¾" 30.00 40.00
☐ **EEL RIVER VALLEY SODA WORKS**
In center "SPRINGVILLE, CAL.," aqua, 7" 8.00 11.00
☐ **E.K.B.**
On base, over it "soda water," on shoulder "aer-
ated," all in 3 lines, tapered blob top, cobalt, 6¾" 90.00 110.00
☐ **EL DORADO**
Tapered top, aqua, 7¼" 9.00 12.00
☐ **ELECTRO BRAND**
"Jackson, Tenn." on back, "R.O. Co." under bot-
tom 7.00 10.00
☐ **ELEPHANT BOTTLING CO.**
D under bottom, aqua, 7¾" 6.00 9.00
☐ **ELLIOTT**
Trenton, NJ, blob top, aqua, 7¼" 12.00 18.00
☐ **EL RENO, B. W.**
Aqua, 7¼" 12.00 18.00
☐ **ELSBERRY BOTTLING WORKS**
"Elsberry, MO." on front in oval slug plate, ABM,
crown top, 8" 3.00 5.00
☐ **EMPIRE SODA WORKS**
Vallejo, CA, crown top, aqua, 6½" 6.00 9.00
☐ **EMPSORRS**
In fancy script, tall blob top, panel base, amber,
9¼" 8.00 12.00

Price Range

☐ **F. ENGLE**
Big "E" in back, aqua, 7½" 12.00 18.00

☐ **ENSLEY BOTTLING WORKS**
Ensley, AL, crown top, clear or aqua, 7½" 4.00 6.00

☐ **ENTERPRISE BOTTLING WORKS, DAVIS & CO. PROP.**
"Lincoln, Ill." on panels, ten panels, aqua, 6¾" 9.00 12.00

☐ **EPPS-COLA**
"John C Epping, Louisville, Ky, Reg. 7 Fluid Oz." around bottle, "E" under bottom, snap-on top, aqua, 8" 7.00 10.00

☐ **C. ERNE'S CITY BOTTLING WORKS**
348 & 350 Pienville St. N.O., T.B.N.T.B.S. Blob top, 8¼" 12.00 18.00

☐ **CHARLES EUKER**
Reverse "T.B.N.T.B.S. 1866, Richmond, Va.," blob top, light blue, 7" 18.00 24.00

☐ **M. FAIRBANKS & CO.**
"Howard St., Boston, Mass." on front, large "F & Co." on back, aqua 6.00 9.00

☐ **F.B.W.**
Fairfield, IA, tenpin type, blob top, aqua, 6½" .. 12.00 18.00

☐ **J. A. FALSONE**
Clear or amethyst, 6¾" 5.00 8.00

☐ **S. H. FARNHAM**
In center, "AMERICAN FLA., WESTERLY, R.I." vertical, aqua, 7½" 10.00 15.00

☐ **J. E. FARRELL**
"Main St., Cold Spring" on front in oval slug plate, clear, 9⅛" 6.00 9.00

☐ **FEIGENSON BROS.**
"Reg. Detroit, Mich." on front in oval slug plate, aqua, 6⅛" 7.00 10.00

☐ **FEIHENSPAN P.O.N. TRADEMARK AGENCY**
"Newburgh, N.Y." in oval slug plate, crown top, aqua, 9¼" 6.00 9.00

☐ **E.M. FERRY**
Essex, CT, blob top, clear, 9¼" 6.00 9.00

☐ **FIELDS SUPERIOR SODA WATER**
Charleston, SC, eight sided, blue, 7⅝" 90.00 110.00

☐ **FIELDS SUPERIOR SODA WATER**
Charleston, SC, eight sided, green, 7⅝" 110.00 135.00

Price Range

☐ **S.C. FIELDS SUPERIOR SODA WATER**
Eight panels, ground pontil, cobalt, 7¼" 80.00 100.00

☐ **B.H. FINK**
"J" instead of "F" in back "To Be Returned,"
ground pontil, blue green, 7¼" 60.00 70.00

☐ **HENRY FINKS SONS**
Harrisburg, PA, clear or amethyst, 9½" 7.00 10.00

☐ **FLEMING BROS.**
"Meadville, PA." in four lines, aqua, 6½" 7.00 10.00

☐ **J.C. FOX & CO., FOX T.M.**
Seattle, WA, aqua, 7½" 8.00 12.00

☐ **WM. FREIDMAN, CHAMPION SODA
FACTORY**
Key West, FL, T.B.N.T.B.S., clear or amber, 6½" 6.00 9.00

☐ **GADSDEN**
In center "BOTTLING WORKS, GADSEN, ALA.,"
clear, 6¾" 7.00 10.00

☐ **GAFFNEY & MORGAN**
"Amsterdam, N.Y." in a circle, panel base, aqua,
7½" 7.00 10.00

☐ **GALLITZIN BOTTLING CO.**
"326" under bottom, aqua 6.00 9.00

☐ **GALVESTON BREWING CO.**
Guaranteed Pure, Galveston, TX, aqua, round,
7¾" 6.00 9.00

☐ **HENRY GARDENER TRADEMARK**
West Bromwish, emerald green, 7½" 7.00 10.00

☐ **GEO. GEMENDEN**
"Savannah, Ga" on front, eagle, shield and flag
on back, improved pontil, green, blob top, 7¼" 50.00 60.00

☐ **WILLIAM GENAUST**
"Wilmington, N.C." in a circle, blob top, reverse
side "T.B.N.T.B.S.," aqua, 9¼" 8.00 12.00

☐ **E. M. GATCHELL AND CO.**
Charleston, SC, soda water, green, round, pint,
7¾" 90.00 110.00

☐ **GEYSER SODA**
In back "Natural Mineral Water, From Litton
Springs, Sonoma Co. Calif.," blob top, aqua, 7" 16.00 23.00

☐ **GHIRARD ELLIS BRANCH**
"Oakland" three lines on front, blob top, blue,
7¾" 9.00 12.00

Price Range

☐ **CHAS. GIBBONS**
"Philad." in a horseshoe shape, reverse a star,
long neck, blob top, amber, 8" 16.00   23.00

☐ **T.W. GILLETT**
New Haven, eight panels, graphite pontil, blue,
7½" 60.00   80.00

☐ **GLOBE BOTTLING WORKS**
"Savannah, Ga.," in a circle in center on bottom,
in back "This Bottle Is Never Sold," clear, 8½"   5.00   8.00

☐ **G.M.S. CO.**
Crown in center, "REGISTERED, ALLIANCE,
OHIO," panel base, aqua, 7⅜" 8.00   11.00

☐ **GOLDEN GATE BOTTLING WORK**
In a horseshoe, under it "SAN FRANCISCO,"
7¾" 9.00   12.00

☐ **GOLDEN WEST S. & E. SODA WORKS**
San Jose, CA, four-piece mold, aqua green, 8⅜"   7.00   10.00

☐ **JOHN GRAF**
Milwaukee, panel base, reverse "T.B.N.T.B.S.,"
blue, 8½" 15.00   25.00

☐ **JOHN GRAF**
On other panels "This bottle never sold, Please
Return, When Empty, To The Owner, Cor. 17th
& Greenfield Ave., Trademark The Best What
Gives" 20.00   30.00

☐ **JOHN GRAF**
"Milwaukee, WI." on front, reverse "T.B.N.T.B.S.,
The Best What Gives," trademark, eight panels
on base, aqua green, 6⅜" 8.00   12.00

☐ **GRANT & UPTON**
In a horseshoe shape, under it "COLUMBUS,
OHIO," aqua, 6½" 11.00   15.00

☐ **J & J GRANTHAM**
Star under bottom, "Kiner Bros Ltd" on back,
green, 8" 18.00   24.00

☐ **JOHN GRANZ**
"Croton Falls, N.Y." on front, "T.B.N.T.B.S." on
reverse side, blob top, aqua, 7½" 7.00   10.00

☐ **GRAPE PRODUCTS CO. WALKERS**
On bottom, clear or amethyst, 11" 4.00   6.00

☐ **GRATTAN & CO. LTD.**
Aqua, 9" 6.00   9.00

Price Range

☐ **GREAT BEAR SPRINGS**
Fulton, NY, round bottom, aqua, 12″ 9.00 12.00
☐ **GREENWOOD BOTTLING & SUPPLY CO.**
"Greenwood, S.C." In a circle, crown top, aqua,
7½″ 8.00 11.00
☐ **G.T.B.**
Under bottom, marble in center, aqua, 7¾″ ... 5.00 8.00
☐ **W. GUBNER & SONS**
"New York" all on front. Shield design on back
with "G" embossed in center. Small "G" on bot-
tom. Blob top. Aqua, 7¼″ 10.00 15.00
☐ **GUYETTE & COMPANY**
Detroit, MI, "REGISTERED" in center, "G" under
bottom, cobalt, 6¾″ 30.00 40.00
☐ **H**
In hollow letter, also **"SAC."** with hollow "P,"
clear or aqua, 7″ 7.00 10.00
☐ **HABENICHT BOTTLING WORKS**
"Columbia, S.C." in sunken panel, aqua, 9″ ... 6.00 9.00
☐ **HABENICHT**
Next line "Bottling Works, Columbia, S.C." in
round sunken circle, blob top, amber, 9½″ 15.00 25.00
☐ **HAIGHT & O BRIEN**
Graphite pontil, aqua, 7½″ 30.00 40.00
☐ **H. HALL, HILLTOWN**
"Ireland & New York" at base in three lines, in
center a hand in shield, under it "Trademark," ta-
pered top, semi-round, aqua, 9″ 10.00 15.00
☐ **HANNE BROTHERS**
"This Bottle Not To Be Sold" in back, clear, 7½″ 8.00 12.00
☐ **HANSSEN BROS.**
Grass Valley, CA, in center "G.W.B.," aqua, 7¼″ 8.00 12.00
☐ **C. J. HARGAN & CO.**
Memphis, TN, blob top, aqua, 6¾″ 9.00 12.00
☐ **P. HARRINGTON**
Manchester, NH, "P.H." monogram all inside slug
plate, blob top, clear, 9¼″ 12.00 18.00
☐ **J. HARRISON**
In center "197 FULTON, N.Y.," reverse, "Phila.
XXX Porter & Ale," squat type, green, 6½″ ... 40.00 50.00
☐ **C. HARTMAN**
Cleveland, OH, light blue and blue green 10.00 15.00

Price Range

☐ **F. HARVEY & CO.**
"This Bottle Not To Be Sold" on back, amber,
8½" 6.00   9.00

☐ **J. HARVEY & CO.**
In hollow letters, 65½ Canal St., Providence, RI,
graphite pontil, tapered top, green, 7¾" 60.00   80.00

☐ **J. HARVEY & CO.**
In hollow letters, 65½ Central St., Providence, RI,
blob top, graphite pontil, green, 7½" 60.00   70.00

☐ **J. & J.W. HARVEY**
Norwich, CT, reverse hollow letter "H," graphite
pontil, blob top, green, 7¾" 60.00   70.00

☐ **HARVEY & BRO.**
In a dome shape, under it "HACKETTSTOWN,
N.J.," in back, hollow letter "H," green, 7" 20.00   30.00

☐ **HAWAIIAN SODA WORKS**
Honolulu, TH, aqua, 7½" 9.00   12.00

☐ **J.S. HAZARD**
Westerly, RI, reverse side "XX" in hollow letters,
blob top, aqua, 7¼" 20.00   30.00

☐ **H & D**
In raised letters 1½" tall, under this in two lines
"Savannah, Geo," squat bottle, aqua, 7", blob
top, 7" 18.00   24.00

☐ **HEADMAN**
Phila, reverse "F.W.H." in hollow letters, graphite
pontil, green, 7¼" 55.00   75.00

☐ **M.C. HEALD & CO. (M.C.H. CO)**
"Lynn, Mass." inside of slug plate on front, crown
top, amethyst, 7½" 7.00   10.00

☐ **HEATLY BROS., MAGNUM**
"This Bottle Not To Be Sold" reverse side, aqua,
6¾" 20.00   30.00

☐ **JOHN HEINZERLING**
Baltimore, MD, aqua, 7½" 8.00   12.00

☐ **GEO. N. HEMBT**
"Monticello, N.Y., Reg." on front in slug plate,
aqua, 6¾" 6.00   9.00

☐ **HEMPSTEAD BOTTLING WORK**
"Hempstead, Tx." in a circle, amethyst, fluted
bottom, 8" 6.00   9.00

☐ **HENNESSY & NOLAN GINGER ALE**
"Albany, N.Y." in panels, reverse "H. & N."
monogram, 1876, blob top, aqua, 7¼" 12.00 18.00

☐ **ED HENRY**
Napa, CA, monogram in center, aqua, 6¾" ... 6.00 9.00

☐ **GEO. HENRY**
Aqua, 7½" 7.00 11.00

☐ **F. T. HELLER**
Aqua, 7½" 7.00 11.00

☐ **HERANCOURT BRG. CO.**
Amber, 8¼" 6.00 9.00

☐ **J.C. HERRMANN**
Sharon, PA, Hutchinson, aqua, 9" 15.00 25.00

☐ **HEWLETT BROS.**
Salt Lake City, UT, reverse "T.B.N.T.B.S.," aqua,
6½" 7.00 10.00

☐ **E. HIGGINS**
"OROVILLE" in two lines, blob top, aqua, 7" .. 9.00 12.00

☐ **E. HINECKE**
Louisville, KY, "H" under bottom, aqua, 7" 7.00 10.00

☐ **HIPPO SIZE SODA WATER**
"Prop. Of Alamo Bottling Wks., San Antonio, Tx.,
Nov. 2–1926," picture of hippopotamus, clear,
9½" 3.00 5.00

☐ **HIRE'S**
On bottom, old crown top, aqua, 9¾" 5.00 10.00

☐ **H.L. & J.W.**
Hartford, CT, amber, 6½" 6.00 9.00

☐ **LAWRENCE L. HOLDEN**
"Fall River, Mass." written at an angle, fancy,
blob top, clear, 9¼" 7.00 10.00
☐ Same as above except amber, 8½" 8.00 12.00

☐ **E. K. HORNER BOTTLING WORKS**
Charleston, SC, aqua, round 4.00 7.00

☐ **E.L. HUSTING**
"Milwaukee, Wis." vertical on side, aqua, 6½" 6.00 9.00

☐ **HYDE PARK**
St. Louis, crown top, amber, 9¾" 4.00 6.00

☐ **HYGEIA SODA WORKS**
"Kahului, H." in three lines, star under bottom,
7¼" 15.00 25.00

Price Range

☐ **HYGENIC DISTILLED WATER CO.**
In horseshoe shape, lines under it "BROOKLYN,
AND FAR ROCKAWAY, L.I.," in back "H.D.W.
Co." interlocking hollow letters, aqua, 7" 12.00 18.00

☐ **IMBESCHEID & CO.**
In center, "Registered Jamaica Plain, Mass" all
in a circle, on base "Registered," in back
"T.B.N.T.B.S.," under bottom "Kare Hutter, 33 N,
N.Y.," blob top, aqua, 9" 20.00 30.00

☐ **INGALL'S BROS.**
Portland, ME, squat type, green, 7" 15.00 25.00

☐ **INGALL'S BROS.**
"Portland, Me, Belfast Ale," vertical lines, round
bottom, aqua, 8¼" 11.00 15.00

☐ **ITALIAN, SODA WORKS, MANUFACTURING**
"San Francisco" all in 4 lines, blob top, dark
green, 7" 48.00 62.00

☐ **ITALIAN SODA WATER MANUFACTOR**
"San Francisco" in a horizontal line, reverse
"Union Glass Works, Phila," graphite pontil, em-
erald green, 7½" 75.00 95.00

☐ **JACKSON BOTTLING WORKS**
Jackson, TN, aqua, 8" 6.00 9.00

☐ **J. L. JACOBS**
"Cairo, N.Y." in a round sunken panel, green, 7" 12.00 18.00

☐ **J.L. JACOBS**
Cairo, NY, reverse side "This Bottle Not To Be
Sold," blob top, 7¾" 7.00 10.00

☐ **THE JAMES BOTTLING CO.**
Aqua, 6¾" 8.00 11.00

☐ **F.W. JESSEN BOTTLING WORKS**
Amber, 9½" 7.00 10.00

☐ **J.L. & C. LDC 1449**
Under bottom, aqua, 9½" 4.00 6.00

☐ **JOHNSON & CORBETT**
"Socorro, N.M." in a circle, Hutchinson, aqua, 7" 15.00 25.00

☐ **S. N. JOHNSON BOTTLING WORK**
Laredo, TX, blob top, aqua, 7½" 9.00 12.00

☐ **JOHNSTON BROS.**
"J" on bottom, clear, 7½" 8.00 12.00

☐ **JOHNSTON & CO.**
Phila, squat type, blob top, green, 7" 50.00 60.00

Price Range

☐ **D. JOHNSTON**
"Atlantic City, N.J." in back, "J" in hollow letter,
blob top, aqua, 7" 15.00 25.00

☐ **A. JONES**
Aqua, 6¾" 7.00 10.00

☐ **G. W. JONES & CO.**
Vicksburg, MS, blob top, cobalt blue 200.00 250.00

☐ **GEO. JONES**
Aqua, 7" 6.00 9.00

☐ **GEO. JONES**
"Fonda, N.Y." on front, "G-J Co." monogram on
back, clear, 7¼" 7.00 10.00

☐ **DANIEL KAISER**
"Keokuk, Iowa, P.A. & Co." in four lines, aqua,
7½" 9.00 12.00

☐ **NICK KARL**
"Gloversville, N.Y." on front in oval slug plate,
"This Bottle Not To Be Sold" on back, aqua, 9¼" 7.00 10.00

☐ **K.B. LD 7-122-1**
Under bottom, aqua, 7½" 3.00 5.00

☐ **M.F. KEELER**
"M.F. Keeler" appears in an arc, "Auburn, N.Y."
appears as two straight lines, blob top, aqua, 7⅜" 9.00 12.00

☐ **P. KELLETT**
Newark, NJ, squat type, graphite pontile, green,
6¾" 38.00 48.00

☐ **P. KELLETT**
"Newark, NJ," reverse "K", 1857, green, 7½" 30.00 40.00

☐ **T. M. KERR**
Jackson, MS, blob top, aqua, 7⅛" 200.00 250.00

☐ **KERYER & CO., EST. 1851**
"Belfast" in center, in center of Trademark a five-
leaved flower, round bottom, aqua, tapered top,
9½" 7.00 10.00

☐ **KIA-ORA. T.M. REG. BEVERAGES LEMON
ORANGE & LIME MADE FROM REAL FRUIT
JUICE, O-T LTD. INC.**
S.F., CA, Clear or amber, 11" 10.00 15.00

☐ **H.B. KILMER**
N.Y., "Philada Porter & Ale" in back, graphite
pontil, green, 6½" 60.00 70.00

Price Range

☐ **GEORGE KIMMERER**
"Canajoharie, N.Y." on front in oval slug plate,
aqua, 9½" 5.00   8.00

☐ **KINSELLA & HENNESSY**
Albany, NY, blob top, aqua, 6¾" 8.00   12.00

☐ **KINSELLA & HENNESSY**
In a dome shape under it "ALBANY", blob top,
aqua, 7½" 7.00   10.00

☐ **CHAS. KOLSHORN & BRO.**
Savannah, GA, blob top, aqua, 8" 7.00   10.00

☐ **C. L. KORNAHRENS**
Aqua, "C.L.K." in back, 7½" 8.00   11.00

☐ **C.L. KORNAHRENS**
"Charleston, S.C." in circle, Trademark in center,
in back "This Bottle Not To Be Sold," aqua, 7¾" 7.00   10.00

☐ **C.L. KORNAHRENS**
In a horseshoe shape, under it "Charleston,
S.C.," blob top, aqua, 7" 6.00   9.00

☐ **C. L. KORNAHRENS**
Charleston, SC, round, aqua, $7^{9/16}$" 4.00   8.00

☐ **J. L. KORNAHRENS**
Charleston, SC, round, iron pontil, blue, $7^{7/16}$" 40.00   50.00

☐ **KROGER BROS**
"Butte, MT." in a slug plate, aqua, 6¾" 10.00   15.00

☐ **H.O. KRUEGER**
Grand Forks, ND, aqua, 7½" 9.00   13.00

☐ **A. KRUMENAKER**
"New York" in a slug plate circle, in center two
lines "512 & 514 West 166th St.," under it "Registered," in back "This Bottle Not To Be Sold,"
blob top, aqua, 7¼" 7.00   10.00

☐ **HENRY KUCK, 1878**
"Savannah, Ga." in four lines on front, green,
blob top, 7½" 25.00   35.00

☐ Same as above, no date 40.00   30.00

☐ **HENRY KUCK**
"Savannah, Ga" in a slug plate on front, blob top,
short neck, aqua, 7½" 20.00   30.00

☐ **HENRY KUCK**
"Savannah, Ga." in three lines, green, blob top,
7" 12.00   17.00

☐ Same except no "Ga" 13.00   19.00

☐ **THE JOHN KUHLMANN BREWING CO.**
"Ellenville, N.Y." on front in oval slug plate, aqua,
6¾" **6.00 9.00**

☐ **J. H. KUMP**
In hollow letters "MEMPHIS, TENN.", blob top,
aqua, 7½" **8.00 12.00**

☐ **L & V**
In large hollow letters, blob top, pontil, aqua and
green, 7" **65.00 85.00**

☐ **Le LAGHTLEBEN**
"Hackensack, N.J. REGISTERED" slanted on
front, blob top, aqua, 9¼" **7.00 10.00**

☐ **J. LAKE**
In hollow letters, Schenectady, NY, semi-round
bottom, graphite pontil, cobalt, 8" **55.00 65.00**

☐ **LANCASTER GLASS WORKS**
NY, graphite pontil, blue, 7¼" **55.00 65.00**

☐ **E. LESTER**
St. Louis, skinny neck, concave bottom, graphite
pontil, tear shaped bubbles, early soda, aqua,
7½" tall, 2⅝" diam. at base, 2½" diam. at neck **20.00 35.00**

☐ **LOS ANGELES SODA CO.**
In a dome shape, line under it "MINERAL
WATER FACTORY," reverse side "H.W. Stoll,"
blob top, aqua, 6¾" **15.00 25.00**

☐ **LOS BANOS**
In center "L & B SODA WORKS," crown top,
clear, 6½" **6.00 9.00**

☐ **HENRY LUBS & CO.**
1885, Savannah, GA, green, blob top, 7½" ... **18.00 24.00**

☐ **HENRY LUBS & CO.**
1885, Savannah, GA, short neck, aqua, blob top **18.00 24.00**

☐ **LYMAN ASTLEY**
Cheyenne, WY, aqua, 7" **8.00 12.00**

☐ **M.B. & CO.**
145 West 35th St., NY, 1861, early blob top,
smooth bottom, aqua, 7½" **12.00 17.00**

☐ **MACON MEDICINE CO.**
"Guinn's Pioneer Blood Renerver on other side,
amber, 11" **12.00 18.00**

☐ **M. MADISON**
Laramie, WT, blob top, aqua, 7" **55.00 65.00**

Price Range

☐ **MAGNOLIA BOTTLING CO.**
Paso, TX, "Contents 7 fl. oz." around bottom and
shoulder, crown top, aqua, 7⅝" 4.00 6.00

☐ **THOS MAHER**
In small letters on slug plate, ground pontil, dark
green, 7½" 15.00 25.00

☐ Same, except larger ½" size letters 15.00 25.00

☐ **THOS MAHER**
Slug plate, green, 6¾" 25.00 35.00

☐ **THOS MAHER**
Slug plate, dark green, 7" 20.00 28.00

☐ **MANUEL BROS.**
"New Bedford, Mass" on front in slug plate, blob
top, amethyst, 9¼" 7.00 11.00

☐ **MARBLE BOTTLE**
Japan, two round holes on shoulder, green, 7½" 8.00 11.00

☐ **MARBLE TEARDROP TYPE BOTTLE**
Aqua, 9¾" 15.00 25.00

☐ **THE MAR-COLA CO.**
Aqua, 7¾" 6.00 9.00

☐ **MARION-BOTTLE WORKS**
In center "M. & B." monogram, Marion, NC, aqua,
6½" 15.00 25.00

☐ **A. MAROTTA**
249–251 North St., Boston, MA, clear, 9¼" ... 6.00 9.00

☐ **MARQUEZ & MOLL**
Ground pontil, aqua, 7¼" 50.00 60.00

☐ **C.H. MARTIN & CO., SODA WORKS**
Avon, WA, aqua, 7¼" 7.00 10.00

☐ **B. MARSH & SON**
Detroit, MI, ten panels, blob top, aqua, 7½" ... 12.00 17.00

☐ **MASON & BURNS**
Richmond, VA, 1859, blob top, dark green, 7" 25.00 35.00

☐ **S.M. MATTEAWAN**
NY, "S.M.M." monogram on back, ten panels at
base, clear, 6¼" 7.00 10.00

☐ **MAU & CO. H.**
"Eureka, Nevada" in 3 lines, blob top, plain bottom, aqua, 6½" 38.00 48.00

☐ **M. B. & CO.**
145 W. 35th St., N.Y., 1862, blob top, aqua, 7¼" 11.00 15.00

☐ **J.W. McADAMS TRADEMARK**
In center of a bunch of grapes, Richmond, VA,
panel base, aqua, 7″ 10.00 14.00

☐ **M. McCORMACK**
"W. McC & CO." on back, amber, 7″ 15.00 25.00

☐ **McGEE, BENICEA**
In 2 lines, blob top, plain bottom, 6¾″ 55.00 65.00

☐ **THOS. McGOVERN**
Albany, NY, blob top, aqua, 7½″ 8.00 12.00

☐ **J. McLAUGLIN**
Green, 7½″ 20.00 30.00

☐ **McMAHONS WELL'S**
Ft. Edward, NY, T.B.N.T.B.S., blob top, clear or
amber, 7½″ 8.00 12.00

☐ **McMINNVILLE BOTTLING WORKS**
"This Bottle Not To Be Sold" in back, amber,
7½″ 6.00 9.00

☐ **MEEHAN BROS.**
"Barberton, Ohio" in script, aqua, 6½″ 12.00 18.00

☐ **MEINCKE & EBBERWEIN**
In horseshoe shape, in center "1882", under it
in two lines "Savannah, Geo," "Ginger Ale" vertical on back, amber, short neck, blob top, 8¼″ 30.00 40.00

☐ **JOSEPH MENTZE**
Milton, PA, blob top, aqua, 7¼″ 12.00 17.00

☐ **MERCER BOTTLING CO.**
"This Bottle Is Registered Not To Be Sold" on
back, aqua, 9½″ 8.00 11.00

☐ **MERRITT & CO.**
Helena, MT, blob top, aqua, 7¼″ 10.00 15.00

☐ **A. METTE & BRO.**
Chicago, "M. Bros." embossed on bottom, back
"I.G. Co." light blue, 6½″ 8.00 12.00

☐ **MEXOTA**
Root under bottom, 11½″ 7.00 10.00

☐ **A.W. MEYER 1885**
"Savannah, GA." in four lines on front, green,
blob top, 8″ 15.00 25.00

☐ Same except aqua 15.00 25.00

☐ **JOHN P. MEYER**
"Freehold, N.Y." on front in oval slug plate, clear,
9″ 7.00 10.00

Price Range

☐ **MIAMI BOTTLING WORKS**
Clear or amethyst, 7½" 6.00   9.00
☐ **MIGUEL PONS & CO.**
Mobile, blob top, graphite pontil, teal blue, 7½"   40.00   50.00
☐ **MILLERS BOTTLING WORKS**
Aqua, M under bottom, 8" 5.00   8.00
☐ **MILLER, BECKER & CO., M.B. & CO.**
Cleveland, OH, apple green, blob top, 6¾" 7.00   10.00
☐ **MILVILLE GLASS WORK**
In ½ moon circle, dark green, 7" 40.00   55.00
☐ **M. MINTZ, M.M.**
In center "GLOVERSVILLE, N.Y., REGIS-
TERED," blob top, clear, 8" 6.00   9.00
☐ **MIRRIANS**
On shoulder, graphite pontil, cobalt, 7¼" 40.00   50.00
☐ **MISSION ORANGE DRY REG.**
Under bottom, black glass, 9½" 5.00   8.00
☐ **C.A. MOELLER**
"Karl Hutter 33 in New York" under bottom, aqua,
9¼" 9.00   12.00
☐ **CHAS MOHR & SON**
5¢ for return of bottle, Mobile, AL, clear, 7" . . .   7.00   10.00
☐ **MONTANA BOTTLING CO.**
Butte City, MT, blob top, clear or aqua, 6¾" . .   12.00   18.00
☐ **MONROE CIDER & VINEGAR CO.**
Eureka, CA, clear or aqua, 7¼" 7.00   10.00
☐ **MORGAN & BRO.**
232 W. 47th St., NY, reverse "M.B. Trademark,"
blob top, aqua, 7" 12.00   18.00
☐ **MORLEY C.**
"Victoria, B.C." in 4 lines vertical, blob top, 6½"   60.00   80.00
☐ **MORRILL G.P.**
In 2 lines, blob top, plain bottom, aqua, 7" 25.00   34.00
☐ **T. & R. MORTON**
"Newark, N.J." in three lines, squat type, graphite
pontil, green, 6¾" 55.00   75.00
☐ **L.C. MOSES BOTTLER**
Parsons, Kansas and Bartlesville, Crown top,
aqua 15.00   25.00
☐ **MOUNT BOTTLING CO.**
"This Bottle Not To Be Sold" on back, "3" under
bottom, aqua, 9½" 8.00   11.00

Price Range

☐ **C. MOTEL**
Aqua, big "M" on bottom, 7" 8.00 11.00

☐ **E. MOYLE**
Aqua, 7¼" 7.00 10.00

☐ **EDWARD MOYLE**
"Savannah, GA" on front, "Ginger Ale" vertical
on back, amber, 7½" 25.00 35.00

☐ **E. MOYLE**
"Savannah, GA." in sunken circle, blob top,
1880, aqua, 7¼" 7.00 10.00

☐ **JOHN E. MUELHLECK**
"Nelliston, N.Y." on front in arch slug plate,
"T.B.N.T.B.S." on reverse side, aqua, 6¾" 6.00 9.00

☐ **MUFF CO.**
Label, marble in center of neck, aqua, 7¼" ... 5.00 8.00

☐ **JAS. MULHOLLAND**
"South Amboy, N.J." on front in oval slug plate,
reverse side "T.B.N.T.B.S.," blue aqua, 9½" .. 7.00 10.00

☐ **B.J.E. MULLENS**
Eagle in center, "STANDARD GRADE BOT-
TLING WORK, ALBANY, N.Y." in script, crown
top, aqua, 9¼" 7.00 10.00

☐ **T.F. MURPHY**
"Brookfield, Mass." on front in slug plate, blob
top, aqua, 9¼" 5.00 8.00

☐ **P.C. MURRAY**
"Monticello, N.Y." on front in slug plate, aqua, 7" 7.00 10.00

☐ **N.A. PA. (star under it), WOODS (star under
it), SODA**
In back "Natural Mineral Water," blob top, blue,
7¼" 20.00 30.00

☐ **OTIS S. NEALE CO,**
"Howard St., Boston, Registered 1893" with
"OSN" monogram, all on front, blob top, ame-
thyst, 9¼" 7.00 10.00

☐ **NERVE PEPSIN CO.**
"Trademark Registered" on shoulder, clear, 8" 6.00 9.00

☐ **NEUMANN & FUNKE**
Detroit, MI, Hutchinson, aqua, 7" 15.00 25.00

☐ **NEVADA CITY SODA WORKS**
"L. Seibert" in 4 lines, blob top, plain bottom,
aqua, 7" 35.00 45.00

Price Range

☐ **NEW ALAMADEN/MINERAL WATER, W & W, 1870**
Same on reverse in large letters, blob top, aqua, 7½" 7.00 10.00

☐ **NEW CASTLE BOTTLING CO.,**
"Mt. Kisco, N.Y." on front in oval slug plate, amethyst, 9" 5.00 8.00

☐ **NONPAREIL, SODA WATER CO.**
"S.F." in 3 lines, blob top, aqua, 6¾" 20.00 28.00

☐ **NO. MAIN ST. WINE CO.**
"208–212 No. Main St., Providence, R.I." with "H" in center inside of slug plate, blob top, clear, 9¼" 6.00 9.00

☐ **NORTHERN COCA-COLA BOTTLING WORKS, INC.**
Massena, NY, seltzer bottle type with pewter nozzle, cobalt, 9¼" 55.00 65.00

☐ **NOVA KOLA**
"This Bottle Not To Be Sold" on base, clear or amethyst, 7¾" 5.00 8.00

☐ **OAKLAND PIONEER SODA WORK CO., TRADEMARK**
Embossed bottle inside of "O", aqua, 8¼" 6.00 9.00

☐ **OAKLAND STEAM SODA WORKS INC.**
In center in a wheel, on base "Bottle Not To Be Sold" 10.00 15.00

☐ **OCCIDENTAL BOTTLE WORKS**
Occidental, CA, "O.B.W." monogram, aqua or clear, 6¾" 7.00 10.00

☐ **ODIORNE'S**
Clear, 8½" 4.00 6.00

☐ **O'KEEFE BROS. BOTTLERS**
"Matteawan, N.Y. Registered" on front, "O.K.B." monogram on back, ten panels at base, aqua or clear, 6½" 7.00 10.00

☐ Same as above except 9¼" 8.00 11.00

☐ **O.K. SODA WORKS**
In three lines, aqua, 7" 7.00 10.00

☐ **OLSEN & CO.**
Memphis, TN, blob top, cobalt, 7½" 75.00 95.00

Price Range

☐ **D.L. ORMSBY**
In 2″ hollow letters, graphite pontil, blob top, cobalt, 7½″ 60.00 70.00

☐ **OWEN CASE**
"Eagle Soda Work" in 3 lines, on back "Sac City," tapered top, cobalt, 7½″ 42.00 58.00

☐ **OZARK FRUIT CO.**
"Memphis, Tenn" in a circle, panels around base, aqua, 7½″ 12.00 18.00
☐ Same except crown top 7.00 10.00

☐ **OZO-OLA THE HAPPY DRINK**
Clear, 7½″ 4.00 6.00

☐ **J. PABLO & CO., SELTZ, & MINERAL WATER MANUFACTORY**
Biloxi, embossed picture of man and dog in rowboat, blob top, aqua, 7⅛″ 100.00 150.00

☐ **J. PABST & SON**
"Hamilton, Ohio" in a circle, aqua, 6½″ 8.00 11.00

☐ **PACIFIC & PUGET SOUND SODA WORKS**
Seattle, WA, aqua, 7″ 9.00 12.00

☐ **PACIFIC BOTTLING WORKS**
Pacific, MO, ABM, aqua, 8″ 4.00 6.00

☐ **PACIFIC GLASS WORK**
All under bottom, blob top, label bottle, aqua, 6¾″ 35.00 45.00

☐ **PACIFIC SODA WORKS**
Santa Cruz, "R" in a hollow letter in center ... 7.00 10.00

☐ **D. PALLISER**
Mobile, AL, aqua, 6¾″ 7.00 10.00

☐ **D. PALLISER**
"Arthur Christian, 1875 Pat. April 13" under bottom, glass plunger for stopper, aqua 12.00 18.00

☐ **D. PALLISER**
Aqua, 7½″ 8.00 11.00

☐ **D. PALLISIER**
Palliser misspelled, aqua, 7½″ 15.00 25.00

☐ **PALMETTO BOTTLING WORKS**
Clear or amethyst, 9¼″ 9.00 12.00

☐ **PARKER**
Graphite pontil, blue, 5″ 50.00 60.00

Price Range

☐ **E. PARMENTER**
"Glenham, N.Y." on front in crude slug plate,
aqua, 9¼" 7.00 10.00

☐ **E. PARMENTER**
"Matteawan, N.Y." on front in slug plate,
"T.B.N.T.B.S." reverse side, blob top, aqua ... 6.00 8.00

☐ **PATTERSONS T.**
In ½ moon circle in center of it "140," under it
in 2 lines "Church St., New York," 7" blob top,
dark blue 38.00 50.00

☐ **PEARSON'S SODAWORKS**
Aqua, 7" 6.00 8.00

☐ **PEPSI-COLA**
In center in script, also on bottom, "7" on top of
shoulder, clear or aqua, crown top, not machine
made 6.00 8.00

☐ **PEPSI-COLA**
In script, "Trademark" on top, "Memphis, Tenn."
under it on slug plate, on back "Registered,"
"2322" under bottom, crown top, not machine
made, amber 20.00 30.00

☐ **PORT BYRON BOTTLING WORKS**
Name and location appear as a circle, "N.Y." in
center of circle, old blob top, aqua, 8½" 9.00 12.00

☐ **PORTLAND**
Picture of an eagle, above that "TRADEMARK,
THE EAGLE SODA WORKS, P.O.," blob top,
aqua, 7¼" 13.00 18.00

☐ **POST E.A.**
In center a eagle, under it "Portland, Org.," all in
watermelon circle, blob top, plain bottom, aqua 50.00 60.00

☐ **POST EXCHANGE BOTTLING WORKS**
"Fort Riley, KAN." in a circle, crown top, aqua,
7" 7.00 10.00

☐ **PRESCOTT BOTTLING WORKS**
"Prescott, A.T." in four lines, aqua, 6½" 70.00 90.00

☐ **S. PRIESTER & BRO.**
Houston, TX, aqua, 7¼" 10.00 15.00

☐ **PURITY BOTTLING & MFG. CO.**
Clear or amethyst, purity on bottom, 8" 6.00 9.00

Price Range

☐ **M.T. QUINAN**
In horseshoe shape, in center "1884," under it
in two lines "Savannah, Geo," in back, 2″ monogram "MTQ," on top "Mineral" and under
"Water" under bottom monogram "MTQ," co-
balt, blob top, 7¾″ 40.00 50.00

☐ **QUINAN & STUDER 1888**
Savannah, GA, aqua, blob top, 7½″ 15.00 25.00

☐ **RADIUM SPRINGS BOTTLING CO.**
Machine made, "R" on bottom, clear, 7¾″ 4.00 6.00

☐ **RANDALL**
Clear or amethyst, 5¼″ 4.00 6.00

☐ **JAMES RAY'S SONS**
"Savannah, GA," in center, "Hayo-Kola" in
sunken circle, blob top, clear, 8″ 9.00 12.00

☐ **JAMES RAY**
"Savannah, Geo." in sunken circle, on back in
one vertical line "Ginger Ale," cobalt, blob top,
8″ 30.00 40.00

☐ **JAMES RAY**
"Savannah, GA." in watermelon circle on back,
monogram "JR," dark amber, 7½″ 30.00 40.00

☐ **JAMES RAY**
"Savannah, GA." in watermelon circle on back,
monogram "JR," aqua, 7½″ 30.00 40.00

☐ **JAMES RAY & SONS 1876**
"Savannah, GA." in a sunken circle on back,
"This Bottle Registered, Not To Be Sold," under
bottom, "B," clear or amethyst, 7½″ 13.00 18.00

☐ **JAMES RAY**
"Savannah, GA." in a sunken circle, aqua, blob
top, under bottom C24, 7½″ 9.00 13.00

☐ **JAMES RAY**
"Savannah, GA." in a sunken circle on front, blob
top, aqua, 7½″ 8.00 12.00

☐ **JAMES RAY & SONS 1876**
Same except on back "RJ," hollow letters 30.00 40.00

☐ **RAYNERS SPECIALTIES**
Aqua, 7½″ 9.00 12.00

☐ **R.C. & T.**
New York, graphite pontil, aqua, 7½″ 65.00 85.00

Price Range

☐ **R CROWN SODA WORKS**
In large slug plate, ABM, aqua, 7⅞" 4.00   6.00

☐ **READ'S DOG'S HEAD**
"London" on front around base, crown top, ABM,
emerald green, 9¼" 4.00   6.00

☐ **REGISTERED**
In oval slug plate, T.B.N.T.B.S., crown top, amethyst, 9¼" 4.00   6.00

☐ **C.H. RICHARDSON**
In a dome shape, under it "TRENTON, N.J.,"
green, 7" 16.00   23.00

☐ **N. RICHARDSON**
Trenton, NJ, graphited pontil, dark green, 7" .. 55.00   75.00

☐ **THE RICHARDSON BOTTLING CO.**
"Mansfield, Ohio" in a circle, aqua, 6¾" 6.00   9.00

☐ **RICHMOND PEPSI COLA BOTTLING CO.**
"Richmond, Va." in a circle, slim shape, aqua, 9"   12.00   18.00

☐ **W.R. RIDDLE**
Phila., reverse large monogram, graphite pontil,
blob top, blue, 7½" 55.00   70.00

☐ **C.W. RIDER**
Watertown, NY, frost green, 6¾" 17.00   23.00

☐ **T. & H. ROBER**
Savannah, GE., graphite pontil, green, 7" 55.00   75.00

☐ **JAMES M. ROBERTSON**
Phila., reverse side "T.B.N.T.B.S.," blob top,
aqua, 7¼" 7.00   10.00

☐ **A.B. ROBINSON**
In a dome shape, under it "BANGOR, ME.," blob
top, aqua, 7¾" 11.00   15.00

☐ **J.P. ROBINSON**
Salem, NJ, on reverse side hollow letter "R," blob
top, green, 6½" 15.00   25.00

☐ **R ROBINSON'S**
"402 Atlantic Av., Brooklyn, N.Y." on back, aqua,
7¼" 10.00   15.00

☐ **ROBINSON, WILSON & LEGALLSE**
102 Sudsburys, Boston, blob top, ice blue, 6⅜"   11.00   16.00

☐ **ROCKY MOUNTAIN BOTTLING CO.**
"Butte, Mont." in large letters, aqua, 6⅜" 15.00   25.00

☐ **A.I. ROE**
"Arcadia, Fla." on panel, "Coca Cola Bottling
Co." on bottom, clear, machine made, 7¾" ... **5.00 8.00**

☐ **HENRY ROWOHLT**
"HR Trademark Registered" on back, aqua, 7½" **7.00 10.00**

☐ **JOHN RYAN**
In 2" letters around bottle, hollow letters under
it "Savannah, Geo," ground pontil, cobalt, 7" .. **60.00 80.00**

☐ **JOHN RYAN**
In 2" letters around bottle, under it "Savannah,
Geo," under it "1859," cobalt, 7" **70.00 90.00**

☐ **JOHN RYAN**
Savannah, GA. in vertical line, in back, also vertical line "Gingerale," on shoulder "1852 Excelsior," amber or golden, 7½" **35.00 45.00**

☐ **JOHN RYAN 1866**
In front, in back "Excelsior Soda-works, Savannah, Geo.," cobalt, olive, blue, green and red,
7¼" **45.00 65.00**

☐ **JOHN RYAN**
In small no. "1866," blue, 7¼" **38.00 48.00**

☐ **JOHN RYAN**
On front "J.R.S. 1852. T. Columbus, Ga.," on
back "This bottle is Never Sold 1883," on bottom
"R," cobalt, 7¾", round **60.00 80.00**

☐ **JOHN RYAN 1866**
"Savannah, GA." on front, in back, 1" letters
"Cider," amber, 7½" **28.00 38.00**

☐ **JOHN RYAN**
"Savannah, GA." in center of it, "1852," blue,
7½" **45.00 55.00**

☐ **JOHN RYAN**
"Savannah, GA." in three vertical lines, round
bottom, 8" **75.00 110.00**

☐ **CHAS SCHEPEGRELL**
Charleston, SC, green, round, pint, 7⅜" **140.00 165.00**

☐ **P. SCHILLE**
In center monogram "S. P.," under it "COLUM-
BUS, O.," aqua, 6¾" **7.00 10.00**

Price Range

☐ **SCHOONMAKER & WILKLOW**
In center, "ELLENVILLE, N.Y." in a sunken circle,
blob top, aqua, 7½" 10.00   15.00

☐ **ALEX SCHOONMAKER**
"Ellenville, N.Y." in an oval slug plate, clear, 6¾"   7.00   10.00

☐ **CARL H. SCHULT**
Top vertical line, in center "C-P", monogram "M-
S", three lines "Pat. May 4, 1868 New York," ten-
pin type, aqua, 8½" 10.00   15.00

☐ **CHRISTIAN SCHLEPEGRELL AND CO.
SODA WATER,**
Charleston, SC, Return This Bottle, eight sided,
iron pontil, blue, 8¼" 140.00   160.00

☐ **CHRISTIAN SCHLEPEGRALL AND CO.
SODA WATER**
Charleston, SC, "Return This Bottle," eight sided,
iron pontil, dark olive green, 8¼" 165.00   185.00

☐ **FRANK SCUTT BOTTLER**
"Verband Village, N.Y. 702" inside of slug plate,
crown top, amethyst, 7½" 5.00   8.00

☐ **H. C. SEEDORFF**
Charleston, SC, slug plate, round, iron pontil,
blue, 7⁷/₁₆" 40.00   50.00

☐ **H.C. SEEDORFF**
Charleston, SC slug plate, round, iron pontil,
green, 7⁷/₁₆" 40.00   50.00

☐ **JOHN SEEDORFF**
Charleston, SC, slug plate, round, iron pontil,
blue, 7¹/₁₆" 40.00   50.00

☐ **JOHN SEEDORFF**
Ground pontil, blue, 7½" 48.00   58.00

☐ **SEITZ BROS**
Easton, PA, large "S" on reverse side, blob top,
graphite pontil, cobalt, 7½" 60.00   70.00

☐ **SEITZ BR. CO.**
Large "S" in back, amber, 7¼" 40.00   50.00

☐ **SEITZ BROS.**
Easton, PA, large "S" on reverse side, blob top,
green, 7¼" 45.00   55.00

☐ **SEITZ BROS**
Large "S" on back, blue green, 7" 55.00   75.00

☐ **F. SETZ**
Easton, PA, on back, ground pontil, green, 7¼″   **40.00**   **50.00**

☐ **7-UP**
Crown top, brown, squat type bottle, 6″ **7.00**   **10.00**

☐ **E.P. SHAW'S**
Label, marble in center of neck, aqua, 7¼″ . . .   **8.00**   **11.00**

☐ **E. SHEEHAN 1880**
Augusta, GA, blob top, "Return This Bottle" reverse side, aqua, 9″ **13.00**   **18.00**

☐ **E. SHEEHAN 1880**
Augusta, Ga, blob top, amber, 7¼″ **40.00**   **50.00**

☐ **E. SHEEHAN 1880**
Augusta, GA, in an oval slug plate, reverse side "R.T.B.," cobalt, 7½″ **120.00**   **150.00**

☐ **E. SHEEHAN**
Augusta, GA, blob top, amber, 7½″ **25.00**   **35.00**

☐ **E. SHEEHAN, 1880**
Augusta, GA, blob top, green, 7¼″ **25.00**   **35.00**

☐ **E. SHEEHAN, 1880**
Augusta, GA, reverse side "R.T.B.," amber, 8¼″   **25.00**   **35.00**

☐ **SHEYENNE BOTTLING**
Valley City, ND

☐ **SHINER BOTTLING WORKS**
"Shiner, TEX." in a circle slug plate, aqua, 6½″   **7.00**   **10.00**

☐ **SINALCO**
"C" in a triangle and "8" under bottom, snap-on, machine made, amber, 7½″ **5.00**   **8.00**

☐ **CHARLES SINGER**
Peoria, IL, "C. S." on bottom, squat blob top, medium blue, 7⅝″ **12.00**   **18.00**

☐ **SIOUX BOTTLING WORKS**
Watertown, SD, clear, 7″ **9.00**   **12.00**

☐ **SIP DRINKS TASTE LIKE MORE**
Around base "SIP BOTTLING CORP.," reverse side, a hand with crossed fingers and embossing reading "Make This Sign," crown top, clear, 7½″   **10.00**   **15.00**

☐ **A.P. SMITH**
Ground pontil, 7¼″ **40.00**   **50.00**

☐ **B. SMITH**
"Reg. Poughkeepsie, N.Y." in a slug plate, blob top, clear, 9¼″ **6.00**   **9.00**

Price Range

☐ **D. SMITH**
"Yonkers, N.Y." on front in shield slug plate,
T.B.N.T.B.S., aqua, 9" 7.00 10.00

☐ **D.H. SMITH**
"Yonkers, N.Y." in shield slug plate, blob top,
clear, 11½" 7.00 10.00

☐ **A. P. SMITH**
Charleston, SC, blue, round, pint, 7½" 38.00 47.00

☐ **A. P. SMITH**
Charleston, SC, green, round, pint, 7½" 38.00 47.00

☐ **A. P. SMITH SLUG PLATE**
Charleston, blue, round, pint, 7½" 35.00 43.00

☐ **A. P. SMITH SLUG PLATE**
Charleston, green, round, pint, 7½" 37.00 43.00

☐ **SMITH & CO.**
Panels around base, blue 25.00 35.00

☐ **SMITH & CO.**
Seven panels, ground pontil, green 60.00 70.00

☐ **SMITH AND CO. PREMIUM SODA WATER**
Charleston, SC, eight sided, iron pontil, blue, 7⅝" 90.00 110.00

☐ **SMITH & SWEENEY**
"Middletown, N.Y." on front in oval slug plate,
blob top, aqua, 7" 7.00 10.00

☐ **SODA**
Label, graphite pontil, green, 7½" 25.00 34.00

☐ **SODA**
Plain, blob top with sunken circle, under it, "Reg-
is-tered," aqua, 7½" 6.00 9.00

☐ **SODA**
Label, "1589 C" on bottom, aqua, 7½" 4.00 6.00

☐ **SODA**
Label, clear or amethyst, 7½" 4.00 6.00

☐ **SODA**
Label, aqua, marble in neck, 9" 7.00 10.00

☐ **SODA**
Label, tear drop, flat top, aqua, 8½" 20.00 30.00

☐ **SODA**
Label, small kick-up, dark green, 7½" 4.00 6.00

☐ **SODA**
Label, "This Bottle Not To Be Sold" on back,
aqua, 9¼" 4.00 6.00

Price Range

☐ **SODA**
Label, "Reg. This Bottle Not To Be Sold" on
back, anchor under bottom, clear or amethyst,
7½" 6.00 9.00

☐ **SODA WATER BOTTLING CO.**
"Property of Coca Cola, Pat'd June 1, 1926,
Memphis" on four panels on center, six panels
on neck with stars, ABM, green, 9¼" 5.00 8.00

☐ **SOLANO SODA WORKS**
"Vacaville, Calif." in four lines, aqua, 6¾" 8.00 12.00

☐ **SOUTHERN BOTTLING CO.**
Atlanta, GA, aqua, 6¼" 20.00 30.00

☐ **THE SOUTHWESTERN BOTTLING CO.**
Tulsa, crown top, aqua, 7¾" 12.00 17.00

☐ **SOUTHWICK & TUPPES**
"New York" on eight panels, graphite pontil,
green, 7½" 55.00 75.00

☐ **SQUEEZE**
Clear or amethyst, "Ybor City, Fla" on bottom,
machine made, 8" 7.00 10.00

☐ **STANDARD BOTTLING & EXTRACT CO.**
Aqua, 9¼" 4.00 6.00

☐ **STANDARD BOTTLING CO.**
Machine made, a star on bottom, aqua 4.00 6.00

☐ **STANDARD BOTTLING CO., PETER ORELLO
PROP.**
Silverton, CO, aqua, 6¾" 9.00 12.00

☐ **STANDARD BOTTLING WORKS,**
Minneapolis, Minn, amber, 6¾" 11.00 15.00

☐ **STAR**
Under bottom, aqua, 9½" 5.00 8.00

☐ **STAR BOTTLING WORKS**
"Houston, Texas" written in a circle around a
large star, tear drop shape, blob top, aqua, 8" 55.00 65.00

☐ **STAR MAIL ORDER HOUSE**
"243" under bottom, clear or amethyst, 12¼" 11.00 15.00

☐ **M & M STAR BOTTLING CO**
Oskaloosa, LA, clear or aqua, 6¾" 8.00 11.00

☐ **STAR SODA WORKS, GRIBLE & CO.**
In a circle, in center "Nevada City," 7", clear .. 8.00 11.00

☐ **E.B. STARSNEY**
Clear or amethyst, 8¼" 4.00 6.00

Price Range

☐ **STEINKE & KORNAHRNES**
On one panel, "Charleston, S.C." other panel,
eight panels, dark olive, ground pontil, 8½" ...   70.00   80.00

☐ **STEINKE AND KORNAHRENS SODA WATER**
Charleston, SC, "Return This Bottle," eight sided,
iron pontil, green, 8½" 135.00 165.00

☐ **H. STEWART**
253 Room St., NO, blob top, graphite pontil, aqua,
7½" 65.00   75.00

☐ **STILLMAN BOTTLING CO.**
"42 Stillman St., Boston" in a slug plate, blob top,
9¼" 6.00   9.00

☐ **PETER STONITSCH**
Aqua, 9" 6.00   9.00

☐ **STRAWHORN & SLAGO, REGISTERED**
Greenwood, SC, T.B.N.T.B.S. & "MUST BE RE-
TURNED," crown top, aqua, 7¾" 9.00   12.00

☐ **P. STUMPF & CO**
"This Bottle Not To Be Sold" on back, amber,
8½" 20.00   30.00

☐ **J.P. SLLIVAN**
Santa Rosa, blob top, aqua, 6½" 6.00   9.00

☐ **SUMMERS & ALLEN**
"Alexandria, Virginia" in three vertical lines, aqua,
7½" 12.00   18.00

☐ **SUPERIOR BOTTLING WORK**
Superior, Wash, aqua, 6½" 12.00   18.00

☐ **SUPERIOR SODA WATER, J.F. MILLER**
Davenport, Iowa, blob top, fancy shoulder, five
panels, blue 17.00   23.00

☐ **SUPERIOR SODA WATER**
Other side, ground pontil, blue, 7½" 55.00   70.00

☐ **SUPERIOR SODA WATER**
Eagle on shield and flags, "Superior Soda Water"
on back, round, iron pontil, blue, 7¾" 115.00 135.00

☐ **SUPREME BOTTLING CO.**
"Waukesha, Wis." on front in a slug plate, aqua,
6¾" 7.00   10.00

☐ **ALBERT H. SYDNEY**
"Providence, R.I.," "AHS" monogram all inside
slug plate, blob top, clear, 9¼" 7.00   10.00

Price Range

☐ **SYPHON CORP. OF FLORIDA**
"Bottle made in Czechoslovakia" under bottom,
emerald green, 9" **17.00 23.00**

☐ **TAMPA BOTTLING WORKS**
Pale green, 8" **7.00 10.00**

☐ **THE TAMPA PEPSI COLA BOTTLING CO.**
Semi-round bottom, aqua, 6" **8.00 11.00**

☐ **TANGO-COLA**
Richmond, VA. Reg., star around neck, clear,
7½" **7.00 10.00**

☐ **B.F. TATMAN**
"OWENSBORO, KY." in center on 3-4" panel,
other panels are plain, semi-round bottom, aqua **7.00 10.00**

☐ **TAYLOR SODA WATER MFG. CO.**
Boise, ID, panel base, clear, 6¾" **10.00 15.00**

☐ **TAYLOR & CO.**
"Valparaiso Chile" in 3 lines, blob top, dark
green, 7¼" **45.00 62.00**

☐ **TAYLOR & WILSON**
Aqua, round bottom, 8½" **11.00 16.00**

☐ **TEAR DROP**
Or sunbeam, aqua, there are three or four different sizes, 8½" **11.00 15.00**

☐ **TEAR DROP**
Shape, crude blob top, dark olive 8" **50.00 70.00**

☐ **THORNTON & CO.**
In ¼ moon letters, under it in 2 lines "Hudson,
N.Y.," blob top, aqua **20.00 30.00**

☐ **TOLLE BOTTLING WORKS**
In center big "T," Litchfield, IL, clear or amethyst,
6½" **8.00 12.00**

☐ **C.A. TOLLE**
In a circle, in the center "A" big "C" in center,
"REGISTERED LITCHFIELD, ILL.," aqua, 6½" **7.00 10.00**

☐ **TONOPAH SODA WORKS**
"TONOPAH, NEV." in three lines, Hutchinson,
clear, 6" **15.00 25.00**

☐ **TRI STATE BOTTLING CO.**
"D.O.C. 1209" around base in back, 7½" **11.00 15.00**

☐ **TRY-ME BEVERAGE CO.**
Machine made, clear, 9" **1.50 2.25**

Price Range

☐ **T S**
"SAVANNAH, GEO." in three lines, on back, "This Bottle Is Never Sold," emerald green, improved pontil, blob top, 6½" 28.00 40.00

☐ **TUCSON BOTTLING WORKS**
Tucson, Ariz., I.P.G. CO. crown top, 7¼" 5.00 8.00

☐ **T. & W.**
In hollow letter, under it "1875," reverse side "141 Franklin St. N.Y.," blob top, aqua, 6½" .. 10.00 15.00

☐ **TWITCHELL**
Aqua, 7½" 10.00 15.00

☐ **G.S. TWITCHELL**
In center, hollow letter "T," under it "PHILA.," reverse hollow letter "T," blob top, green, 7" 10.00 15.00

☐ **TWITCHELL**
"Philada," in center, hollow letter "T," same on back, green, 7½" 10.00 15.00

☐ **TYLER BOTTLING WORKS**
Aqua, 7¼" 4.00 6.00

☐ **TYLER UNION BOTTLING WORKS T.B.N.T.B.S.,**
Tyler, TX, panel base, clear or amethyst, 7" ... 8.00 11.00

☐ **U.C.B. CO.**
"Contents 8 Fl. Oz." under bottom, clear, machine made, 8" 4.00 6.00

☐ **WM. UNDERWOOD & CO.**
"Boston" around base, amber or aqua, 7½" .. 10.00 15.00

☐ **UNION BEVERAGE CO., JITNEY-COLA**
Knoxville, TENN., 6½ FLU OZ." on shoulder, amber, 7¾" 7.00 10.00

☐ **UNION BOTTLING WORK**
In dome shape, under it "VICTOR, COLO.," aqua, 6¾" 17.00 23.00

☐ **UNION GLASS WORK**
Phila, blob top, graphite pontil, green, 7" 50.00 68.00

☐ **UNION SODA WATER CO.**
"W & C" under bottom, "This Bottle never Sold Please Return" on back, aqua, 7½" 5.00 8.00

☐ **W.H.H.**
Large lettering on front, "Chicago" in small letters below, graphite pontil, tear-shaped bubbles in glass, sapphire-blue, 7½" tall, 2⅝" diam. 30.00 40.00

SPIRITS

This is, unquestionably, the largest single category in the bottle hobby in terms of the number of different bottles available. Among the spirits bottles you will find an enormous variety of sizes, colors, designs, and shapes—including the ornate figurals. In terms of age, they date well back into the 19th century up to modern times. Because collecting activity has been strong on spirits bottles for many years, the prices in general have gotten high and most of the scarcer and handsomer ones are well up into the double-digit range. The beginner may be best advised to specialize if he chooses to collect spirits bottles either by manufacturer, age, or in some other way, since this field as a whole is enormous. Flasks and bitters bottles, which are also spirits, are collected as a specialty in themselves and are listed in their own section in this book.

In 1860, E. G. Booz of Philadelphia manufactured a whiskey bottle in the shape of a cabin. His name, the year 1840, the phrase "Old Cabin Whiskey," and the company's address were embossed on the bottle. Many believe that the popularity of Booz's product was responsible for hard liquor gaining the colloquial name "booze." As logical as that sounds, there is an alternative theory: a Dutch word, bouse, meaning liquor, was adopted into the English language in the 17th century. Local dialectic pronounciation could easily have transformed "bouse" into "booze."

The Booz bottle is credited with starting the practice of embossing brand names on spirits bottles.

Jack Daniel is one of the more popular brands. As a child, young Jack ran away from home and succeeded in obtaining a partnership in a distillery. By 1866, only three years later, he owned his own whiskey company in Tennessee.

Other spirits bottles are found in the figural shapes of cannons, clocks, and barrels. These and other figurals are the most sought-after spirits bottles among collectors.

After the repeal of Prohibition in 1933, all liquor bottles bore the inscription "Federal Law Forbids Sale or Re-Use of this Bottle." That practice was discontinued in 1964. It was designed to prevent cheap liquors from being sold as famous brands.

NOTE: A license is necessary to sell any liquor bottle containing alcoholic spirits.

Price Range

☐ **F.P. ADAMS AND CO.**
"Boston, Mass., USA" under bottom, decanter
with handle, ring top, clear 22.00   32.00

☐ **ADAMS, TAYLOR & CO.**
"Full Qt. Registered" on back, clear, 12½" ... 17.00   22.00

☐ **ADAMS, TAYLOR & CO.**
Boston, MA., Royal Hand Made Sour Mash Whis-
key, clear, quart 11.00   17.00

☐ **ADAM-BOOTH CO.**
In center anchor lean-to toward left, "Sacramento, Cal." all in a circle, tapered top and ring,
clear, 12" 40.00   50.00

☐ **AGCS CO.**
Birds or eagle all around bottle on base, clear,
12" 12.00   17.00

☐ **ALAMEDA COMPANY**
"Tremont and Bromfield Streets, Boston" on
front written in slug plate, flask, ring collar, side
bands, amethyst, 8" 8.00   11.00

☐ Same as above except ½ pint, monogram on center, 6⅛" 8.00   11.00

☐ **ALCOHOL**
In label, also "Brandy," square bottle, clear, 8¼"   5.00   7.00

☐ **ALDERNEY OLD RYE WHISKEY**
Around a cow, Chris Gallagher, 806 Lombard
Street, Philadelphia, 7½" 22.00   32.00

☐ **ALMADEN VINEYARDS**
Green, 10" 2.00   3.00

☐ **AMBROSIAL B.M. & EAW & CO.**
In a seal on shoulder, pontil, amber, 9" 90.00   120.00

☐ **AMERICAN CORDIAL & DISTILLING CO.**
"San Francisco" embossed vertically, square,
amber, 10" 28.00   32.00

☐ **AMERICAN SUPPLY CO.**
Quart, cork, amethyst, 12" 5.00   8.00

☐ **AMERICUS CLUB**
Amber, 7½" 20.00   30.00

☐ **AMERICUS CLUB PURE WHISKEY**
Clear or amethyst, 9½" 10.00   13.00

☐ **AMIDON'S UNION**
Ginger Brandy Registered, in center lady with
long hair, clear or amethyst, 11¾" 12.00   17.00

Price Range

☐ **E.L. ANDERSON DISTILLING CO.**
"Newport, Ky." on front in circle, round, tapered,
graduated top and ring, clear 9.00   13.00

☐ **ANDRESEN & SON**
"Western Importers, Minneapolis, Minn. & Winni-
peg" on back, amber, 5" x 4¾" x 3" 360.00   460.00

☐ **B.B. EXTRA SUPERIOR WHISKEY**
In center a hand holding playing cards, blob neck,
amber, 4½" 22.00   32.00

☐ **SOL. BEAR & CO.**
Wilmington, North Carolina, ring top, clear or
aqua, 6" x 2½" x 1½" 12.00   17.00

☐ **BEECH HILL DISTILLING CO.**
"B" under bottom, amber, 12" 12.00   17.00

☐ Same as above except letters closer together and
longer neck 19.00   25.00

☐ **BELFAST MALT WHISKEY FOR MEDICINE
USE**
In a circle, aqua, 11" 40.00   52.00

☐ **BELLE OF NELSON**
Label, whiskey, top one full quart, "M.M." under
bottom, clear, 12" 7.00   10.00

☐ **BELSINGER & CO. DISTILLERS**
"Grar. Full Qt." on back, clear, 10" 10.00   13.00

☐ **BENEDICTINE**
Round, cork, green, 8" 3.00   5.00

☐ **BININGER'S**
Barrel-shaped, quart 150.00   175.00

☐ **BININGER'S**
Barrel-shaped, ¾" quart 140.00   160.00

☐ **W.E. BONNEY**
In center of barrel-shaped bottle, two rings encircling bottle, three rings on top and bottom, stands
up on one side, aqua, 3" long x 1½" wide, 2½"   12.00   17.00

☐ **BONNIE BROS.**
On top of circle, "Louisville, Ky." on bottom, in
center circle "Bonnie & Twiges," whiskey, clear,
quart, 6½" 9.00   13.00

☐ **BONNIE BROS.**
In circle, foliage and "BONNIE" in center, "LOU-
ISVILLE, KY." on front, rectangular, amethyst,
½" pint, 7" 9.00   13.00

Price Range

☐ **E.C. BOOZ'S**
Broad sloping collar, smooth with circular depression, "Old Cabin Whiskey" on one roof, on back roof "1840," short neck on front door, three windows on back, plain on one side, "120 Walnut St.," two dots under "St.," "Philadelphia" on other side, "E.C. Booz's Old Cabin Whiskey" on another side 250.00 340.00

☐ Same as above except no dot under "St.," very short neck with large round collar, smooth with circular depression, pale green. 195.00 240.00

☐ Same as above except reproduction or machine made 6.00 9.00

☐ **BOURBON**
In center, over it inside a diamond "131 F," amber, 3" round bottle, 7½" body, 2¾" neck with a handle from neck to shoulder 50.00 60.00

☐ **BOURBON WHISKEY**
Bitters, 1875, amber, 9¼" 120.00 155.00

☐ Same as above except puce 160.00 190.00

☐ **JOHN BOWMAN AND CO.**
Old Jewell Bourbon, San Francisco, amber 75.00 95.00

☐ Same except flask 330.00 390.00

☐ **BUREAU, THE**
In center crown, "Portland, Or." all in a circle, pumpkin seed flask, double ring top, amethyst or clear, pt. 75.00 95.00

☐ **SURSH BROWN**
Label, "R.B.J. & Co." under bottom, clear, 8" 19.00 26.00

☐ **BROWNSVILLE FRUIT DISTILLING CO.**
Native Wine Maker, Brooklyn, NY, clear, 13¼" 13.00 18.00

☐ **BUFFALO OLD BOURBON**
George Dierssen & Co. of Sacramento, CA, clear, quart 140.00 185.00

☐ **BUFFALO SPRING**
With buffalo in center, Stomping Ground, KY Co., 7" 12.00 17.00

☐ **SIR R. BURNETT & CO., TRADEMARK**
Between "Co." and "Trade" is a circle with a crown in it on top of shoulder, under it "This Bottle Not To Be Sold But Remains Property of Sir

Price Range

R. Burnett & Co. London, England," under the bottom "B & Co.," in center of bottom "K B 57," whiskey, clear or aqua, 12" **10.00** **15.00**

☐ **SIR R. BURNETT & CO.**
London England Trademark, Crown, "This Bottle Is Not To Be Sold But Remains Property of," bulbous neck, gloppy square and ring top, round, aqua, 11¾" **10.00** **17.00**

☐ **BURNS & O'DONOHUE**
Amber, 10¼" **14.00** **20.00**

☐ **BURROW MARTIN & CO.**
Norfolk, Virginia, round ring top, clear or aqua, 6" **14.00** **20.00**

☐ **CAHN, BELT & CO.**
Clear, 8½" **7.00** **10.00**

☐ **CAHN, BELT & CO.**
Embossed, applied lip, amethyst, 7" **6.00** **9.00**

☐ **CALEDONIA WHISKEY, B.C. DISTILLER CO. L.T.D.**
New Westminister, BC, oval shape, graduated top, emerald green, quart **7.00** **10.00**

☐ **CALLAHAN WHISKEY**
Clear or amethyst, 12⅛" **8.00** **10.00**

☐ **CALLAHAN WHISKEY J. CALLAHAN & COMPANY**
Written fancy, "Boston, Mass Registered," round, amethyst, 12⅛" **8.00** **11.00**

☐ **J.F. CALLAHAN & COMPANY**
"Boston, Mass" at a slant, clear, ½ pint, 6⅝" **7.00** **10.00**

☐ **JOHN F. CALLAHAN, BOTTLED ONLY BY**
Boston, MA, round, slug plate, graduated top and ring, amethyst, 11" **12.00** **17.00**

☐ **D. CANALE & CO.**
"Memphis, Tenn. Old Dominick Bourbon" other side, clear or amethyst, 11" **16.00** **21.00**

☐ **T.F. CANNON & COMPANY**
Boston, Mass, Guaranteed Full Pint all in slug, plate, "12 Devonshire St." on side, "28–30 Exchange St." on opposite side, rectangular, clear, pint, 8" **9.00** **13.00**

Price Range

☐ **CARLSBAD**
In large letters on bottom, "LS" in center of bottom, whittlemarked, cylinder, olive green, 3¾" x 10¾" 10.00 18.00

☐ **CARLSON-BROS.**
In center "Wholesale and Retail" in three lines, "Astoria" are all in a circle, applied ring top, clear, ½" pint 18.00 25.00

☐ **CARTAN, McCARTHY & CO.**
San Francisco, amber, 11¼" 14.00 17.00

☐ **CARTAN, McCARTHY & CO.**
San Francisco, CA, rectangular, amber, 10⅝" 12.00 14.00

☐ **CARTAN, McCARTHY & CO.**
San Francisco, Calif., "Full Quart," embossed vertically, rectangular, graduated top and ring, amber 10¾" 35.00 43.00

☐ **CASCADE**
Clear, 9½" 14.00 20.00

☐ **J.W. CASHIN FAMILY LIQUOR STORE**
Clear or amethyst, 9½" 8.00 12.00

☐ **CASPERS WHISKEY**
Cobalt, 10½" 185.00 300.00

☐ **CATTO'S WHISKEY**
Olive-green, 9" 6.00 9.00

☐ **CEDARHURST**
"Cont. 8 Oz." on back shoulder, amber, ½ pint, 7" 9.00 13.00

☐ **CENTURY LIQUOR CO., OLD OVERTON**
Memphis, TN, round, cylinder whiskey, amber, 11½" 25.00 30.00

☐ **CENTURY LIQUOR & CIGAR CO.**
"B-8" under bottom, amber, pint 10.00 14.00

☐ **CHAMPAGNE**
Cylindrical, 2" indented bottom, pale green, 11⅞" 8.00 12.00

☐ **CHAMPAGNE**
Plain, kick-up, opalescent, green 12" x 10" x 9" 6.00 10.00

☐ **CHAMPAGNE**
Plain, green, 4¼" 5.00 7.00

☐ **CHAMPAGNE**
Plain, kick-up, dark green, 8" 5.00 7.00

Price Range

☐ **J. LABORDE CHAMPAGNE**
"1815 Cosmac Bordraux" in seal on shoulder,
ring top, blob neck, green, 1 qt. 16.00 21.00

☐ **CHAPIN & GORE**
Chicago, "Hawley Glass Co." under bottom,
amber, 8¼" 85.00 110.00

☐ **CHAPIN & GORE**
Diamond shape on back for label, amber, 8¾" 65.00 75.00

☐ **HENRY CHAPMAN & COMPANY**
"Sole agents, Montreal" in circle, pumpkin seed
type, inside screw, "Patent 78" on screw cap,
amber, 5¼" 60.00 70.00

☐ **CHEATHAM & KINNEY**
"W. Mc & Co." under bottom, aqua, 8¾" 18.00 25.00

☐ **CHESLEYS JOCKEY CLUB**
In center a jockey and running horse, under it
"Whiskey" all in a circle, tapered top and ring,
amber, 12" 185.00 250.00
☐ Same except clear 120.00 170.00

☐ **CHESTNUT BOTTLE**
Kick-up, handle, ring around top neck, squat,
amber, 2" neck, 4" body, 3" x 4" 25.00 32.00
☐ Same as above except larger, amber 18.00 25.00
☐ Same as above except machine made 8.00 12.00
☐ Same as above except clear or blue 18.00 26.00

☐ **CHESTNUT BOTTLE**
Kick-up, ring around top, pontil, blue, 4" body, 2"
neck 65.00 85.00

☐ **CHESTNUT BOTTLE**
25 ribs, Midwestern, l.h. swirl, sheared top, green,
7½" 80.00 110.00

☐ **CHESTNUT BOTTLE**
24 vertical ribs, sheared neck, attributed to
Zanesville, golden amber, 5¼" 155.00 185.00

☐ **CHESTNUT BOTTLE**
Light vertical rib plus 18 r.h. swirl ribs, sheared
neck, attributed to Kent, green 85.00 110.00

☐ **CHESTNUT BOTTLE**
16 vertical ribs, sheared neck, 6½" 110.00 140.00

☐ **CHESTNUT BOTTLE**
Swirl tooled top, pontil, green, 5¾" 90.00 120.00
☐ Same as above except deep amber, 5¼" 135.00 160.00

Price Range

☐ **CHESTNUT BOTTLE**
Diamond, ¼" ground off top, attributed to Zanesville, yellow green, 10" 72.00 82.00

☐ **CHESTNUT BOTTLE**
Aqua, 5½" 30.00 40.00

☐ **CHESTNUT BOTTLE**
Twelve diamonds quilted over 24 vertical ribs,
tooled mouth, clear, 5¾" 200.00 245.00

☐ **CHESTNUT BOTTLE**
Diamond, yellow green or clear, 5¼" 28.00 39.00

☐ **CHESTNUT BOTTLE**
Sixteen ribs, sheared neck, mantua, 6¼" 85.00 110.00

☐ **CHESTNUT BOTTLE**
Sixteen ribs, l.h. swirl, mantua, aqua, 6½" 85.00 110.00

☐ **CHESTNUT BOTTLE**
Kick-up, ring around top, pontil, amber, 6" 21.00 28.00

☐ **CHESTNUT GROVE WHISKEY**
C.W., flat chestnut-shaped bottle, applied handle,
open pontil, collared mouth, amber, 8¾" 140.00 170.00

☐ **CHIANTI BOTTLE**
Green glass, wicker wrapped, 3' 4" 11.00 16.00

☐ **VERY OLD CORN**
From Casper Winston, North Carolina, Lowest
Price Whiskey House, write for private terms,
fancy with handle and glass top 70.00 90.00

☐ **COWIE & CO. LTD.**
Clear, 8¾" 18.00 25.00

☐ **S. CRABFELDER & CO.**
Amber, 7", 4" x 2" 9.00 12.00

☐ **CREAMDALE**
Hulling, Mobile, Alabama, Cincinnati, Ohio, Refilling of This Bottle Will Be Prosecuted By Law"
under bottom, amber, 11¼" 14.00 19.00

☐ **CREAM OF KENTUCKY "THEE WHISKEY"**
Clear, 11¼" 32.00 42.00

☐ **THE CRIGLER & CRIGLER CO.**
Clear or amethyst, 4½" 7.00 10.00

☐ **CRIGLER & CRIGLER DISTILLERS**
"Full Qt. Union Made" other side, clear or amethyst, quart. 10.00 14.00

Price Range

☐ **CRIGLER & CRIGLER DISTILLERS**
"Covington, KY." vertical on one panel, "Full Quart Union Made" on next side, square body, lady's leg neck, graduated top and ring, amethyst, 10⅛" **18.00 26.00**

☐ **M. CRONAN & CO.**
Sacramento, CA., light amber, 11¾" **18.00 26.00**

☐ **GET THE BEST, ORDER YOUR WHISKEY FROM J. CROSSMAN SONS**
New Orleans, LA, amber, quart **11.00 17.00**

☐ **CROWN**
Label, whiskey pinch bottle, machine made, amber, 8½" **9.00 13.00**

☐ **CROWN DISTILLERIES CO.**
Around monogram "Crown & Co." in center, inside screw thread, amber, 10" **11.00 17.00**

☐ **CROWN DISTILLERIES COMPANY**
Under bottom "Sample Whiskey," round, clear or amethyst **9.00 14.00**

☐ **CROWN DISTILLERIES COMPANY**
In circle, "CROWN & SHIELD, DC CO." monogram, on center "S.F. Whiskey," inside threads, embossed cork, round, amber, 11¼" **22.00 33.00**
☐ Same as above except reddish amber, quart ... **15.00 19.00**

☐ **CROWN DISTILLERIES COMPANY**
Crown and shield, inside threads, tooled lip, amber, 11¾" **27.00 33.00**
☐ Same as above, light amber, 11⅛" **15.00 19.00**
☐ Same as above, amber, 9⅝" **15.00 19.00**
☐ Same as above, without inside threads, amber, 9⅝" **15.00 19.00**

☐ **CUCKOO**
Clear or amethyst, 11¾" **24.00 32.00**

☐ **CUCKOO**
bird, branches, leaves on center "Whiskey M. Burke Boston Trademark" flask, clear, ½ pint, 6½" **17.00 25.00**

☐ **CUCKOO/WHISKEY/M. BURKE/BOSTON/TRADEMARK**
All with embossed cuckoo bird in branches and leaves, "Full M.B. Quart" on back, graduated top, round, amethyst, 12" **28.00 38.00**

Price Range

☐ **CURNER & COMPANY**
80 Cedar Street, New York, three-part mold, olive, amber, 11½" 34.00 45.00

☐ **J.H. CUTTER OLD BOURBON**
A.P. Hotaling & Company, Portland, Oregon, pewter screw cap, round top, amber 350.00 440.00

☐ **J.H. CUTTER OLD BOURBON**
A.P. Hotaling & Co., Portland, Oregon, 5th 48.00 61.00

☐ **J.H. CUTTER OLD BOURBON**
Moorman, Mfg. Louisville, KY, A.P. Hotaling & Company amber, quart 90.00 120.00

☐ **J.H. CUTTER OLD BOURBON**
E. Martin & Company, amber, quart 130.00 160.00

☐ **CUTTER, J.H.**
"Old Bourbon," under it a crown, around it "bottled by A. P. Hotaling & Co." all in a watermelon circle, tapered top and ring, amber, 12" 45.00 55.00

☐ **CUTTER, J.H.**
"Old Bourbon, A.P. Hotaling & Co. sale agents" all in five lines, on shoulder a crown, tapered top and ring, chip mold, light amber, 11¾" 270.00 320.00

☐ **J.H. CUTTER TRADEMARK**
Star and Shield E. MARTIN & COMPANY San Francisco, CAL." in circle, slug plate, graduated top, round, amber, 11" 20.00 24.00

☐ **J.H. CUTTER OLD BOURBON**
Round, amber, 12" 15.00 20.00

☐ **J.H. CUTTER OLD BOURBON**
Louisville, KY, amber, 5th 44.00 62.00

☐ **J.H. CUTTER OLD BOURBON**
Barrel and crown in center, C.P. Moorman Mfg., Louisville, KY, A.P. Hotaling & Co., amber, quart 85.00 120.00

☐ **CUTTER HOTALING**
Coffin type, 1886, amber 120.00 150.00

☐ **CUTTY SARK**
Blended Scot's Whiskey, green, 12" 1.75   3.75

☐ **DALLEMAND & CO., INC.**
"Chicago" around bottom, brandy, fancy, blob neck, amber, 11¼" 9.00 13.00

☐ **DALLEMAND & CO.**
Creme Rye, amber, sampler, 3" 7.00 10.00

Price Range

☐ **DALLEMAND & CO.**
"Cream Rye" around bottom, fancy shoulders,
amber, 2¾" 9.00 13.00

☐ **DALLEMAND & CO. CHICAGO**
"Design Pat 21509 Apr. 26, 1892" under bottom,
amber, 11" 15.00 22.00

☐ **B.B. DAVIS & COMPANY**
New York, Contents 8 fl. ozs., flask, graduated
collar and ring, amethyst, ½ pint, 6¾" 8.00 11.00

☐ **DAVIS' MARYLAND**
Label, "Guaranteed Full Pint" in back, Davis &
Drake, clear, 8½" 7.00 10.00

☐ **PETER DAWSON LTD, DISTILLERS**
On bottom, graduated and flared collar, concave
and convex circles (thumb prints) around shoulder and base, green, 11¾" 7.00 10.00

☐ **DEEP SPRING**
Tennessee Whiskey, amber, quart, 7" 37.00 47.00

☐ **DeFREMERY JAMES & CO.**
Round, amber, 11" 1.50 3.50

☐ **DeKUYPER'S SQUAREFACE, WHO**
DeKUYPER'S NIGHTLY TAKES, SOUNDLY
SLEEPS AND FIT AWAKES
On two panels, vertical at slant, vase gin shape,
ABM, thread top, grass green, 7⅞" 8.00 11.00

☐ **R. DENNER WINE & SPIRIT MERCHANT**
"Bridgewater" in three lines on one side shoulder, crock with handle, coffin flask type, ring top,
short neck, tan and cream, 2¼" x 3", 8½" ... 20.00 30.00

☐ **DEVIL'S ISLAND ENDURANCE GIN**
Clear or amethyst, pint 7.00 10.00

☐ **DEVIL'S ISLAND**
"V" missing from Devil's, clear, 9" 13.00 18.00

☐ **DIAMOND PACKING CO.**
Bridgeton, NJ, "Pat. Feb 11th 1870" on shoulder,
aqua, 8" 12.00 17.00

☐ **DIAMOND QUILTED FLASK**
Double collar, very light aqua, almost clear, quart,
9" 17.00 25.00

☐ **DIEHL & FORD**
"Nashville, Tennessee" around bottle, each letter in a panel, light amber, 9" 22.00 32.00

Price Range

☐ **DIP MOLD WINE**
Kick-up, pontil, dark amber 9.00 13.00

☐ **J.E. DOHERTY COMPANY**
"Boston, Mass" written vertically, flask, clear, ½
pint, 6¾" 6.00 9.00

☐ **J.E. DOHERTY CO.**
"Boston, Mass" on shoulder, "Regist. Full Qt."
on back, three-piece mold, graduated top, lady's
leg neck, amethyst, 11" 9.00 13.00

☐ **N.F. DOHERTY**
"181–185 Cambridge St., Boston, Guaranteed
Full Pint" vertically in slug plate, rectangular,
graduated, collar and ring, amethyst, pint, 8¾" 8.00 11.00

☐ **NEIL DOHERTY**
"176 North St., Boston" in circle, in center of circle "Wine & Liquors," strap flask, light amber,
9⅝" 8.00 12.00

☐ **DONALDSON & COMPANY FINE OLD**
MADERA, MADCIRA HOUSE, FOUNDED
1783
Label, aqua, quart, 12¼" 8.00 11.00

☐ **DREYFUSS-WEIL & COMPANY, DISTILLERS**
Paducah, KY, USA clear, ½ pint 7.00 10.00

☐ **DREYFUSS-WEIL & CO.**
Clear or amethyst, 6½" 6.00 9.00

☐ **D.S.G. COMPANY**
Under bottom, light amber, 7¾" 33.00 44.00

☐ **DUFF GORDON SHERRY**
Three-part mold, aqua, 12" 10.00 14.00

☐ **THE DUFFY MALT WHISKEY CO.**
"Rochester, N.Y., U.S.A." on front in watermelon
circle, in center monogram "D.M.W. Co.," under
bottom "pat'd Aug. 24-1886," different number or
letter on bottom, round, amber, 10¼" 6.00 9.00
☐ Same as above except ½ pint or pint 32.00 42.00
☐ Same as above except miniature 19.00 28.00
☐ Same as above except machine made 4.00 5.00

☐ **EL MONTE DISTILLING CO.**
"San Francisco, Cal." embossed vertically, rectangular, inside threads, aqua, 10⅝" 24.00 28.00

Price Range

☐ **ESSENCE OF JAMAICA**
Label, clear or amethyst, 5″ 8.00 11.00
☐ Same as above except 7½″ 13.00 18.00
☐ **N.J. ETHRIDGE**
Macon, GA, pure old Winchester rye whiskey,
label, clear, 6½″ 14.00 20.00
☐ **EUREKA**
Clear or amethyst, 7¾″ 8.00 11.00
☐ **EVERETT-LIQUOR CO.**
"Everett, Wash." all in a circle, applied ring top,
amber, 11″ 34.00 44.00
☐ **EVANS & O'BRIEN**
1870 Stockton, amber or green 140.00 185.00
☐ **FARMVILLE DISPENSARY**
"Farmville, VA." in a circle, "REGISTERED FULL
PINT," ring collar, and below it tapered ring top,
clear or amethyst 14.00 20.00
☐ **GALLO**
Wine, green screw-top, ⁴/₅ quart, 10½″ .... .75 1.25
☐ **GELLERT, J.M.**
In center "230 Washington St., Portland, Ore-
gon," bulb neck and applied tapered top, amber,
10¾″ 80.00 100.00
☐ **C.R. GIBSON**
"Salamanca, New York" in shield, amber, pint 12.00 17.00
☐ **OLD JOE GIDEON WHISKEY**
Amber, 11½″ 43.00 55.00
☐ **OLD JOE GIDEON**
Amber, ½ pint 10.00 13.00
☐ **GILBERT BROS. & CO.**
"Baltimore, MD" on front, oval, graduated collar
and ring, thick glass, aqua, pint, 8¼″ 9.00 12.00
☐ **THEO. GIER**
Oakland, Cal., amber, 11⅛″ 14.00 19.00
☐ **J.A. GILKA**
Vertically, "J.A. GILKA BERLIN" vertically on
side, "THIS BOTTLE D" vertically on corner
panel, "NOT TO BE SOLD" on corner panel,
"SCHUTZEN STR. NO. 9" on side, graduated
collar and ring, light amber, quart, 9¾″ 30.00 40.00

Price Range

☐ **J.A. GILKA**
"Berlin" on side, "J.A. GILKA" on back, "SCHUTZEN STR. NO. 9" on opposite side, same as above except embossing, gloppy collar, red amber, quart, 9¾" 30.00 40.00

☐ **W. GILMORE & SON**
Pavilion, NY, kick-up, teal blue, 10¼" 14.00 20.00

☐ **GINOCCHIO & CO.**
In center "Importers 287-First St." in two lines, "Portland" all in a circle, pumpkin seed flask, clear, pt. 132.00 160.00

☐ **GLENBROOK DISTILLING CO.**
"Boston, Mass" vertically, oval flask, aqua, ½ pint, 6¾" 10.00 14.00

☐ **GLENBROOK**
On bottom, flask, amber, ½ pint 8.00 11.00

☐ **GORDON'S DRY GIN**
Embossed horizontally on front, "LONDON ENG-LAND" is embossed on the sides, oval, aqua, 11" 5.00 7.00

☐ **GORDONS DRY GIN**
London, England, square with wide beveled corners, boar on bottom, graduated and flared collar, aqua, quart, 8⅝" 8.00 11.00
☐ Same as above except oval back, old 6.00 9.00
☐ Same as above except ABM 6.00 9.00

☐ **G.P.R.**
Whiskey label, clear or amethyst, 7½" 6.00 9.00

☐ **G.P.R.**
"Baltimore, G. Gump & Sons" on shoulder, clear, 10¾" 11.00 17.00

☐ **S. GRABFELDER & CO.**
"I" on bottom, amber, 5¾" 8.00 10.00

☐ **S. GRABFELDER & CO.**
"99A" on bottom, amber, 7" 9.00 12.00

☐ **S. GRABFELDER & CO.**
"J" on bottom, amber, 7¼" 10.00 13.00

☐ **S. GRABFELDER & CO.**
Clear or amethyst, 6" 6.00 9.00

☐ **GRAFFING & CO.**
"N.Y." under bottom, boy and girl climbing trees, clear, 12¼" 33.00 44.00

Price Range

☐ **HANLEY MERCANTILE CO.**
Amber, 10″ 5.00 8.00

☐ **I.W. HARPER**
With like-new wicker, name shows through window in wicker, graduated collar, light amber, quart, 9¾″ 32.00 44.00

☐ **I.W. HARPER**
"Medal Whiskey" in center; gold on front, anchor in gold, rope around neck, 3″ pottery, very light tan, 4″ square tapering to 3½″ on shoulder ... 42.00 54.00

☐ **I.W. HARPER**
Cork, amber, 10″ 10.00 15.00

☐ **I.W. HARPER**
Cork, amber, 9½″ 17.00 22.00

☐ **I.W. HARPER**
Clear or amethyst, 4″ 18.00 25.00

☐ **ADOLPH HARRIS AND CO.**
San Francisco, amber, quart 32.00 43.00

☐ **ANDOLPH HARRIS & CO.**
Deer Head, San Francisco, cylindrical, amber, fifth 95.00 125.00

☐ **ALBERT H. HARRIS**
NY, label, turn mold, amber, quart 8.00 11.00

☐ **HARVARD RYE**
With interlocking "HR," inside of rectangle, slug plate, vertical panels on neck and shoulder, fancy, graduated collar, round, amethyst, quart, 12″ 8.00 11.00

☐ **HARVARD RYE**
With interlocking "HR" monogram in center, rectangular, double band collar, heavy glass, clear pint, 7½″ 8.00 11.00

☐ **HARVARD RYE**
Clear or amethyst, 7½″ 11.00 16.00

☐ **HARVEST KING DISTILLING CO.**
Embossed, cork, aqua, 12″ 27.50 33.50

☐ **HAWKINS RYE**
Rectangular, aqua, 10⅝″ 19.00 22.00

☐ **THE HAYNER DISTILLING CO.**
"Dayton, Ohio & St. Louis, Mo. Distillers, W" on bottom, also "Nov. 30th 1897," Whiskey, amethyst, 11½″ 22.00 32.00

Price Range

☐ **THE HAYNER DISTILLING CO.**
Dayton, St. Louis, Atlanta, St. Paul, Distillers, Design Patented Nov. 30th, 1897" under bottom,
amber, 11½" 11.00 16.00

☐ **HAYNER RICH PRIVATE STOCK PURE
WHISKEY**
In back "H.W. Distillers, Troy, Ohio," under bottom "Distillers, Pat. Nov 30th, 1897-F," clear,
11½" 9.00 12.00

☐ **THE HAYNER WHISKEY DISTILLERS**
Troy, Ohio, "Designed Patented Nov. 30th,
1897" on bottom, fluting around the base 1" high,
also on shoulder and neck, graduated collar and
ring, round, ABM, clear, quart, 11½" 8.00 11.00

☐ **HAYNER WHISKEY DISTILLERY**
Troy, OH, lower trunk and paneled shoulder, Nov.
30th 1897, "F" on bottom, round, amethyst ... 17.00 27.00

☐ **HAYNERS DISTILLING CO.**
Dayton, Ohio, USA, Distillers & Importers, in circle, design patented Nov. 30th, 1897 on bottom,
14 fancy vertical panels on shoulder and neck,
14 vertical 1" panels around base, graduated collar and ring, amethyst, liter, 12" 8.00 11.00

☐ **W.H. HECKENDORN & CO.**
Label, 2 under bottom, three-part, mold, golden
amber, 12" 11.00 18.00

☐ **EDWARD HEFFERMAN**
In center, "REG. FULL PINT" at top, "8 PORT-
LAND ST. BOSTON, MASS" all on front in slug
plate, rectangular, light green, pint, 8½" 6.00 9.00

☐ **W.H. HENNESSEY**
"38 to 44 Andrew St., Lynn, Mass" vertically, slug
plate, rectangular, graduated collar and ring, amethyst, ½ pint, 6¾" 8.00 11.00

☐ **HERE'S A SMILE TO THOSE I LOVE**
Clear, 5½" 16.00 27.00

☐ **HERE'S A SMILE TO THOSE I LOVE**
Clear or amethyst, 5½" 22.00 30.00

☐ **HERE'S HOPING—**
Clear, 8" 11.00 17.00

☐ **HEWONTS SQUEAL**
Hog bottle 38.00 48.00

Price Range

☐ **HIGHCLIFF WHISKEY**
　Cincinnati, OH, label, amber, ½ pint .... 7.00　10.00

☐ **HILDEBRANDT, POSNER & CO.**
　"S.F., Cal.," inside threads, amber, 11¼" ..... 23.00　26.00

☐ Same as above, without inside threads .... 17.00　20.00

☐ **HOCK WINE**
　Label sheared top and ring, red ground pontil,
　mold, 14" .... 20.00　28.00

☐ Same as above except old teal blue, 11½" .... 8.00　11.00

☐ Same as above except old teal blue, 14" ...... 10.00　13.00

☐ Same as above except old red amber, 11½" ... 6.00　9.00

☐ Same as above except old light amber, 7" ..... 8.00　11.00

☐ Same as above except old ABM light amber, 14" 6.00　9.00

☐ Same as above except old ABM green, 13½" .. 5.00　7.00

☐ **HOFFMAN**
　Pure Rye, round quart, amber, 10½" .... 24.00　31.00

☐ **HOFHEIMER'S EAGLE RYE BLEND M.**
　HOFHEIMER & CO.
　Norfolk, VA, large eagle embossed on shield, rec-
　tangular, clear, ½ pint, 6" .... 8.00　11.00

☐ **HOFHEIMER'S EAGLE RYE BLEND**
　Clear or amethyst, 6" .... 7.00　10.00

☐ **HOLBERG MERCANTILE CO.**
　Amber, 11" .... 13.00　19.00

☐ **HOLLANDS**
　In gold letters, around it gold circle, glass top with
　"H" fancy, 9½" .... 55.00　72.00

☐ **HOLLYWOOD WHISKEY**
　Round, graduated collar and ring, amber, quart,
　11" .... 11.00　17.00

☐ Same as above except golden amber .... 30.00　40.00

☐ **HOLLYWOOD WHISKEY**
　Amber, 12" .... 12.00　17.00

☐ **HOLLYWOOD WHISKEY**
　Kick-up, amber, 11¼" .... 12.00　17.00

☐ **HOLTON, CHAS. F.**
　In center in hollow letters "Hover lap C., Olympia,
　W.T.," all in a circle, Shoo Fly Flask, pt., clear,
　ring top .... 150.00　180.00

☐ **HOME SUPPLY CO.**
　Wine label three-part mold, amber, 11¼" ..... 8.00　11.00

Price Range

☐ **HOME SUPPLY CO.**
Whiskey label three-part mold, amber, 11¼″ ..   8.00   11.00

☐ **HONEST MEASURE**
Clear, 4¾″ 9.00   12.00

☐ **HONEST MEASURE**
Half pint on shoulder saddle flask, amber, ½ pint   8.00   11.00
☐ Same as above except clear 5.00   7.00
☐ Same as above except clear, pint 7.00   10.00

☐ **W. HONEY GLASS WORKS**
Under bottom amber, 7½″ 33.00   45.00

☐ **L.P. HOSSLEY, FINE WHISKIES**
Canton, Miss, clear cylinder whiskey, quart, 11½″   80.00   100.00

☐ **HOTALING CO. THE A.P.**
In center a crown, under it "Portland, Or., sole
agents" all in a watermellon circle, applied top,
amber, 11″ 260.00   310.00

☐ **HOTEL DONNELLY, TACOMA, (MINIATURE)**
3″, Pu top, clear 20.00   26.00

☐ **HOTEL WORTH BAR**
"Fort Worth, Texas" inside screw, amber, 6″ ..   95.00   125.00

☐ **HUBER KUEMMEL LIQUEUR, B.S.**
FLERSHEIM MERC. CO.
Label, amber, 10″ 14.00   20.00

☐ **H.W. HUGULEY CO.**
134 Canal St., Boston, "Full Quart" on back,
round, graduated collar and ring, amethyst, 12″   11.00   16.00

☐ **H.W. HUGULEY CO.**
Clear or amethyst, 11¾″ 11.00   16.00

☐ **HURDLE RYE**
Clear panels, neck, letters etched, 3″ 10.00   13.00

☐ **ELIAS HYMAN & SON**
"Cincinnati, USA" all in square slug plate, paneled design, round corker, clear glass, 3½″ x
11¾″ 12.00   16.00

☐ **IMPERIAL COCKTAILS CO.**
San Francisco, CA & New York, amethyst, 12″   39.00   43.00

☐ **IMPERIAL DISTILLING CO.**
"Kansas City, MO." in center, IDCO fancy shoul-
der, clear, 4″ 12.00   16.00

☐ **IMPERIAL**
In ribbon, "pint" on back in ribbon, oval, aqua, 9″   7.00   10.00

Price Range

☐ **IMPERIAL**
In back, aqua, ½ pint, 7¾″ 23.00 33.00
☐ **IMPERIAL WEDDING WHISKEY BLEND**
Label, clear or amethyst, 8″ and other sizes ... 10.00 13.00
☐ **IMPORTERS**
Vertically, flask, clear, ½ pint, 6½″ 9.00 12.00
☐ **G. INNSEN & SONS**
"Pittsburgh" under bottom, green, quart 17.00 25.00
☐ **JACK CRANSTON'S DIODORA CORN WHISKEY**
"Jack Cranston Co., Baltimore, Md." in back, U
blank seal, clear, 12″ 14.00 20.00
☐ **JACK DANIEL'S GOLD MEDAL OLD NO. 7**
Clear, 7¾″ 30.00 40.00
☐ **JAMES BUCHANAN & CO. LTD.**
½ ring on each side, "106" under bottom dark
green, 7¼″ 19.00 26.00
☐ **JESSE MOORE-HUNT CO.**
Amber, 11¾″ 11.00 16.00
☐ **J.F.T. & Co.**
Phila, vertically ribbed mellon-shaped bottle, ap-
plied handle, open pontil, collared mouth, yellow-
amber, 6″ 300.00 330.00
☐ **J.M. & CO.**
"Boston, Mass" in slug plate, oval flask, aqua,
10″ 9.00 12.00
☐ **JOHANN MARIA FARINA NO. 4, JULICRSPLATZ NO. 4**
Clear or amethyst, 4″ 9.00 12.00
☐ **JOHN HART & CO.**
On each side amber, 7¼″ 43.00 55.00
☐ **W.L. JOHNSON**
Kentucky, pontil, amber, 8¼″ 80.00 103.00
☐ **W.H. JONES & CO. ESTABLISHED 1851 IMPORTERS**
"Hanover and Blackstone Sts Boston, Mass,"
shield with bear, all on front flask, light green slug
plate, pint, 8¾″ 19.00 26.00
☐ **W.H. JONES AND CO.**
Clear, 9½″ 14.00 20.00

Price Range

☐ **JUG**
Round base, bulbous neck, light green, gallon,
5¾" across, 13½" **22.00 29.00**

☐ **L.E. JUNG & CO. PURE MALT WHISKEY**
New Orleans, LA, amber, 10¾" **14.00 21.00**

☐ **J & W HARDIE**
"Edinburgh" on bottom, three-piece mold, large
square collar, emerald green, 10¼" **9.00 12.00**

☐ **J&W.N. & CO.**
Under bottom, aqua, 11" **8.00 11.00**
☐ Same as above except clear, 10" **6.00 9.00**

☐ **J. KELLENBERGER WHOLESALE WINES &
LIQUORS**
Durango, CO, clear, 11⅜" **60.00 68.00**

☐ **KANE, O'LEARY & CO.**
In center, "221 & 223," under it, "Bush St. S.F.,"
inside of square box enclosing, tapered top and
ring, amber, 12" **190.00 255.00**

☐ **J. KELLENBERGER WHOLESALE WINES &
LIQUORS**
Durango, CO, clear, 11⅜" **60.00 65.00**

☐ **KELLY & KERR**
222 College St., Springfield, MO, C.W. Stuart's,
machine made, clear, amber, or aqua, quart. .. **6.00 10.00**

☐ **KELLY & KERR**
222 College St., Springfield, MO, machine made,
clear or aqua **5.00 7.00**

☐ **KENTUCKY GEM, S.M. COPPER
DISTILLERS, WHISKEY**
T.G. Cockrill, San Francisco, quart **9.00 13.00**

☐ **KEYSTONE BURGUNDY**
Tapered top, amber, 8¾" **50.00 72.00**

☐ **KEYSTONE**
Whiskey label, clear or amethyst, 7½" **14.00 20.00**

☐ **KING BEE**
Ten panels, clear, 11¾" **19.00 26.00**

☐ **KIRBY'S**
243 College St., Springfield, MO, 1870, quart,
clear or aqua **11.00 17.00**

☐ **H.B. KIRK & CO.**
Amber, 11⅛" **14.00 20.00**

Price Range

☐ **REMAINS THE PROPERTY OF H.S. KIRK & CO.**
NY, "Registered U.S." on front, on back three Indian heads embossed in a circle on the shoulder, graduated collar and ring, round, amber, quart, 11¼" 20.00 30.00

☐ **HENRY KLINKER, JR.**
"The Owl, 748-10th Ave., SE corner 51st Street, N.Y." in circle, under it "Full Measure," double collar, under bottom "LCMG, 182 Fulton Street, N.Y.," amber, 1½" pint 24.00 35.00

☐ **C.F. KNAPP**
Philadelphia, pig slope, clear or amethyst, 3¼" x 2" 38.00 49.00

☐ **CHATEAU LAFIETE 1896**
In circle, blob seal on shoulder, crude band collar, kick-up, green, 12" 10.00 13.00

☐ **LAKE DRUMMOND PURE RYE, J & E MAHONEY**
Rectangular, clear, ½ pint, 6½" 8.00 11.00

☐ **LAKE KEUKA VINTAGE CO., BATH, NEW YORK WINERY NO. 25**
Same shape and design as a Hayner Whiskey, graduated collar and ring, amethyst, 12" 11.00 18.00

☐ **LAMBE & DENMARKE FINE WHISKEY**
Arkansas City, AR, under bottom "L.C. & R CO.," tapered top and ring, fancy bottom, clear or aqua, 8" 30.00 40.00

☐ **LANGERT WINE CO.**
"422-Sprague Ave. Spokane, Wash." all in a circle, applied ring top, amethyst and clear, qt. 13.00 19.00

☐ **JOHN LATREYTE**
Under bottom "C. Pat'd, April 1, '84," clear or aqua, 7¼" 13.00 19.00

☐ **LEIPPS**
In script, Chicago, tapered top, amber, 4½" ... 12.00 17.00

☐ **LILIENTHAL**
Cincinnati, San Francisco & New York, 1885, yellow amber 185.00 240.00

☐ **LILIENTHAL DISTILLERS**
Coffin type with crown, amber 185.00 240.00

Price Range

☐ **LICKING VALLEY CO.**
Clear, quart size **11.00 17.00**

☐ **LEVAGGI COMPANY**
SF, CA, rectangular, amber, 10⅛" **19.00 22.00**

☐ **MACY & JENKINS**
NY, applied handle, embossed, amber 10" **24.00 28.00**

☐ **McAVDY BREW CO.**
Amber, 8½" **7.00 10.00**

☐ **McDONALD & COHN**
San Francisco, CA, amber, quart **19.00 25.00**

☐ **McDONALD & COHN**
San Francisco embossed on a slant, inside
threads, amber, 11¼" **23.00 26.00**

☐ **McHENRY**
Amber, 10½" **12.00 17.00**

☐ **McKNIGHTS**
Amber, 10½" **14.00 20.00**
☐ Same as above except clear, 9¼" **11.00 17.00**

☐ **JOHN A. McLAREN**
In center, "PERTH MALT WHISKEY, PERTH,
ONT," saddle flask, "193" under bottom, two-
ring top, 8" **14.00 20.00**

☐ **Mc. LAUGHLIN H.**
In center "The Magnolia, San Nateo" all in a cir-
cle, double ring top, picnic flask, clear, 5¼" ... **39.00 49.00**

☐ **MERIDITH'S CLUB PURE RYE WHISKEY**
East Liverpool, Ohio, white, 7¼" **14.00 20.00**

☐ **MERRY CHRISTMAS HAPPY NEW YEAR**
Quilted back, sheared top, clear, 6" **33.00 43.00**

☐ **MERRY CHRISTMAS & HAPPY NEW YEAR**
In center, clear or amethyst, 5" **22.00 30.00**

☐ **MERRY CHRISTMAS & HAPPY NEW
CENTURY**
In back a watch with Roman letters and "B I Co"
in center, pocket watch type, milk glass **30.00 38.00**

☐ **MEXICAN DRINKING BOTTLE**
Clear, 10" tall, 7" round **12.00 17.00**

☐ **MEYER PITTS & CO.**
Clear or amethyst, 6" **5.00 7.00**

☐ **H. MICHELSEN**
In center, on top "Bay Rum," under it "St.
Thomas," clear or amethyst, fifth **7.00 10.00**

Price Range

☐ **I. MICHELSON & BROS.**
Clear or amethyst, 11" 22.00 33.00

☐ **MIDLAND HOTEL**
Kansas City, MO, panels on neck, clear, 3" ... 8.00 11.00

☐ **MILK GLASS**
7¼" 37.00 48.00

☐ **J.A. MILLER**
Houston, Texas, clear or amethyst, ½ pint 12.00 17.00

☐ **MONK LABEL**
Amber, 10" 59.00 79.00

☐ **MONOGRAM**
No. 6, clear, 8¼" 100.00 130.00

☐ **M & M T CO.**
Clear or amethyst, 3¼" 7.00 10.00

☐ **J. MOORE OLD BOURBON**
Amber, 12" 65.00 86.00

☐ **J. MOORE**
Amber, 11" 72.00 93.00

☐ **JESSE MOORE & CO.**
Louisville, KY, ringdeer trademark, Bourbon &
Rye, Moore Hunt & Co., sole agents, flask, amber 180.00 230.00

☐ **JESSE MOORE & CO.**
"Louisville, KY" outer circle, "C.H. MOORE
BOURBON & RYE" center, "JESSE MOORE
HUNT CO./SAN FRANCISCO" at base, gradu-
ated collar and ring, quart, 11½" 88.00 110.00

☐ Same as above except golden amber, 11¾" ... 88.00 110.00

☐ **G.T. MORRIS**
A bunch of flowers on back, amber, 12" 185.00 235.00

☐ **MOSES IN BULRUSH**
Clear or amethyst, 5" 42.00 53.00

☐ **MOUNT VERNON**
Machine made, amber, 8¼" 11.00 17.00

☐ **MOUNT VERNON**
Pure Rye, square quart, embossed, amber 12.00 16.00

☐ **MOUNT VERNON PURE RYE WHISKEY**
In three lines, back "Hannis Dist'l'G Co., Full
Five" in two lines, two more lines "Re-Use of Bottle Prohibited," under bottom "Patented March
25, 1890," amber, 3¼" square, neck 4", 4¼" 22.00 32.00

☐ Same as above except sample, 3¼" 22.00 32.00

☐ Same as above except machine made 26.00 28.00

Griffith Hyatt & Co./Baltimore,
applied handle, open pontil,
applied collar amber, 7¼".
$150.00

	Price Range	
☐ **MULFORD'S DISTILLED MALT EXTRACT**		
Embossed, J.F. Mulford & Co., chemists, Philadelphia, amber, 8¾"	7.00	9.00
☐ **MUNRO, DALUHINNIL**		
Scotland, reuse of bottle prohibited in 5 lines on front, in back, "House of Lords," whiskey, 2½" x 2½" square, blob neck, double ring top, improved pontil, dr. aqua, 12½"	40.00	50.00
☐ **MURPHY THE**		
In center, "Wine & Liquor Co., 308–310-Pike St., Seattle, Wash." all in a circle, applied ring top, amber, qt.	63.00	85.00
☐ **MURRAY HILL MARYLAND RYE**		
Sherbrook Distilling Co., Cincinnati, label, clear or amethyst, 6"	9.00	12.00
☐ **JOHN MURRAY (JM) RYE WHISKEY**		
Label only, flask, amber, ½ pint, 7"	7.00	10.00
☐ **ANGELO MYERS**		
Clear or amethyst, 6¼"	8.00	11.00

Price Range

☐ **H.C. MYERS COMPANY**
New York, N.Y. and Covington, KY, Guaranteed
Full ½ pint, all on front, flask, amethyst, 6⅜″   **8.00   11.00**

☐ **NABOB**
Four-part mold, amber, 10½″ **50.00   58.00**

☐ **NEALS AMB PHTH**
In a seal on shoulder, cobalt blue, 9⅛″ **88.00 120.00**

☐ **NEWMAN'S COLLEGE**
San Francisco and Oakland, round like football,
amber, 4¼″ **30.00   35.00**

☐ **NIXON & CO. J.C.**
In center, "Seattle, W.T." all in a circle, flask,
amber, ½ pt. **150.00 185.00**

☐ **O'HARE MALT, H. ROSENTHAL & SONS**
"#1" under bottom, amber, 10¾″ **18.00   25.00**

☐ **O'HEARN'S WHISKEY**
"#1919" under bottom, side mold, inside screw,
amber, 10¼″ **25.00   35.00**

☐ **OHIO**
Expanded swirl bottle, 24 rib pattern, vertical over
swirl to left, club shaped, deep blue aqua, 7¾″ **80.00 110.00**

☐ **OLD ASHTON**
Clear, 8½″ **9.00   13.00**

☐ **THE OLD BUSHMILLS DISTILLING CO.,**
LIMITED TRADEMARK
Pure malt, established 1734, to 1903, 10″ **10.00   13.00**

☐ 1915 up **7.00   10.00**

☐ **OLD CHARTER WHISKEY**
Louisville, KY, label, amber, 11¾″ **28.00   39.00**

☐ **OLD CROW**
Paper label, clear, 11″ **3.00   6.00**

☐ **OLD DUFFY'S 1842 APPLE JUICE, VINEGAR**
STERILIZED 5 YEARS
Around shoulder, amber, 10″ **9.00   12.00**

☐ **OLD EDGEMONT WHISKEY**
Label, clear, ½ pint, 6½″ **9.00   13.00**

☐ **OLD EDGEMONT WHISKEY, THE I TRAGER**
CO.
Cincinnati, Ohio, label, clear, ¼ pint, 5″ **9.00   13.00**

Price Range

☐ **OLD FAMILY WINE STORE (diamond design) ESTABLISHED 1857 JOS. CLEVE & CO 19821**
"Cambridge St., Boston" in slug plate, narrow flask, ring collar, clear, ½ pint, 6½" 9.00 12.00

☐ **OLD HENRY RYE**
In script, ring top, clear or aqua, 9½" 11.00 16.00

☐ **OLD HUDSON**
Pinch bottle, clear, 6½" 32.00 43.00

☐ **OLD IRISH WHISKEY**
Trademark—shield and crown, "This is the property of Mitchell & Co. of Belfast, Ltd, Imperial Pint" all on front, flask shape, graduated collar and flared band, ABM, aqua, 9½" 5.00 7.00

☐ **OLD IRISH WHISKEY**
Imperial Pint on back, aqua, 10" 24.00 32.00

☐ **OLD J.H. CUTTER V.F.O. RYE**
Louisville, KY, label, clear or amethyst, 11" 7.00 10.00

☐ **OLD JOE GIDEON WHISKEY BROS.**
"F" under bottom, 11½" 20.00 27.00

☐ **OLD KAINTUCK BOURBON**
Clear, 3¾" 10.00 14.00

☐ **OLD KENTUCKY BOURBON**
Cork, amber, 8" 10.00 15.00

☐ **THE OLD KENTUCKY CO.**
Clear or amethyst, 11" 30.00 40.00

☐ **OLD PLANTATION DISTILLING CO.**
Los Angeles, CA, amber, 10" 35.00 44.00

☐ **OLD PORT HALEY WHISKEY**
Swope & Mangold, Dallas, Texas, clear or aqua, quart 25.00 35.00

☐ **OLD PRENTICE WHISKEY**
Label, in back embossed "J.T.S. Brown & Sons, Distillers, Louisville, Ky.," clear, 11" 7.00 10.00

☐ **OLD QUAKER**
"1234" under bottom, clear, 6½" 57.00 68.00

☐ **OLD SERVITOR DISTRIBUTING CO.**
NY, amber, 11" 7.00 10.00

☐ **THE OLD SPRING DISTILLING CO.**
Clear or amethyst, 8½" 8.00 11.00

☐ **OLD SPRING WHISKEY**
Clear or amethyst, 9¼" 11.00 17.00

Price Range

☐ **OLD TIME**
First Prize Worlds Fair 1893, clear, 9½" ...... | 19.00 | 25.00

☐ **PAUL JONES**
Embossed, labeled, rectangular, cork, amber, 10" .... | 10.00 | 14.00

☐ **S.F. PETTS & CO. IMPORTERS**
"Boston U.S.A., Registered" horizontally, round, graduated collar and ring, amethyst, 12½" .... | 9.00 | 12.00

☐ **PICNIC FLASK or PUMPKIN SEED**
There are many different sizes and colors, some embossed, some not .... | 8.00 | 11.00

☐ **S.N. PIKES MAGNOLIA**
Cincinnati, Ohio, the Fleischman, clear or amethyst, 12¼" .... | 15.00 | 21.00

☐ **PIKES PEAK OLD RYE**
Aqua, pint .... | 60.00 | 78.00

☐ **PIKESVILLE RYE**
Clear, 4" .... | 7.00 | 10.00
☐ Same as above except "Patented" under bottom | 8.00 | 11.00

☐ **PLANTER RYE, REGISTERED, ULLMAN & CO.**
Ohio, amethyst, ½ pint .... | 15.00 | 21.00

☐ **PLANTER MARY LOU RYE**
Ullman & Co., Cincinnati, ground top, clear, 5½" | 11.00 | 17.00

☐ **PLANTER MARY LOU RYE**
Ullman & Co., Cincinnati, clear, 5½" .... | 11.00 | 17.00

☐ **POND'S ROCK & RYE WITH HOREHOUND**
"R" missing in Rock, "E" missing in Rye, aqua, 10" .... | 19.00 | 25.00

☐ **PREACHER WHISKEY**
Curved bottle, 3" round sides, off-center neck, clear or amethyst, ½ pint, 6½" .... | 30.00 | 40.00

☐ **P & SP**
Under bottom, three-part mold, dark olive, 9½" | 12.00 | 17.00
☐ Same as above except 11½", pontil .... | 28.00 | 37.00

☐ **PUMPKIN SEED**
Small, on back and front, sunburst pattern, clear or amethyst, 5" .... | 19.00 | 27.00

☐ **PUMPKIN SEED**
Plain, clear or amethyst, all sizes .... | 10.00 | 13.00

☐ **PUMPKIN SEED PICNIC FLASK**
Double band collar, amethyst, 5½" .... | 6.00 | 9.00

Price Range

☐ **PUMPKIN SEED**
Amethyst, 6″ 7.00 10.00
☐ **PUMPKIN SEED**
Label, amber, 4″ 19.00 25.00
☐ Same as above except dark aqua, 4½″ 40.00 50.00
☐ **PURE MALT WHISKEY, PRIDE OF CANADA**
Tapered top, amber, 10½″ 19.00 25.00
☐ **QUAKER MAID WHISKEY**
Girl in center of label, S. Hirsch & Co. Kansas
City, MO, fancy shoulder, clear, 3½″ 29.00 39.00
☐ **QUAKER MAID WHISKEY**
In center, "S.C.H. & Co." in circle, embossed,
fancy shoulder, clear, 3½″ 29.00 39.00
☐ **QUAKER MAID WHISKEY**
"Patented" under bottom, clear or aqua, quart 22.00 35.00
☐ **QUARTERBACK RYE WHISKEY**
S. Silberstein, Philadelphia, PA, clear, quart ... 27.00 37.00
☐ **QUEEN MARY SCOTCH WHISKEY**
Amber, quart 27.00 37.00
☐ **QUEENSDALE WHISKEY**
Label, amber, quart 7.00 10.00
☐ **QUININE WHISKEY CO.**
"Louisville, KY." on bottom, amber, 5¼″ 11.00 17.00
☐ **F.R. QUINN**
"This Bottle Not To Be Sold" on back base, aqua,
11½″ 10.00 14.00
☐ **RCV NP**
On shoulder, on top a crown, 3 pt. mold, applied
top, kick up, dark green, 9½″ 38.00 51.00
☐ **W.J. RAHILY CO.**
"W.J.R." on back shoulder, three-part mold, clear
or amethyst, 11″ 12.00 17.00
☐ **FRED RASCHEN CO.**
"Sacramento, Cal." in form of circle, "F.R. CO."
monogram, round, graduated collar and ring,
amber, fifth, 12″ 19.00 25.00
☐ **FRED RASCHEN**
Sacramento, CA, amber, fifth 24.00 33.00
☐ **REBECCA AT THE WELL**
Pontil, clear or amethyst, 8″ 65.00 87.00

Price Range

☐ **RECORDS AND GOLDBOROUGH**
"Baltimore, MD." vertically on slug plate, rectangular, ring collar, clear, pint, 6" 7.00 10.00

☐ **RED CHIEF**
Fort Hood, Indiana, Ballina Rye, clear, 12" 15.00 21.00

☐ **RED TOP**
With "Top" on shoulder, "R.D. Westheimer & Sons" on bottom, under bottom, different numbers, flask, extra ring on bottom of neck, amber, ½ pint 7.00 10.00

☐ **RED TOP RYE**
Embossed, amber, 12" 9.00 14.00

☐ **REGISTERED HONEST ONE PINT**
At top half, rectangular, graduated collar and ring, amethyst, pint and ½ pint 5.00 7.00

☐ **REGISTERED**
Clear or amethyst, 8" 9.00 12.00

☐ **E. REMY**
Champagne, cognac, machine made, "A.R." on bottom, green, 4" 2.50 3.00

☐ **RHEINSTROM BROS. PROPRIETORS**
On other side "Mother Putnam's Blackberry Cordial," amber, 11" 32.00 44.00

☐ **RICHARDSON, BRUNSING CO.**
San Francisco, CA., amber, 11" 32.00 44.00

☐ **J. RIEGER & CO.**
Kansas City, MO, flute shoulder, clear or aqua, 11½" 15.00 21.00

☐ **W.R. RILEY DISTILLING CO.**
Kansas City, MO, clear, quart 11.00 16.00

☐ **RIFLE FIGURAL**
Italian wine bottle, wide base is made by stock of rifle, green, 16" 10.00 14.00

☐ **H.H. ROBINSON, BOSTON**
Label, "Guaranteed Full Pt" on back, clear or amethyst, 8¾" 4.00 6.00

☐ **ROMA CALIFORNIA WINE, PRIDE OF THE VINYARD, R.C.W. CO.**
Monogram all on front, ABM, thread top, amber, 12⅛" 4.00 5.00

Price Range

☐ **L. ROSE & CO.**
Rose and wine bottle, applied crown, tapered,
aqua, 7½" 8.00 11.00

☐ **ROSEDALE OK WHISKEY**
Siebe Bros. & Plagermann, San Francisco,
amber, quart 190.00 240.00

☐ **ROSSKAM GERSTLEY & CO.**
"Old Saratoga Extra Fine Whiskey" on back,
"Philadelphia" in seal, small kick-up, clear or am-
ethyst, 9¼" 12.00 17.00

☐ **ROSSKAM GERSTLEY & CO.**
Monogram No. 6, clear, 8¼" 38.00 49.00

☐ **ROSSKAM GERSTLEY & CO.**
Clear, 9½", amber 24.00 33.00

☐ **ROSS'S BRAND**
Aqua, 14¼" 11.00 16.00

☐ **ROTH & CO.**
San Francisco, CA, pocket flask 13.00 19.00

☐ **ROTH & CO.**
San Francisco, amber, quart 55.00 70.00

☐ **THE ROTHENBERG CO. WHOLESALE
LIQUOR DEALERS**
San Francisco, CA., rectangular, amber, 10¼" 24.00 27.00

☐ **ROTHENBERG & CO.**
Embossed figure of a judge, rectangular, quart,
deep amber, 10" 40.00 50.00

☐ **ROXBORO LIQ. CO.**
Clear or amethyst, 8" 9.00 12.00

☐ **AQUA DE RUBINAT**
Aqua, 11" 4.00 6.00

☐ **CHAS. RUGERS, WINE & LIQUORS**
Houston, TX, "#181" under bottom, amber, 6" 12.00 17.00

☐ **RUM**
Five rings, clear, 3¾" 7.00 10.00

☐ **RUSCONI, FISHER & CO.**
"San Francisco" in 3 lines, back full quart on
shoulder, inside threads top, flask type bottle,
amber, 11" 34.00 45.00

☐ **RYE**
Three-part mold, clear, 11" 12.00 17.00

☐ **RYE**
Ground pontil, silk glass, hand painted, 11" ... 30.00 40.00

	Price Range	

☐ **RYE**
Decanter, gold trim, clear, 9¼" 30.00 40.00

☐ **SAFE WHISKEY**
Aqua, 9¼" 36.00 48.00

☐ **SAILOR'S FLASK**
Crock, tan and brown, 8¼" 95.00 122.00

☐ **JARED SPENCER**
Flask, flared top, green, pint 900.00 1200.00

☐ **R.A. SPLAINE & CO.**
"Haverhill, Mass." on shoulder, "It Pays To Buy
the Best" written on shoulder on opposite sides,
three-piece mold, round, graduated collar and
ring, amethyst, quart, 11½" 9.00 12.00

☐ **SPRUANCE, STANLEY & CO.**
Sunflower Pennsylvania Rye, San Francisco, CA,
four-part mold, amber, 10⅜" 21.00 27.00

☐ **S.S.T. PATENT**
Amber, quart 10.00 13.00

☐ **STAR**
In center with stars circling, clear, 4¾" 9.00 12.00

☐ **STAR WHISKEY LABEL**
Saddle strap, amber, pint 7.00 10.00

☐ **STAR WHISKEY**
Handled jug, applied seal, yellow-amber, 7½" 350.00 425.00

☐ **STEIN BROS.**
"Chicago" on bottom, round, graduated rows of
beads swirled around on shoulder, graduated
band and ring collar, amethyst, quart, 11¾" ... 19.00 25.00

☐ **C.B. STEWART**
Atlanta, GA, double top, clear, pint 12.00 17.00

☐ **C.B. STEWART**
Atlanta, GA, clear or aqua, pint 8.00 11.00

☐ **STODDARD**
Label, wine, iron pontil, olive or amber, 8½" ... 45.00 56.00

☐ **STODDARD**
Willington Glassworks, olive-amber, 10" 25.00 35.00

☐ **STONEBROOK**
Turn mold, amber, 9½" x 4" 8.00 11.00

☐ **OLD HENRY WHISKEY, STRAUS GUNST & CO.**
Richmond, VA, panels on shoulder, clear or amethyst, 11" 18.00 25.00

Price Range

☐ **STRAUS GUNST & CO., PROPRIETORS**
Richmond, VA, amber, ½ pint 18.00 25.00

☐ **STRAUSS BROS. CO.**
Chicago, U.S.A., deep green, 12¼″ 18.00 25.00

☐ **STRAUSS PRITZ & CO.**
Sheared top, clear or amethyst, 5½″ 8.00 11.00

☐ **THE STRAUSS PRITZ CO.**
Clear or amethyst, 6¼″ 4.00 6.00

☐ **C.W. STUARTS**
Amber, quart 18.00 25.00

☐ **SWANS G.**
"The-owl, 5160 Ballard Ave. Ballard, Wash." all
in a circle, double ring top and neck flask, clear
and amethyst, ½ pt. 14.00 20.00

☐ **TACOMA, WASH.**
In a double circle in center "Monty's," flask Pu
top, clear, ½ pt. 14.00 20.00

☐ **LOUIS TAUSSIG & CO.**
San Francisco, embossed, clear, 11½″ 8.00 11.00

☐ **LOUIS TAUSSIG & CO.**
"San Francisco, New York" vertically on one
side, "Union Made C.B.B.A. Branch No. 22" on
opposite side, square, graduated collar, clear,
scant quart, 10¼″ 8.00 11.00

☐ **LOUIS TAUSSIG & CO.**
In script on top, "San Francisco," under bottom,
"New York" all in 2 vertical lines, square, tapered
top and ring, 10″ 18.00 25.00

☐ **LOUIS TAUSSIG**
Main Street, San Francisco, flask, amber 190.00 240.00

☐ **LT & CO**
Inside of circle, "Patented Feb. 4th, 1902" on
bottom, oval front paneling, ribbed, panels at
base on back, rectangular, graduated collar and
ring, amber, quart, 10½″ 8.00 11.00

☐ **TAYLOR & WILLIAMS**
Embossed, cork, amethyst color, 12″ 10.00 15.00

☐ **TAYLOR & WILLIAMS**
Clear or amethyst, 3¼″ 7.00 10.00

☐ **TAYLOR & WILLIAMS**
Side strap, clear, 6½″ 4.00 5.00

Price Range

☐ **TAYLOR & WILLIAMS**
In a horseshoe shape, under it "Louisville, Ky,"
in center "Whiskey," ring top, clear or amethyst,
4¾" round 7.00 10.00
☐ Same as above except 11⅜" 8.00 11.00
☐ **TEA CUP**
Old Bourbon, Shea Bacqueraz & Co., San Fran-
cisco, amber, quart 260.00 340.00
☐ **TEAKETTLE OLD BOURBON**
San Francisco, amber, quart 190.00 240.00
☐ **TEXAS**
Flask, tapered top, whiskey, clear, quart, 11" tall,
1¾" neck, 8" wide at center, 4" x 3" at bottom 11.00 16.00
☐ **JAS. THARP'S SONS**
In center, Wine & Liquor, Washington, D.C., sad-
dle flask, ring top, amber, 7¾" 21.00 28.00
☐ **A. THELLER**
On shoulder, under bottom of bottle in a circle,
"Theller Arnold," applied top, kick-up, dark olive,
9½" 7.00 10.00
☐ **THEODORE NETTER**
1232 Market St., Phila., PA, 6", clear 16.00 21.00
☐ **TOKJ**
In seal, small kick-up, clear, 11" 8.00 11.00
☐ **TONSMEIRE & CRAFT**
Mobile AL, amber, 11" 35.00 47.00
☐ **THE I. TRAGER CO.**
Amber, 12" 11.00 17.00
☐ **THE I. TRAGER CO.**
"Cincinnati, Ohio" inverted "V" instead of "A" in
"Cincinnati," amber, 12" 33.00 43.00
☐ **THE I. TRAGER CO.**
Ring top, amber, ½ pint..................... 7.00 10.00
☐ **THE I. TRAGER CO.**
Ring top, amber, ½ pint..................... 5.00   7.00
☐ **THE I. TRAGER CO.**
Amber, ½ pint 6.00   9.00
☐ **TROST BROS.**
Clear, 6½" 7.00 10.00
☐ **TUCKER ALA**
On one panel, four running legs in circle on back
panel, amber, 9¼" 60.00 72.00

Price Range

☐ **F.G. TULLEDGE & CO, PURE POP CORN WHISKEY**
Cincinnati, OH, clear, quart 8.00   11.00

☐ **TWO FISH WHISKEY**
Clear or amethyst, 7½" 55.00 72.00

☐ **ULLMAN & CO.**
Planter Rye Registered on back, clear or amethyst, 6¼" 11.00 17.00

☐ **UNION MADE C.B.B.A. OF US & C TRADEMARK**
In circle, flask, clear, pint, 8¾" 6.00   9.00

☐ Same as above except ½ pint 8.00 11.00

☐ **UNION SQUARE COMPANY**
"239 Union St., Lynn, Mass. Guaranteed Full ½ Pint" all in slug plate, rectangular, clear, 7" ...   4.00   5.00

☐ **N.M. URI & CO.**
"B" on bottom, amber, 4¾" x 1½" 11.00 17.00

☐ **N.M. URI & CO.**
Louisville, KY, amber, 5¾" 11.00 17.00

☐ **U.S. MAIL**
Clear, 5½" 80.00 110.00

☐ **W.B. VAIL**
Golden amber, 11½" 22.00 31.00

☐ **VARWIG & SON**
Portland, OR, monogram in center, Full Measure, round, graduated collar and ring, amber, 12¼"   33.00 44.00

☐ **L. VERETERRA OVIEDO**
On bottom, ring top, 12" 4.00   6.00

☐ **THE NORTH VERNON DISTILLING CO., DISTILLERY OFFICE**
Cincinnati, OH, round, ten fancy vertical panels on neck and shoulder, graduated collar and ring, amethyst 13.00 20.00

☐ **VIEUX COGNAC**
Three-part mold, small kick-up, old top, aqua, 8¾" 8.00 11.00

☐ **VINOL**
"Private Mold Pat April 18, 1898" under bottom, amber, 6½" 9.00 12.00

☐ **VIOLIN**
Plain back, different colors and sizes 11.00 17.00

Mohawk Whiskey Figural Bottle, *full figure of Indian, amber, 12¼".*
$25.00–$35.00

Old Continental Whiskey Bottle, *full figure of Continental soldier, amber, 9".*
$20.00–$30.00

Price Range

☐ **VIOLIN**
Label, plain back, different colors and sizes ... **20.00 27.00**

☐ **VIOLIN**
Label, amber, 8½" **27.00 38.00**

☐ **VIOLIN**
Label, music score on back, pontil, different colors, 9¾" **33.00 44.00**

☐ **VIOLIN**
In back, musical score, plain bottom, many colors, various sizes **10.00 13.00**

☐ **VIOLIN FLASK**
Ring top, clear, 6" x 3" **15.00 21.00**

☐ **WALKERS KILMARNOOK WHISKEY 1807**
On bottom, square, square band and ring, ABM, emerald green, 10¼" **8.00 11.00**

☐ **WALTERS & CO.**
"Baltimore" on back base, amber, 11¾" **33.00 44.00**

☐ **WARRANTED**
Flask, dark amber and golden amber, pint or ½ pint **8.00 11.00**

☐ **WARRANTED**
Flask, side bands, double band collar, amethyst, pint and ½ pint **8.00 11.00**

☐ **LOUIS WEBER**
Louisville, KY, "H.W.M. Colly & Co., Pittsburg" under bottom, three-part mold, olive, 10" **40.00 50.00**

☐ **WEIL BROS. & SONS**
San Francisco, amethyst, 12" **28.00 31.00**

☐ **EDWARD WEISS**
Leading West End Liquor House, corner of West and Calvert, Annapolis, MD, ring top, clear or aqua, 6" **9.00 13.00**

☐ **WEST BEND OLD TIMERS LAGER BEER**
Label, aqua, 9¼" **4.00 6.00**

☐ **WEST END WINE & SPIRITS CO.**
"Full Qt. Registered" on back, amber, 12¼" .. **40.00 52.00**

☐ **FERDINAND WESTHEIMER & SONS**
"Cincinnati, USA" in circle, Rectangular, graduated collar and ring, amber, ½ pint **5.00 7.00**

☐ **FERDINAND WESTHEIMER & SONS**
Amber, 6" **9.00 13.00**

Price Range

☐ **FERDINAND WESTHEIMER & SONS**
Amber, 9½″ 15.00 21.00
☐ **WHISKEY**
Vertical ribbing, applied handle, open pontil, gold-
amber, 9½″ 130.00 150.00
☐ **WHITE HORSE WHISKEY**
Embossed, cork, olive-green, 11″ 4.50 6.50
☐ **WILD TURKEY**
Tom Turkey in the Straw, #1, turkey figural ... 225.00 265.00
☐ **WILD TURKEY**
Turkey on a Log, #2, turkey figural 315.00 355.00
☐ **WILD TURKEY**
Turkey on the Wing, #3, turkey figural 110.00 130.00
☐ **WRIGHT & TAYLOR**
Round quart, amber 10.00 15.00

NEW BOTTLES

AVON

Avon has been calling for more than 50 years, and the call from collectors for imaginative, decorative toiletries and cosmetic bottles has brought a stampede upon the antique shops. As the modern leader in the non-liquor bottle field, Avon's vast range of bottles offers almost unlimited opportunities for the collector. Since none of their figurals are extremely rare, a complete collection of them is possible though it would contain hundreds of specimens.

Today, the Avon figurals—shaped as animals, people, cars, and numerous other objects—are the most popular of the company's bottles, but not always the most valuable. Some of the early non-figurals of the pre-World War II era sell for high prices because of their scarcity. Since there were virtually no Avon collectors in those days, very few specimens were preserved.

Avon collecting has become such a science that all of its bottles, and even the boxes that they came in, have been carefully catalogued. In fact, everything relating to Avon is now regarded as collectible, including brochures, magazines ads, and anything bearing the Avon name. Of course, the older material is more sought after than items of recent vintage.

Avon bottles are readily obtainable through specialized dealers and numerous other sources. Since some people who sell the Avons are unaware of their value, the collector can often find bargain prices at garage sales or flea markets.

Although it seems that every possible subject has been exhausted, Avon continues to bring out original bottles with a variety in sizes, colors, and decorative designs. The new figurals in its line are issued in limited editions with editions being rather large in order to accommodate the collector as well as the general public. Collectors of new Avons should purchase the new issues as soon as they reach the market since they often sell out quickly. When an Avon product has sold out, its price begins rising and can double in less than a year depending on its popularity. Even though this does not always happen, the original retail price will be lower than can be expected later on in the collector's market.

Although Avon is the oldest toiletry company issuing decorative bottles, collecting interest in its products did not become wide-spread until stimulated by the release in 1965 of an after shave lotion in a stein decanter and a men's cologne in an amber boot. The interest created by those tolletries led many people to investigate the earlier Avon products, partly for collecting and partly for use as decorations. At that time they could be purchased inexpensively from secondhand shops and thrift bazaars. Unfortunately, by then many of the older ones had perished and were just not to be found.

By the late sixties, Avons were plentiful in antique shops with prices on the rise. Some collecting clubs were established. The early seventies saw further increases in collecting activity. The company, well aware of what was happening, expanded its line of figurals to meet public demand.

Many collectors doubt that modern Avon figurals can ever become really valuable because of the large quantities made. But with natural loss, passage of time, and increasing collector demand, Avon figurals may well reach respectable prices in five or ten years, making the 1984 prices look like great bargains.

Just as with many other collectibles, the Avons that prove least popular when issued sometimes end up being the scarcest and costliest. This is why collectors automatically buy each one as they come out.

Avon began as the California Perfume Company, founded by D.H. McConnell, a door-to-door salesman who gave away perfume samples to prevent doors from being slammed in his face. Eventually he started selling perfume and abandoned bookselling. Although it was located in New York, the name "Avon" was initially used in 1929 in conjunction with the California Perfume Company or C.P.C. After 1939 it was known exclusively as Avon. The C.P.C. bottles are naturally very desirable, having been issued in relatively small quantities and not having been well preserved. These bottles are impossible to date accurately because many designs were used with various preparations. In most cases, sales do not occur frequently enough to establish firm price levels. Therefore, the prices listed in this book should be regarded only as being approximate. All C.P.C. bottles in this section are indicated with a cross (+).

There are numerous possible approaches to Avon collecting. The most popular is to amass as many figurals as one's budget, time and energy (not to mention luck) allows. They can also be collected by subject matter, or according to the type of product they originally contained—such as making specialized collection of perfume bottles, or after shave bottles. Another favorite specialty is Avons with figural stoppers.

Price Range

☐ **ATOMIZER PERFUME** (1908)
Six-sided bottle, cork stopper, green label on
front and neck, 1 oz., sold in CPC Atomizer Sets.
Original price $.50 .... **92.00 105.00**

☐ **CALIFORNIA ROSE TALCUM** (1921)
Clear glass, brass cap, 3½ oz. Original price $.33 **73.00 85.00**

☐ **CHRISTMAS PERFUME** (1907)
Clear glass, glass stopper, paper label, ribbon at
neck, 2 oz. Original price $.75 .... **125.00 145.00**

☐ **CPC PERFUME** (1918)
Clear glass, glass and cork stopper, sold in gift
box set, ½ oz. **77.00 97.00**

☐ **CRAB APPLE BLOSSOM** (1908)
Clear glass, round bottle, glass stopper, paper
label with Eureka trademark, 1 oz. Original price
$.50 to $.75 .... **145.00 200.00**

☐ **CUT GLASS PERFUME** (1915–20)
Square-shaped bottle of clear glass, round neck,
round cut glass stopper, two different labels with
gold embossing, 2 oz. Original price $2.25 .... **175.00 200.00**

☐ **EXTRA CONCENTRATED PERFUME** (1916)
Glass stopper, paper labels on front and neck, 1
oz. Original price $.75 .... **170.00 190.00**

☐ **EXTRACT ROSE GERANIUM PERFUME** (1887)
Narrow clear bottle, glass stopper with floral de-
sign, paper label, 1 oz. Original price $.40 ..... **185.00 220.00**

☐ **EXTRACT PERFUME** (1908)
Clear glass, glass stopper, paper label, 1 oz. Original price $.50 .... **175.00 200.00**

☐ **EXTRACT PERFUMES** (1896)
Clear glass, round glass stopper, 2 oz. Original
price $.90 to $1.40 .... **145.00 190.00**

☐ **EIGHT OUNCES PERFUME**
Clear glass, glass stopper, paper labels on front
and neck, 8 oz. Original price $3.25 .... **170.00 195.00**

☐ **FRENCH PERFUME** (1896–1908)
Clear glass, glass stopper, paper label with Eu-
reka trademarks, ½ oz. Original price $.55 .... **145.00 160.00**

☐ **FRENCH PERFUME** (1896)
Clear glass with embossing, cork stopper, ¼ oz.
Original price $.25 .... **125.00 135.00**

Price Range

☐ **FRENCH PERFUME** (1890)
Clear glass, glass stopper, paper label, ¼ oz.
Original price $.25 . . . .   **125.00 140.00**

☐ **HALF OUNCE PERFUME** (1919)
Clear glass, glass stopper with crown on top, ½
oz. Original price $.75 . . . .   **80.00   95.00**

☐ **HALF OUNCE PERFUME** (1915)
Clear glass, glass stopper set in cork, paper la-
bels on front and neck, ½ oz. Original price $.25   **95.00 110.00**

☐ **CPC PERFUME** (1906)
Clear glass, glass stopper, gold label on front and
neck, 1 oz. **145.00 190.00**

☐ **CPC PERFUME** (1916)
Glass stopper, paper label on front and neck, 1
oz. Original price $.50 . . . .   **125.00 140.00**

☐ **FLORIDA WATER** (1887)
Glass stopper, labels on front and neck, 2 or 4
oz. **95.00 110.00**

☐ **CPC TOILET WATER** (1890)
Glass stopper, front and neck labels of various
designs, 2 oz. or 4 oz. **95.00 110.00**

☐ **EAU DE COLOGNE** (1890)
Glass stopper, paper labels on front and neck in
various designs, 4 oz. Original price $.65 . . . . . .   **95.00 110.00**

☐ **FLORIDA WATER** (1900)
Glass stopper, ribbed bottle, 2 oz. Original price
$.35 . . . .   **170.00 185.00**

☐ **LAVENDER WATER** (1910)
Glass stopper, paper label on front with Eureka
trademark, 2 oz. Original price $.35 . . . .   **145.00 160.00**

☐ **BABY TOILET WATER** (1923)
Clear bottle, brass and cork stopper, soldier on
front label, blue label on neck, 2 or 4 oz. Original
price $.48 or $.89 . . . .   **67.00   85.00**

☐ **LILAC VEGETAL** (1928–29)
Clear glass ribbed, cork stopper with metal crown
on top, paper front and neck labels are pink, 2 oz.   **67.00   85.00**

☐ **LITTLE FOLKS PERFUME** (1908)
Clear glass, cork stopper, front label, sold in Little
Folks Set only **67.00   85.00**

Price Range

☐ **LITTLE FOLKS PERFUME** (1912)
Clear glass, cork stopper, sold in Little Folks Set, various labels on front **67.00   85.00**

☐ **LITTLE FOLKS PERFUME** (1915)
Small bottle, cork stopper, front label, ribbon on neck **67.00   85.00**

☐ **LITTLE FOLKS PERFUME** (1925–32)
Clear glass with brass screw on cap, sold in Little Folks Set, ½ oz. **64.00   80.00**

☐ **MUSK PERFUME** (1896)
Clear glass, glass stopper, paper label, 1 oz. . .   **95.00 120.00**

☐ **MUSK PERFUME** (1915)
Clear glass, glass stopper, paper labels on front and neck, 1 oz. Original price $.75 . . . .   **145.00 160.00**

☐ **ONE OUNCE PERFUME** (1908)
Clear glass, glass stopper, paper label with Eureka trademark, 1 oz. Original price $.50 . . . . . .   **145.00 190.00**

☐ **PERFUME** (1890)
Clear glass, glass stopper, different labels, neck ribbons, 1 oz. Original price $.25 . . . .   **95.00 110.00**

☐ **PERFUME** (1896)
Clear glass, octagonally shaped, labels on front and neck with Eureka trademark, cork stopper, 1 oz. **145.00 160.00**

☐ **PERFUME** (1906)
Clear glass, round bottle, sold with Atomizer Perfume Set, cork stopper, 1 oz. **95.00 110.00**

☐ **PERFUME** (1908)
Clear glass, various designs of glass stoppers, gold labels, band around neck, 1 oz. **145.00 170.00**

☐ **PERFUME** (1908–18)
Clear glass, glass stopper, gold embossed design on front and neck, 4 oz. Original price $2.75   **145.00 190.00**

☐ **PERFUME** (1923)
Clear glass, glass stopper with crown on top, labels on front and neck, ½ oz. Original price $.59   **95.00 100.00**

☐ **PERFUME** (1925)
Ribbed bottle, glass stopper, paper labels on front and neck, 1 oz. Original price $1.17 . . . . .   **95.00 110.00**

☐ **PERFUME AND ATOMIZER** (1918)
Clear bottle with atomizer, cork stopper, green label on front and neck, 1 oz. Original price $1.50   **85.00 100.00**

Price Range

☐ **PERFUME "FLORAL EXTRACTS"** (1908)
Clear glass, glass stopper, paper label with Eureka trademark, 1 oz. Original price $.50 ...... **145.00 190.00**

☐ **PERFUME FALCONETTE** (1923)
Clear glass, octagonal shaped bottle, long glass stopper, with or without brass cap, neck label. Original price $.49 .... **75.00 95.00**

☐ **PERFUME FALCONETTE** (1925)
Clear glass embossed, glass stopper, brass cap that fits over stopper. Original price $1.10 ..... **85.00 100.00**

☐ **PERFUME FALCONETTE** (1925)
Frosted glass with ribbing, long glass stopper, brass cap that fits over stopper, paper label. Original price $.59 .... **75.00 90.00**

☐ **PERFUME FALCONETTE** (1930–35)
Clear glass with embossing, glass stopper, brass cap that fits over stopper, "Avon" on cap. Original price $1.10 .... **85.00 100.00**

☐ **PERFUME—HIGHLY CONCENTRATED** (1918)
Clear glass, glass stopper set in cork with crown on top, paper labels on front and neck, ½ oz. Original price $.50 .... **85.00 100.00**

☐ **POWDER SACHET** (1886–1912)
Clear glass, gold cap, front label. Original price $.25 .... **93.00 110.00**

☐ **CPC POWDER SACHETS** (1886–1912)
Clear glass, round bottle, gold cap, front label. Original price $.25 .... **93.00 110.00**

☐ **CPC POWDER SACHET** (1890)
Round glass, aluminum cap, front label. Original price $.25 .... **93.00 110.00**

☐ **POWDER SACHET** (1915)
Clear glass, gold cap, paper label. Original price $.25 .... **65.00 90.00**

☐ **POWDER SACHET** (1919)
Clear glass, gold cap, yellow label on front **85.00 100.00**

☐ **POWDER SACHET** (1922–25)
Clear glass, brass cap, black label on front. Original price $72 .... **77.00 95.00**

☐ **POWDER SACHET** (1922–25)
Clear glass, brass cap, black label on front, small bottle. Original price $.49 .... **68.00 85.00**

	Price Range	

☐ **POWDER SACHET** (1923)
Clear glass, brass cap, front label **78.00   95.00**

☐ **ROSE PERFUME SAMPLE** (1900)
Clear glass, cork stopper, ½ oz. **120.00 135.00**

☐ **SWEET COLOGNE** (1905)
Cork stopper, paper labels on front and neck, or
4 oz. Original price $.65 . . . .   **125.00 160.00**

☐ **SMOKERS TOOTH POWDER** (1918)
Cork stopper with metal top, 2¾″ oz. Original
price $.50 . . . .   **95.00 100.00**

☐ **SMOKERS TOOTH POWDER** (1920)
Cork stopper with metal top, paper labels on front
and neck, 2¾″ oz. Original price $.50 . . . .   **95.00 100.00**

☐ **TOILET WATER** (1896)
Clear glass ribbed, glass stopper set in cork,
paper labels on front and neck with Eureka trade-
mark, 2 oz. Original price $.35 . . . .   **170.00 185.00**

☐ **TOILET WATER** (1906)
Clear glass ribbed, glass and cork stopper, 2 oz.
Original price $.35 . . . .   **170.00 185.00**

☐ **TOILET WATER** (1910)
Clear glass, glass stopper, paper labels on front
and neck, 8 oz. Original price $1.25 . . . .   **145.00 160.00**

☐ **TOILET WATER** (1916)
Clear glass, metal spout cap set in cork, paper
labels on front and neck, 2 oz. Original price $.35   **95.00 110.00**

☐ **TOILET WATER** (1916)
Clear glass, cork stopper with crown made of
metal, front labels in two different designs, 2 oz.
Original price $.35 . . . .   **95.00 110.00**

☐ **TOILET WATER** (1916)
Clear glass, cork stopper with plain metal top,
paper labels on front and neck, 4 oz. Original
price $.65 . . . .   **85.00 100.00**

WOMEN'S FRAGRANCES

☐ **APPLE BLOSSOM COLOGNE MIST** (1974–76)
Clear glass, clear cap with inner pink and white
cap, 2 oz. Original price $3.00 . . . .   **.50   1.00**

☐ **APPLE BLOSSOM PERFUME** (1941–42)
Clear glass, gold cap, ⅛ oz. Original price $.75   **50.00 55.00**

Price Range

☐ **APPLE BLOSSOM PERFUME** (1941–43)
Clear glass, gold cap and label, ⅛ oz. Original
price $.75 .... **25.00   35.00**

☐ **APPLE BLOSSOM TOILET WATER** (1941–42)
Pink, white and blue glass, 2 oz. Original price
$1.04 .... **30.00   40.00**

☐ **APPLE BLOSSOM TOILET WATER** (1941–42)
Clear glass, blue label on front, pink cap, 2 oz.
Original price $1.04 .... **30.00   40.00**

☐ **ATTENTION TOILET WATER** (1942)
Clear glass, purple cap, 2 oz. Original price $.25   **35.00   45.00**

☐ **BALLAD PERFUME** (1945)
Small bottle, clear glass, gold neck cord and
label, 3 drams. Original price $3.50 .... **120.00 145.00**

☐ **BALLAD PERFUME** (1945–53)
Clear glass, small bottle, glass stopper, gold neck
cord and label, 3 drams. Original price $3.50 .. **120.00 130.00**

☐ **BIRD OF PARADISE COLOGNE DECANTER**
(1970–72)
Clear glass in shape of bird with gold head, 5 oz.   **7.00   9.00**

☐ **BIRD OF PARADISE PERFUME ROLLETTE**
(1970–76)
Clear glass, gold cap ⅓ oz. Original price $3.00   **1.00   2.00**

☐ **BLUE LOTUS AFTER BATH FRESHENER**
(1967–72)
Clear glass with blue cap, 6 oz. Original price
$3.00 .... **4.00   6.00**

☐ **BLUE LOTUS CREAM SACHET** (1968–72)
Blue frosted glass, blue cap, .66 oz. Original price
$2.50 .... **1.00   3.00**

☐ **BRIGHT NIGHT COLOGNE** (1954–61)
Clear glass, gold speckled cap, gold neck cord
and white paper label, 4 oz. Original price $2.50   **16.00   20.00**

☐ **BRIGHT NIGHT COLOGNE MIST** (1958–61)
Clear glass coated with white plastic, gold speckled gold cap, gold neck cord with white label, 3
oz. Original price $2.75 .... **16.00   22.00**

☐ **BRIGHT NIGHT PERFUME** (1954–59)
Clear glass, glass stopper, white label on gold
neck cord, ½ oz. Original price $7.50 .... **70.00 115.00**

Price Range

☐ **BRIGHT NIGHT TOILET WATER** (1955–61)
Clear glass, gold speckled cap, gold neck cord
with white label, 2 oz. Original price $2.00 ..... **16.00** **22.00**

☐ **BRISTOL BLUE BATH OIL** (1975–76)
Blue opaline glass, plastic inner bottle, 5 oz. Original price $6.00 .... **2.00** **4.00**

☐ **BRISTOL BLUE COLOGNE** (1975)
Blue glass with raised designs, 5 oz. Original price
$6.00 .... **3.00** **5.00**

☐ **BROCADE PERFUME ROLLETTE** (1967–72)
Brown frosted glass, gold cap, ribbed. Original
price $3.00 .... **2.00** **4.00**

☐ **BUTTERFLY COLOGNE** (1972–73)
Clear glass, gold cap with two prongs for an-
tenna, 1.5 oz. Original price $3.00 .... **2.00** **4.00**

☐ **BUTTONS 'N BOWS COLOGNE** (1960–63)
Clear glass, white cap, pink lettering on front, pink
ribbon around neck, 2 oz. Original price $1.35 **14.00** **16.00**

☐ **CHARISMA COLOGNE** (1969–72)
Red glass, red plastic cap trimmed in gold, 4 oz.
Original price $6.00 .... **2.00** **4.00**

☐ **CHARISMA COLOGNE MIST** (1968–76)
Clear glass coated with red plastic, gold trimming,
3 oz. Original price $8.00 .... **.50** **3.00**

☐ **CHARISMA COLOGNE SILK** (1969)
Frosted glass, red cap, 3 oz. Original price $4.50 **3.00** **5.00**

☐ **CHARISMA COLOGNE SILK** (1970–71)
Clear glass, red cap, 3 oz. Original price $4.50 **1.00** **3.00**

☐ **CHARISMA PERFUME ROLLETTE** (1968–76)
Red glass, gold trimming, .33 oz. Original price
$4.50 .... **.50** **3.00**

☐ **COLOGNE ELEGANTE** (1971–72)
Tall bottle with red rose on gold cap, clear glass
painted gold, 4 oz. Original price $5.00 .... **2.00** **4.00**

☐ **COME SUMMER COLOGNE MIST** (1975–76)
Clear glass, green band, white cap with green
band, 2 oz. Original price $3.00 .... **.50** **2.00**

☐ **CORNUCOPIA SKIN-SO-SOFT** (1971–76)
White glass, gold cap, 6 oz. **4.00** **6.00**

Price Range

☐ **COUNTRY GARDEN FOAMING BATH OIL**
(1971–73)
White glass, white cap, green ribbon around
neck. Original price $5.50 .... **4.00** **6.00**

☐ **COUNTRY KITCHEN MOISTURIZED HAND
LOTION** (1974–76)
Red glass, plastic top, 10 oz. Original price $6.00 **5.00** **7.00**

☐ **COURTSHIP PERFUME** (1937)
Clear glass, gold cap, ribbed cap, paper label with
flower, 2 drams **45.00** **55.00**

☐ **COURTSHIP PERFUME** (1938)
Clear glass, gold cap, paper label, 2 drams. Original price $.20 .... **45.00** **55.00**

☐ **COTILLION BATH OIL** (1950–53)
Clear glass, pink cap, pink and white paper label,
6 oz. Original price $.95 .... **18.00** **24.00**

☐ **COTILLION BATH OIL** (1954–59)
Clear glass with pink lettering, pink cap, 4½ oz.
Original price $1.35 .... **8.00** **12.00**

☐ **COTILLION BODY POWDER** (1958–59)
Frosted glass, pink cap, pink paper label, 3 oz.
Original price $1.00 .... **8.00** **12.00**

☐ **COTILLION COLOGNE** (1950–53)
Clear glass, pink cap, pink paper label, 4 oz. Original price $1.75 .... **18.00** **24.00**

☐ **COTILLION COLOGNE** (1946–50)
Clear glass, pink cap, scallops along sides of bot-
tle, 6 oz. Original price $1.50 .... **50.00** **60.00**

☐ **COTILLION COLOGNE** (1957)
Clear glass, white cap, lettering painted on front,
3 drams **10.00** **15.00**

☐ **COTILLION COLOGNE** (1960)
Clear glass, pink paper label around neck, pink
lettering on front, pink cap, 4 oz. Original price
$2.50 .... **18.00** **22.00**

☐ **COTILLION COLOGNE** (1961)
Clear glass, gold cap, pink band around neck, let-
tering painted on front, 2 oz. Original price $1.50 **18.00** **24.00**

☐ **COTILLION COLOGNE** (1961–63)
Frosted glass, white cap, 4 oz. Original price
$3.00 .... **8.00** **12.00**

Price Range

☐ **COTILLION COLOGNE** (1961–71)
Frosted glass, white pointed cap, 2 oz. Original
price $2.00 .... 1.00 2.00

☐ **COTILLION COLOGNE** (1969–72)
Clear glass, white pointed cap, ½ oz. Original
price $1.50 .... 1.00 2.00

☐ **COTILLION COLOGNE MIST** (1961–74)
Clear glass coated with white plastic, white cap,
3 oz. Original price $4.00 .... 8.00 12.00

☐ **COTILLION CREAM LOTION** (1950–53)
Clear glass, pink cap, pink and white paper label,
4 oz. Original price $.89 .... 18.00 24.00

☐ **COTILLION CREAM LOTION** (1954–61)
Clear glass, pink lettering, pink cap, 4½ oz. Original price $.95 .... 6.00 10.00

☐ **COTILLION FOUR OUNCES COLOGNE**
(1953–61)
Clear glass, gold cap, pink band at neck, pink
label, 4 oz. Original price $2.00 .... 8.00 12.00

☐ **COTILLION PERFUME** (1935)
Clear glass, metal cap, paper label on front, ½
oz. Original price $.20 .... 50.00 60.00

☐ **COTILLION PERFUME** (1935)
Clear glass, gold cap, green and gold paper label,
¼ oz. Original price $.20 .... 50.00 60.00

☐ **COTILLION PERFUME** (1968–76)
Clear glass, gold cap, 2 drams. Original price $.20 45.00 55.00

☐ **COTILLION PERFUME** (1939)
Clear glass, ribbed cap, paper label on front, 2
drams 50.00 60.00

☐ **COTILLION PERFUME** (1940)
Clear glass, ribbed gold cap, paper label on front,
2 drams.................................... 50.00 60.00

☐ **COTILLION PERFUME** (1951–52)
Clear glass, swirl bottle, glass stopper, white, pink
and blue floral neck tag at neck, 3 drams. Original
price $3.50 .... 100.00 140.00

☐ **COTILLION PERFUME OIL FOR THE BATH**
(1963–64)
Frosted glass, white pointed cap, ½ oz. Original
price $4.00 .... 8.00 12.00

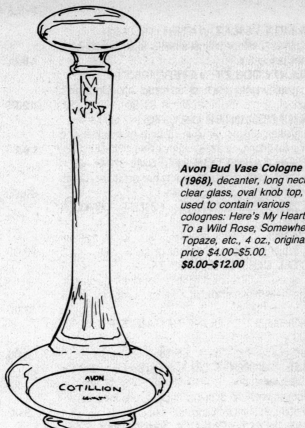

Avon Bud Vase Cologne (1968), decanter, long neck, clear glass, oval knob top, used to contain various colognes: Here's My Heart, To a Wild Rose, Somewhere, Topaze, etc., 4 oz., original price $4.00–$5.00. **$8.00–$12.00**

	Price Range	
☐ **COTILLION SWIRL PERFUME** (1948–50) Clear glass, swirl bottle, gold neck band, dome lid, paper label, 3 drams. Original price $3.00 ..	70.00	80.00
☐ **COTILLION TALC** (1956–58) Frosted glass, pink cap, pink paper label, 3 oz. Original price $1.00	8.00	12.00
☐ **COTILLION TOILET WATER** (1939) Clear glass, ribbed cap, paper label on front, with flowered design	30.00	40.00

Price Range

☐ **COTILLION TOILET WATER** (1950–53)
Clear glass, pink cap and white paper label, 2 oz.
Original price $1.25 . . . .   **18.00   24.00**

☐ **COTILLION TOILET WATER** (1953–61)
Clear glass, gold cap, pink band around neck,
pink label, 2 oz. Original price $1.50 . . . .   **12.00   16.00**

☐ **CREAMY DECANTER** (1973–75)
Clear glass painted yellow, design of basket and
flowers on front, 8 oz. Original price $5.00 . . . .   **4.00   6.00**

☐ **CRIMSON CARNATION PERFUME** (1946–47)
Clear glass, white cap, paper label on front. Origi-
nal price $3.75 . . . .   **90.00 110.00**

☐ **CRIMSON CARNATION TOILET WATER**
(1946–48)
Clear glass, gold or plastic cap, long narrow
paper label on front. Original price $1.19 . . . . . .   **40.00   50.00**

☐ **CRYSTAL COLOGNE** (1966–70)
Clear glass, patterned glass, matching plastic
cap, gold trim at shoulder, 4 oz. Original price
$3.50 to $5.00 . . . .   **3.00   5.00**

☐ **DACHSHUND COLOGNE DECANTER**
(1973–74)
Frosted glass, gold cap, 1.5 oz. **2.00   4.00**

☐ **DAISIES WON'T TELL BUBBLE BATH**
(1957–58)
Clear glass with rib around middle, painted letter-
ing, white cap, 4 oz. Original price $1.10 . . . . . .   **6.00   10.00**

☐ **DAISIES WON'T TELL COLOGNE** (1958–62)
Clear glass, white cap, painted lettering on front,
lace bow around neck, 2 oz. Original price $1.19   **6.00   8.00**

☐ **DAISIES WON'T TELL COLOGNE** (1962–64)
Clear glass, white cap, lettering painted on front,
daisies on front, 2 oz. Original price $1.19 . . . . .   **5.00   7.00**

☐ **DEW KISS DECANTER** (1974–75)
Clear glass painted, pink lid, 4 oz. Original price
$3.00 . . . .   **2.00   4.00**

☐ **ELEGANTE COLOGNE** (1956–59)
Clear glass, silver cap and neck tag, red ribbon,
4 oz. Original price $2.50 . . . .   **35.00   45.00**

☐ **ELEGANTE PERFUME** (1956–59)
Clear glass, silver cap and neck tag, red neck rib-
bon ½ oz. Original price $7.50 . . . .   **100.00 140.00**

Price Range

☐ **ELEGANTE TOILET WATER** (1957–59)
Clear glass, silver cap and neck tag, red neck ribbon, 2 oz. Original price $2.00 .... 30.00 40.00

☐ **EMERALD BUD VASE COLOGNE** (1971)
Green glass, glass lid, 3 oz. Original price $5.00 2.00 4.00

☐ **FLORAL BUD VASE** (1973–75)
White milk glass, 5 oz. 4.00 6.00

☐ **FLOWERTIME COLOGNE** (1949–53)
Clear glass, pink cap, paper label on front, 4 oz.
Original price $1.75 .... 15.00 25.00

☐ **FOREVER SPRING CREAM** (1956–59)
Clear glass, yellow cap, lettering painted on front,
4 oz. Original price $.95 .... 10.00 14.00

☐ **FOREVER SPRING ONE DRAM PERFUME**
(1951–52)
Clear glass, ribbed, gold cap, 1 dram. Original
price $1.75 .... 15.00 18.00

☐ **FOREVER SPRING PERFUME** (1951–56)
Clear glass, glass stopper, blue ribbon and tag on
neck, 3 drams. Original price $5.00 .... 75.00 85.00

☐ **FOREVER SPRING PERFUME** (1956–59)
Yellow cap with blue bird on top, lettering painted
on front, ½ oz. Original price $5.00 .... 80.00 90.00

☐ **FOREVER SPRING TOILET WATER** (1939)
Clear glass with leaflet design in the glass, yellow
plastic cap in design of tulip, 2 oz. Original price
$1.50 .... 15.00 18.00

☐ **FOREVER SPRING TOILET WATER** (1956–59)
Clear glass, yellow cap, blue bird on cap, lettering
painted on front, 2 oz. Original price $1.50 .... 12.00 16.00

☐ **FLOWERTIME TALC** (1949–53)
Clear glass, brass shaker lid, 5 oz. Original price
$.89 .... 15.00 25.00

☐ **FLOWERTIME TOILET WATER** (1949–53)
Clear glass, pink cap, paper label on front, 2 oz.
Original price $1.25 .... 18.00 25.00

☐ **GARDEN OF LOVE SWIRL PERFUME** (1948)
Clear glass, swirl design, glass stopper, gold neck
tag, 3 drams. Original price $3.00 .... 85.00 95.00

Price Range

☐ **GOLDEN PROMISE COLOGNE** (1947–56)
Clear glass, large gold dome shaped cap, lettering painted on front around shoulder, 4 oz. Original price $2.25 .... 16.00   22.00

☐ **GOLDEN PROMISE PERFUME** (1947–50)
Clear glass, gold cap, lettering painted on front,
½ oz. Original price $3.95 .... 160.00   185.00

☐ **GOLDEN PROMISE PERFUME** (1949)
Clear glass, some ribbing, large gold cap in dome
shape, ¼ oz. 20.00   30.00

☐ **GOLDEN PROMISE PERFUME** (1950–54)
Clear glass, glass stopper dome shaped, faceted
bottle, gold base label and neck cord, 3 drams.
Original price $4.00 .... 90.00   110.00

☐ **GOLDEN PROMISE PERFUME** (1954–56)
Clear glass, glass stopper with flat top, gold and
white label, ½ oz. Original price $3.95 .... 110.00   140.00

☐ **GOLDEN PROMISE PERFUME GIFT** (1947)
Clear glass, large gold cap dome shaped, gold
paper label with red lettering 45.00   55.00

☐ **GOLDEN PROMISE TOILET WATER** (1953–56)
Clear glass, large dome shaped cap, lettering
painted on around shoulder, 2 oz. Original price
$1.50 .... 18.00   22.00

☐ **HAPPY HOURS COLOGNE** (1948–49)
Clear glass, pink cap, paper label on front 20.00   25.00

☐ **HAPPY HOURS PERFUME** (1948–49)
Clear glass, pink cap, paper label on front 60.00   70.00

☐ **HAPPY HOURS TALC** (1948–49)
Clear glass, metal shaker cap, small paper label
on front, 2¾ oz. 20.00   30.00

☐ **HAWAIIAN WHITE GINGER ALE AFTER BATH
FRESHENER** (1965–67)
Clear glass, pedestal foot, large white flat cap,
painted lettering in white, 5 oz. Original price
$2.00 .... 4.00   6.00

☐ **HAWAIIAN WHITE GINGER COLOGNE MIST**
(1971–72)
Green glass, large white cap, wide decorative
band around neck, 2 oz. Original price $4.25 .. 1.00   2.00

Price Range

☐ **HAWAIIAN WHITE GINGER COLOGNE MIST**
(1972–76)
Clear glass, textured, clear plastic cap, green, red
and white inner cap, 2 oz. Original price $5.00   **.50**   **1.00**

☐ **HERE'S MY HEART COLOGNE** (1970–71)
Clear glass, white plastic cap with scalloped and
beaded rim, lettering painted on front, 4½ oz.
Original price $1.50 . . . .   **1.00**   **3.00**

☐ **HERE'S MY HEART CREAM LOTION** (1958–68)
Clear glass, white plastic cap with scalloped and
beaded rim, lettering painted on front, 4 oz. Origi-
nal price $1.00 . . . .   **2.00**   **4.00**

☐ **HERE'S MY HEART LOTION SACHET** (1958)
Clear glass, fan shaped, blue cap, also came in
Persian Wood **6.00**   **10.00**

☐ **HERE'S MY HEART PERFUME** (1946–48)
Clear glass, glass stopper with dome shape, pink
ribbon around neck, lettering painted on front, ½
oz. Original price $7.50 . . . .   **90.00** **120.00**

☐ **HERE'S MY HEART PERFUMED CREAM
ROLLETTE** (1963–65)
Clear glass, embossed, gold cap, .33 oz. Original
price $1.75 . . . .   **2.00**   **4.00**

☐ **HERE'S MY HEART PERFUME ROLLETTE**
(1967–68)
Clear glass, ribbed, gold cap, .33 oz. Original
price $3.00 . . . .   **2.00**   **4.00**

☐ **HERE'S MY HEART PERFUME** (1948–49)
Clear glass, glass stopper, heart shaped bottle,
pink satin ribbon around neck, lettering painted
on front, ½ oz. Original price $7.50 . . . .   **110.00** **140.00**

☐ **HERE'S MY HEART PERFUME OIL** (1964–68)
Clear glass, white plastic cap with scalloped rim
and beading, lettering painted on front, ½ oz.
Original price $3.50 . . . .   **5.00**   **8.00**

☐ **HERE'S MY HEART PERFUME OIL FOR THE
BATH** (1963)
Clear glass, white plastic cap with scalloped rim
and beading, lettering painted on the front, ½ oz.
Original price $3.50 . . . .   **10.00**   **14.00**

Price Range

☐ **HERE'S MY HEART TOILET WATER** (1959–62)
Clear glass, heart shaped bottle, white cap with
scalloped and beaded rim, lettering painted on
front, 2 oz. Original price $2.50 . . . .   8.00   12.00

☐ **HERE'S MY HEART TWO OUNCES COLOGNE**
(1961–68)
Clear glass, white plastic cap with scalloped rim
and beading, lettering painted on front, 2 oz. Orig-
inal price $1.75 . . . .   1.00   2.00

☐ **HONEYSUCKLE AFTER BATH FRESHENER**
(1967–72)
Clear glass, orange cap, orange band around
center of bottle, 8 oz. Original price $3.00 . . . . .   1.00   3.00

☐ **HONEYSUCKLE COLOGNE MIST** (1971–72)
Yellow glass, yellow cap, 2 oz. Original price
$4.25 . . . .   1.00   3.00

☐ **HONEYSUCKLE COLOGNE MIST** (1972–76)
Clear glass, clear plastic cap, inner cap of yellow
and green, 2 oz. Original price $3.25 . . . .   2.00   5.00

☐ **HONEYSUCKLE CREAM SACHET** (1967–75)
Yellow glass, frosted, orange cap, .66 oz. Original
price $2.50 50   2.00

☐ **JARDIN D'AMOUR PERFUME** (1929–33)
Clear stopper, black label at neck, 1 or 2 oz. Origi-
nal price $3.50 or $6.50 . . . .   90.00   120.00

☐ **JARDIN D'AMOUR PERFUME** (1954)
Clear glass bottle that sits in a blue and gold
bucket with gold cord that ties around the top of
the bottle, clear plastic cap, gold label, 1 dram.
Original price $15.00 . . . .   160.00   195.00

☐ **JASMINE AFTER BATH FRESHENER**
(1964–68)
Clear glass, tall shaped bottle, yellow cap, letter-
ing painted on front, 8 oz. Original price $2.50   1.00   3.00

☐ **JASMINE BATH SALTS** (1945–52)
Clear glass, black cap and label, 9 oz. Original
price $.75 . . . .   25.00   35.00

☐ **JASMINE POWDER SACHET** (1949)
Clear glass, black cap and label, 1½ oz. Original
price $1.25 . . . .   35.00   45.00

Price Range

☐ **JASMINE TOILET WATER** (1946–48)
Clear glass, gold cap, long narrow black label on
front of bottle, 2 oz. Original price $1.19 ...... **25.00   35.00**

☐ **JASMINE TOILET WATER** (1949)
Clear glass, black cap and label, 2 oz. Original
price $1.25 .... **35.00   45.00**

☐ **LEMON VELVET COLOGNE MIST** (1972–76)
Clear glass, clear plastic cap, yellow and green
inner cap, 2 oz. Original price $4.25 .... **1.00   3.00**

☐ **LEMON VELVET CREAM SACHET** (1971–75)
Yellow glass and cap, .66 oz. Original price $3.00 **1.00   3.00**

☐ **LEMON VELVET ROLLETTE** (1972–74)
Clear glass, green and yellow cap, .33 oz. Original
price $2.50 .... **.50   1.50**

☐ **LEMON VELVET MOISTURIZED FRICTION
LOTION** (1973)
Yellow glass, gold cap, 8 oz. Original price $4.00 **1.00   3.00**

☐ **LAVENDER POWDER SACHET** (1961–68)
Clear glass, glass and plastic stopper, pink and
white labels on front and around neck, 9 oz. .. **4.00   6.00**

☐ **LAVENDER TOILET WATER** (1934–37)
Clear glass, ribbed, blue or gold cap, lavender
label, 4 oz. Original price $.75 .... **55.00   65.00**

☐ **LAVENDER TOILET WATER** (1938–43)
Clear glass, lavender cap, small paper label on
front, 4 oz. Original price $.78 .... **35.00   45.00**

☐ **LAVENDER TOILET WATER** (1945–46)
Clear glass, lavender cap, small paper label, 4 oz.
Original price $.89 .... **40.00   50.00**

☐ **LAVENDER TOILET WATER** (1946)
Clear glass, pink cap, small paper label on front,
4 oz. Original price $1.19 .... **45.00   55.00**

☐ **LILAC AFTER BATH FRESHENER** (1964–68)
Clear glass, pink cap and label, 8 oz. Original
price $2.50 .... **20.00   30.00**

☐ **LILAC CREAM SACHET** (1967–75)
Purple frosted glass, gold and white cap, .66 oz.
Original price $2.50 .... **1.00   3.00**

☐ **LILAC CREAM SACHET** (1975–76)
Clear glass, white cap with lilacs, .66 oz. Original
price $1.00 .... **.50   1.00**

Price Range

☐ **LILY OF THE VALLEY AFTER BATH FRESHENER** (1964–68)
Clear glass, green domed shaped cap, lettering painted on front, 8 oz. Original price $2.50 ....   2.00   4.00

☐ **LILY OF THE VALLEY TOILET WATER** (1946–49)
Clear glass, gold cap and label, 2 oz. Original price $1.19 ....   40.00   50.00

☐ **LILY OF THE VALLEY TOILET WATER** (1949–52)
Clear glass, white flat cap, paper label on front, 2 oz. Original price $1.25 ....   30.00   40.00

☐ **LIQUID MILK BATH** (1975–76)
Frosted glass, gold cap, paper label on front, 6 oz. Original price $5.00 ....   4.00   6.00

☐ **LULLABYE BABY OIL** (1946–50)
Clear glass, flat on the back, pink cap, lettering painted pink on front, 6 oz. Original price $1.00   1.00   2.00

☐ **LUSCIOUS PERFUME** (1950)
Clear glass, gold cap and label, 1 dram. Original price $1.75 ....   10.00   14.00

☐ **LUSCIOUS PERFUME** (1950)
Clear glass, glass stopper, either painted on lettering or gold neck tag label, 3 dams. Original price $2.25 ....   110.00   140.00

☐ **LUSCIOUS PERFUME** (1950–55)
Clear glass, embossed gold cap, lettering painted on front, 1 dram. Original price $1.75 ....   8.00   14.00

☐ **LUSCIOUS PERFUME AWARD** (1950)
Clear circular bottle, glass stopper, 3 drams ...   90.00   120.00

☐ **MARIONETTE PERFUME** (1938)
Clear glass, gold cap with ribbing, ½ oz. Original price $.20 ....,.............................   35.00   45.00

☐ **MARIONETTE TOILET** (1939–40)
Clear glass, plastic cap, long narrow label on front, 2 oz. Original price $.20 ....   30.00   40.00

☐ **ORCHARD BLOSSOMS** (1941–45)
Clear glass, bubble side bottle, white flat cap, paper label on front with tree and flowers, 6 oz. Original price $1.50 ....   50.00   60.00

Price Range

☐ **ORCHARD BLOSSOMS** (1945–46)
Clear glass, bubbled sided bottle, pink flat cap,
paper label on front, 6 oz. Original price $1.50   **65.00   75.00**

☐ **PEAR LUMIERE** (1975–76)
Pear shape, clear glass, plastic gold leaf, 2 oz.
Original price $5.00 . . . .   **4.00   6.00**

☐ **PERFUME CONCENTRE** (1975–76)
Clear glass with gold cap, 1 oz. **3.00   5.00**

☐ **PERSIAN WOOD COLOGNE** (1960–63)
Clear glass, gold cap, gold lettering painted on
front, 4 oz. Original price $2.75 . . . .   **8.00   14.00**

☐ **PERSIAN WOOD COLOGNE** (1961–66)
Clear glass, gold cap, gold lettering painted on
front, 2 oz. Original price $1.75 . . . .   **4.00   6.00**

☐ **PERSIAN WOOD CREAM LOTION** (1961–63)
Clear glass, gold cap, gold lettering and floral de-
sign painted on front, 4 oz. Original price $1.25   **6.00   10.00**

☐ **PERSIAN WOOD PERFUME** (1964–66)
Clear glass, gold cap lettering painted on front,
½ oz. Original price $3.50 . . . .   **10.00   14.00**

☐ **PERSIAN WOOD PERFUME OIL FOR THE
BATH** (1963)
Clear glass, gold domed shaped cap with decorative design, lettering painted on front, ½ oz. Origi-
nal price $3.50 . . . .   **10.00   14.00**

☐ **PERSIAN WOOD TOILET WATER** (1959–61)
Clear glass, gold cap with decorative dome
shape, floral design and lettering painted on front,
2 oz. Original price $2.50 . . . .   **10.00   14.00**

☐ **PETTI FLEUR COLOGNE** (1969–70)
Flower shaped, clear glass, gold cap, 1 oz. Origi-
nal price $2.50 . . . .   **3.00   5.00**

☐ **PINE BATH OIL** (1942–51)
Clear glass, flat sided bottle, turquoise cap, paper
label on front, 6 z. Original price $.95 . . . .   **20.00   26.00**

☐ **PINE BATH OIL** (1944–45)
Clear glass, green cap, flat sided bottle, brown
label, 6 oz. Original price $1.00 . . . .   **20.00   28.00**

☐ **PINE BATH OIL** (1955–57)
Clear glass, green cap, paper label on front with
pine needles and cones, 4 oz. **25.00   34.00**

Price Range

☐ **PRETTY PEACH COLOGNE** (1964–67)
Clear glass, large cap in shape of peach with green leaf, lettering painted on front, 2 oz. Original price $1.50 ....   6.00   10.00

☐ **PURSE PETITE COLOGNE** (1971)
Purse shaped, embossed, gold trim, gold cap and chain, 1½ oz. Original price $4.00 ....   5.00   7.00

☐ **QUAINTANCE BATH OIL** (1949–56)
Clear glass, rose shaped and colored cap, lettering painted on front, 4 oz. Original price $1.25   18.00   24.00

☐ **QUAINTANCE COLOGNE** (1955–56)
Clear glass, blue cap with narrow ribbing, large paper label on front, 2 oz. 12.00   18.00

☐ **QUAINTANCE CREAM LOTION** (1949–56)
Clear glass, rose shaped and colored cap, lettering and decorative border painted on front, 4 oz. Original price $.89 ....   10.00   14.00

☐ **QUAINTANCE FOUR OUNCES COLOGNE** (1948–56)
Clear glass, ribbed corners, rose shaped and colored cap, with green leaf neck band, lettering painted on front, 4 oz. Original price $1.75 ....   20.00   18.00

☐ **QUAINTANCE PERFUME** (1948–50)
Clear glass, with ribbed corners, large rose shaped cap, lettering and decorative borders painted on front, 1 dram. Original price $1.50 ..   65.00   75.00

☐ **QUAINTANCE PERFUME** (1950)
Clear glass, small dome shaped red cap with green leaf, 3 drams. 110.00   140.00

☐ **QUAINTANCE TOILET WATER** (1953–56)
Clear glass, ribbed corners, rose shaped and colored cap, with green leaf neck band, green painted lettering on front, 2 oz. Original price $1.25 ....   16.00   24.00

☐ **RAPTURE HALF OUNCE COLOGNE** (1969–72)
Clear glass, bulbous shaped, large tulip shaped green cap, ½ oz. Original price $1.50 ....   1.00   3.00

☐ **RAPTURE PERFUMED ROLLETTE** (1965–69)
Blue glass, ribbed, large cylinder shaped cap, 1/3 oz. Original price $2.50 ....   5.00   7.00

Price Range

☐ **REGENCE PERFUME ROLLETTE** (1967–68)
Clear glass, ribbed, large cylinder shaped gold cap, .33 oz. Original price $3.00 . . . .   2.00   4.00

☐ **REGENCE PERFUME ROLLETTE** (1969–70)
Clear glass, ribbed, large cylinder green cap, .33 oz. Original price $3.00 . . . .   1.00   3.00

☐ **REGENCE BATH OIL SKIN SO SOFT** (1967–71)
Clear glass, faceted bottle, large domed shaped gold cap, 6 oz. Original price $5.00 . . . .   2.00   4.00

☐ **REGENCE COLOGNE** (1967–69)
Clear glass, faceted, gold cap in dome shape, 2 oz. Original price $3.00 . . . .   1.00   3.00

☐ **REGENCE HALF OUNCE COLOGNE** (1970–71)
Clear glass, gold domed cap with decorative designs, ½ oz. Original price $1.75 . . . .   2.00   4.00

☐ **REGENCE PERFUME** (1966–69)
Frosted glass, gold plastic cap, urn shaped bottle, gold band around shoulder, gold neck tag, ½ oz. Original price $15.00 . . . .   12.00   18.00

☐ **REGENCE PERFUME** (1966–69)
Frosted glass, glass stopper, urn shaped bottle, gold and green trimmings around neck and shoulder, 1 oz. Original price $30.00 . . . .   25.00   35.00

☐ **REGENCE PERFUME OIL** (1968–69)
Clear glass, domed shaped cap with decorative designs, either clear bottom label or gold neck tag, ½ oz. Original price $6.00 . . . .   6.00   10.00

☐ **ROSE GERANIUM AFTER BATH FRESHENER** (1964–68)
Clear glass, rose colored dome cap, lettering painted on front, 8 oz. Original price $2.50 . . . .   5.00   8.00

☐ **ROSE GERANIUM BATH OIL** (1943–50)
Clear glass, flat sided bottle, pink cap, 6 oz. Original price $.95 . . . .   20.00   28.00

☐ **ROSE GERANIUM BATH OIL** (1956–57)
Clear glass, red cap, oval shaped paper label on front, 8 oz. Original price $1.95 . . . .   15.00   20.00

☐ **ROYAL JASMINE BATH OIL** (1958–59)
Clear glass, yellow cap, flowered label on front, 8 oz. Original price $1.95 . . . .   18.00   22.00

☐ **ROYAL JASMINE BATH SALTS** (1954–57)
Clear glass, yellow cap, 8 oz. Original price $.89   18.00   22.00

Price Range

☐ **ROYAL PINE BATH OIL** (1957–59)
Clear glass, green cap, paper label with pine
cones, 8 oz. Original price $1.95 . . . .   22.00   28.00

☐ **ROYAL PINE BATH SALTS** (1954–57)
Clear glass, green cap, green and brown label
with pine cone and needles, 8 oz. Original price
$.75 . . . .   18.00   24.00

☐ **391 PERFUME** (1931–33)
Clear glass, glass stopper, ribbon at neck, 1 oz.
Original price $2.60 . . . .   10.00   140.00

☐ **391 PERFUME** (1933–36)
Clear glass, ribbed, large flat plastic cap with oc-
tagon shape, large label on front, ½ oz. 40.00   50.00

☐ **391 PERFUME FALCONETTE** (1931–33)
Clear glass with embossing, glass stopper with
long dabber, brass cap. Original price $1.30 . . .   80.00   90.00

☐ **TO A WILD ROSE BATH OIL** (1953–55)
Clear glass, contoured bottle, blue cap, with or
without embossed roses, 4 oz. Original price
$1.25 . . . .   16.00   20.00

☐ **TO A WILD ROSE BATH OIL** (1956)
Clear glass, large flat white cap, large paper label,
2 oz. 18.00   22.00

☐ **TO A WILD ROSE BATH OIL** (1956–59)
White glass, large domed pink cap, paper label
on front, 4 oz. Original price $1.35 . . . .   10.00   15.00

☐ **TO A WILD ROSE BODY POWDER** (1955–59)
White glass, white flat cap with rose design,
paper label border around base, lettering painted
on front, 4 oz. Original price $1.00 . . . .   12.00   16.00

☐ **TO A WILD ROSE BODY POWDER** (1955–59)
White glass, white flat cap with rose design on
top, paper label on front, 4 oz. Original price $1.00   10.00   15.00

☐ **TO A WILD ROSE COLOGNE** (1950–55)
Clear glass, contoured bottle, blue cap, blue
label, 4 oz. Original price $2.00 . . . .   18.00   22.00

☐ **TO A WILD ROSE COLOGNE** (1954)
Clear glass, white flat cap, blue paper label on
front, 2 oz. 18.00   22.00

☐ **TO A WILD ROSE COLOGNE** (1955)
Clear glass, white flat cap, large paper label on
front, 2 oz. 18.00   22.00

Price Range

☐ **TO A WILD ROSE COLOGNE** (1955–63)
White glass, large pink domed cap, paper border
around base with floral design, lettering painted
on front, 4 oz. Original price $2.50 .... **12.00** **18.00**

☐ **TO A WILD ROSE COLOGNE** (1956)
Clear glass, large white flat cap, large paper label
on front, 2 oz. **18.00** **22.00**

☐ **TO A WILD ROSE COLOGNE** (1957)
White glass, pink domed cap, paper label on
front, 2 oz. **16.00** **20.00**

☐ **TO A WILD ROSE COLOGNE** (1970–71)
White glass, domed pink cap, lettering painted on
front, ½ oz. Original price $1.75 .... **1.00** **3.00**

☐ **TO A WILD ROSE CREAM LOTION** (1954)
Clear glass, blue cap, paper label, 2 oz. **18.00** **22.00**

☐ **TO A WILD ROSE CREAM** (1956–65)
White glass, large domed pink cap, paper label
on front, 4 oz. Original price $1.25 .... **6.00** **10.00**

☐ **TO A WILD ROSE CREAM LOTION** (1965–68)
White glass, large domed pink cap, lettering
painted on front, floral border around the base,
4 oz. Original price $1.25 .... **5.00** **8.00**

☐ **TO A WILD ROSE FOUR OUNCES COLOGNE**
(1960–61)
White glass, pink cap and neck ribbon, lettering
painted on front, 4 oz. Original price $2.50 .... **22.00** **28.00**

☐ **TO A WILD ROSE LOTION** (1957)
White glass, paper label on front, large domed
pink cap **16.00** **20.00**

☐ **TO A WILD ROSE PERFUME** (1950–56)
Clear glass, large blue cap, flower around the
neck, 2 drams. Original price $4.50 .... **70.00** **80.00**

☐ **TO A WILD ROSE PERFUME** (1955–59)
White glass, large domed pink cap, lettering
painted on front, floral border around base ½ oz.
Original price $5.00 .... **90.00** **120.00**

☐ **TO A WILD ROSE PERFUME OIL** (1964–68)
White glass, large domed pink cap, lettering
painted on front, ½ oz. Original price $3.50 ... **6.00** **8.00**

Price Range

☐ **TO A WILD ROSE PERFUME OIL FOR THE BACH** (1963)
White glass, large domed pink cap, lettering painted on front, ½ oz. Original price $1.50 ... **8.00 12.00**

☐ **TO A WILD ROSE TOILET WATER** (1950–55)
Clear glass, contoured bottle, blue cap with or without embossed roses, 4 oz. Original price $1.50 .... **18.00 22.00**

☐ **TO A WILD ROSE TOILET WATER** (1956)
White glass, large domed pink cap, lettering painted on front, ½ oz. **22.00 28.00**

☐ **TO A WILD ROSE TOILET WATER** (1956–72)
White glass, large domed pink cap, paper border around base with floral design, lettering painted on front, 2 oz. Original price $1.50 .... **8.00 15.00**

☐ **TO A WILD ROSE TWO OUNCES COLOGNE** (1961–68)
White glass, large domed pink cap, lettering painted on front, 2 oz. Original price $1.50 .... **2.00 4.00**

☐ **SOMEWHERE COLOGNE** (1966–71)
Clear glass, gold domed shaped cap, 2 oz. Original price $2.50 .... **1.00 3.00**

☐ **SOMEWHERE COLOGNE** (1961–66)
Clear glass, pink cap with jeweled trim, sculptured bottle, lettering painted around shoulder, 2 oz. Original price $2.00 .... **4.00 6.00**

☐ **SOMEWHERE CREAM LOTION** (1963–66)
Clear glass, pink cap, sculptured bottle, lettering painted around shoulder, 4 oz. Original price $1.50 .... **4.00 6.00**

☐ **SOMEWHERE CREAM LOTION** (1967–68)
Clear glass, large dome shaped gold cap, front paper label, 4 oz. Original price $1.50 .... **5.00 8.00**

☐ **SOMEWHERE PERFUME** (1961–63)
Clear glass, pink cap, sculptured bottle, lettering painted around shoulder, jeweled trim around cap and base of bottle, 1 oz. Original price $20.00 **50.00 60.00**

☐ **SOMEWHERE PERFUMED OIL** (1964–66)
Clear glass, pink glass, sculptured bottle, lettering painted around shoulder, ½ oz. Original price $4.00 .... **6.00 10.00**

Price Range

☐ **SOMEWHERE PERFUME OIL** (1966–69)
Clear glass, gold domed cap, front paper label,
1/3 oz. Original price $4.00 .... 5.00   8.00

☐ **SOMEWHERE PERFUMED OIL FOR THE BATH**
(1963)
Clear glass, pink cap, sculptured bottle, lettering
painted around shoulder, ½ oz. Original price
$4.00 .... 8.00   12.00

☐ **SONNET TOILET WATER** (1941)
Clear glass, purple cap and label, narrow paper
label down the center, 2 oz. Original price $.20   30.00   40.00

☐ **SWAN LAKE BATH OIL** (1947–49)
Clear glass, flat sided bottle, pink cap, lettering
and swan painted on front, 6 oz. Original price
$1.25 .... 50.00   60.00

☐ **SWAN LAKE COLOGNE** (1947–50)
Clear glass, pink cap, lettering and decorative
border painted on front, 4 oz. Original price $1.35   40.00   50.00

☐ **SWEET HONESTY COLOGNE MIST** (1973–74)
Clear glass, horizontal ribbing, inner and outer
caps, 2 oz. 1.00   3.00

☐ **TOPAZE FOUR OUNCES COLOGNE** (1959–63)
Gold cap, faceted bottle, lettering painted on
front, 4 oz. 8.00   12.00

☐ **TOPAZE FOUR OUNCES GIFT COLOGNE**
(1959–61)
Clear glass, gold cap, 4 oz. 10.00   15.00

☐ **TOPAZ HALF OUNCE COLOGNE** (1970–71)
Clear glass, gold cap, lettering painted on front,
½ oz. Original price $1.50 .... 2.00   4.00

☐ **TOPAZ CREAM LOTION** (1959–67)
Clear glass, tall narrow shaped bottle, yellow cap,
4 oz. Original price $1.50 .... 6.00   10.00

☐ **TOPAZ PERFUME** (1959–63)
Amber glass, amber jeweled glass stopper, fac-
eted bottle, 1 oz. Original price $20.00 .... 90.00   120.00

☐ **TOPAZ PERFUME OIL** (1964–69)
Clear glass, gold cap, lettering painted on front,
½ oz. Original price $4.00 .... 50.00   60.00

☐ **TOPAZ PERFUME OIL FOR THE BATH** (1963)
Clear glass, gold cap, lettering painted on front,
½ oz. Original price $4.00 .... 50.00   60.00

Price Range

☐ **TOPAZ TWO OUNCES COLOGNE** (1960–71)
Gold cap, faceted bottle, lettering painted on
front, 2 oz. Original price $2.00 . . . .   1.00   3.00
☐ **ULTRA COLOGNE** (1975–76)
Clear glass, gold cap, 1 oz. Original price $2.50   2.00   4.00
☐ **UNFORGETTABLE COLOGNE** (1966–71)
Clear glass, domed shaped bottle, large flat dec-
orative cap, lettering painted on front, 2 oz. Origi-
nal price $2.50 . . . .   1.00   3.00
☐ **UNFORGETTABLE PERFUME OIL** (1965–69)
Clear glass, large decorative gold cap, lettering
painted on front. Original price $5.00 . . . .   6.00   10.00
☐ **VIOLET BOUQUET COLOGNE** (1946–49)
Clear glass, bubble sides, caps in different colors,
6 oz. Original price $1.00 . . . .   80.00 100.00
☐ **WINTER GARDEN** (1975–76)
Tall bottle, clear glass, gold cap, 6 oz. Original
price $5.00 . . . .   4.00   6.00

WOMEN'S FIGURALS

☐ **BABY OWL** (1975–76)
Clear glass, gold cap, 1 oz. Original price $2.00   2.00   4.00
☐ **BATH URN** (1971–73)
White glass and cap with gold top band under the
cap, 5 oz. 4.00   6.00
☐ **BATH TREASURE SNAIL DECANTER**
(1973–76)
Clear glass, gold head, 6 oz. Original price $6.00   6.00   8.00
☐ **BEAUTIFUL AWAKENING** (1973–74)
Clear glass, painted gold in shape of an alarm
clock, with clock face on front, 3 oz. 5.00   7.00
☐ **BETSY ROSS DECANTER** (1976)
Clear glass painted white, 4 oz. Original price
$10.00 . . . .   8.00   12.00
☐ **BIRD OF HAPPINESS COLOGNE** (1975–76)
Blue glass, gold cap, 1.5 oz. Original price $3.00   3.00   5.00
☐ **BLUE DEMI-CUP BATH OIL** (1968–70)
White glass, blue cap and floral design, 3 oz. Orig-
inal price $3.50 . . . .   6.00   9.00

Price Range

☐ **BLUE EYES** (1975–76)
Kitten figurine, opal glass, blue eyes 1.5 oz. Original price $4.00 .... | **3.50** | **5.50**

☐ **BON BON COLOGNE** (1972–73)
Poodle figurine, white glass, white cap, 1 oz. Original price $2.00 .... | **2.50** | **4.50**

☐ **BON BON COLOGNE** (1973)
Poodle figurine, black milk glass, black plastic cap, 1 oz. Original price $2.00 .... | **1.50** | **3.50**

☐ **BRIDAL MOMENTS** (1976)
Clear glass painted white, figurine of a bride, gold cap, 4 oz. Original price $9.00 .... | **6.50** | **8.50**

☐ **CANDLESTICK COLOGNE** (1966)
Clear glass coated silver, silver cap, 3 oz. Original price $3.75 .... | **8.50** | **12.50**

☐ **CANDLESTICK COLOGNE** (1970–71)
Red glass, gold cap with wide plastic collar, 4 oz. Original price $6.00 .... | **6.00** | **8.00**

☐ **CANDLESTICK COLOGNE** (1972–75)
Clear glass painted silver, 5 oz. .... | **6.00** | **8.00**

☐ **CHARMLIGHT DECANTER** (1975–76)
Clear glass in shape of lamp with white shade, 8.8 oz. Original price $7.00 .... | **7.00** | **9.00**

☐ **CHIMNEY LAMP COLOGNE MIST DECANTER** (1973–74)
Clear glass, white plastic shade with pink floral design, 2 oz. .... | **6.00** | **8.00**

☐ **CHRISTMAS BELLS COLOGNE** (1974–75)
Clear glass painted red, gold cap, 1 oz. .... | **2.00** | **4.00**

☐ **CHRISTMAS TREE** (1968–70)
Clear glass painted red, green, gold and silver, 4 oz. Original price $2.50 .... | **7.00** | **9.00**

☐ **CLASSIC DECANTER** (1969–70)
Figurine of women with bowl on her head, white glass, gold cap, 8 oz. .... | **7.00** | **9.00**

☐ **COLOGNE AND CANDLELIGHT** (1975)
Clear glass, short, round bottle, gold cap and clear plastic collar, 2 oz. Original price $3.00 .. | **2.50** | **4.50**

☐ **COLOGNE ROYALE** (1972–74)
Clear glass in shape of a crown, god cap, 1 oz. | **2.50** | **4.50**

☐ **COMPOTE COLOGNE DECANTER** (1972–75)
White milk glass, gold cap, 5 oz. .... | **4.50** | **6.50**

Price Range

☐ **COUNTRY CHARM BUTTER CHURN DECANTER** (1973–74)
Clear glass, gold band around the body, gold cap, 1.5 oz. 4.50   6.50

☐ **COUNTRY KITCHEN DECANTER** (1973–75)
Rooster figurine, white milk glass, red plastic head, 6 oz. 4.50   6.50

☐ **COUNTRY STORE COFFEE MILL** (1972–76)
White milk glass, white plastic cap and handles, gold rim, 5 oz. 6.00   8.00

☐ **COURTING CARRIAGE** (1973–74)
Clear glass in the shape of a carriage, gold cap, 1 oz. 3.00   5.00

☐ **COURTING LAMP COLOGNE** (1970–71)
Blue glass base, white milk glass shade, blue velvet ribbon, 5 oz. Original price $6.00 . . . . 9.00   12.00

☐ **CRYSTALIER COLOGNE DECANTER** (1975)
Clear glass, large glass stopper, 2 oz. Original price $4.00 . . . . 4.00   6.00

☐ **CRYSTALLITE COLOGNE** (1970–71)
Clear glass, gold cap, tall, textured. Original price $5.50 . . . . 5.00   7.00

☐ **CRYSTAL SONG** (1975–76)
Red glass, frosted bow and handle, in shape of bell, 4 oz. Original price $6.00 . . . . 4.00   6.00

☐ **CRYSTAL TREE COLOGNE DECANTER** (1975)
Clear glass in shape of tree, gold plastic cap shaped like a star, 3 oz. Original price $6.00 . . 4.00   7.00

☐ **DEAR FRIEND COLOGNE DECANTER** (1974)
Seated girl holding cat, clear glass painted pink, light pink plastic top, 4 oz. 6.00   8.00

☐ **DEMI-CUP BATH OIL** (1969–70)
White milk glass, floral design in red, red cap, 3 oz. Original price $3.50 . . . . 6.00   8.00

☐ **DOLPHIN MINIATURE** (1973–74)
Clear glass, gold tail, 1.5 oz. Original price $3.00   3.00   5.00

☐ **DREAM GARDEN** (1972–73)
Pink frosted glass in design of a watering can, gold cap, ½ oz. Original price $5.00 . . . . 7.00   9.00

Price Range

☐ **DR. HOOT DECANTER** (1975)
Opal white glass, black cap shaped like a graduate's cap with a gold tassel, 4 oz. Original price
$5.00 . . . .   **5.00**   **7.00**

☐ **DUTCH GIRL FIGURINE COLOGNE** (1973–74)
Clear glass painted blue, white plastic top, 3 oz.   **6.00**   **8.00**

☐ **DUTCH TREAT DEMI-CUPS** (1971)
White glass, floral designs on front, yellow, blue,
or pink cap, 3 oz. Original price $3.50 . . . .   **6.00**   **8.00**

☐ **EIFFEL TOWER COLOGNE** (1970)
Clear glass, gold cap, 3 oz. **7.00**   **9.00**

☐ **EIGHTEENTH CENTURY CLASSIC FIGURINE
YOUNG BOY** (1974–75)
Clear glass painted white, white plastic head, 4
oz. Original price $5.00 . . . .   **5.00**   **7.00**

☐ **EIGHTEENTH CENTURY CLASSIC FIGURINE
YOUNG GIRL** (1974–75)
Clear glass painted white, white plastic head, 4
oz. Original price $5.00 . . . .   **5.00**   **8.00**

☐ **ELIZABETHAN FASHION FIGURINE** (1972)
Clear glass painted pin on lower portion, top portion pink plastic, 4 oz. **10.00**   **12.00**

☐ **ENCHANTED FROG CREAM SACHET**
(1973–76)
Colored milk glass, plastic lid, 1.25 oz. Original
price $3.00 . . . .   **4.00**   **6.00**

☐ **ENCHANTED HOURS** (1972–73)
Blue glass, gold cap, 5 oz. **8.00**   **10.00**

☐ **EVENING GLOW PERFUME DECANTER**
(1974–75)
White milk glass, in shape of old-fashioned lamp,
green floral design on front, white and gold cap,
3.3 oz. Original price $6.00 . . . .   **6.00**   **8.00**

☐ **FAIRYTALE FROG** (1976)
Clear glass, gold frog, 1 oz. Original price $3.00   **1.50**   **3.50**

☐ **FASHION FIGURINE COLOGNE** (1971–72)
Clear glass painted white on lower portion, top
portion white plastic, 4 oz. **8.00**   **11.00**

☐ **FLAMINGO DECANTER** (1971–72)
Clear glass shaped like a bird, gold cap, tall and
narrow shaped, 5 oz. **7.00**   **9.00**

Price Range

☐ **FLOWER MAIDEN COLOGNE DECANTER**
(1973–74)
Figurine of a girl, clear glass painted yellow for
the skirt, white plastic top, 4 oz. 6.00   8.00

☐ **FLY-A-BALLOON** (1975–76)
Clear glass painted blue, boy figurine holding balloon on a string, white top, red balloon, 3 oz. Original price $7.00 ....   7.00   9.00

☐ **FRAGRANCE BELL COLOGNE** (1965–66)
Clear glass, plastic handle, neck tag, 4 oz. Original price $3.50 ....   13.00 17.00

☐ **FRAGRANCE BELL COLOGNE** (1968–69)
Clear glass ribbed in shape of bell that actually
rings, gold handle, 1 oz. Original price $2.00 ..   3.50   5.50

☐ **FRAGRANCE HOURS COLOGNE** (1971–73)
White glass in shape of grandfather's clock, gold
cap, 6 oz. 6.00   8.00

☐ **FRAGRANCE SPLENDER** (1971–74)
Clear glass, gold cap, frosted plastic handle, 4½
oz. Original price $5.00 ....   5.00   7.00

☐ **FRAGRANCE TOUCH** (1969–70)
White milk glass, tall shaped bottle, 3 oz. Original
price $5.00 ....   6.00   8.00

☐ **FRENCH TELEPHONE** (1971)
White milk glass base, gold cap and trim, 6 oz.
Original price $22.00 ....   20.00 26.00

☐ **GARDEN GIRL COLOGNE** (1975)
Clear glass painted yellow, figurine of girl, yellow
plastic top, 4 oz. Original price $3.50 ....   4.00   7.00

☐ **GAY NINETIES COLOGNE** (1974)
Clear bottle painted orange in figurine of woman,
white top, orange hat, 3 oz. Original price $4.00   5.00   8.00

☐ **GOLDEN THIMBLE** (1972–74)
Clear glass on lower portion, gold cap, 2 oz. ..   4.00   6.00

☐ **GOOD LUCK ELEPHANT** (1975–76)
Frosted glass, gold cap, 1.5 oz. Original price
$3.00 ....   3.00   5.00

☐ **GRACEFUL GIRAFFE** (1976)
Clear glass, plastic top, 1.5 oz. Original price
$4.00 ....   4.00   6.00

Price Range

☐ **GRECIAN PITCHER** (1972–76)
Bust of woman with jar on her head, white glass,
white stopper, 5 oz. 5.00 7.00

☐ **HANDY FROG MOISTURIZED HAND LOTION**
(1975–76)
Large frog with red hat, white milk glass, 8 oz.
Original price $6.00 .... 5.50 7.50

☐ **HEARTH LAMP COLOGNE DECANTER**
(1973–74)
Black glass, gold handle, yellow and white shade,
daisies around neck, 8 oz. 8.00 11.00

☐ **HEAVENLY ANGEL COLOGNE** (1974–75)
Clear glass, white top, 2 oz. Original price $4.00 2.50 4.50

☐ **HIGH-BUTTONED SHOE** (1975–76)
Clear glass in shape of a shoe, gold cap, 2 oz.
Original price $3.00 .... 2.50 4.50

☐ **HOBNAIL BELL COLOGNE DECANTER**
(1973–74)
White milk glass, gold handle, gold bell clapper,
2 oz. 4.00 6.00

☐ **HOBNAIL BUD VASE** (1973–74)
White milk glass, red and yellow roses on front,
long neck, 4 oz. 6.00 8.00

☐ **HOBNAIL DECANTER FOAMING BATH OIL**
(1972–74)
White opal glass, 4 oz. 6.00 8.00

☐ **HURRICANE LAMP COLOGNE DECANTER**
(1973–74)
White glass lower portion, clear glass for top portion, gold cap, 6 oz. 9.00 13.00

☐ **KEY NOTE PERFUME** (1967)
Clear glass in shape of key with gold plastic cap,
¼ oz. Original price $5.50 and $6.50 .... 9.00 13.00

☐ **KOFFEE KLATCH** (1971–74)
Clear glass painted yellow in shape of coffee pot,
gold top, 5 oz. 5.00 7.00

☐ **LA BELLE TELEPHONE** (1974–76)
Telephone figurine, clear glass, gold top, 1 oz.
Original price $7.00 .... 7.00 9.00

☐ **LADY BUG PERFUME DECANTER** (1975–76)
Frosted glass, gold cap, ½ oz. Original price
$4.00 .... 3.00 5.00

Price Range

☐ **LADY SPANIEL** (1974–76)
Opal glass, plastic head, 1.5 oz. Original price
$3.00 .... 3.00   5.00

☐ **LEISURE HOURS** (1970–72)
White milk glass in shape of clock with face of
clock design on the front, gold cap, 5 oz. Original
price $4.00 .... 4.00   6.00

☐ **LEISURE HOURS MINIATURE** (1974)
White milk glass in shape of clock with face of
clock on front, gold cap, 1.5 oz. Original price
$3.00 .... 3.00   5.00

☐ **LIBRARY LAMP DECANTER** (1976)
Clear glass with base covered with gold foil, gold
cap, 4 oz. Original price $9.00 .... 5.00   7.00

☐ **LITTLE DUTCH KETTLE** (1972–73)
Shaped like coffee pot, clear glass painted orange, gold cap, 5 oz. 4.50   6.50

☐ **LITTLE GIRL BLUE** (1972–73)
Clear glass painted blue, blue plastic cap, 3 oz. 5.50   7.50

☐ **LITTLE KATE** (1973–74)
Clear glass painted orange, figurine of girl, orange
plastic hat over the cap, 3 oz. 6.00   8.00

☐ **LOOKING GLASS COLOGNE** (1970)
Yellow glass model of a hand-held mirror, 1½".
Original price $3.50 .... 7.00   10.00

☐ **LOVE BIRD PERFUME** (1969–70)
Frosted glass in design of a bird, head as gold
cap, ¼ oz. Original price $7.50 .... 8.00   10.00

☐ **LOVE SONG DECANTER** (1973–75)
Frosted glass, gold cap, 6 oz. Original price $6.00 5.50   7.50

☐ **MAGIC PUMPKIN COACH** (1976)
Clear glass, gold cap, 1 oz. Original price $5.00 2.50   4.50

☐ **MING BLUE LAMP** (1974–76)
Blue glass in shape of lamp, white plastic shade,
5 oz. Original price $6.00 .... 6.00   8.00

☐ **MING CAT COLOGNE** (1971)
Tall seated cat, white glass, blue trim, neck ribbon, 6 oz. 8.00   11.00

☐ **ONE DRAM PERFUME** (1974–76)
Clear glass with ribbing, gold cap. Original price
$4.25 .... 3.00   5.00

Price Range

☐ **PARISIAN GARDEN PERFUME** (1974–75)
White milk glass, in shape of pitcher with floral design on front, gold cap, 3.3 oz. Original price $5.00 .... 5.00   7.00

☐ **PARLOR LAMP** (1971–72)
Lower portion in white milk glass, top portion in light amber glass, gold cap 3 oz. Original price $7.00 .... 8.00   11.00

☐ **PARTRIDGE COLOGNE DECANTER** (1973–75)
White milk glass, white plastic lid, 5 oz. Original price $5.00 .... 5.00   7.00

☐ **PERFUME PETITE MOUSE** (1970)
Frosted glass, gold head and tail, ¼ oz. Original price $7.50 .... 15.00   17.00

☐ **PERT PENGUIN** (1975–76)
Clear glass, gold cap, 1 oz. Original price $2.00   1.50   3.50

☐ **PETITE PIGLET** (1972)
Clear glass, embossed, gold cap, in design of pig. Original price $5.00 .... 8.00   10.00

☐ **PINEAPPLE PETITE COLOGNE** (1972–74)
Clear glass in the shape of a pineapple, large gold cap, 1 oz. 2.50   4.50

☐ **PRECIOUS SLIPPER** (1973–74)
Frosted glass, gold cap as bow on shoe, .25 oz. Original price $4.00 .... 5.00   7.00

☐ **PRECIOUS SWAN PERFUME DECANTER** (1974–76)
Frosted glass, gold cap, ⅛ oz. Original price $4.00 .... 2.50   4.50

☐ **PRETTY GIRL PINK** (1974–75)
Clear glass painted pink on lower portion, top portion light pink, 6 oz. Original price $4.00 ...... 4.00   6.00

☐ **QUEEN OF SCOTS** (1973–75)
White milk glass, figurine of dog, white plastic head, 1 oz. 2.50   4.50

☐ **REGENCY CANDLESTICK COLOGNE** (1973–74)
Clear glass, faceted, tall bottle, 4 oz. 6.50   8.50

☐ **REMEMBER WHEN SCHOOL DESK DECANTER** (1972–74)
Black glass, light brown plastic seat and desk top, red apple for cap, 4 oz. 7.50   9.50

Price Range

☐ **ROARING TWENTIES FASHION FIGURINE**
(1972–74)
Clear glass painted purple, plastic purple top, 3
oz. 6.00   8.00

☐ **ROBIN RED-BREAST COLOGNE DECANTER**
(1974–75)
Red frosted glass, silver plastic cap, 2 oz. Original
price $4.00 . . . .   4.00   6.00

☐ **ROYAL COACH** (1972–73)
White milk glass, in shape of coach with gold cap
on top, 5 oz. Original price $5.00 . . . .   5.00   7.00

☐ **ROYAL PEKINGNESE** (1974–75)
White milk glass, white plastic head, 1.5 oz. Origi-
nal price $3.00 . . . .   3.00   5.00

☐ **ROYAL SWAN COLOGNE** (1971–72)
White glass, gold crown cap on swan's head, 1
oz. 4.00   6.00

☐ **ROYAL SWAN COLOGNE** (1974)
Blue glass, gold crown on swan's head, 1 oz.   3.00   5.00

☐ **SALT SHAKERS** (1968–70)
White glass with floral designs either in pink or
yellow, pink or yellow ribbon, 3 oz. Original price
$2.50 . . . .   5.00   7.00

☐ **SCENT WITH LOVE** (1971–72)
Frosted glass, cap is gold pen, gold and white
label around bottle, ¼ oz. Original price $6.00   9.00   13.00

☐ **SCENT WITH LOVE** (1975–76)
Glass base painted gold with plastic amber top,
.66 oz. Original price $4.00 . . . .   4.00   6.00

MEN'S FIGURALS

☐ **ALASKAN MOOSE** (1974)
Glass figure with white antlers, 8 oz. Original price
$8.00 . . . .   7.00   10.00

☐ **AMERICAN BUFFALO** (1975)
Amber glass model of a buffalo, white horns, 5
oz. Original price $7.50 . . . .   5.00   8.00

Price Range

☐ **AMERICAN EAGLE**
Glass model of the bald eagle, made in amber
and black glass, 5 oz. Original price $5.00
amber (1971) 6.00 9.00
black (1973) 4.00 7.00

☐ **APOTHECARY DECANTER** (1972–73)
Glass, in yellow, gold, or green, plastic stopper,
8 oz. Original price $4.00 .... 3.00 5.00

☐ **AVON CALLING 1905** (1973)
Brown glass antique telephone with receiver and
mouthpiece, 7 oz. Original price $10.00 .... 9.00 14.00

☐ **THE AVON OPEN** (1972)
Green glass model of a golf cart, golf clubs are
in the back, 5 oz. Original price $6.00 .... 8.00 11.00

☐ **BIG MACK** (1973)
Green glass model of a truck, 6 oz. Original price
$6.00 .... 7.00 10.00

☐ **BLACKSMITH'S ANVIL** (1972)
Brown anvil with silver hammer on top, 4 oz. Original price $5.00 .... 5.00 8.00

☐ **BOOT** (1965)
Glass, in violet or amber, silver stopper, 8 oz.
Original price $5.00 .... 10.00 15.00

☐ **BREAKER 19** (1977)
Brown plastic bottle in the shape of a CB radio
microphone, 2 oz. Original price $5.00 .... 2.00 4.00

☐ **CANNONBALL EXPRESS 4-6-0** (1976)
Glass model of a locomotive, 3¼ oz. Original
price $8.00 .... 7.00 10.00

☐ **DEFENDER** (1966)
Brown glass with plastic base, in the shape of a
cannon, 6 oz. Original price, $5.00 .... 19.00 24.00

☐ **DINGO BOOT** (1979)
Western boot, brown, 6 oz. Original price $5.50 5.00 7.00

☐ **EIGHT BALL** (1973)
Black billiard ball, 3 oz. Original price $4.00 ... 3.00 5.00

☐ **FIELDER'S CHOICE** (1971)
Glass model of a baseball glove with a ball, 5 oz.
Original price $4.00 .... 5.00 7.00

☐ **FIRM GRIP** (1977)
Model of a wrench, 1½ oz. Original price $5.00 2.50 4.50

Price Range

☐ **FUTURA** (1969)
Running figure of a man, head is the stopper, no
arms, 5 oz. Original price $7.00 . . . .   **25.00   30.00**

☐ **HOMESTEAD** (1974)
Brown glass in the shape of a log cabin, chimney,
4 oz. Original price $4.00 . . . .   **4.00   6.00**

☐ **HUGGABLE HIPPO** (1980)
White glass hippo figurine with red top hat as
stopper, comes with a sheet of decals, 1¾ oz.
Original price $6.00 . . . .   **3.00   5.00**

☐ **INDIAN CHIEFTAIN** (1972)
Brown glass, the head of an Indian Chief, silver
stopper, 4 oz. Original price $3.50 . . . .   **3.00   5.50**

☐ **INDIAN TEPEE** (1974)
Brown glass Indian tepee, the very top of the bot-
tle is a silver stopper, 4 oz. Original price $4.00   **4.00   6.50**

☐ **IT ALL ADDS UP** (1978)
Brown plastic calculator, 4 oz. Original price
$8.50 . . . .   **5.00   8.00**

☐ **JAGUAR** (1973)
Glass model of a classic Jaguar automobile, 5 oz.
Original price $6.00 . . . .   **7.00   10.00**

☐ **JUKE BOX** (1977)
Body of juke brown and white with some blue-
yellow, and red markings, 4½ oz. Original price
$6.50 . . . .   **5.00   7.00**

☐ **LITTLE BROWN JUG** (1978)
Brown glass with cork and "XXX" marking, 2 oz.
Original price, $4.50 . . . .   **3.00   4.50**

☐ **LOCKER TIME** (1977)
Green gym locker, stopper is yellow towels on
top, 6 oz. Original price $5.50 . . . .   **4.00   6.00**

☐ **MINI-BIKE** (1972)
Yellow glass model, 4 oz. Original price $6.00   **5.00   8.00**

☐ **MODEL "A"** (1972)
Yellow model of the automobile, 4 oz. Original
price $6.00 . . . .   **7.00   9.00**

☐ **ONE GOOD TURN** (1976)
Yellow glass model of a screwdriver, 3 oz. Origi-
nal price $6.00 . . . .   **3.50   5.50**

Price Range

☐ **ON THE MARK** (1978)
Amber glass model of a hammer, 2½ oz. Original
price, $7.50 .... 4.00　7.00

☐ **PASS-PLAY DECANTER** (1973)
Figure of a football player about to throw the ball,
bottom of body is blue glass, top of body is white
plastic, 5 oz. Original price $5.75 .... 7.00　9.00

☐ **PIPE FULL** (1971–72)
Amber or green glass model of a pipe, 2 oz. Original price $3.50
amber .... 5.00　8.00
green .... 4.00　7.00

☐ **ROLLIN' GREAT** (1980)
Golden roller skate with red ball on top as the
stopper, 2 oz. Original price $6.00 .... 3.00　5.00

☐ **SCIMITAR** (1968)
Brown glass with gold-colored plastic ornamenta-
tion, in the figure of a sword, 6 oz. Original price
$6.00 .... 18.00　22.00

☐ **SEA TROPHY** (1972)
Green glass figure of a swordfish, 5½ oz. Original
price $6.00 .... 6.00　9.00

☐ **STAMP DECANTER** (1970)
Amber glass model of a stamper marked "PAID,"
the stopper is the knob of the handle, 4 oz. Original price $4.00 .... 5.00　8.00

☐ **STAR SIGNS DECANTERS** (1975)
Circular bottles with a sign of the horoscope embossed on it, made in both black glass and black-
painted glass, 4 oz. Original price $7.00
black glass .... 5.00　7.00
painted glass .... 8.00　11.00

☐ **STEIN** (1979)
Car Classics, stoneware, engraved designs of automobiles, the stein itself is lidded, 16 oz. Original
price $37.50 .... 32.00　37.00

☐ **STEIN** (1976)
Stoneware, contains an 8 oz. plastic bottle of cologne, the stein itself is lidded, 16 oz. Original
price $30.00 .... 35.00　40.00

	Price Range	

☐ **TEE-OFF DECANTER** (1973)
Model of a golf ball on the tee, 3 oz. Original price
$4.00 .... **4.00** **6.00**

☐ **TENNIS ANYONE** (1975)
Tennis racket, gray with black handle, 5 oz. Original price $5.00 .... **2.00** **4.00**

☐ **VANTASTIC** (1979)
Model of a custom van, 5 oz. Original price $9.50 **6.00** **9.00**

☐ **VIKING HORN** (1966)
Brown glass, gold-colored plastic cap shaped like
crown, 7 oz. Original price $7.00 .... **20.00** **25.00**

☐ **VINTAGE YEAR** (1978)
Modeled after a bottle of wine, green glass, 2 oz.
Original price $6.00 .... **4.50** **6.50**

☐ **WESTERN CHOICE** (1967)
Yellow glass, two horns on a brown base, each
horn has its own stopper, 6 oz. Original price
$6.00 .... **20.00** **25.00**

☐ **WILDERNESS CLASSIC** (1976)
Running deer with antlers, 6 oz. Original price
$10.00 .... **7.00** **10.00**

BALLANTINE

Ballantine figural bottles are made to contain Ballantine imported Scotch whiskey. These ceramic bottles are brightly colored, generally reading "Blended Scotch Whiskey, 14 Years Old." When the bottle represents an animal or human figure, the head is the cap. Most of the Ballantine figurals are on sporting themes, such as Fisherman, Duck, and Golf Bag. Also collectible are the older Ballantine bottles which are non-figurals but are often very decorative, such as a 3-inch pottery jug in which the company's product was marketed around 1930.

	Price Range	

☐ **BALLANTINE**
Duck **10.00** **15.00**

☐ **BALLANTINE**
Fisherman **14.00** **20.00**

☐ **BALLANTINE**
Golf Bag **10.00** **15.00**

Price Range

☐ **BALLANTINE**
Mallard Duck 5.00   8.00
☐ **BALLANTINE**
Old Crow Chessman 10.00   15.00
☐ **BALLANTINE**
Scottish Knight 10.00   15.00
☐ **BALLANTINE**
Seated Fisherman 15.00   22.00
☐ **BALLANTINE**
Silver Knight 17.00   24.00
☐ **BALLANTINE**
Zebra 17.00   24.00

BARSOTTINI

The Barsottini bottle manufacturers from Italy, unlike other foreign companies, do not use American or non-geographic themes for the avid U.S. market. Barsottini bottles mostly represent European subjects, such as architectural bottles of the Arc de Triomphe, the Eiffel Tower, and the Florentine Steeple. Subjects from European history included an antique Florentine cannon from the early days of gunpowder. Most Barsottini bottles are large ceramics, often in gray and white to represent the brickwork of buildings. Prices vary depending on quantities imported to this country and the extent of their distribution.

Price Range

☐ **ALPINE PIPE**
Ceramic, 10″ 7.00   11.00
☐ **ANTIQUE AUTOMOBILE**
Ceramic, Coupe 5.00   8.00
☐ **ANTIQUE AUTOMOBILE**
Open Car 5.00   8.00
☐ **CLOWNS**
Ceramic, 12″ each 8.00   11.00
☐ **EIFFEL TOWER**
Gray & White, 15″ 7.00   11.00
☐ **FLORENTINE CANNON**
Length, 15″ 13.00   19.00
☐ **FLORENTINE STEEPLE**
Gray & White 8.00   11.00
☐ **MONASTERY CASK**
Ceramic, 12″ 13.00   19.00

*Right: **Ballantine Knight,**
(1969) $10.00–$15.00; Bottom:
Ballantine Zebra, (1970).
$17.00–$24.00*

Price Range

☐ **PARIS ARC DE TRIOMPHE**
7½" 9.00 12.00
☐ **PISA'S LEANING TOWER**
Gray & White 9.00 12.00
☐ **ROMAN COLISEUM**
Ceramic 7.00 11.00
☐ **TIVOLI CLOCK**
Ceramic, 15" 13.00 19.00
☐ **CLOCK**
With cherub 31.00 39.00

JIM BEAM

In their variety of styles, shapes, subjects, colors, and approaches to modeling, Jim Beam bottles are unrivaled. They provide a feast for the collector. With such a wide selection, the hobbyist can choose to collect them topically, such as Beam operas, trophies, or figurals.

Jim Beam figurals were first issued in the 1950s, prior to the initial collecting interest in Avons. The history of the James B. Beam Distilling Company dates to the late 1700s following the Revolutionary War. Founded in Kentucky in 1778 by Jacob Beam, the company now bears the name of Colonel James B. Beam, Jacob's grandson. Beam whiskey was popular throughout most of the south during the 19th and 20th centuries, though it was not manufactured on a large scale. Since it was difficult to obtain in the North during the 19th century, Northerners often boasted of possessing "genuine Kentucky whiskey" when they were able to purchase it.

The early Beam bottles, though they bear little resemblance to the company's modern figurals, are collectible, of course. Some are worth more because of their scarcity.

In 1953, the Beam Distilling Co. produced and sold bourbon in a special ceramic decanter for the Christmas and New Year holiday season. At that time, special packaging by any spirits distiller was rare. When the decanters sold widely, Beam realized that creative bottling could indeed increase sales. His development of decorative packaging on a large scale led to a variety of series in the 1950s.

They appeared in the following order:

Ceramics 1953   Customer specialities ... 1956
Executive 1955   Trophy 1957
Regal china 1955   State 1958
Political figures 1956

The Executive Series, which consists of 22K gold decorated bottles, was issued to mark the corporation's 160th anniversary which distinguished the Beam Distilling Co. as one of the oldest American business enterprises.

In the same year, Beam started its Regal china series, one of the most popular series of Beam bottles. The Regal china bottles, issued annually at intervals, honor significant people, places, or events, concentrating on subjects based on Americana and the contemporary scene. The sport figurals, a frequent subject for Beam Regal chinas, are handsome, striking, and very decorative. The first Regal china bottle, the *Ivory Ash Tray,* still sells in a modest price range.

The following year in 1956 the Beam Political Figures series started off with the traditional elephant and donkey, representing the Republican and Democratic parties, and has been issued with variations every four years for the presidential election.

Customer Specialties, bottles made on commission for customers who are usually liquor dealers or distributors, had its inception with a bottle created for Foremost Liquor Stores of Chicago.

In 1958 and 1959, the State series commemorated the admittance of Alaska and Hawaii into the Union during the 1950s. The Beam Distilling Co. continues to issue bottles in honor of other states with the intention of making bottles for each of the 50 states.

Over 500 types of Beam bottles have been issued since 1953. Beam's ceramic bottles, produced by the Wheaton Glass Co. of Millville, New Jersey, are considerably more popular than the glass bottles, probably because of their pleasing coloration.

	Price Range	
□ **AC SPARK PLUG** (1977)		
Replica of a spark plug in white, green, and gold	**13.00**	**17.00**
□ **AIDA** (1978)		
Figurine of character from the opera of the same name. Woman is dressed in blue and yellow with black cone-shaped hat. The first in the Opera Series, this bottle comes with a music box which plays a selection from the "Egyptian March." Bottle and base make up 2-piece set	**150.00**	**200.00**
□ **AHEPA 50TH ANNIVERSARY** (1972)		

This striking Regal China bottle was designed in honor of AHEPA'S (American Hellenic Education Progressive Association) 50th anniversary. The Order's anniversary logo is reproduced on the front. Current officers listed on the back. The

Price Range

"Greek Key" design appears on both the bottle and the stopper which is a hollow vase. The bottle's neck is a traditional Greek column. 12" ...   5.00   8.00

☐ **AKRON RUBBER CAPITAL** (1973)
A unique Regal China creation honoring Akron, Ohio, the Rubber Producing Capital of the World. This creation is in the shape of an automobile tire, and features a Mag Wheel. In the center of the wheel is the inscription Rubber Capital Jim Beam Bottle Club 17.00   22.00

☐ **ALASKA** (1958)
Star-shaped bottle in turqoise blue and gold. Symbols of Alaskan industry in corners of star, gold "49" in center. Regal China, 9½" 60.00   70.00

☐ **ALASKA** (1964–65)
Re-issued as above 55.00   62.00

☐ **ALASKA PURCHASE** (1966)
Blue and gold bottle with star-shaped stopper. Mt. McKinley pictured with State flag on top. Regal China, 10" 9.00   13.00

☐ **AMERICAN SAMOA** (1973)
The enchantment of one of America's outside territorial possessions is captured in this genuine Regal China bottle. The Seal of Samoa signifies friendship, the whip and staff signify authority and power held by the great chiefs. 5.00   9.00

☐ **ANTIOCH** (1967)
The Regal China Company is located in Antioch, Illinois. This decanter commemorates the Diamond Jubilee of Regal. Large Indian head ("Sequoit") on one side. Blue and Gold diamond on reverse. Regal China, 10" 6.00   7.50
With arrow package 6.00   8.00

☐ **ANTIQUE COFFEE GRINDER** (1979)
Replica of a box coffee mill used in the mid 19th century. Brown with black top and crank which moves, gold lettering 12.00   15.00

☐ **ANTIQUE GLOBE** (1980)
Represents the Martin Behaim globe of 1492. The globe is blue and rotates on the wooden cradle stand 12.00   18.00

Price Range

☐ **ANTIQUE TELEPHONE 1897** (1978)
Gold base with black speaker and ear phone.
Replica of an 1897 desk phone. The second in
the series of antique telephones 62.00   72.00

☐ **ANTIQUE TRADER** (1968)
The widely read ANTIQUE TRADER weekly
newspaper forms this bottle with the front page
clearly shown in black and red, along side the
"1968 NATIONAL DIRECTORY OF ANTIQUE
DEALERS" both are on a black base. Regal
China, 10½" 4.00   7.00

☐ **APPALOOSA** (1974)
The appaloosa was the favorite horse of the old
west and is shown on this bottle trotting along
above an embossed horseshoe marked "AP-
PALOOSA." His body is brown and white while
his tail and mane are black. The stopper is formed
by his head. Regal China, 10" 14.50   19.50

☐ **ARIZONA** (1968)
Embossed scene of canyon, river, and cactus in
blue, yellow and brown, "THE GRAND CANYON
STATE" "ARIZONA" in gold. Map embossed on
stopper. Reverse has scenes of Arizona life.
Regal China, 12" 4.00   7.00

☐ **ARMANETTI AWARD WINNER** (1969)
A pale blue bottle in the shape of the number "1,"
to honor Armanetti Inc. of Chicago as "LIQUOR
RETAILER OF THE YEAR" in 1969. In shield,
gold and blue lettering proclaims "ARMANETTI
LIQUORS 1969 AWARD WINNER". Heavily em-
bossed gold scrolls decorate the bottle 6.50   9.00

☐ **ARMANETTI SHOPPER** (1971)
The front of the bottle has a man pushing a shopping cart and the slogan "It's Fun to Shop Armanetti—Self Service Liquor Store." On the back of
the bottle, there is an embossed view of the store
with other Illinois locations of Armanetti stores.
11¾" 6.00   9.00

☐ **ARMANETTI VASE** (1968)
Yellow toned decanter embossed with many
flowers and a large letter "A" for Armanetti . . .   5.50   8.50

Price Range

☐ **BACCHUS** (1970)
This bottle was issued by the Armanetti Liquor
Stores of Chicago, Illinois. The body of the bottle
is made of a circular medallion showing Bacchus.
The medallion is topped by grapes. The stopper
is circular and bears the symbol of Armanetti Liquors. Regal China, 11¾" 7.00 10.00

☐ **BARNEY'S SLOT MACHINE** (1978)
Replica of the world's largest slot machine which
is located in Barney's Casino on the South Shore
at Lake Tahoe, Nevada. Red with small black
stopper at the top 22.00 28.00

☐ **BARTENDER'S GUILD** (1973)
A commemorative Regal China bottle honoring
the International Bartenders' Association on the
first International Cocktail Competition in the
United States 7.00 10.00

☐ **BASEBALL** (1969)
To commemorate the 100th Anniversary of the
professional sport, this baseball shaped bottle
was issued. "PROFESSIONAL BASEBALL'S
100th ANNIVERSARY—1869–1969" in gold and
black on the front. Decal of player in action on
top. Reverse has history of growth of baseball   10.00 14.00

☐ **BEAM POT** (1980)
Shaped like a New England bean pot, a colonial
scene is depicted on the front. On the back, there
is a large map of the New England states. The
stopper is a large gold dome. This is the club bottle for the New England Beam Bottle and Specialties Club 12.00 17.00

☐ **BEAVER VALLEY CLUB** (1977)
Figurine of a beaver sitting on a stump wearing
blue pants, a white shirt, a red jacket, black bow
and hat. The beaver is saluting. A club bottle to
honor the Beaver Valley Jim Beam Club of Rochester 10.00 15.00

☐ **BELL SCOTCH** (1970)
Tan center, gold base, brown top with coat-of-
arms of Arthur Bell & Sons on front. Bottle is in
the shape of a large handbell. Regal China, 10½"   5.00 10.00

Price Range

☐ **THE BIG APPLE** (1979)
Apple shaped bottle with embossed Statue of Liberty on the front with New York City in the background and the lettering "The Big Apple" over the top **10.00   15.00**

☐ **BING'S 31ST CLAM BAKE BOTTLE** (1972)
An inspired Regal China bottle heavily decorated in gold. The front features a three dimensional reproduction of the famous Pebble Beach, California wind-swept tree overlooking the Pacific Ocean. The back commemorates the 31st Bing Crosby National Pro-Amateur Golf Tournament at the World Famous Pebble Beach course, January, 1972. The stopper is the official seal of the Tourney. 10¾" **30.00   35.00**

☐ **BING CROSBY NATIONAL PRO-AM** (1973)
The fourth in its series honoring the Bing Crosby Gold Tournament, genuine Regal China bottle in luxurious fired 22 karat gold with a white stopper, featuring replicas of the famous Crosby hat, pipe and gold club **30.00   35.00**

☐ **BING CROSBY 36TH** (1976)
Same as the Floro de Oro except for the medallion below the neck. Urn-shaped bottle with pastel wide band and flowers around the middle. Remainder of bottle is shiny gold with fluting and designs **17.00   25.00**

☐ **BLACK KATZ** (1968)
Same Kitty, different color: black cat, green eyes, red tongue, white base. Both Katz are Regal China, 14½" **8.00   14.00**

☐ **BLUE CHERUB EXECUTIVE** (1960)
Blue and white decanter with heavily embossed figures of cherubs with bow & arrow gold details. Scrolls and chain holding Beam Label around neck. Regal China, 12½" **140.00 160.00**

☐ **BLUE DAISY** (1967)
Also known as "Zimmerman Blue Daisy." Light blue with embossed daisies and leaves around bottle. Background resembles flower basket . . .   **11.00   15.00**

Price Range

☐ **BLUE JAY** (1969)
Tones of sky blue on the birds body with black
& white markings. Black claws grip "oak tree
stump" with acorns and leaves embossed 8.00   12.00

☐ **BLUE GOOSE** (1979)
Replica of a blue goose with its characteristic
greyish-blue coloring. Authenticated by Dr. Lester
Fisher, director of Lincoln Park Zoological Gardens in Chicago 4.00   8.00

☐ **BLUE SLOT MACHINE** (1967) 12.00   15.00

☐ **BOBBY UNSER OLSONITE EAGLE** (1975)
Replica of the racing car used by Bobby Unser.
White with black accessories and colored decals   45.00   55.00

☐ **BOB HOPE DESERT CLASSIC** (1973)
The first genuine Regal China bottle created in
honor of the Bob Hope Desert Classic, an annual
charity fund raising golf tournament. A profile of
Bob Hope is shown on the front side, with a golf
ball and tee perched at the tip of his nose 12.00   18.00

☐ **BOB HOPE DESERT CLASSIC** (1974)
This Regal China creation honors the famous
Bob Hope Desert Classic. Bob Hope silhouette
and the sport of golf is a color feature of the bottle   8.00   12.00

☐ **BOHEMIAN GIRL** (1974)
This bottle was issued for the Bohemian Cafe in
Omaha, Nebraska to honor the Czech and Slovak
immigrants in the United States. She is wearing
a white skirt decorated with flowers; also a white
skirt and blue vest. Her white cap is the stopper.
Regal China, 14¼" 15.00   20.00

☐ **BONDED MYSTIC** (1979)
Urn shaped bottle with fluting on sides and lid.
Small scroll handles, open work handle on lid.
Burgundy colored 10.00   16.00

☐ **BOOT HILL**
See Dodge City

☐ **BOYS TOWN OF ITALY** (1973)
A handsome genuine Regal China bottle created
in honor of the Boys Town of Italy. This home for
Italian orphans began after World War II. The bottle features a map of Italy, showing the various
provinces of that country 8.00   12.00

Price Range

☐ **BROADMOOR HOTEL** (1968)
To celebrate the 50th Anniversary of this famous hotel in Colorado Springs, Colorado, Beam issued this bottle replica complete with details of windows, doors, roof tiles and tower capped with a "roof" stopper. The base bears the legend "1918—THE BROADMOOR—1968" in white ovals on a black background 5.00 9.00

☐ **BUFFALO BILL** (1971)
The front of this bottle shows a bust of Buffalo Bill with his name above. The back illustrates his adventures as an Indian fighter and Pony Express rider. The stopper is a small figure of a buffalo. The bottle is beige and gold. Regal China, 10½" 5.00 8.00

☐ **BULL DOG** (1979)
Bull dog with yellow infantry helmet with "Devil Dogs" embossed on front. Real leather collar with metal studding around his neck. The mascot of the United States Marine Corps, this bottle honors their 204th anniversary. 18.00 22.00

☐ **CABLE CAR** (1968)
A gray-green bottle in the form of a San Francisco cable car, complete with doors, windows and wheels. A gold label with "Van Ness Ave., CALIFORNIA & MARKET STREETS" in black on one end, "POWELL & MASON STREETS" on the side. The stopper is the front light. Regal China, 4½" high, 7" long 4.00 6.00

☐ **CABOOSE** (1980)
Red caboose with black trim. Sign on side reads "New Jersey Central." Has movable wheels and gold lanterns on each side 42.00 50.00

☐ **CALIFORNIA MISSION** (1970)
This bottle was issued for the Jim Beam Bottle Club of Southern California in honor of the 200th anniversary of the California Missions. A priest is shown leaning with one hand on his staff and the other around an Indian boy. Above them is a doorway and the steeple of the mission. The stopper is the very top of the mission. Regal China, 14" 15.00 20.00

☐ **CALIFORNIA RETAIL LIQUOR DEALERS ASSOCIATION** (1973)
Made of genuine Regal China, this bottle was designed to commemorate the 20th Anniversary of the California Retail Liquor Dealers Association. The bottle depicts the emblem of the association showing a liquor store superimposed on the State of California 8.00 12.00

☐ **CAL-NEVA** (1969)
This is a standard square bottle, green toned with "RENO 100 YEARS" deeply embossed and "CAL-NEVA, CASINO—HOTEL, RENO—LAKE TAHOE" in the oval shaped emblem, Regal China, 9½" 6.00 9.00

☐ **CAMELLIA CITY CLUB** (1979)
Replica of the cupola of the State Capitol building in Sacramento surrounded with camellias since the capitol is known as "The Camellia Capitol of the World." 25.00 30.00

☐ **CAMEO BLUE** (1965)
Also known as the Shepherd Bottle, Scenes of shepherd and dog in white, on the sky blue, square-shaped bottle. White glass stopper, 12¾" 4.00 8.00

☐ **CANNON** (1970)
This bottle was issued to commemorate the 175th anniversary of the Jim Beam Co. The bottle is octogonal with the muzzle of the cannon at a 45 degree angle with the base. The stopper is the end of the muzzle. Some of these bottles have a small chain shown on the cannon and some do not. Those without the chain are harder to find and more valuable. 8"
Chain 2.00 4.00
No chain 10.50 14.50

☐ **CANTEEN** (1979)
Replica of the exact canteen used by the armed forces with simulated canvas covering which has snap flaps and chained cap 12.00 16.00

☐ **CAPTAIN AND MATE** (1980)
A sea faring captain with blue jacket, white cap, and yellow duffel bag over his shoulder. The cap-

Price Range

tain has his other arm around the shoulder of a small boy dressed in a red jacket and blue pants. He holds a toy boat **15.00 20.00**

☐ **CARDINAL—(KENTUCKY CARDINAL)** (1968)
A bright red bird with a black mask, tail, and markings, perched on a dark tree stump shaped base **45.00 55.00**

☐ **CARMEN** (1978)
Figurine of Carmen from the character in the opera of the same name, the third issue in the Opera Series, it is a woman dressed in Spanish clothes of white, blue, gold and red. She wears a small black coned-shaped hat. Music box plays "Habanera" which is from the opera, part of three-piece set, which includes base and paperweight **240.00 300.00**

☐ **CATHEDRAL RADIO** (1979)
Replica of one of the earlier dome-shaped radios. Brown with gold trim and a large domed-shaped lid **13.00 17.00**

☐ **CATS** (1967)
Trio of cats, Siamese, Burmese, and Tabby. Colors: gray with blue eyes, dark brown and white with yellow eyes, and white with tan and blue eyes. Regal China, 11½" high, ea. **10.00 15.00**

☐ **CEDARS OF LEBANON** (1971)
This bottle shows a green tree rising above a background of a gray and gold colored building. This bottle was issued in honor of the "Jerry Lewis Muscular Dystrophy" telethon held in 1971. Near the base of the bottle, the words "TALL CEDARS OF LEBANON" appear. The stopper is the upper half of the tree. Regal China, 9¾" **5.00 7.00**

☐ **CHARLIE MCCARTHY** (1976)
Replica of Edgar Bergen's puppet from the 1930s. A black ribbon is attached to his monocle **28.00 34.00**

☐ **CHERRY HILLS COUNTRY CLUB** (1973)
A very handsome genuine Regal China bottle, commemorating the 50th Anniversary of the famous Cherry Hills Country Club. Located in Denver, Colorado, Cherry Hills has hosted some of the top professional golf tournaments. The front

Price Range

of the bottle illustrates the many activities available at Cherry Hills, while the name of the club circles the bottom in luxurious 22 karat gold . . .   4.00   8.00

□ **CHEYENNE, WYOMING** (1977)
Circular decanter in shape of a wheel. Spokes separate scenes of Cheyenne history. Regal China 4.00   8.00

□ **CHICAGO SHOW BOTTLE** (1977)
Stopper is a gold loving cup standing on a black pedestal. Commemorates the 6th Annual Chicago Jim Beam Bottle Show 24.00   32.00

□ **CHURCHILL DOWN—PINK ROSES** (1969)
Same as below, pink embossed roses 6.00   8.00

□ **CHURCHILL DOWNS—RED ROSES** (1969)
"CHURCHILL DOWNS—HOME OF THE 95th KENTUCKY DERBY" is embossed in gold on the front, around the main paddock building. The shell-shaped bottle comes with red roses framing the scene. Reverse: "ARISTEDES," 1st Derby winner in 1875, on a decal. Regal China, 10¾"   10.00   14.00

□ **CIRCUS WAGON** (1979)
Replica of a circus wagon from the late 19th century. Blue with gold embossing, white wheels with red trim which are movable 26.00   36.00

□ **CIVIL WAR NORTH** (1961)
Blue and gray bottle depicting Civil War battle scenes. Stopper has Lee's face on one side, Grant's on the other. Regal China, 10¾" (when sold as a pair) 48.00   58.00

□ **CIVIL WAR SOUTH** (1961)
One side portrays the meeting of Lee and Jackson at Chancellorville. On the other side a meeting of southern Generals. Regal China, 10¾" (when sold as a pair) 48.00   58.00

□ **CLEAR CRYSTAL SCOTCH** (1966)
The original patterned embossed bottle. Glass stopper ("DOORKNOB"). Bottom is unpatterned and has number and date of issue, 11½" 10.00   15.00

□ **CLEAR CRYSTAL BOURBON** (1967)
Patterned embossed with "swirl" stopper. Starburst design on base of the bottle. Clear Glass, 11½" 6.00   10.00

Price Range

☐ **CLEAR CRYSTAL VODKA** (1967)
Same as above 6.00 10.00

☐ **CLEOPATRA RUST** (1962)
Same as Cleopatra Yellow. Scene with Mark Anthony and Cleopatra in white on rust-red background 3.00 7.00

☐ **CLEOPATRA YELLOW** (1962)
Black and purple, two handled, amphora-
decanter. Yellow figures of Mark Anthony in
armor, and Cleopatra beside the Nile, Pyramid
and Sphinx background. Egyptian border design
circles bottles, white stopper. Rarer than Cleopatra Rust. Glass, 13¼ " 9.00 14.00

☐ **CLINT EASTWOOD** (1973)
A handsome genuine Regal China bottle, commemorating the Clint Eastwood Invitational Ce-
lebrity Tennis Tournament held in Pebble Beach.
The bottle features two tennis rackets across the
front while the stopper features an exact likeness
of Clint Eastwood. Two ribbons adorn the front
of the bottle, one with stars on a field of blue, the
other in red with the name of the tournament em-
blazoned in 22 karat gold 5.00 10.00

☐ **COCKTAIL SHAKER** (1953)
Glass, Fancy Diz. Bottle, 9¼ " 3.00 6.00

☐ **COFFEE WARMERS** (1954)
Four types are known in red, black, gold and
white necks, plastic cord over cork. The Corning
Glass Company made the Pyrex bottles. Round
stoppers are made of wood. Pyrex Glass, 9" .. 8.00 14.00

☐ **COFFEE WARMERS** (1956)
Two types with metal necks and handles, black
and gold stripes on one, gold neck with black
handle on the other. White Star design on sides
of Pyrex glass on both. Round black plastic tops.
Some have holder type candle warmers. Pyrex
Glass, 10" 3.00 6.00

☐ **COHO SALMON** (1976)
Gray with black speckles. Official seal of the National Fresh Water Fishing Hall of Fame is on the
back 12.00 16.00

Price Range

☐ **COLLECTOR'S EDITION** (1966)
Set of six, glass, famous painting, The Blue Boy,
on the Terrace, Mardi Gras, Austide Bruant, The
Artist Before His Easel, Laughing Cavalier each   3.00   7.00

☐ **COLLECTORS EDITION VOLUME II** (1967)
A set of six flask type bottles painted gold with
pictures from the Renaissance period, i.e.
George Gisze, Soldier and Girl, Night Watch, The
Jester, Nurse and Child and Man on Horse each   2.50   6.50

☐ **COLLECTORS EDITION VOLUME III** (1968)
A set of eight bottles covered with a blue velvet
finish and picturing a famous American painting
on each; i.e. On the Trail, Indian Maiden, Buffalo,
Whistlers Mother, American Gothic, The Ken-
tuckian, The Scout and Hauling in the Gill Net
each 2.50   5.50

☐ **COLLECTORS EDITION VOLUME IV** (1969)
A set of eight bottles with a brown leather-like finish and setting on an angle. Each has a picture
of a painting by a famous French artist. They are
Balcony, The Judge, Fruit Basket, Boy with Cherries, Emile Zola, The Guitarist Zouave and Sun-
flowers each 2.50   5.50

☐ **COLLECTORS EDITION VOLUME V** (1970)
A set of six bottles finished in a gold flecked red
paint with more French paintings featured. These
include Au Cafe, Old Peasant, Boaring Party,
Gare Saint Lazare, The Jewish Bride and Titus at
Writing Desk each 2.50   5.50

☐ **COLLECTORS EDITION VOLUME VI** (1971)
This set of three bottles look like green picture
frames around three more art masterpieces.
They are Charles I by Van Dyck, The Merry Lute
Player and Boy Holding Flute by Frans Hals each   2.50   6.50

☐ **COLLECTORS EDITION VOLUME VII** (1972)
Again, this set of three bottles is three different
colored-frame oval pictures of famous European
paintings. These are The Bag Piper, Prince Balta-
sor and Maidservant Pouring Milk each 2.50   5.50

Price Range

☐ **COLLECTORS EDITION VOLUME VIII** (1973)
This selection of three bottles features contemporary American artist, Edward H. Weiss' portraits of Ludwig Van Beethoven, Wolfgang Mozart and Frederic Francis Chopin each 2.50   5.50

☐ **COLLECTORS EDITION VOLUME IX** (1974)
This set of three bottles have a wood-tone finish and features scenes of bird-life designed and painted by James Lockhart, one of the finest wild-life artist in America today. The birds include the Cardinal, Ring-neck Pheasant and the Woodcock each 3.50   6.50

☐ **COLLECTORS EDITION VOLUME X** (1975)
A set of three different colored bottles featuring diamond shaped pictures of the Sailfish, Rainbow Trout and Largemouth Bass as painted by the esteemed naturalist, Jim Lockhart each 3.50   6.50

☐ **COLLECTORS EDITION VOLUME XI** (1976)
Each of this set of three bottles features one of three reproductions of Jim Lockhart's paintings of the Chipmunk, Bighorn Sheep or Pronghorn Antelope each 3.50   6.50

☐ **COLLECTORS EDITION VOLUME XII** (1977)
A set of four bottles of painted glass, each painted a different color and having a different reproduction of James Lockhart's on the front. Each picture is framed with a gold border. German Shorthaired Pointer is black with gold matting and black stopper, Labrador Retriever is dark purple 3.50   6.50

☐ **COLLECTORS EDITION VOLUME XIV** (1978)
A set of four flask type bottles. Glass made to appear like brown leather with framed wildlife scenes on the front which are reproductions of paintings by James Lockhart. Each picture has embossed details. The names and themes of the bottles are: Raccoon, Mule Deer, Red Fox, and Cottontail Rabbit each 3.50   6.50

Price Range

☐ **COLLECTORS EDITION VOLUME XV** (1979)
A set of three flasks each with a different repro-
duction of Frederic Remington's paintings titled:
The Cowboy 1902, The Indian Trapper 1902, and
Lieutenant S.C. Robertson 1890 each 2.50   5.50

☐ **COLLECTORS EDITION VOLUME XVI** (1980)
Set of three flasks with each depicting scenes of
ducks in flight on the front with an oval background and a bamboo styled frame. Large domed
lids. The Mallard, The Redhead, The Canvasback. Artwork by James Lockhart, one of the best
known wildlife artists in America each 3.50   6.50

☐ **COLLECTORS EDITION VOLUME XVII** (1981)
Three flask bottles with ball type lids, featuring
three more paintings by Jim Lockhart. These triangular pictures are of the Great Elk, Pintail Duck
and the Horned Owl (also known as the Car Owl)
each 3.50   6.50

☐ **COLORADO** (1959)
Light turquoise showing pioneers crossing the
rugged mountains with snow capped peaks in
background. "COLORADO" and "1859–1959" in
gold. Bottle has a leather thong. Regal China,
10¾″ 40.00 50.00

☐ **COLORADO CENTENNIAL** (1976)
Replica of Pike's Peak with a miner and his mule
in front with the word "Colorado" above the base 10.00 16.00

☐ **CONVENTION BOTTLE** (1971)
Created to commemorate the occasion of the 1st
National Convention of the National Association
of Jim Beam Bottle and Specialty Clubs hosted
by the Rocky Mountain Club, Denver, Colorado,
June 1971. 11″ 12.00 16.00

☐ **CONVENTION NUMBER 2** (1972)
This beautiful Regal China creation honors the
second annual convention of the National Association of Jim Beam Bottle and Specialty Clubs,
held June 19 through 25 in Anaheim, California.
Stopper features the national symbol of the Beam
Bottle Clubs. 13″ 60.00 70.00

Price Range

☐ CONVENTION NUMBER 3—DETROIT (1973)
Round blue bottle designed like the world with a
green U.S. outstanding and a large numeral 3.
The stopper is a bust of a golden fox. Commemo-
rates the 3rd Annual Convention of Beam Bottle
Collectors held in Detroit. 14" 22.00   27.00

☐ CONVENTION NUMBER 4—PENNSYLVANIA
(1974)
A black and gold Amish wagon commemorating
the annual convention of the Jim Beam Bottle
Clubs held in Lancaster, Pa. On the back is listed
in gold, all the member clubs. A green fox is in
the driver's seat. 7½" 110.00   120.00

☐ CONVENTION NUMBER 5—SACRAMENTO
(1975)
The famous gold pan frames an embossed scene
of Sutter's Fort in Sacramento, Ca. Gold nuggets
gleam in the miner's pan and in the transparent
stopper of the bottle. On the back: "Hosted by
Camellia City Jim Beam Bottle Club 1975." 10¾"   12.00   16.00

☐ CONVENTION NUMBER 6—HARTFORD (1976)
Chart Oak and gold lettering on the front. A map
of the U.S. is on the back. Commemorates the
annual convention of the Jim Beam Bottle Club
held in Hartford, Connecticut 15.00   21.00

☐ CONVENTION NUMBER 7—LOUISVILLE
(1978). 10.00   15.00

☐ CONVENTION NUMBER 8—CHICAGO (1978)
Embossed scene with the Sears Tower, Hancock
Building. Marina City, and Water Tower with Lake
Michigan at the base. Commemorates the 8th
Beam convention held in Chicago 14.00   18.00

☐ CONVENTION NUMBER 9—HOUSTON (1979)
The mascot of the Beam Clubs, a gray poodle
named Tiffany—sits on the side of a space capsule. Commemorates the 9th Beam convention
which was held in Houston 45.00   55.00

☐ CONVENTION NUMBER 10—NORFOLK (1980)
The sailing ship USS Beam passing between the
spokes of ship's helm, with a gold flag atop the
mast. The USS Beam is located at the Norfolk
naval base where the 10th convention was held   22.00   29.00

Price Range

☐ **CONVENTION NUMBER 11—LAS VEGAS** (1981)
A Las Vegas dealer fox stands behind a barrel marked "Jim Beam since 1795" dealing poker to two players while the chips are stacked by their hands. On the dealer's back is the logo of the International Association of Jim Beam Bottle and Specialty Clubs, 10" **32.00 37.00**

☐ **CONVENTION NUMBER 12—NEW ORLEANS** (1982)
An unusual bottle that represents a Mardi Gras float with Rex, the King of the Mardi Gras waving to the crowd. This is a green bottle, embellished with gold and "1982 Mardi Gras Rex" on the front. The bottle is open through the center around Rex. 9¼" **38.00 44.00**

☐ **COWBOY** (1979)
Either antique tan or multicolored. Cowboy leaning on a fence with one hand on his belt buckle and the other holding a rifle. His cowboy hat is the stopper. Awarded to collectors who attended the 1979 convention for the International Association of Beam Clubs **135.00 165.00**

☐ **CRAPPIE** (1979)
Figure of a silver and black speckled crappie commemorates the National Fresh Water Fishing Hall of Fame **13.00 18.00**

☐ **DARK EYES BROWN JUG** (1978)
Beige, both flecked with color, the brown jug has red flecks, the beige jug has brown flecks. Regular jug shape with small handle at neck with black stopper **5.00 8.00**

☐ **DELAWARE BLUE HEN BOTTLE** (1972)
This diamond shaped bottle, fashioned of genuine hand crafted Regal China commemorates the state of Delaware. "The first state of the Union." The front of the bottle depicts the act of ratification of the Federal Constitution on December 7, 1787. The back shows the Delaware State House, a state map and the famous Twin Bridges **6.00 10.00**

Price Range

☐ **DELCO FREEDOM BATTERY** (1978)
Replica of a Delco battery. Entire plastic top is removable 10.00 15.00

☐ **DELFT BLUE** (1963)
"Windmill Bottles" a reverse has scene of embossed Dutch windmills, on grey-white bottle. Dutch fishing boats under sail on front in "Delft" in dark blue handle and stopper, 13″ 4.00 7.00

☐ **DELFT ROSE** (1963)
Rarer than Delft Blue, same as above, sailing scene in pale blue and pink. Windmill scene embossed on reverse. Glass, 13″ 5.00 8.00

☐ **DEL WEBB MINT** (1970)
A large gold "400" and "DEL WEBB'S LAS VEGAS", embossed under crossed checkered flags. Stopper is gold dune buggy. Checkered flags on edge of bottle. "MINT" on front for the Vegas Hotel that originally had the bottle. Regal China, China or metal stopper, 13″
Metal stopper 10.00 15.00
China stopper 62.00 70.00

☐ **DIAL TELEPHONE** (1980)
Black reproduction of a 1919 desk model telephone with a movable dial. The fourth in a series of Beam telephone designs 20.00 25.00

☐ **DODGE CITY** (1972)
This bottle was issued to honor the centennial of Dodge City. The bottle is roughly triangular and depicts the city as it must have looked a century ago. Above the town, the famous cemetery BOOT HILL appears. A circular plaque on the bottle acknowledges the centennial. The stopper is a six-pointed sherriff's badge. Regal China, 10″ 7.00 10.00

☐ **DOE** (1963)
Pure white neck markings, natural brown body. "Rocky" base. Regal China, 13½″ 26.00 32.00

☐ **DOE—RE-ISSUED** (1967)
As Above 26.00 32.00

☐ **DOG** (1959)
Long-eared Setter Dog, soft brown eyes, black and white coat. Regal China, 15¼″ 42.00 52.00

Price Range

☐ **DON GIOVANNI** (1980)
Figurine of Don Giovanni from the Mozart opera
of the same name. The fifth in the Operatic series,
this bottle has a music box which plays the duet
"La ci darem la mano." .... | 180.00 240.00

☐ **DONKEY & ELEPHANT ASH TRAYS** (1956)
They were made to be used as either ash trays
w/coaster, or book ends. The stylized Elephant
and Donkey heads are in lustrous gray china. The
"Beam" label fits the round coaster section of the
bottle. Regal China, 10". PAIR .... | 12.00 16.00

☐ **DONKEY & ELEPHANT CAMPAIGNERS** (1960)
Elephant is dressed in a brown coat, blue vest
with a gold chain, he carries a placard stating
"REPUBLICANS—1960" and the state where
the bottle is sold. Donkey is dressed in black coat,
tan vest and gray pants. His placard reads "DEM-
OCRATS—1960" and state where sold. Regal
China, 12". PAIR .... | 12.00 16.00

☐ **DONKEY & ELEPHANT BOXERS** (1964)
The G.O.P. elephant has blue trunks with red
stripes, white shirt and black top hat with stars on
the band. His gloves are brown. The donkey has
red trunks with a blue stripe, black shoes and top
hat. The hat band is white with red and blue stars.
PAIR .... | 14.00 18.00

☐ **DONKEY & ELEPHANT CLOWNS** (1968)
Both are dressed in polka dot clown costumes.
Elephant has red ruffles and cuffs, with blue dots.
Donkey has blue with red dots. Yellow styrofoam
straw hat, and clown shoes on both elephant and
donkey. Their heads are the stoppers. Regal
China, 12". PAIR .... | 5.00 9.00

☐ **DONKEY & ELEPHANT FOOTBALL ELECTION
BOTTLES** (1972)
"Pick the winning team." The Democratic donkey
and the G.O.P. elephant are depicted in football
costumes atop genuine Regal China footballs in
this 1972 version of Beam's famous election bot-
tle series. Each is 9½". PAIR .... | 3.00 7.00

Price Range

☐ **DONKEY NEW YORK CITY** (1976)
Donkey wearing blue coat and black patriot hat
stands inside broken drum decorated with stars,
banner, and plaque in red, white, and blue. Commemorates the National Democratic Convention
in New York City 10.00   16.00

☐ **DUCK** (1957)
Green-headed Mallard, bright yellow bill, brown
breast, black wings. Regal China, 14¼" 20.00   26.00

☐ **DUCKS & GEESE** (1955)
A scene of wild ducks and geese flying up from
marshes in white is featured on this clear glass
decanter. A round, tall bottle with a large base
and slender tapering neck. Tall gold stopper sits
in a flared top, 13½" 6.00   10.00

☐ **DUCKS UNLIMITED BLUE WINGED TEAL**
(1980)
Two ducks made of bisque, dark brown coloring
with blue markings. The sixth in a series, 9½" 30.00   35.00

☐ **DUCKS UNLIMITED CANVASBACK DRAKE**
(1979)
Replica of a canvasback drake preparing to take
off in flight with his wings spread. Light gray with
black and burgundy coloring on wings and neck.
8" 22.00   28.00

☐ **DUCKS UNLIMITED 40TH MALLARD HEN**
(1977)
White bottle with base designed to appear as if
it is floating in water which also has a brown mallard hen sitting on it. The number "40" in green
is on the front, plaques on the base and at the
neck of the bottle 20.00   25.00

☐ **DUCKS UNLIMITED MALLARD** (1978)
Head of a Mallard duck on a semi-circular shaped
bottle with a medallion type stopper. Ducks Unlimited is a conservation organization, 9¼" 22.00   28.00

☐ **DUCKS UNLIMITED WOOD DUCK** (1975)
Wood duck nestled against a tree stump with
Ducks Unlimited logo on front, 9" 20.00   28.00

Price Range

☐ **EAGLE** (1966)
White head, golden beak, deep rich brown plumage, yellow claws on "tree trunk" base. Regal China, 12½" 13.00 18.00

☐ **ELDORADO** (1978)
Gray-blue or beige, tear drop shaped bottle on pedestal stand, domed-shaped stopper, mottled, 13" 8.00 12.00

☐ **ELEPHANT AND DONKEY SUPERMEN** (1980)
Set of two. Representing the Democratic and Republican political parties, the elephant and the donkey are both dressed as Superman in yellow and gray outfits. Each carries the world on his shoulders 10.00 14.00

☐ **ELEPHANT KANSAS CITY** (1976)
Elephant standing inside broken drum decorated in red, white, and blue with stars, banner and coat and black patriot hat stands inside broken drum decorated with stars, banner, and plaque in red, white, and blue. Commemorates the National Democratic Convention in New York City 5.00 9.00

☐ **EMERALD CRYSTAL BOURBON** (1968)
Emerald green bottle, patterned embossed glass. Flat stopper, "swirl" embosses. Green glass, 11½" 4.00 7.00

☐ **EMMETT KELLY** (1973)
A delightful genuine Regal China creation. An exact likeness of the original Emmett Kelly, as sad-faced Willie the Clown, who has captivated and won the hearts of millions from the Big Top of television, 14" 22.00 28.00

☐ **ERNIE'S FLOWER CART** (1976)
Replica of an old-fashioned flower cart used in San Francisco. Wooden cart with movable wheels. In honor of Ernie's Wines and Liquors of Northern California 28.00 34.00

☐ **EXPO 74** (1974)
This bottle was issued on the occasion of the World's Fair held at Spokane, Washington in 1974. A very unusual bottle; six-sided panels form

Price Range

the bottle's sides. The top of the bottle is a clock
tower. The stopper is the roof of the tower. Regal
China, 7¼ " **11.00   15.00**

☐ **FALSTAFF** (1979)
Replica of Sir John Falstaff with blue and yellow
outfit holding a gold goblet. Second in the Australian Opera Series. Music box which plays "Va,
vecchio, John." Limited edition of 1000 bottles,
comes with base **200.00 265.00**

☐ **FANTASIA BOTTLE** (1971)
This tall, delicately handcrafted Regal China decanter is embellished with 22 karat gold and
comes packaged in a handsome midnight blue
and gold presentation case lined with red velvet.
16¼ " **12.00   18.00**

☐ **FEMALE CARDINAL** (1973)
The body of the bird is mostly brown with a red
beak and some red on the tail feathers. The stopper is the upper part of the bird. Regal China,
13½ " **21.00   25.00**

☐ **FIESTA BOWL** (1973)
The second bottle created for the Fiesta Bowl.
This bottle is made of genuine Regal China, fea-
turing a football player on the front side, 13¼ " **9.00   15.00**

☐ **FIGARO** (1977)
Figurine of the character Figaro from the opera
Barber of Seville. Spanish costume in beige, rose,
and yellow. Holds a brown guitar on the ground
in front of him. Music box plays an aria from the
opera **235.00 270.00**

☐ **FIRST NATIONAL BANK OF CHICAGO** (1964)
Note: Beware of reproductions
Issued to commemorate the 100th anniversary of
the First National Bank of Chicago, about 130
were issued, 117 were given as momentoes to
the bank directors, none for public distribution.
This is the most valuable Beam bottle known. Sky
blue color, circular shape, gold embossed design
around banner lettered "THE FIRST NATIONAL
BANK OF CHICAGO." Center oval was ornate
bank logo "1st", and "100th Anniversary" in gold.
Gold embossed "1st" on stopper. Bottom

Price Range

marked "CREATION OF JAMES B. BEAM DIS-
TILLING CO.—GENUINE REGAL CHINA". Re-
verse: Round paper label inscribed "BEAM CON-
GRATULATES THE FIRST NATIONAL BANK OF
CHICAGO—100th ANNIVERSARY. 100 YEARS
OF SUCCESSFUL BANKING" **3000.00 3800.00**

☐ **FISH** (1957)
Sky blue sailfish, pink underside, black dorsal fin
and side markings on "ocean waves" base.
Regal China, 14" **30.00 40.00**

☐ **FIVE SEASONS** (1980)
The club bottle for the Five Seasons Club of
Cedar Rapids honors their home state, Iowa. The
bottle is shaped like Iowa with a large ear of corn.
The top of the corn is the lid **14.00 18.00**

☐ **FLEET RESERVE ASSN.** (1974)
This bottle was issued by the Fleet Reserve Association to honor the Career Sea Service on
their 50th anniversary. The bottle is roughly triangular with the words "LOYALTY PROTECTION
SERVICE" embossed on the front. The stopper
is plain. Regal China, 9" **6.00 9.00**

☐ **FLORIDA SHELL** (1968)
Shell shaped bottles made in two colors, mother
of pearl, and iridescent bronze, for a shimmering
luminescent effect. Reverse has map of Florida,
and "SEA SHELL HEADQUARTERS OF THE
WORLD." Regal China, 9¾" **3.00 7.00**

☐ **FLORO DE ORO** (1976)
Urn-shaped bottle with pastel band around middle and yellow and blue flowers, remainder of the
bottle is gold with fluting and designs, gold handle, 12" **12.00 18.00**

☐ **FLOWER BASKET** (1962)
Blue Basket filled with embossed pastel flowers
and green leaves resting on gold base, gold de-
tails and stopper. Regal China, 12¼" **45.00 55.00**

☐ **FOREMOST—BLACK & GOLD** (1956)
Pylon shaped decanter with a deep black body
embossed with gold nuggets. The square white
stopper doubles as a jigger. This is the first Beam

Price Range

bottle issued for a liquor retailer. Foremost Liquor
Store of Chicago, many others have followed.
Regal China 330.00 350.00
☐ **FOREMOST GRAY AND GOLD** (1956)
Same as above. Tapered decanter with gray body
and gold nuggets. Both decanters are 15½" high
and are Regal China 325.00 350.00
☐ **FOREMOST—SPECKLED BEAUTY** (1956)
The most valuable of the "Foremost" bottles.
Also known as the "Pink Speckled Beauty", was
created in the shape of a Chinese vase and spat-
tered in various colors of pink, gold, black and
gray. The spattered colors may vary from bottle
to bottle since it was hand applied. Regal China,
14½" 600.00 675.00
☐ **FOOTBALL HALL OF FAME** (1972)
This bottle is a reproduction of the striking new
Professional Football Hall of Fame Building, executed in genuine Regal China. The stopper is in
the shape of half a football, 9¾" 4.00 8.00
☐ **FOX** (1967)
blue coat 110.00 120.00
☐ **FOX** (1971)
gold coat 60.00 70.00
☐ **FRENCH CRADLE TELEPHONE** (1979)
Replica of a French cradle telephone. The third
in the Telephone Pioneers of America series,
7¼" 22.00 27.00
☐ **GALAH BIRD** (1979)
Rose colored Galah bird which is part of the cock-
atoo family from South Australia. It has a white
plume on its head and touches of gray and white
feathers 12.00 18.00
☐ **GEORGE WASHINGTON COMMEMORATIVE
PLATE** (1976)
Plate-shaped bottle with a painting of George
Washington in the center bordered by a band of
gold. The bottle is blue with lettering around the
outside rim. Commemorates the U.S. Bicenten-
nial, 9½" 15.00 20.00

Price Range

☐ **GERMAN BOTTLE—WEISBADEN** (1973)
This bottle, of genuine Regal China, depicts a map of the famous Rhine wine-growing regions of Germany. Special attention is given to the heart of this wine country at Weisbaden, 11" ..   4.00   8.00

☐ **GERMANY** (1970)
This bottle was issued to honor the American Armed Forces in Germany. The body of the bottle is made up of a plaque on both sides showing rustic German scenes. The stopper is plain. Regal China, 10" 4.00   7.00

☐ **GLEN CAMPBELL 51ST** (1976)
Guitar-shaped bottle with a bust of Glen Campbell sculptured at top of guitar. Lid is the ends of gold clubs. Honors the 51st Los Angeles Open, a golf tournament held at the Rivera Country Club between February 16 to 20. 12¾" 8.00   14.00

☐ **GOLDEN CHALICE** (1961)
Chalice with gray-blue body, gold accents. Band of embossed pastel flowers on the neck. Gold scrolled neck and base. Regal China, 12¼" ...   54.00   65.00

☐ **GOLDEN GATE** (1969)
This almond-shaped bottle has "LAS VEGAS" embossed in bright gold in a banner on the front. Mountains, a helicopter, a golfer, and gambling montage, with "GOLDEN GATE CASINO" in gold on a shield are featured. Regal China, 12½" ..   45.00   55.00

☐ **GOLDEN NUGGET** (1969)
Same as above "GOLDEN NUGGET" in gold on shield in front. Regal China, 12½" 50.00   60.00

☐ **GOLDEN ROSE** (1978)
Three versions of this urn-shaped bottle, yellow embossed rose with a blue background framed in gold band, remainder of bottle gold mottled with two handles. Yellow Rose of Texas version has the name of this bottle beneath the rose, the Harolds Club VIP version has its title lettered under the rose also, 11½" 18.00   24.00

☐ **GRAND CANYON** (1969)
"GRAND CANYON NATIONAL PARK 50th ANNIVERSARY" in a circle around a scene of the Canyon in black with "1919–1969" in earth-red.

Price Range

A round bottle (same as Arizona) with a "stick up" spout and round stopper embossed with map of Arizona. Regal China, 12½" 8.00 12.00

☐ **GRANT LOCOMOTIVE** (1979)
Replica of Grant Locomotive, black engine with gold trim and bells, red wheels that move. 9" .. 45.00 55.00

☐ **GRAY CHERUB** (1958)
Checkered design, bordered with scroll work, accented with 22 karat gold. Three embossed cherubs on neck. Regal China, 12" 290.00 320.00

☐ **GREAT CHICAGO FIRE BOTTLE** (1971)
This historical decanter was created to commemorate the great Chicago fire of 1871, and to salute Mercy Hospital which rendered service to the fire victims. This first hospital of Chicago was started in 1852 by the Sisters of Mercy. The new Mercy Hospital and Medical Center, opened in 1968, is depicted on the reverse side. The front of the bottle shows towering flames engulfing Chicago's waterfront as it appeared on the evening of October 8, 1871. The look of actual flames has been realistically captured in this Regal China masterpiece, 7½" 20.00 25.00

☐ **GREAT DANE** (1976)
White with black markings and gold collar, 7" 8.00 12.00

☐ **GREEN CHINA JUG** (1965)
Deep mottled green china jug, with embossed branches and buds on side. Solid handle Regal Glass, 12½" 4.00 8.00

☐ **HANNAH DUSTIN** (1973)
A beautiful Regal China creation designed after the granite monument erected in her memory on Contoocook Island, in the Merrimack River north of Concord. This was where in 1697 Hannah Dustin, her nurse and a young boy made their famous frantic escape from Indians, who held them captive for two weeks. 14½" 30.00 35.00

☐ **HANSEL AND GRETEL BOTTLE** (1971)
The forlorn, lost waifs from the Brothers Grimm's beloved fable *Hansel and Gretel* are depicted on the front of this charming and beautiful Regal

Price Range

China bottle. Above them, the words "GERMANY
... LAND OF HANSEL AND GRETEL" stand out
in gold. 10¼" 4.00 8.00

☐ **HAROLDS CLUB—BLUE SLOT MACHINE**
(1967)
A blue-toned "One Armed Bandit" with 2 gold
bells showing in the window, and a gold colored
handle, the money slot is the stopper. "HAR-
OLDS CLUB RENO" and a large "H" on a pinwheel emblem are on the front. Regal China,
10⅜" 10.00 16.00

☐ **HAROLDS CLUB—COVERED WAGON**
(1969–70)
A Conestoga wagon with "HAROLDS CLUB"
embossed on the side pulled by a galloping ox,
driven by a cowboy. The bottle is "arch" shaped,
framing Nevada's mountains and the wagon.
Regal China, 10" 4.00 8.00

☐ **HAROLDS CLUB—GRAY SLOT MACHINE**
(1968)
Same as above but with an overall gray tone.
Regal China, 10⅜" 6.00 10.00

☐ **HAROLDS CLUB (MAN-IN-A BARREL)** (1957)
This was the first in a series made for the famous
Harolds Club in Reno, Nevada. The man-in-a-
barrel was an advertising logo used by the club.
In 1957, Jim Beam issued a bottle using the figure
of "Percy" in a barrel with "HAROLDS CLUB"
embossed on the front. "Percy" has a top hat, a
monocle, a mustache, a white collar and a bright
red tie, and spats. He stands on a base of "Bad
News" dice cubes. Regal China, 14" 425.00 485.00

☐ **HAROLDS CLUB (MAN-IN-A-BARREL-2)**
(1958)
Twin brother of Percy No. 1. No mustache, "HAR-
OLDS CLUB" inscribed on base of the bottle.
Regal China, 14" 225.00 260.00

☐ **HAROLDS CLUB—NEVADA (GRAY)** (1963)
"HAROLDS CLUB OF RENO" inscribed on base
of bottle created for the "Nevada Centennial—1864–1964" as a state bottle. Embossed picture of miner and mule on the "HAROLDS" side,

Price Range

crossed shovel and pick are on stopper. Embossed lettering on base is gray-toned and not bold. This is a rare and valuable bottle **165.00 190.00**

☐ **HAROLDS CLUB—NEVADA (SILVER)** (1964)
Same as above. Base lettering now reads "HAROLDS CLUB RENO." The letters are bolder and are bright silver. **165.00 190.00**

☐ **HAROLDS CLUB—PINWHEEL** (1965)
A round bottle supporting a design of a spinning pinwheel of gold and blue, with gold dots on the edge. "HAROLDS CLUB RENO" embossed in gold in the center, "FOR FUN" on the stopper. Regal China, 10½" **60.00 70.00**

☐ **HAROLDS CLUB—SILVER OPAL** (1957)
Issued to commemorate the 25th Anniversary of Harolds Club, bright silver color with a snowflake design center and a red label. Glass, 11⅛" . . . **20.00 28.00**

☐ **HAROLDS CLUB—VIP EXECUTIVE** (1967)
An Alladin's Lamp shaped decanter. "HAROLDS CLUB RENO" embossed gold label on bottle. Over-all gold and green color on bottle. Limited quantity issued. Regal China, 12½" **55.00 65.00**

☐ **HAROLDS CLUB—VIP EXECUTIVE** (1968)
An overall bubble pattern in cobalt blue with silver trim and handle distinguishes this bottle. "HAROLDS CLUB RENO" in silver, on an embossed oval emblem, is in the center of the bottle. Regal China, 12¾" **60.00 70.00**

☐ **HAROLDS CLUB—VIP EXECUTIVE** (1969)
An oval shaped decanter with an overall motif of roses. "HAROLDS CLUB RENO" is embossed in gold on the yellow-toned bottle. The bottle was used as a Christmas gift to the Casino's executives. Regal China, 12½" **240.00 260.00**

☐ **HAROLDS CLUB VIP** (1976)
Same as Floro de Oro except for the Harold's Club patch on the base. Urn-shaped bottles with pastel band of blue and yellow flowers around the middle. Remainder of the bottle has very shiny gold with fluting and designs. 12" **22.00 30.00**

Price Range

☐ **HAROLD'S CLUB VIP** (1979)
Double urn shaped bottle with wide alternating
bands of gold and mother-of-pearl with double
scroll handles on large screw lid. 11½" **30.00   36.00**

☐ **HARRAH'S CLUB NEVADA—GRAY** (1963)
This is the same round bottle used for the Nevada
Centennial and Harolds Club with the miner, and
mule and lettered "NEVADA CENTENNIAL."
The base has "HARRAH'S RENO AND LAKE
TAHOE" embossed on the gray-tone base. Regal
China, 11½" **570.00 620.00**

☐ **HARRAH'S CLUB NEVADA—SILVER** (1963)
Same as above. Nevada Centennial bottle,
"HARRAH'S RENO AND LAKE TAHOE" em-
bossed on base in silver. Regal China, 11½" ..**1000.00 1100.00**

☐ **HARVEY'S RESORT HOTEL AT LAKE TAHOE**
Glass, 11½" **10.00   18.00**

☐ **HATFIELD** (1973)
The character of Hatfield from the famous story
of the Hatfield and McCoy feud. Hatfield is shown
standing holding a rifle at his side. He is dressed
all in black. On the base of the bottle, he is referred to as "DEVIL ANSE HATFIELD." His hat
is the stopper. Regal China, 14" **24.00   28.00**

☐ **HAWAII** (1959)
Tribute to 50th State. Panorama of Hawaiian
scenes, palm trees, the blue Pacific, outriggers,
and surf boarders. Gold "50" in star. Regal China,
8½" **45.00   55.00**

☐ **HAWAII—RE-ISSUED** (1967)
As above **50.00   60.00**

☐ **HAWAII** (1971) **6.00   10.00**

☐ **HAWAII ALOHA** (1971)
Pear shaped bottle with picture of Hawaiian King
on the front and a scene of mountain and palm
tree on reverse. 11" **10.00   20.00**

☐ **HAWAIIAN OPEN BOTTLE** (1972)
Cleverly decorated to simulate a pineapple with
the famous "Friendly Skies" logo in gold, this
genuine Regal China Bottle honors the 1972 Hawaiian Open Golf Tournament. The reverse side

Price Range

commemorates United Air Lines' 25th year (1972) of air service to Hawaii. The stopper is designed to look like pineapple leaves. 10" 6.00 10.00

□ **HAWAIIAN OPEN** (1973)
The second bottle created in honor of the United Hawaiian Open Golf Classic. Of genuine Regal China designed in the shape of a golf ball featuring a pineapple and airplane on front. 11" 6.00 10.00

□ **HAWAIIAN OPEN** (1974)
Genuine Regal China bottle commemorating the famous 1974 Hawaiian Open Golf Classic. 15" 6.00 10.00

□ **HAWAIIAN OPEN OUTRIGGER** (1975)
A very unusual bottle. Two native girls are paddling an outrigger canoe on a wave beautifully colored in different shades of blue. The bottle is shaped like the wave. The stopper is the very top of the wave. Regal China, 8½" 9.00 13.00

□ **HAWAII PARADISE** (1978)
Commemorates the 200th Anniversary of the landing of Captain Cook. Embossed scene of a Hawaiian resort framed by a pink garland of flowers. Black stopper, 8¾" 20.00 28.00

□ **HEMISFAIR** (1968)
The Lone Star of Texas crowns the tall gray and blue "TOWER OF THE AMERICAS." "THE LONE STAR STATE" is lettered in gold over a rustic Texas scene. The half map of Texas has "HEMISFAIR 68—SAN ANTONIO." Regal China, 13" 6.00 10.00

□ **HOFFMAN** (1969)
The bottle is in the shape of Harry Hoffman Liquor Store with the Rocky Mountains in the background. Beam bottles, and "SKI COUNTRY—USA" are in the windows. Reverse: embossed mountain and ski slopes with skier. Regal China, 9" 4.00 8.00

□ **HOME BUILDERS** (1978)
Replica of a Rockford Builders Bungalow, brown with touches of black. Oval medallion on the roof reads "Your Best Bet—A Home Of Your Own." This bottles commemorates the 1979 convention of the Home Builders 22.00 28.00

Price Range

☐ **HONGA HIKA** (1980)
Honga Hika is the most famous warchief of the
Ngapuki Tribe. This is the first in a series of au-
thentic Maori Warrior bottles **200.00 225.00**

☐ **HORSE (BLACK)** (1962)
Black horse with white on blaze nose, white
hooves, and black tail. Regal China, 13½" **20.00 28.00**

☐ **HORSE (BLACK)—RE-ISSUED** (1967)
As above **19.00 23.00**

☐ **HORSE (BROWN)** (1962)
Brown horse with white blaze on nose, black
hooves and tail. Regal China, 13½" high **22.00 26.00**

☐ **HORSE (BROWN)—RE-ISSUED** (1967)
As above **19.00 23.00**

☐ **HORSE (WHITE)** (1962)
White mustang with white flowing mane and tail.
Regal China, 13½" **20.00 28.00**

☐ **HORSE (WHITE)—RE-ISSUED** (1967)
As above **16.00 22.00**

☐ **HORSESHOE CLUB** (1969)
Same as Reno and Cal-Neva bottles with
"RENO'S HORSESHOE CLUB" and a horse-
shoe in yellow and black on the emblem. 9¼" **4.00 8.00**

☐ **HULA BOWL** (1975)
Brown football resting on a stand with a red helmet on the top. Medallion type plaque on the
front, football player in the center **7.00 11.00**

☐ **IDAHO** (1963)
Bottle in the shape of Idaho. Skiier on slope on
one side and farmer on other side. Pick and
shovel on stopper. Regal China, 12¼" **40.00 50.00**

☐ **ILLINOIS** (1968)
The log cabin birth place of "Abe Lincoln" embossed on front, oak tree, and banner with 21
stars (21st state) and "Land of Lincoln." Made
to honor the Sesquicentennial 1818–1968 of Illinois, home of the James B. Beam Distilling Company. Regal China, 12¾" **4.00 8.00**

☐ **INDIAN CHIEF** (1979)
Seated Indian chief with a peace pipe across his
arm. Tan colored with touches of brown, green,
and red **18.00 23.00**

Price Range

☐ **INTERNATIONAL CHILI SOCIETY** (1976)
Upper body of a chef with recipe of C.V. Wood's
World Championship Chili Recipe 6.00 10.00

☐ **IVORY ASH TRAY** (1955)
Designed for a dual purpose, as a bottle, and as
an ash tray. Bottle lies flat with cigarette grooves
and round coaster seat. Ivory color. Regal China,
12¾" 20.00 28.00

☐ **JACKALOPE** (1971)
The fabulous Wyoming Jackalope, a rare cross
between a jackrabbit and antelope. It has the
body and ears of the Western Jackrabbit and the
head and antlers of an antelope. Golden brown
body on prairie grass base. Regal China, 14" .. 9.00 13.00

☐ **JOHN HENRY** (1972)
This bottle commemorates the legendary Steel
Drivin' Man. He is black and is shown bare-
chested. In each hand he holds a steel hammer.
Embossed on the base is "BIG BEND TUNNEL
WEST VIRGINIA." Regal China, 12¾" 45.00 55.00

☐ **JOLIET LEGION BAND** (1978)
Shield-shaped bottle with embossed details resembling a coat of arms in blue, green, and gold.
Commemorates the 26 national championships
won by the band. 12¼" 15.00 19.00

☐ **KAISER INTERNATIONAL OPEN BOTTLE**
(1971)
This handsome Regal China creation commemorates the Fifth Annual Kaiser International Open
Golf Tournament played that year at Silverado in
California's beautiful Napa Valley. The stopper is
a "golf ball" decorated with the Kaiser International Open logo suspended over a red tee. The
logo is repeated, in gold against a blue field, in
the center of the front panel and is surrounded
by a ring of decorated golf balls. Listed on the
back are the particulars of the tournament. 11¼" 4.00 8.00

☐ **KANGAROO** (1977)
Kangaroo with its baby in its pouch on a green
pedestal. The head is the stopper. 11¾" 16.00 20.00

Price Range

☐ **KANSAS** (1960)
Round, yellow-toned bottle shows harvesting of wheat on one side and "KANSAS 1861–1961 CENTENNIAL" embossed in gold. On the other side, symbols of the modern age with aircraft, factories, oil wells, and dairies. Leather thong. Regal China, 11¾" 48.00 55.00

☐ **KENTUCKY BLACK HEAD—BROWN HEAD** (1967)
The stopper is a horse's head, some are made in brown, some black. State map on bottle shows products of Kentucky. Tobacco, distilling, farming, coal, oil, and industries. Regal China, 11½"
black head 12.00 18.00
brown head 20.00 28.00
white head 20.00 25.00

☐ **KENTUCKY DERBY BOTTLE** (1972)
Designed to commemorate the 98th Run For The Roses at Churchill Downs showing Canonero II, 1971 winner, garlanded with the traditional American Beauty Roses. The reverse side depicts famous Churchill Downs Clubhouse in relief and etched in gold. The stopper is a replica of an American Beauty Rose. 11" 10.00 15.00

☐ **KENTUCKY DERBY 100th** (1974)
This bottle commemorates the 100th anniversary of the running of the Kentucky Derby. The number "100" is embossed very large on the bottle and the interior of the numbers is decorated with pink flowers with green leaves and stems. Also on the front of the bottle are embossings of the first Derby winner, Aristides, and the one-hundreth winner, Cannonade. Both horse's portraits are framed by horseshoes. 7½" 9.00 12.00

☐ **KEY WEST** (1972)
This bottle was issued to honor the 150th anniversary of Key West, Florida. It is roughly triangular with embossed details such as palm trees and surf. Regal China, 9¾" 7.50 12.00

☐ **KING KAMEHAMEHA** (1972)
A replica of the famous King Kamehameha statue, this genuine Regal China bottle has been

Price Range

designed to commemorate the 100th Anniversary of King Kamehameha Day. A hero of the Hawaiian people, King Kamehameha is credited for uniting the Hawaiian Islands 12.00 20.00

☐ **KING KONG** (1976)
Three-quarters body of King Kong. Commemorates the Paramount Picture movie release in December 1976. 9¾" 10.00 16.00

☐ **KIWI** (1974)
The Kiwi bird is shown protecting its egg near a tree stump. The Kiwi's feathers are brown and the egg is white. The stopper is plain. Regal China, 8½" 8.00 13.00

☐ **KOALA BEAR** (1973)
The koala bear, the native animal of Australia. A genuine Regal China creation. The bottle features two koala bears on a tree stump, the top of the stump is its pourer, with the name Australia across the front of the bottle. 9" 15.00 20.00

☐ **LARAMIE** (1968)
"CENTENNIAL JUBILEE LARAMIE WYO. 1868–1968" embossed around cowboy on bucking bronco. Locomotive of 1860's on reverse. 10½" 4.00 8.00

☐ **LARGEMOUTH BASS TROPHY BOTTLE** (1973)
Created in honor of the National Fresh Water Fishing Hall of Fame, located in Hayward, Wisconsin, scheduled for completion in 1974. A genuine Regal China creation designed after the Largemouth Bass. Its stopper features the official seal of the Hall of Fame 12.00 16.00

☐ **LAS VEGAS** (1969)
This bottle was also used for CUSTOMER SPECIALS—CASINO SERIES. Almond shaped with gold embossed "LAS VEGAS" in a banner, and scenes of Nevada, and a gambling montage. Reverse: Hoover Dam and Lake Mead. Regal China, 12½" 3.00 7.00

☐ **LIGHT BULB** (1979)
Regular bottle shape with replica of a light bulb for the stopper, picture of Thomas Edison in an oval, letter of tribute to Edison on the back. 11¼" 10.00 15.00

Price Range

☐ **LOMBARD** (1969)
A pear-shaped decanter, embossed with lilacs and leaves around a circular motto "VILLAGE OF LOMBARD, ILLINOIS—1869 CENTENNIAL 1969" lilac shaped stopper. Reverse has an embossed outline map of Illinois. Colors are lavender and green. 12¼" 3.00 7.00

☐ **LOUISVILLE DOWNS RACING DERBY** (1978)
Short, oblong-shaped bottle, scene with horse, buggy and rider on the front framed by wide white band with gold lettering. Medallion type stopper, 9½" 4.00 8.00

☐ **MADAME BUTTERFLY** (1977)
Figurine of Madame Butterfly character from the opera of the same name. Female dressed in blue and black kimono holding a realistic fan made of paper and wood. Music box plays *One Fine Day* from the opera, includes base and paperweight, 16½" 425.00 475.00

☐ **THE MAGPIES** (1977)
Black magpie sitting on tip of a football with the name "The Magpies" on the front, honors an Australian football team. 10½" 12.00 16.00

☐ **MAINE** (1970)
A green triangular bottle with the outline of the state on the front and wording "The Pine Tree State." 12" 3.00 7.00

☐ **MAJESTIC** (1966)
Royal blue decanter with handle, on a base of golden leaves. Gold scrolled stopper, and lip. Regal China, 14½" 27.00 34.00

☐ **MARBLED FANTASY** (1965)
Decanter on a blue marbled base, set in a cup of gold with a heavy gold ring around the center. Gold lip and handle, blue and gold stopper. Regal China, 15" 53.00 65.00

☐ **MARINA CITY** (1962)
Commemorating modern apartment complex in Chicago. Light blue with "Marina City" in gold on the sides. Regal China, 10¾" 30.00 40.00

Jim Beam Kentucky Derby Bottle (c.1972), designed to commemorate the 98th "Run for the Roses," showing Canonero II, 1971 winner, garlanded with the traditional American Beauty Roses. Reverse: Churchill Downs Clubhouse in relief and etched in gold. The stopper is a replica of an American Beauty Rose, 11".
$10.00–$15.00

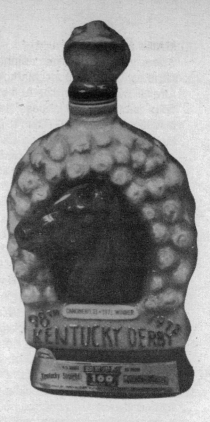

Jim Beam Glen Campbell 51st (1976), guitar shaped bottle with a bust of Glen Campbell sculptured at top of guitar. Lid is the ends of golf clubs. Honors the 51st Los Angeles Open, a golf tournament held at the Riviera Country Club, 12".
$8.00–$14.00

Price Range

☐ **MARK ANTHONY** (1962)
Same as Cleo bottles, amphora-decanter, two
handles, white stopper. Mark Anthony alone before Nile scene, white on rust background. Bottle
color is black-purple. Glass, 13¼″ 20.00 28.00

☐ **MARTHA WASHINGTON** (1976)
Designed like a collector's plate, with a portrait
of Martha Washington encircled by a band of
white with the outside rim in light blue and gold
embossed lettering. 9½″ 7.00 11.00

☐ **McCOY** (1973)
The character of McCoy from the famous story
of the Hatfield and McCoy feud. McCoy is shown
seated holding a rifle. On the base of the bottle,
he is referred to as "RANDOLPH McCOY." The
stopper is his hat. Regal China, 12″ 24.00 28.00

☐ **MEPHISTOPHELES** (1979)
Part of the Opera series, this figurine depicts
Mephistopheles from the opera *Faust.* The music
box plays *Soldier's Chorus,* bottle and base make
up two-piece set, 14½″ 180.00 230.00

☐ **MICHIGAN BOTTLE** (1972)
The map of the "Great Lakes State" adorns the
front of this striking commemorative Regal China
bottle. The state flower and the major cities are
shown along with an inset plaque of an antique
automobile, one of Michigan's traditional symbols. A capsule description of the state, a drawing
of the magnificent Mackinac Bridge and the state
motto of the "Wolverine State" appear on a scroll
on the back. The stopper depicts an antique
wooden wheel on one side and a modern automobile wheel on the other. 11⅞″ 6.00 10.00

☐ **MINNESOTA VIKING** (1973)
A strikingly handsome Regal China creation designed after the famous Viking statue in Alexandria, Minnesota, known as the Largest Viking in
the World. The bottle features a helmet as its
stopper. The back depicts a replica of the Kensington Runestone. 14″ 12.00 16.00

Price Range

☐ **MINT 400** (1971)
The annual Del Webb Mint 400 was commemorated by a striking Regal China sculpture which
captures the feeling of the desert, surrounded by
mountains, beneath a blue Las Vegas sky. It is
the home of one of the racing world's most gruel-
ing off-road events. The bottle's most prominent
feature is the gold-painted motorcycle racer on
the stopper. Black and white checkered flags are
crossed on the front above large gold letters.
Black and white checks edge the sides. A decal
on the reverse details information about the race.
8¼" 8.00   12.00
Same as above (1970) 8.00   12.00
☐ **MINT 400** (1972)
This bottle commemorates the fifth annual Greatest Off Road Race held by Del Webb and Mint
400. A black and white checkered flag has the
name in large gold letters across the flag. 11¼"   6.00   9.00
☐ **MINT 400** (1973)
An all gold bottle honors the sixth annual Mint
400 Sahara Desert Rally, the world's greatest off-
road race. An embossed scene is on the back.
13" 5.00   8.00
☐ **MINT 400, SEVENTH ANNUAL** (1975)
The checkerboard finish flag serves as a background for the emblem of the Mint 400 Desert
Race. This $100,000 purse event includes both
auto and cycle contests and they are shown on
the gold-embossed back of the bottle. 8¼" ...   6.00   10.00
☐ **MINT 400 8TH ANNUAL** (1976)
Medallion-shaped bottle. White bottle with gold
lettering and gold center with black lettering.
Commemorates the Mint 400, a road race spon-
sored by Del Webb's Hotel and Casino in Las
Vegas. 10" 12.00   18.00
☐ **MISSISSIPPI FIRE ENGINE** (1978)
Replica of the 1867 Fire Engine, red and black
with brass simulated fittings. Bells, lanterns,
water pump, and engine mountings are authentic.
11¾" 70.00   80.00

Price Range

☐ **MODEL A FORD 1903** (1978)
Replica of Henry Ford's Model A Ford in red with
black trim or black with red trim. Simulated brass
and trim. Stopper at the rear of the car, 8" 35.00   42.00

☐ **MODEL A FORD 1928** (1980)
Beige Model A with black accessories, authentic
details for the headlights, trim, and interior. Stopper underneath the rear trunk and spare tire. 6½"   50.00   60.00

☐ **MONTANA** (1963)
Tribute to gold miners. Names of "ALDER
GULCH," "LAST CHANCE GULCH, BANNACK"
and "MONTANA, 1864 GOLDEN YEARS CEN-
TENNIAL 1964" are embossed on bottle. Regal
China, 11½" 60.00   70.00

☐ **MONTEREY BAY CLUB** (1977)
Based on the band stand in Watsonville city park,
honors the Monterey Bay Beam Bottle and Specialty Club. 7½" 13.00   17.00

☐ **MORTIMER SNERD** (1976)
Country boy with buck teeth, straw hat, and bow
tie, replica of famous character, created by Edgar
Bergen, 12" 28.00   34.00

☐ **MOTHER OF PEARL** (1979)
Double urn-shaped bottle with wide alternating
bands of gold and mother-of-pearl with double
scroll handles on large screw lid. Identical to the
Harold's Club VIP bottle except no lettering on
the front. 11½" 20.00   28.00

☐ **MOUNT ST. HELENS** (1980)
Depicts the eruption of St. Helens on May 18,
1980. A small vial of ash from the explosion is attached on the back. 9¼" 28.00   36.00

☐ **MR. GOODWRENCH** (1978)
Half-figure of Mr. Goodwrench based on the General Motors advertisement. The figure is the stopper which sits on a rectangular base. Blue and
white, 13½" 15.00   19.00

☐ **MUSICIANS ON A WINE CASK** (1964)
Old time tavern scene: musicians, guitar and ac-
cordian, embossed on cask-shaped embossed
bottle. Wooden barrel effect, and wood base.
Gray china color. Regal China, 9¾" 4.00   8.00

Price Range

☐ **MUSKIE** (1971)
The Muskie is the state fish of Wisconsin. The bottle is a figure of the fish, the stopper is the head, the fish rests on a platform of water. Also on the bottle is a plaque indicating the Muskie as the Wisconsin state fish. The bottle was issued in honor of the National Fresh Water Fishing Hall of Fame. Regal China, 14½" 20.00 25.00

☐ **NATIONAL TOBACCO FESTIVAL** (1973)
Regal China bottle commemorating the 25th Anniversary of the National Tobacco Festival. The festival was held in Richmond, Virginia, on October 6 through the 13th. On the base of the special bottle, historic data of the growth and development of the tobacco industry is featured. The unique closure is the bust of an American Indian 8.00 12.00

☐ **NEBRASKA** (1967)
Round bottle bears the words, "WHERE THE WEST BEGINS" with a picture of a covered wagon drawn by oxen. Regal China, 12¼" 4.00 8.00

☐ **NEBRASKA FOOTBALL** (1972)
This strikingly handsome genuine Regal China creation commemorates the University of Nebraska's national championship football team of 1970–71 season. The stopper features an exact likeness of Bob Devaney, the Cornhuskers head coach. 8¾" 6.00 10.00

☐ **NEVADA** (1963)
Circular silver and gray bottle, with silver "NEVADA," bearing outline of state with embossed mountain peaks, forests, and a factory. Reverse is a miner and donkey. Same bottle used by Harold's Club and Harrah's Regal China, 11½" ... 38.00 46.00

☐ **NEW HAMPSHIRE** (1967)
Blue-tone bottle in the shape of the state. Decal of state motto, seal, flower and bird. Stopper in the shape of the Old Man of the Mountain. Regal China, 13½" 4.00 8.00

☐ **NEW HAMPSHIRE EAGLE BOTTLE** (1971)
Under the New Hampshire banner on this beautiful Regal China bottle, a solid gold eagle against a blue field stands as a proud reminder of the

Price Range

original symbol, a great carved wooden bird, which was placed atop the New Hampshire State House when it was built in 1818. On the back of the bottle, beneath the slogan "Granite State," a decal recounts the history of the first New Hampshire Eagle. 12½" **25.00** **33.00**

☐ **NEW JERSEY** (1963)
Gray map of state filled with embossed colorful fruits, vegetables, and flowers, set on pyramid shaped bottle. "NEW JERSEY—THE GARDEN STATE, FARM & INDUSTRY" in gold. Regal China, 13½" **65.00** **75.00**

☐ **NEW JERSEY YELLOW** (1963)
Same as above, yellow toned map of New Jersey, 13½" **55.00** **65.00**

☐ **NEW MEXICO BICENTENNIAL** (1976)
Square-shaped bottle with blue center. White lettering and gold eagle embossed on front. The Governor's home is on the back. 10½" **8.00** **12.00**

☐ **NEW MEXICO STATEHOOD** (1972)
Commemorating New Mexico's 60 years of statehood, this dramatic genuine Regal China bottle has been designed to represent the historical Indian Ceremonial Wedding Vase which was used through the centuries by the New Mexico Indians in tribal wedding ceremonies. 9½" **11.00** **15.00**

☐ **NEW YORK WORLD'S FAIR** (1964)
The emblem of the NY World's Fair of 1964, The Unisphere forms the shape of this bottle. Blue tone oceans, gray continents crossed by space flight routes. Emblem embossed in gold "1964 WORLD'S FAIR—1965." Stopper has Unisphere. Regal China, 11½" **12.00** **16.00**

☐ **NORTH DAKOTA** (1964)
Embossed memorial picture of a pioneer family in NORTH DAKOTA—75" embossed in gold in banner. Yellows, greens and browns. Regal China, 11¾" **45.00** **55.00**

Price Range

☐ **NORTHERN PIKE** (1977)
Replica of the Northern Pike. Green and yellow
with pointed head. The sixth in a series of bottles
designed for the National Fresh Water Fishing
Hall of Fame. 9″ 10.00 18.00

☐ **NUTCRACKER TOY SOLDIER** (1978)
Figurine based on the character the toy soldier
in the ballet *The Nutcracker Suite.* This is not part
of the opera series. Small man dressed in red,
white uniform with blue suspenders and gold trim.
The music box plays a selection from *The Parade
of the Toy Soldiers.* 12½″ 215.00 250.00

☐ **OHIO** (1966)
Bottle in shape of state. One side bears state
seal, other side has pictures of state industries.
Regal China, 10″ 8.00 14.00

☐ **OHIO STATE FAIR** (1973)
A handsome bottle made of genuine Regal
China, created in honor of the 120th Ohio State
Fair, 10¾″ 5.00 9.00

☐ **OLYMPIAN** (1960)
Green urn decanter. Chariot horses, and warriors
design in white on light blue bottle. White glass
stopper, embossed base. Glass, 14″ 3.00 6.00

☐ **ONE HUNDRED FIRST AIRBORNE DIVISION**
(1977)
Honors the division known during World War II as
the Screaming Eagles. A gold flying eagle on top
a white pedestal. 14″ 7.00 11.00

☐ **OPALINE CRYSTAL** (1969)
Milk glass bottle, same pattern and embossing,
and stopper. Milk glass, 11½″ 4.00 8.00

☐ **OREGON** (1959)
Green-tone bottle to honor centennial of the
state. Depicting famous scenery on both sides.
Two beavers on bottle neck. Regal China, 8¾″ 30.00 40.00

☐ **PANDA** (1980)
Adult panda on the ground with two cubs climbing
the stump of a tree. Authenticated by Dr. Lester
Fisher, Director of the Lincoln Park Zoological
Gardens in Chicago 20.00 28.00

Price Range

☐ **PEARL HARBOR MEMORIAL** (1972)
Honoring the Pearl Harbor Survivors Association,
this handsome genuine Regal China bottle is em-
blazoned with the motto: "REMEMBER PEARL
HARBOR—KEEP AMERICA ALERT." The stop-
per features the official seal of the armed serv-
ices that were present December 7, 1941, those
were Army, Navy, Marine Corps, and Coast
Guard. The stopper is set off by an American
eagle. 11½" 17.00 23.00

☐ **PEARL HARBOR SURVIVORS ASSOCIATION**
(1976)
Medallion-shaped bottle with flying eagle in the
center with a blue background and white lettering
around the border. On the back, a scene of the
island, Oahu, with three battleships. 9¾" 8.00 12.00

☐ **PENNSYLVANIA** (1967)
Keystone-shaped bottle in blue tones. Decal of
state seal "HISTORIC PENNSYLVANIA—THE
KEYSTONE STATE" on front. Reverse: scenes
of history and industry. Keystone stopper with
gold "1776." Regal China, 11½" 3.00 7.00

☐ **PERMIAN BASIN OIL SHOW** (1972)
This dramatic genuine Regal China bottle is fashioned after an oil derrick and its attendant buildings. Commemorates the Permian Basin Oil
Show in Odessa, Texas, October 18 through 21,
1972. The building is inscribed: "The E. E. "Pop"
Harrison No. 1 well." The back of the flag says
"The oil industry provides energy, enterprise, em-
ployment for the nation." The stopper is fashioned in the shape of the logo for the Oil Field
Workers Show with their motto "let's go." 13" 4.00 8.00

☐ **PHEASANT** (1960)
Ring-necked pheasant with red-circled eyes,
green and blue head, and soft brown plumage
perched on a fence base. Regal China, 13" ... 18.00 26.00

☐ **PHEASANT** (1961)
Re-issued also: '63, '66, '67, '68. As above ... 11.00 15.00

☐ **PHI SIGMA KAPPA (CENTENNIAL SERIES)**
(1973)
A Regal China creation commemorating the

Price Range

100th Anniversary of this national fraternity dedicated to the promotion of brotherhood, the stimulation of scholarship, and the development of character. The fraternity insignia is in silver on a magenta background outlined in white and lavender **4.00 8.00**

☐ **PHOENICIAN** (1973)
An elegantly handcrafted genuine Regal China, heavily embellished with 22 karat gold and features a floral design on the front. Each bottle comes in its own handsome presentation case lined with velvet **6.00 10.00**

☐ **PIED PIPER OF HAMLET** (1974)
This charming bottle of genuine Regal China was especially produced for the United States Armed Forces in Europe as a commemorative of the famous German legend, the Pied Piper of Hamlet. 10¼" **4.00 8.00**

☐ **PONDEROSA** (1969)
The home of the Cartwrights of *Bonanza* TV fame. A replica of the Ponderosa Ranch log cabin in brown tones. Reverse: Lake Tahoe. Bottles in green lined box are worth more. Regal China, 7½" high, 10" wide **3.00 7.00**

☐ **PONDEROSA RANCH TOURIST** (1972)
Commemorating the one millionth tourist to the Ponderosa Ranch. This horseshoe shaped bottle of genuine Regal China features the Ponderosa Pine and "P" symbol that has made the ranch famous. The stopper is traditional ten gallon hat made famous by Dan Blocker. 11" **10.00 16.00**

☐ **PONY EXPRESS** (1968)
Clearly embossed figure of horse and Pony Express Rider with "SACRAMENTO, CALIF.—OCTOBER 1861" and "ST. JOSEPH, MO.—APRIL 1860" and stars around figure. Reverse: Map of the Pony Express route. Yellow & brown tones, 11" **3.00 7.00**

☐ **POODLE—GRAY & WHITE** (1970)
Both poodles sit up with one paw on a ball. The gray has a green banded ball embossed

Price Range

"PENNY," the white has a blue banded ball. Black eyes, and nose with a gold color on each. Regal China, 12", Pair **8.00 12.00**

☐ **PORTLAND ROSE FESTIVAL** (1972)
To commemorate the 64th Portland, Oregon Rose Festival which began in 1889. The Regal China bottle is encompassed in a garland of red roses which is commemorative of the oldest and largest rose show in America. On the reverse side, there is a brief description of the festival with the very poignant line, "For You A Rose In Portland Grows." 10¼" **6.00 10.00**

☐ **PORTOLA TREK** (1969)
This gold glass bottle has a painting of the Portola Trek reproduction in full color on the front. This bottle was issued to celebrate the 200th Anniversary of San Diego. 11" **4.00   8.00**

☐ **POULAN CHAIN SAW** (1979)
Replica of the Poulan Chain Saw with a plastic handle and blade. Green body with silver blade and black trim. 7" **20.00 24.00**

☐ **POWELL EXPEDITION** (1969)
Gold glass bottle with a full color painting depicting John Wesley Powell's survey of the Colorado River and his traversing the Grand Canyon. 11" **4.00   8.00**

☐ **PRETTY PERCH** (1980)
Spiny-finned fish with dark bands, touches of orange on the fins, the eighth in a series, this fish is used as the official seal of the National Fresh Water Fishing Hall of Fame. 9" **16.00 20.00**

☐ **PREAKNESS** (1970)
This bottle was issued to honor the 100th anniversary of the running of the Preakness. The body of the bottle is made up of a horseshoe surrounding the trophy awarded the Preakness winner, the Woodlawn Vase. In lettering on the horseshoe is "PIMLICO RACE COURSE". A wreath of daisies tops the horseshoe. The stopper is plain. Regal China, 11" **5.00   7.00**

☐ **PRIMA-DONNA** (1969)
Same as CAL-NEVA with PRIMA-DONNA CASINO and show girls on the emblem. 9¼" **4.00   8.00**

Price Range

☐ **QUEENSLAND** (1978)
In the shape of the province, Queensland, the
Sunshine State of Australia. Embossed lettering
and details, gold star on the back Medallion type
stopper with "Australia" in center. 8½" 16.00 22.00

☐ **RAINBOW TROUT** (1975)
Rainbow trout mounted on an oval plaque made
to look like wood. Produced for the National
Fresh Water Fishing Hall of Fame. Their official
seal is on the back. 7½" 10.00 14.00

☐ **RALPH CENTENNIAL** (1973)
Made of genuine Regal China, this bottle was designed to commemorate the 100th Anniversary
of the Ralph Grocery Company in California. The
bottle depicts two sides of a coin struck especially for the occasion and an early version of a
Ralphs delivery wagon. 7¾" 12.00 16.00

☐ **RAM** (1958)
Stylized Ram in soft tans and browns. Calender
mounted on green base, and a round thermometer in the curve of the horn (without thermometer,
value is less). Regal China, 12½" 88.00 95.00

☐ **RAMADA INN** (1976)
A Ramada Inn attendant is shown as a sentinel
at the door to a small narrow building of red,
white, and blue. Gold shingles with a black lid on
the chimney. 11" 5.00 10.00

☐ **REDWOOD** (1967)
Pyramid shaped bottle, Coast Redwoods embossed on front in tones of brown and green.
"REDWOOD EMPIRE OF CALIFORNIA" lettered
below tree. Reverse: scenes of Redwood country. Regal China, 12¾" 4.50 7.00

☐ **REGENCY** (1972)
This elegantly handcrafted Regal China bottle is
heavily embellished with fired 22 karat gold and
features a bouquet of tiny flowers about its mid-
section. Each bottle comes in its own handsome
dark red presentation case lined with velvet ... 8.00 12.00

☐ **REIDSVILLE** (1973)
This bottle was issued to honor the city of Reidsville, North Carolina on the occasion of its centen-

Price Range

nial. The bottle is circular with leaves surrounding a central plaque bearing the slogan "YESTER-DAY TODAY TOMORROW." The bottle is blue and the stopper is circular and bears the date "1973." Regal China, 12" 7.00 10.00

☐ **RENEE THE FOX** (1974)
This interesting Regal China bottle represents the companion for the International Association of Jim Beam Bottle and Specialty Group's mascot. Renee the Fox is the life long companion of Ren-nie the Fox. 12½" 11.00 14.00

☐ **RENNIE THE SURFER** (1975)
Rennie the fox dressed in an old-fashioned bath-ing suit and a black top hat rides a small surf-board. He holds a bottle of Beam behind him with one hand. 12½" 20.00 24.00

☐ **RENNIE THE RUNNER** (1974)
Rennie the fox is shown running in his brown run-ning suit, white running shoes, and black top hat. On a string around his neck is the seal of the In-ternational Association of Beam Clubs. 12½" .. 10.00 15.50

☐ **RENO** (1968)
"100 YEARS—RENO" embossed over skyline of downtown Reno. "THE BIGGEST LITTLE CITY IN THE WORLD" lettered over skyline. Reverse: "RENO 100 YEARS" and scenes of Reno. Regal China, 9¼" 4.00 8.00

☐ **REPUBLIC OF TEXAS** (1980)
Star-shaped bottle with gold spout, handle and top. White with a red border, symbols of the state are represented on the front. The stopper is a gold star. 12¾" 20.00 25.00

☐ **RICHARDS—NEW MEXICO** (1967)
Created for Richards Distributing Company of Al-buquerque, New Mexico. Lettered "NEW MEX-ICO" and "RICHARD SAYS DISCOVER NEW MEXICO," in blue. Embossed scene of Taos Rueblo. Picture of Richard on stopper and front. Regal China, 11" 3.00 7.00

Price Range

☐ **ROBIN** (1969)
An olive gray bird with a soft red breast, dark
toned head and tail. The robin has a yellow beak
and stands on a tree trunk with an embossed
branch and leaves. Regal China, 13½" 8.00   12.00

☐ **ROCKY MARCIANO** (1973)
A handsome genuine Regal China bottle in honor
of Rocky Marciano, the world's only undefeated
boxing champion. The bottle takes the shape of
a rock, with a likeness of Rocky Marciano on the
front. The back of the bottle features Marciano's
complete professional record of 49 fights, all vic-
tories, 43 knockouts and 6 decisions 13.00   17.00

☐ **ROYAL CRYSTAL** (1959)
Starburst design embossed on both sides on this
clear flint glass decanter. Gold label on neck and
flat black stopper. Starburst theme appears on
label and stopper. Glass, 11½" 4.00   8.00

☐ **ROYAL DI MONTE** (1957)
Mottled design, black and white bottle. Hand
painted with 22 karat gold and bordered in gold.
Gold & black stopper. Regal China, 15½" 70.00   80.00

☐ **ROYAL EMPEROR** (1958)
Made in the shape of a classic Greek urn. Warrior
figure with spear, helmet and fret design in white
on purple-black glass. White glass stopper.
Glass, 14" 4.00   8.00

☐ **ROYAL GOLD DIAMOND** (1964)
Diamond-shaped decanter set on a flaring base,
all in mottled gold. Gold-chain holds label. Regal
China, 12" 50.00   60.00

☐ **ROYAL GOLD ROUND** (1956)
Mottled with 22 karat gold, in classic round shape
with graceful pouring spout, and curved handle.
Gold neck chain holds label. Regal China, 12"   125.00   175.00

☐ **ROYAL OPAL** (1957)
A round, handled bottle, of Opal glass. Embossed
geometric design on one side. White glass stop-
per. Bottle made by Wheaton Glass of Millville,
New Jersey. Same bottle in silver was used for
Harolds Club, 25th Anniversary. Glass, 10¾" . .   6.00   10.00

Price Range

☐ **ROYAL PORCELAIN** (1955)
Gleaming black decanter, tapered with a large flared pouring lip, white stopper, gold cord and tassel. Regal China, 14½" 420.00 520.00

☐ **ROYAL ROSE** (1963)
Decanter, gold embossed with hand painted roses on a background of soft blue, gold spout, stopper, base and handle. Regal China, 17" ... 45.00 55.00

☐ **RUBY CRYSTAL** (1967)
Amethyst colored, patterned embossed bottle. Swirl glass stopper. When bottle is filled with bourbon it's ruby red. Sunburst pattern on bottom. Amethyst glass, 11½" 7.00 11.00

☐ **RUIDOSO DOWNS** (1968)
A round decanter with a unique "horsehead" stopper. Embossed silver horseshoe, branding iron and cowboy hat, "RUIDOSO DOWNS—NEW MEXICO, WORLD'S RICHEST HORSE RACE" on front. Reverse: Red, white and blue emblem. The bottle is known in "Pointed & Flat Ears". Regal China, 12¾" 18.00 22.00
Flat Ears 3.00 6.00

☐ **SAHARA INVITATIONAL BOTTLE** (1971)
Introduced in honor of the Del Webb 1971 Sahara Invitational Pro-Am Golf Tournament. The prominent feature of this Regal China Bottle is a large "Del Webb Pro-Am 1971" golf ball atop a red tee on the face. Listed on the back are the winners of this annual contest from 1958 through 1970. 12" 3.00 7.00

☐ **SAN DIEGO** (1968)
Issued by the Beam Company for the 200th Anniversary of its founding in 1769. Honoring Junipero Serra, Francisca missionary. Serra and Conquistador embossed on gold front. Regal China, 10" 3.00 7.00

☐ **SANTA FE** (1960)
Governor's Palace blue-toned sky, date 1610–1960 (350th Anniversary). Navaho woman with Indian basket on reverse. Gold lettering. Regal China, 10" 205.00 250.00

Price Range

☐ **SCREECH OWL** (1979)
Either red or gray shading. Birds are bisque replicas of screech owls, authenticated by Dr. Lester Fisher, director of the Lincoln Zoological Gardens in Chicago. 9¾" 18.00 26.00

☐ **SEAFAIR TROPHY RACE** (1972)
This dramatic genuine Regal China creation commemorates the Seattle Seafair Trophy Race, August 6, 1972, and features an unlimited hydroplane at speed with picturesque Mt. Rainier in the background. 11½" 8.00 12.00

☐ **SEATTLE WORLD'S FAIR** (1962)
The Space Needle, as this bottle is known, embossed in gold on one side, "CENTURY 21" on the other. Pylon shaped with color scenes of fruit, airplanes over mountains, salmon, etc. Stopper is the Fair's revolving restaurant. Regal China, 13½" 18.00 23.00

☐ **SHORT DANCING SCOT** (1963)
A short barrel-shaped bottle with the dancing Scot, and music box in the base. Square shaped stopper, a rare bottle. Glass, 11" 70.00 80.00

☐ **SHORT TIMER** (1975)
Brown army shoes with army helmet sitting on top. Produced for all who have served in the armed forces. 8" 33.00 40.00

☐ **SHRINERS** (1975)
Embossed camel on front of bottle in blue, green, and brown with bright red blanket flowing from the camel's saddle. A gold scimitar and star centered with a fake ruby is on the back. 10½" ... 15.00 20.00

☐ **SHRINERS PYRAMID** (1975)
This bottle was issued by the El Kahir Temple of Cedar Rapids, Iowa. It is shaped like a pyramid with embossing on the sides of the various insignia of the Shriners. The bottle is white and brown and made to look as if it were made of brick. The stopper is the very top of the pyramid. Regal China, 5" 14.00 18.00

Price Range

☐ **SHRINERS RAJAH** (1977)
Pretzel-shaped bottle with a Shriner's sword in the center. Stopper is red and shaped like a Shriner's cap with a black tassel. 8¾″ **18.00**   **26.00**

☐ **SHRINER'S TEMPLE** (1972)
This beautiful Regal China bottle features the traditional symbols of Moila Templei the scimitar, star and crescent, the fez and the pyramid with the stopper as the head of a Sphinx. This bottle is unique in that it features three simulated precious stones, two of them in the handle of the sword and the third is the center point of the star. 11½″ **30.00**   **40.00**

☐ **SIGMA NU FRATERNITY** (1977)
Rectangular bottle with the badge and coat of arms of the Sigma Nu Fraternity embossed on the front. White and gold lettering and designs. Medallion type stopper **9.00**   **13.00**

☐ **SMITH'S NORTH SHORE CLUB** (1972)
Commemorating Smith's North Shore Club, at Crystal Bay, Lake Tahoe. This striking genuine Regal China bottle features the anchor, symbol of the club and is topped by a giant golden golf ball. 12″ **10.00**   **16.00**

☐ **SMOKED CRYSTAL** (1964)
Dark green in tone, and resembling a Genie's magic bottle, this tall bottle has a bulbous embossed base, and a slender tapering shape, topped by an embossed glass topper. Glass, 14″   **7.00**   **11.00**

☐ **SNOW GOOSE** (1979)
Replica of a white goose with black wingtips. Authenticated by Dr. Lester Fisher, director of Lincoln Park Zoological Gardens in Chicago. 11½″   **15.00**   **20.00**

☐ **SOUTH CAROLINA** (1970)
The Palmetto State celebrated its tri-centennial, 1670–1970. Palmetto trees are embossed on the outline map of the state which is outlined in gold. The South Carolina Dispensary is on the back. 9¼″ **3.00**   **7.00**

☐ **SOUTH DAKOTA—MOUNT RUSHMORE** (1969)
The faces of Washington, Jefferson, T. Roosevelt, and Lincoln are shown in relief in white with

	Price Range	

blue sky and green forest. This landmark is the Mount Rushmore National Memorial. Reverse: scroll with information about Memorial. Regal China, 10½" **4.00** **8.00**

☐ **SOUTH FLORIDA FOX ON DOLPHIN** (1980)
A fox dressed in hunting garb rides a dolphin. This bottle was sponsored by the South Florida Beam Bottle and Specialties Club which is located in Miami. 14½" **16.00** **20.00**

☐ **SPENGER'S FISH GROTTO** (1977)
Designed as a small boat with the captain at the helm. Brown, yellow and blue, made in conjunction with Spenger's Fish Grotto Restaurant in Berkeley, California. **22.00** **28.00**

☐ **SPORTS CAR CLUB OF AMERICA** (1976)
Six-sided front with a Ridge-Whetworth wire wheel in the center on pedestal foot. Brief history of the club on the back. 11" **5.00** **10.00**

☐ **STATUE OF LIBERTY** (1975)
Figural bottle with gold embossed Statue of Liberty on the front with light blue background. Green base with plaque. 12½" **8.00** **12.00**

☐ **ST. BERNARD** (1979)
Replica of a St. Bernard with a small cask of Beam around his neck held by a real leather collar. 6½" **50.00** **60.00**

☐ **ST. LOUIS ARCH** (1964)
The silhouette of St. Louis with the Mississippi River flowing past. The famous stainless steel arch frames the bottle "ST. LOUIS, GATEWAY TO THE WEST" and "200 YEARS" embossed in gold. The ferry boat "ADMIRAL" is on the back. Regal China 11" **20.00** **30.00**

☐ **ST. LOUIS ARCH—RE-ISSUE** (1967)
Same as above **18.00** **24.00**

☐ **ST. LOUIS STATUE** (1972)
This handsome Regal China bottle features the famous statue of St. Louis on horseback atop its pedestal base. The entire statue is fired gold. The back bears the inscription, "Greater St. Louis Area Beam and Specialties Club." 13¼" **10.00** **14.00**

Price Range

☐ **STURGEON** (1980)
Exclusive issue for a group that advocates the
preservation of sturgeons. Long brown colored
fish. 6¼" **15.00   20.00**

☐ **STUTZ BEARCAT 1914** (1977)
Either yellow and black or gray and black. Replica
of the 1914, 4-cylinder Stutz Bearcat. Authentic
details with movable windshield. Stopper is under
plastic trunk and spare wheel. 7" **55.00   64.00**

☐ **SUBMARINE REDFIN** (1970)
Embossed submarine on ocean-blue background. "MANITOWOC SUBMARINE MEMO-
RIAL ASSOCIATION" in black. Round stopper
with map of Wisconsin. Regal China. 11½" . . . **5.00   9.00**

☐ **SUPERDOME** (1975)
Replica of the Louisiana Superdome which
opened in August 1975. White and gold with
black lettering around the top. 6½" **6.00   10.00**

☐ **SWAGMAN** (1979)
Replica of an Australian hobo called a Swagman
who roamed that country looking for work during
the depression. He wears a grayish outfit with red
kerchief around his neck. A brown dog and a
sheep are curled around his feet. 14" **14.00   19.00**

☐ **SYDNEY OPERA HOUSE** (1977)
Replica of the building housing the Sydney Opera
in Sydney, Australia. Music box is in the base.
8½" **23.00   29.00**

☐ **TALL DANCING SCOT** (1964)
A small Scotsman encased in a glass bubble in
the base dances to the music of the base. A tall
pylon shaped glass bottle with a tall stopper. No
dates on these bottles. Glass, 17" **12.00   18.00**

☐ **TAVERN SCENE** (1959)
Two "beer stein" tavern scenes are embossed
on sides, framed in wide gold band on this round
decanter. Regal China, 11½" **65.00   75.00**

☐ **TELEPHONE** (1975)
Replica of a 1907 phone of the Magneto Wallset
type which was used from 1890 until the 1930's.
9½" **55.00   65.00**

Price Range

☐ **TEN-PIN** (1980)
Designed as a bowling pin with two red bands around the shoulder and the neck. Remainder of the pin is white, screw lid. 12″ 4.00 8.00

☐ **THAILAND** (1969)
Embossed elephant in the jungle and "THAILAND—A NATION OF WONDERS" on the front. Reverse: A map of Thailand and a dancer. Regal China, 12½″ 2.00 6.00

☐ **THOMAS FLYER 1907** (1976)
Replica of the 1907 Thomas Flyer, 6-70 Model K Flyabout which was a luxury car of its day. Comes in blue or white. Plastic rear trunk covers the lid to the bottle 50.00 60.00

☐ **TIFFINY POODLE** (1973)
Genuine Regal China bottle created in honor of Tiffiny, the poodle mascot of the National Association of the Jim Beam Bottle & Specialties Clubs. 8½″ 20.00 25.00

☐ **THE TIGERS** (1977)
Tiger head on top of a football which reads "The Tigers." Honors an Australian football team. 7¾″ 20.00 24.00

☐ **TITIAN** (1980)
Urn-shaped bottle, reproduces the designs created by the Venetian artist Titian in his oil paintings. Long fluted neck, with double scrolled handle. 12½″ 12.00 16.00

☐ **TREASURE CHEST** (1979)
Partially opened treasure chest with gold coins, pearls, and jewelry. The lid is a screw top. 6″ 13.00 18.00

☐ **TROUT UNLIMITED** (1977)
Large traditionally shaped bottle with a large yellow trout placed across the front of the bottle at the shoulder. Stopper reads "Limit Your Kill, Don't Kill Your Limit." To honor the Trout Unlimited Conservation Organization. 12″ 11.00 16.00

☐ **TRUTH OR CONSEQUENCES FIESTA** (1974)
A ruggedly handsome Regal China bottle in honor of Ralph Edward's famous radio and television show and the city of Truth or Consequences, New Mexico. 10″ 5.00 9.00

Price Range

☐ **TURQUOISE CHINA JUG** (1966)
Alternating bands of scrolled designs spiral up
the turquoise decanter. Regal China, 13¼″ ...   4.00   8.00

☐ **TWIN BRIDGES BOTTLE** (1971)
Designed to commemorate the largest twin
bridge complex of its kind in the world. The twin
bridges connect Delaware and New Jersey and
serve as major link between key east coast cities.
Handsomely accented in gold and bearing the
shield of the Twin Bridges Beam Bottle and Specialty Club, this Regal China bottle portrays the
twin spans on the front and provides a descriptive
story on the back. The stopper is a replica of the
bridge toll house. 10½″ 42.00   52.00

☐ **U.S. OPEN** (1972)
Whimsically depicts Uncle Sam's traditional hat
holding a full set of golf clubs. This charming
Regal China creation honors the U.S. Open Golf
Tourney at the famous Pebble Beach course in
California. 10½″ 10.00   14.00

☐ **VENDOME DRUMMER'S WAGON** (1975)
Replica of a delivery wagon, green and cream
wood with yellow wheels which are plastic. Honored the Vendomes of Beverly Hills, California, a
food chain store which was first established in
1937. 8½″ 60.00   70.00

☐ **V.F.W. BOTTLE** (1971)
A handsome Regal China creation designed to
commemorate the 50th Anniversary of the Department of Indiana V.F.W. This proclamation is
made on the neck of the bottle, in a plaque in the
shape of the state of Indiana, over a striking reproduction of the medal insignia of the V.F.W.
9¾″ 7.00   11.00

☐ **VIKING** (1973)
The Viking is holding a shield and sword and is
leaning against a stone. The words "MINNE-
SOTA, LAND OF THE VIKINGS" appear on the
shield. On the stone is recorded the Viking exploration of 1362. The stopper is his helmet. Regal
China, 14″ 14.00   18.00

Price Range

☐ **VOLKSWAGEN COMMEMORATIVE BOTTLE (2) COLORS** (1977)
Commemorating the Volkswagen Beetle, the largest selling single production model vehicle in automotive history. Handcrafted of genuine Regal China, this unique and exciting bottle will long remain a memento for bottle collectors the world over, 14½" 30.00 36.00

☐ **WALLEYE PIKE** (1977)
Tall blue bottle with a large figurine of a yellow pike at the base. Designed for the National Fresh Water Fishing Hall of Fame in Hayward, Wisconsin 8.00 12.00

☐ **WASHINGTON** (1975)
A state series bottle to commemorate the Evergreen State, which was honored with this green bottle featuring an apple and a fir tree in bas-relief, 10" 13.00 17.00

☐ **WASHINGTON—THE EVERGREEN STATE** (1974)
The club bottle for the Evergreen State Beam Bottle and Specialties Club is contoured to the shape of the state. The green bottle has evergreen trees embossed on it and a unique stopper with an exact replica of a small evergreen branch in a transparent enclosure, 10" 12.00 18.00

☐ **WASHINGTON STATE BICENTENNIAL** (1976)
Patriot dressed in black and orange holding drum. Liberty bell and plaque in front of drummer, 10" 12.00 20.00

☐ **WATERMAN** (1980)
In pewter or glazed. Boatman at helm of his boat wearing rain gear. Glazed version in yellow and brown, 13½" 150.00 200.00

☐ **WESTERN SHRINE ASSOCIATION** (1980)
Designed to commemorate the Shriners' convention in 1980 which was held in Phoenix, Arizona. Rounded surface with a desert scene, red stopper designed as a fez with a tassel 28.00 32.00

☐ **WEST VIRGINIA** (1963)
Waterfall scene in blue and green with gold embossed "BLACKWATER FALLS—WEST VIRGINIA—1863 CENTENNIAL 1963" surrounded

Price Range

by scrolled picture frame bottle. Reverse: State bird-red cardinal and gold "35" in a star. Bear's head and maple leaf on each side of stopper, 10¼" 170.00 195.00

☐ **WHITE FOX** (1969)
This bottle was issued for the second anniversary of the Jim Beam Bottles and Specialties Club, Berkeley, California. It shows a standing fox with his arms folded behind him. He is wearing a white jacket and a gold medallion and chain. The medallion displays a happy birthday message to the Berkeley Club. 12½" 40.00 50.00

☐ **WISCONSIN MUSKIE BOTTLE** (1971)
This striking Regal China sculpture pays tribute to the state fish of Wisconsin, as the mighty Muskellunge dances on his powerful tail in a burst of gold flecked blue water. 14" 18.00 26.00

☐ **WOODPECKER** (1969)
Bright glazed red head, white breast and markings, black beak and dark wings and tails. Woody grips a tree trunk base. Regal China, 13½" ... 7.00 11.00

☐ **WYOMING** (1965)
An embossed bucking bronco with a cowboy 'hanging' on with mountains in the background and "WYOMING—THE EQUALITY STATE" in gold on tones of blue and tan. A rectangle shape of a pyramid, with a gold buffalo on the stopper. Reverse: State bird, flower, and Old Faithful. Regal China, 12" 55.00 65.00

☐ **YELLOW KATZ** (1967)
The emblem of the Katz Department Stores (Missouri), a green-eyed meowing cat, is the head (and stopper) of this bottle. The pylon shaped, orange color body has a curved tail. The Katz commemorates the 50th birthday of the store, 14½" 20.00 28.00

☐ **YOSEMITE** (1967)
Oval shaped bottle with scenes from the Park, and trees, embossed on the front. "YOSEMITE CALIFORNIA" lettered on front. Gold pine tree on stopper, 11" 3.00 7.00

Price Range

☐ **ZIMMERMAN BELL—COLBALT** (1976)
Bell-shaped bottle in colbalt blue with flowers and
foliage embossed in blue and gold. Designed for
Zimmerman Liquor Store of Chicago, 12½" ...　**10.00　15.00**

☐ **ZIMMERMAN BELL—LIGHT BLUE** (1976)
Bell-shaped bottle in light blue with lavender lid.
Floral and foliage designs embossed on the front,
12½" ....　**10.00　15.00**

☐ **ZIMMERMAN BLUE BEAUTY** (1969)
The name "ZIMMERMAN'S LIQUORS" is embossed in bright gold on a sky blue bottle decorated with flowers and scrolls. Reverse has Chicago skyline embossed on blue toned bottle.
Arrow with "ZIMMERMAN'S" points to store.
Regal China, 10" ....　**9.00　13.00**

☐ **ZIMMERMAN CHERUBS PINK & LAVENDER**
(1968)
Winged cherubs and leaves and vines are embossed over the surface of these slender round
bottles. They were issued for the Zimmerman Liquor Stores of Chicago. Regal China, 11½" ....　**4.00　8.00**

☐ **ZIMMERMAN—GLASS** (1969)
A white outline of the Chicago skyline with "ZIM-
MERMAN'S" store on front of this glass bottle.
White stopper has Max Zimmerman's portrait.
Glass, 11¼" ....　**8.00　14.00**

☐ **ZIMMERMAN'S THE PEDDLER BOTTLE** (1971)
This unusual bottle in genuine Regal China was
made in honor of Zimmerman's, the world's largest liquor store, in Chicago, Illinois. Max Zimmerman, The Peddler himself, who specializes in personal service and works the counters of the store
himself, is famous for his Stetson hat and cowboy
boots. He is affectionately known in the trade as
Max the Hat. Zimmerman's has always been active in merchandising Beam's collector's bottles.
12" ....　**12.00　16.00**

☐ **ZIMMERMAN—TWO HANDLED JUG** (1965)
Shaped and colored like an avocado, this dark
green bottle has embossed grapes and grape
leaves on the front, and two side handles. Regal
China, 10¼" ....　**85.00　120.00**

BISCHOFF

Founded at Trieste, Italy in 1777, Bischoffs was issuing decorative figurals in the 18th century long before the establishment of most companies who presently issue figural bottles. The early specimens are extremely rare, because of limited production and the loss over the years. Since sales do not occur often enough for firm values to be established, they are not included in this listing further.

Imported into the U.S. in 1949, the modern Bischoffs attracted little notice at first due to lack of interest of Americans in bottle collecting at that time. Most sales were made for gift giving. The bottles are produced by the foremost glass, pottery, and porcelain companies in Bohemia, Czechoslovakia, Murano, Italy, Austria, and Germany.

KORD BOHEMIAN DECANTERS

Handblown, hand painted glass bottles were created in Czechoslovakia by the Kord Company, based on a long tradition of Bohemian cut, engraved, etched, and flashed glass. Typical Bohemia themes were used to decorate the decanters. Complete bottles with stoppers and labels are very difficult to find today.

Cut glass and ruby-etched decanters, traditional forms of Bohemian glass, were imported into the U.S. in the early 1950s. Cut glass specimens are of lead crystal with hand cutting. The ruby-etched decanters are executed in the usual two-layer manner with the exterior ruby glass etched through to show the clear glass beneath. Designs are quite elaborate including leaping deer, castles, scrolls, foliage, wild birds, grapes, and latticework. The overall color can be amber or topaz with ruby the most common.

When the under layer of glass is opaque, the cut designs show very distinctly. Several of the etched decanters, made in Austria and Germany, should have labels indicating the place of origin. Most Bischoff Kord Bohemian decanters had matching sets of glasses.

The Double Dolphin, Hunter & Lady, and Horse's Head decanters are thick, handblown glass made in Czechoslovakia. Not as rare as the ruby-etched decanter since importation continues, they have value only when complete with stoppers.

□ **AMBER FLOWERS** (1952)
 A two-toned glass decanter. Amber flowers, stems and leaves on a Pale Amber background.

Price Range

The long tapering neck is etched in panels and circles. The stopper is dark amber and hand-ground to fit, 15½ " 30.00 40.00

☐ **AMBER LEAVES** (1952)
Multi-tone bottle with dark amber leaves, and flowers, on pale amber etched background. Stopper neck and base are cut in circles and panels. Round bottle with long neck, 13½" 30.00 40.00

☐ **ANISETTE** (1948–51)
Clear glass bottle with two handles and a ground glass stopper. Clear glass ribbing on sides of bottle, 11" 20.00 30.00

☐ **BOHEMIAN RUBY ETCHED** (1949–51)
Etched design in typical Bohemian style, castle, birds, deer and scrolls and curlecues in clear glass, ruby-red color flashed on bottle, except for etching and cut neck. Ground glass, etched stoppers on this tall, round, decanter, 15½", tapered neck. 30.00 40.00

☐ **CORONET CRYSTAL** (1952)
A broad band of flowers, leaves and scrolls circle this multi-toned bottle. The designs are cut in dark amber glass revealing the opaque pale amber background. Stopper neck and base are cut in circles and panels. A round tall bottle 14" 30.00 40.00

☐ **CUT GLASS DECANTER (BLACKBERRY)** (1951)
A geometric design hand-cut over-all on this lead glass decanter. The stopper is cut and ground to fit the bottle, 10½" 32.00 42.00

☐ **CZECH HUNTER** (1958)
Round thick clear glass body with green collar and green buttons and heavy round glass base. The stopper-head is of glass with a jaunty green Bohemian hat with feather crowning, pop-eyes, white mustache and red button nose, 8½" 18.00 26.00

☐ **CZECH HUNTER'S LADY** (1958)
"Mae West" shaped decanter of cracked clear glass. Green collar at neck of bottle with amber glass stopper-head. Brown hair, glasses and yellow earrings make up the lady's head. She's taller than the Hunter, 10" 18.00 26.00

Price Range

☐ **DANCING—COUNTRY SCENE** (1950)
Clear glass hand-blown decanter with hand-painted and signed colorful scene of peasant boy and girl doing a country dance beside a tree, Bohemian village background. Spider bold white lines painted on bottle and stopper, 12¼" **25.00 35.00**

☐ **DANCING—PEASANT SCENE** (1950)
Colorful peasants in costume, dancing to music of bagpipes, hand painted and signed. The decanter is of pale amber glass, fine black lines painted on bottle. Stopper is ground to fit and fine line painted, 12" **25.00 35.00**

☐ **DOUBLE-DOLPHIN** (1949–69)
Fish-shaped twin bottles joined at the bellies. They are made of handblown clear glass and have fins and "fish tail" ground glass stoppers, each has fish eyes and mouth **20.00 30.00**

☐ **FLYING GEESE PITCHER** (1952)
Same as below, but with green glass handle and stopper. This pitcher has a glass base **15.00 25.00**

☐ **FLYING GEESE PITCHER** (1957)
Clear crystal, handled pitcher. Hand-painted and signed, colorful scene of wild geese flying over Czech marshes. Gold neck, pouring lip, and stopper, 9½" **15.00 25.00**

☐ **HORSE HEAD** (1947–69)
Pale amber colored bottle in the shape of a horse's head. Embossed details of horse's features are impressed on this hand-blown bottle. Round pouring spout on top, 8" **15.00 25.00**

☐ **JUNGLE PARROT—AMBER GLASS** (1952)
Same as below, except bottle is flashed a yellow-amber color **25.00 35.00**

☐ **JUNGLE PARROT—RUBY GLASS** (1952)
Profusely hand-etched jungle scene with parrot, monkeys, insects, flowers, leaves, cut through the ruby flashed body. A tall round decanter with tapering etched neck, 15½" **20.00 30.00**

Price Range

☐ **OLD COACH BOTTLE** (1948)
Old time coach and white horses hand-painted on
a handblown Bohemian glass bottle pale amber
color. Round ground glass stopper. Bottle and
stopper are both numbered, 10" 25.00   35.00

☐ **OLD SLEIGH BOTTLE** (1949)
Hand painted, signed, Czech winter old-time
sleigh scene. Driver sits on lead horse and blows
trumpet, passengers on top of coach are pouring
drinks. Glass decanter has fine white trace lines.
Glass stopper is clear and painted, 10" 22.00   32.00

☐ **WILD GEESE—AMBER GLASS** (1952)
Same as below, except bottle is a flashed yellow-
amber color 25.00   35.00
Matching glasses were made for both the Ruby
& Amber.

☐ **WILD GEESE—RUBY GLASS** (1952)
Etched design of wild geese rising above the
marshes. A tall round decanter with tapering,
etched neck, and etched hand-ground stopper.
Ruby-red color "flashed" on bottle, 15½" 25.00   35.00

VENETIAN GLASS FIGURALS

Bischoff's Venetian Glass Figurals are made in limited editions by
the Serguso Glass Company in Murano, Italy, a town historically famous for its artistic glass. The Bischoff figurals, originally containing
the firm's liquors, are quite unique in design and color. Chief themes
depict natural subjects such as birds, mammals, and fish.

☐ **BLACK CAT** (1969)
Glass black cat, with curled tail, 12" long 18.00   25.00

☐ **DOG—ALABASTER** (1969)
Seated alabaster glass dog, 13" 28.00   38.00

☐ **DOG—DACHSHUND** (1966)
Alabaster long dog with brown tones, 19" long   35.00   45.00

☐ **DUCK** (1964)
Alabaster glass tinted pink & green, long neck,
up-raised wings, 11" long 42.00   52.00

☐ **FISH—MULTICOLOR** (1964)
Round fat fish, alabaster glass. Green, rose, yel-
low 18.00   25.00

Price Range

☐ **FISH—RUBY** (1969)
Long, flat, ruby glass fish, 12″ long **18.00   25.00**

CERAMIC DECANTERS & FIGURALS

Many of the most interesting, attractive and valuable Bischoff bottles are made of ceramic, stoneware or pottery. They have a "rougher" surface appearance than the glass or porcelain bottles. Values quoted are for complete bottles with handles, spouts and stoppers in mint condition.

	Price Range	
☐ **AFRICAN HEAD** (1962)	**14.00**	**20.00**
☐ **BELL HOUSE** (1960)	**30.00**	**40.00**
☐ **BELL TOWER** (1960)	**15.00**	**30.00**
☐ **BOY (CHINESE) FIGURAL** (1962)	**30.00**	**40.00**
☐ **BOY (SPANISH) FIGURAL** (1961)	**25.00**	**35.00**
☐ **CLOWN WITH BLACK HAIR** (1963)	**30.00**	**40.00**
☐ **CLOWN WITH RED HAIR** (1963)	**18.00**	**25.00**
☐ **DEER FIGURAL** (1969)	**21.00**	**27.00**
☐ **EGYPTIAN DANCING FIGURAL** (1961)	**13.00**	**19.00**
☐ **EGYPTIAN PITCHER 2 MUSICIANS** (1969) . . .	**18.00**	**25.00**
☐ **EGYPTIAN PITCHER 3 MUSICIANS** (1959) . . .	**20.00**	**28.00**
☐ **FLORAL CANTEEN** (1969)	**20.00**	**28.00**
☐ **FRUIT CANTEEN** (1969)	**13.00**	**19.00**
☐ **GIRL IN CHINESE COSTUME** (1962)	**30.00**	**40.00**
☐ **GIRL IN SPANISH COSTUME** (1961)	**30.00**	**40.00**
☐ **GREEK VASE DECANTER** (1969)	**13.00**	**19.00**
☐ **MASK—GRAY FACE** (1963)	**16.00**	**26.00**
☐ **OIL & VINEGAR CRUETS BLACK & WHITE** (1959)	**18.00**	**25.00**
☐ **VASE—BLACK & GOLD** (1959)	**21.00**	**27.00**
☐ **WATCHTOWER** (1960)	**13.00**	**19.00**

BORGHINI

Borghini bottles, exported from Pisa, Italy, are ceramics of modernistic style, dealing mostly with historical themes. Their sizes vary more than bottles from other manufacturers. Easily obtainable in the U.S., as is often the case with imported bottles, their prices vary greatly in different parts of the country. The lowest values tend to be in areas either closest to the points of distribution or heaviest in retail sale. Most of the recent Borghini bottles are stamped "BORGHINI COLLECTION MADE IN ITALY."

	Price Range	
☐ **CATS**		
Black with red ties, 6″	11.00	15.00
☐ **CATS**		
Black with red ties, 12″	10.00	13.00
☐ **FEMALE HEAD**		
Ceramic, 9½″	11.00	15.00
☐ **PENGUIN**		
Black & white, 6″	8.00	11.00
☐ **PENGUIN** (1969)		
Black & white, 12″	12.00	16.00

MARIE BRIZARD

The Marie Brizard bottles are ceramics, usually deep brown in color with distinctive modeling. New editions are issued only occasionally. The Chessman series, which consists of bottles representing figures from the chessboard, are their most popular products. Among the more valuable of the Brizard bottles is a large model of a Parisian kiosk or newsstand, standing 11½″ high.

	Price Range	
☐ **BISHOP**		
Ceramic chessmen, dark brown	11.00	14.00
☐ **CASTLE**		
Ceramic chessmen, dark brown	6.00	9.00
☐ **KIOSK**		
Colorful Parisian signpost, 11½″	13.00	19.00
☐ **KNIGHT**		
Ceramic chessmen, dark brown	7.00	10.00
☐ **LADY IN ERMINE CAPE**		
7″	9.00	13.00
☐ **PAWN**		
Ceramic chessman, dark brown	7.00	10.00

Left to Right: **Brizard Castle (1952),** *ceramic chessman, dark brown, 6 oz.* **$6.00–$9.00; Brizard Pawn (1962),** *ceramic chessman, dark brown, 6 oz.* **$7.00–$10.00; Brizard Knight (1962),** *ceramic chessman, dark brown, 6 oz.* **$7.00–$10.00**

EZRA BROOKS BOTTLES

Ezra Brooks rivals Jim Beam as one of the chief whiskey companies in America manufacturing figural bottles. First issuing figurals in 1964, Brooks started a decade later than Beam, but became competitive because of effective promotion and a heavy production schedule. Due to the creative design, imaginative choice of subjects and an efficient distribution network, the Ezra Brooks bottles are collected throughout the country.

Some of the Brooks figurals deal with traditional themes for bottles such as sports and transportation. But Brooks has designed bottles based on subjects that are both surprising and striking. The very realistic *Maine Lobster* is among its masterpieces—a bottle that looks good enough to eat. One of the most popular series of their bottles represents various antiques, a subject neglected by most manufacturers. These include an Edison phonograph, a grandfather clock, and a Spanish cannon.

While the number of bottles produced fluctuates each year, Brooks usually adds new editions annually, often highlighting an American historical event or anniversary.

The Ezra Brooks Distilling Co., located in Frankfort, Kentucky, manufactures bottles containing Kentucky bourbon. Before 1968 their most brisk sales occurred around the Christmas/New Year season as the majority were bought for gift giving. When interest grew in the U.S. for figural bottles, most sales were to collectors.

	Price Range	
☐ **ALABAMA BICENTENNIAL** (1976)	10.00	15.00
☐ **AMERICAN LEGION** (1971)		
Distinguished embossed star emblem born out of WWI struggle. Combination blue and gold. On blue base	25.00	34.00
☐ **AMERICAN LEGION** (1972)		
Ezra Brooks salutes the American Legion, its Illinois Department, and Land of Lincoln and the city of Chicago, host of the Legion's 54th National Convention	60.00	70.00
☐ **AMERICAN LEGION** (1973)		
Hawaii, our fiftieth state, hosted the American Legion's 1973 annual Convention. It was the largest airlift of a mass group ever to hit the islands. Over		

Price Range

15,000 Legionnaires visited the beautiful city of Honolulu to celebrate the Legion's fifty-fourth anniversary	10.00	15.00
☐ **AMERICAN LEGION** (1977)		
Denver	20.00	30.00
☐ **AMERICAN LEGION** (1973)		
Miami Beach	8.00	12.00
☐ **AMVETS** (1974)		
Dolphin	16.00	20.00
☐ **AMVET** (1973)		
Polish Legion	36.00	22.00
☐ **ANTIQUE CANNON** (1969)	5.00	8.00
☐ **ANTIQUE PHONOGRAPH** (1970)		
Edison's early contribution to home entertainment. White, black, Morning Glory horn, red. Richly detailed in 24k gold	8.00	12.00
☐ **ARIZONA** (1969)		
Man with burro in search of Lost Dutchman Mine, golden brown mesa, green cactus, with 22k gold base, "ARIZONA" imprinted	4.00	8.00
☐ **AUBURN 1932** (1978)		
Classic Car	13.00	17.00
☐ **BADGER NO. 1** (1973)		
Boxer	10.00	14.00
☐ **BADGER NO. 2** (1974)		
Football	16.00	24.00
☐ **BADGER NO. 3** (1974)		
Hockey	16.00	24.00
☐ **BALTIMORE ORIOLE WILD LIFE** (1979)	35.00	45.00
☐ **BARE KNUCKLE FIGHTER** (1971)	6.00	10.00
☐ **BASEBALL HALL OF FAME** (1973)		
Baseball fans everywhere will enjoy this genuine Heritage China ceramic of a familiar slugger of years gone by	18.00	21.00
☐ **BASKETBALL PLAYER** (1974)	8.00	12.00
☐ **BEAR** (1968)	5.00	9.00
☐ **BENGAL TIGER WILD LIFE** (1979)	25.00	35.00
☐ **BETSY ROSS** (1975)	9.00	13.00
☐ **BIG BERTHA**		
Nugget Casino's very-own elephant with a raised trunk, gray, red, white and black, yellow & gold trim. Blanket and stand	10.00	15.00

Price Range

☐ **BIG DADDY LOUNGE** (1969)
Salute to South Florida's state liquor chain, and
Big Daddy's lounges. White, green, red 5.00 10.00
☐ **BIGHORN RAM** (1973) 8.00 11.00
☐ **BIRD DOG** (1971) 10.00 18.00
☐ **BORDERTOWN**
Borderline Club where California and Nevada
meet for a drink. Brown, red, white. Club building
with vulture on roof stopper, and outhouse 5.00 10.00
☐ **BOWLER** (1973) 5.00 10.00
☐ **BRAHMA BULL** (1972) 12.00 18.00
☐ **BUCKET OF BLOOD** (1970)
Fabled Virginia City, Nevada saloon. Bucket
shape bottle. Brown, red with gold lettering on re-
verse side 5.00 10.00
☐ **BUCKING BRONCO** (1973)
Rough Rider 9.00 14.00
☐ **BUCKY BADGER**
Football 22.00 28.00
☐ **BUCKY BADGER** (1975)
Hockey 20.00 26.00
☐ **BUCKY BADGER** (1973)
No. 1, Boxer 12.00 18.00
☐ **BUFFALO HUNT** (1971) 7.00 13.00
☐ **BULLDOG** (1972)
Mighty canine mascot and football symbol. Red,
white 16.00 22.00
☐ **BULL MOOSE** (1973) 10.00 15.00
☐ **BUSY BEAVER**
This genuine Heritage China ceramic is a salute
to the beaver 5.00 10.00
☐ **CABIN STILL**
Hillbilly, Papers From Company, Gallon 35.00 45.00
☐ **CABLE CAR** (1968)
San Francisco's great trolley car ride in bottle
form. Made in three different colors, green, gray
and blue, with red, black & gold trim. Open Cable
Car with passengers clinging to sides 5.00 9.00
☐ **CALIFORNIA QUAIL** (1970)
Widely admired game bird shape bottle. Crested
head stopper. Unglazed finish. Green, brown,
white, black, gray 12.00 18.00

	Price Range	
☐ **CANADIAN HONKER** (1975)	11.00	15.00
☐ **CANADIAN LOON WILD LIFE** (1979)	40.00	48.00
☐ **CARDINAL** (1972)	20.00	25.00
☐ **CASEY AT BAT** (1973)	6.00	10.00
☐ **CEREMONIAL INDIAN** (1970)	18.00	28.00
☐ **C.B. CONVOY RADIO** (1976)	5.00	9.00
☐ **CHAROLAIS BEEF** (1973)		
The Charolais have played an important role in raising the standards of quality in today's cattle	10.00	14.00
☐ **CHEYENNE SHOOT OUT** (1970)		
Honoring the Wild West and her Cheyenne Frontier Days. Sheriff and outlaw shoot-out over mirrored bar. Brown tone with multi-colors	6.00	10.00
☐ **CHICAGO FIRE** (1974)	17.00	24.00
☐ **CHICAGO WATER TOWER** (1969)	8.00	12.00
☐ **CHRISTMAS DECANTER** (1966)	5.00	8.00
☐ **CHRISTMAS TREE** (1979)	16.00	23.00
☐ **CHURCHILL** (1970)		
Commemorating *Iron Curtain* speech at Westminster College, Churchhill at lectern with hand raised in *V* sign. Fulton, Mo. Gold color	5.00	9.00
☐ **CIGAR STORE INDIAN** (1968)		
Sidewalk statue in bottle form. The original Wooden Indian first appeared in 1770. Dark Tan	6.00	10.00
☐ **CLASSIC FIREARMS** (1969)		
Embossed gun set consisting of: Derringer, Colt 45, Peacemaker, Over & Under Flintlock, Pepper box. Green, blue violet, red	17.00	23.00
☐ **CLOWN BUST** (1979)		
No. 1, Smiley	22.00	28.00
☐ **CLOWN BUST** (1979)		
No. 2, Cowboy	24.00	28.00
☐ **CLOWN BUST** (1979)		
No. 3, Pagliacci	17.00	24.00
☐ **CLOWN WITH ACCORDIAN** (1971)	20.00	26.00
☐ **CLOWN WITH BALLOON** (1973)	30.00	36.00
☐ **CLOWN** (1978)		
Imperial Shrine	20.00	28.00
☐ **CLUB BOTTLE** (1973)		
The third commemorative Ezra Brooks Collector Club bottle is created in the shape of America.		

Price Range

Each gold star on the new club bottle represents
the location of an Ezra Brooks Collectors Club   **21.00**   **28.00**

☐ **CLYDESDALE HORSE** (1973)
In the early days of distilling, Clydesdales carted
the bottles of whiskey from the distillery to towns
all across America **10.00**   **16.00**

☐ **COLT PEACEMAKER** (1969)
Flask **4.00**   **8.00**

☐ **CONQUISTADORS**
Tribute to a great drum & Bugle Corps. Silver col-
ored trumpet attached to drum **6.00**   **12.00**

☐ **CONQUISTADOR'S DRUM & BUGLE** (1972) ..   **10.00**   **18.00**

☐ **CORVETTE INDY PACE CAR** (1978) **40.00**   **50.00**

☐ **CORVETTE** (1976)
1957 Classic **100.00**   **120.00**

☐ **COURT JESTER**
A common sight in the throne rooms of Europe.
Yellow and blue suit, pointed cap **6.00**   **10.00**

☐ **DAKOTA COWBOY** (1975) **34.00**   **44.00**

☐ **DAKOTA COWGIRL** (1976) **20.00**   **26.00**

☐ **DAKOTA GRAIN ELEVATOR** (1978) **20.00**   **30.00**

☐ **DAKOTA SHOTGUN EXPRESS** (1977) **24.00**   **33.00**

☐ **DEAD WAGON** (1970)
To carry gunfight losers to Boot Hill, old-time
hearse with Tombstones on side. Vulture adorn-
ment on stopper. White, with black details **5.00**   **10.00**

☐ **DELTA BELLE** (1969)
Proud paddlewheel boat on the New Orleans to
Louisville passage, steamboat shape with embossed details. White, brown, red with 22k gold
trim **6.00**   **11.00**

☐ **DEMOCRATIC CONVENTION** (1976) **10.00**   **16.00**

☐ **DERRINGER** (1969)
Flask **4.00**   **8.00**

☐ **DISTILLERY—CLUB BOTTLE** (1970)
Reproduction of the Ezra Brooks Distillery in Kentucky, complete with smokestack. Beige, black,
brown with 22k gold color **4.00**   **8.00**

☐ **DUESENBERG**
Jaunty vintage convertible. Famous SJ model reproduction complete with superchargers and
white sidewalls. Blue and gold, or solid gold color   **24.00**   **33.00**

Price Range

☐ **ELEPHANT** (1973)
Based on an Asian elephant which has small ears
and tusks 8.00 12.00
☐ **ELK** (1973)
While the elk herd is still relatively scarce in the
United States, the elk name flourishes as a sym-
bol for many worthwhile organizations, especially
those whose primary object is the practice of be-
nevolence and charity in its broadest sense. Ezra
Brooks salutes these organizations with this gen-
uine Heritage China Ceramic bottle 20.00 28.00
☐ **ENGLISH SETTER—BIRD DOG** (1971)
Happy hunting dog retrieving red pheasant. White
flecked with black, yellow base 10.00 15.00
☐ **EQUESTRIENNE** (1974) 6.00 11.00
☐ **ESQUIRE**
Ceremonial Dancer 10.00 16.00
☐ **FARTHINGTON BIKE** (1972) 6.00 10.00
☐ **FIRE ENGINE** (1971) 11.00 15.00
☐ **FIREMAN** (1975) 20.00 28.00
☐ **FISHERMAN** (1974) 16.00 22.00
☐ **FLINTLOCK** (1969)
Dueling pistol rich in detail. Japanese version has
wooden rack, "Made in Japan" on handle. Herit-
age China gun has plastic rack, less detail. Gun-
metal gray and brown, silver and gold trim.
Japanese 4.00 8.00
Heritage 10.00 15.00
☐ **FLORIDA 'GATORS'** (1973)
Tribute to the University of Florida Gators football
team 13.00 18.00
☐ **F.O.E. EAGLE** (1978) 15.00 20.00
☐ **F.O.E. FLYING EAGLE** (1979) 25.00 30.00
☐ **F.O.E. EAGLE** (1980) 35.00 44.00
☐ **F.O.E. EAGLE** (1981) 18.00 28.00
☐ **FOREMOST ASTRONAUT** (1970)
Tribute to major liquor supermart, Foremost Liq-
uor Store. Smiling "Mr. Bottle-Face" clinging to
space rocket on white base 6.00 11.00
☐ **FOOTBALL PLAYER** (1974) 7.00 11.00
☐ **FORD THUNDERBIRD** (1976)
1956 .... 45.00 55.00

Price Range

☐ **FRESNO DECANTER**
Map of famed California grape center. Stopper
and inscription has gold finish. Blue, white .... | 5.00 | 12.00
☐ **FRESNO GRAPE WITH GOLD** .... | 48.00 | 60.00
☐ **FRESNO GRAPE** (1970) .... | 6.00 | 11.00
☐ **GAMECOCK** (1970)
All feathers and fury against rival birds. Red with
yellow base .... | 9.00 | 13.00
☐ **GO BIG RED** #1, #2 and #3
Football shaped bottle with white bands and
laces on base embossed "GO BIG RED." Brown,
white, gold detail.
No. 1 with football (1972) .... | 25.00 | 32.00
No. 2 with hat (1971) .... | 25.00 | 32.00
No. 3 with rooster (1972) .... | 12.00 | 18.00
☐ **GOLD PROSPECTOR** (1969)
Rugged miner with white beard panning for gold.
Black, pink and gold trim .... | 5.00 | 9.00
☐ **GOLDEN ANTIQUE CANNON** (1969)
Symbol of Spanish power. Embossed details on
barrel, wheels and carriage. Dark brown, with lav-
ish 22k gold trim .... | 5.00 | 5.00
☐ **GOLDEN EAGLE** (1971)
Rich plummage, sitting on a branch. Gold color | 12.00 | 18.00
☐ **GOLDEN GRIZZLY BEAR** (1970)
A bear-shaped bottle, on haunches. Brown with
gold highlights .... | 7.00 | 11.00
☐ **GOLDEN HORSESHOE** (1970)
Salute to Reno's Horseshoe Club. Good luck
symbol on horseshoe. 24k gold covered, in a blue
base .... | 10.00 | 15.00
☐ **GOLDEN ROOSTER** #1
A replica of the famous solid gold rooster on dis-
play at Nugget Casino in Reno, Nevada. Glowing
rooster in 22k gold on black base .... | 35.00 | 45.00
☐ **GO TIGER GO** (1973) .... | 12.00 | 18.00
☐ **GOLD SEAL** (1972) .... | 10.00 | 15.00
☐ **GOLD TURKEY** .... | 45.00 | 55.00
☐ **GRANDFATHER CLOCK** (1970)
Brown with gold highlights, embossed detail ... | 8.00 | 14.00

	Price Range	
☐ **GRANDFATHER'S CLOCK** (1970)	**12.00**	**20.00**
☐ **GREAT STONE FACE—OLD MAN OF THE MOUNTAIN** (1970)		
Famous profile found in mountain of New Hampshire. Stopper has seal of New Hampshire	**12.00**	**18.00**
☐ **GREATER GREENSBORO OPEN** (1972)		
To commemorate this event, Ezra Brooks has designed this genuine Heritage Ceramic bottle ...	**25.00**	**30.00**
☐ **GREAT WHITE SHARK** (1977)	**8.00**	**14.00**
☐ **GREATER GREENSBORO OPEN** (1973)		
Golfer	**18.00**	**26.00**
☐ **GREATER GREENSBORO OPEN** (1974)		
Map	**29.00**	**36.00**
☐ **GREATER GREENSBORO OPEN** (1975)		
Cup	**27.00**	**33.00**
☐ **HAMBLETONIAN** (1971)		
Harness Racer honors the N.Y. town and race track that sired harness racing, trotting, horse pulling driver and sulky. Green, brown, white, yellow, blue, gold base	**8.00**	**14.00**
☐ **HAPPY GOOSE** (1975)	**16.00**	**26.00**
☐ **HAROLD'S CLUB DICE** (1968)		
Lucky 7 dice combination topped with H-cube stopper, on round white base. Red and white with gold trim	**5.00**	**10.00**
☐ **HEREFORD** (1971)	**9.00**	**13.00**
☐ **HEREFORD** (1972)		
Brown, white face	**9.00**	**12.00**
☐ **HISTORICAL FLASK** (1970)		
Eagle Blue	**2.00**	**4.00**
☐ **HISTORICAL FLASK** (1970)		
Flagship, Purple	**2.00**	**4.00**
☐ **HISTORICAL FLASK** (1970)		
Liberty, Amber	**2.00**	**4.00**
☐ **HISTORICAL FLASK** (1970)		
Old Ironside, Green	**2.00**	**4.00**
☐ **HISTORICAL FLASK** (1970)		
Set of 4	**2.00**	**4.00**
☐ **HOLLYWOOD COPS** (1972)	**15.00**	**25.00**
☐ **HOPI INDIAN** (1970)		
"KACHINA DOLL." Creative tribe doing ritual song-and-dance. White, red ornamental trim ...	**18.00**	**22.00**

Price Range

☐ **HOPI KACHINA** (1973)
Genuine Heritage China ceramic reproduction of
a Hummingbird Kachina Doll 62.00 72.00
☐ **IDAHO—SKI THE POTATO** (1973)
Ezra Brooks salutes the beautiful state of Idaho,
its ski resorts and famous Idaho potatoes, with
this genuine Heritage China Ceramic bottle 10.00 14.00
☐ **INDIAN HUNTER** (1970)
Traditional buffalo hunt. Indian on horseback
shooting buffalo with bow and arrow. White
horse, brown buffalo, yellow base 11.00 15.00
☐ **INDIAN CEREMONIAL**
Colorful tribal dancer from New Mexico Reserva-
tion. Multi-colored, gold trim 13.00 18.00
☐ **INDIANAPOLIS 500**
Sleek, dual-exhaust racer. White, blue, black, sil-
ver trim 21.00 28.00
☐ **IOWA FARMER** (1977) 65.00 75.00
☐ **IOWA GRAIN ELEVATOR** (1978) 30.00 40.00
☐ **IRON HORSE LOCOMOTIVE**
Replica of old-time locomotive, complete with
funnel, cow-catcher and oil burning headlamp.
Black and red with 22k gold trim 8.00 14.00
☐ **JACK O' DIAMONDS** (1969)
The symbol of good luck, a bottle in the shape
of the "Jack" right off the card. A Royal Flush
decorates the front. White, Red, Blue & Black 8.00 10.00
☐ **JAY HAWK** (1969)
Funny bird with a large head perched on a "tree
trunk" base. Symbol of Kansas during and after
Civil War. Yellow, red, blue and brown 8.00 12.00
☐ **JESTER** (1971) 8.00 10.00
☐ **JUG, OLD TIME**
1.75 Liter 12.00 18.00
☐ **KACHINA DOLL** (1971)
No. 1 . . . . 125.00 150.00
☐ **KACHINA DOLL** (1973)
No. 2, Hummingbird 68.00 78.00
☐ **KACHINA DOLL** (1974)
No. 3 . . . . 50.00 60.00
☐ **KACHINA DOLL** (1975)
No. 4 . . . . 27.00 33.00

**Ezra Brooks Groucho Marx
(1977),** *head adorned with
famous bush helmet.*
$27.00–$35.00

**Ezra Brooks Sphinx (1980).
$30.00–$38.00**

Price Range

☐ **KACHINA DOLL** (1976)
No. 5 . . . .   30.00   40.00
☐ **KACHINA DOLL** (1977)
No. 6, White Buffalo 25.00   35.00
☐ **KACHINA DOLL** (1978)
No. 7, Mud Head 20.00   30.00
☐ **KACHINA DOLL** (1979)
No. 8 . . . .   50.00   60.00
☐ **KANSAS JAYHAWK** (1969) 8.00   16.00
☐ **KATZ CATS** (1969)
Seal point and blue point. Siamese cats are symbolic of Katz Drug Company of Kansas City, Kansas. Gray and blue, tan and brown 8.00   12.00
☐ **KATZ CATS PHILHARMONIC** (1970)
Commemorating its 27th Annual star night, devoted to classical and pop music. Black tuxedo, brown face, pair 6.00   10.00
☐ **KEYSTONE COP** (1980) 30.00   38.00
☐ **KEYSTONE COPS** (1971) 20.00   24.00
☐ **KILLER WHALE** (1972) 11.00   16.00
☐ **KING OF CLUBS** (1969)
Figure of card symbol. Sword and orb symbolize wisdom and justice. Royal flush in clubs in front. Yellow, red, blue, black and white with gold trim   6.00   10.00
☐ **KING SALMON** (1971)
Bottle in shape of leaping salmon, natural red   18.00   24.00
☐ **LIBERTY BELL** (1970)
Replica of the famous bell complete with wooden support. Dark copper color, embossed details   5.00   8.00
☐ **LINCOLN CONTINENTAL MARK I** (1941) 17.00   23.00
☐ **LION ON THE ROCK** (1971) 8.00   12.00
☐ **LIQUOR SQUARE** (1972) 5.00   9.00
☐ **LITTLE GIANT** (1971)
Replica of the first horse-drawn steam engine to arrive at the Chicago fire in 1871. Red, black with gold trim 11.00   16.00
☐ **MAINE LOBSTER** (1970)
Bottle in Lobster shape, complete with claws. Pinkish-red color. Bottle is sold only in Maine . .   18.00   25.00

	Price Range	

☐ **MAINE LIGHTHOUSE** (1971) 20.00 25.00

☐ **MAN-O-WAR** (1969)
Big Red captured just about every major horse-racing prize in turfdom. Replica of famous horse in brown and green, 22k gold base. Embossed "MAN-O-WAR" 10.00 16.00

☐ **M & M BROWN JUG** (1975) 18.00 24.00

☐ **MAP** (1972)
U.S.A. Club Bottle 8.00 14.00

☐ **MASONIC FEZ** (1976) 10.00 18.00

☐ **MAX** (1976)
The Hat, Zimmerman 24.00 30.00

☐ **MILITARY TANK** (1971) 15.00 22.00

☐ **MINNESOTA HOCKEY PLAYER** (1975) 18.00 22.00

☐ **MINUTEMAN** (1975) 10.00 15.00

☐ **MISSOURI MULE** (1972)
Brown 8.00 12.00

☐ **MOOSE** (1973) 20.00 28.00

☐ **MR. MAINE POTATO** (1973)
From early beginnings the people of Maine have built the small potato into a giant industry. Today potatoes are the number one agricultural crop in the state. Over thirty-six billion pounds are grown every year 6.00 10.00

☐ **MR. FOREMOST** (1969)
An authentic reproduction of the famous bottle-shaped symbol of Foremost Liquor stores, Mr. Foremost known for good wines and spirits. Red, white and black 9.00 12.00

☐ **MR. MERCHANT** (1970)
Jumping Man, whimsical, checkered-vest carica-ture of amiable shopkeeper, leaping into the air, arms outstretched. Yellow, black 6.00 10.00

☐ **MOTORCYCLE**
Motorcycle rider and machine. Rider dressed in Blue pants, red jacket, with stars 'n stripes hel-met. Motorcycle black with red tank on silver base 6.00 10.00

Price Range

☐ **MOUNTAINEER** (1971)
Figure dressed in buckskin, holding rifle. "MOUN-
TAINEERS ARE ALWAYS FREE" embossed on
base. Bottle is hand-trimmed in platinum. One of
the most valuable Ezra Brooks figural bottles .. **40.00** **60.00**

☐ **MUSTANG INDY PACE CAR** (1979) **20.00** **25.00**

☐ **NEW HAMPSHIRE STATE HOUSE** (1970)
150-year old State House. Embossed doors, windows, steps. Eagle topped stopper. Gray building
with gold **9.00** **13.00**

☐ **NEBRASKA—GO BIG RED!** (1972)
Genuine Heritage China reproduction of a game
ball and fan, trimmed in genuine 24k gold **10.00** **14.00**

☐ **NORTH CAROLINA BICENTENNIAL** (1975) .. **8.00** **12.00**

☐ **NUGGET CLASSIC**
Replica of golf pin presented to golf tournament
participants. Finished in 22k gold **7.00** **12.00**

☐ **OIL GUSHER**
Bottle in shape of oil drilling rig. All silver, jet black
stopper in shape of gushing oil **6.00** **10.00**

☐ **OLD CAPITAL** (1971)
Bottle in shape of Iowa's seat of government
when the corn state was still frontier territory. Embossed windows, doors, pillars. "OLD CAPITAL
IOWA 1840–1857" on base, Reddish color with
gold dome stopper **15.00** **22.00**

☐ **OLD EZ** (1977)
No. 1, Barn Owl............................. **45.00** **55.00**

☐ **OLD EZ** (1978)
No. 2, Eagle Owl **62.00** **68.00**

☐ **OLD EZ** (1979)
No. 3, Show Owl **40.00** **45.00**

☐ **OLD MAN OF THE MOUNTAIN** (1970) **10.00** **18.00**

☐ **OLD WATER TOWER** (1969)
Famous land mark. Survived the Chicago fire of
1871. Embossed details, towers, doors, stones,
windows. Gray and brown gold base **12.00** **16.00**

☐ **ONTARIO 500** (1970)
California 500 is a speedway classic with an
"Indy" style racing oval. Red, white, blue and
black with silver trim **18.00** **22.00**

Price Range

☐ **OVERLAND EXPRESS** (1969)
Brown stagecoach bottle 8.00 12.00
☐ **OVER-UNDER FLINTLOCK** (1969)
Flask 4.00 8.00
☐ **PANDA—GIANT** (1972)
Giant Panda ceramic bottle 12.00 17.00
☐ **PENGUIN** (1972)
Ezra Brooks salutes the penguin with a genuine
Heritage China ceramic figural bottle 7.00 11.00
☐ **PENNY FARTHINGTON HIGH WHEELER**
(1973)
Ezra Brooks salutes the millions of cyclists every-
where, and the new cycling boom with this genu-
ine Heritage China ceramic of the Penny Farth-
ington bicycle 10.00 15.00
☐ **PEPPERBOX** (1969)
Flask 4.00 6.00
☐ **PHOENIX BIRD** (1971)
Famous mythical bird reborn from its own ashes
honoring Arizona. Blue bird with outstretched
wings arising from gold flames 20.00 26.00
☐ **PHOENIX JAYCEES** (1973)
Ezra Brooks is proud to honor the Phoenix Jay-
cees and the Rodeo of Rodeos with this Heritage
China reproduction of a silver saddle 12.00 17.00
☐ **PIANO** (1970)
An old time piano player and his upright piano.
Player wears blue pants, striped shirt, red bow tie,
black derby, and yellow vest. Piano is brown in
gold trim 10.00 15.00
☐ **PIRATE** (1971)
A swashbuckling sailor with beard and eye-patch
and hook hand, who flew the Jolly Roger (skull
and crossbones) o'er the 7-seas. Black hat,
jacket, boots, yellow striped shirt, pistol, sword
and treasure chest on gold base 6.00 10.00
☐ **POLISH LEGION AMERICAN VETS** (1978) ... 18.00 26.00
☐ **PORTLAND HEAD LIGHTHOUSE** (1971)
It's guided ships safely into Maine Harbor since
1791. White, red trim, gold Light stopper.
"MAINE" embossed on rock base 15.00 22.00

Price Range

☐ **POT-BELLIED STOVE** (1968)
Old time round coal burning stove with ornate
legs and fire in the grate. Black and red 8.00 10.00

☐ **QUEEN OF HEARTS** (1969)
Playing card symbol with royal flush in hearts on
front of bottle 6.00 10.00

☐ **RACCOON WILD LIFE** (1978) 40.00 50.00

☐ **RAM** (1973) 13.00 18.00

☐ **RAZORBACK HOG** (1969)
Bright red hog with white tusks and hooves running on green grass 18.00 24.00

☐ **RAZORBACK HOG** (1979) 15.00 25.00

☐ **RED FOX** (1979)
Wild Life 40.00 46.00

☐ **RENO ARCH** (1968)
Honoring the biggest little city in the world, Reno,
Nevada. Arch shape with "RENO" embossed on
yellow. Front of bottle multi-color decal of: dice,
rabbits foot, roulette wheel, slot machine, etc.
White and yellow, purple stopper 4.00 8.00

☐ **SAN FRANCISCO CABLE CAR** (1968) 10.00 16.00

☐ **SAILFISH** (1971)
Leaping deep water Sailfish with a sword-like
nose and large spread fin. Blue-green luminous
tones on green waves base 7.00 11.00

☐ **SALMON** (1971)
Washington King 20.00 26.00

☐ **SAN FRANCISCO CABLE CAR** (1968) 10.00 16.00

☐ **SEA CAPTAIN** (1971)
Salty old seadog, white hair and beard, in blue
captains jacket with gold buttons and sleeve
stripes, white cap, gold band. Holding pipe, on
wooden stanchion base 10.00 14.00

☐ **SENATOR** (1971)
Cigar-chomping, whistle-stopping state senator,
stumping on a platform of pure nostalgia. Black
western hat and swallow-tail coat, red vest, string
tie, gold, black red, white 9.00 15.00

☐ **SENATORS OF THE U.S.** (1972)
Ezra Brooks honors the senators of the United
States of America with this genuine Heritage Ce-
ramic old time courtly Senator 12.00 16.00

Price Range

☐ **SETTER** (1974) 12.00 18.00
☐ **SHRINE KING TUT GUARD** (1979) 16.00 24.00
☐ **SILVER SADDLE** (1973) 24.00 30.00
☐ **SILVER SPUR BOOT** (1971)
Cowboy-boot shaped bottle with silver spur buckled on. "SILVER SPUR—CARSON CITY NEVADA" embossed on side of boot. Brown boot
with platinum trim 7.00 11.00
☐ **1804 SILVER DOLLAR** (1970)
Commemorates the famous and very valuable 1804 silver dollar. Embossed replica of the Liberty Head dollar. Platinum covered round dollar
shaped bottle on black or white base 5.00 8.00
☐ **SIMBA** (1971)
Beautifully detailed Lion is reddish-brown color. Head of Lion is stopper. Rock base is dark gray 9.00 12.00
☐ **SKI BOOT** (1972)
Ezra Brooks salutes the exciting sport of skiing
with this genuine Heritage Ceramic Ski Boot ... 7.00 12.00
☐ **SLOT-MACHINE** (1971)
A tribute to the slots of Las Vegas, Nevada. A replica of the original nickle LIBERTY BELL slot machine invented by Charles Fey in 1895. The original is in Reno's Liberty Belle Saloon. Top window shows two horseshoes and a bell, bottom panel
shows prizes. Gray body with gold trim 20.00 26.00
☐ **SNOWMOBILES** (1972)
A tribute to the chief means of transportation in
Alaska and Canada 10.00 15.00
☐ **SOUTH DAKOTA AIR NATIONAL GUARD**
(1976) 22.00 30.00
☐ **SPIRIT OF '76** (1974) 6.00 11.00
☐ **SPIRIT OF ST. LOUIS** (1977)
50th Anniversary 6.00 11.00
☐ **SPRINT CAR RACER**
A decanter replica of the race car sponsored by Ezra Brooks. Supercharged racer with black Firestone racing tires, and silver and blue trim. Goggled driver in white and red jump suit at wheel.
Cream colored car with silver and blue trim ... 20.00 26.00

	Price Range	
☐ **STAN LAUREL BUST** (1976)	10.00	16.00
☐ **STOCK MARKET TICKER** (1970)		
A unique replica of a ticker tape machine. Gold colored mechanism with white market tape under plastic dome. Black base with embossed plaque "STOCK MARKET QUOTATIONS"	8.00	11.00
☐ **STONEWALL JACKSON** (1974)	17.00	23.00
☐ **STRONGMAN** (1974)	6.00	10.00
☐ **STURGEON** (1975)	20.00	28.00
☐ **JOHN L. SULLIVAN** (1970)		
The great John L. mustached, last of the bare nuckle fighters, in fighting stance. Red tights, gold belt cord, white gym shirt. John stands on a gold base	12.00	17.00
☐ **SEALION-GOLD** (1972)		
Ezra Brooks commemorates the state of California and her world-famous marine showmen, with the California Sealion ceramic bottle, hand detailed in 24K gold	10.00	15.00
☐ **SYRACUSE—NEW YORK** (1973)		
Ezra Brooks salutes the great city of Syracuse, its past and its present	11.00	16.00
☐ **TANK PATTON** (1972)		
Reproduction of a U.S. Army tank. Turret top with cannon is the stopper. Embossed details on tracks, tools, etc. Camouflage green and brown	18.00	24.00
☐ **BOWLING TEN PINS** (1973)		
In Colonial days, Massachusetts and Connecticut banned bowling at nine pins along with dice and cards. But bowlers avoided the law by simply adding a 10th pin. Thus 10 pin bowling was born. Today the sport of bowling is enjoyed by more than 30,000,000 Americans	10.00	15.00
☐ **TECUMSEH** (1969)		
The figure head of the U.S.S. Delaware, this decanter is an embossed replica of the statue at the United States Naval Academy in Annapolis, M.D. Feathers in quiver form stopper. Gold figure on brown wood base	6.00	10.00

Price Range

☐ **TELEPHONE** (1971)
A replica of the old time upright handset telephone. 24k. gold body, mouth piece, and base
trim, black receiver, wires, base and head. Mouth-
piece and head form the stopper **12.00   17.00**

☐ **TENNIS PLAYER** (1972)
Ezra Brooks salutes tennis lovers everywhere,
with this genuine Heritage China ceramic tennis
player bottle **8.00   12.00**

☐ **TERRAPIN** (1974)
Maryland **16.00   20.00**

☐ **TEXAS LONGHORN** (1971)
Realistic longhorn on tall green Texas grass
base. Long-horned head is stopper. Reddish-
brown body, white horns and mask, gold trimmed
base **10.00   15.00**

☐ **TICKER TAPE** (1970) **8.00   14.00**

☐ **TOM TURKEY**
Replica of the American White Feathered Turkey.
Tail spread, red head and wattles, yellow feet and
beak. On a brown tree trunk base **18.00   24.00**

☐ **TONOPAH** (1972) **14.00   20.00**

☐ **TOTEM POLE** (1972)
Ezra Brooks commemorates the totem art of the
American Indian with this genuine Heritage China
reproduction of an ornate, intricately designed In-
dian totem pole **10.00   14.00**

☐ **TOTEM POLE** (1973)
The Indians of North America have a proud history. And in many instances, that history is beautifully portrayed in totem pole art. It is a truly remarkable art form that will enrich the world for
generations to come. Ezra Brooks commemorates the totem pole art of the North American Indian with this genuine Heritage China reproduction of an ornate, intricately designed Indian
totem pole **12.00   18.00**

☐ **TIGER ON STADIUM** (1973)
To commemorate college teams who have cho-
sen the tiger as their mascot **12.00   17.00**

Price Range

☐ **TRACTOR** (1971)
A model of the 1917 Fordson made by Henry Ford. Embossed details of engine and hood seat and steering wheel. Red tractor wheels, gray body with silver trim **10.00   14.00**

☐ **TRAIL BIKE RIDER** (1972)
Ezra Brooks salutes the trail bike riders of America with this genuine Heritage China ceramic bottle **7.00   13.00**

☐ **TROJAN HORSE** (1974) **15.00   21.00**

☐ **TROJANS—U.S.C. FOOTBALL** (1973)
A tribute to the Trojans who have given U.S.C. seven Pacific-Eight Conference titles, six Rose Bowl teams, 23 All-Americans, two Heisman Trophy winners (Mike Garrett and O.J. Simpson), three undefeated seasons, and three national championships **8.00   20.00**

☐ **TRUCKIN & VANNIN** (1977) **7.00   12.00**

☐ **TROUT & FLY** (1970)
The Rainbow Trout leaping and fighting the McGinty Fly. A luminescent replica of this angler's dream on a blue water base, complete with scales, fins and flashing tail **7.00   11.00**

☐ **V.F.W.—VETERANS OF FOREIGN WARS** (1973)
Ezra Brooks salutes the Veterans of Foreign Wars of the United States and the 1.8 million fighting men of five wars who wear the Cross of Malta **6.00   10.00**

☐ **VERMONT SKIER** (1972) **12.00   18.00**

☐ **VIRGINIA—RED CARDINAL** (1973)
A glorious bird, the cardinal represents this illustrious state **10.00   15.00**

☐ **WALGREEN DRUGS** (1974) **16.00   24.00**

☐ **WEIRTON STEEL** (1973) **16.00   22.00**

☐ **WESTERN RODEOS** (1973)
Ezra Brooks salutes the rodeo, from its early pioneers to its professional circuit riders, with this genuine Heritage China bottle **17.00   23.00**

☐ **WEST VIRGINIA—MOUNTAINEER** (1971) **78.00   85.00**

☐ **WEST VIRGINIA—MOUNTAIN LADY** (1972) .. **14.00   20.00**

	Price Range	
☐ **WHALE** (1972)	**14.00**	**20.00**
☐ **WHEAT SHOCKER** (1971)		
The mascot of the Kansas football team in a fighting pose. Wheat-yellow figure, with black turtleneck sweater, "WHEAT SHOCKER" embossed in yellow on front. Wheat stalk tops are the stopper, wheat plants are the base	**6.00**	**10.00**
☐ **WHISKEY FLASKS** (1970)		
Reproductions of collectible American patriotic whiskey flasks of the 1800's, Old Ironsides, Miss Liberty, American Eagle, Civil War Commemorative. Embossed designs in gold, on blue, amber, green and red	**10.00**	**15.00**
☐ **WHITE TAIL DEER** (1947)	**20.00**	**26.00**
☐ **WHITE TURKEY** (1971)	**20.00**	**25.00**
☐ **WICHITA**	**4.00**	**8.00**
☐ **WICHITA CENTENNIAL** (1970)		
Replica of the Wichita's center of culture and commerce, Century II, the round building with the square base. Blue roof with gold airliner on top symbol of "Air Capital of the World." Blue, brown, black and gold	**4.00**	**10.00**
☐ **WINSTON CHURCHILL** (1969)	**6.00**	**10.00**
☐ **ZIMMERMAN'S HAT** (1968)		
A salute to "Zimmerman's—WORLD'S LARGEST LIQUOR STORE." A replica of the store, embossed windows, doors, and roof. The Zimmerman Hat caps the store and is the bottle stopper. Red, white, brown and gold	**5.00**	**8.00**

J. W. DANT BOTTLES

The bottles of J.W. Dant Distilling Company from Louisville, Kentucky, are not as numerous as those of Ezra Brooks and Jim Beam, the other major Kentucky distilleries, but their following is strong. Introduced in 1968, the Dant figurals carry American themes, including patriotic events, folklore, and animal species such as the mountain quail, woodcock, and prairie chicken. Dant's preoccupation with American history originates from the period of its establishment in 1863 during the Civil War.

Most Dant bottles are conventionally shaped with historical scenes in full color. The back of all rectangular bottles carries an embossed American eagle and shield with stars. Several of the *Boston Tea Party* bottles have an error: the eagle's head faces his left side instead of his right.

All Dant bottles are limited editions and the company assures customers that the molds will not be reused.

	Price Range	
☐ **ALAMO**	4.00	6.00
☐ **AMERICAN LEGION**	3.00	7.00
☐ **ATLANTIC CITY**	4.00	6.00
☐ **BOBWHITE**	4.00	7.00
☐ **BOEING 747**	5.00	9.00
☐ **BOSTON TEA PARTY**		
Eagle to left	4.00	6.00
☐ **BOSTON TEA PARTY**		
Eagle to right	8.00	10.00

Dant Boeing 747.
$5.00–$9.00

	Price Range	
☐ BOURBON	3.00	4.00
☐ PAUL BUNYAN	4.00	7.00
☐ CALIFORNIA QUAIL	4.00	6.00
☐ CHUKAR PARTRIDGE	5.00	8.00
☐ CLEAR TIP PINCH	7.00	9.00
☐ CONSTITUTION & GUERRIERE	4.00	6.00
☐ DUEL BETWEEN BURR & HAMILTON	8.00	10.00
☐ EAGLE	5.00	8.00
☐ FORT SILL CENTENNIAL (1969)	7.00	11.00
☐ PATRICK HENRY	4.00	7.00
☐ INDIANAPOLIS 500	7.00	11.00
☐ MT. RUSHMORE	5.00	9.00
☐ MOUNTAIN QUAIL	5.00	8.00
☐ PRAIRIE CHICKEN	3.00	4.00
☐ REVERSE EAGLE	4.00	6.00
☐ RING-NECKED PHEASANT	3.75	5.75
☐ RUFFED GROUSE	3.75	5.75
☐ SAN DIEGO	5.00	8.00
☐ SPEEDWAY 500	5.00	8.00
☐ STOVE-POT BELLY	9.00	11.00
☐ WASHINGTON CROSSING DELAWARE	3.00	5.00
☐ WOODCOCK	4.50	7.00
☐ WRONG WAY CHARLIE	14.00	19.00

GARNIER BOTTLES

The prestigious figural bottles of the Garnier firm are among the oldest ones issued continuously since 1899 by a spirits company. But during the American Prohibition and World War II, which eliminated the majority of the Garnier market, production ceased temporarily. Garnet et Cie, a French firm founded in 1858, is recognized as the pioneer of the modern "collector" bottle for liquor. Of course, figural and other decorative bottles for liquor existed before the Garnier products but these were not issued in the form of a series which encouraged the building up of a collection. Garnier actually had a line of figural bottles 50 years before Jim Beam. Some antique historians claim to have found a relationship between Garnier bottles and the later Hummel porcelain figurines, believing that the former inspired the latter. The two companies' figurals are similar.

The older Garniers, produced prior to World War II, are scarce and valuable. They are not listed because their price levels are difficult to establish. Some of the better known "old Garniers" are the Cat

(1930), Clown (1910), Country Jug (1937), Greyhound (1930), Penguin (1930), and Marquise (1931). Garnier released its new figurals gradually with only 52 available within a 31 year span. But since 1930, new figurals have been produced more frequently.

	Price Range	
☐ **ALADDIN'S LAMP** (1963)		
Silver. 6½″	38.00	48.00
☐ **ALFA ROMEO 1913** (1970)		
Red body, yellow seats, black trim, 4″ x 10½″	15.00	25.00
☐ **ALFA ROMEO 1929** (1969)		
Pale blue body, red seat, black trim, 4″ x 10½″	15.00	25.00
☐ **ALFA ROMEO RACER** (1969)		
Maroon body, black tires and trim, 4″ x 10″	15.00	25.00
☐ **ANTIQUE COACH** (1970)		
Multicolor pastel tones, 8″ x 12″	15.00	25.00
☐ **APOLLO** (1969)		
Yellow quarter-moon, blue clouds, silver Apollo Spaceship, 13½″	17.00	22.00
☐ **AZTEC VASE** (1965)		
Stone tan, multicolor aztec design, 11¾″	8.00	14.00
☐ **BABY FOOT-SOCCER SHOE** (1963)		
Black with white trim, 3¾″ x 8½″	10.00	20.00
1962 soccer shoe—large	7.00	11.00
☐ **BABY TRIO** (1963)		
Clear glass, gold base, 6¼″	7.00	10.00
☐ **BACCUS—FIGURAL** (1967)		
Purple, brown, flesh tones, 13″	12.00	16.00
☐ **BAHAMAS**		
Black policeman, white jacket, and hat, black pants, red stripe, gold details	16.00	26.00
☐ **BALTIMORE ORIOLE** (1970)		
Multicolor, green, yellow, blue, approx. 11″	10.00	16.00
☐ **BANDIT—FIGURAL** (1958)		
Pin ball shape, multicolor, 11½″	10.00	14.00
☐ **BEDROOM CANDLESTICK** (1967)		
White with hand painted flowers, 11½″	32.00	42.00
☐ **BELLOWS** (1969)		
Gold and red, 4″ x 14½″	14.00	21.00
☐ **BIRD ASHTRAY** (1958)		
Clear glass, gold stopper, 3″	3.00	4.00
☐ **BURMESE MAN VASE** (1965)		
Stone gray, multicolor eastern design, 12″	15.00	25.00

Price Range

☐ **BLUEBIRD** (1970)
Two blue birds, multicolor green, brown and yellow, approx. 11″ **12.00 18.00**

☐ **BOUQUET** (1966)
White basket, multicolor flowers, 10¾″ **15.00 25.00**

☐ **BULL (& MATADOR)—ANIMAL FIGURAL** (1963)
A Rocking bottle, bronze and gold, 12½″ x 12½″ **17.00 23.00**

☐ **CANADA**
Mountie in red jacket, black jodphur, brown boots **11.00 14.00**

☐ **CANDLESTICK** (1955)
Yellow candle, brown holder with gold ring, 10¾″ **11.00 15.00**

☐ **CANDLESTICK GLASS** (1965)
Ornate leaves and fluting, 10″ **16.00 23.00**

☐ **CANNON** (1964)
With wheels and carriage, mottled yellow-brown, 7½″ x 13½″ **48.00 58.00**

☐ **CARDINAL STATE BIRD—ILLINOIS** (1969)
Bright red bird, green and brown tree, 11½″ .. **10.00 14.00**

☐ **CAT, BLACK** (1962)
Black cat with green eyes, 11½″ **15.00 25.00**

☐ **CAT, GRAY** (1962)
Grayish-white cat with yellow eyes, 11½″ **15.00 25.00**

☐ **CHALET** (1955)
White, red, green and blue, 9″ **40.00 50.00**

☐ **CHIMNEY** (1956)
Red bricks and fire, white mantel with picture, 9¾″ **55.00 65.00**

☐ **CHINESE DOG** (1965)
Foo Dogs, carved, embossed, ivory white on dark blue base, 11″ **15.00 25.00**

☐ **CHINESE STATUETTE, MAN** (1970)
Yellow robe, dark skin, blue base, 12″ **15.00 25.00**

☐ **CHINESE STATUETTE, WOMAN** (1970)
Ebony skin tones, lavender robe, blue base, 12″ **15.00 25.00**

☐ **CHRISTMAS TREE** (1956)
Dark green tree, gold decorated, white candles, red flame, 11½″ **58.00 68.00**

☐ **CITROEN, 1922** (1970)
Yellow body, black trim wheels, 4″ x 10½″ **14.00 24.00**

☐ **CLASSIC ASHTRAY** (1958)
Clear glass, round with pouring spout, 2½″ ... **5.00 8.00**

Price Range

☐ **CLOCK** (1958)
Clear glass, round on black base. Working clock
in center, 9″ 20.00   30.00

☐ **CLOWN HOLDING TUBA** (1955)
Green clown with gold trim, 12¾″ 15.00   25.00

☐ **COFFEE MILL** (1966)
White with blue flowers 20.00   30.00

☐ **COLUMBINE FIGURAL** (1968)
Female partner to Harlequin, green and blue,
black hair and mask, 13″ 10.00   14.00
HARLEQUIN 16.00   22.00

☐ **DRUNKARD—DRUNK ON LAMPOST**
Figure in top hat and tails holding "wavy" lampost, black, red, blue and white, 14¾″ 20.00   30.00

☐ **DUCKLING FIGURAL** (1956)
Yellow duckling, white basket and red flowers,
pink hat 18.00   26.00

☐ **DUO** (1954)
Two clear glass bottles stacked, two pouring
spouts, 7¼″ 12.00   18.00

☐ **EGG FIGURAL** (1956)
White egg shape house, pink, red, green, 8¾″ 68.00   78.00

☐ **EIFFEL TOWER** (1951)
Ivory with yellow tones, 13½″ 15.00   25.00
EIFFEL TOWER 12½″ 14.00   20.00

☐ **ELEPHANT FIGURAL** (1961)
Black with ivory white tusks, 6¾″ 20.00   30.00

☐ **EMPIRE VASE** (1962)
Green and white, gold design and trim, 11½″ 10.00   18.00

☐ **FIAT 500, 1913** (1970)
Yellow body, red hub caps, black trim, 4″ x 10¾″ 15.00   25.00

☐ **FIAT NEUVO, 1913** (1970)
Open top, blue body and hub caps, yellow and
black trim, 4″ x 10¾″ 20.00   30.00

☐ **FLASK GARNIER** (1958)
Clear glass, embossed cherries, 3″ 9.00   12.00

☐ **FLYING HORSE PEGASUS** (1958)
Black horse, gold mane and tail, red "marble"
candle holder, 12″ 50.00   60.00

☐ **FORD, 1913** (1970)
Green open body and wheels, black trim, 4″ x
10¾″ 20.00   30.00

Price Range

☐ **FOUNTAIN** (1964)
Brown with Gold Lion Head spout and embossing, 12½" 24.00 34.00

☐ **GIRAFFE** (1961)
Yellow marble, modern animal figure, 18" 15.00 21.00

☐ **GOLDFINCH** (1970)
Yellow bird, black wings and tail, green and brown
leaves and limbs, 12" 12.00 16.00

☐ **GOOSE** (1955)
White with gold decoration, modern swirl shaped
goose, 9¼" 14.00 24.00

☐ **GRENADIER** (1949)
Light blue soldier with sword in uniform of 1880's.
(Faceless Figure), 13¾" 55.00 65.00

☐ **HARLEQUIN WITH MANDOLIN** (1958)
Seated comedy figure, mandolin and mask, white
with multicolored circles, black buttons and
shoes, 14½" 30.00 40.00

☐ **HARLEQUIN STANDING** (1968)
Columbine's mate, brown costume, blue cape,
black cap and shoes, 13¼" 13.00 19.00

☐ **HORSE PISTOL** (1964)
Embossed brown antique pistol, gold details, 18" 11.00 14.00

☐ **HUNTING VASE** (1964)
Tan and gold with embossed hunting scene,
12¼" 25.00 35.00

☐ **HUSSAR** (1949)
French Cavalry Soldier of 1800's holding sword,
maroon color, 13¾" 25.00 33.00

☐ **INDIA**
Turbaned figure, white jacket, blue kilts, red sash 10.00 14.00

☐ **INDIAN** (1958)
Big Chief with headdress, bowling pin shape,
bright indian design colors, 11¾" 13.00 17.50

☐ **JOCKEY** (1961)
Bronzed gold horse and jockey rocking bottle,
12½" x 12" 20.00 26.00

☐ **LANCER** (1949)
Light green soldier holding drum, 13" 15.00 22.00

☐ **LOCOMOTIVE** (1969)
Tan, old fashioned locomotive, 9" 11.00 15.00

Price Range

☐ **LOG—ROUND** (1958)
Brown and tan log shape, silver handle and
spout, 10″ **20.00 30.00**

☐ **LONDON—BOBBY**
Dark blue uniform, silver helmet shield **12.00 18.00**

☐ **LOON** (1970)
Sitting bird, white, brown, tan, blue base, 11″ .. **10.00 18.00**

☐ **MAHARAJAH** (1958)
White and gold, Indian ruler with turban, 11¾″ **68.00 78.00**

☐ **M.G. 1933** (1970)
Green body, orange trim, white wheels, 4″ x 11″ **15.00 25.00**

☐ **MOCKINGBIRD** (1970)
Black and white bird on tree stump, 11″ **8.00 14.00**

☐ **MONTMARTRE JUG** (1960)
Colorful Parisian Bohemian scene, green, 11″ **12.00 18.00**

☐ **MONUMENTS** (1966)
A cluster of Parisian monuments, Eiffel Tower
spout, multicolor, 13″ **15.00 25.00**

☐ **NAPOLEON ON HORSEBACK** (1969)
Rearing white horse, Napoleon in red cloak, black
hat and uniform, 12″ **20.00 30.00**

☐ **NATURE GIRL** (1959)
Native girl under palm tree, black with bronze, 13″ **10.00 14.00**

☐ **NEW YORK POLICEMAN**
Dark blue uniform with gold shield and buttons **9.00 13.00**

☐ **PAINTING** (1961)
Multicolor painting of girl, in tan wood frame, 12″ **20.00 30.00**

☐ **PACKARD, 1930** (1970)
Orange body, cream roof and wheels, black trim,
4″ x 10″ **15.00 25.00**

☐ **PARIS**
French policemen in black, white gloves, hat and
garness **10.00 14.00**

☐ **PARIS TAXI** (1960)
Old time cab, yellow body, red windows and
headlights, black wire frame, 9″ x 10½″ **20.00 30.00**

☐ **PARTRIDGE** (1961)
Multicolor game bird, on leaf base, 10″ **32.00 38.00**

☐ **PHEASANT** (1969)
Multicolor game bird on rocking tree trunk base,
12″ **17.00 23.00**

Garnier Strawberries (1982) decanter basket of ceramic strawberries, contained Strawberry liqueur. **$18.00–$26.00**

Garnier Chanticleer or Rooster (1982), ceramic decanter. **$18.00–$26.00**

Price Range

☐ **PIGEON—CLEAR GLASS** (1958)
Bird-shape bottle, gold stopper, 8″ 10.00   14.00
☐ **PONY** (1961)
Modern shaped horse, wood grain tan, 8¾″ . . .   15.00   25.00
☐ **POODLE** (1954)
Begging poodles in white or black with red trim,
8½″ 14.00   18.00
☐ **RENAULT, 1911** (1969)
Green body and hood, red hubs, black trim, 4″
x 10¾″ 15.00   25.00
☐ **ROAD RUNNER** (1969)
Multicolor bird, green cactus pouring spout, 12″   10.00   15.00
☐ **ROBIN** (1970)
Multicolor bird on tree stump with leaves, 12″   9.00   12.00
☐ **ROCKET** (1958)
Rocket shape bottle, wire holder, yellow nose,
10¾″ 11.00   14.00
☐ **ROLLS ROYCE 1908** (1970)
Open touring car in yellow, red seats and hubs,
black trim, 4″ x 10½″ 15.00   25.00
☐ **ROOSTER** (1952)
Crowing rooster with handle, black or maroon
with gold trim, 12″ 15.00   25.00
☐ **SAINT TROPEZ JUG** (1961)
Colorful French Riviera scene, tan jug, black han-
dle 12.00   18.00
☐ **SCARECROW** (1960)
Yellow straw body and hat, green jacket, red
stripe face and tie, bird on shoulder, 12″ 18.00   26.00
☐ **SHERIFF** (1958)
Two guns, badge and cowboy hat, pin-ball shape,
white and gold, 12″ 15.00   25.00
☐ **SNAIL** (1950)
White and brown with spiral shell, 6½″ x 10″ . .   58.00   68.00
☐ **SOCCER SHOE** (1962)
Black shoe, white laces, 10″ long 30.00   40.00
☐ **S.S. FRANCE—LARGE** (1962)
Commemorative model of ocean liner, black hull,
blue-green decks, red and black stacks, with gold
labels, 5″ x 19″ 80.00   130.00
☐ **S.S. FRANCE—SMALL** (1962)
Same as above, 4½″ x 14″ 50.00   60.00

	Price Range	

☐ **S.S. QUEEN MARY** (1970)
Black hull, green-blue decks, blue water, 3 red
and black stacks, 4″ x 16″ 24.00   32.00

☐ **STANLEY STEAMER 1907** (1970)
Open blue car, yellow and black trim, 4″ x 10½″   14.00   20.00

☐ **TEAPOT** (1961)
Yellow and black striped body, black handle and
spout, 8½″ 15.00   25.00

☐ **TEAPOT, 1935** 20.00   30.00

☐ **TROUT** (1967)
Gray-blue speckled leaping trout, water base, 11″   17.00   22.00

☐ **VALLEY QUAIL** (1969)
Black marked bird on wood base, 11″ 8.00   12.00

☐ **VIOLIN** (1966)
White violin, hand painted flowers and details,
14″ 15.00   25.00

☐ **WATCH-ANTIQUE** (1966)
Antique pocket watch, tan and gold, 10″ 20.00   30.00

☐ **WATER PITCHER** (1965)
Glass body, silver base, handle and top, 14″ .. 12.00   18.00

☐ **WATERING CAN** (1958)
Hand painted design, handle and pouring spout,
7″ 12.00   18.00

☐ **YOUNG DEER VASE** (1964)
Embossed figures, tan color, 12″ 25.00   35.00

HOFFMAN

The Hoffman bottles are limited editions ceramics. Each issue is restricted in the number of bottles made and when this designated number is reached the mold is destroyed to prevent reproductions in the future. Consequently, the "out of production" designs quickly become collectors' items achieving high prices on the market. Hoffmans have sometimes been called the Hummels of the bottle world because they often depict figures in European dress at various kinds of occupations. These include a shoemaker, a doctor, and a bartender. However, the firm also focused upon American themes, such as its 1976 centennial bottles with "Pioneer of 1876" and "Hippie of 1976."

	Price Range	

☐ **MR. BARTENDER with Music Box**
He's a Jolly Good Fellow 25.00   30.00

	Price Range	
☐ **MR. CHARMER with Music Box**		
Glow Little Glow Worm	25.00	30.00
☐ **MR. DANCER with Music Box**		
The Irish Washerwoman	24.00	29.00
☐ **MR. DOCTOR with Music Box**		
As Long As He Needs Me	30.00	42.00
☐ **MR. FIDDLER with Music Box**		
Hearts and Flowers	30.00	42.00
☐ **MR. GUITARIST with Music Box**		
Johnny Guitar	30.00	42.00
☐ **MR. HARPIST with Music Box**		
Do—Re—Mi	20.00	32.00
☐ **MR. LUCKY with Music Box**		
When Irish Eyes Are Smiling	20.00	32.00
☐ **MRS. LUCKY with Music Box**		
The Kerry Dancer	30.00	42.00
☐ **MR. POLICEMAN with Music Box**		
Don't Blame Me	30.00	42.00
☐ **MR. SANDMAN with Music Box**		
Mr. Sandman	40.00	55.00
☐ **MR. SAXAPHONIST with Music Box**		
Tiger Rag	30.00	42.00
☐ **MR. SHOE COBBLER with Music Box**		
Danny Boy	26.00	37.00

BICENTENNIAL SERIES—4/5 QUART SIZE.

☐ **BETSY ROSS with Music Box**		
Star Spangled Banner	30.00	40.00
☐ **GENERATION GAP**		
Depicting "100 Years of Progress"—2 ounce size	28.00	40.00
☐ **MAJESTIC EAGLE with Music Box**		
America the Beautiful	55.00	65.00

C. M. RUSSELL SERIES—4/5 QUART SIZE.

☐ **BUFFALO MAN**	18.00	23.00
☐ **FLATHEAD SQUAW**	19.00	22.00
☐ **LAST OF FIVE THOUSAND**	23.00	34.00
☐ **RED RIVER BREED**	17.00	21.00
☐ **THE SCOUT**	23.00	27.00
☐ **THE STAGE DRIVE**	17.00	23.00
☐ **TRAPPER**	18.00	22.00

Top: **Hoffman Swan (1978),** part of the Duck Decoy Series, **$18.00–$26.00;** Right: **Hoffman Cowboy (1978),** part of the C.M. Russell Series #2, **$23.00–$34.00**

DECOY DUCKS LIMITED (DOES NOT INCLUDE MUSIC BOX)

	Price Range	
☐ CANADA GOOSE		
8 ounce capacity	18.00	26.00
☐ GREEN-WINGED TEAL	18.00	26.00
☐ MALLARDS		
2 ounce capacity	18.00	26.00
☐ PINTAIL	14.00	20.00
☐ WOOD DUCKS	18.00	26.00

MR. LUCKY SERIES—2 OUNCE MINIATURE SIZE. (DOES NOT INCLUDE MUSIC BOX)

☐ MR. DOCTOR	23.00	28.00
☐ MR. HARPIST	25.00	30.00
☐ MR. LUCKY	40.00	50.00
☐ MRS. LUCKY	22.00	27.00
☐ MR. SANDMAN	22.00	26.00
☐ SHOE COBBLER	22.00	27.00

JAPANESE BOTTLES

Bottlemaking in Japan is an ancient art. Although the collectible bottles presently produced in Japan are mainly for exportation, they still reflect native designing in their characteristic shapes and handsome enameling. Japanese bottles are increasing in numbers on the American market but prices remain modest. Japan produces figural bottles also. The popular Kamotsuru bottles picture characters from Japanese mythology.

	Price Range	
☐ DAUGHTER	12.00	18.00
☐ FAITHFUL RETAINER	15.00	25.00
☐ GOLDEN PAGODA	12.00	18.00
☐ "KIKU" GEISHA		
Blue, 13¼"	20.00	30.00
☐ MAIDEN	12.00	18.00
☐ NOH MASK	12.00	18.00
☐ OKAME MASK	35.00	45.00
☐ PLAYBOY	14.00	24.00
☐ PRINCESS	14.00	24.00
☐ RED LION MAN	20.00	30.00

	Price Range	
☐ **SAKE GOD**		
Colorful robe, porcelain 10″	10.00	14.00
☐ **SAKE GOD**		
White, Bone China, 10″	10.00	14.00
☐ **WHITE LION MAN**	35.00	45.00
☐ **WHITE PAGODA**	12.00	18.00
☐ **"YURI" GEISHA**		
Pink, red sash, 13¼″	35.00	45.00

HOUSE OF KOSHU

☐ **ANGEL**		
With book, 7 oz.	5.00	8.00
☐ **ANGEL**		
Sitting on a barrel, 17 oz.	5.00	8.00
☐ **BEETHOVEN BUST**		
7 oz.	5.00	8.00
☐ **CENTURIAN BUST**		
7 oz.	5.00	8.00
☐ **CHILDREN**		
7 oz.	7.00	10.00
☐ **DECLARATION OF INDEPENDENCE**	4.00	6.00
☐ **GEISHA**		
Blue	40.00	45.00
☐ **GEISHA**		
Cherry Blossom	25.00	30.00
☐ **GEISHA**		
Lily	23.00	28.00
☐ **GEISHA**		
Violet	27.00	32.00
☐ **GEISHA**		
Wisteria	25.00	30.00
☐ **GEISHA**		
Lavender, with fan	45.00	50.00
☐ **GEISHA**		
Reclining	60.00	70.00
☐ **GEISHA**		
Sitting	45.00	50.00
☐ **LIONMAN**		
Red	35.00	40.00
☐ **LIONMAN**		
White	65.00	70.00

	Price Range	
□ **PAGODA**		
Green	25.00	30.00
□ **PAGODA**		
White	20.00	25.00
□ **PAGODA**		
Gold	15.00	20.00
□ **SAILOR**		
With a pipe	4.00	7.00

KAMOTSURU BOTTLES

	Price Range	
□ **DAOKOKU**		
God of wealth	9.00	13.00
□ **EBISU**		
God of fishermen	9.00	13.00
□ **GODDESS OF ART**	7.00	11.00
□ **HOTEI**		
God of wealth	8.00	11.00

KENTUCKY GENTLEMAN BOTTLES

Kentucky Gentleman, another Kentucky whiskey distiller, issues figural bottles. Their figurals are released less frequently than those of Beam or Brooks. To date, they have concentrated on ceramics, picturing costumes worn at various times in American history, especially from the Civil War period. Large sized, more than a foot high, they are impressively modeled and colored. Each stands on a rectangular base, the front of which reads "Kentucky Gentleman."

	Price Range	
□ **CONFEDERATE INFANTRY**		
In gray uniform, with sword, 13½″	10.00	15.00
□ **FRONTIERS MAN** (1969)		
Coonskin cap, fringed buckskin, powder horn and long rifle, tan, 14″	13.00	18.00
□ **PINK LADY** (1969)		
Long bustle skirt, feathered hat, parasol, pink, 13¾″	25.00	35.00
□ **KENTUCKY GENTLEMEN** (1969)		
Figural bottle, frock coat, top hat and cane, "Old Colonel", gray ceramic, 14″	7.00	11.00

Japanese "yuri" Geisha,
pink, red sash, 13¼".
$35.00–$45.00

	Price Range	
☐ **REVOLUTIONARY WAR OFFICER** In dress uniform and boots, holding sword, 14"	11.00	14.00
☐ **UNION ARMY SARGEANT** In dress blue uniform, with sword, 14"	9.00	13.00

Kentucky Gentleman Pink Lady (1969), long, bustle skirt, feathered hat, parasol, 13¾". $25.00–$35.00

LIONSTONE BOTTLES

Lionstone Distillery, a relative newcomer into the ranks of figural bottle makers, has already garnered a substantial reputation. Their bottles stress realism in design with a great variety of subjects. Lionstone combines the better elements of classical porcelain-making with the traditional art of bottle manufacturing in their creations. Prices of the more popular issues have increased rapidly. Lionstone produced the most ambitious of all collector bottles in terms of components and detail. Their "Shootout At O.K. Corral," based upon an authentic incident in Old West history, consists of three bottles with nine human figures and two horses.

Lionstone issues all their bottles in series form, including the Oriental Worker series, Dog series, Sports series, Circus series, and Bicentennial series, with new ones added periodically. The most popular with collectors are the Western Figurals, a lengthy series depicting various characters from Western American history such as: Jesse James, Sod Buster, Mountain Man, Highway Robber, and Gentleman Gambler. Lionstone's Annie Oakley bottle comes complete with guns and sharpshooter medals.

Since prices of Lionstones on the collector market continue to be firm, buyers should investigate the possibility of spirits dealers still having some old unsold stock on hand.

	Price Range	
☐ BARTENDER	27.00	37.00
☐ BELLY ROBBER	15.00	20.00
☐ BLACKSMITH	25.00	32.00
☐ MOLLY BROWN	26.00	34.00
☐ BUFFALO HUNTER	32.00	38.00
☐ CALAMITY JANE	18.00	23.00
☐ CAMP COOK	22.00	28.00
☐ CAMP FOLLOWER	20.00	25.00
☐ CASUAL INDIAN	12.00	16.00
☐ CAVALRY SCOUT	10.00	14.00
☐ CHERRY VALLEY CLUB	50.00	65.00
☐ CHINESE LAUNDRYMAN	16.00	22.00
☐ ANNIE CHRISTMAS	16.00	24.00
☐ CIRCUIT JUDGE	10.00	15.00
☐ CORVETTE		
1.75 liters	50.00	55.00
☐ COUNTRY DOCTOR	15.00	22.00
☐ COWBOY	14.00	18.00
☐ FRONTIERSMAN	17.00	22.00
☐ GAMBELS QUAIL	8.00	12.00
☐ GENTLEMEN GAMBLER	32.00	47.00
☐ GOD OF LOVE	17.00	22.00
☐ GOD OF WAR	17.00	22.00
☐ GOLD PANNER	37.00	45.00
☐ HIGHWAY ROBBER	45.00	60.00
☐ JESSE JAMES	10.00	15.00
☐ JUDGE ROY BEAN	20.00	24.00
☐ JOHNNY LIGHTNING	67.00	77.00

	Price	Range
☐ LONELY LUKE	55.00	75.00
☐ LUCKY BUCK	24.00	31.00
☐ MINIATURES WESTERN (6)	85.00	110.00
☐ MINT BAR WITH FRAME	700.00	900.00
☐ MINT BAR w/nude & Fr.	1000.00	1250.00
☐ MOUNTAIN MAN	45.00	60.00
☐ ANNIE OAKLEY	18.00	22.00
☐ PROUD INDIAN	15.00	20.00
☐ RAILROAD ENGINEER	35.00	47.00
☐ RENEGADE TRADER	20.00	25.00
☐ RIVERBOAT CAPTAIN	45.00	55.00
☐ ROADRUNNER	28.00	36.00
☐ SHEEPHERDER	30.00	40.00
☐ SHERIFF	32.00	43.00
☐ SOD BUSTER	8.00	13.00
☐ STP TURBOCAR	35.00	47.00
☐ STP TUBOCAR w/gold & plt, PAIR	130.00	165.00
☐ SQUAWMAN	14.00	19.00
☐ STAGECOACH DRIVER	45.00	60.00
☐ TELEGRAPHER	15.00	20.00
☐ TINKER	25.00	30.00
☐ TRIBAL CHIEF	30.00	37.00
☐ AL UNSER #1	15.00	20.00
☐ WOODHAWK	22.00	30.00

BICENTENNIAL SERIES

☐ FIREFIGHTERS NO. 1 (Old Item)	90.00	110.00
☐ MAIL CARRIER	23.00	29.00
☐ MOLLY PITCHER	22.00	27.00
☐ PAUL REVERE	20.00	25.00
☐ BETSY ROSS	25.00	30.00
☐ SONS OF FREEDOM	32.00	38.00
☐ GEORGE WASHINGTON	25.00	30.00
☐ WINTER AT VALLEY FORGE	24.00	28.00

BICENTENNIAL WESTERNS

☐ BARBER	30.00	40.00
☐ FIREFIGHTER NO. 3	60.00	70.00

Price Range

☐ INDIAN WEAVER	18.00	22.00
☐ PHOTOGRAPHER	34.00	40.00
☐ RAINMAKER	27.00	33.00
☐ SATURDAY NIGHT	27.00	38.00
☐ TRAPPER	30.00	36.00

BIRD SERIES
(1972–74)

☐ BLUEBIRD—WISCONSIN	45.00	60.00
☐ BLUEJAY	45.00	60.00
☐ PEREGRINE FALCON	45.00	60.00
☐ MEADOWLARK	40.00	55.00
☐ SCREECH OWL	50.00	70.00
☐ SWALLOW	50.00	65.00

CIRCUS SERIES
(MINIATURES)

☐ THE BAKER	12.00	17.00
☐ BURMESE LADY	14.00	19.00
☐ FAT LADY	13.00	17.00
☐ FIRE EATER	13.00	17.00
☐ GIANT WITH MIDGET	13.00	17.00
☐ SNAKE CHARMER	13.00	17.00
☐ STRONG MAN	13.00	17.00
☐ SWORD SWALLOWER	13.00	17.00
☐ TATTOOED LADY	13.00	17.00

DOG SERIES
(MINIATURES)

☐ BOXER	14.00	20.00
☐ COCKER SPANIEL	12.00	17.00
☐ COLLIE	14.00	20.00
☐ POINTER	14.00	20.00
☐ POODLE	14.00	20.00

EUROPEAN WORKER SERIES

☐ THE COBBLER	50.00	65.00
☐ THE HORSESHOER	50.00	65.00

	Price Range	
☐ THE POTTER	50.00	65.00
☐ THE SILVERSMITH	50.00	65.00
☐ THE WATCHMAKER	50.00	65.00
☐ THE WOODWORKER	50.00	65.00

ORIENTAL WORKER SERIES

☐ BASKET WEAVER	22.00	30.00
☐ EGG MERCHANT	22.00	30.00
☐ GARDNER	22.00	30.00
☐ SCULPTOR	22.00	30.00
☐ TEA VENDOR	22.00	30.00
☐ TIMEKEEPER	22.00	30.00

SPORTS SERIES

☐ BASEBALL	22.00	30.00
☐ BASKETBALL	22.00	30.00
☐ BOXING	22.00	30.00
☐ FOOTBALL	22.00	30.00
☐ HOCKEY	22.00	30.00

TROPICAL BIRD SERIES (MINIATURES)

☐ BLUE CROWNED CHLOROPHONIA	12.00	16.00
☐ EMERALD TOUCANET	12.00	16.00
☐ NORTHERN ROYAL FLYCATCHER	12.00	16.00
☐ PAINTED BUNTING	12.00	16.00
☐ SCARLET MACAW	12.00	16.00
☐ YELLOW HEADED AMAZON	12.00	16.00

OTHER LIONSTONE BOTTLES

☐ BUCCANEER	50.00	70.00
☐ COWGIRL	50.00	70.00
☐ DANCE HALL GIRL	50.00	70.00
☐ FALCON	55.00	75.00
☐ FIREFIGHTER NO. 2	85.00	105.00
☐ FIREFIGHTER NO. 4		
Emblem	22.00	27.00

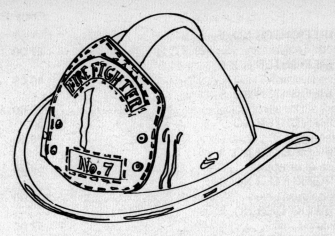

Top: **Lionstone Fire Fighter No. 7 (1982)**, *firefighter's
helmet, $20.00–$30.00;* Bottom Left to Right: **Lionstone
Fireman Emblem #5 (1979)**, *commemorating 60th anniversary
of The International Association of Fire Fighters $40.00–$50.00;*
Lionstone Indian Chief (1980) *$30.00–$50.00*

Price Range

☐ **FIREFIGHTER NO. 5**
60th Anniversary 22.00 27.00
☐ **FIREFIGHTER NO. 6**
Fire hydrant 40.00 45.00
☐ **FIREFIGHTER NO. 6**
In gold or silver 280.00 320.00
☐ **FIREFIGHTER NO. 7**
Helmet 70.00 80.00
☐ **FIREFIGHTER NO. 8**
Fire alarm box 50.00 55.00
☐ **FIREFIGHTER NO. 8**
In gold or silver 100.00 115.00
☐ **FIREFIGHTER NO. 9**
Extinguisher 55.00 60.00
☐ **FIREFIGHTER NO. 10**
Trumpet................................... 55.00 60.00
☐ **FIREFIGHTER NO. 10**
Gold 220.00 245.00
☐ **FIREFIGHTER NO. 10**
Silver 130.00 145.00
☐ **INDIAN MOTHER & PAPOOSE** 55.00 75.00
☐ **ROSES ON PARADE** 80.00 110.00
☐ **SCREECH OWLS** 50.00 65.00
☐ **THE PERFESSER** 50.00 65.00
☐ **UNSER-OLSONITE EAGLE** 55.00 70.00

OTHER MINIATURES

☐ **CLIFF SWALLOW MINIATURE** 13.00 18.00
☐ **DANCE HALL GIRL MINIATURE** 15.00 22.00
☐ **FIREFIGHTER EMBLEM** 24.00 31.00
☐ **FIREFIGHTER ENGINE NO. 8** 24.00 31.00
☐ **FIREFIGHTER ENGINE NO. 10** 24.00 31.00
☐ **HORSESHOE MINIATURE** 14.00 20.00
☐ **KENTUCKY DERBY RACE HORSE**
(Cannanade)............................... 33.00 43.00
☐ **SAHARA INVITATIONAL NO. 1** 33.00 43.00
☐ **SAHARA INVITATIONAL NO. 2** 33.00 43.00
☐ **SHOOT OUT AT THE OK CORRAL** (Set of three) 250.00 300.00

LUXARDO BOTTLES

Made in Torreglia, Italy, the Girolamo Luxardo bottles boast a long and distinctive history. Imported into the U.S. in 1930, the bottles gradually acquired an impressive following among American collectors. Chiefly a manufacturer of wine, Luxardo also sells liquors.

The Luxardo line, extremely well modeled and meticulously colored, captures the spirit of Renaissance glass. Varying hues of color are blended on most specimens which radiate brilliantly when light shines through the bottles. The effective coloring techniques of the Luxardo bottles compare to those of ancient Egypt where color was the most important consideration. While Egyptian bottles were often colored garishly, the Luxardos carefully balance splashiness and restraint—the dominant colors never obscure the pastel shades.

Many of Luxardo's bottles, both glass and majolica, are figural. Natural history subjects as well as classical themes predominate. Most of the majolica decanters can be reused as vases, jars, lamp bases, or ash trays.

The firms maintains a regular schedule for its bottle production. Between three to six new designs are chosen each January for that year's production. The most popular, such as the *Cellini* bottle introduced in the early 1950s, continue to be used. Occasionally a design is discontinued after just one year. The Chess Set, produced in 1959, was discontinued because of manufacturing difficulty.

Unfortunately, the names and dates of production of the earlier Luxardo decanters are mostly unknown, due to many owners removing the paper identification labels.

The rare Zara decanters, made before World War II, are expected to increase further in value and scarcity. The *"First Born"* of the Murano Venetion glass, if ever located, will command a very strong price. Eventually, all the Naponelli "signed" decanters should rise markedly in value because of the small quantities issued.

Although the knowledgeable dealers are aware of the Luxardo prices, remarkable bargains are sometimes obtainable by shopping at garage sales, thrift stores and charity outlets.

Specimens in mint condition with the original manufacturer's label always command the highest sums. All prices listed are for empty bottles, in Fine to Mint condition.

If current or recent Luxardo bottles are not available at your local spirits dealer, the dealer can order them from the American distributor, Hans Schonewalk, American Beverage Brokers, 420 Market Street, San Francisco, California 94111.

Price Range

☐ **ALABASTER FISH FIGURAL** (1960–67–68) . . .	19.00	26.00
☐ **ALABASTER GOOSE FIGURAL** (1960–67–68)		
Green and white, wings, etc.	19.00	26.00
☐ **AMPULLA FLASK** (1958–59)	14.00	19.00
☐ **APOTHECARY JAR** (1960)		
Hand painted multicolor, green and black	11.00	16.00
☐ **AUTUMN LEAVES DECANTER** (1952)		
Hand painted, 2 handles	30.00	40.00
☐ **ASSYRIAN ASHTRAY DECANTER** (1961)		
Gray, tan and black	16.00	22.00
☐ **AUTUMN WINE PITCHER** (1958)		
Hand painted country scene, handled pitcher . .	30.00	40.00
☐ **BABYLON DECANTER** (1960)		
Dark green and gold	16.00	23.00
☐ **BIZANTINA** (1959)		
Gold embossed design, white body	28.00	38.00
☐ **BLUE FIAMMETTA or VERMILLIAN** (1957)		
Decanter	20.00	27.00
☐ **BLUE & GOLD AMPHORA** (1968)		
Blue and gold with pastoral scene in white oval	14.00	19.00
☐ **BROCCA (PITCHER)** (1958)		
White background pitcher with handle, multicolor flowers, green leaves	28.00	37.00
☐ **BUDDHA GODDESS FIGURAL** (1961)		
Goddess head in green-gray stone	14.00	19.00
Miniature	11.00	16.00
☐ **BURMA ASH TRAY SPECIALTY** (1960)		
Embossed white dancing figure, dark green background	13.00	18.00
☐ **BURMA PITCHER SPECIALTY** (1960)		
Green and gold, white embossed dancing figure	14.00	19.00
☐ **CALYPSO GIRL FIGURAL** (1962)		
Black West Indian girl, flower headdress in bright color	14.00	19.00
☐ **CANDLESTICK ALABASTER** (1961)	20.00	28.00
☐ **CELLINI VASE** (1958–68)		
Glass and silver decanter, fancy	14.00	19.00
☐ **CELLINI VASE** (1957)		
Glass and silver handled decanter, fancy, with serpent handle	14.00	19.00

Price Range

☐ **CERAMIC BARREL** (1968)
Barrel shape, barrel color, painted flowers, embossed scroll with cameo head on decorative stand **14.00   19.00**

☐ **CHERRY BASKET FIGURAL** (1960)
White basket, red cherries **14.00   19.00**

☐ **CLASSICAL FRAGMENT SPECIALTY** (1961)
Embossed Classic Roman female figure and vase **25.00   33.00**

☐ **COCKTAIL SHAKER** (1957)
Glass and silver decanter, silver plated top **14.00   19.00**

☐ **COFFEE CARAFE SPECIALTY** (1962)
Old time coffee pot, with handle and spout, white with blue flowers **14.00   19.00**

☐ **CURVA VASO VASE** (1961)
Green, green and white, ruby red **22.00   29.00**

☐ **DERUTA CAMEO AMPHORA** (1959)
Colorful floral scrolls and cameo head on eggshell white, twohandled vase **25.00   35.00**

☐ **DERUTA AMPHORA** (1956)
Colorful floral design on white, two handled decanter **11.00   16.00**

☐ **DERUTA PITCHER** (1953)
Multicolor flowers on base perugia, white single-handled pitcher **11.00   16.00**

☐ **DIANA DECANTER** (1956)
White figure of Diana with deer on black, single-handled decanter **11.00   16.00**

☐ **DOGAL SILVER & GREEN DECANTER** (1952–56)
Hand painted gondola **14.00   19.00**

☐ **DOGAL SILVER SMOKE DECANTER** (1952–55)
Hand painted gondola **14.00   19.00**

☐ **DOGAL SILVER SMOKE DECANTER** (1953–54)
Hand painted gondola **11.00   16.00**

☐ **DOGAL SILVER RUBY** (1952–56)
Hand painted gondola, silver band neck **14.00   18.00**

☐ **DOGAL SILVER SMOKE DECANTER** (1956)
Hand painted silver clouds and gondola **11.00   16.00**

☐ **DOGAL SILVER SMOKE DECANTER** (1956)
Hand painted gondola, buildings, flowers, neck bands **14.00   18.00**

Price Range

☐ **DOGAL SILVER RUBY DECANTER** (1956)
Hand painted Venetian scene and flowers **17.00   22.00**
☐ **DOLPHIN FIGURAL** (1959)
Yellow, green, blue **42.00   57.00**
☐ **"DOUGHNUT" BOTTLE** (1960) CLOCK BOTTLE
(1959)
Cherry este working clock in doughnut shape bot-
tle **14.00   18.00**
☐ **DRAGON AMPHORA** (1953)
Two handled white decanter with colorful dragon
and flowers **14.00   18.00**
☐ **DRAGON PITCHER** (1958)
One handle, white pitcher, color dragon and
scroll work **14.00   18.00**
☐ **DUCK-GREEN GLASS FIGURAL** (1960)
Green and amber duck, clear glass base **20.00   27.00**
☐ **EAGLE** (1970) **45.00   55.00**
☐ **EGYPTIAN SPECIALTY** (1960)
Two handle amphora, Egyptian design on tan and
gold background **14.00   19.00**
☐ **EUGANEAN BRONZE** (1952–55) **14.00   19.00**
☐ **EUGANEAN COPPERED** (1962–55)
Majolica **13.00   18.00**
☐ **ETRUSCAN DECANTER** (1959)
Single handle black Greek design on tan back-
ground **14.00   19.00**
Except A, earthen brown **13.00   18.00**
☐ **FAENZA DECANTER** (1952–56)
Colorful country scene on white single handle de-
canter **21.00   28.00**
☐ **FIGHTING COCKS** (1962)
Combination decanter and ashtray, black and red
fighting birds **14.00   19.00**
☐ **FISH GREEN & GOLD GLASS FIGURAL** (1960)
Green, silver and gold, clear glass base **16.00   21.00**
☐ **FISH RUBY MURANO GLASS FIGURAL** (1961)
Ruby red tones of glass **26.00   37.00**
☐ **FLORENTINE MAJOLICA** (1956)
Round handled decanter, painted pitcher, yellow,
dragon, blue wings **21.00   27.00**

Price Range

☐ **GAMBIA** (1961)
Black princess, kneeling holding tray, gold trim,
10¾" **14.00   19.00**

☐ **GOLDEN FAKIR**
Seated snake charmer, with flute and snakes,
gold **26.00   37.00**
1961—Fakir 1960, black and gray **26.00   37.00**

☐ **GONDOLA** (1959)
Highly glazed abstract gondola and gondolier in
black, orange and yellow, stopper on upper prow,
12¾" **21.00   27.00**

☐ **GONDOLA** (1960)
Same as 1959, stopper moved from prow to stern **14.00   19.00**

☐ **GRAPES, PEAR FIGURAL** **24.00   34.00**

☐ **MAYAN** (1960)
A Mayan temple god head mask, brown, yellow,
black, white, 11" **15.00   25.00**

☐ **MOSAIC ASHTRAY** (1959)
Combination decanter ashtray, mosaic pattern of
rearing horse, black, yellow, green, 11½" **15.00   25.00**
Miniature 6", black, green **10.00   14.00**

☐ **NUBIAN**
Kneeling black figure, gold dress and headress,
9½" **14.00   19.00**
Miniature, as above, 4¾" **8.00   11.00**

☐ **OPAL MAJOLICA** (1957)
Two gold handles, translucent opal top, pink
base, also used as lamp base, 10" **14.00   19.00**

☐ **PENGUIN MURANO GLASS FIGURAL** (1968)
Black and white penguin, crystal base **26.00   37.00**

☐ **PHEASANT RED & GOLD FIGURAL** (1960)
Red and gold glass bird on crystal base **23.00   35.00**

☐ **PHEASANT MURANO GLASS FIGURAL** (1960)
Red and clear glass on a crystal base **26.00   37.00**

☐ **PRIMAVERA AMPHORA** (1958)
Two handled vase shape, with floral design in yellow, green and blue, 9¾" **14.00   19.00**

☐ **PUPPY CUCCIOLO GLASS FIGURAL** (1961)
Amber and green glass **26.00   37.00**

☐ **PUPPY MURANO GLASS FIGURAL** (1960)
Amber glass, crystal base **26.00   37.00**

Price Range

☐ **SILVER BLUE DECANTER** (1952–55)
Hand painted silver flowers and leaves **22.00 28.00**
☐ **SILVER BROWN DECANTER** (1952–55)
Hand painted silver flowers and leaves **26.00 37.00**
☐ **SIR LANCELOT** (1962)
Figure of English knight in full armor with embossed shield, tan-gray with gold, 12″ **14.00 19.00**
☐ **SPRINGBOX AMPHORA** (1952)
Vase with handle, leaping African deer with floral and lattice background, black, brown, 9¾″ **14.00 19.00**
☐ **SQUIRREL GLASS FIGURAL** (1968)
Amethyst colored squirrel on crystal base **30.00 40.00**
☐ **SUDAN** (1960)
Two handle classic vase, incised figures, African motif in browns, blue, yellow and gray, 13½″ .. **14.00 19.00**
☐ **TOWER OF FRUIT MAJOLICAS TORRE BIANCA** (1962)
White and gray tower of fruit, 10¼″ **16.00 24.00**
☐ **TORRE ROSA** (1962)
Rose tinted tower of fruit, 10¼″ **16.00 24.00**
☐ **TORRE TINTA** (1962)
Multicolor tower of fruit, natural shades **14.00 20.00**
☐ **TOWER OF FRUIT** (1968)
Various fruits in natural colors, 22¼″ **16.00 24.00**

McCORMICK

The McCormick bottles are made for retailing McCormick Irish Whiskey. There are four different series: Cars, Famous Americans, Frontiersman Decanters and Gunfighters. The category for cars includes various forms of transportation. The lengthiest series has been the Famous American, encompassing celebrities from colonial times to the 20th century. Released in limited numbers, the prices on all of the McCormick's are automatically higher than most figurals.

Price Range

BARREL SERIES

☐ **BARREL** (1958)
With stand and shot glasses **28.00 36.00**
☐ **BARREL** (1968)
With stand and plain hoops **14.00 18.00**

Price Range

☐ **BARREL** (1968)
With stand and gold hoops 18.00   26.00

BIRD SERIES

☐ **BLUE JAY** (1971)	16.00	20.00
☐ **WOOD DUCK** (1980)	23.00	30.00
☐ **GAMBEL'S QUAIL** (1982)	40.00	50.00
☐ **RING NECK PHEASANT** (1982)	35.00	45.00

BULL SERIES

☐ **CHARLOLAIS** (1974)	35.00	42.00
☐ **BRAHMA** (1973)	40.00	46.00
☐ **HERFORD** (1972)	42.00	48.00
☐ **MEXICAN FIGHTING** (1974)	30.00	38.00
☐ **TEXAS LONGHORN** (1974)	34.00	40.00

CAR SERIES

☐ **PACKARD** (1937)	36.00	42.00
☐ **THE PONY EXPRESS**	30.00	42.00
☐ **THE SAND BUGGY COMMEMORATIVE DECANTER**	35.00	50.00

CONFEDERATE SERIES

☐ **JEFFERSON DAVIS**	18.00	25.00
☐ **STONEWALL JACKSON**	18.00	25.00
☐ **ROBERT E. LEE**	25.00	35.00
☐ **JEB STUART**	18.00	25.00

COUNTRY & WESTERN SERIES

☐ **HANK WILLIAMS, SR.** (1980)	35.00	42.00
☐ **HANK WILLIAMS, JR.** (1980)	40.00	50.00
☐ **TOM T. HALL** (1980)	32.00	42.00

ELVIS PRESLEY SERIES

☐ **ELVIS '77** (1978)	65.00	80.00
☐ **ELVIS BUST** (1978)	24.00	35.00

	Price	Range
☐ **ELVIS '55** (1979)	26.00	37.00
☐ **ELVIS '68** (1980)	25.00	35.00
☐ **ELVIS '77** (1979)		
Mini	32.00	40.00
☐ **ELVIS '55** (1980)		
Mini	32.00	40.00
☐ **ELVIS GOLD** (1979)	195.00	220.00
☐ **ELVIS SILVER** (1980)	145.00	155.00
☐ **ELVIS '68** (1981)		
Mini	40.00	50.00
☐ **ELVIS KARATE**	90.00	105.00
☐ **ELVIS DESIGNER I**		
Music box plays *Are You Lonesome Tonight?*	85.00	100.00
☐ **ELVIS, DESIGNER II**		
Music box plays *It's Now or Never*	85.00	100.00
☐ **ELVIS SERGEANT**	130.00	150.00

FAMOUS AMERICAN PORTRAIT SERIES

☐ **ALEXANDER GRAHAM BELL**		
With apron	15.00	25.00
☐ **GEORGE WASHINGTON CARVER**	28.00	40.00
☐ **WILLIAM CLARK**	23.00	31.00
☐ **THOMAS EDISON**	33.00	44.00
☐ **HENRY FORD**	30.00	42.00
☐ **ULYSSES S. GRANT**		
With coffee pot and cup	20.00	30.00
☐ **LEWIS-MERIWEATHER**	20.00	30.00
☐ **ABE LINCOLN**		
With law book in hand	26.00	35.00
☐ **CHARLES LINDBERGH**	35.00	47.00
☐ **ROBERT E. PERRY**	26.00	35.00
☐ **POCAHANTAS**	30.00	42.00
☐ **ELEANOR ROOSEVELT**	20.00	27.00
☐ **CAPTAIN JOHN SMITH**	29.00	39.00

FOOTBALL MASCOTS

☐ **ALABAMA BAMA**	26.00	34.00
☐ **ARIZONA WILDCATS**	21.00	27.00
☐ **ARIZONA SUN DEVILS**	39.00	48.00
☐ **ARKANSAS HOGS** (1972)	42.00	48.00

Price Range

☐ AUBURN WAR EAGLES	16.00	24.00
☐ BAYLOR BEARS (1972)	24.00	30.00
☐ CALIFORNIA BEARS	20.00	25.00
☐ DRAKE BULLDOGS (1974)		
Blue helmet and jersey	14.00	19.00
☐ GEORGIA BULLDOGS		
Black helmet and red jersey	12.00	19.00
☐ GEORGIA TECH YELLOWJACKETS	12.00	18.00
☐ HOUSTON COUGARS (1972)	18.00	25.00
☐ INDIANA HOOSIERS (1974)	14.00	24.00
☐ IOWA CYCLONES (1974)	45.00	55.00
☐ IOWA HAWKEYES (1974)	55.00	65.00
☐ IOWA PURPLE PANTHERS	32.00	42.00
☐ LOUISIANA STATE TIGERS (1974)	14.00	19.00
☐ MICHIGAN STATE SPARTANS	15.00	20.00
☐ MICHIGAN WOLVERINES (1974)	14.00	19.00
☐ MINNESOTA GOPHERS (1974)	13.00	17.00
☐ MISSISSIPPI REBELS (1974)	13.00	17.00
☐ MISSISSIPPI STATE BULLDOGS (1974)		
Red helmet and jersey	12.00	18.00
☐ MISSOURI UNIVERSITY TIGERS (1974)		
☐ NEBRASKA CORNHUSKERS (1974)	12.00	18.00
☐ NEW MEXICO LOBO	32.00	40.00
☐ OKLAHOMA SOONERS WAGON (1974)	20.00	28.00
☐ OKLAHOMA SOUTHER COWBOY (1974)	11.00	15.00
☐ OREGON BEAVERS (1974)	12.00	18.00
☐ OREGON DUCKS (1974)	12.00	18.00
☐ PURDUE BOILERMAKER (1974)	22.00	27.00
☐ RICE OWLS (1972)	18.00	23.00
☐ S.M.U. MUSTANGS (1972)	17.00	24.00
☐ TCU HORNED FROGS (1972)	25.00	30.00
☐ TENNESSEE VOLUNTEERS (1974)	11.00	15.00
☐ TEXAS A&M AGGIES (1972)	22.00	30.00
☐ TEXAS TECH RAIDERS (1972)	20.00	26.00
☐ TEXAS HORNS (1972)	23.00	33.00
☐ WASHINGTON COUGARS (1974)	11.00	15.00
☐ WASHINGTON HUSKIES (1974)	11.00	15.00
☐ WISCONSIN BADGERS (1974)	11.00	15.00

McCormick, *Oklahoma Sooners Wagon (1974).* **$22.00–$26.00**

McCormick Airplane, *Spirit of St. Louis (1969).* **$80.00–$90.00**

FRONTIERSMEN COMMEMORATIVE DECANTERS 1972

Price Range

☐ **DANIEL BOONE**	25.00	31.00
☐ **JIM BOWIE**	25.00	31.00
☐ **KIT CARSON**	16.00	24.00
☐ **DAVIE CROCKETT**	17.00	25.00

GENERAL

☐ **A & P WAGON**	50.00	56.00
☐ **AIRPLANE** (1969)		
Spirit of St. Louis	80.00	90.00
☐ **AMERICAN BALD EAGLE** (1982)	30.00	40.00
☐ **BUFFALO BILL** (1979)	45.00	55.00
☐ **CABLE CAR**	28.00	32.00
☐ **CAR** (1980)		
Packard 1937 Black or cream, first in a series of classic cars, rolling wheels and vinyl seats	50.00	60.00
☐ **CHAIR**		
Queen Anne	28.00	32.00
☐ **CIAO BABY** (1978)	25.00	35.00
☐ **CLOCK** (1971)		
Cuckoo	25.00	35.00
☐ **DE WITT CLINTON ENGINE** (1970)	40.00	50.00
☐ **FRENCH TELEPHONE** (1969)	28.00	34.00
☐ **GLOBE** (1971)		
Angelica	25.00	32.00
☐ **HUTCHINSON KANSAS CENTENNIAL** (1972)	12.00	18.00
☐ **JESTER** (1972)	20.00	28.00
☐ **JIMMY DURANTE** (1981)		
With music box, plays *Inka Dinka Do*	31.00	40.00
☐ **J.R. EWING** (1980)		
With music box, plays theme song from *Dallas.*	22.00	27.00
☐ **J.R. EWING**		
Gold colored	63.00	67.00
☐ **JOPLIN MINER** (1972)	13.00	20.00
☐ **JULIA BULETTE** (1974)	150.00	180.00
☐ **LAMP**		
Hurricane	13.00	18.00
☐ **LARGE MOUTH BASS** (1982)	20.00	28.00
☐ **LOBSTERMAN** (1979)	30.00	35.00

	Price	Range
☐ LOUIS ARMSTRONG	35.00	40.00
☐ McCORMICK CENTENNIAL (1956)	125.00	150.00
☐ MIKADO (1980)	75.00	100.00
☐ MO. SESQUICENTENNIAL CHINA (1970)	5.00	11.00
☐ MO. SESQUICENTENNIAL GLASS (1971)	3.00	7.00
☐ U.S. MARSHAL (1979)	35.00	45.00
☐ OZARK IKE (1979)	22.00	27.00
☐ PAUL BUNYAN (1979)	35.00	40.00
☐ PONY EXPRESS (1978)	20.00	25.00
☐ PIONEER THEATRE (1972)	8.00	12.00
☐ RENAULT RACER (1969)	40.00	50.00
☐ THELMA LU (1982)	20.00	28.00
☐ YACHT AMERICANA (1971)	30.00	38.00
☐ MARK TWAIN (1977)	24.00	28.00
☐ WILL ROGERS (1977)	28.00	38.00
☐ HENRY FORD (1977)	28.00	38.00
☐ STEPHEN F. AUSTIN (1977)	17.00	22.00
☐ SAM HOUSTON (1977)	22.00	28.00
☐ TELEPHONE OPERATOR	52.00	60.00

GUNFIGHTER SERIES

☐ BLACK BART	26.00	35.00
☐ WYATT EARP	21.00	30.00
☐ WILD BILL HICKOK	21.00	30.00
☐ DOC HOLIDAY	28.00	37.00
☐ JESSE JAMES	26.00	35.00
☐ CALAMITY JANE	28.00	37.00
☐ BILLY THE KID	26.00	35.00
☐ BAT MASTERSON	28.00	37.00

JUG SERIES

☐ BOURBON JUG	62.00	70.00
☐ PLATTE VALLEY (1953)		
Traditional jug shape with two small handles from shoulders to neck	5.00	12.00
☐ GIN JUG	6.00	10.00
☐ VODKA JUG	6.00	10.00
☐ OLD HOLIDAY BOURBON (1956)		
Embossed lettering in various sizes	6.00	18.00

KING ARTHUR SERIES

Price Range

☐ KING ARTHUR ON THRONE 30.00 40.00
☐ MERLIN THE WIZARD WITH HIS WISE OLD
   MAGICAL ROBE (c. 1979) 17.00 25.00
☐ QUEEN GUINEVERE, THE GEM OF ROYAL
   COURT 12.00 18.00
☐ SIR LANCELOT OF THE THE LAKE IN ARMOR
   A KNIGHT OF ROUNDTABLE 12.00 18.00

THE LITERARY SERIES

☐ HUCK FINN (1980)
   Sets fishing, leaning on a tree trunk and smoking
   a pipe 15.00 22.00
☐ TOM SAWYER (1980)
   Stands in front of a fence scratching his head 22.00 26.00

MINIATURES

☐ PATRIOT MINIATURE SET (8) (1976) 175.00 200.00
☐ MINIATURE SPIRIT OF '76 (1977) 20.00 30.00
☐ MINIATURE GUNFIGHTERS (8) (1977) 110.00 140.00
☐ CONFEDERATES MINIATURE SET (4) (1978) 50.00 75.00
☐ MINIATURE NOBLE (1978) 14.00 20.00
☐ MARK TWAIN MINIATURE (1978) 12.00 18.00
☐ WILL ROGERS MINIATURE (1978) 12.00 16.00
☐ HENRY FORD MINIATURE (1978) 10.00 14.00
☐ CHARLES LINDBERGH MINIATURE (1978) .. 8.00 12.00
☐ ROSE COLLECTION (1980) 80.00 90.00
☐ PONY EXPRESS MINIATURE (1980) 12.00 15.00
☐ MINIATURE JUPITER 60 TRAIN (1980) 65.00 75.00

THE PATRIOTS

☐ BENJAMIN FRANKLIN (1975) 17.00 25.00
☐ JOHN HANCOCK (1975) 18.00 24.00
☐ PATRICK HENRY (1975) 16.00 24.00
☐ THOMAS JEFFERSON (1975) 18.00 24.00
☐ JOHN PAUL JONES (1975) 20.00 27.00
☐ PAUL REVERE (1975) 32.00 40.00
☐ BETSY ROSS (1975) 25.00 34.00
☐ SPIRIT OF '76 (1976) 65.00 75.00
☐ GEORGE WASHINGTON (1975) 30.00 40.00

PIRATES SERIES

<table>
<tr><td></td><td></td><td>Price Range</td></tr>
</table>

	Price	Range
☐ **PIRATE, NO. 1** (1972)	12.00	16.00
☐ **PIRATE, NO. 2** (1972)	12.00	16.00
☐ **PIRATE, NO. 3** (1972)	8.00	12.00
☐ **PIRATE, NO. 4** (1972)	8.00	12.00
☐ **PIRATE, NO. 5** (1972)	8.00	12.00
☐ **PIRATE, NO. 6** (1972)	8.00	12.00
☐ **PIRATE, NO. 7** (1972)	8.00	12.00
☐ **PIRATE, NO. 8** (1972)	8.00	12.00
☐ **PIRATE, NO. 9** (1972)	8.00	12.00
☐ **PIRATE, NO. 10** (1972)	20.00	28.00
☐ **PIRATE, NO. 11** (1972)	20.00	28.00
☐ **PIRATE, NO. 12** (1972)	20.00	28.00

RURAL AMERICANA SERIES

☐ **WOMAN FEEDING CHICKENS** (1980) Young woman with white bonnet and apron tossing feed, two chickens at her feet	40.00	50.00
☐ **WOMAN WASHING CLOTHES** (1980) Setting on a low table	40.00	50.00

SHRINE SERIES

☐ **CIRCUS**	48.00	53.00
☐ **IMPERIAL COUNCIL**	40.00	45.00
☐ **JESTER (MIRTH KING)** (1972)	40.00	50.00
☐ **THE NOBLE** (1976)	25.00	32.00
☐ **DUNE BUGGY** (1976)	55.00	60.00

SPORTS SERIES

☐ **AIR RACE PROPELLER** (1971)	15.00	20.00
☐ **AIR RACE PYLON** (1970)	7.00	12.00
☐ **MUHAMMID ALI** (1980)	32.00	37.00
☐ **JOHNNY RODGERS NO. 1** (1972)	160.00	195.00
☐ **JOHNNY RODGERS NO. 2** (1973)	70.00	85.00
☐ **K.C. CHIEFS** (1969)	35.00	45.00

	Price Range	
☐ **K.C. ROYALS** (1971)	8.00	13.00
☐ **NEBRASKA FOOTBALL PLAYER** (1972)	22.00	30.00
☐ **SKIBOB** (1971)	12.00	18.00

TRAIN SERIES

☐ **JUPITER ENGINE** (1969)	32.00	42.00
☐ **MAIL CAR** (1970)	43.00	55.00
☐ **PASSENGER CAR** (1970)	63.00	75.00
☐ **WOOD TENDER** (1969)	22.00	28.00

WARRIOR SERIES

☐ **BERSAGLIERI** (1969)	16.00	24.00
☐ **CENTURION** (1969)	16.00	24.00
☐ **GARIBALDI** (1969)	16.00	24.00
☐ **NAPOLEON** (1969)	16.00	24.00

THE BOTTLES LISTED BELOW WERE DESTROYED

☐ **GUNFIGHTER SERIES** (c. 1972)
☐ **FAMOUS AMERICANS** (c. 1976)
☐ **FRONTIERSMEN SERIES** (c. 1975)
☐ **PATRIOT DECANTERS** (C. 1976)

OBR BOTTLES (OLD BLUE RIBBON)

Old Blue Ribbon (OBR) bottles are made to contain the company's liquors. With a relatively late start in issuing figural bottles, this firm has released a large number in recent years. The OBR bottles with historical themes are distinctive for their realism, such as the "Jupiter '60" series depicting various railroad cars from the 19th century. OBR is the only bottle maker with a Hockey Series; each bottle in this group relates to a different professional hockey team. The company also issues a Transportation Series, which includes such diverse representations as a hot-air balloon and a 5th Avenue New York Bus.

	Price Range	
☐ **AIR RACE DECANTER (PYLON)**	15.00	22.00
☐ **BLUE BIRD**	14.00	19.00
☐ **CABOOSE MKT**	13.00	17.00
☐ **EASTERN KENTUCKY UNIVERSITY**	15.00	21.00

	Price Range	
□ JUPITER '60 MAIL CAR	13.00	17.00
□ JUPITER '60 PASSENGER CAR	16.00	23.00
□ JUPITER '60 WOOD TENDER	13.00	17.00
□ JUPITER '60 LOCOMOTIVE	15.00	22.00
□ K.C. ROYALS	18.00	24.00
□ PIERCE ARROW	15.00	20.00
□ SANTA MARIA COLUMBUS SHIP	10.00	15.00
□ TITANIC OCEAN LINER	30.00	37.00

OBR TRANSPORTATION SERIES

□ BALLOON	9.00	12.00
□ 5TH AVE. BUS	14.00	21.00
□ PRAIRIE SCHOONER	12.00	20.00
□ RIVER QUEEN	10.00	15.00
□ RIVER QUEEN, GOLD	22.00	28.00

OBR HOCKEY SERIES

□ BOSTON BRUINS.........................	13.00	17.00
□ CHICAGO BLACK HAWKS	10.00	15.00
□ DETROIT RED WINGS	14.00	19.00
□ MINNESOTA NORTH STARS	13.00	17.00
□ NEW YORK RANGERS	17.00	24.00
□ ST. LOUIS BLUES	17.00	24.00

1972–74

□ AGING BARREL WITH SPIGOT	11.00	15.00
□ ROBERT E. LEE	24.00	32.00
□ PIRATES		
Different types of costumes, each	14.00	19.00
□ PLATTE VALLEY POTTERY JUG	13.00	17.00
□ YACHT AMERICA	13.00	17.00

OLD COMMONWEALTH

The brand name, Old Commonwealth, is produced by J. P. Van Winkle and Son. Opening in 1974, it was one of the newer companies involved in producing collector decanters with high-quality whiskey. The company presently bottles its products at the Hoffman Distilling

Company, located in Lawrenceburg, Kentucky. Their ceramic decanters are manufactured in the Orient, but they brew their own 80 proof Kentucky bourbon whiskey, which is distributed nationally.

Their decanters are easily identified because the titles of most pieces appear on front plaques. The first Old Commonwealth mini piece was made in 1980 when a small version of Coal Miner #1 was offered. Today, the majority of the decanters are produced in regular and miniature sizes.

	Price Range	
☐ **ALABAMA CRIMSON TIDE** (1981)		
University of Alabama symbol, front of elephant thrusting through a large red "A," elephant's foot propped on top of a football, "Crimson Tide" printed on the front	23.00	30.00
☐ **BULLDOGS** (1982)		
The mascot of the Georgia Bulldogs, front portion of a bulldog stands in the center of a large "G" with one front paw propped on a football	25.00	35.00
☐ **CHIEF ILLINI** (1979)		
#1, the mascot for the University of Illinois, warrior stands with arms up and spread wide, dressed in beige buckskin and ceremonial warbonnet	78.00	87.00
☐ **CHIEF ILLINI** (1981)		
#2, the mascot of the University of Illinois, warrior running with arms flung back to the sides, dressed in beige buckskins and orange feathered headdress, a large letter "I" in orange and blue stands behind him	55.00	65.00
☐ **CHIEF ILLINI** (1979)		
#3	65.00	75.00
☐ **COTTONTAIL** (1981)		
Jumping rabbit lands on front feet with hind feet extended in the air, short stump	25.00	35.00
☐ **COAL MINER** (1975)		
#1, man stands holding shovel in one hand, and other hand on jacket, bucket of coal at his feet	97.00	110.00
Mini (1980)	30.00	38.00
☐ **COAL MINER** (1976)		
#2, man stands with pick in one hand and a lantern in the other, wears blue mining outfit with red kerchief, plaque reads "Old Time Coal Miner"	28.00	34.00
Mini (1982)	19.00	28.00

Old Commonwealth Western Boot Decanter (1982), replica of a brown leather boot with exact shading, 10½".
$42.00–$52.00

Old Commonwealth U.S.C. Trojan, (1980), the mascot for the University of Southern California, a warrior stands at base of pillar with sword, shield and Trojan helmet.
$45.00–$55.00

Price Range

☐ **COAL MINER** (1977)
#3, miner kneels on one leg, holding a shovel
in one hand and coal in the other hand, bucket
of coal at his feet **28.00** **36.00**
Mini (1981) **30.00** **38.00**

☐ **COAL MINER-LUNCH TIME** (1980)
#4, miner sits eating lunch, red apple in one
hand, wears blue overalls and red miner's hat **33.00** **43.00**
Mini **20.00** **27.00**

☐ **ELUSIVE LEPRECHAUN** (1980)
Leprechaun sits on top of a pot of gold with arms
wrapped around bent knees, wears dark green
hat and boots, and red jacket **24.00** **30.00**

☐ **FISHERMAN, "A KEEPER"** (1980)
Old man sits holding fish in both hands, his pole
tucked in one arm, fishing tackle sits on the
ground **32.00** **40.00**

☐ **GOLDEN RETRIEVER** (1979)
Dog sits with game laying between front feet .. **30.00** **40.00**

☐ **KENTUCKY THOROUGHBREDS** (1976)
Red mare and colt with dark manes and tails,
prancing on blue grass **30.00** **40.00**

☐ **L.S.U. TIGER** (1979)
The mascot for Louisiana State University, fero-
cious tiger stands with front legs resting on stone
structure, a football under one paw, "LSU" in yellow on structure **45.00** **55.00**

MODERN FIREFIGHTERS SERIES

☐ **MODERN HERO** (1982)
#1, stands clutching an axe and oxygen mask,
wears black firefighting outfit with yellow stripes,
number "1" on helmet, 12″ **40.00** **47.00**
Mini **15.00** **21.00**

☐ **THE NOZZLEMAN** (1982)
#2, firefighter kneels on rubble of bricks, holding
fire hose, wears oxygen mask over face and yel-
low tank on his back, number "2" on helmet, 9½″ **41.00** **49.00**
Mini, 5″ **17.00** **24.00**

Price Range

☐ **ON CALL** (1982)
#3, pair of black firefighting boots with yellow
toes, red helmet rests on top of boots, number
"3" on helmet, 8½" 40.00 50.00
Mini 15.00 24.00

☐ **FALLEN COMRADE** (1982)
#4, pair of firefighters with one unconscious on
his back, the other kneels next to him while placing an oxygen mask over the victim's face, kneeling firefighter wears helmet with the number "4,"
7" 45.00 55.00
Mini, 3½" 17.00 25.00

☐ **OLD RIP VAN WINKLE** (1974)
#1, old man sits on stump with legs crossed and
musket held across his lap, wears green hat and
jacket, and red pants 40.00 50.00

☐ **OLD RIP VAN WINKLE** (1975)
#2, old man sprawled with his back resting
against a stump, sleeping, musket held between
crossed hand 35.00 45.00

☐ **OLD RIP VAN WINKLE** (1977)
#3, old man stands stroking his long white beard,
musket propped on ground, held in crook of arm,
wears tattered clothes 30.00 40.00

☐ **TENNESSEE WALKING HORSE** (1977)
Black, prancing horse, red and yellow bridle,
stands on aqua green grass 24.00 35.00

☐ **U.S.C. TROJAN** (1980)
The mascot for the University of Southern California, a warrior stands at base of pillar with sword,
shield and Trojan helmet 45.00 55.00
Mini 11.00 16.00

WATERFOWLER SERIES

☐ **WATERFOWLER** (1979)
#1, hunter with shotgun slung under one arm
and two ducks held in the other hand, wears
beige hunter's jacket and hat 40.00 50.00

☐ **HERE THEY COME** (1980)
#2, hunter kneels in front on log, aiming his shot-
gun, black hunting dog sits at his side 32.00 42.00

Price Range

☐ **GOOD BOY** (1981)
#3, hunter kneels beside tree stump with shot-
gun in one hand and the other hand cradling a
retrieved duck hanging from the mouth of a black
bird dog **32.00   42.00**

☐ **WESTERN BOOT DECANTER** (1982)
Replica of a brown leather booth with exact shad-
ing, 10½" **26.00   34.00**
Mini, 4" **12.00   19.00**

☐ **WESTERN LOGGER** (1980)
Man stands on log, holding a logger's tool in one
hand and an axe in the other hand **25.00   34.00**

☐ **WILDCATS** (1982)
The mascot for Kansas State, front portion of figure thrusts through a large letter "K" with front
paw propped on a football **40.00   46.00**

☐ **YANKEE DOODLE**
Yankee figure wearing blue pants, white shirt, yellow vest, and black hat rides brown pony, on large
stand with brick fence, plaque on front with part
of the song, music box plays *Yankee Doodle*, 11"   **25.00   32.00**

OLD FITZGERALD

Old Fitzgerald bottles are made by the Old Fitzgerald Distilling
Co., to contain their whiskey and bourbon. Old Fitzgeralds are sometimes called Old Cabin Still bottles after one of the brand names under
which they are sold. The company issues both decanter style and figural bottles. The decanters are ceramics in various styles and colors.
Its figurals portray many different Irish and American subjects. New
figurals are added to the line irregularly. The number of bottles issued
by this firm is small.

Price Range

☐ **AMERICA'S CUP COMMEMORATIVE** (1970) . .   **15.00   22.00**
☐ **BLARNEY CASTLE** (1970)
Porcelain **12.00   19.00**
☐ **BROWSING DEER DECANTER** (1967)
Deer and woods scene, brown, tan and white,
amber stopper **15.00   22.00**

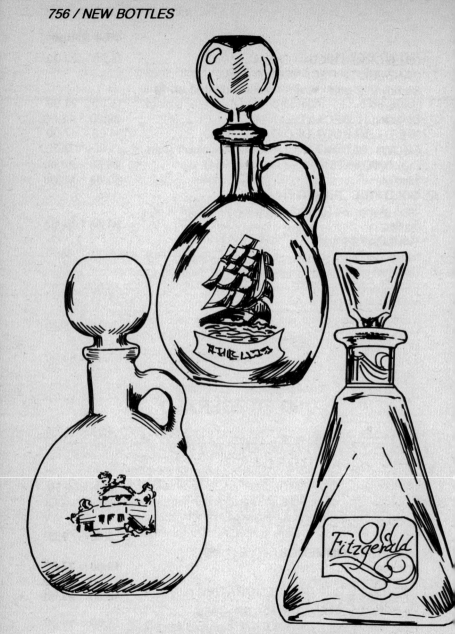

Top: **Old Fitzgerald Old Flagship (1967)**, glass decanter
$7.00–$11.00; Bottom Left to Right: **Old Fitzgerald Monticello
(1968)**, glass decanter $7.00–$11.00; **Old Fitzgerald Triangle
Prime (1976)**, glass decanter in shape of triangle. $7.00–$11.00

	Price Range	
☐ **CALIFORNIA BICENTENNIAL** (1970)	15.00	22.00
☐ **CANDLELITE DECANTER** (1955)		
Removable gold candle holder mounted on flint glass, pair	15.00	21.00
☐ **COLONIAL DECANTER** (1969)		
Glass	4.00	7.00
☐ **CROWN DECANTER**	5.00	9.00
☐ **GOLD COASTER DECANTER** (1954)		
Flint glass decanter, gold metal coaster	7.00	11.00
☐ **GOLD WEB DECANTER** (1953)		
Flint glass, gold web and frame fused onto decanter	10.00	16.00
☐ **"GOLDEN BOUGH" DECANTER** (1971)		
Glass	4.00	9.00
☐ **HILLBILLY BOTTLE** (1954)		
Pint, Hillbilly on Barrel with rifle, in brown, tan, black and green, 9⅛"	13.00	18.00
☐ **HILLBILLY BOTTLE** (1954)		
Quart, Same as above, 11⅜"	13.00	18.00
☐ **HILLBILLY BOTTLE** (1954)		
Same as above, gallon size, very rare	60.00	85.00
☐ **HILLBILLY** (1969)		
Same bottle as 1954 HILLBILLY, more detail and color, 11½"	13.00	18.00
☐ **JEWEL DECANTER** (1951–52)		
Flint glass, beveled neck	9.00	15.00
☐ **LEAPING TROUT DECANTER** (1969)	11.00	16.00
☐ **LEPRECHAUN BOTTLE** (1968)		
Porcelain bottle, gold band, green shamrocks, Irish verse, 10⅛"	25.00	32.00
☐ **LSU ALUMNI DECANTER** (1970)	25.00	32.00
☐ **MAN O'WAR DECANTER** (1969)		
Glass	5.00	9.00
☐ **MEMPHIS COMMEMORATIVE** (1969)		
porcelain	19.00	27.00
☐ **NEBRASKA** (1971)	27.00	32.00
☐ **NEBRASKA** (1972)	18.00	25.00
☐ **OLD CABIN STILL DECANTER** (1958)		
Gold letters "OLD CABIN STILL" infused on flint glass bottle, solid faceted stopper	16.00	23.00
☐ **OHIO STATE CENTENNIAL** (1970)	14.00	24.00
☐ **PILGRIM LANDING COMMEMORATIVE** (1970)	14.00	24.00

	Price Range	
☐ **POINTING SETTER DECANTER** (1965)		
Dog on point, brown, tan and white, glass, 12"	16.00	23.00
☐ **QUAIL ON THE WING DECANTER** (1968)		
Round glass bottle, three color design, 12" ...	7.00	12.00
☐ **REBEL YELL RIDER** (c. 1970)		
Figurine, Confederate cavalryman bottle in six colors, sold only in the South, 9¾"	23.00	32.00
☐ **RIP VAN WINKLE FIGURINE** (1970)		
Famous Catskill character with blunderbuss and elf, multicolor, 9¼"	32.00	40.00
☐ **SONGS OF IRELAND** (1972)		
Porcelain	15.00	20.00
☐ **SONS OF ERIN** (1969)		
Porcelain	9.00	14.00
☐ **SOUTH CAROLINA TRICENTENNIAL** (1970)	12.00	19.00
☐ **WELLER MASTER PIECE** (1963)		
White, porcelain apothecary bottle, rebus design, gold bands, 10⅝"	26.00	35.00
☐ **WINGS ACROSS THE CONTINENT** (1972)		
Porcelain, duck finial	16.00	23.00

SKI COUNTRY

Ski Country produces limited edition bottles in two sizes, regular and miniature. The company offers many different bottle series including Indians, owls, game birds, Christmas and customer specialties. The bottles manufactured by Ski Country are exquisitely detailed and highly sought after by collectors.

ANIMALS

	Price Range	
☐ **BADGER FAMILY**	27.00	36.00
Mini	17.00	22.00
☐ **BOBCAT FAMILY**	40.00	50.00
Mini	20.00	25.00
☐ **COYOTE FAMILY**	46.00	55.00
Mini	20.00	25.00
☐ **KANGAROO**	25.00	30.00
Mini	24.00	29.00

	Price Range	
☐ **KOALA**	28.00	33.00
☐ **RACCOON**	53.00	60.00
Mini	25.00	30.00
☐ **SKUNK FAMILY**	50.00	56.00
Mini	22.00	26.00
☐ **SNOW LEOPARD**	52.00	57.00
Mini	12.00	18.00

BIRDS

☐ **BLACKBIRD**	34.00	40.00
Mini	20.00	25.00
☐ **BLACK SWAN**	27.00	33.00
Mini	22.00	27.00
☐ **BLUE JAY**	50.00	60.00
Mini	42.00	49.00
☐ **CARDINAL**	50.00	60.00
Mini	50.00	60.00
☐ **CONDOR**	40.00	45.00
Mini	25.00	30.00
☐ **GAMECOCKS**	125.00	145.00
Mini	40.00	46.00
☐ **GILA WOODPECKER**	75.00	85.00
Mini	26.00	32.00
☐ **PEACE DOVE**	45.00	55.00
Mini	30.00	35.00
☐ **PEACOCK**	68.00	77.00
Mini	60.00	68.00
☐ **PENGUIN FAMILY**	45.00	55.00
Mini	21.00	27.00
☐ **WOOD DUCK**	70.00	80.00
Mini	25.00	30.00

CHRISTMAS

☐ **BOB CRATCHIT**	40.00	50.00
Mini	25.00	30.00
☐ **MRS. CRATCHIT**	40.00	50.00
Mini	25.00	30.00
☐ **SCROOGE**	40.00	50.00
Mini	15.00	20.00

Right: **Ski Country P.T. Barnum (1976),** *bust,* **$32.00–$40.00,** *Bottom:* **Ski Country Ahrens-Fox Fire Engine. $200.00–$230.00**

CIRCUS

Price Range

☐ **P.T. BARNUM**	32.00	40.00
Mini	20.00	25.00
☐ **CLOWN**	44.00	52.00
Mini	27.00	33.00
☐ **ELEPHANT ON DRUM**	35.00	45.00
Mini	35.00	45.00
☐ **JENNY LIND**		
Blue dress	85.00	95.00
Mini	64.00	74.00
☐ **LION ON DRUM**	31.00	36.00
Mini	23.00	28.00
☐ **PALOMINO HORSE**	43.00	50.00
Mini	40.00	45.00
☐ **RINGMASTER**	20.00	25.00
Mini	18.00	23.00
☐ **TOM THUMB**	20.00	25.00
Mini	16.00	21.00
☐ **TIGER ON BALL**	35.00	44.00
Mini	31.00	37.00

CUSTOMER SPECIALTIES

☐ **AHRENS-FOX FIRE ENGINE**	200.00	230.00
☐ **BONNIE AND CLYDE, PAIR**	60.00	70.00
Mini, pair	55.00	62.00
☐ **CAVEMAN**	16.00	23.00
Mini	13.00	18.00
☐ **MILL RIVER COUNTRY CLUB**	38.00	47.00
☐ **OLYMPIC SKIER**		
Gold	100.00	120.00
☐ **OLYMPIC SKIER**		
Red	27.00	34.00
Mini, red	37.00	44.00
☐ **OLYMPIC SKIER**		
Blue	30.00	35.00
Mini, blue	35.00	40.00
☐ **POLITICAL DONKEY AND ELEPHANT**	50.00	60.00

DOMESTIC ANIMALS

	Price Range	
☐ BASSET HOUND	55.00	65.00
Mini	25.00	30.00
☐ HOLSTEIN COW	50.00	60.00

EAGLES, FALCONS AND HAWKS

☐ BIRTH OF FREEDOM	85.00	95.00
Mini	65.00	70.00
☐ EAGLE ON THE WATER	75.00	85.00
Mini	33.00	40.00
☐ EASTER SEALS EAGLE	60.00	66.00
Mini	25.00	31.00
☐ FALCON GALLON	200.00	220.00
☐ GYRFALCON	35.00	43.00
Mini	22.00	28.00
☐ HARPY EAGLE	105.00	125.00
Mini	90.00	100.00
☐ MOUNTAIN EAGLE	130.00	150.00
Mini	100.00	120.00
☐ OSPREY HAWK	140.00	160.00
Mini	100.00	120.00
☐ PEREGRINE FALCON	85.00	95.00
Mini	13.00	17.00
☐ PRAIRIE FALCON	45.00	54.00
Mini	27.00	33.00
☐ RED SHOULDER HAWK	74.00	81.00
Mini	34.00	40.00
☐ REDTAIL HAWK	60.00	70.00
Mini	33.00	40.00
☐ WHITE FALCON	68.00	75.00
Mini	30.00	35.00

FISH

☐ MUSKELLUNGE	25.00	30.00
Mini	17.00	21.00
☐ RAINBOW TROUT	52.00	57.00
Mini	20.00	27.00
☐ SALMON	30.00	35.00
Mini	16.00	22.00

	Price Range	
☐ **TROUT**		
Mini, brown	27.00	32.00

GAME BIRDS

☐ **BANDED MALLARD**	55.00	65.00
☐ **CHUKAR PARTRIDGE**	33.00	40.00
Mini	16.00	21.00
☐ **KING EIDER DUCK**	55.00	65.00
☐ **MALLARD,** (1973)	60.00	70.00
☐ **PHEASANT**		
Standing, mini	65.00	75.00
☐ **PHEASANT**		
Golden	50.00	60.00
Mini	22.00	26.00
☐ **PHEASANT IN THE CORN**	48.00	55.00
Mini	34.00	43.00
☐ **PHEASANTS FIGHTING**	69.00	75.00
Mini	24.00	29.00
☐ **PHEASANTS FIGHTING**		
½ gallon	160.00	180.00
☐ **PINTAIL**	70.00	80.00
☐ **PRAIRIE CHICKEN**	60.00	70.00
☐ **RUFFED GROUSE**	35.00	45.00
Mini	22.00	28.00
☐ **TURKEY**	135.00	150.00
Mini	110.00	125.00

GRAND SLAM SERIES

☐ **DESERT SHEEP**	60.00	70.00
Mini	21.00	28.00
☐ **MOUNTAIN SHEEP**	55.00	60.00
Mini	16.00	23.00
☐ **STONE SHEEP**	40.00	50.00
Mini	27.00	34.00

HORNED AND ANTLERED ANIMALS

☐ **ANTELOPE**	48.00	56.00
☐ **BIG HORN RAM**	55.00	65.00
Mini	30.00	35.00

	Price Range	
☐ **MOUNTAIN GOAT**	55.00	65.00
Mini	45.00	52.00
☐ **MOUNTAIN GOAT**		
Gallon	800.00	900.00
☐ **WHITE TAIL DEER**	60.00	70.00
Mini	30.00	35.00

INDIANS

☐ **CEREMONIAL ANTELOPE DANCER**	52.00	62.00
Mini	32.00	42.00
☐ **CEREMONIAL BUFFALO DANCER**	105.00	125.00
Mini	20.00	28.00
☐ **CEREMONIAL DEER DANCER**	70.00	80.00
Mini	42.00	50.00
☐ **CEREMONIAL EAGLE DANCER**	185.00	205.00
Mini	20.00	30.00
☐ **CEREMONIAL FALCON DANCER**	78.00	88.00
Mini	35.00	45.00
☐ **CEREMONIAL WOLF DANCER**	50.00	60.00
Mini	32.00	40.00
☐ **CHIEF #1**	105.00	125.00
Mini	14.00	20.00
☐ **CHIEF #2**	105.00	125.00
Mini	14.00	20.00
☐ **CIGAR STORE INDIAN**	35.00	45.00
☐ **DANCERS OF THE SOUTHWEST**		
Set	350.00	400.00
Mini	170.00	200.00

OWLS

☐ **BARN OWL**	70.00	80.00
Mini	22.00	30.00
☐ **GREAT GRAY OWL**	60.00	68.00
Mini	27.00	33.00
☐ **HORNED OWL**	70.00	80.00
Mini	86.00	94.00
☐ **HORNED OWL**		
Gallon	1000.00	1200.00
☐ **SAW WHET OWL**	48.00	54.00
Mini	28.00	34.00

	Price Range	
☐ SCREECH OWL FAMILY	85.00	95.00
Mini	74.00	84.00
☐ SPECTACLED OWL	100.00	110.00
Mini	74.00	82.00

RODEO

☐ BARREL RACER	48.00	56.00
Mini	22.00	28.00
☐ BULL RIDER	48.00	56.00
Mini	25.00	30.00
☐ WYOMING BRONCO	50.00	60.00
Mini	30.00	35.00

WHEATON/NULINE DECANTERS

One of the oldest American manufacturers of decorative bottles, the Wheaton Company was founded in 1888. At first, it produced a general line of hand-blown and pressed glassware. Wheaton Commemorative and Nuline bottles often illustrate portraits in the 19th century manner on flasks with raised designs. These honor famous Americans as well as American historical events. Created in the style of 19th century flasks, the designs do not reproduce any actual antique bottles. Wheaton/Nuline bottles include the Campaign Series, Great American Series and Presidential Series. The Presidential Series includes recent chief executives as well as past ones. Issued in no particular order, the series began with a memorial issue for President Kennedy in 1967. The well-known Astronaut Series was instituted in 1969, concentrating on Moon Missions.

	Price Range	

ASTRONAUT SERIES

☐ APOLLO 11 (1969)		
Blue	16.00	23.00
☐ APOLLO 12 (1969)		
Ruby	33.00	43.00
☐ APOLLO 13 (1970)		
Burley	14.00	21.00
☐ APOLLO 14 (1971)		
Aqua	3.00	7.00

Price Range

☐ **APOLLO 15** (1971)
Green 12.00   16.00
☐ **APOLLO 16** (1972)
Iridescent Flint 10.00   13.00

CAMPAIGN SERIES

☐ **HUMPHREY** (1969)
Muskie Green 16.00   23.00
☐ **NIXON-AGNEW** (1968)
Topaz 20.00   30.00

CHRISTMAS DECANTER SERIES

☐ **MERRY CHRISTMAS** (1971)
Green 13.00   18.00
☐ **SEASON'S GREETINGS** (1972)
Topaz 9.00   12.00

GREAT AMERICAN SERIES

☐ **HUMPHREY BOGART** (1971)
Star Decanter, Green 7.00   10.00
☐ **THOMAS EDISON** (1969)
Blue 7.00   10.00
☐ **BEN FRANKLIN** (1970)
Aqua 12.00   17.00
☐ **REV. BILLY GRAHAM** (1970)
Green 3.00   7.00
☐ **JEAN HARLOW (Star Decanter)** (1972)
Topaz 4.00   8.00
☐ **CHARLES EVANS HUGHES** (1971)
Blue 7.00   10.00
☐ **JOHN PAUL JONES** (1970)
Green 9.00   12.00
☐ **HELEN KELLER** (1970)
Frosty Flint 7.00   10.00
☐ **ROBERT KENNEDY** (1967)
Green 13.00   18.00
☐ **MARTIN LUTHER KING** (1968)
Amber 7.00   10.00

	Price Range	
☐ **ROBERT E. LEE** (1969)		
Green	13.00	18.00
☐ **CHARLES LINDBERGH** (1968)		
Blue	7.00	10.00
☐ **DOUGLAS MacARTHUR** (1968)		
Amethyst	13.00	18.00
☐ **PAUL REVERE** (1971)		
Blue	9.00	18.00
☐ **WILL ROGERS** (1969)		
Topaz	6.00	10.00
☐ **BETSY ROSS** (1969)		
Ruby	10.00	15.00

THE PRESIDENTIAL SERIES

	Price Range	
☐ **GENERAL EISENHOWER** (Special Memorial Issue)	16.00	23.00
☐ **PRESIDENT EISENHOWER** (1969)		
Green	9.00	12.00
☐ **PRESIDENT GRANT** (1972)		
Topaz	7.00	10.00
☐ **ANDREW JACKSON** (1971)		
Green	13.00	18.00
☐ **THOMAS JEFFERSON** (1970)		
Ruby	15.00	22.00
☐ **JOHN F. KENNEDY*** (c. 1967) Blue	20.00	30.00
☐ **ABRAHAM LINCOLN** (1968)		
Topaz	9.00	12.00
☐ **FRANKLIN D. ROOSEVELT** (1967)		
Green	9.00	12.00
☐ **THEODORE ROOSEVELT** (1970)		
Blue	8.00	11.00
☐ **WOODROW WILSON** (1969)		
Blue	9.00	12.00
☐ **GEORGE WASHINGTON** (1970)		
Blue (1969) Frosty Mint	16.00	23.00

*HAS BEEN "QUOTED" AS HIGH AS $100.00

Wheaton-Nuline, George Washington (c. 1970), *flask decanter, blue or frosty mint.* **$16.00–$23.00**

Wheaton-Nuline, Thomas Jefferson (c. 1970), *flask decanter, ruby.* **$15.00–$25.00**

MINIATURE BOTTLES

A lot of bottle collectors don't know it, but miniature bottles have been manufactured in the United States for quite a while.

The first minis appeared on the U.S. market in the 1890s. They were non-figural beers and whiskeys, and they were generally a little larger than the minis in use today. A lot of standard or "common" bottles were made, but jugs were also popular.

Mini bottle production stayed constant through the beginning of the 1890s until 1920 when prohibition became law. During prohibition, a very small number of mini liquor bottles may have been made for medicinal use, but if they still exist, they are extremely rare.

When prohibition ended in 1933, minis came back strong. The five-year period of 1933–1938 was a "golden age" to many collectors. American production was back in full swing, and for the first time, Americans saw the European minis.

Some of the manufacturers active in that period were: Garnier, Rynbende, Bols, Riemerschmid, Manhattan, and Miniature Sales. Many standard bottles were made, but it was then that the figurals were first produced.

Miniature beer production stopped at the beginning of World War II. Manhattan Distributors Inc., long a prolific manufacturer of very creative figural designs, went out of business in 1944, but despite these setbacks, mini bottle production remained strong through the 1940s. It was in the 1950s that Luxardo and Drioli joined the ranks of mini bottle manufacturers and produced some very beautiful items. Since that time, McLech and Mead have begun production and have also produced attractive figurals.

As in all bottle specialties, collectors are interested in different aspects of the hobby. Many people collect only figurals or only standards. Others will collect bottles containing only a certain liquor. Many collectors are interested only in bottles with the original contents and stamps. Many other collectors feel they'll miss out on a lot of fine old bottles if they insist on original contents. It's these friendly disagreements that make the hobby fun. Whatever your specialty is, mini bottles is a challenging and relatively inexpensive hobby. Be sure to check our club section for a mini bottle club in your area.

Price Range

☐ **AALBORG AKRAVIT**
  Est. 1846, Denmark, 4½" 1.50   2.50

Price Range

☐ **ABBOTT'S BITTERS**
Copyright 1931, label shows figure of a bartender
pouring, 2¾" 4.00 6.00

☐ **ACME BEER**
Stubby, San Francisco, foliage on label, 3" 6.00 9.00

☐ **ACME LAGER**
San Francisco, foliage on label, 4¼" 6.00 9.00

☐ **AINSLIE'S**
Scotland, Royal Edinburgh Brand, Glasgow, 5½" 6.00 10.00

☐ **AMBASSADOR**
Est. 1820, Blended Scotch Whisky, 25 years old,
Scotland, screw cap, 4" 6.00 9.00

☐ **AMBASSADOR**
Deluxe Scotch, embossed, 4½" 2.00 4.00

☐ **AMERICAN BEER**
Embossed "NO DEPOSIT, NO RETURN," 1947,
3" 6.00 9.00

☐ **ARROW**
Sloe Gin, Heublein, 1968, 4" .... .75 1.75

☐ **ASBACH VXOP**
Urait, Germany, 4½" .... .75 1.75

☐ **BACARDI**
Souvenir of 1940 Rotary Convention-Havana,
Cuba, 4½" 4.00 6.00

☐ **BACARDI**
Clear bottle, oval label, Mexico, 5" 10.00 15.00

☐ **BALLANTINE BEER**
Mini beer bottle, 4¼" 6.00 8.00

☐ **BALLANTINE BEER**
Mug, lidded, has Ballantine Beer seal on the side,
2¾" 10.00 14.00

☐ **BALLANTINE'S**
Finest Scotch Whisky, ceramic jug, Scotland,
3½" 8.00 12.00

☐ **BALLANTINE'S**
Est. 1827, Cognac Brancy, Scotland, 1937, 3¾" 4.00 6.00

☐ **BAL TABARIN**
Figure of a Cocker Spaniel with her pup, the
mother is brown and tan, the pup is white with
brown spots, 3" 22.00 28.00

Price Range

☐ **BAL TABARIN**
Figure of a St. Bernard with her pup, the mother
is white with brown spots, the pup is white with
black spots, 3″ **22.00** **28.00**

☐ **BAL TABARIN**
A figure of a Scottish Terrier with her pup, both
are yellow, mother has some brown around her
eye, 3″ **22.00** **28.00**

☐ **BAL TABARIN**
Figure of a cat with her kitten on her head, both
are yellow and brown, 2½″ **22.00** **28.00**

☐ **BAL TABARIN**
Figure of a baseball player with a bat leaning over
an oversized playing glove, the bat is brown as
is the player's cap, his shirt is brown and his
socks are white, 4″ **22.00** **28.00**

☐ **BAL TABARIN**
Figure of a saxophone player, his jacket is green,
his pants are yellow and the saxophone is brown,
5″ **22.00** **28.00**

☐ **BAL TABARIN**
Figure of a tuba player, the player's top hat is
brown, his coat is gray and his pants are tan, 5″ **22.00** **28.00**

☐ **BAL TABARIN**
Figure of a flute player, his coat is tan, his pants
are gray, 5″ **22.00** **28.00**

☐ **BAL TABARIN**
Figure of a Bluejay, distributed by John Miner &
Sons, New York, 3″ **22.00** **28.00**

☐ **BAL TABARIN**
Figure of a squirrel with an acorn, 3¾″ **22.00** **28.00**

☐ **BAL TABARIN**
Figure of a satyr, the base is brown, the satyr is
yellow, and his hooves are black, he is playing the
pipes, 3¾″ **22.00** **28.00**

☐ **BAL TABARIN**
Figure of a deer, the deer's body is white with
brown spots, 4″ **22.00** **28.00**

☐ **BAL TABARIN**
Figure of a tennis player leaning over an oversize
racket, the tennis player's shirt is green, his pants
are brown, and his cap is also brown, 4″ **22.00** **28.00**

Price Range

☐ **BAL TABARIN**
Figure of a skier leaning over the rest of the bottle, the skier's sweater is green, his scarf is yellow, his cap his brown and his pants also brown, 4" 22.00 28.00

☐ **BAL TABARIN**
Figure of a golfer leaning over the nineteenth hole (which is actually the rest of the bottle), the golfer's sweater is green, his pants are brown and his cap is black, 4" 22.00 28.00

☐ **BALTIMORE CLUB**
Grape brandy, 4½" 1.00 3.00

☐ **BARDINET**
Embossed, France, 4¼" 2.00 4.00

☐ **BARDINET**
Rhum Negrita, applied neck, comes with jigger glass, hip flask, France, 4½" 10.00 15.00

☐ **Wm. BARKER & SON**
Bishopsgate, London, 5¾" 1.00 3.00

☐ **BASS RIVER**
Skipper's Choice, Bottled by Allen's Ltd., Boston, 4½" 4.00 6.00

☐ **JOHN BEGG**
Est. 1845, laid on ring, Blended Scotch Whisky, Scotland, 3¾" 8.00 12.00

☐ **BELL'S**
Est. 1825, Scotland, 1969 (1960 bottle was brown), 3¾" 3.00 5.00

☐ **BONDED BELMONT**
Embossed "CLEAR AS A BELL," 1938, 4¾" .. 10.00 15.00

☐ **BEN AROS**
Label shows Scottish Shepherd, Blended Scotch Whisky, 5" 13.00 17.00

☐ **BENGIT SERRES**
France, cylindrical bottle with handle and pouring spout, green over blue, 3½" 4.00 6.00

☐ **BLACK DIAMOND**
Rye Whisky, Melchers Distilleries, Canada, 5" 6.00 8.00

☐ **BLACK & WHITE TWELVE**
Scotch, James Buchanan Co., Scotland, 4½" 6.00 9.00

☐ **BLACK & WHITE**
Label is in Spanish, Mexico, 4¾" 18.00 23.00

Price Range

☐ **BLATZ BEER**
  Mug, lidded, has Blatz Beer seal on the side, 2¾″ **10.00 14.00**

☐ **BOLS**
  Claeryn, embossed, waisted bottle, 5¼″ **2.00 5.00**

☐ **BOLS**
  Embossed "B," Alter Weinbrand, Neuss, Germany, 3″ **1.00 3.00**

☐ **BOLS**
  Embossed "B," dry Gin, Neuss, Germany, 3″ .. **2.00 4.00**

☐ **BOLS**
  Embossed "BOLS," Creme de Cacao, Tsaoula, Holland 4″ **1.00 3.00**

☐ **BOLS**
  Embossed "ERVEN LUCAS BOLS," Krauter Likor, Neuss, Germany, 3″ **1.00 3.00**

☐ **DR. C. BOUVIER'S BUCHU GIN**
  Embossed, hand blown, clear glass, 4″ **17.00 23.00**

☐ **BRANCA**
  Bremen, Germany, 4″ **1.00 4.00**

☐ **MARIE BRIZARD**
  Anisette, France, 1969, 3½″ .... **.75 1.75**

☐ **MARIE BRIZARD**
  Blackberry liqueur, 1969, 3½″ .... **.75 1.75**

☐ **MARIE BRIZARD**
  Creme de Cacao-chouao, applied top, label shows plants, France, 3½″ **2.00 4.00**

☐ **BRONTE**
  Beam import, with ½″ kickup, England 1969, 2¾″ **2.00 4.00**

☐ **BROOK HILL**
  Nelson County, Kentuck, Friedman and Keiler, Est. 1890, Pre 1920, jug-style bottle, 3″ **21.00 28.00**

☐ **BROWN-FORMAN**
  Bottoms up, Kentucky Straight Whisky, 4″ **10.00 15.00**

☐ **BRUGAL**
  Est. 1888, superior Puerto Rican Rum, 3″ **2.00 4.00**

☐ **BUCHANAN's LIQUEUR**
  Scotland, 1935, 3½″ **6.00 10.00**

☐ **CALIDAD SUPERIOR**
  Crema de Cacao, Spain, 5″ **1.00 3.00**

☐ **CALVERT GIN**
  Distilled London Dry Gin, 1940, clear glass, 3¾″ **4.00 7.00**

	Price Range	
☐ **CALVERT RESERVE**		
Blended Whisky, 1940, 3¾"	6.00	9.00
☐ **CARIOCA**		
Puerto Rican Rum, 5"	1.00	3.00
☐ **CASANOVA**		
Embossed, applied top, upside-down figure of a woman, 3-piece mold, clear glass, France, 6"	12.00	17.00
☐ **COINTREAU**		
Signed, France, tan and brown, 1936, 4½"	8.00	12.00
☐ **COINTREAU**		
Creme de Banane, hand blown, France, 1936, 4"	5.00	8.00
☐ **COINTREAU**		
Blackberry liqueur, hand blown, France, 1936, 4"	5.00	8.00
☐ **COINTREAU**		
Creme of Cacao-Chouva, hand blown, France, 1937, 3¾"	4.00	7.00
☐ **COINTREAU**		
Signature on bottom, Veritable Guignolet D'Angers, brown, France, 3"	7.00	10.00

Cointreau, liqueur, blue to gray, 3".
$7.00–$10.00

Price Range

☐ **COINTREAU LIQUEUR**
Embossed, hand blown, France, 1937, 3″ 4.00 6.00

☐ **COINTREAU LIQUEUR**
Embossed, France, 1937, 3″ 4.00 6.00

☐ **COORS**
Mini beer mug, Coors logo on side, white, applied
handle, 1½″ 4.00 6.00

☐ **DALMAU HERMANOS**
Spanish Lady, Tarragona, Spain, white figure with
red sweater and white dress with red markings,
6″ 32.00 38.00

☐ **DON Q**
Puerto Rican Rum, 1936, 5″ 2.00 4.00

☐ **DRIOLI**
Smoking Oriental, figure is standing and smoking
from a water pipe, bearded, yellow shirt, red vest,
green pants, stamped "1970 Exclusive Drioli,
Made in Italy", 4¾″ 4.00 6.50

☐ **DRIOLI**
Oriental snake charmer, seated figure with red
turban playing a flute in front of a basket,
stamped "1970 Exclusive Drioli, Made in Italy",
4½″ 4.00 6.50

☐ **DRIOLI**
Donkey, shown braying, wearing a black cap,
"1970 Exclusive Drioli, Made in Italy," 5¼″ ... 4.00 6.50

☐ **DRIOLI**
Pitcher, in the shape of a ewer, red figures on a
brown background on the body, yellow mottled
handle, stamped "1970 Exclusive Drioli, Made in
Italy." 4½″ 2.50 3.75

☐ **DRIOLI**
Vase, red figure of a discus thrower against a
brown background on the body, stamped "1970
Exclusive Drioli, Made in Italy," 4¾″ 2.50 3.75

☐ **DRIOLI**
Pitcher, in the shape of a ewer, red figures on a
brown background on the body, yellow handle,
stamped "1970 Exclusive Drioli, Made in Italy,"
5″ 2.50 3.75

	Price Range	

☐ **DRIOLI**
Venus, figure is of a statue, no arms, loose cloth covering the lower half of her body, stamped "1970 Exclusive Drioli, Made in Italy," 6" **4.00 6.50**

☐ **DRIOLI**
Oriental, comic figure, blue turban, red jacket, yellow robe, stamped "1970 Exclusive Drioli, Made in Italy," 5½" **4.00 6.50**

☐ **DRIOLI**
Vase, with pastoral scene, brown, uneven rim, stamped "Drioli, Marmaca, Italy," 1958, 4½" .. **10.00 15.00**

☐ **DRIOLI**
Turkey, red and yellow plumage, red head, brown body, green base, stamped "1970 Exclusive Drioli, Made in Italy," 4¾" **4.00 6.50**

☐ **DRIOLI**
Indian girl, her robe is yellow, green and red, she is leaning on a portrait of an Indian girl in a canoe, stamped "Exclusive Drioli, Made in Italy," c. 1962, 5" **17.00 22.00**

☐ **DRIOLI**
Cat and birdhouse, cat is embracing the base of the birdhouse, stamped "Exclusive Drioli, Made in Italy," c. 1962, 5" **17.00 22.00**

☐ **DRIOLI**
Elephant, blue seat on elephant's back with yellow cloth underneath, stamped "1970 Exclusive Drioli, Made in Italy," 5" **4.00 6.50**

☐ **DRIOLI**
Jazz singer, from the 1959–60 minstrel set, figure is of a black woman, arms crossed on her breast, with white gown, stamped "Exclusive Drioli, Made in Italy," 5" **12.00 17.00**

☐ **DRIOLI**
Oriental merchant, his jacket is red, his hands are folded on his chest, he is sitting in front of two baskets, stamped "1970 Exclusive Drioli, Made in Italy," 4½" **4.00 6.50**

All A. DROZ bottles are marked "Made in France" on the bottom

☐ **A. DROZ**
Rabbit, white with brown markings, porcelain, 1948, 3¾" **21.00 26.00**

Price Range

☐ **A. DROZ**
Fish, white with brown markings and blue base, porcelain, 1948, 4″ 21.00 26.00

☐ **A. DROZ**
Parrot, white with blue and green markings, porcelain, 1948, 4½″ 21.00 26.00

☐ **A. DROZ**
Squirrel, brown with white markings, porcelain, 1948, 3¾″ 21.00 26.00

☐ **A. DROZ**
Dog, white with brown markings, porcelain, 1948, 4″ 21.00 26.00

☐ **A. DROZ**
Owl, white with black markings, owl is wearing small cap, porcelain, 1948, 4¼″ 21.00 26.00

☐ **A. DROZ**
Penguin, white with black wings and yellow beak and feet, porcelain, 1948, 4¼″ 21.00 26.00

☐ **A. DROZ**
Cat, white with yellow collar, porcelain, 1948, 4″ 21.00 26.00

☐ **A. DROZ**
Frog, green and white, porcelain, 1948, 4″ 21.00 26.00

☐ **FOUR ROSES**
Rye, Frankfort Distilling, Louisville, Kentucky, 1941, 4½″ 7.00 10.00

☐ **FOUR SEASONS**
Bourbon Whiskey, Distilled by Clifton Springs Distilling Co., Terre Haute, Indiana, reduced in proof and bottled by Paramount Distilling Corp., Chicago, 1937, 4½″ 12.00 17.00

☐ **FOUR SEASONS**
Bourbon Whiskey, Distilled by Clifton Springs, bottled by Paramount Distilling, 1937, 4″ 12.00 17.00

☐ **FOX HEAD BEER**
Mug lidded, has Fox Head Beer seal on the side, 2¾″ 10.00 14.00

☐ **GARNIER**
Playing cards, King, Queen and Jack of Hearts or Clubs; front of bottle is face of card, back of bottle is designed like back of standard playing card, issued with blue or brown backs, 4½″ For each bottle 10.00 14.00

Dubouchett, Rock and Rye, Many Blanc & Co., Chicago, 1937, 4¾". **$2.50–$3.50**

Escat, Anis Extra, bull fiddle, embossed, "Escat Barcelona," 4½". **$4.00–$7.00**

Price Range

☐ **GARNIER**
Eiffel tower, incised "Garnier, Liqueurs, Enghien,
Paris, France," 1951, 5¼" 26.00 33.00

☐ **GARNIER**
Bottle is in the shape of an amphora, black and
tan, France, 1936, 3½" 8.00 12.00

☐ **GARNIER**
#485, bottle is in the shape of a ewer, blue and
green, wide-footed base, 4½" 8.00 12.00

☐ **GARNIER**
Vase, white and brown, #5, France, 1936, 3½" 8.00 12.00

☐ **GARNIER**
Skittle, #98, France, c. 1939, white figure of
young girl with a blue cap and collar, blonde hair,
4¾" 13.00 18.00

☐ **GARNIER**
Figure of a white dog with paws folded in front,
ears are brown, 4½" 13.00 18.00

☐ **GARNIER**
Figure of a white duck, brown cap and beak, beak
tilted downward, France, 4½" 13.00 18.00

☐ **GARNIER**
Figure of white hen and chicks, #255, some yellow and red markings, France, 1934, 3½" 13.00 18.00

☐ **GARNIER**
Skittle, France, c. 1939, white figure of a young
boy, gray cap and buttons, 4½" 13.00 18.00

☐ **GARNIER**
Apricot Liqueur, hand blown, embossed "Aprico-
tine," France, 1934, 4" 2.00 3.00

☐ **GARNIER**
Bricotine, embossed "Abricotine," France, imported 1970, 4" .... .75 1.50

☐ **GARNIER**
Orange Curacao, France, imported 1970, 3¼" .75 1.50

☐ **GARNIER**
Prunelle, France, imported, 1970, 3¼" 1.50 2.50

☐ **GARNIER**
Triple sec, France, imported 1970, 3¼" .... .75 1.50

☐ **GLAD HAND**
"GLAD" embossed on palm of hand, blue, 4 oz.,
Germany, 6" 4.00 6.00

Price Range

☐ **GLEN GARRY**
Bottled for the New Haven Railroad by S. S.
Pierce Company, Est. 1831, 3½" 13.00 17.00

☐ **GODET FRERES**
#H3, bottle is in the shape of an amphora, black,
4" 6.00 10.00

☐ **GOEBEL BEER**
Mini beer bottle, 4¼" 6.00 9.00

☐ **HELDENS**
Embossed "LIQUEURS HELDENS," Belgium, 4" 1.00 3.00

☐ **HENNESSY**
Est. 1765, France, 1937, 4" 1.00 3.00

☐ **HEUBLEIN'S COCKTAILS**
The Club, Dry Martini Cocktails, 3½" 2.00 4.00

☐ **HOPPE**
Jug-style bottle, delft, Holland, 4" 8.00 12.00

☐ **HOPPE**
Vase-style, delft, Holland, 4"

☐ **HOPPE**
Vase with handle, delft, Holland, 4" 8.00 12.00

☐ **HOUSE OF KOSHU**
Boy, clear glass, 6" 4.00 6.00

☐ **IBARRA Y. ALVAREZ**
Anisado Refined, clear glass, 4½" 1.00 2.00

☐ **JACK DANIEL'S**
1964 counter display with one-day old whiskey,
5" 8.00 12.00

☐ **JAMAICA RHUM**
Blue Seal, Mexico, 3¾" 2.00 4.00

☐ **JAX BEER**
Mini beer bottle, 3¾" 6.00 8.00

☐ **KORD**
Blackberry Liqueur, Czechoslovakia, 1951, 4" . . 1.00 3.00

☐ **LANG'S**
Est. 1861, Scotland, Blended Scotch Whisky,
Eight Years Old, 5¼" 13.00 18.00

☐ **LARSEN**
Viking ship, white with gold trim, banner on the
stopper is embossed "INVINCIBLE," Limoges
China, France, 1970, 4¾" 10.00 14.00

Price Range

☐ **LEROUX**
Creme de Cafe, ewer-style bottle, dark brown,
3¾" **3.00   5.00**

☐ **LEROUX**
Figaro rum, 1955, 5" **3.00   5.00**

☐ **LEROUX**
Ginger brandy, 1937, 5" **1.50   2.50**

☐ **LEROUX**
Kummel, 1937, 4" **1.50   2.50**

☐ **LEROUX**
Triple Sec, hand blown, embossed "BELGIUM"
on the bottom, 1937, 3½" **1.50   2.50**

☐ **LIONEL**
Embossed, Cherie Brand Beneteux, Type Li-
queur, 1934, 4" **4.00   6.00**

☐ **LIONEL**
Embossed, Woodmont Straight Whiskey, 1934,
4½" **17.00 23.00**

☐ **LIONEL**
Embossed, Auld MacGregor Scotch Whiskey,
1934, 3¾" **18.00 24.00**

☐ **LIONEL**
Embossed, cocktail, 1934, 5¼" **4.00   6.00**

☐ **LIONEL**
Embossed, English Castle, Dry Gin, 1934, 4" .. **8.00 12.00**

☐ **LIONEL**
Orange brandy, Cordialized, 1934, 5¼" **4.00   6.00**

☐ **LUXARDO**
Creme Cacao, clear glass, label shows small
branch with leaves, made in Italy, 4" **4.00   6.00**

☐ **LUXARDO**
Embossed "LUXARDO 1821," cherry, 4" **1.00   2.00**

☐ **LUXARDO**
Embossed "LUXARDO 1821," triplum, 3" **1.00   2.00**

☐ **LUXARDO**
Embossed "LUXARDO 1821," maraschino, 5¾" **1.00   2.00**

☐ **LUXARDO**
Baroque pitcher, issued in ruby, green and turquoise, shaped like an ewer, gold handle, approximately 3,173 issued, 1958, 3½" **13.00 17.00**

Price Range

☐ **LUXARDO**
Baroque amphora, issued in green and ruby, gold
handles, approximately 3,173 issued, 1958, 3½″   **13.00 17.00**

☐ **LUXARDO**
White majolica pitcher, approximately 3,173 is-
sued, gold trim, 1958, 4″ **13.00 17.00**

☐ **LUXARDO**
Opal majolica vase, approximately 3,173 issued,
gold trim, 1958, 3½″ **13.00 17.00**

☐ **LUXARDO**
Nacreous majolica amphora, approximately
3,173 issued, 1958, 3¾″ **13.00 17.00**

☐ **LUXARDO**
Apple, 740 imported, total production 1,160,
1960–61, 3½″ **45.00 55.00**

☐ **LUXARDO**
Pear, 740 imported, total production 1,080,
1960–61, 3½″ **45.00 55.00**

☐ **LUXARDO**
Queen chess piece, 278 imported, 1960, 5¾″   **80.00 90.00**

☐ **LUXARDO**
Orange, 740 imported, total production 1,110,
1960–61, 2½″ **45.00 55.00**

☐ **LUXARDO**
Banana, 740 imported, total production 1,124,
1960–61, 3″ **45.00 55.00**

☐ **LUXARDO**
Pitcher, smooth glaze, mottled blue, c-scroll handle, stamped "Marmaca, Made in Rep. S. Ma-
rino," 1953–56, 3¾″ **14.00 20.00**

☐ **LUXARDO**
Amphora, white with flowers, stamped "Marmaca, Made in Rep. S. Marino," two handles,
3¾″ **17.00 23.00**

☐ **LUXARDO**
Vase, white with flowers, stamped "Marmaca,
Made in Rep. S. Marino," 1953–56, 3¾″ **17.00 23.00**

☐ **LUXARDO**
Pitcher, Perugia, Italy painted on the bottom, 12
Perugia varieties, 393 made of each, total produc-
tion 4,716, 1955, 3¾″ **27.00 33.00**

	Price Range	
☐ **LUXARDO**		
Bird, brown with black feathers, 4″	**22.00**	**28.00**
☐ **LUXARDO**		
Turkey, made in Italy, 2,900 turkeys were imported, green body, black and green plumage, 1961, 4½″	**22.00**	**28.00**
☐ **LUXARDO**		
Fish, green with yellow markings, light blue tailfins, 4½″	**22.00**	**28.00**
☐ **LUXARDO**		
Dog, white with black and yellow markings, dog is holding blue jar, 5″	**22.00**	**28.00**
☐ **LUXARDO**		
Bishop, blue with black markings, waisted, approximately 278 pieces imported, 1960, 5½″ ..	**80.00**	**90.00**
☐ **LUXARDO**		
Chess King, blue with black markings, waisted, bearded, approximately 278 pieces imported, 1960, 6″	**80.00**	**90.00**
☐ **LUXARDO**		
Horse, blue with black mane and eyes, approximately 278 pieces imported, 1960, 5″	**80.00**	**90.00**
☐ **LUXARDO**		
Grapes, dark blue with green leaves, approximately 1,060 of these bottles were imported, 1960, 2¾″	**45.00**	**55.00**
☐ **LUXARDO**		
Embossed, tears of gold, a recipe from 1685, 4″	**.75**	**1.75**
☐ **LUXARDO**		
Gondola, boat is black and yellow, gondolier is dressed in traditional red and white striped shirt, and blue pants, 1959, 4½″	**10.00**	**15.00**
☐ **LUXARDO**		
Lemon, yellow, approximately 1,060 imported, 1960, 2¼″	**45.00**	**55.00**
☐ **LA MADRILENA**		
Crema de Amor, Mexico, label shows mandarintype figure, 4½″	**1.00**	**3.00**
☐ **LA MADRILENA**		
Crema de Menta, Mexico, label shows mandarintype figure, 4½″	**1.00**	**3.00**

Price Range

☐ **MAMPE**
Grune Pomeranze, embossed, Berlin, 5½″ 1.00 3.00
☐ **MAMPE-HALB u. HALB**
Embossed, Schimmelgespann, Berlin, 6½″ 1.00 3.00
☐ **MARTINI PRATI**
Chianti style bottle, 4¼″ 1.00 3.00
☐ **McLECH**
Golf ball, shite, Scotland, 1969, 1½″ 4.00 6.00
☐ **McLECH**
Scotch Tam, blue with red markings, red ball on
top, 1¾″ 4.00 6.00
☐ **McLECH**
Chick, clear glass, 2½″ 3.00 5.00
☐ **McLECH**
Rabbit, brown, one ear up, one down, 3″ 4.00 6.00
☐ **McLECH**
Lighthouse, red and white, 4″ 4.00 6.00
☐ **McLECH**
Tennis ball, white, marked "BULLFIGHTER,
SPANISH SHERRY," 2″ 4.00 6.00
☐ **McLECH**
Soccer ball, brown, 2″ 4.00 6.00
☐ **McLECH**
Ship's running light, port side, 3″ 3.00 5.00
☐ **McLECH THISTLE**
Ball-like body of bottle with crown-like top, clear
glass, 3¼″ 2.00 4.00
☐ **MEIER'S**
Ohio Port blue, 4¾″ 6.00 10.00
☐ **MEIER'S**
Muscatel, 1934, two-handled jug, 3½″ 4.00 6.00
☐ **MEIER'S**
Port, one-handled jug, 3¾″ 4.00 6.00
☐ **MEIER'S**
Wild cherry wine, embossed with three bunches
of grapes on the vine, 1942, 6″ 1.00 3.00
☐ **MILLER HIGH LIFE**
Mini beer bottle, clear bottle, 4¼″ 6.00 8.00
☐ **MOLLFULLEDA**
Callisay, embossed "FERROQUINA," Spain,
3¾″ 1.00 3.00

	Price Range	
☐ **MOLLFULLEDA**		
Anisette, Spain, 3¾"	1.00	3.00
☐ **MOLLFULLEDA**		
Crema Cacao Chouva, Spain, 4¼"	1.00	3.00
☐ **MOLLFULLEDA**		
Crema Cacao Chouao, Spain, 3½"	1.00	3.00
☐ **MOLLFULLEDA**		
Curacao, Spain, 3½"	1.00	3.00
☐ **MOLLFULLEDA**		
Gin, hand blown, Spain, 4½"	6.00	9.00
☐ **MOLLFULLEDA**		
Kirsch Pur, Spain, 4½"	1.00	3.00
☐ **MOLLFULLEDA**		
Rhum San Juan, Spain, 4"	2.00	4.00
☐ **MOLLFULLEDA**		
Embossed "TRIPLE SEC LICOR," Spain, 3½"	1.00	3.00
☐ **MONTANA**		
Anis Dulce, 3 piece mold, clear glass, Spain, 4½"	1.00	3.00
☐ **MONTANA**		
Curacao, Spain, 4"	1.00	3.00
☐ **MONTANA**		
Drake's Dry Gin, Through Distillation, Spain, clear glass, 4"	4.00	6.00
☐ **MONTANA**		
Peppermint, Est. 1839, Spain, 4"	1.00	3.00
☐ **NADWISLANSKI**		
Honey Drink, Poland, 1969, 3¾"	1.00	3.00
☐ **NALTET-MENAND & FILS**		
France, Prunelle Naltet Liqueur, slightly waisted bottle, 4"	2.00	4.00
☐ **NATIONAL DISTILLERY**		
Embossed, Smirice, Czechoslovakia, Creme de Menthe, 3¾"	2.00	4.00
☐ **NATIONAL DISTILLERY**		
Embossed, Smirice, Czechoslovakik, Griotte, 4"	1.00	3.00
☐ **NASSAU ROYALE**		
Embossed, Bahama Islands, 1969, 4½"	1.00	2.00
☐ **NG G PY**		
Chinese Liqueur, Taiwan, the Republic of China, flared rim, 3"	2.00	4.00

	Price Range	

☐ **E. NORMANDIN & CO.**
Est. 1844, Grande Reserve Cognac, hand blown,
France, 3″ **4.00** **6.00**

☐ **NUYENS & CO.**
Dry French Vermouth, turn mold, France, 1936,
4″.. **.75** **1.75**

☐ **OLLA**
Applied lip, Mexico, bulbous body, Mexico, 3½″ **2.00** **4.00**

☐ **OLD KAINTUCK BOURBON**
Embossed, applied top, clear glass, 3¾″ **17.00** **23.00**

☐ **OLD MISTER LONDON**
Three G Distillery, 5″ **3.00** **5.00**

☐ **OLD MR. BOSTON**
Anisette, label shows small portrait of a man,
4¼″ .... **.75** **1.75**

☐ **ORENDAIN**
Tequila, gold label, Guadalajara, 4½″ **1.00** **3.00**

☐ **PADUCAH CLUB**
John L. Bernecker, Est. 1871, "Handmade," Fin-
est Whisky, pre-1920, jug-style bottle, 3½″ **22.00** **28.00**

☐ **PAPILLON**
Embossed "DESTILERIA FRANCESA MEXICO,
D.F.," 1947, 4″ **1.00** **3.00**

☐ **PAPILLON**
Embossed "DESTILERIA FRANCESA MEXICO,
D.F.," Anisette, 3-piece mold, 5″ **2.00** **4.00**

☐ **PAUL JONES**
Embossed "PAUL JONES PURE RYE, LOUIS-
VILLE," hand blown, opaque 4¼″ **17.00** **23.00**

☐ **PECHUGA ALMENDRADO**
Guadalajara, Mexico, 4″ **2.00** **4.00**

☐ **WILLIAM PENN**
Blended Whiskey, label shows signature, 4¼″ **2.00** **4.00**

☐ **POWER'S GIN**
Special Dry, clear glass, 5½″ **1.00** **3.00**

☐ **PRESIDENTE**
No seams, bulbous body, aqua color, 4″ **2.00** **4.00**

☐ **PRETZEL**
Made in Italy, brown body of pretzel with white
salt, 1 oz., 1926, 5¾″ **22.00** **28.00**

☐ **J. REIGER & CO.**
Embossed, applied top, Kansas City, MO, 4½″ **22.00** **28.00**

Pinch, by Mr. Boston, called the "Thin Man," basically a test-tube shaped bottle with plastic stopper, label bears Mr. Boston portrait, 6½". **$5.00–$8.00**

Price Range

☐ **RIEMERSCHMID**
Bavarian Enzian, Germany, white vase with floral markings, 3½" with red or black cap, 1969, 3½" — 2.00 — 4.00

☐ **RIEMERSCHMID**
Cherry with rum, cylindrical vase with red and green floral markings, red cap, 1969, 4" ...... — 2.00 — 4.00

☐ **RIEMERSCHMID**
Goldwasser, clear glass with red, blue, and yellow floral markings, red cap, 3½" .... — 1.00 — 3.00

☐ **RIEMERSCHMID**
Flask, white with brown design of antique automobiles on the sides, 6½" .... — 2.00 — 4.00

☐ **RIEMERSCHMID**
Flask with map of Munich on the side, 1969, 5¼" — 2.00 — 4.00

☐ **RIEMERSCHMID**
Royal coffee, bottle is shaped like a coffee pot, 1969, 5" .... — 2.00 — 4.00

☐ **RITTENHOUSE SQUARE RYE**
Embossed "CONTINENTAL DIST. CORP.," clear glass, etched design, 3¾" .... — 10.00 — 15.00

Price Range

☐ **ROBERTSON**
Bottle is black and in the shape of a still, Scotland, 1969, 3½" 5.00 8.00

☐ **RODERICK DHU**
Scotland, jug-style bottle, floral design, 4" 35.00 45.00

☐ **ROMATE**
Dry Solera, Full Pale Dry Sherry, Spain, 1934, 5" .75 1.75

☐ **ROMATE**
Spanish Port Wine, 1934, 5" .... .75 1.75

☐ **L. ROSE & CO. LTD.**
Embossed, orange squash, England, 4½" ..... .75 1.75

☐ **RYEBROOK**
Rye, label shows two diamond-shaped figures, 5" 10.00 15.00

☐ **RYNBENDE**
Delft farmhouse, #3, front view shows one door and no windows, one chimney, 1968, Holland, 2½" 4.00 6.00

☐ **RYNBENDE**
Delft farmhouse, #2, front view shows one door and four windows, two chimneys, 1968, Holland, 2¼" 4.00 6.00

☐ **RYNBENDE**
Delft farmhouse, #5, front view shows one door and two windows, two chimneys, 1968, Holland, 3" 4.00 6.00

☐ **RYNBENDE**
Delft farmhouse, #6, front view shows one door and three windows two chimneys, 1968, Holland, 2¼" 4.00 6.00

☐ **RYNBENDE**
Delft farmhouse, #1, front view shows one door and one window, two chimneys, 1968, Holland, 2¼" 4.00 6.00

☐ **RYNBENDE**
Delft farmhouse, #4, front view shows one door and three windows, two chimneys, 1968, Holland, 2¼" 4.00 6.00

☐ **SAMOVAR VODKA**
Dry, clear glass, slightly waisted body, 1967, 5" .75 1.75

☐ **SANDEMAN**
Est. 1790, bottle by Royal Doulton, England, 1937, 4½" 55.00 65.00

	Price Range	

☐ **SANDEMAN**
Est. 1790, Portugal, Partner's Port, label shows
painting, 5¾" **1.00** **3.00**

☐ **SAUZA COMMEMORATIVE-1873–1965**
Embossed "TEQUILA SAUZA," 1965, 4¼" ... **1.00** **3.00**

☐ **SCHWARZER KATER**
Fritz Lehment, Est. 1868, label shows a black cat,
Germany, 3" **1.00** **3.00**

☐ **SEAGRAM'S ANCIENT BOTTLE**
Rye, Canada, Straight Rye Whiskey, 1936, 4" **8.00** **12.00**

☐ **SEAGRAM'S KING ARTHUR GIN**
Clear glass, distilled London Dry Gin, 4" **4.00** **6.00**

☐ **SEAGRAM'S SEVEN CROWN**
Blended Whiskey, clear glass, 1937, 4" **8.00** **12.00**

☐ **SOUTHERN SALES**
Black Horse, contents 3 grams, 3¾" **4.00** **6.00**

☐ **SOUTHERN SALES**
Apricot Cordial, 3¾" **1.00** **3.00**

☐ **SOUTHERN SALES**
Apricot Cordial, with mini nozzle attached, 2¾" **2.00** **4.00**

☐ **STEWARTS DUNDEE**
Embossed, Blended Scotch Whisky, Beam im-
port, 1969, 3½" **1.00** **3.00**

☐ **SUPERIOR RON**
Mexico, bulbous body, 4½" **2.00** **4.00**

☐ **TRIUNFO**
Embossed "VINOS LA MEXICANA," 3" .... **.75** **1.75**

☐ **UCAGCO**
Itlay, Chianti style decanter, 3½" .... **.75** **1.75**

☐ **UNCLE SAM**
Figure of Uncle Sam with knees slightly bent, red
coat, white pants, black shoes, stars and stripes
on hat, in his right hand is a cocktail glass, 6" **160.00** **190.00**

☐ **HENRI VALLET BRANDY**
Mexico, 5½" **1.00** **3.00**

☐ **HENRI VALLET RHUM**
Mexico, bulbous body, 3¼" **2.00** **4.00**

☐ **HENRI VALLET PEPPERMINT**
Mexico, 6½" .... **.75** **1.75**

☐ **VIRREYES**
Embossed, Mexico, ovoid shape, 3¼" **1.00** **3.00**

Price Range

☐ **HIRAM WALKER'S RYE**
"Twin Seal," 1937, 4" 10.00 15.00

☐ **HIRAM WALKER'S TEN HIGH**
Straight Bourbon Whiskey, 1937, 4" 7.00 10.00

☐ **WING FUNG HONG**
Embossed, China, bulbous body, green, 1937,
3½" 5.00 7.00

☐ **WING FUNG HONG**
Embossed, China, bulbous body, flared lip,
brown, 1937, 2¾" 5.00 7.00

☐ **ZWACK**
Embossed, Cacao Chouva, applied top, 1937,
4½" 10.00 15.00

☐ **ZWACK**
Est. 1840, embossed, blackberry, applied top, 4" 10.00 15.00

☐ **ZWACK**
Kummel, applied top and handle, 1937, 3½" .. 10.00 15.00

☐ **ZWACK**
Embossed, Mandarinette, applied top, clear
glass, Budapest, 1935, 3½" 10.00 15.00

☐ **ZWACK**
Embossed, Mandarinette, applied top, brown bottle, Budapest, 1935, heart-shaped bottle, 3¾" 10.00 15.00

☐ **ZWACK**
Embossed, mocca, long neck, 4½" 10.00 15.00

☐ **ZWACK**
Embossed, strawberry, applied neck and handle,
Budapest, 1937, 4" 13.00 18.00

☐ **ZWACK**
Embossed, peach, applied top, neck used 4-
piece mold, Budapest, 1936, 3½" 13.00 18.00

☐ **ZWACK**
Embossed, royal orange, applied top and handles, 1935, 3½" 13.00 18.00

☐ **ZWACK**
Embossed, Yvette, flared lip, 1937, 4¼" 13.00 18.00

☐ **ZWACK**
Tulip, applied top, 4½" 1.00 14.00

BOTTLE CLUBS

ALABAMA

Alabama Bottle Collectors Society— 2768 Hanover Circle, Birmingham, AL 35205, (205) 933–7902.

Azalea City Beamers Bottle & Spec. Club— 100 Bienville Avenue, Mobile, AL 36606, (205) 473–4251.

Bama Beamers Bottle & Spec. Club— Rt. 1, P.O. Box 72, Sheffield, AL 35660, (205) 383–6884.

Choctaw Jim Beam Bottle & Spec. Club —218 S. Hamburg Street, Butler, AL 36904, (205) 459–3140.

Heart of Dixie Beam Bottle & Spec. Club— 2136 Rexford Road, Montgomery, AL 36116.

Mobile Bottle Collectors Club— 7927 Historic Mobile Parkway, Theodore, AL 36582, (205) 653–0713.

Montgomery, Alabama Bottle Club— 1940A Norman Bridge Court, Montgomery, AL 36104.

Montgomery Bottle & Insulator Club— 2021 Merrily Drive, Montgomery, AL 36111, (205) 288–7937.

Mobile Bottle Collectors Club— Rt. 4, P.O. Box 28, Theodore, AL 36582.

North Alabama Bottle & Glass Club— P.O. Box 109, Decatur, AL 35601.

Tuscaloosa Antique Bottle Club— 1617 11th Street, Tuscaloosa, AL 35401.

Southern Beamers Bottle & Spec. Club —1400 Greenbrier Road, Apt. G-3, Anniston, AL 36201, (205) 831–5151

Vulcan Beamers Bottle & Spec. Club— 5817 Avenue Q, Birmingham, AL 35228, (205) 831–5151.

ALASKA

Alaska Bottle Club—(formerly The Anchorage Beam Club)— 8510 E. 10th, Anchorage, AK 99504.

ARIZONA

Avon Collectors Club— P.O. Box 1406, Mesa, AZ 86201.

Fort Smith Area Bottle Collectors Association— 4618 S. "Q", Fort Smith, AZ 72901.

Kachina Ezra Brooks Bottle Club— 3818 W. Cactus Wren Drive, Phoenix, AZ 85021.

Pick & Shovel A.B.C. of Arizona, Inc.— P.O. Box 7020, Phoenix, AZ 85011. Meets 8:00 P.M. first Wednesday at 531 E. Bethany Home Rd., Phoenix. (Stuckey Ins.

Agency) Newsletter: The Blister. Club formed 1969, has 40 family members.

Southern AZ Historical Collector's Association, Ltd.— 6211 Piedra Seca, Tucson, AZ 85718.

Tri-City Jim Beam Bottle Club— 2701 E. Utopia Road, Sp. #91, Phoenix, AZ 85024, (602) 867–1375.

Valley of the Sun Bottle & Specialty Club— 212 E. Minton, Tempe, AZ 85281.

White Mountain Antique Bottle Collectors Association— P.O. Box 503, Eager, AZ 85925.

Wildcat Country Beam Bottle & Spec. Club— 2601 S. Blackmoon Drive, Tucson, AZ 85730, (602) 298–5943.

ARKANSAS

Fort Smith Area Bottle Collectors Assn.— 2201 S. 73rd Street, Ft. Smith, AR 72903.

Hempsted County Bottle Club— 710 S. Hervey, Hope, AR 71801.

Little Rock Antique Bottle Collectors Club— #12 Martin Drive, North Little Rock, AR 72118, (501) 753–2623.

Madison County Bottle Collectors Club —Rt. 2, Box 304, Huntsville, AR 72740.

Razorback Jim Beam Bottle & Spec. Club— 2609 S. Taylor, Little Rock, AR 72204, (501) 664–1335.

Southwest Arkansas Bottle Club— Star Route, Delight, AR 71940.

CALIFORNIA

A.B.C. of Orange County— P.O. Box 10424, Santa Ana, CA 92711. Meet first Monday at 7:30 P.M. Willard Jr. High School, Santa Ana. Newsletters: The Bottle Bulletin, Club formed 1968, has 60 members.

Amethyst Bottle Club— 3245 Military Avenue, Los Angeles, CA 90034.

Antique Bottle Collectors of Orange County— 223 E. Ponona, Santa Ana, CA 92707.

Antique Bottle Club Association of Fresno— P.O. Box 1932, Fresno, CA 93718.

A, OK Beamers— 7650 Balboa Blvd., Van Nuys, CA 91406, (213) 787–2674.

Argonaut Jim Beam Bottle Club— 8253 Citadel Way, Sacramento, CA 95826, (916) 383–0206.

Avon Bottle & Specialties Collectors—

Southern California Division, 9233 Mills Avenue, Montclair, CA 91763.

Bay Area Vagabonds Jim Beam Club—224 Castleton Way, San Bruno, CA 94066, (415) 355–4356.

Beach Cities Beamers—3111 Highland Avenue, Manhattan Beach, CA 90266.

Beaming Beamers Jim Beam Bottle & Spec. Club—3734 Lynhurst Way, North Highlands, CA 95660, (916) 482–0359.

Beam Bottle Club of Southern California—3221 N. Jackson, Rosemead, CA 91770.

Beam's Orange County Bottle & Spec. Club—1516 E. Harmony Lane, Fullerton, CA 92631, (714) 526–5137.

Bidwell Bottle Club—Box 546, Chico, CA 95926.

Bishop Belles & Beaux Bottle Club—P.O. Box 1475, Bishop, CA 93514.

Blossom Valley Jim Beam Bottle & Spec. Club—431 Grey Ghost Avenue, San Jose, CA 95111, (408) 227–2759.

Bodfish Beamers Jim Beam Bottle Club—19 Dow Drive, P.O. Box 864-A, Bodfish, CA 93205, (714) 379–3280.

California Ski Country Bottle Club—212 South El Molino Street, Alhambra, CA 91801.

Camellia City Jim Beam Bottle Club—3734 Lynhurst Way, North Highlands, CA 95660.

Central Calif. Avon Bottle & Collectible Club—P.O. Box 232, Amador City, CA 95601.

Cherry Valley Beam Bottle & Specialty Club—6851 Hood Drive, Westminster, CA 92683.

Chief Solano Bottle Club—4-D Boynton Avenue, Sulsun, CA 94585.

Curiosity Bottle Association—Box 103, Napa, CA 94558.

Fiesta City Beamers—329 Mountain Drive, Santa Barbara, CA 93103.

First Double Springs Collectors Club—13311 Illinois Street, Westminster, CA 92683.

Five Cities Beamers—756 Mesa View Drive, Sp. 57, Arroyo Grande, CA 93420.

Fresno Raisin Beamers—3850 E. Ashian #A, Fresno, CA 93726, (209) 224–3086.

Glass Belles of San Gabriel—518 W. Neuby Avenue, San Gabriel, CA 91776.

Glasshopper Figural Bottle Association—P.O. Box 6642, Torrance, CA 90504.

Golden Bear Ezra Brooks Bottle Club—8808 Capricorn Way, San Diego, CA 92162.

Golden Bear Jim Beam Bottle & Specialty Club—8808 Capricorn Way, San Diego, CA 92126.

Golden Gate Beam Club—35113 Clover Street, Union City, CA 94587, (415) 487–4479.

Golden Gate Historical Bottle Society—P.O. Box 2129, Alameda, CA 94501.

Greater Cal. Antique Bottle Collectors—P.O. Box 55, Sacramento, CA 95801.

Grizzly Guzzlers Jim Beam Bottle Club—40080 Francis Way, P.O. Box 3725, Big Bear Lake, CA 92351.

High Desert Bottle Hunters—P.O. Box 581, Ridgecrest, CA 93558.

Highland Toasters Beam Bottle & Spec. Club—1570 E. Marshall, San Bernardino, CA 92404, (714) 883–2000.

Hoffman's Mr. Lucky Bottle Club—2104 Rhoda Street, Simi Valley, CA 93065.

Hollywood Stars-Ezra Brooks Bottle Club—2200 N. Beachwood Drive, Hollywood, CA 90028.

Humboldt Antique Bottle Club—P.O. Box 6012, Eureka, CA 95501.

Insulator Collectors Club, San Diego County, Inc.

Jim Beam Bottle Club—139 Arlington, Berkeley, CA 94707.

Jim Beam Bottle Club of So. Calif.—1114 Coronado Terrace, Los Angeles, CA 90066.

Juniper Hills Bottle Club—Rt. 1, Box 18, Valyerma, CA 93563.

Jewels of Avon—2297 Maple Avenue, Oroville, CA 95965.

Kern County Antique Bottle Club—P.O. Box 6724, Bakersfield, CA 93306.

Lilliputian Bottle Club—5119 Lee Street, Torrance, CA 90503.

Lionstone Bottle Collector's of America—P.O. Box 75924, Los Angeles, CA 90075.

Livermore Avon Club—6385 Claremont Avenue, Richmond, CA 94805.

Lodi Jim Beam Bottle Club—429 E. Lodi Avenue, Lodi, CA 95240.

Los Angeles Historical Bottle Club—P.O. Box 60762, Terminal Annex, Los Angeles, CA 90060, (213) 332–6751.

Mission Bells (Beams)—1114 Coronada Terrace, Los Angeles, CA 90026.

Mission Tesore Jim Beam Bottle & Spec. Club—7701 E. Zayante Road, Felton, CA 95018, (408) 335–4317.

Mission Trails Ezra Brooks Bottles & Specialties Club, Inc.—4923 Bel Canto Drive, San Jose, CA 95124.

Mission Trail Historical Bottle Club—P.O. Box 721, Seaside, CA 93955, (408) 394-3257.

Modesto Beamers—1429 Glenwood Drive, Modesto, CA 95350, (209) 523-3440.

Modesto Old Bottle Club (MOBC)—P.O. Box 1791, Modesto, CA 95354.

Monterey Bay Beam Bottle & Specialty Club—P.O. Box 258, Freedom, CA 95019.

M. T. Bottle Club—P.O. Box 608, Solana Beach, CA 92075.

Mt. Bottle Club—422 Orpheus, Encinitas, CA 92024.

Mt. Diablo Bottle Club—4166 Sandra Circle, Pittsburg, CA 94565.

Mt. Diablo Bottle Society—1699 Laguna #110, Concord, CA 94520.

Mt. Whitney Bottle Club—P.O. Box 688, Lone Pine, CA 93545.

Motherlode Bottle Club—P.O. Box 337, Angels Camp, CA 95222.

Napa-Solano Bottle Club—1409 Delwood, Vallejo, CA 94590.

National Jim Beam Bottle & Spec. Club—5005 Cochrane Avenue, Oakland, CA 94618, (415) 655-5005.

Northern California Jim Beam Bottle & Specialty Club—P.O. Box 186, Montgomery Creek, CA 96065.

Northwestern Bottle Club—P.O. Box 1121, Santa Rosa, CA 95402. Meet 4th Tuesday January, April, June, September, October, Coddingtown Community Meeting Room, Santa Rosa. Newsletter: The Glassblower. Club formed 1966, has 29 family members.

Northwestern Bottle Collectors Association—1 Keeler Street, Petaluma, CA 94952.

Ocean Breeze Beamers—4841 Tacayme Drive, Oceanside, CA 92054, (714) 757-9081.

Original Sippin Cousins Ezra Brooks Specialties Club—12206 Malone Street, Los Angeles, CA 90066.

Palomar Jim Bean Club—246 S. Las Posas, P.O. Box 125, San Marcos, CA 92069, (714) 744-2924.

Pebble Beach Jim Beam Bottle Club—419 Alvarado Street, Monterey, CA 93940, (408) 373-5320.

Peninsula Bottle Club—P.O. Box 886, Belmont, CA 94002.

Petaluma Bottle & Antique Club—P.O. Box 1035, Petaluma, CA 94952.

Quail Country Jim Beam Bottle & Spec. Club—625 Pleasant, Coalinga, CA 93210.

Queen Mary Beam & Specialty Club—P.O. Box 2054, Anaheim, CA 92804.

Relic Accumulators—P.O. Box 3513, Eureka, CA 95501.

Santa Barbara Beam Bottle Club—5307 University Drive, Santa Barbara, CA 93111.

Santa Barbara Bottle Club—P.O. Box 30171, Santa Barbara, CA 93105.

San Bernardino County Historical Bottle and Collectible Club—P.O. Box 127, Bloomington, CA 92316. Meets 4th Tuesday, 7:30 P.M. San Bernardino Co. Museum, Redlands, CA, phone (714) 244-5863. Newsletter: Bottle Nooz. Club formed 1967, has 60 members.

San Diego Antique Bottle Club—P.O. Box 536, San Diego, CA 92112.

San Diego Jim Beam Bottle Club—2620 Mission Village Drive, San Diego, CA 92112.

San Joaquin Valley Jim Beam Bottle & Specialties Club—4085 N. Wilson Avenue, Fresno, CA 93704.

San Jose Antique Bottle Collector's Assn.—P.O. Box 5432, San Jose, CA

San Francisco Bay Area Miniature Bottle Club—160 Lower Via Casitas #8, Kentfield, CA 94904.

San Luis Obispo Antique Bottle Club—124-21 Street Paso Robles, CA 93446. Meets 3rd Saturday, private homes. Phone (238) 1848. Club formed in 1965, has 30 family members.

Santa Maria Beam & Spec. Club—528 E. Harding, Santa Maria, CA 93454, (805) 922-1238.

Sequoia Antique Bottle Society—1900 4th Avenue, Kingsburg, CA 93631.

Shasta Antique Bottle Collectors Association—Rt. 1, Box 3147-A, Anderson, CA 96007.

Sierra Gold Ski Country Bottle Club—5081 Rio Vista Avenue, San Jose, CA 95129.

Ski-Country Bottle Club of Southern California—3148 N. Walnut Grove, Rosemead, CA 91770.

Solar Country Beamers—940 Kelly Drive, Barstow, CA 92311, (714) 256-1485.

South Bay Antique Bottle Club—2589½ Valley Drive, Manhattan Beach, CA 90266.

Southern California Miniature Bottle Club—5626 Corning Avenue, Los Angeles, CA 90056.

Southwestern Wyoming Avon Bottle Club—301 Canyon Highlands Drive, Oroville, CA 95965.

Stockton Historical Bottle Society, Inc.—P.O. Box 8584, Stockton, CA 95204.

Sunnyvale Antique Bottle Collectors Association—613 Torrington, Sunnyvale, CA 94087.

Superior California Bottle Club—P.O. Box 555, Anderson, CA 96007.

Taft Antique Bottle Club—P.O. Box 334, Taft, CA 93268.

Teen Bottle Club—Rt. 1, Box 60-TE, Eureka, CA 95501.

Tehama County Antique Bottle Club—Rt. 1 Box 775, Red Bluff, CA 96080. Meets 7:30 P.M. 1st Wednesday at Lassen View School. Phone 916–527–1680. Club formed 1960, has 55 family members.

Tinseltown Beam Club—4117 E. Gage Avenue, Bell, CA 90201, (213) 699–8787.

Western World Collectors Assn.—P.O. Box 409, Ontario, CA 91761. Meets every 3rd Wednesday, 7:30 P.M. at Upland Lumber Co., 85 Euclid Avenue, Upland, CA. Phone (714) 984–0614. Club formed in 1971, has 150 family members.

Wildwind Jim Beam Bottle & Specialties Club—905 Eaton Way, Sunnyvale, CA 94087, (408) 739–1558.

World Wide Avon Collectors Club—44021 Seventh Street E. Lancaster, CA 93534, (805) 948–8849.

COLORADO

Alamosa Bottle Collectors—Rt. 2, Box 170, Alamosa, CO 81101.

Avon Club of Colorado Springs, CO—707 N. Farragut, Colorado Springs, CO 80909.

Colorado Mile-High Ezra Brooks Bottle Club—7401 Decatur Street, Westminster, CO 80030.

Foot-Hills Jim Beam Bottle & Spec. Club—1303 Kilkenny Street, Boulder, CO 80303, (303) 665–3957.

Four Corners Bottle & Glass Club—P.O. Box 45, Cortez, CO 81321.

Horsetooth Antique Bottle Collectors, Inc.—P.O. Box 944, Ft. Collins, CO 80521.

Lionstone Western Figural Club—P.O. Box 2275, Colorado Springs, CO 80901.

Mile-Hi Jim Beam Bottle & Spec. Club—13196 W. Green Mountain Drive, Lakewood, CO 80228, (303) 986–6828.

National Ski Country Bottle Club—1224 Washington Avenue, Golden, CO 80401, (303) 279–3373.

Northeastern Colorado Antique Bottle Club—P.O. Box 634, Ft. Morgan, CO 80701.

Northern Colorado Antique Bottle Club—227 W. Beaver Avenue, Ft. Morgan, CO 80701.

Northern Colorado Beam Bottle & Spec. Club—3272 Gunnison Drive, Ft. Collins, CO 80526, (303) 226–2301.

Ole Foxie Jim Beam Club—P.O. Box 560, Westminster, CO 80020.

Peaks & Plains Antique Bottle Club—P.O. Box 814, Colorado Springs, CO 80901.

Rocky Mountain Jim Beam Bottle & Specialty Club—Alcott Station, P.O. Box 12162, Denver, CO 80212.

Telluride Antique Bottle Collectors—P.O. Box 344, Telluride, CO 8143.

Western Figural & Jim Beam Specialty Club—P.O. Box 4331, Colorado Springs, CO 80930.

Western Slope Bottle Club—607 Belford Avenue, Grand Junction, CO 81501.

CONNECTICUT

The Milk Route—4 Ox Bow Road, Westport, CT. 06880.

Connecticut Specialty Bottle Club, Inc.—P.O. Box 624, Stratford, CT.

Somers Antique Bottle Club—Somers, CT 06071, (203) 487–1071.

Southern Connecticut Antique Bottle Collectors Association, Inc.—c/o Tom Harris—22 Sawmill Road, Norwalk, CT. 06851.

Western Connecticut Jim Beam Bottle & Spec. Club—Rt. 1, Box 442, Old Hawleyville Road, Bethel, CT 06801, (203) 744–6118.

DELAWARE

Blue Hen Jim Beam Bottle & Spec. Club—303 Potomac Drive, Wilmington, DE 19803, (302) 652–6378.

Mason-Dixon Bottle Collectors Association—P.O. Box 505, Lewes, DE 19958.

Tri-State Bottle Collectors and Diggers Club—730 Paper Mill Road, Newark, DE 19711.

FLORIDA

Antique Bottle Collectors Assn. of Florida—5901 S.W. 16th Street, Miami, FL 33144. Meets 2nd Tuesday, 7:30 P.M. School. Phone 305–266–4854. Newsletter: Whittlemark. Club formed 1965, has 55 members.

Antique Bottle Collectors of North Florida—P.O. Box 14796, Jacksonville, FL 32210.

Antique Bottle Collectors of Florida, Inc.—2512 Davie Boulevard, Ft. Lauderdale, FL 33312.

Bay Area Historical Bottle Collector—
P.O. Box 3454, Apollo Beach, FL 33570.
Central Florida Insulator Club—3557
Nicklaus Drive, Titusville, FL 32780, 305
267–9170.
Central Florida Jim Beam Bottle Club—
1060 W. French Avenue, Orange City, FL
32763, (904) 775–7392.
Crossarms Collectors Club—1756 N.W.
58th Avenue, Lauderhill, FL 33313. Meets
every other month, 3rd Wednesday at
above address. Phone (733) 1053. News-
letter: Crossarms. Club formed 1975.
Deep South Jim Beam Bottle & Spec.
Club—16100 S.W. 278th Street, Home-
stead, FL 33031, (305) 248–7301.
Everglades A.B.C.—6981 S.W. 19th
Street, Pompano, FL 33068. Club formed
1977, has 44 members.
Everglades Antique Bottle & Collec-
tors Club—400 S. 57 Terrace, Holly-
wood, FL 33023, (305) 962–3434.
Florida Panhandle Jim Beam Bottle &
Spec. Club—706 James Court, Ft. Wal-
ton Beach, FL 32548, (904) 862–3469.
Gateway of the Palms Beam Bottle &
Spec. Club—6621 Katherine Road, West
Palm Beach, FL 33406, (305) 683–3900.
Gold Coast Collectors Club—Joseph I.
Frakes, P.O. Box 10183, Wilton Manors,
FL 33305.
Halifax Historical Society—224½ S.
Beach Street, Daytona Beach, FL 32018.
Harbor City—1232 Causeway, Eau, FL
32935.
Longwood Bottle Club—P.O. Box 437,
Longwood, FL 32750.
M. T. Bottle Collectors Assn., Inc.—P.O.
Box 581, Deland, FL 32720.
Mid-State Antique Bottle Collectors—
88 Sweetbriar Branch, Longwood, FL
32750, 834–8914.
Northwest Florida Regional Bottle
Club—P.O. Box 282, Port St. Joe, FL
32456.
Original Florida Keys Collectors Club—
P.O. Box 212, Islamorada, FL 33036.
Oviedo Bottling Works—Maitland, FL
32751.
Pensacola Bottle & Relic Collectors
Association—1004 Freemont Avenue,
Pensacola, FL 32505.
Ridge Area Antique Bottle Collectors
—1219 Carlton, Lake Wales, FL 33853.
Sanford Antique A.B.C.—2656 Grand-
view Avenue, Sanford, FL. Meets 2nd
Tuesday, 8:00 P.M. (305) 322–7181. News-
letter: Probe. Club formed 1966, has 50
members.
Sarasota-Manatee A.B.C. Assn.—Rt. 1,

Box 74–136, Sarasota, FL 33583. Phone
(813) 924–5995. Meets 3rd Wednesday,
7:30 P.M. in member's homes. Newsletter:
The Glass Habit. Club formed 1969, has
20 members.
South Florida Jim Beam Bottle & Spe-
cialty Club—7741 N.W. 35th Street,
West Hollywood, FL 33024.
Suncoast Antique Bottle Club—P.O.
Box 12712, St. Petersburg, FL 33733.
Suncoast Jim Beam Bottle & Spec.
Club—P.O. Box 5067, Sarasota, FL
33579.
Tampa Antique Bottle Collectors—P.O.
Box 4232, Tampa, FL 33607.
West Coast Florida Ezra Brooks Bottle
Club—1360 Harbor Drive, Sarasota, FL
33579.

GEORGIA
Bulldog Double Springs Bottle Collec-
tor Club of Augusta, Georgia—1916
Melrose Drive, Augusta, GA 30906.
Coastal Empire Bottle Club—P.O. Box
3714, Station B, Savannah, GA 31404.
The Desoto Trail Bottle Collectors Club
—406 Randolph Street, Cuthbert, GA
31740.
Flint Antique Bottle & Coin Club—c/o
Cordele-Crisp Co., Recreation Depart-
ment, 204 2nd Street North, Cordele, GA
31015.
Flint River Jim Beam Bottle Club—Rt. 3,
P.O. Box 6, Camilla, GA 31730, (912)
336–7034.
Georgia Bottle Club—2996 Pangborn
Road, Decatur, GA 30033.
Georgia-Carolina Empty Bottle Club—
P.O. Box 1184, Augusta, GA 30903.
Macon Antique Bottle Club—P.O. Box
5395, Macon, GA 31208. Meets 7:30 P.M.
2nd Monday, Robert Train Recreation
Center. Newsletter: Glass Heart of
Georgia. Club formed 1968, has 20 mem-
bers.
Macon Antique Bottle Club—c/o 5532
Jane Run Circle, Macon, GA 31206.
Meets 7:30 P.M. 2nd Monday at Robert
Train Rec. Newsletter: Heart of Georgia
News, has 30 members.
The Middle Georgia Antique Bottle
Club—2746 Alden Street, Macon, GA
31206.
Peachstate Bottle & Specialty Club—
5040 Vallo Vista Court, Atlanta, GA
30342.
Peachtree Jim Beam Bottlers Club—
224 Lakeshore Drive, Daluth, GA 30136,
(404) 448–9013.
Peanut State Jim Beam Bottle & Spec.

Club—767 Timberland Street, Smyrna, GA 30080. (404) 432–8482.
Southeastern Antique Bottle Club—P.O. Box 657, Decatur, GA 30033.

HAWAII

Hauoli Beam Bottle Collectors Club of Hawaii—45–027 Ka-Hanahou Place, Kaneohe, HI 96744.
Hawaii Bottle Collectors Club—6770 Hawaii Kal Drive, Apt. 708, Hawaii Kai, HI 96825.

IDAHO

Buhl Antique Bottle Club—500 12th N. Buhl, ID 83316.
Eagle Rock Beam & Spec. Club—3665 Upland Avenue, Idaho Falls, ID 83401, (208) 522–7819.
Em Tee Bottle Club—P.O. Box 62, Jerome, ID 83338.
Fabulous Valley Antique Bottle Club—P.O. Box 769, Osburn, ID 83849.
Gem Antique Bottle Collectors Assn., Inc.—P.O. Box 8051, Boise, ID 83707.
Idaho Beam & Spec. Club—2312 Burrell Avenue, Lewiston, ID 83501, (208) 743–5997.
Idaho Bottle Collectors Association—4530 S. 5th Street, Pocatello, ID 83201.
Inland Empire Jim Beam Bottle & Collectors' Club—1117 10th Street, Lewiston, ID 83501.
Rock & Bottle Club—Rt. 1, Fruitland, ID 83619.
Treasure Valley Beam Bottle & Spec. Club—2324 Norcrest Drive, Boise, ID 83705, (208) 343–6207.

ILLINOIS

A.B.C. of Northern Illinois—P.O. Box 23, Ingleside, IL 60041. Phone (815) 338–2567. Meets 1st Wednesday 8:00 P.M. at Jones Island Meeting House, Grayslake, IL. Newsletter: Pick & Probe. Formed 1973, has 29 members.
Alton Area Bottle Club—2448 Alby Street, Alton, IL. (618) 462–4285.
Blackhawk Jim Beam Bottle & Specialties Club—2003 Kishwaukee Street, Rockford, IL 61101.
Central & Midwestern States Beam & Specialties Club—44 S. Westmore, Lombard, IL 60148.
Central Illinois Jim Beam Bottle & Spec. Club—3725 S. Sand Creek Road, Decatur, IL 62521.
Chicago Ezra Brooks Bottle & Specialty Club—3635 W. 82nd Street, Chicago, IL 60652.

Chicago Jim Beam Bottle & Specialty Club—1305 W. Marion Street, Joliet, IL 60436.
Dreamer Beamers—5721 Vial Parkway, LaGrange, IL 60525, (312) 246–4838.
Eagle Jim Beam Bottle & Spec. Club—1015 Hollycrest, P.O. Box 2084 CFS, Champaign, IL 61820, (217) 352–4035.
1st Chicago A.B.C.—P.O. Box A-3382, Chicago, IL 60690. Meets 3rd Friday, 7:00 P.M. at St. Daniels Church, 5400 S. Nashville, Chicago. Newsletter: Mid-West Bottled News. Formed 1969, has 50 members.
Heart of Illinois Antique Bottle Club—2010 Bloomington Road, East Peoria, IL 61611.
Illinois Bottle Club—P.O. Box 181, Rushville, IL 62681.
Illini Jim Beam Bottle & Specialty Club—P.O. Box 13, Champaign, IL 61820.
International Association of Jim Beam—4338 Saratoga Ave., Downers Grove, IL 60515.
Kelly Club—147 North Brainard Avenue, La Grange, IL 60525.
Land of Lincoln Bottle Club—2515 Illinois Circle, Decatur, IL 62526.
Lewis & Clark Jim Beam Bottle & Specialty Club—P.O. Box 451, Wood River, IL 62095.
Lionstone Bottle Collectors of America—P.O. Box 2418, Chicago, IL 60690.
Little Egypt Jim Beam Bottle & Spec. Club—Rt. 2, Flat Rock, IL 62427, (618) 584–3338.
Louis Joliet Bottle Club—12 Kenmore, Joliet, IL 60433.
Metro East Bottle & Jar Association—309 Bellevue Drive, Belleville, IL, (618) 233–8841. Meets 2nd Tuesday at O'Fallon Township Bldg., 801 E. State Street, O'Fallon, IL. Newsletter: Metro-East Bottle & Jar & Insulator Relater. Club formed 1971, has 26 members.
Metro East Bottle & Jar Association—1702 North Keesler, Collinsville, IL 62234.
Metro East Bottle & Jar Association—P.O. Box 185, Mascoutah, IL.
National Ezra Brooks Club—645 N. Michigan Avenue, Chicago, IL 69611.
North Shore Jim Beam Bottle & Spec. Club—542 Glendale Road, Glenview, IL 60025.
Pekin Bottle Collectors Assn.—P.O. Box 372, Pekin, IL 61554. Phone (309) 347–4441. Meets 3rd Wednesday, Pekin Chamber of Commerce. Club formed 1970, has 80 members.
Rock River Valley Jim Beam Bottle &

Spec. Club—1107 Avenue A., Rock Falls, IL 61071, (815) 625-7075.
Starved Rock Jim Beam Bottle & Spec. Club—P.O. Box 177, Ottawa, IL 61350, (815) 433-3269.
Sweet Corn Capital Bottle Club—1015 W. Orange, Hoopeston, IL 60942.
Tri County Jim Beam Bottle Club—3702 W. Lancer Road, Peoria, IL 61615, (309) 691-8784.

INDIANA

City of Bridges Jim Beam Bottle & Spec. Club—1017 N. 6th Street, Logansport, IN 46947. (219) 722-3197.
Crossroads of American Jim Beam Bottle Club—114 S. Green Street, Brownsburg, IN 46112. (317) 852-5168.
Fort Wayne Historical Bottle Club—5124 Roberta Drive, Fort Wayne, IN 46306. Meets 2nd Wednesday at Library Branches. Club formed 1970, has 20 members.
Hoosier Jim Beam Bottle & Specialties Club—P.O. Box 24234, Indianapolis, IN 46224.
Indiana Ezra Brooks Bottle Club—P.O. Box 24344, Indianapolis, IN 46224.
Lafayette Antique Bottle Club—3664 Redondo Drive, Lafayette, IN 47905. Phone 477-0038. Meets 4:00 P.M. 1st Sunday at Jenks Rest, Columbian Park, Lafayette, IN. Club formed in 1977, has 8 members.
Michiana Jim Beam Bottle & Specialty Club—58955 Locust Road, South Bend, IN 46614.
Mid-West Antique Fruit Jar & Bottle Club—P.O. Box 38, Flat Rock, IN 47234.
The Ohio Valley Antique Bottle and Jar Club—214 John Street, Aurora, IN 47001.
Steel City Ezra Brooks Bottle Club—Rt. 2, Box 32A, Valparaiso, IN 46383.
Three Rivers Jim Beam Bottle & Spec. Club—Rt. 4, Winchester Road, Ft. Wayne, IN 46819. (219) 639-3041.
We Found 'Em Bottle & Insulator Club—P.O. Box 578, Bunker Hill, IN 46914.

IOWA

Five Seasons Beam & Spec. Club of Iowa—609 32nd Street, NE, Cedar Rapids, IA 52402, (319) 365-6089.
Gold Dome Jim Beam Bottle & Spec. Club—2616 Hull, Des Moines, IA 50317, (515) 262-8728.
Hawkeye Jim Beam Bottle Club—658 Kern Street, Waterloo, IA 60703, (319) 233-9168.
Iowa Antique Bottlers—1506 Albia Road, Ottumwa, IA 52501, (319-377) 6041. Meets 4 times a year at various places. Newsletter. The Iowa Antique Bottleers. Club formed 1968, has 60 members.
Iowa Great Lakes Jim Beam Bottle & Spec. Club—Green Acres Mobile Park, Lot 88, Estherville, IA 51334, (712) 362-2759.
Larkin Bottle Club—107 W. Grimes, Red Oak, IA 51566.
Midlands Jim Beam Bottle & Spec. Club—Rt. 4, Harlan, IA 51537, (712) 744-3686.
Quad Cities Jim Beam Bottle & Spec. Club—2425 W. 46th Street, Davenport, IA 52806, (319) 391-4319.
Shot Tower Beam Club—284 N. Booth Street, Dubuque, IA 52001, (319) 583-6343.

KANSAS

Air Capital City Jim Beam Bottle & Spec. Club—3256 Euclid, Wichita, KS 67217, (316) 942-3162.
Bud Hastin's National Avon Collector's Club—P.O. Box 12088, Overland Park, KS 66212.
Cherokee Strip Ezra Brooks Bottle & Specialty Club—P.O. Box 631, Arkansas City, KS 67005.
Flint Hills Beam & Specialty Club—201 W. Pine, El Dorado, KS 67042.
Jayhawk Bottle Club—7919 Grant, Overland Park, KS 66212.
Kansas City Antique Bottle Collectors—5528 Aberdeen, Shawnee Mission, KS 66205. Phone (816) 433-1398. Meets 6 P.M. 2nd Sunday at 1131 E. 77th, Kansas City, MO 64125. Newsletter: Privy Primer. Club formed 1974, has 15 family members.
Southeast Kansas Bottle & Relics Club—115 N. Lafayette, Chanute, KS 66720, (316) 431-1643. Meets 7:30 P.M. 1st Wednesday at First National Bank Community Room. Newsletter: S.E. Kantique News. Club formed 1973, has 40 members.
Walnut Valley Jim Beam Bottle & Spec. Club—P.O. Box 631, Arkansas City, KS 67005, (316) 442-0509.
Wichita Ezra Brooks Bottle & Specialties Club—8045 Peachtree Street, Wichita, KS 67207.

KENTUCKY

Derby City Jim Beam Bottle Club—4105 Spring Hill Road, Louisville, KY 40207.

Gold City Jim Beam Bottle Club—286 Metts Court, Apt. 4, Elizabethtown, KY 42701, (502) 737–9297.

Kentuckiana A.B. & Outhouse Society—5801 River Knolls Drive, Louisville, KY 40222, 425–6995.

Kentucky Bluegrass Ezra Brooks Bottle Club—6202 Tabor Drive, Louisville, KY 40218.

Kentucky Cardinal Beam Bottle Club—428 Templin, Bardstown, KY 41104.

Land by the Lakes Beam Club—Rt. 6, Box 320, Cadiz KY 42211, (502) 522–8445.

Louisville Bottle Collectors—11819 Garrs Avenue, Anchorage, KY 40223.

Pegasus Jim Beam Bottle & Spec. Club—9405 Cornflower Road, Valley Station, KY 40272, (502) 937–4376.

LOUISIANA

Ark-La-Tex Jim Beam Bottle & Spec. Club—1902 Carol Street, Bossier City, LA 71112, (318) 742–3550.

Bayou Bottle Bugs—216 Dahlia, New Iberia, LA 70560.

"Cajun Country Cousins" Ezra Brooks Bottle & Specialties Club—1000 Chevis Street, Abbeville, LA 70510.

Cenia Bottle Club—c/o Pam Tullos, Rt. 1, Box 463, Dry Prong, LA 71423.

Crescent City Jim Beam Bottle & Spec. Club—733 Wright Avenue, Gretna, LA 70053, (504) 367–2182.

Dixie Diggers Bottle Club—P.O. Box 626, Empire, LA 70050.

Historical Bottle Association of Baton Rouge—1843 Tudor Drive, Baton Rouge, LA 70815.

Ken Tally Jim Beam Bottle Club—110 Kin Tally Estates, Hammond, LA 70401, (504) 345–6186.

New Albany Glass Works Bottle Club—732 N. Clark Boulevard, Parksville, LA 47130.

New Orleans Antique Bottle Club—c/o Ralph J. Luther, Jr., 4336 Palmyra Street, New Orleans, LA 70119. Meets 7:30 P.M. last Friday of the month at Banks St. Social Club, 423 S. Lopez St. Newsletter: Crescent City Comments. Club formed 1969, has 42 family members.

North East Louisiana A.B.C.—P.O. Box 4192, Monroe, LA 71291, 322–8359. Meets 7:00 P.M. 3rd Thursday at Ouachita Valley Library. Newsletter: Glass Treasures. Club formed 1972, has 25 family members.

Red Stick Jim Beam Bottle Club—2127 Beaumont, Suite 4, Baton Rouge, LA 70806.

Sanford's Night Owl Beamers—Rt. 2, Box 102, Greenwell Springs, LA 70739, (504) 261–3658.

Shreveport Antique Bottle Club—1157 Arncliffe Drive, Shreveport, LA 71107, 221–0089.

MAINE

Dirigo Bottle Collectors Club—R.F.D. 3, Dexter, ME, (207) 924–3443. Meets 1st Tuesday at Eastern Maine Vocational Tec. Institute, Hogan Road, Bangor, ME. Newsletter: The Paper Label. Club formed 1969, has 21 members.

Dover Foxcroft Bottle Club—50 Church Street, Dover Foxcroft, ME 04426.

The Glass Bubble Bottle Club—P.O. Box 91, Cape Neddick, ME 03902.

Jim Beam Collectors Club—10 Lunt Road, Falmouth, ME 04105.

Kennebec Valley Bottle Club—9 Glenwood Street, Augusta, ME 04330.

Mid Coast Bottle Club—c/o Miriam Winchenbach, Waldoboro, ME 04572.

New England Bottle Club—45 Bolt Hill Road, Eliot, ME 03903.

Paul Bunyan Bottle Club—237 14th Street, Bangor, ME 04401.

Pine Tree Antique Bottle Club—Buxton Road, Saco, ME 04072.

Pine Tree State Beamers—15 Woodside Avenue, Saco, ME 04072, (207) 284–8756.

Tri-County Bottle Collectors Association—RFD 3, Dexter, ME 04930.

Waldo County Bottlenecks Club—Head-of-the-Tide, Belfast, ME 04915.

MARYLAND

Antique Bottle Club of Baltimore—c/o Fred Parks, 10 S. Linwood Avenue, Baltimore, MD 21224, (301) 732–2404. Club meets 2nd Friday of every month at 7:30 P.M. at Ridgely Middle School, corner of Ridgely Rd. and Charmuth Rd., Lutherville, MD. Club formed 1970.

Blue & Gray Ezra Brooks Bottle Club—2106 Sunnybrook Drive, Frederick, MD 21201.

Catoctin Jim Beam Bottle Club—c/o Ron Danner, I North Chatham Rd. Ellicott City, MD 21063, (301) 465–5773. Club meets 3rd Monday of every month at Ernie's Restaurant in Frederick, MD.

Mason Dixon Bottle Collectors Association—601 Market Street, Denton, MD 21629.

Mid-Atlantic Miniature Whiskey Bottle Club—208 Gloucester Drive, Glen Burnie, MD 21061, (301) 766–8421.
South County Bottle Collector's Club—Bast Lane, Shady Side, MD 20867.

MASSACHUSETTS
Baystate Beamers Bottle & Spec. Club—27 Brookhaven Drive, Ludlow, MA 01056, (413) 589–0446.
Berkshire Antique Bottle Assoc.—RD #1, West Stockbridge, MA 01266.
The Cape Cod Antique Bottle Club—c/o Mrs. John Swanson, 262 Setucket Rd., Yarmouth, MA 02675.
Merrimack Valley Antique Bottle Club—c/o M. E. Tarleton, Hillside Road, Boxford, MA.
New England Beam & Specialty Club—1104 Northampton Street, Holyoke, MA 01040.
Scituate Bottle Club—54 Cedarwood Road, Scituate, MA 02066.
Yankee Pole Cat Insulator Club—105 Richards Avenue, North Attleboro, MA 02760.

MICHIGAN
Central Michigan Krazy Korkers Bottle Club—Mid-Michigan Community College, Clare Ave., Harrison, MI 48625.
Chief Pontiac Antique Bottle Club—13880 Neal Rd., Davisburg, MI 48019. c/o Larry Blascyk. (313) 634–8469.
Dickinson County Bottle Club—717 Henford Avenue, Iron Mountain, MI 49801.
Flint Antique Bottle Collectors Association—450 Leta Avenue, Flint, MI 48507.
Flint Eagles Ezra Brooks Club—1117 W. Remington Avenue, Flint, MI 48507.
Grand Valley Bottle Club—31 Dickinson S.W., Grand Rapids, MI 49507.
Great Lakes Jim Beam Bottle Club of Michigan—1010 South Harvey, Plymouth, MI 48170, (313) 453–0579.
Great Lakes Miniature Bottle Club—P.O. Box 245, Fairhaven MI 48023.
Huron Valley Bottle Club—12475 Saline-Milan Road, Milan, MI 48160.
Kalamazoo A.B.C.—628 Mill St., Kalamazoo, MI 49001, (616) 342–5077. Meets 2nd Monday at 628 Mill St. in Kalamazoo at 7 P.M. Club formed 1979, has 42 members.
Lionstone Collectors Bottle & Specialties Club of Michigan—3089 Grand Blanc Road, Swartz Creek, MI 48473.
Manistee Coin & Bottle Club—207 E. Piney Road, Manistee, MI 49660.

Metro & East Bottle and Jar Assn.—309 Bellevue Park Drive, Fairview Heights, MI
Metro Detroit Antique Bottle Club—28860 Balmoral Way, Farmington Hills, MI 48018. Meets 3rd Thursday, 7:30 P.M. at Hazel Park Recreation Center. Has 50 family members.
Michigan Bottle Collectors Association—144 W. Clark Street, Jackson, MI 49203.
Michigan's Vehicle City Beam Bottles & Specialties Club—907 Root Street, Flint, MI 48503.
Mid-Michee Pine Beam Club—609 Webb Drive, Bay City, MI 48706.
Northern Michigan Bottle Club—P.O. Box 421, Petoskey, MI 49770.
Old Corkers Bottle Club—Rt. 1, Iron River, MI 49935.
Red Run Jim Beam Bottle & Spec. Club—172 Jones Street, Mt. Clemens, MI 48043, (313) 465–4883.
Traverse Area Bottle & Insulator Club—P.O. Box 205, Acme, MI 49610.
W.M.R.A.C.C.—331 Bellevue S.W., Grand Rapids, MI 49508.
West Michigan Avon Collectors—331 Bellevue S.W., Wyoming, MI 49508.
Wolverine Beam Bottle & Specialty Club of Michigan—36009 Larchwood, Mt. Clemens, MI 48043.
World Wide Avon Bottle Collectors Club—22708 Wick Road, Taylor, MI 48180.
Ye Old Corkers—c/o Janet Gallup, Box 7, Gastr, MI 49927. Meets 7:15 P.M. at Bates Twp. School. Club formed 1968, has 20 members.

MINNESOTA
Arnfalt Collectors Beam Club—New Richard, MN 56072.
Dump Diggers—P.O. Box 24, Dover, MN 55929.
Gopher State Jim Beam Bottle & Spec. Club—1216 Sheridan Avenue N., Minneapolis, MN 55411, (612) 521–4150.
Heartland Jim Beam Bottle & Spec. Club—Box 633, 245 Elm Drive, Foley, MN 56329, (612) 968–6767.
Hey! Rube Jim Beam Bottle Club—1506 6th Avenue N.E., Austin, MN 55912, (507) 433–6939.
Lake Superior Antique Bottle Club—P.O. Box 67, Knife River, MN 55609.
Minnesota's First Antique B.C.—5001 Queen Avenue, N. Minneapolis, MN 55430. Meets 8:00 P.M. 1st Thursday in member's homes. Newsletter: Bottle Dig-

gers Dope. Club formed 1966, has 48 members.

North Star Historical Bottle Association, Inc.—P.O. Box 30343, St. Paul, MN 55175.

Paul Bunyan Jim Beam Bottle & Spec. Club—Rt. 8, Box 656, Bemidji, MN 56601, (218) 751–6635.

Truman Minnesota Jim Beam Bottle & Spec. Club—Truman, MN 56088, (507) 776–3487.

Viking Jim Beam Bottle & Spec. Club—8224 Oxborough Avenue S., Bloomington, MN 55437, (612) 831–2303.

MISSISSIPPI

Middle Mississippi Antique Bottle Club—P.O. Box 233, Jackson, MS 39205.

Oxford Antique Bottlers—128 Vivian Street, Oxford, MS 38633.

South Mississippi Antique Bottle Club—203 S. 4th Avenue, Laurel, MS 39440.

South Mississippi Historical Bottle Club—165 Belvedere Dr., Biloxi, MS, 388–6472.

Magnolia Beam Bottle & Spec. Club—2918 Larchmont, Jackson, MS 39209, (601) 354–1350.

Gum Tree Beam Bottle Club—104 Ford Circle, Tupelo, MS 38801.

MISSOURI

A.B.C. of Central Missouri—726 W. Monroe, Mexico, MO 65265. Phone (314) 581–1391. Meets 7:30 P.M. 1st Wednesday at Farm & Home Bldg., E. Broadway, Columbia, MO. Newsletter: No Deposit No Return. Club formed in 1974, has 20 family members.

Antique Bottle & Relic Club of Central Missouri—c/o Ann Downing, Rt. 10, Columbia, MO 65210.

Arnold, Missouri Jim Beam Bottle & Spec. Club—1861 Jean Drive, Arnold, MO 63010, (314) 296–0813.

Barnhart, Missouri Jim Beam Bottle & Spec. Club—2150 Cathlin Court, Barnhart, MO 63012.

Bud Hastin's National Avon Club—P.O. Box 9868, Kansas City, MO 64134.

Chesterfield Jim Beam Bottle & Spec. Club—2066 Honey Ridge, Chesterfield, MO 63017.

"Down in the Valle" Jim Beam Bottle Club—528 St. Louis Avenue, Valley Park, MO 63088.

Festus, Missouri Jim Beam Bottle & Spec. Club—Rt. 3, Box 117H, Frederick Road, Festus, MO 63028.

First Capital Jim Beam Bottle & Spec. Club—731 McDonough, St. Charles, MO 63301.

Florissant Valley Jim Beam Bottles & Spec. Club—25 Cortez, Florissant, MO 63031.

Greater Kansas City Jim Beam Bottle & Specialty Club—P.O. Box 6703, Kansas City, MO 64123.

Kansas City Antique Bottle Collectors Association—1131 E. 77 Street, Kansas City, MO 64131.

Maryland Heights Jim Beam Bottle & Spec. Club—2365 Wesford, Maryland Heights, MO 63043.

Mineral Area Bottle Club—Knob Lick, MO 63651.

Missouri Arch Jim Beam Bottle & Spec. Club—2900 N. Lindbergh, St. Ann, MO 63074, (314) 739–0803.

Mound City Jim Beam Decanter Collectors—42 Webster Acres, Webster Groves, MO 63119.

North-East County Jim Beam Bottle & Spec. Club—10150 Baron Drive, St. Louis, MO 63136.

Northwest Missouri Bottle & Relic Club—3006 S. 28th Street, St. Joseph, MO 64503.

Rock Hill Jim Beam Bottle & Spec. Club—9731 Graystone Terrace, St. Louis, MO 63119, (314) 962–8125.

Sho Me Jim Beam Bottle & Spec. Club—Rt. 7, Box 314-D, Springfield, MO 65802, (417) 831–8093.

St. Charles, Mo. Jim Beam Bottle & Spec. Club—122 S. Cardinal, St. Charles, MO 63301.

St. Louis Antique Bottle Collectors Assn.—306 N. Woodlawn Avenue, Kirkwood, MO 63122.

St. Louis Ezra Brooks Ceramics Club—Webster Acres, Webster Groves, MO 63119.

St. Louis Jim Beam Bottle & Spec. Club—2900 Lindbergh, St. Ann, MO 63074, (314) 291–3256.

The Federation of Historical Bottle Clubs—10118 Schuessler, St. Louis, MO 63128, (314) 843–7573.

Troy, Missouri Jim Beam Bottle & Spec. Club—121 E. Pershing, Troy, MO 63379, (314) 528–6287.

Valley Bank Park Jim Beam Bottle & Spec. Club—614 Benton Street, Valley Park, MO 63088.

Walnut Park Jim Beam Bottle & Spec. Club—5458 N. Euclid, St. Louis MO 63114.

West County Jim Beam Bottle & Spec. Club—11707 Momarte Lane, St. Louis, MO 63141.

MONTANA
Hellgate Antique Bottle Club—P.O. Box 411, Missoula, MT 59801.

NEBRASKA
Cornhusker Jim Beam Bottle & Spec. Club—5204 S. 81st Street, Ralston, NB 68127, (402) 331-4646.
Mini-Seekers—"A" Acres, Rt. 8, Lincoln, NE 68506.
Nebraska Antique Bottle and Collectors Club—P.O. Box 37021, Omaha, NE 68137.
Nebraska Big Red Bottle & Specialty Club—N Street Drive-in, 200 S. 18th Street, Lincoln, NE 68508.

NEVADA
Jim Beam Bottle Club of Las Vegas—212 N. Orland Street, Las Vegas, NV 89107.
Las Vegas Bottle Club—3115 Las Vegas Boulevard, N. Space 56, North Las Vegas, NV 89030, (702) 643-1101. Meets 7:30 P.M. 1st Wednesday at 2832 E. Flamingo Road, Las Vegas. Newsletter: The Front Line. Club formed 1976, has 45 members.
Las Vegas Bottle Club—884 Lulu Avenue, Las Vegas, NV 89119.
Lincoln County A.B.C.—P.O. Box 191, Calente, NV 89008, 726-3655. Meets 7:30 P.M. 2nd Tuesday at Pioche Housing Admin. Bldg. Newsletter: Bottle Talk. Club Formed 1971, has 30 members.
Nevada Beam Club—P.O. Box 426, Fallon, NV 89406.
Reno/Sparks A.B.C.—P.O. Box 1061, Verdi, NV 89439. Meets 3rd Wednesday at McKinley Park School. Newsletter: Diggers Dirt. Club formed 1965, has 30 members.
Southern Nevada Antique Bottle Club—431 N. Spruce Street, Las Vegas, NV 89101.
Virginia & Truckee Jim Beam Bottle & Specialties Club—P.O. Box 1596, Carson City, NV 89701.
Wee Bottle Club International—P.O. Box 1195, Las Vegas, NV 89101.

NEW HAMPSHIRE
Bottleers of New Hampshire—125A Central Street, Farmington, NH 03835.

Granite State Bottle Club—R.F.D.-1, Belmont, NH 03220.
Yankee Bottle Club—P.O. Box 702, Keene, NH 03431.

NEW JERSEY
Antique Bottle Collectors Club of Burlington County—18 Willow Road, Bordentown, NJ 08505.
Artifact Hunters Association Inc.—c/o 29 Lake Road, Wayne, NJ 07470.
Jersey Jackpot Jim Beam Bottle & Spec. Club—197 Farley Avenue, Fanwood, NJ 07023, (201) 322-7287.
Jersey Shore Bottle Collectors—Box 95, Toms River, NJ 08753.
Lakeland A.B.C.—18 Alan Lane, Mine Hill, Dover, NJ 07801. Phone (201) 366-7482. Meets 3rd Friday except July and August at Roosevelt School on Hillside Avenue, Succasuna, NJ in the cafeteria. Has 50 members.
Lionstone Collectors Club of Delaware Valley—R.D. 3, Box 93, Sewell, NJ 08080.
Meadowland Beamers—413 24th Street, Union City, NJ 07087, (201) 865-3684.
New Jersey Ezra Brooks Bottle Club—S. Main Street, Cedarville, NJ 08311.
North Jersey Antique Bottle Collectors Assoc.—560 Overlook Drive, Wyckoff, NJ 07481.
South Jersey's Heritage Bottle & Glass Club Inc.—P.O. Box 122, Glassboro, NJ 08028, (609) 423-5038. Meets 7:30 P.M. 4th Wednesday, September through June, at Owen's III. Club House, 70 Sewell Street, Glassboro, NJ. Newsletter. Club formed 1970, has 200 members.
Sussex County Antique Bottle Collectors—Division of Sussex County Historical Society, 82 Main Street, Newton, NJ 07860.
The Jersey Devil Bottle Diggers Club—14 Church Street, Mt. Holly, NJ 08060.
The Jersey Shore Bottle Club—P.O. Box 995, Toms River, NJ 08753.
Trenton Jim Beam Bottle Club, Inc.—17 Easy Street, Freehold, NJ 07728.
Twin Bridges Beam Bottle & Specialty Club—P.O. Box 347, Pennsville, NJ 08070.
West Essex Bottle Club—76 Beaufort Avenue, Livingston, NJ 07039.

NEW MEXICO
Roadrunner Bottle Club of New Mexico—2341 Gay Road S.W., Alburquerque, NM 87105.

Cave City Antique Bottle Club—Rt. 1 Box 155, Carlsbad, NM 88220.

NEW YORK

Auburn Bottle Club—297 S. Street Road, Auburn, NY 13021.

Big Apple Beamers Bottle & Spec. Club —2901 Long Branch Road, Oceanside, NY 11572, (516) 678-3414.

Catskill Mountains Jim Beam Bottle Club—Six Gardner Avenue, Middletown, NY 10940.

Chautauqua County Bottle Collectors Club—Morse Motel, Main Street, Sherman, NY 14781.

Eastern Monroe County Bottle Club— c/o Bethlehem Lutheran Church, 1767 Plank Road, Webster, NY 14580.

Empire State Bottle Collectors Association—c/o Donald Tupper—8780 Oswego Rd., Clay, NY 13041.

Empire State Jim Beam Bottle Club— P.O. Box 561, Farmingdale Post Office, Main Street, Farmingdale, NY 11735.

Finger Lakes Bottle Club Association —P.O. Box 815, Ithaca, NY 14850.

Genessee Valley Bottle Collectors Assn.—P.O. Box 7528, West Ridge Station, Rochester, NY 14610, (716) 872-4015. Meets 7:30 P.M. 3rd Thursday at Klem Road School, Webster, NY. Newsletter: Applied Seats. Club formed 1969, has 155 family members.

Greater Catskill Antique Bottle Club— P.O. Box 411, Liberty, NY.

Hudson River Jim Beam Bottle and Specialties Club—48 College Road, Monsey, NY 10952.

Hudson Valley Bottle Club—c/o Robert Jordy, 255 Fostertown Road, Newburgh, NY 12550.

Long Island Antique Bottle Assoc.— P.O. Box 147, Bayport, NY 11705.

National Bottle Museum—c/o Marilyn Stephenson, Pres., 45 West High St., Ballston Spa, NY 12020.

Niagara Frontier Beam Bottle & Spec. Club—17 Ravensbrook Court, Getzville, NY 14066, (716) 688-6624.

North Country Bottle Collectors Association—Rt. 1, Canton, NY 13617.

Rensselaer County Antique Bottle Club—P.O. Box 792, Troy, NY 12180.

Rochester New York Bottle Club— 7908 West Henrietta Road, Rush, NY 14543.

Southern Tier Bottle & Insulator Collectors Association—47 Dickinson Avenue, Port Dickinson, NY 13901.

Suffolk County Antique Bottle Association of Coney Island, Inc.—P.O. Box 943, Melville, NY 11746.

Tryon Bottle Badgers—P.O. Box 146, Tribes Hill, NY 12177.

Twin Counties Old Bottle Club—Don McBride, Star Route, Box 242, Palenville, NY 12463, (518) 943-5399.

Upper Susquehanna Bottle Club—P.O. Box 183, Milford, NY 13807.

Warwick Valley Bottle Club—Box 393, Warwick, NY 10990.

Western New York B.C.A.—c/o 62 Adams Street, Jamestown, NY 14701 (716) 487-9645. Meets 7:30 P.M. 4th Wednesday except January Ell South Campus, Rt. 20, Orchard Park. Newsletter: Traveler's Companion. Club formed 1967, has 40 club members.

Western New York Bottle Collectors— 87 S. Bristol Avenue, Lockport, NY 14094.

West Valley Bottleique Club—Box 204, Killbuck, NY 14748, (716) 945-5769. Meets 8:00 P.M. 3rd Thursday at West Valley American Legion, Rt. 240, West Valley, NY. Newsletter: The Bottleique Banner. Club formed 1967, has 36 family members.

NORTH CAROLINA

Blue Ridge Bottle and Jar Club—Dogwood Lane, Black Mountain, NC 28711.

Carolina Bottle Club—c/o Industrial Piping Co., Anonwood, Charlotte, NC 28210.

Carolina Jim Beam Bottle Club—1014 N. Main Street, Burlington, NC 27215.

Catawba Valley Jim Beam Bottle & Spec. Club—265 5th Avenue, N.E., Hickory, NC 28601, (704) 322-5268.

Goldsboro Bottle Club—2406 E. Ash Street, Goldsboro, NC 27530.

Greater Greensboro Moose Ezra Brooks Bottle Club—217 S. Elm Street, Greensboro, NC 27401.

Kinston Collectors Club, Inc.—325 E. Lenoir, Kinston, NC 28501.

Pelican Sand Dunners Jim Beam Bottle & Spec. Club—Lot 17-J, Paradise Bay Mobile Home Park, P.O. Box 344, Salter Path, NC 28575, (919) 247-3290.

Tar Heel Jim Beam Bottle & Spec. Club —6615 Wake Forest Road, Fayetteville, NC 28301, (919) 488-4849.

Wilmington Bottle & Artifact Club—183 Arlington Drive, Wilmington, NC 28401, (919) 763-3701. Meets 1st Wednesday, Carolina Savings & Loan Board Room. Club formed 1977, has 25 members.

Wilson Antique Bottle & Artifact Club— Rt. 5 Box 414, Wilson, NC 27893.

Yadkin Valley Bottle Club—General Delivery, Gold Hill, NC 28071.

OHIO
Beam on the Lake Bottle & Spec. Club—9151 Mentor Avenue, F 15, Mentor, OH 44060, (215) 255–0320.
Buckeye Bottle Club—229 Oakwood Street, Elyria, OH 44035.
Buckeye Bottle Diggers—Rt. 2 P.O. Box 77, Thornville, OH.
Buckeye Jim Beam Bottle Club—1211 Ashland Avenue, Columbus, OH 43212.
Carnation City Jim Beam Bottle Club—135 W. Virginia, Sebring, OH 44672, (216) 938–6817.
Central Ohio Bottle Club—931 Minerva Avenue, Columbus, OH 43229.
Diamond Pin Winners Avon Club—5281 Fredonia Avenue, Dayton, OH 45431.
The Federation of Historical Bottle Clubs—c/o Gary Beatty, Treasurer, 9326 Ct. Rd. 3C, Galion, OH 44833.
Findlay Antique Bottle Club—P.O. Box 1329, Findlay, OH 45840, (419) 422–3183. Meets 2nd Sunday at 7:00 P.M. at Findlay College Croy Center, Findlay, OH. Newsletter: Whittlemarks. Club formed 1976, has 35 members.
First Capitol B.C.—c/o Maxie Harper, Rt. 1, Box 94, Laurelville, OH 43135.
Gem City Beam Bottle Club—1463 E. Stroop Road, Dayton, OH 45429.
Greater Cleveland Jim Beam Club—5398 W. 147th Street Brook Park, OH 44142, (216) 267–7665.
Heart of Ohio Bottle Club—P.O. Box 353, New Washington, OH 44854, (419) 492–2829.
Jeep City Beamers—531A Durango, Toledo, OH 43609, (419) 382–2515.
Jefferson County A.B.S.—1223 Oakgrove Avenue, Steubenville, OH 43952.
Lakeshore Beamers—2681 Douglas Road, Ashtabula, OH 44004, (216) 964–3457.
Maple Leaf Beamers—8200 Yorkshire Road, Mentor, OH 44060, (216) 255–9118.
Northern Ohio Jim Bottle Club—43152 Hastings Road, Oberlin, OH 44074, (216) 775–2177.
North Eastern Ohio Bottle Club—P.O. Box 57, Madison, OH 44057, (614) 282–8918.
Northwest Ohio Bottle Club—104 W. Main, Norwalk, OH 44857.
Ohio Bottle Club—c/o Linda Koch—4248 Reimer Rd., Norton, OH 44203.

Ohio Ezra Brooks Bottle Club—8741 Kirtland Chardon Road, Kirtland Hills, OH 44094.
Pioneer Beamers—38912 Buttermut Ridge, Elyria, OH 44035, (216) 458–6621.
Queen City Jim Beam Bottle Club—4327 Greenlee Avenue, Cincinnati, OH 45217, (513) 641–3362.
Rubber Capitol Jim Beam Club—151 Stephens Road, Akron, Ohio 44312.
Sara Lee Bottle Club—27621 Chagrin Boulevard, Cleveland, OH 44122.
Southwestern Ohio Antique Bottle and Jar Club—P.O. Box 53, North Hampton, OH. Meets 1st Sunday at 1:30 P.M. at Meat Cutters Local 430 Hall, 1325 E. 3rd Street, Dayton, OH. Newsletter: Shards. Formed 1976, has 29 family members.
Tri State Historical Bottle Club—817 E. 7th Street, Dewey, OK 74029.

OKLAHOMA
Bar-Dew Antique Bottle Club—817 E. 7th Street, Dewey, OK 74029.
Frontier Jim Beam Bottle & Spec. Club—P.O. Box 52, Meadowbrook Trailer Village, Lot 101, Ponca City, OK 74601, (405) 765–2174.
Green Country Jim Beam Bottle & Spec. Club—Rt. 2, P.O. Box 233, Chouteau, OK 74337, (918) 266–3512.
McDonnel Douglas Antique Club—5752 E. 25th Place, Tulsa, OK 74114.
Ponca City Old Bottle Club—2408 Juanito, Ponca City, OK 74601.
Sooner Jim Beam Bottle & Spec. Club—5913 S.E. 10th, Midwest City, OK 73110, (405) 737–5786.
Southwest Oklahoma Antique Bottle Club—35 S. 49th Street, Lawton, OK 73501.
Tulsa Antique Bottle & Relic Club—P.O. Box 4278, Tulsa, OK 74104.

OREGON
Central Oregon Bottle & Relic Club—671 N.E. Seward, Bend, OR 97701.
Central Oregon Bottle & Relic Club—1545 Kalama Avenue, Redmond, OR 97756.
Central South Oregon Antique Bottle Club—708 S. F. Street, Lakeview, OR 97630.
Emerald Empire Bottle Club—P.O. Box 292, Eugene, OR 97401.
Frontier Collectors—504 N.W. Bailey, Pendleton, OR 97801.
Gold Diggers Antique Bottle Club—1958 S. Stage Road, Medford, OR 97501.

Lewis & Clark Historical Bottle & Collectors Soc.—8018 S.E. Hawthorne Blvd., Portland, OR.

Lewis & Clark Historical Bottle Society—4828 N.E. 33rd, Portland, OR.

Molalla Bottle Club—Rt. 1 Box 205, Mulino, OR 97042.

Oregon Antique Bottle Club—Rt. 3 Box 23, Molalla, OR 97038.

Oregon Beamer Beam Bottle & Specialties—P.O. Box 7, Sheridan, OR 97378.

Oregon B.C.A.—3661 S.E. Nehalem Street, Portland, OR 97202. Meets 8:00 P.M. every 3rd Saturday, except July and August. Newsletter: The Bottle Examiner. Club formed 1966, has 60 family members.

Pioneer Fruit Jar Collectors Association—P.O. Box 175, Grand Ronde, OR 97347.

Siskiyou Antique Bottle Collectors Assn.—P.O. Box 1335, Medford, OR 97501.

PENNSYLVANIA

Anthracite Jim Beam Bottle Club—406 Country Club Apartments, Dallas, PA 18612.

Antique Bottle Club of Burlington County—8445 Walker Street, Philadelphia, PA 19136.

Beaver Valley Jim Beam Club—1335 Indiana Avenue, Monaca, PA 15061.

Bedford County Antique Bottle Club—107 Seifert Street, Bedford, PA 15522.

Camoset Bottle Club—P.O. Box 252, Johnstown, PA 15901.

Christmas Valley Beamers—150 Second Street, Richlandtown, PA 18955, (215) 536-4636.

Classic Glass Bottle Collectors—2, Cogan Station, PA 17728.

Cumberland Valley Jim Beam Club—P.O. Box 132 (219 Adelia Street), Middletown, PA 17057, (717) 944-5376.

Delaware Valley Bottle Club—12 Belmar Road, Hatboro, PA 19040.

Del-Val Bottle Club—Rt. 152 & Hilltown Pike, Hilltown, PA. Mailing address: Duffield's, 12 Belmar Road, Hatboro, PA 19040.

East Coast Double Springs Specialty Bottle Club—P.O. Box 419, Carlisle, PA 17013.

East Coast Ezra Brooks Bottle Club—2815 Fiddler Green, Lancaster, PA 17601.

Endless Mountain Antique Bottle Club—P.O. Box 75, Granville Summit, PA 16926.

Erie Bottle Club—P.O. Box 373, Erie, PA 16512.

Flood City Jim Beam Bottle Club—231 Market Street, Johnston, PA 15901.

Forks of the Delaware Bottle Collectors, Inc.—Box 693, Easton, PA 18042.

Friendly Jim's Beam Club—508 Benjamin Franklin H.W. East, Douglasville, PA 19518.

Indiana Bottle Club—240 Oak Street, Indiana, PA 15701.

Keystone Flyers Jim Beam Bottle Club—288 Hogan Boulevard, Box 42, Lock Haven, PA 17745, (717) 748-6741.

Kiski Mini Beam and Spec. Club—816 Cranberry Drive, Monroeville, PA 15146.

Laurel Valley Bottle Club—618 Monastery Drive, Latrobe, PA 15650, (412) 537-4800. Meets at 8:00 P.M. last Saturday at Oak Grove Civil Center. Newsletter: Digger's Delight. Formed 1975, has 35 members.

Middletown Area B.C.A.—P.O. Box 1, Middletown, PA 17057. (717) 939-0288. Meets 2nd Tuesday, 7:30 P.M. at Middletown Elks Lodge, Emaus Street, Middletown. Club formed 1973, has 54 members.

Pagoda City Beamers—735 Florida Avenue, Riverview Park, Reading, PA 19605, (215) 929-8924.

Penn Beamers' 14th—15 Gregory Place, Richboro, PA 18954.

The Pennsylvania Bottle Collectors Association—825 Robin Road, Lancaster, PA 17601.

Pennsylvania Dutch Jim Beam Bottle Club—812 Pointview Avenue, Ephrate, PA 17522.

Philadelphia Coll. Club—8445 Walker Street, Philadelphia, PA. Meets 1st Monday at 8:00 P.M. at Trevose Savings Bank, L Street and Hunting Park Avenue Club has 25 members.

Philadelphia Bottle Club—8203 Elberon Avenue, Philadelphia, PA 19111.

Pittsburgh Bottle Club—P.O. Box 401, Ingomar, PA 15127.

Pittsburgh Bottle Club—1528 Railroad Street, Sewickley, PA 15143.

Susquehanna Valley Jim Beam Bottle & Spec. Club—64 E. Park Street, Elizabethtown, PA 17022, (717) 367-4256.

Tri-County Antique Bottle & Treasure Club—R. D. 2 P.O. Box 30, Reynoldsville, PA 15851.

Valley Forge Jim Beam Bottle Club— 1219 Ridgeview Drive, Phoenixville, PA 19460, (215) 933–5789.

Washington County Bottle & Insulator Club—R.D. 2 P.O. Box 342, Carmichaels, PA 15320. Phone (412) 966–7996. Meets 7:30 P.M. 1st Tuesday at Washington County City Building. Newsletter: Bottle Nut News. 40 Members.

Whitetail Deer Jim Beam Bottle Club— 94 Lakepoint Drive, Harrisburgh, PA 17111, (717) 561–2517.

RHODE ISLAND
Little Rhody Bottle Club—c/o Ted Baldwin 3161 West Shore Road, Warwick, RI 02886.

Seaview Jim Beam Bottle & Spec. Club —362 Bayview Avenue, Cranston, RI 02905, (401) 461–4952.

SOUTH CAROLINA
Greer Bottle Collectors Club—P.O. Box 142, Greer, SC 29651.

Lexington County Antique Bottle Club —201 Roberts Street, Lexington, SC 29072.

Palmetto State Beamers—908 Alton Circle, Florence, SC 29501, (803) 669–6515.

Piedmont Bottle Collectors—c/o R. W. Leizear, Rt. 3, Woodruff, SC 29388.

South Carolina Bottle Club—1119 Greenbridge Lane, Columbia, SC 29210. Meets 8:00 P.M. 1st Thursday at Dewey's Antique. Newsletter: South Carolina Bottle News. Club formed 1970, has 35 members.

Union Bottle Club—107 Pineneedle Road, Union, SC 29379.

Upper Piedmont Bottle and Advertising Collectors Club—Rt. 3, Woodruff, SC, c/o R. W. Leizear.

TENNESSEE
Cotton Carnival Beam Club—P.O. Box 17951, Memphis, TN 38117.

Memphis Bottle Collectors Club—232 Tifton Road, Memphis, TN 38111, (901) 272–8998.

Middle Tenn. Bottle Collector's Club— P.O. Box 120083, Nashville, TN 37212, (615) 269–4402. Meets 2nd Tuesday at 7:00 P.M. Donelson Branch Public Library. Newsletter: Notes From a Bottle Bug. Club formed March 1969, has 45 members.

Music City Beam Bottle Club—2008 June Drive, Nashville, TN 37214, (615) 883–1893.

TEXAS
Alamo City Jim Beam Bottle & Spec. Club—5785 FM 1346, P.O. Box 20442, San Antonio TX 78220.

Alamo Chapter Antique Bottle Club Association—701 Castano Avenue, San Antonio, TX 78209.

Austin Bottle & Insulator Collectors Club—1614 Ashberry Drive, Austin, TX 78723.

Cowtown Jim Beam Bottle Club—2608 Roseland, Ft. Worth, TX 76103, (817) 536–4335.

El Paso Insulator Club—Martha Stevens, Chairman, 4556 Bobolink, El Paso, TX 79922.

The Exploration Society—603 9th Street NAS, Corpus Christie, TX 78419, 992–2902.

Foard C. Hobby Club—P.O. Box 625, Crowell, TX 79227.

Fort Concho Bottle Club—1703 W. Avenue, N. San Angelo, TX 76901.

Foursome (Jim Beam)—1208 Azalea Drive, Longview, TX 75601.

Golden Spread Jim Beam Bottle & Spec. Club—1104 S. Maddox, Dumas, TX 79029, (806) 935–3690.

Gulf Coast Beam Club—128 W. Bayshore Drive, Baytown, TX 77520.

Gulf Coast Bottle & Jar Club—P.O. Box 1754, Pasadena, TX 77501, (713) 592–3078. Meets 7:30 P.M. 1st Monday at 1st Pasadena State Bank, Corner of Southmore and Tarter. Newsletter: Gulf Coast Bottle & Jar Club News. Club formed 1969, has 55 family members.

Oil Patch Beamers—1300 Fairmont -112, Longview, TX 75604, (214) 758–1905.

Republic of Texas Jim Beam Bottle & Specialty Club—616 Donley Drive, Euless, TX 76039.

San Antonio Antique Bottle Club—c/o 3801 Broadway, Witte Museum-Auditorium, San Antonio, TX 78209.

UTAH
Utah Antique Bottle and Relic Club— 1594 W. 500 No., Salt Lake City, UT 84116, 328–4142.

Utah Antique Bottle Club—P.O. Box 15, Ogden, UT 84402.

VIRGINIA
Apple Valley Bottle Collectors Club— P.O. Box 2201, Winchester, VA 22601. Meets 2 P.M. 3rd Sunday at Gore-Volunteer Fire Hall, U.S. 50. Newsletter: Bottle

Worm. Club formed 1973, has 36 members.

Bottle Club of the Virginia Peninsula—P.O. Box 5456, Newport News, VA 23605.

Buffalo Beam Bottle Club—P.O. Box 434, Buffalo Junction, VA 24529, (804) 374–2041.

Chesapeake Bay Beam Bottle & Spec. Club—515 Briar Hill Road, Norfolk, VA 23502, (804) 461–3763.

Country Cousins Beam Bottle & Spec. Club—Rt. 2, Box 18C, Dinwiddle, VA 23841, (804) 469–7414.

Dixie Beam Bottle Club—Rt. 4, Box 94-4, Glen Allen, VA 23060.

Hampton Roads Area Bottle Collector's Assn.—Virginia Beach Federal Savings & Loan, 4848 Virginia Beach Boulevard in Va. Beach.

Merrimac Beam Bottle & Spec. Club—433 Tory Road, Virginia Beach, VA 23462, (804) 497–0969.

Metropolitan Antique Bottle Club—109 Howard Street, Dumfries, VA 22026, 221–8055.

Potomac Bottle Collectors—6602 Orland Street, Falls Church, VA 22043, (703) 534–7271 or 534–5619. Meets 8:00 P.M. 1st Monday at Coca-Cola Plant, Seminary Road. Club formed 1972, has 156 members.

Old Dominion Beam Bottle & Spec. Club—624 Brandy Creek Drive, Mechanicsville, VA 23111, (804) 746–7144.

Richmond Area B.C. Assn.—7 N. 8th Street, Richmond, VA 23219. Meets 7:30 P.M. 3rd Monday at Bank of Virginia, 8th and Main. Newsletter: The Bottle Digger. Club formed 1970, has 20 members.

Shenandoah Valley Beam Bottle & Spec. Club—11 Bradford Drive, Front Royal, VA 22630, (703) 743–6316.

Tidewater Beam Bottle & Specialty Club—P.O. Box 14012, Norfolk, VA 23518.

Ye Old Bottle Club—General Delivery, Clarksville, VA 23927.

WASHINGTON

Antique Bottle and Glass Collectors—P.O. Box 163, Snohomish, WA 98290.

Apple Capital Beam Bottle & Spec. Club—300 Rock Island Road, E. Wenatchee, WA 98801, (509) 884–6895.

Blue Mountain Jim Beam Bottle & Spec. Club—P.O. Box 147, Russet Road, Walla Walla, WA 99362, (509) 525–1208.

Capitol Collectors & Bottle—P.O. Box 202, Olympia, WA 98507.

Cascade Treasure Club—254 N.E. 45th, Seattle, WA 98105.

Chinook Ezra Brooks Bottle Club—233 Kelso Drive, Kelso, WA 98626.

Evergreen State Beam Bottle & Specialty Club—P.O. Box 99244, Seattle, WA 98199.

Klickital Bottle Club Association—Goldendale, WA 98620.

Inland Empire Bottle & Collectors Club —7703 E. Trent Avenue, Spokane, WA 99206.

Mt. Rainer Ezra Brooks Bottle Club—P.O. Box 1201, Lynwood, WA 98178.

Northwest Jim Beam Bottle Collectors Association—P.O. Box 7401, Spokane, WA 99207.

Northwest Treasure Hunter's Club—E. 107 Astor Drive, Spokane, WA 99208.

Pacific Northwest Avon Bottle Club—25425 68th S. Kent, WA 98031.

Seattle Jim Beam Bottle Collectors Club—8015 15th Avenue N.W., Seattle, WA 98107.

Skagit Bottle & Glass Collectors—1314 Virginia, Mt. Vernon, WA 98273.

South Whedley Bottle Club—c/o Juanita Clyde, Langley, WA 98260.

Washington Bottle Collectors Association—P.O. Box 80045, Seattle, WA 98108. Meets 5 P.M. 2nd Saturday at King Co. Recreations Center, 46th and 188th Street Newsletter: Ghost Town Echo. Club formed 1966, has 30 family members.

WEST VIRGINIA

Blennerhassett Jim Beam Club—Rt. 1 - 26 Popular Street, Davisville, WV 26142, (304) 428–3184.

Wild & Wonderful West Virginia Ezra Brooks Bottle & Specialty Club—1924 Pennsylvania Avenue, Weirton, WV 26062.

Wild Wonderful W. VA. Jim Beam Bottle & Spec. Club—3922 Hanlin Way, Weirton, WV 20062, (304) 748–2675.

WISCONSIN

Badger Bottle Diggers—1420 McKinley Road, Eau Claire, WI 54701.

Badger Jim Beam Club of Madison—P.O. Box 5612, Madison, WI 53705.

Belle City Jim Beam Bottle Club—8008 104th Avenue, Kenosha, WI 53140, (414) 694–3341.

Bucken Beamers Bottle Club of Milw. WI.—N 95th Street, W. 16548 Richmond

Drive, Menomonee Falls, WI 53051, (414) 251–1772.

Cameron Bottle Diggers—P.O. Box 276, 314 South 1st Street, Cameron, WI 54822.

Central Wisconsin Bottle Collectors—1608 Main Street, Stevens Point, WI 54481.

Heart of the North Beam Bottle and Bottle Club—1323 Eagle Street, Rhinelander, WI 54501, (715) 362–6045.

Hooten Beamers—2511 Needles Lane, Wisconsin Rapids, WI 54494, (715) 423–7116.

Indianhead Jim Beam Club—5112 Berry Street, Rt. 7, Menomonee, WI 54751, (715) 235–5627.

Lumberjack Beamers—414 N. 5th Avenue, Wausau, WI 54401, (715) 842–3793.

Milwaukee Antique Bottle Club—N 88 W 15211 Cleveland Avenue, Menomonee Falls, WI 53051.

Milwaukee Jim Beam Bottle and Specialties Club, Ltd.—N. 95th Street W. 16548 Richmond Drive, Menomonee Falls, WI 53051.

Milwaukee Antique Bottle Club, Inc.—2343 Met-To-Wee Lane, Wauwatosa, WI 53226, (414) 257–0156. Meets 7:30 P.M. 1st Wednesday, 8701 W. Chambers Street, Cooper Park. Newsletter: Cream City Courier. Club formed 1973, has 57 members.

Packerland Beam Bottle & Spec. Club—1366 Avondale Drive, Green Bay, WI 54303, (414) 494–4631.

Shot Tower Jim Beam Club—818 Pleasant Street, Mineral Point, WI 53565.

South Central Wisconsin Bottle Club—c/o Dr. T. M. Schwartz, Rt. 1, Arlington, WI 53911.

Sportsman's Jim Beam Bottle Club—6821 Sunset Strip, Wisconsin Rapids, WI 54494, (715) 325–5285.

Sugar River Beamers—Rt. 1, Box 424, Brodhead, WI 53520, (608) 897–2681.

WYOMING
Cheyenne Antique Bottle Club—4417 E. 8th St., Cheyenne, WY 82001.

Insubott Bottle Club—P.O. Box 34, Lander, WY 82520.

CANADA
St. John B.C.—25 Orange Street, St. John. N.B. E2L 1L9, 652–3537. Meets 8 P.M. 1st Monday at N.B. Museum. Newsletter: The Historical Flask. Club formed 1969, has 25 members.

BOTTLE DEALERS

ALABAMA
BIRMINGHAM—Steve Holland, 1740 Serene Dr., Birmingham, AL 35215. 853–7929. *Bottles dug around Alabama.*

BIRMINGHAM—Walker's Antique Bottles, 2768 Hanover Circle, Birmingham, AL 35205. (205) 933–7902. *Medicines, crown sodas.*

FORT PAYNE—Terry & Katie Gillis, 115 Mountain Dr., Fort Payne, AL 35967. (205) 845–4541.

FORT PAYNE—C. B. and Barbara Meares, Rt. 3, Box 161, Ft. Payne, AL (205) 638–6225.

MOBILE—Bottles and Stuff, Clinton P. King, 4075 Moffatt Road, Mobile, AL 36618. (205) 344–2959. *Pontiled medicines, local bottles, black glass, pottery.*

MOBILE—Loretta and Mack Wimmer, 3012 Cedar Cresent Dr., Mobile, AL 36605.

OZARK—Old Time Bottle House and Museum, 306 Parker Hills Dr., Ozark, AL 36360. *Old bottles, stone jugs, fruit jars.*

SPANISH FORT—Elroy and Latrelle Webb, 203 Spanish Main, Spanish Fort, AL 36527, (205) 626–1067.

THEODORE—Ed's Lapidary Shop, 7927 Historic Mobile Parkway, US HWY #90, 36582. Call (205) 653–0713. *Locally dug bottles.*

ARIZONA
PHOENIX—The Brewery, 1605 N. 7th Ave., Phoenix, AZ 85007. 252–1415. *Brewery items.*

PHOENIX—Tom and Kay Papa, 3821 E. Mercer Lane, Phoenix, AZ 85028, (602) 996–3240.

PINETOP—Ray and Dyla Lawton, Box 374, Pinetop, AZ 85935, (602) 366–4449.

ARKANSAS
JACKSONVILLE—Charles and Mary Garner, 620 Carpenter Dr., Jacksonville, AR 72076, (501) 982–8381.

RISON—Rufus Buie, P.O. Box 226, Rison, AR 71665. (501) 325–6816.

ASHDOWN—Buddy's Bottles, 610 Park Ave., Ashdown, AR 71822, (501) 898-5877. *Hutchinson sodas, medicines. Arkansas bottles always wanted.*

CALIFORNIA

AROMAS—Bobbie's Country Store, in the Big Red Barn, 1000 El Camino Real, HWY 101, P.O. Box 1761, Carmel, CA 93921, (408) 394-3257.

BEVERLY HILLS—Alex Kerr, 9584 Wilshire Blvd., Beverly Hills, CA 90212, (213) 762-6320.

BUENA PARK—Walter Yeargain, 6222 San Lorenzo Dr., Buena Park, CA 90620, (714) 826-5264.

BUTLER—Wayne Hortman, P.O. Box 183, Butler, CA 31006, (912) 862-3699.

CHICO—Randy Taylor, 566 E. 12th St., (916) 342-4928.

CITRUS HEIGHTS—Duke Jones, P.O. Box 642, Citrus Heights, CA 95610, (916) 725-1989. *California embossed beers.*

CONCORD—Stoney and Myrt Stone, 1925 Natoma Dr., Concord, CA 94519, (415) 685-6326.

CORONA—Russell Brown, P.O. Box 441, Corona, CA 91720, (714) 737-7164.

CYPRESS—Gary and Harriet Miller, 5034 Oxford Dr., Cypress, CA 90630, (714) 828-4778.

FILLMORE—Mike and Joyce Amey, 625 Clay St., Fillmore, CA 93015, (805) 524-3364.

HESPERIA—Gene and Phyllis Kemble, 14733 Poplar St., Hesperia, CA 92345, (714) 244-5863.

HUNTINGTON BEACH—Larry Caddell, 15881 Malm Circle, Huntington Beach, CA 92647, (714) 897-8133.

LOS ALTOS—Louis and Cindy Pellegrini, 1231 Thurston, Los Altos, CA 94022, (415) 965-9060.

MARIETTA—John and Estelle Hewitt, 366 Church St., Marietta, CA 30060, (404) 422-5525.

REDDING—Byrl and Grace Rittenhouse, 3055 Birch Way, Redding, CA 96002, (916) 243-0320.

REDDING—Ralph Hollibaugh, 2087 Gelnyose Dr., Redding, CA 96001, (916) 243-4672.

SACRAMENTO—George and Rose Reidenbach, 2816, - "P" St., Sacramento, CA 95816, (916) 451-0063.

SACTO—Peck and Audie Markota, 4627 Oakhallow Dr. Sacto, CA 95842, (916) 334-3260.

SAN FRANCISCO—Bill Groves, 2620 Sutter St., San Francisco, CA 94115, (415) 922-6248.

SAN JOSE—Terry and Peggy Wright, 6249 Lean Ave., San Jose, CA 95123, (408) 578-5580.

SOLANA BEACH—T.R. Schweighart, 1123 Santa Luisa Dr., Solana Beach, CA 92075.

STOCKTON—Frank and Judy Brockman, 104 W. Park, Stockton, CA 95202, (209) 948-0746.

SUTTER CREEK—The Glass Bottle, now in "Creekside Shops," 22 Main St., Sutter Creek, HWY 49. Mailing address, P.O. Box 374, Sutter Creek, CA 95685, (209) 267-0122. *Old figural, perfumes, whiskey, milk.*

WESTWOOD—Whitman's Bookkeeping Service, 219 Fir St., P. O. Drawer KK 96147, (916) 256-3437. *Soda.*

WINDSOR—Betty and Ernest Zumwalt, 5519 Kay Dr., Windsor, CA 95492, (707) 545-8670.

YREKA—Sleep's Siskiyou Specialties, 217 West Miner, P.O. Box 689, Yreka, CA. 96097.

COLORADO
SNOWMASS VILLAGE—Jim Bishop, Box 5554, Snowmass Village, CO 81615. 923-2348. *Miniature liquor.*

CONNECTICUT
ASHFORD—Woodlawn Antiques, P.O. Box 277, Mansfield Center, Ashford, CT 06250, (203) 429-2983. *Flasks, bitters, inks.*

FAIRFIELD—Stephen Link, 953 Post Rd., Fairfield, CT 06430.

HARTFORD—B'Thea's Cellar, 31 Kensington St., Hartford, CT 06112. 249-4686.

LIME ROCK—Mary's Old Bottles. White Hollow Road, Lakeville, CT 06039, (203) 435-2961. *Bottles.*

MYSTIC—Bob's Old Bottles, 656 Noank Rd. RT. 215, Mystic, CT 06355, (203) 536-8542.

NEW HAVEN—Gerald "J." Jaffee and Lori Waldeck, P.O. Box 1741, New Haven, CT 06507, (203) 787-4232. *Poisons (bottles), insulators.*

NIANTIC—Albert Corey, 153 W. Main St., Niantic, CT 06357, (203) 739-7493. *No. Eastern bottles, jars, stoneware.*

SAYBROOK—Bill Stankard, 61 Old Post Rd., Saybrook, CT 06475, (203) 388-4235.

WATERTOWN—George E. Johnson, 2339 Litchfield Rd., Watertown, CT 06795, (203) 274–1785.
WOODSTOCK—Norman and Elizabeth Heckler, Woodstock Valley, CT 06282, (203) 974–1634.

FLORIDA
BROOKSVILLE—E.S. and Romie MacKenzie, Box 57, Brooksville, FL 33512, (904) 796–3400.
FORT MEADE—M and S Bottles and Antiques, Marlaine and Steve, 421 Wilson St., Mail address: Rt. 2, Box 84B3, Fort Meade, FL 33841, 285–9421.
FT. PIERCE—Gore's Shoe Repair, 410 Orange Avenue, Ft. Pierce, FL 33450. *Old bottles, Florida bottles, black glass.*
HOLLISTER—This-N That Shop (Albert B. Coleman), P.O. Box 185, Hollister, FL 32047, (904) 328–3658.
HOLLYWOOD—Hickory Stick Antiques, 400 So. 57 Terr., Hollywood, FL 33023, 962–3434. *Canning jars, black glass, household.*
JACKSONVILLE—The Browns, 6512 Mitford Rd., Jacksonville, FL 32210, 771–2091. *Sodas, min. waters, milk, glass, black glass.*
KEY LARGO—Dwight Pettit, 33 Sea Side Dr. Key Largo, FL 33037, (305) 852–8338.
NEW PORT RICHEY—Gerae and Lynn McLarty, 6705 Dogwood Ct, New Port Richey, FL 33552, (813) 849–7166.
ORMOND BEACH—Mike Kollar, 50 Sylvania Pl., Ormond Beach, FL 32074.
PALMETTO—Jon Vander Schouw, P.O. Box 1151, Palmetto, FL 33561, (813) 722–1375.
SANFORD—Hidden-Bottle-Shop, 2656 Grandview, Sanford, FL 32771, 322–7181.
TALLAHASSEE—Harry O. Thomas, 2721 Parson's Rest., Tallahassee, FL 32308, (904) 893–3834.
TITUSVILLE—Insulators - L. L. Linscott, 3557 Nicklaus Drive, Titusville, FL 32780, (305) 267–9170. *Fruit jars, porcelain insulators.*

GEORGIA
BUTLER—Wayne's Bottles, Box 183, Butler, GA 31006, (912) 862–3699. *Odd colors, odd shapes.*
DUNWOODY—Carlo and Dot Sellari, Box 888553. Dunwoody, GA 30338, (404) 451–2483.
EATONTON—James T. Hicks, Rt. 4, Box 265, Eatonton, GA 31024, (404) 485–9280.

LAURENCEVILLE—Dave and Tia Janousek, 2293 Mulligan Circle, Laurenceville, GA 30245.
MACON—Schmitt House Bottle Diggers, 5532 Jane Rue Circle, Macon, GA 31206, (912) 781–6130. *Indiana, Kentucky bottles.*
NEWNAN—Bob and Barbara Simmons, 152 Greenville St., Newnan, GA 30263, (404) 251–2471.

HAWAII
HONOLULU—The Hawaiian Antique Bottle Shop, Kahuku Sugar Mill, P.O. Box 495, Honolulu, HI 96731, 293–5581. *Hawaiian soda, whiskey, medicine, milk.*
HONOLULU—The Hawaii Bottle Museum, 1044 Kalapaki St., P.O. Box 25153, Honolulu, HI 96825, (808) 395–4671. *Hawaiian bottles, Oriental bottles and pottery.*

IDAHO
SILVER CITY—Idaho Hotel, Jordan Street, Box 75, Murphy, ID 83650, (208) 495–2520.
BUHL—John Cothern, Rt. #1, Buhl, ID 83316, (208) 543–6713.

ILLINOIS
ADDISON—Ronald Selcke, 4N236 8th Ave., Addison, IL 60101, (312) 543–4848.
ALTON—Sean Mullikin, 5014 Alicia Dr., Alton, IL 62002, (312) 466–7506.
ALTON—Mike Spiiroff, 1229 Alton St., Alton, IL 62002, (618) 462–2283.
BELLEVILLE—Wayne and Jacqueline Brammer, 309 Bellevue Dr., Belleville, IL 62223, (618) 233–8841.
CERRO GORDO—Marvin and Carol Ridgeway, 450 W. Cart, Cerro Gordo, IL 61818, (217) 763–3271.
CHAMPAIGN—Casad's Antiques, 610 South State St., Champaign, IL 61820, (217) 356–8455. *milk bottles,*
CHICAGO—Tom and Gladys Bartels, 5315 W. Warwick, Chicago, IL 60641, (312) 725–2433.
CHICAGO—Ernest Brooks, 9023 S. East End, Chicago, IL 60617, (312) 375–9233.
CHICAGO—1st Chicago Bottle Club, P.O. Box A3382, Chicago, IL 60690.
CHICAGO—Fruit Jars, 5003 West Berwyn, Chicago, IL 60630, (312) 777–0443. *Fruit jars.*
CHICAGO—Joe Healy, 3421 W. 76th St. Chicago, IL 60652.

CHICAGO—William Kiggans, 7747 South Kedzle, Chicago, IL 60652, (312) 925–6148.

CHICAGO—Carl Malik, 8655 S. Keeler, Chicago, IL 60652, (312) 767–8568.

CHICAGO—Jerry and Aryliss McCann, 5003 W. Berwyn, Chicago, IL 60630, (312) 777–0443.

CHICAGO—Louis Metzinger, 4140 N. Mozart, Chicago, IL 60618, (312) 478–9034.

CHICAGO—L. D. and Barbara Robinson, 1933 So. Homan, Chicago, IL 60623, (312) 762–6096.

CHICAGO—Paul R. Welko, 5727 S. Natoma Ave., Chicago, IL 60638, (312) 582–3564. *Blob top and Hutchinson sodas.*

CHICAGO HTS.—Al and Sue Verley, 486 Longwood Ct., Chicago Hts., IL 60411, (312) 754–4132.

DEERFIELD—Jim Hall, 445 Partridge Lane, Deerfield, IL 60014, (312) 541–5788.

DEERFIELD—John and Claudia Panek, 816 Holmes, Deerfield, IL 60015, (312) 945–5493.

DIETERICH—Ray's and Betty's Antiques, Dieterich, IL 62424, (217) 925–5449. *Bitters.*

ELMWOOD PARK—Keith and Ellen Leeders, 1728 N. 76th Ave., Elmwood Park, IL 60635, (312) 453–2085.

GODFREY—Jeff Cress, 3403 Morkel Dr., Godfrey, IL 62035, (618) 466–3513.

HICKORY HILLS—Doug and Eileen Wagner, 9225 S. 88th Ave., Hickory Hills, IL 60457, (312) 598–4570.

HILLSBORO—Jim and Penny Lang, 628 Mechanic, Hillsboro, IL 62049, (217) 532–2915.

INGELSIDE—Art and Pat Besinger, 611 Oakwood, Ingelside, IL 60041, (312) 546–2367.

LAGRANGE—John Murray, 301 Hillgrove, LaGrange, IL 60525, (312) 352–2199.

LAKE VILLA—Lloyd Bindscheattle, P.O. Box 11, Lake Villa, IL 60046.

LEMONT—Russ and Lynn Sineni, 1372 Hillcrest Rd., Lemont, IL 60439, (312) 257–2648.

MOKENA—Neal and Marianne Vander Zande, 18830 Sara Rd., Mokena, IL 60448, (312) 479–5566.

MORRISON—Emma's Bottle Shop, Emma Rosenow, Rt.3, Morrison, IL 61270, (815) 778–4596. *Beers, inks, bitters, sodas.*

O'FALLON—Tom and Ann Feltman, 425 North Oak St., O'Fallon, IL 62269, (618) 632–3327.

PARK FOREST—Vern and Gloria Nitchie, 300 Indiana St., Park Forest, IL 60466, (312) 748–7198.

PARK RIDGE—Ken's Old Bottles, 119 East Lahon, Park Ridge, IL 60068, (312) 823–1267. *Milks, inks, sodas and whiskies.*

PEKIN—Harry's Bottle Shop, 612 Hillyer St., Pekin, IL 61555, (309) 346–3476. *Pottery, beer, sodas and medicines.*

PEKIN—Oertel's Bottle House, Box 682, Pekin, IL 61555, (309) 347–4441. *Peoria pottery, embossed picnic beer bottles, fruit jars.*

RIVERDALE—Bob and Barbara Harms, 14521 Atlantic, Riverdale, IL 60627, (312) 841–4068.

SAUK VILLAGE—Ed McDonald, 3002 23rd St., Sauk Village, IL 60511, (312) 758–0373.

TRENTON—Jon and Char Granda, 631 S. Main, Trenton, IL 62293, (618) 224–7308.

WHEATON—Ben Crane, 1700 Thompson Dr., Wheaton, IL 60187, (312) 665–5662.

WHEATON—Scott Garrow, 2 S. 338 Orchard Rd., Wheaton, IL

WHEELING—Hall, 940 E. Old Willow Rd., Wheeling, IL 60090, (312) 541–5788. *Sodas, inks, medicines, etc.*

WHEELING—Steve Miller, 623 Ivy Ct., Wheeling, IL 60090, (312) 398–1445.

WOODSTOCK—Michael Davis, 1652 Tappan, Woodstock, IL 66098, (815) 338–5147.

WOODSTOCK—Mike Henrich, 402 McHenry Ave., Woodstock, IL 60098, (815) 338–5008.

QUINCY—Bob Rhinberger, Rt. 7, Quincy, IL 62301, (217) 223–0191.

INDIANA

BOGGSTOWN—Ed and Margaret Shaw, Rt. 1, Box 23, Boggstown, IN 46110, (317) 835–7121.

CLINTON—Tony and Dick Stringfellow, 714 Vine, Clinton, IN 47842, (317) 832–2355.

FLORA—Bob and Morris Wise, 409 E. Main, Flora, IN 46929, (219) 967–3713.

FORT WAYNE—Annett's Antiques, 6910 Lincoln HWY-East, Fort Wayne, IN 46803, (219) 749–2745.

GOSHEN—Gene Rice, 61935 CR37, Rt. 1, Goshen, IN 46526.

GOSHEN—Wayne Wagner, 23558 Creek Park Dr., Goshen, IN 46526.

GREENFIELD—George and Nancy Reilly, Rt. 10, Box 67, Greenfield, IN 46140, (317) 462–2441.

INDIANAPOLIS—John and Dianna Atkins, 3168 Beeler Ave., Indianapolis, IN 46224, (317) 299–2720.

NOBELSVILLE—Rick and Becky Norton, Rt. G, Box 166, Noblesville, IN 46060, (317) 844–1772.

PERU—Herrell's Collectibles, 265 E. Canal St., Peru, IN 46970, 473–7770.

SCOTTSBURG—Fort Harrod Glass Works, 160 N. Gardner St., Scottsburg, IN 47170, (812) 752–5170.

TERRE HAUTE—Harry and Dorothy Frey, 5210 Clinton Rd., Terre Haute, IN 47805, (812) 466–4642.

WESTFIELD—Doug Moore, #9 Northbrook Circle Westfield, IN 46074, (317) 896–3015.

IOWA

ELKADER—The Bottle Shop, 206 Chestnut, S.E., Mailing address, Box 188, Max Hunt, Elkader, IA 52043, (319) 245–2359. *Sarsaparilla and bitters.*

STORM LAKE—Ralph and Helen Welch, 804 Colonial Circle, Storm Lake, IA 50588, (712) 732–4124.

KANSAS

HALSTEAD—Doanald Haury, Rt. #2, Halstead, KS 67056, (316) 283–5876.

LAWRENCE—Mike Elwell, Rt. 2, Box 30, Lawrence, KS 66044, (913) 842–2102.

MERRIAM—Dale Young, 9909 West 55th St., Merriam, KS 66203, (913) 677–0175.

PAOLA—Stewart and Sons Old Bottle Shop, 610 E. Kaskaskia, Paola, KS 66071, (913) 294–3434. *Drugstore bottles, blob top beers.*

TOPEKA—Joe and Alyce Smith, 4706 West Hills Dr., Topeka, KS 66606, (913) 272–1892.

KENTUCKY

ALEXANDRIA—Michael and Kathy Kolb, 6 S. Jefferson, Alexandria, KY 41001, (606) 635–7121.

JEFFERSONTOWN—Paul Van Vactor, 10004 Cardigan Dr., Jeffersontown, KY 40299.

LOUISVILLE—Gene Blasi, 5801 River Knolls Dr., Louisville, KY 40222. (502) 425–6995.

LOUISVILLE—Jerry and Joyce Phelps, 6013 Innes Trace Rd., Louisville, KY 40222.

LOUISVILLE—Paul and Paulette Van Vactor, 300 Stilz Ave., Louisville, KY 40299, (502) 895–3655.

PADUCAH—Earl and Ruth Cron 808 N. 25th St., Paducah, KY 42001, (502) 443–5005.

LOUISIANA

BATON ROUGE—Sidney and Eulalle Genius, 1843 Tudor Dr., Baton Rouge, LA 70815, (504) 925–5774.

BATON ROUGE—Bobby and Ellen Kirkpatrick, 7313 Meadowbrook Ave., Baton Rouge, LA 70808.

BATON ROUGE—Sheldon L. Ray, Jr. (Summer address): 2316 Amalie, Monroe, LA 71201. Mail address: P.O. Box 17238 LSU, Baton Rouge, LA 70893, (504) 388–3814.

JENNINGS—Cajun Pop Factory, P.O. Box 1113, Jennings, LA 70546, (318) 824–7078. *Hutchinsons, Blob-tops and pontil sodas.*

MONROE—Everett L. Smith, 100 Everett Dr., Monroe, LA 71202, 325–3534. *Embossed whiskies.*

NATCHITOCHES—Ralph and Cheryl Green, 515 Elizabeth St., Natchitoches, LA 71457.

NEW ORLEANS—Bep's Antiques, 3923 Magazine St., New Orleans, LA 70115, 891–3468. *Antique bottles, import bottles.*

NEW ORLEANS—Dr. Charles and Jane Aprill, 484 Chestnut, New Orleans, LA 70118, (504) 899–7441.

RUSTON—The Dirty Digger, 1804 Church St., Ruston, LA 71270, 255–6112.

RUSTON—Bob and Vernell Willett, 1804 Church St., Ruston, LA 71270, (318) 255–6112.

MAINE

BETHEL—F. Barrie Freeman, antiques, Paradise Hill Rd., Bethel, ME 04217, (207) 824–3300.

BRYANT POND—John and Althea Hathaway, Bryant Pond, ME 04219.

EAST WILTON—Don McKeen Bottles, McKeen Way. P.O. Box 5A, E. Wilton, ME 04234.

MILFORD—Spruce's Antiques, Main St., P.O. Box 295, Milford, ME 04461, 827–4756.

SEARSPORT—Morse and Applebee Antiques, U.S. Rt. 1. Box 164, Searsport, ME 04974, 548–6314, *Early American glass.*

WALDOBORO—Wink's Bottle Shop, Rt. 235, Waldoboro, ME 04572, (207) 832–4603.

WALDOBORO—Daniel R. Winchenbaugh, RFD #4, Box 21, Waldoboro, ME 04572, (207) 832–7702.

MARYLAND
NORTH EAST—Pete's Diggins, Rt. 40 West, RR #3, Box 301, North East, MD 21901, (301) 287–9245.
SUDLERSVILLE—Fran and Bill Lafferty, Box 142, Sudlersville, MD 21668.

MASSACHUSETTS
DUXBURY—Joe and Kathy Wood, 49 Surplus St., Duxbury, MA 02332, (617) 934–2221.
LEVERETT—Metamorphosis, 46 Teewaddle Rd., RFD #3, Leverett, MA 01002. *Hairs, medicines.*
LITTLETON—The Thrift & Gift Shop, Littleton Common, Box 21, Littleton, MA, (617) 486–4464.
MANSFIELD—Shop in my home, 211 East St., Mansfield, MA 02048, (617) 339–6086. *Historic flasks.*
NORTH EASTON—The Applied Lip Place, 26 Linden St., North Easton, MA 02356, (617) 238–1432. *Medicines, whiskies.*
WELLESLEY—Carlyn Ring, 59 Livermore Road, Wellesley, MA 02181, (617) 235–5675.
WEST SPRINGFIELD—Leo A. Bedard, 62 Craig Dr., Apt. 7A, West Springfield, MA 01089. *Bitters, whiskeys, medicines.*
YARMOUTH—Gloria Swanson Antiques, 262 Setucket RD., Yarmouth, MA 02675, 398–8848. *Inks.*

MICHIGAN
ANN ARBOR—John Wolfe, 1622 E. Stadium Blvd., Ann Arbor, MI 48104, (313) 665–6106.
BLOOMFIELD HILLS—Jim and Robin Meehan, 25 Valley Way, Bloomfield Hills, MI 48013, (313) 642–0176.
BUCHANAN—Old Chicago, 316 Ross Dr., Buchanan, MI 49107, (616) 695–5896. *Hutchinson sodas, blob beers.*
CLARKLAKE—Fred and Shirley Weck, 8274 S. Jackson Rd., Clarklake, MI 49234, (517) 529–9631.
DAVISBURG—Chief Pontiac Antique Bottle Shop, 13880 Neal Rd., Davisburg, MI 48019, (313) 634–8469.
DETROIT—Michael and Christina Garrett, 19400 Stout, Detroit, MI 48219, (313) 534–6067.
DUNDEE—Ray and Hillaine Hoste, 366 Main St., Dundee, MI 48131, (313) 529–2193.

GAINES—E & E Antiques, 9441 Grand Blanc Road, Gaines, MI 48436, (517) 271–9063. *Fruit jars, beer bottles, milks.*
GRAND RAPIDS—Dewey and Marilyn Heetderks, 21 Michigan N.E., Grand Rapids, MI 49503, (616) 774–9333.
IRON RIVER—Sarge's, 111 E. Hemlock, Iron River, MI 49935, (906) 265–4223. *Old mining town bottles, Hutchinsons.*
KALAMAZOO—Mark and Marty McNee, 1009 Vassar Dr., Kalamazoo, MI 49001, (616) 343–9393.
KALAMAZOO—Lew and Leon Wisser, 2837 Parchmount, Kalamazoo, MI 49004, (616) 343–7479.
LATHRUP VILLAGE—The Jar Emporium, Ralph Finch, 19420 Saratoga, Lathrup Village, MI 48076, (313) 569–6749. *Fruit jars.*
MANISTEE—Chris and Becky Batdorff, 516 Maple St., Manistee, MI 49660, (616) 723–7917.
MONROE—Don and Glennie Burkett, 3942 West Dunbar Rd., Monroe, MI 48161, (313) 241–6740.
STAMBAUGH—Copper Corner Rock & Bottle Shop, 4th & Lincoln, Stambaugh, MI 49964, (906) 265–3510. *Beer, Hutch's, medicines.*
ST. JOSEPH—Anvil Antiques, 2 blocks So. of exit 27, I-94, 3439 Hollywood Rd., St. Joseph, MI 49085, (616) 429–5132. *Bottles, insulators.*
STUGIS—John and Kay Petruska, 21960 Marathon Rd., Sturgis, MI 49091, (616) 651–6400.
WUCHANAN—James Clengenpeel, 316 Ross Dr., Wuchanan, MI 49107, (616) 695–5896.

MINNESOTA
EXCELSIOR—Jim Conley, P.O. Box 351, Excelsior, MN 55331, (612) 935–0964.
MINNEAPOLIS—Steve Ketcham, P.O. Box 24114, Minneapolis, MN 55424, (612) 920–4205.
MINNEAPOLIS—Neal and Pat Sorensen, 132 Peninsula Rd., Minneapolis, MN 55441, (612) 545–2698.
RICHFIELD—Ron and Vernie Feldhaus, 6904 Upton Ave., S. Richfield, MN 55423, (612) 866–6013.
ST. PAUL—J & E, 1000 Arcade St., St. Paul, MN 55106, 771–9654.

MISSISSIPPI
BILOXI—Vieux Beloxie Bottlery Factory Restaurant, US 90 E., Biloxi, MS 39530, 374–0688. *Mississippi bottles.*

COLUMBIA—Robert A. Knight, 516 Dale St., Columbia, MS 39429, (601) 736–4249. *Mississippi bottles & jugs.*

McCOMB—Robert Smith, 623 Pearl River Ave., McComb, MS 39648, (601) 684–1843.

STARKVILLE—Jerry Drott, 710 Persimmon Dr., P.O. Box 714, Starkville, MS 39759, 323–8796. *Liniments, drug stores.*

VICKSBURG—Ted and Linda Kost, 107 Columbia Ave., Vicksburg, MS 39180, (601) 638–8780.

MISSOURI
ELSBERRY—Dave Hausgen, Rt. 1, Box 164, Elsberry, MO 63343, (314) 898–2500.

GLENCOE—Sam and Eloise Taylor, 3002 Woodlands Terrace, Glencoe, MO 63038, (314) 273–6244.

HANNIBAL—Bob and Debbi Overfield, 2318 Chestnut St., Hannibal, MO 63401, (314) 248–9521.

INDEPENDENCE—Mike and Carol Robison, 1405 N. River, Independence, MO 64050, (816) 836–2337.

KANSAS CITY—Donald Kimrey, 1023 W. 17th St., Kansas City, MO 64108, (816) 741–2745.

KANSAS CITY—Robert Stevens, 1131 E. 77th, Kansas City, MO 64131, (816) 333–1398.

LINN CREEK—The Bottle House, 1 mile north of Linn Creek on HWY 54, Rt. 1, Box 111, Linn Creek, MO 65052, (314) 346–5890.

ST. LOUIS—Gene and Alberta Kelley, 1960 Cherokee, St. Louis, MO 63126, (314) 664–7203.

ST. LOUIS—Jerry Mueller, 4520 Langtree, St. Louis, MO 63128, (314) 843–8357.

ST. LOUIS—Terry and Luann Phillips, 1014 Camelot Gardens, St. Louis, MO 63125, (314) 892–6864.

ST. LOUIS—Hal and Vern Wagner, 10118 Schuessler, St. Louis, MO 63128, (314) 843–7573. *Historical flasks, colognes, early glass.*

TAYLOR—Barkely Museum, one mile South Taylor, MO on U.S. 61 (service road), (314) 393–2408. 10,000 old bottles for sale, plus thousands of other collector items.

TIPTON—Joseph and Jean Reed, 237 E. Morgan, Tipton, MO 65081, (816) 433–5937.

WESTPHALIA—Randy and Jan Haviland, American Systems Antiques, Westphalia, MO 65085, (314) 455–2525.

NEBRASKA
OMAHA—Born Again Antiques, 1402 Williams St., Omaha, NE 68108, 341–5177.

OMAHA—Karl Person, 10210 "W" St., Omaha, NE 68127, (402) 331–2666.

OMAHA—Fred Williams, 5712 N. 33rd St., Omaha, NE 68111, (402) 453–4317.

NEVADA
FALLON—Don and Opal Wellman, P.O. Box 521, Fallon, NV 89406, (702) 423–3490.

SPARKS—Don and Bonnie McLane, 1846 F. St., Sparks, NV 89431, (702) 359–2171.

NEW HAMPSHIRE
AMHERST—Dave and Carol Waris, Boston Post Rd., Amherst, NH 03031, (603) 882–4409.

DOVER—Bob and Betty Morin, RD 3, Box 280, Dover, NH 03820.

EXETER—Lucille Stanley, 9 Oak St., Exeter, NH 03833, (603) 772–2296.

HAMPSTEAD—Murray's Lakeside Bottle Shop, Benson Shores, Hampstead, NH 03841, P.O. Box 57, (603) 329–6969. *All types, pontils, bitters, sarsaparillas, balsams, hairs, labeled, medicines, general line. Open 7 days, mail order too.*

MANCHESTER—Jim and Joyce Rogers, Harvey Road, Rt. 10, Manchester, NH 03103, (603) 623–4101.

TROY—House of Glass, 25 High St., Troy, NH 03465, (603) 242–7947.

NEW JERSEY
BRANCHVILLE—Richard and Lesley Harris, Box 400, Branchville, NY 07826, (201) 948–3935.

CALIFON—Phil and Flo Alvarez, P.O. Box 107, Califon, NJ 07830, (201) 832–7438.

ENGLEWOOD—Ed and Carole Clemens, 81 Chester Pl. Apt. D–2, Englewood, NJ 07631, (201) 569–4429.

FLEMINGTON—John Orashen, RD 6, Box 345–A, Flemington, NJ 08822, (201) 782–3391.

HOPEWELL—Tom and Marion McCandless, 62 Lafayette St., Hopewell, NJ 08525, (609) 466–0619.

HOWELL—Howell Township, Bruce and Pat Egeland, 3 Rustic Drive, Howell, NJ. 07731, (201) 363–0556. *Second shop open 7 days a week at shop #106, build-*

ing #3, Red Bank Antique Center, West Front St., and Bridge Ave., Red Bank, N.J.

MICKLETON—Sam Fuss, Harmony Rd., Mickleton, NJ 08056, (609) 423–5038.

SALEM—Old Bottle Museum, 4 Friendship Dr., Salem, NJ. 08079, (609) 935–5631. *10,000 old bottles for sale, plus thousands of other collector items.*

NEW MEXICO

ALBUQUERQUE—Irv and Ruth Swalwell, 8826 Fairbanks NE, Albuquerque, NM 87112, (505) 299–2977.

DEMING—Krol's Rock City & Mobile Park, 5 miles east of Deming on State HWY 26, Star Rt. 2, Box 15A, Deming, NM. 88030. *Hutch sodas, inks, Avons.*

NEW YORK

AUBURN—Brewster Bottle Shop, 297 South St. Road, Auburn, NY. 13021, (315) 252–3246. *Milk bottles.*

BALLSTON LAKE—Tom and Alice Moulton, 88 Blue Spruce Lane, RD 5, Ballston Lake, NY 12019.

BINGHAMTON—Jim Chamberlain, RD 8, 607 Nowland Rd., Binghamton, NY 13904, (607) 772–1135.

BINGHAMTON—Jo Ann's Old Bottles, RD 2, Box 638, Port Crane, NY 13833, (607) 648–4605.

BLODGETT MILLS—Edward Pettet, P.O. Box 1, Blodgett Mills, NY 13738, (607) 756–7891. *Inks.*

BLOOMING GROVE—Old Bottle Shop, Horton Rd., P.O. Box 105, Blooming Grove, NY 10914, (914) 496–6841.

CENTRAL VALLEY—J. J.'s Pontil Place, 1001 Dunderberg RD., Central Valley, NY, (914) 928–9144.

CLIFTON PARK—John Kovacik, 11 Juniper Dr., Clifton Park, NY 12065, (518) 371–4118.

CLIFTON PARK—Richard Strunk, Rd. 4, Grooms Rd., Clifton Park, NY 12065. *Bottles, flasks, bitters, Saratogas.*

CRANBERRY LAKE—The Bottle Shop Antiques, P.O. Box 503, Cranberry Lake, NY, (315) 848–2648.

ELMA—Leonard and Joyce Blake, 1220 Stolle Rd., Elma, NY 14059, (716) 652–7752.

LEROY—Kenneth Cornell, 78 Main, Leroy, NY 14482, (716) 768–8919.

LOCH SHELDRAKE—The Bottle Shop, P.O. Box 24, Loch Sheldrake, NY 12759, (914) 434–4757.

MONTICELLO—Manor House Collectibles, Rt. 42, South Forestburgh, RD 1, Box 67, Monticello, NY 12701, (914) 794–3967. *Whiskeys, beers, sodas.*

NEW WINDSOR—David Byrd, 43 E. Kenwood Dr., New Windsor, NY 12550, (914) 561–7257.

NEW YORK CITY—Chuck Moore, 3 East 57th St., N.Y.C., NY 10022.

NEW YORK CITY—Bottles Unlimited, 245 East 78th St., N.Y.C., NY 10021, (212) 628–8769. *19th and 18th century.*

ROCHESTER—Burton Spiller, 169 Greystone Lane, Apt. 31, Rochester, NY 14618, (716) 244–2229.

ROCHESTER—Robert Zorn, 23 Knickerbocker Ave., Rochester, NY 14615, (716) 254–7470.

WEBSTER—Dick and Evelyn Bowman, 1253 LaBaron Circle, Webster, NY 14580, (716) 872–4015.

NORTH CAROLINA

BLOWING ROCK—Vieve and Luke Yarbrough, P.O. Box 1023, Blowing Rock, NC 28605, (704) 963–4961.

CHARLOTTE—Bob Morgan, P.O. Box 3163, Charlotte, NC 28203, (704) 527–4841.

DURHAM—Clement's Bottles, 5234 Willowhaven Dr., Durham, NC. 27712, 383–2493. *Commemorative soft drink bottles.*

GOLDSBORO—Vernon Capps, Rt. 5, Box 529, Goldsboro, NC 27530, (919) 734–8964.

GOLD HILL—Howard Crowe, P.O. Box 133, Gold Hill, NC 28071, (704) 279–3736.

RALEIGH—Rex D. McMillan, 4101 Glen Laurel Dr., Raleigh, NC. 27612, (919) 787–0007. *N.C. blobs, saloon bottles, colored drug store.*

NORTH DAKOTA

MANDAN—Robert Barr, 102 N. 9th Ave. N.W., Mandan, ND 58554.

OHIO

AKRON—Don and Barb Dzuro, 5113 W. Bath Rd., Akron, OH 44313, (216) 666–8170.

AKRON—Jim Salzwimmer, 3391 Tisen Rd., Akron, OH 44312, (216) 699–3990.

BEACHWOOD—Allan Hodges, 25125 Shaker Blvd., Beachwood, OH 44122, (216) 464–8381.

BLUFFTON—Schroll's Country Shop, 3 mi. east of county line on Co. Rd. 33, (419) 358–6121.

BYESVILLE—Albert and Sylvia Campbell, RD. 1, Box 194, Byesville, OH 43723, (614) 439–1105.

CINCINNATI—Kenneth and Dudie Roat, 7755 Kennedy Lane, Cincinnati, OH 45242, (513) 791–1168.

CLEVELAND—Joe and Mary Miller, 2590 N. Moreland Blvd., Cleveland, OH 44120, (216) 721–9919.

DAYTON—Don and Paula Spangler, 2554 Loris Dr., Dayton, OH 45449, (513) 435–7155.

DUBLIN—Roy and Barbara Brown, 8649 Dunsinane Dr., Dublin, OH 43017, (614) 889–0818.

FRANKFORT—Roger Durflinger, P.O. Box 2006, Frankfort, OH 45628, (614) 998–4849.

HANNIBAL—Gilbert Nething, P.O. Box 96, Hannibal, OH. 43931. *Hutchinson sodas.*

LANCASTER—R. J. and Freda Brown, 125 S. High St., Lancaster, OH 43130, (614) 687–2899.

LEWISTOWN—Sonny Mallory, P.O. Box 134, Lewistown, OH 43333, (513) 686–2185.

NORTH HAMPTON—John and Margie Bartley, 160 South Main, North Hampton, OH 45319, (513) 964–1080.

POWHATAN POINT—Bob and Dawn Jackson, 107 Pine St., Powhatan Point, OH 43942, (614) 795–5567.

REYNOLDSBURG—Bob and Phyllis Christ, 1218 Creekside Place, Reynoldburg, OH 43068, (614) 866–2156.

SPRINGFIELD—Ballentine's Bottles, 710 W. First St., Springfield, OH 45504, 399–8359. *Antique bottles.*

SPRINGFIELD—Larry R. Henschen, 3222 Delrey Rd., Springfield, OH, (513) 399–1891.

STEUBENVILLE—Tom and Deena Caniff, 1223 Oak Grove Ave., Steubenville, OH 43952, (614) 282–8918.

STEUBENVILLE—Bob and Mary Ann Villamagna, 711 Kendall Ave., Steubenville, OH 43952, (614) 282–9029.

STOW—Doug and Joann Bedore, 1483 Ritchie Rd., Stow, OH 44224, (216) 688–4934.

TORONTO—Bob Villamagna, 1518 Madison Ave., P.O. Box 56, Toronto, OH. 43964, (614) 537–4503. *Tri-state area bottles, stoneware.*

WASHINGTONVILLE—Al and Beth Bignon, 480 High St., Washingtonville, OH 44490, (216) 427–6848.

WARREN—Michael Cetina, 3272 Northwest Blvd. N.W., Warren, OH 44485, (216) 898–1845.

WAYNESVILLE—The Bottleworks, 70 N. Main St., P.O. Box 446, Waynesville, OH 45068, (513) 897–3861.

WELLINGTON—Elvin and Cherie Moody, Trails End, Wellington, OH 44090, (216) 647–4917.

XENIA—Bill and Wanda Dudley, 393 Franklin Ave., Xenia, OH 45385, (513) 372–8567.

OKLAHOMA

ENID—Ronald and Carol Ashby, 831 E. Pine, Enid, OK 73701. *Rare and scarce fruit jars.*

OKLAHOMA CITY—Joe and Hazel Nagy, 3540 NW 23, Oklahoma City, OK 73107, (405) 942–0882.

SANDSPRINGS—Larry and Linda Shope, 310 W. 44th, Sandsprings, OK 74063, (918) 363–8481.

OREGON

HILLSBORO—Robert and Marguerite Ornduff, Rt. 4, Box 236–A, Hillsboro, OR 97123, (503) 538–2359.

PORTLAND—Alan Amerman, 2311 S.E. 147th, Portland, OR 97233, (503) 761–1661. *Fruit jars.*

PORTLAND—The Glass House, 4620 S.E. 104th, Portland, OR 97266, (503) 760–3346. *Fruit jars.*

PENNSYLVANIA

ALBURTIS—R. S. Riovo, 686 Franklin St., Alburtis, PA 18011, (215) 965–2706. *Milk bottles, dairy go-withs.*

BRADFORD—Ernest Hurd, 5 High St., Bradford, PA 16701, (814) 362–9915.

BRADFORD—Dick and Patti Mansour, 458 Lambert Dr., Bradford, PA 16701, (814) 368–8820.

CANONSBURG—John and Mary Schultz, RD 1, Box 118, Canonsburg, PA 15317, (412) 745–6632.

EAST GREENVILLE—James A. Hagenbach, 102 Jefferson St., East Greenville, PA 18041, (215) 679–5849.

COUDERSPORT—The Old Bottle Corner, 508 South Main St. Mailing address: 102 West Maple St., Coudersport, PA 16915, (814) 274–7017. *Fruit jars, blob tops.*

EAST PETERSBURG—Jere and Betty Hambleton, 5940 Main St., East Petersburg, PA 17520, (717) 569–0130.

HATBORO—Al and Maggie Duffield, 12 Belmar Rd., Hatboro, PA 19040, (215) 675–5175. *Hutchinson's and inks.*

LANCASTER—Barry and Mary Hogan, 3 Lark Lane, Lancaster, PA 17603.

LEVITTOWN—Ed Lasky, 43 Nightingale LN., Levittown, PA 19054, (215) 945–1555.

MARIENVILLE—Harold Bauer Antique Bottles, 136 Cherry St., Marienville, PA 16239.

McKEES ROCKS—Chuck Henigin, 3024 Pitch Fork Lane, McKees Rocks, PA 15136, (412) 331–6159.

MUNCY—Harold Hill, 161 E. Water St., Muncy, PA 17756, (717) 546–3388.

PIPERSVILLE—Allen Holtz, RD 1, Pipersville, PA 18947, (215) 847–5728.

PITTSBURGH—Carl & Gail Onufer, 210 Newport Rd., Pittsburgh, PA 15221, (412) 371–7725. *Milk bottles.*

ROULETTE—R. A. and Esther Heimer, P.O. Box 153, Roulette, PA 16746, (814) 544–7713.

STRONGSTOWN—Butch and Gloria Kim, RD 2, Box 35, Strongstown, PA 15957.

RHODE ISLAND

KENYON—Wes and Diane Seemann, Box 49, Kenyon, RI 02836, (203) 599–1626.

SOUTH CAROLINA

EASHEY—Bob Durham, 704 W. Main St., Eashey, SC 29640.

MARION—Tony and Marie Shank, P.O. Box 778, Marion, SC 29571, (803) 423–5803.

TENNESSEE

KNOXVILLE—Ronnie Adams, 7005 Charlotte Dr., Knoxville, TN 37914, (615) 524–8958.

McMINNVILLE—Terry Pennington, 415 N. Spring St., McMinnville, TN 37110. *Jack Daniels, amber Coca Cola.*

MEMPHIS—Bluff City Bottlers, 4630 Crystal Springs Dr., Memphis, TN 38123, (901) 353–0541. *Common American bottles.*

MEMPHIS—Larry and Nancy McCage, 3772 Hanna Dr., Memphis, TN 38128, (901) 388–9329.

MEMPHIS—Tom Phillips, 2088 Fox Run Cove, Memphis, TN 38138, (901) 754–0097.

TEXAS

AMARILLO—Robert Synder, 4235 W. 13th St., Amarillo, TX 79106.

EULESS—Mack and Alliene Landers, P.O. Box 5, Euless, TX 76039, (817) 267–2710.

HOUSTON—Bennie and Harper Leiper, 2800 W. Dallas, Houston, TX 77019, (713) 526–2101.

PASADENA—Gerald Welch, 4809 Gardenia Trail, Pasadena, TX 77505, (713) 487–3057.

PORT ISABEL—Jimmy and Peggy Galloway, P.O. Drawer A, Port Isabel, TX 78578, (512) 943–2437.

RICHARDSON—Chuck and Reta Bukin, 1325 Cypress Dr., Richardson, TX 75080, (214) 235–4889.

SAN ANTONIO—Sam Greer, 707 Nix Professional Bldg., San Antonio, TX 78205, (512) 227–0253.

VERMONT

BRATTLEBORO—Kit Barry, 88 High St., Brattleboro, VT 05301, (802) 254–2195.

VIRGINIA

ALEXANDRIA—A. E. Steidel, 6167 Cobbs Rd., Alexandria, VA 22310.

ARLINGTON—Dick and Margie Stockton, 2331 N. Tuckahoe St., Arlington, VA 22205, (703) 534–5619.

CHESTERFIELD—Tom Morgan, 3501 Slate Ct., Chesterfield, VA 23832.

FREDERICKSBURG—White's Trading Post, Boutchyards Olde Stable, Falmouth, VA. 1903 Charles St., Fredericksburg, VA 22401, (703) 371–6252. *Fruit jars, new and old bottles.*

HINTON—Vic and Betty Landis, Rt. 1, Box 8A, Hinton, VA 22801, (703) 867–5959.

HUNTLY—Early American Workshop, Star Route, Huntly, VA 22640, (703) 635–8252. *Milk bottles.*

MARSHALL—John Tutton, Rt. 1, Box 261, Marshall, VA 22115, (703) 347–0148.

RICHMOND—Lloyd and Carrie Hamish, 2936 Woodworth Rd., Richmond, VA 23234, (804) 275–7106.

RICHMOND—Jim and Connie Mitchell, 5106 Glen Alden Dr., Richmond, VA.

WASHINGTON
BELLEVUE—Don and Dorothy Finch, 13339 Newport Way, Bellevue, WA 98006, (206) 746–5640.
BREMERTON—Ron Flannery, 423 NE Conifer Dr., Bremerton, WA 98310, (206) 692–2619.
SEATTLE—John W. Cooper, 605 N.E. 170th St., Seattle, WA 96155, (206) 364–0858.

WISCONSIN
ARLINGTON—Mike and Carole Schwartz, Rt. 1, Arlington, WI 53911, (608) 846–5229.
MEQUON—Jeff Burkhardt, 12637 N. River Forest Cir., Mequon, WI 53092, (414) 243–5643.
MEQUON—Bor Markiewicz, 11715 W. Bonniwell Rd., Mequon, WI 53092, (414) 242–3968.
OSKOSH—Richard Schwab, 65–5 Lareen Rd., Oskosh, WI 54901, (414) 235–9962.
STEVENS POINT—Bill and Kathy Mitchell, 703 Linwood Ave., Stevens Point, WI 55431, (715) 341–1471.

WAUTOMA—George and Ruth Hansen, Rt. 2, Box 26, Wautoma, WI 54962, (414) 787–4893.

FOREIGN

CANADA
BADEN, ONTARIO—John and Sara Moore, Rt. 2, Baden, ONT.
DOLLARD-DES-ORMEAUX, P.Q.—Richard Davis, 39 Brunswick #115, Dollard-Des-Ormeaux, P.Q, (314) 683–8522.
OTTAWA, ONT.—Paul Hanrahan, 292 Byron Ave. #2, Ottawa, ONT, Canada, (613) 929–56–75.

CENTRAL AMERICA
BELIZE CITY, BELIZE—Emory King, #9 Regent Street, Belize City, Belize.
BELIZE CITY, BELIZE—Paul Hunt, Managing Director, Fort George Hotel, Belize Hotels Limited, Belize City, Belize.

ENGLAND
TRENT—David Geduhon, Box 85, Cayuga Ind. & Burton-on-Trent, England, (317) 494–3027.
YORKSHIRE—John Morrison, 33 Ash Grove, Leeds G., Yorkshire, England.